Compiled from *Billboard's* Pop Singles charts 1940-1954
and *Billboard's* Pop Albums charts 1945-1954.

Record Research Inc.
P.O. Box 200
Menomonee Falls, Wisconsin 53052-0200   U.S.A.

Phone: (262) 251-5408
Fax: (262) 251-9452
E-Mail: books@recordresearch.com
Website: www.recordresearch.com

Dedicated to...

...The Great MGM Musical Soundtracks

From *Till The Clouds Roll By* (MGM 1) in March of 1947 through *Brigadoon* in November of 1954, MGM supplied 22 of the 28 charted movie soundtracks in this book. Among this musical bounty were *Show Boat*, *An American In Paris*, *Three Little Words*, *Singin' In The Rain*, *Annie Get Your Gun*, *Words And Music*, *The Merry Widow*, and *Seven Brides For Seven Brothers*. There really is "No Business Like Show Business" (or music business for that matter).

The author wishes to extend a special note of thanks to:

The staff of Record Research....

Top: Joel Whitburn, Bill Hathaway, Jeanne Olynick, Kay Wagner; Middle: Frances Whitburn, Sue Hustad, Kim Bloxdorf, Paul Haney; Bottom: Brent Olynick, Nestor Vidotto

From pastime to passion to profitable enterprise, the growth of Record Research has been the outgrowth of Joel Whitburn's hobby. Joel began collecting records as a teenager in the 1950s. As his collection grew, he began to sort, categorize and file each record according to the highest position it reached on *Billboard's* Hot 100 charts. He went on to publish this information in 1970 and a business was born.

Today, Joel leads a team of researchers who delve into all of *Billboard's* music charts to an unmatched degree of depth and detail. Joel is widely recognized as the most authoritative historian on charted music. Joel's own record collection remains unrivaled the world over and includes every charted Hot 100 and pop single (back to 1920), every charted pop album (back to 1945), collections of nearly every charted Country, R&B, Bubbling Under The Hot 100 and Adult Contemporary records. Ever the consummate collector, Joel also owns one of the world's largest picture sleeve collections.

In person, this walking music encyclopedia stands 6'6" — a definite advantage when he played high school, college and semi-pro basketball. An avid sports fan, Joel actively engages in a wide variety of water, winter and motor sports. A native of Wisconsin, Joel has been married for 38 years to Fran, a native of Honduras; their daughter, Kim Bloxdorf, is part of the Record Research team, as are two of Joel's friends and key employees of 30 years, Bill Hathaway and Brent Olynick. Joel's lifelong passion for music, old and new, and his penchant for accurate detail continues into the 21st century.

CONTENTS

I am happy to introduce this second edition of *Pop Hits*. Actually, this complete revision contains so many additions, updates and new features that it is really now four books in one. *Pop Hits Singles & Albums 1940-1954* explores one of the greatest eras in music, artist by artist, single by single, album by album, week by week and year by year.

The book's starting point, 1940, is the year that *Billboard* introduced its first definitive weekly singles sales ranking, the Best Sellers chart. This is also when pop music suddenly gained a great deal of rhythm, energy and volume, and thus commenced the "modern" era of pop music. This new tide brought the great orchestras and vocalists whose classic songs now stir the waves of nostalgia. The musical impact of those years is measured more fully than ever in the pages ahead. You will notice the following new features to this all-encompassing retrospective.

The Singles Section is up to par with my other recent books with an easier-to-read font and many new special symbols. There are twice as many titles since I've included the B-side of every record. The ❶ now indicates all #1 hits. All Top 5 hits stand out with shading. The peak positions within an artist's string of five or more consecutive Top 10 hits are also shaded. As expected, the price guide shows some dramatic increases and many artist bios now contain death dates that have occurred since the previous edition.

A new feature unique to *Pop Hits Singles & Albums* is the index of contributing orchestras and vocalists below artist biographies. For example, following Doris Day's bio is a listing of her orchestra conductors, such as Les Brown and Percy Faith, and a reference to the hits on which they appeared. Following Les Brown's bio is a listing of his vocalists, such as the Ames Brothers and Doris Day.

The Pop Annual Section now includes the songwriter(s) of every song, a revealing new complement that highlights this great age of classic songwriters. In the yearly wrap-ups, you'll see rankings of the legendary tunesmiths such as Irving Berlin, Rodgers & Hammerstein, Cole Porter, Sammy Cahn, Jule Styne, Johnny Mercer, Harold Arlen, Hoagy Carmichael, and more.

The Top 10 Singles Section displays, for the first time anywhere, the consecutive week by week Top 10 charts from 1940 through 1954. This completely new addition is the same format as my *Top 10 Singles 1955-2000* book. I found it fun following the progress of the five different versions of "Open The Door, Richard!" as they competed on the Best Sellers chart and watching the three different versions of "To Each His Own" take turns at #1.

The Albums Section is back in print after a 30-year hiatus. I first published the history of the early albums chart in *Top LP's 1945-1972*, back in 1973. This was the only publication with the research of the early era of the albums chart. This research has been significantly enhanced with many new features, including an index of all of the cuts for each album that charted. In addition to my initial research of the Best Selling 33-1/3 R.P.M. album chart, I've now added the research of the Best Selling 45 R.P.M. chart and its sequel, the Best Selling Popular E.P.'S chart. For albums that hit both charts, their configurations, different prefixes and label numbers, and number of records in the package are also shown for the first time anywhere.

Finally, you can trust the accuracy within as the label number, spelling and punctuation of every title and every artist have been proofed against the singles and albums in my collection. I have strived to create a comprehensive account of this wonderful era of pop music. My hope is that the following pages will jog the musical memories of those who lived through these years and acquaint the younger generations with this rich and invigorating music.

JOEL WHITBURN

THE SINGLES

Record Buying Guide

An Analysis of Current Songs and Recordings From the Standpoint of Their Value to Phonograph Operators

GOING STRONG

Recordings listed below are currently the biggest money-makers in automatic phonographs. Selections are the consensus of reports gathered each week by representatives of The Billboard from at least four leading phonograph operators in each of the 30 most important phonograph operating centers in the country. Recordings listed without an explanation are those that have appeared under this heading for one week or more and have thus become such established successes that they require no further explanation.

Stop, It's Wonderful. The history of this song, as far as music boxes are concerned, proves again what has often been demonstrated in the past. That is simply that when a band clicks in a big way with the nickel droppers its success carries along many another recording of the same ork that might be lost in the shuffle if it weren't for the band's initial hit. Orrin Tucker made a national menace out of the oldie, *Oh, Johnny, Oh,* and now he finds himself with another hit disk on his hands. This song had been around for some time, getting no place very successfully until ops jumped on the Tucker record. Now, in only a couple of weeks, it has climbed up into the big time. You're missing out on plenty of buffalo heads if you're not playing this one.

Scatterbrain. Frankie Masters, Freddy Martin, Benny Goodman, Guy Lombardo.

South of the Border. Shep Fields, Ambrose, Guy Lombardo, Tony Martin, Sammy Kaye, Horace Heidt.

Oh, Johnny, Oh. Orrin Tucker.

My Prayer. Glenn Miller, Ink Spots.

Yodelin' Jive. Andrews Sisters-Bing Crosby.

In the Mood. Glenn Miller.

COMING UP

Recordings listed below are those which operators report are not yet top-notch money-makers but which are growing in popularity on automatic phonographs. Selections are the consensus of reports gathered each week by representatives of The Billboard from at least four leading phonograph operators in each of the 30 most important phonograph operating centers in the country.

Careless. A "possibility" last week and now the fastest rising recording on the phono network is Dick Jurgen's version of his own (with Eddy Howard and Lou Quadling) ballad. There is something about this melody, title and lyric that cannot possibly miss hitting universal favor. From its progress in the machines in only one week it looks certain to be a smash very soon, not only under the needles but in the other departments of song popularization, radio and sheet music. This is practically a must for operators right now.

Bluebirds in the Moonlight. Also indulging in a gargantuan hop, skip and jump up the ladder of phono popularity this week is this hit tune from *Gulliver's Travels.* It's mentioned on 90 per cent of the reports received during the last seven days as being among the strongest potentialities on the list of currently rising numbers. Dick Jurgens is very much in the record picture again with this item, leading Benny Goodman by a two-to-one ratio on reports coming in this week.

Billy. Tho continuing to give a good enough account of itself, this follow-up to *Oh, Johnny, Oh* from the Orrin Tucker factory (altho it actually preceded that hit by a number of weeks) is not as big as it might be, operators and patrons apparently preferring to hear from Tucker again on a different sort of song like his new reigning success, *Stop, It's Wonderful.* Some ops are finding *Billy* a profitable enough venture tho, and it has a good chance of growing in favor.

I Didn't Know What Time It Was. Still garnering more than its share of nickels in a nice, quiet, refined way is this superior ballad, whose very aura of sophistication takes away from its commercial appeal and therefore lessens its chances of becoming a front-running hit in the machines. It's doing surprisingly well, with a second surprise coming from reports this week mentioning Artie Shaw's recording as threatening the supremacy of the Jimmy Dorsey and Benny Goodman disks.

Chatterbox. The second of last week's "possibilities" to depart that nebulous state and forge ahead into the more tangible classification of a number that is definitely on its way up. This may be operators' follow-up to the tremendously successful *Scatterbrain,* it's more or less similar title seeming to help it along rather than hinder it. Kay Kyser takes the lead in the matter of the most favored records, with Dick Jurgens, Guy Lombardo and Sammy Kaye.

Last Night. Still pretty much in the running is this ballad. It's not setting any high-water marks but going along to good enough returns to keep it around for a little while yet. Glenn Miller and Bob Crosby are the most important contributing factors to its success.

The Little Red Fox. Climbing, albeit slowly, this tune from Kay Kyser's *That's Right, You're Wrong* movie is worth space in the machines. It's still a little too soon to tell whether it will be a quick fizzle or whether it will live up to advance expectations. Kyser has the leading disk, followed by Van Alexander and Hal Kemp.

POSSIBILITIES

Recordings listed below have not as yet shown any strength in automatic phonographs but are the most likely prospects for music machine success among new record releases. These suggestions are based upon radio performances, sheet music sales, reports from music publishers as to the relative importance of certain songs in their catalogs as well as on the judgment of The Billboard's music department.

Woodpecker. Here is a new one by Will Glahe, who gave you—need we mention the name?—the immortal *Beer Barrel Polka.* No one can say with accuracy just what the future of this new one will be, but if it's only a quarter as good for the boxes as its predecessor, that will be enough to land it among the blue-ribbon winners.

Johnson Rag. With oldtimers the rage among popular songs of the day, this is one that may have a good chance for future hitdom. As recorded by either Larry Clinton or Glenn Miller it makes excellent listening in a style that fits very nicely with the demands of phono addicts.

Your Feet's Too Big. One of the best recordings turned out by Fats Waller in many a month. It should be a natural in colored locations, and its humor and expert Waller projection ought to do equally well in almost any other type of location.

(Double-meaning records are purposely omitted from this column)

National and Regional List of BEST SELLING RETAIL RECORDS

This compilation is based upon reports from the following retail stores, of their 10 best selling records of the past week. New York City: Center Music Store; Bloomfield Music Shop; Liberty Music Shop; Vesey Music Shop. Boston: Boston Music Co.; The Melody Shop; Mosher Music Co., Inc. Buffalo: Broadway Music Shop; Avenue Record Shop. Pittsburgh: Volkwein Bros., Inc. Washington: George's Radio Co., Inc. Denver: Knight-Campbell Music Co.; The Record Shop; Charles E. Wells Music Co. Salt Lake City: Z. C. M. I. Record Dept. Portland, Ore.: Meir and Frank Co., Inc.; Sherman Clay & Co. Los Angeles: Birkel-Richardson. Chicago: Sears, Roebuck & Co.; Garrick Music Shop; Goldblatt Bros. Cincinnati: Clifton Music Shop; Song Shop; Willis Music Co.; Wurlitzer; Steinberg's, Inc. Milwaukee: Schuster's; Record Library (Ed Drum's); Broadway House of Music; J. B. Bradford Piano Co. Des Moines: Des Moines Music House; Davidson Co. Detroit: Grinnell Bros. Kansas City, Mo.: Music Box. St. Louis: Famous & Barr, St. Paul: Mayflower Novelty Co. Cleveland: Halle Bros. Co. Birmingham: Nolen's Radio Service Shop. E. E. Forbes & Sons; Monarch Sales Co.; Louis Pizitz Dry Goods Co. Atlanta: Cox Prescription Shop. Raleigh, N. C.: James E. Thiem; C. H. Stephenson Music Co. Miami: Burdine's, Inc. New Orleans: Louis Grunewald Co., Inc.; G. Schirmer, Inc. Fort Worth, Tex.: McCrory's; Kemble Bros. Furniture Co. San Antonio: Thomas Acuna; Alamo Piano Co.; San Antonio Music Co.

NATIONAL

POSITION
This Wk.

1. I'LL NEVER SMILE AGAIN
   —TOMMY DORSEY

2. THE BREEZE AND I
   —JIMMY DORSEY

3. IMAGINATION
   —GLENN MILLER

4. PLAYMATES
   —KAY KYSER

5. FOOLS RUSH IN
   —GLENN MILLER

6. WHERE WAS I?
   —CHARLIE BARNET

7. PENNSYLVANIA 6-5000
   —GLENN MILLER

8. IMAGINATION
   —TOMMY DORSEY

9. SIERRA SUE
   —BING CROSBY

10. MAKE BELIEVE ISLAND
    —MITCHELL AYRES

EAST

POSITION
This Wk.

1. I'll Never Smile Again
   —Tommy Dorsey

2. The Breeze and I
   —Jimmy Dorsey

3. Playmates
   —Kay Kyser

4. Imagination
   —Tommy Dorsey

5. Make Believe Island
   —Mitchell Ayres

6. Imagination
   —Glenn Miller

7. Pennsylvania 6-5000
   —Glenn Miller

8. Sierra Sue
   —Bing Crosby

9. Six Lessons from Madame La
   Zonga —Jimmy Dorsey

10. The Woodpecker Song
    —Will Glahe

MIDWEST

1. I'll Never Smile Again
   —Tommy Dorsey

2. The Breeze and I
   —Jimmy Dorsey

3. Fools Rush In
   —Glenn Miller

4. Pennsylvania 6-5000
   —Glenn Miller

5. God Bless America
   —Kate Smith

6. Imagination
   —Glenn Miller

7. Playmates
   —Kay Kyser

8. Sierra Sue
   —Bing Crosby

9. I Can't Love You Any More
   Than I Do —Benny Goodman

10. Six Lessons From Madame La
    Zonga —Jimmy Dorsey

WEST COAST

POSITION
This Wk.

1. I'll Never Smile Again
   —Tommy Dorsey

2. The Breeze and I
   —Jimmy Dorsey

3. Where Was I?
   —Charlie Barnet

4. Fools Rush In
   —Glenn Miller

5. The Breeze and I
   —Charlie Barnet

6. The Nearness of You
   —Glenn Miller

7. Imagination
   —Glenn Miller

8. Playmates
   —Kay Kyser

9. Make Believe Island
   —Sammy Kaye

10. Imagination
    —Tommy Dorsey

SOUTH

1. I'll Never Smile Again
   —Tommy Dorsey

2. Friendship
   —Artie Shaw

3. The Breeze and I
   —Jimmy Dorsey

4. Where Was I?
   —Charlie Barnet

5. Imagination
   —Glenn Miller

6. Playmates
   —Kay Kyser

7. When the Swallows Come
   Back To Capistrano
   —Ink Spots

8. Fools Rush In
   —Glenn Miller

9. Devil May Care
   —Glenn Miller

10. Make Believe Island
    —Mitchell Ayres

The chart data contained in this section of the book is compiled primarily from *Billboard's* three Pop Singles charts: Best Sellers, Juke Box and Disk Jockey. An extensive breakdown of the history of these charts follows. In the chart synopsis' below, <u>Date</u> refers to the debut date of the chart or the date of change to the chart title and/or the chart size (number of positions).

BEST SELLERS CHARTS

Chart Title	Date	# of Positions
Best Selling Retail Records	*7/27/40 (first chart)*	*10*
Best-Selling Popular Retail Records	*3/24/45*	*10*
Best-Selling Popular Retail Records	*11/15/47*	*15*
Best-Selling Popular Retail Records	*6/12/48*	*30*
Best-Selling Pop Singles	*10/8/49*	*30*
Best Selling Singles	*11/15/52*	*20*
Best Sellers In Stores	*2/20/54*	*20*
Best Sellers In Stores	*5/29/54*	*30*

The Best Sellers chart was the first chart to show only one artist for each title at every chart position. Prior to this, *Billboard* combined all versions of a hit tune into one chart position. In fact, their early Song Plug charts and Record Buying Guides did not list artists, only song titles.

From July 27, 1940 through July 1, 1944, five Top 10 Best Sellers charts were published each week: a National chart and four Regional charts: East, Midwest, South and West Coast. From July 8, 1944 through January 6, 1945, *Billboard* listed, each week, between two and five Regional titles as "Other Records Reported in Best Selling List by Sections." The Regional charts ended on January 6, 1945. (See page 10 to view a sample chart.)

The Regional charts were researched <u>only</u> for titles that never made the National charts. For these Regional-only hits, 10 points (or 10 positions) were added to their weekly Regional ranking. The abbreviations for these charts are:

e = East Coast
mw = Midwest
s = South
wc = West Coast

These Best Seller regional chart abbreviations are shown across from the song title along with their peak position. For example, '**S(wc): 17**' listed to the right of a song title indicates that the song peaked at #17 on the Best Sellers (S) West Coast (wc) chart.

Ties were common on *Billboard's* Best Sellers charts, especially from April 14, 1945 through January 3, 1948. During this period, *Billboard* used the following numbering system for ties: 6-7-7-7-8. Because of this numbering system, the Top 10 chart often listed 15 hits, while the Top 15 chart may have listed 20. After January 3, 1948, ties were shown as follows: 6-7-7-7-10, which kept the chart closer to the position size as shown in the above synopsis.

RECORD BUYING GUIDE

Chart Title	Date	# of Positions
Record Buying Guide	*1/6/40 through 7/20/40*	*10*

Billboard introduced the Record Buying Guide on February 19, 1938 in the back of the magazine, in the Coin Operators section, as "a value to phonograph operators" (juke box dealers). This was the first juke box chart. The first 10 weeks were a written analysis of the top tunes of the day; artists were not listed.

On April 30, 1938, the Record Buying Guide was listed in an unnumbered chart form of approximately 18 titles without listing the artists. On October 22, 1938, the chart took shape and listed approximately 20 tunes in rank order, although chart positions were not shown. This was the first chart to list artist names, although all versions of a hit tune were combined into one listing. Also a sales analysis of each title was listed for the benefit of operators. These analyses reported the sales action of each song; the artist with the most action on the song was listed first.

In order for this book to include the <u>complete chart history of 1940</u> we researched <u>all</u> of the Top 10 songs listed on the first Record Buying Guide of 1940, and not only the titles that made their debut on that January 6, 1940 chart. In other words, we included the songs on this chart that made their debut, and possibly hit their peak, in 1939 but were still on the charts in 1940.

The Record Buying Guide combined all versions of a hit title into one listing at an unnumbered position. In order to compile a Top 10 chart, we sequentially numbered the songs, according to the chart's top-to-bottom listing. The artist listed first in the song analysis is the artist credited for the hit in this book. (See page 10 to view a sample chart.)

Our research of the Record Buying Guide ends with the July 20, 1940 chart. We did not continue the research of the Record Buying Guide, until it evolved into the Juke Box chart in 1944, since the more definitive National Best Sellers chart was introduced on July 27, 1940. January through July of 1940 was an important period in the Big Band era. The Record Buying Guide was the only *Billboard* pop chart published during those months. And, although it was not a definitive chart, it did chronicle the popularity of several very significant hits, such as Glenn Miller's "In The Mood."

JUKE BOX CHARTS

Chart Title	Date	# of Positions
Most-Played In Juke Boxes	*1/8/44 (first chart)*	*15-20*
Most-Played In Juke Boxes	*5/7/48*	*30*
Most Played In Juke Boxes	*11/15/52*	*20*

The Record Buying Guide became the Most-Played In Juke Boxes chart on January 8, 1944. Compared to its predecessor, this Juke Box chart was much more precise. From January 8, 1944 through October 25, 1947, the Most-Played Juke Box Records chart listed the Top 15-20 songs under the caption "Going Strong." Generally, two to five titles were listed at the bottom of the chart under the caption, "Coming Up." Also, from January 8, 1944 through January 6, 1945, two to four titles were listed after the "Coming Up" section as "Territorial Favorites With Juke Box Operators."

For the research in this book, we numbered the titles from those two sections as a continuation from the last chart position of the "Going Strong" section; a song that hit the lower reaches of the Juke Box chart as a Territorial Favorite is indicated to the right of the song title as '**J (terr.)**' and includes its peak position (ex.: J(terr.): 19). The "Going Strong" and "Coming Up" captions were deleted after the October 25, 1947 chart. (See page 306 to view a sample chart.)

Ties were common on *Billboard's* Juke Box charts. From January 8, 1944 through March 1, 1947, with the chart size fluctuating from 15 to 20 positions, and with *Billboard* using the following numbering system for ties—5-6-6-6-7—the chart size was not consistent. On March 8, 1947, it became a steady 15-position chart.

DISK JOCKEY CHARTS

Chart Title	Date	# of Positions
Disks With Most Radio Plugs	*1/27/45 (first chart)*	15
Record Most-Played On The Air	*2/3/45*	15
Records Most Played By Disk Jockeys	*2/14/48*	15
Records Most Played By Disk Jockeys	*8/7/48*	30
Most Played By Jockeys	*11/15/52*	20

From January 27, 1945 through October 26, 1947, the Top 15 ranking was headed by the caption "Going Strong." At the bottom of the chart was a section captioned "Coming Up." Generally, two to five titles were listed there without chart positions. For the research in this book, we numbered those titles as a continuation from the last chart position of the "Going Strong" section. The last chart showing the "Going Strong" and "Coming Up" captions was on October 25, 1947.

Ties were common on *Billboard's* Disk Jockey charts. From January 27, 1945 through January 3, 1948, ties were shown as follows: 3-4-4-4-5. Because of this numbering system, often the Top 15 chart would list 18 to 24 hits. After January 3, 1948, ties were shown as follows: 3-4-4-4-7, making the chart size more consistent.

Billboard spelled Disk Jockey with a 'k' during the above era; however, the modern spelling is Disc Jockey.

Sample of Disk Jockey chart (10/6/45)

13

USER'S GUIDE TO SINGLES BY ARTIST SECTION

The artist section lists each artist's charted hits in chronological order. Each of an artist's song titles is sequentially numbered. All **Top 5 hits** are **shaded** with a light gray background for quick identification.

EXPLANATION OF COLUMNAR HEADINGS

DEBUT: Date single first charted; taken from the chart on which it first appeared. The date shown is *Billboard's* issue date.

PEAK: Highest charted position (highlighted in **bold type**) taken from the chart on which it achieved its highest ranking. All #1 singles are identified by a special #1 symbol (**❶**).

WKS: Total weeks charted; taken from the chart on which it achieved its highest total.

Gold: ● Gold single (million seller)*

A-side: Song title of chart hit

B-side: Flip side of single

$: Current value of near-mint commercial copy

LABEL & NUMBER: Original label and number of single

*Before the Recording Industry Association of America (RIAA) began certifying gold records in 1958, *Billboard* and other entertainment trade magazines would periodically publish a list of million-selling singles. These lists were compiled primarily from reports submitted by the record companies; they were not audited.

EXPLANATION OF SYMBOLS

★30★ Number next to the artist name denotes an artist's ranking among the Top 150 Artists (see ranking on pages 297-298)

2^3 Superior number to the right of the #1 or #2 peak position is the total weeks the single held that position; taken from the chart on which it achieved its highest total

+ Indicates that a title peaked in the year after it first charted

/ Divides a two-sided hit; highest peak side listed first with the lower peak side indented beneath it

LETTER(S) IN BRACKETS AFTER TITLES

C - Comedy
F - Foreign language
I - Instrumental
N - Novelty

R - Re-entry, reissue or re-release of a previously recorded single by that artist
S - Spoken
X - Christmas

14

PEAK POSITIONS ATTAINED ON VARIOUS POP CHARTS

Billboard published three weekly Pop singles charts from 1940 to 1954: Best Sellers, Disk Jockey and Juke Box. The peak position shown in the Peak column for these charts is taken from the chart on which it achieved its highest position. The individual peak positions attained on these three charts is listed to the right of the A-side title. The following letter designations precede the peak position attained on these charts:

- **S:** Best Sellers (<u>S</u>ales)
- **A:** Disk Jockey (<u>A</u>irplay)
- **J:** Juke Box

See "Reseaching *Billboard's* Pop Singles Charts" on page 11 for a complete explanation of the above charts.

B-SIDES

If an A-side is recorded by a duo and its B-side is recorded by a solo artist, then the solo artist's name is shown in parentheses after the B-side.

ARTIST'S TOP YEAR

The year of an artist's peak popularity (based on yearly pop chart performance) is listed in **bold type** to the right of the artist's name. The same point system used to determine an artist's overall rank (see page 296) is also used to determine their top year. This top year is based on their peak year and not the year they first charted. For example, an artist may chart a record with a debut date of 12/29/51+. The plus sign after the date indicates the record peaked in 1952; and, therefore, the record is considered a 1952 hit.

Although the year from which an artist generates the most points is generally considered the top year, some exceptions are made. For example, if an artist has a lone major hit in one year, and a few minor hits in another year which collectively accumulate more points, the year of the major hit is considered the artist's top year.

Artist's hits listed in our *Pop Memories* book (from 1890 to 1940) and our *Top Pop Singles 1955-1999* book were also used to determine their top year on the pop charts.

PICTURES OF THE TOP 100 ARTISTS

A picture of each of the Top 100 artists is shown next to their bio in the artist section. Each Top 100 artist's overall ranking is listed to the right of their name. The overall ranking of artists from 101 through 150 is listed to the left of their name.

#1 HITS ON OTHER CHARTS

Singles that peaked at #1 on the *R&B* or *Country* charts are indicated in the title notes, along with each single's total weeks at #1.

ARTIST & TITLE NOTES

Below nearly every artist name is a brief biography about the artist. Most song titles have a line or two of notes indicating backing vocalists, backing orchestras, guest instrumentalists, the title of the movie in which the song was featured and its stars, etc. Duets and other important name variations, as they appear on the record label, are shown in bold capital letters. Shown in italics are titles of movies, TV programs, Broadway shows, symphonies and other major works. In the title notes, "#" refers to peak chart position. If a song charted earlier than 1940 or later than 1954, the artist, peak position and year of popularity are shown in a title note. Various versions of the same song that charted from 1940-54 are not noted, but can be seen listed together in the song title section.

Names of artists mentioned in the artist and title notes that have pop-charted hits of their own are highlighted in bold type. For example, since **Count Basie** is mentioned in Tab Smith's artist biography, his name is shown in bold type. A name is only shown in bold the <u>first</u> time it appears in an artist's biography and in bold every time it appears in a title note.

ORCHESTRA and VOCALIST GUIDE

The orchestras and/or vocalists featured on recordings by an artist with 10 or more chart hits are listed below the artist's biography. The artist must have a combined total of at least six different orchestras and/or vocalists to warrant this listing. The number(s) to the immediate right of the orchestra/vocalist refers to the sequential count shown to left of the chart hit(s) on which they appear. The name of the orchestra/vocalist is highlighted in bold type if they have their own chart hits in the book.

CONSECUTIVE TOP 10 HITS

The peak positions of an artist's string of five or more consecutive Top 10 hits are shaded in a box, so you can quickly spot their hot streaks. Reissues or early label affiliation releases and B-side chart hits do not break a string nor count within a string. The peak position of a non-Top 10 B-side chart hit (of a Top 10 A-side chart hit) is shaded in a string even if it appears at the end of a string.

ARTIST'S BIGGEST HITS

Listed in bold type right below the artist's biography in rank order are:

>   the Top 3 hits of every artist with 10 to 19 charted hits and
>   the Top 5 hits of every artist with 20 or more charted hits.

<u>Underlined</u> is the highest-charting title for an artist who charted five or more titles. The top hit is a reflection of chart performance only and may or may not relate to an artist's best seller or most popular song over the years. A tie is broken based on total weeks at the peak position, total weeks in the Top 5, total weeks in the Top 10, and finally, total weeks charted. To qualify as the artist's top hit, <u>the artist must be the lead singer</u> on the song and not a secondary or "featuring" artist. For example, "Cry" by Johnnie Ray & The Four Lads is not underlined as The Four Lads top hit because Johnnie Ray is the main vocalist with The Four Lads supplying backing vocals. Their song "Skokiaan (South African Song)" is underlined as their top hit.

COMPLETE RECORD PRICE GUIDE

The values listed in the price ($) column reflect the current estimated value of an original commercial copy in near-mint condition. You will note that the very collectible records such as hard-to-find, small independent label hits and early R&B singles reflect a much higher price than most.

Please consider that everyone's estimate of value may be different, especially when considering geographics. A $10 record in this book may be worth $20 in New York City, but only $5 in the South. Also, variations of the original commerical release, such as promotional copies, mistakes or differentiations on the label, etc. can vastly increase, or in rare cases, decrease the price of a record.

The 7" 45 rpm record was introduced in 1948 by RCA Victor. Within three years, all of the major labels and most of the smaller independent labels were issuing both 45s and 78s. These early 45s are hard to find and their values are much greater than their counterpart 78s. You will see a dramatic increase in value when an artist's label switches from 78 to 45 numbers.

RECORD LABELS AND NUMBERS

For all hits prior to 1950 (with a few exceptions), the record label, label numbers and prices are for the 78 rpm release.

For any hit beginning in 1949, the record label and number is for the 45 rpm release if it was issued as such. By late 1950, most labels were issuing 45s (see prefix listing below). If the 45 and 78 label numbers were different, then the 78 number is listed in title trivia.

Our abbreviation of Capitol Americana is Capitol Amer. in this section.

The following is a basic guide of the label number prefixes used by the major record companies for their configurations. These prefixes will help you determine whether a record was issued as a 45 or 78.

For small independent labels that did not use prefixes to indicate 45 or 78, a bracketed 45 '(45)' after the label number indicates its issuance as a 45.

Record Company	Label # Prefix	Configuration	Genre
Bluebird	54-	45 rpm	all
Bluebird	30-	78 rpm	all
Capitol*	54- and F	45 rpm	all
Capitol	57-	78 rpm	all
Columbia	1-	7" 33-1/3 rpm	all
Columbia**	6- and 4-	45 rpm	all
Coral	9-	45 rpm	all
Decca	9-	45 rpm	all
Mercury	-X45	45 rpm	all
MGM	K	45 rpm	all
RCA	47-	45 rpm	pop
RCA	48-	45 rpm	country
RCA	49-	45 rpm	classical
RCA	20-	78 rpm	pop
RCA	21-	78 rpm	country
RCA	10-	78 rpm	classical

*Capitol initially used a 54- for the 45 rpm, before adopting the F- prefix.

**Columbia was one of the last record companies to produce the 45 rpm. They initially manufactured seven-inch singles on the 33-1/3-speed as the microgroove record with a small hole in the middle. When they began to produce the seven-inch record on 45-rpm-speed, they initially used the 6- prefix followed by a three-digit number, before going to the 4- prefix and their regular five-digit number.

A bit of history...Beginning in the late '40s, RCA and Columbia battled over the standard for record configurations. In 1948, Columbia introduced, into a market dominated by the 78 rpm, their microgroove long-play record album at 33-1/3 rpm. Six months later, RCA introduced their 45 rpm, unbreakable, seven-inch single, with a large hole in the middle. Columbia then began issuing 7" microgroove singles on the new 33-1/3-speed with a small hole in the middle. By mid-1950, the record-buying public made the 45 rpm single the winner over the 33-1/3 single. Thirty-three and one-third became the standard speed of the record album. By the mid-50's, the 45 rpm single dominated the 78 rpm single, which were phased out by the end of the decade.

RCA Victor 45 RPM Records

Series	Size	*Suggested List Price	Record Color	Remarks
47-0000 to 47-1999	7″	$0.65	Yellow	Children's
47-2000	7″	.65	Black	Popular
48-0000	7″	.65	Green	Country-Western
49-0000	7″	.95	Red	Classical (Red Seal)
50-0000	7″	.65	Rose	Blues-Rhythm
51-0000	7″	.65	Blue-Green	International
52-0000	7″	.65	Blue	Popular Classics

Chart of RCA Victor's 45 RPM label numbers with prefixes
(taken from an RCA Victor 1949 catalog)

SINGLES BY ARTIST

Lists, alphabetically by artist name, every single that made *Billboard's* Pop Singles charts from 1940-1954.

Here's a quick reference guide to our symbols. Refer to *RESEARCHING BILLBOARD'S POP SINGLES CHARTS* and *USER'S GUIDE* for complete descriptions. (The artist and titles below are NOT real.)

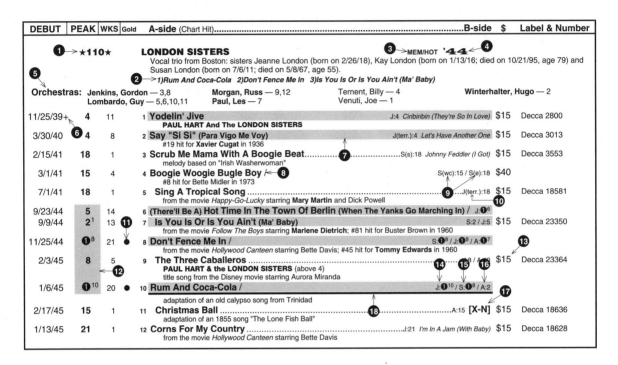

1. artist's ranking within the Top 150 artists
2. artist's top 3 or top 5 hits
3. more hits in *Top Pop Singles* (HOT) *book* and/or *Pop Memories* (MEM) *book*
4. artist's peak year of popularity
5. index of backing orchestras and/or vocalists for major artists
6. peaked in the following year
7. Top 5 hit (shaded)
8. 2-sided hit separator
9. Regional Best Sellers chart (e=East Coast, mw=Midwest, s=South, wc=West Coast)
10. Juke Box territorial chart (terr.)
11. Gold record • (million seller)
12. Top 10 hit streak (shaded)
13. current value of near-mint commercial single
14. peak position on Juke box charts (J:)
15. peak position on Best Sellers charts (S:)
16. peak position on Disk Jockey charts (A:)
17. Christmas/Novelty song [X-N]
18. artist's biggest hit (underlined)

A

ACUFF, Roy
MEM '38

Born on 9/15/03 in Maynardville, Tennessee. Died of heart failure on 11/23/92 (age 89). The Smoky Mountain Boys consisted of Pete "Bashful Brother Oswald" Kirby (dobro), Howard "Howdy" Forrester (fiddle; died on 8/1/87, age 65) and Jimmie Riddle (harmonica, piano; died on 12/10/82, age 64). Formed Acuff-Rose music publishing company in 1942 and the Hickory record label in 1953 with Fred Rose. Twice ran for governor of Tennessee. Elected to the Country Music Hall of Fame in 1962. Won Grammy's Lifetime Achievement Award in 1987. Known as "The King Of Country Music."

ROY ACUFF and his SMOKY MOUNTAIN BOYS:

2/12/44	13	1	1 The Prodigal Son ....J:13 *Not A Word From Home* $25	Okeh 6716
12/30/44	21	1	2 I'll Forgive You But I Can't Forget..........................J(terr.):21 *Write Me Sweetheart* (C&W #6) $25	Okeh 6723

above 2 were Top 5 Country hits

ALEXANDER BROTHERS
'50

9/2/50	26	1	Goodnight Irene ....A:26 *Home Cookin'* $20	Mercury 5465-X45

#75 hit for Billy Williams in 1959

ALLEN, Rex
HOT '62

Born on 12/31/20 in Willcox, Arizona. Died after being struck by a car on 12/17/99 (age 78). Country singer/guitarist/actor. Professional rodeo rider as a teenager. Starred in numerous western movies. Narrator for several Disney nature movies. Played "Bill Baxter" on TV's *Frontier Doctor*. Father of country singer Rex Allen Jr.

2/10/51	20	4	1 The Roving Kind..A:20 *Wreck Of The John B* $25	Mercury 5573-X45

adapted from the English folk song "The Pirate Ship"

4/28/51	28	2	2 Sparrow In The Tree Top ....J:28 *Always You* $25	Mercury 5597-X45

Jud Conlon Singers (backing vocals); Harry Geller (orch.)

8/1/53	8	15	●	3 Crying In The Chapel ....J:8 / S:10 / A:12 *I Thank The Lord* $20	Decca 9-28758

#3 hit for Elvis Presley in 1965; above 2 were Top 10 Country hits

ALLISON, Fran
'51

Born on 11/20/07 in La Porte City, Iowa. Died of bone marrow failure on 6/13/89 (age 81). Former school teacher. Host of the children's TV series *Kukla, Fran & Ollie.*

4/22/50	26	1	1 Peter Cottontail ....A:26 *Stars Are The Windows Of Heaven* $20	RCA Victor 47-3727
7/14/51	20	2	2 Too Young ....A:20 *Lies* $20	RCA Victor 47-4105

#13 hit for Donny Osmond in 1972; Jack Fascinato (orch., above 2)

AMECHE, Lola
'51

5/26/51	21	10	1 Pretty Eyed Baby ....J:21 / S:24 *That's The One For Me* $20	Mercury 5609-X45

AL TRACE and His Orchestra; Vocal by Lola Ameche
new lyrics to the R&B song "Satchelmouth Baby" recorded by Deek Watson and The Brown Dots on Manor 1026 in 1946

7/28/51	24	3	2 Hitsity Hotsity...J:24 *Josephine* $20	Mercury 5675-X45

LOLA AMECHE; Al Trace Orchestra

AMES BROTHERS ★36★
MEM/HOT '50

Pop vocal group from Malden, Massachusetts: brothers Ed (born on 7/9/27), Gene (born on 2/13/23), Joe (born on 5/3/21) and Vic (born on 5/20/25; died in a car crash on 1/23/78, age 52) Urick. Changed last names professionally to Ames. Own TV series in 1955. Ed recorded solo and played "Mingo" on TV's *Daniel Boone.* Also see **Milt Herth Trio.**

1)You You You 2)Rag Mop 3)Sentimental Me 4)Undecided 5)The Naughty Lady Of Shady Lane

Orchestras: Bloch, Ray — 18-20   Manning, Marty — 16,17   **Ross, Roy** — 2-12   Winterhalter, Hugo — 21-23
Brown, Les — 14,15   Osborne, Mary, Trio — 1   Smeck, Roy — 13

8/21/48	21	3		1 A Tree In The Meadow........................A:21 / S:22 / J:28 *On The Street Of Regret* $15	Decca 24411
				MONICA LEWIS and AMES BROTHERS	
2/26/49	23	4		2 You, You, You Are The One ....S:23 / A:26 / J:27 *More Beer* $15	Coral 60015
				adaptation of the German folk song "Du, Du Liegst Mir Im Herzen"	
4/16/49	29	1		3 Cruising Down The River....................A:29 *Clancy Lowered The Boom!* $15	Coral 60035
1/14/50	❶²	14	●	4 Rag Mop A:❶² / S:❶¹ / J:2 *Sentimental Me* $15	Coral 60140
1/28/50	❶¹	27	●	5 Sentimental Me A:❶¹ / J:2 / S:3 *Blue Prelude* $15	Coral 60173
				charted its first 7 weeks on Coral 60140; then on Coral 60173 from 3/18/50 on; charted by Elvis Presley in 1961 on the album Something for Everybody	
3/18/50	13	6		6 (Put Another Nickel In) Music! Music! Music!...............A:13 / J:18 / S:30 *I Love Her Oh! Oh! Oh!* $15	Coral 60153
				#54 hit for The Sensations in 1961	
6/24/50	17	4		7 Stars Are The Windows Of Heaven ....J:17 *Hoop Dee Doo* $25	Coral 9-60209
8/12/50	5	19		8 Can Anyone Explain? (No, No, No!) J:5 / S:7 / A:8 *Sittin' 'N Starin' 'N Rockin'* $25	Coral 9-60253
11/11/50	26	2		9 Thirsty For Your Kisses ....J:26 *I Don't Mind Being Alone (When I'm All Alone With You)* $25	Coral 9-60300
11/25/50	20	6		10 Oh Babe!..J:20 *To Think You've Chosen Me* $25	Coral 9-60327
12/23/50	29	1		11 The Thing ....J:29 *Music By The Angels* **[N]** $25	Coral 9-60333
				uses melody of the traditional song "The Tailor's Boy"	
6/23/51	16	3		12 Wang Wang Blues.....................................A:16 / J:20 / S:30 *Who'll Take My Place* $25	Coral 9-60489
				#1 hit for Paul Whiteman in 1921	
9/8/51	21	4		13 Hawaiian War Chant (Ta-Hu-Wa-Hu-Wai) ....J:21 / S:25 *Sweet Leilani* $25	Coral 9-60510
				#89 hit for Billy Vaughn in 1959	
9/29/51	2¹	21	●	14 Undecided / A:2 / J:4 / S:6	
				AMES BROTHERS And LES BROWN And His Band Of Renown	
				#8 hit for Ella Fitzgerald & Chick Webb in 1939	
10/6/51	23	4		15 Sentimental Journey.....................................J:23 $20	Coral 9-60566
				LES BROWN And His Band Of Renown And AMES BROTHERS	
				#1 hit for Les Brown (with Doris Day) in 1945	
1/19/52	19	4		16 I Wanna Love You / A:19 / S:21 / J:25	
				melody is similar to "Muskrat Ramble"	
3/29/52	29	1		17 I'll Still Love You J:29 $20	Coral 9-60617

AMES BROTHERS — Cont'd

8/16/52	13	8		18 **Aufwiederseh'n Sweetheart** ....J:13 / A:26 *Break The Bands That Bind Me*	$20	Coral 9-60773
				The Sweetland Singers (backing vocals)		
8/23/52	18	7		19 **String Along** ....A:18 / J:19 / S:28 *Absence Makes The Heart Grow Fonder (For Somebody Else)*	$20	Coral 9-60804
10/18/52	15	5		20 **My Favorite Song** ....A:15 / J:27 *Al-Lee-O! Al-Lee-Ay!*	$20	Coral 9-60846
6/27/53	❶8	31	●	21 **You You You** ....A:❶8 / J:❶6 / S:2 *Once Upon A Tune*	$15	RCA Victor 47-5325
				#49 hit for Mel Carter in 1966		
3/20/54	6	18		22 **The Man With The Banjo** ....J:6 / A:6 / S:7 *Man, Man, Is For The Woman Made*	$15	RCA Victor 47-5644
11/20/54	3	15	●	23 **The Naughty Lady Of Shady Lane** ....S:3 / A:3 / J:3 *Addio*	$15	RCA Victor 47-5897

ANDERS, Laurie — see GODFREY, Arthur

ANDERSON, Ivie '44

Born on 7/10/05 in Gilroy, California. Died of asthma on 12/28/49 (age 44). Black female vocalist with **Duke Ellington**'s band from 1931-42. Appeared in the 1937 movie *A Day At The Races*.

4/8/44	16	1		**Mexico Joe**..J(terr.):16 *When The Ships Come Sailing Home Again* (Burke)	$50	Exclusive 3113
				IVIE ANDERSON with CEELE BURKE'S ORCH.		

ANDERSON, Leroy MEM '52

Born on 6/29/08 in Cambridge, Massachusetts. Died on 5/18/75 (age 66). Composer of the Christmas standard "Sleigh Ride." Served as an arranger for the **Boston Pops Orchestra**.

ANDERSON, Leroy, And His "Pops" Concert Orchestra:

3/31/51	12	14	●	1 **The Syncopated Clock** ....S:12 / A:26 *The Waltzing Cat* [I]	$15	Decca 9-40201
				famous as the theme song of TV's *Late Show*; also released on Decca's Gold Label Series #16005		
12/29/51+	❶5	38	●	2 **Blue Tango** ....S:❶5 / A:2 / J:3 *Belle Of The Ball* [I]	$15	Decca 9-27875
				#16 hit for Bill Black's Combo in 1960		

ANDREWS SISTERS ★4★ MEM '44

Vocal trio from Minneapolis: sisters **Patty Andrews** (born on 2/26/18), Maxene Andrews (born on 1/13/16; died on 10/21/95, age 79) and LaVerne Andrews (born on 7/6/11; died on 5/8/67, age 55). The trio appeared together in several movies; Patty and Maxene starred in the 1974 Broadway musical *Over There*. The Andrews Sisters pre-1940 #1 hit: "Bei Mir Bist Du Schön."

1)Rum And Coca-Cola 2)Shoo-Shoo Baby 3)Don't Fence Me In
4)(There'll Be A) Hot Time In The Town Of Berlin (When The Yanks Go Marching In) 5)I Can Dream, Can't I?

Orchestras: Harmonica Gentlemen — 44-46   Lombardo, Guy — 30,37,52,61   Schoen, Vic — 2-29,31-34,36,   Venuti, Joe — 1
Heywood, Eddie — 35   Morgan, Russ — 56,59,60   38-43,49-51,54,62-64,67-69   Young, Victor — 70
Jenkins, Gordon —   Paul, Les — 36   Ternent, Billy — 47,48
57,58,65,66,71

11/25/39+	4	11		1 **Yodelin' Jive** ....J:4 *Ciribiribin (They're So In Love)*	$15	Decca 2800
				BING CROSBY And The ANDREWS SISTERS		
3/30/40	4	8		2 **Say "Si Si" (Para Vigo Me Voy)** ....J(terr.):4 *Let's Have Another One*	$15	Decca 3013
				#19 hit for **Xavier Cugat** in 1936		
4/13/40	7	2		3 **The Woodpecker Song** ....J:7 *Down By The Ohio*	$15	Decca 3065
10/12/40	19	1		4 **Beat Me Daddy, Eight To A Bar**.................................S(mw):19 *Pennsylvania 6-5000*	$15	Decca 3375
12/7/40	8	3		5 **Ferryboat Serenade (La Piccinina)** ....S:8 *Hit The Road*	$15	Decca 3328
2/15/41	18	1		6 **Scrub Me Mama With A Boogie Beat**..............................S(s):18 *Johnny Feddler (I Got)*	$15	Decca 3553
				melody based on "Irish Washerwoman"		
3/1/41	15	4		7 **Boogie Woogie Bugle Boy**......................S(wc):15 / S(e):18 *Bounce Me Brother With A Solid Four*	$40	Decca 3598
				#8 hit for Bette Midler in 1973		
5/3/41	5	11		8 **I'll Be With You In Apple Blossom Time** ....S:5 *I, Yi, Yi, Yi, Yi (I Like You Very Much)*	$15	Decca 3622
				#2 hit for Charles Harrison in 1920; #31 hit for Tab Hunter in 1959; above 2 from the movie *Buck Privates* starring Abbott & Costello		
1/10/42	17	3		9 **The Shrine Of Saint Cecilia** ....S(s):17 *Jack Of All Trades*	$15	Decca 4097
				#96 hit for Faron Young in 1957		
8/15/42	19	1		10 **Three Little Sisters** ....S(wc):19 *(Toy Balloon) Boolee Boolee Boon*	$15	Decca 18319
				from the movie *Private Buckaroo* starring the Andrews Sisters		
10/31/42	6	4		11 **Strip Polka** / S:6		
12/19/42	17	2		12 **Mister Five By Five**.........................S(wc):17 / S(s):20	$15	Decca 18470
				from the movie *Behind The Eight Ball* starring the Ritz Brothers		
11/6/43	2⁴	9	●	13 **Pistol Packin' Mama** / ....S:2 / J:7		
1/8/44	6	5		14 **Vict'ry Polka** J:6	$15	Decca 23277
				BING CROSBY and the ANDREWS SISTERS (above 2)		
1/1/44	❶9	19		15 **Shoo-Shoo Baby** / ....J:❶9 / S:2		
1/29/44	17	3		16 **Down In The Valley** J:17	$15	Decca 18572
				from the movie *Moonlight And Cactus* starring the Andrews Sisters; traditional tune written in 1845; #71 hit for Solomon Burke in 1962		
6/17/44	8	13		17 **Straighten Up And Fly Right** / J:8		
				#73 hit for the DeJohn Sisters in 1958		
7/8/44	18	1		18 **Tico-Tico** ....J(terr.):18	$15	Decca 18606
				Brazilian samba featured in the Disney movie *Saludos Amigos*		
7/1/44	18	1		19 **Sing A Tropical Song** ....J(terr.):18 *There'll Be A Jubilee*	$15	Decca 18581
				from the movie *Happy-Go-Lucky* starring **Mary Martin** and Dick Powell		
9/23/44	❶6	14		20 **(There'll Be A) Hot Time In The Town Of Berlin (When The Yanks Go Marching In)** / J:❶6		
9/9/44	2¹	13		21 **Is You Is Or Is You Ain't (Ma' Baby)** ....S:2 / J:5	$15	Decca 23350
				from the movie *Follow The Boys* starring **Marlene Dietrich**; #81 hit for Buster Brown in 1960		
11/25/44	❶8	21	●	22 **Don't Fence Me In** ....S:❶8 / J:❶8 / A:❶7	$15	Decca 23364
				from the movie *Hollywood Canteen* starring Bette Davis; #45 hit for **Tommy Edwards** in 1960		
2/3/45	8	5		23 **The Three Caballeros** ....J:8 / A:10		
				BING CROSBY & the ANDREWS SISTERS (above 4)		
				title song from the Disney movie starring Aurora Miranda		

DEBUT	PEAK	WKS	Gold	A-side (Chart Hit) .... B-side	$	Label & Number
				ANDREWS SISTERS — Con'td		
1/6/45	❶¹⁰	20	●	24 **Rum And Coca-Cola** / J:❶¹⁰ / S:❶⁸ / A:2		
				adaptation of an old calypso song from Trinidad		
2/17/45	15	1		25 **One Meat Ball** A:15	$15	Decca 18636
				adaptation of an 1855 song "The Lone Fish Ball"		
1/13/45	21	1		26 **Corns For My Country** ....J:21 *I'm In A Jam (With Baby)*	$15	Decca 18628
				from the movie *Hollywood Canteen* starring Bette Davis		
2/3/45	2¹	12		27 **Ac-Cent-Tchu-Ate The Positive** S:2 / A:3 / J:3 *There's A Fellow Waiting In Poughkeepsie*	$15	Decca 23379
				from the movie *Here Come The Waves* starring Crosby and **Betty Hutton**		
9/15/45	2¹	11		28 **Along The Navajo Trail** J:2 / A:4 / S:5 *Good, Good, Good (That's You—That's You)*	$15	Decca 23437
				BING CROSBY and the ANDREWS SISTERS (above 2)		
9/29/45	8	8		29 **The Blond Sailor** ....J:8 / A:10 *Lily Belle*	$15	Decca 18700
2/2/46	9	5		30 **Money Is The Root Of All Evil** (Take It Away, Take It Away, Take It Away) ..A:9 *Johnny Fedora*	$15	Decca 23474
				ANDREWS SISTERS and GUY LOMBARDO And His Royal Canadians		
3/16/46	12	1		31 **Patience And Fortitude** ....A:12 *Red River Valley*	$15	Decca 18780
8/3/46	2¹	19	●	32 **South America, Take It Away** / S:2 / A:3 / J:3		
				from the Broadway musical *Call Me Mister* starring Betty Garrett		
8/10/46	14	2		33 **Get Your Kicks On "Route 66!—"** ....J:14 / A:15	$15	Decca 23569
				BING CROSBY and the ANDREWS SISTERS (above 2)		
				#61 hit for Depeche Mode in 1988		
8/31/46	17	1		34 **I Don't Know Why (I Just Do)** ....J:17 *Azusa*	$15	Decca 18899
				#2 hit for **Wayne King** in 1931; #12 hit for Linda Scott in 1961		
9/28/46	15	5		35 **The House Of Blue Lights** ....J:15 *A Man Is A Brother To A Mule*	$15	Decca 23641
				ANDREWS SISTERS and EDDIE HEYWOOD and HIS ORCHESTRA		
				#9 hit for Chuck Miller in 1955		
10/19/46	4	13		36 **Rumors Are Flying** J:4 / S:6 / A:7 *Them That Has—Gets* (Andrews Sisters & Eddie Heywood)	$15	Decca 23656
				ANDREWS SISTERS with LES PAUL		
12/21/46	7	4	●	37 **Christmas Island** ....J:7 / A:13 *Winter Wonderland* [X]	$15	Decca 23722
				ANDREWS SISTERS and GUY LOMBARDO And His Royal Canadians		
7/5/47	10	10		38 **Tallahassee** ....J:10 / A:13 *Go West, Young Man!*	$15	Decca 23885
				BING CROSBY and the ANDREWS SISTERS		
				from the movie *Variety Girl* starring Mary Hatcher		
9/27/47	2¹	17		39 **Near You** J:2 / A:3 / S:4 *How Lucky You Are*	$15	Decca 24171
				#10 hit for Roger Williams in 1958		
10/18/47	7	2		40 **The Lady From 29 Palms**........................J:7 *The Turntable Song ('Round, An' 'Round, An' 'Round)*	$15	Decca 23976
11/22/47+	3	11		41 **Civilization (Bongo, Bongo, Bongo)** S:3 / J:3 / A:7 *Bread And Butter Woman* [N]	$15	Decca 23940
				DANNY KAYE - ANDREWS SISTERS		
				from the Broadway musical *Angel In The Wings* starring Hank Ladd		
4/17/48	3	17		42 **Toolie Oolie Doolie (The Yodel Polka)** / J:3 / S:4 / A:9		
6/12/48	14	7		43 **I Hate To Lose You** J:14	$15	Decca 24380
5/15/48	21	5		44 **Heartbreaker** / J:21		
5/22/48	21	3		45 **(Every Time They Play The) Sabre Dance** J:21	$15	Decca 24427
				based on Khatchaturian's "Gayne Ballet Suite"		
7/17/48	18	6		46 **The Woody Woodpecker**	$15	Decca 24462
				J:18 / S:19 *Put 'Em In A Box, Tie 'Em With A Ribbon (And Throw 'Em In The Deep Blue Sea)* [N]		
				DANNY KAYE - ANDREWS SISTERS		
				from the Walter Lanz cartoon; different than #3 above		
9/4/48	5	14		47 **Underneath The Arches** / J:5 / S:10 / A:16		
				#11 hit for George Olsen in 1933		
9/4/48	8	12		48 **You Call Everybody Darling** ....J:8 / S:16 / A:19	$15	Decca 24490
10/9/48	12	14		49 **Cuanto La Gusta** ....S:12 / J:13 / A:27 *The Matador*	$15	Decca 24479
				CARMEN MIRANDA - ANDREWS SISTERS		
				from the movie *A Date With Judy* starring Wallace Beery and Jane Powell		
11/6/48	23	2		50 **A Hundred And Sixty Acres** ....J:23 *At The Flying "W"*	$15	Decca 24481
				BING CROSBY and the ANDREWS SISTERS		
11/20/48	23	2		51 **Bella Bella Marie** ....J:23 / S:24 *The Money Song*	$15	Decca 24499
				from the movie *Music Man* starring **Phil Brito**		
1/8/49-	26	1		52 **Christmas Island** ....J:26 *Winter Wonderland* [X-R]	$15	Decca 23722
				ANDREWS SISTERS and GUY LOMBARDO And His Royal Canadians		
1/22/49	12	6		53 **The Pussy Cat Song**		
				(Nyow! Nyot Nyow!).....................S:12 / J:13 / A:14 *Don't Worry 'Bout Strangers* (Andrews Sisters) [N]	$15	Decca 24533
				PATTY ANDREWS and BOB CROSBY		
1/29/49	30	3		54 **More Beer!**........................J:30 *Let A Smile Be Your Umbrella (On A Rainy Day)*	$15	Decca 24548
5/7/49	30	1		55 **I'm Bitin' My Fingernails And Thinking Of You** ..J:30 *Don't Rob Another Man's Castle* (C&W #6)	$20	Decca 24592
				ANDREWS SISTERS and ERNEST TUBB with The Texas Troubadors		
7/16/49	21	1		56 **Now! Now! Now! Is The Time** ....S:21 *Oh, You Sweet One (The Schnitzelbank Song)*	$15	Decca 24664
				ANDREWS SISTERS - RUSS MORGAN And His Orchestra		
9/24/49+	❶⁵	25	●	57 **I Can Dream, Can't I?** / A:❶⁵ / S:❶⁴ / J:❶³		
				from the Broadway musical *Right This Way* starring Guy Robertson; #5 hit for **Tommy Dorsey** in 1938		
10/1/49	20	2		58 **The Wedding Of Lili Marlene** J:20	$15	Decca 24705
12/17/49+	15	4		59 **Charley My Boy** / ....J:15 / S:17		
				#3 hit for **Eddie Cantor** in 1924		
12/10/49	22	2		60 **She Wore A Yellow Ribbon** ....S:22 / J:24 / A:29	$15	Decca 24812
				ANDREWS SISTERS - RUSS MORGAN And His Orchestra (above 2)		
				title song from the movie starring John Wayne; written in 1917		
1/7/50-	18	1		61 **Merry Christmas Polka**................................S:18 *Christmas Candles* [X]	$15	Decca 24748
				ANDREWS SISTERS and GUY LOMBARDO And His Royal Canadians		
1/28/50	6	17		62 **Quicksilver** / ....J:6 / S:8		
1/21/50	24	4		63 **Have I Told You Lately That I Love You?**...........................J:24	$15	Decca 24827
				BING CROSBY & the ANDREWS SISTERS (above 2)		
				#29 hit for Ricky Nelson in 1957		
1/28/50	23	3		64 **The Wedding Samba** ....S:23 / J:23 *I See, I See (Asi Asi)*	$15	Decca 24841
				CARMEN MIRANDA and ANDREWS SISTERS		

DEBUT	PEAK	WKS	Gold	A-side (Chart Hit) .... B-side	$	Label & Number

ANDREWS SISTERS — Cont'd

DEBUT	PEAK	WKS		A-side	B-side	$	Label & Number
5/13/50	**❶**²	21		65 **I Wanna Be Loved**	A:**❶**² / J:2 / S:3 *I've Just Got To Get Out Of The Habit*	$20	Decca 9-27007
9/23/50	22	1		66 **Can't We Talk It Over**	J:22 *There Will Never Be Another You*	$20	Decca 9-27115
				#10 hit for **Bing Crosby** & the **Mills Brothers** in 1932			
12/9/50+	22	4		67 **A Bushel And A Peck**	J:22 *Guys And Dolls*	$20	Decca 9-27252
				from the Broadway musical *Guys And Dolls* starring Robert Alda and Vivian Blaine			
3/3/51	17	7		68 **A Penny A Kiss–A Penny A Hug**	J:17 *Zing Zing-Zoom Zoom*	$20	Decca 9-27414
3/10/51	8	15		69 **Sparrow In The Tree Top**	J:8 / A:9 / S:12 *Forsaking All Others*	$20	Decca 9-27477
				BING CROSBY And ANDREWS SISTERS			
6/16/51	19	6		70 **Too Young**	J:19 / A:28 / S:30 *Gotta Find Somebody To Love*	$20	Decca 9-27569
				PATTY ANDREWS			
				#13 hit for Donny Osmond in 1972			
6/30/51	24	1		71 **I'm In Love Again**	S:24 *It Never Entered My Mind*	$20	Decca 9-27635
				featured in the Broadway musical *The Greenwich Village Follies Of 1925* starring Tom Howard			

ANTHONY, Ray, and His Orchestra ★39★ MEM/HOT '50

Born Raymond Antonini on 1/20/22 in Bentleyville, Pennsylvania; raised in Cleveland. Trumpeter/bandleader. Joined **Al Donahue** in 1939, then with **Glenn Miller** and **Jimmy Dorsey** from 1940-42. Led U.S. Army band. Own band in 1946. Own TV series in 1956. Appeared in the movie *Daddy Long Legs*. Wrote "Bunny Hop." Married for a time to actress Mamie Van Doren.

1)At Last 2)Dragnet 3)Count Every Star 4)Harbor Lights 5)Can Anyone Explain

Vocalists: Anthony Choir, The — 14,16,21   Deauville, Ronnie — 3,5-10   Miller, Marcie — 15,19   Skyliners, The — 2,6,8,11,13,18
Craig, Gloria — 13   Mercer, Tommy — 11-16,18,19   Noel, Dick — 1,2,4

DEBUT	PEAK	WKS		A-side	B-side	$	Label & Number
11/19/49+	11	10		1 **A Dreamer's Holiday**	A:11 / J:15 *Bye Bye Baby*	$10	Capitol 57-761
1/28/50	21	1		2 **Sitting By The Window**	A:21 *Dixie*	$20	Capitol F794
4/22/50	7	15		3 **Sentimental Me**	A:7 / J:18 / S:22 *Spaghetti Rag*	$15	Capitol F923
				recorded by Elvis Presley in 1961 on the album *Something for Everybody*			
5/27/50	4	21		4 **Count Every Star**	A:4 / S:17 / J:19 *The Darktown Strutters' Ball*	$15	Capitol F979
				#35 hit for Donnie & The Dreamers in 1961			
7/29/50	19	2		5 **Roses**	A:19 *National Emblem March*	$15	Capitol F1001
9/2/50	5	13		6 **Can Anyone Explain**	A:5 / S:27 *Skycoach*	$15	Capitol F1131
9/30/50	4	17		7 **Harbor Lights /**	A:4 / S:15 / J:15	$15	Capitol F1190
				#6 hit for Frances Langford in 1937; #8 hit for The Platters in 1960			
10/21/50	9	14		8 **Nevertheless (I'm In Love With You)**	A:9 / S:15 / J:19		
				featured in the movie *Three Little Words* starring Fred Astaire; #5 hit for Jack Denny in 1931			
1/13/51	26	1		9 **The Night Is Young And You're So Beautiful**	A:26 *All Anthony And No Cleopatra*	$15	Capitol F1310
				from the stage show *Casa Manana*; #5 hit for **Jan Garber** in 1937			
1/27/51	13	16		10 **Be My Love**	A:13 / J:22 *I Wonder What's Become Of Sally?*	$15	Capitol F1352
				from the movie *The Toast Of New Orleans* starring **Mario Lanza**			
6/2/51	17	7		11 **These Things I Offer You (For A Lifetime)**	A:17 *Here's To Your Illusions*	$15	Capitol F1522
7/28/51	28	1		12 **My Truly, Truly Fair**	J:28 / A:30 *Pretty Eyed Baby*	$15	Capitol F1583
11/10/51	10	11		13 **Undecided**	A:10 *Just A Moment More*	$15	Capitol F1824
				#8 hit for **Ella Fitzgerald** & Chick Webb in 1939			
2/9/52	2¹	15		14 **At Last**	A:2 / S:22 / J:22 *I'll See You In My Dreams*	$15	Capitol F1912
				from the movie *Orchestra Wives* starring George Montgomery; #47 hit for Etta James in 1961			
2/23/52	24	2		15 **Bermuda**	A:24 *(Here Am I) Broken Hearted*	$15	Capitol F1956
6/28/52	10	4		16 **As Time Goes By**	A:10 *Scatterbrain*	$15	Capitol F2104
				written in 1931; from the Broadway musical *Everybody's Welcome* starring Frances Williams and featured in the movie *Casablanca* starring Humphrey Bogart			
7/26/52	21	4		17 **Slaughter On Tenth Avenue (Parts I & II)**	A:21 **[I]**	$15	Capitol 6F2085
				from the Broadway musical *On Your Toes* starring **Ray Bolger**; featured in the movie *Words And Music* starring Mickey Rooney; #35 hit for The Ventures in 1964; issued with a picture sleeve			
10/11/52	20	1		18 **Marilyn**	A:20 *Randle's Island*	$25	Capitol F2207
				song dedicated to Marilyn Monroe			
11/1/52	13	5		19 **Bunny Hop**	A:13 *Blow, Man, Blow!*	$15	Capitol F2251
				an instrumental version issued on Capitol F2427 with a picture sleeve in 1953; #70 hit for The Applejacks in 1959			
8/29/53	2¹	13		20 **Dragnet**	A:2 / S:3 / J:4 *Dancing In The Dark* **[I]**	$20	Capitol F2562
				theme from the TV series *Dragnet* starring Jack Webb ('52-'59 and '67-'70); also see the "Dragnet" parodies by **Stan Freberg**			
12/26/53+	15	4		21 **O Mein Papa (Oh! My Papa)**	A:15 *Secret Love*	$15	Capitol F2678
				Ray Anthony (trumpet); from the Swiss musical comedy *Fireworks*; #94 hit for Dick Lee in 1961			
9/25/54	18	5		22 **Skokiaan**	A:18 / S:24 *Say Hey* **[I]**	$15	Capitol F2896
				South African song, named for a Zulu tribal drink; #70 hit for **Bill Haley & His Comets** in 1960			

ARDEN, Toni HOT '50

Born Antoinette Aroizzone in New York City. Female singer. Sang with **Al Trace** in 1945 and Joe Reichman in 1946.

DEBUT	PEAK	WKS		A-side	B-side	$	Label & Number
11/19/49+	7	14		1 **I Can Dream, Can't I?**	A:7 / J:29 *A Little Love, A Little Kiss*	$10	Columbia 38612
				TONI ARDEN with HUGO WINTERHALTER and his ORCHESTRA and Choir			
				7" 33-1/3 rpm: 1-377; from the Broadway musical *Right This Way* starring Guy Robertson; #5 hit for **Tommy Dorsey** in 1938			
6/2/51	15	9		2 **Too Young**	A:15 *Too Late Now*	$15	Columbia 4-39271
				#13 hit for Donny Osmond in 1972			
5/24/52	14	8		3 **Kiss Of Fire /**	A:14 / S:27		
				adapted from the 1913 Argentine tango "El Choclo"			
6/21/52	24	2		4 **I'm Yours**	A:24	$15	Columbia 4-39737
				Percy Faith (orch., above 3)			

ARMEN, Kay   MEM/HOT '44

Born in Chicago. Singer/actress. Appeared in the 1955 movie musical *Hit The Deck*.

KAY ARMEN And The Balladiers:

DEBUT	PEAK	WKS	Gold	A-side	$	Label & Number
1/8/44	7	3		1 **The Dreamer** /..J:7		
1/15/44	10	9		2 **How Sweet You Are**..S:10 / J:10	$10	Decca 18566

above 2 from the movie Thank Your Lucky Stars starring Eddie Cantor and Dennis Morgan

★109★ ARMSTRONG, Louis   MEM/HOT '32

Born Daniel Louis Armstrong on 8/4/01 in New Orleans. Died of heart failure on 7/6/71 (age 69). Legendary jazz singer/trumpet player. Nicknamed "Satchmo." Moved to Chicago in 1922 to join King Oliver's band. Formed own band in 1926. Known for his uniquely raspy, scat-tinged vocals. Numerous appearances on radio, TV and in movies. Won Grammy's Lifetime Achievement Award in 1972. Inducted into the Rock and Roll Hall of Fame in 1990. Armstrong's pre-1940 #1 hit: "All Of Me."

1)(When We Are Dancing) I Get Ideas 2)You Won't Be Satisfied (Until You Break My Heart) 3)A Kiss To Build A Dream On

DEBUT	PEAK	WKS	Gold	A-side	$	Label & Number
4/6/46	10	2		1 **You Won't Be Satisfied (Until You Break My Heart)**......J:10 / A:14 *The Frim Fram Sauce* (R&B #4)	$20	Decca 23496
				ELLA FITZGERALD AND LOUIS ARMSTRONG Bob Haggart (orch.)		
10/22/49	19	3		2 **That Lucky Old Sun (Just Rolls Around Heaven All Day)**............J:19 / A:22 / S:24 *Blueberry Hill*	$20	Decca 24752
				Gordon Jenkins (orch.); #20 hit for Ray Charles in 1964; B-side charted in 1956 on Decca 30091 (#29)		
10/14/50	28	1		3 **La Vie En Rose**...J:28 *C'est Si Bon*	$25	Decca 9-27113
11/18/50	30	1		4 **Can Anyone Explain? (No, No, No!)**......................J:30 *Dream A Little Dream Of Me*	$25	Decca 9-27209
				ELLA FITZGERALD-LOUIS ARMSTRONG		
6/30/51	19	2		5 **Gone Fishin'**.....................................A:19 *We All Have A Song In Our Heart* (Crosby)	$25	Decca 9-27623
				BING CROSBY And LOUIS ARMSTRONG John Scott Trotter (orch.)		
9/1/51	10	16		6 **(When We Are Dancing) I Get Ideas** / J:10 / A:11 / S:13		
				adapted from the Argentine tango "Adios Muchachos"		
11/24/51+	16	11		7 **A Kiss To Build A Dream On**..................................A:16 / S:17 / J:19	$25	Decca 9-27720
				from the movie *The Strip* starring Mickey Rooney; Sy Oliver (orch.: #3, 4, 6 & 7)		
1/12/52	19	3		8 **When It's Sleepy Time Down South**.................A:19 / J:27 *It's All In The Game*	$25	Decca 9-27899
				LOUIS ARMSTRONG And GORDON JENKINS And His Orchestra Armstrong's theme song; he originally recorded it in 1931 on Okeh 41504; #6 hit for Paul Whiteman in 1931		
6/7/52	20	2		9 **Kiss Of Fire**..A:20 *I'll Walk Alone*	$20	Decca 9-28177
				adapted from the 1913 Argentine tango "El Choclo"		
10/18/52	19	2		10 **Takes Two To Tango**.................................A:19 / S:28 *I Laughed At Love*	$20	Decca 9-28394

★113★ ARNOLD, Eddy   MEM/HOT '48

Born Richard Edward Arnold on 5/15/18 in Henderson, Tennessee. Legendary country singer/songwriter/guitarist. Lead singer of **Pee Wee King**'s Golden West Cowboys from 1940-43. Hosted own TV show from 1952-56. Nicknamed "The Tennessee Plowboy" on all RCA recordings through 1954. Elected to the Country Music Hall of Fame in 1966.

1)Bouquet Of Roses 2)Just A Little Lovin' (Will Go A Long, Long Way) 3)Anytime

EDDY ARNOLD, The Tennessee Plowboy and his Guitar:

DEBUT	PEAK	WKS	Gold	A-side	$	Label & Number
5/15/48	17	1	●	1 **Anytime** /...J:17		
				written in 1921		
5/15/48	29	1		2 **What A Fool I Was**...J:29	$30	RCA Victor 20-2700
				45 rpm: 48-0002		
6/19/48	13	27	●	3 **Bouquet Of Roses** / J:13 / S:21 / A:26		
7/3/48	18	1		4 **Texarkana Baby**...J:18	$30	RCA Victor 20-2806
				45 rpm: 48-0001; issued with RCA's first text sleeve: "One Of The 101 Best Sellers"		
9/11/48	13	9	●	5 **Just A Little Lovin' (Will Go A Long, Long Way)**..........J:13 *My Daddy Is Only A Picture* (C&W #5)	$30	RCA Victor 20-3013
				45 rpm: 48-0026		
12/11/48	23	2		6 **A Heart Full Of (For a Handful of Kisses)** /..................................J:23		
1/8/49	30	1		7 **Then I Turned And Walked Slowly Away**..............................J:30	$30	RCA Victor 20-3174
				45 rpm: 48-0025		
3/19/49	23	2		8 **Don't Rob Another Man's Castle**..........J:23 *There's Not A Thing (I Wouldn't Do For You)* (C&W #3)	$30	RCA Victor 21-0002
				45 rpm: 48-0042		
5/28/49	23	1		9 **One Kiss Too Many**...................................J:23 / S:27 *The Echo Of Your Footsteps* (C&W #2)	$35	RCA Victor 48-0083
				78 rpm: 21-0051		
8/20/49	19	2		10 **I'm Throwing Rice (At the Girl That I Love)**......J:19 *Show Me The Way Back To Your Heart* (C&W #7)	$35	RCA Victor 48-0080
				78 rpm: 21-0083; all of above were #1 Country hits (59 weeks total - except #2 and 7 both hit #2)		

AUGUST, Jan   HOT '50

Born Jan Augustoff on 9/24/04 in New York City. Died on 1/17/76 (age 71). Male pianist.

DEBUT	PEAK	WKS	Gold	A-side	$	Label & Number
12/28/46	7	2		1 **Misirlou**...A:7 / J:16 *Babalu* [I]	$30	Diamond 2009
				song published in 1934		
5/20/50	8	12		2 **Bewitched**.......................................J:8 / A:12 / S:17 *Blue Prelude* [I]	$20	Mercury 5399-X45
				JAN AUGUST & Jerry Murad's HARMONICATS from the Broadway musical *Pal Joey* starring Gene Kelly; #50 hit for the Betty Smith Group in 1958		
6/3/50	22	2		3 **Buffalo Billy**...A:22 *I Never Had A Worry In The World*	$20	Mercury 5420-X45
				ROBERTA QUINLAN, JERRY MURAD'S HARMONICATS & JAN AUGUST adaptation of the 1844 tune "Buffalo Gals (Won't You Come Out Tonight)"; also see **Russ Morgan**'s "Dance With A Dolly"		
11/18/50	30	1		4 **Molasses, Molasses It's Icky Sticky Goo**...................A:30 *Orange Colored Sky* [N]	$20	Mercury 5504-X45
				ROBERTA QUINLAN with JAN AUGUST Orchestra Marty Manning (choral group); variation on the melody of "A-Tisket, A-Tasket"		

AUTRY, Gene ★62★   MEM/HOT **'50**
Born Orvon Gene Autry on 9/29/07 in Tioga, Texas. Died of respiratory failure on 10/2/98 (age 91). Country singer/songwriter/guitarist/actor. Sang on KVOO in Tulsa in 1929 as "The Oklahoma Yodeling Cowboy." Joined the WLS *National Barn Dance* in 1930. Hosted own *Melody Ranch* radio series. Acted in over 90 western movies. Starred in own TV western series from 1950-56. Later owned several businesses (including the California Angels major league baseball team). Elected to the Country Music Hall of Fame in 1969.

1)Rudolph, The Red-Nosed Reindeer 2)Peter Cottontail 3)Frosty The Snow Man

DEBUT	PEAK	WKS	Gold	A-side	B-side	$	Label & Number
8/15/42	17	1		1 **Jingle Jangle Jingle** ....S(wc):17 *I'm A Cow Poke Pokin' Along*		$25	Okeh 6690
				from the movie *The Forest Rangers* starring Fred MacMurray			
1/15/44	16	1		2 **Tweedle-O-Twill** ....J:16 *Take Me Back Into Your Heart*		$20	Columbia 36587
				originally released on Okeh 6680 in 1942			
12/27/47	9	2	●	3 **Here Comes Santa Claus (Down Santa Claus Lane)** ....S:9 / A:13 *An Old-Fashioned Tree* **[X]**		$20	Columbia 37942
11/20/48	17	3		4 **Buttons And Bows** ....J:17 / A:26 *Can't Shake The Sands Of Texas From My Shoes*		$20	Columbia 20469
				from the movie *The Paleface* starring **Bob Hope**; #104 hit for The Browns in 1962			
12/11/48	8	5		5 **Here Comes Santa Claus (Down Santa Claus Lane)** ....S:8 / A:9 / J:20 *An Old-Fashioned Tree* **[X-R]**		$20	Columbia 20377
12/3/49	❶¹	6	●	6 **Rudolph, The Red-Nosed Reindeer** S:❶¹ / A:3 / J:4 *If It Doesn't Snow On Christmas* **[X]**		$15	Columbia 38610
				The Pinafores (backing vocals); 7" 33-1/3 rpm: 1-375; issued with a picture sleeve on Columbia's Children's Series MJV 4-56; new version charted by Autry in 1957 on Challenge 1010 (#70)			
1/7/50-	24	1		7 **Here Comes Santa Claus (Down Santa Claus Lane)** ....S:24 *An Old-Fashioned Tree* **[X-R]**		$20	Columbia 20377
				7" 33-1/3 rpm: 2-392; issued with a picture sleeve on Columbia's Children's Series MJV 4-84			
4/1/50	5	5	●	8 **Peter Cottontail** ....S:5 / A:7 / J:19 *The Funny Little Bunny (With The Powder Puff Tail)*		$20	Columbia 38750
				7" 33-1/3 rpm: 1-575; issued with a picture sleeve on Columbia's Children's Series MJV 4-68			
12/2/50	3	7		9 **Rudolph, The Red-Nosed Reindeer** S:3 / J:6 / A:9 *If It Doesn't Snow On Christmas* **[X-R]**		$15	Columbia 38610
12/9/50	7	6	●	10 **Frosty The Snow Man** ....S:7 *When Santa Claus Gets Your Letter* **[X]**		$20	Columbia 6-742
				The Cass County Boys (vocals); 78 rpm: 38907; issued with a picture sleeve on Columbia's Children's Series MJV 4-75			
3/31/51	19	2		11 **Peter Cottontail** ....S:19 *The Funny Little Bunny (With The Powder Puff Tail)* **[R]**		$20	Columbia 38750
12/22/51	16	3		12 **Rudolph, The Red-Nosed Reindeer** ....S:16 *Here Comes Santa Claus* **[X-R]**		$20	Columbia 4-39463
12/20/52	9	2		13 **The Night Before Christmas Song** ....A:9 *Look Out The Window (The Winter Song)* **[X]**		$20	Columbia 4-39876
				ROSEMARY CLOONEY & GENE AUTRY			
				issued with a picture sleeve on Columbia's Children's Series MJV 4-149; Carl Cotner (orch.: #10 & 13)			
12/27/52	13	1		14 **Rudolph, The Red-Nosed Reindeer** ....A:13 *Here Comes Santa Claus* **[X-R]**		$20	Columbia 4-39463

AYRES, Mitchell   MEM **'40**
Born Mitchell Agress on 12/24/10 in Milwaukee. Died after being struck by a car on 9/5/69 (age 58). Formerly with Little Jack Little's band. Musical director for **Perry Como** from 1948-61.

       MITCHELL AYRES and his Fashions in Music:

DEBUT	PEAK	WKS	Gold	A-side	B-side	$	Label & Number
6/8/40	❶²	11		1 **Make-Believe Island** ....J:❶² / S:10 *Poor Ballerina*		$10	Bluebird 10687
6/28/41	13	1		2 **Just A Little Bit South Of North Carolina** ....S(wc):13 *And The Band Played On*		$10	Bluebird 11101
				Mary Ann Mercer (vocal, above 2)			
10/11/41	19	1		3 **I Don't Want To Set The World On Fire** ....S(wc):19 *When Are We Going To Land Abroad?*		$10	Bluebird 11275
				Meredith Blake and the Four Trumpet-Ayres (vocals)			

B

BAILEY, Pearl   **'52**
Born on 3/29/18 in Newport News, Virginia. Died of heart disease on 8/17/90 (age 72). Vocalist with **Cootie Williams**. Appeared in several movies and Broadway shows. Married to drummer Louis Bellson from 1952 until her death.

DEBUT	PEAK	WKS	Gold	A-side	B-side	$	Label & Number
9/27/52	7	17		**Takes Two To Tango** ....S:7 / J:9 / A:16 *Let There Be Love*		$20	Coral 9-60817
				Don Redman (orch.)			

BAKER, Dick "Two Ton"   MEM **'47**
Born Richard Baker on 5/2/16 in Chicago. Died in May 1975 (age 59). Pianist/bandleader.

      DICK "TWO TON" BAKER And His Music Makers:

DEBUT	PEAK	WKS	Gold	A-side	B-side	$	Label & Number
10/11/47	12	5		1 **Near You** ....J:12 *I'm A Lonely Little Petunia*		$10	Mercury 5066
				#10 hit for Roger Williams in 1958			
1/10/48	13	1		2 **Too Fat Polka** ....J:13 *With A Hey And A Hi And A Ho-Ho-Ho* **[N]**		$10	Mercury 5079

BAKER, Kenny   MEM **'42**
Born on 9/30/12 in Monrovia, California. Died of a heart attack on 8/10/85 (age 72). Singer/actor. Appeared in several movies and Broadway shows.

DEBUT	PEAK	WKS	Gold	A-side	B-side	$	Label & Number
12/28/40	18	1		1 **There I Go** ....S(s):18 *You And Your Kiss*		$10	Victor 27207
2/8/41	15	3		2 **You Walk By** ....S(e):15 / S(s):15 / S(wc):18 / S(mw):20 *Chapel In The Valley*		$10	Victor 27250
				Leonard Joy (orch., above 2)			
6/27/42	14	4		3 **Johnny Doughboy Found A Rose In Ireland** ....S(mw):14 / S(wc):15 / S(e):20 *There Are Rivers To Cross (Before We Meet Again)*		$10	Decca 18274
7/25/42	18	1		4 **Always In My Heart** ....S(mw):18 *Blue Tahitian Moon*		$10	Decca 18262
				title song from the movie starring Kay Francis; #82 hit for Los Indios Tabajaras in 1964; Harry Sosnik (orch., above 2)			
2/8/47	11	2		5 **The Old Lamp-Lighter** ....J:11 *Love Walked In*		$10	Decca 23781
				#5 hit for The Browns in 1960			
5/24/47	16	1		6 **My Adobe Hacienda** ....J:16 *This Is The Night*		$10	Decca 23846
				KENNY BAKER and RUSS MORGAN And His Orchestra (above 2)			

BALLADIERS, The — see **ARMEN, Kay**

BALLANTINE, Eddie — see **OWENS, Jack**

BARBER, Ray '51
Baritone ballad singer.

| 9/29/51 | 23 | 1 | | **Because Of You** ....A:23 *The Girls We Never Did Wed* | $15 | Mercury 5643-X45 |

78 rpm: 5625; **Russ Case** (orch.); song published in 1940; featured in the 1951 movie *I Was An American Spy* starring Ann Dvorak; #71 hit for Chris Montez in 1967

BARBOUR, Dave, And His Orchestra '50
Born on 5/28/12 in Flushing, Long Island, New York. Died on 12/11/65 (age 53). Guitarist with Red Norvo, **Hal Kemp**, **Artie Shaw** and **Benny Goodman**. Married to **Peggy Lee** from 1943-51; co-wrote several of her biggest hits.

| 9/9/50 | 27 | 1 | | **Mambo Jambo**...S:27 *Dave's Boogie* [I] | $20 | Capitol F973 |

written by Perez Prado; first pressings labeled as "The Mambo (Qué Rico El Mambo)"

BARKER, Blue Lu MEM '49
Born Louise Dupont on 11/13/13 in New Orleans. Died of cancer on 5/7/98 (age 84). Black female jazz singer. Married New Orleans jazz guitarist/banjo player Danny Barker in 1930. First recorded with Erskine Butterfield as "Lu Blue" in 1938.

| 12/18/48+ | 4 | 14 | | **A Little Bird Told Me** A:4 / J:10 / S:16 *What Did You Do To Me?* | $20 | Capitol 15308 |

#4 R&B hit; accompanied by husband Danny Barker's band

BARNET, Charlie, and his Orchestra ★69★ MEM '40
Born on 10/26/13 in New York City. Died of pneumonia on 9/4/91 (age 77). Saxophonist/vocalist/bandleader. Nicknamed "Mad Mab." First led his own band at age 16. One of the first white band leaders to feature black musicians. Married six times. His most famous recording is 1939's "Cherokee."

1)Where Was I? 2)I Hear A Rhapsody 3)Pompton Turnpike

| **Vocalists:** | Andrews, Huck — 11 | Leary, Ford, & The | McCall, Mary Ann — 1,2,4 | Taylor, Larry — 3 |
| | **Carroll, Bob** — 8 | Three Moaxes — 9 | Robey, Art — 12 | Wayne, Frances — 10 |

7/6/40	**❶²**	9		1	**Where Was I?** J:❶² / S:6 *'Deed I Do*	$10	Bluebird 10669
					from the movie *'Til We Meet Again* starring Merle Oberon and George Brent		
7/27/40	15	1		2	**The Breeze And I** ....S(wc):15 *The Fable Of The Rose*	$10	Bluebird 10696
					adapted from the Spanish song "Andalucia"; #8 hit for Caterina Valente in 1955		
8/3/40	16	3		3	**All This And Heaven Too** ....S(wc):16 *Where Do You Keep Your Heart?*	$10	Bluebird 10751
					title song from the movie starring Bette Davis		
9/7/40	13	1		4	**Six Lessons From Madame La Zonga** ....S(wc):13 *Lament For May*	$10	Bluebird 10743
10/26/40	3	6		5	**Pompton Turnpike** S:3 *I Don't Want To Cry Any More* [I]	$10	Bluebird 10825
					Billy May (trumpet)		
12/28/40	17	1		6	**Redskin Rhumba** / ....S(e):17 [I]		
2/8/41	17	1		7	**Southern Fried** ....S(wc):17 [I]	$10	Bluebird 10944
1/11/41	**2⁶**	11		8	**I Hear A Rhapsody** S:2 *The Moon Is Cryin' For Me*	$10	Bluebird 10934
3/15/41	18	1		9	**Whatcha Know Joe** ....S(mw):18 *Isola Bella (That Little Swiss Isle)*	$10	Bluebird 10918
4/17/43	15	4		10	**That Old Black Magic** / ....S(e):15	$10	
					from the movie *Star Spangled Rhythm* starring **Bing Crosby** and **Bob Hope**; #13 hit for **Sammy Davis, Jr.** in 1955		
12/9/44	22	1		11	**I Don't Want Anybody At All (If I Can't Have You)** J:22	$10	Decca 18541
					from the movie *Sleepytime Gal* starring Judy Canova		
6/8/46	13	2		12	**Cement Mixer (Put-ti, Put-ti)** ....J:13 *Madame Butterball* [N]	$10	Decca 18862

BARRON, Blue, and his Orchestra ★90★ MEM '49
Born Harry Friedland on 3/22/11 in Cleveland. Sweet-band leader. Singer Tommy Ryan took over the band while Barron served in WWII. Continued performing at hotels and ballrooms into the 1960s.

1)Cruising Down The River 2)You Were Only Fooling 3)Darn That Dream

| **Vocalists:** | Beers, Bobby — 9 | Burke, Clyde — 4,5 | Goodfellow, Johnny — 10 | ensemble — 3,6-8 |
| | **Blue Notes, The** — 9,10 | Carlyle, Russ — 1,2 | Hawkins, Dolores — 5 | |

3/9/40	10	2		1	**Darn That Dream**...J:10 *Peace, Brother!*	$10	Bluebird 10525
					from the Broadway musical *Swingin' The Dream* starring **Louis Armstrong**		
1/25/41	19	3		2	**You Walk By**...S(s):19 / S(wc):20 *It's Eight O'Clock*	$10	Bluebird 10894
					"Music of Yesterday and Today Styled the Blue Barron Way" (above 2)		
5/24/47	14	3		3	**Chi-Baba Chi-Baba ("My Bambino Go To Sleep")** ....S:14 *Oh! My Aching Heart*	$10	MGM 10027
7/3/48	9	17		4	**You Were Only Fooling** ....S:9 / A:11 / J:26 *It's Easy When You Know How*	$10	MGM 10185
					#30 hit for **Vic Damone** in 1965		
11/27/48	20	2		5	**A Strawberry Moon (In A Blueberry Sky)**.................J:20 *There's A Quaker Down In Quaker Town*	$10	MGM 10297
1/29/49	**❶⁷**	20	●	6	**Cruising Down The River** / A:❶⁷ / J:❶³ / S:❶²	$10	MGM 10346
2/26/49	18	6		7	**Powder Your Face With Sunshine (Smile! Smile! Smile!)** ....J:18 / A:19	$10	MGM 10346
7/2/49	25	1		8	**Whose Girl Are You** ....S:25 *Open The Door Polka*	$10	MGM 10412
4/1/50	19	8		9	**Are You Lonesome Tonight** ....S:19 / A:26 / J:26 *Penny Wise And Love Foolish*	$15	MGM K10628
					John McCormick (narration); #4 hit for Vaughn Deleath in 1927; #1 hit for Elvis Presley in 1960		
4/7/51	26	1		10	**Let Me In** ....J:26 *Somebody's Thinking Of You Tonight*	$15	MGM K10923

BARTON, Eileen ★128★   MEM '50

Born on 11/24/29 in Brooklyn, New York. Started in the late 1930s as a child performer on Milton Berle's radio show.

3/11/50	❶10	16	●	1 **If I Knew You Were Comin' (I'd've Baked A Cake)** A:❶10 / J:❶3 / S:❶2 *Poco, Loco In The Coco*	$50	National 9103
				the New Yorkers (backing vocals); also released on Mercury 5392		
7/15/50	25	3		2 **May I Take Two Giant Steps?** ....A:25 *If You Saw What I Saw*	$30	National 9112
12/8/51+	10	11		3 **Cry**...A:10 *Hold Me Just A Little Longer, Daddy*	$20	Coral 9-60592
				Neal Hefti (orch.); #18 hit for Ronnie Dove in 1966		
3/22/52	30	1		4 **Wishin'**..A:30 *When You're Near Me*	$20	Coral 9-60651
				Paul Neilson (orch.)		
2/28/53	17	3		5 **Pretend**...J:17 / S:18 / A:19 *Too Proud To Cry*	$20	Coral 9-60927
				Jack Pleis (orch.)		

BASIE, Count, and his Orchestra ★72★   MEM/HOT '47

Born William Basie on 8/21/04 in Red Bank, New Jersey. Died of cancer on 4/26/84 (age 79). Legendary jazz, big-band leader/pianist/organist. Learned organ from **Fats Waller**. First recorded with own band for Decca in 1937. Appeared in several movies. His best-known recording, "One O'Clock Jump" (1937), is in the Grammy Hall of Fame. Won Grammy's Lifetime Achievement Award in 2002.

1)Open The Door, Richard! 2)I Ain't Mad At You (You Ain't Mad At Me) 3)Free Eats

Vocalists: Donnelly, Ted — 12   Johnson, Bill — 8   Moore, Ann — 4   Sherman, Lynne — 1
           Edison, Harry — 8   Miller, Taps — 12   Rushing, Jimmy — 2,3,6,7   ensemble — 9,12

7/3/43	17	1		1 **All Of Me** ....S(wc):17 *Rusty Dusty Blues* (R&B #6)	$15	Columbia 36675
				#1 hit for both **Louis Armstrong** and Paul Whiteman in 1932; #3 Country hit for Willie Nelson in 1978		
1/22/44	16	1		2 **For The Good Of Your Country**...........................J:16 *Time On My Hands*	$15	Columbia 36685
10/6/45	10	1		3 **Jimmy's Blues** ....A:10 *Taps Miller*	$15	Columbia 36831
1/26/46	12	1		4 **Jivin' Joe Jackson**...A:12 *Queer Street*	$15	Columbia 36889
4/6/46	10	10		5 **The Mad Boogie /**...A:10 **[I]**	$15	
3/23/46	14	2		6 **Patience And Fortitude** A:14	$15	Columbia 36946
9/14/46	8	4		7 **Blue Skies** ....A:8 *The King*	$15	Columbia 37070
				featured in the movie *Blue Skies* starring Fred Astaire and **Bing Crosby**; #1 hit for Ben Selvin in 1927		
2/8/47	❶1	7		8 **Open The Door, Richard!** S:❶1 / A:❶1 / J:2 *Me And The Blues* **[N]**	$15	RCA Victor 20-2127
4/19/47	7	3		9 **Free Eats** ....A:7 *Bill's Mill*	$15	RCA Victor 20-2148
6/14/47	12	2		10 **One O'Clock Jump** ....A:12 *John's Idea* **[I]**	$20	Decca 25056
				Basie's theme song; selected for NARAS Hall of Fame; originally charted in 1937 (#15) on Decca 1363; also see the 1941 version by **Metronome All Star Band** featuring Basie		
6/28/47	8	4		11 **One O'Clock Boogie** ....A:8 *Meet Me At No Special Place (And I'll Be There At No Particular Time)* **[I]**	$15	RCA Victor 20-2262
8/2/47	7	4		12 **I Ain't Mad At You (You Ain't Mad At Me)** ....A:7 *The Jungle King (You Ain't a Doggone Thing)*	$15	RCA Victor 20-2314

BAXTER, Les, and His Orchestra ★91★   MEM/HOT '56

Born on 3/14/22 in Mexia, Texas. Died of a heart attack on 1/15/96 (age 73). Orchestra leader/arranger. Began as a conductor on radio shows in the 1930s. Member of **Mel Torme**'s vocal group, the Mel-Tones. Musical arranger for Capitol Records in the 1950s. Composed numerous movie scores.

3/17/51	12	14		1 **Beautiful Brown Eyes**...................J:12 / S:23 / A:27 *At The Close Of A Long Long Day*	$20	Capitol F1393
				JIMMY WAKELY and the LES BAXTER CHORUS		
7/14/51	4	21		2 **Because Of You** A:4 / S:9 / J:14 *Somewhere, Somehow, Someday*	$15	Capitol F1760
				song published in 1940; featured in the 1951 movie *I Was An American Spy* starring Ann Dvorak; #71 hit for Chris Montez in 1967		
3/15/52	10	17		3 **Blue Tango**..A:10 / S:22 / J:25 *Please, Mr. Sun* **[I]**	$15	Capitol F1966
				#16 hit for Bill Black's Combo in 1960		
6/28/52	26	3		4 **Lonely Wine** ....A:26 *Lost In Meditation*	$15	Capitol F2106
7/26/52	20	6		5 **Auf Wiederseh'n, Sweetheart** ....A:20 *Padam..Padam..*	$15	Capitol F2143
4/4/53	2³	22		6 **April In Portugal** S:2 / A:2 / J:2 *Suddenly* **[I]**	$15	Capitol F2374
				Portuguese song originally published as "Coimbra"		
5/23/53	7	12		7 **Ruby** ....A:7 / S:9 / J:12 *A Little Love (Can Go A Long, Long Way)* **[I]**	$15	Capitol F2457
				Danny Welton (harmonica solo); theme from the movie *Ruby Gentry* starring Jennifer Jones and Charlton Heston; #28 hit for Ray Charles in 1960		
10/3/53	13	3		8 **I Love Paris** ....A:13 *Gigi*	$15	Capitol F2479
				from the Broadway musical *Can Can* starring Lilo		
7/31/54	4	13		9 **The High And The Mighty** ....A:4 / S:6 / J:16 *More Love Than Your Love* **[I]**	$15	Capitol F2845
				title song from the movie starring John Wayne		

BEE, Molly   '52

Born Molly Beachboard on 8/18/39 in Oklahoma City. Country singer/actress. Appeared in several movies and Broadway shows.

| 1/3/53- | 19 | 1 | | **I Saw Mommy Kissing Santa Claus** ....A:19 *Willy Claus (Little Son of Santa Claus)* **[X-N]** | $20 | Capitol F2285 |
| | | | | Van Alexander (orch.) | | |

BELAFONTE, Harry   MEM/HOT '57

Born on 3/1/27 in Harlem, New York (Jamaican mother and West Indian father). Calypso singer/actor. Rode the crest of the calypso craze to worldwide stardom. Acted in several movies. Replaced **Danny Kaye** in 1987 as UNICEF goodwill ambassador. Father of actress Shari Belafonte. Won Grammy's Lifetime Achievement Award in 2000.

| 4/11/53 | 19 | 1 | | **Gomen Nasai (Forgive Me)**...........................J:19 *Springfield Mountain (Too-Roo-De-Nay)* | $15 | RCA Victor 47-5210 |

BELL SISTERS, The '52

Vocal duo of Cynthia (born in 1935) and Kay (born in 1940) Strother. Both were born in Kentucky and raised in Seal Beach, California. Bell is their mother's maiden name.

DEBUT	PEAK	WKS		A-side		$	Label & Number
1/5/52	7	16		1 **Bermuda** ....A:7 / S:8 / J:8 *June Night*		$15	RCA Victor 47-4422
3/1/52	10	11		2 **Wheel Of Fortune**.......................................A:10 / J:17 *Poor Whip-Poor-Will (Move Over, Move Over)*		$15	RCA Victor 47-4520
				#83 hit for LaVern Baker in 1960			
3/15/52	19	6		3 **Hambone** ....A:19 / J:24 *Mama's On The Warpath* [N]		$20	RCA Victor 47-4584
				PHIL HARRIS and THE BELL SISTERS			
				Henri René (orch., above 3)			

BELLTONES, The '51

9/8/51	30	1		**Way Up In North Carolina** ....A:30 *Stop Worryin' (You'll Never Get Out Of This World Alive)*		$25	Mercury 5692-X45
				originally released on the regional Colonial label in North Carolina			

BENEKE, Tex ★66★ MEM '46

Born Gordon Beneke on 2/12/14 in Fort Worth, Texas. Died of respiratory failure on 5/30/2000 (age 86). Featured tenor saxophonist for **Glenn Miller** from 1938-42. Fronted Miller's band for one year after Miller's death. Went on to form his own band which continued to play in the Miller style.

1)*Anniversary Song* 2)*Give Me Five Minutes More* 3)*Hey! Ba-Ba-Re-Bop*

Vocalists: Beneke, Tex — 1,3,6,8   Douglas, Glenn — 12   Malvin, Artie — 2,4,9   Stevens, Garry — 10
     Crew Chiefs, The — 2-5,8   Lane, Lillian — 4,7   Mello Larks, The — 10

TEX BENEKE with THE GLENN MILLER ORCHESTRA:

DEBUT	PEAK	WKS		A-side		$	Label & Number
5/25/46	4	9		1 **Hey! Ba-Ba-Re-Bop** /	S:4 / A:7 / J:9		
6/22/46	19	1		2 **The Whiffenpoof Song** *Baa! Baa! Baa!*...J:19		$10	RCA Victor 20-1859
				theme song of the Yale University Glee Club since 1909; #96 hit for Bob Crewe in 1960			
6/1/46	12	1		3 **It Couldn't Be True! (Or Could It?)** ....A:12 *One More Tomorrow*		$10	RCA Victor 20-1835
6/15/46	15	2		4 **Cynthia's In Love** ....A:15 *Strange Love*		$10	RCA Victor 20-1858

TEX BENEKE and the MILLER ORCHESTRA:

8/3/46	9	3		5 **I Know**..A:9 *Ev'rybody Loves My Baby (My Baby)*		$10	RCA Victor 20-1914
8/17/46	4	18		6 **Give Me Five Minutes More** ....J:4 / S:6 / A:6 *Texas Tex*		$10	RCA Victor 20-1922
				featured in the movie *Sweetheart Of Sigma Chi* starring Elyse Knox			
10/19/46	9	5		7 **Passe** ....A:9 / J:18 *The Woodchuck Song*		$10	RCA Victor 20-1951
12/21/46+	6	8		8 **A Gal In Calico** / ....S:6 / J:6 / A:7			
2/1/47	11	3		9 **Oh, But I Do** A:11		$10	RCA Victor 20-1991
				above 2 from the movie *The Time, The Place And The Girl* starring Dennis Morgan			
2/22/47	3	11		10 **Anniversary Song** ....A:3 / S:3 / J:4 *Hoodle Addle*		$10	RCA Victor 20-2126
				from the movie *The Jolson Story* starring Larry Parks; based on Ivanovic's 1880 song "Danube Waves"			

TEX BENEKE and his ORCHESTRA:

4/10/48	5	17		11 **St. Louis Blues March** ....S:5 / J:6 / A:8 *Cherokee Canyon* [I]		$10	RCA Victor 20-2722
				Glenn Miller's Army Air Force Band made famous this arrangement of the W.C. Handy classic			
11/12/49+	12	12		12 **I Can Dream, Can't I** ....A:12 / J:18 / S:27 *Over Three Hills*		$10	RCA Victor 20-3553
				45 rpm: 47-3046; from the Broadway musical *Right This Way* starring Guy Robertson; #5 hit for **Tommy Dorsey** in 1938			

BENNETT, Tony ★45★ MEM/HOT '51

Born Anthony Benedetto on 8/3/26 in Queens, New York. **Bob Hope** gave him his first important concert engagement in 1949 and suggested that he change his then-stage name, Joe Bari, to Tony Bennett. Has remained in the forefront of American jazz and ballad vocalists from 1951 to the present. Appeared in the movie *The Oscar*. Won Grammy's Lifetime Achievement Award in 2001.

1)*Because Of You* 2)*Rags To Riches* 3)*Cold, Cold Heart*

DEBUT	PEAK	WKS		A-side		$	Label & Number
6/23/51	❶¹⁰	32	●	1 **Because Of You** /	J:❶¹⁰ / S:❶⁸ / A:❶⁸		
				song published in 1940; featured in the 1951 movie *I Was An American Spy* starring Ann Dvorak; #71 hit for Chris Montez in 1967			
6/30/51	12	17		2 **I Won't Cry Anymore** ....J:12 / S:14		$20	Columbia 4-39362
7/28/51	❶⁶	27	●	3 **Cold, Cold Heart** ....S:❶⁶ / J:❶³ / A:3 *While We're Young*		$20	Columbia 4-39449
				#1 Country hit for **Hank Williams** in 1951; #96 hit for **Dinah Washington** in 1962			
10/13/51	16	11		4 **Blue Velvet** / ....A:16 / S:18 / J:18			
				#1 hit for Bobby Vinton in 1963			
10/27/51	17	5		5 **Solitaire** ....A:17 / S:24 / J:25		$20	Columbia 4-39555
5/24/52	15	10		6 **Here In My Heart** ....J:15 / A:17 / S:20 *I'm Lost Again*		$20	Columbia 4-39745
8/16/52	16	5		7 **Have A Good Time** ....J:16 / S:27 *Please, My Love*		$20	Columbia 4-39764
				#31 hit for Sue Thompson in 1962			
3/7/53	20	1		8 **Congratulations To Someone** ....A:20 *Take Me*		$20	Columbia 4-39910
9/19/53	❶⁸	25	●	9 **Rags To Riches** ....J:❶⁸ / A:❶⁷ / S:❶⁶ *Here Comes That Heartache Again*		$20	Columbia 4-40048
				#45 hit for Sunny & The Sunliners in 1963			
11/28/53+	2²	19	●	10 **Stranger In Paradise** ....A:2 / S:3 / J:3 *Why Does It Have To Be Me?*		$20	Columbia 4-40121
				from the Broadway musical *Kismet* starring **Alfred Drake**; song based on a theme from "Polovetsian Dances" in the 1888 opera *Prince Igor*; issued with a picture sleeve ('45' hole in the middle)			
3/13/54	7	12		11 **There'll Be No Teardrops Tonight**......................J:7 / A:9 / S:11 *My Heart Won't Say Good-Bye*		$15	Columbia 4-40169
				written by **Hank Williams** in 1949			
8/7/54	8	7		12 **Cinnamon Sinner**..A:8 / S:19 *Take Me Back Again*		$15	Columbia 4-40272
				Percy Faith (orch., all of above)			

BLANC, Mel '48

Born on 5/30/08 in San Francisco. Died of heart disease on 7/10/89 (age 81). Long famous as the voice of Bugs Bunny, Daffy Duck, Porky Pig and numerous other popular cartoon characters.

7/17/48	2⁵	9		1 **Woody Woodpecker** A:2 / S:2 / J:6 *I'd Love To Live In Loveland With A Girl Like You* (Sportsmen) **[N]**	$20	Capitol 15145

THE SPORTSMEN and MEL BLANC And His Original Woody Woodpecker Voice
from the Walter Lantz cartoon

12/3/49	26	1		2 **Toot, Toot, Tootsie (Good-Bye)** ....A:26 *I've Got A Lovely Bunch Of Coconuts* **[N]**	$20	Capitol 57-780

Blanc parodies Al Jolson's hit version of 1923

1/27/51	9	11		3 **I Taut I Taw A Puddy Tat** ....S:9 / A:13 *Yosemite Sam* **[N]**	$30	Capitol F1360

voices of cartoon characters Sylvester and Tweety Pie; **Billy May** (orch., above 2)

BLEYER, Archie HOT '54

Born on 6/12/09 in Corona, New York. Died of Parkinson's disease on 3/20/89 (age 79). Arranger/music director for the radio and TV versions of **Arthur Godfrey** and His Friends from 1949-54. Founded Cadence Records. Married Chordettes member Janet Ertel in 1954.

5/22/54	2²	17		1 **Hernando's Hideaway** S:2 / A:3 / J:3 *S'il Vous Plait*	$15	Cadence 1241

Maria Alba (castanet soloist); from the Broadway musical *The Pajama Game* starring John Raitt

12/4/54+	17	6		2 **The Naughty Lady Of Shady Lane** ....A:17 / J:20 / S:26 *While The Vesper Bells Were Ringing*	$15	Cadence 1254

BLOCH, Ray, and his Orchestra MEM '47

Born on 8/3/02 in Alsace-Lorraine, France. Died on 3/29/82 (age 79). Conductor for the Jackie Gleason and Ed Sullivan TV programs in the 1950s and 1960s.

9/20/47	11	2		**Kate (Have I Come Too Early Too Late)**...........................A:11 *If My Heart Had A Window*	$15	Signature 15114

Alan Dale and ensemble (vocals)

BOB and JEANNE '49

5/21/49	21	1		**Careless Hands** ....J:21 *Don't Gamble With Romance*	$15	Decca 24563

BOLGER, Ray '50

Born Raymond Bulcao on 1/10/04 in Dorchester, Massachusetts. Died of cancer on 1/15/87 (age 83). Singer/dancer/actor. Appeared in several movies and Broadway shows. Best remembered as the "Scarecrow" in the movie *The Wizard of Oz*.

4/16/49	16	7		1 **Once In Love With Amy** ....S:16 / J:24 / A:26 *Make A Miracle* (w/Allyn McLerie)	$15	Decca DU 40065

from the Broadway musical *Where's Charley* starring Bolger; one of the first hit singles over 4 minutes in length (4:17) since the Edison Amberols; reissued on Decca 1-191 with a picture sleeve in 1952

3/4/50	12	11		2 **Dearie /** J:12 / S:13 / A:19		

RAY BOLGER And ETHEL MERMAN
from the stage production *The Copacabana Show Of 1950*

3/11/50	20	2		3 **I Said My Pajamas (And Put On My Pray'rs)** ....J:20 / S:25 / A:30	$15	Decca 24873
4/29/50	15	3		4 **If I Knew You Were Comin' I'd've Baked A Cake** ..J:15 *It's So Nice To Have A Man Around The House*	$15	Decca 24944

ETHEL MERMAN and RAY BOLGER (above 2)

5/5/51	29	1		5 **Once Upon A Nickel** ....A:29 *Oldies* **[N]**	$20	Decca 9-27506

RAY BOLGER And ETHEL MERMAN
Sy Oliver (orch., all of above)

BONES — see BROTHER BONES / MR. FORD

BOSTON POPS ORCHESTRA MEM/HOT '38

An American institution founded in 1885 by Henry Lee Higginson, conductor of the Boston Symphony Orchestra. Arthur Fiedler (born on 12/17/1894 in Boston, trained in Germany; died on 7/10/79, age 84) joined the orchestra in 1915 as a violist; began his reign as its conductor in 1930 and remained until his death. Local radio broadcasts of concerts began in 1952, then syndicated nationally from 1962-92. National public TV program *Evening at Pops* began in 1969. John Williams succeeded Fiedler in 1980. Keith Lockhart (former Cincinnati Pops conductor) succeeded Williams in 1995.

12/24/49	24	1		1 **Sleigh Ride**..S:24 *Serenata* **[X-I]**	$20	RCA Victor 49-0515

78 rpm: 10-1484

6/9/51	28	2		2 **Syncopated Clock** ....S:28 *Classical Juke Box* **[I]**	$15	RCA Victor 49-3044

famous as the theme song of TV's *Late Show*; above 2 composed by the orchestra's former arranger, **Leroy Anderson**; both records are on RCA Victor Red Seal

BOSWELL, Connee MEM '38

Born on 12/3/07 in New Orleans. Died of cancer on 10/11/76 (age 68). Member of the Boswell Sisters (Connee, Martha and Helvetis), the most popular female group of the 1930s. Overcame polio which restricted her to a wheelchair. Boswell's pre-1940 #1 hits: "Alexander's Ragtime Band," "The Object Of My Affection" and "Bob White (Whatcha Gonna Swing Tonight?)."

3/30/40	3	8		1 **On The Isle Of May** J:3 *Gotta Get Home*	$10	Decca 3004

CONNIE BOSWELL
based on Tchaikovsky's *D Major String Quartette*; **Victor Young** (orch.)

2/2/46	9	5		2 **Let It Snow! Let It Snow! Let It Snow!** ...J:9 / A:20 *Walkin' With My Honey (Soon, Soon, Soon)* **[X]**	$10	Decca 18741

CONNEE BOSWELL and RUSS MORGAN and HIS ORCHESTRA

11/9/46	14	3		3 **Ole Buttermilk Sky** ....J:14 *Love Doesn't Grow On Trees*	$10	Decca 18913

Bob Haggart (orch.); from the movie *Canyon Passage* starring Dana Andrews; #25 hit for Bill Black's Combo in 1961

9/11/54	10	11		4 **If I Give My Heart To You**..A:10 / S:20 *T-E-N-N-E-S-S-E-E*	$15	Decca 9-29148

George Siravo (orch.); #34 hit for **Kitty Kallen** in 1959

BOWERS, Richard — see COLUMBIA TOKYO ORCH.

BOYD, Jimmy MEM '52

Born on 1/9/39 in McComb, Mississippi. Played "Howard Meechim" on TV's *Bachelor Father* (1958-61).

12/6/52	❶²	5	●	1 **I Saw Mommy Kissing Santa Claus** S:❶² / A:3 / J:3 *Thumbelina* **[X-N]**	$20	Columbia 4-39871

reportedly sold 250,000 copies in one day; issued with a picture sleeve on Columbia's Children's Series MJV 4-152

3/14/53	4	12	●	2 **Tell Me A Story** S:4 / J:5 / A:8 *The Little Boy And The Old Man* **[N]**	$20	Columbia 4-39945

JIMMY BOYD - FRANKIE LAINE
Norman Luboff (accompaniment, above 2)

BRADFORD and ROMANO '50

Vocal duo of John Bradford and Tony Romano. Bradford was born on 7/2/19 in Long Branch, New Jersey. Romano was born on 9/26/15 in Fresno, California.

2/25/50	17	3		**Chattanoogie Shoe-Shine Boy** ....A:17 *Rag Mop*	$20	RCA Victor 47-3208

78 rpm: 20-3685; #34 hit for Freddy Cannon in 1960

BRADLEY, Owen, And His Quintet HOT '49

Born on 10/21/15 in Westmoreland, Tennessee. Died on 1/7/98 (age 82). Bandleader/producer/organist/combo leader. Country A&R director for Decca from 1958-68. Became vice president of MCA in 1968. Elected to the Country Music Hall of Fame in 1974.

12/17/49	11	7	1 **Blues Stay Away From Me** ....J:11 / S:15 / A:17 *Fairy Tales*	$15	Coral 60107
			Jack Shook and Dottie Dillard (vocals); #36 hit for Ace Cannon in 1962		
5/20/50	23	3	2 **The 3rd Man Theme**..J:23 *Cafe Mozart Waltz* [I]	$15	Coral 60159
			from the movie *The Third Man* starring Orson Welles; #47 hit for Herb Alpert & The Tijuana Brass in 1965		
1/13/51	18	8	3 **I Still Feel The Same About You**.............................S:18 / J:20 / A:28 *Get Out Those Old Records*	$20	Coral 9-60353
			"HER NIBS" Sings With GEORGIA GIBBS With OWEN BRADLEY SEXTET		

BRADLEY, Will, And His Orchestra ★117★ MEM '40

Born Wilbur Schwichtenberg on 7/12/11 in Newton, New Jersey. Died on 7/15/89 (age 78). Played trombone with Red Nichols and **Ray Noble**, among other bands, before starting his own in 1939, featuring boogie-woogie pianist **Freddie Slack** and drummer/vocalist **Ray McKinley**. Later played with the *Tonight Show* band.

9/28/40	2[1]	15	1 **Beat Me Daddy (Eight To The Bar) Parts I & II** S:2	$15	Columbia 35530
			WILL BRADLEY and his ORCHESTRA featuring RAY McKINLEY and Freddie Slack		
12/21/40	10	1	2 **Down The Road A Piece /** S:10		
			WILL BRADLEY TRIO		
			Ray McKinley (drums); "Doc" Goldberg (bass); **Freddie Slack** (piano); Ray McKinley and Will Bradley (vocals)		
11/30/40	18	1	3 **Celery Stalks At Midnight**...S(mw):18 [I]	$15	Columbia 35707
12/7/40+	2[1]	7	4 **Scrub Me, Mama, With A Boogie Beat /** S:2		
			melody based on "Irish Washerwoman"		
12/28/40+	5	3	5 **There I Go** S:5	$15	Columbia 35743
2/8/41	9	1	6 **High On A Windy Hill** ....S:9 *Love Of My Life*	$15	Columbia 35912
			WILL BRADLEY AND HIS ORCHESTRA FEATURING RAY McKINLEY (above 4)		
			Jimmy Valentine (vocal, above 2)		
1/29/44	18	1	7 **Cryin' The Boogie Blues**..J(terr.):18 *Jingle Bells Boogie Woogie* [I]	$40	Beacon 7013
			WILL BRADLEY and his Boogie Woogie Boys		
			Billy Butterfield (trumpet)		

BREWER, Teresa ★63★ MEM/HOT '53

Born Theresa Breuer on 5/7/31 in Toledo, Ohio. Debuted on *Major Bowes Amateur Hour* at age five, toured with show until age 12. Appeared on *Pick & Pat* radio show. First recorded for London in 1949. Appeared in the movie *Those Redheads From Seattle*.

1)Till I Waltz Again With You 2)Music! Music! Music! 3)Ricochet (Rick-O-Shay)

2/4/50	❶[4]	17 ●	1 **Music! Music! Music!** S:❶[4] / J:❶[1] / A:2 *Copenhagen*	$25	London 30023
			TERESA BREWER with THE DIXIELAND ALL STARS		
			78 rpm: 604; #54 hit for The Sensations in 1961		
4/22/50	17	5	2 **Choo'n Gum**..S:17 / A:17 / J:23 *Honky Tonkin'* [N]	$25	London 30100
			TERESA BREWER with JIMMY LYTELL AND THE DIXIELAND ALL STARS		
			78 rpm: 678; melody adapted from George Gershwin's "An American In Paris"; Jack Pleis (piano solo, above 2)		
9/15/51	28	1	3 **Longing For You**..S:28 *Jazz Me Blues*	$25	London 45-1086
			with Male Quartet and The All Stars conducted by Jack Pleis		
5/31/52	25	2	4 **Gonna Get Along Without Ya Now** ....J:25 *Roll Them Roly Boly Eyes*	$25	Coral 9-60676
			Ray Bloch (orch.); #11 hit for Patience & Prudence in 1956		
9/27/52	17	6	5 **You'll Never Get Away**..A:17 / S:18 / J:20 *The Hookey Song* [N]	$20	Coral 9-60829
			DON CORNELL And TERESA BREWER		
			featuring Cornell singing the title line from his hit "I'm Yours"		
12/13/52+	❶[7]	24 ●	6 **Till I Waltz Again With You** J:❶[7] / A:❶[6] / S:❶[5] *Hello Bluebird*	$20	Coral 9-60873
4/11/53	17	2	7 **Dancin' With Someone (Longin' For You)**.............................J:17 *Breakin' In The Blues*	$20	Coral 9-60953
10/3/53	2[2]	20 ●	8 **Ricochet (Rick-O-Shay)** J:2 / S:4 / A:4 *Too Young To Tango*	$20	Coral 9-61043
12/12/53	12	1	9 **Baby Baby Baby** ....A:12 *I Guess It Was You All The Time*	$20	Coral 9-61067
			from the movie *Those Redheads From Seattle* starring Rhonda Fleming and Gene Barry		
2/20/54	17	3	10 **Bell Bottom Blues**...S:17 *Our Heartbreaking Waltz*	$20	Coral 9-61066
4/24/54	6	9	11 **Jilted**...J:6 / A:12 / S:14 *Le Grand Tour De L'Amour*	$20	Coral 9-61152
12/18/54+	6	12 ●	12 **Let Me Go, Lover!** ....J:6 / A:7 / S:8 *The Moon Is On Fire*	$20	Coral 9-61315
			TERESA BREWER with The Lancers		
			Jack Pleis (orch., above 8)		

BRITO, Phil '45

Born Philip Colombrito on 9/15/15 in Boomer, West Virginia. Vocalist with **Al Donahue**'s band from 1939-42. Appeared in the movie *Sweetheart of Sigma Chi*. Known as "The Balladier of the Blues."

12/23/44+	14	2	1 **I Don't Want To Love You (Like I Do) /** ....A:14 / J:18		
9/2/44	17	1	2 **You Belong To My Heart Solamente Una Vez**...............................J:17	$15	Musicraft 15018
			from the Disney movie *The Three Caballeros* starring Aurora Miranda; **Paul Lavalle** (orch., above 2)		

BRITT, Elton '42

Born James Elton Baker on 6/27/13 in Zack, Arkansas. Died of a heart attack on 6/23/72 (age 58). Country singer/songwriter/ guitarist. Appeared in several movies.

9/26/42	17	2 ●	1 **There's A Star Spangled Banner Waving**		
			Somewhere..S(wc):17 / S(s):17 *When The Roses Bloom Again*	$30	Bluebird 9000
			new version by Red River Dave charted in 1960 (#64)		
3/16/46	19	1	2 **Wave To Me, My Lady** ....J:19 *Blueberry Lane* (C&W #4)	$30	Victor 20-1789
			#3 Country hit		

BROOKS, Norman MEM '53

Born Norman Arie in 1928 in Canada. Singer/actor. Played **Al Jolson** in the 1956 movie *The Best Things In Life Are Free*.

4/4/53	20	1	**Hello Sunshine**..A:20 *You're My Baby*	$25	Zodiac 45Z-101
			Lou Harold (orch.)		

BROTHER BONES And His Shadows   '49

Born Herbert Kern in New York City. Nicknamed "Brother Bones" because of his unique knuckle bones and whistling style. Also see **Mr. Ford** & **Mr. Goon-Bones**.

11/27/48+	10	16		Sweet Georgia Brown..S:10 / J:13 / A:19 *Margie* **[I]**	$25	Tempo TR 652

the original Harlem Globetrotters "warm-up" theme; #1 hit for Ben Bernie in 1925; #100 hit for the Carroll Bros. in 1962

BROWN, Les, and his Orchestra ★33★   MEM '45

Born on 3/14/12 in Reinerton, Pennsylvania. Died of cancer on 1/4/2001 (age 88). Clarinetist/bandleader. Worked as an arranger for **Jimmy Dorsey**, **Larry Clinton**, and other bands before his own orchestra took off. Brown's leading musicians during the 1940s included trumpeter **Billy Butterfield**, tenor saxophonist Ted Nash, and trombonists Si Zentner and Warren Covington. Vocalist **Doris Day** was the band's biggest star. In the 1950s, Brown's band was featured on Steve Allen's TV show, and has since accompanied **Bob Hope** on Bob's TV shows and overseas tours. Theme song: "Leap Frog."

1)*Sentimental Journey*   2)*My Dreams Are Getting Better All The Time*   3)*I've Got My Love To Keep Me Warm*
4)*You Won't Be Satisfied (Until You Break My Heart)*   5)*Undecided*

Vocalists: Ames Brothers — 23,24   Day, Doris — 5,7-12,14-16,19,20   4 Hits and A Miss — 22   Stone, Butch — 3,13,18
          Bonney, Betty — 1   Drake, Gordon — 4   Haskell, Jack — 17   Young, Ralph — 2

10/11/41	16	3		1 Joltin' Joe DiMaggio.............................S(e):16 *The Nickel Serenade (The Coin Machine Song)* **[N]**	$50	Okeh 6377
12/13/41	19	2		2 'Tis Autumn ....S(mw):19 / S(e):20 *That Solid Old Man*	$15	Okeh 6430
2/24/45	12	1		3 Robin Hood / A:12		
3/3/45	18	1		4 Sleigh Ride In July ....J:18 / A:19	$15	Columbia 36763
				from the movie *Belle Of The Yukon* starring Randolph Scott		
3/3/45	❶⁹	28	●	5 **Sentimental Journey /** S:❶⁹ / A:❶⁷ / J:❶⁷		
				also see #24 below		
3/17/45	16	1		6 Twilight Time ....J:16 **[I]**	$15	Columbia 36769
				#1 hit for The Platters in 1958		
3/17/45	❶⁷	16		7 **My Dreams Are Getting Better All The Time** S:❶⁷ / J:❶⁷ / A:❶³ *He's Home For A Little While*	$15	Columbia 36779
				from the movie *In Society* starring Abbott & Costello		
6/30/45	10	1		8 'Tain't Me ....A:10 *I'll Always Be With You*	$15	Columbia 36804
8/18/45	3	13		9 **Till The End Of Time** A:3 / J:11 *He'll Have To Cross The Atlantic (To Get To The Pacific)*	$15	Columbia 36828
				song based on Chopin's "Polonaise"; #83 hit for the Ray Charles Singers in 1964		
11/24/45+	11	4		10 Aren't You Glad You're You? ....A:11 *The Last Time I Saw You*	$15	Columbia 36875
				from the movie *The Bells Of St. Mary's* starring **Bing Crosby** and Ingrid Bergman		
1/12/46	2²	15		11 **You Won't Be Satisfied (Until You Break My Heart) /** J:2 / A:4 / S:5		
12/29/45+	11	3		12 Come To Baby, Do! A:11	$15	Columbia 36884
3/9/46	6	4		13 Doctor, Lawyer, Indian Chief / ....S:6 / A:11 / J:14		
				from the movie *The Stork Club* starring **Betty Hutton**		
3/30/46	15	2		14 Day By Day A:15	$15	Columbia 36945
6/15/46	10	5		15 I Got The Sun In The Morning...............A:10 / J:13 *It Couldn't Be True! (Or Could It?)*	$15	Columbia 36977
				from the Broadway musical *Annie Get Your Gun* starring **Ethel Merman**		
10/19/46	6	11		16 The Whole World Is Singing My Song / ....A:6 / J:9		
9/14/46	11	2		17 I Guess I'll Get The Papers (And Go Home)..........................A:11	$15	Columbia 37066
12/7/46	15	1		18 The Best Man ....A:15 *My Serenade*	$15	Columbia 37086
1/4/47-	12	2		19 The Christmas Song (Merry Christmas To You) ......A:12 *When You Trim Your Christmas Tree* **[X]**	$15	Columbia 37174
1/25/47	8	1		20 Sooner Or Later ....J:8 / A:13 *Years And Years Ago*	$15	Columbia 37153
				introduced by Hattie McDaniel in the animated/live-action movie *Song Of The South*		
12/25/48+	❶¹	17	●	21 **I've Got My Love To Keep Me Warm** A:❶¹ / S:7 / J:11 *I'm A-Tellin' You, Sam* **[I]**	$15	Columbia 38324
				the last great instrumental hit of the Big Band Era; recorded on 9/16/46; from the 1937 movie *On The Avenue* starring Dick Powell and Alice Faye; #3 hit for **Ray Noble** in 1937		
5/13/50	22	2		22 It Isn't Fair ....A:22 *Solid As A Rock*	$15	Columbia 38735
				LES BROWN and his Band of Renown		
				7" 33-1/3 rpm: 1-558; written in 1933		
9/29/51	2¹	21	●	23 **Undecided /** A:2 / J:4 / S:6		
				AMES BROTHERS And LES BROWN And His Band Of Renown		
				#8 hit for **Ella Fitzgerald** & Chick Webb in 1939		
10/6/51	23	4		24 Sentimental Journey J:23	$20	Coral 9-60566
				LES BROWN And His Band Of Renown And AMES BROTHERS		

BROWNE, Sam   '48

Born in England. Lead vocalist with the Ambrose Orchestra.

9/18/48	24	3		A Tree In The Meadow ....A:24 / J:28 *An Old Sombrero*	$10	London 123
				Bert Thompson (orch.)		

BULAWAYO SWEET RHYTHMS BAND   '54

Group from South Africa.

8/28/54	17	8		Skokiaan..S:17 / A:20 *In The Mood* **[I]**	$15	London 45-1491
				South African song, named for a Zulu tribal drink; #70 hit for **Bill Haley & His Comets** in 1960		

BURKE, Sonny — see CHERRY, Don

BUTLER, Champ   HOT '51

Born on 12/21/26 in St. Louis; raised in Los Angeles. Died on 3/8/92 (age 65). Pop singer.

5/26/51	29	1		1 I Apologize ....A:29 *There'll Be Mournin' In The Mornin'*	$15	Columbia 4-39189
				Skippy Martin (orch.); #3 hit for **Bing Crosby** in 1931; #72 hit for Timi Yuro in 1961		
7/21/51	22	2		2 Them There Eyes ....S:22 *At Your Beck And Call*	$15	Columbia 4-39434
				Paul Weston (orch.); #7 hit for Gus Arnheim in 1931		
9/29/51	17	16		3 Down Yonder ....A:17 / J:18 / S:18 *Way Up In North Carolina* (w/Lee Brothers)	$15	Columbia 4-39533
				#5 hit for Ernest Hare & Billy Jones in 1921; #48 hit for Johnny & The Hurricanes in 1960		
5/17/52	26	1		4 Be Anything (But Be Mine) ....S:26 *When I Look Into Your Eyes*	$15	Columbia 4-39690
				Percy Faith (orch.); #25 hit for Connie Francis in 1964		

BUTLER, Daws — see FREBERG, Stan

BUTTERFIELD, Billy, And His Orchestra   MEM '46
Born Charles William Butterfield on 1/14/17 in Middleton, Ohio. Died on 3/18/88 (age 71). Legendary trupeter. Played with **Bob Crosby**, **Artie Shaw**, **Benny Goodman** and **Les Brown**.

7/24/43+	11	19		1 **My Ideal**..S(wc):11 / S(mw):20 *Without Love*	$10	Capitol 134
				#12 hit for Maurice Chevalier in 1931
1/20/45	10	2		2 **There Goes That Song Again**..................................A:10 / J:13 *Moonlight In Vermont*	$10	Capitol 182
				from the movie *Carolina Blues* starring **Kay Kyser**; **Margaret Whiting** (vocal, above 2)
10/26/46	6	7		3 **Rumors Are Flying**...A:6 / J:14 *The Sharp Scarf*	$10	Capitol 282
				Pat O'Connor (vocal)

BUTTONS, Red   '53
Born Aaron Chwatt on 2/5/19 in New York City. Comedian/actor. Hosted own TV show from 1952-54. Appeared in several movies.

5/2/53	9	9		1 **The Ho Ho Song** / ....A:9 / J:9 / S:10 [N]
5/9/53	15	3		2 **Strange Things Are Happening (Ho Ho, Hee Hee, Ha Ha)**..................S:15 / J:20 [N]	$15	Columbia 4-39981
				Elliot Lawrence (orch., above 2); both tunes are very similar, like Parts 1 and 2 of a song

BYRD, Jerry   HOT '50
Born on 3/9/20 in Lima, Ohio. Steel guitarist.

9/23/50	19	4		**Harbor Lights**..J:19 *At Sundown* [I]	$15	Mercury 5461-X45
				JERRY BYRD & His Steel Guitar & JERRY MURAD'S Harmonicats
				#6 hit for Frances Langford in 1937; #8 hit for The Platters in 1960

BYRNE, Bobby, And His Orchestra   MEM '40
Born on 10/10/18 in Columbus, Ohio. Trombonist. Formerly with **Jimmy Dorsey**. Bandleader for Steve Allen's *Tonight Show* (1953-54).

10/19/40	19	1		1 **Maybe**...S(wc):19 *One Look At You*	$10	Decca 3392
				Jimmy Palmer (vocal)
3/29/41	20	1		2 **You Walk By**..S(s):20 *Chapel In The Valley*	$10	Decca 3613
				Jerry Wayne (vocal)

C

CALLOWAY, Cab   MEM/HOT '31
Born Cabell Calloway on 12/25/07 in Rochester, New York; raised in Baltimore. Died of a stroke on 11/18/94 (age 86). Nicknamed "His Hi-De-Ho Highness Of Jive." Black vocalist/bandleader/alto saxophonist/drummer. Gained fame at New York's Cotton Club in the 1930s. Appeared in several movies. Calloway's pre-1940 #1 hit: "Minnie The Moocher (The Ho De Ho Song)."

3/14/42	8	1		1 **Blues In The Night (My Mama Done Tol' Me)**.........................S:8 *Says Who? Says You, Says I!*	$25	Okeh 6422
				Cab Calloway and The Palmer Brothers (vocals); Dizzy Gillespie (trumpet); from the movie *Blues In The Night* starring Priscilla Lane
11/11/44	24	1		2 **The Moment I Laid Eyes On You**.......................................J(terr.):24 *Lordy*	$20	Columbia 36751
				Cab Calloway (vocal)

CALVERT, Eddie   '54
Born on 3/15/22 in Preston, Lancashire, England. Died of a heart attack on 8/7/78 (age 56). Trumpet player.

EDDIE CALVERT and His Golden Trumpet:

| 12/5/53+ | 6 | 14 | | **Oh, Mein Papa**..J:6 / A:7 / S:9 *Mystery Street* [I] | $20 | Essex 336 |
| | | | | Norrie Paramor (backing music); from the Swiss musical comedy *Fireworks*; #94 hit for Dick Lee in 1961 |

CAMARATA, Music By   MEM '52
Born Salvatore Tutti Camarata on 5/11/13 in Glen Ridge, New Jersey. Played trumpet for **Charlie Barnet** and **Jimmy Dorsey**; arranged many of the Dorsey band's top hits. Conducted for **Ella Fitzgerald**, **Bing Crosby**, **Dick Haymes** and many others. Served as musical director at Walt Disney Studios.

11/24/51+	16	7		1 **Shrimp Boats**...J:16 / A:18 / S:25 *More! More! More!*	$15	Decca 9-27832
				DOLORES GRAY With MUSIC BY CAMARATA
12/29/51	30	1		2 **You Better Go Now**...A:30 *Baby Did You Hear?*	$15	Decca 9-27840
				JERI SOUTHERN With MUSIC BY CAMARATA
10/25/52	28	1		3 **Veradero**..A:28 *Brief Interlude* [I]	$15	Decca 9-28376

CANTOR, Eddie   MEM '23
Born Edward Iskowitz on 1/31/1892 in New York City. Died of a heart attack on 10/10/64 (age 72). One of the most popular entertainers in vaudeville and musical comedy history. Founded the March of Dimes charity with President Franklin Roosevelt. Celebrated in the 1953 movie *The Eddie Cantor Story*. Cantor's pre-1940 #1 hits: "If You Knew Susie," Margie" and "No, No, Nora."

| 6/24/50 | 27 | 1 | | **The Old Piano Roll Blues**.......................................J:27 / S:29 *Juke Box Annie (Doodle-Oodle-Oo)* | $20 | RCA Victor 47-3751 |
| | | | | **EDDIE CANTOR, LISA KIRK, and the SAMMY KAYE ORCHESTRA** |

CAPTAIN STUBBY — see IVES, Burl

CARLE, Frankie, and his Orchestra ★48★   MEM '46
Born Francis Carlone on 3/25/03 in Providence, Rhode Island. Died on 3/7/2001 (age 97). Prolific pianist. Played with Mal Hallet and **Horace Heidt**. Daughter **Marjorie Hughes** was his main vocalist.

1)Oh! What It Seemed To Be   2)Rumors Are Flying   3)A Little On The Lonely Side

10/7/44	20	1		1 **Charmaine**...J(terr.):20 *Diane* [I]	$10	Columbia 36690
				#1 hit for Guy Lombardo in 1927; #69 hit for The Four Freshmen in 1956
2/3/45	4	14		2 **A Little On The Lonely Side** J:4 / A:5 / S:5 *I Had A Little Talk With The Lord*	$10	Columbia 36760
2/10/45	8	1		3 **Saturday Night (Is The Loneliest Night In The Week)**.....................S:8 *Carle Boogie*	$10	Columbia 36777
				Phyliss Lynne (vocal)

CARLE, Frankie, and his Orchestra — Cont'd

DEBUT	PEAK	WKS		A-side / B-side	$	Label & Number
2/24/45	19	1		4 **Evelina** ....J:19 *Right As The Rain*	$10	Columbia 36764
				from the Broadway musical *Bloomer Girl* starring Celeste Holm		
7/14/45	17	1		5 **Counting The Days** ....J:17 *Missouri Waltz*	$10	Columbia 36805
				Paul Allen (vocal: #2, 4 & 5)		
1/26/46	❶[11]	20		6 **Oh! What It Seemed To Be** ....J:❶[11] / S:❶[6] / A:2 *As Long As I Live*	$10	Columbia 36892
				#91 hit for The Castells in 1962		
6/8/46	10	8		7 **One More Tomorrow** ....J:10 / A:12 *I'm Gonna Make Believe*	$10	Columbia 36978
				title song from the movie starring Ann Sheridan		
8/17/46	14	2		8 **I'd Be Lost Without You** ....J:14 *Cynthia's In Love*	$10	Columbia 36994
9/21/46	❶[9]	18		9 **Rumors Are Flying** ....A:❶[9] / S:❶[8] / J:❶[8] *Without You*	$10	Columbia 37069
11/30/46	6	4		10 **It's All Over Now** ....A:6 / J:13 *Either It's Love Or It Isn't*	$10	Columbia 37146
4/12/47	9	2		11 **Roses In The Rain** ....A:9 / J:15 *You Are There*	$10	Columbia 37252
2/7/48	5	16		12 **Beg Your Pardon** ....J:5 / A:5 / S:6 *The Dream Peddler*	$10	Columbia 38036
				Marjorie Hughes (vocal: #6-12)		
12/4/48	10	1		13 **Twelfth Street Rag** ....J:10 *Sweet Lorraine* [I]	$10	Columbia 35572
				At The Piano...Horace Heidt Presents FRANKIE CARLE; recorded and first released in 1940; #7 hit for Earl Fuller in 1917		
3/19/49	8	12		14 **Cruising Down The River (On A Sunday Afternoon)** ....A:8 / S:28 *Mississippi Flyer*	$10	Columbia 38411
				Marjorie Hughes and The Sunrise Serenaders (vocals)		

CARMICHAEL, Hoagy ★121★   MEM '47

Born on 11/22/1899 in Bloomington, Indiana. Died on 12/27/81 (age 82). Legendary songwriter (including the standard "Stardust"). Acted in several movies. Played "Jonesy" in the TV series *Laramie*.

DEBUT	PEAK	WKS		A-side / B-side	$	Label & Number
8/25/45	6	3		1 **Hong Kong Blues** ....A:6 *How Little We Know*	$20	ARA 123
				from the movie *To Have And Have Not* starring Humphrey Bogart; other versions recorded by Carmichael in 1938 (Brunswick 8255) and 1942 (Decca 18395)		
3/16/46	18	1		2 **Doctor Lawyer Indian Chief** ....J:18 *Am I Blue*	$20	ARA 128
				from the movie *The Stork Club* starring Betty Hutton		
10/12/46+	2[4]	19		3 **Ole Buttermilk Sky** ....S:2 / J:2 / A:4 *Ginger And Spice*	$20	ARA 155
				from the movie *Canyon Passage* starring Dana Andrews; new version by Carmichael was recorded in 1947 on Decca 23769; #25 hit for Bill Black's Combo in 1961		
11/23/46+	❶[2]	15		4 **Huggin' And Chalkin'** .....J:❶[2] / S:2 / A:5 *I May Be Wrong, But, I Think You're Wonderful* [N]	$15	Decca 23675
				The Chickadees (backing vocals); Vic Schoen (orch.)		
5/13/50	11	10		5 **The Old Piano Roll Blues** ....J:11 / S:15 *Stay With The Happy People*	$20	Decca 9-24977
4/14/51	23	3		6 **The Aba Daba Honeymoon** ....J:23 / A:29 *The Golden Rocket*	$20	Decca 9-27474
				HOAGY CARMICHAEL And CASS DALEY (above 2); from the movie *Two Weeks With Love* starring Debbie Reynolds and Carleton Carpenter; #1 hit for Arthur Collins & Byron Harlan in 1914; Matty Matlock's All Stars (orch., above 2)		

CARPENTER, Carleton — see REYNOLDS, Debbie

CARR, Joe "Fingers"   MEM/HOT '50

Born Lou Busch on 7/18/10 in Louisville. Died on 9/19/79 (age 69). Honky-tonk pianist. Played with George Olsen and Hal Kemp. Married singer Margaret Whiting. Also recorded under his real name.

DEBUT	PEAK	WKS		A-side / B-side	$	Label & Number
6/17/50	7	13		1 **Sam's Song** ....J:7 / S:8 / A:12 *Ivory Rag*	$15	Capitol F962
				JOE "FINGERS" CARR And The Carr-Hops; #94 hit for Dean Martin & Sammy Davis, Jr. in 1962		
10/20/51	14	17		2 **Down Yonder** ....S:14 / J:17 / A:19 *Ivory Rag* [I]	$15	Capitol F1777
				#5 hit for Ernest Hare & Billy Jones in 1921; #48 hit for Johnny & The Hurricanes in 1960		

CARROLL, Bob   MEM/HOT '53

Born on 6/18/18 in New York City. Baritone singer. Sang with Charlie Barnet, Jimmy Dorsey, Kay Kyser and Gordon Jenkins bands.

DEBUT	PEAK	WKS		A-side / B-side	$	Label & Number
2/21/53	14	3		**Say It With Your Heart** ....J:14 / A:17 / S:20 *Where*	$20	Derby 45-814
				Jimmy Leyden (orch. and chorus)		

CARROLL, Helen   '46

DEBUT	PEAK	WKS		A-side / B-side	$	Label & Number
11/16/46	7	6		1 **Ole Buttermilk Sky** ....S:7 / J:10 *Let's Sail To Dreamland*	$10	RCA Victor 20-1982
				HELEN CARROLL and THE SATISFIERS; Russ Case (orch.); from the movie *Canyon Passage* starring Dana Andrews; #25 hit for Bill Black's Combo in 1961		
4/2/49	29	1		2 **Cruising Down The River** ....J:29 *The Gang That Sang Heart Of My Heart*	$10	Mercury 5249
				HELEN CARROLL And The Carolers		

CARSON, Ken   '51

Born on 11/14/14 in Coalgate, Oklahoma. Died of ALS (Lou Gehrig's disease) on 4/7/94 (age 79). Singer featured on TV's *Garry Moore Show* (1950-51).

DEBUT	PEAK	WKS		A-side / B-side	$	Label & Number
6/30/51	30	1		**Wondrous Word (of the Lord)** ....A:30 *Hometown U.S.A.*	$40	Bibletone 770 (45)
				Hal Kanner (orch. and chorus)		

CARSON, Mindy   MEM/HOT '50

Born on 7/16/27 in New York City. Sang with Paul Whiteman in the 1940s.

DEBUT	PEAK	WKS		A-side / B-side	$	Label & Number
10/19/46	12	2		1 **Rumors Are Flying** ....A:12 / J:14 *The Whole World Is Singing My Song* (Cool)	$15	Signature 15043
				HARRY COOL and MINDY CARSON		
4/29/50	6	11		2 **My Foolish Heart** / ....A:6 / J:7 / S:13		
				title song from the movie starring Susan Hayward		
3/11/50	12	7		3 **Candy And Cake** ....J:12 / S:16 / A:24	$15	RCA Victor 47-3204
				78 rpm: 20-3681; Henri René (orch., above 2)		
6/30/50	20	1		4 **Bewitched** ....A:20 *Hoop-Dee-Doo*	$15	RCA Victor 47-3782
10/28/50	24	1		5 **A Rainy Day Refrain** ....A:24 *Looks Like A Cold, Cold Winter*	$15	RCA Victor 47-3921
				Andrew Ackers (orch.)		
7/21/51	25	1		6 **Lonely Little Robin** ....A:25 *You Only Want Me When You're Lonesome*	$15	RCA Victor 47-4151
				Norman Leyden (orch.); #105 hit for The Browns in 1960		
11/1/52	26	2		7 **'Cause I Love You That's A-Why** ....S:26 *Train Of Love*	$20	Columbia 4-39879
				GUY MITCHELL - MINDY CARSON; Mitch Miller (orch.)		

CARTER, Benny, And His Orchestra   MEM '44

Born Bennett Lester Carter on 8/8/07 in New York City. Black alto saxophonist/trumpeter/clarinetist/pianist. Played in several bands, including **Duke Ellington**, until 1935. Own band to 1946. Moved to Los Angeles and did movie soundtrack work. Appeared in the movie *The Snows of Kilimanjaro*. Won Grammy's Lifetime Achievement Award in 1987.

| 2/5/44 | 12 | 6 | | 1 **Poinciana (Song of the Tree)** / ....S(wc):12 **[I]** | | |
| 3/11/44 | 23 | 1 | | 2 **Hurry, Hurry!** ....J:23 | $20 | Capitol 144 |

Savannah Churchill (vocal); #2 Country hit; above 2 were Top 10 R&B hits

CARTER, June — see HOMER and JETHRO

CARUSO, Marian — see OVERTURES, The

CASE, Russ, and his Orchestra   '49

Born on 3/19/12 in Hamburg, Iowa. Died on 10/10/64 (age 52). Played trumpet with Frankie Trumbauer, Paul Whiteman, **Hal Kemp** and **Raymond Scott**. Orchestra conductor for such singers as **Perry Como** and **Dinah Shore**.

| 10/1/49 | 26 | 1 | | **You're Breaking My Heart** ....A:26 *One More Time* | $10 | MGM 10478 |

The Quintones (vocals); based on the Italian song "La Mattinata"

CATS and the FIDDLE, The   '40

Black vocal group from Chicago: Austin Powell, Jimmy Henderson, Ernie Price and Chuck Barksdale. Henderson died in 1940 (after recording "I Miss You So"); replaced by Herbie Miles. Barksdale died in 1942; replaced by George Steinback.

| 9/21/40 | 20 | 1 | | **I Miss You So** ....S(e):20 *Public Jitterbug No. 1* | $40 | Bluebird 8429 |

#33 hit for Paul Anka in 1959

CAVALLARO, Carmen, And His Orchestra ★99★   '45

Born on 5/6/13 in New York City. Died of cancer on 10/12/89 (age 76). Classically-trained pianist. Played in the 1930s with **Al Kavelin**, **Rudy Vallee** and **Abe Lyman**. Provided the 1956 movie soundtrack *The **Eddy Duchin** Story*.

| 6/30/45 | 3 | 19 | ● | 1 **Chopin's Polonaise**   S:3 / A:3 / J:3 *Enlloro (Voodoo Moon)* **[I]** | $10 | Decca 18677 |

Perry Como's #1 hit in 1945 "Till The End Of Time" also based on Chopin's "Polonaise"

| 11/17/45 | ❶⁶ | 20 | ● | 2 **I Can't Begin To Tell You**   J:❶⁶ / S:❶¹ / A:2 *I Can't Believe That You're In Love With Me* | $15 | Decca 23457 |

BING CROSBY with **CARMEN CAVALLARO** At The Piano
from the movie *The Dolly Sisters* starring **Betty Grable**

| 11/8/47+ | 6 | 14 | | 3 **How Soon (Will I Be Seeing You)** / ....J:6 / S:8 / A:13 | | |
| 11/1/47 | 8 | 8 | | 4 **You Do**...J:8 / S:10 / A:15 | $15 | Decca 24101 |

BING CROSBY and **CARMEN CAVALLARO** At The Piano (above 2)
from the movie *Mother Wore Tights* starring **Betty Grable**

| 9/17/49 | 29 | 1 | | 5 **There's Yes! Yes! In Your Eyes** ....J:29 *Twenty Four Hours Of Sunshine* | $10 | Decca 24678 |

ensemble (vocals)

| 3/11/50 | 5 | 9 | | 6 **(Put Another Nickel In) Music! Music! Music!**   J:5 / S:17 / A:18 *O, Katharina* | $10 | Decca 24881 |

Bob Lido, The Cavaliers and ensemble (vocals); #54 hit for The Sensations in 1961

| 9/27/52 | 28 | 1 | | 7 **Meet Mister Callaghan** ....S:28 / J:28 *Runnin' Wild Boogie* **[I]** | $15 | Decca 9-28373 |

CHACKSFIELD, Frank, And His Orchestra   HOT '53

Born on 5/9/14 in Battle, Sussex, England. Died on 6/9/95 (age 81). Pianist/bandleader.

| 5/30/53 | 5 | 13 | | 1 **Terry's Theme From "Limelight"**   A:5 / S:6 / J:10 *Limelight* **[I]** | $15 | London 45-1342 |

written by Charlie Chaplin for his movie *Limelight*; #92 hit for Mr. Acker Bilk in 1962; **Vic Damone**'s #12 hit in 1953 "Eternally" used the melody from "Limelight"

| 8/29/53 | 2⁴ | 23 | ● | 2 **Ebb Tide**   S:2 / A:2 / J:8 *Waltzing Bugle Boy* **[I]** | $15 | London 45-1358 |

#5 hit for The Righteous Brothers in 1966

CHANDLER, Karen   MEM/HOT '53

Born Eva Nadauld in Rexburg, Idaho. Married to conductor/arranger Jack Pleis. Sang with **Benny Goodman** in 1946 and also recorded solo under pseudonym **Eve Young**.

| 12/11/48 | 29 | 1 | | 1 **Cuanto Le Gusta** ....A:29 *Say Something Sweet To Your Sweetheart* | $10 | RCA Victor 20-3077 |

EVE YOUNG "The Girlfriend" and The Drugstore Cowboys
from the movie *A Date With Judy* starring Wallace Beery and Jane Powell

| 1/29/49 | 26 | 1 | | 2 **My Darling, My Darling** ....J:26 *You're The First Cup Of Coffee* | $10 | RCA Victor 20-3187 |

EVE YOUNG and **JACK LATHROP**
from the Broadway musical *Where's Charley?* starring **Ray Bolger**

| 10/25/52+ | 5 | 18 | ● | 3 **Hold Me, Thrill Me, Kiss Me**   A:5 / S:7 / J:8 *One Dream (Tells Me)* | $15 | Coral 9-60831 |

Jack Pleis (orch.); #8 hit for Mel Carter in 1965

CHARIOTEERS, The   ★139★   MEM '47

Black vocal group from Ohio: **Billy Williams**, Howard Daniel, Edward Jackson and Ira Williams. First recorded for Decca in 1935. Immensely popular on radio with **Bing Crosby** on the Kraft Music Hall. Four years with Ole Olsen and Chic Johnson in the Broadway revue *Hellzapoppin'*. Billy Williams left in January 1950 to form his own quartet. Billy Williams died on 10/17/72 (age 61).

| 11/10/45 | 9 | 4 | | 1 **Don't Forget Tonight Tomorrow** ....A:9 / J:13 *Lily Belle* | $50 | Columbia 36854 |

FRANK SINATRA and **THE CHARIOTEERS**

| 10/12/46 | 12 | 1 | | 2 **On The Boardwalk (In Atlantic City)** ....A:12 *You Make Me Feel So Young* | $50 | Columbia 37074 |

from the movie *Three Little Girls In Blue* starring June Haver

| 3/8/47 | 6 | 3 | | 3 **Open The Door, Richard** ....A:6 *You Can't See The Sun When You're Cryin'* **[N]** | $50 | Columbia 37240 |

Mannie Klein (orch.)

| 7/19/47 | 16 | 3 | | 4 **Chi-Baba Chi-Baba (My Bambino Go To Sleep)** ....A:16 *Say No More* | $50 | Columbia 37384 |

Mitchell Ayres (orch.)

| 3/27/48 | 6 | 5 | | 5 **Now Is The Hour (Maori Farewell Song)**   A:6 / J:26 *Peculiar (Clark)* | $50 | Columbia 38115 |

BUDDY CLARK and **THE CHARIOTEERS**
#59 hit for Gale Storm in 1956

| 7/2/49 | 19 | 1 | | 6 **A Kiss And A Rose** ....A:19 *A Cottage In Old Donegal* | $50 | Columbia 38438 |

7" 33-1/3 rpm: 1-168; #8 R&B hit

CHARMS, The   HOT '55

R&B vocal group from Cincinnati: Otis Williams, Richard Parker, Donald Peak, Joe Penn and Rolland Bradley. Group first recorded for Rockin' in 1953. Otis, not to be confused with the same-named member of The Temptations, later recorded country music.

| 11/27/54+ | 15 | 15 | | Hearts Of Stone..S:15 / J:15 / A:20 Who Knows | $100 | DeLuxe 6062 |

#1 R&B hit (9 weeks)

CHEERS, The   HOT '55

Pop vocal trio from Los Angeles: Bert Convy, Gil Garfield and Sue Allen. Convy later became a popular TV personality; died of a brain tumor on 7/15/91 (age 58).

| 10/16/54 | 15 | 11 | | (Bazoom) I Need Your Lovin'...S:15 / A:18 Arivederci | $30 | Capitol F2921 |

Buddy Bregman (orch.)

CHERRY, Don   HOT '56

Born on 1/11/24 in Wichita Falls, Texas. Vocalist with Jan Garber's band in the late 1940s. Not to be confused with the jazz trumpeter.

| 7/1/50 | 7 | 15 | | 1 Mona Lisa / ....J:7 / S:10 | | |

from the movie Captain Carey, U.S.A. starring Alan Ladd; #25 hit for Carl Mann in 1959

| 7/8/50 | 22 | 2 | | 2 The 3rd Man Theme..J:22 / S:25 | $15 | Decca 9-27048 |

VICTOR YOUNG And His Orchestra And Chorus And DON CHERRY (above 2)
from the movie The Third Man starring Orson Welles; #47 hit for Herb Alpert & The Tijuana Brass in 1965

| 9/23/50 | 4 | 21 | | 3 Thinking Of You   S:4 / A:7 / J:9 Here In My Arms | $15 | Decca 9-27128 |

Dave Terry (orch.); from the Broadway musical The Five O'Clock Girl starring Mary Eaton; featured in the movie Three Little Words starring Fred Astaire; #5 hit for Nat Skilkret in 1928

| 7/28/51 | 11 | 13 | | 4 Vanity...A:11 / S:17 / J:29 Powder Blue | $15 | Decca 9-27618 |

Sy Oliver (orch.)

| 9/1/51 | 25 | 1 | | 5 Belle, Belle, My Liberty Belle..A:25 Cara Cara Bella Bella | $15 | Decca 9-27717 |

DON CHERRY And SONNY BURKE And His Orchestra

CHESTER, Bob, and his Orchestra   MEM '40

Born on 3/20/08 in Detroit. Tenor saxophonist. Played with Ben Bernie, Ben Pollack and Russ Morgan.

| 10/12/40 | 6 | 6 | | 1 Practice Makes Perfect ....S:6 Don't Let It Get You Down | $10 | Bluebird 10838 |

Al Stuart (vocal)

| 3/8/41 | 17 | 2 | | 2 May I Never Love Again ....S:(mw):17 Buzz Buzz Buzz (Lookin' For My Honey) | $10 | Bluebird 10904 |

Dolores O'Neill (vocal)

| 5/31/41 | 19 | 1 | | 3 My Sister And I ....S:(s):19 Slow Down | $10 | Bluebird 11088 |

Bill Darnel (vocal)

CHORDETTES, The   HOT '54

Female vocal group from Sheboygan, Wisconsin: Janet Ertel, Carol Buschman, Lynn Evans and Margie Needham. With Arthur Godfrey from 1949-53. Ertel married Cadence owner Archie Bleyer in 1954; her daughter Jackie was married to Phil Everly of The Everly Brothers. Ertel died of cancer on 11/22/88 (age 75).

| 10/30/54 | ❶7 | 20 | ● | Mr. Sandman   S:❶7 / A:❶7 / J:❶4 I Don't Wanna See You Cryin' | $20 | Cadence 1247 |

Archie Bleyer (orch.); #37 hit for Emmylou Harris in 1981

CHORDS, The   '54

R&B vocal group from the Bronx, New York: Carl Feaster, Jimmy Keyes, Floyd McRae, Claude Feaster, William Edwards and Rupert Branker. Keyes died on 7/22/95 (age 65).

| 7/3/54 | 5 | 16 | | Sh-Boom   J:5 / S:9 / A:13 Cross Over The Bridge | $125 | Cat 45-104 |

#2 R&B hit

CHURCHILL, Savannah   MEM '51

Born Savannah Valentine on 8/21/20 in Colfax, Louisiana; raised in Brooklyn, New York. Died of pneumonia on 4/20/74 (age 53). Black vocalist/violinist. With Benny Carter, recorded for Capitol in 1943. Also see Benny Carter and Jimmy Lytell.

| 5/22/48 | 24 | 3 | | 1 Time Out For Tears ....J:24 All My Dreams (If All My Dreams Would Only Come True) | $30 | Manor 1116 |

SAVANNAH CHURCHILL And THE FOUR TUNES
#10 R&B hit

| 10/6/51 | 5 | 17 | | 2 (It's No) Sin   A:5 / S:9 / J:9 I Don't Believe In Tomorrow | $30 | RCA Victor 47-4280 |

CLARK, Buddy   ★40★   MEM '47

Born Samuel Goldberg on 7/26/12 in Dorchester, Massachusetts. Died in a plane crash on 10/1/49 (age 37). Popular vocalist. First wide exposure came via the Benny Goodman radio show. Featured on radio's Your Hit Parade. Hosted own radio show. Recorded with Ray Noble ("Linda") and Johnny Hodges. Also see Xavier Cugat.

1)Peg O' My Heart   2)Love Somebody   3)Linda

Orchestras: Ayres, Mitchell — 2-4,13   Hagen, Earle — 12   Noble, Ray — 1,5   Zimmerman, Harry — 15
Dale, Ted — 14,16   Jones, Dick — 6   Siravo, George — 8-11

| 2/15/47 | ❶2 | 23 | | 1 Linda   A:❶2 / S:2 / J:2 Love Is A Random Thing | $10 | Columbia 37215 |

RAY NOBLE and his ORCHESTRA with BUDDY CLARK
Anita Gordon (female vocal); written for then six-year-old Linda Eastman McCartney (Paul's late wife); #28 hit for Jan & Dean in 1963

| 3/1/47 | 6 | 8 | | 2 How Are Things In Gloca Mora...A:6 / J:10 If This Isn't Love | $10 | Columbia 37223 |

from the Broadway musical Finian's Rainbow starring David Wayne

| 6/28/47 | ❶6 | 15 | | 3 Peg O' My Heart   A:❶6 / S:4 / J:13 Come To Me, Bend To Me | $10 | Columbia 37392 |

#1 hit for Charles Harrison in 1913; #64 hit for Robert (Bobby) Maxwell in 1964

| 11/8/47 | 14 | 1 | | 4 An Apple Blossom Wedding ....A:14 Passing By | $10 | Columbia 37488 |

| 12/6/47+ | 3 | 15 | | 5 I'll Dance At Your Wedding   S:3 / A:3 / J:4 Those Things Money Can't Buy | $10 | Columbia 37967 |

RAY NOBLE and his ORCHESTRA with BUDDY CLARK
Anita Gordon (female vocal)

| 1/10/48 | 5 | 7 | | 6 Ballerina   A:5 / S:10 / J:13 It Had To Be You | $10 | Columbia 38040 |

#18 hit for Nat "King" Cole in 1957

DEBUT	PEAK	WKS	Gold	A-side (Chart Hit)..B-side	$	Label & Number

CLARK, Buddy — Cont'd

DEBUT	PEAK	WKS	Gold	A-side / B-side	$	Label & Number
3/27/48	6	5		7 **Now Is The Hour** (Maori Farewell Song) ....A:6 / J:26 *Peculiar* (Clark) **BUDDY CLARK and THE CHARIOTEERS** #59 hit for Gale Storm in 1956	$50	Columbia 38115
5/29/48	❶5	24	●	8 **Love Somebody** / ....A:❶5 / J:5 / S:6		
6/26/48	16	11		9 **Confess** ....S:16 / A:17 / J:21	$10	Columbia 38174
11/20/48	7	13		10 **My Darling My Darling** ....S:7 / A:7 / J:8 *That Certain Party* from the Broadway musical *Where's Charley?* starring **Ray Bolger**	$10	Columbia 38353
2/26/49	16	3		11 **Powder Your Face With Sunshine** (Smile! Smile! Smile!) ...A:16 / J:28 *I'll String Along With You* **DORIS DAY and BUDDY CLARK** (above 4) 7" 33-1/3 rpm: 1-113	$10	Columbia 38394
3/19/49	24	2		12 **I Love You So Much It Hurts** ....A:24 *Love Me! Love Me! Love Me! (Or Leave Me Alone)* #71 hit for Charlie Gracie in 1957	$10	Columbia 38406
3/19/49	25	4		13 **It's A Big, Wide, Wonderful World** ....A:25 *The Song Of Long Ago* from the 1940 Broadway musical *All In Fun* starring Imogene Coca	$10	Columbia 38370
5/7/49	3	19		14 **Baby, It's Cold Outside** ....A:3 / S:4 / J:6 *My One And Only Highland Fling* **DINAH SHORE and BUDDY CLARK** 7" 33-1/3 rpm: 1-200; from the movie *Neptune's Daughter* starring Esther Williams	$10	Columbia 38463
8/20/49	4	16		15 **You're Breaking My Heart** ....A:4 / S:9 / J:12 *Song Of Surrender* 7" 33-1/3 rpm: 1-296; based on the Italian song "La Mattinata"	$10	Columbia 38546
11/5/49	12	11		16 **A Dreamer's Holiday** ....A:12 / S:15 / J:18 *Envy* **BUDDY CLARK With the Girl Friends** 7" 33-1/3 rpm: 1-360	$10	Columbia 38599

CLARK SISTERS, The — see SMITH, Jack

CLINTON, Larry, And His Orchestra   MEM '38

Born on 8/17/09 in New York City. Died on 5/2/85 (age 75). Composer/arranger for Isham Jones, **Tommy Dorsey**, **Jimmy Dorsey** and Glen Gray. Clinton's top 3 pre-1940 #1 hits: "Deep Purple," "My Reverie" and "Cry, Baby, Cry."

DEBUT	PEAK	WKS	Gold	A-side / B-side	$	Label & Number
5/29/48	22	2		1 **The Dickey-Bird Song** ....J:22 / S:25 *Ooh! Look-A There, Ain't She Pretty?* from the movie *Three Darling Daughters* starring Jeanette MacDonald	$10	Decca 24301
12/4/48	25	1		2 **On A Slow Boat To China** ....J:25 / S:27 *This Is The Moment* Helen Lee and The Dipsy Doodlers (vocals, above 2)	$10	Decca 24482

CLOONEY, Rosemary ★38★   MEM/HOT '54

Born on 5/23/28 in Maysville, Kentucky. Died of cancer on 6/29/2002 (age 74). Sang with her sister Betty in **Tony Pastor**'s orchestra in the late 1940s. Became one of the most popular singers of the early 1950s. Acted in several movies including *White Christmas*. Re-emerged in the late 1970s as a successful jazz and ballad singer and as a TV commercial actress. Married twice to actor **Jose Ferrer** (1953-61 and 1964-67); their son Gabriel married Debby Boone. Her nephew, George Clooney, is a popular TV and movie actor. Won Grammy's Lifetime Achievement Award in 2002. Also see **Jose Ferrer** and **Tony Pastor**.

1)Come On-a My House 2)Hey There 3)This Ole House

DEBUT	PEAK	WKS	Gold	A-side / B-side	$	Label & Number
2/24/51	24	2		1 **You're Just In Love** ....A:24 / S:29 *Marrying For Love* **GUY MITCHELL & ROSEMARY CLOONEY** from the Broadway musical *Call Me Madam* starring **Ethel Merman**	$20	Columbia 4-39052
3/3/51	11	14		2 **Beautiful Brown Eyes** ....S:11 / A:11 / J:11 *Shot Gun Boogie* **Mitch Miller** (orch.)	$20	Columbia 4-39212
7/7/51	❶8	20	●	3 **Come On-a My House** ....A:❶8 / J:❶8 / S:❶6 *Rose Of The Mountain* from the off-Broadway musical *The Son*	$20	Columbia 4-39467
9/15/51	22	1		4 **Mixed Emotions** ....J:22 *Kentucky Waltz* also released as the B-side of #7 below	$20	Columbia 4-39333
9/22/51	21	4		5 **I'm Waiting Just For You** / ....J:21 #27 hit for Pat Boone in 1957		
9/22/51	24	1		6 **If Teardrops Were Pennies** ....S:24 / A:30 / J:30	$20	Columbia 4-39535
9/22/51	27	2		7 **I Wish I Wuz** ....A:27 *Mixed Emotions* from the movie *Slaughter Trail* starring Brian Donlevy and Gig Young	$20	Columbia 4-39536
2/9/52	18	3		8 **Be My Life's Companion** ....S:18 / A:21 / J:29 *Why Don't You Love Me*	$20	Columbia 4-39631
3/1/52	17	6	●	9 **Tenderly** ....A:17 / S:30 *Did Anyone Call* "Tenderly" was voted the #2 all-time favorite song in *Billboard*'s 1953 Disk Jockey poll; Clooney's recording was voted the #6 all-time favorite record in 1956; #31 hit for Bert Kaempfert in 1961	$20	Columbia 4-39648
5/3/52	❶3	27	●	10 **Half As Much** ....J:❶3 / A:2 / S:2 *Poor Whip - Poor-Will* #2 Country hit for **Hank Williams** in 1952	$20	Columbia 4-39710
6/28/52	2³	17	●	11 **Botch-A-Me** (Ba-Ba-Baciami Piccina) ....S:2 / A:2 / J:3 *On The First Warm Day* from the Italian movie *Una Famiglia Impossibile*	$20	Columbia 4-39767
8/23/52	12	6		12 **Too Old To Cut The Mustard** ....A:12 / J:19 / S:22 *Good For Nothin'* **MARLENE DIETRICH & ROSEMARY CLOONEY**	$20	Columbia 4-39812
9/27/52	17	3		13 **Blues In The Night** ....A:17 / J:27 / S:29 *Who Kissed Me Last Night* title song from the movie *Priscilla Lane*; **Percy Faith** (orch.: #1, 4, 8-10 & 13)	$20	Columbia 4-39813
12/20/52	9	2		14 **The Night Before Christmas Song** ....A:9 *Look Out The Window (The Winter Song)* [X] **ROSEMARY CLOONEY & GENE AUTRY** Carl Cotner (orch.); issued with a picture sleeve on Columbia's Children's Series MJV 4-149	$20	Columbia 4-39876
1/10/53	18	1		15 **You'll Never Know** ....J:18 *The Continental (You Kiss While You're Dancing)* **ROSEMARY CLOONEY-HARRY JAMES** from the movie *Hello Frisco, Hello* starring Alice Faye	$20	Columbia 4-39905
7/17/54	❶6	27	●	16 **Hey There** / ....S:❶6 / A:❶5 / J:❶4 from the Broadway musical *The Pajama Game* starring John Raitt		
8/7/54	❶3	27		17 **This Ole House** ....J:❶3 / S:❶1 / A:5	$15	Columbia 4-40266
11/13/54	9	12	●	18 **Mambo Italiano** ....J:9 / S:10 / A:13 *We'll Be Together Again* The Mellomen (backing vocals); Buddy Cole (orch., above 3)	$15	Columbia 4-40361

COLE, Nat "King" ★17★   MEM/HOT '55

Born Nathaniel Adams Coles on 3/17/17 in Montgomery, Alabama; raised in Chicago. Died of cancer on 2/15/65 (age 47). First recorded in 1936 in band led by brother Eddie. Toured with "Shuffle Along" musical revue. Formed **The King Cole Trio** in 1939: Cole (piano), Oscar Moore (guitar) and Wesley Prince (bass; replaced several years later by Johnny Miller). Long series of top-selling records led to his solo career in 1950. Appeared in several movies. Hosted own TV variety series from 1956-57. Father of Natalie Cole. Won Grammy's Lifetime Achievement Award in 1990. Inducted into the Rock and Roll Hall of Fame in 2000 as an early influence.

1)Mona Lisa 2)Nature Boy 3)(I Love You) For Sentimental Reasons 4)Too Young 5)Pretend

Orchestras: **Baxter, Les** — 17,22,23,25,33   Lipman, Joe — 21   Riddle, Nelson —
            DeVol, Frank — 13   **May, Billy** — 28,36,40   26,27,30-32,34,35,37-39,41-45
            Kenton, Stan — 19   Rugolo, Pete — 18,20,24,29

KING COLE'S TRIO:

DEBUT	PEAK	WKS	Gold	A-side / B-side	$	Label & Number
12/11/43	**19**	1		**1 All For You** ....S(wc):19 *Vom, Vim, Veedle*	$20	Capitol 139
				#1 R&B hit (2 weeks)		
				THE KING COLE TRIO:		
6/3/44	**9**	5		**2 Straighten Up And Fly Right /** ....S:9 / J:14		
				#1 R&B hit (10 weeks); #73 hit for the DeJohn Sisters in 1958		
5/6/44	**24**	1		**3 I Can't See For Lookin'** J:24	$15	Capitol 154
11/18/44	**20**	1		**4 Gee, Baby, Ain't I Good To You** ....J:20 *I Realize Now* (R&B #9)	$15	Capitol 169
				#1 R&B hit (4 weeks)		
1/5/46	**19**	1		**5 The Frim Fram Sauce**...A:19 *Come To Baby, Do!* (R&B #3)	$15	Capitol 224
8/3/46	**11**	2		**6 (Get Your Kicks On) Route 66** ....A:11 / J:16 *Everyone Is Sayin' Hello Again (Why Must We Say Goodbye?)*	$15	Capitol 256
				the Trio's most renowned jazz/R&B song, celebrating the famous westward highway; #61 hit for Depeche Mode in 1988		
9/7/46	**10**	1		**7 You Call It Madness (But I Call It Love)**......................................A:10 *Oh, But I Do*	$15	Capitol 274
				#5 hit for Russ Columbo in 1931		
11/9/46	**❶⁶**	25		**8 (I Love You) For Sentimental Reasons /** ....A:❶⁶ / S:❶¹ / J:4		
				#17 hit for Sam Cooke in 1958		
11/16/46	**14**	3		**9 The Best Man** A:14	$15	Capitol 304
11/30/46	**3**	7	●	**10 The Christmas Song** (Merry Christmas		
				To You) A:3 / S:7 / J:16 *The Little Boy That Santa Claus Forgot* **[X]**	$15	Capitol 311
				Cole's classic Christmas tune re-charted with a new version in 1960 (#80) and 1962 (#65)		
10/25/47	**12**	1		**11 Save The Bones For Henry Jones** ('Cause Henry Don't Eat No Meat) /...................A:12		
11/8/47	**12**	1		**12 Harmony**...A:12	$15	Capitol 15000
				JOHNNY MERCER And THE KING COLE TRIO (above 2)		
				from the movie *Variety Girl* starring Mary Hatcher		
4/17/48	**❶⁸**	18	●	**13 Nature Boy** A:❶⁸ / S:❶⁷ / J:2 *Lost April*	$15	Capitol 15054
				KING COLE		
				#40 hit for Bobby Darin in 1961		
7/17/48	**30**	1		**14 Put 'Em In A Box, Tie 'Em With A Ribbon**		
				(And Throw 'Em In The Deep Blue Sea)...............................J:30 *It's The Sentimental Thing To Do*	$15	Capitol 15080
				from the movie *Romance On The High Seas* starring Jack Carson		
1/8/49-	**24**	1		**15 The Christmas Song** (Merry Christmas		
				To You) ....A:24 *The Little Boy That Santa Claus Forgot* **[X-R]**	$15	Capitol 15201
				NAT "KING" COLE:		
4/1/50	**26**	1		**16 I Almost Lost My Mind** ....A:26 *Baby Won't You Say You Love Me*	$30	Capitol F889
				#1 R&B hit for Ivory Joe Hunter in 1950; #1 hit for Pat Boone in 1956		
6/10/50	**❶⁸**	27	●	**17 Mona Lisa** A:❶⁸ / S:❶⁵ / J:❶⁵ *The Greatest Inventor (Of Them All)*	$25	Capitol F1010
				from the movie *Captain Carey, U.S.A.* starring Alan Ladd; #1 R&B hit (4 weeks); #25 hit for Carl Mann in 1959		
9/2/50	**22**	1		**18 Home** (When Shadows Fall) ....A:22 *Tunnel Of Love*	$25	Capitol F1133
				#2 hit for Peter Van Steeden in 1932		
9/30/50	**5**	14		**19 Orange Colored Sky** A:5 / J:10 / S:11 *Jam-Bo*	$25	Capitol F1184
				NAT "KING" COLE and STAN KENTON		
1/6/51-	**❶⁸**	1		**20 Frosty The Snow Man**...A:9 *Little Christmas Tree* **[X-N]**	$40	Capitol F1203
				The Singing Pussy Cats (Chipmunk voices)		
2/10/51	**20**	2		**21 Jet** ....S:20 / A:29 *The Magic Tree*	$25	Capitol F1365
				The Ray Charles Singers (backing vocals)		
4/7/51	**28**	2		**22 Always You**..A:28 *Destination Moon*	$25	Capitol F1401
				adapted from Tchaikovsky's "Romance"		
4/14/51	**❶⁵**	29	●	**23 Too Young** S:❶⁵ / A:❶⁴ / J:❶⁴ *That's My Girl*	$25	Capitol F1449
				#13 hit for Donny Osmond in 1972		
5/19/51	**24**	2		**24 Red Sails In The Sunset** ....S:24 / A:29 *Little Child*	$25	Capitol F1468
				from the Broadway musical *Provincetown Follies Of 1935* starring **Beatrice Kay**; #1 hit for both **Bing Crosby** and **Guy Lombardo** in 1935; #36 hit for The Platters in 1960		
6/9/51	**17**	4		**25 Because Of Rain** ....J:17 / A:19 *Song Of Delilah*	$25	Capitol F1501
11/3/51+	**12**	15		**26 Unforgettable** ....A:12 / S:14 / J:22 *My First And My Last Love*	$25	Capitol F1808
				the 1961 remake of this song by Cole charted in 1991 with Natalie Cole's vocals dubbed in (#14)		
5/31/52	**8**	25		**27 Somewhere Along The Way** ....A:8 / S:8 / J:12 *What Does It Take*	$20	Capitol F2069
				#67 hit for Steve Lawrence in 1961		
7/5/52	**8**	12		**28 Walkin' My Baby Back Home /**..A:8 / J:11 / S:12		
				NAT KING COLE and BILLY MAY and His Orchestra		
				#8 hit in 1931 for both Nick Lucas and **Ted Weems**		
8/16/52	**26**	1		**29 Funny** (Not Much)...S:26	$20	Capitol F2130
9/27/52	**16**	5		**30 Because You're Mine /** ....A:16 / S:17 / J:19		
				title song from the movie starring **Mario Lanza**		
10/18/52	**22**	1		**31 I'm Never Satisfied** A:22	$20	Capitol F2212

DEBUT	PEAK	WKS	Gold	A-side (Chart Hit)..B-side	$	Label & Number

COLE, Nat "King" — Cont'd

DEBUT	PEAK	WKS	Gold	A-side / B-side	$	Label & Number
10/11/52	24	4		32 Faith Can Move Mountains / S:24		
10/11/52	25	2		33 The Ruby And The Pearl ....S:25 / A:25	$20	Capitol F2230
				from the movie Thunder In The East *starring Alan Ladd*		
1/31/53	20	1		34 Strange ....A:20 *How (How Do I Go About It?)*	$20	Capitol F2309
2/7/53	2[1]	21		35 Pretend ....J:2 / A:3 / S:3 *Don't Let Your Eyes Go Shopping (For Your Heart)*	$20	Capitol F2346
4/4/53	16	3		36 Can't I ....A:16 / S:17 / J:18 *Blue Gardenia*	$20	Capitol F2389
				NAT "KING" COLE and BILLY MAY and His Orchestra		
6/27/53	19	1		37 I Am In Love ....A:19 *My Flaming Heart*	$20	Capitol F2459
				from the Broadway musical Can-Can *starring Lilo*		
7/25/53	15	1		38 Return To Paradise ....A:15 *Angel Eyes*	$20	Capitol F2498
				title song from the movie starring Gary Cooper		
8/22/53	17	1		39 A Fool Was I ....A:17 *If Love Is Good To Me*	$20	Capitol F2540
11/14/53	16	3		40 Lover, Come Back To Me! ....A:16 *That's All*	$20	Capitol F2610
				NAT "KING" COLE and BILLY MAY and His Orchestra		
				from the Broadway musical The New Moon *starring Evelyn Herbert; #3 hit for Paul Whiteman in 1929; #95 hit for The Cleftones in 1962*		
2/13/54	6	19	●	41 Answer Me, My Love ....S:6 / A:7 / J:7 *Why*	$20	Capitol F2687
5/1/54	16	2		42 It Happens To Be Me ....A:16 *Alone Too Long*	$20	Capitol F2754
7/24/54	19	2		43 Make Her Mine ....A:19 *I Envy*	$20	Capitol F2803
9/18/54	10	11		44 Smile ....A:10 / S:14 / J:20 *It's Crazy*	$20	Capitol F2897
				music written by Charlie Chaplin, based on the theme from his 1936 movie Modern Times*; #42 hit for Timi Yuro in 1961*		
11/13/54	14	7		45 Hajji Baba (Persian Lament) ....S:14 / A:16 / J:19 *Unbelievable*	$20	Capitol F2949
				from the movie The Adventures Of Hajji Baba *starring John Derek*		

COLONNA, Jerry   MEM '45

Born on 9/17/04 in Boston. Died of kidney failure on 11/21/86 (age 82). Popular comedian. Hosted own TV show in 1951.

| 7/21/45 | 7 | 4 | | Bell Bottom Trousers ....A:7 / S:9 *I Cried For You* [N] | $10 | Capitol 204 |
| | | | | *based on a traditional sea chantey published in 1907* | | |

COLUMBIA TOKYO ORCH.   '53

| 3/14/53 | 15 | 2 | | Gomen-Nasai (Forgive Me) ....J:15 / A:16 *Tokyo Boogie Woogie* | $15 | Columbia 4-39954 |
| | | | | *Richard Bowers (vocal)* | | |

COMO, Perry ★3★   MEM/HOT '46

Born Pierino Como on 5/18/12 in Canonsburg, Pennsylvania. Died on 5/12/2001 (age 88). Owned barbershop in hometown. With Freddy Carlone band in 1933; with **Ted Weems** from 1936-42. Appeared in several movies. Hosted own TV shows from 1948-63. One of the most popular singers of the 20th century. Won Grammy's Lifetime Achievement Award in 2002.

1)Till The End Of Time   2)Wanted   3)If   4)Some Enchanted Evening   5)Don't Let The Stars Get In Your Eyes

Orchestras: Ayres, Mitchell — 38-57,59-71,82-84   Case, Russ — 10-24,27,31-34   René, Henri — 35,37,77   Romberg, Sigmund — 58   Shaffer, Lloyd — 25,26,28-30   Steele, Ted — 9   Weems, Ted — 30   Winterhalter, Hugo — 73,74,78-81

Vocalists: Charles, Ray, Chorus — 82,83   Fontane Sisters, The — 36,40,46, 47,50,51,53,56,59,61,63,66,71   Ramblers, The — 72,75   Satisfiers, The — 13,14,16,17,27-29,34

DEBUT	PEAK	WKS	Gold	A-side / B-side	$	Label & Number
10/16/43	20	1		1 Goodbye, Sue ....S(wc):20 *There'll Soon Be A Rainbow*	$10	Victor 20-1538
1/15/44	14	2		2 Have I Stayed Away Too Long? ....J(terr.):14 *I've Had This Feeling Before (But Never Like This)*	$10	Victor 20-1548
				#94 hit for Bobby Bare in 1964		
5/6/44	8	7		3 Long Ago (And Far Away) / ....S:8 / J:8		
				from the movie Cover Girl *starring Rita Hayworth*		
4/29/44	16	3		4 I Love You J:16	$10	Victor 20-1569
				from the Broadway musical Mexican Hayride *starring Bobby Clark*		
8/26/44	13	3		5 Lili Marlene ....J:13 *First Class Private Mary Brown*	$10	Victor 20-1592
				song usually identified with **Marlene Dietrich**		
1/27/45	10	2		6 I Dream Of You (More Than You Dream I Do) / ....S:10 / A:16		
3/3/45	12	1		7 I'm Confessin' (That I Love You) A:12	$10	Victor 20-1629
				#2 hit for Guy Lombardo in 1930; #58 hit for Frank Ifield in 1963		
3/17/45	14	2		8 More And More ....A:14 *I Wish We Didn't Have To Say Goodnight*	$10	Victor 20-1630
				from the movie Can't Help Singing *starring Deanna Durbin*		
6/16/45	15	1	●	9 Temptation ....A:15 *I'll Always Be With You*	$10	Victor 20-1658
				from the movie Going Hollywood *starring* **Bing Crosby***; #3 hit for Bing Crosby in 1934; #27 hit for The Everly Brothers in 1961; also see* **Red Ingle***'s novelty version of 1947*		
7/28/45	3	13	●	10 If I Loved You / S:3 / A:3 / J:3		
				from the Broadway musical Carousel *starring John Raitt; #23 hit for Chad & Jeremy in 1965*		
7/21/45	4	17		11 I'm Gonna Love That Gal (Like She's Never Been Loved Before) J:4 / S:7 / A:7	$10	Victor 20-1676
8/18/45	❶[10]	19	●	12 Till The End Of Time S:❶[10] / A:❶[9] / J:❶[9]		
				song based on Chopin's "Polonaise" (also see **Carmen Cavallaro***'s instrumental version in 1945); #83 hit for the Ray Charles Singers in 1964*		
8/25/45	9	11		13 (Did You Ever Get) That Feeling In The Moonlight ....J:9 / A:10	$10	Victor 20-1709
12/8/45+	3	14	●	14 Dig You Later (A Hubba-Hubba-Hubba) / S:3 / A:3 / J:5 [N]		
				featuring Como singing the title line from his hit "Till The End Of Time"		
12/29/45	12	3		15 Here Comes Heaven Again A:12	$10	Victor 20-1750
				above 2 from the movie Doll Face *starring Como and Vivian Blaine*		
2/2/46	5	8	●	16 I'm Always Chasing Rainbows / J:5 / S:7 / A:8		
				from the movie The Dolly Sisters *starring* **Betty Grable***; melody adapted from Chopin's "Fantasie Impromptu"; #1 hit for Charles Harrison in 1918*		
2/9/46	5	14		17 You Won't Be Satisfied (Until You Break My Heart) J:5 / A:8	$10	Victor 20-1788

DEBUT	PEAK	WKS	Gold	A-side (Chart Hit)..B-side	$	Label & Number
				COMO, Perry — Cont'd		
3/30/46	**❶**³	21	●	18 **Prisoner Of Love** / S:**❶**³ / A:**❶**² / J:2		
				#16 hit for Russ Columbo in 1932; #18 hit for James Brown in 1963		
5/11/46	8	5		19 **All Through The Day**...A:8 / J:13	$10	RCA Victor 20-1814
				from the movie *Centennial Summer* starring Cornel Wilde		
6/1/46	4	13		20 **They Say It's Wonderful** / S:4 / J:4 / A:7		
				from the Broadway musical *Annie Get Your Gun* starring **Ethel Merman**		
6/8/46	14	4		21 **If You Were The Only Girl** ....A:14 / J:15	$10	RCA Victor 20-1857
6/29/46	**❶**¹	17		22 **Surrender** / S:**❶**¹ / A:2 / J:2		
8/17/46	19	1		23 **More Than You Know** J:19	$10	RCA Victor 20-1877
				from the Broadway musical *Great Day* starring Allan Pryor; #9 hit for Ruth Etting in 1930		
11/16/46	19	1		24 **If I'm Lucky** ....J:19 *One More Vote (One More Kiss)*	$10	RCA Victor 20-1945
				title song from the movie starring Como and Vivian Blaine		
12/28/46+	9	7		25 **Sonata** / ....A:9 / J:15		
2/1/47	19	1		26 **That's The Beginning Of The End** J:19	$10	RCA Victor 20-2033
12/28/46	10	1		27 **Winter Wonderland** ....S:10 *That Christmas Feeling* **[X]**	$10	RCA Victor 20-1968
				#2 hit for Guy Lombardo in 1934		
5/24/47	**❶**³	13	●	28 **Chi-Baba Chi-Baba (My Bambino Go To Sleep)** / S:**❶**³ / J:2 / A:8		
7/12/47	2¹	19		29 **When You Were Sweet Sixteen** ....S:2 / J:4 / A:6	$10	RCA Victor 20-2259
				from the movie *The Great John L.* starring Greg McClure; #1 in 1900 for both George J. Gaskin and Jere Mahoney		
8/2/47	2⁵	17		30 **I Wonder Who's Kissing Her Now** A:2 / J:2 / S:3 *That Old Gang Of Mine*	$10	Decca 25078 and
				TED WEEMS And His Orchestra; Perry Como, vocal		RCA Victor 20-2315
				Billboard listed both the Decca and RCA versions at one chart position (the Decca version charted alone for the first 11 weeks; it was recorded on 10/5/39 and originally issued on Decca 2919); the RCA release (Como's solo version) features Lloyd Shaffer's orchestra (B-side: "When Tonight Is Just A Memory"); title song from the 1947 movie starring June Haven; #1 hit for Henry Burr in 1909; #93 hit for Bobby Darin in 1964		
10/25/47	11	2		31 **So Far** ....A:11 *A Fellow Needs A Girl*	$10	RCA Victor 20-2402
				from the Broadway musical *Allegro* starring John Battles		
3/13/48	4	18	●	32 **Because** S:4 / A:10 / J:11 *If You Had All The World And Its Gold*	$10	RCA Victor 20-2653
				#4 hit for Enrico Caruso in 1913		
6/5/48	23	2		33 **Haunted Heart** ....S:23 *Carolina Moon*	$10	RCA Victor 20-2713
				from the Broadway musical *Inside U.S.A.* starring Jack Haley		
7/31/48	18	14		34 **Rambling Rose** ....S:18 / J:19 / A:21 *There Must Be A Way*	$10	RCA Victor 20-2947
1/8/49	4	17		35 **Far Away Places** ....A:4 / S:6 / J:7 *Missouri Waltz*	$10	RCA Victor 20-3316
1/15/49	20	6		36 **N'yot N'yow (The Pussycat Song)** ....A:20 / S:21 *Roses Of Picardy*	$10	RCA Victor 20-3288
2/26/49	18	3		37 **Blue Room** ....S:18 *With A Song In My Heart*	$10	RCA Victor 20-3329
				from the movie *Words And Music* starring Mickey Rooney; #3 hit for the Revelers in 1926		
3/19/49	2¹	25		38 **Forever And Ever** / A:2 / S:3 / J:3		
				adapted from a Swiss waltz		
5/14/49	11	15		39 **I Don't See Me In Your Eyes Anymore** ....S:11 / J:16 / A:26	$25	RCA Victor 47-2892
				78 rpm: 20-3347; #47 hit for Charlie Rich in 1974		
4/9/49	**❶**²	15		40 **"A"-You're Adorable** A:**❶**² / J:3 / S:4 *When Is Sometime?*	$20	RCA Victor 47-2899
				78 rpm: 20-3381		
4/30/49	**❶**⁵	26		41 **Some Enchanted Evening** / S:**❶**⁵ / J:**❶**⁵ / A:**❶**²		
				#13 hit for Jay & The Americans in 1965		
4/30/49	5	16		42 **Bali Ha'i** S:5 / J:9 / A:14	$20	RCA Victor 47-2896
				78 rpm: 20-3402; above 2 from the Broadway musical *South Pacific* starring **Mary Martin** and **Ezio Pinza**		
7/16/49	15	10		43 **Let's Take An Old-Fashioned Walk** / ....S:15 / A:20 / J:30		
7/9/49	23	2		44 **Just One Way To Say I Love You** S:23	$20	RCA Victor 47-2931
				78 rpm: 20-3469; above 2 from the Broadway musical *Miss Liberty* starring Eddie Albert		
9/3/49	23	2		45 **Give Me Your Hand** ....A:23 / J:24 / S:25 *I Wish I Had A Record (Of The Promises You Made)*	$20	RCA Victor 47-2997
				78 rpm: 20-3521		
10/8/49+	3	19		46 **A Dreamer's Holiday** A:3 / S:4 / J:5 *The Meadows Of Heaven*	$20	RCA Victor 47-3036
				78 rpm: 20-3543		
11/26/49	18	8		47 **I Wanna Go Home (With You)** ....A:18 / S:22 / J:26 *Hush Little Darlin'* **[N]**	$20	RCA Victor 47-3082
				78 rpm: 20-3586		
12/24/49	22	3		48 **Ave Maria** / ....S:22 / A:22 **[X]**		
				Franz Schubert version		
12/17/49	28	2		49 **The Lord's Prayer** ....S:28 **[X]**	$25	RCA Victor 52-0071
				78 rpm: 28-0436; reissued in 1959 on RCA Victor 7650 with a picture sleeve; new version of Biblical text charted by Sister Janet Mead in 1974 (#4)		
1/28/50	14	6		50 **Bibbidi-Bobbidi-Boo (The Magic Song)** ....J:14 / S:17 / A:23 *A Dream Is A Wish Your Heart Makes*	$20	RCA Victor 47-3113
				78 rpm: 20-3607; from the Disney animated feature movie *Cinderella*		
4/29/50	**❶**²	17		51 **Hoop-Dee-Doo** / A:**❶**² / S:4 / J:4		
4/29/50	16	5		52 **On The Outgoing Tide**...A:16	$20	RCA Victor 47-3747
8/12/50	25	2		53 **I Cross My Fingers** ....S:25 *If You Were My Girl*	$20	RCA Victor 47-3846
9/30/50	7	12		54 **Patricia** ....S:7 / J:11 / A:28 *Watchin' The Trains Go By*	$20	RCA Victor 47-3905
10/21/50	3	18		55 **A Bushel And A Peck** A:3 / S:6 / J:7 *She's A Lady* **[N]**	$20	RCA Victor 47-3930
				PERRY COMO and BETTY HUTTON		
				from the Broadway musical *Guys And Dolls* starring Robert Alda and Vivian Blaine		
12/9/50+	5	17		56 **You're Just In Love** S:5 / A:6 / J:7 *It's A Lovely Day Today*	$20	RCA Victor 47-3945
				from the Broadway musical *Call Me Madam* starring **Ethel Merman**		
1/13/51	**❶**⁸	24	●	57 **If** / A:**❶**⁸ / S:**❶**⁶ / J:**❶**⁵		
				#82 hit for The Paragons in 1961		
1/13/51	12	9		58 **Zing Zing—Zoom Zoom**..................................J:12 / A:13 / S:17	$20	RCA Victor 47-3997
6/23/51	20	2		59 **There's No Boat Like A Rowboat** / ....J:20 / A:30		
6/23/51	25	2		60 **There's A Big Blue Cloud (Next to Heaven)** ....A:25 / S:28	$20	RCA Victor 47-4158
10/13/51	24	4		61 **Rollin' Stone** / ....A:24 / J:29		
				Como's backing vocalists, **The Fontane Sisters**, had a 1955 hit of the same title, but it was a completely different song		
10/20/51	28	1		62 **With All My Heart And Soul** A:28	$20	RCA Victor 47-4269
12/15/51	19	3		63 **It's Beginning To Look Like Christmas**........................A:19 / S:23 *There Is No Christmas Like A Home Christmas* **[X]**	$20	RCA Victor 47-4314

				COMO, Perry — Cont'd		
2/16/52	12	10		64 Please Mr. Sun / ....A:12 / J:29		
				#11 hit for **Tommy Edwards** in 1959		
1/26/52	16	11		65 Tulips And Heather ....J:16 / S:17 / A:24	$20	RCA Victor 47-4453
3/8/52	23	1		66 Noodlin' Rag ....J:23 *Play Me A Hurtin' Tune*	$20	RCA Victor 47-4542
5/3/52	18	8		67 One Little Candle ....J:18 *It's Easter Time*	$20	RCA Victor 47-4631
6/14/52	3	18		68 Maybe /	J:3 / A:7 / S:8		
6/14/52	19	6		69 Watermelon Weather ....A:19 / J:20 / S:28	$20	RCA Victor 47-4744
				PERRY COMO and EDDIE FISHER (above 2)		
10/4/52	22	1		70 My Love And Devotion ....A:22 *Sweethearts Holiday*	$20	RCA Victor 47-4877
11/1/52	19	1		71 To Know You (Is to Love You)...............J:19 / A:25 *My Lady Loves To Dance*	$20	RCA Victor 47-4959
12/6/52+	❶5	21	●	72 Don't Let The Stars Get In Your Eyes	S:❶5 / J:❶4 / A:❶3 *Lies*	$20	RCA Victor 47-5064
				#1 Country hit for both **Skeets McDonald** and **Slim Willet** in 1952		
2/14/53	6	12		73 Wild Horses / ....J:6 / A:6 / S:7		
				adapted from Robert Schumann's "Wilder Reiter"		
3/28/53	17	1		74 I Confess A:17	$20	RCA Victor 47-5152
4/25/53	3	16		75 Say You're Mine Again /	J:3 / A:4 / S:5		
6/6/53	11	7		76 My One And Only Heart ....J:11 / A:14	$20	RCA Victor 47-5277
6/20/53	❶4	22		77 No Other Love	A:❶4 / S:2 / J:4 *Keep It Gay*	$20	RCA Victor 47-5317
				melody based on Richard Rodgers' "Beneath the Southern Cross" from the TV documentary series *Victory At Sea*; lyrical version from the Broadway musical *Me And Juliet* starring Bill Hayes; issued with a picture sleeve		
10/31/53	9	13		78 You Alone (Solo Tu) / ....J:9 / S:10 / A:11		
10/24/53	11	5		79 Pa-Paya Mama ....J:11 / A:12 / S:19	$20	RCA Victor 47-5447
3/6/54	❶8	22	●	80 Wanted	S:❶8 / J:❶8 / A:❶7 *Look Out The Window (And See How I'm Standing in the Rain)*	$20	RCA Victor 47-5647
				issued with a picture sleeve: "Pop Si Hit Record of the Month"		
7/3/54	15	2		81 Hit And Run Affair.........................A:15 / J:18 / S:30 *There Never Was A Night So Beautiful*	$20	RCA Victor 47-5749
10/2/54	4	18	●	82 Papa Loves Mambo	S:4 / A:4 / J:4		
11/13/54	27	1		83 The Things I Didn't Do S:27	$20	RCA Victor 47-5857
12/25/54	8	3		84 There's No Place Like Home For The Holidays ....A:8 / S:18 *Silk Stockings* **[X]**	$20	RCA Victor 47-5950
				CONTINO, Dick HOT **'54**		
				Born on 1/17/30 in Fresno, California. Accordion virtuoso. Discovered by bandleader **Horace Heidt** and featured on his radio show in the late 1940s.		
12/4/54	27	1		Yours (Quireme Mucho)...S:27 *Ooh! Mambo* **[I]**	$15	Mercury 70455-X45
				David Carroll (orch.).		
				COOK, Lawrence (Piano Roll) **'50**		
				Boogie-woogie pianist.		
4/15/50	13	11		1 The Old Piano Roll Blues ....J:13 / A:19 / S:23 *Why Do They Always Say "No"?*	$25	Abbey 15003-X45
				The Jim Dandies (vocals)		
9/29/51	22	2		2 Down Yonder ....J:22 / S:23 *Tiger Rag* **[I]**	$25	Abbey 15053-X45
				#5 hit for Ernest Hare & Billy Jones in 1921; #48 hit for Johnny & The Hurricanes in 1960		
				COOL, Harry, and His Orchestra **'46**		
				Born on 6/28/13 in Chicago. Died in June 1979 (age 66). Vocalist with **Dick Jurgens**' band from 1939-43.		
10/19/46	12	2		Rumors Are Flying ....A:12 / J:14 *The Whole World Is Singing My Song* (Cool)	$15	Signature 15043
				HARRY COOL and MINDY CARSON		
				COOLEY, Spade — see SHORE, Dinah		
				COPAS, Cowboy — see LAWRENCE, Elliot		

				CORNELL, Don ★85★ MEM/HOT **'52**		
				Born Louis Varalo on 4/21/19 in New York City. Popular singer/guitarist. From the late 1930s, worked with **Al Kavelin** and Red Nichols. Achieved greatest success with **Sammy Kaye**, charting 14 hits from 1942-50.		
				1)Hold My Hand 2)I'm Yours 3)I'll Walk Alone		
6/18/49	12	10		1 Baby, It's Cold Outside..A:12 / S:13 / J:17 *Whispering Waters*	$20	RCA Victor 47-2914
				DON CORNELL and LAURA LESLIE **Sammy Kaye** (orch.); from the movie *Neptune's Daughter* starring Esther Williams		
9/30/50	25	1		2 I Need You So ....J:25 / A:28 *It Couldn't Happen To A Sweeter Girl (It Couldn't Happen to a Nicer Guy)*	$20	RCA Victor 47-3884
				Hugo Winterhalter (orch.); #1 R&B hit for Ivory Joe Hunter in 1950		
3/22/52	5	19		3 I'll Walk Alone ....A:5 / S:7 / J:7 *That's The Chance You Take*	$20	Coral 9-60659
				featured in the movie *With A Song In My Heart* starring Susan Hayward		
4/26/52	3	17	●	4 I'm Yours ....A:3 / S:5 / J:9 *My Mother's Pearls*	$20	Coral 9-60690
7/19/52	20	3		5 This Is The Beginning Of The End ....A:20 / S:30 *(I've Cried Until) I Can't Cry Anymore*	$20	Coral 9-60748
				from the movie *Johnny Apollo* starring Tyrone Power		
9/27/52	17	6		6 You'll Never Get Away ....A:17 / S:18 / J:20 *The Hookey Song* **[N]**	$20	Coral 9-60829
				DON CORNELL And TERESA BREWER featuring Cornell singing the title line from his hit "I'm Yours"		
11/1/52	7	8		7 I ....J:7 / A:11 / S:15 *Be Fair*	$20	Coral 9-60860
				the shortest song title ever charted; melody based on the semi-classical "Serenade" by Drigo; lyrics written by Milton Berle		
9/5/53	18	2		8 Please Play Our Song (Mister Record Man) ....A:18 *If I Should Love Again*	$20	Coral 9-61030
				Norman Leyden (orch.): #3-5, 7 & 8)		
12/5/53+	10	10		9 The Gang That Sang "Heart Of My Heart" ....J:10 / A:14 / S:18 *I Think I'll Fall In Love Today*	$20	Coral 9-61076
				DON CORNELL, ALAN DALE AND JOHNNY DESMOND Jack Pleis (orch.: #6 & 9); song written in 1926		
9/11/54	2¹	18	●	10 Hold My Hand ....A:2 / S:5 / J:7 *I'm Blessed*	$20	Coral 9-61206
				Jerry Carr (orch.); from the movie *Susan Slept Here* starring Dick Powell and **Debbie Reynolds**		

COTÉ, Emile, Serenaders — '48
A cappella vocal group directed by Bob Evans.

7/17/48	23	1		**Tea Leaves** ....S:23 *In Martha's Eyes* (Nick De Frances)	$15	Columbia 38230

originally issued on Algene 1933 in 1948; #9 hit for Nora Bayes in 1921

★133★ CRAIG, Francis, and His Orchestra — '47
Born on 9/10/1900 in Dickson, Tennessee. Died on 11/20/66 (age 66). Pianist/songwriter/bandleader.

8/9/47	❶17	25	●	1 **Near You** ....A:❶17 / J:❶13 / S:❶12 *Red Rose*	$15	Bullet 1001

the most weeks at #1 in Pop chart history, until Bryan Adams had 17 weeks at #1 on the Sales chart with "(Everything I Do) I Do It For You"; #10 hit for Roger Williams in 1958

1/17/48	3	20		2 **Beg Your Pardon** ....J:3 / S:4 / A:4 *I'm Looking For A Sweetheart*	$15	Bullet 1012

Bob Lamm (vocal, above 2)

★146★ CREW-CUTS, The — MEM/HOT '54
Pop vocal group from Toronto: brothers John and Ray Perkins, Pat Barrett and Rudi Maugeri.

5/8/54	8	18		1 **Crazy 'Bout Ya Baby** ....S:8 / J:11 / J:12 *Angela Mia*	$25	Mercury 70341-X45
7/10/54	❶9	20		2 **Sh-Boom** ....A:❶9 / J:❶8 / S:❶7 *I Spoke Too Soon*	$25	Mercury 70404-X45

considered by many to be the first #1 rock and roll record; issued with a picture sleeve: "Pop Si Hit Record of the Month"

9/25/54	13	7		3 **Oop-Shoop** ....J:13 / S:18 *Do Me Good Baby*	$20	Mercury 70443-X45

#8 R&B hit for Shirley Gunter in 1954; David Carroll (orch., above 3)

CROSBY, Bing ★1★ — MEM/HOT '44

Born Harry Lillis Crosby on 5/3/03 in Tacoma, Washington. Died of a heart attack on 10/14/77 (age 74). Bing and singing partner Al Rinker were hired in 1926 by Paul Whiteman; with Harry Barris they became the Rhythm Boys and gained an increasing following. The trio split from Whiteman in 1930, and Bing sang briefly with Gus Arnheim's band. It was his early-1931 smash with Arnheim, "I Surrender, Dear," which earned Bing a CBS radio contract and launched an unsurpassed solo career. Over the next three decades the resonant Crosby baritone and breezy persona sold more than 300 million records and was featured in over 50 movies (won Academy Award for *Going My Way*, 1944). Won Grammy's Lifetime Achievement Award in 1962. Ranked as the #1 artist in *Joel Whitburn's Pop Memories 1890-1954* book, Bing had over 150 hits from 1931-39. Married to actress Dixie Lee from 1930 until her death in 1952; their son **Gary Crosby** began recording in 1950. Married to actress Kathryn Grant from 1957 until his death; their daughter Mary became an actress. Bing's youngest brother, **Bob Crosby**, was a popular swing-era bandleader. Crosby's top 5 pre-1940 #1 hits: "Sweet Leilani," "Pennies From Heaven," "June In January," "Please" and "Love In Bloom."

1)White Christmas 2)Swinging On A Star 3)Only Forever 4)Don't Fence Me In 5)Sunday, Monday Or Always

Orchestras: Barbour, Dave — 127
Blackton, Jay — 79
Botkin, Perry — 99,100,103,104,133,134
Burke, Sonny — 121
Camarata — 54
Cavallaro, Carmen — 68,88,89
Condon, Eddie — 78
Crosby, Bob — 10,11,85
Cugat, Xavier — 61,62

Dorsey, Jimmy — 73
Haggart, Bob — 75,77,87
Herman, Woody — 16,20
Jordan, Louis — 63
Lilley, Joseph — 60
Martin, Grady — 131
Matlock, Matty — 111,112,123,124,126
McIntire, Dick — 6
Murray, Lyn — 116,117

Oliver, Sy — 110
Paul, Les — 67
Schoen, Vic — 32,33,44,45,49,50,55,66,80,81,86,94,107-109,122,130
Sosnik, Harry — 18
Stordahl, Axel — 113,114

Trotter, John Scott — 2-5,7,9,12,14,15,17,21-27,34-43,46-48,52,53,56,57,59,64,65,69,70,71,74,82-84,91,92,95,101,102,106,118-120,125,128,129,135
Venuti, Joe — 1
Waring, Fred — 90,105
Young, Victor — 8,13,19,58,72,97,98,115

Vocalists: Alexander, Jeff, Chorus — 115,120
Andrews Sisters — 1,32,33,44,45,49,50,55,66,80,81,86,94,107,108,122
Aristokats, The — 110
Armstrong, Louis — 125
Calico Kids, The — 84
Cass County Boys — 134

Chickadees, The — 85
Conlon, Jud, Rhythmaires — 92,98,103,118,132,133
Crosby, Gary — 111,112,120,123,124
Crosby, Phillip, Dennis & Lindsay — 120

Darby, Ken, Singers — 25,28,29,35,52,58,69,83,91,93,95,96,99,100,106,119,129,135
Ervin, Judy — 30,31
Garland, Judy — 60
Gordon, Lee, Singers — 121
Guardsmen Quartette — 8,19
Jesters, The — 75,77,87
Lane, Muriel — 16

Lee, Peggy — 130
Merry Macs, The — 11
Music Maids And Hal — 17
Six (4) Hits And A Miss — 64,126
Sportsmen Glee Club — 30,31
Tormé, Mel — 76
Williams Brothers Quartet — 40
Wyman, Jane — 126,132

11/25/39+	4	11		1 **Yodelin' Jive** ....J:4 *Ciribiribin (They're So In Love)*	$15	Decca 2800

BING CROSBY And The ANDREWS SISTERS

4/20/40	2³	14		2 **The Singing Hills** ....J(terr.):2 *Devil May Care*	$15	Decca 3064

#56 hit for Billy Vaughn in 1958

6/22/40	10	2		3 **April Played The Fiddle** ....J(terr.):10 *I Haven't Time To Be A Millionaire*	$15	Decca 3161

from the movie *If I Had My Way* starring Crosby and Gloria Jean

7/20/40	❶4	12		4 **Sierra Sue** ....J(terr.):❶4 / S:3 *Marcheta*	$15	Decca 3133
9/7/40	14	3		5 **That's For Me** ....S(wc):14 / S(e):18 *Rhythm On The River*	$15	Decca 3309
9/21/40	2²	15		6 **Trade Winds** ....S:2 *A Song Of Old Hawaii*	$15	Decca 3299
9/28/40	❶9	16		7 **Only Forever** S:❶9 *When The Moon Comes Over Madison Square Or (The Love Lament Of A Western Gent)*	$15	Decca 3300

#4 & 6 from the movie *Rhythm On The River* starring Crosby and Mary Martin

1/4/41-	19	1	●	8 **Silent Night** ....S(e):19 *Adeste Fideles (O Come, All Ye Faithful)* [X]	$10	Decca 621

originally released and charted in 1935 (#7); new version recorded in 1942 and charted in 1957 and 1960 (both #54) on Decca 23777

2/15/41	18	1		9 **Along The Santa Fe Trail** ....S(wc):18 *I'd Know You Anywhere*	$15	Decca 3565

title song from the movie

3/29/41	7	3	●	10 **New San Antonio Rose** ....S:7 *It Makes No Difference Now*	$15	Decca 3590

vocal version of **Bob Wills'** 1938 classic Country hit "San Antonio Rose"; #8 hit for Floyd Cramer in 1961

4/26/41	2¹	9		11 **Dolores** ....S:2 *De Camptown Races*	$15	Decca 3644

Eddie Miller (sax solo); from the movie *Las Vegas Nights* starring **Tommy Dorsey**

8/9/41	6	5		12 **'Til Reveille** ....S:6 *My Old Kentucky Home*	$15	Decca 3886
8/30/41	20	1		13 **You Are My Sunshine** ....S(mw):20 *Ridin' Down The Canyon (When The Desert Sun Goes Down)*	$15	Decca 3952

written and recorded by Jimmie Davis in 1940; #7 hit for Ray Charles in 1962

9/13/41	6	4		14 **You And I** ....S:6 *Brahms' Lullaby*	$15	Decca 3840
9/13/41	20	1		15 **Be Honest With Me** ....S(s):20 *Goodbye, Little Darlin', Goodbye*	$15	Decca 3856
11/29/41	18	1		16 **The Whistler's Mother-In-Law** ....S:18 *I Ain't Got Nobody (And Nobody Cares For Me)*	$15	Decca 3971

BING CROSBY With Muriel Lane

11/29/41	20	1		17 **Clementine** ....S(e):20 *Day Dreaming*	$15	Decca 4033

#21 hit for Bobby Darin in 1960

CROSBY, Bing — Cont'd

DEBUT	PEAK	WKS	Gold	A-side (Chart Hit) / B-side	$	Label & Number
12/13/41	5	6		18 **Shepherd Serenade** S:5 *The Anniversary Waltz*	$15	Decca 4065
12/27/41	16	1		19 **Silent Night**.................................S(wc):16 / S(mw):20 *Adeste Fideles (O Come, All Ye Faithful)* **[X-R]**	$10	Decca 621
3/7/42	3	6		20 **Deep In The Heart Of Texas** S:3 *Let's All Meet At My House*	$15	Decca 4162
				#78 hit for Duane Eddy in 1962		
4/4/42	9	1		21 **I Don't Want To Walk Without You**..............................S:9 *Moonlight Cocktail*	$15	Decca 4184
				from the movie *Sweater Girl* starring Eddie Bracken; #36 hit for Barry Manilow in 1980		
6/6/42	9	1		22 **Miss You**....................................S:9 *Blues In The Night (My Mama Done Tol' Me)*	$15	Decca 4183
				featured in the movie *Strictly In The Groove* starring Mary Healy; #78 hit for Jaye P. Morgan in 1959		
7/18/42	19	1		23 **Skylark**..S(s):19 *Blue Shadows And White Gardenias*	$15	Decca 4193
				#101 hit for Linda Ronstadt in 1984		
9/5/42	14	6		24 **Be Careful It's My Heart**.....................S(wc):14 / S(s):18 *Happy Holiday*	$15	Decca 18424
				from the movie *Holiday Inn* starring Crosby and Fred Astaire		
10/10/42	❶11	15	●	25 **White Christmas** S:❶11 *Let's Start The New Year Right* **[X]**	$10	Decca 18429
				from the movie *Holiday Inn* starring Crosby and Fred Astaire; #1 R&B hit (3 weeks); the #1-selling single of all time (over 30 million sold)		
1/16/43	3	11		26 **Moonlight Becomes You** / S:3		
2/20/43	17	1		27 **Constantly**..S(s):17	$15	Decca 18513
				above 2 from the movie *Road To Morocco* starring Crosby and **Bob Hope**		
8/28/43	❶7	18	●	28 **Sunday, Monday Or Always** / S:❶7		
10/23/43	17	3		29 **If You Please**...........................S(mw):17 / S(s):18 / S(e):20	$15	Decca 18561
				above 2 from the movie *Dixie* starring Crosby and Dorothy Lamour		
10/16/43	2¹	14		30 **People Will Say We're In Love** / S:2		
11/13/43	5	9		31 **Oh! What A Beautiful Mornin'** S:5 / J:9	$15	Decca 18564
				BING CROSBY And TRUDY ERWIN (above 2)		
				above 2 from the Broadway musical *Oklahoma!* starring **Alfred Drake**		
11/6/43	2⁴	9	●	32 **Pistol Packin' Mama** / S:2 / J:7		
1/8/44	6	5		33 **Vict'ry Polka**..J:6	$15	Decca 23277
				BING CROSBY and the ANDREWS SISTERS (above 2)		
12/11/43	3	5	●	34 **I'll Be Home For Christmas (If Only In My Dreams)** S:3 / J:6 *Danny Boy* **[X]**	$15	Decca 18570
1/1/44-	7	1		35 **White Christmas**.................................J:7 / S:9 *Let's Start The New Year Right* **[X-R]**	$10	Decca 18429
3/11/44	❶5	22		36 **San Fernando Valley** / J:❶5 / S:2		
2/26/44	3	15		37 **Poinciana (Song Of The Tree)** J:3 / S:5	$15	Decca 18586
4/15/44	❶5	18		38 **I Love You** / S:❶5 / J:❶2		
				from the Broadway musical *Mexican Hayride* starring Bobby Clark		
4/22/44	❶4	25		39 **I'll Be Seeing You** S:❶4 / J:❶1	$15	Decca 18595
				#58 hit for **Frank Sinatra** in 1961		
5/13/44	❶9	27	●	40 **Swinging On A Star** / S:❶9 / J:❶8		
				#38 hit for Big Dee Irwin with Little Eva in 1963		
9/9/44	12	1		41 **Going My Way**..S(s):12	$15	Decca 18597
7/8/44	2³	16		42 **Amor** / J:2 / S:4		
				from the movie *Broadway Rhythm* starring George Murphy and **Ginny Simms**; #18 hit for Ben E. King in 1961		
7/8/44	5	5		43 **Long Ago (And Far Away)** S:5 / J:9	$15	Decca 18608
				from the movie *Cover Girl* starring Rita Hayworth		
9/23/44	❶6	14		44 **(There'll Be A) Hot Time In The Town Of Berlin (When The Yanks Go Marching In)** / J:❶6		
9/9/44	2¹	13		45 **Is You Is Or Is You Ain't (Ma' Baby)** S:2 / J:5	$15	Decca 23350
				BING CROSBY and the ANDREWS SISTERS (above 2)		
				from the movie *Follow The Boys* starring **Marlene Dietrich**; #81 hit for Buster Brown in 1960		
9/23/44	12	1		46 **The Day After Forever** /................................S(mw):12 / S(e):13		
12/16/44	13	1		47 **It Could Happen To You**..........................S(wc):13	$15	Decca 18580
				from the movie *And The Angels Sing* starring Dorothy Lamour; #53 hit for Dinah Washington in 1960		
10/14/44	4	12	●	48 **Too-Ra-Loo-Ra-Loo-Ral (That's An Irish Lullaby)** S:4 / J:5 *I'll Remember April*	$15	Decca 18621
				#1 hit for Chauncey Olcott in 1914; #40, 41, 46 & 48 from the movie *Going My Way* starring Crosby		
11/25/44	❶8	21	●	49 **Don't Fence Me In** / S:❶8 / J:❶8 / A:❶7		
				from the movie *Hollywood Canteen* starring Bette Davis; #45 hit for **Tommy Edwards** in 1960		
2/3/45	8	5		50 **The Three Caballeros** ....J:8 / A:10	$15	Decca 23364
				BING CROSBY & the ANDREWS SISTERS (above 2)		
				title song from the Disney movie starring Aurora Miranda		
12/2/44	21	1		51 **Sweet And Lovely**..........................J(terr.):21 *I Apologize*	$20	Brunswick 80057
				originally recorded and charted by Bing in 1931 (#9) on Brunswick 6179; revived due to inclusion in the movie *Two Girls And A Sailor* starring Van Johnson; #1 hit for Gus Arnheim in 1931; #77 hit for Nino Tempo & April Stevens in 1962		
12/16/44	5	3		52 **White Christmas** J:5 / S:6 *Let's Start The New Year Right* **[X-R]**	$10	Decca 18429
12/30/44	19	1		53 **I'll Be Home For Christmas (If Only In My Dreams)** ....J:19 *Danny Boy* **[X-R]**	$15	Decca 18570
1/27/45	9	5		54 **Evelina**.......................................A:9 / J:12 *The Eagle And Me*	$15	Decca 18635
				from the Broadway musical *Bloomer Girl* starring Celeste Holm		
2/3/45	2¹	12		55 **Ac-Cent-Tchu-Ate The Positive** S:2 / A:3 / J:3 *There's A Fellow Waiting In Poughkeepsie*	$15	Decca 23379
				BING CROSBY and the ANDREWS SISTERS		
				from the movie *Here Come The Waves* starring Crosby and **Betty Hutton**		
2/24/45	14	3		56 **Sleigh Ride In July** / A:14		
3/3/45	15	1		57 **Like Someone In Love**...........................J:15	$15	Decca 18640
				above 2 from the movie *Belle Of The Yukon* starring Randolph Scott		
4/14/45	4	10		58 **Just A Prayer Away** S:4 / A:6 / J:6 *My Mother's Waltz*	$15	Decca 23392
				Ethel Smith (organ)		
5/5/45	12	1		59 **All Of My Life**...................................A:12 *A Friend Of Yours*	$15	Decca 18658
5/12/45	5	7		60 **Yah-Ta-Ta Yah-Ta-Ta (Talk, Talk, Talk)** A:5 *You've Got Me Where You Want Me* **[N]**	$20	Decca 23410
				BING CROSBY and JUDY GARLAND		
6/2/45	3	14		61 **You Belong To My Heart** / J:3 / S:4 / A:4		
6/16/45	6	2		62 **Baía**...A:6	$15	Decca 23413
				BING CROSBY and XAVIER CUGAT And His Orchestra (above 2)		
				above 2 from the Disney movie *The Three Caballeros* starring Aurora Miranda		
7/21/45	14	1		63 **(Yip Yip De Hootie) My Baby Said Yes**........................J:14 *Your Socks Don't Match*	$15	Decca 23417
				BING CROSBY and LOUIS JORDAN And His Tympany Five		

DEBUT	PEAK	WKS	Gold	A-side (Chart Hit) .... B-side	$	Label & Number
				CROSBY, Bing — Cont'd		
7/28/45	**3**	15		64 **On The Atchison, Topeka And The Santa Fe** A:3 / J:3 / S:4 *I'd Rather Be Me*	$15	Decca 18690
				from the movie *The Harvey Girls* starring **Judy Garland**		
8/18/45	**8**	6		65 **If I Loved You** ....A:8 / J:10 *Close As Pages In A Book*	$15	Decca 18686
				from the Broadway musical *Carousel* starring John Raitt; #23 hit for Chad & Jeremy in 1965		
9/15/45	**2**[1]	11		66 **Along The Navajo Trail** J:2 / A:4 / S:5 *Good, Good, Good (That's You—That's You)*	$15	Decca 23437
				BING CROSBY and the ANDREWS SISTERS		
10/13/45	**❶**[2]	16		67 **It's Been A Long Long Time** J:❶[2] / S:❶[1] / A:3 *Whose Dream Are You*	$15	Decca 18708
				BING CROSBY with LES PAUL And His Trio		
11/17/45	**❶**[6]	20	●	68 **I Can't Begin To Tell You** J:❶[6] / S:❶[1] / A:2 *I Can't Believe That You're In Love With Me*	$15	Decca 23457
				BING CROSBY with CARMEN CAVALLARO At The Piano		
				from the movie *The Dolly Sisters* starring **Betty Grable**		
12/15/45	**❶**[2]	4		69 **White Christmas** A:❶[2] / J:4 / S:9 *Let's Start The New Year Right* **[X-R]**	$10	Decca 18429
12/22/45+	**8**	9		70 **Aren't You Glad You're You? /** ....A:8 / J:13		
1/5/46	**18**	1		71 **In The Land Of Beginning Again** A:18	$15	Decca 18720
				above 2 and #74 below from the movie *The Bells Of St. Mary's* starring Crosby and Ingrid Bergman; #6 hit for Charles Harrison in 1919		
1/5/46	**3**	12		72 **Symphony** S:3 / A:4 / J:5 *Beautiful Love*	$15	Decca 18735
1/19/46	**16**	1		73 **Give Me The Simple Life** ....A:16 *It's The Talk Of The Town*	$15	Decca 23469
				BING CROSBY and JIMMY DORSEY And His Orchestra		
				from the movie *Wake Up And Dream* starring June Haver		
2/2/46	**13**	1		74 **The Bells Of St. Mary's** ....A:13 *I'll Take You Home Again, Kathleen*	$15	Decca 18721
				#7 hit for Frances Alda in 1920		
3/16/46	**10**	4	●	75 **McNamara's Band** ....J:10 *Dear Old Donegal*	$15	Decca 23495
				BING CROSBY and THE JESTERS		
				The Jesters released their own version of this tune in 1940 on Decca 3268		
3/23/46	**15**	1		76 **Day By Day** ....A:15 *Prove It By The Things You Do*	$15	Decca 18746
				BING CROSBY with MEL TORME And His Mel-Tones		
3/30/46	**3**	16		77 **Sioux City Sue** J:3 / A:5 / S:6 *You Sang My Love Song To Somebody Else*	$15	Decca 23508
				BING CROSBY and THE JESTERS		
4/6/46	**9**	3		78 **Personality** ....J:9 / A:13 *Would You?*	$15	Decca 18790
				Wild Bill Davis (cornet); from the movie *Road To Utopia* starring Crosby and **Bob Hope**		
6/8/46	**12**	4		79 **They Say It's Wonderful** ....A:12 / J:14 *These Foolish Things (Remind Me Of You)*	$15	Decca 18829
				from the Broadway musical *Annie Get Your Gun* starring **Ethel Merman**		
8/3/46	**2**[1]	19	●	80 **South America, Take It Away /** S:2 / A:3 / J:3		
				from the Broadway musical *Call Me Mister* starring **Betty Garrett**		
8/10/46	**14**	2		81 **Get Your Kicks On "Route 66!—"** ....J:14 / A:15	$15	Decca 23569
				BING CROSBY and the ANDREWS SISTERS (above 2)		
				#61 hit for Depeche Mode in 1988		
11/16/46	**12**	2		82 **You Keep Coming Back Like A Song** ....A:12 / J:13 *(Running Around In Circles) Getting Nowhere*	$15	Decca 23647
				from the movie *Blue Skies* starring Crosby and Fred Astaire		
12/7/46	**❶**[1]	6		83 **White Christmas** A:❶[1] / S:2 / J:3 *God Rest Ye Merry Gentlemen* **[X-R]**	$10	Decca 23778
				same version as Decca 18429 but with new label number and new B-side		
1/11/47	**8**	6		84 **A Gal In Calico** ....J:8 / S:9 / A:11 *Oh, But I Do*	$15	Decca 23739
				BING CROSBY with The Calico Kids		
				from the movie *The Time, The Place And The Girl* starring Dennis Morgan		
4/26/47	**17**	1		85 **That's How Much I Love You** ....J:17 *Rose Of Santa Rosa*	$15	Decca 23840
				BING CROSBY and BOB CROSBY And His BOB CATS		
				#2 Country hit for **Eddy Arnold** in 1946; #39 hit for Pat Boone in 1958		
7/5/47	**10**	10		86 **Tallahassee** ....J:10 / A:13 *Go West, Young Man!*	$15	Decca 23885
				BING CROSBY and the ANDREWS SISTERS		
				from the movie *Variety Girl* starring Mary Hatcher		
9/13/47	**9**	4		87 **Feudin' And Fightin'** ....J:9 *Goodbye, My Lover, Goodbye*	$15	Decca 23975
				BING CROSBY and THE JESTERS		
				from the Broadway musical *Laffing Room Only* starring **Betty Garrett**		
11/8/47+	**6**	14		88 **How Soon (Will I Be Seeing You) /** ....J:6 / S:8 / A:13		
11/1/47	**8**	8		89 **You Do** ....J:8 / S:10 / A:15	$15	Decca 24101
				BING CROSBY and CARMEN CAVALLARO At The Piano (above 2)		
				from the movie *Mother Wore Tights* starring **Betty Grable**		
11/15/47	**7**	7	●	90 **Whiffenpoof Song** ....S:7 *Kentucky Babe*	$15	Decca 23990
				BING CROSBY with FRED WARING and the GLEE CLUB		
				theme song of the Yale University Glee Club since 1909; #96 hit for Bob Crewe in 1960		
12/6/47	**3**	5		91 **White Christmas** S:3 / J:3 / A:4 *God Rest Ye Merry Gentlemen* **[X-R]**	$10	Decca 23778
				new version recorded on 3/19/47 (version on all subsequent releases) but released with same number as earlier version above		
1/17/48	**10**	8		92 **Ballerina** ....S:10 / J:12 *Golden Earrings*	$15	Decca 24278
				#18 hit for Nat "King" Cole in 1957		
1/31/48	**❶**[3]	23	●	93 **Now Is The Hour (Maori Farewell Song)** J:❶[3] / S:2 / A:3 *Silver Threads Among The Gold*	$15	Decca 24279
				#59 hit for Gale Storm in 1956		
11/6/48	**23**	2		94 **A Hundred And Sixty Acres** ....J:23 *At The Flying "W"*	$15	Decca 24481
				BING CROSBY and the ANDREWS SISTERS		
12/11/48	**6**	6		95 **White Christmas** ....S:6 / A:6 / J:12 *God Rest Ye Merry Gentlemen* **[X-R]**	$10	Decca 23778
1/8/49	**2**[3]	19		96 **Far Away Places** S:2 / J:2 / A:11 *Tarra Ta-Lara Ta-Lar*	$15	Decca 24532
1/22/49	**3**	17		97 **Galway Bay** S:3 / J:6 / A:11 *My Girl's An Irish Girl*	$15	Decca 24295
4/23/49	**27**	1		98 **If You Stub Your Toe On The Moon** ....A:27 *Once And For Always*	$15	Decca 24524
				from the movie *A Connecticut Yankee In King Arthur's Court* starring Crosby		
5/7/49	**12**	10		99 **Careless Hands** ....J:12 / S:21 *Memories*	$15	Decca 24616
5/14/49	**14**	10		100 **Riders In The Sky A Cowboy Legend** ....S:14 / J:14 / A:15 *Lullaby Land*	$15	Decca 24618
				#30 hit for The Ramrods in 1961		
5/28/49	**3**	20		101 **Some Enchanted Evening /** J:3 / S:5 / A:17		
				#13 hit for Jay & The Americans in 1965		
6/18/49	**12**	7		102 **Bali Ha'i** ....J:12 / S:19	$15	Decca 24609
				above 2 from the Broadway musical *South Pacific* starring **Mary Martin** and **Ezio Pinza**		
12/3/49+	**2**[4]	17	●	103 **Dear Hearts And Gentle People /** J:2 / S:2 / A:4		
11/19/49	**4**	12		104 **Mule Train** A:4 / J:4 / S:5	$15	Decca 24798
				featured in the 1950 movie *Singing Guns* starring **Vaughn Monroe**		

DEBUT	PEAK	WKS	Gold	A-side (Chart Hit)..B-side	$	Label & Number
				CROSBY, Bing — Cont'd		
11/19/49	21	2		105 'Way Back Home...S:21 / A:30 *The Iowa Indian Song (I-O-Wuh)*	$15	Decca 24800
				BING CROSBY with FRED WARING AND HIS PENNSYLVANIANS #6 hit for Victor Young in 1935		
12/17/49	5	4		106 White Christmas A:5 / S:7 / J:10 *God Rest Ye Merry Gentlemen* **[X-R]**	$10	Decca 23778
1/28/50	6	17		107 Quicksilver / ....J:6 / S:8		
1/21/50	24	4		108 Have I Told You Lately That I Love You?...J:24	$15	Decca 24827
				BING CROSBY & the ANDREWS SISTERS (above 2) #29 hit for Ricky Nelson in 1957		
2/4/50	4	13		109 Chattanoogie Shoe Shine Boy A:4 / S:9 / J:10 *Bibbidi - Bobbidi - Boo*	$15	Decca 24863
				#34 hit for Freddy Cannon in 1960		
7/8/50	22	2		110 I Didn't Slip, I Wasn't Pushed, I Fell...............................J:22 *So Tall A Tree*	$25	Decca 9-27018
7/29/50	2²	19	●	111 Play A Simple Melody / J:2 / A:3 / S:3 **[N]**		
				from the Broadway musical *Watch Your Step* starring Irene and Vernon Castle; #4 hit for Billy Murray and Elsie Baker in 1916		
7/29/50	3	19		112 Sam's Song (The Happy Tune) S:3 / A:3 / J:3 **[N]**	$25	Decca 9-27112
				GARY CROSBY and FRIEND (above 2) #94 hit for Dean Martin & Sammy Davis, Jr. in 1962		
8/5/50	13	6		113 La Vie En Rose / ....J:13 / S:18		
8/5/50	22	4		114 I Cross My Fingers..J:22	$20	Decca 9-27111
10/7/50	11	12		115 All My Love ....J:11 / S:14 / A:17 *The Friendly Islands*	$20	Decca 9-27117
11/11/50	8	13		116 Harbor Lights / ....J:8 / S:10 / A:20		
				#6 hit for Frances Langford in 1937; #8 hit for The Platters in 1960		
10/28/50	26	1		117 Beyond The Reef J:26	$20	Decca 9-27219
12/16/50	14	4		118 Rudolph The Red-Nosed Reindeer ....S:14 / A:30 *The Teddy Bear's Picnic* **[X-N]**	$20	Decca 9-27159
				issued with a picture sleeve on Decca's Children's Series K-15		
12/23/50	13	4		119 White Christmas...............................J:13 / S:16 / A:25 *God Rest Ye Merry Gentlemen* **[X-R]**	$10	Decca 9-23778
12/23/50	22	2		120 A Crosby Christmas (Parts 1 & 2)..S:22 **[X]**	$25	Decca 9-40181
				GARY, PHILLIP, DENNIS, LINDSAY and BING CROSBY medley: That Christmas Feeling/I'd Like To Hitch A Ride With Santa Claus/The Snowman; Lindsay shot himself to death on 12/11/89; also issued with a picture sleeve on Decca 1-134 in 1950		
1/6/51-	24	1		121 A Marshmallow World ....S:24 *Looks Like A Cold, Cold Winter* **[X]**	$25	Decca 9-27230
3/10/51	8	15		122 Sparrow In The Tree Top ....J:8 / A:9 / S:12 *Forsaking All Others*	$20	Decca 9-27477
				BING CROSBY And ANDREWS SISTERS		
4/21/51	8	10		123 When You And I Were Young Maggie Blues / ....A:8 / J:10 / S:10 **[N]**		
				#4 hit for Frank Stanley & Corrine Morgan in 1905		
4/21/51	14	6		124 Moonlight Bay...A:14 / S:15 / J:15 **[N]**	$20	Decca 9-27577
				BING and GARY CROSBY (above 2) #1 hit for the American Quartet in 1912; #72 hit for The Drifters in 1958		
6/30/51	19	2		125 Gone Fishin'...A:19 *We All Have A Song In Our Heart* (Crosby)	$25	Decca 9-27623
				BING CROSBY And LOUIS ARMSTRONG		
8/4/51	11	6		126 In The Cool, Cool, Cool Of The Evening ....A:11 / S:23 *Misto Cristofo Columbo*	$20	Decca 9-27678
				BING CROSBY And JANE WYMAN from the movie *Here Comes The Groom* starring Crosby and Wyman		
9/8/51	21	1		127 Why Did I Tell You I Was Going To Shanghai ....A:21 *I've Got To Fall In Love Again*	$20	Decca 9-27653
11/3/51	15	6		128 Domino....................................A:15 / J:23 / S:26 *When The World Was Young (Le Chevalier de Paris)*	$20	Decca 9-27830
12/22/51	13	3		129 White Christmas...........................A:13 / S:16 / J:21 *God Rest Ye Merry Gentlemen* **[X-R]**	$10	Decca 9-23778
7/26/52	28	2		130 Watermelon Weather...................................A:28 *The Moon Came Up With A Great Idea Last Night*	$20	Decca 9-28238
				BING CROSBY And PEGGY LEE		
8/2/52	16	6		131 Till The End Of The World ....J:16 *Just A Little Lovin' (Will Go A Long Way)*	$20	Decca 9-28265
				BING CROSBY And GRADY MARTIN And His Slew Foot Five #4 Country hit for Ernest Tubb in 1949		
8/9/52	18	5		132 Zing A Little Zong ....A:18 / J:28 *The Maiden Of Guadalupe*	$20	Decca 9-28255
				BING CROSBY and JANE WYMAN from the movie *Just For You* starring Crosby and Wyman		
1/30/54	13	2		133 Changing Partners / ....J:13 / S:17		
1/30/54	20	3		134 Y'all Come A:20	$20	Decca 9-28969
				#7 Country hit for Arlie Duff in 1954		
12/25/54	13	3		135 White Christmas...................................A:13 / J:19 / S:21 *God Rest Ye Merry Gentlemen* **[X-R]**	$10	Decca 9-23778

CROSBY, Bob, And His Orchestra ★68★   MEM '39

Born George Robert Crosby on 8/25/13 in Spokane, Washington. Died of cancer on 3/9/93 (age 79). Younger brother of **Bing Crosby**. Popular swing-era bandleader, specializing in Dixieland jazz. His own band, the Bobcats, featured tenor saxophonist/leader Gil Rodin, trumpet stars **Billy Butterfield** and Muggsy Spanier, clarinet virtuoso Irving Fazola, tenor saxophonist Eddie Miller, trombonists **Buddy Morrow** and Ray Conniff (both briefly), pianists Bob Zurke and Jess Stacy, and bassist Bobby Haggart. Crosby's pre-1940 #1 hits: "Whispers In The Dark," "In A Little Gypsy Tea Room" and "Day In-Day Out."

1)Down Argentina Way 2)With The Wind And The Rain In Your Hair 3)Leanin' On The Ole Top Rail

Vocalists: Andrews, Patty — 11   **Crosby, Bing** — 10   **Gibbs, Georgia** — 13   Mann, Marion — 2,3
Bob-o-links, The — 4,6,9   **Crosby, Bob** — 1,4,6,8,9,12,14   King, Bonnie — 5   Morgan, Marion — 12
Chickadees, The — 10

DEBUT	PEAK	WKS		A-side	$	Label & Number
4/20/40	7	4		1 Leanin' On The Ole Top Rail ....J(terr.):7 *Shake Down The Stars*	$10	Decca 3027
4/20/40	9	2		2 I've Got My Eyes On You...J(terr.):9 *Gotta Get Home*	$10	Decca 2991
				from the movie *Broadway Melody Of 1940* starring Fred Astaire		
4/27/40	7	3		3 With The Wind And The Rain In Your Hair...................J(terr.):7 *You, You Darlin'*	$10	Decca 3018
				#21 hit for Pat Boone in 1959		
11/23/40+	15	6		4 You Forgot About Me...........................S(wc):15 / S(e):17 *Gone But Not Forgotten*	$10	Decca 3417
				from the movie *Let's Make Music* starring Crosby and Jean Rogers		
12/14/40+	2¹	4		5 Down Argentina Way S:2 *Two Dreams Met*	$10	Decca 3404
				from the movie *Down Argentine Way* starring Don Ameche and **Betty Grable**		

CROSBY, Bob, And His Orchestra — Cont'd

DEBUT	PEAK	WKS	A-side / B-side	$	Label & Number
10/25/41	18	1	6 **Do You Care?** ....S(wc):18 *Will You Still Be Mine?*	$10	Decca 3860
7/3/43	19	2	7 **Blue Surreal** ....S(wc):19 *Black Zephyr* [I] Eddie Miller (tenor sax)	$10	Decca 4415
2/16/46	14	1	8 **Let It Snow; Let It Snow; Let It Snow** ....J:14 *In The Valley* [X]	$10	ARA 129
9/28/46	12	5	9 **Five Minutes More** ....J:12 *I've Never Forgotten* featured in the movie *Sweetheart Of Sigma Chi* starring Elyse Knox	$10	Decca 18909
4/26/47	17	1	10 **That's How Much I Love You** ....J:17 *Rose Of Santa Rosa* **BING CROSBY and BOB CROSBY And His BOB CATS**	$15	Decca 23840
1/22/49	12	6	11 **The Pussy Cat Song** (Nyow! Nyot Nyow!)................S:12 / J:13 / A:14 *Don't Worry 'Bout Strangers* (Andrews Sisters) [N] **PATTY ANDREWS and BOB CROSBY**	$15	Decca 24533
10/8/49	22	3	12 **Maybe It's Because** ....A:22 *Be My Little Baby Bumble Bee* **BOB CROSBY - MARION MORGAN** Jerry Gray (orch.); from the Broadway musical *Along Fifth Avenue* starring Jackie Gleason	$10	Columbia 38504
8/26/50	25	2	13 **Simple Melody** ....A:25 / J:25 *A Little Bit Independent* **GEORGIA GIBBS and BOB CROSBY and his Orchestra** from the Broadway musical *Watch Your Step* starring Irene and Vernon Castle; #4 hit for Billy Murray & Elsie Baker in 1916	$20	Coral 9-60227
7/21/51	22	1	14 **Shanghai** ....A:22 *That Naughty Waltz*	$15	Capitol F1525

CROSBY, Gary — see CROSBY, Bing

CROWS, The '54
R&B vocal group from Harlem, New York: Bill Davis, Daniel Norton (died in 1972), Harold Major, Gerald Hamilton (died in 1967) and Mark Jackson.

DEBUT	PEAK	WKS	A-side / B-side	$	Label & Number
4/10/54	14	5	**Gee**...A:14 / J:15 / S:17 *I Love You So* #81 hit for Jan & Dean in 1960	$125	Rama 5

CUGAT, Xavier ★60★ MEM '45
Born on 1/1/1900 in Barcelona, Spain; raised in Havana, Cuba. Died of heart failure on 10/27/90 (age 90). Bandleader/vocalist/composer/arranger. Specialized in Latin American music since forming own band in the late 1920s. Many appearances in movies, on radio and TV. Married to Abbe Lane (1952-63) and Charo (1964-78).

1)*Brazil (Aquarela Do Brasil)* 2)*Perfidia* 3)*You Belong To My Heart*

Vocalists: Campo, Del — 9 Clark, Buddy — 12 Shore, Dinah — 1,4
Castillo, Carmen — 8 Crosby, Bing — 10,11 Valdez, Miguelito — 7

CUGAT, Xavier, and his Waldorf-Astoria Orchestra:

DEBUT	PEAK	WKS	A-side / B-side	$	Label & Number
8/10/40	18	1	1 **The Breeze And I**...........................S(s):18 / S(mw):20 *When The Swallows Come Back To Capistrano* adapted from the Spanish song "Andalucia"; #8 hit for Caterina Valente in 1955	$10	Victor 26641
2/1/41	3	13	2 **Perfidia** S:3 *Nana* [I] #15 hit for The Ventures in 1960	$10	Victor 26334
7/5/41	20	1	3 **Intermezzo (A Love Story)** ....S(mw):20 *A Rendezvous In Rio* [I] from the movie *Intermezzo* starring Ingrid Bergman	$10	Columbia 36041
9/6/41	19	1	4 **Quierme Mucho (Yours)**...........................S(wc):19 *One, Two, Three, Kick*	$10	Victor 26384
9/20/41	17	1	5 **Green Eyes (Ojos Verdes)** ....S(wc):17 *Perdon* [I] **XAVIER CUGAT and his ORCHESTRA** originally issued on Victor 26794	$10	Victor 27443
1/30/43	2⁷	19	6 **Brazil (Aquarela Do Brasil)** S:2 *Chiu-Chiu* [I] featured in the movie *Saludos Amigos*; #11 hit for The Ritchie Family in 1975	$10	Columbia 36651
4/29/44	21	1	7 **Babalu** ....J(terr.):21 *Bambarito* [F] **XAVIER CUGAT and his ORCHESTRA** song later associated with Desi Arnaz	$10	Columbia 36068
7/15/44	10	9	8 **Amor** ....J:10 *Let Me Love You Tonight* [F] from the movie *Broadway Rhythm* starring George Murphy and **Ginny Simms**; #18 hit for Ben E. King in 1961	$10	Columbia 36718
6/2/45	6	7	9 **Good, Good, Good (That's You - That's You)**...................A:6 / J:18 *Toca-Tu Samba*	$10	Columbia 36793
6/2/45	3	14	10 **You Belong To My Heart** / J:3 / S:4 / A:4		
6/16/45	6	2	11 **Baía** ....A:6 **BING CROSBY and XAVIER CUGAT And His Orchestra** (above 2) above 2 from the Disney movie *The Three Caballeros* starring Aurora Miranda	$15	Decca 23413
8/17/46	6	13	12 **South America, Take It Away!** ....A:6 / J:8 / S:9 *Chiquita Banana (The Banana Song)* from the Broadway musical *Call Me Mister* starring Betty Garrett	$10	Columbia 37051
1/1/49	27	1	13 **Cuanto Le Gusta** ....S:27 *Take It Away (Tomalu Tu)* [I] **XAVIER CUGAT and his ORCHESTRA** from the movie *A Date With Judy* starring Wallace Beery and Jane Powell	$10	Columbia 38239

D

DAGMAR — see SINATRA, Frank

DALE, Alan MEM/HOT '55
Born Aldo Sigismondi on 7/9/28 in Brooklyn, New York. Died on 4/20/2002 (age 73). Baritone singer formerly with **Carmen Cavallaro**. Hosted his own TV show in 1951. Starred in the 1956 movie *Don't Knock The Rock*. Also see **Ray Bloch**.

DEBUT	PEAK	WKS	A-side / B-side	$	Label & Number
8/28/48	29	1	1 **The Darktown Strutters' Ball**...J:29 *Little Boy Blues* **CONNIE HAINES and ALAN DALE** **Ray Bloch**'s Swing Eight (Dixieland jazz band); #1 hit for Arthur Collins & Byron Harlan in 1918	$20	Signature 15197
12/5/53+	10	10	2 **The Gang That Sang "Heart Of My Heart"** ....J:10 / A:14 / S:18 *I Think I'll Fall In Love Today* **DON CORNELL, ALAN DALE AND JOHNNY DESMOND** Jack Pleis (orch.); song written in 1926	$20	Coral 9-61076

DALEY, Cass '50

Born Catherine Dailey on 7/17/15 in Philadelphia. Died on 3/22/75 (age 59). Singer/comedian. Appeared in several movies.

5/13/50	11	10		1 **The Old Piano Roll Blues**.......................................J:11 / S:15 *Stay With The Happy People*	$20	Decca 9-24977
4/14/51	23	3		2 **The Aba Daba Honeymoon**...............................J:23 / A:29 *The Golden Rocket*	$20	Decca 9-27474

HOAGY CARMICHAEL And CASS DALEY (above 2)
from the movie *Two Weeks With Love* starring **Debbie Reynolds** and **Carleton Carpenter**; #1 hit for Arthur Collins & Byron Harlan in 1914; Matty Matlock's All Stars (orch., above 2)

DAMONE, Vic ★28★   MEM/HOT '49

Born Vito Farinola on 6/12/28 in Brooklyn, New York. Among the most popular of postwar ballad singers. Appeared in the movies *Kismet*, *Meet Me In Las Vegas* and *Hell To Eternity*. Hosted own TV series (1956-57). Married to actress Diahann Carroll from 1987-96.

1)You're Breaking My Heart 2)My Truly, Truly Fair 3)My Heart Cries For You 4)Again 5)Tzena, Tzena, Tzena

Orchestras: Bassman, George — 21,22,24,25   Hayman, Richard — 31,32   Osser, Glenn — 5-12   Selby, Ronnie — 14
Carroll, David — 29,30   Leyden, Norman — 27,28   Robinson, Eric — 4   Siravo, George — 17-20,23
Gray, Jerry — 1,2   Marterie, Ralph — 15,16

8/30/47	7	7		1 **I Have But One Heart** "O Marinariello".............................J:7 / S:8 / A:11 *Ivy*	$10	Mercury 5053
				Damone sings English and Italian verses on #1 and 6		
11/1/47	7	9		2 **You Do**...A:7 / J:11 *Angela Mia*	$10	Mercury 5056
				from the movie *Mother Wore Tights* starring **Betty Grable**		
9/18/48	24	1		3 **It's Magic**...J:24 *It's You Or No One*	$10	Mercury 5138
				from the movie *Romance On The High Seas* starring **Doris Day** and Jack Carson; #91 hit for The Platters in 1962		
10/30/48	23	4		4 **Say Something Sweet To Your Sweetheart**.............................A:23 *Isn't It Romantic*	$15	Mercury 5192
				VIC DAMONE—PATTI PAGE		
4/9/49	6	21	●	5 **Again**..A:6 / J:9 / S:11 *I Love You So Much It Hurts*	$10	Mercury 5261
				from the movie *Road House* starring Ida Lupino and Cornel Wilde		
6/18/49	❶⁴	26	●	6 **You're Breaking My Heart** / S:❶⁴ / A:❶⁴ / J:❶³		
				based on the Italian song "La Mattinata"		
7/23/49	16	3		7 **Four Winds And Seven Seas**..A:16 / S:25	$10	Mercury 5271
8/27/49	10	6		8 **My Bolero**.............................S:10 / A:26 / J:29 *Through A Long And Sleepless Night*	$10	Mercury 5313
10/29/49	20	7		9 **Why Was I Born?**.............................A:20 / S:21 *Lonely Night*	$10	Mercury 5326
				from the Broadway musical *Sweet Adeline* starring Helen Morgan; #8 hit for Helen Morgan in 1930		
1/28/50	29	1		10 **Sitting By The Window**.............................A:29 *Nice To Know You Care*	$10	Mercury 5343
3/18/50	27	1		11 **God's Country**.............................A:27 *Where I Belong*	$15	Mercury 5374-X45
7/1/50	17	13		12 **Vagabond Shoes**.............................J:17 / S:18 / A:21 *I Hadn't Anyone Till You*	$20	Mercury 5429-X45
7/22/50	7	11		13 **Tzena, Tzena, Tzena**.............................A:7 / S:8 / J:11 *I Love That Girl*	$20	Mercury 5454-X45
				adaptation of a popular Israeli song		
8/26/50	13	2		14 **Just Say I Love Her** /.............................A:13 / J:23 / S:26		
10/14/50	25	1		15 **Can Anyone Explain (No! No! No!)**.............................A:25	$15	Mercury 5474-X45
9/16/50	11	3		16 **Cincinnati Dancing Pig**.............................A:11 / J:25 *Forbidden Love*	$15	Mercury 5477-X45
				Meadowlarks (backing vocals)		
12/30/50+	4	15		17 **My Heart Cries For You** / A:4 / J:6 / S:12		
				adapted from the 18th-century French melody "Chanson de Marie Antoinette"; #38 hit for Ray Charles in 1964		
12/30/50+	18	2		18 **Music By The Angels**.............................A:18	$15	Mercury 5563-X45
2/3/51	21	4		19 **Tell Me You Love Me**.............................A:21 *Little Cafe Paree*	$15	Mercury 5572-X45
				adapted by **Sammy Kaye** from the opera *Pagliacci*		
2/17/51	28	3		20 **If**.............................A:28 *You And Your Beautiful Eyes*	$15	Mercury 5565-X45
				#82 hit for The Paragons in 1961; Ken Lane Singers (backing vocals: #17 & 20)		
6/2/51	4	17		21 **My Truly, Truly Fair**.............................A:4 / J:12 / S:18 *My Life's Desire*	$15	Mercury 5646-X45
8/4/51	12	11		22 **Longing For You**.............................J:12 / A:13 / S:19 *The Son Of A Sailor*	$15	Mercury 5655-X45
9/22/51	21	1		23 **Wonder Why**.............................A:21 *I Can See You*	$15	Mercury 5669-X45
				from the movie *Rich, Young And Pretty* starring Damone and Jane Powell		
10/6/51	13	3		24 **Calla Calla**.............................A:13 / S:24 *It's A Long Way (From Your House To My House)*	$15	Mercury 5698-X45
5/10/52	22	1		25 **Jump Through The Ring**.............................A:22 *My Funny Valentine*	$15	Mercury 5785-X45
6/14/52	8	9		26 **Here In My Heart**.............................A:8 *Tomorrow Never Comes*	$15	Mercury 5858-X45
7/26/52	23	2		27 **Rosanne** /.............................A:23		
7/12/52	30	3		28 **Take My Heart**.............................A:30	$15	Mercury 5877-X45
2/7/53	13	2		29 **Sugar**.............................A:13 *Amor*	$15	Mercury 70054-X45
				The Jack Halloran Singers (backing vocals); #9 hit for Ethel Waters in 1926		
5/16/53	10	7		30 **April In Portugal**.............................A:10 / J:15 / S:16 *I'm Walking Behind You*	$15	Mercury 70128-X45
				Portuguese song originally published as "Coimbra"		
8/8/53	12	5		31 **Eternally The Song From Limelight**.............................A:12 *Simonetta*	$15	Mercury 70186-X45
				written by Charlie Chaplin for his movie *Limelight*; #92 hit for Mr. Acker Bilk in 1962		
10/17/53	10	11		32 **Ebb Tide**.............................A:10 / J:16 *If I Could Make You Mine*	$15	Mercury 70216-X45
				#5 hit for The Righteous Brothers in 1966; above 2 are vocal versions of Top 5 instrumental hits by **Frank Chacksfield**		

DARDANELLE TRIO, The '46

Dardanelle was a female pianist/vibraphonist/singer. Her trio included Tal Farrow (guitar) and Paul Edenfield (bass).

12/14/46	11	2		**September Song**.............................A:11 *When A Woman Loves A Man*	$10	RCA Victor 20-1993

from the movie *Knickerbocker Holiday* starring Nelson Eddy; #12 hit for Walter Huston in 1939; #51 hit for **Jimmy Durante** in 1963

DARNEL, Bill   MEM '50

Born in Lorain, Ohio. Singer formerly with the Red Nichols, **Bob Chester** and **Al Kavelin** bands.

2/25/50	18	2		1 **Chattanoogie Shoe Shine Boy**.............................A:18 / J:24 / S:26 *Sugarfoot Rag*	$15	Coral 60147
				#34 hit for Freddy Cannon in 1960		
7/8/50	26	1		2 **M-I-S-S-I-S-S-I-P-P-I**.............................A:26 *Gone Fishin'*	$15	Coral 60220
				The Heathertones (backing vocals); **Roy Ross** (orch., above 2)		

DAVIS, Janette '49
Born on 11/2/18 in Memphis. Regular on **Arthur Godfrey**'s TV show.

| 1/29/49 | 15 | 5 | | A Little Bird Told Me ....A:15 / S:26 *If That Isn't Love, What Is?* | $10 | Columbia 38386 |

JANETTE DAVIS and JERRY WAYNE

DAVIS, Sammy Jr. MEM/HOT '55
Born on 12/8/25 in New York City. Died of cancer on 5/16/90 (age 64). Singer/dancer/actor. With father and uncle in dance act the Will Mastin Trio from the early 1940s. First recorded for Capitol in 1950. Lost his left eye and had his nose smashed in an auto accident near San Bernardino, California on 11/19/54; returned to performing in January 1955. Frequent appearances on TV, Broadway and in movies. Won Grammy's Lifetime Achievement Award in 2001.

| 8/21/54 | 16 | 10 | | Hey There ....S:16 / A:16 / J:16 *And This Is My Beloved* | $15 | Decca 9-29199 |

Sy Oliver (orch.); from the Broadway musical *The Pajama Game* starring John Raitt

DAVIS SISTERS, The '53
Vocal duo from Lexington, Kentucky: Skeeter Davis and Betty Jack Davis. The two were not related. Betty Jack was killed and Skeeter was seriously injured in a car crash on 8/2/53. Betty Jack was replaced by her sister Georgia.

| 10/10/53 | 18 | 2 | | I Forgot More Than You'll Ever Know ....J:18 *Rock-A-Bye Boogie* | $25 | RCA Victor 47-5345 |

#1 Country hit (8 weeks); #80 hit for Sonny James in 1960

DAY, Dennis ★125★ '50
Born Eugene Dennis McNulty on 5/21/18 in New York City. Died of ALS (Lou Gehrig's disease) on 6/22/88 (age 70). Tenor who sang and performed in comedy sketches on Jack Benny's radio and TV shows from 1939-65; also appeared in several movies.

| 5/3/47 | 8 | 5 | | 1 Mam'selle | S:8 / A:10 / J:10 *Stella By Starlight* | $10 | RCA Victor 20-2211 |

from the movie *The Razor's Edge* starring Tyrone Power

| 3/26/49 | 23 | 1 | | 2 Clancy Lowered The Boom ....S:23 / A:29 *The Romance Of The Rose* | $10 | RCA Victor 20-2810 |
| 1/14/50 | 14 | 4 | | 3 Dear Hearts And Gentle People ....A:14 / S:19 *I Must Have Done Something Wonderful* | $15 | RCA Victor 47-3102 |

78 rpm: 20-3596; The Rhythmaires (backing vocals)

| 8/19/50 | 25 | 1 | | 4 Mona Lisa ....S:25 / J:29 *A Shawl Of Galway Grey* | $15 | RCA Victor 47-3753 |

The Ray Charles Choir (backing vocals); **Henri René** (orch.); from the movie *Captain Carey, U.S.A.* starring Alan Ladd; #25 hit for Carl Mann in 1959

| 8/19/50 | 17 | 8 | | 5 Goodnight, Irene / ....A:17 / S:22 | | |

#75 hit for **Billy Williams** in 1959

| 10/14/50 | 22 | 4 | | 6 All My Love ....S:22 / A:28 *Charles Dant* | $15 | RCA Victor 47-3870 |

based on the French song "Bolero"; Charles Dant (orch.: #1-3, 5 & 6)

| 12/30/50 | 10 | 3 | | 7 Christmas In Killarney ....S:10 *I'm Praying To St. Christopher* [X] | $20 | RCA Victor 47-3970 |

The Mellowmen (backing vocals); **Henri René (orch.)**

| 6/9/51 | 13 | 11 | | 8 Mister And Mississippi..........................A:13 / S:15 / J:22 *A Trinket Of Shiny Gold* | $15 | RCA Victor 47-4140 |

Norman Luboff Choir (backing vocals)

DAY, Doris ★26★ MEM/HOT '48
Born Doris Kappelhoff on 4/3/22 in Cincinnati. Sang briefly with **Bob Crosby** in 1940 and shortly thereafter became a major star with the **Les Brown** band (she had 12 charted hits with Les). Starred in several movies; own TV series from 1968-73. Her husband, Marty Melcher, owned Arwin Records; their son, Terry, was a member of the Rip Chords and Bruce & Terry, and a prolific producer (The Beach Boys).

1)Love Somebody 2)Secret Love 3)A Guy Is A Guy 4)Again 5)It's Magic

Orchestras: Faith, Percy — 24
Fisher, Carl — 23
Heindorf, Ray — 30,31

James, Harry — 19
Rarig, John — 6,7,9,10,16

Siravo, George — 1-5,11
Stordahl, Axel — 8

Weston, Paul — 20-22,25-29
Wyle, George — 13-15,17

Vocalists: Country Cousins — 12
Lane, Ken, Singers — 8

Luboff, Norman, Choir — 23,24,27
Mellowmen, The — 6,7,9,15-17,32

male quartet — 10

| 5/29/48 | ❶⁵ | 24 | ● | 1 Love Somebody / | A:❶⁵ / J:5 / S:6 | | |
| 6/26/48 | 16 | 11 | | 2 Confess...S:16 / A:17 / J:21 | $10 | Columbia 38174 |

DORIS DAY and BUDDY CLARK (above 2)

| 7/17/48 | 2¹ | 21 | ● | 3 It's Magic S:2 / A:4 / J:4 *Put 'Em In A Box, Tie 'Em With A Ribbon (And Throw 'Em In The Deep Blue Sea)* | $10 | Columbia 38188 |

from the movie *Romance On The High Seas* starring Day and Jack Carson; #91 hit for The Platters in 1962

| 11/20/48 | 7 | 13 | | 4 My Darling My Darling ....S:7 / A:7 / J:8 *That Certain Party* | $10 | Columbia 38353 |

from the Broadway musical *Where's Charley?* starring **Ray Bolger**

| 2/26/49 | 16 | 3 | | 5 Powder Your Face With Sunshine (Smile! Smile! Smile!)...A:16 / J:28 *I'll String Along With You* | $10 | Columbia 38394 |

DORIS DAY and BUDDY CLARK (above 2)
7" 33-1/3 rpm: 1-113

| 5/21/49 | 2² | 19 | | 6 Again / | A:2 / S:14 / J:17 | | |

from the movie *Road House* starring Ida Lupino and Cornel Wilde

| 6/11/49 | 22 | 1 | | 7 Everywhere You Go ....A:22 | $10 | Columbia 38467 |

7" 33-1/3 rpm: 1-211

| 8/6/49 | 17 | 6 | | 8 Let's Take An Old-Fashioned Walk..................A:17 *(Just One Way To Say) I Love You* (Sinatra) | $15 | Columbia 38513 |

FRANK SINATRA and DORIS DAY
7" 33-1/3 rpm: 1-260; from the Broadway musical *Miss Liberty* starring Eddie Albert

| 8/27/49 | 20 | 7 | | 9 (Where Are You) Now That I Need You ....S:20 / A:23 / J:26 *Blame My Absent-Minded Heart* | $10 | Columbia 38507 |

7" 33-1/3 rpm: 1-251; from the Broadway musical *Red Hot And Blue* starring **Ethel Merman**

| 10/22/49 | 15 | 10 | | 10 Canadian Capers (Cuttin' Capers) ....S:15 / J:18 *It's Better To Conceal Than Reveal* | $10 | Columbia 38595 |

7" 33-1/3 rpm: 1-353; from the movie *My Dream Is Yours* starring Day and Jack Carson; #4 hit for Paul Whiteman in 1922

| 11/5/49 | 19 | 2 | | 11 There's A Bluebird On Your Windowsill......................A:19 / S:30 *The River Seine* | $10 | Columbia 38611 |

7" 33-1/3 rpm: 1-376

| 1/21/50 | 20 | 3 | | 12 Quicksilver ....S:20 / A:25 / J:27 *Crocodile Tears* | $10 | Columbia 38638 |

7" 33-1/3 rpm: 1-407

| 3/4/50 | 21 | 6 | | 13 I Said My Pajamas (And Put On My Pray'rs) / ....A:21 / S:27 / J:27 | | |
| 3/4/50 | 24 | 3 | | 14 Enjoy Yourself (It's Later Than You Think) ....J:24 | $10 | Columbia 38709 |

7" 33-1/3 rpm: 1-497

DEBUT	PEAK	WKS	Gold	A-side (Chart Hit)..B-side	$	Label & Number
				DAY, Doris — Cont'd		
5/6/50	17	12		15 **Hoop-Dee-Doo** ....A:17 / J:17 / S:18 *Marriage Ties*	$10	Columbia 38771
				7" 33-1/3 rpm: 1-591		
5/13/50	9	15		16 **Bewitched** ....A:9 / J:9 / S:10 *Imagination*	$10	Columbia 38698
				7" 33-1/3 rpm: 1-480; from the Broadway musical *Pal Joey* starring **Gene Kelly**; #50 hit for the Betty Smith Group in 1958		
6/24/50	19	4		17 **I Didn't Slip - I Wasn't Pushed - I Fell** ....A:19 / J:19 / S:28 *Before I Loved You*	$10	Columbia 38818
				7" 33-1/3 rpm: 1-637		
11/4/50	16	8		18 **A Bushel And A Peck** ....A:16 / J:21 / S:30 *The Best Thing For You*	$20	Columbia 4-39008
				from the Broadway musical *Guys And Dolls* starring Robert Alda and Vivian Blaine		
3/10/51	10	10		19 **Would I Love You (Love You, Love You)** ....A:10 / S:19 / J:26 *Lullaby Of Broadway*	$20	Columbia 4-39159
				HARRY JAMES & his ORCH. with DORIS DAY		
6/30/51	7	17		20 **(Why Did I Tell You I Was Going To) Shanghai** ....A:7 / J:7 / S:9 *My Life's Desire*	$20	Columbia 4-39423
11/17/51	21	4		21 **Domino** ....A:21 *If That Doesn't Do It!*	$20	Columbia 4-39596
3/15/52	❶¹	19	●	22 **A Guy Is A Guy** ....J:❶¹ / A:2 / S:4 *Who Who Who*	$15	Columbia 4-39673
				adapted from the World War II soldiers' song "A Gob Is A Slob," which in turn was based on the 1719 British tune "I Went To The Alehouse (A Knave Is A Knave)"		
6/21/52	7	14	●	23 **Sugarbush** ....J:7 / S:10 / A:15 *How Lovely Cooks The Meat*	$15	Columbia 4-39693
				DORIS DAY - FRANKIE LAINE		
8/2/52	20	3		24 **When I Fall In Love** ....J:20 *Take Me In Your Arms*	$15	Columbia 4-39786
				from the movie *One Minute To Zero* starring Robert Mitchum; #7 hit for The Lettermen in 1962		
10/25/52	25	2		25 **No Two People** ....A:25 *You Can't Lose Me*	$15	Columbia 4-39863
				DORIS DAY - DONALD O'CONNOR		
				from the movie *Hans Christian Andersen* starring **Danny Kaye**		
12/13/52	20	1		26 **A Full Time Job** ....A:20 *Ma Says, Pa Says*	$15	Columbia 4-39898
				DORIS DAY - JOHNNIE RAY		
1/17/53	10	7		27 **Mister Tap Toe** ....A:10 / S:15 / J:15 *Your Mother And Mine*	$15	Columbia 4-39906
6/20/53	17	1		28 **Candy Lips** ....A:17 *Let's Walk That-A-Way*	$15	Columbia 4-40001
				JOHNNIE RAY - DORIS DAY		
9/26/53	20	1		29 **Choo Choo Train (Ch— Ch— Foo)** ....A:20 *This Too Shall Pass Away* [N]	$15	Columbia 4-40063
				adapted from the French song "Le Petit Train"		
1/9/54	❶⁴	22	●	30 **Secret Love** ....A:❶⁴ / S:❶³ / J:2 *The Deadwood Stage (Whip-crack - Away!)*	$15	Columbia 4-40108
				from the movie *Calamity Jane* starring Day; #20 hit for Freddy Fender in 1975		
4/24/54	16	4		31 **I Speak To The Stars** ....A:16 *The Blue Bells Of Broadway*	$15	Columbia 4-40210
				from the movie *Lucky Me* starring Day		
9/11/54	3	17		32 **If I Give My Heart To You** ....J:3 / S:4 / A:4 *Anyone Can Fall In Love*	$15	Columbia 4-40300
				#34 hit for **Kitty Kallen** in 1959		
				DEAN, Alan '52		
				Born in 1921 in London. Leader of **The Keynotes** vocal group in England.		
8/23/52	26	4		**Luna Rossa (Blushing Moon)** ....S:26 *I'll Forget You*	$15	MGM K11269
				Joe Lipman (orch.)		
				DeCASTRO SISTERS, The HOT '55		
				Female vocal trio from Cuba: Peggy, Babette and Cherie DeCastro.		
10/9/54+	2¹	20		**Teach Me Tonight** ....J:2 / A:3 / S:3 *It's Love*	$25	Abbott 3001
				Skip Martin (orch.); #25 hit for George Maharis in 1962		
				DEEP RIVER BOYS '48		
				Black vocal group formed at Virginia's Hampton Institute: Harry Douglas (born on 5/6/16), Vernon Gardner, George Lawson and Edward Ware (died in 1956), with Cameron Williams (piano).		
11/20/48	18	5		**Recess In Heaven** ....A:18 *It's Too Soon To Know*	$25	RCA Victor 20-3203
				DeHAVEN, Gloria '51		
				Born on 7/23/25 in Los Angeles. Starred in several Hollywood musicals. Started as a band singer with **Bob Crosby** and **Jan Savitt**.		
9/8/51	11	12		**Because Of You** ....J:11 / S:27 *Out O' Breath*	$15	Decca 9-27666
				GLORIA DeHAVEN and GUY LOMBARDO And His Royal Canadians		
				song published in 1940; featured in the 1951 movie *I Was An American Spy* starring Ann Dvorak; #71 hit for Chris Montez in 1967		
				DeJOHN SISTERS HOT '55		
				Pop vocal duo from Chester, Pennsylvania: Julie (born on 3/18/31) and Dux (born on 1/21/33) DeGiovanni.		
12/25/54+	6	13		**(My Baby Don't Love Me) No More** ....A:6 / S:8 / J:11 *Theresa (The Little Flower)*	$20	Epic 9085
				O.B. Masingill (orch.)		
				DELTA RHYTHM BOYS '45		
				R&B vocal group formed at Langston University in Oklahoma; later transferred to Dillard University in New Orleans: Carl Jones, Traverse Crawford, Kelsey Pharr and Lee Gaines, with Rene DeKnight (piano). Pharr died in 1960. Crawford died in 1975. Gaines died on 7/15/87 (age 73).		
8/25/45	9	3		1 **It's Only A Paper Moon** ....J:9 *(I'm Gonna Hurry You Out Of My Mind And) Cry You Out Of My Heart*	$30	Decca 23425
				ELLA FITZGERALD and DELTA RHYTHM BOYS		
				originally featured in the Broadway production *The Great Magoo* under the title "If You Believe In Me"; also featured in the movie *Take A Chance* starring James Dunn; #9 hit for Paul Whiteman in 1933		
11/24/45	10	3		2 **The Honeydripper** ....S:10 / A:17 *Baby, Are You Kiddin'?*	$30	Decca 23451
				JIMMIE LUNCEFORD And His Orchestra and DELTA RHYTHM BOYS		
				#2 R&B hit		
2/23/46	17	1		3 **Just A-Sittin' And A-Rockin'** ....A:17 *Don't Knock It*	$40	Decca 18739
				#3 R&B hit		
12/7/46+	8	14		4 **(I Love You) For Sentimental Reasons** ....J:8 / A:10 *It's A Pity To Say Goodnight*	$30	Decca 23670
				ELLA FITZGERALD And DELTA RHYTHM BOYS		
				#17 hit for Sam Cooke in 1958		
				DENNIS, Clark MEM '47		
				Singer/pianist. Briefly with Ben Pollack and Paul Whiteman bands.		
6/21/47	8	10		1 **Peg O' My Heart** ....A:8 / J:8 / S:10 *Bless You (For Being An Angel)*	$10	Capitol 346
				from the Broadway musical *Ziegfeld Follies Of 1913* starring Elizabeth Brice; #1 hit for Charles Harrison in 1913; #64 hit for Robert (**Bobby**) Maxwell in 1964		
3/26/49	23	1		2 **Galway Bay** ....A:23 *O'Leary Is Leery Of Fallin' In Love*	$10	Capitol 15403
				Buddy Cole (orch.)		

DENNIS, Matt — see WESTON, Paul

DERWIN, Hal   MEM '46
Born on 8/7/14 in Chicago. Died on 2/9/98 (age 83). Baritone singer. Previously with **Shep Fields** and **Les Brown** bands.

| 11/30/46 | 5 | 10 | | **The Old Lamplighter**   A:5 / S:6 / J:7 *I Guess I'll Get The Papers And Go Home* | $10 | Capitol 288 |

Frank DeVol (orch.); #5 hit for The Browns in 1960

DESMOND, Johnny ★96★   MEM/HOT '55
Born Giovanni Desimons on 11/14/20 in Detroit. Died on 9/6/85 (age 64). Sang with **Bob Crosby**, **Gene Krupa** and **Glenn Miller**'s military band. Featured on the *Breakfast Club* radio show in the 1950s. Regular on TV's *Your Hit Parade* (1958-59).

1)Woman 2)(The Gang That Sang) "Heart Of My Heart" 3)Guilty

| 3/22/47 | 12 | 3 | | 1 **Guilty**..A:12 / J:13 *I'll Close My Eyes* | $15 | RCA Victor 20-2109 |

Page Cavanaugh Trio (piano, guitar and bass); #4 hit for Ruth Etting in 1931

| 12/24/49 | 22 | 1 | | 2 **Don't Cry Joe (Let Her Go, Let Her Go, Let Her Go)** ....J:22 *The Last Mile Home* | $15 | MGM 10518 |

Bobby Hackett (trumpet solo)

| 3/25/50 | 25 | 2 | | 3 **C'est Si Bon (It's So Good)** ....S:25 *If You Could Care* | $15 | MGM 10613 |

The Quintones (backing vocals); #22 hit for Conway Twitty in 1961

7/1/50	20	1		4 **The Picnic Song** ....A:20 *I've Got A Heart Filled With Love (For You Dear)* [N]	$20	MGM K10703
8/26/50	24	1		5 **Just Say I Love Her (Dicitencello Vuie)** ....A:24 *If Anybody Does*	$20	MGM K10758
12/9/50	29	1		6 **A Bushel And A Peck** ....A:29 *So Long Sally*	$20	MGM K10800

from the Broadway musical *Guys And Dolls* starring Robert Alda and Vivian Blaine

| 9/8/51 | 17 | 8 | | 7 **Because Of You** ....A:17 *Andiamo* | $20 | MGM K10947 |

song published in 1940; featured in the 1951 movie *I Was An American Spy* starring Ann Dvorak; #71 hit for Chris Montez in 1967

| 9/22/51 | 30 | 1 | | 8 **I Want To Be Near You** ....A:30 *I Will Never Change* | $20 | MGM K11027 |

The Ray Charles Singers (backing vocals; #4 & 6-8)

| 11/1/52 | 19 | 3 | | 9 **Nina Never Knew** ....A:19 *Stay Where You Are* | $20 | Coral 9-60848 |

Tony Mottola (orch.: #2-9)

| 12/5/53+ | 10 | 10 | | 10 **The Gang That Sang "Heart Of My Heart"** ....J:10 / A:14 / S:18 *I Think I'll Fall In Love Today* | $20 | Coral 9-61076 |

DON CORNELL, ALAN DALE AND JOHNNY DESMOND
Jack Pleis (orch.); song written in 1926

| 1/2/54 | 9 | 7 | | 11 **Woman**   J:9 *The River Seine* | $15 | Coral 9-61069 |

| 8/7/54 | 17 | 5 | | 12 **The High And The Mighty** ....J:17 / S:28 *Got No Time* | $15 | Coral 9-61232 |

George Cates (orch.); originally released on Coral 61204; title song from the movie starring John Wayne

DeVOL, Frank, and his Orchestra   HOT '50
Born on 9/20/11 in Moundsville, West Virginia. Died on 10/27/99 (age 88). Lead alto saxophonist/arranger with **Horace Heidt** and **Alvino Rey**. Conductor/arranger for many top singers, radio and TV shows. Received several Academy Award nominations for movie scores; composed the TV theme for <My Three Sons>. Married **Helen O'Connell** in 1991.

| 3/4/50 | 21 | 3 | | 1 **I Said My Pajamas (And Put On My Pray'rs)** ....A:21 / S:24 *Be Mine* (Whiting) | $20 | Capitol F841 |

MARGARET WHITING and FRANK DeVOL (vocal duet)

| 9/23/50 | 28 | 1 | | 2 **Dream Awhile**..A:28 *Powder And Paint* | $15 | Capitol F1143 |

#15 hit for **Eddy Duchin** in 1936

DEWAN, Emil, Quintones   '51
Born on 1/13/23 in Danbury, Conecticut. Died in October 1980 (age 57). Vibes player. His Quintones: Mike Cuseta (guitar), Sam Blake (piano) and Sam Bari (bass).

| 8/11/51 | 22 | 1 | | **Butcher Boy (Aeluna Mezzumare)**..A:22 *The Lady Is A Tramp* [F] | $20 | Mercury 5537-X45 |

#5 hit for **Rudy Vallee** in 1938; #12 hit in 1958 for **Lou Monte** entitled "Lazy Mary"

DEXTER, Al, and his Troopers   '43
Born Clarence Albert Poindexter on 5/4/05 in Troup, Texas. Died on 1/28/84 (age 78). Country singer/songwriter/guitarist/violinist. Owned his own Round-Up club in Longview, Texas. His Troopers included Aubrey Gass, Paul Sells and Holly Hollinger.

| 8/28/43 | ❶¹ | 17 | ● | 1 **Pistol Packin' Mama /**   S:❶¹ / J:2 | | |

#5 R&B hit

| 4/22/44 | 22 | 1 | | 2 **Rosalita** ....J:22 | $30 | Okeh 6708 |
| 4/1/44 | 18 | 1 | | 3 **Too Late To Worry** ....J(terr.):18 *So Long Pal* (C&W #1) | $30 | Okeh 6718 |

#76 hit for Glen Campbell in 1962

| 3/2/46 | 16 | 1 | | 4 **Guitar Polka**..J:16 *Honey Do You Think It's Wrong* (C&W #2) [I] | $25 | Columbia 36898 |

all of above are #1 Country hits

DIAMOND, Leo   HOT '53
Born on 6/29/15 in New York City. Died on 9/15/66 (age 51). Arranger/lead harmonica player for The Borrah Minevitch Harmonica Rascals (1930-46).

| 11/28/53 | 14 | 1 | | **Off Shore** ....A:14 *Easy Melody* [I] | $20 | Ambass. 45-1005 |

DIETRICH, Marlene   '52
Born on 12/27/01 in Schöneberg, Germany. Died of kidney failure on 5/6/92 (age 90). Legendary movie star.

| 8/23/52 | 12 | 6 | | **Too Old To Cut The Mustard**..A:12 / J:19 / S:22 *Good For Nothin'* | $20 | Columbia 4-39812 |

MARLENE DIETRICH & ROSEMARY CLOONEY

DINNING SISTERS, The   '48
Vocal trio from Wichita, Oklahoma: twin sisters Jean and Ginger Dinning, with Jayne Bundeson (had replaced Lucille Dinning in 1946). Regulars on radio's *National Barn Dance*. Their brother Mark hit #1 in 1960 with "Teen Angel."

| 5/3/47 | 9 | 4 | | 1 **My Adobe Hacienda** ....A:9 *If I Had My Life To Live Over* | $10 | Capitol 389 |
| 10/11/47 | 12 | 1 | | 2 **I Wonder Who's Kissing Her Now**..A:12 *Lolita Lopez* | $10 | Capitol 433 |

title song from the movie starring June Haver; #1 hit for Henry Burr in 1909; #93 hit for Bobby Darin in 1964

| 2/28/48 | 12 | 3 | | 3 **Beg Your Pardon** ....A:12 *Melancholy* | $10 | Capitol 490 |

Jack Fascinato (orch.)

| 10/30/48 | 5 | 16 | ● | 4 **Buttons And Bows**   J:5 / S:7 / A:7 *San Antonio Rose* | $10 | Capitol 15184 |

from the movie *The Paleface* starring **Bob Hope**; #104 hit for The Browns in 1962; Art Van Damme Quintet (instrumental backing: #1, 2 & 4)

DOMINOES, The   HOT '51

R&B vocal group from New York City: Clyde McPhatter, Charlie White, Joe Lamont and Bill Brown, with Billy Ward (piano). McPhatter died of a heart attack on 6/13/72 (age 39). Ward died on 2/16/2002 (age 80).

| 8/25/51 | 17 | 9 | | Sixty Minute Man ....J:17 / S:23 *I Can't Escape From You* | $500 | Federal 45-12022 |

#1 R&B hit (14 weeks); #65 Pop hit for Clarence Carter in 1973

DONAHUE, Al, and his Orchestra   MEM '39

Born on 6/12/04 in Boston. Died on 2/20/83 (age 78). Bandleader/songwriter/arranger.

| 3/1/41 | 19 | 1 | | 1 I Hear A Rhapsody ....S(mw):19 *Frenesi* | $10 | Okeh 5888 |

Phil Brito (vocal)

| 4/19/41 | 7 | 2 | | 2 The Wise Old Owl ....S:7 *You Should Be Set To Music* | $10 | Okeh 6037 |

Dee Keating (vocal)

DONAHUE, Sam, And His Orchestra ★71★   MEM '47

Born on 3/8/18 in Detroit. Died on 3/22/74 (age 56). Tenor saxophonist. Played with **Gene Krupa** and (briefly) with **Harry James** and **Benny Goodman**. Took over **Artie Shaw**'s Navy band after Shaw's discharge. Later led the **Billy May** Orchestra. Played with **Stan Kenton**. In the 1960s became leader of the late **Tommy Dorsey**'s band.

1)I Never Knew 2)My Melancholy Baby 3)The Whistler

Orchestras:	Allen, Mynell — 3	Daye, Irene — 1	Lloyd Shirley — 8,9
	Blue Hues, The — 7	**Donahue, Sam** — 5	Lockwood, Bill — 4,7,11

| 9/13/41 | 19 | 1 | | 1 Do You Care? ....S(s):19 *Six Mile Stretch* | $10 | Bluebird 11198 |
| 7/13/46 | 9 | 6 | | 2 Dinah ....A:9 *Take Five* [I] | $10 | Capitol 260 |

#1 hit in 1932 for both **Bing Crosby** and the **Mills Brothers**

8/3/46	8	7		3 Just The Other Day...A:8 *I Left My Heart In Mississippi*	$10	Capitol 275
10/26/46	8	2		4 Put That Kiss Back Where You Found It ....A:8 *Scufflin'*	$10	Capitol 293
12/14/46+	7	7		5 A Rainy Night In Rio ....A:7 *It's Anybody's Love Song*	$10	Capitol 325

from the movie *The Time, The Place And The Girl* starring Dennis Morgan

| 4/19/47 | 5 | 7 | | 6 My Melancholy Baby   A:5 *I Can't Believe It Was All Make Believe* [I] | $10 | Capitol 357 |

#3 hit for Gene Austin in 1928

| 5/10/47 | 2¹ | 23 | | 7 I Never Knew   A:2 *Why Did It Have To End So Soon* | $10 | Capitol 405 |

#8 hit for Gene Austin in 1926

| 11/8/47 | 6 | 7 | | 8 The Whistler / ....A:6 | | |
| 11/1/47 | 9 | 2 | | 9 Red Wing ....A:9 | $10 | Capitol 472 |

#2 hit for Frank Stanley & Henry Burr in 1907; #64 hit in 1960 by Sammy Masters as "Rockin' Red Wing"

8/21/48	24	1		10 Saxa-Boogie / ....A:24 [I]		
10/16/48	26	3		11 I'll Get Along Somehow A:26	$15	Capitol 15081
12/11/48	26	1		12 September In The Rain ....A:26 *Constellation* [I]	$10	Capitol 15172

from the movie *Melody For Two* starring James Melton

DON, DICK & JIMMY   MEM/HOT '54

Vocal trio: Don Ralke, Dick Crowe and Jimmy Styne. Ralke died on 1/26/2000 (age 80).

| 10/23/54 | 14 | 6 | | That's What I Like.................................J:14 / S:20 *You Can't Have Your Cake And Eat It Too* | $20 | Crown 45x125 |

DOREY, Ray   '47

Singer with **Larry Green**'s Orchestra.

| 5/3/47 | 7 | 8 | | Mam'selle...A:7 / J:16 *The Man Who Paints The Rainbow* | $10 | Majestic 7217 |

Paul Baron (orch.); from the movie *The Razor's Edge* starring Tyrone Power

DORSEY, Jimmy, And His Orchestra ★12★   MEM/HOT '41

Born on 2/29/04 in Shenandoah, Pennsylvania. Died of cancer on 6/12/57 (age 53). Legendary alto sax and clarinet soloist/bandleader. Jimmy and brother **Tommy Dorsey** recorded together as the Dorsey Brothers Orchestra from 1928-35 and 1953-56. They hosted a musical variety TV show, *Stage Show*, from 1954-56. Jimmy's band featured popular vocalists **Bob Eberly** and **Helen O'Connell**. Dorsey's pre-1940 #1 hits: "Is It True What They Say About Dixie" and "Change Partners."

1)Amapola (Pretty Little Poppy) 2)Besame Mucho (Kiss Me Much) 3)Tangerine 4)Green Eyes (Aquellos Ojos Verdes) 5)Maria Elena

Vocalists:	Carroll, Bob — 49-51	Eberly, Bob — 1,3,6-8,10-21,23,	Kallen, Kitty — 34-36,38	Parker, Dee — 48,50
	Cromwell, Jean — 46	24,26,27,29-33,35-37,39	O'Connell, Helen — 2,4,5,10,11,	Tell, Gladys — 41
	Crosby, Bing — 47	Hogan, Claire "Shanty" — 52,53	14,17-19,22,23,28,30	Walters, Teddy — 42-45

| 7/6/40 | ❶¹ | 10 | | 1 The Breeze And I   J:❶¹ / S:2 *Little Curly Hair In A High Chair* | $10 | Decca 3150 |

adapted from the Spanish song "Andalucia"; #8 hit for Caterina Valente in 1955

| 8/17/40 | 4 | 3 | | 2 Six Lessons From Madame La Zonga ....S:4 *Boog-It* | $10 | Decca 3152 |
| 8/24/40 | 20 | 1 | | 3 All This And Heaven Too..S:20 *If I Forget You* | $10 | Decca 3259 |

title song from the movie starring Bette Davis

| 1/11/41 | 16 | 1 | | 4 You've Got Me This Way / ....S(wc):16 | | |
| 1/11/41 | 19 | 1 | | 5 The Bad Humor Man ....S(e):19 [N] | $10 | Decca 3435 |

above 2 from the movie *You'll Find Out* starring **Kay Kyser**

1/18/41	3	10		6 I Hear A Rhapsody S:3 *The Mem'ry Of A Rose*	$10	Decca 3570
2/22/41	7	1		7 High On A Windy Hill / S:7		
4/12/41	14	11		8 I Understand ....S(e):14 / S(mw):19 / S(wc):19 / S:20	$10	Decca 3585
3/22/41	15	2		9 Tonight (Perfidia) ....S(mw):15 *Contrasts* [I]	$10	Decca 3198

record also labeled as "Perfidia (Tonight)"; #15 hit for The Ventures in 1960

DORSEY, Jimmy, And His Orchestra — Cont'd

DEBUT	PEAK	WKS	Gold	A-side (Chart Hit) .... B-side	$	Label & Number
3/22/41	❶10	14	●	10 **Amapola (Pretty Little Poppy)** S:❶10 *Donna Maria*	$10	Decca 3629
				adaptation of a Spanish song featured in the movie *First Love* starring Deanna Durbin; #63 hit for Jacky Noguez in 1960		
5/17/41	❶4	21	●	11 **Green Eyes (Aquellos Ojos Verdes)** / S:❶4		
5/24/41	❶2	17		12 **Maria Elena** S:❶2	$10	Decca 3698
				#6 hit for Los Indios Tabajaras in 1963		
5/17/41	❶2	10		13 **My Sister And I** S:❶2 *In The Hush Of The Night*	$10	Decca 3710
5/31/41	2²	13		14 **Yours (Quiereme Mucho)** S:2 *When The Sun Comes Out*	$10	Decca 3657
7/5/41	7	3		15 **The Things I Love** ....S:7 *Once And For All*	$10	Decca 3737
				#60 hit for The Fidelity's in 1958		
8/2/41	❶1	14		16 **Blue Champagne** S:❶1 *All Alone And Lonely*	$10	Decca 3775
10/4/41	5	9		17 **Jim** S:5 *A New Shade Of Blue*	$10	Decca 3963
10/25/41	10	1		18 **Time Was (Duerme)** ....S:10 *Isle Of Pines*	$10	Decca 3859
1/31/42	10	1		19 **I Said No** / S:10		
				from the movie *Sweater Girl* starring Eddie Bracken		
2/7/42	19	1		20 **This Is No Laughing Matter** ....S(wc):19	$10	Decca 4102
2/7/42	16	1		21 **The White Cliffs Of Dover** S(e):16 / S(mw):20 *I Got It Bad (And That Ain't Good)*	$10	Decca 4103
3/28/42	19	1		22 **Arthur Murray Taught Me Dancing In A Hurry** ....S(e):19 *Not Mine*	$10	Decca 4122
4/18/42	❶6	15		23 **Tangerine** S:❶6 *Ev'rything I Love*	$10	Decca 4123
				#18 hit for the Salsoul Orchestra in 1976		
4/25/42	9	1		24 **I Remember You** ....S:9 *If You Build A Better Mousetrap*	$10	Decca 4132
				#2 hit in 1909 for Ada Jones; #5 hit in 1962 for Frank Ifield; above 3 from the movie *The Fleet's In* starring Dorothy Lamour		
6/13/42	9	1		25 **Jersey Bounce** ....S:9 *My Little Cousin* [I]	$10	Decca 4288
6/27/42	20	1		26 **Always In My Heart** S:20 *Last Night I Said A Prayer*	$10	Decca 4277
				title song from the movie starring Kay Francis; #82 hit for Los Indios Tabajaras in 1964		
7/25/42	17	5		27 **This Is Worth Fighting For** / S(e):17 / S(wc):20		
				from the movie *When Johnny Comes Marching Home* starring **Donald O'Connor**		
8/15/42	17	4		28 **Take Me** S(mw):17 / S(wc):18	$10	Decca 18376
8/29/42	10	1		29 **My Devotion** ....S:10 *Sorghum Switch*	$10	Decca 18372
12/26/42+	17	3		30 **Brazil (Aquarela Do Brasil)** / S(wc):17	$10	Decca 18460
				featured in the movie *Saludos Amigos*; #11 hit for The Ritchie Family in 1975		
10/31/42	19	1		31 **Daybreak** ....S(wc):19	$10	Decca 18460
				based on the theme of "Mardi Gras" from Ferde Grofe's *Mississippi Suite* of 1926		
10/31/42	20	1		32 **Ev'ry Night About This Time** ....S(s):20 *I'm Getting Tired So I Can Sleep*	$10	Decca 18462
5/29/43	14	3		33 **Let's Get Lost** ....S(e):14 / S(mw):15 *Murder! He Says*	$10	Decca 18532
				from the movie *Happy-Go-Lucky* starring **Mary Martin**		
12/4/43+	2¹	9		34 **They're Either Too Young Or Too Old** / J:2 / S:3		
				from the movie *Thank Your Lucky Stars* starring **Eddie Cantor**		
1/8/44	3	13		35 **Star Eyes** S:3 / J:5	$10	Decca 18571
				from the movie *I Dood It* starring Red Skelton		
1/15/44	❶7	23	●	36 **Besame Mucho (Kiss Me Much)** / S:❶7 / J:❶1		
				#70 hit for the Coasters in 1960		
1/8/44	5	11		37 **My Ideal** J:5 / S:8	$10	Decca 18574
				#12 hit for Maurice Chevalier in 1931		
2/5/44	4	16		38 **When They Ask About You** / S:4 / J:7		
				from the movie *Stars On Parade* starring Larry Parks		
2/26/44	22	1		39 **My First Love** J:22	$10	Decca 18582
4/8/44	13	2		40 **Holiday For Strings** ....J:13 *Ohio* [I]	$10	Decca 18593
				Si Zentner (trombone)		
9/23/44	17	2		41 **An Hour Never Passes** ....J(terr.):17 *Two Again*	$10	Decca 18616
12/23/44	24	1		42 **Moon On My Pillow** ....J(terr.):24 *Sweet Dreams, Sweetheart*	$10	Decca 18627
				from the movie *She Has What It Takes* starring Jinx Falkenburg		
4/21/45	13	2		43 **I Should Care** ....A:13 *Twilight Time*	$10	Decca 18656
				from the movie *Thrill Of A Romance* starring Esther Williams		
6/16/45	8	6		44 **There! I've Said It Again** / A:8 / J:12		
				#1 hit for Bobby Vinton in 1964		
6/2/45	13	3		45 **Dream** J:13	$10	Decca 18670
				originally heard as the closing theme for composer **Johnny Mercer**'s radio show; #19 hit for Betty Johnson in 1958		
6/30/45	8	1		46 **Can't You Read Between The Lines?** ....A:8 *Negra Consentida (My Pet Brunette)*	$10	Decca 18676
1/19/46	16	1		47 **Give Me The Simple Life** ....A:16 *It's The Talk Of The Town*	$15	Decca 23469
				BING CROSBY and JIMMY DORSEY And His Orchestra		
				from the movie *Wake Up And Dream* starring June Haver		
6/15/46	8	10		48 **Doin' What Comes Natur'lly** ....J:8 / A:10 *All That Glitters Is Not Gold*	$10	Decca 18872
				from the Broadway musical *Annie Get Your Gun* starring **Ethel Merman**		
12/7/46	12	1		49 **The Whole World Is Singing My Song** ....A:12 *Apache Serenade*	$10	Decca 18917
3/29/47	11	1		50 **Heartaches** ....A:11 *There Is No Greater Love*	$10	MGM 10001
				#12 hit for **Guy Lombardo** in 1931; #7 hit for The Marcels in 1961		
1/17/48	10	1		51 **Ballerina** ....A:10 *(Love's Got Me In A) Lazy Mood*	$10	MGM 10035
				#18 hit for Nat "King" Cole in 1957		
				JIMMY DORSEY and his Original "Dorseyland" Jazz Band:		
1/14/50	13	11		52 **Johnson Rag** ....A:13 / J:13 / S:14 *Charley, My Boy*	$10	Columbia 38649
				7" 33-1/3 rpm: 1-426		
3/11/50	15	5		53 **Rag Mop** ....A:15 / J:23 *That's A Plenty*	$10	Columbia 38710
				7" 33-1/3 rpm: 1-499; Charlie Teagarden, trumpet and Cutty Cutshall, trombone (above 2)		

DORSEY, Tommy, and his Orchestra ★8★   MEM/HOT '37

Born on 11/19/05 in Mahanoy Plane, Pennsylvania. Choked to death on 11/26/56 (age 51). Legendary trombonist/bandleader. Played with brother **Jimmy Dorsey** from 1928-35. Tommy's band launched the career of vocalist **Frank Sinatra**. Band's theme song was "I'm Getting Sentimental Over You" (#8 in 1936). The brothers appeared in the 1947 movie *The Fabulous Dorseys*. Reunited with Jimmy in the Dorsey Brothers Orchestra in 1953. They hosted the musical variety TV program, *Stage Show*, 1954-56. Dorsey's top 5 pre-1940 #1 hits: "Once In A While," "Music, Maestro, Please," "Dipsy Doodle," "Alone" and "The Music Goes 'Round And 'Round."

1)I'll Never Smile Again 2)There Are Such Things 3)In The Blue Of Evening 4)Oh! Look At Me Now 5)Indian Summer

Vocalists:
Clark Sisters — 65
Dennis, Denny — 66
Dorsey, Tommy — 35
Foster, Stuart — 55,56,60,61,63,64
Haines, Connie — 14,18,19,23,26,32,49

Herfurt, "Skeets" — 59
Leonard, Jack — 1,2
Lutes, Marcy — 68
Oliver, Sy — 24
Pied Pipers, The — 3,7,16-21,23,27,33-35,40,42,46
Polk, Lucy Ann — 66

Prime, Harry — 65
Sentimentalists, The — 54,57,61,62,66
Shavers, Charlie — 67
Sinatra, Frank — 3-9,11-13,15,16,18-23,25,27-31,33-35,37,38,40-44,48

Stafford, Jo — 24,39,46
Storr, Alan — 10
Stewart, Freddie — 50
Town Criers — 65
Williams, Bonnie Lou — 52-54

DEBUT	PEAK	WKS		#	A-side / B-side	$	Label & Number
1/13/40	3	8		1	**All The Things You Are** J:3 *That Lucky Fellow*	$10	Victor 26401
					from the Broadway musical *Very Warm For May* starring Grace McDonald		
2/3/40	2[2]	12	•	2	**Indian Summer** J:2 *A Lover Is Blue*	$10	Victor 26390
7/20/40	❶[12]	18	●	3	**I'll Never Smile Again** S:❶[12] / J:❶[6] *Marcheta*	$15	Victor 26628
					record selected for the NARAS Hall of Fame; #25 hit for The Platters in 1961		
7/27/40	8	1		4	**Imagination** S:8 *Charming Little Faker*	$15	Victor 26581
8/10/40	17	2		5	**Fools Rush In (Where Angels Fear To Tread)** S(e):17 / S:19 *Devil May Care*	$15	Victor 26593
					#12 hit for Rick Nelson in 1963		
8/10/40	15	2		6	**All This And Heaven Too** S(e):15 / S(s):16 *Where Do You Keep Your Heart?*	$15	Victor 26653
					title song from the movie starring Bette Davis		
8/31/40	15	4		7	**The One I Love (Belongs To Somebody Else)** S(e):15 / S(s):19 *And So Do I*	$15	Victor 26660
					new version of #16 hit for Dorsey in 1938 on Victor 25741; #2 hit for Al Jolson in 1924		
8/31/40	17	1		8	**Love Lies** / S(e):17		
9/21/40	18	3		9	**The Call Of The Canyon** S(e):18	$15	Victor 26678
					title song from the movie starring Gene Autry		
10/26/40	7	3		10	**Only Forever** / S:7		
					from the movie *Rhythm On The River* starring Bing Crosby and Mary Martin		
9/21/40	10	4		11	**Trade Winds** S:10	$15	Victor 26666
10/12/40	18	1		12	**I Could Make You Care** S(e):18 *The World Is In My Arms*	$15	Victor 26717
					from the movie *Ladies Must Live* starring Wayne Morris		
11/9/40	5	3		13	**Our Love Affair** S:5 *That's For Me*	$15	Victor 26736
					from the movie *Strike Up The Band* starring Mickey Rooney and Judy Garland		
11/16/40	16	2		14	**Two Dreams Met** S(e):16 / S(s):20 *When You Awake*	$10	Victor 26764
					from the movie *Down Argentine Way* starring Don Ameche and Betty Grable		
11/30/40	3	5		15	**We Three (My Echo, My Shadow and Me)** S:3 *Tell Me At Midnight*	$15	Victor 26747
1/4/41	7	1		16	**Star Dust** S:7 *Swanee River*	$15	Victor 27233
					new version of #8 hit for Dorsey in 1936 on Victor 25320; #1 hit for Isham Jones in 1931; #12 hit for Billy Ward & His Dominoes in 1957		
1/4/41	14	1		17	**You've Got Me This Way** S(wc):14 *I'd Know You Anywhere*	$10	Victor 26770
					from the movie *You'll Find Out* starring Kay Kyser		
3/1/41	2[6]	12		18	**Oh! Look At Me Now** / S:2		
3/22/41	16	1		19	**You Might Have Belonged To Another** S(s):16	$15	Victor 27274
					above 2 tunes were contest winners in Dorsey's *Fame And Fortune* program		
4/12/41	4	3		20	**Do I Worry?** S:4 *Little Man With A Candy Cigar*	$15	Victor 27338
4/26/41	7	2		21	**Dolores** S:7 *I Tried*	$15	Victor 27317
					from the movie *Las Vegas Nights* starring Dorsey		
5/3/41	9	1		22	**Everything Happens To Me** S:9 *Whatcha Know Joe?*	$15	Victor 27359
5/10/41	7	2		23	**Let's Get Away From It All-Parts 1 & 2** S:7	$15	Victor 27377
					The Pied Pipers (vocals - Part 1); **Connie Haines, Frank Sinatra** and **The Pied Pipers** (vocals - Part 2)		
7/12/41	4	14		24	**Yes Indeed!** S:4 *Will You Still Be Mine?*	$10	Victor 27421
8/30/41	16	3		25	**You And I** S(mw):16 / S(wc):16 / S(e):18 *Free For All*	$15	Victor 27532
8/30/41	16	2		26	**Kiss The Boys Goodbye** S(wc):16 *I'll Never Let A Day Pass By*	$10	Victor 27461
					title song from the movie starring Mary Martin		
10/4/41	15	3		27	**I Guess I'll Have To Dream The Rest** S(e):15 *Loose Lid Special*	$15	Victor 27526
10/25/41	3	16		28	**This Love Of Mine** S:3 *Neiani*	$15	Victor 27508
12/20/41	9	1		29	**Two In Love** / S:9		
12/20/41	20	1		30	**A Sinner Kissed An Angel** S(mw):20	$15	Victor 27611
2/28/42	16	3		31	**How About You?** S(wc):16 *Winter Weather*	$15	Victor 27749
					from the movie *Babes On Broadway* starring Mickey Rooney and Judy Garland		
3/28/42	16	1		32	**What Is This Thing Called Love?** S(wc):16 *Love Sends A Little Gift Of Roses*	$10	Victor 27782
					from the Broadway musical *Wake Up And Dream* starring Tilly Losch; #5 hit for Leo Reisman in 1930		
6/20/42	20	1		33	**The Last Call For Love** S(s):20 *Poor You*	$15	Victor 27849
					from the movie *Ship Ahoy* starring Eleanor Powell (also #35 below)		
7/25/42	3	9		34	**Just As Though You Were Here** S:3 *Street Of Dreams*	$15	Victor 27903
8/8/42	18	1		35	**I'll Take Tallulah** S(e):18 *Not So Quiet Please*	$15	Victor 27869
8/22/42	20	1		36	**Well, Git It!** S(mw):20 *Somewhere A Voice Is Calling* [I]	$10	Victor 27887
					Ziggy Elman (trumpet)		
9/26/42	5	3		37	**Take Me** / S:5		
8/29/42	15	3		38	**Be Careful, It's My Heart** S(e):15 / S(mw):15 / S(s):20	$15	Victor 27923
					from the movie *Holiday Inn* starring Bing Crosby and Fred Astaire		
10/17/42	15	3		39	**Manhattan Serenade** S(wc):15 / S(mw):16 / S(s):16 *Blue Blazes*	$10	Victor 27962

DORSEY, Tommy, and his Orchestra — Cont'd

DEBUT	PEAK	WKS	Gold	A-side / B-side	$	Label & Number
11/14/42+	**❶**⁵	24	●	40 **There Are Such Things** / S:**❶**⁵		
11/7/42	10	2		41 **Daybreak** S:10	$15	Victor 27974
				based on the theme of "Mardi Gras" from Ferde Grofe's *Mississippi Suite* of 1926		
2/13/43	4	13		42 **It Started All Over Again** S:4 *Mandy, Make Up Your Mind*	$15	Victor 20-1522
7/10/43	**❶**³	17		43 **In The Blue Of Evening** S:**❶**³		
				originally released on Victor 27947 in 1942		
7/17/43	6	7		44 **It's Always You**..S:6	$15	Victor 20-1530
				originally released on Victor 27345 in 1941; from the movie *The Road To Zanzibar* starring **Bing Crosby** and **Bob Hope**		
10/23/43+	5	6	●	45 **Boogie Woogie** S:5 *Weary Blues* **[I]**	$10	Victor 26054
				Tommy's instrumental classic featuring Howard Smith on piano; originally charted at #3 in 1938; **Jimmy Dorsey**'s version "Jay-Dee's Boogie Woogie" hit #77 in 1957; also see #58 below		
1/22/44	18	1		46 **Embraceable You** ....J(terr.):18 *The Sunshine Of Your Smile*	$10	Victor 27638
				originally released in 1941; #2 hit for Red Nichols in 1929		
3/25/44	19	1		47 **Another One Of Them Things**..................J(terr.):19 *The Night We Called It A Day* **[I]**	$10	Victor 20-1553
				originally released on Victor 27208 and 27374 in 1940		
5/27/44	4	17		48 **I'll Be Seeing You** S:4 / J:7 *Let's Just Pretend*	$15	Victor 20-1574
				from the Broadway musical *Right This Way* starring Guy Robertson		
11/25/44	24	1		49 **Will You Still Be Mine?** ....J(terr.):24 *None But The Lonely Heart*	$10	Victor 20-1576
				originally released on Victor 27421 in 1941		
1/6/45	4	9	●	50 **I Dream Of You (More Than You Dream I Do)** / S:4 / J:7 / A:9		
3/3/45	8	3		51 **Opus No. I** ....A:8 **[I]**	$10	Victor 20-1608
				featuring Buddy DeFranco (clarinet) and Nelson Riddle (trombone); voted the #12 all-time record in *Billboard's* 1956 Disk Jockey poll		
2/10/45	15	2		52 **Sleigh Ride In July** ....A:15 *Like Someone In Love*	$10	Victor 20-1622
				from the movie *Belle Of The Yukon* starring Randolph Scott		
3/3/45	10	4		53 **More And More** ....A:10 / J:17 *You're Drivin' Me Crazy*	$10	Victor 20-1614
				from the movie *Can't Help Singing* starring Deanna Durbin		
4/28/45	11	3		54 **I Should Care** ....A:11 *Please Don't Say No*	$10	Victor 20-1625
				from the movie *Thrill Of A Romance* starring Esther Williams		
7/21/45	12	1		55 **Out Of This World** ....A:12 *June Comes Around Every Year*	$10	Victor 20-1669
				title song from the movie starring Eddie Bracken		
7/28/45	9	1		56 **A Friend Of Yours** ....A:9 *There's No You*	$10	Victor 20-1657
				from the movie *The Great John L.* starring Greg McClure		
8/11/45	6	6		57 **On The Atchison, Topeka & Santa Fe** ......S:6 / A:7 / J:7 *In The Valley*	$10	Victor 20-1682
				from the movie *The Harvey Girls* starring **Judy Garland**		
9/15/45	4	4		58 **Boogie Woogie** S:4 / J:12 / A:14 *There You Go* **[I-R]**	$10	Victor 20-1715
				originally written and recorded by Clarence "Pine Top" Smith in 1929 as "Pine Top's Boogie Woogie"; also see #45 above		
10/6/45	8	3		59 **Hong Kong Blues** ....A:8 / S:9 / J:16 *You Came Along*	$10	Victor 20-1722
				from the movie *To Have And Have Not* starring Humphrey Bogart		
1/19/46	14	1		60 **Aren't You Glad You're You?** / J:14		
				from the movie *The Bells Of St. Mary's* starring **Bing Crosby**		
12/1/45	15	4		61 **A Door Will Open** A:15	$10	Victor 20-1728
1/26/46	11	3		62 **The Moment I Met You**............................A:11 *That Went Out With Button Shoes*	$10	Victor 20-1761
7/20/46	16	5		63 **I Don't Know Why (I Just Do)** ....J:16 / A:16 *Remember Me*	$10	RCA Victor 20-1901
				#2 hit for **Wayne King** in 1931; #12 hit for Linda Scott in 1961		
3/15/47	9	5		64 **How Are Things In Glocca Morra?** ....J:9 *When I'm Not Near The Girl I Love*	$10	RCA Victor 20-2121
				from the Broadway musical *Finian's Rainbow* starring David Wayne		
9/11/48	4	21		65 **Until** A:4 / S:6 / J:10 *After Hour Stuff*	$10	RCA Victor 20-3061
1/22/49	11	9		66 **Down By The Station** ....S:11 / A:19 / J:26 *How Many Tears Must Fall*	$10	RCA Victor 20-3317
				#13 hit for The Four Preps in 1960		
6/4/49	5	21		67 **The Huckle-Buck** / S:5 / J:10 / A:11		
				Charlie Shavers (trumpet); based on the Charlie Parker jazz instrumental "Now's The Time"; #14 hit for Chubby Checker in 1960		
6/4/49	6	15		68 **Again** ....A:6 / J:10 / S:22 **[I]**	$20	RCA Victor 47-3028
				78 rpm: 20-3427; from the movie *Road House* starring Ida Lupino and Cornel Wilde; Louis Bellson (drummer, above 4)		

DOUGLAS, Larry   '47

Born Lawrence Duckat on 2/17/14 in Philadelphia. Died on 9/15/96 (age 82). Singer with **Carmen Cavallaro**.

5/3/47	14	1		**Linda**..A:14 *Beware My Heart*	$15	Signature 15106
				Ray Bloch's Radio Seven (orch.); #28 hit for Jan & Dean in 1963		

DOWNEY, Morton   MEM '29

Born on 11/14/01 in Wallingford, Connecticut. Died on 10/25/85 (age 83). Popular tenor balladeer. Sang in the early 1920s with Paul Whiteman and hosted various radio shows from 1931 through the 1940s. His son was a popular TV talkshow host (died of cancer on 3/11/2001, age 67).

12/14/46	16	1		**The Old Lamp-Lighter** ....A:16 *The Whole World Is Singing My Song*	$10	Majestic 1061
				Jimmy Lytell (orch.); #5 hit for The Browns in 1960		

DRAKE, Alfred — see OKLAHOMA! Original Cast Album

DRAPER, Rusty   MEM/HOT '55

Born Farrell Draper on 1/25/25 in Kirksville, Missouri. Male singer/songwriter/guitarist.

2/28/53	10	8		1 **No Help Wanted** ....J:10 / A:12 / S:15 *Texarkana Baby*	$20	Mercury 70077-X45
				Jack Halloran Singers (backing vocals); #1 Country hit for The Carlisles in 1953		
7/4/53	6	18	●	2 **Gambler's Guitar** ....A:6 / J:8 / S:10 *Free Home Demonstration*	$20	Mercury 70167-X45
				written by Jim ("Green Door") Lowe; David Carroll (orch., above 2)		

DREW, Doris   '51

8/11/51	22	2		**Sweet Violets**..J:22 *Them There Eyes*	$15	Mercury 5673-X45
				Jack Halloran Singers (backing vocals); Cliff Parman (orch.)		

DUCHIN, Eddy, and his Orchestra   ★126★   MEM '34

Born on 4/10/10 in Cambridge, Massachusetts. Died of leukemia on 2/9/51 (age 40). The famous pianist/bandleader first became known with **Leo Reisman** before starting his own orchestra. Five years after his death Hollywood produced *The Eddy Duchin Story*. Son Peter Duchin became a successful society pianist/bandleader. Eddy's famous theme "My Twilight Dream" (based on Chopin's "Nocturne In E-Flat") was recorded in 1939. Duchin's top 3 pre-1940 #1 hits: "Let's Fall In Love," "Lovely To Look At" and "I Won't Dance."

DEBUT	PEAK	WKS		A-side		B-side	$	Label & Number
11/2/40	18	1		1 Only Forever ....S(mw):18	*Who Are You?*		$10	Columbia 35624
				from the movie *Rhythm On The River* starring **Bing Crosby** and Mary Martin				
11/23/40	13	4		2 Down Argentina Way / ....S(wc):13				
				The Earbenders (vocals)				
11/30/40	19	1		3 Two Dreams Met ....S(wc):19			$10	Columbia 35774
				above 2 from the movie *Down Argentine Way* starring Don Ameche and **Betty Grable**				
12/28/40	16	1		4 Dream Valley ....S(s):16	*Let's Be Buddies*		$10	Columbia 35780
1/25/41	14	3		5 So You're The One / ....S(mw):14				
1/25/41	14	2		6 I Give You My Word ....S(mw):14 / S(s):15 / S(e):18			$10	Columbia 35812
2/1/41	6	6		7 You Walk By	S:6 *Here's My Heart*		$10	Columbia 35903
				Johnny Drake (vocal: #3, 4 & 7)				
2/15/41	16	1		8 It All Comes Back To Me Now ....S(wc):16	*The Old Jalop*		$10	Columbia 35867
				June Robbins (vocal: #1, 5, 6 & 8)				

DURANTE, Jimmy   MEM/HOT '34

Born on 2/10/1893 in New York City. Died of pneumonia on 1/29/80 (age 86). Legendary comedian. Appeared in several movies and TV shows.

DEBUT	PEAK	WKS		A-side		B-side	$	Label & Number
10/21/44	19	1		1 Umbriago ....J(terr.):19	*Inka Dinka Doo* [N]		$15	Decca 23351
				Six Hits And A Miss (backing vocals); Ray Bargy (orch.); from the movie *Music For Millions* starring Margaret O'Brien				
9/22/51	29	1		2 Black Strap Molasses ....J:29 / A:30	*How D' Ye Do And Shake Hands* [N]		$25	Decca 9-27748
				DANNY KAYE-JIMMY DURANTE-JANE WYMAN-GROUCHO MARX				
				4 Hits And A Miss (backing vocals); **Sonny Burke** (orch.)				

E

EBERLY, Bob   MEM '48

Born Robert Eberle on 7/24/16 in Mechanicsville, New York. Died of a heart attack on 11/17/81 (age 65). Sang with Dorsey Brothers band in 1935. Vocalist with **Jimmy Dorsey** from 1935-43. Appeared in the movies *The Fleet's In*, *I Dood It* and *The Fabulous Dorseys*. Own TV series in 1955. Older brother of Ray Eberle, vocalist with **Glenn Miller**'s band.

DEBUT	PEAK	WKS		A-side		B-side	$	Label & Number
10/30/48	25	3		Hair Of Gold (Eyes Of Blue) J:25	*Rendezvous With A Rose*		$10	Decca 24491
				The Sunshine Serenaders (backing vocals); from the movie *Singing Spurs* starring Kirby Grant				

ECKSTINE, Billy   ★55★   MEM/HOT '50

Born on 7/8/14 in Pittsburgh. Died of heart failure on 3/8/93 (age 78). R&B singer/guitarist/trumpeter. One of the most distinctive baritones in popular music. Sang with **Earl Hines** from 1939-43. Nicknamed "Mr. B." His son Ed was the president of Mercury Records.

1)My Foolish Heart   2)I Apologize   3)I Wanna Be Loved

BILLY ECKSTINE And His Orchestra:

DEBUT	PEAK	WKS		A-side		B-side	$	Label & Number
10/6/45	8	2	●	1 A Cottage For Sale A:8	*(I Love The) Rhythm In A Riff*		$15	National 9014
				#4 hit for **Guy Lombardo** in 1930; #63 hit for Little Willie John in 1960				
1/26/46	12	3		2 I'm In The Mood For Love A:12	*Long Long Journey*		$15	National 9016
				from the movie *Every Night At Eight* starring George Raft; #1 hit for Little Jack Little in 1935				
4/6/46	10	10	●	3 Prisoner Of Love A:10	*All I Sing Is Blues*		$15	National 9017
				#16 hit for Russ Columbo in 1932; #18 hit for James Brown in 1963				
7/27/46	13	2		4 You Call It Madness But I Call It Love A:13	*Tell Me Pretty Baby*		$15	National 9019
				#5 hit for Russ Columbo in 1931				

BILLY ECKSTINE:

DEBUT	PEAK	WKS		A-side		B-side	$	Label & Number
3/5/49	21	3	●	5 Blue Moon J:21	*Fools Rush In* (R&B #6)		$10	MGM 10311
				featured in the movie *Words And Music* starring Mickey Rooney and **Judy Garland**; #1 hit for Glen Gray in 1935; #1 hit for The Marcels in 1961				
3/5/49	27	1		6 Bewildered S:27	*No Orchids For My Lady*		$10	MGM 10340
				#9 hit for **Tommy Dorsey** in 1938				
4/23/49	27	1	●	7 Caravan S:27	*A Senorita's Bouquet*		$10	MGM 10368
				#4 hit for **Duke Ellington** in 1937; #48 hit for Santo & Johnny in 1960				
8/6/49	27	3		8 Crying S:27	*Temptation* (R&B #7)		$10	MGM 10458
9/3/49	25	2		9 Somehow S:25	*What's My Name*		$10	MGM 10383
				Hugo Winterhalter (orch.: #5-7 & 9)				
9/24/49	27	1		10 Body And Soul S:27	*If Love Is Trouble (That's What I'm Lookin' For)*		$10	MGM 10501
				from the Broadway musical *Three's A Crowd* starring Fred Allen; #1 hit for Paul Whiteman in 1930				
12/3/49	24	1		11 Fool's Paradise S:24	*A:24 You're Wonderful*		$10	MGM 10562
				Buddy Baker (orch.: #8, 10 & 11)				
2/4/50	23	3		12 Sitting By The Window A:23	*S:30 Lost In A Dream*		$10	MGM 10602
				The Quartones (backing vocals: #6, 9 & 12)				
3/11/50	6	19	●	13 My Foolish Heart	S:6 / J:6 / A:8 *(We've Got A) Sure Thing*		$20	MGM K10623
				title song from the movie starring Susan Hayward				
6/17/50	7	15		14 I Wanna Be Loved A:7	*S:9 / J:17 Stardust*		$20	MGM K10716
2/17/51	10	8		15 If A:10	*S:26 When You Return*		$20	MGM K10896
				#82 hit for The Paragons in 1961				
3/3/51	6	20	●	16 I Apologize J:6	*A:7 / S:8 Bring Back The Thrill*		$20	MGM K10903
				#3 hit for **Bing Crosby** in 1931; #72 hit for Timi Yuro in 1961; Pete Rugolo (orch., above 2)				

DEBUT	PEAK	WKS	Gold	A-side (Chart Hit)..B-side	$	Label & Number

ECKSTINE, Billy — Cont'd

| 3/10/51 | 26 | 2 | | 17 **Be My Love** ....A:26 / J:28 *Only A Moment Ago* | $20 | MGM K10799 |

from the movie *The Toast Of New Orleans* starring **Mario Lanza**; **Russ Case** (orch.: #12-14 & 17)

| 4/26/52 | 16 | 13 | | 18 **Kiss Of Fire** ....J:16 / S:17 / A:18 *Never Like This* | $20 | MGM K11225 |

Nelson Riddle (orch.); adapted from the 1913 Argentine tango "El Choclo"

EDWARDS, Tommy MEM/HOT **'58**

Born on 2/17/22 in Richmond, Virginia. Died on 10/23/69. R&B singer/pianist/songwriter.

| 7/28/51 | 24 | 1 | | 1 **The Morningside Of The Mountain** ....S:24 / A:29 *F'r Instance* | $25 | MGM K10989 |

#8 hit for Donny & Marie Osmond in 1975; new version by Edwards charted in 1959 (#27) on MGM 12757

| 9/15/51 | 18 | 9 | | 2 **It's All In The Game** ....A:18 / S:18 / J:19 *All Over Again* (R&B #10) | $30 | MGM K11035 |

written by U.S Vice President Charles Dawes in 1912; new version by Edwards hit #1 for 6 weeks in 1958 on MGM 12688

| 2/9/52 | 22 | 4 | | 3 **Please, Mr. Sun** ....A:22 *Where I May Live With My Love* | $25 | MGM K11134 |

new version by Edwards charted in 1959 (#11) on MGM 12757

| 12/13/52 | 13 | 4 | | 4 **You Win Again** ....A:13 *Sinner Or Saint* | $25 | MGM K11326 |

#10 Country hit for **Hank Williams** in 1952; #22 hit for Fats Domino in 1962; **Leroy Holmes** (orch., all of above)

| | ★120★ | | | **ELLINGTON, Duke, and his Famous Orchestra** MEM **'38** | | |

Born Edward Kennedy Ellington on 4/29/1899 in Washington DC. Died on 5/24/74 (age 75). Jazz music's leading bandleader/composer/arranger. Studied piano since age seven; formed first band around 1918. To New York in 1923 at **Fats Waller**'s suggestion. In late 1927 began five-year association with New York's Cotton Club. Worked with noted arranger/composer Billy Strayhorn from 1939 on. His 50-minute suite *Black, Brown and Beige* was introduced at Carnegie Hall in 1943. Won Grammy's Lifetime Achievement Award (1966) and Trustees Award (1968). Ellington's pre-1940 #1 hits: "Cocktails For Two," "I Let A Song Go Out Of My Heart" and "Three Little Words."

| 6/14/41 | 13 | 4 | | 1 **Flamingo** ....S(wc):13 *The Girl In My Dreams Tries To Look Like You* | $15 | Victor 27326 |

Herb Jeffries (vocal); #28 hit for Herb Alpert & The Tijuana Brass in 1966

| 7/26/41 | 13 | 7 | | 2 **Take The "A" Train** ....S(wc):13 *The Sidewalks Of New York* [I] | $15 | Victor 27380 |

the unforgettable Ellington theme of later years written by Billy Strayhorn; selected for the NARAS Hall of Fame

| 1/10/42 | 17 | 1 | | 3 **I Got It Bad (And That Ain't Good)** ....S(e):17 / S(wc):18 / S(mw):20 *Chocolate Shake* | $20 | Victor 27531 |

Ivie Anderson (vocal); from Ellington's West Coast revue *Jump For Joy*

| 7/3/43 | 8 | 2 | | 4 **Don't Get Around Much Anymore (Never No Lament)** ....S:8 *Cotton Tail* [I] | $15 | Victor 26610 |

originally released in 1940 as "Never No Lament" on Victor 26610; #57 hit for The Belmonts in 1961

| 2/5/44 | 6 | 7 | | 5 **Do Nothin' Till You Hear From Me** ....J:6 / S:10 *Chlo-E (Song of the Swamp)* [I] | $15 | Victor 20-1547 |

Cootie Williams (trumpet); originally released in 1940 as "Concerto For Cootie" on Victor 26598

| 3/25/44 | 20 | 1 | | 6 **Main Stem** ....J:20 *Johnny Come Lately* [I] | $15 | Victor 20-1556 |

above 3 were #1 R&B hits

| 2/3/45 | 6 | 12 | | 7 **I'm Beginning To See The Light** | $15 | Victor 20-1618 |

S:6 / A:6 / J:9 *Don't You Know I Care (Or Don't You Care to Know)* (R&B #10)

| 2/2/46 | 13 | 1 | | 8 **Come To Baby, Do!** ....A:13 *Tell Ya What I'm Gonna Do* | $15 | Victor 20-1748 |

Joya Sherrill (vocal, above 2)

EMERSON, Jack **'48**

| 8/21/48 | 18 | 9 | | **Hair Of Gold** ....A:18 / J:18 / S:24 *The Moonrise Song (It Just Dawned On Me)* | $15 | Metrotone 2018 |

Chet Howard (orch. & trio); from the movie *Singing Spurs* starring Kirby Grant

ERWIN, Trudy — see CROSBY, Bing

F

FAITH, Percy, & his Orch. ★84★ MEM/HOT **'53**

Born on 4/7/08 in Toronto. Died of cancer on 2/9/76 (age 67). Orchestra leader. Moved to the U.S. in 1940. Joined Columbia Records in 1950 as conductor/arranger.

| 6/3/50 | 20 | 4 | | 1 **I Cross My Fingers**...S:20 / A:29 / J:29 *Valencia* | $10 | Columbia 38786 |

7" 33-1/3 rpm: 1-607; Russ Emery (vocal)

| 9/2/50 | 7 | 11 | | 2 **All My Love** ....A:7 / S:18 / J:27 *This Is The Time* | $15 | Columbia 4-38918 |

45 rpm: 6-752

| 12/23/50 | 28 | 1 | | 3 **Christmas In Killarney** ....A:28 *Norah* [X] | $20 | Columbia 4-39048 |

45 rpm: 6-899; Shillelagh Singers (vocals)

| 5/12/51 | 10 | 9 | | 4 **On Top Of Old Smoky** ....A:10 / J:17 / S:18 *The Syncopated Clock* | $20 | Columbia 4-39328 |

PERCY FAITH and his Orchestra and Chorus with BURL IVES
adaptation of a traditional Southern Highlands folk song; Tom Glazer's parody "On Top Of Spaghetti" peaked at #14 in 1963

| 9/15/51 | 29 | 1 | | 5 **When The Saints Go Marching In** / ....A:29 | | |

with the All Star Dixielanders (feat. **Will Bradley**, Terry Snyder and Red Solomon); #18 hit for **Bill Haley & His Comets** in 1956 ("The Saints Rock 'N Roll")

| 9/22/51 | 30 | 1 | | 6 **I Want To Be Near You** ....A:30 | $15 | Columbia 4-39528 |

Peter Hanley (vocal)

| 4/26/52 | ❶¹ | 22 | | 7 **Delicado** ....S:❶¹ / A:3 / J:4 *Festival* [I] | $15 | Columbia 4-39708 |

Stan Freeman (harpsichord)

| 4/4/53 | ❶¹⁰ | 24 | ● | 8 **The Song From Moulin Rouge (Where Is Your Heart)** | $15 | Columbia 4-39944 |

S:❶¹⁰ / A:❶⁹ / J:❶⁶ *Midsummer Vigil (Swedish Rhapsody)*

Felicia Sanders (vocal); from the movie *Moulin Rouge* starring **Jose Ferrer**

| 6/20/53 | 19 | 1 | | 9 **Return To Paradise (Parts 1 & 2)** ....A:19 [I] | $15 | Columbia 4-39998 |

from the movie *Return To Paradise* starring Gary Cooper

FARNEY, Dick '47
Born Farnésio Dutra Silva on 11/14/21 in Rio de Janeiro. Died on 8/4/87 (age 65). Singer/pianist. Regular on Milton Berle's radio show.

11/1/47	13	1		I Wish I Didn't Love You So...A:13 *My Young And Foolish Heart*	$10	Majestic 7225

Paul Baron (orch.); from the movie *The Perils Of Pauline* starring **Betty Hutton**

FARRELL, Bill '51
Born William Fiorelli in 1926 in Cleveland. Regular singer on **Bob Hope**'s radio show.

9/24/49	26	1		1 Circus...A:26 / J:30 *Through A Long And Sleepless Night*	$10	MGM 10488

Earle Hagen (orch.)

4/1/50	20	6		2 It Isn't Fair ....A:20 / J:28 *Bamboo*	$15	MGM K10637

written in 1933

1/6/51	18	4		3 My Heart Cries For You ....J:18 / A:23 *You Love Me*	$15	MGM K10868

adapted from the 18th-century French melody "Chanson de Marie Antoinette"; #38 hit for Ray Charles in 1964; **Russ Case** (orch., above 2)

FENNELLY, Paul, and his Orchestra '48

9/4/48	21	2		A Tree In The Meadow ....J:21 *Reflections In The Water ("Looking Down At Me")*	$10	MGM 10211

Reggie Goff (vocal)

FERRER, Jose MEM '54
Born on 1/8/09 in Santurce, Puerto Rico. Died of cancer on 1/26/92 (age 83). Prolific movie actor. Married twice to **Rosemary Clooney** (1953-61 and 1964-67). Father of actor Miguel Ferrer; uncle of actor George Clooney.

1/30/54	16	7		Woman (Uh-Huh).................................J:16 / S:18 *Man (Uh-Huh)* (**Rosemary Clooney**) [N]	$15	Columbia 4-40144

Norman Leyden (orch. and chorus); **Rosemary Clooney** sings "Uh-Huh's"; issued with a picture sleeve on Columbia 4-48004

FIELDS, Gracie '48
Born Grace Stansfield on 1/9/1898 in Rochdale, Lancashire, England. Died of pneumonia on 9/27/79 (age 81). Female singer/actress. Appeared in several movies.

1/31/48	3	21		1 Now Is The Hour A:3 / S:4 / J:5 *Come Back To Sorrento*	$10	London 110

Phil Green (orch.); #59 hit for Gale Storm in 1956

4/2/49	23	3		2 For Ever And Ever ....J:23 *Underneath The Linden Tree*	$10	London 362

The Wardour Singers (chorus); Bob Farnon (orch.)

FIELDS, Herbie, and his Orchestra MEM '47
Born on 5/24/19 in Elizabeth, New Jersey. Committed suicide on 9/17/58 (age 39). Saxophonist. Played with **Lionel Hampton** from 1944-46.

1/18/47	14	1		A Huggin' And A Chalkin'.................................A:14 / J:17 *Blue Fields* [N]	$10	RCA Victor 20-2036

Herbie Fields (vocal)

FIELDS, Shep, and his Rippling Rhythm Orchestra MEM '37
Born on 9/12/10 in Brooklyn, New York. Died of a heart attack on 2/23/81 (age 70). Formed own band in 1929. Fields's top 3 pre-1940 #1 hits: "That Old Feeling," "Thanks For The Memory" and "Did I Remember."

10/21/39	❶⁵	13		1 South Of The Border (Down Mexico Way) J:❶⁵ *It's All Over Town*	$15	Bluebird 10376

Hal Derwin (vocal)

11/16/40	18	3		2 Down Argentine Way ....S(mw):18 / S(wc):19 / S(s):19 *Moon Over Burma*	$10	Bluebird 10886

Sonny Washburn (vocal); title song from the movie starring Don Ameche and **Betty Grable**

SHEP FIELDS and his NEW MUSIC:

6/6/42	17	1		3 Breathless ....S(mw):17 *I Threw A Kiss In The Ocean*	$15	Bluebird 11497

Ken Curtis (vocal - actor, later starred as Festus on TV's *Gunsmoke*, d: 4/28/91, age 74)

7/11/42	19	1		4 Jersey Bounce ....S(e):19 *Long May We Love* [I]	$10	Bluebird 11490
3/27/43	18	3		5 Please Think Of Me ....S(s):18 *Take It Slow*	$10	Bluebird 30-0807

Ralph Young (vocal)

FISHER, Eddie ★21★ MEM/HOT '52
Born Edwin Jack Fisher on 8/10/28 in Philadelphia. At Copacabana night club in New York at age 17. With **Buddy Morrow** and Charlie Ventura in 1946. On **Eddie Cantor**'s radio show in 1949. In the Armed Forces Special Services, 1952-53. Married to **Debbie Reynolds** from 1955-59. Other marriages to Elizabeth Taylor and Connie Stevens. Daughter with Debbie is actress/author Carrie Fisher. Daughters with Connie are singer Tricia Leigh Fisher and actress Joely Fisher. Own *Coke Time* 15-minute TV series, 1953-57. In movies *All About Eve* (1950), *Bundle Of Joy* (1956) and *Butterfield 8* (1960). Eddie was the #1 idol of bobbysoxers during the early 1950s.

1)Oh! My Pa-Pa (O Mein Papa) 2)I'm Walking Behind You 3)I Need You Know 4)Wish You Were Here 5)Any Time

6/12/48	19	4		1 You Can't Be True, Dear ....S:19 / J:22 *Toolie Oolie Doolie (The Yodel Polka)* (Marlin Sisters - #48)	$20	Columbia 38211

THE MARLIN SISTERS with EDDIE FISHER
The Columbians (harmonica backing); #75 hit for the Mary Kaye Trio in 1959

10/14/50	5	18		2 Thinking Of You A:5 / S:8 / J:16 *If You Should Leave Me*	$25	RCA Victor 47-3901

featured in the movie *Three Little Words* starring Fred Astaire; #5 hit for Nat Shilkret in 1928; **Hugo Winterhalter** (orch., all RCA records, except #14 & 15); Winterhalter received equal billing on the label for the first 6 RCA hits

2/3/51	14	14		3 Bring Back The Thrill ....S:14 / J:20 / A:22 *If It Hadn't Been For You*	$25	RCA Victor 47-4016
5/5/51	17	11		4 Unless ....S:17 / A:21 / J:24 *I Have No Heart*	$25	RCA Victor 47-4120
7/21/51	18	9		5 I'll Hold You In My Heart ('Til I Can Hold You In My Arms).................................J:18 / S:27 *I Heard A Song*	$25	RCA Victor 47-4191
9/29/51	8	14		6 Turn Back The Hands Of Time ....S:8 / A:10 / J:12 *I Can't Go On Without You*	$20	RCA Victor 47-4257
12/8/51+	2²	30	●	7 Any Time J:2 / S:3 / A:4 *Never Before*	$20	RCA Victor 47-4359
1/5/52	4	19	●	8 Tell Me Why / A:4 / S:7 / J:8		

#13 hit for Bobby Vinton in 1964

2/2/52	25	2		9 Trust In Me ....A:25 / J:28 / S:29	$20	RCA Victor 47-4444

#4 hit for Mildred Bailey in 1937; #30 hit for Etta James in 1961

3/22/52	7	17		10 Forgive Me / ....S:7 / J:9 / A:9		

#1 hit for Gene Austin in 1927

4/5/52	10	10		11 That's The Chance You Take ....A:10 / J:18 / S:25	$20	RCA Victor 47-4574

DEBUT	PEAK	WKS	Gold	A-side (Chart Hit)..B-side	$	Label & Number
				FISHER, Eddie — Cont'd		
5/3/52	3	19		12 **I'm Yours /** J:3 / A:3 / S:5		
6/14/52	20	4		13 **Just A Little Lovin' (Will Go a Long Way)**............J:20 / A:29	$20	RCA Victor 47-4680
				#1 Country hit (8 weeks) for **Eddy Arnold** in 1948		
6/14/52	3	18		14 **Maybe /** J:3 / A:7 / S:8		
6/14/52	19	6		15 **Watermelon Weather**............................A:19 / J:20 / S:28	$20	RCA Victor 47-4744
				PERRY COMO and EDDIE FISHER (above 2)		
				Mitchell Ayres (orch., above 2)		
6/14/52	29	1		16 **I Remember When**........................A:29 *Am I Wasting My Time On You*	$20	RCA Victor 47-4618
7/19/52	❶¹	21	●	17 **Wish You Were Here /** A:❶¹ / S:3 / J:3	$20	RCA Victor 47-4830
				title song from the Broadway musical starring Jack Cassidy		
7/26/52	24	1		18 **The Hand Of Fate**..S:24	$20	RCA Victor 47-4830
9/27/52	6	17	●	19 **Lady Of Spain**.......................................A:6 / J:6 / S:9		
				#5 hit for **Ray Noble** in 1931		
10/4/52	8	13		20 **Outside Of Heaven**........................J:8 / A:9 / S:10	$20	RCA Victor 47-4953
1/17/53	7	8		21 **Even Now**.............................A:7 / J:7 / S:12 *If It Were Up To Me*	$20	RCA Victor 47-5106
2/7/53	5	12		22 **Downhearted /** A:5 / J:8 / S:15		
3/14/53	14	2		23 **How Do You Speak To An Angel?**.............A:14 / J:16	$20	RCA Victor 47-5137
				from the Broadway musical *Hazel Flagg*		
5/9/53	❶⁷	25	●	24 **I'm Walking Behind You** J:❶⁷ / A:❶³ / S:❶² *Just Another Polka*	$20	RCA Victor 47-5293
				Sally Sweetland (female vocal)		
7/11/53	7	14		25 **With These Hands**....................A:7 / S:8 / J:9 *When I Was Young*	$20	RCA Victor 47-5365
				#27 hit for Tom Jones in 1965		
10/10/53	4	16		26 **Many Times /** A:4 / J:5 / S:7		
10/24/53	18	1		27 **Just To Be With You**...A:18	$20	RCA Victor 47-5453
12/12/53+	❶⁸	19	●	28 **Oh! My Pa-Pa (O Mein Papa)** S:❶⁸ / A:❶⁷ / J:❶⁶ *I Never Missed Your Sweet "Hello" Until You Said "Goodbye"*	$20	RCA Victor 47-5552
				English version of song from the Swiss musical comedy *Fireworks*; #94 hit for Dick Lee in 1961		
3/27/54	6	14		29 **A Girl, A Girl (Zoom-Ba Di Alli Nella) /** J:6 / S:7 / A:8		
4/10/54	14	4		30 **Anema E Core (With All My Heart and Soul)**...........S:14 / A:16 / J:18	$15	RCA Victor 47-5675
				from the Broadway musical *Murray Anderson's Almanac* starring Jimmy Savo		
6/12/54	8	8		31 **Green Years /** A:8 / S:16 / J:20		
6/12/54	15	8		32 **My Friend**...S:15 / A:16 / J:18	$15	RCA Victor 47-5748
7/3/54	9	11		33 **The Little Shoemaker /** S:9 / A:9 / J:9		
7/31/54	25	3		34 **The Magic Tango**..S:25	$15	RCA Victor 47-5769
				HUGO WINTERHALTER'S ORCHESTRA and CHORUS and a Friend (above 2)		
				Eddie Fisher (a Friend) leads the chorus on above 2		
9/4/54	❶³	24	●	35 **I Need You Now** S:❶³ / A:❶² / J:❶² *Heaven Was Never Like This*	$15	RCA Victor 47-5830
				#93 hit for Ronnie Dove in 1969		
10/30/54+	5	15		36 **Count Your Blessings (Instead of Sheep)** S:5 / J:9 / A:10 *Fanny*	$15	RCA Victor 47-5871
				from the movie *White Christmas* starring **Bing Crosby**; picture sleeve with a hole in the middle and crediting Fisher as the star of *Coke Time* were issued for many of his records during his 1953-57 TV show		

FITZGERALD, Ella ★41★ MEM/HOT **'44**

Born on 4/25/18 in Newport News, Virginia. Died of diabetes on 6/15/96 (age 78). The most-honored jazz singer of all time. Discovered after winning on the *Harlem Amateur Hour* in 1934, she was hired by Chick Webb and in 1938 created a popular sensation with "A-Tisket, A-Tasket." Following Webb's death in 1939, Ella took over the band for three years. Appeared in several movies. Won Grammy's Lifetime Achievement Award in 1967. Winner of the *Down Beat* poll as top female vocalist more than 20 times and winner of 12 Grammys, she remains among the undisputed royalty of 20th-century popular music.

1)*Into Each Life Some Rain Must Fall* 2)*I'm Making Believe* 3)*I'm Beginning To See The Light*

Orchestras: Haggart, Bob — 10 | Jordan, Louis — 11,15 | Long, Johnny — 7
Heywood, Eddie — 13 | Kirkland, Leroy — 18 | Oliver, Sy — 16,19

Vocalists: Armstrong, Louis — 10,16 | Delta Rhythm Boys — 9,12 | Song Spinners, The — 7,14
Charles, Ray, Singers — 17,19 | Ink Spots — 5,6,8

DEBUT	PEAK	WKS	Gold	A-side / B-side	$	Label & Number
1/4/41	9	1		1 **Five O'Clock Whistle**......................S:9 *So Long*	$20	Decca 3420
				ELLA FITZGERALD And Her Famous Orchestra		
3/11/44	10	8		2 **Cow-Cow Boogie (Cuma-Ti-Yi-Ay) /** J:10		
				INK SPOTS And ELLA FITZGERALD		
				from the movie *Ride 'Em Cowboy* starring Abbott & Costello		
3/11/44	22	1		3 **When My Sugar Walks Down The Street**....................J(terr.):22	$20	Decca 18587
				ELLA FITZGERALD And Her Famous Orchestra		
				#3 hit for Aileen Stanley & Gene Austin in 1925		
7/8/44	20	2		4 **Once Too Often**..................J(terr.):20 *Time Alone Will Tell*	$20	Decca 18605
				from the movie *Pin-Up Girl* starring Betty Grable		
11/4/44	❶²	18	●	5 **Into Each Life Some Rain Must Fall /** J:❶² / S:5		
11/4/44	❶²	17		6 **I'm Making Believe** S:❶² / J:3 / A:5	$20	Decca 23356
				INK SPOTS and ELLA FITZGERALD (above 2)		
				from the movie *Sweet And Lowdown* starring **Benny Goodman**		
1/6/45	10	5		7 **And Her Tears Flowed Like Wine**..............J:10 *Confessin' (That I Love You)*	$20	Decca 18633
4/28/45	5	6		8 **I'm Beginning To See The Light** J:5 / S:7 / A:11 *That's The Way It Is*	$20	Decca 23399
				ELLA FITZGERALD and INK SPOTS		
8/25/45	9	3		9 **It's Only A Paper Moon** ....J:9 *(I'm Gonna Hurry You Out Of My Mind And) Cry You Out Of My Heart*	$30	Decca 23425
				ELLA FITZGERALD and DELTA RHYTHM BOYS		
				originally featured in the Broadway production *The Great Magoo* under the title "If You Believe In Me"; also featured in the movie *Take A Chance* starring James Dunn; #9 hit for Paul Whiteman in 1933		
4/6/46	10	2		10 **You Won't Be Satisfied (Until You Break My Heart)**......J:10 / A:14 *The Frim Fram Sauce (R&B #4)*	$20	Decca 23496
				ELLA FITZGERALD and LOUIS ARMSTRONG		

DEBUT	PEAK	WKS	Gold	A-side (Chart Hit) ....B-side	$	Label & Number

FITZGERALD, Ella — Cont'd

DEBUT	PEAK	WKS		A-side / B-side	$	Label & Number
7/6/46	7	6		11 **Stone Cold Dead In The Market** (He Had It Coming)..........A:7 / S:9 / J:13 *Petootie Pie* (R&B #3)	$20	Decca 23546
				ELLA FITZGERALD and LOUIS JORDAN And His Tympany Five #2, 5 & 11: #1 R&B hits		
12/7/46+	8	14		12 **(I Love You) For Sentimental Reasons**...........................J:8 / A:10 *It's A Pity To Say Goodnight*	$30	Decca 23670
				ELLA FITZGERALD And DELTA RHYTHM BOYS #17 hit for Sam Cooke in 1958		
4/12/47	11	4		13 **Guilty**..J:11 *Sentimental Journey*	$20	Decca 23844
				ELLA FITZGERALD and EDDIE HEYWOOD AND HIS ORCHESTRA #4 hit for Ruth Etting in 1931		
6/19/48	6	21		14 **My Happiness**...J:6 / S:8 / A:10 *Tea Leaves*	$20	Decca 24446
				#2 hit for Connie Francis in 1959		
6/11/49	9	13		15 **Baby, It's Cold Outside**......................................J:9 / S:17 *Don't Cry, Cry Baby*	$20	Decca 24644
				ELLA FITZGERALD and LOUIS JORDAN And His Tympany Five from the movie *Neptune's Daughter* starring Esther Williams		
11/18/50	30	1		16 **Can Anyone Explain?** (No, No, No!) ....J:30 *Dream A Little Dream Of Me*	$25	Decca 9-27209
				ELLA FITZGERALD–LOUIS ARMSTRONG		
9/8/51	23	6		17 **Smooth Sailing**..S:23 *Love You Madly*	$25	Decca 9-27693
				one of Fitzgerald's most popular scat-singing performances		
9/27/52	22	2		18 **Trying**...A:22 / J:24 *My Bonnie Lies Over The Ocean*	$25	Decca 9-28375
				Billy Vaughn had an instrumental version in 1958 (#77)		
9/5/53	15	2		19 **Crying In The Chapel**....................................A:15 *When The Hands Of The Clock Pray At Midnight*	$25	Decca 9-28762
				#3 hit for Elvis Presley in 1965; Bill Doggett (organ: #17 & 19)		

FIVE GEMS — see WINTERHALTER, Hugo

FIVE KEYS, The   HOT '56

R&B vocal group formed in Newport News, Virginia. Consisted of two sets of brothers: Rudy & Bernie West and Ripley & Raphael Ingram. In 1949, added Maryland Pierce and changed group name to The Five Keys. Dickie Smith replaced Raphael Ingram. Smith replaced by Ramon Loper in 1953. Rudy West sings lead on the ballads, Maryland Pierce lead on the rhythm tunes. Ripley Ingram died on 3/23/95 (age 65). Rudy West died of a heart attack on 5/14/98 (age 65).

| 12/25/54 | 28 | 2 | | **Ling, Ting, Tong** ....S:28 *I'm Alone* | $60 | Capitol F2945 |

5 RED CAPS   HOT '44

R&B vocal group formed in Los Angeles: **Steve Gibson**, Emmett Matthews, Dave Patillo, Jimmy Springs and Romaine Brown. Later known as Steve Gibson's Red Caps. Damita Jo, married to Gibson for a time, was in the group from 1950-53. Patillo died in September 1967 (age 53). Springs died on 10/4/87 (age 75). Brown died in January 1988 (age 73).

7/22/44	14	2		1 **I Learned A Lesson, I'll Never Forget**...J:14 *Words Can't Explain*	$30	Beacon 7120
				#2 Country hit; #3 R&B hit		
10/11/52	20	1		2 **I Went To Your Wedding** ....J:20 / A:23 *Wait*	$40	RCA Victor 47-4835
				STEVE GIBSON and the Original Red Caps Damita Jo (vocal)		

FLANAGAN, Ralph, and his Orchestra ★42★   MEM '50

Born on 4/7/19 in Lorain, Ohio. Pianist/arranger for **Sammy Kaye**. Also arranged for various other bands and singers. His band was credited with stimulating a 1950s revival of the **Glenn Miller** sound. Voted America's #1 Band in *Billboard's* 1953 Disk Jockey poll.

1)Rag Mop 2)I Should Care 3)Harbor Lights 4)Slow Poke 5)Hot Toddy

9/24/49	14	9		1 **You're Breaking My Heart**....................................A:14 / J:19 *You're So Understanding*	$10	RCA Victor 30-0001
				based on the Italian song "La Mattinata"		
11/12/49	9	8		2 **Don't Cry Joe** (Let Her Go, Let Her Go, Let Her Go) ....A:9 / J:23 *Swing To 45*	$15	RCA Victor 54-0002
				78 rpm: 30-0007		
11/26/49	27	2		3 **My Hero** ....A:27 *Tell Me Why* [I]	$10	RCA Victor 30-0006
				from the Broadway musical *The Chocolate Soldier* starring Ida Brooks Hunt; #2 hit for Lucy Isabelle Marsh in 1910; #78 hit for The Blue Notes in 1960		
1/14/50	24	3		4 **Dear Hearts And Gentle People** ....A:24 / J:24 *Where Or When*	$15	RCA Victor 54-0011
				78 rpm: 30-0016; all of above labeled as RCA Victor Bluebird Series		
2/11/50	3	10		5 **Rag Mop** A:3 / J:9 / S:10 *You're Always There*	$15	RCA Victor 47-3212
				78 rpm: 20-3688		
4/29/50	17	3		6 **Joshua** ....A:17 *Spring Will Be A Little Late This Year* [I]	$15	RCA Victor 47-3724
				Flanagan arrangement of the spiritual "Joshua Fought De Battle Of Jericho"		
6/3/50	28	1		7 **Stars And Stripes Forever** ....A:28 *Giannina Mia* [I]	$15	RCA Victor 47-3762
				famous march; #1 in 1897 and again in 1901 for Sousa's Band		
8/5/50	16	5		8 **Tzena Tzena Tzena** ....A:16 / J:27 *Pink Champagne*	$15	RCA Victor 47-3847
				adaptation of a popular Israeli song		
9/2/50	16	3		9 **Mona Lisa** ....A:16 / J:23 *Toreador*	$15	RCA Victor 47-3888
				from the movie *Captain Carey, U.S.A.* starring Alan Ladd; #25 hit for Carl Mann in 1959		
9/23/50	9	14		10 **Nevertheless** / ....J:9 / A:10 / S:16		
				featured in the movie *Three Little Words* starring Fred Astaire; #5 hit for Jack Denny in 1931; Harry Prime (vocal: #1, 2, 4, 9 & 10)		
9/9/50	13	3		11 **The Red We Want Is The Red We've Got** (In the Old Red, White and Blue) ....A:13 / J:23 / S:30	$15	RCA Victor 47-3904
9/23/50	27	1		12 **La Vie En Rose** ....A:27 *Dancing Tambourine* [I]	$15	RCA Victor 47-3889
10/7/50	5	17		13 **Harbor Lights** A:5 / S:27 / J:28 *Singing Winds* [I]	$15	RCA Victor 47-3911
				#6 hit for Frances Langford in 1937; #8 hit for The Platters in 1960		
11/25/50	27	2		14 **Oh Babe!** ....A:27 *Halls Of Ivy*	$15	RCA Victor 47-3954
				Steve Benoric and Band (vocals)		
9/29/51	15	5		15 **The Blues from An American In Paris** ....A:15 *Love Is Here To Say* [I]	$15	RCA Victor 47-4247
				from the movie *An American In Paris* starring **Gene Kelly**		
12/8/51+	6	14		16 **Slow Poke** ....A:6 / S:29 *Charmaine*	$15	RCA Victor 47-4373
				The Singing Winds (vocals)		

FLANAGAN, Ralph, and his Orchestra — Cont'd

DEBUT	PEAK	WKS	Gold	A-side	$	Label & Number
7/19/52	26	2		17 **Delicado** ....A:26 *The Blacksmith Blues* [I]	$15	RCA Victor 47-4706
9/6/52	4	12		18 **I Should Care** ....A:4 *Tippin' In*	$15	RCA Victor 47-4885
				Harry Prime and The Singing Winds (vocals)		
1/17/53	7	16		19 **Hot Toddy** ....A:7 / S:12 / J:13 *Serenade* [I]	$15	RCA Victor 47-5095
5/2/53	18	1		20 **A-L-B-U-Q-U-E-R-Q-U-E** ....A:18 *Moon*	$15	RCA Victor 47-5237
				Ralph Flanagan and the Singing Winds (vocals)		
9/5/53	19	1		21 **Rub-A-Dub-Dub**..J:19 *The Stop And Kiss Dance*	$15	RCA Victor 47-5361
				the Band (vocals: #5, 8, 11 & 21)		

FLETCHER, "Dusty"   **'47**

Born Clinton Fletcher in 1897 in Des Moines, Iowa. Died on 3/15/54 (age 57). Black comedian; long-time favorite at the Apollo Theater.

DEBUT	PEAK	WKS	Gold	A-side	$	Label & Number
2/8/47	3	7	●	**Open The Door, Richard! (Parts 1 & 2)** ....S:3 / J:4 / A:8 [N]	$25	National 4012
				Fletcher had performed this routine in vaudeville since the early 1930s; Jimmy Jones (backing band and backing vocal)		

FOLEY, Red ★74★   MEM **'50**

Born Clyde Foley on 6/17/10 in Blue Lick, Kentucky. Died of a heart attack on 9/19/68 (age 58). On the WLS *National Barn Dance* from 1930-37 and the *Renfro Valley Show* from 1937-39. Member of the *Grand Ole Opry* from 1946-54. Hosted the *Ozark Jubilee* series on ABC-TV from 1954-60. Regular on TV's *Mr. Smith Goes To Washington.* **Pat Boone** married his daughter Shirley in 1953. Elected to the Country Music Hall of Fame in 1967.

1)Chattanoogie Shoe Shine Boy   2)Cincinnati Dancing Pig   3)Smoke On The Water

DEBUT	PEAK	WKS	Gold	A-side	$	Label & Number
9/30/44	7	11		1 **Smoke On The Water**.................J:7 *There's A Blue Star Shining Bright (In A Window Tonight)* (C&W #5)	$20	Decca 6102
9/29/45	13	1		2 **Shame On You** ....J:13 *At Mail Call Today* (C&W #3)	$20	Decca 18698
				LAWRENCE WELK AND HIS ORCHESTRA with RED FOLEY		
1/21/50	❶[8]	16	●	3 **Chattanoogie Shoe Shine Boy /** J:❶[8] / S:❶[4] / A:❶[2]		
				#34 hit for Freddy Cannon in 1960		
2/4/50	24	1		4 **Sugarfoot Rag** J:24	$20	Decca 46205
				Hank "Sugarfoot" Garland (guitar solo)		
5/13/50	14	4		5 **Birmingham Bounce** ....J:14 *Choc'late Ice Cream Cone* (C&W #5)	$25	Decca 9-46234
6/10/50	22	3		6 **Mississippi** ....J:22 *Old Kentucky Fox Chase*	$25	Decca 9-46241
				The Dixie Dons (female backing vocals)		
8/12/50	10	10		7 **Goodnight Irene**......................................J:10 *Hillbilly Fever #2* (C&W #9)	$25	Decca 9-46255
				RED FOLEY-ERNEST TUBB		
				The Sunshine Trio (female backing vocals); #75 hit for **Billy Williams** in 1959		
9/2/50	7	9		8 **Cincinnati Dancing Pig** ....J:7 / S:24 *Somebody's Crying*	$25	Decca 9-46261
9/2/50	16	9		9 **Our Lady Of Fatima** ....S:16 *The Rosary*	$25	Decca Faith 9-14526
				Anita Kerr Singers (backing vocals)		
2/10/51	28	6		10 **My Heart Cries For You** ....J:28 *'Tater Pie*	$25	Decca 9-27378
				EVELYN KNIGHT and RED FOLEY		
				Alcyone Beasley Singers (backing vocals); adapted from the 18th-century French melody "Chanson de Marie Antoinette"; #38 hit for Ray Charles in 1964		
12/15/51	28	1		11 **Alabama Jubilee** ....J:28 *Dixie*	$25	Decca 9-27810
				The Nashville Dixielanders (dixieland backing - feat. **Francis Craig** on bones); #2 hit for Arthur Collins & Byron Harlan in 1915; #14 hit for the Ferko String Band in 1955; all of above were Top 10 Country hits		

FONTANE, Tony   **'51**

DEBUT	PEAK	WKS	Gold	A-side	$	Label & Number
11/10/51	28	2		**Cold, Cold Heart**..................................A:28 *Why Do I Love You*	$15	Mercury 5693-X45
				Lew Douglas (orch.); #96 hit for **Dinah Washington** in 1962		

FONTANE SISTERS, The   MEM/HOT **'55**

Female vocal trio from New Milford, New Jersey: sisters Marge, Bea and Geri Rossi. Frequent backing vocalists for **Perry Como**.

DEBUT	PEAK	WKS	Gold	A-side	$	Label & Number
6/3/50	11	9		1 **I Wanna Be Loved** ....A:11 / J:21 / S:24 *I Didn't Know What Time It Was*	$20	RCA Victor 47-3772
				THE FONTANE SISTERS with HUGO WINTERHALTER'S Orchestra and Chorus		
1/6/51	20	4		2 **Tennessee Waltz**.....................A:20 / J:25 / S:29 *I Guess I'll Have To Dream The Rest*	$20	RCA Victor 47-3979
				#35 hit for Sam Cooke in 1964		
3/31/51	24	1		3 **Let Me In** ....A:24 *Hurry Home To Me*	$25	RCA Victor 47-4077
				THE FONTANE SISTERS with TEXAS JIM ROBERTSON		
9/8/51	27	1		4 **Castle Rock**..A:27 *Makin' Like A Train*	$20	RCA Victor 47-4213
				Norman Leyden (orch.)		
11/3/51	16	3		5 **Cold, Cold Heart**....................A:16 / J:22 *I Get The Blues When It Rains*	$20	RCA Victor 47-4274
				Mitchell Ayres (orch.); #96 hit for **Dinah Washington** in 1962		
8/7/54	18	2		6 **Happy Days And Lonely Nights** ....J:18 *If I Didn't Have You*	$20	Dot 45-15171
				#9 hit for Ruth Etting in 1928		
12/11/54+	❶[3]	20	●	7 **Hearts Of Stone** J:❶[3] / S:❶[1] / A:2 *Bless Your Heart*	$20	Dot 45-15265
				Billy Vaughn (orch., above 2)		

FORD, Tennessee Ernie   ★106★   HOT **'55**

Born on 2/13/19 in Fordtown, Tennessee. Died of liver failure on 10/17/91 (age 72). Country singer. Revered as America's favorite hymn singer. Began career as a DJ. Host of musical variety TV shows, 1955-65. Elected to the Country Music Hall of Fame in 1990.

TENNESSEE ERNIE:

DEBUT	PEAK	WKS	Gold	A-side	$	Label & Number
11/26/49	9	9		1 **Mule Train** ....A:9 / S:10 / J:12 *Anticipation Blues* (C&W #3)	$20	Capitol 57-40258
2/18/50	15	6		2 **The Cry Of The Wild Goose** ....A:15 / S:21 *The Donkey Serenade*	$25	Capitol F40280
8/19/50	3	20		3 **I'll Never Be Free /** S:3 / J:6 / A:8		
8/19/50	22	2		4 **Ain't Nobody's Business But My Own** J:22	$25	Capitol F1124
				KAY STARR and TENNESSEE ERNIE (above 2)		
1/27/51	14	13	●	5 **The Shot Gun Boogie**..........................J:14 / S:21 *I Ain't Gonna Let It Happen No More*	$25	Capitol F1295

DEBUT	PEAK	WKS	Gold	A-side (Chart Hit)...B-side	$	Label & Number

FORD, Tennessee Ernie — Cont'd

6/16/51	**18**	7		6 Mr. And Mississippi ....J:18 *She's My Baby*	$25	Capitol F1521
				all of above were Top 5 Country hits		
6/30/51	**15**	6		7 Oceans Of Tears / J:15		
6/30/51	**22**	2		8 You're My Sugar J:22	$25	Capitol F1567
				KAY STARR and TENNESSEE ERNIE (above 2)		
6/19/54	**16**	2		9 The Honeymoon's Over...J:16 *This Must Be The Place*	$20	Capitol F2809
				BETTY HUTTON and "TENNESSEE" ERNIE FORD		
				Billy May (orch.)		

FORREST, Helen ★75★   MEM '44

Born on 4/12/17 in Atlantic City, New Jersey. Died of heart failure on 7/11/99 (age 82). Between 1938 and 1943, was a featured vocalist with **Artie Shaw** ("They Say"), **Benny Goodman** ("Taking A Chance On Love") and **Harry James** ("I've Heard That Song Before"), placing her in the forefront of all female band singers. Hosted a successful radio show with **Dick Haymes** in the mid-1940s.

4/29/44	**2**[1]	18		1 Long Ago (And Far Away) S:2 / J:2 *Look For The Silver Lining*	$10	Decca 23317
				HELEN FORREST And DICK HAYMES		
				from the movie *Cover Girl* starring Rita Hayworth		
8/5/44	**2**[1]	10		2 Time Waits For No One S:2 / J:9 *In A Moment Of Madness*	$10	Decca 18600
				from the movie *Shine On Harvest Moon* starring Ann Sheridan; **Camarata** (orch., above 2)		
10/7/44	**3**	12		3 Together / S:3 / J:9		
				HELEN FORREST & DICK HAYMES		
				from the movie *Since You Went Away* starring Claudette Colbert; #1 hit for Paul Whiteman in 1928; #6 hit for Connie Francis in 1961		
9/16/44	**4**	9		4 It Had To Be You S:4 / J:8	$10	Decca 23349
				DICK HAYMES & HELEN FORREST		
				from the movie *Show Business* starring **Eddie Cantor**; #1 hit for Isham Jones in 1924		
9/8/45	**2**[1]	13		5 I'll Buy That Dream / S:2 / J:3 / A:3		
				HELEN FORREST And DICK HAYMES		
				from the movie *Sing Your Way Home* starring Jack Haley		
9/8/45	**9**	5		6 Some Sunday Morning...A:9 / J:11	$10	Decca 23434
				from the movie *San Antonio* starring Errol Flynn; #4 hit for Ada Jones & M.J. O'Connell in 1917; **Victor Young** (orch., above 4)		
1/19/46	**7**	5		7 I'm Always Chasing Rainbows............A:7 / J:10 / S:10 *Tomorrow Is Forever*	$10	Decca 23472
				from the movie *The Dolly Sisters* starring **Betty Grable**; melody adapted from Chopin's "Fantasie Impromptu"; #1 hit for Charles Harrison in 1918		
3/2/46	**4**	11		8 Oh! What It Seemed To Be S:4 / J:6 / A:7 *Give Me A Little Kiss, Will You Huh?*	$10	Decca 23481
				#91 hit for The Castells in 1962		
8/10/46	**12**	2		9 In Love In Vain...A:12 *All Through The Day*	$10	Decca 23528
				DICK HAYMES and HELEN FORREST (above 4)		
				from the movie *Centennial Summer* starring Jeanne Crain and Cornel Wilde; **Earle Hagen** (orch., above 3)		

FOSTER, Sally — see HOOSIER HOT SHOTS

FOUR ACES Featuring Al Alberts ★49★   MEM/HOT '55

Vocal group from Chester, Pennsylvania: Al Alberts (lead singer), Dave Mahoney (tenor), Sol Vaccaro (baritone) and Lou Silvestri (bass). Worked Ye Olde Mill near Philadelphia, late 1940s. First recorded for Victoria in 1951. Group has undergone several personnel changes over the years.

1)Three Coins In The Fountain 2)Tell Me Why 3)Stranger In Paradise

9/15/51	**4**	22	●	1 Sin S:4 / A:5 / J:5 *Arizona Moon*	$30	Victoria 101 (45)
				also released on Flash 101 in 1951		
12/8/51+	**2**[6]	24	●	2 Tell Me Why / S:2 / J:2 / A:2		
				#13 hit for Bobby Vinton in 1964		
1/5/52	**14**	11		3 A Garden In The Rain ....S:14 / J:15 / A:20	$20	Decca 9-27860
				#15 hit for Gene Austin in 1929; #97 hit for Vic Dana in 1964		
2/23/52	**7**	16		4 Perfidia ....S:7 / J:10 / A:14 *You Brought Me Love*	$20	Decca 9-27987
				#15 hit for The Ventures in 1960		
3/8/52	**29**	1		5 Two Little Kisses ....J:29 *Whose To Blame*	$25	Flash 103 (45)
				both Victoria and Flash labels are from the independent Palda Record Co.		
5/31/52	**17**	3		6 I'm Yours ....A:17 / S:21 / J:27 *I Understand*	$20	Decca 9-28162
8/9/52	**9**	10		7 Should I ....J:9 / A:15 / S:20 *There's Only Tonight*	$20	Decca 9-28323
				from the movie *Lord Byron Of Broadway* starring Charles Kaley; #3 hit for the Arden-Ohman Orchestra in 1930; #42 hit for The String-A-Longs in 1961		
10/25/52	**11**	10		8 Heart And Soul / ....J:11 / A:12 / S:15		
				#1 hit for **Larry Clinton** in 1938; #18 hit for The Cleftones in 1961		
11/1/52	**20**	2		9 Just Squeeze Me (But Don't Tease Me) ....J:20 / S:27	$20	Decca 9-28390
6/6/53	**17**	1		10 Organ Grinder's Swing.....................................J:17 *Honey In The Horn*	$20	Decca 9-28691
				Owen Bradley (orch.); #2 hit for **Jimmie Lunceford** in 1936		
12/5/53+	**3**	16	●	11 Stranger In Paradise ....A:3 / S:5 / J:6		
				from the Broadway musical *Kismet* starring **Alfred Drake**		
12/5/53+	**7**	18		12 The Gang That Sang "Heart Of My Heart" ....J:7 / S:8 / A:14	$20	Decca 9-28927
				song written in 1926		
5/22/54	**❶**[1]	18	●	13 Three Coins In The Fountain / J:**❶**[1] / A:2 / S:2		
				title song from the movie starring Clifton Webb and Dorothy McGuire		
5/29/54	**26**	5		14 Wedding Bells (Are Breaking Up That Old Gang Of Mine) S:26	$20	Decca 9-29123

FOUR ACES Featuring Al Alberts — Cont'd

DEBUT	PEAK	WKS		A-side / B-side	$	Label & Number
9/4/54	17	3		15 **Dream** ....J:17 *It Shall Come To Pass*	$15	Decca 9-29217
				originally heard as the closing theme for composer **Johnny Mercer**'s radio show; #19 hit for Betty Johnson in 1958		
10/23/54	11	7		16 **It's A Woman's World** ....A:11 / J:15 / S:19 *The Cuckoo Bird In The Pickle Tree*	$15	Decca 9-29269
				from the movie *Woman's World* starring Clifton Webb		
11/27/54+	5	14		17 **Mister Sandman**　　　A:5 / J:6 / S:9 *(I'll Be With You) In Apple Blossom Time*	$15	Decca 9-29344
				#37 hit for Emmylou Harris in 1981; Jack Pleis (orch.: #11-17)		

FOUR FRESHMEN, The　　　MEM/HOT **'56**

Vocal group from Indianapolis: brothers Ross and Don Barbour, their cousin Bob Flanigan and Ken Albers. Don Barbour died in a car crash on 10/5/61 (age 32).

DEBUT	PEAK	WKS		A-side / B-side	$	Label & Number
8/23/52	30	1		**It's A Blue World** ....S:30 *Tuxedo Junction*	$20	Capitol F2152
				from the movie *Music In My Heart* starring Tony Martin		

4 HITS AND A MISS — see SIX HITS AND A MISS

★101★ FOUR KING SISTERS　　　MEM **'44**

Family vocal group from Salt Lake City. Consisted of sisters Alyce, Yvonne, Donna and Louise Driggs. Professional name taken from their father's middle name: William King Driggs. Worked with **Horace Heidt** from 1935-38. Much radio and club work from 1938-39. Worked with **Alvino Rey** (husband of Luise) from 1939-43. In the movies *Sing Your Worries Away*, *Follow The Band*, *Larceny With Music* and *On Stage Everybody*. Own TV series, *The King Family Show*, 1965-66. Alyce died on 8/21/96 (age 80). Louise died on 8/4/97 (age 83).

1)It's Love-Love-Love   2)The Hut-Sut Song (A Swedish Serenade)   3)I'll Get By (As Long As I Have You)

DEBUT	PEAK	WKS		A-side / B-side	$	Label & Number
7/5/41	7	2		1 **The Hut-Sut Song (A Swedish Serenade)** ....S:7 *Music Makers*	$10	Bluebird 11154
1/17/42	18	1		2 **Rose O'Day (The Filla-ga-dusha-Song)** ....S(s):18 *Jack And Jill*	$10	Bluebird 11349
9/5/42	13	3		3 **My Devotion** ....S(s):13 / S(wc):15 *Conchita, Marquita, Lolita, Pepita, Rosita, Juanita Lopez*	$10	Bluebird 11555
				The Rhythm "Reys" (**Alvino Rey**, backing band, above 3)		
4/15/44	4	11		4 **It's Love-Love-Love /**　　　　　　　　　　　　　　　S:4 / J:6		
				from the movie *Stars Over Broadway* starring James Melton		
4/15/44	21	1		5 **Mairzy Doats And Dozy Doats (Mares Eat Oats and Does Eat Oats)** ....J:21 **[N]**	$10	Bluebird 30-0822
				#75 hit for The Innocence in 1967		
4/29/44	12	4		6 **I'll Get By (As Long As I Have You)** ....J:12 *Behind Those Swinging Doors* (**Spike Jones**)	$10	Bluebird 30-0821
				Alvino Rey (orch.); #3 hit for Ruth Etting in 1929; #87 hit for **Billy Williams** in 1958		
6/10/44	13	5		7 **Milkman, Keep Those Bottles Quiet** ....J:13 *San Fernando Valley*	$10	Bluebird 30-0824
				from the movie *Broadway Rhythm* starring George Murphy and **Ginny Simms**		
11/25/44	13	7		8 **The Trolley Song** ....J:13 *(All Of A Sudden) My Heart Sings*	$10	Bluebird 30-0829
				from the movie *Meet Me In St. Louis* starring **Judy Garland**		
3/31/45	15	2		9 **Candy /**　　　　　　　　　　　　　　　　　　　　　　　　J:15		
3/31/45	15	1		10 **Saturday Night (Is The Loneliest Night In The Week)** J:15	$10	Victor 20-1633
				Buddy Cole (orch., above 2)		

★145★ FOUR KNIGHTS, The　　　MEM/HOT **'54**

R&B vocal group formed in Charlotte, North Carolina: Gene Alford (lead; died in 1960), Clarence Dixon (baritone), Oscar Broadway (bass) and John Wallace (tenor; died in 1978).

DEBUT	PEAK	WKS		A-side / B-side	$	Label & Number
7/28/51	23	1		1 **I Love The Sunshine Of Your Smile** ....A:23 *Sentimental Fool*	$40	Capitol F1587
10/27/51	14	10		2 **(It's No) Sin** ....A:14 / J:15 / S:24 *The Glory Of Love*	$40	Capitol F1806
12/15/51+	21	4		3 **Cry** ....J:21 *Charmaine*	$40	Capitol F1875
				#18 hit for Ronnie Dove in 1966		
1/24/53	8	6		4 **Oh, Happy Day** ....A:8 / J:11 / S:11 *A Million Tears*	$30	Capitol F2315
				Bobby Page and His Musical Pages (instrumental backing); Oscar Broadway (bass solo)		
1/23/54	2[1]	24	●	5 **I Get So Lonely (When I Dream About You)**　　J:2 / S:3 / A:3 *I Couldn't Stay Away From You*	$25	Capitol F2654
				tune also known as "Oh Baby Mine"		

FOUR LADS, The　★82★　　　MEM/HOT **'56**

Vocal group from Toronto: Bernie Toorish (lead tenor), Jimmie Arnold (second tenor), Frankie Busseri (baritone) and Connie Codarini (bass). Sang in choir at St. Michael's Cathedral in Toronto. Worked local hotels and clubs. Worked Le Ruban Bleu in New York City. Signed as backup singers by Columbia in 1950. Backed **Johnnie Ray** on several of his hits, including his #1 hit "Cry."

DEBUT	PEAK	WKS		A-side / B-side	$	Label & Number
11/24/51	❶[11]	27	●	1 **Cry /**　　　　　　　　　　　　　　S:❶[11] / A:❶[10] / J:❶[9]		
				#18 hit for Ronnie Dove in 1966		
11/24/51+	2[2]	22		2 **The Little White Cloud That Cried**　　　　S:2 / A:2 / J:3	$30	Okeh 4-6840
				JOHNNIE RAY & the Four Lads (above 2)		
				#99 hit for Wayne Newton in 1964		
7/26/52	23	4		3 **The Mocking Bird** ....S:23 *I May Hate Myself In The Morning*	$25	Okeh 4-6885
				melody also known as "Going Home"; taken from Dvorak's "New World Symphony"; re-charted in 1956 (#67) on Epic 9150; new version charted in 1958 (#32) on Columbia 41266		
10/18/52	22	1		4 **Somebody Loves Me** ....A:22 *Thanks To You*	$20	Columbia 4-39865
				Mitch Miller (orch.); from the Broadway musical *George White's Scandals Of 1924* starring Lester Allen; #1 hit for Paul Whiteman in 1924		
8/8/53	17	1		5 **Down By The River Side** ....J:17 *Take Me Back*	$20	Columbia 4-40005
				traditional Black American spiritual written in 1865; #60 hit for Les Compagnons De La Chanson in 1960		
10/17/53	10	13		6 **Istanbul (Not Constantinople)** ....S:10 / A:11 / J:11 *I Should Have Told You Long Ago*	$20	Columbia 4-40082
7/3/54	18	1		7 **Gilly Gilly Ossenfeffer Katzenelle Bogen By The Sea**.........J:18 *I Hear It Everywhere* **[N]**	$20	Columbia 4-40236
				Norman Leyden (orch., above 3)		
9/4/54	7	12		8 **Skokiaan (South African Song)**　　　S:7 / A:8 / J:9 *Why Should I Love You?*	$20	Columbia 4-40306
				Neal Hefti (orch.); South African song, named for a Zulu tribal drink; #70 hit for **Bill Haley & His Comets** in 1960		
10/23/54	30	1		9 **Rain, Rain, Rain** ....S:30 *Your Heart - My Heart (Sehnsucht)*	$20	Columbia 4-40295
				FRANKIE LAINE & THE FOUR LADS		
				The Buddy Cole Quartet (instrumental backing)		

DEBUT	PEAK	WKS	Gold	A-side (Chart Hit)..B-side	$	Label & Number

FOUR TUNES, The   MEM **'54**

R&B vocal group from New York City: Ivory "Deek" Watson (formerly with the **Ink Spots**), Pat Best, Jimmy Gordon and Jimmie Nabbie. First recorded for Regis in 1945. Recorded for Manor in 1946 as The Sentimentalists. Best and Watson wrote "I Love You For Sentimental Reasons" hit for **Nat King Cole** and others. Nabbie wrote hit "You Are My Love" for **Joni James**. Group active until 1963. Nabbie later fronted an "Ink Spots" group. Watson died on 11/4/69 (age 60). Nabbie died on 9/12/92 (age 72). Gordon died on 10/27/93 (age 80).

5/22/48	24	3		1 **Time Out For Tears**.............................J:24 *All My Dreams (If All My Dreams Would Only Come True)*	$30	Manor 1116
				SAVANNAH CHURCHILL And THE FOUR TUNES		
				#10 R&B hit		
11/21/53+	13	6	●	2 **Marie**...J:13 / S:18 *I Gambled With Love*	$40	Jubilee 45-5128
				#1 hit for **Tommy Dorsey** in 1937; #15 hit for The Bachelors in 1965		
5/29/54	6	15	●	3 **I Understand Just How You Feel**..................................J:6 / S:8 / A:9 *Sugar Lump*	$40	Jubilee 45-5132
				#9 hit for The G-Clefs in 1961; Sid Bass (orch., above 2)		

FOUR VAGABONDS, The   MEM **'43**

R&B vocal group from St. Louis: John Jordan, Robert O'Neal, Norval Taborn and Ray Grant. Jordan died on 6/16/88 (age 74). Taborn died on 1/23/90 (age 74).

7/24/43	20	1		**Comin' In On A Wing And A Prayer**....................................S(s):20 *It Can't Be Wrong* (R&B #3)	$50	Bluebird 30-0815

FREBERG, Stan ★95★   MEM/HOT **'53**

Born on 8/7/26 in Pasadena, California. Began career doing impersonations on Cliffie Stone's radio show in 1943. Did cartoon voices for the major movie studios. Wrote and did voices for the children's TV show *Time For Beany*. Hosted own radio show in 1957. Had a long string of brilliant satirical recordings. Launched highly successful advertising career in the early 1960s.

1)St. George And The Dragonet 2)Little Blue Riding Hood 3)I've Got You Under My Skin

Orchestras: Baxter, Les — 2,3   May, Billy — 4,10   Scott, Nathan — 7
              Bruns, George — 8,9   Schumann, Walter — 5,6   Stone, Cliffie — 1

2/10/51	21	3		1 **John And Marsha**...S:21 / A:21 *Ragtime Dan* [N]	$35	Capitol F1356
				a soap opera parody using only the words John - Marsha		
8/4/51	11	5		2 **I've Got You Under My Skin** /...A:11 / S:20 [N]		
				parody of the call and response arrangement used in "On Top Of Old Smoky" by **The Weavers**; #3 hit for **Ray Noble** in 1936; #9 hit for The 4 Seasons in 1966		
8/11/51	30	1		3 **That's My Boy**...A:30 [N]	$35	Capitol F1711
4/5/52	15	3		4 **Try**..A:15 / S:20 *Pass The Udder Udder* [N]	$35	Capitol F2029
				Buddy Cole (piano); parody of **Johnnie Ray**'s version of "Cry"		
10/3/53	❶⁴	10	●	5 **St. George And The Dragonet** / S:❶⁴ / A:❶¹ / J:7 [N]		
10/10/53	9	4		6 **Little Blue Riding Hood** ....A:9 / S:12 [N]	$40	Capitol F2596
				above 2 use TV's *Dragnet* theme song and the monotone style of its star character Sgt. Joe Friday to lampoon 2 children's fables: "St. George And The Dragon" and "Little Red Riding Hood"; June Foray (female voice, above 2)		
12/19/53	13	3		7 **Christmas Dragnet (Parts I & II)**..S:13 / A:16 [X-N]	$50	Capitol F2671
				another *Dragnet* parody — a take-off on "Scrooge" ("Grudge"); re-issued in 1954, entitled "Yulenet" on Capitol 2986		
1/2/54	13	3		8 **C'est Si Bon (It's So Good)**..A:13 *A Dear John And Marsha Letter* [N]	$30	Capitol F2677
				parody of **Eartha Kitt**'s 1953 hit version of the classic French song		
6/26/54	15	3		9 **Point Of Order**..S:15 *Person To Pearson* [N]	$30	Capitol F2838
				STAN FREBERG and DAWS BUTLER		
				take-off on the Senate's Army-McCarthy hearings (using "Baa, Baa, Black Sheep"); Daws Butler (writer and voice, with Freberg, on above 5 - except #8)		
10/23/54	14	1		10 **Sh-Boom**...A:14 *Wide-Screen Mama Blues* [N]	$35	Capitol F2929
				The Toads (chorus)		

FRIZZELL, Lefty   HOT **'51**

Born William Orville Frizzell on 3/31/28 in Corsicana, Texas. Died of a stroke on 7/19/75 (age 47). Country singer/songwriter/guitarist. Elected to the Country Music Hall of Fame in 1982.

8/25/51	29	1		**I Want To Be With You Always**..J:29 *My Baby's Just Like Money*	$25	Columbia 4-20799
				#1 Country hit (11 weeks)		

FROMAN, Jane   MEM **'52**

Born Ellen Jane Froman on 11/10/07 in University City, Missouri. Died on 4/22/80 (age 72). Featured in many Broadway musicals and radio programs during the 1930s and 1940s. Recovered from serious injuries in a 1943 plane crash. Honored by Hollywood in the 1952 movie *With A Song In My Heart*.

5/3/52	14	13		1 **I'll Walk Alone**...S:14 / A:24 / J:25 *With A Song In My Heart*	$20	Capitol F2044
				featured in Froman's biographical movie *With A Song In My Heart* starring Susan Hayward		
9/27/52	25	2		2 **Wish You Were Here**...A:25 *Mine*	$20	Capitol F2154
				title song from the Broadway musical starring Jack Cassidy		
4/4/53	11	10		3 **I Believe**...S:11 / A:14 *Ghost Of A Rose*	$20	Capitol F2332
				introduced on Froman's TV show *U.S.A. Canteen*; #33 hit for The Bachelors in 1964; Sid Feller (orch., above 3)		

FULTON, Jack   **'49**

Born on 6/13/03 in Philipsburg, Pennsylvania. Sang and played trombone for Paul Whiteman from 1926-34. Wrote such songs as "Until," "Ivory Tower" and "Silence Is Golden."

3/12/49	12	6		**Sunflower**...A:12 / S:15 / J:27 *Tell Me The Truth*	$15	Tower 1454
				Eddie Ballantine (orch.); a court ruling found the 1964 hit "Hello, Dolly!" to be directly based on this song		

G

GAILLARD, Slim, Trio   '46

Born Bulee Gaillard on 1/4/16 in Detroit. Died on 2/26/91 (age 75). Black singer/multi-instrumentalist. Formed duo with bassist Leroy "Slam" Stewart in 1937. Became known as the "Flat Foot Floogie Boys" from big hit of the same title. Gaillard invented "voot," a comical scat language he used on many recordings. Trio included Gaillard, Bam Brown and Zutty Singleton.

| 5/25/46 | 21 | 1 | | Cement Mixer (Put-Ti-Put-Ti) ....J:21 *Scotchin' With The Soda* [N] | $30 | Cadet 201 |
| | | | | #5 R&B hit | | |

★150★   GALE, Sunny   MEM/HOT '52

Born Selma Segal on 2/20/27 in Clayton, New Jersey; raised in Philadelphia. Pop singer. Formerly with **Hal McIntyre**'s band.

2/9/52	13	6		1 Wheel Of Fortune ....J:13 / S:14 / A:22 *You Showed Me The Way*	$25	Derby 45-787
				EDDIE WILCOX ORCH. with SUNNY GALE		
9/13/52	14	8		2 I Laughed At Love ....J:14 *Father Time*	$15	RCA Victor 47-4789
1/24/53	12	3		3 Teardrops On My Pillow / J:12		
1/31/53	18	2		4 A Stolen Waltz J:18	$15	RCA Victor 47-5103
				Ralph Burns (orch., above 3)		
7/31/54	27	2		5 Goodnight, Sweetheart, Goodnight...S:27 *Call Off The Wedding*	$15	RCA Victor 47-5746
				Joe Reisman (orch.); #5 R&B hit for The Spaniels in 1954		
10/9/54	19	1		6 Smile ....A:19 *An Old Familiar Love Song*	$15	RCA Victor 47-5836
				Hugo Winterhalter (orch.); music written by Charlie Chaplin, based on the theme from his 1936 movie *Modern Times*; #42 hit for Timi Yuro in 1961		

GALLAGHER, Frank   '48

| 12/25/48 | 25 | 1 | | You're All I Want For Christmas ....A:25 *Merry Christmas* [X] | $35 | Dana 2026 |
| | | | | Dana Serenaders (backing vocals) | | |

★108★   GARBER, Jan, And His Orchestra   MEM '36

Born on 11/5/1897 in Morristown, Pennsylvania. Died on 10/5/77 (age 79). Popular dance bandleader in mellow "sweet" style. Had over 50 charted hits from 1923-39. Garber's top 3 pre-1940 #1 hits: "Baby Face," "Melody From The Sky" and "All I Do Is Dream Of You."

1)Shoo-Shoo Baby   2)My Heart Tells Me   3)The Gypsy

Vocalists:	Cordell, Roy — 10,11	Kleeb, Bill — 8	O'Brien, Dottie — 9	Tilton, Liz — 1,3
	Davis, Bob, & Quintet — 2	Mathias, Ernie — 8	Reardon, Tim, & orchestra — 5	Traynor, Tommy — 4
	Grabeau, Bob — 6,7			

2/26/44	12	2		1 Shoo-Shoo Baby J:12 *They're Either Too Young Or Too Old*	$15	Hit 7069
				from the movie *Three Cheers For The Boys*		
2/26/44	14	1		2 My Heart Tells Me / J:14		
				from the movie *Sweet Rosie O'Grady* starring **Betty Grable**		
5/13/44	19	1		3 No Love, No Nothin' J:19	$15	Hit 7070
				from the movie *The Gang's All Here* starring Alice Faye		
6/22/46	14	1		4 The Gypsy ....A:14 *Doing What Comes Natur'lly*	$25	Black & White 774
1/8/49	28	1		5 Bella Bella Marie ....J:28 *How Could I Know*	$10	Capitol 15181
				from the movie *Music Man* starring **Phil Brito**		
9/24/49	19	10		6 You're Breaking My Heart ....J:19 / S:26 / A:28 *(Where Are You?) Now That I Need You*	$10	Capitol 57-719
				based on the Italian song "La Mattinata"		
11/5/49	22	1		7 Jealous Heart ....S:22 / A:29 *The Hop-Scotch Polka*	$10	Capitol 57-759
				#47 hit for Connie Francis in 1965		
7/15/50	30	1		8 The Old Piano Roll Blues ....A:30 *Clodhopper*	$15	Capitol F970
8/5/50	23	2		9 I Wanna Be Loved ....A:23 / J:28 *Remember Me (When The Candlelights Are Gleaming)*	$15	Capitol F1044
				DOTTIE O'BRIEN & JAN GARBER and His Orchestra		
3/17/51	26	2		10 If ....J:26 *Castles In The Sand*	$15	Capitol F1351
				#82 hit for The Paragons in 1961		
10/6/51	29	2		11 The Morningside Of The Mountain ....J:29 *Moon, June, Spoon*	$15	Capitol F1594
				#8 hit for Donny & Marie Osmond in 1975		

★118★   GARLAND, Judy   MEM '44

Born Frances Gumm on 6/10/22 in Grand Rapids, Minnesota. Died of an accidental sleeping pill overdose on 6/22/69 (age 47). Star of MGM movie musicals from 1935-54. Most famous movie role was "Dorothy" in 1939's *The Wizard Of Oz*. Hosted own TV variety series, 1963-64. Married to David Rose from 1941-45. Married to director Vincente Minnelli from 1945-51; their daughter is Liza Minnelli. Won Grammy's Lifetime Achievement Award in 1997.

8/10/40	3	10		1 I'm Nobody's Baby S:3 *Buds Won't Bud*	$25	Decca 3174
				Bobby Sherwood (orch.); from the movie *Andy Hardy Meets Debutante* starring Garland and Mickey Rooney; #3 hit for Marion Harris in 1921		
1/30/43	3	10		2 For Me And My Gal S:3 *When You Wore A Tulip (And I Wore A Big, Red Rose)*	$20	Decca 18480
				JUDY GARLAND and GENE KELLY		
				David Rose (orch.); title song from the movie starring Garland and Kelly; #1 hit for Van & Schenck in 1917; #71 hit for Freddy Cannon in 1961		
3/18/44	22	1		3 A Journey To A Star ....J(terr.):22 *No Love, No Nothin'*	$20	Decca 18584
				from the movie *The Gang's All Here* starring Alice Faye		
11/25/44	4	10		4 The Trolley Song S:4 / J:6 / A:10 *Boys And Girls Like You*	$20	Decca 23361
12/23/44	22	1		5 Meet Me In St. Louis, Louis ....J:22 *Skip To My Lou*	$20	Decca 23360
				#1 hit for Billy Murray in 1904; above 2 from the movie *Meet Me In St. Louis* starring Garland; Georgie Stoll (orch., above 3)		
5/12/45	5	7		6 Yah-Ta-Ta Yah-Ta-Ta (Talk, Talk, Talk) A:5 *You've Got Me Where You Want Me* [N]	$20	Decca 23410
				BING CROSBY and JUDY GARLAND		
				Joseph Lilley (orch.)		
9/29/45	9	1		7 On The Atchison, Topeka And The Santa Fe...........................A:9 / S:10 / J:10 *If I Had You*	$20	Decca 23436
				JUDY GARLAND and THE MERRY MACS		
				Lyn Murray (orch.); from the movie *The Harvey Girls* starring Garland		

DEBUT	PEAK	WKS	Gold	A-side (Chart Hit) ....B-side	$	Label & Number

GARRETT, Betty   '48

Born on 5/23/19 in St. Joseph, Missouri. Actress/singer. Starred in several movies and Broadway shows. Regular on TV's *All In The Family* (1973-75) and *Laverne & Shirley* (1976-81). Married to actor Larry Parks from 1944-75 (his death).

| 11/6/48 | **8** | 11 | | **Buttons And Bows** ....A:8 / J:20 / S:27 *The Matador* | $10 | MGM 10244 |

Harold Mooney (orch.); from the movie *The Paleface* starring **Bob Hope**; #104 hit for The Browns in 1962

★**102**★ **GAYLORDS, The**   MEM/HOT '54

Italian-American trio: **Ronnie Gaylord** (Vincent), Burt Holiday (Bonaldi) and Don Rea. Formed trio while students at the University of Detroit. Hosted own *Melodies In Money* and *Club Polka* TV shows in Detroit.

| 12/20/52+ | **2**[1] | 22 | ● | 1 **Tell Me You're Mine** ....A:2 / J:3 / S:3 *Cuban Love Song* | $20 | Mercury 70067-X45 |

first released on Mercury 70030-X45; Italian song "Per un Bacio d'amor"

| 4/11/53 | **12** | 8 | | 2 **Ramona** / ....J:12 / A:13 | | |

#1 hit in 1928 for both Gene Austin and Paul Whiteman; #72 hit for The Blue Diamonds in 1960

| 4/25/53 | **16** | 1 | | 3 **Spinning A Web** ....S:16 | $20 | Mercury 70112-X45 |
| 2/6/54 | **7** | 12 | | 4 **From The Vine Came The Grape** ....J:7 / S:8 / A:11 *Stolen Moments* | $15 | Mercury 70296-X45 |

George Annis (orch.); also released on Mercury 70308

| 2/20/54 | **13** | 15 | | 5 **Cuddle Me** ....S:13 / J:15 / A:19 *Oh, Am I Lonely* | $15 | Mercury 70285-X45 |

RONNIE GAYLORD
David Carroll (orch.)

| 5/15/54 | **14** | 10 | | 6 **Isle Of Capri** / ....J:14 / S:15 | | |

#1 hit for **Ray Noble** in 1935

| 6/5/54 | **23** | 3 | | 7 **Love I You** ....S:23 [N] | $15 | Mercury 70350-X45 |
| 7/3/54 | **2**[1] | 19 | | 8 **The Little Shoemaker** ....S:2 / A:3 / J:3 *Mecque, Mecque* | $15 | Mercury 70403-X45 |

THE GAYLORDS, Three Friends and a Stranger
George Annis (orch.)

GIBBS, Georgia ★**67**★   MEM/HOT '55

Born Fredda Gibbons on 8/17/20 in Worcester, Massachusetts. Sang on the *Lucky Strike* radio show from 1937-38. With Hudson-DeLange band, then with Frankie Trumbauer (1940) and **Artie Shaw** (1942). On Garry Moore's radio show in the late 1940s, where Moore dubbed her "Her Nibs, Miss Gibbs."

1)Kiss Of Fire 2)Seven Lonely Days 3)(If I Knew You Were Comin') I'd've Baked A Cake

| 3/25/50 | **5** | 11 | | 1 **If I Knew You Were Comin' I'd've Baked A Cake** ......A:5 / J:11 / S:21 *Stay With The Happy People* | $20 | Coral 60169 |

Max Kaminsky's Dixielanders (dixieland backing)

| 8/26/50 | **25** | 2 | | 2 **Simple Melody** ....A:25 / J:25 *A Little Bit Independent* | $20 | Coral 9-60227 |

GEORGIA GIBBS and BOB CROSBY
from the Broadway musical *Watch Your Step* starring Irene and Vernon Castle; #4 hit for Billy Murray & Elsie Baker in 1916

| 1/13/51 | **18** | 8 | | 3 **I Still Feel The Same About You** ....S:18 / J:20 / A:28 *Get Out Those Old Records* | $20 | Coral 9-60353 |

"HER NIBS" Sings With GEORGIA GIBBS Vocal With OWEN BRADLEY SEXTET

6/16/51	**21**	2		4 **Tom's Tune** ....A:21 *I Wish, I Wish*	$20	Mercury 5644-X45
7/21/51	**21**	2		5 **Good Morning Mister Echo** ....A:21 *Be Doggone Sure You Call*	$20	Mercury 5662-X45
8/18/51	**6**	9		6 **While You Danced, Danced, Danced** ....A:6 / S:20 / J:28 *While We're Young*	$20	Mercury 5681-X45

also released on Mercury 5718-X45

| 12/8/51 | **24** | 3 | | 7 **Cry** ....A:24 / J:25 *My Old Flame* | $20 | Mercury 5749-X45 |

#18 hit for Ronnie Dove in 1966

| 4/19/52 | ❶[7] | 20 | ● | 8 **Kiss Of Fire** ....A:❶[7] / J:❶[6] / S:2 *A Lasting Thing* | $20 | Mercury 5823-X45 |

adapted from the 1913 Argentine tango "El Choclo"

7/26/52	**21**	3		9 **So Madly In Love** ....A:21 / J:29 *Make Me Love You*	$20	Mercury 5874-X45
10/25/52	**25**	2		10 **My Favorite Song** ....A:25 / J:25 / S:28 *Sinner Or Saint*	$20	Mercury 5912-X45
3/14/53	**5**	24		11 **Seven Lonely Days** ....A:5 / J:5 / S:11 *If You Take My Heart Away*	$15	Mercury 70095-X45

the Yale Brothers (backing vocals)

| 3/20/54 | **18** | 4 | | 12 **Somebody Bad Stole De Wedding Bell (Who's Got de Ding Dong)** ....A:18 *Baubles, Bangles And Beads* | $15 | Mercury 70298-X45 |

from the stage production *The Copacabana Show Of 1954*; Glenn Osser (orch.: #4-12)

GIBSON, Steve — see 5 RED CAPS

GILKYSON, Terry — see WEAVERS

GLAHÉ, Will   MEM/HOT '39

Born on 2/12/02 in Elberfeld, Germany. Died on 11/21/89 (age 87). Accordionist/composer/conductor.

| 7/27/40 | **20** | 1 | | 1 **Woodpecker** ....S(e):20 *Tavern Waltz* | $15 | Victor V-743 |

GLAHÉ MUSETTE ORCHESTRA

| 6/12/48 | **17** | 5 | | 2 **You Can't Be True** ....J:17 *Turnpike Polka* | $10 | RCA Victor 25-1117 |

WILL GLAHÉ and his Orchestra with Chorus
#75 hit for the Mary Kaye Trio in 1959

GLENN, Darrell   '53

Born on 12/7/35 in Waco, Texas. Died of cancer on 4/9/90 (age 54). Country singer. Son of Artie Glenn who wrote "Crying In The Chapel." Became a recording engineer and producer.

| 7/18/53 | **6** | 13 | | **Crying In The Chapel** ....J:6 / S:9 / A:12 *Hang Up That Telephone* | $40 | Valley 105 (45) |

#4 Country hit; #3 hit for Elvis Presley in 1965

GODFREY, Arthur ★80★ MEM '47

Born on 8/31/03 in New York City. Died on 3/16/83 (age 79). One of the best-known stars in TV and radio history. His CBS radio show *Arthur Godfrey Time* and his CBS-TV shows *Arthur Godfrey And His Friends* and *Talent Scouts* were all top-rated shows in the 1950s. Also see **Archie Bleyer, Janette Davis, Julius LaRosa** and **The Mariners**.

1)Too Fat Polka (I Don't Want Her) (You Can Have Her) (She's Too Fat For Me)   2)Dance Me Loose
3)Slap 'Er Down, Agin, Paw

11/1/47	2⁸	18	●	1	**Too Fat Polka (I Don't Want Her) (You Can Have Her)** (She's Too Fat For Me)	A:2 / S:2 / J:2 *For Me And My Gal* [N]	$10	Columbia 37921
2/21/48	7	9		2	**Slap 'Er Down, Agin, Paw**.....A:7 / S:8 / J:10 *I'd Give A Million Tomorrows (For Just One Yesterday)* [N]		$10	Columbia 38066
					The Too Fat Trio (backing vocals); #10 Country hit for Esmereldy in 1948			
3/13/48	14	3		3	**I'm Looking Over A Four Leaf Clover** ....A:14 *The Thousand Islands Song*		$10	Columbia 38081
					The Mariners (chorus); #2 hit for Nick Lucas in 1927			
3/18/50	16	5		4	**Candy And Cake**...J:16 / S:17 / A:19 *Dear Old Girl*		$10	Columbia 38721
					7" 33-1/3 rpm: 1-547; The Chordettes (backing vocals)			
3/25/50	8	7		5	**Go To Sleep, Go To Sleep, Go To Sleep**....................S:8 / A:12 / J:17 *But Me, I Love You* [N]		$10	Columbia 38744
					MARY MARTIN and ARTHUR GODFREY			
					7" 33-1/3 rpm: 1-569			
12/9/50	24	5		6	**The Thing**...A:24 *Yea—Boo* [N]		$15	Columbia 4-39068
					7" 33-1/3 rpm: 1-919; uses melody of the traditional song "The Tailor's Boy"			
5/19/51	13	6		7	**I Like The Wide Open Spaces** ....S:13 / A:27 / J:28 *Love Is The Reason* [N]		$15	Columbia 4-39404
					ARTHUR GODFREY & LAURIE ANDERS			
					Anders: TV's Glamour Cowboy on *The Ken Murray Show*			
8/11/51	27	2		8	**What Is A Boy** ....S:27 *What Is A Girl* [S]		$15	Columbia 4-39487
					Mitch Miller (orch.); also issued with a picture sleeve on Columbia's Children's Series (4-120); updated version by Tom Edwards,			
					"What Is A Teenage Boy?", charted in 1957 (#96)			
12/22/51+	6	14		9	**Dance Me Loose** / ....J:6 / A:9 / S:12			
					The Chordettes (backing vocals)			
1/5/52	12	11		10	**Slow Poke**...S:12 / A:14 / J:22		$15	Columbia 4-39632
8/9/52	17	2		11	**I Love Girls**..A:17 *(I'm In Love With You) Honey* [N]		$15	Columbia 4-39792
					Archie Bleyer (orch., all of above - except #8)			

GOFF, Reggie '49

Baritone singer. Known as "the English **Vaughn Monroe**." Also see **Paul Fennelly**.

2/5/49	13	2			**I Love You So Much It Hurts** ....A:13 *Maria Mia*	$10	London 312
					REGGIE GOFF with CYRIL STAPLETON AND HIS ORCHESTRA		
					#71 hit for Charlie Gracie in 1957		

GOODMAN, Benny, and his Orchestra ★23★ MEM/HOT '36

Born on 5/30/09 in Chicago. Died of a heart attack on 6/13/86 (age 77). Began playing clarinet professionally at age 16 with **Art Kassel**. Made his reputation with Ben Pollack from 1925-29. After several years of studio work, formed his own band in 1934. The band's hard-driving sound, fueled by Fletcher Henderson's arrangements, hit big in 1936, the dawn of the Swing Era. The band's 1/16/38 Carnegie Hall concert was a historic triumph. Theme song: "Let's Dance." Hollywood's *The Benny Goodman Story* in 1956 honored the "King Of Swing" who provided more than 50 years of classic jazz. Won Grammy's Lifetime Achievement Award in 1986. Goodman's top 5 pre-1940 #1 hits: "The Glory Of Love," "Goody-Goody," "And The Angels Sing," "Don't Be That Way" and "Goodnight My Love."

1)Taking A Chance On Love   2)Jersey Bounce   3)Gotta Be This Or That (Part 1)   4)Symphony   5)Why Don't You Do Right

Vocalists:
Bailey, Mildred — 1	Haymes, Dick — 14-16	McGarrity, Lou — 9	Tobin, Louise — 5
Forrest, Helen — 2,4,7,8,18	Hendrickson, Al — 35	Morrow, Liza — 27-29	**Young, Eve** — 33
Goodman, Benny — 24	**Lee, Peggy** — 9,12,13,17,34	Reed, Nancy — 37	
Greco, Buddy — 36	**Lund, Art** — 30-32	Reid, Dottie — 25,26	
Harvey, Jane — 23	Mann, Peggy — 22	Ricks, Jimmy — 37	
		Tilton, Martha — 21	

2/10/40	8	5		1	**Darn That Dream** ....J:8 *Peace, Brother!*	$10	Columbia 35331
					Fletcher Henderson (piano); from the Broadway musical *Swingin' The Dream* starring **Louis Armstrong**		
7/20/40	8	5		2	**I Can't Love You Any More (Any More Than I Do)** ....J:8 *The Moon Won't Talk*	$10	Columbia 35487
8/17/40	19	1		3	**The Hour Of Parting** ....S(wc):19 *Cocoanut Grove* [I]	$10	Columbia 35527
					Charlie Christian (guitar, above 3)		
3/29/41	12	1		4	**Perfidia (Tonight)** ....S(wc):12 *Let The Door Knob Hitcha*	$10	Columbia 35962
					#15 hit for The Ventures in 1960		
4/5/41	6	3		5	**There'll Be Some Changes Made**............................S:6 *Jumpin' At The Woodside*	$10	Columbia 35210
					originally recorded and released in 1939; revived through play in the 1940 movie *Play Girl* starring Kay Francis;		
					#5 hit for Ethel Waters in 1922		
5/3/41	17	1		6	**Intermezzo (A Love Story)**...................S(mw):17 / S(e):20 *Amapola (Pretty Little Poppy)* [I]	$10	Columbia 36050
					from the movie *Intermezzo* starring Ingrid Bergman		
5/17/41	19	1		7	**My Sister And I**...S(mw):19 *I'm Not Complainin'*	$10	Columbia 36022
8/16/41	19	1		8	**Yours**..S(wc):19 *Take It*	$10	Columbia 36067
2/14/42	18	1		9	**Blues In The Night**...S(s):18 *Where Or When*	$10	Okeh 6553
					BENNY GOODMAN & his SEXTET		
					title song from the movie starring Priscilla Lane		
4/4/42	2⁶	20		10	**Jersey Bounce** / ....S:2 [I]		
3/21/42	18	1		11	**A String Of Pearls** ....S(e):18 / S(s):19 [I]	$10	Okeh 6590
3/28/42	5	9		12	**Somebody Else Is Taking My Place** S:5 *That Did It, Marie*	$10	Okeh 6497
					Billy Butterfield (trumpet: #6 & 12)		
4/11/42	18	3		13	**My Little Cousin**.................................S(e):18 *A Zoot Suit (For My Sunday Gal)*	$10	Okeh 6606
8/29/42	4	3		14	**Idaho** / S:4		
8/22/42	10	1		15	**Take Me** S:10	$10	Columbia 36613

DEBUT	PEAK	WKS	Gold	A-side (Chart Hit)..B-side	$	Label & Number
				GOODMAN, Benny, and his Orchestra — Cont'd		
10/17/42	17	2		16 **Serenade In Blue**...S(wc):17 *I've Got A Gal In Kalamazoo*	$10	Columbia 36622
				from the movie *Orchestra Wives* starring George Montgomery		
1/9/43	4	12	●	17 **Why Don't You Do Right**...S:4 *Six Flats Unfurnished*	$10	Columbia 36652
5/8/43	❶³	11		18 **Taking A Chance On Love**...S:❶³ *Cabin In The Sky*	$10	Columbia 35869
				originally recorded and released in 1940; from the movie *Cabin In The Sky* starring Lena Horne; **Cootie Williams** (trumpet: #4, 7, 8, 14-16 & 18)		
10/9/43	16	1		19 **Mission To Moscow**...S(wc):16 *It's Always You* [I]	$10	Columbia 36680
1/8/44	16	1		20 **Solo Flight**...J(terr.):16 *The World Is Waiting For The Sunrise* [I]	$10	Columbia 36684
				Charlie Christian (guitar); recorded on 3/4/41; #1 R&B hit (1 week)		
10/28/44	23	1		21 **And The Angels Sing**......................J(terr.):23 *Sent For You Yesterday And Here You Come Today* [R]	$10	Victor 26170
				Ziggy Elman (trumpet); re-issue of Goodman's #1 hit (5 weeks) in 1939; #70 hit for the **Three Chuckles** in 1956		
3/10/45	12	3		22 **Ev'ry Time We Say Goodbye**..A:12 *Only Another Boy And Girl*	$10	Columbia 36767
				BENNY GOODMAN QUINTET		
				from the Broadway musical *Seven Lively Arts* starring Bert Lahr		
5/12/45	11	4		23 **Close As Pages In A Book**.................................A:11 *You Brought A New Kind Of Love To Me*	$10	Columbia 36787
				from the Broadway musical *Up In Central Park* starring Noah Beery		
6/30/45	2¹	17		24 **Gotta Be This Or That (Part 1)**...A:2 / S:4 / J:4 *(Part 2)*	$10	Columbia 36813
10/13/45	9	1		25 **I'm Gonna Love That Guy** /...J:9 / A:12		
9/29/45	10	1		26 **It's Only A Paper Moon**..S:10 / A:12	$10	Columbia 36843
				originally featured in the Broadway production *The Great Magoo* under the title "If You Believe In Me"; also featured in the movie *Take A Chance* starring James Dunn		
12/8/45+	2¹	14		27 **Symphony** /..A:2 / J:4 / S:5		
12/8/45	12	3		28 **My Guy's Come Back**...A:12	$10	Columbia 36874
3/16/46	13	1		29 **Give Me The Simple Life**...A:13 *I Wish I Could Tell You*	$10	Columbia 36908
				Kai Winding (trombone); from the movie *Wake Up And Dream* starring June Haver		
5/25/46	11	1		30 **Don't Be A Baby, Baby**..A:11 *All The Cats Join In*	$10	Columbia 36967
				BENNY GOODMAN SEXTET		
8/17/46	9	1		31 **Blue Skies** /...A:9		
				featured in the movie *Blue Skies* starring Fred Astaire and Bing Crosby; #1 hit for Ben Selvin in 1927		
8/3/46	12	1		32 **I Don't Know Enough About You**..A:12 / J:14	$10	Columbia 37053
				Stan Getz (tenor sax: #29 & 32)		
1/11/47	6	6		33 **A Gal In Calico**...A:6 *Benjie's Bubble*	$10	Columbia 37187
				from the movie *The Time, The Place And The Girl* starring Dennis Morgan		
6/19/48	30	1		34 **Somebody Else Is Taking My Place**.............................J:30 *Why Don't You Do Right* [R]	$15	Columbia 38198
				BENNY GOODMAN and his ORCHESTRA with PEGGY LEE		
				re-issue of #12 above		
11/13/48+	7	12	●	35 **On A Slow Boat To China**...............J:7 / S:10 / A:14 *I Hate To Lose You (I'm So Used To You Now)*	$10	Capitol 15208
4/22/50	13	3		36 **It Isn't Fair**..A:13 *You're Always There*	$20	Capitol F860
12/2/50	25	3		37 **Oh Babe**...A:25 *Walkin' With The Blues*	$20	Columbia 39045
				BENNY GOODMAN & his SEXTET		
				7" 33-1/3 rpm: 1-889		
8/4/51	27	1		38 **The Wang Wang Blues**..................................A:27 *It Never Entered My Mind* [I]	$20	Columbia 4-39478
				BENNY GOODMAN SEXTET		
				originally released on Columbia 36594 in 1942; #1 hit for Paul Whiteman in 1921		
				GOODMAN, Hal, and his Orchestra '43		
9/11/43	17	3		**People Will Say We're In Love**...........................S(mw):17 / S(e):18 *I Need A Guy To Tie My Tie*	$15	Hit 7059
				from the Broadway musical *Oklahoma!* starring **Alfred Drake**		
				GORDON, Gray, and his Tic-Toc Rhythm MEM '38		
				Born on 5/4/04 in New York City. Died on 7/23/76 (age 72). Sweet-band leader. Began career playing jazz saxophone and clarinet.		
12/7/40	18	1		**Ferry-Boat Serenade**...S(wc):18 / S(mw):19 *I Could Make You Care*	$10	Bluebird 10819
				Meredith Blake and chorus (vocals)		
				GRABLE, Betty — see JAMES, Harry		
				GRANDE, "Tex", And His Range Riders '44		
4/29/44	22	1		**Have I Stayed Away Too Long?**.................................J(terr.):22 *Sweetheart, I Still Remember*	$25	DeLuxe 5004
				#94 hit for Bobby Bare in 1964		
				GRAY, Dolores MEM '52		
				Born on 6/7/24 in Chicago. Died on 6/26/2002 (age 78). Starred in the London production of *Annie Get Your Gun*.		
11/24/51+	16	7		**Shrimp Boats**..J:16 / A:18 / S:25 *More! More! More!*	$15	Decca 9-27832
				DOLORES GRAY With MUSIC BY CAMARATA		

GRAY, Glen, And The Casa Loma Orchestra ★100★ MEM '35

Born Glen Gray Knoblaugh on 6/7/06 in Metamora, Illinois. Died on 8/23/63 (age 57). Alto saxophonist/bandleader. Formed the Casa Loma Orchestra in 1927. Gray's top 3 pre-1940 #1 hits: "When I Grow Too Old To Dream," "Blue Moon" and "Sunrise Serenade."

DEBUT	PEAK	WKS		A-side	$	Label & Number
6/1/40	9	2		1 **No Name Jive (Parts 1 & 2)**..J:9 [I]	$10	Decca 3089
6/13/42	8	3		2 **One Dozen Roses**..S:8 *The Mem'ry Of This Dance*	$10	Decca 4299
				Pee Wee Hunt (vocal)		
5/8/43	7	8		3 **Don't Get Around Much Anymore**.............................S:7 *Don't Do It, Darling*	$10	Decca 18479
				Kenny Sargent and LeBrun Sisters (vocals); #57 hit for The Belmonts in 1961		

GRAY, Glen, And The Casa Loma Orchestra — Cont'd

DEBUT	PEAK	WKS	Gold	A-side	$	Label & Number
11/27/43+	❶⁵	20		4 **My Heart Tells Me (Should I Believe My Heart?)** / S:❶⁵ / J:2		
				from the movie *Sweet Rosie O'Grady* starring **Betty Grable**		
1/22/44	4	6		5 **My Shining Hour** S:4 / J:9	$10	Decca 18567
				from the movie *The Sky's The Limit* starring Fred Astaire		
5/13/44	12	7		6 **Suddenly It's Spring** ....J:12 *Sure Thing*	$10	Decca 18596
				from the movie *Lady In The Dark* starring Ginger Rogers		
10/7/44	21	1		7 **Don't Take Your Love From Me** ....J(terr.):21 *Forget-Me-Nots In Your Eyes*	$10	Decca 18615
				Eugenie Baird (vocal, above 4)		
9/8/45	9	2		8 **Gotta Be This Or That** ....J:9 / S:10 *While You're Away*	$10	Decca 18691
				"Fats" Daniels (vocal)		

GRECO, Buddy   MEM/HOT '47

Born Armando Greco on 8/14/26 in Philadelphia. Former pianist/vocalist with **Benny Goodman**.

DEBUT	PEAK	WKS	Gold	A-side	$	Label & Number
12/20/47	15	1	●	1 **Ooh! Look-A There, Ain't She Pretty** ....A:15 *Don't You Think I Ought To Know*	$20	Musicraft 515
				BUDDY GRECO and his THREE SHARPS		
11/10/51	30	1		2 **I Ran All The Way Home** ....S:30 *The Glory Of Love*	$25	Coral 9-60573
				The Heathertones (female chorus)		

GREEN, Barry   '48

DEBUT	PEAK	WKS	Gold	A-side	$	Label & Number
11/6/48	16	2		**Brush Those Tears From Your Eyes** ....J:16 *I Gotta Know (Whose Baby Are You)*	$20	Rainbow 10090

GREEN, Larry, and his Orchestra   MEM '47

Born in Boston. Pianist/bandleader.

DEBUT	PEAK	WKS	Gold	A-side	$	Label & Number
10/11/47	3	13		1 **Near You** S:3 / J:5 / A:6 *Pic-A-Nic-In*	$10	RCA Victor 20-2421
				#10 hit for Roger Williams in 1958		
3/6/48	8	7		2 **Beg Your Pardon** ....S:8 / J:9 / A:12 *Can It Ever Be The Same?*	$10	RCA Victor 20-2647
				The Trio (vocals, above 2)		
11/13/48	21	2		3 **Bella Bella Marie** ....S:21 *Whistling In The Dark*	$10	RCA Victor 20-3072
				Male Quartet (vocals); from the movie *Music Man* starring **Phil Brito**		
6/3/50	13	9		4 **Bewitched** ....J:13 / S:15 / A:18 *If I Had You On A Desert Island*	$15	RCA Victor 47-3726
				from the Broadway musical *Pal Joey* starring **Gene Kelly**; #50 hit for the Betty Smith Group in 1958		
10/21/50	28	1		5 **Can Anyone Explain? (No! No! No!)** ....A:28 *All Dressed Up To Smile*	$15	RCA Victor 47-3902
				The Honeydreamers (vocals, above 2)		

★111★   **GRIFFIN, Ken, at the Organ**   '48

Born on 12/28/09 in Columbia, Missouri. Died on 3/11/56 (age 46). Organist.

DEBUT	PEAK	WKS	Gold	A-side	$	Label & Number
4/10/48	❶⁷	23	●	1 **You Can't Be True, Dear** J:❶⁷ / S:2 / A:2 *Doodle Doo Doo*	$10	Rondo 228
				Jerry Wayne (vocal - his singing was dubbed on to the original instrumental version below); #75 hit for the Mary Kaye Trio in 1959		
7/10/48	2⁷	15	●	2 **You Can't Be True, Dear** / J:2 / S:2 / A:7 **[I]**		
6/5/48	19	8		3 **Cuckoo Waltz** ....J:19 **[I]**	$10	Rondo 128
4/30/49	29	1		4 **You, You, You Are The One** ....J:29 *Five Foot Two* **[I]**	$10	Rondo 186
				adaptation of the German folk song "Du, Du Liegst Mir Im Herzen"		
8/20/49	26	1		5 **Beautiful Wisconsin** ....S:26 *By The Waters of The Minnetonka*	$10	Rondo 192
				Johnny Hill (vocal)		
9/30/50	11	20		6 **Harbor Lights** ....J:11 / A:26 / S:27 *Josephine* **[I]**	$15	Columbia 4-38889
				45 rpm: 6-710; organ and Hawaiian guitar; #6 hit for Frances Langford in 1937; #8 hit for The Platters in 1960		

GRIFFIN, Merv   HOT '51

Born on 7/6/25 in San Mateo, California. Popular TV talk show host/TV producer. Featured singer with **Freddy Martin** from 1948-52 ("I've Got A Lovely Bunch Of Coconuts").

DEBUT	PEAK	WKS	Gold	A-side	$	Label & Number
8/4/51	27	1		1 **The Morningside Of The Mountain** ....A:27 *I Love The Sunshine Of Your Smile*	$20	RCA Victor 47-4181
				#8 hit for Donny & Marie Osmond in 1975		
8/25/51	25	1		2 **Belle, Belle, My Liberty Belle** ....A:25 *I Fall In Love With You Ev'ry Day*	$20	RCA Victor 47-4217
11/3/51	30	1		3 **Twenty Three Starlets (And Me)** ....A:30 *The Lord's Ridin' With Me Tonight* **[N]**	$20	RCA Victor 47-4270
				Hugo Winterhalter (orch., above 3)		

GRIFFITH, Andy   MEM/HOT '54

Born on 6/1/26 in Mount Airy, North Carolina. Actor/comedian. Starred in several movies and Broadway shows. Star of TV's *The Andy Griffith Show* and *Matlock*.

DEBUT	PEAK	WKS	Gold	A-side	$	Label & Number
1/9/54	9	6		**What It Was, Was Football (Parts I & II)** ....S:9 / A:11 **[C]**	$30	Capitol F2693
				DEACON ANDY GRIFFITH		
				first released on Colonial 3 in 1953		

GROVE, Harry, Trio   '52

DEBUT	PEAK	WKS	Gold	A-side	$	Label & Number
9/6/52	11	7		**Meet Mr. Callahan** ....S:11 / A:13 *Intermezzo from "Escape to Happiness"* **[I]**	$15	London 451248

H

HAINES, Connie   MEM '49

Born Yvonne Marie Jamais on 1/20/22 in Savannah, Georgia. Sang with **Tommy Dorsey** ("Kiss The Boys Goodbye"). Also see **Gordon Jenkins**.

DEBUT	PEAK	WKS	Gold	A-side	$	Label & Number
8/28/48	29	1		1 **The Darktown Strutters' Ball** ....J:29 *Little Boy Blues*	$20	Signature 15197
				CONNIE HAINES and ALAN DALE		
				Ray Bloch's Swing Eight (Dixieland jazz band); #1 hit for Arthur Collins & Byron Harlan in 1918		
4/23/49	19	2		2 **How It Lies, How It Lies, How It Lies!** ....A:19 *You Told A Lie*	$10	Coral 60044
				4 Hits And A Miss (chorus)		
9/24/49	20	1		3 **Maybe It's Because** ....J:20 *Hang On The Bell, Nellie*	$10	Coral 60070
				The Highlighters (backing vocals); **Roy Ross** (orch.); from the Broadway musical *Along Fifth Avenue* starring Jackie Gleason		

HALEY, Bill, And His Comets   MEM/HOT '55
Born on 7/6/25 in Highland Park, Michigan. Died of a heart attack on 2/9/81 (age 55). Began career as a singer with the Down Homers. Formed the Four Aces of Western Swing in 1948. In 1949 formed the Saddlemen, who recorded on various labels before signing with the Essex label (as Bill Haley and the Saddlemen) in 1952; signed with Decca in 1954. Inducted into the Rock and Roll Hall of Fame in 1987.

5/23/53	12	10		1 Crazy Man, Crazy..J:12 / S:15 *Whatcha Gonna Do*	$75	Essex 321
				BILL HALEY With HALEY'S COMETS		
8/21/54	7	27	●	2 Shake, Rattle And Roll..S:7 / J:8 / A:9 *A.B.C. Boogie*	$30	Decca 29204
				#1 R&B hit for Joe Turner in 1954		
11/20/54+	11	15		3 Dim, Dim The Lights (I Want Some Atmosphere) ....S:11 / A:16 / J:16 *Happy Baby*	$30	Decca 29317

HALL, Juanita   '49
Born Juanita Long on 11/6/01 in Keyport, New Jersey. Died on 2/28/68 (age 66). Black singer/actress. Played "Bloody Mary" in both the Broadway and movie versions of *South Pacific*.

11/5/49	22	4		Don't Cry Joe (Let Her Go, Let Her Go, Let Her Go) ....A:22 *Love's A Precious Thing*	$40	RCA Victor 47-3050
				78 rpm: 20-3557; Bennie Morton (orch.)		

HAMBLEN, Stuart   '54
Born Carl Stuart Hamblen on 10/20/08 in Kellyville, Texas. Died of a brain tumor on 3/8/89 (age 80). Singer/actor. Appeared in many western movies and on radio with own band. Wrote "It Is No Secret (What God Can Do)," "This Ole House," "Open Up Your Heart (And Let The Sunshine In)," and many others. Ran for president on the Prohibition Party ticket in 1952.

11/13/54	26	4		This Ole House ....S:26 *When My Lord Picks Up The 'Phone*	$20	RCA Victor 47-5739
				#2 Country hit		

HAMPTON, Lionel, And His Orchestra   MEM '37
Born on 4/20/08 in Louisville, Kentucky; raised in Birmingham and Chicago. Died of heart failure on 8/31/2002 (age 94). Legendary black jazz vibraphonist. First recorded with the Reb Spikes band for Hollywood in 1924. Started as a drummer, added vibes in 1930. Worked with Les Hite, then **Benny Goodman** from 1936-40; own band thereafter. The first jazz musician to feature vibes. Appeared in several movies. Theme song: "Flying High."

9/30/44	18	1		1 Hamp's Boogie Woogie ....J(terr.):18 *Chop-Chop* [I]	$20	Decca 18613
				Earl Bostic (alto sax)		
3/2/46	9	8		2 Hey! Ba-Ba-Re-Bop ....S:9 / J:9 *Slide, Hamp, Slide*	$20	Decca 18754
				Lionel Hampton (vocal); **Herbie Fields** (alto sax)		
2/4/50	7	10		3 Rag Mop ....J:7 / S:10 / A:13 *For You My Love*	$20	Decca 24855
				The Hamptones (vocals); Wes Montgomery (guitar); above 3 were Top 5 R&B hits		

HANLEY, Pete   MEM '53
Born in New York City. Featured vocalist with Sonny Durham's band.

5/16/53	19	2		Big Mamou ....A:19 / J:19 *Should You Change Your Mind*	$25	Okeh 4-6956
				Leyden Brothers (orch.); Cajun song with French and English choruses		

HANNA, Phil   '44
Born on 10/9/10 in River Forest, Illinois. Died on 7/20/57 (age 46). Sang briefly with **Russ Morgan**.

9/9/44	13	4		A Fellow On A Furlough ....J:13 *You May Not Remember*	$10	Decca 4445
				Leonard Joy (orch.); from the movie *Meet Miss Bobby Socks* starring Bob Crosby		

HARMONICATS, The   ★110★   MEM/HOT '47
Harmonica trio formed in Chicago: Jerry Murad (died on 5/11/96, age 80), Al Fiore (died on 10/25/96, age 73) and Don Les (died on 8/25/94, age 79).

4/26/47	❶8	26	●	1 Peg O' My Heart J:❶8 / S:❶4 / A:3 *Fantasy Impromptu* [I]	$15	Vitacoustic 1
				also issued on Universal 7503 in 1947; the first major hit on an independent label; #1 hit for Charles Harrison in 1913; #64 hit for Robert (**Bobby**) Maxwell in 1964		
8/14/48	15	9		2 Hair Of Gold ....J:15 / S:22 *Harmonicats Blues*	$10	Universal 121
				JERRY MURAD'S HARMONICATS		
				from the movie *Singing Spurs* starring Kirby Grant		
5/20/50	8	12		3 Bewitched ....J:8 / A:12 / S:17 *Blue Prelude* [I]	$20	Mercury 5399-X45
				JAN AUGUST & Jerry Murad's HARMONICATS		
				from the Broadway musical *Pal Joey* starring **Gene Kelly**; #50 hit for the Betty Smith Group in 1958		
6/3/50	22	2		4 Buffalo Billy ....A:22 *I Never Had A Worry In The World*	$20	Mercury 5420-X45
				ROBERTA QUINLAN, JERRY MURAD'S HARMONICATS & JAN AUGUST		
				adaptation of the 1844 tune "Buffalo Gals (Won't You Come Out Tonight)"; also see **Russ Morgan**'s "Dance With A Dolly"		
9/23/50	19	4		5 Harbor Lights ....J:19 *At Sundown* [I]	$15	Mercury 5461-X45
				JERRY BYRD & His Steel Guitar & JERRY MURAD'S Harmonicats		
				#6 hit for Frances Langford in 1937; #8 hit for The Platters in 1960		
12/29/51	21	2		6 Charmaine ....J:21 *Domino* [I]	$15	Mercury 5747-X45
				Jerry Murad's HARMONICATS		
				#1 hit for Guy Lombardo in 1927; #69 hit for The Four Freshmen in 1956		
9/26/53	14	8		7 The Story Of Three Loves ....S:14 / A:14 *Sweet Leilani* [I]	$15	Mercury 70202-X45
				JERRY MURAD Of The Harmonicats		
				Richard Hayman (orch.); title song from the movie starring Kirk Douglas; tune based on Rachmaninoff's "Paganini"		

HARRIS, Phil   ★92★   MEM '50
Born on 6/24/04 in Linton, Indiana. Died of heart failure on 8/11/95 (age 91). Best known as a movie/radio/TV personality. Also a popular bandleader, having previously played drums in **Francis Craig**'s 1920s band. Co-hosted a radio program with his wife, actress Alice Faye, 1947-54.

PHIL HARRIS and his Orchestra:

3/16/46	2²	10		1 One-Zy Two-Zy A:2 / S:7 / J:13 *Some Little Bug* [N]	$15	ARA 136
				Phil Harris and daughter (vocals)		
3/23/46	10	3		2 The Dark Town Poker Club ....A:10 *Jelly Bean* [N]	$15	ARA 116
				Phil Harris (vocal); #3 hit for Bert Williams in 1914		
8/23/47	8	4		3 Smoke, Smoke, Smoke (That Cigarette)........................S:8 / J:10 *Crawdad Song* [N]	$10	RCA Victor 20-2370
				Phil Harris and The Sportsmen (vocals); #94 hit for Commander Cody & His Lost Planet Airmen in 1973		

DEBUT	PEAK	WKS	Gold	A-side (Chart Hit)..B-side	$	Label & Number
				HARRIS, Phil — Cont'd		
12/31/49+	10	8		4 **The Old Master Painter** ....A:10 / S:14 / J:14 *St. James Infirmary*	$20	RCA Victor 47-3114
				78 rpm: 20-3608		
3/11/50	8	6		5 **Chattanoogie Shoe-Shine Boy**.........................A:8 / S:26 / J:27 *That's A Plenty* [N]	$20	RCA Victor 47-3216
				78 rpm: 20-3692; #34 hit for Freddy Cannon in 1960		
				PHIL HARRIS:		
9/2/50	30	1		6 **Simple Melody** ....A:30 *On The Mississippi*	$20	RCA Victor 47-3781
				from the Broadway musical *Watch Your Step* starring Irene and Vernon Castle; #4 hit for Billy Murray & Elsie Baker in 1916		
11/25/50	❶⁵	15	●	7 **The Thing** ....A:❶⁵ / S:❶⁴ / J:❶² *Goofus* [N]	$20	RCA Victor 47-3968
				uses melody of the traditional song "The Tailor's Boy"; reissued in 1959 on RCA's Children's Series WBY-87 with a picture sleeve; Walter Scharf (orch., above 2)		
9/1/51	24	2		8 **The Musicians** ....A:24 *How D'Ye Do And Shake Hands* [N]	$20	RCA Victor 47-4225
				DINAH SHORE, BETTY HUTTON, TONY MARTIN, PHIL HARRIS		
3/15/52	19	6		9 **Hambone** ....A:19 / J:24 *Mama's On The Warpath* [N]	$20	RCA Victor 47-4584
				PHIL HARRIS and THE BELL SISTERS		
				Henri René (orch., above 2)		
				HART, Gloria **'52**		
				Sang with **Art Kassel** in the 1940s.		
9/15/51	28	2		1 **Oh! How I Love You** ....J:28 *Red Rose Waltz*	$30	Sharp 45-36
				GLORIA HART and the HEARTBEATS		
8/2/52	18	2		2 **I Would Rather Look At You** ....J:18 / A:24 *Nickels, Quarters And Dimes*	$20	Mercury 5881-X45
				based on Offenbach's *Barcarolle* from the opera *Tales Of Hoffmann*; same melody used for Elvis Presley's "Tonight Is So Right For Love" on his 1960 album *G.I. Blues*; **Art Kassel** (orch., above 2)		
	★**124**★			**HAWKINS, Erskine** MEM **'45**		
				Born on 7/26/14 in Birmingham, Alabama. Died on 11/11/93 (age 79). Black trumpeter/composer/band leader. Nicknamed the "Twentieth Century Gabriel." Member of the 'Bama State Collegians, at State Teacher's College, in Montgomery, which became the Erskine Hawkins band in 1934. Very popular at the Savoy Ballroom in New York City. Featured brothers Dud and Paul Bascomb on trumpet and tenor sax. Hawkins wrote "Tuxedo Junction." Active with own quartet into the 1970s.		
				ERSKINE HAWKINS (The Twentieth Century Gabriel) and his Orchestra:		
8/3/40	16	1		1 **Whispering Grass** ....S(s):16 *Gabriel Meets The Duke*	$20	Bluebird 10671
				Jimmy Mitchelle (vocal)		
9/14/40	10	1		2 **Dolimite**...S:10 *Too Many Dreams* [I]	$20	Bluebird 10812
11/9/40	16	2		3 **Five O'Clock Whistle** ....S(s):16 *Sweet Georgia Brown* [I]	$20	Bluebird 10854
3/15/41	18	2		4 **Nona**...S(e):18 *I Know A Secret* [I]	$20	Bluebird 10979
8/28/43	15	9		5 **Don't Cry, Baby** ....S(s):15 / S(wc):16 *Bear-Mash Blues*	$20	Bluebird 30-0813
2/26/44	17	1		6 **Cherry**...J:17 *Country Boy*	$20	Bluebird 30-0819
				recorded on 7/18/39; Jimmy Mitchelle (vocal, above 2)		
				ERSKINE HAWKINS and his Orchestra:		
4/28/45	9	8		7 **Tippin' In** J:9 / A:14 *Remember* [I]	$15	Victor 20-1639
5/12/45	12	3		8 **Caldonia**...J:12 / A:13 *I Hope To Die (If I Told a Lie)*	$15	Victor 20-1659
				Ace Harris and band (vocals); #95 hit for James Brown in 1964		
				HAWKINS, Hawkshaw HOT **'52**		
				Born Harold Franklin Hawkins on 12/22/21 in Huntington, West Virginia. Died in a plane crash on 3/5/63 (age 41) near Camden, Tennessee (with Patsy Cline and **Cowboy Copas**). Singer/songwriter/guitarist. Joined the *Grand Ole Opry* in 1955. Married **Jean Shepard** on 11/26/60.		
1/12/52	26	1		**Slow Poke** ....J:26 *Two Roads*	$30	King 45-998
				#7 Country hit		
				HAYES, Bruce **'48**		
				Sang briefly with Vincent Lopez in the 1940s.		
7/24/48	18	10		**You Call Everybody Darlin'** ....J:18 / A:30 *Lonesome For Someone*	$15	DeLuxe 1178
				HAYES, Peter Lind **'49**		
				Born on 6/25/15 in San Francisco. Died on 4/21/98 (age 82). Comedian/singer. Host of TV variety and comedy shows, with wife, Mary Healy, from 1949-60.		
1/1/49	20	2		**My Darling, My Darling**...................................S:20 / J:25 / A:30 *Dainty Brenda Lee*	$10	Decca 24519
				The Stardusters (backing vocals); from the Broadway musical *Where's Charley?* starring **Ray Bolger**		

HAYES, Richard ★**83**★   MEM **'50**

Born on 1/5/30 in Passaic, New Jersey. Attended Julliard on a scholarship. Sang briefly with **Teddy Phillips**. Big break came when he won first place on **Arthur Godfrey**'s Talent Scouts. Emceed TV's *Name That Tune* from 1970-71.

1)The Old Master Painter 2)Out In The Cold Again 3)The Aba Daba Honeymoon

Orchestras:	Bassman, George — 5-7		**Miller, Mitch** — 1,2	Sauter, Eddie — 9		
	Carroll, Jimmy — 3,11		Reisman, Joe — 8,10	Siravo, George — 4		
12/17/49+	2¹	12		1 **The Old Master Painter** A:2 / S:7 / J:9 *Open Door — Open Arms*	$10	Mercury 5342
5/27/50	21	2		2 **My Foolish Heart**..A:21 *The Flying Dutchman*	$10	Mercury 5362
				title song from the movie starring Susan Hayward		
9/9/50	10	12		3 **Our Lady Of Fatima** ....S:10 / J:15 / A:19 *Honestly I Love You*	$20	Mercury 5466-X45
3/3/51	9	10		4 **The Aba Daba Honeymoon** ....A:9 / J:18 / S:24 *I Don't Want To Love You*	$20	Mercury 5586-X45
				RICHARD HAYES & KITTY KALLEN (above 2)		
				from the movie *Two Weeks With Love* starring **Debbie Reynolds** and **Carleton Carpenter**; #1 hit for Arthur Collins & Byron Harlan in 1914		
7/14/51	24	1		5 **Too Young** ....A:24 *Shenandoah Waltz*	$20	Mercury 5599-X45
				#13 hit for Donny Osmond in 1972		

DEBUT	PEAK	WKS	Gold	A-side (Chart Hit)...B-side	$	Label & Number

HAYES, Richard — Cont'd

DEBUT	PEAK	WKS		A-side / B-side	$	Label & Number
8/11/51	14	1		6 **Come On-A My House** / A:14		
				from the off-Broadway musical *The Son*		
8/11/51	23	1		7 **Go Go Go Go** A:23	$20	Mercury 5671-X45
10/27/51	9	10		8 **Out In The Cold Again** ....J:9 / S:18 / A:22 *Once*	$15	Mercury 5724-X45
				#4 hit for **Glen Gray** in 1934		
5/3/52	15	11		9 **Junco Partner A Worthless Cajun** ....J:15 / A:17 / S:23 *Summertime*	$15	Mercury 5833-X45
				tune labeled as "An Authentic Cajun Folk Song"		
5/3/52	24	1		10 **I'll Walk Alone** ....A:24 *Tattletale*	$15	Mercury 5821-X45
				featured in the movie *With A Song In My Heart* starring Susan Hayward		
7/12/52	23	1		11 **The Mask Is Off** ....J:23 *Never Leave Me*	$15	Mercury 5872-X45
11/1/52	15	2		12 **Forgetting You** ....A:15 / J:20 *Forgive And Forget*	$15	Mercury 5910-X45
				#18 hit for **Kitty O'Connor** in 1928		

HAYMAN, Richard   MEM/HOT **'53**

Born on 3/27/20 in Cambridge, Massachusetts. Orchestra leader/harmonica soloist. Helped arrange background music for *Meet Me In St. Louis* and other movies. Also arranger for **Vaughn Monroe**. Long-time associate conductor of the **Boston Pops Orchestra**.

DEBUT	PEAK	WKS		A-side / B-side	$	Label & Number
4/11/53	3	19		1 **Ruby** A:3 / S:3 / J:6 *Love Mood* [I]	$15	Mercury 70115-X45
				theme from the movie *Ruby Gentry* starring Jennifer Jones and Charlton Heston; #28 hit for Ray Charles in 1960		
5/2/53	12	11		2 **April In Portugal** ....S:12 / J:16 / A:17 *Anna* [I]	$15	Mercury 70114-X45
				Portuguese song originally published as "Coimbra"		
6/27/53	13	3		3 **Terry's Theme (From Limelight)** ....A:13 *Eyes Of Blue* [I]	$15	Mercury 70168-X45
				written by Charlie Chaplin for his movie *Limelight*; #92 hit for Mr. Acker Bilk in 1962; Hayman also conducted on **Vic Damone**'s vocal version of this tune, "Eternally"		
1/2/54	16	1		4 **Off Shore** ....A:16 *Joeys' Theme* [I]	$15	Mercury 70252-X45
2/6/54	20	1		5 **Sadie Thompson's Song (Blue Pacific Blues)**......A:20 *Drive In* [I]	$15	Mercury 70237-X45
				theme from the movie *Miss Sadie Thompson* starring Rita Hayworth		

HAYMES, Dick ★14★   MEM/HOT **'45**

Born on 9/13/16 in Buenos Aires, Argentina; raised in America. Died of cancer on 3/28/80 (age 63). Ballad singer with **Harry James**, **Benny Goodman** and **Tommy Dorsey** in the early 1940s. Appeared in various movies from 1944-53. Hosted a successful radio show with **Helen Forrest** in the mid-1940s. Married to actress Rita Hayworth from 1953-55. His daughter Stephanie (with singer Fran Jeffries) married rock songwriter Bernie Taupin in 1993.

1)*You'll Never Know* 2)*It Can't Be Wrong* 3)*Little White Lies* 4)*Long Ago (And Far Away)* 5)*I'll Buy That Dream*

Orchestras: Burke, Sonny — 40   Jenkins, Gordon —   Newman, Emil — 10,11   Shaw, Artie — 42
  Camarata — 9   28,29,31,32,35,39,41,44   Schoen, Vic — 36   Young, Victor — 12-23,25,43,45
  Hagen, Earle — 24,26,27

Vocalists: 4 Hits And A Miss —   Song Spinners, The — 1-8,33,34   Troubadours, The — 37
  32,40,41,43,45   Tattlers, The — 39   mixed quartet — 30

DEBUT	PEAK	WKS		A-side / B-side	$	Label & Number
7/3/43	2⁴	11		1 **It Can't Be Wrong** / S:2		
				from the movie *Now Voyager* starring Bette Davis		
7/31/43	7	7		2 **In My Arms** S:7	$10	Decca 18557
7/10/43	❶⁴	16	●	3 **You'll Never Know** / S:❶⁴		
				from the movie *Hello Frisco, Hello* starring Alice Faye; #1 R&B hit (4 weeks)		
8/28/43	17	3		4 **Wait For Me Mary** ....S(s):17 / S(wc):19 / S(mw):20	$10	Decca 18556
9/11/43	14	2		5 **I Never Mention Your Name (Oh, No!)** /...S(s):14 / S(mw):20 / S(wc):20		
11/13/43	19	1		6 **I Heard You Cried Last Night (And So Did I)**............S(mw):19	$10	Decca 18558
				from the movie *Cinderella Swings It* starring Guy Kibbee		
10/30/43	5	6		7 **Put Your Arms Around Me, Honey (I Never Knew Any Girl Like You)** / S:5		
				from the movie *Coney Island* starring **Betty Grable**; #1 hit for Arthur Collins & Byron Harlan in 1911; #58 hit for Fats Domino in 1960		
12/18/43+	17	3		8 **For The First Time (I've Fallen In Love)** ....S(s):17 / S(mw):19	$10	Decca 18565
4/29/44	2¹	18		9 **Long Ago (And Far Away)** S:2 / J:2 *Look For The Silver Lining*	$10	Decca 23317
				HELEN FORREST And DICK HAYMES
starring Rita Hayworth		
6/24/44	11	10		10 **How Blue The Night** / J:11		
6/17/44	22	1		11 **How Many Times Do I Have To Tell You** J:22	$10	Decca 18604
				above 2 from the movie *Four Jills In A Jeep* starring Kay Francis		
10/7/44	3	12		12 **Together** / S:3 / J:9		
				HELEN FORREST & DICK HAYMES
from the movie *Since You Went Away* starring Claudette Colbert; #1 hit for Paul Whiteman in 1928; #6 hit for Connie Francis in 1961		
9/16/44	4	9		13 **It Had To Be You** S:4 / J:8	$10	Decca 23349
				DICK HAYMES & HELEN FORREST
from the movie *Show Business* starring **Eddie Cantor**; #1 hit for Isham Jones in 1924		
11/4/44	22	1		14 **Janie** ....J(terr.):22 *Our Waltz*	$10	Decca 18623
				title song from the movie starring Joyce Reynolds		
5/26/45	9	3		15 **Laura** ....S:9 / A:10 / J:17 *The Night Is Young And You're So Beautiful*	$10	Decca 18666
				title song from the movie starring Gene Tierney and Dana Andrews		
7/14/45	6	6		16 **I Wish I Knew** / ....A:6 / S:10		
6/9/45	7	3		17 **The More I See You** A:7	$10	Decca 18662
				#16 hit for Chris Montez in 1966; above 2 from the movie *Billy Rose's Diamond Horseshoe* starring Haymes and **Betty Grable**		
9/8/45	2¹	13		18 **I'll Buy That Dream** / S:2 / J:3 / A:3		
				HELEN FORREST And DICK HAYMES
from the movie *Sing Your Way Home* starring Jack Haley		
9/8/45	9	5		19 **Some Sunday Morning** A:9 / J:11	$10	Decca 23434
				DICK HAYMES And HELEN FORREST
from the movie *San Antonio* starring Errol Flynn		

DEBUT	PEAK	WKS	Gold	A-side (Chart Hit)..B-side	$	Label & Number

HAYMES, Dick — Cont'd

DEBUT	PEAK	WKS	Gold	A-side	B-side	$	Label & Number
9/15/45	3	9		20 **Till The End Of Time** /	S:3 / A:6 / J:6		
				song based on Chopin's "Polonaise"; #83 hit for the Ray Charles Singers in 1964			
9/29/45	11	1		21 **Love Letters** A:11		$10	Decca 18699
				title song from the movie starring Jennifer Jones; #5 hit for Ketty Lester in 1962			
11/17/45	5	12		22 **It Might As Well Be Spring** /	S:5 / J:5 / A:6		
10/13/45	6	10		23 **That's For Me** .... S:6 / A:6 / J:14		$10	Decca 18706
				above 2 from the movie *State Fair* starring Haymes and Dana Andrews			
1/19/46	7	5		24 **I'm Always Chasing Rainbows** .... A:7 / J:10 / S:10 *Tomorrow Is Forever*		$10	Decca 23472
				DICK HAYMES And HELEN FORREST			
				from the movie *The Dolly Sisters* starring **Betty Grable**; melody adapted from Chopin's "Fantasie Impromptu";			
				#1 hit for Charles Harrison in 1918			
2/16/46	12	1		25 **Slowly** .... A:12 *I Wish I Could Tell You*		$10	Decca 18747
3/2/46	4	11		26 **Oh! What It Seemed To Be** S:4 / J:6 / A:7 *Give Me A Little Kiss, Will You Huh?*		$10	Decca 23481
				#91 hit for The Castells in 1962			
8/10/46	12	2		27 **In Love In Vain** .... A:12 *All Through The Day*		$10	Decca 23528
				DICK HAYMES and HELEN FORREST (above 2)			
				from the movie *Centennial Summer* starring Jeanne Crain and Cornel Wilde			
3/29/47	9	5		28 **How Are Things In Glocca Morra** .... S:9 / J:12 *'Twas Only An Irishman's Dream*		$10	Decca 23830
				from the Broadway musical *Finian's Rainbow* starring David Wayne			
5/3/47	3	11		29 **Mam'selle** J:3 / S:4 / A:5 *Stella By Starlight*		$10	Decca 23861
				from the movie *The Razor's Edge* starring Tyrone Power			
10/25/47	9	7		30 **I Wish I Didn't Love You So** .... S:9 / J:10 / A:11 *Naughty Angeline*		$10	Decca 23977
				from the movie *The Perils Of Pauline* starring **Betty Hutton**			
11/22/47	15	1		31 **—And Mimi** .... A:15 *When I'm Not Near The Girl I Love*		$10	Decca 24172
4/10/48	2¹	23	●	32 **Little White Lies** A:2 / S:3 / J:3 *The Treasure Of Sierra Madre*		$10	Decca 24280
				#1 hit for **Fred Waring** in 1930; #25 hit for Betty Johnson in 1957			
6/5/48	9	13		33 **You Can't Be True, Dear** / .... S:9 / A:9 / J:9			
				#75 hit for the Mary Kaye Trio in 1959			
6/5/48	11	5		34 **Nature Boy** .... J:11 / A:14 / S:16		$10	Decca 24439
				#40 hit for Bobby Darin in 1961			
7/24/48	9	18		35 **It's Magic** .... J:9 / S:13 / A:19 *It's You Or No One*		$10	Decca 23826
				from the movie *Romance On The High Seas* starring **Doris Day** and Jack Carson; #91 hit for The Platters in 1962			
9/25/48	24	2		36 **Every Day I Love You** .... S:24 *Hankerin'*		$10	Decca 24457
				from the movie *Two Guys From Texas* starring Dennis Morgan and Jack Carson			
3/19/49	22	1		37 **Bouquet Of Roses** .... J:22 *Any Time*		$10	Decca 24506
6/25/49	6	20		38 **Room Full Of Roses** .... J:6 / A:8 / S:10 *A Chapter In My Life Called Mary*		$10	Decca 24632
				#50 hit for Mickey Gilley in 1974			
7/16/49	5	18		39 **Maybe It's Because** S:5 / J:13 / A:13 *It Happens Every Spring*		$10	Decca 24650
				from the Broadway musical *Along Fifth Avenue* starring Jackie Gleason			
12/10/49+	4	13		40 **The Old Master Painter** J:4 / S:5 / A:9 *Why Was I Born?*		$10	Decca 24801
5/27/50	28	2		41 **Roses** .... A:28 / S:29 *I Still Get A Thrill (Thinking Of You)*		$20	Decca 9-27008
7/22/50	10	11		42 **Count Every Star** .... J:10 / S:15 / A:27 *If You Were Only Mine*		$20	Decca 9-27042
				DICK HAYMES and ARTIE SHAW			
				#35 hit for Donnie & The Dreamers in 1961			
9/9/50	23	2		43 **Can Anyone Explain? (No, No, No!)** .... J:23 *If I Had A Magic Carpet*		$20	Decca 9-27161
4/7/51	30	1		44 **You're Just In Love** .... S:30 *Something To Dance About* (Merman)		$20	Decca 9-27317
				ETHEL MERMAN and DICK HAYMES			
				from the Broadway musical *Call Me Madam* starring Merman			
10/27/51	28	3		45 **And So To Sleep Again** .... A:28 *Long Ago*		$20	Decca 9-27731

HAYTON, Lennie   MEM '49

Born on 2/13/08 in New York City. Died on 4/24/71 (age 63). Pianist/arranger for Paul Whiteman, 1928-30. Musical director for various radio shows and MGM studios. Married Lena Horne in 1947.

DEBUT	PEAK	WKS	Gold	A-side	B-side	$	Label & Number
4/23/49	19	6		**Slaughter On Tenth Avenue (Parts 1 & 2)** .... S:19 **[I]**		$15	MGM 30174

LENNY HAYTON And The M-G-M Studio Orchestra
from the Broadway musical *On Your Toes* starring **Ray Bolger**; featured in the movie *Words And Music* starring Mickey Rooney; #35 hit for The Ventures in 1964

HEARTBEATS — see HART, Gloria

HEIDT, Horace, and his Musical Knights ★86★   MEM '38

Born on 5/21/01 in Alameda, California. Died of pneumonia on 12/1/86 (age 85). Sweet-band leader who featured vocalist/movie star **Gordon MacRae**, vocalist/comedian Art Carney, tenor saxophonist **Frank DeVol**, pianist **Frankie Carle** and guitarist **Alvino Rey**. Host of radio show *Pot O' Gold* (1938-41). Also hosted a TV talent show from 1950-51. Heidt's pre-1940 #1 hits: "Ti-Pi-Tin" and "Gone With The Wind."

1)I Don't Want To Set The World On Fire 2)G'bye Now 3)The Hut-Sut Song (A Swedish Serenade)

Vocalists: Bowne, Jerry & Gang — 9   Kemper, Ronnie — 1,3   Walsh, Gene — 10   glee club — 5,10
Cotton, Larry — 4,5   Lowery, Fred — 5   Wood, Donna (& her Don
Farrington, Red (marine) — 7   O'Toole, Ollie (sailor) — 7   Juans) — 2-4
Goodman, Charles — 7 (soldier),8   Sweetswingsters — 10   band ensemble — 6

DEBUT	PEAK	WKS	Gold	A-side	B-side	$	Label & Number
5/3/41	2¹	6		1 **G'bye Now** S:2 *Do You Believe In Fairy Tales?*		$10	Columbia 36026
				starring Ole Olsen and Chic Johnson			
6/14/41	3	6		2 **The Hut-Sut Song (A Swedish Serenade)** S:3 *The Way You Look At Me*		$10	Columbia 36138
7/26/41	8	2		3 **Good Bye Dear, I'll Be Back In A Year** .... S:8 *Walkin' Round In Circles*		$10	Columbia 36148
9/27/41	2²	11		4 **I Don't Want To Set The World On Fire** S:2 *Mama*		$10	Columbia 36295
12/6/41	7	5		5 **Shepherd Serenade** S:7 *Delilah*		$10	Columbia 36370
3/14/42	7	4	●	6 **Deep In The Heart Of Texas** .... S:7 *Loretta*		$10	Columbia 36525
				#78 hit for Duane Eddy in 1962			

HEIDT, Horace, and his Musical Knights — Cont'd

DEBUT	PEAK	WKS		A-side / B-side	$	Label & Number
6/20/42	20	1		7 **Three Little Sisters** ....S(mw):20 *Mary* **[N]**	$10	Columbia 36576
				from the movie *Private Buckaroo* starring the **Andrews Sisters**		
4/3/43	14	2		8 **That Old Black Magic** ....S(wc):14 / S(s):19 *If I Cared A Little Bit Less*	$10	Columbia 36670
				from the movie *Star Spangled Rhythm* starring **Bing Crosby** and **Bob Hope**; #13 hit for **Sammy Davis, Jr.** in 1955		
3/25/44	18	1		9 **Friendly Tavern Polka**...J(terr.):18 *Broadway Caballero*	$10	Columbia 36006
2/3/45	10	2		10 **Don't Fence Me In** ....S:10 *I Promise You*; #45 hit for **Tommy Edwards** in 1960	$10	Columbia 36761
				from the movie *Hollywood Canteen* starring Bette Davis; #45 hit for **Tommy Edwards** in 1960		

HENDERSON, Skitch   MEM '46

Born Lyle Henderson on 1/27/18 in Halstad, Minnesota. Conductor for TV's *The Tonight Show* from 1962-66.

| 10/12/46 | 9 | 9 | | **Five Minutes More** ....A:9 / J:13 *You'll See What A Kiss Can Do* | $10 | Capitol 287 |
| | | | | Ray Kellogg (vocal); featured in the movie *Sweetheart Of Sigma Chi* starring Elyse Knox | | |

HERMAN, Woody, And His Orchestra ★31★   MEM/HOT '45

Born on 5/16/13 in Milwaukee. Died of heart failure on 10/29/87 (age 74). Played clarinet and saxophone for Harry Sosnik, Gus Arnheim and Isham Jones before assembling his own "Band That Plays The Blues" in 1936. "Woodchopper's Ball" was his trademark hit and "Blue Flame" his theme. Sax stars Stan Getz and Zoot Sims led his famous jazz ensemble in the late 1940s. Won Grammy's Lifetime Achievement Award in 1987. One of the most innovative and contemporary of all bandleaders.

1)Blues In The Night (My Mama Done Tol' Me)   2)Caldonia   3)Sabre Dance   4)Laura   5)Blue Flame

Vocalists: Blue Flames, The — 24   **Herman, Woody** —   Rogers, Billie — 14   ensemble — 8,9
Grey, Carolyn — 7   1,2,6-11,13,16-18,21-29   **Shore, Dinah** — 28
Lane, Muriel — 4,5   Wayne, Frances — 12,15,20

DEBUT	PEAK	WKS	Gold	A-side / B-side	$	Label & Number
1/4/41	13	1		1 **There I Go** ....S(mw):13 / S(wc):16 *Beat Me Daddy, Eight To A Bar*	$10	Decca 3454
1/25/41	16	1		2 **Frenesí** ....S(e):16 *A Song Of Old Hawaii*	$10	Decca 3427
4/5/41	5	4		3 **Blue Flame** S:5 *Fur Trappers' Ball* **[I]**	$10	Decca 3643
				the band's theme song		
6/28/41	10	1		4 **G'bye Now** ....S:10 *Until Tomorrow*	$10	Decca 3745
				from the movie *Hellzapoppin* starring Ole Olsen and Chic Johnson		
12/6/41	20	1		5 **By-U By-O (The Lou'siana Lullaby)**.............................S(wc):20 / S(s):20 *Misirlou*	$10	Decca 4024
1/10/42	❶¹	11		6 **Blues In The Night (My Mama Done Tol' Me)** S:❶¹ *This Time The Dream's On Me*	$10	Decca 4030
				from the movie *Blues In The Night* starring Priscilla Lane		
3/7/42	18	1		7 **Rose O'Day** ....S(s):18 *Someone's Rocking My Dream Boat*	$10	Decca 4113
9/5/42	5	4		8 **Amen** S:5 *Deliver Me To Tennessee*	$10	Decca 18346
				from the movie *What's Cookin'* starring the **Andrews Sisters**		
7/10/43	17	1		9 **Four Or Five Times** ....S(wc):17 *Hot Chestnuts*	$10	Decca 18526
				#17 hit for King Oliver in 1928		
2/5/44	7	11		10 **Do Nothin' Till You Hear From Me** / ....J:7 / S:9	$10	Decca 18578
4/8/44	12	7		11 **By The River Of The Roses**..J:12		
3/25/44	10	8		12 **The Music Stopped** ....J:10 *I Couldn't Sleep A Wink Last Night*	$10	Decca 18577
				from the movie *Higher And Higher* starring **Frank Sinatra**		
6/24/44	10	5		13 **Milkman, Keep Those Bottles Quiet** ....J:10 *Irresistible You*	$10	Decca 18603
				from the movie *Broadway Rhythm* starring George Murphy and **Ginny Simms**		
12/30/44	18	1		14 **Let Me Love You Tonight (No Te Importe Saber)** ....J:18 *Who Dat Up Dere?*	$10	Decca 18619
2/24/45	18	1		15 **Saturday Night (Is The Loneliest Night In The Week)** ....J:18 *I Didn't Know About You*	$10	Decca 18641
4/14/45	4	12	●	16 **Laura** ....A:4 / S:7 / J:14 *I Wonder*	$10	Columbia 36785
				title song from the movie starring Gene Tierney and Dana Andrews		
5/5/45	2²	14		17 **Caldonia** A:2 / S:6 / J:15 *Happiness Is A Thing Called Joe*	$10	Columbia 36789
				top 1944-45 sidemen: Bill Harris (trombone), Flip Phillips (tenor sax), Pete Candoli (trumpet), Dave Tough (drummer), pianist/arranger Ralph Burns, trumpet/arranger Neal Hefti; #95 hit for James Brown in 1964		
7/14/45	9	6		18 **A Kiss Goodnight**..A:9 *Goosey Gander*	$10	Columbia 36815
9/29/45	13	1		19 **Northwest Passage** ....A:13 *June Comes Around Every Year* **[I]**	$10	Columbia 36835
1/5/46	17	1		20 **Gee, It's Good To Hold You** ....A:17 *Your Father's Mustache*	$10	Columbia 36870
2/16/46	7	4		21 **Let It Snow! Let It Snow! Let It Snow!** / ....A:7 / S:8 / J:14 **[X]**	$10	Columbia 36909
2/16/46	11	1		22 **Everybody Knew But Me** A:11		
4/13/46	11	2		23 **Atlanta, G.A.** ....A:11 *Wild Root*	$10	Columbia 36949
6/29/46	8	10		24 **Surrender** ....A:8 / J:12 *The Good Earth*	$10	Columbia 36985
8/31/46	12	1		25 **Mabel! Mabel!**...............................A:12 *Linger In My Arms A Little Longer, Baby*	$10	Columbia 36995
				based on the 1894 tune by Anton Dvorak, "Humoresque"; Red Norvo (vibraphone, above 2)		
5/3/47	12	2		26 **Across The Alley From The Alamo**......................A:12 *(There Is) No Greater Love*	$10	Columbia 37289
6/14/47	13	3		27 **That's My Desire** ....A:13 *Ivy*	$10	Columbia 37329
				WOODY HERMAN Accompanied by The Four Chips (above 2)		
				The Four Chips: Andy Lambert-bass, Gene Sargent-guitar, Dick Kane-piano, Don Lamond-drums; #69 hit for The Sensations in 1962		
7/12/47	15	2		28 **Tallahassee** ....A:15 *Natch*	$10	Columbia 37387
				DINAH SHORE and WOODY HERMAN		
				Sonny Burke (orch.); from the movie *Variety Girl* starring Mary Hatcher		
1/3/48	15	1		29 **Civilization (Bongo, Bongo, Bongo)** ....S:15 *Boulevard Of Memories*	$10	Columbia 37885
				WOODY HERMAN With Orchestral Acc.		
				from the Broadway musical *Angel In The Wings* starring Hank Ladd		
3/20/48	3	12		30 **Sabre Dance** A:3 / S:7 / J:10 *Swing Low, Sweet Clarinet* **[I]**	$10	Columbia 38102
				based on Khatchaturian's "Gayne Ballet Suite"; Stan Getz (tenor sax, above 2)		

HERTH, Milt, Trio   MEM '38

Born on 11/3/02 in New York City. Died on 6/18/69 (age 66). White organist. His trio included pianist Willie "The Lion" Smith (died on 4/18/73, age 76) and drummer O'Neill Spencer (died on 6/24/44, age 34).

7/28/45	12	7		1 Fuzzy Wuzzy ....J:12 Please No Squeeza Da Banana	$10	Decca 18688
				MILT HERTH TRIO and THE JESTERS		
2/21/48	6	13		2 I'm Looking Over A Four Leaf Clover ....J:6 / S:7 / A:11 Bye Bye Blackbird	$10	Decca 24319
				RUSS MORGAN And His ORCHESTRA with MILT HERTH At The Organ		
				Ames Brothers & Ensemble (vocals); #2 hit for Nick Lucas in 1927		

HEYWOOD, Eddie   MEM/HOT '56

Born on 12/4/15 in Atlanta. Died on 1/2/89 (age 73). Jazz pianist. Played professionally by age 14. Own band in New York City in 1941. Worked with Billie Holiday. To the West Coast in 1947, with own trio. Active into the 1970s.

9/28/46	15	5		1 The House Of Blue Lights ....J:15 A Man Is A Brother To A Mule	$15	Decca 23641
				ANDREWS SISTERS and EDDIE HEYWOOD and HIS ORCHESTRA		
				#9 hit for Chuck Miller in 1955		
4/12/47	11	4		2 Guilty ....J:11 Sentimental Journey	$20	Decca 23844
				ELLA FITZGERALD and EDDIE HEYWOOD AND HIS ORCHESTRA		
				#4 hit for Ruth Etting in 1931		
12/25/54	30	1		3 Land Of Dreams ....S:30 Song Of The Barefoot Contessa (Winterhalter - #25) [I]	$15	RCA Victor 47-5888
				HUGO WINTERHALTER/EDDIE HEYWOOD		

HILDEGARDE   ★141★   MEM '46

Born Hildegarde Loretta Sell on 2/1/06 in Adell, Wisconsin. Popular radio singer.

4/29/44	15	2		1 Suddenly It's Spring / J:15		
				from the movie Lady In The Dark starring Ginger Rogers		
3/4/44	25	1		2 Leave Us Face It (We're In Love)...J:25	$10	Decca 23297
9/9/44	16	1		3 Lili Marlene ....J:16 (All Of A Sudden) My Heart Sings	$10	Decca 23348
				song usually identified with Marlene Dietrich; Harry Sosnik (orch., above 3)		
8/18/45	6	2		4 June Is Bustin' Out All Over A:6 / J:11 This Was A Real Nice Clambake	$10	Decca 23428
				HILDEGARDE with GUY LOMBARDO AND HIS ROYAL CANADIANS		
				The Song Spinners (backing vocals); from the Broadway musical Carousel starring John Raitt		
5/11/46	7	14		5 The Gypsy / ....J:7 / A:11		
4/13/46	15	2		6 One-Zy Two-Zy (I Love You-zy).............................A:15 / J:15	$10	Decca 23511
				HILDEGARDE and GUY LOMBARDO And His Royal Canadians (above 2)		

HILL, Tiny, And His Orchestra   MEM '39

Born Harry Hill on 7/19/06 in Sullivan Township, Illinois. Died in 1972 (age 66). Nicknamed "Tiny" because of his weight (350 pounds). Formed his own trio in 1931, later had The Five Jacks. Own big band in 1933. Worked as drummer with Byron Dunbar in the mid-1930s.

10/28/44	14	4		1 How Many Hearts Have You Broken (With Those Great Big		
				Beautiful Eyes) ....J:14 Rose Of Santa Rosa	$10	Decca 4447
1/27/51	29	2		2 Hot Rod Race ....J:29 Lovebug Itch [N]	$30	Mercury 5547-X45
				original version of Johnny Bond and Charlie Ryan's 1960 hit "Hot Rod Lincoln"		
1/12/52	28	2		3 Slow Poke ....J:28 / S:30 Don't Put A Tax On Love	$15	Mercury 5740-X45

HILLTOPPERS, The   ★88★   MEM/HOT '53

Vocal group formed in Bowling Green, Kentucky: Jimmy Sacca, Don McGuire, Seymour Spiegelman and **Billy Vaughn**. Vaughn left for own conducting career in 1955. Spiegelman died on 2/13/87 (age 56). Vaughn died of cancer on 9/26/91 (age 72).

1)P.S. I Love You 2)Trying 3)From The Vine Came The Grape

    THE HILL TOPPERS Featuring Jimmy Sacca:

8/16/52	7	19		1 Trying ....S:7 / J:9 / A:10 You Made Up My Mind	$20	Dot 45-15018
				group member Billy Vaughn had an instrumental hit version in 1958 (#77)		
				THE HILLTOPPERS Featuring Jimmy Sacca:		
1/10/53	15	2		2 Must I Cry Again...A:15 / J:18 I Keep Telling Myself	$15	Dot 45-15034
6/13/53	4	21	●	3 P.S. I Love You / S:4 / A:4 / J:5		
				#12 hit for Rudy Vallee in 1934		
6/6/53	8	12		4 I'd Rather Die Young (Than Grow Old Without You) ....A:8 / S:12 / J:15	$15	Dot 45-15085
10/24/53	8	11		5 To Be Alone / ....J:8 / A:9 / S:12		
10/24/53	8	10		6 Love Walked In ....A:8 / S:11 / J:13	$15	Dot 45-15105
				#1 hit for Sammy Kaye in 1938; #30 hit for Dinah Washington in 1960		
1/30/54	10	11		7 Till Then ....A:10 / S:10 / J:13 I Found Your Letter	$15	Dot 45-15132
				#20 hit for The Classics in 1963		
2/13/54	8	11		8 From The Vine Came The Grape ....J:8 / S:12 / A:13 Time Will Tell	$15	Dot 45-15127
				sung in English and Italian		
4/24/54	12	5		9 Poor Butterfly ....J:12 / S:15 / A:15 Wrapped Up In A Dream	$15	Dot 45-15156
				#1 hit for the Victor Military Band in 1917		
8/28/54	17	2		10 If I Didn't Care ....J:17 Bettina	$15	Dot 45-15220
				#2 hit for the Ink Spots in 1939; #22 hit for Connie Francis in 1959		

HINES, Earl, and his Orchestra   MEM '40

Born on 12/28/05 in Duquesne, Pennsylvania. Died of a heart attack on 4/22/83 (age 72). Black singer/pianist/bandleader. Nicknamed "Fatha" or "Father." Piano style inspired by **Louis Armstrong**'s trumpet work. Recorded solo for QRS in 1928. Own bands until 1948. With Louis Armstrong from 1948-51, then own sextet.

8/3/40	14	4		1 Boogie Woogie On St. Louis Blues ....S(s):14 Number 19 [I]	$20	Bluebird 10674
8/12/44	18	1		2 It Had To Be You...J:18 Body And Soul (Coleman Hawkins)	$25	Bluebird 30-0825
				Madeline Greene and The Three Varieties (vocals); originally released on Bluebird 11308 in 1941; from the movie Show Business		
				starring Eddie Cantor; #1 hit for Isham Jones in 1924		

HODGES, Johnny, and His Orchestra   MEM '38
Born on 7/25/06 in Cambridge, Massachusetts. Died of a heart attack on 5/11/70 (age 63). Black alto saxophonist. With **Duke Ellington** from 1928-51 and 1955-70.

| 9/1/51 | 28 | 1 | | Castle Rock ....S:28 *Jeep's Blues* [I] | $20 | Mercury 8944-X45 |

band features Al Sears on tenor sax and **Ellington** trombonist Lawrence Brown

HOLMES, LeRoy, and his Orchestra   MEM/HOT '54
Born Alvin Holmes on 9/22/13 in Pittsburgh. Died on 7/27/86 (age 72). Orchestra conductor/arranger.

| 7/31/54 | 9 | 14 | ● | The High And The Mighty ....S:9 / A:10 / J:14 *Lisa* [I] | $15 | MGM K11761 |

Fred Lowery (whistling); title song from the movie starring John Wayne

HOMER AND JETHRO   HOT '59
Comedy duo from Knoxville, Tennessee: Henry "Homer" Haynes (guitar) and Kenneth "Jethro" Burns (mandolin). Homer was born on 7/27/20; died of a heart attack on 8/7/71 (age 51). Jethro was born on 3/10/20; died of cancer on 2/4/89 (age 68). Regulars on the WLS *National Barn Dance* from 1950-58. Elected to the Country Music Hall of Fame in 2001.

| 8/20/49 | 22 | 1 | | 1 Baby, It's Cold Outside ....A:22 *Country Girl* [N] | $35 | RCA Victor 48-0075 |

    HOMER and JETHRO with June Carter
78 rpm; 21-0078; from the movie *Neptune's Daughter* starring Esther Williams

| 6/6/53 | 17 | 3 | | 2 (How Much Is) That Hound Dog In The Window ....J:17 *Pore Ol' Koo-Liger* [N] | $25 | RCA Victor 47-5280 |

parody of **Patti Page**'s "Doggie In The Window"

HOOSIER HOT SHOTS   MEM '38
Novelty group from Fort Wayne, Indiana: brothers Paul "Hezzie" (song whistle, washboard, drums, alto horn; born on 4/11/05; died on 4/27/80, age 75) and Kenneth "Rudy" Triesch (banjo, bass horn; born on 9/13/03; died on 9/17/87, age 84), with Charles Otto "Gabe" Ward (clarinet, saxophone, fife; born on 11/26/04; died on 1/14/92, age 87) and Frank Kettering (banjo, guitar, flute, piano, bass fiddle; born on 1/1/09; died in 6/73, age 64). Regulars on the WLS *National Barn Dance* from 1933-42. Also appeared in several western movies.

| 6/17/44 | 21 | 1 | | 1 She Broke My Heart In Three Places ....J(terr.):21 *Don't Change Horses* [N] | $20 | Decca 4442 |
| 2/9/46 | 12 | 1 | | 2 Someday (You'll Want Me To Want You) ....J:12 *You Two-Timed Me One Time Too Often* [N] | $20 | Decca 18738 |

    HOOSIER HOT SHOTS and SALLY FOSTER
Sally Foster and Gil Taylor (vocals); #56 hit for Della Reese in 1960; above 2 were #3 Country hits

HOPE, Bob — see WHITING, Margaret

HOPE, Lynn, Quintet   '50
Born on 9/26/26 in Birmingham, Alabama. Male saxophonist.

| 8/26/50 | 19 | 3 | | Tenderly ....J:19 *Song Of The Wanderer* [I] | $20 | Premium 851 |

78 rpm only; #31 hit for Bert Kaempfert in 1961

HORTON, Vaughn, And His Polka Debs   '48
Born George Vaughn Horton on 6/6/11 in Broad Top, Pennsylvania. Died on 3/1/88 (age 76). Singer/prolific songwriter. Member of **The Pinetoppers**.

| 5/8/48 | 11 | 4 | | Toolie Oolie Doolie The Yodel Polka...S:11 / J:16 *The Skaters Waltz* | $20 | Continental 1223 |

HOUR OF CHARM CHOIR   '50
Female choir conducted by Russian-born bandleader Phil Spitalny who came to the U.S. in 1917. In 1934, he formed an "all-girl" orchestra. His *Hour Of Charm* radio show was a long-running hit through the 1940s. Phil was born on 11/7/1890; died on 10/11/70 (age 79).

| 10/28/50 | 23 | 5 | | Our Lady Of Fatima ....S:23 *Ave Maria* | $20 | RCA Victor 47-3920 |

    Phil Spitalny (conductor)

HOUSTON, Bob   MEM '49
Vocalist with the **Johnny Long** band.

| 11/19/49 | 27 | 1 | | That Lucky Old Sun (Just Rolls Around Heaven All Day).............J:27 *The Meadows Of Heaven* | $10 | MGM 10509 |

    Russ Case (orch.); The Quartones (backing vocals); #20 hit for Ray Charles in 1964

HOWARD, Don   '53
Born Donald Howard Koplow on 5/11/35 in Cleveland.

| 12/6/52+ | 4 | 15 | ● | Oh Happy Day   S:4 / A:6 / J:6 *You Went Away* | $25 | Essex 45-311 |

originally released on Triple A 45-2503 in 1952

HOWARD, Eddy, And His Orchestra   ★20★   MEM/HOT '47
Born on 9/12/14 in Woodland, California. Died on 5/23/63 (age 48). Singer with the **Dick Jurgens** band from 1934-40. Composer of "My Last Goodbye" and "Careless."

    1)To Each His Own   2)Sin   3)I Wonder, I Wonder, I Wonder   4)My Adobe Hacienda
    5)(I Love You) For Sentimental Reasons

| 6/29/46 | ❶8 | 25 | ● | 1 To Each His Own   A:❶8 / J:❶6 / S:❶5 *Cynthia's In Love* | $10 | Majestic 7188 |

Eddy Howard (vocal on all recordings); written for, but not included in the movie starring Olivia de Havilland; also released on Majestic 1070; #21 hit for The Platters in 1960

| 8/24/46 | 6 | 14 | | 2 The Rickety Rickshaw Man ....A:6 / J:9 *She's Funny That Way* | $10 | Majestic 7192 |

also released on Majestic 1078

| 11/16/46+ | 2¹ | 20 | | 3 (I Love You) For Sentimental Reasons   A:2 / J:2 / S:6 *Why Does It Get Late So Early* | $10 | Majestic 7204 |

also released on Majestic 1071; #17 hit for Sam Cooke in 1958

| 11/16/46 | 17 | 1 | | 4 My Best To You ....A:17 *Missouri Waltz* | $10 | Majestic 1074 |
| 2/8/47 | 23 | 1 | | 5 The Girl That I Marry ....J:23 *You Are Everything To Me* | $10 | Majestic 1083 |

from the Broadway musical *Annie Get Your Gun* starring **Ethel Merman**

| 4/5/47 | 2⁵ | 15 | | 6 My Adobe Hacienda   J:2 / A:3 / S:4 *Midnight Masquerade* | $10 | Majestic 1117 |
| 4/19/47 | 11 | 5 | | 7 Heartaches...A:11 *Don't Tell Her What Happened To Me* | $10 | Majestic 1111 |

#12 hit for **Guy Lombardo** in 1931; #7 hit for The Marcels in 1961

| 5/17/47 | 2⁵ | 19 | | 8 I Wonder, I Wonder, I Wonder   J:2 / A:2 / S:3 *Ask Anyone Who Knows* | $10 | Majestic 1124 |
| 7/26/47 | 16 | 3 | | 9 Ragtime Cowboy Joe ....J:16 *On The Old Spanish Trail* | $10 | Majestic 1155 |

from the movie *Hello Frisco, Hello* starring Alice Faye; #1 hit for Bob Roberts in 1912; #16 hit for The Chipmunks in 1959

DEBUT	PEAK	WKS	Gold	A-side (Chart Hit) .... B-side	$	Label & Number
				HOWARD, Eddy, And His Orchestra — Cont'd		
9/20/47	7	3		10 **Kate (Have I Come Too Early, Too Late)** ....J:7 / A:8 *On The Avenue*	$10	Majestic 1160
10/18/47	9	4		11 **An Apple Blossom Wedding** ....J:9 / S:14 *Blue Tail Fly*	$10	Majestic 1156
2/14/48	8	16		12 **Now Is The Hour (Maori Farewell Song)** ....J:8 / S:8 / A:11 *True*	$10	Majestic 1191
				based on the traditional New Zealand song "Hearere Ra"; #59 hit for Gale Storm in 1956		
5/22/48	20	4		13 **Just Because** ....J:20 *Encore, Cherie*	$10	Majestic 1231
				#99 hit for **The McGuire Sisters** in 1961		
6/12/48	23	2		14 **Put 'Em In A Box, Tie 'Em With A Ribbon (And Throw 'Em In The Deep Blue Sea)** ....J:23 *Dainty Brenda Lee*	$10	Majestic 1252
				from the movie *Romance On The High Seas* starring Jack Carson		
11/27/48	6	12		15 **I'd Love To Get You On A Slow Boat To China** ....A:6 / J:9 / S:12 *I'd Love To Live In Loveland*	$10	Mercury 5210
12/11/48	27	1		16 **Dainty Brenda Lee** ....A:27 *Bella Bella Marie*	$10	Mercury 5208
				originally released as the B-side of #14 above		
4/23/49	24	1		17 **Love Me! Love Me! Love Me!** ....J:24 *A Rosewood Spinet*	$10	Mercury 5238
4/23/49	20	2		18 **Candy Kisses** ....J:20 *Judy*	$10	Mercury 5272
				#1 Country hit for **George Morgan** in 1949		
6/4/49	29	1		19 **Red Head** ....J:29 *Single Saddle*	$10	Mercury 5274
7/9/49	4	23		20 **Room Full Of Roses /** ....J:4 / A:4 / S:11		
				#50 hit for Mickey Gilley in 1974		
8/20/49	21	3		21 **Yes, Yes, In Your Eyes** J:21	$10	Mercury 5296
				#5 hit for Paul Whiteman in 1924		
8/27/49	9	14		22 **Maybe It's Because /** ....J:9 / A:13 / S:17		
				from the Broadway musical *Along Fifth Avenue* starring Jackie Gleason		
10/29/49	25	1		23 **Tell Me Why** J:25	$10	Mercury 5314
				#13 hit for Bobby Vinton in 1964		
2/4/50	28	1		24 **Half A Heart Is All You Left Me (When You Broke My Heart in Two)**...J:28 *Peggy Dear*	$10	Mercury 5349
3/11/50	24	1		25 **Rag Mop** ....J:24 *Daddy's Little Girl*	$10	Mercury 5371
7/15/50	21	1		26 **American Beauty Rose** ....J:21 *Seems Like Yesterday*	$15	Mercury 5433-X45
11/4/50	9	11		27 **To Think You've Chosen Me** ....A:9 / J:12 / S:23 *The One Rose (That's Left In My Heart)*	$15	Mercury 5517-X45
2/17/51	14	7		28 **A Penny A Kiss–A Penny A Hug** ....J:14 *I Still Feel The Same About You*	$15	Mercury 5567-X45
6/2/51	27	1		29 **What Will I Tell My Heart /** A:27	$15	
				#2 hit for **Andy Kirk** in 1937		
6/2/51	28	3		30 **The Strange Little Girl** J:28	$15	Mercury 5630-X45
7/21/51	22	2		31 **A Woman Is A Deadly Weapon** ....A:22 / J:24 *I'm In Love Again*	$15	Mercury 5663-X45
				also released on Mercury 5676 in 1951		
9/22/51	❶[8]	24	●	32 **Sin** ....A:❶[8] / S:❶[2] / J:❶[1] *My Wife And I*	$15	Mercury 5711-X45
2/2/52	11	14		33 **Stolen Love**.......................J:11 / A:17 / S:24 *I'll See You In My Dreams*	$15	Mercury 5771-X45
				also released as the B-side of "Wishin'" below		
3/8/52	17	14		34 **Wishin'** ....J:17 *Stolen Love*	$15	Mercury 5784-X45
				also released on Mercury 5791-X45 in 1952		
3/29/52	7	16		35 **Be Anything (But Be Mine)** ....A:7 / J:13 / S:13 *She Took*	$15	Mercury 5815-X45
				#25 hit for Connie Francis in 1964		
6/28/52	4	16		36 **Auf Wiederseh'n, Sweetheart /** ....A:4 / J:7 / S:16		
				Jack Halloran Choir (backing vocals, above 2)		
9/13/52	26	1		37 **I Don't Want To Take A Chance** A:26	$15	Mercury 5871-X45
9/6/52	14	6		38 **Mademoiselle** ....A:14 *I Don't Know Any Better*	$15	Mercury 5898-X45
11/22/52	11	5		39 **It's Worth Any Price You Pay** ....A:11 *Kentucky Babe*	$15	Mercury 70015-X45
3/28/53	17	3		40 **Gomen Nasai** *Forgive Me* ....A:17 *Someone To Kiss Your Tears Away*	$15	Mercury 70107-X45
4/3/54	16	2		41 **Melancholy Me** ....A:16 *I Wonder What's Become Of Sally*	$15	Mercury 70304-X45

HOWARD, Rosetta '48

Born in 1914 in Chicago. Died in 1974 (age 60). Blues singer.

DEBUT	PEAK	WKS	Gold	A-side	$	Label & Number
8/14/48	23	1		**Ebony Rhapsody** ....J:23 *When I Been Drinking*	$30	Columbia 37573
				accompanied by the Big Three Trio, including great blues bassist/songwriter Willie Dixon; also released on Columbia 30053		

HUGHES, Marjorie '49

Daughter and featured vocalist of **Frankie Carle**'s orchestra.

DEBUT	PEAK	WKS	Gold	A-side	$	Label & Number
7/23/49	18	5		**You Told A Lie (I Believed You)** ....A:18 / J:20 *You're Mine*	$10	Columbia 38500
				7" 33-1/3 rpm: 1-235; Hugo Winterhalter (orch.)		

HUNT, Pee Wee, And His Orchestra   MEM '48   ★148★

Born Walter Hunt on 5/10/07 in Mt. Healthy, Ohio. Died on 6/22/79 (age 72). Singer/trombonist with **Glen Gray** from 1929-43. Own Dixieland band featured Carl Fischer on piano.

DEBUT	PEAK	WKS	Gold	A-side	$	Label & Number
6/26/48	❶[8]	32	●	1 **Twelfth Street Rag** ....S:❶[8] / J:❶[6] / A:❶[4] *Somebody Else, Not Me* [I]	$10	Capitol 15105
				#7 hit for Earl Fuller in 1917		
7/4/53	3	25	●	2 **Oh!** ....J:3 / S:3 / A:4 *San* [I]	$15	Capitol F2442
				#13 hit for Ted Lewis in 1920		

HUSKY, Ferlin — see SHEPARD, Jean

HUTTON, Betty   ★78★   MEM '50

Born Elizabeth June Thornburg on 2/26/21 in Battle Creek, Michigan. Actress/singer. Appeared in several movies and Broadway shows. Sang with Vincent Lopez from 1938-39.

1)Doctor, Lawyer, Indian Chief 2)A Bushel And A Peck 3)Stuff Like That There

DEBUT	PEAK	WKS	Gold	A-side	$	Label & Number
8/5/44	5	12		1 **It Had To Be You /** ....S:5 / J:8		
				from the movie *Show Business* starring **Eddie Cantor**; #1 hit for Isham Jones in 1924		
7/29/44	7	7		2 **His Rocking Horse Ran Away** ....S:7 / J:15 [N]	$10	Capitol 155
				from the movie *And The Angels Sing* starring Hutton		

HUTTON, Betty — Cont'd

DEBUT	PEAK	WKS	Gold	A-side / B-side	$	Label & Number
4/7/45	4	10		3 **Stuff Like That There** A:4 / J:6 / S:7 *Blue Skies*	$10	Capitol 188
				from the movie *On Stage Everybody* starring Jack Oakie		
10/13/45	15	2		4 **What Do You Want To Make Those Eyes At Me For**.........J:15 / A:17 *Doin' It The Hard Way*	$10	Capitol 211
				from the movie *Incendiary Blonde* starring Hutton; #3 hit for Ada Jones & Billy Murray in 1917; #104 hit for Ray Peterson in 1960		
12/1/45+	❶²	20		5 **Doctor, Lawyer, Indian Chief** A:❶² / S:❶¹ / J:2 *A Square In The Social Circle*	$10	Capitol 220
				from the movie *The Stork Club* starring Hutton; **Paul Weston** (orch.: #1-5)		
9/20/47	5	12	●	6 **I Wish I Didn't Love You So** A:5 / S:6 / J:10 *The Sewing Machine*	$10	Capitol 409
				Joe Lilley (orch.); from the movie *The Perils Of Pauline* starring Hutton		
10/21/50	3	18		7 **A Bushel And A Peck** A:3 / S:6 / J:7 *She's A Lady* [N]	$20	RCA Victor 47-3930
				PERRY COMO and BETTY HUTTON		
				Mitchell Ayres (orch.); from the Broadway musical *Guys And Dolls* starring Robert Alda and Vivian Blaine		
12/2/50	24	2		8 **Orange Colored Sky**...A:24 *Can't Stop Talking*	$20	RCA Victor 47-3908
9/1/51	24	2		9 **The Musicians** ....A:24 *How D'Ye Do And Shake Hands* [N]	$20	RCA Victor 47-4225
				DINAH SHORE, BETTY HUTTON, TONY MARTIN, PHIL HARRIS		
				Henri René (orch.)		
6/19/54	16	2		10 **The Honeymoon's Over** ....J:16 *This Must Be The Place*	$20	Capitol F2809
				BETTY HUTTON and "TENNESSEE" ERNIE FORD		
				Billy May (orch.)		

INGLE, Red, & The Natural Seven   MEM '47

Born Ernest Ingle on 11/7/06 in Toledo, Ohio. Died on 9/7/65 (age 58). Comic singer/violinist/clarinetist/saxophonist. Worked with **Ted Weems** (1931-41) and **Spike Jones** (1943-46). Formed group The Natural Seven: Luke "Red" Roundtree (guitar), Noel Boggs (steel guitar), Herman "The Hermit" Snyder (banjo), Art Wenzel (accordion), Joseph "Country" Washbourne (suitcase), Rull Hall (bass) and Ray Hagan (drums).

DEBUT	PEAK	WKS	Gold	A-side / B-side	$	Label & Number
6/14/47	❶¹	15		1 **Temptation (Tim-Tayshun)** A:❶¹ / S:2 / J:5		
				(I Love You) For Sentimental Reasons (I Love You) For Seventy Mental Reasons [N]	$15	Capitol 412
				RED INGLE AND THE NATURAL SEVEN with Cinderella G. Stump (Jo Stafford)		
				novelty hillbilly version of song that was a #3 hit for **Bing Crosby** in 1934 and a #27 hit for The Everly Brothers in 1961		
4/24/48	15	1	●	2 **Cigareetes, Whuskey, And Wild, Wild Women** ....A:15 *Pearly Maude* [N]	$15	Capitol 15045
				Red Ingle and the Might And Main Street Choral Society (vocals)		
10/9/48	12	6		3 **Serutan Yob (A Song For Backward Boys And**		
				Girls Under 40) ....A:12 / S:24 *Oh! Nick-O-Deemo* [N]	$15	Capitol 15210
				THE UNNATURAL SEVEN		
				Karen Tedder and Enrohtwah (vocals); parody of **Nat King Cole**'s "Nature Boy"		

INK SPOTS ★24★   MEM '46

R&B vocal group from Indianapolis: Ivory "Deek" Watson, Charlie Fuqua, Orville "Hoppy" Jones and Bill Kenny. Jones died on 10/18/44 (age 39); replaced by Bill Kenny's brother, Herb Kenny. Watson left in 1945 to form **The Four Tunes**. The Kenny brothers left in 1952. Watson died on 11/4/69 (age 60). Fuqua died on 12/21/71 (age 61). Bill Kenny died on 3/23/78 (age 67). Herb Kenny died on 7/11/92 (age 78). Group inducted into the Rock and Roll Hall of Fame in 1989 as forefathers of rock 'n' roll. The Ink Spot's biggest pre-1940 hits: "Address Unknown" (#1) and "If I Didn't Care" (#2).

1)The Gypsy 2)Into Each Life Some Rain Must Fall 3)I'm Making Believe 4)To Each His Own 5)Maybe

DEBUT	PEAK	WKS	Gold	A-side / B-side	$	Label & Number
8/3/40	4	11		1 **When The Swallows Come Back To Capistrano** S:4 *What Can I Do*	$15	Decca 3195
				#80 hit for Pat Boone in 1957		
9/7/40	2⁶	14		2 **Maybe** / S:2		
10/5/40	10	1		3 **Whispering Grass (Don't Tell The Trees)** S:10	$15	Decca 3258
9/28/40	18	2		4 **Stop Pretending (So Hep You See)** ....S(e):18 *You're Breaking My Heart All Over Again*	$15	Decca 3288
10/12/40	3	14		5 **We Three (My Echo, My Shadow And Me)** / S:3		
10/19/40	17	1		6 **My Greatest Mistake** ....S(e):17	$15	Decca 3379
5/10/41	14	4		7 **Do I Worry?** / ....S(mw):14 / S(wc):15 / S(s):19		
3/1/41	17	2		8 **Java Jive** ....S(mw):17	$15	Decca 3432
10/18/41	4	8		9 **I Don't Want To Set The World On Fire** S:4 *Hey Doc!*	$15	Decca 3987
1/3/42	20	1		10 **Someone's Rocking My Dream Boat**...............................S(wc):20 *Nothin'*	$15	Decca 4045
2/20/43	2¹	16		11 **Don't Get Around Much Anymore** S:2 *Street Of Dreams*	$15	Decca 18503
				#57 hit for The Belmonts in 1961		
3/4/44	14	9		12 **Don't Believe Everything You Dream** / J:14		
				from the movie *Around The World* starring **Kay Kyser**		
3/11/44	17	1		13 **A Lovely Way To Spend An Evening** ....S(wc):17	$15	Decca 18583
				from the movie *Higher And Higher* starring **Frank Sinatra**		
3/11/44	10	8		14 **Cow-Cow Boogie (Cuma-Ti-Yi-Yi-Ay)** ....J:10 *When My Sugar Walks Down The Street* (Fitzgerald - #22)	$20	Decca 18587
				INK SPOTS And ELLA FITZGERALD		
				from the movie *Ride 'Em, Cowboy* starring Abbott & Costello		
5/6/44	7	10		15 **I'll Get By (As Long As I Have You)** / ....S:7 / J:8	$15	Decca 18579
				#3 hit for Ruth Etting in 1929 and #87 hit for **Billy Williams** in 1958		
7/29/44	11	1		16 **Someday I'll Meet You Again** ....S(s):11		
				from the movie *Passage To Marseille* starring Humphrey Bogart		
11/4/44	❶²	18	●	17 **Into Each Life Some Rain Must Fall** / ....J:❶² / S:5		
11/4/44	❶²	17		18 **I'm Making Believe** S:❶² / J:3 / A:5	$20	Decca 23356
				INK SPOTS and ELLA FITZGERALD (above 2)		
				from the movie *Sweet And Lowdown* starring **Benny Goodman**		
4/28/45	5	6		19 **I'm Beginning To See The Light** J:5 / S:7 / A:11 *That's The Way It Is*	$20	Decca 23399
				ELLA FITZGERALD and INK SPOTS		
5/4/46	❶¹³	23	●	20 **The Gypsy** J:❶¹³ / S:❶¹⁰ / A:❶² *Everyone Is Saying Hello Again (Why Must We Say Goodbye?)*	$15	Decca 18817

INK SPOTS — Cont'd

DEBUT	PEAK	WKS	Gold	A-side	$	Label & Number
6/1/46	9	11		21 **Prisoner Of Love** ....J:9 / S:10 / A:14 *I Cover The Waterfront*	$15	Decca 18864
				#16 hit for Russ Columbo in 1932; #18 hit for James Brown in 1963		
8/31/46	❶¹	14	●	22 **To Each His Own** S:❶¹ / J:3 / A:5 *I Never Had A Dream Come True*	$15	Decca 23615
				written for, but not included in the movie starring Olivia de Havilland; #21 hit for The Platters in 1960		
12/4/48+	8	8		23 **You Were Only Fooling (While I Was Falling In Love)** / ....J:8 / S:18		
				#30 hit for Vic Damone in 1965		
11/27/48	22	2		24 **Say Something Sweet To Your Sweetheart**...J:22	$15	Decca 24507
8/20/49	6	16		25 **You're Breaking My Heart** / ....J:6 / S:9 / A:10		
				based on the Italian song "La Mattinata"		
9/24/49	21	1		26 **Who Do You Know In Heaven (That Made You The Angel You Are?)** J:21	$15	Decca 24693
1/21/50	24	1		27 **Echoes**...J:24 *Land Of Love (Come My Love And Live With Me)*	$15	Decca 24741
9/2/50	26	2		28 **Sometime**..S:26 / J:28 *I Was Dancing With Someone*	$25	Decca 9-27102
				#3 hit for the Green Brothers Novelty Band in 1925		
2/10/51	18	11		29 **It Is No Secret** ....S:18 / A:21 / J:24 *I Hear A Choir*	$25	Decca 9-27326
				Bill Kenny of THE INK SPOTS and The Song Spinners		
3/3/51	23	5		30 **If** ....J:23 *A Friend Of Johnny's*	$25	Decca 9-27391
				#82 hit for The Paragons in 1961		

IVES, Burl
MEM/HOT '**62**

Born on 6/14/09 in Huntington Township, Illinois. Died of cancer on 4/14/95 (age 85). Actor/singer. Acted in several movies.

DEBUT	PEAK	WKS	Gold	A-side	$	Label & Number
2/12/49	16	1		1 **Lavender Blue (Dilly Dilly)** ....A:16 *Billy Boy*	$20	Decca 24547
				BURL IVES with Captain Stubby & The Buccaneers		
				from the Disney movie *So Dear To My Heart* starring Ives; #3 hit for Sammy Turner in 1959		
4/30/49	21	6		2 **Riders In The Sky (Cowboy Legend)** ....S:21 / A:21 *Wayfaring Stranger / Woolie Boogie Bee*	$15	Columbia 38445
				#30 hit for The Ramrods in 1961		
5/12/51	10	9		3 **On Top Of Old Smoky** ....A:10 / J:17 / S:18 *The Syncopated Clock*	$20	Columbia 4-39328
				PERCY FAITH and his Orchestra and Chorus with BURL IVES		
				adaptation of a traditional Southern Highlands folk song; Tom Glazer's parody "On Top Of Spaghetti" peaked at #14 in 1963		
7/26/52	30	1		4 **Wild Side Of Life**..J:30 *It's So-Long And Good-Bye To You*	$20	Decca 9-28055
				BURL IVES And GRADY MARTIN And His Slew Foot Five		
				#1 Country hit for Hank Thompson in 1952		

J

JACKSON, Bull Moose
HOT '**48**

Born Benjamin Jackson on 4/22/19 in Cleveland. Died of cancer on 7/31/89 (age 70). R&B singer/saxophonist.

DEBUT	PEAK	WKS	Gold	A-side	$	Label & Number
5/15/48	24	1		**I Love You Yes I Do** ....J:24 *Sneaky Pete (R&B #10)*	$40	King 4181
				BULL MOOSE JACKSON and his Buffalo Bearcats		
				new version by Jackson charted in 1961 on 7 Arts 705 (#98); #1 R&B hit in 1947		

JAMES, Dick
'**48**

Born Isaac Vapnick in 1921 in London. Died on 2/1/86 (age 65). Later became a successful music publisher.

DEBUT	PEAK	WKS	Gold	A-side	$	Label & Number
7/3/48	19	2		**You Can't Be True, Dear**.....................................S:19 / J:23 *Nature Boy (To Love and Be Loved in Return)*	$10	RCA Victor 20-2944
				with instrumental trio; #75 hit for the Mary Kaye Trio in 1959		

JAMES, Harry ★11★
MEM '**43**

Born on 3/15/16 in Albany, Georgia. Died of cancer on 7/5/83 (age 67). Star trumpet player/bandleader. Played with Ben Pollack from 1935-36 before gaining fame with **Benny Goodman** the following two years. His own band started slowly despite vocalist **Frank Sinatra**, but soon became one of the 1940s' most popular. Also featured trombonist Juan Tizol (1945), drummer Buddy Rich (1950s), and arrangers Ray Conniff & Neal Hefti. Theme song: "Ciribiribin." Married to movie star **Betty Grable** from 1943-65. He remained active until his death.

1)I've Heard That Song Before 2)I'll Get By (As Long As I Have You) 3)Sleepy Lagoon
4)It's Been A Long, Long Time 5)I Had The Craziest Dreams

Vocalists:	Clooney, Rosemary — 57	Forrest, Helen —	Kallen, Kitty — 35-37,40-42,45	Saunders, Jimmy — 10
	Day, Doris — 55	6,9,12-16,18,19,24	McAfee, Johnny — 17,20	**Sinatra, Frank** — 23,29,30,34,56
	DiVito, Buddy — 38,39,46,49-51	**Grable, Betty** — 44	Morgan, Marion — 52	Smith, Willie — 47
		Haymes, Dick — 2,5,28	Powell, Ginnie — 48	Williams, Dick — 54

DEBUT	PEAK	WKS	Gold	A-side	$	Label & Number
4/12/41	9	1		1 **Music Makers** ....S:9 *Montevideo (Mon-te-vi-DAY-o)* [I]	$10	Columbia 35932
8/30/41	10	1		2 **Lament To Love** ....S:10 *Dodgers' Fan Dance*	$10	Columbia 36222
10/18/41	19	1		3 **Trumpet Rhapsody (Parts I & II)** ....S:(wc):19 [I]	$10	Columbia 36160
11/1/41	5	10	●	4 **You Made Me Love You (I Didn't Want To Do It)** / S:5 [I]		Columbia 36296
				#1 hit for Al Jolson in 1913; #45 hit for Nat King Cole in 1959		
12/13/41	19	1		5 **A Sinner Kissed An Angel** ....S:(e):19	$10	Columbia 36296
2/28/42	2⁵	13		6 **I Don't Want To Walk Without You** S:2 *B-19*	$10	Columbia 36478
				from the movie *Sweater Girl* starring Eddie Bracken; #36 hit for Barry Manilow in 1980		
4/4/42	16	1	●	7 **Easter Parade** ....S:(wc):16 / S:(e):20 *Crazy Rhythm* [I]	$10	Columbia 36545
				#5 hit for Leo Reisman & Clifton Webb in 1933; from Broadway's *As Thousands Cheer* starring Webb; melody originally written by Irving Berlin in 1918 as "Smile And Show Your Dimple"		
4/25/42	❶⁴	18		8 **Sleepy Lagoon** S:❶⁴ *Trumpet Blues* [I]	$10	Columbia 36549
				adapted from a symphonic composition by Eric Coates		
5/2/42	16	3		9 **Skylark** ....S:(e):16 / S:(s):18 *The Clipper*	$10	Columbia 36533
				#101 hit for Linda Ronstadt in 1984		
6/6/42	4	10		10 **One Dozen Roses** S:4 *You're Too Good For Good-For-Nothing Me*	$10	Columbia 36566
8/8/42	5	7		11 **Strictly Instrumental** S:5 *When You're A Long, Long Way From Home* [I]	$10	Columbia 36579
8/8/42	16	1		12 **But Not For Me** ....S:(wc):16 *The Mole*	$10	Columbia 36599
				from the Broadway musical *Girl Crazy* starring **Ethel Merman**; #41 hit for Ketty Lester in 1962		
9/26/42	18	2		13 **I Cried For You (Now It's Your Turn To Cry Over Me)** ....S:(e):18 *Let Me Up*	$10	Columbia 36623
				#2 hit for Benny Krueger in 1923		

DEBUT	PEAK	WKS	Gold	A-side (Chart Hit) ....B-side	$	Label & Number
				JAMES, Harry — Cont'd		
10/3/42	9	1		14 **He's My Guy** ....S:9 *You're In Love With Someone Else*	$10	Columbia 36614
11/28/42	2¹	9		15 **Mister Five By Five** S:2 *That Soldier Of Mine*	$10	Columbia 36650
				from the movie *Behind The Eight Ball* starring the Ritz Brothers		
11/28/42	9	1		16 **Manhattan Serenade** / S:9		
12/12/42	19	2		17 **Daybreak** ....S(wc):19	$10	Columbia 36644
				based on the theme of "Mardi Gras" from Ferde Grofe's *Mississippi Suite* of 1926		
12/5/42+	❶²	18	●	18 **I Had The Craziest Dream** S:❶² *A Poem Set To Music*	$10	Columbia 36659
				from the movie *Springtime In The Rockies* starring **Betty Grable**		
1/30/43	❶¹³	20	●	19 **I've Heard That Song Before** / S:❶¹³		
				from the movie *Youth On Parade* starring John Hubbard; #1 R&B hit (1 week)		
1/16/43	17	2		20 **Moonlight Becomes You** ....S(e):17 / S(wc):20	$10	Columbia 36668
				from the movie *Road To Morocco* staring **Bing Crosby** and **Bob Hope**		
4/17/43	2²	13		21 **Velvet Moon** / S:2 **[I]**		
5/8/43	15	4		22 **Prince Charming** ....S(wc):15 **[I]**	$10	Columbia 36672
6/19/43	2¹	18	●	23 **All Or Nothing At All** S:2 *Flash* (James - R&B #10)	$15	Columbia 35587
				FRANK SINATRA with HARRY JAMES and his ORCHESTRA		
				recorded on 9/17/39 (originally released July 1940)		
7/31/43	4	18		24 **I Heard You Cried Last Night** S:4 *James Session*	$10	Columbia 36677
				recorded on 7/15/42; from the movie *Cinderella Swings It* starring Guy Kibbee		
1/15/44	4	10		25 **Cherry** / J:4 / S:10 **[I]**		
1/8/44	20	1		26 **Jump Town** ....S(wc):20 **[I]**	$10	Columbia 36683
				above 2 recorded on 7/22/42		
4/1/44	19	1		27 **Back Beat Boogie** ....J(terr.):19 *Night Special* **[I]**	$10	Columbia 35456
				recorded on 11/30/39 (originally released May 1940)		
4/15/44	❶⁶	28		28 **I'll Get By (As Long As I Have You)** J:❶⁶ / S:❶⁴ *Flatbush Flanagan*	$10	Columbia 36698
				recorded on 4/7/41 (originally released on Columbia 36285); #3 hit for Ruth Etting in 1929; #87 hit for **Billy Williams** in 1958		
5/27/44	17	2		29 **Every Day Of My Life** / J:17		
5/13/44	20	1		30 **On A Little Street In Singapore** J:20	$15	Columbia 36700
				FRANK SINATRA with HARRY JAMES and his Orchestra (above 2)		
				above 2 recorded in 1939		
7/8/44	15	2		31 **Memphis Blues** / ....J:15 **[I]**		
				recorded in July 1942; #4 hit for Prince's Orchestra in 1914		
8/5/44	21	1		32 **Sleepy Time Gal** ....J:21 **[I]**	$10	Columbia 36713
				recorded on 10/13/39 (Harry James, solo); #1 hit for Ben Bernie in 1926		
9/16/44	12	3		33 **Estrellita (My Little Star)** ....J:12 *My Beloved Is Rugged* **[I]**	$10	Columbia 36729
				recorded on 3/19/42; #9 hit for McKee's Orchestra in 1915		
10/28/44	21	1		34 **It's Funny To Everyone But Me** ....J:21 *Don't Take Your Love From Me*	$15	Columbia 36738
				FRANK SINATRA with HARRY JAMES and his ORCHESTRA		
				recorded in 1939		
1/27/45	❶²	19		35 **I'm Beginning To See The Light** A:❶² / J:4 / S:4 *The Love I Long For*	$10	Columbia 36758
4/7/45	8	1		36 **I Don't Care Who Knows It**...................A:8 *Guess I'll Hang My Tears Out To Dry*	$10	Columbia 36778
				from the movie *Nob Hill* starring George Raft		
5/5/45	11	2		37 **Yah-Ta-Ta, Yah-Ta-Ta** ....A:11 *All Of My Life*	$10	Columbia 36788
5/26/45	12	3		38 **The More I See You** ....A:12 *I Wish I Knew*	$10	Columbia 36794
				from the movie *Billy Rose's Diamond Horseshoe* starring **Dick Haymes** and **Betty Grable**; #16 hit for Chris Montez in 1966		
7/28/45	8	3		39 **If I Loved You** ....A:8 / J:15 *Oh, Brother!*	$10	Columbia 36806
				from the Broadway musical *Carousel* starring John Raitt; #23 hit for Chad & Jeremy in 1965		
9/8/45	8	4		40 **11:60 P.M.** ....S:8 / A:8 / J:8 *Carnival*	$10	Columbia 36827
9/22/45	2¹	14		41 **I'll Buy That Dream** ....J:2 / A:3 / S:6 *Memphis In June*	$10	Columbia 36833
				from the movie *Sing Your Way Home* starring Jack Haley		
10/13/45	❶³	17		42 **It's Been A Long, Long Time** / S:❶³ / A:❶² / J:2		
11/3/45	15	2		43 **Autumn Serenade** ....A:15 **[I]**	$10	Columbia 36838
12/8/45+	5	12		44 **I Can't Begin To Tell You** / A:5 / J:7 / S:9		
				Betty Grable (vocal, under pseudonym "Ruth Haag" - James' wife); from the movie *The Dolly Sisters* starring Grable		
11/24/45	6	10		45 **Waitin' For The Train To Come In** ....J:6 / A:8 / S:10	$20	Columbia 36867
2/2/46	9	4		46 **I'm Always Chasing Rainbows** ....A:9 / J:11 *Baby, What You Do To Me*	$10	Columbia 36899
				from the movie *The Dolly Sisters* starring **Betty Grable**; melody adapted from Chopin's "Fantasie Impromptu"; #1 hit for Charles Harrison in 1918		
6/8/46	18	2		47 **Who's Sorry Now?** ....J:18 *I Didn't Mean A Word I Said*	$10	Columbia 36973
				#3 hit for Isham Jones in 1923; #4 hit for Connie Francis in 1958		
7/13/46	15	1		48 **Do You Love Me** ....A:15 *As If I Didn't Have Enough On My Mind*	$10	Columbia 36965
				title song from the movie starring **Dick Haymes**		
9/21/46	13	2		49 **And Then It's Heaven** ....J:13 *I Guess I Expected Too Much*	$10	Columbia 37060
				from the movie *Sweetheart Of Sigma Chi* starring Elyse Knox		
9/28/46	10	2		50 **This Is Always** ....A:10 / J:14 *I've Never Forgotten*	$10	Columbia 37052
				from the movie *Three Little Girls In Blue* starring June Haver		
1/25/47	12	2		51 **Oh, But I Do** ....A:12 *Life Can Be Beautiful*	$10	Columbia 37156
				from the movie *The Time, The Place And The Girl* starring Dennis Morgan		
4/5/47	4	9		52 **Heartaches** A:4 / S:8 / J:8 *I Tipped My Hat (And Slowly Rode Away)*	$10	Columbia 37305
				#12 hit for Guy Lombardo in 1931; #7 hit for The Marcels in 1961		
4/5/47	17	1		53 **Jalousie (Jealousy)**...................................J:17 *The Man With The Horn* **[I]**	$10	Columbia 37218
				#7 hit for Leo Reisman in 1932		
8/5/50	14	8		54 **Mona Lisa**..J:14 / A:21 *La Vie En Rose*	$10	Columbia 38768
				7" 33-1/3 rpm: 1-588; from the movie *Captain Carey, U.S.A.* starring Alan Ladd; #25 hit for Carl Mann in 1959		
3/10/51	10	10		55 **Would I Love You (Love You, Love You)** ....A:10 / S:19 / J:26 *Lullaby Of Broadway*	$20	Columbia 4-39159
				HARRY JAMES & his ORCH. with DORIS DAY		
9/1/51	8	8		56 **Castle Rock**....................................A:8 / S:26 / J:26 *Deep Night*	$25	Columbia 4-39527
				FRANK SINATRA & HARRY JAMES		

JAMES, Harry — Cont'd

DEBUT	PEAK	WKS	Gold	A-side	$	Label & Number
1/10/53	18	1		57 **You'll Never Know** ....J:18 *The Continental (You Kiss While You're Dancing)*	$20	Columbia 4-39905
				ROSEMARY CLOONEY-HARRY JAMES from the movie *Hello Frisco, Hello* starring Alice Faye		
7/18/53	20	1		58 **Ruby** ....A:20 *Palladium Party* **[I]**	$15	Columbia 4-39994
				Tommy Gumina (accordion); theme from the movie *Ruby Gentry* starring Jennifer Jones and Charlton Heston; #28 hit for Ray Charles in 1960		

JAMES, Joni ★89★ MEM/HOT **'53**

Born Joan Carmello Babbo on 9/22/30 in Chicago. Worked as a dancer from age 12; model during high school. Toured Canada as a dancer in the late 1940s. First recorded for Sharp in 1952. Married to her orchestral arranger/conductor (1958-61) Tony Acquaviva (died on 9/27/86, age 61).

DEBUT	PEAK	WKS	Gold	A-side	$	Label & Number
10/18/52	**❶**[6]	23	●	1 **Why Don't You Believe Me** ....A:**❶**[6] / S:**❶**[4] / J:**❶**[3] *Purple Shades*	$25	MGM K11333
				#37 hit for The Duprees in 1963		
1/3/53	4	16	●	2 **Have You Heard /** ....A:4 / S:5 / J:6		
				#18 hit for The Duprees in 1963		
1/17/53	17	2		3 **Wishing Ring** ....J:17 / S:20 / A:20	$20	MGM K11390
2/21/53	**2**[3]	17	●	4 **Your Cheatin' Heart** ....J:2 / A:4 / S:7 *I'll Be Waiting For You*	$20	MGM K11426
				#1 Country hit for **Hank Williams** in 1953; #29 hit for Ray Charles in 1962		
5/2/53	9	9		5 **Almost Always /** ....J:9 / A:14 / S:18		
5/9/53	16	4		6 **Is It Any Wonder** ....A:16 / S:20	$20	MGM K11470
8/22/53	8	12		7 **My Love, My Love /** ....A:8 / S:10 / J:18		
				The Jack Halloran Choir (backing vocals: #2 & 7)		
8/22/53	11	12		8 **You're Fooling Someone** ....J:11 / A:18	$20	MGM K11543
				Lew Douglas (orch., all of above)		

JARRETT, Art, and his Orchestra MEM **'41**

Born on 7/20/07 in Brooklyn, New York. Died on 7/23/87 (age 80). Singer/guitarist/trombonist formerly with Earl Burtnett and **Ted Weems**; took over the late **Hal Kemp**'s band in 1941. Married to Olympic swimming champion Eleanor Holm from 1933-38.

DEBUT	PEAK	WKS	Gold	A-side	$	Label & Number
8/23/41	15	3		1 **Foolish /** ....S(mw):15		
				Gale Robbins (vocal - future movie actress)		
11/29/41	17	1		2 **Shepherd Serenade** ....S(mw):17	$10	Victor 27527
				The Smoothies (vocals)		

JEFFRIES, Herb MEM **'49**

Born on 9/24/11 in Detroit. Black baritone who sang with **Earl Hines** (1934) and **Duke Ellington** (1940-42).

DEBUT	PEAK	WKS	Gold	A-side	$	Label & Number
7/16/49	18	3		**The Four Winds And The Seven Seas** ....A:18 *Never Be It Said*	$15	Columbia 38511
				7" 33-1/3 rpm: 1-256; **Hugo Winterhalter** (orch.)		

JENKINS, Gordon, And His Orchestra ★34★ MEM/HOT **'50**

Born on 5/12/10 in Webster Groves, Missouri. Died of ALS (Lou Gehrig's disease) on 5/1/84 (age 73). Pianist/arranger in the early 1930s with Isham Jones, **Benny Goodman** and others. Musical director/conductor for Decca Records beginning in 1945. Composer of many popular songs ("San Fernando Valley," "Goodbye") and larger works (*Manhattan Tower Suite*, the *Future* song cycle for **Frank Sinatra**'s 1980 *Trilogy* album). Orchestral accompanist for Sinatra, **Louis Armstrong**, **Dick Haymes**, and many other singers.

1)Goodnight Irene 2)Again 3)Tzena Tzena Tzena 4)Maybe You'll Be There
5)Don't Cry Joe (Let Her Go, Let Her Go, Let Her Go)

Vocalists:
Armstrong, Louis — 18
Brewer, Betty — 6
Carroll, Bob — 2,17
Evans, Sandy — 8
Haines, Connie — 1
Houston, Cisco — 14
Graydon, Joe — 5
LaVere, Charles — 4
Lee, Peggy — 21-23
Stevens, Bob — 15
Weavers, The — 10,11,13,19,20
Williams, Bonnie Lou — 9
Wilson, Eileen — 7

DEBUT	PEAK	WKS	Gold	A-side	$	Label & Number
8/29/42	20	1		1 **He Wears A Pair Of Silver Wings** ....S(wc):20 *I'm Always Chasing Rainbows*	$10	Capitol 106
				from George Black's musical revue *Black Vanities*		
11/14/42	16	2		2 **White Christmas**.................................S(wc):16 *Heaven For Two* **[X]**	$10	Capitol 124
				from the movie *Holiday Inn* starring **Bing Crosby**		
12/30/44	11	1		3 **Always** ....S(wc):11 *I'm Glad There Is You* **[I]**	$10	Capitol 125
				#1 hit for both Vincent Lopez and **George Olsen** in 1926; revived popularity due to inclusion in the movie *Christmas Holiday* starring Deanna Durbin; #19 hit for Sammy Turner in 1959		
6/19/48	3	30	●	4 **Maybe You'll Be There** ....S:3 / A:3 / J:6 *Dark Eyes*	$10	Decca 24403
4/23/49	**2**[3]	23		5 **Again** ....S:2 / A:2 / J:2 *Skip To My Lou*	$10	Decca 24602
				from the movie *Road House* starring Ida Lupino and Cornel Wilde		
9/24/49	3	19		6 **Don't Cry Joe (Let Her Go, Let Her Go, Let Her Go)** .....J:3 / S:4 / A:4 *Perhaps, Perhaps, Perhaps (Quizas, Quizas, Quizas)*	$10	Decca 24720
12/17/49	26	2		7 **A Dreamer's Holiday** ....J:26 *Tell Me Why*	$10	Decca 24738
				EILEEN WILSON And GORDON JENKINS And His Orchestra		
2/18/50	3	23		8 **My Foolish Heart** ....S:3 / A:3 / J:6 *Don't Do Something To Someone Else (That You Wouldn't Want Done To You)*	$20	Decca 9-24830
				title song from the movie starring Susan Hayward		
4/29/50	4	18		9 **Bewitched** ....J:4 / S:6 / A:8 *Where In The World*	$20	Decca 9-24983
				from the Broadway musical *Pal Joey* starring **Gene Kelly**; #50 hit for the Betty Smith Group in 1958		
7/8/50	**❶**[13]	25	●	10 **Goodnight Irene /** ....S:**❶**[13] / J:**❶**[12] / A:**❶**[8]	$20	Decca 9-27077
				#75 hit for **Billy Williams** in 1959		
7/1/50	**2**[1]	17		11 **Tzena Tzena Tzena** ....S:2 / A:4 / J:5		
				GORDON JENKINS and his Orchestra and THE WEAVERS (above 2) adaptation of a popular Israeli song		

DEBUT	PEAK	WKS	Gold	A-side (Chart Hit)..B-side	$	Label & Number

JENKINS, Gordon, And His Orchestra — Cont'd

DEBUT	PEAK	WKS	Gold	A-side / B-side	$	Label & Number
9/16/50	10	10		12 **I'm Forever Blowing Bubbles**........................J:10 / S:14 / A:15 *You're Mine, You!*	$20	Decca 9-27186
				GORDON JENKINS and ARTIE SHAW		
				from the Broadway musical *The Passing Show Of 1918* starring Fred Astaire; #1 hit in 1919 for both Henry Burr & Albert Campbell, and Ben Selvin		
1/13/51	4	14		13 **So Long** (It's Been Good to Know Yuh) J:4 / S:6 / A:7 *Lonesome Traveler*	$20	Decca 9-27376
				GORDON JENKINS and his Orchestra and THE WEAVERS		
				GORDON JENKINS And His Chorus And Orchestra:		
6/9/51	21	4		14 **Rose, Rose, I Love You** / ....S:21 / J:23 / A:28		
6/23/51	30	1		15 **Unless**...S:30	$20	Decca 9-27594
10/27/51	27	1		16 **Whispering** ....S:27 *Song Of The Bayou* [I]	$20	Decca 9-27585
				Gordon Jenkins (piano solo); #1 hit for Paul Whiteman in 1920; #11 hit for Nino Tempo & **April Stevens** in 1964		
12/1/51	18	9		17 **Charmaine**...A:18 / J:22 / S:26 *When A Man Is Free*	$20	Decca 9-27859
				written to promote the 1926 movie *What Price Glory?* starring Victor McLaglen; #1 hit for **Guy Lombardo** in 1927; #69 hit for The Four Freshmen in 1956		
1/12/52	19	3		18 **When It's Sleepy Time Down South**...............A:19 / J:27 *It's All In The Game*	$25	Decca 9-27899
				LOUIS ARMSTRONG And GORDON JENKINS And His Orchestra		
				#6 hit for Paul Whiteman in 1931		
2/16/52	14	11		19 **Wimoweh**...S:14 / A:19 *Old Paint (Ride Around Little Dogies)* [F]	$20	Decca 9-27928
				adapted from the South African Zulu song "Mbube"; revised version by The Tokens hit #1 in 1961 as "The Lion Sleeps Tonight"		
4/26/52	19	1		20 **Around The Corner** (Beneath The Berry Tree)...........................A:19 *The Gandy Dancers' Ball*	$20	Decca 9-28054
				THE WEAVERS And GORDON JENKINS And His Chorus And Orchestra (above 2)		
5/24/52	21	3		21 **Be Anything** (But Be Mine) ....A:21 *Forgive Me*	$20	Decca 9-28142
				PEGGY LEE And GORDON JENKINS And His Chorus And Orchestra		
				#25 hit for Connie Francis in 1964		
6/7/52	3	13	●	22 **Lover** ....A:3 / S:10 / J:15 *You Go To My Head*	$20	Decca 9-28215
				from the movie *Love Me Tonight* starring Maurice Chevalier; #3 hit for Paul Whiteman in 1933		
8/2/52	14	4		23 **Just One Of Those Things** ....A:14 *I'm Glad There Is You (In This World Of Ordinary People)*	$20	Decca 9-28313
				PEGGY LEE And GORDON JENKINS And His Orchestra (above 2)		
				from the Broadway musical *Jubilee* starring Melville Cooper; #10 hit for Richard Himber in 1935		

JEROME, Jerry, and his Cats and Jammers   '44

Born on 6/19/12 in Brooklyn, New York. Died on 11/17/2001 (age 89). Tenor saxophonist. Played with Red Norvo, Benny Goodman, Artie Shaw, and **Lionel Hampton**.

DEBUT	PEAK	WKS	Gold	A-side / B-side	$	Label & Number
6/17/44	19	1		**Arsenic And Old Face**...................................J(terr.):19 *When I Grow Too Old To Dream* [I]	$35	Asch 501
				boogie instrumental featuring Jerome (tenor sax), Yank Lawson (trumpet) and Ray Conniff (trombone); title adapted from the 1944 movie *Arsenic And Old Lace* starring Cary Grant		

JESTERS, The   ★122★   MEM '46

White vocal trio: Dwight "Red" Latham, Walter "Wamp" Carlson and Guy Bonham. Not to be confused with the 1950s R&B group.

DEBUT	PEAK	WKS	Gold	A-side / B-side	$	Label & Number
6/14/41	20	1		1 **The Band Played On** ....S(wc):20 *Mister Gallagher And Mister Shean*	$10	Decca 3676
				from the movie *The Strawberry Blonde* starring James Cagney and Rita Hayworth; #1 hit for Dan Quinn in 1895		
6/9/45	11	3		2 **Bell Bottom Trousers**.........................A:11 / J:14 *The Bunion Brigadiers (The Infantry, The Infantry)*	$10	Decca 4452
				melody based on a traditional sea chantey		
7/28/45	12	7		3 **Fuzzy Wuzzy**...J:12 *Please No Squeeza Da Banana*	$10	Decca 18688
				MILT HERTH TRIO and THE JESTERS		
12/15/45+	10	5		4 **Chickery Chick** ....S:10 / J:13 / A:14 *Let Him Go—Let Him Tarry*	$10	Decca 18725
				EVELYN KNIGHT and THE JESTERS		
3/16/46	10	4	●	5 **McNamara's Band**..J:10 *Dear Old Donegal*	$15	Decca 23495
				The Jesters released their own version of this tune in 1940 on Decca 3268		
3/30/46	3	16		6 **Sioux City Sue** J:3 / A:5 / S:6 *You Sang My Love Song To Somebody Else*	$15	Decca 23508
9/13/47	9	4		7 **Feudin' And Fightin'** ....J:9 *Goodbye, My Lover, Goodbye*	$15	Decca 23975
				BING CROSBY and THE JESTERS (above 3)		
				from the Broadway musical *Laffing Room Only* starring **Betty Garrett**; Bob Haggart (orch., above 4)		

JOHNSON, Bill   '48

DEBUT	PEAK	WKS	Gold	A-side / B-side	$	Label & Number
11/20/48	27	1		**A Tree In The Meadow** ....J:27 *Galway Bay*	$15	Columbia 38279

JOHNSON, Buddy, And His Orchestra   HOT '49

Born Woodrow Wilson Johnson on 1/10/15 in Darlington, South Carolina. Died of a brain tumor on 2/9/77 (age 62). Black orchestra leader/painist.

DEBUT	PEAK	WKS	Gold	A-side / B-side	$	Label & Number
4/8/44	18	1		1 **When My Man Comes Home** ....J(terr.):18 *I'll Always Be With You*	$20	Decca 8655
9/1/45	14	1		2 **That's The Stuff You Gotta Watch** ....J:14 *One Of Them Good Ones*	$20	Decca 8671
				Ella Johnson (vocal, above 2)		
9/11/48	28	1		3 **Far Cry** ....A:28 *Li'l Dog* [I]	$20	Decca 48076
7/30/49	17	8		4 **Did You See Jackie Robinson Hit That Ball?**....................A:17 *Down Yonder*	$50	Decca 24675
				Buddy Johnson (vocal)		

JOHNSON, Lonnie   '48

Born Alonzo Johnson on 2/8/1889 in New Orleans. Died of a stroke on 6/16/70 (age 81). Blues singer/guitarist. Staff musician at Okeh from 1925-32. Recorded with **Louis Armstrong** and **Duke Ellington**. Guitar style highly influential to later jazz and blues guitarists.

DEBUT	PEAK	WKS	Gold	A-side / B-side	$	Label & Number
6/26/48	19	3	●	**Tomorrow Night**..J:19 *What A Woman*	$20	King 4201
				#1 R&B hit (Lonnie's theme song); #16 hit for **Horace Heidt** in 1939		

| --- | --- | --- | --- | --- | --- | --- |

JOHNSTON, Johnnie '45

Born on 12/1/15 in St. Louis. Died of heart failure on 1/6/96 (age 80). Baritone singer. Gained fame at age 15 as a junior pocket billiards champion. Hosted own CBS-radio program in the 1940s. Appeared in several movies.

11/7/42	15	5		1 **Dearly Beloved** ....S(wc):15 *Easy To Love*	$10	Capitol 120
				Gordon Jenkins (orch.); from the movie *You Were Never Lovelier* starring Fred Astaire and Rita Hayworth		
3/24/45	7	1		2 **(All Of A Sudden) My Heart Sings**..A:7 *What A Sweet Surprise*	$10	Capitol 186
				from the movie *Anchors Aweigh* starring **Frank Sinatra**; #15 hit for Paul Anka in 1959		
6/2/45	5	5		3 **Laura** / S:5 / A:9 / J:15		
				title song from the movie starring Gene Tierney and Dana Andrews		
7/14/45	9	2		4 **There Must Be A Way** ....A:9 / J:11	$10	Capitol 196
				#33 hit for **Joni James** in 1959; Paul Baron (orch., above 3)		
1/26/46	13	2		5 **One More Dream (And She's Mine)** ....A:13 *As Long As I Live*	$10	Capitol 228
				The Satisfiers (backing vocals); Lloyd Shaffer (orch.)		

JOLSON, Al MEM '28

Born Asa Yoelson on 3/26/1886 in St. Petersburg, Russia; raised in Washington DC. Died on 10/23/50 (age 64). One of the most popular entertainers of the 20th century. Starred in several movies and Broadway shows. Married to actress Ruby Keeler from 1928-39. Jolson's top 5 pre-1940 #1 hits: "Sonny Boy", "April Showers", "Swanee", "Rock-A-Bye Your Baby With A Dixie Melody" and "You Made Me Love You, I Didn't Want To Do It."

2/15/47	2[6]	14	●	1 **Anniversary Song** S:2 / A:5 / J:6 *Avalon*	$10	Decca 23714
				Morris Stoloff (orch.); based on Ivanovic's 1880 song "Danube Waves"		
5/17/47	16	1	●	2 **April Showers**..A:16 *Swanee*	$10	Decca 23470
				Carmen Dragon (orch.); new recording of Jolson's #1 hit from 1922 on Columbia 3500; originally featured in the the Broadway musical *Bombo* starring Jolson; above 2 featured in the 1946 movie *The Jolson Story* starring Larry Parks		

JONES, Spike, & His City Slickers ★46★ MEM '48

Born Lindley Armstrong Jones on 12/14/11 in Long Beach, California. Died of emphysema on 5/1/65 (age 53). Novelty bandleader. Known as "The King of Corn." His City Slickers included **Red Ingle**, **Mickey Katz**, Carl Grayson, Freedie Morgan, George Rock and Doodles Weaver.

1)*All I Want For Christmas (Is My Two Front Teeth)* 2)*Der Fuehrer's Face* 3)*Cocktails For Two*

Vocalists: Berner, Sara — 15	Ingle, Red— 5	Morgan, Fleddy — 13	Rock, George — 9,10,12,17
Grayson, Carl — 1,3	Manners, Judy — 5	Porter, Del — 2,4	Sir Fredric Gas — 15,18

10/24/42	3	10	●	1 **Der Fuehrer's Face** S:3 *I Wanna Go Back To West Virginia* [N]	$25	Bluebird 11586
				Willie Spicer (birdaphone); from the Disney animated short *In Nutzi Land*		
6/17/44	20	1		2 **Behind Those Swinging Doors**....J(terr).:20 *I'll Get By (As Long As I Have You)* (**Four King Sisters**) [N]	$20	Bluebird 30-0821
1/27/45	4	9	●	3 **Cocktails For Two** / S:4 / A:5 / J:9 [N]	$20	
				from the movie *Murder At The Vanities* starring Jack Oakie; #1 hit for **Duke Ellington** in 1934		
3/3/45	14	1		4 **Leave The Dishes In The Sink, Ma** J:14	$20	Victor 20-1628
4/28/45	5	6		5 **Chloe** S:5 / A:11 *A Serenade To A Jerk* [N]	$20	Victor 20-1654
				featured in the movie *Bring On The Girls* starring Veronica Lake; #7 hit for Paul Whiteman in 1928 (as "Chloe (Song Of The Swamp)")		
11/24/45	10	1		6 **Holiday For Strings**..S:10 *Drip, Drip, Drip-(Sloppy Lagoon)* [I-N]	$20	Victor 20-1733
7/27/46	8	1		7 **Hawaiian War Chant (Ta-Hu-Wa-Hu-Wai)** ....S:8 / A:14 / J:19 *The Glow-Worm* [N]	$20	RCA Victor 20-1893
				SPIKE JONES and his WACKY WAKAKIANS		
				#89 hit for **Billy Vaughn** in 1959		
6/12/48	6	15		8 **William Tell Overture** ....S:6 / A:10 / J:17 *The Man On The Flying Trapeze* [N]	$25	RCA Victor 20-2861
				horse race ("Feetlebaum") commentary by Doodles Weaver, backed by the "Lone Ranger Theme"; #3 hit for Sousa's Band in 1901; released with 2 different B-sides		
11/27/48	❶[3]	8	●	9 **All I Want For Christmas (Is My Two Front Teeth)** A:❶[3] / S:❶[1] / J:4 *Happy New Year* [X-N]	$20	RCA Victor 20-3177
4/16/49	24	2		10 **Ya Wanna Buy A Bunny?** ....S:24 *Knock Knock (Who's There?)* [N]	$30	RCA Victor 47-2894
				78 rpm: 20-3359		
8/27/49	13	9		11 **Dance Of The Hours** ....S:13 / A:13 *None But The Lonely Heart* [N]	$30	RCA Victor 47-2992
				78 rpm: 20-3516; Indianapolis car race commentary by Doodles Weaver; same melody as Allen Sherman's 1963 hit "Hello Mudduh, Hello Faddum!"; #9 hit for Arthur Pryor's Band in 1905		
1/7/50-	18	1		12 **My Two Front Teeth (All I Want for Christmas)**.......................S:18 *Happy New Year* [X-N-R]	$25	RCA Victor 47-2963
				78 rpm: 20-3177; new title - same recording as #9 above		
4/29/50	13	3		13 **Chinese Mule Train** ....S:13 *Riders In The Sky* [N]	$25	RCA Victor 47-3741
				from the movie *Singing Guns* starring **Vaughn Monroe**; parody of **Frankie Laine**'s "Mule Train"		
12/23/50	7	3		14 **Rudolph The Red-Nosed Reindeer** ....A:7 / S:11 / J:21	$25	RCA Victor 47-3934
				Mommy, Won't You Buy A Baby Brother (Or Sister For Me) [X-N]		
				Rudolph (himself) with Santa Claus and The Four Reindeer (vocals); 9 & 14: reissued in 1953 on RCA Victor's Junior Series #417 with a picture sleeve		
1/20/51	13	5		15 **Tennessee Waltz**..A:13 / S:16 *I Haven't Been Home For Three Whole Nights* [N]	$25	RCA Victor 47-4011
				#35 hit for Sam Cooke in 1964		
1/5/52-	22	1		16 **Rudolph The Red-Nosed Reindeer** ..A:22 *(All I Want For Christmas Is) My Two Front Teeth* [X-N-R]	$20	RCA Victor 47-4315
12/20/52	4	3		17 **I Saw Mommy Kissing Santa Claus** A:4 / S:7 / J:9 *Winter* [X-N]	$20	RCA Victor 47-5067
1/31/53	20	1		18 **I Went To Your Wedding** ....S:20 *I'll Never Work There Any More* [N]	$20	RCA Victor 47-5107

JORDAN, Louis, And His Tympany Five ★54★   MEM '44

Born on 7/8/08 in Brinkley, Arkansas. Died of a heart attack on 2/4/75 (age 66). R&B vocalist/saxophonist/bandleader. First recorded for Brunswick in 1929, with the Jungle Band. With Clarence Williams in New York, early 1930s, and Chick Webb from 1936-38. Formed own band at Elk's Rendezvous in 1938; later known as the Tympany Five, his backing band. Innovative, extremely popular vocal style paved the way for later R&B styles. In movies *Follow The Boys*, *Beware*, *Meet Miss Bobby Sox*, and *Swing Parade Of 1946*. Active into the early '60s. Inducted into the Rock and Roll Hall of Fame in 1987 as a rock 'n' roll forefather.

1)*G.I. Jive* 2)*Is You Is Or Is You Ain't (Ma' Baby)* 3)*Caldonia*

DEBUT	PEAK	WKS	Gold	A-side	$	Label & Number
2/12/44	16	1		1 Ration Blues ....J:16 *Deacon Jones* (C&W #7)	$20	Decca 8654
				#1 Country hit (3 weeks)		
5/6/44	❶²	25	●	2 G.I. Jive / J:❶² / S:3		
7/29/44	2³	19		3 Is You Is Or Is You Ain't (Ma' Baby) J:2 / S:5	$20	Decca 8659
				from the movie *Follow The Boys* starring **Marlene Dietrich**; #1 Country hit (5 weeks); #81 hit for Buster Brown in 1960		
3/24/45	11	2		4 You Can't Get That No More...A:11 *Mop! Mop!* (R&B #1) **[N]**	$15	Decca 8668
5/26/45	6	8	●	5 Caldonia................................S:6 / J:9 / A:16 *Somebody Done Changed The Lock On My Door* (R&B #3)	$15	Decca 8670
				#95 hit for James Brown in 1964		
7/21/45	14	1		6 (Yip Yip De Hootie) My Baby Said Yes...........................J:14 *Your Socks Don't Match*	$15	Decca 23417
				BING CROSBY and LOUIS JORDAN And His Tympany Five		
1/5/46	9	2		7 Buzz Me.......................................S:9 / J:10 *Don't Worry 'Bout That Mule* (R&B #1)	$15	Decca 18734
7/6/46	7	6		8 Stone Cold Dead In The Market (He Had It Coming)..........A:7 / S:9 / J:13 *Petootie Pie* (R&B #3)	$20	Decca 23546
				ELLA FITZGERALD and LOUIS JORDAN And His Tympany Five		
8/31/46	7	16	●	9 Choo Choo Ch'Boogie...............................J:7 / S:8 / A:10 *That Chick's Too Young To Fry* (R&B #3)	$15	Decca 23610
11/2/46	17	2		10 Ain't That Just Like A Woman (They'll Do It		
				Every Time) ....J:17 *If It's Love You Want Baby, That's Me*	$15	Decca 23669
				#33 hit for Fats Domino in 1961		
1/4/47	6	6		11 Ain't Nobody Here But Us Chickens ....J:6 *Let The Good Times Roll* (R&B #2)	$15	Decca 23741
3/8/47	6	4		12 Open The Door, Richard! ....J:6 / S:7 *It's So Easy* **[N]**	$15	Decca 23841
7/3/48	23	3		13 Run Joe...J:23 / A:24 / S:29 *All For The Love Of Lil* (R&B #13)	$15	Decca 24448
				The Calypso Boys (backing vocals)		
6/11/49	9	13		14 Baby, It's Cold Outside...J:9 / S:17 *Don't Cry, Cry Baby*	$20	Decca 24644
				ELLA FITZGERALD And LOUIS JORDAN And His Tympany Five		
				from the movie *Neptune's Daughter* starring Esther Williams		
10/22/49	21	5	●	15 Saturday Night Fish Fry (Parts I & II)...........................J:21 / S:27	$15	Decca 24725
				10 of the above 15 titles hit #1 on the R&B charts (79 weeks total); Louis Jordan (vocal, all of above)		

JUBALAIRES, The   '46

R&B vocal group: Caleb Ginyard, Orville Brooks, Ted Brooks and George McFadden, with Everett Barksdale (guitar). Ginyard died on 8/11/78 (age 68). Orville Brooks died on 8/30/97 (age 78).

DEBUT	PEAK	WKS	A-side	$	Label & Number
5/11/46	14	1	1 I Know..J:14 *Get Together With The Lord*	$25	Decca 18782
			ANDY KIRK AND HIS ORCHESTRA and THE JUBALAIRES		
			#2 R&B hit		
6/17/50	25	1	2 That Old Piano Roll Blues ....J:25 / S:26 *A Dream Is A Wish Your Heart Makes*	$35	Capitol F845

JURGENS, Dick, and his Orchestra ★87★   MEM '40

Born on 1/9/10 in Sacramento, California. Died of cancer on 10/5/95 (age 85). Own big band from 1928. Wrote "Elmer's Tune," "Careless," "One Dozen Roses," "If I Knew Then," and many others. Vocalist **Eddy Howard** had over 40 Pop hits. Started an electronics business with brother Will in the mid-1950s.

1)*Careless* 2)*In An Old Dutch Garden (By An Old Dutch Mill)* 3)*Elmer's Tune*

Vocalists: Castle, Jimmy — 11,12   Galante, Al — 11   Kemper, Ronnie — 4
            Cool, Harry — 5,6,9,10   **Howard, Eddy** — 1-3   Moreno, Buddy — 8

DEBUT	PEAK	WKS	A-side	$	Label & Number
1/6/40	6	3	1 Careless J:6 *I Only Want A Buddy - Not A Sweetheart*	$15	Vocalion 5235
1/6/40	9	1	2 Bluebirds In The Moonlight..J:9 *Faithful Forever*	$15	Vocalion 5181
			from the animated movie *Gulliver's Travels*		
3/2/40	8	3	3 In An Old Dutch Garden (By An Old Dutch Mill)...J:8 *The Little Red Fox (N'Ya N'Ya Ya Can't Catch Me)*	$15	Vocalion 5263
5/4/40	8	4	4 Cecelia..J(terr.):8 *Love Song Of Renaldo* **[N]**	$15	Vocalion 5405
			#7 hit for "Whispering" Jack Smith in 1926		
8/3/40	18	2	5 Make-Believe Island..S(mw):18 *The Kitten With The Big Green Eyes*	$15	Vocalion 5540
8/10/40	14	6	6 A Million Dreams Ago ....S(wc):14 *Avalon*	$10	Okeh 5628
10/11/41	8	6	7 Elmer's Tune..S:8 *You're The Sunshine Of My Heart* **[I]**	$10	Okeh 6209
4/18/42	17	3	8 One Dozen Roses ....S(mw):17 / S(wc):17 *Always In My Heart*	$10	Okeh 6636
1/30/43	16	2	9 (As Long As You're Not In Love With Anyone Else) Why Don't You		
			Fall In Love With Me? ....S(mw):16 *Hip Hip Hooray*	$10	Columbia 36643
3/20/43	16	3	10 You'd Be So Nice To Come Home To ....S(s):16 *I'm So-So-So-So-So In Love*	$10	Columbia 36669
			from the movie *Something To Shout About* starring Don Ameche		
2/15/47	14	1	11 (Oh Why, Oh Why, Did I Ever Leave) Wyoming.................................A:14 *Bless You*	$10	Columbia 37210
10/4/47	17	1	12 When You Were Sweet Sixteen ....A:17 *On The Avenue*	$10	Columbia 37803
			from the movie *The Great John L.* starring Greg McClure; #1 hit in 1900 for both George J. Gaskin and Jere Mahoney		

PICTURE SLEEVES — EARLY 1950's

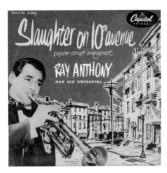

Ray Anthony
Slaughter On 10th Avenue

Gene Autry
Frosty The Snow Man

Gene Autry
Here Comes Santa Claus

Gene Autry
Peter Cottontail

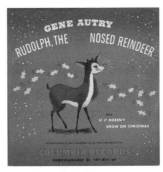

Gene Autry
Rudolph, The Red-Nosed Reindeer

Tony Bennett
Stranger In Paradise

Ray Bolger
Once In Love With Amy

Jimmy Boyd
I Saw Mommy Kissing Santa Claus

Rosemary Clooney & Gene Autry
The Night Before Christmas Song

Perry Como
No Other Love

Bing Crosby
Rudolph The Red-Nosed Reindeer

Vic Damone
Wonder Why

Jose Ferrer
Woman (Uh, Huh)

Eddie Fisher
Generic sleeve — used for many Fisher releases

Arthur Godfrey
What Is A Boy

Phil Harris
The Thing

Spike Jones
I Saw Mommy Kissing Santa Claus

Spike Jones
Rudolph The Red-Nosed Reindeer

Eartha Kitt
Santa Baby

Mario Lanza
If You Were Mine

Mario Lanza
The Loveliest Night Of The Year

Tony Martin
Here

Guy Mitchell
My Heart Cries For You (insert)

Patti Page
The Mama Doll Song

K

★105★   **KALLEN, Kitty**   MEM/HOT '54
Born on 5/25/22 in Philadelphia. Won first amateur contest at age eight. Got her start singing on the *Horn & Hardt Children's Hour* in Philadelphia at age 12. Big band singer with Jack Teagarden, **Jimmy Dorsey**, **Harry James** and **Artie Shaw**.

4/30/49	30	1		1 Kiss Me Sweet...A:30 *I Don't See Me In Your Eyes Anymore* $10	Mercury 5265
				Mitch Miller (orch.)	
5/13/50	17	1		2 Juke Box Annie ....J:17 *Choo'n Gum* $25	Mercury 5417-X45
				Harry Geller (orch.)	
9/9/50	10	12		3 Our Lady Of Fatima ....S:10 / J:15 / A:19 *Honestly I Love You* $20	Mercury 5466-X45
				Jimmy Carroll (orch.)	
3/3/51	9	10		4 The Aba Daba Honeymoon..........................A:9 / J:18 / S:24 *I Don't Want To Love You* $20	Mercury 5586-X45
				RICHARD HAYES & KITTY KALLEN (above 2)	
				George Siravo (orch.); from the movie *Two Weeks With Love* starring **Debbie Reynolds** and **Carleton Carpenter**;	
				#1 hit for Arthur Collins & Byron Harlan in 1914	
4/17/54	**❶**[9]	26	●	5 Little Things Mean A Lot S:**❶**[9] / A:**❶**[8] / J:**❶**[7] *I Don't Think You Love Me Anymore* $15	Decca 9-29037
				#35 hit for **Joni James** in 1960	
7/17/54	4	14	●	6 In The Chapel In The Moonlight A:4 / S:5 / J:5 *Take Everything But You* $15	Decca 9-29130
				#1 hit for **Shep Fields** in 1936; #25 hit for **Dean Martin** in 1967	
11/27/54	30	1		7 I Want You All To Myself (Just You)................................S:30 *Don't Let The Kiddy Geddin* $15	Decca 9-29268
				Jack Pleis (orch., above 3)	

KAPELL, William   '53
Born on 9/20/22 in New York City. Died in a plane crash on 10/29/53 (age 31). Classical pianist.

11/14/53	19	2		Rachmaninoff: The Eighteenth Variation (from the Rhapsody on a	
				Theme of Paganini, Op. 43) ....S:19 *Rachmaninoff: Introduction, Theme And Five Variations* [I] $20	RCA Victor 49-4210
				Fritz Reiner conducting the Robin Hood Dell Orch. of Philadelphia; same tune as the title song from the movie *The Story Of Three*	
				Loves by Jerry Murad Of **The Harmonicats**	

KARAS, Anton   '50
Born on 7/1/06 in Vienna, Austria. Died on 1/9/85 (age 78). Zither player.

| 2/18/50 | **❶**[11] | 27 | ● | "The Third Man" Theme   S:**❶**[11] / A:4 / J:4 *The Cafe Mozart Waltz* [I] $25 | London 45-30005 |
| | | | | 78 rpm: 536; performed by Karas in the movie *The Third Man* starring Orson Welles; #47 hit for Herb Alpert & The Tijuana Brass in 1965 | |

KASSEL, Art, and his Kassels-in-the-Air   MEM '32
Born on 1/18/1896 in Chicago. Died on 2/3/65 (age 69). Orchestra leader. Kassel's biggest pre-1940 hit: "Hell's Bells" (#2).

1/3/42	18	2		1 Angeline ....S(mw):18 *I'm A Little Teapot* $15	Bluebird 11356
				male trio and chorus (vocals)	
6/10/44	22	1		2 I'm In Love With Someone (Who Is Not In Love	
				With Me) ....J(terr.):22 *What A Difference A Day Made* $15	Hit 7090
1/18/47	15	1		3 I Love You (For Sentimental Reasons) ....J:15 *Sooner Or Later* $100	Vogue 781
				ART KASSEL And His Orchestra	
				record is from the Vogue "Picture Record" series; #17 hit for Sam Cooke in 1958; Jimmy Featherstone (vocal, above 2)	

KATZ, Mickey, and His Orchestra   '50
Born on 6/15/09 in Cleveland. Died on 4/30/85 (age 75). Formerly with **Spike Jones**; specialized in Yiddish humor. Father of actor Joel Grey.

3/11/50	18	2		1 (Put Another Nickel In) Music! Music! Music! ....A:18 *The Wedding Samba* [N] $20	Capitol F862
				#54 hit for The Sensations in 1961	
9/29/51	22	3		2 Come On-A My House ....S:22 *Sound Off* [N] $20	Capitol F1788
				from the off-Broadway musical *The Son*	
3/1/52	28	1		3 Herring Boats (Shrimp Boats) ....S:28 *Sin* [N] $20	Capitol F1961

KAVELIN, Al, and his Cascading Chords   '40
Born on 3/21/03 in New York City. Died in January 1982 (age 78). Orchestra leader. **Carmen Cavallaro** was his featured pianist in the 1930s.

| 10/12/40 | 15 | 3 | | Practice Makes Perfect................................S(mw):15 *The Swiss Bellringer* $15 | Okeh 5746 |
| | | | | Bill Darnel (vocal) | |

KAY, Beatrice   '49
Born Hannah Beatrice Kuper on 4/21/07 in New York City. Died on 11/8/86 (age 79). Popular on radio and stage for vocal parodies of turn-of-the-century songs.

2/5/49	21	2		I've Been Waitin' For Your Phone Call For Eighteen	
				Years (Maybe You Don't Love Me Anymore)............A:21 *How Come The Mortgage Got Paid* [N] $15	Columbia 38373
				Mitchell Ayres (orch.)	

KAYE, Buddy, Quintet   MEM '49
Born on 1/3/18 in New York City. Lyricist on many popular songs, including "Till The End Of Time" and " 'A' You're Adorable."

| 5/7/49 | 27 | 1 | | "A" You're Adorable (The Alphabet Song)...................J:27 *Don't Save Your Kisses For Tomorrow* $10 | MGM 10310 |
| | | | | Artie Malvin (vocal) | |

KAYE, Danny   MEM '48
Born David Daniel Kaminsky on 1/18/13 in Brooklyn, New York. Died of heart failure on 3/3/87 (age 74). Legendary comedic actor/singer. Acted in numerous movies and Broadway shows. Married lyricist Sylvia Fine in 1940.

11/22/47+	3	11		1 Civilization (Bongo, Bongo, Bongo) S:3 / J:3 / A:7 *Bread And Butter Woman* [N] $15	Decca 23940
				from the Broadway musical *Angel In The Wings* starring **Hank Ladd**	
7/17/48	18	6		2 The Woody Woodpecker ....J:18 / S:19	Decca 24462
				Put 'Em In A Box, Tie 'Em With A Ribbon (And Throw 'Em In The Deep Blue Sea) [N] $15	
				DANNY KAYE - ANDREWS SISTERS (above 2)	
				The Harmonica Gentlemen (instrumental backing); from the Walter Lantz cartoon	
1/14/50	26	2		3 I've Got A Lovely Bunch Of Cocoanuts...................S:26 *The Peony Bush* [N] $15	Decca 24784
				The Harmonaires (backing vocals)	
6/3/50	21	1		4 C'est Si Bon (It's So Good)......................................J:21 *Wilhelmina* $20	Decca 9-24932
				Lee Gordon Singers (backing vocals); #22 hit for Conway Twitty in 1961; Vic Schoen (orch.: #1, 3 & 4)	
9/22/51	29	1		5 Black Strap Molasses ....J:29 / A:30 *How D' Ye Do And Shake Hands* [N] $25	Decca 9-27748
				DANNY KAYE-JIMMY DURANTE-JANE WYMAN-GROUCHO MARX	
				4 Hits And A Miss (backing vocals); **Sonny Burke** (orch.)	

KAYE, Sammy [Swing and Sway with] ★9★   MEM/HOT '46

Born on 3/13/10 in Rocky River, Ohio. Died of cancer on 6/2/87 (age 77). Leader of popular "sweet" dance band with the slogan "Swing and Sway with Sammy Kaye." Also played clarinet and alto sax. Kaye's pre-1940 #1 hits: "Love Walked In" and "Rosalie."

1)Daddy 2)The Old Lamp-Lighter 3)Harbor Lights 4)Chickery Chick 5)I'm A Big Girl Now

Vocalists:

Alamo, Tony — 53,56,59,60	Cornell, Don —	Leslie, Laura — 51	Three Kadets/Three Kaydets/
Barclay, Betty — 32,36	13,14,39-45,48,49,51,52,55	Marlow, Mary — 33,38	Kaydets, The — 6,16,37,39,
Brown, Jimmy — 5	Cross, Maury (the dragon) — 8	Norman, Nancy —	43-50,52,54,57,59,61
Burke, Clyde — 2	Gingell, George — 8	15,17,21,24-27,29	Williams, Billy —
Cantor, Eddie — 58	Kaye Choir, The —	Russo, Tony — 62,63	18,19,22,23,25-28,30,31,34,35
Clay, Jeffrey — 64	7,22,24,26,48,53,56,64	Ryan, Tommy — 1,3,4,9,12	Wright, Arthur — 10,20
	Kirk, Lisa — 58		choir/chorus — 10,35,37,40,43
			glee club — 11,41,42,60,63

DEBUT	PEAK	WKS		A-side / B-side	$	Label & Number
5/25/40	7	4	1	**Let There Be Love** ....J:7 *The Peasant Serenade*	$10	Victor 26564
8/3/40	13	1	2	**Where Was I?** / ....S(e):13	$10	
				from the movie *'Til We Meet Again* starring Merle Oberon and George Brent		
7/27/40	19	1	3	**Make Believe Island**..S(wc):19	$10	Victor 26594
12/21/40	19	2	4	**A Nightingale Sang In Berkeley Square** ....S(e):19 *Dream Valley*	$10	Victor 26795
				from the London musical *New Faces*		
1/4/41	14	1	5	**Along The Santa Fe Trail** ....S(e):14 *Down The Gypsy Trail*	$10	Victor 27220
				title song from the movie		
5/24/41	10	1	6	**Until Tomorrow (Goodnight My Love)** ....S:10 *The Sidewalk Serenade*	$10	Victor 27262
6/7/41	❶⁸	15	7	**Daddy** ....S:❶⁸ *Two Hearts That Pass In The Night*	$10	Victor 27391
7/26/41	17	4	8	**The Reluctant Dragon** ....S(e):17 *Sleepy Serenade* **[N]**	$10	Victor 27449
				title song from the live-action/animated movie		
12/13/41	18	2	9	**Minka** ....S(mw):18 *Wasn't It You?*	$10	Victor 27567
1/10/42	16	4	10	**There'll Be Blue Birds Over The White Cliffs Of Dover** .....S(mw):16 / S(s):16 / S(e):17 *Madelaine*	$10	Victor 27704
1/31/42	3	5	11	**Remember Pearl Harbor** ....S:3 *Dear Mom*	$10	Victor 27738
7/11/42	17	1	12	**Johnny Doughboy Found A Rose In Ireland** ....S(mw):17 / S(s):19 *Here You Are*	$10	Victor 27870
9/5/42	3	7	13	**I Left My Heart At The Stage Door Canteen** ....S:3 *South Wind*	$10	Victor 27932
				from the Broadway musical *This Is The Army* starring **Burl Ives**		
11/14/42	20	1	14	**I Came Here To Talk For Joe**......................................S(e):20	$10	Victor 27944
				(I'm Headin' for the Blue Horizon) Where The Mountains Meet The Sky		
1/23/43	19	1	15	**There Will Never Be Another You**.........................S(mw):19 *Let's Bring New Glory To Old Glory*	$10	Victor 27949
				from the movie *Iceland* starring Sonja Henie; #33 hit for Chris Montez in 1966		
4/24/43	17	1	16	**Taking A Chance On Love** ....S(s):17 / S(wc):18 / S(mw):20 *You And Your Kiss*	$10	Victor 27239
				originally released in 1940; from the movie *Cabin In The Sky* starring Lena Horne		
12/30/44+	7	8	17	**There Goes That Song Again** / ....J:7 / S:8 / A:11		
				from the movie *Carolina Blues* starring Kay Kyser		
1/13/45	10	3	18	**You Always Hurt The One You Love**...........................J:10	$10	Victor 20-1606
				#12 hit for Clarence Henry in 1961		
1/20/45	4	7	19	**Don't Fence Me In** / ....S:4 / A:4 / J:10		
				from the movie *Hollywood Canteen* starring Bette Davis; #45 hit for **Tommy Edwards** in 1960		
1/13/45	10	4	20	**Always** ....J:10 / A:13	$10	Victor 20-1610
				#1 hit for Vincent Lopez and **George Olsen** in 1926; revived popularity due to inclusion in the movie *Christmas Holiday* starring Deanna Durbin; #19 hit for Sammy Turner in 1959		
2/17/45	6	7	21	**Saturday Night (Is The Loneliest Night In The Week)** ..A:6 / J:8 *I Don't Want To Love You (Like I Do)*	$10	Victor 20-1635
4/14/45	10	5	22	**Just A Prayer Away** / ....S:10 / A:12 / J:13	$10	
4/14/45	10	1	23	**All Of My Life** A:10	$10	Victor 20-1642
8/4/45	6	7	24	**Gotta Be This Or That** / ....J:6 / A:7	$10	
8/11/45	10	1	25	**Good, Good, Good (That's You–That's You)** S:10	$10	Victor 20-1684
10/20/45	❶⁴	16	26	**Chickery Chick** ....A:❶⁴ / S:❶³ / J:❶² *I Lost My Job Again*	$10	Victor 20-1726
10/27/45	10	5	27	**I'll Be Walkin' With My Honey (Soon, Soon, Soon)** / ...A:10 / J:11	$10	
11/10/45	17	1	28	**Promises** A:17	$10	Victor 20-1713
12/8/45+	9	7	29	**I Can't Begin To Tell You**...................................A:9 / J:12 *What Makes The Sunset?*	$10	Victor 20-1720
				from the movie *The Dolly Sisters* starring **Betty Grable**		
12/15/45+	4	10	30	**It Might As Well Be Spring** ....J:4 / S:8 / A:8 *Give Me The Simple Life*	$10	Victor 20-1738
				from the movie *State Fair* starring **Dick Haymes** and Dana Andrews		
3/2/46	6	8	31	**Atlanta, GA.**..A:6 / J:7 *I Didn't Mean A Word I Said*	$10	Victor 20-1795
3/30/46	❶¹	15	32	**I'm A Big Girl Now** ....S:❶¹ / J:2 / A:5 *Put Your Little Foot Right Out*	$10	RCA Victor 20-1812
5/11/46	3	17	33	**The Gypsy** ....A:3 / J:3 / S:4 *(Gee! I'm Glad To Be) The One That I Am*	$10	RCA Victor 20-1844
5/18/46	3	11	34	**Laughing On The Outside, Crying On The Inside** ....J:3 / S:7 / A:11 *I've Never Forgotten*	$10	RCA Victor 20-1856
11/2/46	❶⁷	17	35	**The Old Lamp-Lighter** ....S:❶⁷ / J:❶⁷ / A:❶¹ *Touch-Me-Not*	$10	RCA Victor 20-1963
				#5 hit for The Browns in 1960		
11/16/46	8	8	36	**Sooner Or Later (You're Gonna Be Comin' Around)** / ...J:8 / A:14		
12/21/46+	11	5	37	**Zip-A-Dee Doo-Dah** ....J:11 / A:13	$10	RCA Victor 20-1976
				above 2 from the Disney movie *Song Of The South* starring James Baskett; #8 hit for Bob B. Soxx & The Blue Jeans in 1963		
5/10/47	16	1	38	**The Egg And I** ....A:16 *After Graduation Day*	$10	RCA Victor 20-2209
				title song from the movie starring Claudette Colbert and Fred MacMurray		
5/24/47	2¹	22	39	**That's My Desire** / ....J:2 / S:3 / A:5		
				#69 hit for The Sensations in 1962		
5/24/47	8	8	40	**Red Silk Stockings And Green Perfume**.....................J:8 / A:15	$10	RCA Victor 20-2251
10/4/47	5	5	41	**An Apple Blossom Wedding** / ....J:5 / S:6		
9/20/47	17	1	42	**The Echo Said "No"** J:17	$10	RCA Victor 20-2330

DEBUT	PEAK	WKS	Gold	A-side / B-side	$	Label & Number
				KAYE, Sammy [Swing and Sway with] — Cont'd		
11/15/47+	3	16		43 **Serenade Of The Bells** S:3 / J:7 *That's What Every Young Girl Should Know*	$10	RCA Victor 20-2372
3/20/48	10	4		44 **I Love You, Yes I Do** ....A:10 *The Last Polka*	$10	RCA Victor 20-2674
5/15/48	8	10		45 **Tell Me A Story**.................................J:8 / S:11 *I Wouldn't Be Surprised*	$10	RCA Victor 20-2761
5/29/48	11	7		46 **Baby Face** ....J:11 / S:17 *Miss You*	$10	RCA Victor 20-2879
				#1 hit for **Jan Garber** *in 1926; #14 hit for* **The Wing And A Prayer Fife And Drum Corps.** *in 1976*		
12/11/48+	4	16		47 **Lavender Blue (Dilly Dilly)** / J:4 / S:5 / A:11		
				from the Disney movie So Dear To My Heart *starring* **Burl Ives**; *#3 hit for* **Sammy Turner** *in 1959*		
11/13/48+	14	6		48 **Down Among The Sheltering Palms**.............................J:14 / A:17	$10	RCA Victor 20-3100
				#3 hit for the **Lyrio Quartet** *in 1915*		
2/5/49	3	22		49 **Careless Hands** / J:3 / A:5 / S:7		
2/5/49	13	10		50 **Powder Your Face With Sunshine**........................A:13 / S:14 / J:14	$10	RCA Victor 20-3321
5/28/49	29	1		51 **Kiss Me Sweet**............................J:29 *A Chapter In My Life Called Mary*	$10	RCA Victor 20-3420
6/11/49	2¹	24		52 **Room Full Of Roses** A:2 / J:2 / S:3 *It's Summertime Again*	$15	RCA Victor 47-2908
				78 rpm: 20-3441; #50 hit for **Mickey Gilley** *in 1974*		
6/18/49	3	11		53 **The Four Winds And The Seven Seas** A:3 / S:7 / J:11 *Out Of Love*	$15	RCA Victor 47-2923
				78 rpm: 20-3459		
10/1/49	24	6		54 **Dime A Dozen** ....J:24 *Everything They Said Came True*	$15	RCA Victor 47-3010
				78 rpm: 20-3532		
2/4/50	2⁶	24		55 **It Isn't Fair** A:2 / J:2 / S:3 *My Lily And My Rose*	$15	RCA Victor 47-3115
				78 rpm: 20-3609		
3/25/50	11	10		56 **Wanderin'** ....A:11 / S:11 / J:18 *The Bicycle Song*	$15	RCA Victor 47-3203
				78 rpm: 20-3680; same melody used for **Tom Jones'** *1969 hit "I'll Never Fall In Love Again"*		
5/6/50	5	12		57 **Roses** J:5 / S:13 / A:24 *Tiddley Winkie Woo*	$15	RCA Victor 47-3754
6/24/50	27	1		58 **The Old Piano Roll Blues**........................J:27 / S:29 *Juke Box Annie (Doodle-Oodle-Oo)*	$20	RCA Victor 47-3751
				EDDIE CANTOR, LISA KIRK, and the SAMMY KAYE ORCHESTRA		
9/9/50	❶⁴	27		59 **Harbor Lights** J:❶⁴ / S:❶² / A:2 *Sugar Sweet*	$15	Columbia 4-38963
				#6 hit for **Frances Langford** *in 1937; #8 hit for* **The Platters** *in 1960*		
8/18/51	16	8		60 **Longing For You** ....J:16 / S:25 *Mary Rose (Bloesem Van Seringen)*	$15	Columbia 4-39499
11/17/51	25	2		61 **(It's No) Sin** ....A:25 *Jealous Eyes*	$15	Columbia 4-39567
6/7/52	28	1		62 **You** ....S:28 / A:30 *Oh, How I Miss You Tonight*	$15	Columbia 4-39724
				SAMMY KAYE with The Swing & Sway Strings		
				based on "Musetta's Waltz" from La Boheme *- same melody as* **Della Reese's** *1959 hit "Don't You Know"*		
8/2/52	11	13		63 **Walkin' To Missouri** ....J:11 / A:14 / S:18 *One For The Wonder*	$15	Columbia 4-39769
10/17/53	15	7		64 **In The Mission Of St. Augustine**........................S:15 / J:19 *No Stone Unturned*	$15	Columbia 4-40061
				KELLY, Gene — see GARLAND, Judy		
				KELLY, Monty, And His Orchestra MEM/HOT **'60**		
				Born on 6/8/10 in Modesto, California. Died on 3/15/71 (age 60). Conductor/arranger. Trumpeter with Paul Whiteman in the early 1940s.		
8/15/53	19	1		**Tropicana** ....A:19 *Life In New York* **[I]**	$20	Essex 325 (45)
				KELLY, Paula — see MODERNAIRES, The		
				KELLY, Willie, and his Orchestra MEM **'43**		
6/12/43	6	4		1 **You'll Never Know** / S:6		
				from the movie Hello Frisco, Hello *starring* Alice Faye		
7/10/43	18	2		2 **Comin' In On A Wing And A Prayer** ....S(e):18	$15	Hit 7046
				KEMP, Hal, and his Orchestra MEM **'36**		
				Born James Harold Kemp on 3/27/05 in Marion, Alabama. Died in a car crash on 12/21/40 (age 35). Popular sweet-band leader and saxophonist. Charted over 50 hits in the 1930s. Kemp's top 3 pre-1940 #1 hits: "This Year's Kisses," "There's A Small Hotel" and "When I'm With You."		
2/15/41	5	2		1 **It All Comes Back To Me Now** S:5 *Talkin' To My Heart*	$10	Victor 27255
				Bob Allen (vocal)		
2/15/41	17	2		2 **So You're The One** / ....S(e):17		
5/24/41	19	1		3 **Walkin' By The River** ....S(s):19	$10	Victor 27222
				movie star Janet Blair (vocal, above 2)		
				KENNY, Bill — see INK SPOTS		

KENTON, Stan, And His Orchestra ★50★   MEM/HOT **'45**

Born on 2/19/12 in Wichita, Kansas. Died of a stroke on 8/25/79 (age 67). One of the most consistently successful bandleaders of the postwar era. Began as a pianist for Gus Arnheim and other bands before becoming composer ("Artistry In Rhythm") and arranger to his own big band. A leader in the "progressive jazz" movement; his orchestras always featured top musicians and vocalists (particularly June Christy). Third person named to the Jazz Hall of Fame.

1)*Tampico*   2)*And Her Tears Flowed Like Wine*   3)*Orange Colored Sky*

Vocalists: Christy, June — 5,6,8-13   Dorris, Red — 1   O'Day, Anita — 3   the band — 3,5,15,16
Cole, Nat King — 14   Howard, Gene — 4   Pastels, The — 11

DEBUT	PEAK	WKS	Gold	A-side / B-side	$	Label & Number
4/1/44	10	1		1 **Do Nothin' 'Till You Hear From Me** ....S:10 *Harlem Folk Dance*	$10	Capitol 145
8/19/44	14	1		2 **Eager Beaver**........................S(wc):14 *Artistry In Rhythm* **[I]**	$10	Capitol 159
9/16/44	4	18		3 **And Her Tears Flowed Like Wine** / S:4 / J:8 / A:11		
11/4/44	9	4		4 **How Many Hearts Have You Broken** ....S:9 / J:14	$10	Capitol 166
				Stan Getz (alto sax, above 2)		
7/28/45	2¹	15	●	5 **Tampico** A:2 / J:3 / S:4 *Southern Scandal*	$10	Capitol 202
11/3/45	6	9		6 **It's Been A Long, Long Time** ....S:6 / A:8 / J:10 *Don't Let Me Dream*	$10	Capitol 219

DEBUT	PEAK	WKS	Gold	A-side (Chart Hit)..B-side	$	Label & Number
				KENTON, Stan, And His Orchestra — Cont'd		
1/26/46	13	3		7 **Artistry Jumps** / ....A:13 [I]		
				new version of Kenton's theme song "Artistry In Rhythm"		
3/2/46	16	1		8 **Just A-Sittin' And A-Rockin'** A:16	$15	Capitol 229
3/9/46	6	11	●	9 **Shoo Fly Pie (And Apple Pan Dowdy)** ....A:6 / J:7 / S:8 *I Been Down In Texas*	$10	Capitol 235
11/16/46	12	2		10 **It's A Pity To Say Goodnight** ....A:12 *Intermission Riff*	$10	Capitol 298
3/29/47	12	1		11 **His Feet Too Big For De Bed** ....A:12 *After You*	$10	Capitol 361
5/3/47	11	5		12 **Across The Alley From The Alamo** ....A:11 *There Is No Greater Love*	$10	Capitol 387
				Kai Winding (trombone, above 2); Vido Musso (tenor sax, above 4)		
7/17/48	27	1		13 **How High The Moon** ....S:27 *Interlude*	$10	Capitol 15117
				from the 1940 Broadway musical *Two For The Show* starring Betty Hutton; #76 hit for Ella Fitzgerald in 1960		
9/30/50	5	14		14 **Orange Colored Sky** A:5 / J:10 / S:11 *Jam-Bo*	$25	Capitol F1184
				NAT "KING" COLE and STAN KENTON		
4/28/51	17	11		15 **September Song** ....A:17 / S:20 *Artistry In Tango*	$15	Capitol F1480
				from the movie *Knickerbocker Holiday* starring Nelson Eddy; #12 hit for Walter Huston in 1939; #51 hit for Jimmy Durante in 1963		
8/4/51	12	5		16 **Laura** ....A:12 / S:17 *Jump For Joe*	$15	Capitol F1704
				title song from the movie starring Gene Tierney and Dana Andrews; Bud Shank (alto sax); Maynard Ferguson and Shorty Rogers (trumpets, above 3)		
6/7/52	25	2		17 **Delicado** ....S:25 / J:28 *Bags And Baggage* [I]	$15	Capitol F2040
				KEYNOTES, The — see SCALA, Primo		
				KILTY, Jack **'49**		
				Sang briefly with **Leo Reisman**. Host of TV's *Musical Merry-Go-Round* (1947-49).		
4/30/49	28	1		**Sunflower** ....J:28 *Brush Those Tears From Your Eyes*	$10	MGM 10339
				a court ruling found the 1964 hit "Hello, Dolly!" to be directly based on this song		
				KING, Henry, And His Orchestra MEM **'35**		
				Born on 2/8/05 in New York City. Died on 8/8/74 (age 69). Orchestra leader/pianist.		
5/15/48	14	4		**Baby Face** ....J:14 *Oh, You Beautiful Doll*	$10	Decca 25356
				Siggy Lane (vocal); #1 hit for Jan Garber in 1926; #14 hit for The Wing And A Prayer Fife And Drum Corps in 1976		
				KING, Pee Wee, and his Band MEM **'52**		
				Born Julius Frank Kuczynski on 2/18/14 in Abrams, Wisconsin; raised in Milwaukee. Died of a heart attack on 3/7/2000 (age 86). Country singer/songwriter/accordionist/fiddle player. Elected to the Country Music Hall of Fame in 1974.		
11/3/51+	❶³	24	●	1 **Slow Poke** J:❶³ / S:3 / A:8 *Whisper Waltz*	$25	RCA Victor 48-0489
				PEE WEE KING and his Golden West Cowboys		
3/8/52	18	4		2 **Silver And Gold** ....J:18 *Ragtime Annie Lee*	$20	RCA Victor 47-4458
6/14/52	27	1		3 **Busybody** ....J:27 *I Don't Mind*	$20	RCA Victor 47-4655
				Redd Stewart (vocal, above 3); above 3 were Top 10 Country hits		
	★135★			**KING, Wayne, and his Orchestra** MEM **'31**		
				Born on 2/16/01 in Savannah, Illinois. Died on 7/16/85 (age 84). Known as "The Waltz King." Alto saxophonist/vocalist. Featured orchestra for years at Chicago's Aragon Ballroom. Theme song: "The Waltz You Saved For Me." King's pre-1940 #1 hits: "Good-night, Sweetheart" and "Dream A Little Dream Of Me."		
8/10/40	19	1		1 **Where Was I?** ....S(s):19 *Cornsilk*	$10	Victor 26424
				from the movie *'Til We Meet Again* starring Merle Oberon and George Brent		
6/7/41	2¹	3		2 **Maria Elena** / S:2 [I]		
				#6 hit for Los Indios Tabajaras in 1963		
11/30/40	20	1		3 **You Are My Sunshine** ....S(s):20	$10	Victor 26767
				Wayne King and Trio (vocals); #7 hit for Ray Charles in 1962		
3/1/41	14	1		4 **You Walk By** ....S(e):14 *Goodnight Mother* [I]	$10	Victor 27206
4/19/41	5	13		5 **Souvenir De Vienne** S:5 *Because* [I]	$10	Victor 26659
				tune best known as "Intermezzo" (title song from the movie starring Ingrid Bergman)		
8/23/41	20	1		6 **'Til Reveille** ....S(s):20 *Dawn*	$10	Victor 27511
				KING SISTERS — see FOUR KING SISTERS		
				KIRK, Andy, And His Clouds Of Joy MEM **'36**		
				Born on 5/28/1898 in Newport, Kentucky. Died on 12/11/92 (age 94). Black singer/saxophonist/bandleader. Kirk's pre-1940 #1 hits: "Until The Real Thing Comes Along" and "I Won't Tell A Soul (I Love You)."		
11/16/40	19	1		1 **Now I Lay Me Down To Dream** ....S(s):19 *What's Your Story Morning Glory*	$20	Decca 3306
				Pha Terrell (vocal)		
5/11/46	14	1		2 **I Know** ....J:14 *Get Together With The Lord*	$25	Decca 18782
				ANDY KIRK AND HIS ORCHESTRA and THE JUBALAIRES		
				#2 R&B hit		
				KIRK, Lisa MEM **'50**		
				Born on 2/25/25 in Charleroi, Pennsylvania. Died of cancer on 11/11/90 (age 65). Actress/singer. Starred in several Broadway shows.		
3/18/50	22	5		1 **Dearie** ....A:22 / S:29 *Just A Girl That Men Forget* [N]	$20	RCA Victor 47-3220
				LISA KIRK and FRAN WARREN		
				78 rpm: 20-3696; Henri René (orch.); from the stage production *The Copacabana Show Of 1950*		
6/24/50	27	1		2 **The Old Piano Roll Blues** ....J:27 / S:29 *Juke Box Annie (Doodle-Oodle-Oo)*	$20	RCA Victor 47-3751
				EDDIE CANTOR, LISA KIRK, and the SAMMY KAYE ORCHESTRA		
				KITT, Eartha MEM **'53**		
				Born on 1/17/27 in Columbia, South Carolina. Black singer/actress. Appeared in several movies and as "Catwoman" on TV's *Batman*.		
7/18/53	8	14		1 **C'est Si Bon (It's So Good)** ....S:8 / A:8 / J:12 *African Lullaby* [F]	$20	RCA Victor 47-5358
				#22 hit for Conway Twitty in 1961; also see **Stan Freberg**'s 1954 parody of this hit		
12/5/53	4	5		2 **Santa Baby** S:4 / A:6 / J:13 *Under The Bridges Of Paris* [X]	$20	RCA Victor 47-5502
2/13/54	16	4		3 **Somebody Bad Stole De Wedding Bell** / .....A:16 / S:17 / J:18		
				from the stage production *The Copacabana Show Of 1954*		
3/20/54	20	1		4 **Lovin' Spree** A:20	$20	RCA Victor 47-5610
				Henri René (orch., all of above)		

KNIGHT, Evelyn ★59★ '49

Born in 1920 in Reedsville, Virginia. Singer with Paul Whiteman, **Tony Martin** and **Gordon MacRae**. Also worked with the Herman Chittison Trio. Nicknamed "The Lass With The Delicate Air."

1)A Little Bird Told Me   2)Powder Your Face With Sunshine (Smile! Smile! Smile!)
3)Dance With A Dolly (With A Hole In Her Stocking)

Orchestras: **Burke, Sonny** — 8,10   Haggart, Bob — 2   **Young, Victor** — 9
    Camarata — 1   Klein, Mannie — 5

Vocalists: Beasley, Alcyone, Singers — 13   **Foley, Red** — 13   Gordon, Lee, Singers — 11   **Stardusters, The** — 3,4,6
    Charles, Ray, Singers — 12   **4 Hits And A Miss** — 7,8,10   **Jesters, The** — 2

8/26/44	6	17		1 **Dance With A Dolly (With A Hole In Her Stocking)**......................J:6 / S:10 *Without A Sweetheart*	$10	Decca 18614

adaptation of the 1844 tune "Buffalo Gals (Won't You Come Out Tonight)"; also see **Jan August**'s "Buffalo Billy"; updated version by The Olympics in 1961 hit #47 as "Dance By The Light Of The Moon"

12/15/45+	10	5		2 **Chickery Chick**..S:10 / J:13 / A:14 *Let Him Go—Let Him Tarry*	$10	Decca 18725

EVELYN KNIGHT and THE JESTERS

11/20/48+	**❶**7	21	●	3 **A Little Bird Told Me /** S:**❶**7/J:**❶**7/A:**❶**6		
11/27/48+	9	15		4 **Brush Those Tears From Your Eyes**...J:9 / S:24	$10	Decca 24514
11/20/48	14	8		5 **Buttons And Bows**...J:14 / S:22 / A:26 *I Know Where I'm Going*	$10	Decca 24489

from the movie *The Paleface* starring **Bob Hope**; #104 hit for The Browns in 1962

12/25/48+	**❶**1	20		6 **Powder Your Face With Sunshine (Smile!**		
				Smile! Smile!) J:**❶**1 / A:2 / S:3 *One Sunday Afternoon*	$10	Decca 24530
8/6/49	21	3		7 **You're So Understanding /** ....S:21 / J:25		
6/18/49	22	2		8 **It's Too Late Now** J:22	$10	Decca 24636
7/30/49	22	3		9 **A Wonderful Guy**...J:22 *A Cock-Eyed Optimist*	$10	Decca 24640

from the Broadway musical *South Pacific* starring **Mary Martin** and **Ezio Pinza**

8/13/49	29	1		10 **Be Goody Good Good To Me**..........J:29 *Don't Ever Marry For Money (You Must Only Marry For Love)*	$10	Decca 24655
4/15/50	20	1		11 **Candy And Cake**...J:20 *A Woman Likes To Be Told*	$10	Decca 24943
8/19/50	25	1		12 **All Dressed Up To Smile**...J:25 *Cherry Stones*	$20	Decca 9-27103
2/10/51	28	6		13 **My Heart Cries For You**...J:28 *'Tater Pie*	$25	Decca 9-27378

EVELYN KNIGHT and RED FOLEY
adapted from the 18th-century French melody "Chanson de Marie Antoinette"; #38 hit for Ray Charles in 1964

KRUPA, Gene, and his Orchestra ★70★   MEM '41

Born on 1/15/09 in Chicago. Died on 10/16/73 (age 64). Legendary drummer. Gained fame with **Benny Goodman** from 1934-38.

1)High On A Windy Hill   2)It All Comes Back To Me Now   3)Along The Navajo Trail

Vocalists: Daye, Irene — 1,5   Eldridge, Roy — 8   Soots, Bobby — 12
    DuLany, Howard — 2-4   **O'Day, Anita** — 6-8,10,11   Stewart, Buddy — 9

12/14/40	16	1		1 **Down Argentina Way** ....S(e):16 / S(wc):20 *Two Dreams Met*	$15	Okeh 5826

from the movie *Down Argentine Way* starring Don Ameche and **Betty Grable**

2/1/41	13	2		2 **Tonight (Perfidia)**...S(e):13 / S(mw):16 *Never Took A Lesson In My Life*	$15	Okeh 5715

#15 hit for The Ventures in 1960

2/15/41	2¹	6		3 **High On A Windy Hill /** S:2		
2/22/41	2¹	5		4 **It All Comes Back To Me Now** S:2	$15	Okeh 5883
3/29/41	13	1		5 **There'll Be Some Changes Made** ....S(wc):13 / S(s):17 *These Things You Left Me*	$15	Okeh 6021

featured in the 1940 movie *Play Girl* starring Kay Francis; #5 hit for Ethel Waters in 1922

6/28/41	18	1		6 **Georgia On My Mind** ....S(mw):18 *Alreet*	$15	Okeh 6118

#10 hit for Frankie Trumbauer in 1931; #1 hit for Ray Charles in 1960

8/2/41	9	1		7 **Just A Little Bit South Of North Carolina** ....S:9 *Let's Get Away From It All*	$15	Okeh 6130
9/6/41	10	1		8 **Let Me Off Uptown**...S:10 *Flamingo*	$15	Okeh 6210
10/13/45	7	2		9 **Along The Navajo Trail** ....A:7 *A Tender Word Will Mend It All*	$10	Columbia 36846
12/8/45+	10	5		10 **Chickery Chick**...A:10 / J:19 *Just A Little Fond Affection*	$10	Columbia 36877
7/6/46	9	6		11 **Boogie Blues**...A:9 / J:15 *Lover*	$10	Columbia 36986

Charlie Ventura (tenor sax, above 3)

6/10/50	9	15		12 **Bonaparte's Retreat**...J:9 / A:15 / S:16 *My Scandinavian Baby*	$20	RCA Victor 47-3766

GENE KRUPA and his CHICAGO JAZZ
#50 hit for Billy Grammer in 1959

KUHN, Dick, And His Orchestra   MEM '43

10/23/43	8	3		**Put Your Arms Around Me, Honey (I Never Knew Any**		
				Girl Like You) ....S:8 *I've Got Rings On My Fingers or, Mumbo Jumbo Jijjiboo J. O'Shea* **[I]**	$10	Decca 4337

instrumental except for a 30-second vocal chorus; from the movie *Coney Island* starring **Betty Grable**; #1 hit for Arthur Collins & Byron Harlan in 1911; #58 hit for Fats Domino in 1960

KYSER, Kay, and his Orchestra ★15★　　MEM '42

Born James Kyser on 6/18/06 in Rocky Mount, North Carolina. Died on 7/23/85 (age 79). Among the most popular of the "sweet" dance bands. Best known as the "Old Professor" on his radio and TV shows *Kollege Of Musical Knowledge*. Featured performers included singers Harry Babbitt and **Ginny Simms**, and trumpet comic Ish Kabibble. Kyser's pre-1940 #1 hits: "(Boop-Boop Dit-Tem Dot-Tem What-Tem Chu!) Three Little Fishies (Itty Bitty Poo)" and "The Umbrella Man."

1)Jingle Jangle Jingle 2)Woody Wood-Pecker 3)Ole Buttermilk Sky 4)Who Wouldn't Love You 5)On A Slow Boat To China

Vocalists: Babbitt, Harry — 1,2,5-8,10-12, 14,16,17,21,22,38,40　Campus Kids, The — 31,32,34-38　Carroll, Georgia — 25　Conway, Julie — 16,21-23　Douglas, Michael — 29,31,32,34,35　Erwin, Trudy — 13,14,21,22　Ferdy, Slim & Quartet — 27　Kabibble, Ish — 5　**Kyser, Kay** — 1　Little Audrey — 1　Martin, Jack — 5,7,8,10,13,18,21,22,36　Mason, Sully (& his Playmates) — 3,9,13　Mitchell, Dolly, & Trio — 26,28　Moonbeams, The — 33　Pokey — 1　Rogers, Clyde — 30　**Simms, Ginny** — 2,4,5,7,8,10,11　Williams, Max — 7,8,10,13,21,22　Wood, Gloria — 37,39,40　glee club — 12,15,18-20　group — 16,29

DEBUT	PEAK	WKS	Gold	#	A-side (Chart Hit) / B-side	$	Label & Number
12/30/39+	4	5		1	The Little Red Fox (N'Ya N'Ya Ya Can't Catch Me)　J:4 *I'm Fit To Be Tied* [N]	$10	Columbia 35295
1/20/40	6	4		2	Chatterbox ....J:6 *This Changing World*	$10	Columbia 35307
					above 2 from the movie *That's Right-You're Wrong* starring Kyser		
5/4/40	2²	13		3	Playmates　J:2 / S:4 *On The Isle Of May* [N]	$10	Columbia 35375
5/18/40	4	7		4	With The Wind And The Rain In Your Hair　J:4 *Way Back In 1939 A.D.*	$10	Columbia 35350
					#21 hit for Pat Boone in 1959		
7/27/40	12	1		5	Friendship ....S(s):12 *Palms Of Paradise* [N]	$10	Columbia 35368
					from Broadway's *DuBarry Was A Lady* starring **Ethel Merman**		
9/21/40	15	2		6	Blueberry Hill ....S(s):15 *Who's Yehoodi?*	$10	Columbia 35554
11/2/40+	6	5		7	Ferry-Boat Serenade ....S:6 *The Call Of The Canyon*	$10	Columbia 35627
4/26/41	3	3		8	Alexander The Swoose (Half Swan–Half Goose)　S:3 *Why Cry Baby?* [N]	$10	Columbia 36040
5/10/41	19	1		9	The Wise Old Owl ....S(e):19 / S(s):19 *Tell It To The Marines*	$10	Columbia 36051
7/26/41	6	4		10	'Til Reveille ....S:6 *Say When*	$10	Columbia 36137
11/15/41	18	2		11	Why Don't We Do This More Often? ....S(wc):18 *I've Been Drafted (Now I'm Drafting You)*	$10	Columbia 36253
1/10/42	7	3		12	(There'll Be Bluebirds Over) The White Cliffs Of Dover ....S:7 *The Nadocky*	$10	Columbia 36445
3/21/42	8	1		13	A Zoot Suit (For My Sunday Gal) ....S:8 *When The Roses Bloom Again*	$10	Columbia 36517
4/18/42	2⁸	22	●	14	Who Wouldn't Love You　S:2 *How Do I Know It's Real*	$10	Columbia 36526
6/20/42	8	3		15	Johnny Doughboy Found A Rose In Ireland ....S:8 *Me And My Melinda*	$10	Columbia 36558
7/4/42	❶⁸	13		16	Jingle Jangle Jingle /　S:❶⁸	$10	Columbia 36604
					from the movie *The Forest Rangers* starring Fred MacMurray		
8/8/42	2⁴	11		17	He Wears A Pair Of Silver Wings　S:2	$10	
					from George Black's musical revue *Black Vanities*		
10/3/42	5	3	●	18	Strip Polka　S:5 *Ev'ry Night About This Time*	$10	Columbia 36635
10/17/42	2⁷	13	●	19	Praise The Lord And Pass The Ammunition!　S:2 *I Came Here To Talk For Joe*	$10	Columbia 36640
2/20/43	17	3		20	Moonlight Mood / ....S(wc):17	$10	Columbia 36657
11/28/42+	18	2		21	Can't Get Out Of This Mood ....S(mw):18 / S(wc):19	$10	
					from the movie *Seven Days Leave* starring Lucille Ball		
6/26/43	4	5		22	Let's Get Lost /　S:4	$10	Columbia 36673
7/3/43	16	1		23	The Fuddy Duddy Watchmaker ....S(mw):16		
					above 2 from the movie *Happy-Go-Lucky* starring **Mary Martin**		
7/10/43	18	1		24	Pushin' Sand ....S(wc):18 *You're So Good To Me* [I]	$10	Columbia 36676
1/20/45	7	4		25	There Goes That Song Again ....S:7 / J:12 / A:15 *I'm Gonna See My Baby*	$10	Columbia 36757
					from the movie *Carolina Blues* starring Kyser		
2/24/45	12	2		26	Ac-Cent-Tchu-Ate The Positive ....J:12 *Like Someone In Love*	$10	Columbia 36771
					from the movie *Here Come The Waves* starring **Bing Crosby** and **Betty Hutton**		
6/9/45	3	10		27	Bell Bottom Trousers　A:3 / S:5 / J:6 [N]	$10	
					based on a traditional sea chantey		
7/7/45	10	1		28	Can't You Read Between The Lines ....A:10 / J:16	$10	Columbia 36801
8/18/45	10	4		29	Rosemary / ....A:10 / J:12		
8/25/45	11	2		30	Horses Don't Bet On People ....A:11 [N]	$10	Columbia 36824
11/3/45	12	2		31	That's For Me ....J:12 *Choo Choo Polka*	$10	Columbia 36844
					from the movie *State Fair* starring **Dick Haymes** and Dana Andrews		
2/9/46	11	1		32	Slowly ....A:11 *I Don't Wanna Do It Alone*	$10	Columbia 36900
4/20/46	5	2		33	One-Zy Two-Zy (I Love You-zy)　A:5 / J:12 *There's No One But You*	$10	Columbia 36960
9/21/46	❶²	19		34	Ole Buttermilk Sky　S:❶² / J:2 / A:2 *On The Wrong Side Of You*	$10	Columbia 37073
					from the movie *Canyon Passage* starring Dana Andrews; #25 hit for Bill Black's Combo in 1961		
11/30/46	3	13		35	The Old Lamp-Lighter /　S:3 / A:3 / J:4	$10	
					#5 hit for The Browns in 1960		
11/16/46+	8	9		36	Huggin' And Chalkin' ....A:8 / J:14 [N]	$10	Columbia 37095
2/1/47	6	12		37	Managua, Nicaragua (Manag-wa, Nicarag-wa) ....A:6 / S:9 / J:11 *That's The Beginning Of The End*	$10	Columbia 37214
1/3/48	13	1		38	Serenade Of The Bells ....S:13 *Pass That Peace Pipe*	$10	Columbia 37956
6/5/48	❶⁶	15	●	39	Woody Wood-Pecker　S:❶⁶ / A:❶⁶ / J:❶⁶ *When Veronica Plays The Harmonica* [N]	$10	Columbia 38197
					from the Walter Lantz cartoon		
10/23/48	2⁷	20	●	40	On A Slow Boat To China　J:2 / S:2 / A:2 *In The Market Place Of Old Monterey*	$10	Columbia 38301

DEBUT	PEAK	WKS	Gold	A-side (Chart Hit)..B-side	$	Label & Number

L

LAINE, Frankie ★18★   MEM/HOT '49

Born Frank Paul LoVecchio on 3/30/13 in Chicago. To Los Angeles in the early 1940s. First recorded for Exclusive in 1945. Signed to the Mercury label in 1947. Dynamic singer whose popularity lasted well into the rock era.

1)That Lucky Old Sun 2)Mule Train 3)The Cry Of The Wild Goose 4)I Believe 5)Jezebel

Orchestras: Carroll, Jimmy — 32,33,36   Fischer, Carl — 3-5,7,9,18,31   Klein('s), Mannie, All Stars — 1   **Weston, Paul** —
Cole, Buddy, Quartet — 44   Geller, Harry — 2,6,10-14,17   **Miller, Mitch**— 19   20-30,34,35,37,38,40,41,43

Vocalists: **Boyd, Jimmy** — 39   **Day, Doris** — 31   Luboff, Norman, Choir —   **Stafford, Jo** — 21,22,25,26,28,35
Conlon('s), Jud, Rhythmaires —   **Four Lads, The** — 44   19,20,24,26,28-31,34,38-40,42
6,11   Norman, Loulie Jean — 11,12

DEBUT	PEAK	WKS			A-side / B-side	$	Label & Number
3/29/47	4	25	●	1	**That's My Desire** A:4 / S:7 / J:7 *By The River Sainte Marie*	$15	Mercury 5007
					FRANKIE LAINE And MANNIE KLEIN'S ALL STARS		
					#69 hit for The Sensations in 1962		
5/17/47	14	2		2	**Mam'selle** ....J:14 *All Of Me*	$15	Mercury 5048
					from the movie *The Razor's Edge* starring Tyrone Power		
1/24/48	9	9	●	3	**Shine** ....J:9 / S:12 / A:13 *We'll Be Together Again*	$15	Mercury 5091
					#7 hit for **Bing Crosby** & the **Mills Brothers** in 1932		
8/21/48	21	1		4	**Ah But It Happens** ....S:21 / A:29 *Hold Me*	$15	Mercury 5158
12/18/48	11	3		5	**You're All I Want For Christmas**...........................S:11 / A:22 *Tara Talara Tala* [X]	$15	Mercury 5177
8/27/49	❶[8]	22	●	6	**That Lucky Old Sun** S:❶[8] / A:❶[7] / J:❶[5] *I Get Sentimental Over Nothing*	$15	Mercury 5316
					#20 hit for Ray Charles in 1964		
9/24/49	20	5		7	**Now That I Need You** ....J:20 / S:23 *My Own – My Only – My All*	$15	Mercury 5311
					from the Broadway musical *Red Hot And Blue* starring Ethel Merman		
11/12/49	❶[6]	13	●	8	**Mule Train** S:❶[6] / A:❶[6] / J:❶[6] *Carry Me Back To Old Virginny*	$15	Mercury 5345
					FRANKIE LAINE and the Muleskinners		
1/7/50-	29	1		9	**You're All I Want For Christmas**................................A:29 *Tara Talara Tala* [X-R]	$15	Mercury 5177
2/11/50	❶[2]	11	●	10	**The Cry Of The Wild Goose** ....A:❶[2] / S:4 / J:4 *Black Lace*	$25	Mercury 5363-X45
3/25/50	28	1		11	**Satan Wears A Satin Gown** ....A:28 *Baby Just For Me*	$25	Mercury 5358-X45
4/1/50	12	4		12	**Swamp Girl** ....A:12 / S:15 / J:25 *(Give Me) A Kiss For Tomorrow*	$25	Mercury 5390-X45
5/20/50	20	4		13	**Stars And Stripes Forever**........................S:20 / A:25 *Thanks For Your Kisses*	$25	Mercury 5421-X45
					famous march, #1 in 1897 and again in 1901 for Sousa's Band		
8/26/50	13	9		14	**Music, Maestro, Please /** ....A:13 / S:14 / J:19		
					#1 hit for **Tommy Dorsey** in 1938		
9/9/50	18	5		15	**Dream A Little Dream Of Me** ....A:18 / S:23 / J:23	$20	Mercury 5458-X45
					#1 hit for **Wayne King** in 1931; #12 hit for Mama Cass in 1968		
11/11/50	11	10		16	**Nevertheless** ....A:11 / J:13 *I Was Dancing With Someone (But I Was Looking at You)*	$20	Mercury 5495-X45
					featured in the movie *Three Little Words* starring Fred Astaire; #5 hit for Jack Denny in 1931		
11/18/50	30	1		17	**If I Were A Bell** ....A:30 *Sleepy Ol' River*	$20	Mercury 5500-X45
					from the Broadway musical *Guys And Dolls* starring Robert Alda and Vivian Blaine		
4/14/51	19	6		18	**Metro Polka** ....J:19 / S:28 / A:28 *The Jalopy Song*	$20	Mercury 5581-X45
5/5/51	2[2]	21	●	19	**Jezebel /** S:2 / J:2 / A:3		
5/12/51	3	19		20	**Rose, Rose, I Love You** J:3 / A:4 / S:6	$20	Columbia 4-39367
5/19/51	13	10		21	**Pretty Eyed Baby** ....J:13 / A:16 / S:23 *That's The One For Me*	$20	Columbia 4-39388
					new lyrics to the R&B song "Satchelmouth Baby" recorded by Deek Watson & The Brown Dots on Manor 1026 in 1946		
8/11/51	17	4		22	**In The Cool, Cool, Cool Of The Evening**..............A:17 *That's Good! That's Bad!*	$20	Columbia 4-39466
					JO STAFFORD & FRANKIE LAINE (above 2)		
					from the movie *Here Comes The Groom* starring **Bing Crosby** and Jane Wyman		
9/1/51	17	3		23	**Wonderful, Wasn't It? /** J:17		
8/11/51	23	2		24	**The Girl In The Wood** ....S:23 / J:24 / A:27	$20	Columbia 4-39489
10/20/51	9	8		25	**Hey, Good Lookin' /** ....J:9 / A:14 / S:20		
					FRANKIE LAINE - JO STAFFORD		
					#1 Country hit for **Hank Williams** in 1951		
10/27/51	19	4		26	**Gambella (The Gamblin' Lady)**........................J:19 / S:27	$20	Columbia 4-39570
					JO STAFFORD - FRANKIE LAINE		
11/10/51	3	14	●	27	**Jealousy (Jalousie)** S:3 / A:3 / J:6 *Flamenco*	$20	Columbia 4-39585
					#7 hit for Leo Reisman in 1932		
3/8/52	6	10		28	**Hambone** ....J:6 / S:15 / A:18 *Let's Have A Party*	$20	Columbia 4-39672
					FRANKIE LAINE & JO STAFFORD		
3/15/52	21	7		29	**The Gandy Dancers' Ball /** ....S:21 / J:21 / A:23		
5/17/52	30	1		30	**When You're In Love** S:30	$20	Columbia 4-39665
6/21/52	7	14	●	31	**Sugarbush** ....J:7 / S:10 / A:15 *How Lovely Cooks The Meat*	$15	Columbia 4-39693
					DORIS DAY - FRANKIE LAINE		
7/12/52	5	19	●	32	**High Noon (Do Not Forsake Me) /** S:5 / A:8 / J:10		
					from the movie *High Noon* starring Gary Cooper		
7/19/52	20	5		33	**Rock Of Gibraltar** ....S:20 / J:23	$20	Columbia 4-39770
10/4/52	29	1		34	**The Mermaid**.....................................S:29 *The Ruby And The Pearl*	$20	Columbia 4-39862
10/18/52	21	3		35	**Settin' The Woods On Fire** ....J:21 / S:26 *Piece A-Puddin'*	$20	Columbia 4-39867
					JO STAFFORD - FRANKIE LAINE		
					78 rpm recording titled as "Tonight We're Setting The Woods On Fire"; #2 Country hit for **Hank Williams** in 1952		
1/17/53	14	7		36	**I'm Just A Poor Bachelor** ....J:14 *Tonight You Belong To Me*	$20	Columbia 4-39903

LAINE, Frankie — Cont'd

DEBUT	PEAK	WKS	Gold	A-side	B-side	$	Label & Number
2/21/53	2³	23	●	37 **I Believe** /	A:2 / S:2 / J:3		
				#33 hit for The Bachelors in 1964			
5/16/53	18	2		38 **Your Cheatin' Heart**	J:18	$20	Columbia 4-39938
				#1 Country hit for **Hank Williams** in 1953; #29 hit for Ray Charles in 1962			
3/14/53	4	12	●	39 **Tell Me A Story**	S:4 / J:5 / A:8 *The Little Boy And The Old Man* [N]	$20	Columbia 4-39945
				JIMMY BOYD - FRANKIE LAINE			
8/22/53	6	16		40 **Hey Joe!**	J:6 / S:11 / A:11 *Sittin' In The Sun (Countin' My Money)*	$20	Columbia 4-40036
				#1 Country hit for Carl Smith in 1953			
1/23/54	17	4		41 **Granada**	J:17 *I'd Give My Life*	$20	Columbia 4-40136
				from the movie *Two Girls And A Sailor* starring Van Johnson; #64 hit for **Frank Sinatra** in 1961			
5/8/54	20	1		42 **The Kid's Last Fight**	J:20 *Long Distance Love*	$20	Columbia 4-40178
7/3/54	14	7		43 **Some Day**	J:14 / S:18 *There Must Be A Reason*	$20	Columbia 4-40235
				from the movie *The Vagabond King* starring Kathryn Grayson; Carl Fischer (piano: #6, 10-15, 17, 19-22, 24-31, 34-36 & 40-43)			
10/23/54	30	1		44 **Rain, Rain, Rain**	S:30 *Your Heart - My Heart (Sehnsucht)*	$20	Columbia 4-40295
				FRANKIE LAINE & THE FOUR LADS			

LANCERS, The   MEM '53

White vocal group: Jerry Meacham, Dick Burr, Bob Porter and Carlton "Corky" Lindgren. Sang backup for **Kay Starr**. Group is namesake of Hollywood vocal coach Peter Lance.

DEBUT	PEAK	WKS	Gold	A-side	B-side	$	Label & Number
11/21/53	13	3		1 **Sweet Mama Tree Top Tall**	A:13 *Were You Ever Mine To Lose*	$25	Trend 45-63
				Van Alexander (orch.)			
12/18/54+	6	12	●	2 **Let Me Go, Lover!**	J:6 / A:7 / S:8 *The Moon Is On Fire*	$20	Coral 9-61315
				TERESA BREWER with The Lancers			
				Jack Pleis (orch.)			

LANE, Muriel — see CROSBY, Bing

LANSON, Snooky   HOT '55

Born Roy Landman on 3/27/14 in Memphis. Died of cancer on 7/2/90 (age 76). Star of TV's *Your Hit Parade* (1950-57).

DEBUT	PEAK	WKS	Gold	A-side	B-side	$	Label & Number
11/27/48+	24	4		1 **I'm Gonna Get You On A Slow Boat To China**	A:24 *Melancholy Minstrel*	$10	Mercury 5191
12/10/49+	12	8		2 **The Old Master Painter**	J:12 / A:16 / S:22 *Did You Ever See A Dream Walking?*	$15	London 30009
				78 rpm: 555; Beasley Smith (orch.)			

★119★   LANZA, Mario   MEM/HOT '51

Born Alfredo Cocozza on 1/31/21 in Philadelphia. Died of a heart attack on 10/7/59 (age 38). Became the most popular operatic tenor since Caruso, with his voice featured in seven movies, though no theatrical operas.

DEBUT	PEAK	WKS	Gold	A-side	B-side	$	Label & Number
12/16/50+	❶¹	34	●	1 **Be My Love**	S:❶¹ / A:2 / J:4 *I'll Never Love You*	$20	RCA Victor 49-1353
				78 rpm: 10-1561; Ray Sinatra (orch.); Jeff Alexander Choir (backing vocals); from the movie *The Toast Of New Orleans* starring Lanza			
3/17/51	21	3		2 **Vesti La Giubba (On with the Play)**	S:21 *Ave Maria* [F]	$15	RCA Victor 49-3228
				from the opera *I Pagliacci: Act II*; #1 hit for Enrico Caruso in 1907			
4/14/51	3	34	●	3 **The Loveliest Night Of The Year**	S:3 / A:8 / J:8 *La Donna È Mobile*	$15	RCA Victor 49-3300
				melody adapted from the 1888 waltz "Over The Waves" (also see **Guy Lombardo**'s "Merry-Go- Round Waltz"); above 2 from the movie *The Great Caruso* starring Lanza			
6/23/51	16	14		4 **Because**	S:16 / A:27 *For You Alone*	$15	RCA Victor 49-3207
				#4 hit for Enrico Caruso in 1913			
9/13/52	7	19	●	5 **Because You're Mine**	S:7 / A:10 / J:13 *The Song The Angels Sing*	$15	RCA Victor 49-3914
				Jeff Alexander Choir (backing vocals); title song from the movie starring Lanza			
8/22/53	20	1		6 **Song Of India**	A:20 *If You Were Mine*	$15	RCA Victor 49-4209
				adapted from Rimsky-Korsakov's opera *Sadko*; #1 hit for Paul Whiteman in 1921; Constantine Callinicos conducts the RCA Victor Orchestra on above 5; all of above records are on RCA Victor's Red Seal label			

LaROSA, Julius   MEM/HOT '53

Born on 1/2/30 in Brooklyn, New York. Regular singer on **Arthur Godfrey**'s TV show until he was fired on the air on 10/19/53. Popular DJ in New York (WNEW) for many years.

DEBUT	PEAK	WKS	Gold	A-side	B-side	$	Label & Number
2/7/53	4	9		1 **Anywhere I Wander**	S:4 / A:12 / J:14 *This Is Heaven*	$15	Cadence F1230
				from the movie *Hans Christian Andersen* starring **Danny Kaye**			
9/12/53	2¹	20	●	2 **Eh, Cumpari**	S:2 / J:4 / A:5 *Till They've All Gone Home* [F]	$15	Cadence 1232
				adaptation of a traditional Italian song; #72 hit for Gaylord & Holiday in 1976; **Archie Bleyer** (orch., above 2)			

LATHROP, Jack, and The Drugstore Cowboys   '48

Singer/guitarist formerly with the **Glenn Miller** and Hal McIntyre bands.

DEBUT	PEAK	WKS	Gold	A-side	B-side	$	Label & Number
10/23/48	19	3		1 **Hair Of Gold** /	J:19 / A:29		
				from the movie *Singing Spurs* starring Kirby Grant			
9/25/48	27	2		2 **You Call Everybody Darling**	S:27 / J:28	$15	RCA Victor 20-3109
1/29/49	26	1		3 **My Darling, My Darling**	J:26 *You're The First Cup Of Coffee*	$10	RCA Victor 20-3187
				EVE YOUNG and JACK LATHROP			
				from the Broadway musical *Where's Charley?* starring **Ray Bolger**			

LAURENZ, John   '48

Born in 1909 in Brooklyn, New York. Died on 11/7/58 (age 49). Singer/actor. Acted in several movies from 1943-50.

DEBUT	PEAK	WKS	Gold	A-side	B-side	$	Label & Number
8/7/48	26	2		1 **My Happiness**	J:26 / A:27 *Someone Cares*	$10	Mercury 5144
				#2 hit for Connie Francis in 1959			
8/21/48	18	7		2 **A Tree In The Meadow**	A:18 / J:24 / S:28 *Tea Leaves*	$10	Mercury 5148
9/4/48	22	5		3 **Hair Of Gold**	A:22 / J:26 *Just One More Chance*	$10	Mercury 5172
				from the movie *Singing Spurs* starring Kirby Grant			
12/4/48	29	1		4 **The Mountaineer And The Jabberwock**	A:29 *Morning Glory Road*	$10	Mercury 5202
				inspired by Lewis Carroll's "Alice In Wonderland"			
4/9/49	21	5		5 **Red Roses For A Blue Lady**	A:21 *Somebody's Lyin'*	$10	Mercury 5201
				#10 hit for Vic Dana in 1965			
7/16/49	28	1		6 **Some Enchanted Evening**	A:28 *A Kiss And A Rose*	$10	Mercury 5276
				Mitch Miller (orch.); from the Broadway musical *South Pacific* starring **Mary Martin** and **Ezio Pinza**; #13 hit for Jay & The Americans in 1965			

LAVALLE, Paul, and his String Orchestra '44
Born on 9/6/08 in Beacon, New York. Died on 6/24/97 (age 88). Conducted The Cities Service Band of America (1949-50).

| 11/11/44 | 25 | 1 | | **Always**..J(terr.):25 *Let Me Call You Sweetheart* [I] | $15 | Musicraft 297 |

#1 hit for both Vincent Lopez and **George Olsen** in 1926; #19 hit for Sammy Turner in 1959

LAWRENCE, Bill '49
Born in 1926 in East St. Louis, Illinois. Sang in the late 1940s with **Jimmy Dorsey**; later on **Arthur Godfrey**'s TV show.

| 10/1/49 | 14 | 8 | | **Jealous Heart**..J:14 / A:15 / S:23 *If You Ever Fall In Love Again* | $15 | RCA Victor 47-3029 |

78 rpm: 20-3539; #47 hit for Connie Francis in 1965

LAWRENCE, Elliot, and his Orchestra   MEM '47
Born Elliot Lawrence Broza on 2/14/25 in Philadelphia. Hosted a daily CBS radio show in the 1950s. Orchestra leader of many TV variety shows from 1952-76.

| 7/20/46 | 9 | 2 | | 1 **Who Do You Love I Hope**..A:9 *I Know* | $10 | Columbia 37047 |

from the Broadway musical *Annie Get Your Gun* starring **Ethel Merman**

| 11/2/46 | 16 | 1 | | 2 **You Broke The Only Heart That Ever Loved You** ....A:16 / J:18 *Five O'Clock Shadow* | $10 | Columbia 37084 |

Jack Hunter and Rosalind Patton (vocals)

| 10/4/47 | 4 | 13 | | 3 **Near You**   A:4 / S:9 *How Lucky You Are* | $10 | Columbia 37838 |

#10 hit for Roger Williams in 1958; Rosalind Patton (vocal: #1 & 3)

| 12/29/51+ | 15 | 12 | | 4 **Don't Leave My Poor Heart Breaking** ....J:15 *Lovin' Machine* | $25 | King 45-15137 |

Lloyd **"Cowboy" Copas** and Rosalind Patton (vocals)

LAWRENCE, Steve   MEM/HOT '63
Born Sidney Leibowitz on 7/8/35 in Brooklyn, New York. Pop singer. Regular performer on Steve Allen's *Tonight Show* for five years. Married Eydie Gorme on 12/29/57.

| 6/14/52 | 21 | 3 | | **Poinciana**..A:21 / S:24 *Never Leave Me* | $25 | King 45-15185 |

Dewey Bergman (orch.)

LEE, Benny — see NICHOLS, Joy

LEE, Jackie, And His Orchestra   HOT '54
Born in May 1932 in Philadelphia. Nicknamed "Mr. Hot Piano."

| 5/8/54 | 17 | 11 | | **Isle Of Capri**...S:17 / J:18 *By The Light Of The Silvery Moon* [I] | $20 | Coral 9-61149 |

#1 hit for **Ray Noble** in 1935

LEE, Julia, And Her Boy Friends   MEM '48
Born on 10/31/02 in Boonville, Missouri. Died of a heart attack on 12/8/58 (age 56). R&B-jazz vocalist/pianist. With father's band from age four. Joined brother George E. Lee's band from 1920-33. First recorded for Merritt in 1927. Worked up until the time of her death. Noted for her risque style of recordings.

| 3/27/48 | 15 | 3 | | 1 **King Size Papa** ....J:15 *When You're Smiling (The Whole World Smiles With You)* [N] | $20 | Capitol Am. 40082 |

#1 R&B hit (9 weeks); follow-up to Lee's #1 (12 weeks) R&B hit "Snatch And Grab It"

| 4/16/49 | 29 | 1 | | 2 **I Didn't Like It The First Time (The Spinach Song)** ....J:29 *Sit Down And Drink It Over* [N] | $20 | Capitol 15367 |

Benny Carter, alto sax and Dave Cavanaugh, tenor sax (above 2)

LEE, Peggy ★37★   MEM/HOT '48
Born Norma Jean Egstrom on 5/26/20 in Jamestown, North Dakota. Died of a heart attack on 1/21/2002 (age 81). Jazz singer with Jack Wardlow band (1936-40), Will Osborne (1940-41) and **Benny Goodman** (1941-43). Went solo in March 1943. In movies *Mister Music* (1950), *The Jazz Singer* (1953) and *Pete Kelly's Blues* (1955). Co-wrote many songs with husband **Dave Barbour** (married, 1943-52). Awarded nearly $4 million in court for her singing in the animated movie *Lady And The Tramp*. Won Grammy's Lifetime Achievement Award in 1995.

1)*Mañana (Is Soon Enough For Me)* 2)*Golden Earrings* 3)*Riders In The Sky (A Cowboy Legend)*
4)*Lover* 5)*Waitin' For The Train To Come In*

Orchestras: Barbour, Dave — 1-9,11-16,18   Jenkins, Gordon — 20,21,23   Schoen, Vic — 22
Goodman, Benny — 10   May, Billy — 19

Vocalists: Conlon, Jud, Singers — 16   Crosby, Bing — 22   Mellowmen, The — 17   Tormé, Mel — 17

11/10/45	4	14		1 **Waitin' For The Train To Come In**...............A:4 / J:5 / S:6 *I'm Glad I Waited For You*	$15	Capitol 218
5/25/46	7	6		2 **I Don't Know Enough About You** ....A:7 *I Can See It Your Way*	$15	Capitol 236
11/23/46	10	6		3 **It's All Over Now**...A:10 *Aren't You Kind Of Glad We Did?*	$15	Capitol 292
1/18/47	16	1		4 **It's A Good Day**..A:16 *He's Just My Kind*	$15	Capitol 322
6/28/47	10	4		5 **Chi-Baba Chi-Baba (My Bambino Go To Sleep)** ....A:10 / J:16 *Ain'tcha Ever Comin' Back*	$15	Capitol 419
11/15/47+	2[1]	18		6 **Golden Earrings** / S:2 / A:3 / J:3	$15	Capitol 15009

title song from the movie starring Ray Milland and **Marlene Dietrich**

1/3/48	11	3		7 **I'll Dance At Your Wedding**...J:11 / A:12	$15	Capitol 15009
1/24/48	**0**[9]	21	●	8 **Mañana (Is Soon Enough For Me)**..........S:**0**[9] / A:**0**[7] / J:**0**[5] *All Dressed Up With A Broken Heart*	$15	Capitol 15022
4/24/48	13	2		9 **Laroo Laroo Lili Bolero** ....A:13 / J:28 *Talking To Myself About You*	$15	Capitol 15048
6/19/48	30	1		10 **Somebody Else Is Taking My Place** ....J:30 *Why Don't You Do Right* [R]	$15	Columbia 38198

BENNY GOODMAN and his ORCHESTRA with PEGGY LEE
re-issue of Goodman's 1942 hit on Okeh 6497

6/26/48	13	2		11 **Caramba! It's The Samba**...........................A:13 / J:20 *Baby, Don't Be Mad At Me*	$15	Capitol 15090
8/7/48	29	1		12 **Bubble-Loo Bubble-Loo** ....A:29 *Why Don't You Do Right*	$15	Capitol 15118
3/12/49	27	1		13 **Blum Blum (I Wonder Who I Am)** ....A:27 *If You Could See Me Now* [N]	$15	Capitol 15371
4/23/49	17	1		14 **Similau (See-Me-Lo)**..A:17 *While We're Young*	$15	Capitol 15416
5/14/49	13	16		15 **Bali Ha'i**.................................A:13 / S:17 / J:17 *There Is Nothin' Like A Dame*	$15	Capitol 57-543

45 rpm: 54-547; from the Broadway musical *South Pacific* starring **Mary Martin** and **Ezio Pinza**

| 5/28/49 | 2[1] | 9 | | 16 **Riders In The Sky (A Cowboy Legend)**   A:2 *Please Love Me Tonight* | $15 | Capitol 57-608 |

#30 hit for The Ramrods in 1961

| 1/7/50 | 9 | 7 | | 17 **The Old Master Painter**........................A:9 / J:18 *Bless You (For The Good That's In You)* | $20 | Capitol F791 |

PEGGY LEE and MEL TORMÉ

| 8/26/50 | 28 | 1 | | 18 **Show Me The Way To Get Out Of This World** ('Cause That's Where | $20 | Capitol F1105 |
| | | | | Everything Is) ....A:28 *Happy Music* | | |

DEBUT	PEAK	WKS	Gold	A-side (Chart Hit)..B-side	$	Label & Number

LEE, Peggy — Cont'd

| 9/8/51 | 14 | 8 | | 19 **When I Dance With You I Get Ideas** ....A:14 *Tonight You Belong To Me* | $20 | Capitol F1573 |

adapted from the Argentine tango "Adios Muchachos"

| 5/24/52 | 21 | 3 | | 20 **Be Anything (But Be Mine)** ....A:21 *Forgive Me* | $20 | Decca 9-28142 |

PEGGY LEE And GORDON JENKINS And His Chorus And Orchestra
#25 hit for Connie Francis in 1964

| 6/7/52 | 3 | 13 | ● | 21 **Lover**   A:3 / S:10 / J:15 *You Go To My Head* | $20 | Decca 9-28215 |

PEGGY LEE and GORDON JENKINS And His Orchestra
from the movie *Love Me Tonight* starring Maurice Chevalier; #3 hit for Paul Whiteman in 1933

| 7/26/52 | 28 | 2 | | 22 **Watermelon Weather**...................................A:28 *The Moon Came Up With A Great Idea Last Night* | $20 | Decca 9-28238 |

BING CROSBY And PEGGY LEE

| 8/2/52 | 14 | 4 | | 23 **Just One Of Those Things** ....A:14 *I'm Glad There Is You (In This World Of Ordinary People)* | $20 | Decca 9-28313 |

PEGGY LEE And GORDON JENKINS And His Orchestra
from the Broadway musical *Jubilee* starring Melville Cooper; #10 hit for Richard Himber in 1935

LEE, Roberta   **'51**

| 12/8/51 | 13 | 10 | | Slow Poke ....J:13 / A:26 / S:28 *I Wanna Play House With You* | $15 | Decca 9-27792 |

LEONARD, Jack   MEM **'41**

Born on 2/10/13 in New York City. Died on 6/17/88 (age 75). Featured vocalist with **Tommy Dorsey** from 1936-39.

| 8/3/40 | 20 | 1 | | 1 **All This And Heaven Too** ....S(e):20 *When The Swallows Come Back To Capistrano* | $10 | Okeh 5631 |

title song from the movie starring Bette Davis

| 1/18/41 | 17 | 1 | | 2 **I Give You My Word**..................................S(mw):17 *When You're A Long, Long Way From Home* | $10 | Okeh 5886 |

Ray Bloch (orch., above 2)

LES COMPAGNONS DE LA CHANSON   HOT **'52**

"The Companions Of Song." French vocal group who sometimes accompanied **Edith Piaf**.

| 1/19/52 | 14 | 9 | | **The Three Bells (Les Trois Cloches) (The Jimmy Brown Song)**.................S:14 *Whirlwind* | $20 | Columbia 4-39657 |

group backed **Edith Piaf** on her original 1946 French recording of this song; #1 hit for The Browns in 1959

LESLIE, Laura — see CORNELL, Don

LESTER, Jerry   **'50**

Born on 2/16/10 in Chicago. Died on 3/23/95 (age 85). Singer/comedian. Hosted TV talk show *Broadway Open House* (1950-51).

| 12/2/50 | 30 | 1 | | Orange Colored Sky ....S:30 *Time Takes Care Of Everything* [N] | $20 | Coral 9-60325 |

LEWIS, Jerry — see MARTIN, Dean

LEWIS, Monica   **'48**

Born on 5/5/25 in Chicago. Singer/actress. Appeared in several movies and TV shows.

| 4/26/47 | 16 | 1 | | 1 **Midnight Masquerade** ....A:16 *A Thousand And One Nights* | $20 | Signature 15078 |

Ray Bloch (orch.)

| 8/21/48 | 21 | 3 | | 2 **A Tree In The Meadow**.........................A:21 / S:22 / J:28 *On The Street Of Regret* | $15 | Decca 24411 |

MONICA LEWIS and AMES BROTHERS
Mary Osborne Trio (instrumental backing)

LEWIS, Robert Q.   **'51**

Born on 4/5/21 in New York City. Died of emphysema on 12/11/91 (age 70). Popular emcee of various TV variety and game shows.

| 11/3/51 | 22 | 3 | | Where's-A Your House? ....J:22 *There She Goes* [N] | $20 | MGM K11056 |

Leroy Holmes (orch.); answer song to **Rosemary Clooney**'s "Come On-a My House"

LIBERACE   MEM **'52**

Born Wladziu Valentino Liberace on 5/16/19 in Milwaukee. Died of AIDS on 2/4/87 (age 67). The flamboyant pianist became a nationwide sensation in 1952 when he hosted his own TV musical show.

| 5/3/52 | 27 | 1 | | September Song ....S:27 *I Want My Mama (Mama Yo Quiero)* | $15 | Columbia 4-39709 |

George Liberace (orch.); from the movie *Knickerbocker Holiday* starring Nelson Eddy; #12 hit for Walter Huston in 1939; #51 hit for **Jimmy Durante** in 1963

LIGGINS, Joe, And His "Honeydrippers"   **'45**

Born on 7/9/16 in Guthrie, Oklahoma. Died of a stroke on 8/1/87 (age 71). R&B singer/pianist/bandleader.

| 10/20/45 | 13 | 3 | ● | 1 **The Honeydripper (Parts 1 and 2)** ....J:13 | $40 | Exclusive 207 |

the all-time #1 R&B hit (#1 for 18 weeks)

| 2/16/46 | 12 | 1 | | 2 **Got A Right To Cry** ....J:12 *Blue Moods* | $40 | Exclusive 210 |

#2 R&B hit

LOMBARDO, Guy, And His Royal Canadians ★7★ MEM **'37**

Born on 6/19/02 in London, Ontario, Canada. Died on 11/5/77 (age 75). The Lombardo brothers formed their band in 1925, with Guy as leader and Carmen as lead saxophonist/singer; gained fame by decade's end for playing "The Sweetest Music This Side of Heaven." Charted over 140 hits from 1927 to 1940 (including 21 #1 hits). The only dance band ever to sell more than 100 million records. Most remembered for their annual New Year's Eve broadcasts, always climaxed by his theme "Auld Lang Syne." Lombardo's top 5 pre-1940 #1 hits: "Charmaine!," "It Looks Like Rain In Cherry Blossom Lane," "Boo-Hoo," "We Just Couldn't Say Good-bye" and "Red Sails In The Sunset."

1)*The 3rd Man Theme* 2)*It's Love-Love-Love* 3)*Managua - Nicaragua* 4)*Anniversary Song* 5)*Harbor Lights*

Vocalists:
Andrews Sisters — 25,31,38,48
Brown, Jimmy — 16,18,19,21,34
Craig, Tony — 10,12
DeHaven, Gloria — 65
Flanagan, Bill — 56,64
Foster, Stuart — 14,15,17

Gardner, Kenny — 3,5,6,33,42,43,45,49, 51-54, 57,59-62,66,67,69,73
Grass, Cliff — 63
Henry, Fred — 1
Hildegarde — 20,28,29
Leach, Billy — 7

Lombardo, Carmen — 1,2,60
Lombardo, Rose Marie — 22
Lombardo Trio (Quartet), The — 3,8,9,13,15,17,18,23,27,30,32, 35-37,40-42,45-47,49,52-54,59, 61,70,71
Martin, Kenny — 70-72

Nelson, Skip — 9
Owen, Larry — 1
Rodney, Don — 22,23,26,30, 32,35,36,39,40,44
Song Spinners, The — 20

| 3/2/40 | 9 | 4 | | 1 Confucius Say ....J:9 *Run Little Rain Drop Run* | $10 | Decca 2917 |
| 4/20/40 | 4 | 1 | | 2 **When You Wish Upon A Star**   J:4 *Turn On The Old Music Box* | $10 | Decca 2969 |

from the Disney animated movie *Pinocchio*; #30 hit for Dion & The Belmonts in 1960

| 5/17/41 | 6 | 4 | | 3 **The Band Played On** ....S:6 *You Stepped Out Of A Dream* | $10 | Decca 3675 |

from the movie *The Strawberry Blonde* starring James Cagney and Rita Hayworth; #1 hit for Dan Quinn in 1895

DEBUT	PEAK	WKS	Gold	A-side (Chart Hit) ... B-side	$	Label & Number
				LOMBARDO, Guy, And His Royal Canadians — Cont'd		
6/7/41	17	4		4 **Intermezzo (Souvenir de Vienne)**....................S(mw):17 / S(wc):20 / S(s):20 *Star Dust* **[I]**	$10	Decca 3674
				from the movie *Intermezzo* starring Ingrid Bergman		
6/27/42	9	1		5 **Johnny Doughboy Found A Rose In Ireland**........................S:9 *Bless 'Em All*	$10	Decca 4278
4/17/43	20	1		6 **For Me And My Gal**...S(wc):20 *Beale Street Blues*	$10	Decca 4371
				title song from the movie starring **Judy Garland** and **Gene Kelly**; #1 hit for Van & Schenck in 1917; #71 hit for Freddy Cannon in 1961		
1/8/44	5	10		7 **Speak Low** / J:5 / S:6		
				from the Broadway musical *One Touch Of Venus* starring **Mary Martin**		
1/29/44	11	10		8 **Take It Easy**...J:11	$10	Decca 18573
				from the movie *Two Sisters And A Sailor*		
3/18/44	**❶²**	19		9 **It's Love-Love-Love**...........................S:❶² / J:2 *Can't You Do A Friend A Favor*	$10	Decca 18589
6/24/44	11	4	●	10 **Long Ago (And Far Away)** /..J:11		
				from the movie *Cover Girl* starring Rita Hayworth		
7/15/44	13	1		11 **Humoresque**...S(s):13 **[I]**	$10	Decca 18602
				Fred Kreitzer and Francis Vigneau (twin pianos); #7 hit for Mischa Elman in 1910; also see **Woody Herman**'s "*Mabel! Mabel!*"		
9/30/44	7	11		12 **Together**...J:7 *Come With Me My Honey (The Song Of Calypso Joe)*	$10	Decca 18617
				from the movie *Since You Went Away* starring Claudette Colbert; #1 hit for Paul Whiteman in 1928; #6 hit for Connie Francis in 1961		
12/9/44+	13	3		13 **Meet Me In St. Louis, Louis**............................J:13 *The Very Thought Of You*	$10	Decca 18626
				from the movie *Meet Me In St. Louis* starring **Judy Garland** (also #15 below); #1 hit for Billy Murray in 1904		
1/20/45	10	5		14 **Always** /..J:10 / A:14		
				#1 hit for both Vincent Lopez and **George Olsen** in 1926; revived popularity due to inclusion in the movie *Christmas Holiday* starring Deanna Durbin; #19 hit for Sammy Turner in 1959		
1/6/45	19	2		15 **The Trolley Song**..J:19	$10	Decca 18634
2/24/45	5	13		16 **A Little On The Lonely Side**................J:5 / S:8 *(All Of A Sudden) My Heart Sings*	$10	Decca 18642
4/21/45	11	8		17 **Poor Little Rhode Island** /...J:11		
				from the movie *Carolina Blues* starring **Kay Kyser**		
3/31/45	18	1		18 **Oh! Moytle**...J:18 **[N]**	$10	Decca 18651
6/23/45	**2¹**	13		19 **Bell Bottom Trousers**......................J:2 / S:6 / A:7 *Oh! Brother*	$10	Decca 18683
				based on a traditional sea chantey		
8/18/45	6	2		20 **June Is Bustin' Out All Over**......................A:6 / J:11 *This Was A Real Nice Clambake*	$10	Decca 23428
				HILDEGARDE with GUY LOMBARDO AND HIS ROYAL CANADIANS		
				from the Broadway musical *Carousel* starring John Raitt		
9/8/45	17	1		21 **Stars In Your Eyes**......................................J:17 *Small World*	$10	Decca 18696
				from the movie *Pan Americana* starring Eve Arden		
11/10/45	8	6		22 **No Can Do**..J:8 *José Gonzalez*	$10	Decca 18712
3/2/46	7	7		23 **Seems Like Old Times** /..A:7 / J:9		
1/12/46	10	8		24 **Symphony**...A:10 / J:10 **[I]**	$10	Decca 18737
2/2/46	9	5		25 **Money Is The Root Of All Evil (Take It Away, Take It Away, Take It Away)** ..A:9 *Johnny Fedora*	$15	Decca 23474
				ANDREWS SISTERS and GUY LOMBARDO And His Royal Canadians		
4/6/46	6	7		26 **Shoo Fly Pie And Apple Pan Dowdy** /..............................J:6 / A:16		
5/4/46	12	8		27 **Give Me The Moon Over Brooklyn**......................J:12	$10	Decca 18809
5/11/46	7	14		28 **The Gypsy** /..J:7 / A:11		
4/13/46	15	2		29 **One-Zy Two-Zy (I Love You-zy)**......................A:15 / J:15	$10	Decca 23511
				HILDEGARDE and GUY LOMBARDO And His Royal Canadians (above 2)		
8/24/46	14	5		30 **I'd Be Lost Without You**......................J:14 *On The Alamo*	$10	Decca 18901
12/21/46	7	4	●	31 **Christmas Island**......................J:7 / A:13 *Winter Wonderland* **[X]**	$15	Decca 23722
				ANDREWS SISTERS and GUY LOMBARDO And His Royal Canadians		
1/25/47	**❶¹**	15		32 **Managua - Nicaragua**......................J:❶¹ / S:4 / A:7 *What More Can I Ask For?*	$10	Decca 23782
2/22/47	**2³**	13		33 **Anniversary Song**......................J:2 / S:4 / A:9 *Uncle Remus Said*	$10	Decca 23799
				based on Ivanovic's 1880 song "Danube Waves"		
5/3/47	9	4		34 **April Showers**......................J:9 *If I Had My Way*	$10	Decca 23845
				#1 hit for **Al Jolson** in 1922; originally from the Broadway musical *Bombo* starring **Al Jolson**; above 2 featured in the movie *The Jolson Story* starring Larry Parks		
5/24/47	3	17		35 **I Wonder, I Wonder, I Wonder**......................J:3 / S:8 / A:16 *It Takes Time*	$10	Decca 23865
10/11/47	16	1		36 **The Echo Said "No"**......................J:16 *Don't Tell Me*	$10	Decca 24115
1/24/48	10	6		37 **I'm My Own Grandpaw**......................S:10 / J:11 *Frankie And Johnny* **[N]**	$10	Decca 24288
1/8/49-	26	1		38 **Christmas Island**......................J:26 *Winter Wonderland* **[X-R]**	$15	Decca 23722
				ANDREWS SISTERS and GUY LOMBARDO And His Royal Canadians		
2/12/49	8	19		39 **Red Roses For A Blue Lady** /......................J:8 / S:10 / A:28		
				#10 hit for Vic Dana in 1965		
4/9/49	19	9		40 **Everywhere You Go**......................J:19	$10	Decca 24549
2/26/49	20	5		41 **Down By The Station**......................S:20 *Sweet Georgia Brown*	$10	Decca 24555
				#13 hit for The Four Preps in 1960		
5/28/49	18	8		42 **Merry-Go-Round Waltz**......................S:18 / J:25 *Canadian Capers*	$10	Decca 24624
				melody adapted from the 1888 waltz "Over The Waves" (also see **Mario Lanza**'s "The Loveliest Night Of The Year")		
6/11/49	30	1		43 **Need You**......................J:30 *You Can't Buy Happiness*	$10	Decca 24614
8/6/49	19	4		44 **The Four Winds And The Seven Seas**......................J:19 *When My Dream Boat Comes Home*	$10	Decca 24648
10/1/49	11	12		45 **Hop-Scotch Polka (Scotch Hot)**......................S:11 / J:16 *Dangerous Dan McGrew*	$10	Decca 24704
10/15/49	30	1		46 **Homecoming Waltz** /......................S:30		
10/22/49	30	1		47 **The Blue Skirt Waltz**......................J:30	$10	Decca 24714
1/7/50-	18	1		48 **Merry Christmas Polka**......................S:18 *Christmas Candles* **[X]**	$15	Decca 24748
				ANDREWS SISTERS and GUY LOMBARDO And His Royal Canadians		
1/21/50	10	19		49 **Enjoy Yourself (It's Later Than You Think)**......................S:10 / J:10 *Rain Or Shine*	$10	Decca 24825
3/11/50	**❶¹¹**	27	●	50 **The 3rd Man Theme**......................J:❶¹¹ / S:2 / A:3 *The Cafe Mozart Waltz* **[I]**	$10	Decca 24839
				Don Rodney (guitar solo); from the movie *The Third Man* starring Orson Welles; #47 hit for Herb Alpert & The Tijuana Brass in 1965		
3/18/50	28	1		51 **The Wedding Samba**......................J:28 *There's A Lovely Lake In Loveland*	$10	Decca 24838
3/25/50	5	14		52 **Dearie**......................J:5 / S:11 *(She's My Lily Of Laguna) My Lily And My Rose*	$10	Decca 24899
				from the stage production *The Copacabana Show Of 1950*		
6/10/50	24	1		53 **Tiddley Winkie Woo**......................J:24 *Where Are You Gonna Be When The Moon Shines*	$10	Decca 27005
8/26/50	19	3		54 **Our Little Ranch House**......................J:19 *Here, Pretty Kitty*	$15	Decca 9-27092

DEBUT	PEAK	WKS	Gold	A-side (Chart Hit)..B-side	$	Label & Number
				LOMBARDO, Guy, And His Royal Canadians — Cont'd		
9/16/50	25	1		55 **Nola** ....J:25 *Let's Do It Again* [I]	$15	Decca 9-27178
				#3 hit for Vincent Lopez in 1922; #39 hit for **Billy Williams** in 1959		
10/7/50	10	15		56 **All My Love ("Bolero")** ....J:10 / S:15 *The Swiss Bellringer*	$15	Decca 9-27118
				adapted from the French song "Bolero"		
10/14/50	2[1]	20		57 **Harbor Lights /** ....S:2 / J:4 / A:14		
				#6 hit for Frances Langford in 1937; #8 hit for The Platters in 1960		
10/7/50	22	3		58 **The Petite Waltz (La Petite Valse)** ....J:22 / S:24 / A:30 [I]	$15	Decca 9-27208
				Fred Kreitzer and Buddy Brennan (twin pianos: #55 & 58)		
12/16/50+	6	17		59 **Tennessee Waltz /** ....J:6 / S:6 / A:21		
				#35 hit for Sam Cooke in 1964		
2/3/51	29	1		60 **Get Out Those Old Records** J:29	$15	Decca 9-27336
1/6/51-	28	1		61 **Frosty The Snowman** ....A:28 *If I Were Santa Claus* [X]	$20	Decca 9-27257
2/17/51	21	1		62 **Velvet Lips /** J:21		
2/17/51	22	5		63 **The Chicken Song (I Ain't Gonna Take It Settin' Down)** ....S:22 / J:26	$15	Decca 9-27393
3/17/51	20	5		64 **If** ....J:20 *Wait For Me*	$15	Decca 9-27449
				#82 hit for The Paragons in 1961		
9/8/51	11	12		65 **Because Of You** ....J:11 / S:27 *Out O' Breath*	$15	Decca 9-27666
				GLORIA DeHAVEN and GUY LOMBARDO And His Royal Canadians		
				song published in 1940; featured in the 1951 movie *I Was An American Spy* starring Ann Dvorak; #71 hit for Chris Montez in 1967		
12/22/51	28	1		66 **Undecided** ....J:28 *The Lie-De-Lie Song*	$15	Decca 9-27835
				#8 hit for Ella Fitzgerald & Chick Webb in 1939		
1/19/52	20	5		67 **Crazy Heart** ....J:20 *Whispering Shadows*	$15	Decca 9-27888
3/29/52	9	19		68 **Blue Tango** ....J:9 / S:16 / A:23 *At Last, At Last* [I]	$15	Decca 9-28031
				#16 hit for Bill Black's Combo in 1960		
7/26/52	30	1		69 **Kiss Of Fire** ....J:30 *Delicado (Delicate)*	$15	Decca 9-28179
				adapted from the 1913 Argentine tango "El Choclo"		
8/2/52	13	9		70 **Auf Wiederseh'n Sweetheart /** ....J:13 / A:29		
8/16/52	20	6		71 **Half As Much** J:20	$15	Decca 9-28271
				#2 Country hit for **Hank Williams** in 1952		
9/27/52	26	2		72 **Wish You Were Here** ....J:26 *Honky Tonk Sweetheart*	$15	Decca 9-28308
				title song from the Broadway musical starring Jack Cassidy		
7/10/54	14	4		73 **Hernando's Hideaway** ....J:14 / S:28 *Vas Villst Du Haben?*	$15	Decca 9-29173
				William Rodriguez (castanets); from the Broadway musical *The Pajama Game* starring John Raitt		

LONG, Johnny, And His Orchestra ★94★   MEM '45

Born on 8/21/15 in Newell, North Carolina. Died on 11/1/72 (age 57). Orchestra leader.

1)My Dreams Are Getting Better All The Time 2)No Love, No Nothin' 3)Waitin' For The Train To Come In

Vocalists: Brace, Janet, & the glee club — 10   Houston, Bob — 1   Robertson, Dick — 5-7   Young, Helen — 1
Dugan, Patti — 2,4   Lane, Frances — 5   Williams, Gene — 3   ensemble — 6,8,9

1/23/43	10	1		1 **(As Long As You're Not In Love With Anyone Else)** **Why Don't You Fall In Love With Me?**..............S:10 *Then You'll Know You're In The Carolines*	$10	Decca 4375
2/12/44	5	8		2 **No Love, No Nothin'** J:5 *You Better Give Me Lots Of Lovin', Honey*	$10	Decca 4427
				from the movie *The Gang's All Here* starring Alice Faye		
2/26/44	20	2		3 **I've Had This Feeling Before (But Never Like This)** ....J(terr.):20 *In A Friendly Little Harbor*	$10	Decca 4429
7/29/44	8	8		4 **Time Waits For No One**....................................J:8 *Featherhead*	$10	Decca 4439
				from the movie *Shine On Harvest Moon* starring Ann Sheridan		
4/14/45	3	12		5 **My Dreams Are Getting Better All The Time /** J:3 / S:3 / A:8		
				from the movie *In Society* starring Abbott & Costello		
5/5/45	8	8		6 **Candy** J:8	$10	Decca 18661
11/24/45	7	10		7 **Waitin' For The Train To Come In** ....J:7 / A:14 *Fishin' For The Moon*	$10	Decca 18718
				JOHNNY LONG And His Orchestra And DICK ROBERTSON (above 3)		
10/12/46	13	7	●	8 **In A Shanty In Old Shanty Town** ....J:13 *Blue Skies*	$10	Decca 23622
				Long first recorded this famous arrangement in a slightly different version released in 1940 on Decca 3409; #1 hit for Ted Lewis in 1932; #27 hit for Somethin' Smith & The Redheads in 1956		
1/8/49	19	3		9 **Sweet Sue, Just You**....................................A:19 *In The Glow Of Evening*	$15	Signature 15243
				#3 hit for both Earl Burtnett and Ben Pollack in 1928		
1/21/50	22	3		10 **We'll Build A Bungalow**....................................A:22 / J:24 *Skirts*	$15	King 15018

LOR, Denise   '54

Born in California. Singer/actress. Regular on TV's *Garry Moore Show* (1950-51).

9/4/54	8	14		**If I Give My Heart To You** ....A:8 / J:10 / S:13 *Hello Darling*	$20	Majar 27-X45
				Joe Candullo (orch.); #34 hit for **Kitty Kallen** in 1959		

LOSS, Joe, and his Orchestra   '48

Born Joshua Loss on 6/22/09 in Spitalfields, London, England. Died on 6/6/90 (age 80). Bandleader/violinist.

9/18/48	17	1		**A Tree In The Meadow**....................................J:17 / S:30 *My Happiness*	$10	RCA Victor 20-2965
				Howard Jones (vocal)		

LUCAS, Clyde, and his Orchestra   MEM '37

Born on 9/1/01 in Minneapolis, Kansas. Died on 1/15/82 (age 80). Trombonist/bandleader.

6/21/41	19	1		**Intermezzo (A Love Story)**....................................S(wc):19 *When Buddha Smiles* [I]	$10	Columbia 36017
				from the movie *Intermezzo* starring Ingrid Bergman		

DEBUT	PEAK	WKS	Gold	A-side (Chart Hit) / B-side	$	Label & Number
	★144★			**LUNCEFORD, Jimmie, And His Orchestra** MEM **'37**		
				Born on 6/6/02 in Fulton, Mississippi. Died on 7/12/47 (age 45). Leader of one of the most influential black big bands during the swing era. Lunceford's pre-1940 #1 hit: "Rhythm Is Our Business."		
2/7/42	4	5		1 **Blues In The Night (My Mama Done Tol' Me) — Parts 1 & 2** S:4	$20	Decca 4125
				Part 1: instrumental; Part 2: ensemble (vocals); from the movie *Blues In The Night* starring Priscilla Lane		
5/30/42	17	1		2 **I'm Gonna Move To The Outskirts Of Town Parts 1 & 2**........................S(s):17 / S(wc):19	$20	Decca 18324
4/15/44	22	1		3 **Back Door Stuff—Parts 1 & 2**..J(terr.):22 **[I]**	$20	Decca 18594
10/21/44	18	1		4 **I Dream A Lot About You** ....J(terr.):18 *Jeep Rhythm*	$20	Decca 18618
				Dan Grissom (vocal: #2 & 4)		
11/24/45	10	3		5 **The Honeydripper** ....S:10 / A:17 *Baby, Are You Kiddin'?*	$30	Decca 23451
				JIMMIE LUNCEFORD And His Orchestra and DELTA RHYTHM BOYS #2 R&B hit		
6/15/46	13	2		6 **Cement Mixer (Put-Ti-Put-Ti)**..A:13 *Just Once Too Often* **[N]**	$25	Majestic 1045
				Lunceford Quartet (vocals)		
	★104★			**LUND, Art** MEM/HOT **'47**		
				Born on 4/1/15 in Salt Lake City. Died on 5/31/90 (age 75). Attended East Kentucky State College on a sports scholarship. Baritone with **Benny Goodman** during the 1940s as both Art Lund and Art London. Starred in the 1956 Broadway musical *The Most Happy Fella*.		
4/19/47	❶²	13	●	1 **Mam'selle** S:❶² / J:2 / A:3 *Sleepy Time Gal*	$10	MGM 10011
				from the movie *The Razor's Edge* starring Tyrone Power		
6/28/47	4	13		2 **Peg O' My Heart** A:4 / S:6 / J:8 *On The Old Spanish Trail*	$10	MGM 10037
				#1 hit for Charles Harrison in 1913; #64 hit for Robert (**Bobby**) **Maxwell** in 1964		
11/22/47	14	1		3 **—And Mimi** ....S:14 *Jealous*	$10	MGM 10082
9/25/48	20	4		4 **Hair Of Gold, Eyes Of Blue /** A:20	$10	MGM 10258
				from the movie *Singing Spurs* starring Kirby Grant		
9/25/48	22	1		5 **You Call Everybody Darling** ....A:22 / J:30		
				The Crew Chiefs and The Harmonica Gentlemen (accompaniment, above 2)		
11/6/48	12	12		6 **On A Slow Boat To China** ....A:12 / S:13 / J:14 *By The Way*	$10	MGM 10269
2/26/49	22	2		7 **I've Got My Love To Keep Me Warm** ....A:22 *Someone Like You*	$10	MGM 10348
				from the 1937 movie *On The Avenue* starring Dick Powell and Alice Faye; #3 hit for **Ray Noble** in 1937; Johnny Thompson (orch.: #1-3, 6 & 7)		
7/8/50	14	7		8 **Mona Lisa** ....S:14 / J:16 / A:26 *When My Stage Coach Reaches Heaven*	$10	MGM 10689
				from the movie *Captain Carey, U.S.A.* starring Alan Ladd; #25 hit for Carl Mann in 1959		
10/11/52	27	1		9 **Cincinatti Ding Dong**..A:27 / J:29 *Going Down To The River*	$15	Coral 9-60834
				Leroy Holmes (orch., above 2)		
				LUTCHER, Nellie, And Her Rhythm MEM **'47**		
				Born on 10/15/15 in Lake Charles, Louisiana. R&B singer/songwriter/pianist.		
11/1/47	15	1		1 **He's A Real Gone Guy** ....A:15 *Let Me Love You Tonight*	$20	Capitol Am. 40017
				#2 R&B hit		
				LYMAN, Abe, and his Californians MEM **'31**		
				Born Abraham Simon on 8/4/1897 in Chicago. Died on 10/23/57 (age 60). Bandleader/drummer. Charted 25 hits from 1923-40.		
3/22/41	12	2		1 **Help Me (Cuatro Vidas)**..S(mw):12 *I Dream Of Jeanie With The Light Brown Hair* **[F]**	$15	Bluebird 10887
				Dale Evans (Roy Rogers' wife) and Lucio Garcia (vocals)		
9/5/42	4	3		2 **Amen** S:4 *He Wears A Pair Of Silver Wings*	$15	Bluebird 11542
				Rose Blane and Chorus (vocals); from the movie *What's Cookin'* starring the **Andrews Sisters**		
2/26/44	21	1		3 **Besame Mucho**..J:21 *So, Goodnight*	$15	Hit 7072
				Si Zentner (trombone); #70 hit for the Coasters in 1960		
2/26/44	25	1		4 **By The River Of Roses** ....J(terr.):25 *My British Buddy*	$15	Hit 7071
				Frank Connors (vocal)		
3/3/45	4	5		5 **Rum And Coca-Cola** S:4 / J:8 / A:18 *Since You*	$10	Columbia 36775
				ABE LYMAN and his Orchestra adaptation of an old calypso song from Trinidad; Rose Blane (Abe's wife; vocal: #2, 3 & 5)		
	★127★			**LYNN, Vera** MEM/HOT **'52**		
				Born Vera Margaret Welsh on 3/20/17 in London. England's most popular female singer during World War II.		
5/22/48	9	7		1 **You Can't Be True Dear**..A:9 / S:14 / J:15 *Once Upon A Wintertime*	$10	London 202
				Bob Farnon (orch.); with Male Voice Choir; #75 hit for the Mary Kaye Trio in 1959		
1/29/49	23	3		2 **Again** ....S:23 *Lavender Blue (Dilly Dilly)*	$10	London 310
				Bruce Campbell (orch.); from the movie *Road House* starring Ida Lupino and Cornel Wilde		
6/21/52	❶⁹	21	●	3 **Auf Wiederseh'n Sweetheart** S:❶⁹ / A:❶⁶ / J:❶⁴ *From The Time You Say Goodbye (The Parting Song)*	$15	London 451227
10/25/52	7	10		4 **Yours** ....J:7 / S:8 / A:10 *The Love Of My Life*	$15	London 451261
				with Sailors, Soldiers and Airmen of Her Majesty's Forces		
5/29/54	26	2		5 **If You Love Me (Really Love Me) (Hymne A L'Amour)**..S:26 *C'est La Vie*	$15	London 45-1412
				Charles Smart (organ); introduced by **Edith Piaf** in 1950; Roland Shaw (orch., above 3)		
				LYTELL, Jimmy, and his All Star Seven **'43**		
				Born James Sarrapede on 12/1/04 in New York City. Died on 11/26/72 (age 67). Jazz clarinetist/orchestra leader.		
3/6/43	14	3		1 **Fat Meat Is Good Meat**..S(s):14 *He's Commander-In-Chief Of My Heart*	$30	Beacon 104
				Savannah Churchill (vocal)		
4/22/50	17	5		2 **Choo'n Gum**..S:17 / A:17 / J:23 *Honky Tonkin'* **[N]**	$25	London 30100
				TERESA BREWER with JIMMY LYTELL AND THE DIXIELAND ALL STARS 78 rpm: 678; Jack Pleis (piano solo); melody adapted from George Gershwin's "An American In Paris"		

M

MacKENZIE, Gisele   MEM/HOT '55
Born Gisele LaFleche on 1/10/27 in Winnipeg, Canada. Star of TV's *Your Hit Parade* from 1953-57.

2/2/52	20	1		1 **Le Fiacre**..A:20 *Tuh Pocket Tuh Pocket (Mississippi River Boat)* [F]	$20	Capitol F1907
8/9/52	14	4		2 **Adios**...A:14 *Darlin', You Can't Love Two*	$20	Capitol F2156
				Buddy Cole (organ solo)		
12/6/52+	11	2		3 **Don't Let The Stars Get In Your Eyes** ....A:11 / J:18 *My Favorite Song*	$20	Capitol F2256
				Buddy Cole (orch., above 3)		

MacRAE, Gordon ★52★   MEM/HOT '49
Born on 3/12/21 in East Orange, New Jersey. Died of cancer on 1/24/86 (age 64). Sang with **Horace Heidt** (1942-43) and recorded numerous duets with **Jo Stafford**, late 1940s. Starred in the movie musicals *Oklahoma!* and *Carousel.* Married to actress Sheila MacRae from 1941-67; their daughter is actress Meredith MacRae.

    1)My Darling, My Darling 2)Whispering Hope 3)"A" You're Adorable

7/31/48	9	17		1 **It's Magic** ....A:9 / J:12 / S:20 *Spring In December*	$10	Capitol 15072
				Carlyle Hall (orch.); from the movie *Romance On The High Seas* starring **Doris Day** and Jack Carson; #91 hit for The Platters in 1962		
8/28/48	7	14		2 **Hair Of Gold, Eyes Of Blue** / ....J:7 / A:8 / S:10		
				from the movie *Singing Spurs* starring Kirby Grant		
10/23/48	27	1		3 **Rambling Rose** S:27	$10	Capitol 15178
10/16/48	10	6	●	4 **Say Something Sweet To Your Sweetheart** / ....A:10 / S:20		
10/16/48	16	4		5 **Bluebird Of Happiness** ....S:16 / A:21 / J:24	$10	Capitol 15207
11/13/48+	❶¹	17		6 **My Darling, My Darling** A:❶¹ / S:3 / J:4 *Girls Were Made To Take Care Of Boys*	$10	Capitol 15270
				from the Broadway musical *Where's Charley?* starring **Ray Bolger**		
2/12/49	26	2		7 **The Pussy Cat Song (Nyow! Nyot Nyow!)** ....A:26 *I'll String Along With You* [N]	$10	Capitol 15342
				JO STAFFORD AND GORDON MacRAE (above 4)		
				The Starlighters (backing vocals: #2-4, 6 & 7)		
3/5/49	20	9		8 **So In Love** ....S:20 / A:30 *A Rosewood Spinet*	$10	Capitol 15357
				from the Broadway musical *Kiss Me, Kate* starring **Alfred Drake**		
3/19/49	4	15		9 **"A" You're Adorable** / ....S:4 / J:6 / A:12		
4/2/49	7	12		10 **Need You** ....J:7 / S:11 / A:18	$10	Capitol 15393
8/20/49	4	23	●	11 **Whispering Hope** A:4 / S:6 / J:19 *A Thought In My Heart*	$10	Capitol 57-690
				JO STAFFORD AND GORDON MacRAE (above 3)		
				#5 hit for Alma Gluck & Louise Homer in 1912		
11/26/49	14	4		12 **Mule Train** / A:14		
12/24/49+	19	2		13 **Dear Hearts And Gentle People** A:19	$20	Capitol 54-777
				Andy Parker And The Plainsmen (accompaniment)		
12/24/49+	13	7		14 **Bibbidi-Bobbidi-Boo (The Magic Song)** / ....J:13 / A:14 / S:19		
				from the Disney animated feature movie *Cinderella*		
12/24/49+	18	5		15 **Echoes** ....J:18 / S:24 / A:28	$20	Capitol 54-782
3/11/50	10	11		16 **Dearie** ....A:10 / S:12 / J:13 *Monday, Tuesday, Wednesday*	$20	Capitol F858
				JO STAFFORD AND GORDON MacRAE (above 3)		
				from the stage production *The Copacabana Show Of 1950*; **Paul Weston** (orch.: #9-11 & 14-16)		

MADDOX, Johnny, and the Rhythmasters   MEM/HOT '55
Born on 8/4/29 in Gallatin, Tennessee. Honky-tonk pianist.

9/20/52	26	1		1 **Little Grass Shack**..J:26 *Cocoanut Grove* [I]	$15	Dot 45-15020
				#1 hit for Ted Fio Rito in 1934 as "My Little Grass Shack In Kealakekua"		
1/31/53	16	3		2 **In The Mood**...J:16 *By The Light Of The Silvery Moon* [I]	$15	Dot 45-15045
				#4 hit for Ernie Fields in 1959		
11/7/53	15	2		3 **Dipsy Doodle** ....J:15 *Alexander's Ragtime Band* [I]	$15	Dot 45-15102
				#1 hit for **Tommy Dorsey** in 1937		

MADIGAN, Betty   MEM/HOT '54
Born In Washington DC. Female singer.

| 5/29/54 | 12 | 8 | | **Joey**..A:12 / S:23 *And So I Walked Home* | $15 | MGM K11716 |
| | | | | Joe Lipman (orch.) | | |

MADRIGUERA, Enric, and his Orchestra   MEM '34
Born on 2/17/04 in Barcelona, Spain. Died on 9/7/73 (age 69). Violinist/band leader. Helped popularize Latin American music. Madriguera's pre-1940 #1 hit: "Carioca."

4/26/41	19	1		1 **Intermezzo** ....S(mw):19 *A Media Luz* [I]	$10	Victor 27355
				Enric Madriguera (violin solo); title song from the movie starring Ingrid Bergman		
4/8/44	7	3		2 **I Love You** / ....S:7 / J:18		
				from the Broadway musical *Mexican Hayride* starring Bobby Clark		
5/6/44	21	2		3 **Someday I'll Meet You Again** J:21	$15	Hit 7077
4/29/44	23	1		4 **Amor Amor** ....J(terr.):23 *Tico Tico*	$15	Hit 8083
				from the movie *Broadway Rhythm* starring George Murphy and **Ginny Simms**; #18 hit for Ben E. King in 1961; Bob Lido (vocal, above 3)		

MALTBY, Richard, and Orchestra   MEM/HOT '56
Born on 6/26/14 in Chicago. Died on 8/19/91 (age 77). Trumpeter/composer/bandleader.

| 10/2/54 | 21 | 5 | | **St. Louis Blues Mambo** ....S:21 *Beloved, Be True* [I] | $15 | "X" 4X-0042 |
| | | | | mambo version of the W.C. Handy classic | | |

MANGANO, Silvana   '53
Born on 4/21/30 in Rome. Died of cancer on 12/16/89 (age 59). Actress/singer. Appeared in several Italian movies. Married movie producer Dino de Laurentiis in 1949.

| 4/11/53 | 5 | 17 | ● | **Anna (El N. Zumbon)**   J:5 / S:6 / A:15 *I Loved You (Tho Voluto Bene)* [F] | $20 | MGM K11457 |
| | | | | introduced by Mangano in her movie *Anna* (vocal was actually dubbed-in by Flo Sandons); also known as "El Negro Zumbon" | | |

DEBUT	PEAK	WKS	Gold	A-side (Chart Hit)..B-side	$	Label & Number

MANNING, Bob   MEM **'53**
Born on 2/1/27 in Philadelphia. Baritone with **Art Mooney**'s band (replaced by **Al Martino**).

4/11/53	16	2		**The Nearness Of You**..A:16 *Gypsy Girl*	$15	Capitol F2383

Monty Kelly (orch.)

MANTOVANI And His Orchestra   MEM/HOT **'35**
Born Annunzio Paolo Mantovani on 11/15/05 in Venice, Italy. Died on 3/29/80 (age 74). Played classical violin in England before forming his own orchestra in the early 1930s. Had first U.S. chart hit in 1935, "Red Sails In The Sunset." Achieved international fame 20 years later with his 40-piece orchestra and distinctive "cascading strings" sound. Charted 53 albums on *Billboard's* Pop Albums charts.

11/17/51	10	19	●	1 **Charmaine** ....S:10 / A:10 / J:18 *Just For A While* **[I]**	$15	London 45-1020

written to promote the 1926 movie *What Price Glory?* starring Victor McLaglen; #1 hit for **Guy Lombardo** in 1927; #69 hit for The Four Freshmen in 1956

4/19/52	26	1		2 **Dancing With Tears In My Eyes** ....A:26 *Dear Love, My Love* **[I]**	$15	London 45-1175

#1 hit for Nat Shilkret in 1930

5/16/53	8	10		3 **The Moulin Rouge Theme (Where Is Your Heart)**..................A:8 / S:13 / J:14 *Vola Colomba* **[I]**	$15	London 451328

from the movie *Moulin Rouge* starring **Jose Ferrer**

8/14/54	10	18	●	4 **Cara Mia** ....S:10 / A:17 *How, When Or Where*	$20	London 45-1486

DAVID WHITFIELD with MANTOVANI His Orchestra and Chorus
#4 hit for Jay & The Americans in 1965

MARINERS, The   MEM **'53**
Vocal group consisting of former coastguardsmen: Jim Lewis, Tom Lockard, Nat Dickerson and Martin Karl. Regulars on **Arthur Godfrey**'s TV show.

7/29/50	16	10		1 **Sometime** ....S:16 / J:25 *Stars*	$10	Columbia 38781

7" 33-1/3 rpm: 1-600; **Archie Bleyer** (orch.); #3 hit for the Green Brothers Novelty Band in 1925

9/19/53	14	14		2 **I See The Moon** ....S:14 / J:14 *I Just Want You*	$15	Columbia 4-40047

David Rhodes (orch.)

MARLIN SISTERS, The   **'48**
Vocal duo: Trudy and Gloria Marlin (also known as the Beaver Valley Sweethearts). Also see **The Pinetoppers**.

6/12/48	19	4		1 **You Can't Be True, Dear** / ....S:19 / J:22		

THE MARLIN SISTERS with EDDIE FISHER
#75 hit for the Mary Kaye Trio in 1959

6/26/48	30	1		2 **Toolie Oolie Doolie (The Yodel Polka)**...S:30	$20	Columbia 38211
7/24/48	24	4		3 **My Happiness** ....S:24 / J:26 / A:30 *The Man On The Carrousel*	$10	Columbia 38217

#2 hit for Connie Francis in 1959; The Columbians (harmonica backing, above 3)

3/5/49	12	26	●	4 **Blue Skirt Waltz** ....J:12 / S:14 *Charlie Was A Boxer*	$10	Columbia 12394-F

FRANKIE YANKOVIC and his YANKS with THE MARLIN SISTERS
Yankovic, The Marlin Sisters and Johnny Pecon (vocals)

MARTERIE, Ralph, And His Orchestra   MEM/HOT **'53**   ★142★
Born on 12/24/14 in Naples, Italy; raised in Chicago. Died on 10/8/78 (age 63). Trumpeter/bandleader. Played trumpet for **Enric Madriguera**.

3/3/51	26	1		1 **So Long (It's Been Good To Know Yuh)** ....A:26 *Here's To Happiness*	$15	Mercury 5570-X45

Skip Farrell, Ann Andrews and Chorus (vocals)

1/10/53	6	10	●	2 **Pretend** ....A:6 / J:13 / S:16 *After Midnight* **[I]**	$15	Mercury 70045-X45
3/21/53	6	11	●	3 **Caravan** ....A:6 / J:10 / S:11 *While We Dream* **[I]**	$15	Mercury 70097-X45

RALPH MARTERIE and his "Down Beat" Orchestra
#4 hit for Duke Ellington in 1937; #48 hit for Santo & Johnny in 1960

6/20/53	13	4		4 **Crazy, Man, Crazy** ....A:13 *Go Away*	$20	Mercury 70153-X45

Larry Ragon & The Smarty-Airs (vocals)

8/28/54	3	15		5 **Skokiaan** A:3 / S:3 / J:4 *Crazy 'Bout Lollipop* **[I]**	$15	Mercury 70432-X45

South African song, named for a Zulu tribal drink; #70 hit for **Bill Haley & His Comets** in 1960

MARTIN, Dean   MEM/HOT **'56**   ★115★
Born Dino Crocetti on 6/7/17 in Steubenville, Ohio. Died of respiratory failure on 12/25/95 (age 78). Singer/actor. To California in 1937, worked local clubs. Teamed with comedian **Jerry Lewis** in Atlantic City in 1946. First movie, *My Friend Irma*, in 1949. Team broke up after 16th movie, *Hollywood Or Bust*, in 1956. Appeared in many movies since then. Own TV series from 1965-74.

12/4/48	22	1		1 **That Certain Party** ....A:22 *The Money Song* **[N]**	$20	Capitol 15249

DEAN MARTIN AND JERRY LEWIS
#8 hit for Ted Lewis in 1926

2/19/49	10	4		2 **Powder Your Face With Sunshine (Smile! Smile! Smile!)**..........A:10 / J:27 *Absence Makes The Heart Grow Fonder (For Somebody Else)*	$20	Capitol 15351
9/2/50	11	16		3 **I'll Always Love You** ....S:11 / J:16 / A:19 *Baby, Obey Me!*	$25	Capitol F1028

from the movie *My Friend Irma Goes West* starring Martin and **Jerry Lewis**; **Paul Weston** (orch., above 2)

2/10/51	14	6		4 **If** ....J:14 / A:23 / S:26 *I Love The Way You Say Goodnight*	$25	Capitol F1342

Lou Busch (orch.); #82 hit for The Paragons in 1961

9/6/52	12	10		5 **You Belong To Me** ....S:12 / A:13 / J:20 *Hominy Grits*	$25	Capitol F2165

#7 hit for The Duprees in 1962

11/14/53	2[6]	22	●	6 **That's Amore** J:2 / S:2 / A:2 *You're The Right One*	$25	Capitol F2589

from the movie *The Caddy* starring Martin and **Jerry Lewis**

7/24/54	15	10		7 **Sway (Quien Sera)** ....S:15 / A:18 *Money Burns A Hole In My Pocket*	$20	Capitol F2818

#14 hit for Bobby Rydell in 1960; Dick Stabile (orch., above 3)

MARTIN, Freddy, and his Orchestra ★19★ MEM '46

Born on 12/9/06 in Cleveland. Died on 9/30/83 (age 76). Leader of one of the most popular "sweet" bands, his tenor saxophone style led to the nickname "Mr. Silvertone." Pianist Jack Fina was a featured sideman. **Merv Griffin** was his late-1940s singing star. Martin's pre-1940 #1 hit: "I Saw Stars."

1)Piano Concerto In B Flat 2)Managua, Nicaragua 3)To Each His Own 4)Symphony
5)The Hut-Sut Song (A Swedish Serenade)

Vocalists:
Arnold, Murray — 28
Conklin, Gene — 19
Griffin, Merv — 34-3

Hughes, Glenn —
11,13,17,25,32,33
Martin Men, The — 12,19,21,23,
25,29,32,33,35,36,38,39

Rogers, Clyde —
2,5,7-10,20,22,25
Stone, Eddie — 1,4,6,12-14
Wade, Stuart — 9,26,27,30

Wayne, Artie — 16
the band — 40
ensemble — 27,30,34,37

DEBUT	PEAK	WKS	Gold	A-side	$	Label & Number
6/7/41	2[1]	9		1 The Hut-Sut Song (A Swedish Serenade) ⟨S:2 *The Karlstad Ball*⟩	$10	Bluebird 11147
7/5/41	7	2		2 Intermezzo ⟨S:7 *Nice Dreamin' Baby*⟩	$10	Bluebird 11123
				title song from the movie starring Ingrid Bergman		
8/9/41	❶[8]	24	●	3 Piano Concerto In B Flat / ⟨S:❶[8] [I]⟩		
				Jack Fina (piano); pop arrangement of the Tchaikovsky classic; also see #7 below for a vocal adaptation of the same melody		
8/16/41	17	1		4 Why Don't We Do This More Often? ⟨S:(wc):17⟩	$10	Bluebird 11211
9/20/41	19	1		5 'Til Reveille ⟨S:(s):19 *Flamingo*⟩	$10	Bluebird 11167
1/10/42	17	2		6 Rose O'Day (The Filla-Ga-Dusha Song) ⟨S:(wc):17 / S:(mw):18 *Miss You*⟩	$10	Bluebird 11286
1/17/42	8	1		7 Tonight We Love ⟨S:8 *Carmen Carmela*⟩	$10	Bluebird 11320
				vocal version of #3 above; melody also used for Jackie Wilson's 1960 hit "Alone At Last" (#8)		
6/27/42	16	2		8 Johnny Doughboy Found A Rose In Ireland ⟨S:(wc):16 / S:(s):19 *I'll Keep The Lovelight Burning*⟩	$10	Bluebird 11503
8/15/42	17	1		9 Jingle, Jangle, Jingle ⟨S:(e):17 *I Met Her On Monday*⟩	$10	Victor 27909
				from the movie *The Forest Rangers* starring Fred MacMurray		
10/17/42	20	1	●	10 White Christmas / ⟨S:(wc):20 [X]⟩		
				from the movie *Holiday Inn* starring **Bing Crosby**		
2/19/44	15	1		11 Abraham ⟨J:15⟩	$10	Victor 27946
				tribute to Abraham Lincoln		
11/7/42	20	1		12 I Met Her On Monday ⟨S:(mw):20 *Jingle, Jangle, Jingle* [N]⟩	$10	Victor 27909
12/19/42+	16	3		13 A Touch Of Texas ⟨S:(wc):16 / S:(mw):20 *Soft-Hearted*⟩	$10	Victor 20-1504
1/9/43	18	2		14 I Get The Neck Of The Chicken ⟨S:(mw):18 *Can't Get Out Of This Mood*⟩	$10	Victor 20-1515
				above 2 from the movie *Seven Days' Leave* starring Lucille Ball		
8/21/43	16	1		15 (Theme from the) Warsaw Concerto ⟨S:(wc):16 / S:(e):20 *From Twilight 'Til Dawn* [I]⟩	$10	Victor 20-1535
				Jack Fina (piano); from the movie *Suicide Squadron* starring Anton Walbrook; melody used for The Four Coins' 1958 hit "The World Outside" (#28)		
4/14/45	8	8		16 Dream / ⟨A:8 / J:13⟩		
				originally heard as the closing theme for composer **Johnny Mercer**'s radio show; #19 hit for Betty Johnson in 1958		
4/28/45	15	2		17 Everytime ⟨A:15⟩	$10	Victor 20-1645
4/28/45	6	7		18 Laura ⟨A:6 / S:7 / J:12 *A Song To Remember* [I]⟩	$10	Victor 20-1655
				title song from the movie starring Gene Tierney and Dana Andrews		
9/29/45	7	2		19 Lily Belle ⟨A:7 / J:10 *And There You Are*⟩	$10	Victor 20-1712
12/1/45+	❶[2]	17		20 Symphony / ⟨S:❶[2] / A:❶[1] / J:2⟩		
12/1/45	13	4		21 In The Middle Of May ⟨A:13 / J:13⟩	$10	Victor 20-1747
12/22/45	16	1		22 White Christmas ⟨J:16 *Abraham* [X-R]⟩	$10	Victor 27946
3/23/46	4	9		23 One-Zy, Two-Zy (I Love You-zy) ⟨J:4 / A:5 / S:6 *Sleepy Baby*⟩	$10	RCA Victor 20-1826
4/27/46	7	6		24 Bumble Boogie ⟨S:7 / A:9 / J:13 *Now And Forever* [I]⟩	$10	RCA Victor 20-1829
				Jack Fina (piano); based on Rimsky-Korsakov's "Flight Of The Bumble Bee"; #21 hit for B. Bumble & The Stingers in 1961		
6/22/46	2[1]	13		25 Doin' What Comes Natur'lly ⟨A:2 / J:2 / S:4 *Blue Champagne*⟩	$10	RCA Victor 20-1878
				from the Broadway musical *Annie Get Your Gun* starring **Ethel Merman**		
8/10/46	❶[2]	17		26 To Each His Own ⟨S:❶[2] / J:3 / A:3 *You Put A Song In My Heart*⟩	$10	RCA Victor 20-1921
				written for, but not included in the movie starring Olivia de Havilland; #21 hit for The Platters in 1960		
1/18/47	❶[3]	13		27 Managua, Nicaragua ⟨J:❶[3] / S:❶[2] / A:3 *Heaven Knows When*⟩	$10	RCA Victor 20-2026
5/3/47	14	1		28 Moon-Faced, Starry-Eyed ⟨J:14 *What Good Would The Moon Be?*⟩	$10	RCA Victor 20-2176
				from the Broadway musical *Street Scene* starring Norman Cordon		
8/16/47	5	9		29 The Lady From 29 Palms ⟨A:5 / J:6 *Cumana*⟩	$10	RCA Victor 20-2347
9/13/47	16	1		30 Come To The Mardi Gras (Não Tenho Lagrimas) ⟨A:16 *Lolita Lopez (The Belle of El Salvador)*⟩	$10	RCA Victor 20-2288
4/3/48	6	11		31 Sabre Dance Boogie ⟨S:6 / A:7 / J:7 *After You've Gone* [I]⟩	$10	RCA Victor 20-2721
				Barclay Allen (piano); based on Khatchaturian's "Gayne Ballet Suite"		
5/1/48	5	11		32 The Dickey-Bird Song ⟨S:5 / A:8 / J:8 *If Winter Comes*⟩	$10	RCA Victor 20-2617
				from the movie *Three Daring Daughters* starring Jeanette MacDonald		
11/6/48	4	17		33 On A Slow Boat To China ⟨A:4 / J:4 / S:5 *Czardas*⟩	$10	RCA Victor 20-3123
10/29/49	8	17	●	34 I've Got A Lovely Bunch Of Coconuts ⟨S:8 / A:10 / J:11 *(There's a) Bluebird On Your Windowsill* [N]⟩	$15	RCA Victor 47-3047
				78 rpm: 20-3554		
3/11/50	5	10		35 (Put Another Nickel in) Music! Music! Music! ⟨A:5 / J:11 / S:13 *Wilhelmina*⟩	$15	RCA Victor 47-3217
				78 rpm: 20-3693; #54 hit for The Sensations in 1961		
6/10/50	17	6		36 The 3rd Man Theme ⟨A:17 / J:22 *Home Cookin'*⟩	$15	RCA Victor 47-3797
				from the movie *The Third Man* starring Orson Welles; #47 hit for Herb Alpert & The Tijuana Brass in 1965		
3/31/51	12	7		37 The Aba Daba Honeymoon ⟨A:12 / J:17 / S:30 *Beautiful Madness*⟩	$15	RCA Victor 47-4065
				from the movie *Two Weeks With Love* starring **Debbie Reynolds** and **Carleton Carpenter**; #1 hit for Arthur Collins & Byron Harlan in 1914		
4/14/51	19	6		38 Never Been Kissed ⟨J:19 / A:19 / S:27 *Jo-Ann* [N]⟩	$15	RCA Victor 47-4099
7/14/51	18	3		39 Truly Truly Fair ⟨A:18 / J:27 *The Good Humor Man*⟩	$15	RCA Victor 47-4159
10/13/51	15	7		40 Down Yonder ⟨A:15 / S:24 / J:24 *Take Her To Jamaica*⟩	$15	RCA Victor 47-4267
				Murray Arnold (piano solo); #5 hit for Ernest Hare & Billy Jones in 1921; #48 hit for Johnny & The Hurricanes in 1960		
5/16/53	15	3		41 April In Portugal (The Whisp'ring Serenade) ⟨S:15 / J:17 *Penny Whistle Blues* [I]⟩	$10	RCA Victor 47-5052
				Portuguese song originally published as "Coimbra"		

MARTIN, Grady '52

Born on 1/17/29 in Chapel Hill, Tennessee. Died of a heart attack on 12/3/2001 (age 72). Session guitarist in Nashville.

7/26/52	30	1		1 **Wild Side Of Life** ....J:30 *It's So-Long And Good-Bye To You*	$20	Decca 9-28055
				BURL IVES And GRADY MARTIN And His Slew Foot Five		
				#1 Country hit for Hank Thompson in 1952		
8/2/52	16	6		2 **Till The End Of The World** ....J:16 *Just A Little Lovin' (Will Go A Long Way)*	$20	Decca 9-28265
				BING CROSBY And GRADY MARTIN And His Slew Foot Five		
				#4 Country hit for **Ernest Tubb** in 1949		

MARTIN, Mary MEM '44

Born on 12/1/13 in Weatherford, Texas. Died of cancer on 11/3/90 (age 76). Legendary Broadway actress. Mother of actor Larry Hagman.

10/7/44	6	8		1 **I'll Walk Alone**...S:6 / J:11 *Good Night, Wherever You Are*	$10	Decca 23340
				Camarata (orch.); from the movie *Follow The Boys* starring **Marlene Dietrich**		
3/25/50	8	7		2 **Go To Sleep, Go To Sleep, Go To Sleep** ....S:8 / A:12 / J:17 *But Me, I Love You* [N]	$10	Columbia 38744
				MARY MARTIN and ARTHUR GODFREY		
				7" 33-1/3 rpm: 1-569; **Archie Bleyer** (orch.)		

MARTIN, Tony ★30★ MEM/HOT '51

Born Alvin Morris on 12/25/12 in San Francisco. Singer/actor. Appeared in several movies. Hosted own TV show from 1954-56. Married actress/dancer Cyd Charisse in 1948.

1)There's No Tomorrow 2)I Get Ideas 3)I Said My Pajamas (And Put on My Pray'rs)
4)To Each His Own 5)Tonight We Love (Concerto No. 1, B Flat Minor)

Orchestras: Hagen, Earle — 6-8   Martin, Skip — 9   **Rose, David** — 3   Sinatra, Ray — 1,2
Hayton, Lennie — 28   René, Henri — 10-27,30   **Sack, Al** — 4,5   Winterhalter, Hugo — 29

Vocalists: Harris, Phil — 20   Lyttle Sisters, The — 5,8   **Starlighters, The** — 4
Hutton, Betty — 20   Shore, Dinah — 15,16,20   **Warren, Fran** — 12

4/6/40	10	2		1 **It's A Blue World** ....J:10 *All The Things You Are*	$10	Decca 2932
				from the movie *Music In My Heart* starring Martin		
8/3/40	16	1		2 **Fools Rush In (Where Angels Fear To Tread)**.................................S(e):16 *Perfidia (Tonight)*	$10	Decca 3119
				#12 hit for Rick Nelson in 1963		
11/8/41	5	8		3 **Tonight We Love (Concerto No. 1, B Flat Minor)** S:5 *I Guess I'll Have To Dream The Rest*	$10	Decca 3988
				melody also used for Jackie Wilson's 1960 hit "Alone At Last" (#8); also see **Freddy Martin**'s vocal and instrumental versions of this Tchaikovsky classic		
7/27/46	4	16	●	4 **To Each His Own** S:4 / A:4 / J:7 *I'll See You In My Dreams*	$10	Mercury 3022
				written for, but not included in the movie starring Olivia de Havilland; #21 hit for The Platters in 1960		
10/12/46	9	7		5 **Rumors Are Flying** ....S:9 / A:10 / J:10 *And Then It's Heaven*	$10	Mercury 3032
6/12/48	30	1		6 **For Every Man There's A Woman**.....................................S:30 *What's Good About Goodbye*	$10	RCA Victor 20-2689
				from the movie *Casbah* starring Martin		
8/7/48	11	14		7 **It's Magic**...A:11 / S:12 / J:15 *It's You Or No One*	$10	RCA Victor 20-2862
				from the movie *Romance On The High Seas* starring **Doris Day** and Jack Carson; #91 hit for The Platters in 1962		
5/21/49	17	3		8 **If You Stub Your Toe On The Moon**...................................A:17 *Once And For Always*	$10	RCA Victor 20-3383
				from the movie *A Connecticut Yankee In King Arthur's Court* starring **Bing Crosby**		
8/27/49	24	3		9 **Circus** ....S:24 *No No And No*	$20	RCA Victor 47-2947
				78 rpm: 20-3488		
11/12/49+	2[1]	27		10 **There's No Tomorrow** S:2 / A:4 / J:4 *A Thousand Violins*	$20	RCA Victor 47-3078
				78 rpm: 20-3582; #3 hit in 1916 for Enrico Caruso as "O Sole Mio"; #1 hit in 1960 for Elvis Presley as "It's Now Or Never"		
12/24/49+	15	6		11 **Marta (Rambling Rose of the Wildwood)** ....A:15 *Bye Bye Baby*	$20	RCA Victor 47-3104
				78 rpm: 20-3598; #19 hit for Arthur Tracy in 1932		
1/21/50	3	13		12 **I Said My Pajamas (And Put on My Pray'rs)** A:3 / S:5 / J:8 *Have I Told You Lately That I Love You*	$20	RCA Victor 47-3119
				TONY MARTIN and FRAN WARREN		
				78 rpm: 20-3613		
5/13/50	18	6		13 **Valencia** ....S:18 / J:25 / A:29 *I Don't Care If The Sun Don't Shine*	$20	RCA Victor 47-3755
				#1 hit for Paul Whiteman in 1926		
7/15/50	9	17		14 **La Vie En Rose** ....S:9 / J:13 / A:27 *Tonight*	$20	RCA Victor 47-3819
2/3/51	8	12		15 **A Penny A Kiss** / ....A:8 / J:12 / S:14	$20	RCA Victor 47-3755
				TONY MARTIN and DINAH SHORE		
3/3/51	24	2		16 **In Your Arms** ....S:24 / A:26	$20	RCA Victor 47-4019
				DINAH SHORE and TONY MARTIN		
				based on Offenbach's *Barcarolle* from the opera *Tales Of Hoffmann*; same melody used for Elvis Presley's "Tonight Is So Right For Love" on his 1960 album *G.I. Blues*		
3/3/51	19	6		17 **Would I Love You (Love You, Love You)** / ....A:19 / S:25		
6/9/51	20	1		18 **I Apologize** A:20	$20	RCA Victor 47-4056
				#3 hit for **Bing Crosby** in 1931; #72 hit for Timi Yuro in 1961		
6/2/51	3	30		19 **I Get Ideas** S:3 / J:4 / A:4 *Tahiti, My Island*	$20	RCA Victor 47-4141
				adapted from the Argentine tango "Adios Muchachos"		
9/1/51	24	2		20 **The Musicians** ....A:24 *How D'Ye Do And Shake Hands* [N]	$20	RCA Victor 47-4225
				DINAH SHORE, BETTY HUTTON, TONY MARTIN, PHIL HARRIS		
9/15/51	18	1		21 **Vanity** ....A:18 *Oh! Beauty!*	$20	RCA Victor 47-4246
9/22/51	17	4		22 **Over A Bottle Of Wine**...A:17 / S:26 *You'll Know*	$20	RCA Victor 47-4220
11/3/51	9	12		23 **Domino** ....A:9 / S:10 / J:11 *It's All Over But The Memories*	$20	RCA Victor 47-4343
5/3/52	6	15		24 **Kiss Of Fire** ....S:6 / A:11 / J:13 *For The Very First Time*	$20	RCA Victor 47-4671
				adapted from the 1913 Argentine tango "El Choclo"		
8/16/52	24	1		25 **Some Day** / ....J:24 / A:29		
				from the movie *The Vagabond King* starring Kathryn Grayson		
8/30/52	27	1		26 **Luna Rossa (Blushing Moon)** J:27	$15	RCA Victor 47-4836

DEBUG	PEAK	WKS	Gold	A-side (Chart Hit)..B-side	$	Label & Number

MARTIN, Tony — Cont'd

11/8/52	27	1		27 **Dance Of Destiny** ....S:27 *Sleepy Time Gal*	$15	RCA Victor 47-5008
5/30/53	17	1		28 **April In Portugal (The Whisp'ring Serenade)**............................J:17 *Now Hear This*	$15	RCA Victor 47-5279
				Portuguese song originally published as "Coimbra"		
1/2/54	10	11		29 **Stranger In Paradise** ....S:10 / A:10 / J:12 *I Love Paris*	$15	RCA Victor 47-5535
				from the Broadway musical *Kismet* starring **Alfred Drake**		
3/27/54	5	16		30 **Here** ....A:5 / S:7 / J:10 *Philosophy*	$15	RCA Victor 47-5665
				adapted from an Aria in Verdi's opera *Rigoletto*		

MARTINO, Al   MEM/HOT **'63**
Born Alfred Cini on 10/7/27 in Philadelphia. Pop singer. Played singer "Johnny Fontaine" in the 1972 movie *The Godfather*.

5/17/52	❶³	19	●	1 **Here In My Heart** ....S:❶³ / A:❶³ / J:2 *I Cried Myself To Sleep*	$25	BBS 101 (45)
				new version by Martino charted in 1961 on Capitol 4593 (#86)		
6/28/52	12	8		2 **Take My Heart** ....J:12 / S:15 / A:18 *I Never Cared*	$20	Capitol F2122
				Monty Kelly (orch., above 2)		

MARX, Groucho — see KAYE, Danny

MASSEY, Louise, and The Westerners   MEM **'47**
Born Victoria Louise Massey on 8/10/02 in Midland Texas. Died on 6/20/83 (age 80). Country singer. The Westerners: her brothers Curtis (died on 10/20/91, age 81) and Allen (died on 3/3/83, age 75) Massey, her husband Milt Mabie (died in September 1973, age 73) and Larry Wellington.

| 6/14/47 | 16 | 1 | | **My Adobe Hacienda** ....J:16 *Starlight Schottische* | $15 | Columbia 37332 |
| | | | | original version released in 1941 on Okeh 6077 | | |

MASTERS, Frankie, and his Orchestra   MEM **'40**
Born on 4/12/04 in Saint Marys, West Virginia. Died on 1/29/91 (age 86). Singer/songwriter/bandleader. In 1942, **David Rose** served as band's arranger.

11/4/39	❶⁶	12		1 **Scatter-Brain** ....J:❶⁶ *Take Me Out To The Ball Game*	$20	Vocalion 4915
				Frankie Masters (vocal)		
5/18/40	7	5		2 **Alice Blue Gown** ....J:7 *Irene*	$15	Vocalion 5455
				Marion Francis (vocal); from the movie *Irene* starring Anna Neagle and Ray Milland; #1 hit for Edith Day in 1920		
11/2/40	15	6		3 **Ferry-Boat Serenade** ....S(mw):15 / S(wc):15 *The Same Old Story*	$15	Okeh 5716
				Marion Francis and The Masters Voices (vocals)		
7/5/41	19	1		4 **Daddy** ....S(wc):19 *Will You Still Be Mine?*	$15	Okeh 6232
				Swingmasters (vocals)		

MAXWELL, Bobby, And His Swinging Harps   HOT **'64**
Born on 4/19/21 in New York City. Jazz harpist/composer. With NBC Symphony under Toscanini at age 17. Also recorded as Mickey Maxwell and Robert Maxwell in the late 1950s and the mid-60s.

| 2/9/52 | 24 | 2 | | **Chinatown My Chinatown** ....A:24 / J:27 / S:29 *Shuffle Off To Buffalo* [I] | $20 | Mercury 5773-X45 |
| | | | | #1 hit for the American Quartet in 1915 | | |

MAY, Billy, And His Orchestra   HOT **'52**
Born on 11/10/16 in Pittsburgh. Arranger/conductor/sideman for many of the big bands. After leading his own band in the early 1950s, he went on to arrange/conduct for **Frank Sinatra** and compose movie scores.

2/2/52	17	2		1 **Charmaine** ....A:17 *When I Take My Sugar To Tea* [I]	$15	Capitol F1919
				written to promote the 1926 movie *What Price Glory?* starring Victor McLaglen; #1 hit for **Guy Lombardo** in 1927; #69 hit for The Four Freshmen in 1956		
7/5/52	8	12		2 **Walkin' My Baby Back Home** ....A:8 / J:11 / S:12	$20	Capitol F2130
4/4/53	16	3		3 **Can't I** ....A:16 / S:17 / J:18 *Blue Gardenia*	$20	Capitol F2389
11/14/53	16	3		4 **Lover, Come Back To Me!** ....A:16 *That's All*	$20	Capitol F2610
				NAT "KING" COLE and **BILLY MAY and His Orchestra** (above 3) from the Broadway musical *The New Moon* starring Evelyn Herbert; #3 hit for Paul Whiteman in 1929; #95 hit for The Cleftones in 1962		

McGHEE, "Stick," and His Buddies   **'49**
Born Granville McGhee on 3/23/18 in Knoxville, Tennessee. Died of cancer on 8/15/61 (age 43). R&B singer/guitarist.

| 8/27/49 | 26 | 1 | | **Drinkin' Wine Spo-Dee-O-Dee** ....J:26 *Blues Mixture (I'd Rather Drink Muddy Water)* | $75 | Atlantic 873 |
| | | | | the first of Atlantic Records' many R&B hits (#2 R&B hit) | | |

McGUIRE SISTERS, The   MEM/HOT **'55**
Vocal trio from Middletown, Ohio: sisters Phyllis (born on 2/14/31), Christine (born on 7/30/29) and Dorothy (born on 2/13/30) McGuire.

6/26/54	7	15		1 **Goodnight, Sweetheart, Goodnight** ....J:7 / S:8 / A:9 *Heavenly Feeling*	$20	Coral 9-61187
				#5 R&B hit for The Spaniels in 1954		
10/16/54	10	10		2 **Muskrat Ramble** / ....J:10 / S:11 / A:16	$20	Coral 9-61258
				Dick Jacobs (orch.); first released on Coral 9-61258 in 1954; #8 hit for **Louis Armstrong** in 1926; #54 hit for Freddy Cannon in 1961		
11/6/54	28	1		3 **Lonesome Polecat** S:28	$20	Coral 9-61278
				first released on Coral 9-61239; from the movie *Seven Brides For Seven Brothers* starring Howard Keel and Jane Powell; Neal Hefti (orch.: #1 & 3)		

McINTYRE, Hal, and his Orchestra   MEM **'45**
★131★ Born on 11/29/14 in Cromwell, Connecticut. Died in an apartment fire on 5/5/59 (age 44). Alto saxophonist. Played for **Glenn Miller** from 1937-41.

2/17/45	14	1		1 **I'm Making Believe** ....A:14 *I'm In A Jam With Baby*	$15	Bluebird 30-0831
				Ruth Gaylor (vocal); from the movie *Sweet And Lowdown* starring **Benny Goodman**		
4/28/45	3	19		2 **Sentimental Journey** ....J:3 / S:3 / A:3 *I'm Gonna See My Baby* [I]	$10	Victor 20-1643
10/20/45	8	5		3 **I'll Buy That Dream** ....A:8 *I'd Do It All Over Again*	$10	Victor 20-1679
				from the movie *Sing Your Way Home* starring Jack Haley		
6/1/46	8	4		4 **The Gypsy** / A:8		
6/1/46	17	3		5 **Cement Mixer (Put-Ti — Put-Ti)** J:17	$25	Cosmo 475
				Nancy Reed (vocal)		
7/6/46	17	1		6 **There's No One But You** ....A:17 *Patience And Fortitude*	$25	Cosmo 470
				Frankie Lester (vocal: #3, 4 & 6)		

DEBUT	PEAK	WKS	Gold	A-side (Chart Hit) ....B-side	$	Label & Number

★138★ McKINLEY, Ray, and his Orchestra   MEM '47

Born on 6/18/10 in Fort Worth, Texas. Died on 5/7/95 (age 84). Drummer for the Dorsey Brothers, **Jimmy Dorsey** (1935-39), then co-leader of the **Will Bradley** band. Ray played from 1943-45 with **Glenn Miller**'s Army Air Force band before his own postwar band caught on, with Eddie Sauter (of **Sauter-Finnegan**) arrangements. He led the Glenn Miller Orchestra in the late 1950s and early 1960s. Also see **Will Bradley**.

DEBUT	PEAK	WKS		A-side	$	Label & Number
5/8/43	16	4		1 **Big Boy** ....S(wc):16 *Hard Hearted Hannah*	$15	Capitol 131
				Imogene Lynn (vocal)		
3/29/47	15	1		2 **Hoodle-Addle** ....A:15 *Passé*	$15	Majestic 7207
				THE RAY McKINLEY QUARTET		
				McKinley, vocal & drums; Louis Stein, piano; Mundell Lowe, guitar; Ward Erwin, bass		
5/3/47	10	3		3 **Red Silk Stockings And Green Perfume**..A:10 *Jiminy Crickets*	$15	Majestic 7216
11/22/47	8	5		4 **Civilization (Bongo, Bongo, Bongo)** A:8 / J:13 / S:14 *Those Things Money Can't Buy*	$15	Majestic 7274
				from the Broadway musical *Angel In The Wings* starring Hank Ladd; Ray McKinley and band (vocals, above 2)		
8/7/48	13	16		5 **You Came A Long Way (From St. Louis)**...........................S:13 / J:18 / A:23 *For Heaven's Sake*	$10	RCA Victor 20-2913
				RAY McKINLEY and Some of the Boys		
				McKinley, vocal; Johnny Gray, guitar; John Potoker, piano; Johnny Chance, bass; Paul Kashishian, drums		
3/12/49	19	3		6 **Sunflower**..J:19 / A:20 / S:27 *Little Jack Frost Get Lost*	$10	RCA Victor 20-3334
				Jean Friley and Ray McKinley (vocals); a court ruling found the 1964 hit "Hello, Dolly!" to be directly based on this song		

McLAURIN, Bette, and Her Friends   MEM '52

Born in 1929 in Winston-Salem, North Carolina; raised in Jamaica, Long Island, New York. Black singer.

DEBUT	PEAK	WKS		A-side	$	Label & Number
5/10/52	23	3		**I May Hate Myself In The Morning**.................................S:23 / J:23 *I Hear A Rhapsody*	$40	Derby 45-790
				Rex Kearney (orch.)		

McVEA, Jack, And His All Stars   '47

Born on 11/5/14 in Los Angeles. Died of cancer on 12/27/2000 (age 86). R&B singer/saxophonist/clarinetist. With **Lionel Hampton** from 1940-43.

DEBUT	PEAK	WKS		A-side	$	Label & Number
1/25/47	3	9		**Open The Door Richard!** A:3 / S:7 / J:8 *Lonesome Blues* **[N]**	$40	Black & White 792
				#2 R&B hit		

MERCER, Johnny ★35★   MEM '45

Born on 11/18/09 in Savannah, Georgia. Died on 6/25/76 (age 66). Legendary lyricist of more than 1000 songs, including "Blues In The Night," "That Old Black Magic" and "Moon River." Founded Capitol Records in 1942. Won the Grammy's Trustees Award in 1987.

1)On The Atchison, Topeka And Santa Fe   2)Personality   3)Ac-Cent-Tchu-Ate The Positive   4)Candy   5)Baby, It's Cold Outside

DEBUT	PEAK	WKS		A-side	$	Label & Number
9/5/42	7	6		1 **Strip Polka** ....S:7 *The Air-Minded Executive*	$10	Capitol 103
1/16/43	19	1		2 **I Lost My Sugar In Salt Lake City** ....S(wc):19 *The Wreck Of The Old '97*	$10	Capitol 122
				Freddie Slack (orch.); from the movie *Stormy Weather* starring Lena Horne		
1/15/44	13	5		3 **G.I. Jive** ....S:13 / J:15 *(I'm Going To Sit Right Down And) Write Myself A Letter*	$10	Capitol 141
4/29/44	20	1		4 **San Fernando Valley** ....S(wc):20 *Someone's In The Kitchen With Dinah*	$10	Capitol 150
				JOHNNY MERCER and The BARRIES		
9/16/44	19	1		5 **Sam's Got Him** ....J(terr.):19 *Duration Blues*	$10	Capitol 164
1/6/45	❶²	16		6 **Ac-Cent-Tchu-Ate The Positive** A:❶² / S:2 / J:2 *There's A Fellow Waiting In Poughkeepsie*	$10	Capitol 180
				from the movie *Here Come The Waves* starring **Bing Crosby** and **Betty Hutton**		
2/24/45	❶¹	19		7 **Candy /** A:❶¹ / J:❶¹ / S:2	$10	
				JOHNNY MERCER, JO STAFFORD		
3/10/45	12	2		8 **I'm Gonna See My Baby** J:12	$10	Capitol 183
7/14/45	❶⁸	19		9 **On The Atchison, Topeka And Santa Fe** J:❶⁸ / S:❶⁷ / A:❶⁶ *Conversation While Dancing*	$10	Capitol 195
				from the movie *The Harvey Girls* starring Judy Garland		
11/17/45	16	1		10 **Surprise Party** ....A:16 *Camptown Races*	$10	Capitol 217
1/26/46	❶²	15		11 **Personality** A:❶² / S:❶¹ / J:2 *If I Knew Then*	$10	Capitol 230
				from the movie *Road To Utopia* starring **Bing Crosby** and **Bob Hope**		
8/10/46	11	9		12 **My Sugar Is So Refined /** J:11		
9/28/46	22	1		13 **Ugly Chile (You're Some Pretty Doll)** J:22	$10	Capitol 268
12/7/46+	8	8		14 **Zip-A-Dee-Doo-Dah** ....A:8 / J:15 *Ev'rybody Has A Laughing Place*	$10	Capitol 323
				from the Disney movie *Song Of The South* starring James Baskett; #8 hit for Bob B. Soxx & The Blue Jeans in 1963		
1/4/47-	4	1		15 **Winter Wonderland /** A:4 / J:16 **[X]**		
				#2 hit for Guy Lombardo in 1934		
12/14/46+	5	10		16 **A Gal In Calico** ....A:5 / J:7	$10	Capitol 316
				from the movie *The Time, The Place And The Girl* starring Dennis Morgan; **The Pied Pipers** (backing vocals: #6, 7, 9, 11, 12 & 14-16)		
1/11/47	8	7		17 **Huggin' And A-Chalkin'**..............................J:8 / A:9 *Take Me Back To Little Rock (Arkansas)* **[N]**	$10	Capitol 334
4/12/47	13	2		18 **I Do Do Do Like You** ....A:13 *Movie Tonight* **[N]**	$10	Capitol 367
9/20/47	4	8		19 **Sugar Blues** ....J:4 / A:13 / S:15 *Why Should I Cry Over You?*	$10	Capitol 448
				#2 hit for Clyde McCoy in 1931; #92 hit for Ace Cannon in 1962		
10/25/47	12	1		20 **Save The Bones For Henry Jones ('Cause Henry Don't Eat No Meat) /**...................A:12		
11/8/47	12	1		21 **Harmony** A:12	$15	Capitol 15000
				JOHNNY MERCER And THE KING COLE TRIO (above 2)		
				from the movie *Variety Girl* starring Mary Hatcher		
5/14/49	3	19		22 **Baby, It's Cold Outside** A:3 / S:4 / J:8 *I Never Heard You Say*	$10	Capitol 57-567
				MARGARET WHITING AND JOHNNY MERCER		
				45 rpm: 54-582; from the movie *Neptune's Daughter* starring Esther Williams; **Paul Weston** (orch.: #3, 4, 6-19 & 22)		
10/25/52	30	1		23 **The Glow Worm**..A:30 *The New Ashmolean*	$15	Capitol F2248
				The Blue Reys (backing vocals); **Alvino Rey** (orch.); originally released in 1949 on Capitol 15412; #1 hit in 1908 for both Lucy Isabelle Marsh and Victor Orchestra; new lyrics added by Mercer in 1952		

MERMAN, Ethel
MEM **'35**

Born Ethel Zimmerman on 1/16/08 in Astoria, Queens, New York. Died on 2/15/84 (age 76). Legendary Broadway actress. Starred in such shows as *Anything Goes*, *Call Me Madam*, *Annie Get Your Gun* (which provided her trademark song, "There's No Business Like Show Business"), and *Gypsy*.

2/20/43	18	1		1 **Move It Over**..S(wc):18 *(We'll Be Singing Hallelujah)* Marching Thru Berlin	$10	Victor 20-1521
				Male Quintet (backing vocals)		
3/4/50	12	11		2 **Dearie** / J:12 / S:13 / A:19		
				RAY BOLGER And ETHEL MERMAN		
				from the stage production *The Copacabana Show Of 1950*		
3/11/50	20	2		3 **I Said My Pajamas (And Put On My Pray'rs)** ....J:20 / S:25 / A:30	$15	Decca 24873
4/29/50	15	3		4 **If I Knew You Were Comin' I'd've Baked A Cake** ...J:15 *It's So Nice To Have A Man Around The House*	$15	Decca 24944
				ETHEL MERMAN and RAY BOLGER (above 2)		
4/7/51	30	1		5 **You're Just In Love** ....S:30 *Something To Dance About* (Merman)	$20	Decca 9-27317
				ETHEL MERMAN and DICK HAYMES		
				Gordon Jenkins (orch. and chorus); from the Broadway musical *Call Me Madam* starring Merman		
5/5/51	29	1		6 **Once Upon A Nickel** ....A:29 *Oldies* **[N]**	$20	Decca 9-27506
				RAY BOLGER And ETHEL MERMAN		
				Sy Oliver (orch.: #2-4 & 6)		

MERRILL, Joan
'41

Born on 1/2/18 in Baltimore. Died of Alzheimer's disease on 5/10/92 (age 74). Actress/singer. Appeared in several movies.

| 8/23/41 | 17 | 2 | | **Daddy** ....S(s):17 *Intermezzo* | $15 | Bluebird 11171 |

MERRILL, Robert
'47

Born on 6/7/47 in Brooklyn, New York. Legendary opera singer.

| 6/7/47 | 14 | 1 | | **(Baa-Baa-Baa) Whiffenpoof Song**..A:14 *The Sweetheart Of Sigma Chi* | $10 | RCA Victor 10-1313 |
| | | | | Russ Case (orch.) and Male Chorus; theme song of the Yale University Glee Club since 1909; #96 hit for Bob Crewe in 1960 | | |

MERRY MACS, The ★79★
MEM **'44**

Vocal group from Minneapolis: brothers Joe, Ted and Judd McMichael, with Marjory Garland. Judd McMichael and Garland eventually married. Joe McMichael died in action during World War II on 2/12/44 (age 28); replaced by Lynn Allen. Judd McMichael died on 10/30/89 (age 83). Ted McMichael died of pneumonia on 2/27/2001 (age 92).

1)*Mairzy Doats* 2)*Jingle Jangle Jingle* 3)*Sentimental Journey*

6/14/41	15	3		1 **The Hut-Sut Song A Swedish Serenade**.................................S(wc):15 *Mary Lou*	$10	Decca 3810
3/7/42	14	3		2 **Deep In The Heart Of Texas** ....S(wc):14 *Kimaneero Down To Cairo (A Frog Went A Courting)*	$10	Decca 4136
				#78 hit for Duane Eddy in 1962		
7/4/42	4	8		3 **Jingle Jangle Jingle** S:4 *Cheatin' On The Sandman*	$10	Decca 18361
				from the movie *The Forest Rangers* starring Fred MacMurray		
11/14/42	8	4		4 **Praise The Lord And Pass The Ammunition!** ....S:8 *Tweedle O Twill*	$10	Decca 18498
2/26/44	❶[5]	15		5 **Mairzy Doats** J:❶[5] / S:2 *I Got Ten Bucks And Twenty-Four Hours' Leave* **[N]**	$10	Decca 18588
				#75 hit for The Innocence in 1967		
7/29/44	7	14		6 **Pretty Kitty Blue Eyes**...J:7 *Sing Me A Song Of Texas*	$10	Decca 18610
10/21/44	17	1		7 **Let's Sing A Song About Susie**..J(terr.):17 *Up, Up, Up*	$10	Decca 18622
6/30/45	4	12		8 **Sentimental Journey** J:4 / A:6 / S:7 *Choo Choo Polka*	$10	Decca 18684
9/29/45	9	1		9 **On The Atchison, Topeka And The Santa Fe**........................A:9 / S:10 / J:10 *If I Had You*	$20	Decca 23436
				JUDY GARLAND and THE MERRY MACS		
				Lyn Murray (orch.); from the movie *The Harvey Girls* starring Garland		
4/20/46	9	6		10 **Laughing On The Outside (Crying On The Inside)** ....J:9 / A:13 *Ashby De La Zooch (Castle Abbey)*	$10	Decca 18811

METRONOME ALL STAR BAND
'41

All-star group: **Count Basie** (piano); **Harry James**, **Cootie Williams**, Ziggy Elman (trumpets); **Tommy Dorsey** and J.C. Higginbotham (trombones); **Benny Goodman** (clarinet); **Benny Carter** and Toots Mondello (alto sax); Coleman Hawkins and **Tex Beneke** (tenor sax); Charlie Christian (electric guitar); Artie Bernstein (bass); Buddy Rich (drums).

| 4/12/41 | 15 | 1 | | **One O'Clock Jump** ....S(wc):15 *Bugle Call Rag* **[I]** | $20 | Victor 27314 |
| | | | | selected for NARAS Hall of Fame; also see **Count Basie**'s solo version in 1947 | | |

MILLER, Allen, and his Orchestra
'43

| 5/8/43 | 15 | 6 | | **It Can't Be Wrong** ....S(e):15 / S(mw):19 *Do I Love You* | $20 | Hit 7045 |
| | | | | from the movie *Now Voyager* starring Bette Davis | | |

MILLER, Eddie, Orch.
'49

Born Edward Lisbona on 7/16/05 in Manchester, England. Died on 11/30/89 (age 84). Honky-tonk pianist. Nicknamed "Piano."

| 12/10/49 | 14 | 3 | | **(Round Her Neck) She Wore A Yellow Ribbon**...........................J:14 *Part-Time Sweetheart* | $20 | Rainbow 80033 |
| | | | | Phil Ellis Choristers (vocals); from the movie *She Wore A Yellow Ribbon* starring John Wayne | | |

MILLER, Glenn, and his Orchestra ★2★   MEM '40

Born Alton Glenn Miller on 3/1/04 in Clarinda, Iowa. Disappeared on a flight over the English Channel on 12/15/44 (age 40). Leader of the most universally beloved of all big bands. He played trombone for Ben Pollack, Red Nichols, **Benny Goodman**, and the **Dorsey** Brothers, became de facto leader of **Ray Noble**'s 1935 American band, and did arrangements for **Glen Gray** and others before starting his own band in 1937. It failed, as did a 1938 successor, but in 1939 Glenn developed his trademark reed sound (4 saxophones and clarinet) and soared to the top. Vital ingredients in the band's staggering success were arrangers Jerry Gray and Bill Finegan, and featured soloists Bobby Hackett, **Tex Beneke**, **Billy May** and **Hal McIntyre**. At the band's peak after four years of extraordinary popularity, Glenn left to enlist in the Army Air Force in September 1942, and formed the war's most famous service band. After Miller's death, Tex Beneke carried on the legacy with a new Miller orchestra, and Hollywood's 1954 *The Glenn Miller Story* further immortalized the music and the man. Theme song: "Moonlight Serenade" (hit #3 in 1939). Miller's top 5 pre-1940 #1 hits: "Over The Rainbow," "Moon Love," "Wishing (Will Make It So)," "Stairway To The Stars" and "The Man With The Mandolin."

1)In The Mood 2)Moonlight Cocktail 3)Chattanooga Choo Choo 4)Tuxedo Junction 5)(I've Got a Gal in) Kalamazoo

Vocalists: Beneke, Tex — 37,42,46,48, 54,59,63,74,76,79,81 | Eberle, Ray — 2-6,8,9,12-14, 16,18-23,25,26,28,29,32,40,41, | Kelly, Paula — 43,46 | **Modernaires, The** — 36,37, 42-46,48,53,54,59,61-65,67,70
Caceres, Ernie — 48 | 44-47,49,51-53,55-57,60-62,69 | Lane, Lillian — 77,80 | Nelson, Skip — 64,66,67
Claire, Dorothy — 36 | Hutton, Marion — | **Lathrop, Jack** — 24,27 | Stevens, Garry — 83
Crew Chiefs, The — | 10,11,31,54,59,63 | **Malvin, Artie** — 75,77,82 |
 | | Mello Larks, The — 83 |

DEBUT	PEAK	WKS	Gold	A-side (Chart Hit) / B-side	$	Label & Number
10/21/39+	❶13	28	●	1 **In The Mood** — J:❶13 *I Want To Be Happy* [I]	$15	Bluebird 10416
				#4 hit for Ernie Fields in 1959		
12/2/39	3	7		2 **My Prayer** — J:3 *Blue Moonlight*	$15	Bluebird 10404
				#1 hit for The Platters in 1956		
1/27/40	2⁹	11		3 **Careless** — J:2 *Vagabond Dreams*	$15	Bluebird 10520
2/10/40	5	3		4 **Faithful Forever** — J:5 *Bluebirds In The Moonlight (Silly Idea)*	$15	Bluebird 10465
				from the animated movie *Gulliver's Travels*		
4/13/40	2⁵	7		5 **When You Wish Upon A Star** — J:2		
				from the Disney animated movie *Pinocchio*; #30 hit for Dion & The Belmonts in 1960		
2/24/40	7	2		6 **The Gaucho Serenade** — J:7	$15	Bluebird 10570
3/9/40	❶9	17	●	7 **Tuxedo Junction** — J:❶9 *Danny Boy (Londonderry Air)* [I]	$15	Bluebird 10612
				#82 hit for Frankie Avalon in 1960		
3/23/40	8	2		8 **In An Old Dutch Garden (By An Old Dutch Mill)** / — J:8		
4/27/40	10	1		9 **Starlit Hour** — J:10	$15	Bluebird 10553
				from the Broadway musical *Earl Carroll Vanities* starring Lillian Roth		
5/4/40	❶5	14		10 **The Woodpecker Song** — J:❶5 *Let's All Sing Together*	$15	Bluebird 10598
6/1/40	7	5		11 **Boog-It** / — J:7		
7/13/40	10	1		12 **Shake Down The Stars** — J:10	$15	Bluebird 10689
6/15/40	7	4		13 **Say It** — J:7 *My! My!*	$15	Bluebird 10631
				from the movie *Buck Benny Rides Again* starring Jack Benny; #5 hit for Isham Jones in 1934		
6/22/40	2²	8		14 **Imagination** — J:2 / S:3 *Say "Si Si" (Para Vigo Me Voy)*	$15	Bluebird 10622
7/6/40	9	3		15 **Slow Freight** — J:9 *Bugle Call Rag* [I]	$15	Bluebird 10740
7/27/40	3	7		16 **Fools Rush In (Where Angels Fear to Tread)** — S:3 *Yours Is My Heart Alone*	$15	Bluebird 10728
				#12 hit for Rick Nelson in 1963		
7/27/40	5	6	●	17 **Pennsylvania Six-Five Thousand** — S:5 *Rug Cutter's Swing* [I]	$15	Bluebird 10754
				band calls out the telephone number of New York's Hotel Pennsylvania		
7/27/40	16	2		18 **Devil May Care** — S(wc):16 / S(s):19 *I'm Stepping Out With A Memory Tonight*	$15	Bluebird 10717
8/3/40	5	8		19 **The Nearness Of You** — S:5 *Mister Meadowlark*	$15	Bluebird 10745
8/3/40	17	1		20 **Sierra Sue** — S(wc):17 / S:19 *Moments In The Moonlight*	$15	Bluebird 10638
8/10/40	2⁴	14		21 **Blueberry Hill** — S:2 *A Million Dreams Ago*	$15	Bluebird 10768
				#2 hit for Fats Domino in 1957		
8/10/40	17	1		22 **I'll Never Smile Again** — S(s):17 *The Rumba Jumps!*	$15	Bluebird 10673
				#25 hit for The Platters in 1961		
8/31/40	10	1		23 **When The Swallows Come Back To Capistrano** — S:10 *A Cabana In Havana*	$15	Bluebird 10776
				#80 hit for Pat Boone in 1957		
10/5/40	9	1		24 **Crosstown** — S:9 *What's Your Story, Morning Glory*	$15	Bluebird 10832
11/9/40	8	2		25 **Our Love Affair** / — S:8		
				from the movie *Strike Up The Band* starring Mickey Rooney and **Judy Garland**		
11/9/40	10	1		26 **The Call Of The Canyon** — S:10	$15	Bluebird 10845
11/23/40	15	1		27 **Beat Me Daddy, Eight To A Bar** — S(wc):15 / S(mw):17 *Falling Leaves*	$15	Bluebird 10876
11/30/40	10	2		28 **A Handful Of Stars** — S:10 *Yesterthoughts*	$15	Bluebird 10893
				from the movie *Hullabaloo* starring Frank Morgan		
12/21/40	2²	6		29 **A Nightingale Sang In Berkeley Square** — S:2 *Goodbye, Little Darlin', Goodbye*	$15	Bluebird 10931
				from the London musical *New Faces*		
1/11/41	3	10		30 **Anvil Chorus–Parts 1 & 2** — S:3 [I]	$15	Bluebird 10982
				from the opera *Il Trovatore* by Verdi		
1/11/41	6	2		31 **Five O'Clock Whistle** — S:6 *Shadows On The Sand*	$15	Bluebird 10900
1/18/41	7	4		32 **Along The Santa Fe Trail** — S:7 *Yes, My Darling Daughter*	$15	Bluebird 10970
				title song from the movie		
2/15/41	18	2		33 **Frenesi** — S(e):18 / S(wc):19 *My Blue Heaven* [I]	$15	Bluebird 10994
2/22/41	❶1	8		34 **Song Of The Volga Boatmen** — S:❶1 *Chapel In The Valley* [I]	$15	Bluebird 11029
				adaptation of a Russian folk song		
3/22/41	3	4		35 **I Dreamt I Dwelt In Harlem** — S:3 *A Stone's Throw From Heaven* [I]	$15	Bluebird 11063
4/19/41	13	4		36 **Perfidia** — S(mw):13 *Spring Will Be So Sad*	$15	Bluebird 11095
				#15 hit for The Ventures in 1960		
8/2/41	7	5		37 **The Booglie Wooglie Piggy** / — S:7		
6/28/41	19	2		38 **Boulder Buff** — S(wc):19 [I]	$15	Bluebird 11163
8/30/41	17	4		39 **Adios** — S(wc):17 / S(e):20 *Under Blue Canadian Skies* [I]	$15	Bluebird 11219
				same version re-charted in 1948 (#84 below)		

DEBUT	PEAK	WKS	Gold	A-side (Chart Hit) ....B-side	$	Label & Number
				MILLER, Glenn, and his Orchestra — Cont'd		
9/6/41	4	6		40 **You And I** ....S:4 *The Angels Came Thru*	$15	Bluebird 11215
9/6/41	17	2		41 **The Cowboy Serenade (While I'm Rollin' My Last Cigarette)**..........S(wc):17 *Below The Equator*	$15	Bluebird 11235
9/13/41	❶⁹	23	●	42 **Chattanooga Choo Choo** / ....S:❶⁹		
				#32 hit for Tuxedo Junction in 1978; the first record formally certified as a million-seller		
11/29/41	19	1		43 **I Know Why** ....S(s):19	$15	Bluebird 11230
				above 2 and #46 from the movie *Sun Valley Serenade* starring Sonja Henie		
9/20/41	16	3		44 **I Guess I'll Have To Dream The Rest** ......S(e):16 / S(mw):16 / S(wc):19 / S(s):20 *Take The "A" Train*	$15	Bluebird 11187
11/8/41	❶¹	15		45 **Elmer's Tune** ....S:❶¹ *Delilah*	$15	Bluebird 11274
11/15/41	20	1		46 **It Happened In Sun Valley** ....S(e):20 *The Kiss Polka*	$15	Bluebird 11263
11/29/41	20	1		47 **I'm Thrilled** ....S(mw):20 / S(s):20 *From One Love To Another*	$15	Bluebird 11287
12/27/41	5	2		48 **Jingle Bells** ....S:5 *Santa Claus Is Comin' To Town* **[X]**	$15	Bluebird 11353
				#18 hit for Benny Goodman in 1935; #74 hit for Perry Como in 1957		
1/3/42	6	7		49 **(There'll Be Blue Birds Over) The White Cliffs Of Dover** ....S:6 *We're The Couple In The Castle*	$15	Bluebird 11397
1/10/42	❶²	18		50 **A String Of Pearls** ....S:❶² *Day Dreaming* **[I]**	$15	Bluebird 11382
				same version re-charted in 1944 (#72 below)		
1/24/42	7	4		51 **Ev'rything I Love** ....S:7 *Baby Mine*	$15	Bluebird 11365
				from the Broadway musical *Let's Face It* starring **Danny Kaye**		
1/31/42	17	1		52 **This Is No Laughing Matter** ....S(s):17 / S(mw):19 *Humpty Dumpty Heart*	$15	Bluebird 11369
2/21/42	❶¹⁰	15		53 **Moonlight Cocktail** ....S:❶¹⁰ *Happy In Love*	$15	Bluebird 11401
5/2/42	2²	13		54 **Don't Sit Under The Apple Tree (With Anyone Else But Me)** ....S:2 *The Lamplighter's Serenade*	$15	Bluebird 11474
5/2/42	7	11		55 **Skylark** / S:7	$15	Bluebird 11462
				#101 hit for Linda Ronstadt in 1984		
5/2/42	19	1		56 **The Story Of A Starry Night** ....S(e):19		
				adapted from Tchaikovsky's *Pathetique Symphony*; recorded by The Platters in 1959 as "Where" (#44), and by **Steve Lawrence** in 1961 as "In Time" (#94)		
5/23/42	10	1		57 **Always In My Heart** ....S:10 *When The Roses Bloom Again*	$15	Bluebird 11438
				title song from the movie starring Kay Francis; #82 hit for Los Indios Tabajaras in 1964		
7/4/42	19	1	●	58 **American Patrol** ....S(mw):19 / S(e):20 *Soldier, Let Me Read Your Letter* **[I]**	$10	Victor 27873
				#3 hit for Sousa's Band in 1901		
8/1/42	❶⁷	18	●	59 **(I've Got a Gal in) Kalamazoo** / ....S:❶⁷		
10/10/42	14	8		60 **At Last** ....S(s):14 / S(wc):19	$10	Victor 27934
				#47 hit for Etta James in 1961		
8/1/42	8	3		61 **Sweet Eloise** ....S:8 *Sleep Song*	$10	Victor 27879
9/19/42	2¹	15		62 **Serenade In Blue** ....S:2 *That's Sabotage*	$10	Victor 27935
				#59, 60 & 62 from the movie *Orchestra Wives* starring George Montgomery		
12/12/42	7	8		63 **Juke Box Saturday Night** ....S:7 *Sleepy Town Train* **[N]**	$15	Victor 20-1509
				featuring imitations of **Harry James**' "Ciribiribin" and the **Ink Spots**' "If I Didn't Care"; from the Broadway musical *Stars On Ice*; updated version by Nino & The Ebb Tides charted in 1961 (#57)		
12/19/42+	5	8		64 **Moonlight Becomes You** / S:5		
				from the movie *Road To Morocco* starring **Bing Crosby** and **Bob Hope**		
1/16/43	16	2		65 **Moonlight Mood** ....S(s):16 / S(e):20	$10	Victor 20-1520
12/19/42+	5	4		66 **Dearly Beloved** ....S:5 *I'm Old Fashioned*	$10	Victor 27953
				from the movie *You Were Never Lovelier* starring Fred Astaire and Rita Hayworth		
3/13/43	❶¹	14		67 **That Old Black Magic** ....S:❶¹ *A Pink Cocktail For A Blue Lady*	$10	Victor 20-1523
				from the movie *Star Spangled Rhythm* starring **Bing Crosby** and **Bob Hope**; #13 hit for **Sammy Davis, Jr.** in 1955		
10/23/43	15	6		68 **Rhapsody In Blue** ....S(wc):15 / S(mw):19 *Along The Santa Fe Trail* **[I]**	$10	Victor 20-1529
				#3 hit for Paul Whiteman feat. George Gershwin in 1924; #41 for Deodato in 1973		
11/6/43+	9	3		69 **Blue Rain** ....S:9 / J:14 *Caribbean Clipper*	$10	Victor 20-1536
				originally released on Bluebird 10486 in 1939		
1/8/44	12	8		70 **It Must Be Jelly ('Cause Jam Don't Shake Like That)** ....J:12 *Rainbow Rhapsody*	$10	Victor 20-1546
				#68 & 70 recorded on 7/15/42		
1/8/44	18	1		71 **Sunrise Serenade** ....J:18 *Moonlight Serenade* (#3/'39) **[I]**	$15	Bluebird 10214
				originally charted in 1939 (#7)		
3/4/44	22	1		72 **A String Of Pearls** ....J:22 *Tuxedo Junction* **[I-R]**	$10	Victor 20-1552
				reissue of #50 above		
4/1/44	20	1		73 **Here We Go Again** ....J(terr.):20 *Long Time No See, Baby* **[I]**	$10	Victor 20-1563
				recorded on 7/14/42		
				TEX BENEKE with THE GLENN MILLER ORCHESTRA:		
5/25/46	4	9		74 **Hey! Ba-Ba-Re-Bop** / ....S:4 / A:7 / J:9		
6/22/46	19	1		75 **The Whiffenpoof Song** Baa! Baa! Baa! J:19	$10	RCA Victor 20-1859
				theme song of the Yale University Glee Club since 1909; #96 hit for Bob Crewe in 1960		
6/1/46	12	1		76 **It Couldn't Be True! (Or Could It?)** ....A:12 *One More Tomorrow*	$10	RCA Victor 20-1835
6/15/46	15	2		77 **Cynthia's In Love** ....A:15 *Strange Love*	$10	RCA Victor 20-1858
				TEX BENEKE and the MILLER ORCHESTRA:		
8/3/46	9	3		78 **I Know** ....A:9 *Ev'rybody Loves My Baby (My Baby)*	$10	RCA Victor 20-1914
8/17/46	4	18		79 **Give Me Five Minutes More** ....J:4 / S:6 / A:6 *Texas Tex*	$10	RCA Victor 20-1922
				featured in the movie *Sweetheart Of Sigma Chi* starring Elyse Knox		
10/19/46	9	5		80 **Passe** ....A:9 / J:18 *The Woodchuck Song*	$10	RCA Victor 20-1951
12/21/46+	6	8		81 **A Gal In Calico** / ....S:6 / J:6 / A:7		
2/1/47	11	3		82 **Oh, But I Do** A:11	$10	RCA Victor 20-1991
				above 2 from the movie *The Time, The Place And The Girl* starring Dennis Morgan		
2/22/47	3	11		83 **Anniversary Song** ....A:3 / S:3 / J:4 *Hoodle Addle*	$10	RCA Victor 20-2126
				from the movie *The Jolson Story* starring Larry Parks; based on Ivanovic's 1880 song "Danube Waves"		
				GLENN MILLER and his Orchestra:		
7/10/48	28	1		84 **Adios** ....J:28 *Delilah* **[I-R]**	$10	RCA Victor 20-2942
				reissue of #39 above		

MILLER, Mitch, and his Orchestra & Chorus MEM/HOT '55
Born on 7/4/11 in Rochester, New York. Producer/conductor/arranger. A&R executive for both Columbia and Mercury Records. Best known for his sing-along albums and TV show (1961-64). Won Grammy's Lifetime Achievement Award in 2000.

7/15/50	3	12	1 **Tzena Tzena Tzena** A:3 / S:10 / J:17 *The Sleigh*	$10	Columbia 38885
			7" 33-1/3 rpm: 1-706; adaptation of a popular Israeli song		
9/27/52	23	1	2 **Meet Mister Callaghan** A:23 *How Strange* [I]	$15	Columbia 4-39851

MILLINDER, Lucky, And His Orchestra ★143★ MEM '44
Born Lucius Millinder on 8/8/1900 in Anniston, Alabama; raised in Chicago. Died on 9/28/66 (age 66). Black bandleader.

8/22/42	17	1	1 **I Want A Tall Skinny Papa** S(s):17 *Shout, Sister, Shout!*	$20	Decca 18386
			LUCKY MILLINDER And His Orchestra With ROSETTA THARPE		
12/19/42+	14	2	2 **When The Lights Go On Again (All Over The World)** S(s):14 / S(wc):18 *That's All*	$20	Decca 18496
1/15/44	15	2	3 **Sweet Slumber** S(s):15 *Don't Cry Baby*	$20	Decca 18569
			Trevor Bacon (vocal, above 2)		
8/12/44	20	1	4 **Hurry, Hurry** J(terr.):20 *I Can't See For Lookin'*	$20	Decca 18609
			above 2 were Top 5 Country hits		
6/30/45	7	10	5 **Who Threw The Whiskey In The Well** J:7 / S:10 *Shipyard Social Function*	$20	Decca 18674
			Wynonie "Mr. Blues" Harris (vocal, above 2)		
7/28/51	19	8	6 **I'm Waiting Just For You** J:19 *Bongo Boogie*	$75	King 45-4453
			Annisteen Allen and John Carol (vocals); #27 hit for **Pat Boone** in 1957; above 5 (except #4) were #1 or #2 R&B hits		

MILLS BROTHERS ★32★ MEM/HOT '32
Legendary family vocal group from Piqua, Ohio: father John Mills (born on 2/11/1889; died on 12/8/67, age 78), with sons Herbert (born on 4/2/12; died on 4/12/89, age 77), Harry (born on 8/19/13; died on 6/28/82, age 68) and Donald (born on 4/29/15; died on 11/13/99, age 84). Group appeared in several movies. Won Grammy's Lifetime Achievement Award in 1998. The Mills Brothers' pre-1940 #1 hits: "Tiger Rag" and "Dinah."

1)Paper Doll 2)You Always Hurt The One You Love 3)The Glow-Worm 4)Across The Alley From The Alamo
5)Nevertheless (I'm In Love With You)

8/7/43	❶[12]	30	●	1 **Paper Doll /** S:❶[12] / J:❶[1]		
				recorded on 2/18/42		
2/19/44	16	1		2 **I'll Be Around** J:16	$10	Decca 18318
				#78 hit for **Don Cherry** in 1956		
6/3/44	❶[5]	33	●	3 **You Always Hurt The One You Love /** S:❶[5] / J:2		
				#12 hit for **Clarence Henry** in 1961		
6/24/44	8	5		4 **Till Then** S:8 / J:16	$10	Decca 18599
				#20 hit for **The Classics** in 1963		
5/19/45	6	11		5 **I Wish /** J:6 / S:10 / A:11		
5/19/45	14	5		6 **Put Another Chair At The Table** J:14	$10	Decca 18663
4/20/46	12	4		7 **Don't Be A Baby, Baby** J:12 *Never Make A Promise In Vain*	$10	Decca 18753
5/18/46	7	15		8 **I Don't Know Enough About You** J:7 *There's No One But You*	$10	Decca 18834
9/28/46	12	7		9 **I Guess I'll Get The Papers And Go Home** J:12 *Too Many Irons In The Fire*	$10	Decca 23638
5/10/47	2[2]	15		10 **Across The Alley From The Alamo** J:2 / S:4 / A:15 *Dream, Dream, Dream (R&B #5)*	$10	Decca 23863
10/25/47	16	1		11 **When You Were Sweet Sixteen** J:16 *Way Down Home*	$10	Decca 23627
				from the movie *The Great John L.* starring Greg McClure; #1 hit in 1900 for both George J. Gaskin and Jere Mahoney		
11/20/48	17	11		12 **Gloria** J:17 / S:18 *I Want To Be The Only One*	$10	Decca 24509
2/12/49	8	9		13 **I Love You So Much It Hurts /** S:8 / J:12 / A:15	$10	Decca 24550
				#71 hit for **Charlie Gracie** in 1957		
2/19/49	9	11		14 **I've Got My Love To Keep Me Warm** J:9 / S:12	$10	Decca 24550
				from the 1937 movie *On The Avenue* starring Dick Powell and Alice Faye; #3 hit for **Ray Noble** in 1937		
8/20/49	5	15		15 **Someday (You'll Want Me To Want You)** J:5 / S:8 / A:13 *On A Chinese Honeymoon*	$10	Decca 24694
				#56 hit for **Della Reese** in 1960		
12/31/49	24	1		16 **Who'll Be The Next One (To Cry Over You)** J:24 *I Want You To Want Me (To Want You)*	$10	Decca 24749
				#6 hit for **Charles Harrison** in 1921		
2/25/50	5	15		17 **Daddy's Little Girl** J:5 / A:8 / S:9 *If I Live To Be A Hundred*	$15	Decca 9-24872
				#42 hit for **Al Martino** in 1967		
11/11/50	4	17		18 **Nevertheless (I'm In Love With You)** J:4 / S:9 / A:16 *Thirsty For Your Kisses*	$15	Decca 9-27253
				featured in the movie *Three Little Words* starring Fred Astaire; #5 hit for Jack Denny in 1931		
1/19/52	7	12		19 **Be My Life's Companion** A:7 / J:10 / S:21 *Love Lies*	$15	Decca 9-27889
				Sy Oliver (orch.)		
9/27/52	❶[3]	21	●	20 **The Glow-Worm** J:❶[3] / A:2 / S:2 *After All*	$15	Decca 9-28384
				Hal McIntyre (orch.); #1 hit in 1908 for both Lucy Isabelle Marsh and Victor Orchestra; new lyrics added by **Johnny Mercer** in 1952		
3/21/53	14	1		21 **Twice As Much** J:14 / A:20 *(I Want) Someone To Care For*	$15	Decca 9-28586
5/23/53	12	4		22 **Say Si Si** A:12 *I'm With You*	$15	Decca 9-28670
				#19 hit for **Xavier Cugat** in 1936; **Sonny Burke** (orch., above 2)		
1/23/54	15	3		23 **The Jones Boy** S:15 / A:16 *She Was Five And He Was Ten*	$15	Decca 9-28945
				Sy Oliver (orch.)		

MIRANDA, Carmen MEM '48
Born Maria Do Carmo Miranda Da Cunha on 2/9/09 in Marco de Canavezes, Portugal; raised in Rio de Janeiro. Died of a heart attack on 8/5/55 (age 46). Singer/actress. Billed as the "Brazilian Bombshell." Appeared in several movies and Broadway shows. Known for her elaborate costumes and fruit-topped turbans.

10/9/48	12	14	1 **Cuanto La Gusta** S:12 / J:13 / A:27 *The Matador*	$15	Decca 24479
			CARMEN MIRANDA - ANDREWS SISTERS		
			from the movie *A Date With Judy* starring Wallace Beery and Jane Powell		
1/28/50	23	3	2 **The Wedding Samba** S:23 / J:23 *I See, I See (Asi Asi)*	$15	Decca 24841
			CARMEN MIRANDA and ANDREWS SISTERS		
			Vic Schoen (orch., above 2)		

MR. FORD & MR. GOON-BONES '49

Duo of Ralph Ford (Hammond organ) with Ted Goon & His Goon-Bones. Also see **Brother Bones And His Shadows**.

| 7/23/49 | 14 | 7 | | Ain't She Sweet...J:14 / S:19 *The Sheik Of Araby* [I] | $25 | Crystalette 601 |

label also showed artist as MR. GOON-BONES & MR. FORD; #1 hit for Ben Bernie in 1927; #19 hit for The Beatles in 1964

MITCHELL, Guy ★53★   MEM/HOT '56

Born Al Cernik on 2/27/27 in Detroit. Died on 7/1/99 (age 72). Sang briefly with **Carmen Cavallaro**'s orchestra in the late 1940s. Appeared in several TV series. Acted in the movies *Those Redheads From Seattle* (1953) and *Red Garters* (1954).

1)My Heart Cries For You 2)My Truly, Truly Fair 3)The Roving Kind

12/9/50+	2[7]	21	●	1 My Heart Cries For You /	J:2 / A:2 / S:2		
				adapted from the 18-century French melody "Chanson de Marie Antoinette"; #38 hit for Ray Charles in 1964		
12/16/50+	4	17		2 The Roving Kind	J:4 / S:4 / A:5	$20	Columbia 4-39067
				45 rpm: 6-918; adapted from the English folk song "The Pirate Ship"		
2/24/51	24	2		3 You're Just In Love....................................A:24 / S:29 *Marrying For Love*	$20	Columbia 4-39052
				GUY MITCHELL & ROSEMARY CLOONEY		
				Percy Faith (orch.); from the Broadway musical *Call Me Madam* starring **Ethel Merman**		
3/3/51	8	15		4 Sparrow In The Tree Top /	A:8 / J:9 / S:9		
3/17/51	27	2		5 Christopher Columbus A:27	$20	Columbia 4-39190
5/5/51	16	11		6 Unless..J:16 / S:17 / A:24 *A Beggar In Love*	$20	Columbia 4-39331
6/2/51	2[1]	19	●	7 My Truly, Truly Fair	J:2 / A:4 / S:5 *Who Knows Love*	$20	Columbia 4-39415
8/18/51	9	9		8 Belle, Belle, My Liberty Belle /....................................A:9 / S:11 / J:11		
8/18/51	23	1		9 Sweetheart Of Yesterday ....A:23 / J:29	$20	Columbia 4-39512
11/17/51	20	1		10 There's Always Room At Our House /.............................A:20		
11/17/51	28	2		11 I Can't Help It (If I'm Still In Love With You)........................J:28	$20	Columbia 4-39595
				#2 Country hit for **Hank Williams** in 1951; #24 hit for Johnny Tillotson in 1962		
3/15/52	4	21	●	12 Pittsburgh, Pennsylvania	J:4 / S:6 / A:6 *The Doll With A Sawdust Heart*	$20	Columbia 4-39663
6/21/52	26	1		13 The Day Of Jubilo..A:26 *You'll Never Be Mine*	$20	Columbia 4-39753
8/23/52	14	6		14 Feet Up (Pat Him On The Po-Po) ....A:14 / J:22 / S:24 *Jenny Kissed Me*	$20	Columbia 4-39822
11/1/52	26	2		15 'Cause I Love You That's A-Why..............................S:26 *Train Of Love*	$20	Columbia 4-39879
				GUY MITCHELL - MINDY CARSON		
1/31/53	19	1		16 She Wears Red Feathers ....A:19 *Pretty Little Black-Eyed Susie*	$20	Columbia 4-39909
				Mitch Miller (orch. & chorus, all of above - except #3)		

MODERNAIRES, The, with Paula Kelly   ★137★   MEM/HOT '46

Vocal group from Buffalo: husband-and-wife Hal Dickinson and Paula Kelly, Chuck Goldstein, Bill Conway and Ralph Brewster. Dickinson died on 11/18/70 (age 59). Kelly died on 4/2/92 (age 72).

7/21/45	11	1		1 There! I've Said It Again ....A:11 *You Belong To My Heart*	$10	Columbia 36800
				#1 hit for Bobby Vinton in 1964		
7/27/46	18	1		2 Salute To Glenn Miller..J:18 *Juke Box Saturday Night*	$15	Columbia 36992
				medley: Moonlight Serenade / Elmer's Tune / Don't Sit Under The Apple Tree (With Anyone Else But Me) / Chattanooga Choo Choo		
8/17/46	3	14		3 To Each His Own	A:3 / S:5 / J:12 *Holiday For Strings*	$10	Columbia 37063
				Mannie Klein (orch.); written for, but not included in the movie starring Olivia de Havilland; #21 hit for The Platters in 1960		
1/11/47	11	3		4 Zip-A-Dee Doo-Dah..A:11 *Too Many Irons In The Fire*	$10	Columbia 37147
				from the Disney movie *Song Of The South* starring James Baskett; #8 hit for Bob B. Soxx & The Blue Jeans in 1963; **Mitchell Ayres** (orch.: #1, 2 & 4)		
12/24/49+	13	7		5 The Old Master Painter ....A:13 / J:17 / S:21 *Lost In The Stars* (Sinatra)	$10	Columbia 38650
				7" 33-1/3 rpm: 1-427		
1/21/50	28	1		6 Sorry..A:28 *Why Remind Me*	$15	Columbia 38662
				FRANK SINATRA and THE MODERNAIRES (above 2)		
				7" 33-1/3 rpm: 1-440		

MONROE, Vaughn, and his Orchestra ★13★   MEM/HOT '49

Born on 10/7/11 in Akron, Ohio. Died on 5/21/73 (age 61). Big-voiced baritone/trumpeter/bandleader. Very popular on radio, and featured in several movies. Theme song: "Racing With The Moon."

1)Riders In The Sky (A Cowboy Legend) 2)Ballerina 3)There! I've Said It Again
4)Let It Snow! Let It Snow! Let It Snow! 5)Someday

Vocalists:	Calvin, Rosemary — 17	Monroe, Vaughn —	Moon Men, The —	Talent, Ziggy — 32
	Duke, Marilyn — 4-6,8,14	1-3,7,10-12,14-31,33-52	36,38,39,41,43,45	chorus — 8,44,46,47,50
	Four Lee Sisters, The — 12	Moon Maids, The —	Norton Sisters, The — 16-23	
	Four V's, The — 9	24-29,31,34,35,42,45,49	Sons Of The Pioneers — 33	

12/28/40	5	4		1 There I Go	S:5 *Whatever Happened To You*	$15	Bluebird 10848
2/8/41	18	4		2 So You're The One ....S(s):18 / S(e):20 *Is It Love, Or Is It Conscription?*	$15	Bluebird 10901
2/15/41	15	4		3 High On A Windy Hill ....S(e):15 *The Last Time I Saw Paris*	$15	Bluebird 10976
3/1/41	20	1		4 There'll Be Some Changes Made ....S(s):20 *Dardanella*	$15	Bluebird 11025
				featured in the 1940 movie *Play Girl* starring Kay Francis; #5 hit for Ethel Waters in 1922		
6/14/41	14	1		5 G'bye Now..S(mw):14 / S(wc):14 *Music Makers*	$15	Bluebird 11114
				from the movie *Hellzapoppin* starring Ole Olsen and Chic Johnson		
8/9/41	18	2		6 Yours (Quieréme Mucho) ....S(e):18 *What Word Is Sweeter Than Sweetheart*	$15	Bluebird 11146
1/17/42	20	2		7 The Shrine Of Saint Cecilia ....S(e):20 / S(s):20 *'Fraidy Cat*	$15	Bluebird 11344
				#96 hit for Faron Young in 1957		

				MONROE, Vaughn, and his Orchestra — Cont'd		
5/23/42	**16**	1		8 **Tangerine** ....S(e):16 *Tica Ti-Tica Ta*	$15	Bluebird 11433
				#18 hit for the Salsoul Orchestra in 1976		
6/20/42	**18**	2		9 **Three Little Sisters** ....S(e):18 *Be Brave, Beloved*	$15	Bluebird 11508
				from the movie *Private Buckaroo* starring the **Andrews Sisters**		
9/5/42	**5**	4		10 **My Devotion** ....S:5 *When I Grow Up*	$10	Victor 27925
10/31/42	**2**[1]	16		11 **When The Lights Go On Again (All Over the World)** ....S:2 *Hip Hip Hooray*	$10	Victor 27945
6/12/43	**8**	2		12 **Let's Get Lost** ....S:8 *Happy-Go-Lucky*	$10	Victor 20-1524
				from the movie *Happy-Go-Lucky* starring **Mary Martin**		
9/2/44	**20**	1		13 **Take It, Jackson** ....J(terr.):20 *Hawaiian Sunset* [I]	$10	Victor 20-1591
12/9/44+	**4**	7		14 **The Trolley Song /** S:4 / A:7 / J:9		
				from the movie *Meet Me In St. Louis* starring **Judy Garland**		
12/16/44	**14**	1		15 **The Very Thought Of You** ....S(s):14	$10	Victor 20-1605
				#1 hit for **Ray Noble** in 1934; #26 hit for Rick Nelson in 1964		
3/17/45	**❶**[6]	29	●	16 **There! I've Said It Again /** A:❶[6] / S:2 / J:2		
				#1 hit for Bobby Vinton in 1964		
3/3/45	**8**	1		17 **Rum And Coca-Cola** S:8	$10	Victor 20-1637
				adaptation of an old calypso song from Trinidad		
11/10/45	**12**	2		18 **Something Sentimental**.........J:12 / A:16 *(Why Don't You Look Me Up) Down In Chi-Chi Hotcha Watchee*	$10	Victor 20-1714
11/10/45	**17**	1		19 **Just A Blue Serge Suit** ....J:17 *Talkin' To Myself About You*	$10	Victor 20-1725
11/24/45	**11**	1		20 **Fishin' For The Moon /** ....J:11 / A:17		
1/26/46	**12**	1		21 **Are These Really Mine?** A:12	$10	Victor 20-1736
12/22/45+	**❶**[5]	14		22 **Let It Snow! Let It Snow! Let It Snow!** S:❶[5] / A:❶[5] / J:❶[5] *When The Sandman Rides The Trail* [X]	$10	Victor 20-1759
3/30/46	**7**	5		23 **Seems Like Old Times** ....J:7 / A:15 *Gee! I Wish The 'G.I. Wish' Song)*	$10	RCA Victor 20-1811
7/13/46	**15**	3		24 **Who Told You That Lie? /** ....A:15 / J:17	$10	RCA Victor 20-1892
7/20/46	**16**	2		25 **It's My Lazy Day** J:16	$10	
				written by actor Smiley Burnette; from the movie *Bordertown Trail* starring Smiley Burnette		
11/16/46	**13**	4		26 **The Things We Did Last Summer** ....J:13 *More Now Than Ever*	$10	RCA Victor 20-1972
				#46 hit for Shelley Fabares in 1962		
9/20/47	**2**[5]	15		27 **I Wish I Didn't Love You So** S:2 / J:2 / A:5 *Tallahassee*	$10	RCA Victor 20-2294
				from the movie *The Perils Of Pauline* starring **Betty Hutton**		
11/1/47	**5**	8		28 **You Do /** J:5 / S:8 / A:15		
10/25/47	**10**	1		29 **Kokomo, Indiana** S:10	$10	RCA Victor 20-2361
				above 2 from the movie *Mother Wore Tights* starring **Betty Grable**		
11/8/47	**❶**[10]	22	●	30 **Ballerina** S:❶[10] / A:❶[8] / J:❶[7] *The Stars Will Remember*	$10	RCA Victor 20-2433
				#18 hit for Nat "King" Cole in 1957		
11/22/47+	**3**	13		31 **How Soon? (Will I Be Seeing You)** J:3 / S:5 / A:8 *True*	$10	RCA Victor 20-2523
6/26/48	**19**	9		32 **The Maharajah Of Magador**......................S:19 / A:22 / J:23 *Give A Broken Heart A Break* [N]	$15	RCA Victor 20-2851
7/24/48	**9**	14		33 **Cool Water** ....S:9 / J:14 / A:27 *The Legend Of Tiabi*	$15	RCA Victor 20-2923
				VAUGHN MONROE and Sons of the Pioneers		
				written in 1936; recorded by the Sons of the Pioneers in 1941 on Decca 5939 and in 1945 on RCA Victor 1724; #85 hit for Jack Scott in 1960		
10/30/48	**22**	1		34 **Ev'rday I Love You (Just A Little Bit More)**.........................S:22 *There's Music In The Land*	$10	RCA Victor 20-2957
				from the movie *Two Guys From Texas* starring Dennis Morgan and Jack Carson		
11/27/48	**20**	2		35 **In My Dreams** ....J:20 / A:23 *The Chocolate Choo-Choo*	$10	RCA Victor 20-3133
1/15/49	**3**	22		36 **Red Roses For A Blue Lady** A:3 / J:3 / S:4 *Melancholy Minstrel*	$25	RCA Victor 47-2889
				78 rpm: 20-3319; #10 hit for Vic Dana in 1965		
4/23/49	**❶**[12]	22	●	37 **Riders In The Sky (A Cowboy Legend)** A:❶[12] / S:❶[11] / J:❶[10] *Single Saddle*	$25	RCA Victor 47-2902
				78 rpm: 20-3411; #30 hit for The Ramrods in 1961		
8/6/49	**❶**[2]	18		38 **Someday** A:❶[2] / J:❶[2] / S:2 *And It Still Goes*	$25	RCA Victor 47-2986
				78 rpm: 20-3510; #56 hit for Della Reese in 1960		
9/24/49	**6**	17		39 **That Lucky Old Sun (Just Rolls Around Heaven All Day)**......A:6 / J:7 / S:9 *Make Believe (You Are Glad When You're Sorry)*	$20	RCA Victor 47-3018
				78 rpm: 20-3531; #20 hit for Ray Charles in 1964		
11/5/49	**29**	1		40 **Vieni Su (Say You Love Me Too)**.....................................J:29 *Blue For A Boy—Pink For A Girl*	$20	RCA Victor 47-3042
				78 rpm: 20-3549		
11/19/49	**10**	9		41 **Mule Train** ....A:10 / S:10 / J:14 *Singing My Way Back Home*	$20	RCA Victor 47-3106
				78 rpm: 20-3600		
1/28/50	**4**	7		42 **Bamboo** A:4 / J:12 / S:16 *A Little Golden Cross*	$20	RCA Victor 47-3143
				78 rpm: 20-3627		
6/17/50	**20**	1		43 **Thanks, Mister Florist** ....A:20 / J:30 *Tell Her You Love Her*	$20	RCA Victor 47-3773
4/21/51	**3**	17		44 **Sound Off (The Duckworth Chant)** A:3 / S:4 / J:4 *Oh, Marry, Marry Me*	$20	RCA Victor 47-4113
				#77 hit for Titus Turner in 1961		
4/21/51	**8**	16		45 **On Top Of Old Smoky** ....J:8 / A:8 / S:10 *Shall We Dance*	$20	RCA Victor 47-4114
				adaptation of a traditional Southern Highlands folk song; Tom Glazer's parody "On Top Of Spaghetti" peaked at #14 in 1963		
5/12/51	**7**	8		46 **Old Soldiers Never Die** ....A:7 / S:9 / J:13 *Love And Devotion*	$20	RCA Victor 47-4146
				inspired by Douglas MacArthur's "farewell" speech to Congress		
10/20/51	**28**	2		47 **Meanderin'** ....A:28 *They Call The Wind Maria*	$20	RCA Victor 47-4271
1/19/52	**27**	1		48 **Charmaine** ....J:27 *Once*	$20	RCA Victor 47-4375
				written to promote the 1926 movie *What Price Glory?* starring Victor McLaglen; #1 hit for **Guy Lombardo** in 1927; #69 hit for The Four Freshmen in 1956		
3/8/52	**22**	1		49 **Mountain Laurel** ....A:22 *Ooh! What You Did*	$20	RCA Victor 47-4479
4/12/52	**18**	5		50 **Lady Love /** ....J:18 / A:21		
				from the movie *Sound Off* starring Mickey Rooney		
5/3/52	**20**	6		51 **Idaho State Fair** J:20	$20	RCA Victor 47-4611
8/7/54	**7**	16		52 **They Were Doin' The Mambo** ....J:7 / A:11 / S:12 *Mister Sandman*	$15	RCA Victor 47-5767

MONTE, Lou
MEM/HOT '63

Born on 4/2/17 in Lyndhurst, New Jersey. Italian-styled novelty singer/guitarist.

| 2/13/54 | 7 | 11 | | Darktown Strutters Ball (Italian Style) ....J:7 / S:11 / A:12 *I Know How You Feel* | $15 | RCA Victor 47-5611 |

Hugo Winterhalter (orch.); sung in English and Italian; #1 hit for Arthur Collins & Byron Harlan in 1918

MOONEY, Art, and his Orchestra ★61★
MEM/HOT '48

Born on 2/4/11 in Lowell, Massachusetts. Leader of a Detroit-based dance band from the mid-1930s to 1940s. To New York following World War II service. Theme song: "Sunset To Sunrise."

1)I'm Looking Over A Four Leaf Clover 2)Baby Face 3)Blue Bird Of Happiness

Vocalists: Brees, Bud — 3
Brooks, Allan — 13
Fletcher, Tex — 11

Four Clovers — 13
Galli Sisters, The — 3
Harris, Betty — 12

Martin, Johnny — 6
Mooney, Art, Choir — 6,8-12

Russell, Madelyn — 6
ensemble — 1-5,7

| 1/24/48 | ❶⁵ | 18 | ● | 1 **I'm Looking Over A Four Leaf Clover**   J:❶⁵ / A:❶⁴ / S:❶³ *The Big Brass Band From Brazil* | $10 | MGM 10119 |

featuring Mike Pingatore (banjo); #2 hit for Nick Lucas in 1927

| 4/3/48 | 3 | 15 | ● | 2 **Baby Face**   J:3 / A:3 / S:5 *Encore, Cherie* | $10 | MGM 10156 |

#1 hit for **Jan Garber** in 1926; #14 hit for **The Wing And A Prayer Fife And Drum Corps.** in 1976

| 7/3/48 | 5 | 22 | ● | 3 **Blue Bird Of Happiness**   A:5 / S:9 / J:12 *Sunset To Sunrise* | $10 | MGM 10207 |

recitation by Art Mooney

2/26/49	18	8		4 Beautiful Eyes / ....J:18 / S:25 / A:26		
3/12/49	21	2		5 Doo De Doo On An Old Kazoo..J:21	$10	MGM 10357
5/7/49	7	17		6 **Again** ....J:7 / A:12 / S:28 *Five Foot Two, Eyes Of Blue (Has Anybody Seen My Girl)*	$10	MGM 10398

from the movie *Road House* starring Ida Lupino and Cornel Wilde

| 6/4/49 | 29 | 1 | | 7 Merry-Go-Round Waltz ....S:29 *The Heart Of Loch Lomond* | $10 | MGM 10405 |

melody adapted from the 1888 waltz "Over The Waves" (also see **Mario Lanza**'s "Loveliest Night Of The Year")

7/16/49	13	6		8 Twenty-Four Hours Of Sunshine ....J:13 / S:22 *In A Shady Nook By A Babbling Brook*	$10	MGM 10446
9/17/49	16	11		9 Hop-Scotch Polka (Scotch Hot) ....J:16 / S:17 / A:26 *Wouldn't It Be Fun*	$10	MGM 10500
10/29/49	19	4		10 Toot, Toot, Tootsie (Good-Bye) / ....S:19 / J:24 / A:25		

featured in the movie *Jolson Sings Again* starring Larry Parks; #1 hit for **Al Jolson** in 1923

| 11/19/49 | 21 | 1 | | 11 I Never See Maggie Alone..J:21 / S:27 | $10 | MGM 10548 |

#13 hit for Irving Aaronson in 1927

| 4/22/50 | 28 | 2 | | 12 If I Knew You Were Comin' I'd've Baked A Cake ....J:28 *Silver Dollar* | $10 | MGM 10660 |
| 7/1/50 | 23 | 1 | | 13 M-I-S-S-I-S-S-I-P-P-I...................................J:23 *The Breeze Is My Sweetheart* | $10 | MGM 10721 |

MOORE, Phil, Four
'45

Born on 2/20/18 in Portland. Died on 5/13/87 (age 69). Black composer/conductor/arranger of cocktail jazz quartet. Wrote arrangements for Jack Teagarden and Mildred Bailey. Composed the hit "Shoo-Shoo Baby."

| 3/17/45 | 3 | 10 | | 1 **My Dreams Are Getting Better All The Time** /   S:3 / J:4 / A:5 | | |

Phil Moore, Billy Daniels and The Phil Moore Four (vocals); from the movie *In Society* starring Abbott & Costello

| 5/5/45 | 22 | 1 | | 2 A Little On The Lonely Side ....J:22 | $15 | Victor 20-1641 |

Phil Moore and The Phil Moore Four (vocals)

MORGAN, Al
'49

Born in Chicago. Pianist who hosted own TV series from 1949-51. Known as "Mr. Flying Fingers."

| 7/30/49 | 4 | 26 | | 1 Jealous Heart   S:4 / J:4 / A:5 *Turnabout Is Fair Play* | $20 | London 30001 |

originally released on Universal 148 in 1949; 78 rpm: London 500; #47 hit for Connie Francis in 1965

| 1/28/50 | 26 | 1 | | 2 Half A Heart Is All You Left Me (When You Broke My
Heart In Two)..J:26 *I've Come Back To Say I'm Sorry* | $20 | London 30025 |

78 rpm: 571

| 12/2/50 | 29 | 1 | | 3 The Place Where I Worship (Is The Wide Open Spaces)...............A:29 *Hopestar* | $20 | London 30197 |

78 rpm: 784; John McCormick (recitation)

| 1/13/51 | 24 | 2 | | 4 My Heart Cries For You ....J:24 *Get Out Those Old Records* | $20 | London 45877 |

78 rpm: 877; The Key-Tones (backing vocals); Jack Pleis (piano); adapted from the 18th-century French melody "Chanson de Marie Antoinette"; #38 hit for Ray Charles in 1964

MORGAN, George
'49

Born on 6/28/24 in Waverly, Tennessee. Died of a heart attack on 7/7/75 (age 51). Country singer/songwriter/guitarist. Joined the *Grand Ole Opry* in 1948. Father of singer Lorrie Morgan. Elected to the Country Music Hall of Fame in 1998.

| 10/29/49 | 25 | 1 | | Room Full Of Roses ....J:25 *Put All Your Love In A Cookie Jar* | $20 | Columbia 20594 |

#4 Country hit; #50 Pop hit for Mickey Gilley in 1974

MORGAN, Jaye P.
MEM/HOT '55

Born Mary Margaret Morgan on 12/3/31 in Mancos, Colorado. Sang with **Frank DeVol**'s band from 1950-53. Featured on many TV game shows from the 1950s-'70s. Sister of recording group The Morgan Brothers.

| 11/27/54+ | 3 | 21 | | That's All I Want From You   A:3 / S:5 / J:5 *Dawn* | $15 | RCA Victor 47-5896 |

Hugo Winterhalter (orch.)

MORGAN, Marion — see CROSBY, Bob

MORGAN, Russ, And His Orchestra ★27★ MEM/HOT '49

Born on 4/29/04 in Scranton, Pennsylvania. Died on 8/8/69 (age 65). Trombonist/pianist/vocalist/bandleader. Former pianist/arranger for Jean Goldkette, Fletcher Henderson, the **Dorsey** brothers and others. Records labeled as "Music In The Morgan Manner." Morgan's pre-1940 #1 hits: "I've Got A Pocketful Of Dreams" and "The Merry-Go-Round Broke Down."

1)Cruising Down The River 2)Forever And Ever 3)So Tired 4)There Goes That Song Again
5)Dance With A Dolly (With A Hole In Her Stockin')

Vocalists:
- Ames Brothers — 12
- Andrews Sisters — 19,21,22
- Baker, Kenny — 10,11
- Boswell, Connee — 9
- Gay Sisters, The — 30
- Heartbeats, The — 20
- Jennings, Al — 5
- Kay, Carol — 1
- Morgan, Russ — 3,4,6-8,13,20,23-31
- Morganaires, The — 2,23-29,31
- Rhythmaires, The — 18
- Skylarks, The — 14-17
- ensemble — 12

DEBUT	PEAK	WKS	Gold	A-side	B-side	$	Label & Number
9/21/40	17	4		1 Blueberry Hill ....S(s):17 / S(mw):19	I'm Home Again	$10	Decca 3290
4/4/42	5	11		2 Somebody Else Is Taking My Place S:5	Prisionero Del Mar ('Neath A Tropical Moon)	$10	Decca 4098
				from the movie *Strictly In The Groove* starring Mary Healy			
5/27/44	6	16		3 Good Night, Wherever You Are / ....S:6 / J:8			
7/15/44	18	1		4 Louise J:18		$10	Decca 18598
				from the movie *You Can't Ration Love* starring **Betty Rhodes**; #3 hit for Maurice Chevalier in 1929			
11/4/44	3	12		5 Dance With A Dolly (With A Hole In Her Stockin') / S:3 / J:4			
				adaptation of the 1844 tune "Buffalo Gals (Won't You Come Out Tonight)"; also see Jan August's "Buffalo Billy"; updated version by The Olympics in 1961 hit #47 as "Dance By The Light Of The Moon"			
11/18/44+	3	14		6 There Goes That Song Again J:3 / A:4 / S:5		$10	Decca 18625
				from the movie *Carolina Blues* starring **Kay Kyser**			
1/26/46	14	1		7 You're Nobody 'Til Somebody Loves You / ....A:14 / J:17			
				#25 hit for Dean Martin in 1965			
1/12/46	17	1		8 (Did You Ever Get) That Feeling In The Moonlight..........................J:17		$10	Decca 18724
2/2/46	9	5		9 Let It Snow! Let It Snow! Let It Snow! ....J:9 / A:20	Walkin' With My Honey (Soon, Soon, Soon)	[X]	$10	Decca 18741
				CONNEE BOSWELL and RUSS MORGAN and HIS ORCHESTRA			
2/8/47	11	2		10 The Old Lamp-Lighter...J:11	Love Walked In	$10	Decca 23781
				#5 hit for The Browns in 1960			
5/24/47	16	1		11 My Adobe Hacienda J:16	This Is The Night	$10	Decca 23846
				KENNY BAKER and RUSS MORGAN And His Orchestra (above 2)			
2/21/48	6	13		12 I'm Looking Over A Four Leaf Clover ....J:6 / S:17 / A:11	Bye Bye Blackbird	$10	Decca 24319
				RUSS MORGAN And HIS ORCHESTRA with MILT HERTH At The Organ Ames Brothers & Ensemble (vocals); #2 hit for Nick Lucas in 1927			
11/27/48+	3	25		13 So Tired J:3 / A:4 / S:4	I Hear Music	$10	Decca 24521
				previously issued on Decca 24449; #9 hit for Gene Austin in 1928			
2/26/49	❶7	22	●	14 Cruising Down The River / S:❶7 / J:❶6 / A:4			
2/26/49	5	15		15 Sunflower J:5 / S:10 / A:24		$10	Decca 24568
				a court ruling found the 1964 hit "Hello, Dolly!" to be directly based on this song			
3/19/49	❶3	26		16 Forever And Ever / J:❶3 / S:2 / A:6			
3/26/49	17	6		17 You, You, You Are The One....................................S:17 / J:17		$10	Decca 24569
				adaptation of the German folk song "Du, Du Liegst Mir Im Herzen"			
5/7/49	20	5		18 Barroom Polka...J:20	Put Your Shoes On, Lucy	$10	Decca 24608
7/16/49	21	1		19 Now! Now! Now! Is The Time...........................S:21	Oh, You Sweet One (The Schnitzelbank Song)	$15	Decca 24664
				ANDREWS SISTERS - RUSS MORGAN And His Orchestra			
9/3/49	17	6		20 That's My Weakness Now...J:17	Laughing Trombone Polka	$10	Decca 24692
				#5 hit for Helen Kane in 1928			
12/17/49+	15	4		21 Charley My Boy / ....J:15 / S:17			
				#3 hit for Eddie Cantor in 1924			
12/10/49	22	2		22 She Wore A Yellow Ribbon ....S:22 / J:24 / A:29		$15	Decca 24812
				ANDREWS SISTERS - RUSS MORGAN And His Orchestra (above 2) title song from the movie starring John Wayne; written in 1917			
12/24/49	11	3		23 Blue Christmas ....S:11 / J:13 / A:21	The Mistletoe Kiss	[X]	$10	Decca 24766
				#1 hit on *Billboard's* special Christmas charts in 1964 for Elvis Presley			
12/31/49+	7	10		24 Johnson Rag ....J:7 / S:16 / A:21	Where Are You Blue Eyes?	$10	Decca 24819
1/14/50	24	1		25 Careless Kisses J:24	Send Ten Pretty Flowers (To My Girl In Tennessee)	$10	Decca 24814
4/22/50	7	17		26 Sentimental Me ....J:7 / A:9 / S:10	Copper Canyon	$15	Decca 9-24904
				recorded by Elvis Presley in 1961 on the album *Something for Everybody*			
5/27/50	15	4		27 Hoop-Dee-Doo J:15	Down The Lane	$15	Decca 9-24986
6/10/50	28	1		28 You Dreamer You / J:28			
10/7/50	28	1		29 Beloved, Be Faithful J:28		$15	Decca 9-27006
3/31/51	16	10		30 Mockin' Bird Hill ....A:16 / J:17 / S:23	Flying Eagle Polka	$15	Decca 9-27444
2/2/52	30	1		31 Dance Me Loose...A:30	River In The Moonlight	$15	Decca 9-27906

MORROW, Buddy, and his Orchestra MEM/HOT '51

Born Muni Zudecoff on 2/8/19 in New Haven, Connecticut. Trombone star for many top big bands. His own swing band was a hit in the early '50s. Later played with the *Tonight Show* band. Currently leads the **Tommy Dorsey** concert orchestra.

DEBUT	PEAK	WKS	Gold	A-side	B-side	$	Label & Number
5/19/51	8	10		1 Rose, Rose, I Love You A:8	(What Can I Say) After I Say I'm Sorry?	$15	RCA Victor 47-4135
				the band (vocals)			
8/30/52	27	2		2 Night Train..J:27	Vereda Tropical	[I]	$15	RCA Victor 47-4693
				also known as "All Night Long"; #1 R&B hit for Jimmy Forrest in 1952; #35 hit for James Brown in 1962			
12/6/52	19	1		3 Greyhound...J:19	Stairway To The Stars	$15	RCA Victor 47-5041
1/31/53	16	3		4 I Don't Know A:16	Hey Mrs. Jones	$15	RCA Victor 47-5117
				#1 R&B hit for Willie Mabon in 1953; Frankie Lester (vocal, above 2)			
12/4/54	20	1		5 Mr. Sandman..A:20	Rock-A-Beatin' Boogie	$15	Mercury 70477X45
				30-second vocal by Quartet; #37 hit for Emmylou Harris in 1981			

MORSE, Ella Mae ★97★   MEM '44
Born on 9/12/24 in Mansfield, Texas. Died of respiratory failure on 10/16/99 (age 75). White blues-styled singer/actress. Sang on radio since age 12. Briefly with **Jimmy Dorsey**'s band in 1939. With **Freddie Slack**'s band from 1941-42. Appeared in several movies. Also see **Freddie Slack**.

DEBUT	PEAK	WKS	Gold	A-side	$	Label & Number
12/25/43+	4	15		1 **Shoo-Shoo Baby /** S:4 / J:4		
				from the movie Three Cheers For The Boys		
1/29/44	4	12		2 **No Love, No Nothin'** J:4 / S:7	$15	Capitol 143
				from the movie The Gang's All Here starring Alice Faye		
5/13/44	7	16		3 **Milkman, Keep Those Bottles Quiet /** ....J:7 / S:10		
				from the movie Broadway Rhythm starring George Murphy and **Ginny Simms**		
5/20/44	13	5		4 **Tess's Torch Song (I Had A Man)** J:13	$15	Capitol 151
				from the movie Up In Arms starring **Dinah Shore** *and* **Danny Kaye**; Dick Walters (orch., all of above)		
9/9/44	10	5		5 **The Patty Cake Man** ....J:10 *Invitation To The Blues*	$15	Capitol 163
5/26/45	17	1		6 **Captain Kidd** ....A:17 *Ya' Betcha*	$15	Capitol 193
1/19/46	15	1		7 **Buzz Me** ....A:15 *Rip Van Winkle*	$15	Capitol 226
				Billy May (orch., above 2)		
2/16/52	3	22	●	8 **The Blacksmith Blues** S:3 / A:3 / J:3 *Love Me Or Leave Me*	$20	Capitol F1922
6/7/52	23	2		9 **Oakie Boogie** ....J:23 *Love Ya' Like Mad!*	$20	Capitol F2072
				Nelson Riddle (orch., above 2)		

MOTEN('S), Bennie, Kansas City Orch.   MEM '29
Born on 11/13/1894 in Kansas City, Missouri. Died during a tonsillectomy operation on 4/2/35 (age 38). Black jazz pianist/bandleader. **Count Basie** was a member of his early-1930s band.

DEBUT	PEAK	WKS	Gold	A-side	$	Label & Number
12/2/44	22	1		**South** ....J(terr.):22 *She's No Trouble* **[I]**	$15	Victor 24893
				original version charted in 1925 on Okeh 8194 (#12); new version charted in 1929 on Victor 38021 (#10)		

MULLICAN, Moon   MEM '50
Born Aubrey Mullican on 3/29/09 in Corrigan, Texas. Died of a heart attack on 1/1/67 (age 57). Singer/pianist. Member of the *Grand Ole Opry* from 1949-55. Known as the "King Of The Hillbilly Piano Players."

DEBUT	PEAK	WKS	Gold	A-side	$	Label & Number
6/17/50	17	3	●	**I'll Sail My Ship Alone** ....J:17 *Moon's Tune*	$30	King 45-830
				#1 Country hit (4 weeks) in 1950; #93 hit for Jerry Lee Lewis in 1959		

MUNSEL, Patrice   '51
Born on 5/14/25 in Spokane, Washington. Opera singer/actress. Starred in the 1953 movie biography of Nellie Melba.

DEBUT	PEAK	WKS	Gold	A-side	$	Label & Number
10/13/51	27	2		**Bela Bimba** ....A:27 / J:27 *Look Me Over Once*	$20	RCA Victor 47-4255
				Norman Leyden (orch. and chorus)		

MURPHY, Rose   '48
Born on 4/28/13 in Xenia, Ohio. Died on 11/16/89 (age 76). Singer/pianist. Nicknamed "The Chee-Chee Girl" for her unique vocal style.

DEBUT	PEAK	WKS	Gold	A-side	$	Label & Number
1/3/48	13	2		**I Can't Give You Anything But Love** ....A:13 *When I Grow Too Old To Dream* (R&B #10)	$10	Majestic 1204
				#1 hit for Cliff Edwards in 1928; #100 hit for Bert Kaempfert in 1966		

N

NELSON, Ozzie, and his Orchestra   MEM '35
Born Oswald Nelson on 3/20/06 in Jersey City. Died of cancer on 6/3/75 (age 69). Orchestra leader/actor. Became famous for the long-running radio and TV series *The Adventures of Ozzie and Harriet*. Wife Harriet Hilliard (died on 10/2/94, age 85) was his featured vocalist. Son Ricky (died on 12/31/85, age 45) was a leading teenage rock idol. Nelson's pre-1940 #1 hit: "And Then Some."

DEBUT	PEAK	WKS	Gold	A-side	$	Label & Number
8/24/40	16	1		**I'm Nobody's Baby** ....S(s):16 *Miss Johnson 'Phoned Again Today*	$10	Bluebird 10722
				Rose Ann Stevens (vocal); from the movie *Andy Hardy Meets Debutante* starring **Judy Garland** and Mickey Rooney; #3 hit for Marion Harris in 1921		

NICHOLS, Joy, and Benny Lee   '49
Vocal duo. Nichols was born on 2/17/25 in Sydney, Australia; died on 6/23/92 (age 67). Lee was born on 8/11/16 in Glasgow, Scotland; died on 12/9/95 (age 79).

DEBUT	PEAK	WKS	Gold	A-side	$	Label & Number
2/12/49	21	1		**The Pussycat Song (Nyot Nyow)** ....S:21 *Bounce-y Bounce-y Ball-y* **[N]**	$10	London 365
				Stanley Black and his Blacksmiths (orch.)		

NIESEN, Gertrude   MEM '45
Born on 7/8/11 in Brooklyn, New York. Died on 3/27/75 (age 63). Singer/actress. Appeared in several movies.

DEBUT	PEAK	WKS	Gold	A-side	$	Label & Number
3/3/45	10	1		**I Wanna Get Married** ....S:10 / J:16 *Twelve O'Clock And All Is Well*	$10	Decca 23382
				Harry Sosnik (orch.); from the movie *Follow The Girls*		

NOBLE, Ray, and his Orchestra ★98★　　　MEM '35

Born Stanley Raymond Noble on 12/17/03 in Brighton, Sussex, England. Died on 4/2/78 (age 74). Pianist/composer/arranger. In late 1934 **Glenn Miller** assembled a new U.S. orchestra for Noble, filled with top musicians. Noble also accompanied Fred Astaire on several late-1930s hits. Noble's top 3 pre-1940 #1 hits: "Isle Of Capri," "Love Is The Sweetest Thing" and "The Very Thought Of You."

| 12/21/40+ | 15 | 2 | | 1 A Nightingale Sang In Berkeley Square ....S(mw):15 / S(wc):19 / S(e):20 *We Three (My Echo, My Shadow And Me)* | $10 | Columbia 35733 |
from the London musical *New Faces*

| 5/2/42 | 16 | 3 | ● | 2 By The Light Of The Silv'ry Moon ....S(mw):16 / S(s):16 *While My Lady Sleeps* | $10 | Columbia 36479 |
from the movie *Birth Of The Blues* starring **Bing Crosby**; #1 hit for Billy Murray & Haydn Quartet in 1910; #50 hit for Jimmy Bowen in 1958

| 7/1/44 | 17 | 1 | | 3 By The Light Of The Silv'ry Moon ....J(terr.):17 *While My Lady Sleeps* **[R]** | $10 | Columbia 36479 |
Snooky Lanson and **The Boys** (vocals, above 2)

| 3/31/45 | 14 | 2 | | 4 Sweet Dreams, Sweetheart ....J:14 *How Bright The Stars* | $10 | Columbia 36765 |
from the movie *Hollywood Canteen* starring Bette Davis; Larry Stewart (vocal: #4)

| 2/23/46 | 18 | 1 | | 5 Full Moon And Empty Arms ....J:18 *It Might As Well Be Spring* | $10 | Columbia 36893 |
Snooky Lanson (vocal); based on Rachmaninoff's *Piano Concerto No. 2 in C-Minor*

| 2/15/47 | ●² | 23 | | 6 Linda　　　　　　　　　　　　A:●² / S:2 / J:2 *Love Is A Random Thing* | $10 | Columbia 37215 |
RAY NOBLE and his ORCHESTRA with BUDDY CLARK
#28 hit for Jan & Dean in 1963

| 9/20/47 | 11 | 4 | | 7 I Wonder Who's Kissing Her Now...........................A:11 / J:16 *April Showers* | $10 | Columbia 37544 |
Snooky Lanson and **The Sportsmen** (vocals); #1 hit for Henry Burr in 1909; #93 hit for Bobby Darin in 1964

| 12/6/47+ | 3 | 15 | | 8 I'll Dance At Your Wedding　　　　　　　S:3 / A:3 / J:4 *Those Things Money Can't Buy* | $10 | Columbia 37967 |
RAY NOBLE and his ORCHESTRA with BUDDY CLARK
Anita Gordon (female vocal: #6 & 8)

| 2/19/49 | 19 | 7 | | 9 Lady Of Spain ....J:19 / S:21 / A:30 *I've Got My Love To Keep Me Warm* | $10 | RCA Victor 20-3302 |
Al Bowlly and Trio (vocals); originally charted in 1931 (Noble's first chart hit) on Victor 22774 (#5)

NYPE, Russell — see SHORE, Dinah

O

O'BRIEN, Dottie　　　'50

| 8/5/50 | 23 | 2 | | I Wanna Be Loved ....A:23 / J:28 *Remember Me (When The Candlelights Are Gleaming)* | $15 | Capitol F1044 |
DOTTIE O'BRIEN & JAN GARBER and His Orchestra

O'CONNELL, Helen　　　MEM '52

Born on 5/23/20 in Lima, Ohio. Died of cancer on 9/9/93 (age 73). Featured vocalist with **Jimmy Dorsey** from 1939-43. Hosted own TV show in 1957. Married **Frank DeVol** in 1991.

| 3/17/51 | 16 | 10 | | 1 Would I Love You...A:16 *Gypsy Heart* | $15 | Capitol F1368 |
Dave Cavanaugh (orch.)

| 12/8/51+ | 8 | 13 | | 2 Slow Poke......................................J:8 / A:9 / S:16 *I Wanna Play House With You* | $15 | Capitol F1837 |
Cliffie Stone (orch.)

| 5/10/52 | 27 | 1 | | 3 Be Anything (But Be Mine)..........................A:27 / S:30 *Right Or Wrong (My Love Belongs To You)* | $15 | Capitol F2011 |
Harold Mooney (orch.); #25 hit for Connie Francis in 1964

O'CONNOR, Donald — see DAY, Doris

O'DAY, Anita, with The All Stars　　　MEM '51

Born Anita Colton on 10/18/19 in Chicago. Jazz singer. Featured vocalist with **Gene Krupa** and **Stan Kenton**.

| 2/24/51 | 24 | 1 | | Tennessee Waltz ....S:24 *Yea Boo* | $20 | London 45-867 |
Doc Severinsen and Charlie Shavers (trumpet), Al Klink (alto sax), Teddy Wilson (piano), **Will Bradley** and Cutty Cutshall (trombone), Billy Mure (guitar), **Benny Carter** (bass); #35 hit for Sam Cooke in 1964

O'DAY, Pat　　　'53

| 8/29/53 | 17 | 1 | | A Dear John Letter...S:17 *No Stone Unturned* | $20 | MGM K11566 |
The Four Horsemen (instrumentation); Al Rawley (recitation); #44 hit for Pat Boone in 1960

OKLAHOMA! Original Cast Album　　　'43

Also see **Original Casts** in the **Albums** section. The only full-length album to make the singles charts.

| 12/18/43 | 9 | 2 | ● | 1 Oklahoma! ....S:9 | $30 | Decca 359 |
1)Oklahoma Overture (Oklahoma Orchestra) 2)Oh, What A Beautiful Mornin' (**Alfred Drake**) 3)The Surrey With The Fringe On Top (Alfred Drake) 4)Kansas City (Lee Dixon) 5)I Cain't Say No (Celeste Holm) 6)Many A New Day (Joan Roberts) 7)People Will Say We're In Love (Alfred Drake & Joan Roberts) 8)Pore Jud Is Daid (Alfred Drake & Howard da Silva) 9)Out Of My Dreams (Joan Roberts) 10)All Er Nothin' (Celeste Holm & Lee Dixon) 11)Oklahoma (Alfred Drake) 12)Finale (Alfred Drake & Joan Roberts); "Oklahoma" Orchestra and Chorus directed by Jay Blackton

| 1/22/44 | 17 | 1 | | 2 The Surrey With The Fringe On Top...............................J(terr.):17 *All Er Nothin'* | $10 | Decca 23284 |
ALFRED DRAKE With Oklahoma Orchestra
this single is the #3 cut on the *Oklahoma!* album above

OLSEN, George, And His Orchestra　　　MEM '26

Born on 3/18/1893 in Portland, Oregon. Died on 3/18/71 (age 78). Orchestra leader. Charted 48 hits from 1925-34. Olsen's top 3 pre-1940 #1 hits: "The Last Round Up," "Who" and "At Sundown (When Love Is Calling Me Home)."

| 12/22/45 | 12 | 2 | | Chickery Chick...J:12 *Kentucky Babe* | $10 | Majestic 7155 |
Judith Blair, Ray Adams and Ensemble (vocals)

O'NEIL, Danny　　　'46

Tenor ballad singer. Regular on TV's *Windy City Jamboree* in 1950.

| 12/14/46 | 12 | 1 | | Ole Buttermilk Sky..A:12 *Remember Me?* | $10 | Majestic 7199 |
Virg Davis (orch. and choir); from the movie *Canyon Passage* starring Dana Andrews; #25 hit for Bill Black's Combo in 1961

DEBUT	PEAK	WKS	Gold	A-side (Chart Hit)..B-side	$	Label & Number

ORIOLES, The '53

R&B vocal group from Baltimore: Sonny Til, Alexander Sharp, George Nelson and Johnny Reed, with Tommy Gaither (guitar). Gaither died in a car crash on 11/5/50. Til died of a heart attack on 12/9/81 (age 51). Inducted into the Rock and Roll Hall of Fame in 1995 as an early influence.

11/6/48	13	7		1 It's Too Soon To Know ....A:13 *Barbra Lee*	$200	It's A Natural 5000
				reissued on Jubilee 5000 in 1948; #4 hit for Pat Boone in 1958		
8/22/53	11	10	●	2 Crying In The Chapel...S:11 / J:12 *Don't You Think I Ought To Know*	$100	Jubilee 45-5122
				#3 hit for Elvis Presley in 1965; above 2 were #1 R&B hits		

OVERTURES Featuring Marian Caruso, The '52

White vocal group.

| 10/11/52 | 28 | 2 | | My Favorite Song ....S:28 *Balboa* | $25 | Devon 1001 |
| | | | | Don Costa (orch.); some pressings label group as THE OVERTONES Featuring MARIAN CARUSO | | |

★149★ OWENS, Jack '47

Born on 10/17/12 in Tulsa, Oklahoma. Died on 1/26/82 (age 69). Singer featured on Don McNeill's *Breakfast Club* radio show.

9/20/47	2[1]	20		1 How Soon (Will I Be Seeing You)	J:2 / A:3 / S:4 *Begin The Beguine*	$15	Tower 1258
				Eddie Ballantine (orch.)		
10/1/49	11	12		2 Jealous Heart ....J:11 / S:19 *Dime A Dozen*	$10	Decca 24711
				#47 hit for Connie Francis in 1965		
1/7/50	22	2		3 You're The Only One I Care For ....A:22 *I Wish I Had A Record (Of The Promises You Made)*	$10	Decca 24712
				Danny Mendelsohn (orch., above 2)		
4/8/50	29	1		4 You're A Sweetheart ....A:29 *Cross Your Heart*	$10	Decca 24935
				3 Beaus And A Peep (backing vocals); Sy Oliver (orch.); #1 hit for Dolly Dawn in 1938		
9/9/50	14	11		5 Dream A Little Dream Of Me ....A:14 *It Couldn't Happen To A Sweeter Girl (It Couldn't Happen to a Nicer Guy)*	$15	Decca 9-27096
				#1 hit for Wayne King in 1931; #12 hit for Mama Cass in 1968		

P

PAGE, Patti ★16★ MEM/HOT '50

Born Clara Ann Fowler on 11/8/27 in Muskogee, Oklahoma; raised in Tulsa. On radio KTUL with Al Klauser & His Oklahomans, as Ann Fowler, late 1940s. Another singer was billed as "Patti Page" for the Page Milk Company show on KTUL. When she left, Fowler took her place and name. Own TV series *The Patti Page SHow* from 1955-58 and *The Big Record* from 1957-58. Acted in the 1960 movie *Elmer Gantry*. Charted an additional 42 pop hits from 1955-68.

1)The Tennessee Waltz 2)I Went To Your Wedding 3)The Doggie In The Window 4)All My Love (Bolero) 5)Cross Over The Bridge

Orchestras:	Barnes, George, Trio — 1	Masher, Zeb — 4	Rael, Jack —	Robinson, Eric — 2
	D'Artega — 7	**Miller, Mitch** — 5	10,12,13,15,17-32,34-39	
	Geller, Harry — 8,9,11,14		Reisman, Joe — 16,33	

6/26/48	12	8		1 Confess..A:12 / S:20 / J:30 *Twelve O'Clock Flight*	$15	Mercury 5129
10/30/48	23	4		2 Say Something Sweet To Your Sweetheart........................A:23 *Isn't It Romantic*	$15	Mercury 5192
				VIC DAMONE—PATTI PAGE		
2/12/49	13	1		3 So In Love ....A:13 / S:28 *Where's The Man*	$15	Mercury 5230
				from the Broadway musical *Kiss Me, Kate* starring **Alfred Drake**		
4/23/49	27	1		4 Money, Marbles And Chalk.....................................J:27 *Where Is The One*	$15	Mercury 5251
9/3/49	26	1		5 I'll Keep The Love Light Burning (In My Heart)................J:26 *Just One Way To Say I Love You*	$15	Mercury 5310
				Bennie Benjamin and Georgie Weiss (harmony vocals)		
1/7/50	11	11	●	6 With My Eyes Wide Open I'm Dreaming ....A:11 / S:13 / J:18 *Oklahoma Blues*	$15	Mercury 5344
				PATTI PAGE QUARTET		
				from the 1934 movie *Shoot The Works* starring Jack Oakie; #3 hit for **Leo Reisman** in 1934; new version by Page charted in 1959 on Mercury 71469 (#59)		
5/20/50	8	9		7 I Don't Care If The Sun Don't Shine ....J:8 / A:14 *I'm Gonna Paper All My Walls With Love Letters*	$20	Mercury 5396-X45
				#74 hit for Elvis Presley in 1956		
8/26/50	❶[5]	23	●	8 All My Love (Bolero) A:❶[5] / J:2 / S:2 *Roses Remind Me Of You*	$20	Mercury 5455-X45
				adapted from the French song "Bolero"		
10/7/50	23	1		9 Back In Your Own Backyard.......................................J:23 *The Right Kind Of Love*	$20	Mercury 5463-X45
				#5 hit for Ruth Etting in 1928		
11/18/50	❶[13]	26	●	10 The Tennessee Waltz J:❶[13] / S:❶[9] / A:❶[8] *Long Long Ago*	$20	Mercury 5534-X45
				#3 Country hit for **Pee Wee King** in 1948; #35 hit for Sam Cooke in 1964		
2/10/51	4	19	●	11 Would I Love You (Love You, Love You) A:4 / J:4 / S:7 *Sentimental Music*	$20	Mercury 5571-X45
2/24/51	2[1]	22	●	12 Mockin' Bird Hill A:2 / J:3 / S:3 *I Love You Because*	$20	Mercury 5595-X45
5/5/51	17	7		13 Down The Trail Of Achin' Hearts / ....J:17 / S:29 / A:30	$20	Mercury 5579-X45
5/5/51	24	2		14 Evertrue Evermore ....J:24 / S:27		
5/19/51	8	14	●	15 Mister And Mississippi / ....J:8 / A:8 / S:9	$20	Mercury 5645-X45
6/30/51	26	2		16 These Things I Offer You ....J:26 / S:28 / A:28		
8/4/51	5	16	●	17 Detour J:5 / S:12 / A:15 *Who's Gonna Shoe My Pretty Little Feet*	$20	Mercury 5682-X45
				#2 Country hit for **Spade Cooley** in 1946		
9/22/51	4	14		18 And So To Sleep Again A:4 / J:9 / S:10 *One Sweet Letter*	$20	Mercury 5706-X45
2/9/52	9	11		19 Come What May / ....A:9 / J:9 / S:11	$20	Mercury 5772-X45
1/26/52	22	4		20 Retreat (Cries My Heart) ....A:22 / J:22		
3/29/52	16	11		21 Whispering Winds ....J:16 / S:18 *Love, Where Are You Now*	$20	Mercury 5816-X45

PAGE, Patti — Cont'd

DEBUT	PEAK	WKS	Gold	A-side (Chart Hit) ... B-side	$	Label & Number
6/28/52	9	11		22 **Once In Awhile**...J:9 / A:18 / S:24 *I'm Glad You're Happy With Someone Else (But I'm Sorry It Couldn't Be Me)*	$20	Mercury 5867-X45
				#1 hit for **Tommy Dorsey** in 1937; #11 hit for The Chimes in 1961		
8/30/52	❶[10]	22	●	23 **I Went To Your Wedding** / J:❶[10] / S:❶[5] / A:❶[1]		
8/30/52	4	17		24 **You Belong To Me** A:4 / J:5 / S:9	$20	Mercury 5899-X45
				#7 hit for The Duprees in 1962		
11/29/52+	4	13		25 **Why Don't You Believe Me** / A:4 / J:6 / S:11		
				#37 hit for The Duprees in 1963		
12/6/52	18	2		26 **Conquest** J:18	$15	Mercury 70025-X45
1/31/53	❶[8]	21	●	27 **The Doggie In The Window** / S:❶[8] / A:❶[7] / J:❶[7] [N]	$15	Mercury 70070-X45
				dog barks by Joe & Mac; #69 hit for Baby Jane & The Rockabyes in 1963		
3/7/53	17	2		28 **My Jealous Eyes** J:17 / A:18		
5/30/53	16	1		29 **Oo What You Do To Me** / A:16		
5/23/53	18	1		30 **Now That I'm In Love** A:18	$15	Mercury 70127-X45
				melody taken from the William Tell Overture (Lone Ranger theme)		
7/18/53	10	11		31 **Butterflies** / J:10 / A:14 / S:17		
8/8/53	20	1		32 **This Is My Song** A:20	$15	Mercury 70183-X45
				Page's theme for her 1952-53 NBC-TV variety show		
11/28/53	3	19	●	33 **Changing Partners** A:3 / J:3 / S:4 *Where Did My Snowman Go*	$15	Mercury 70260-X45
2/27/54	2[4]	21	●	34 **Cross Over The Bridge** J:2 / S:3 / A:3 *Johnny Guitar*	$15	Mercury 70302-X45
				issued with a picture sleeve: "Pop Si Hit Record of the Month"		
6/5/54	8	8		35 **Steam Heat** ....J:8 / A:11 / S:15 *Lonely Days*	$15	Mercury 70380-X45
				from the Broadway musical *The Pajama Game* starring John Raitt		
8/14/54	10	11		36 **What A Dream** / A:10 / J:15 / S:18		
				#1 R&B hit for Ruth Brown in 1954; #106 hit for Conway Twitty in 1960		
8/21/54	13	8		37 **I Cried** J:13 / A:18 / S:26	$15	Mercury 70416-X45
10/30/54	20	3		38 **The Mama Doll Song** J:20 / S:24 *I Can't Tell A Waltz From A Tango*	$15	Mercury 70458-X45
12/18/54	8	7		39 **Let Me Go, Lover!** A:8 / J:12 / S:24 *Hocus-Pocus*	$15	Mercury 70511-X45

PARAMOR, Norrie — see CALVERT, Eddie

PASTOR, Tony, and his Orchestra ★57★   MEM '45

Born Antonio Pestritto on 10/26/07 in Middletown, Connecticut. Died on 10/31/69 (age 62). Former tenor saxophonist/singer with Irving Aaronson (1928-30), Vincent Lopez, and most importantly **Artie Shaw** (1936-39). Johnny McAfee (alto sax) his featured sideman, with late-1940s arrangements by **Ralph Flanagan**. During later period Betty and **Rosemary Clooney** were band's vocalists.

1)Bell Bottom Trousers 2)Red Silk Stockings And Green Perfume 3)Dance With A Dolly (With a Hole In Her Stocking)

Vocalists: Anderson, Dorsey — 1,2   Clooney Sisters, The — 15   Pastor, Stubby — 8   the band — 9,15
Clooney, Rosemary — 12-14   McCullough, Ruth — 5   **Pastor, Tony** — 3-11,13,15

DEBUT	PEAK	WKS		A-side ... B-side	$	Label & Number
6/28/41	9	1		1 **Maria Elena** S:9 *Made Up My Mind*	$15	Bluebird 11127
				#6 hit for Los Indios Tabajaras in 1963		
7/26/41	20	1		2 **Green Eyes (Aquellos Ojos Verdes)** ....S(mw):20 *Blues (My Naughty Sweetie Gives Me)*	$15	Bluebird 11168
10/28/44	9	10		3 **Dance With A Dolly (With a Hole In Her Stocking)** ....J:9 *Don't Blame Me*	$15	Bluebird 30-0827
				adaptation of the 1844 tune "Buffalo Gals (Won't You Come Out Tonight)"; also see **Jan August**'s "Buffalo Billy"; updated version by The Olympics in 1961 hit as "Dance By The Light Of The Moon"		
12/30/44	20	1		4 **Robin Hood** J(terr.):20 *One Meatball*	$15	Victor 20-1607
5/19/45	2[2]	15		5 **Bell Bottom Trousers** / S:2 / J:2 / A:3		
				based on a traditional sea chantey		
7/14/45	11	3		6 **Five Salted Peanuts** J:11	$10	Victor 20-1661
8/18/45	13	1		7 **Please No Squeeza Da Banana** ....J:13 *José Gonzalez (Hozay Gonzalez)*	$10	Victor 20-1693
3/2/46	10	2		8 **Sioux City Sue** A:10 *Loop-De-Loo*	$25	Cosmo 471
5/31/47	8	2		9 **Red Silk Stockings And Green Perfume** ....A:8 *Get Up Those Stairs, Mademoiselle*	$10	Columbia 37330
6/14/47	11	9		10 **I Wonder, I Wonder, I Wonder** ....A:11 *Meet Me At No Special Place (And I'll Be There At No Particular Time)*	$10	Columbia 37353
8/16/47	10	7		11 **The Lady From Twenty-Nine Palms** ....A:10 *I'm Sorry I Didn't Say I'm Sorry (When I Made You Cry Last Night)*	$10	Columbia 37562
11/27/48	16	3		12 **You Started Something** J:16 *The Click Song*	$15	Columbia 38297
2/5/49	21	1		13 **It's Like Taking Candy From A Baby** A:21 *The Chowder Social*	$15	Columbia 38355
2/19/49	11	5		14 **Grieving For You** A:11 *Saturday Night Mood*	$15	Columbia 38383
				#7 hit for Marion Harris in 1921		
5/7/49	12	8		15 **"A"-You're Adorable (The Alphabet Song)** ....A:12 / S:22 / J:22 *It's A Cruel, Cruel World*	$15	Columbia 38449

DEBUT	PEAK	WKS	Gold	A-side (Chart Hit)	B-side	$	Label & Number

PAUL, Les, and Mary Ford ★22★   MEM/HOT '51

Pop duo. Paul was born Lester Polsfuss on 6/9/15 in Waukesha, Wisconsin. Ford was born Colleen Summers on 7/7/24 in Pasadena, California; died on 9/30/77 (age 49). Les Paul was an innovator in electric guitar and multi-track recordings. Married to vocalist Mary Ford from 1949-63. Les Paul won the Grammy's Trustees Award in 1983 and he was inducted into the Rock and Roll Hall of Fame in 1988.

*1)Vaya Con Dios (May God Be With You) 2)How High The Moon 3)It's Been A Long Long Time
4)Mockin' Bird Hill 5)The World Is Waiting For The Sunrise*

DEBUT	PEAK	WKS	Gold	#	A-side	B-side	$	Label & Number
10/13/45	❶²	16		1	**It's Been A Long Long Time** J:❶² / S:❶¹ / A:3 *Whose Dream Are You*		$15	Decca 18708
					BING CROSBY with LES PAUL And His Trio			
10/19/46	4	13		2	**Rumors Are Flying** J:4 / S:6 / A:7 *Them That Has—Gets* (**Andrews Sisters & Eddie Heywood**)		$15	Decca 23656
					ANDREWS SISTERS with LES PAUL			
6/24/50	9	17		3	**Nola** .... S:9 / J:9 / A:17 *Jealous* (w/Mary Ford) **[I]**		$20	Capitol F1014
					#3 hit for Vincent Lopez in 1922; #39 hit for **Billy Williams** in 1959			
10/7/50	21	2		4	**Goofus** .... S:21 *Sugar Sweet* **[I]**		$20	Capitol F1192
					#5 hit for Dan Russo in 1932; #56 hit for the Carpenters in 1976			
12/30/50+	6	14		5	**Tennessee Waltz** / .... A:6 / S:8 / J:13			
					#35 hit for Sam Cooke in 1964			
12/16/50+	18	7		6	**Little Rock Getaway** .... A:18 / S:24 **[I]**		$20	Capitol F1316
					introduced in 1933 by Joe Sullivan			
2/17/51	2⁵	24	●	7	**Mockin' Bird Hill** A:2 / J:2 / S:3 *Chicken Reel* (Paul)		$20	Capitol F1373
3/31/51	❶⁹	25	●	8	**How High The Moon** S:❶⁹ / A:❶⁹ / J:❶⁹ *Walkin' And Whistlin' Blues*		$20	Capitol F1451
					record selected for NARAS Hall of Fame; from the 1940 Broadway musical *Two For The Show* starring **Betty Hutton**; #76 hit for **Ella Fitzgerald** in 1960			
7/7/51	12	12		9	**Josephine** / .... S:12 / A:17 **[I]**			
					#3 hit for both **Tommy Dorsey** and **Wayne King** in 1937; #18 hit for Bill Black's Combo in 1960			
7/28/51	18	6		10	**I Wish I Had Never Seen Sunshine** J:18		$20	Capitol F1592
8/18/51	2²	16	●	11	**The World Is Waiting For The Sunrise** / A:2 / J:3 / S:3			
					#2 hit for Isham Jones in 1922; #108 hit for Don Gibson in 1961			
8/18/51	7	16		12	**Whispering** .... S:7 / A:7 / J:8 **[I]**		$20	Capitol F1748
					#1 hit for Paul Whiteman in 1920; #11 hit for Nino Tempo & **April Stevens** in 1964			
10/27/51	5	13		13	**Just One More Chance** A:5 / J:10 / S:12			
					#1 hit for **Bing Crosby** in 1931			
11/10/51	23	2		14	**Jazz Me Blues** .... S:23 / J:26 **[I]**		$20	Capitol F1825
					#9 hit for the Original Dixieland Jazz Band in 1921			
12/15/51	10	4		15	**Jingle Bells** .... A:10 / J:18 / S:20 *Silent Night* **[X-I]**		$20	Capitol F1881
					#18 hit for **Benny Goodman** in 1935; #74 hit for **Perry Como** in 1957			
1/19/52	2¹	12		16	**Tiger Rag** A:2 / S:6 / J:6 *It's A Lonesome Old Town*		$20	Capitol F1920
					#1 hit for the Original Dixieland Jazz Band (1918) and the **Mills Brothers** (1931)			
5/17/52	13	11		17	**I'm Confessin' (That I Love You)** / .... J:13 / A:14 / S:20			
					#2 hit for **Guy Lombardo** in 1930; #58 hit for Frank Ifield in 1963			
5/17/52	14	9		18	**Carioca** .... J:14 / A:16 / S:17 **[I]**		$20	Capitol F2080
					from the movie *Flying Down To Rio* starring Dolores Del Rio; #1 hit for **Enric Madriguera** in 1934			
6/28/52	14	7		19	**Smoke Rings** / .... A:14 / J:15 / S:19			
					#8 hit for Clyde McCoy in 1933			
6/21/52	15	7		20	**In The Good Old Summertime** .... A:15 / J:23 / S:28		$20	Capitol F2123
					#1 hit for J.W. Meyers, the Haydn Quartet, and Sousa's Band (all in 1902)			
8/30/52	5	14		21	**Meet Mister Callaghan** / S:5 / J:5 / A:6 **[I]**			
9/6/52	15	8		22	**Take Me In Your Arms And Hold Me** .... J:15 / A:17 / S:19		$15	Capitol F2193
					#1 Country hit for **Eddy Arnold** in 1950			
11/22/52+	7	10		23	**My Baby's Coming Home** / .... A:7 / J:10 / S:11			
11/8/52	8	8		24	**Lady Of Spain** .... A:8 / S:17 / J:18 **[I]**		$15	Capitol F2265
					#5 hit for **Ray Noble** in 1931			
1/3/53	5	7		25	**Bye Bye Blues** J:5 / A:6 / S:11 *Mammy's Boogie* (Paul)		$15	Capitol F2316
					#5 hit for Bert Lown in 1930; #54 hit for Bert Kaempfert in 1966			
3/28/53	10	6		26	**I'm Sitting On Top Of The World** .... J:10 / S:14 / A:15 *Sleep* (Paul)		$15	Capitol F2400
					#1 hit for **Al Jolson** in 1926			
6/20/53	❶¹¹	31	●	27	**Vaya Con Dios (May God Be With You)** / S:❶¹¹ / J:❶⁹ / A:❶³			
					#43 hit for The Drifters in 1964			
7/11/53	15	2		28	**Johnny (Is The Boy For Me)** J:15		$15	Capitol F2486
11/7/53	13	4		29	**Don'cha Hear Them Bells** .... A:13 *The Kangaroo* (Paul)		$15	Capitol F2614
4/3/54	11	10		30	**I Really Don't Want To Know** .... J:11 / A:18 / S:19 *South* (Paul)		$15	Capitol F2735
					#1 Country hit for **Eddy Arnold** in 1954; #18 hit for **Tommy Edwards** in 1960			
7/10/54	6	14		31	**I'm A Fool To Care** .... J:6 / A:7 / S:10 *Auctioneer*		$15	Capitol F2839
					song introduced by Country artist Ted Daffan in 1948; #24 hit for Joe Barry in 1961			
10/16/54	10	9		32	**Whither Thou Goest** / .... A:10 / J:11 / S:14			
11/27/54	19	1		33	**Mandolino** .... J:19 **[I]**		$15	Capitol F2928
					all of above titles with [I] symbols are **Les Paul** guitar solo instrumentals			

PEERCE, Jan   '51

Born Jacob Perlmuth on 6/3/04 in New York City. Died on 12/15/84 (age 80). Operatic tenor.

DEBUT	PEAK	WKS	#	A-side	$	Label & Number
10/2/48	23	2	1	**Bluebird Of Happiness** .... S:23 *Because*	$20	RCA Victor 49-0135
				RCA Victor Orchestra; Sylvan Levin, Conductor; 78 rpm: 11-9007 (Red Seal 12" record)		
7/14/51	12	8	2	**Because Of You** / .... A:12 / S:20		
				song published in 1940; featured in the 1951 movie *I Was An American Spy* starring Ann Dvorak; #71 hit for Chris Montez in 1967		
6/16/51	22	5	3	**What Is A Boy** .... S:22 / A:24 **[S]**	$15	RCA Victor 49-3425
				updated version by Tom Edwards, "What Is A Teenage Boy?," charted in 1957 (#96); **Hugo Winterhalter** (orch., above 2)		

PENGUINS, The   '55

R&B vocal group from Los Angeles: Cleveland Duncan, Dexter Tisby, Bruce Tate and Curtis Williams.

| 12/25/54+ | 8 | 15 | ● | Earth Angel (Will You Be Mine)..S:8 / J:10 / A:13 *Hey Senorita* | $150 | DooTone 348 |

written by Jesse Belvin and Curtis Williams; "Bubbled Under" (#101) on 12/28/59; #1 R&B hit (3 weeks)

PETTY, Frank, Trio   '50

Born on 1/12/16 in Chelsea, Massachusetts. His trio featured pianist Mike DiNapoli.

| 5/6/50 | 17 | 5 | | 1 Rain...S:17 / A:28 *A Precious Little Thing Called Love* | $15 | MGM K10669 |

originally released on Dililia 1010; Frank Petty (vocal); #16 hit for Sam Lanin in 1928

| 11/17/51 | 26 | 1 | | 2 Down Yonder ....S:26 *Precious* [I] | $15 | MGM K11057 |

Mike DiNapoli (piano); #5 hit for Ernest Hare & Billy Jones in 1921; #48 hit for Johnny & The Hurricanes in 1960

PETTY, Norman, Trio   MEM/HOT '54

Born on 5/25/27 in Clovis, New Mexico. Died on 8/15/84 (age 57). His trio: Petty (piano), wife Violet Ann (paino) and Jack Vaughn (guitar). Later became Buddy Holly's producer.

| 9/18/54 | 14 | 9 | | Mood Indigo...J:14 / S:22 *Petty's Little Polka* | $20 | "X" 4X-0040 |

#3 hit for Duke Ellington in 1931

PHILLIPS, Teddy, And His Orchestra   '52

Born on 6/15/16 in Oak Park, Illinois. Died on 3/10/2001 (age 84). Bandleader/saxophonist.

| 3/8/52 | 29 | 1 | | Wishin' ....J:29 *Sunshine And Flowers* | $20 | King 45-15156 |

Lynn Hoyt and Trio (vocals)

PIAF, Edith   HOT '50

Born Edith Giovanna Gassion on 12/19/15 in Belleville, Paris, France. Died of cancer on 10/11/63 (age 47). Legendary music hall/cabaret star. Often accompanied by **Les Compagnons De La Chanson**.

| 10/21/50 | 23 | 3 | | La Vie En Rose ....S:23 *Un Refrain Courait Dans La Rue* | $15 | Columbia 4-38948 |

7" 33-1/3 rpm: 1-776; Robert Chavigny (orch.); original 1947 French version is on Columbia 38912

PIED PIPERS, The ★65★   MEM '45

Vocal group formed in Hollywood. Originally an octet including **Jo Stafford** and her then-husband John Huddleston. Group recorded for **Tommy Dorsey**, often backing **Frank Sinatra**. By 1940, group pared down to a quartet. Stafford and Huddleston left in 1943. Group's lineup during 1944-48 "hit" period: Jane Hutton, Clark Yocum, Chuck Lowry and Hal Hopper. Hutton died on 5/2/73 (age 52). Yocum died on 1/13/93 (age 80).

1)Dream 2)The Trolley Song 3)My Happiness

| 4/8/44 | 8 | 1 | | 1 Mairzy Doats ....S:8 *A Journey To A Star* | $10 | Capitol 148 |

#75 hit for The Innocence in 1967

| 10/21/44 | 2² | 14 | | 2 The Trolley Song   S:2 / J:3 *Cuddle Up A Little Closer* | $10 | Capitol 168 |

from the movie *Meet Me In St. Louis* starring **Judy Garland**

| 3/10/45 | ❶¹ | 18 | ● | 3 Dream   A:❶¹ / S:5 / J:7 *Tabby The Cat* | $10 | Capitol 185 |

originally heard as the closing theme for composer **Johnny Mercer**'s radio show; #19 hit for Betty Johnson in 1958

9/22/45	16	1		4 Lily Belle ....J:16 *We'll Be Together Again*	$10	Capitol 207
1/12/46	14	2		5 In The Middle Of May / A:14		
12/29/45	18	1		6 Aren't You Glad You're You A:18	$10	Capitol 225

from the movie *The Bells Of St. Mary's* starring **Bing Crosby**

4/27/46	8	4		7 In The Moon Mist ....A:8 *Madame Butterball*	$10	Capitol 243
3/1/47	8	3		8 Open The Door Richard................................A:8 *When Am I Gonna Kiss You Good Morning* [N]	$10	Capitol 369
5/3/47	3	11		9 Mam'selle A:3 / S:9 / J:9 *It's The Same Old Dream*	$10	Capitol 396

from the movie *The Razor's Edge* starring Tyrone Power; **Paul Weston** (orch., all of above)

| 6/5/48 | 3 | 27 | ● | 10 My Happiness   A:3 / S:4 / J:4 *Highway To Love* | $10 | Capitol 15094 |

#2 hit for Connie Francis in 1959

| 9/25/48 | 13 | 9 | | 11 Underneath The Arches ....A:13 / S:21 / J:22 *Just For Me* | $10 | Capitol 15183 |

ANDY RUSSELL and THE PIED PIPERS
#11 hit for **George Olsen** in 1933

PIMM, Sir Hubert — see SUTTON, Ellen

PINETOPPERS, The   '51

Country group from Broadtop Mountain, Pennsylvania: brothers Roy and **Vaughn Horton**, Ray Smith, Rusty Keefer and Johnny Browers. Vocals by **The Marlin Sisters** (aka The Beaver Valley Sweethearts). Roy Horton was elected to the Country Music Hall of Fame in 1982.

| 3/3/51 | 10 | 17 | | 1 Mockin' Bird Hill..J:10 / S:21 / A:21 *Big Parade Polka* | $25 | Coral 9-64061 |

Beaver Valley Sweethearts (vocals); #3 Country hit

| 7/14/51 | 14 | 9 | | 2 Lonely Little Robin ....J:14 *Hometown Jubilee* | $25 | Coral 9-60508 |

The Marlin Sisters And Ray Smith (vocals); #105 hit for The Browns in 1960

PINZA, Ezio   '49

Born Fortunato Pinza on 5/8/1892 in Rome. Died of a stroke on 5/9/57 (age 65). Legendary bass vocalist with the New York Metropolitan Opera from 1926-48. Starred in several Broadway shows such as *South Pacific* and *Fanny*.

| 9/10/49 | 7 | 9 | | Some Enchanted Evening.............................S:7 / A:30 *This Nearly Was Mine* | $10 | Columbia 4578 |

performed by Pinza in Broadway's *South Pacific*; Salvatore Dell'Isola (orch.); record issued on Columbia's green Masterworks label (also on Columbia 4559 - from the 78 rpm album package); #13 hit for Jay & The Americans in 1965

POWELL, Teddy, and his Orchestra   MEM '41

Born Alfred Paolella on 3/1/05 in Oakland. Bandleader. Played guitar and banjo for **Abe Lyman** (1926-34).

| 4/19/41 | 18 | 1 | | 1 The Wise Old Owl ....S(e):18 / S(s):20 *Two Hearts That Pass In The Night* | $15 | Bluebird 11089 |
| 6/21/41 | 14 | 1 | | 2 The Things I Love ....S(wc):14 *Friendly Tavern Polka* | $15 | Bluebird 11113 |

#60 hit for The Fidelity's in 1958; Ruth Gaylor (vocal, above 2)

PRIMA, Louis, and his Orchestra ★134★   MEM/HOT '35

Born on 12/7/11 in New Orleans. Died on 8/24/78 (age 66). Jazz trumpeter/singer/bandleader. Married to singer **Keely Smith** from 1952-61. Popular Las Vegas duo. Prima was the voice for the cartoon character King Louis in Disney's *The Jungle Book*, in 1969. Surgery for a brain tumor in 1975 left him in a coma until his death.

DEBUT	PEAK	WKS		A-side / B-side	$	Label & Number
5/13/44	22	1		1 I'll Walk Alone..J(terr.):22 *Robin Hood* (R&B #10)	$20	Hit 7083
				from the movie *Follow The Boys* starring **Marlene Dietrich**		
12/23/44+	17	2		2 Angelina / ....A:17 / J:17		
				Louis Prima and Chorus (vocals); also released on Majestic 1016 and Majestic 1052		
11/25/44	25	1		3 Oh Marie..J:25	$20	Hit 7106
				#12 hit for **Horace Heidt** in 1937; #132 hit for the Village Stompers in 1964; Lily Ann Carol (vocal: #1 & 3)		
5/26/45	6	6		4 **Bell Bottom Trousers** J:6 / S:10 *Caldonia*	$15	Majestic 7134
				Lily Ann Carol, Louis Prima and Chorus (vocals); based on a traditional sea chantey		
10/11/47	8	8		5 Civilization (Bongo, Bongo, Bongo)................................S:8 / A:10 / J:10 *Forsaking All Others* [N]	$10	RCA Victor 20-2400
				Louis Prima and Chorus (vocals); from the Broadway musical *Angel In The Wings* starring Hank Ladd		
11/11/50	12	7		6 Oh Babe!...J:12 / S:16 / A:24 *Piccolina Lena*	$35	Robin Hood 45-101
				LOUIS PRIMA and KEELY SMITH		
5/24/52	27	2		7 The Bigger The Figure ....A:27 *Boney Bones* [N]	$25	Columbia 4-39735
				Louis Prima (vocal); based on *Largo al Factotum* from Rossini's *Barber Of Seville*		

Q

QUINLAN, Roberta   '50

Born in 1923 in St. Louis. Hosted her own NBC-TV musical series from 1949-51.

DEBUT	PEAK	WKS		A-side / B-side	$	Label & Number
6/3/50	22	2		1 Buffalo Billy...A:22 *I Never Had A Worry In The World*	$20	Mercury 5420-X45
				ROBERTA QUINLAN, JERRY MURAD'S HARMONICATS & JAN AUGUST		
				adaptation of the 1844 tune "Buffalo Gals (Won't You Come Out Tonight)"; also see **Russ Morgan**'s "Dance With A Dolly"		
11/18/50	30	1		2 Molasses, Molasses It's Icky Sticky Goo.............................A:30 *Orange Colored Sky* [N]	$20	Mercury 5504-X45
				ROBERTA QUINLAN with JAN AUGUST Orchestra		
				Marty Manning (choral group); variation on the melody of "A-Tisket, A-Tasket"		

R

RAINE, Lorry   MEM '50

Female singer; previously sang with Mark Warnow's Orchestra.

DEBUT	PEAK	WKS		A-side / B-side	$	Label & Number
9/23/50	24	4		Strangers...A:24 *Anna From Havana*	$20	London 30178
				Cliff Parman (orch.); 78 rpm: 753		

RAINS, Gray, and his Orchestra   '44

7/22/44	24	1		Swinging On A Star ....J(terr.):24 *The Day After Forever*	$15	Hit 7086
				Margie Wood and Gray Rains (vocals); from the movie *Going My Way* starring **Bing Crosby**; #38 hit in 1963 for Big Dee Irwin with Little Eva		

RANEY, Wayne   '49

Born on 8/17/20 in Wolf Bayou, Arkansas. Died of cancer on 1/23/93 (age 72). Country singer/harmonica player.

10/1/49	22	4		Why Don't You Haul Off And Love Me...........................J:22 *Don't Know Why*	$30	King 791
				#1 Country hit (3 weeks)		

RAY, Johnnie ★51★   MEM/HOT '51

Born on 1/10/27 in Dallas, Oregon. Died of liver failure on 2/25/90 (age 63). Wore hearing aid since age 14. First recorded for Okeh in 1951. Famous for emotion-packed delivery, with R&B influences. Appeared in three movies.

    1)Cry   2)The Little White Cloud That Cried   3)Walkin' My Baby Back Home

DEBUT	PEAK	WKS		A-side / B-side	$	Label & Number
11/24/51	❶[11]	27	●	1 Cry / S:❶[11] / A:❶[10] / J:❶[9]		
				#1 R&B hit (1 week); #18 hit for Ronnie Dove in 1966		
11/24/51+	2[2]	22		2 The Little White Cloud That Cried S:2 / A:2 / J:3	$30	Okeh 4-6840
				JOHNNIE RAY & The Four Lads (above 2)		
				#99 hit for Wayne Newton in 1964		
1/26/52	6	18	●	3 Please, Mr. Sun / ....J:6 / S:6 / A:11		
				#11 hit for **Tommy Edwards** in 1959		
1/26/52	8	15		4 Here Am I - Broken Hearted ....A:8 / S:9 / J:11	$20	Columbia 4-39636
				#3 hit for Paul Whiteman in 1927 as "Broken Hearted"		
4/12/52	13	8		5 What's The Use? ....S:13 / A:18 / J:20 *Mountains In The Moonlight*	$20	Columbia 4-39698
5/24/52	4	20		6 Walkin' My Baby Back Home ....J:4 / S:6 / A:7 *Give Me Time*	$20	Columbia 4-39750
				#8 hit in 1931 for both Nick Lucas and **Ted Weems**		
7/26/52	12	8		7 All Of Me / ....J:12 / S:26 / A:29		
				#1 hit in 1932 for both **Louis Armstrong** and Paul Whiteman; #3 Country hit for Willie Nelson in 1978		
8/9/52	20	2		8 A Sinner Am I J:20	$20	Columbia 4-39788
9/27/52	25	1		9 Love Me (Baby Can't You Love Me)................................S:25 *Faith Can Move Mountains*	$20	Columbia 4-39837
				The Four Lads (backing vocals: #1-5, 8 & 9); Jimmy Carroll (orch.: #3-5, 8 & 9)		
12/13/52	20	1		10 A Full Time Job ....A:20 *Ma Says, Pa Says*	$15	Columbia 4-39898
				DORIS DAY - JOHNNIE RAY		
4/11/53	8	6		11 Somebody Stole My Gal ....J:8 / A:13 / S:19 *Glad Rag Doll*	$15	Columbia 4-39961
				#1 hit for **Ted Weems** in 1924; The Buddy Cole Quartet (instrumental backing: #6, 7 & 11)		

DEBUT	PEAK	WKS	Gold	A-side (Chart Hit)..B-side	$	Label & Number

RAY, Johnnie — Cont'd

6/20/53	17	1		12 Candy Lips ....A:17 *Let's Walk That-A-Way*	$15	Columbia 4-40001
				JOHNNIE RAY - DORIS DAY **Paul Weston** (orch.: #10 & 12)		
4/17/54	19	1		13 Such A Night...A:19 *Destiny*	$15	Columbia 4-40200
				#2 R&B hit for The Drifters in 1954; #16 hit for Elvis Presley in 1964		
6/12/54	14	7		14 Hernando's Hideaway...J:14 / S:24 *Hey There*	$15	Columbia 4-40224
				Joe Reisman (orch.); from the Broadway musical *The Pajama Game* starring John Raitt		

REID, Don   **'49**

Born on 9/28/15 in Montreal. Singer/songwriter. Creator/writer/producer of TV's *College Bowl*. Wrote **Sammy Kaye**'s 1942 hit "Remember Pearl Harbor."

3/26/49	24	5		1 Hurry! Hurry! Hurry! / A:24		
				DON REID and the Peak-A-Boos (polka band)		
5/7/49	23	3		2 Don't Be Afraid To Dream..A:23	$35	Peak 800
				Dave Mann (conductor, above 2)		

REINER, Fritz — see KAPELL, William

REISMAN, Leo, and his Orchestra   MEM **'32**

Born on 10/11/1897 in Boston. Died on 12/18/61 (age 64). Bandleader/violinist. Charted 76 hits from 1921-40. Reisman's top 3 pre-1940 #1 hits: "Night And Day", "Stormy Weather" and "Paradise."

11/23/40	7	2		1 Down Argentina Way ....S:7 *You're Nearer*	$10	Victor 26765
				Sara Horn (vocal); from the movie *Down Argentine Way* starring Don Ameche and **Betty Grable**		
12/28/40	19	1		2 Ferry-Boat Serenade ....S(e):19 *Now I Lay Me Down To Dream*	$10	Victor 26718
				Anita Boyer (vocal)		

RENARD, Jacques, And His Orchestra   MEM **'30**

Born on 5/15/1897 in Paris. Died on 1/4/73 (age 75). Violinist/orchestra leader. Led a popular radio dance band from the mid-1920s to 1940.

| 3/27/43 | 3 | 16 | | **As Time Goes By** ....S:3 *I'm Sorry, Dear* | $15 | Brunswick 6205 |
| | | | | **Frank Munn** (vocal); originally charted in 1931 (#13); from the Broadway musical *Everybody's Welcome* starring Frances Williams; revived because of the recording ban and of its inclusion in the 1942 movie *Casablanca* starring Humphrey Bogart | | |

RENÉ, Henri   MEM/HOT **'54**

★**129**★

Born on 12/29/06 in Germany. Died on 4/25/93 (age 86). Bandleader/arranger/conductor. Began long career with Victor in 1936 as director of their international branch. Arranger/conductor for **Perry Como**, **Dinah Shore**, **Eartha Kitt**, **Mindy Carson**, and many other singers.

3/13/43	16	1		1 Tap The Barrel Dry..S(s):16 *Happy Pappy* [I]	$15	Standard 2057
				RENÉ MUSETTE ORCHESTRA		
6/19/48	30	1		2 Toolie-Oolie-Doolie (The Yodel Polka)...........................S:30 *Every Little Movement*	$10	RCA Victor 25-1114
				HENRI RENÉ and his MUSETTE ORCHESTRA The Three-O-Niners (vocals)		
6/9/51	6	15		3 I'm In Love Again A:6 / S:10 / J:13 *Roller Coaster*	$20	RCA Victor 47-4148
				HENRI RENÉ and his Orchestra featuring **April Stevens** featured in the Broadway musical *The Greenwich Village Follies Of 1925* starring Tom Howard		
8/11/51	10	5		4 Gimme A Little Kiss, Will Ya Huh?.................................A:10 / S:27 *Dreamy Melody*	$20	RCA Victor 47-4208
				APRIL STEVENS with HENRI RENÉ and his Orchestra #1 hit for "Whispering" Jack Smith in 1926		
10/13/51	27	1		5 And So To Sleep Again..A:27 *Aw C'mon*	$20	RCA Victor 47-4283
				APRIL STEVENS with HENRI RENÉ'S Orchestra and Chorus		
10/3/53	8	5		6 The Velvet Glove.....................................J:8 / S:18 / A:19 *Elaine* [I]	$15	RCA Victor 47-5405
				HENRI RENÉ and HUGO WINTERHALTER		
5/8/54	8	15		7 The Happy Wanderer (Val-De Ri, Val-De Ra) ....S:8 / A:9 / J:14 *My Impossible Love*	$15	RCA Victor 47-5715
				HENRI RENÉ'S MUSETTE and CHORUS		

REVELERS, The — see TRACE, Al

REY, Alvino, and his Orchestra   ★**93**★   MEM **'42**

Born Alvin McBurney on 7/1/11 in Cleveland. Bandleader/electric guitarist. Played with **Horace Heidt** from 1934-39. His band featured alto saxophonist Skeets Herfurt, pianist Buddy Cole and the **Four King Sisters** (Alvino married Louise) on vocals, with arranger **Frank DeVol**. Orchestra leader for TV's *The King Family Show* in the 1960s.

5/31/41	15	2		1 Nighty-Night ....S(wc):15 *My Prodigal*	$15	Bluebird 11041
				Yvonne King and Ensemble (vocals)		
1/17/42	2[1]	10		2 I Said No! / S:2		
				Yvonne King (vocal); from the movie *Sweater Girl* starring Eddie Bracken		
2/14/42	3	9		3 Deep In The Heart Of Texas S:3	$15	Bluebird 11391
				Bill Schallen and Skeets Herfurt (vocals); #78 hit for Duane Eddy in 1962		
8/8/42	16	4		4 Idaho ....S(mw):16 / S(wc):20 *It Isn't A Dream Any More*	$15	Bluebird 11331
				Chorus with Yvonne King (vocals)		
9/26/42	8	2		5 Strip Polka..S:8 *The Major And The Minor* [N]	$15	Bluebird 11573
				The Four King Sisters and Chorus (vocals)		
4/20/46	5	9		6 Cement Mixer (Put-ti Put-ti) A:5 / S:6 / J:11 *We'll Gather Lilacs*	$10	Capitol 248
7/19/47	13	3		7 Bloop-Bleep ....A:13 *Cumaná*	$10	Capitol 428
				Rocky Coluccio (vocal, above 2)		
9/20/47	3	14		8 Near You A:3 / S:9 / J:12 *Oh Peter (You're So Nice)*	$10	Capitol 452
				Jimmy Joyce (vocal); #10 hit for Roger Williams in 1958		
2/21/48	6	8		9 I'm Looking Over A Four Leaf Clover.....................................A:6 *Spanish Cavalier*	$10	Capitol 491
				Ensemble (vocals); #2 hit for Nick Lucas in 1927		

REYNOLDS, Debbie
HOT '57

Born Mary Reynolds on 4/1/32 in El Paso, Texas. Leading movie actress. Married to **Eddie Fisher** from 1955-59; their daughter is actress/author Carrie Fisher.

| 2/3/51 | 3 | 17 | ● | **Aba Daba Honeymoon** S:3 / J:4 / A:5 *Row, Row, Row* | $25 | MGM K30282 |

DEBBIE REYNOLDS and CARLETON CARPENTER
Georgie Stoll and the M-G-M Studio Orchestra and Chorus; from the movie *Two Weeks With Love* starring Reynolds and Carpenter; #1 hit for Arthur Collins & Byron Harlan in 1914

RHODES, Betty
MEM '46

Born on 4/21/21 in Rockford, Illinois. Singer/actress. Appeared in several movies.

| 9/28/46 | 5 | 11 | | 1 **Rumors Are Flying** S:5 / A:6 / J:8 *How Could I?* | $10 | RCA Victor 20-1944 |

Charles Dant (orch.)

| 11/13/48 | 9 | 9 | | 2 **Buttons And Bows**..A:9 / S:15 / J:22 *I Still Get A Thrill* | $10 | RCA Victor 20-3078 |

Harry Zimmerman (orch.); from the movie *The Paleface* starring **Bob Hope**; #104 hit for The Browns in 1962

RICHARDS, Trudy
'53

Singer formerly with **Charlie Barnet**'s orchestra.

| 6/20/53 | 19 | 2 | | **The Breeze "That's Bringin' My Honey Back To Me"**.....................J:19 *I Can't Love You Anymore* | $20 | Derby 45-823 |

Eddie Wilcox (orch.); #7 hit for Anson Weeks in 1934

RITTER, Tex
MEM/HOT '61

Born Maurice Woodward Ritter on 1/12/05 in Murvaul, Texas. Died of a heart attack on 1/3/74 (age 68). Country singer/guitarist/actor. Acted in numerous western movies from 1936-45. Elected to the Country Music Hall of Fame in 1964. Father of actor John Ritter.

| 11/25/44+ | 11 | 4 | | 1 **I'm Wastin' My Tears On You** /..J:11 | | |
| 12/9/44 | 21 | 1 | | 2 **There's A New Moon Over My Shoulder**...J:21 | $20 | Capitol 174 |

TEX RITTER And His Texans (above 2)
A-side #1 and B-side #2 on the Country charts

| 9/20/52 | 12 | 8 | | 3 **High Noon (Do Not Forsake Me)** ....S:12 *Go On! Get Out!* | $25 | Capitol F2120 |

sung by Ritter in the movie *High Noon* starring Gary Cooper

ROBERTS, Kenny
'49

Born George Kingsbury on 10/14/26 in Lenoir City, Tennessee; raised in Greenfield, Massachusetts. Country singer/songwriter/guitarist. Known for his yodeling.

| 9/10/49 | 9 | 13 | ● | **I Never See Maggie Alone** ....S:9 / J:12 / A:17 *Wedding Bells* (C&W #15) | $15 | Coral 64012 |

Roberts originally recorded this with Nancy Lee for Vitacoustic 506; #4 Country hit; #13 hit for Irving Aaronson in 1927

ROBERTSON, Dick — see LONG, Johnny

ROBERTSON, Texas Jim — see FONTANE SISTERS, The

ROBISON, Carson
MEM '31

Born on 8/4/1890 in Oswego, Kansas. Died on 3/24/57 (age 66). Country singer/songwriter/guitarist. Known as "The Kansas Jaybird."

| 10/2/48 | 14 | 9 | | **Life Gits Tee-Jus Don't It**...............................S:14 / A:25 / J:26 *Wind In The Mountains* [N] | $20 | MGM 10224 |

CARSON ROBISON With His Pleasant Valley Boys
#3 Country hit

ROS, Edmundo, And His Orchestra
HOT '50

Born on 12/7/10 in Trinidad. Bandleader/drummer based in London.

| 1/21/50 | 16 | 7 | | **The Wedding Samba** ....S:16 / J:23 / A:30 *Too Much Tempo In My Rumba Beat* | $25 | London 30017 |

78 rpm: 499; Edmundo Ros (vocal)

ROSE, David, and his Orchestra
HOT '62

Born on 6/15/10 in London; raised in Chicago. Died of heart failure on 8/23/90 (age 80). Conductor/composer/arranger. Married to Martha Raye (1938-41) and Judy Garland (1941-45).

2/19/44	2³	19	●	1 **Holiday For Strings** ....S:2 / J:8 *Our Waltz* [I]	$10	Victor 27853
2/19/44	11	6		2 **Poinciana (Song of the Tree)**..................................J:11 *Dancing In The Dark* (**Artie Shaw**) [I]	$10	Victor 20-1554
6/17/50	26	2		3 **Bewitched (Bothered And Bewildered)** ....A:26 *Moon Of Manakoora* [I]	$25	MGM K30120

from the Broadway musical *Pal Joey* starring **Gene Kelly**; #50 hit for the Betty Smith Group in 1958

ROSS, Roy, And His Orchestra
'50

Pianist/accordionist. Frequently accompanied the **Ames Brothers**.

| 6/10/50 | 28 | 1 | | **Bewitched** ....J:28 *Where In The World* [I] | $15 | Coral 60182 |

from the Broadway musical *Pal Joey* starring **Gene Kelly**; #50 hit for the Betty Smith Group in 1958

RUSSELL, Andy ★73★
MEM '46

Born Andres Rabajos on 9/16/19 in Los Angeles. Died of a stroke on 4/16/92 (age 72). Popular romantic singer. Replaced **Frank Sinatra** as lead singer on radio's *Your Hit Parade* in 1947. Hosted own TV show in Argentina from 1956-65. Hit #1 on the Adult Contemporary charts in 1967 with "It's Such A Pretty World Today."

1)Laughing On The Outside (Crying On The Inside) 2)Anniversary Song 3)Amor

| 4/22/44 | 10 | 2 | | 1 **Bésame Mucho (Kiss Me Much)** ....S:10 *You're The Dream, I'm The Dreamer* | $10 | Capitol 149 |

#70 hit for the Coasters in 1960

| 6/3/44 | 5 | 9 | | 2 **Amor** ....S:5 / J:8 *The Day After Forever* | $10 | Capitol 156 |

from the movie *Broadway Rhythm* starring George Murphy and **Ginny Simms**; #18 hit for Ben E. King in 1961; **Al Sack** (orch., above 2)

| 10/21/44 | 15 | 8 | | 3 **What A Diff'rence A Day Made** ....J:15 *Don't You Notice Anything New* | $10 | Capitol 167 |

#5 hit for the Dorsey Brothers in 1934; #8 hit for **Dinah Washington** in 1959

| 12/30/44 | 5 | 5 | | 4 **I Dream Of You** S:5 / A:8 / J:9 *Magic Is The Moonlight* | $10 | Capitol 175 |
| 12/15/45+ | 7 | 9 | | 5 **I Can't Begin To Tell You** ....A:7 / S:8 / J:12 *Love Me* | $10 | Capitol 221 |

from the movie *The Dolly Sisters* starring **Betty Grable**

RUSSELL, Andy — Cont'd

DEBUT	PEAK	WKS	A-side / B-side	$	Label & Number
5/11/46	4	12	6 **Laughing On The Outside (Crying On The Inside)** / S:4 / A:4 / J:8		
6/1/46	10	5	7 **They Say It's Wonderful**..A:10 / J:16 from the Broadway musical *Annie Get Your Gun* starring **Ethel Merman**	$10	Capitol 252
8/17/46	10	8	8 **Pretending**...A:10 / S:10 / J:13 *Who Do You Love I Hope* #10 hit for **Rudy Vallee** in 1929	$10	Capitol 271
3/8/47	4	10	9 **Anniversary Song** A:4 / S:5 / J:8 *My Best To You* from the movie *The Jolson Story* starring Larry Parks; based on Ivanovic's 1880 song "Danube Waves"	$10	Capitol 368
3/8/47	15	1	10 **I'll Close My Eyes**...J:15 *It's Dreamtime* (w/**Pied Pipers**) Paul Weston (orch., above 2)	$10	Capitol 342
9/25/48	13	9	11 **Underneath The Arches**..A:13 / S:21 / J:22 *Just For Me* **ANDY RUSSELL and THE PIED PIPERS** #11 hit for **George Olsen** in 1933	$10	Capitol 15183

S

SACK, Albert, and his Orchestra   **'44**
Born on 1/3/11 in New York City. Died on 12/6/47 (age 36). Orchestra leader.

| 9/30/44 | 14 | 1 | **Fellow On A Furlough**..................................S:14 *Dance Of The Tropical Moonbeams*
 Bob Matthews (vocal); from the movie *Meet Miss Bobby Socks* starring **Bob Crosby** | $60 | Premier 101 |

SATISFIERS, The — see CARROLL, Helen / COMO, Perry

SAUNDERS, Red, & his Orch.   **'52**
Born Theodore Saunders on 3/2/12 in Memphis. Died on 3/5/81 (age 69). Drummer/vibraphonist. Worked with **Duke Ellington** and **Louis Armstrong**.

| 3/15/52 | 20 | 1 | **Hambone**..A:20 / S:30 *Boot 'Em Up*
 Dolores Hawkins & The Hambone Kids (vocals; Dee Clark - one of the Kids); re-recorded and issued with a picture sleeve in 1963 on Okeh 4-7166 | $60 | Okeh 4-6862 |

SAUTER-FINEGAN ORCHESTRA   **MEM '52**
Eddie Sauter was born on 12/2/14 in Brooklyn, New York; died on 4/21/81 (age 66). William Finegan was born on 4/3/17 in Newark. One of the 1950s most innovative bands.

8/23/52	12	10	1 **Doodletown Fifers**...A:12 *Azure-Té* [I] adaptation of the Civil War song "Kingdom Coming And The Year Of Jubilo"; #97 hit for **"Tennessee" Ernie Ford** as "Sunday Barbecue" in 1958	$15	RCA Victor 47-4866
12/20/52+	13	4	2 **Nina Never Knew**...A:13 *Love Is A Simple Thing* Joe Mooney (vocal); Kai Winding (trombone)	$15	RCA Victor 47-5065
8/29/53	20	1	3 **The Moon Is Blue**...A:20 *"O" (Oh!)* title song from the movie starring William Holden; Sally Sweetland and The Doodlers (vocals); Doc Severinsen (trumpet, above 2)	$15	RCA Victor 47-5359

SAVITT, Jan, And His Orchestra   **MEM '40**
Born on 9/4/13 in Petrograd, Russia; raised in Philadelphia. Died on 10/4/48 (age 35). Bandleader/violinist.

| 8/3/40 | 8 | 1 | 1 **Make-Believe Island**...S:8 *Ask Your Heart*
 Bon Bon (vocal; real name: George Tunnell) | $10 | Decca 3188 |
| 7/5/41 | 19 | 1 | 2 **The Things I Love**.................................S(mw):19 *Manhattan Sunrise*
 JAN SAVITT and his TOP HATTERS
 Alan Witt (vocal); #60 hit for The Fidelity's in 1958 | $10 | Victor 27403 |

SCALA, Primo   **'48**
Born Harry Bidgood in 1898 in London. Died in 1955 (age 57). Musical director/producer. His featured vocal group was The Keynotes.

8/14/48	6	16	1 **Underneath The Arches**..............................S:6 / J:6 / A:13 *Side By Side* **PRIMO SCALA'S BANJO AND ACCORDION ORCHESTRA with THE KEYNOTES** #11 hit for **George Olsen** in 1933	$10	London 238
1/1/49-	24	1	2 **Jingle Bells** /..S:24 [X] #18 hit for **Benny Goodman** in 1935; #74 hit for **Perry Como** in 1957		
1/8/49-	27	1	3 **The Mistletoe Kiss**...S:27 [X] **THE KEYNOTES with PRIMO SCALA AND HIS BANJO AND ACCORDIAN ORCHESTRA** (above 2)	$15	London 302
3/12/49	27	1	4 **Cruising Down The River**..................................S:27 / J:29 *Dreaming* **PRIMO SCALA & HIS BANJO & ACCORDION ORCHESTRA with THE KEYNOTES**	$10	London 356

SCOTT, Raymond, and his New Orchestra   **MEM '37**
Born Harry Warnow on 9/10/08 in Brooklyn, New York. Died of pneumonia on 2/8/94 (age 85). Pianist/arranger/composer. Musical director for CBS radio. Conductor of TV's *Your Hit Parade*. His "looney tunes" were incorporated into the scores of numerous Warner Brothers cartoons. Married to singer Dorothy Collins from 1952-65.

| 9/21/40 | 15 | 3 | **Huckleberry Duck**..S(wc):15 *Just A Gigolo* [I] | $10 | Columbia 35363 |

SEIDEL, Toscha   **'41**
Born in 1900 in Russia. Died on 11/15/62 (age 62). Violinist.

| 5/17/41 | 15 | 1 | **Intermezzo**...S(wc):15 / S(mw):20 *Hungarian Dance No. 1* [I]
 Eugene Kusmiak (piano); issued on Victor's Red Seal label; title song from the movie starring Ingrid Bergman | $10 | Victor 4458 |

SHAND, Terry, And His Orchestra   **'40**
Born on 10/1/04 in Uvalde, Texas. Died on 11/11/77 (age 73). Pianist/singer with **Freddy Martin**.

| 8/3/40 | 17 | 1 | **I Can't Love You Any More (Any More Than I Do)**...............................S(mw):17 *Pretty Baby*
 Terry Shand (vocal) | $10 | Decca 3127 |

SHAW, Artie, and his Orchestra ★56★   MEM '39

Born Arthur Arshawsky on 5/23/10 in New York City. Considered to be one of the greatest clarinetists of the swing era. Played with Irving Aaronson, Red Nichols, Vincent Lopez, and Roger Wolfe Kahn before forming his own band in 1936. Fueled by Jerry Gray's arrangements, singer **Helen Forrest**, and featured soloists (in addition to Artie) **Tony Pastor** and George Auld (tenor saxes), the band was one of the nation's hottest by late 1938. A year later Artie abruptly left music, but his 1940 return from Mexico led to even greater success with full-band arrangements with strings, and jazz combo recordings with his "Gramercy 5." Theme song: "Nightmare." Married eight times, including movie stars Lana Turner and Ava Gardner. Later became a theatrical producer. Shaw's pre-1940 #1 hits: "Begin The Beguine," "They Say" and "Thanks For Ev'rything."

1)Frenesi 2)Ac-cent-tchu-ate The Positive 3)Star Dust

8/3/40	❶¹³	23	●	1 **Frenesi /** S:❶¹³ [I]		
9/14/40	20	1		2 Adios, Mariquita Linda...S(e):20	$15	Victor 26542
1/18/41	6	3	●	3 **Star Dust** ....S:6 _Temptation_ [I]	$15	Victor 27230
				voted the #1 all-time favorite record in _Billboard_'s 1956 Disk Jockey poll; #1 hit for Isham Jones in 1931; #12 hit for Billy Ward & His Dominoes in 1957
2/8/41	10	1	●	4 Summit Ridge Drive ....S:10 _Cross Your Heart_ [I]	$10	Victor 26763
				ARTIE SHAW and his GRAMERCY 5
2/15/41	10	2		5 Concerto For Clarinet (Parts 1 & 2)..........................S:10 [I]	$10	Victor 36383
				from the movie _Second Chorus_ starring Fred Astaire; issued as a 12" 78 rpm record
3/15/41	9	2	●	6 Dancing In The Dark..........................S:9 _(When Your Heart's On Fire) Smoke Gets In Your Eyes_ [I]	$10	Victor 27335
				#3 hit in 1931 for both **Bing Crosby** and **Fred Waring**; Billy Butterfield (trumpet, above 4)
11/29/41	10	1		7 Blues In The Night ....S:10 _This Time The Dream's On Me_	$10	Victor 27609
				"Hot Lips" Page (vocal and trumpet); title song from the movie starring Priscilla Lane
3/25/44	21	1		8 Dancing In The Dark ....J:21 _Poinciana (Song of the Tree)_ [I-R]	$10	Victor 20-1554
4/15/44	24	1		9 Summit Ridge Drive ....J:24 _Cross Your Heart_ [I-R]	$10	Victor 26763
				ARTIE SHAW and his GRAMERCY 5
9/9/44	10	2		10 It Had To Be You...............................S:10 / J:18 _Don't Take Your Love From Me_ [I]	$10	Victor 20-1593
				originally released in 1938 on Bluebird 10091; a different version released in 1941 on Victor 27536; from the movie _Show Business_ starring **Eddie Cantor**; #1 hit for Isham Jones in 1924
1/20/45	5	7		11 **Ac-cent-tchu-ate The Positive** S:5 / A:8 / J:9 _Jumpin' On The Merry-Go-Round_	$10	Victor 20-1612
				Imogene Lynn (vocal), Roy Eldridge (trumpet) and Barney Kessel (guitar); from the movie _Here Come The Waves_ starring **Bing Crosby** and **Betty Hutton**
7/20/46	17	1		12 I Got The Sun In The Morning ....A:17 _Along With Me_	$15	Musicraft 365
				ARTIE SHAW and his ORCHESTRA Vocal by MEL TORMÉ and the MELTONES
				from the Broadway musical _Annie Get Your Gun_ starring **Ethel Merman**
7/22/50	10	11		13 Count Every Star ....J:10 / S:15 / A:27 _If You Were Only Mine_	$20	Decca 9-27042
				DICK HAYMES and ARTIE SHAW
				#35 hit for Donnie & The Dreamers in 1961
9/16/50	10	10		14 I'm Forever Blowing Bubbles...........................J:10 / S:14 / A:15 _You're Mine, You!_	$20	Decca 9-27186
				GORDON JENKINS and ARTIE SHAW
				from the Broadway musical _The Passing Show Of 1918_ starring Fred Astaire; #1 hits in 1919 for both Henry Burr & Albert Campbell, and Ben Selvin

SHAW, Georgie   MEM/HOT '54

Born in 1930 in Philadelphia. Male singer.

| 1/23/54 | 7 | 14 | | Till We Two Are One ....A:7 / J:7 / S:8 _Honeycomb_ | $15 | Decca 9-28937 |
| | | | | Jimmy Leyden (orch. and singers); similar to Conway Twitty's 1976 hit "Don't Cry Joni" (#63) |

SHAY, Dorothy   '47

Born Dorothy Sims on 4/11/21 in Jacksonville, Florida. Died of a heart attack on 10/22/78 (age 57). Singer/actress. Known as "The Park Avenue Hillbillie." Acted in the movie _Comin' 'Round The Mountain_.

| 7/12/47 | 4 | 12 | | **Feudin' And Fightin'**   S:4 / A:8 / J:9 _Say That We're Sweethearts Again_ | $15 | Columbia 37189 |
| | | | | Mischa Russell (orch.); from the Broadway musical _Laffing Room Only_ starring **Betty Garrett** |

SHELTON, Anne   HOT '49

Born Patricia Sibley on 11/10/23 in Dulwich, London, England. Died of a heart attack on 7/31/94 (age 70). Vocalist with the Ambrose Orchestra.

1/1/49	25	3		1 Be Mine ....J:25 _Time Out For Tears_	$10	London 239
				based on the 1864 Spanish tune "La Paloma" (#20 hit for Billy Vaughn in 1958); melody also used on Elvis Presley's hit "No More" from his _Blue Hawaii_ soundtrack
2/5/49	27	2		2 Galway Bay ....J:27 _Greensleeves_	$10	London 287
				The Wardour Singers (backing vocals); Roy Robertson (orch., above 2)

SHEPARD, Jean   MEM/HOT '53

Born Ollie Imogene Shepard on 11/21/33 in Pauls Valley, Oklahoma; raised in Visalia, California. Country singer/songwriter/ bassist. Married **Hawkshaw Hawkins** on 11/26/60.

9/5/53	4	10		A Dear John Letter J:4 / S:16 _I'd Rather Die Young_	$25	Capitol F2502
				JEAN SHEPARD with FERLIN HUSKEY
				#1 Country hit (6 weeks); #44 hit for Pat Boone in 1960

SHERWOOD, Bobby, And His Orchestra   '46

Born on 5/30/14 in Indianapolis. Died on 1/23/81 (age 66). Former guitarist for **Bing Crosby** and Artie Shaw. Played trumpet and trombone in his own band.

| 10/12/46 | 11 | 1 | | Sherwood's Forest..A:11 _'Least That's My Opinion_ [I] | $10 | Capitol 286 |
| | | | | Manny Klein (trumpet); Dave Cavanaugh (tenor sax) |

SHINER, Mervin   '50

Born on 2/20/21 in Bethlehem, Pennsylvania. Country singer/songwriter/guitarist.

| 3/25/50 | 8 | 6 | ● | Peter Cottontail...S:8 / A:11 / J:13 _Floppy_ | $25 | Decca 9-46221 |

SHORE, Dinah ★10★   MEM/HOT '46

Born Frances Rose Shore on 3/1/17 in Winchester, Tennessee. Died of cancer on 2/24/94 (age 76). One of the most popular female vocalists of the 1940 to mid-1950s era. Sang with **Xavier Cugat** from 1939-40. Hostess of the 15-minute, award-winning early evening TV variety *The Dinah Shore Show* from 1951-57; then hosted the very popular *Dinah Shore Chevy Show* from 1956-63. Own morning talk show *Dinah's Place*, 1970-80. Married to actor George Montgomery from 1943-62.

1)Buttons And Bows 2)The Gypsy 3)I'll Walk Alone 4)Anniversary Song 5)I Wish I Didn't Love You So

Orchestras:

Blackton, Jay — 56	Cooley, Spade — 30	René, Henri — 52-55,57-60	Weston, Paul — 1,4,13-15
Bourdon, Rosario — 9	Dale, Ted — 45	Sack, Al — 19-22	Winterhalter, Hugo — 62
Burke, Sonny — 26-29,34-38	**Jenkins, Gordon** — 12,16	Schoen, Vic — 61	Zimmerman, Harry —
Case, Russ — 23-25	Joy, Leonard — 2,3,5-8,10,11	Stoloff, Morris — 33	41,43,44,46-50

DEBUT	PEAK	WKS	Gold	A-side	B-side	$	Label & Number
10/12/40	17	2		1 Maybe ....S(wc):17	*The Nearness Of You*	$10	Bluebird 10793
1/25/41	10	1		2 Yes, My Darling Daughter S:10	*Down Argentina Way*	$10	Bluebird 10920
3/15/41	9	1		3 I Hear A Rhapsody ....S:9 *I Do, Do You? (Do You Believe In Love)*		$10	Bluebird 11003
10/11/41	5	3		4 "Jim" ....S:5 *I'm Through With Love*		$10	Bluebird 11204
1/31/42	19	1		5 I Got It Bad And That Ain't Good ....S(s):19 *This Is No Laughing Matter*		$10	Bluebird 11357
				from **Duke Ellington**'s West Coast revue *Jump For Joy*			
2/21/42	4	7	●	6 **Blues In The Night** ....S:4 *Sometimes*		$10	Bluebird 11436
				title song from the movie starring Priscilla Lane			
3/21/42	8	3		7 Miss You ....S:8 *Is It Taboo? (To Fall in Love With You)*		$10	Bluebird 11322
				featured in the movie *Strictly In The Groove* starring Mary Healy; #78 hit for **Jaye P. Morgan** in 1959			
3/21/42	15	3		8 I Don't Want To Walk Without You......................................S(mw):15 *Fooled*		$10	Bluebird 11423
				from the movie *Sweater Girl* starring Eddie Bracken; #36 hit for Barry Manilow in 1980			
5/16/42	20	1		9 Skylark ....S(mw):20 / S(s):20 *Goodnight, Captain Curly-Head*		$10	Bluebird 11473
				#101 hit for Linda Ronstadt in 1984			
6/20/42	8	5		10 One Dozen Roses ....S:8 *All I Need Is You*		$10	Victor 27881
6/20/42	18	1		11 Sleepy Lagoon ....S(mw):18 *Three Little Sisters*		$10	Victor 27875
				adapted from a symphonic composition by Eric Coates			
8/1/42	18	2		12 He Wears A Pair Of Silver Wings ....S(e):18 / S(s):19 *Conchita, Marcheta, Lolita, Pepita, Rosita, Juanita Lopez*		$10	Victor 27931
				from George Black's musical revue *Black Vanities*			
1/16/43	3	8		13 (As Long As You're Not in Love With Anyone Else) **Why Don't You Fall In Love With Me?** / S:3			
12/26/42	10	1		14 **Dearly Beloved** S:10		$10	Victor 27970
				from the movie *You Were Never Lovelier* starring Fred Astaire and Rita Hayworth			
2/13/43	4	12		15 **You'd Be So Nice To Come Home To** S:4 *Manhattan Serenade*		$10	Victor 20-1519
				from the movie *Something To Shout About* starring Don Ameche			
5/8/43	5	2		16 **"Murder," He Says** S:5 *Something To Remember You By*		$10	Victor 20-1525
				from the movie *Happy-Go-Lucky* starring **Mary Martin**			
8/12/44	❶⁴	24		17 I'll Walk Alone S:❶⁴ / J:❶¹ *It Could Happen To You*		$10	Victor 20-1586
				from the movie *Follow The Boys* starring **Marlene Dietrich**			
11/11/44	12	1		18 Together ....S(s):12 *I Learned A Lesson I'll Never Forget*		$10	Victor 20-1594
				from the movie *Since You Went Away* starring Claudette Colbert; #1 hit for Paul Whiteman in 1928; #6 hit for Connie Francis in 1961; Mixed Chorus (only accompaniment, above 2)			
2/24/45	8	1		19 Sleigh Ride In July ....A:8 / J:17 *Like Someone In Love*		$10	Victor 20-1617
				from the movie *Belle Of The Yukon* starring Randolph Scott			
3/10/45	5	11		20 Candy / A:5 / J:8 / S:10			
4/7/45	11	1		21 He's Home For A Little While A:11		$10	Victor 20-1632
9/15/45	7	2		22 Along The Navajo Trail ....A:7 / S:8 *Counting The Days*		$10	Victor 20-1666
11/10/45	16	1		23 But I Did...J:16 *As Long As I Live*		$10	Victor 20-1732
11/24/45	14	3		24 My Guy's Come Back ....A:14 *Honey*		$10	Victor 20-1731
3/2/46	10	4		25 Personality ....A:10 *Welcome To My Dream*		$10	Victor 20-1781
				from the movie *Road To Utopia* starring **Bing Crosby** and Bob Hope			
3/9/46	6	9		26 Shoo-Fly Pie And Apple Pan Dowdy ....A:6 / J:6 / S:7 *Here I Go Again*		$10	Columbia 36943
4/27/46	❶⁸	21		27 The Gypsy / A:❶⁸ / S:2 / J:3			
4/20/46	3	15		28 **Laughing On The Outside (Crying On The Inside)** J:3 / S:3 / A:3		$10	Columbia 36964
5/11/46	9	4		29 All That Glitters Is Not Gold ....A:9 *Come Rain Or Come Shine*		$10	Columbia 36971
6/1/46	3	17		30 **Doin' What Comes Natur'lly** A:3 / J:4 / S:4 *I Got Lost In His Arms*		$10	Columbia 36976
				DINAH SHORE with Spade Cooley and his Orchestra from the Broadway musical *Annie Get Your Gun* starring **Ethel Merman**			
11/9/46	5	3		31 **You Keep Coming Back Like A Song** A:5 / J:17 *(It's Gonna Depend On) The Way That The Wind Blows*		$10	Columbia 37072
				from the movie *Blue Skies* starring Fred Astaire and **Bing Crosby**			
1/4/47	2²	16		32 (I Love You) For Sentimental Reasons A:2 / S:6 / J:7 *You'll Always Be The One I Love*		$10	Columbia 37188
				#17 hit for Sam Cooke in 1958			
3/1/47	❶²	12		33 Anniversary Song A:❶² / S:4 / J:5 *Heartaches, Sadness And Tears*		$10	Columbia 37234
				from the movie *The Jolson Story* starring Larry Parks; based on Ivanovici's 1880 song "Danube Waves"			
4/19/47	16	2		34 The Egg And I ....A:16 *Who Cares What People Say*		$10	Columbia 37278
				title song from the movie starring Claudette Colbert and Fred MacMurray			
7/12/47	15	2		35 Tallahassee...A:15 *Natch*		$10	Columbia 37387
				DINAH SHORE and WOODY HERMAN from the movie *Variety Girl* starring Mary Hatcher			

DEBUT	PEAK	WKS	Gold	A-side (Chart Hit) .... B-side	$	Label & Number
				SHORE, Dinah — Cont'd		
10/11/47	**2**³	12		36 **I Wish I Didn't Love You So** A:2 / J:5 / S:8 *(I've Been So Wrong, For So Long—But) I'm So Right Tonight* from the movie *The Perils Of Pauline* starring **Betty Hutton**	$10	Columbia 37506
10/25/47	**4**	11		37 **You Do** A:4 / S:14 *Kokomo, Indiana* from the movie *Mother Wore Tights* starring **Betty Grable**	$10	Columbia 37587
12/20/47+	**8**	9		38 **How Soon (Will I Be Seeing You)** ....A:8 / S:14 *Fool That I Am*	$10	Columbia 37952
6/19/48	**11**	7		39 **Little White Lies** ....A:11 / S:28 *Crying For Joy* #1 hit for **Fred Waring** in 1930; #25 hit for Betty Johnson in 1957	$10	Columbia 38114
9/18/48	**❶**¹⁰	25	●	40 **Buttons And Bows** S:❶¹⁰ / J:❶⁹ / A:❶⁵ *Daddy-O* **DINAH SHORE and her HAPPY VALLEY BOYS** from the movie *The Paleface* starring **Bob Hope**; #104 hit for The Browns in 1962	$10	Columbia 38284
12/18/48+	**9**	12		41 **Lavender Blue (Dilly Dilly)** ....S:9 / A:13 / J:21 *So Dear To My Heart* from the Disney movie *So Dear To My Heart* starring **Burl Ives**; #3 hit for Sammy Turner in 1959	$10	Columbia 38299
1/22/49	**14**	8		42 **Far Away Places** ....A:14 / J:19 / S:28 *Say It Every Day*	$10	Columbia 38356
3/19/49	**20**	4		43 **So In Love** ....A:20 / S:22 *Always True To You In My Fashion* 7" 33-1/3 rpm: 1-111; from the Broadway musical *Kiss Me, Kate* starring **Alfred Drake**	$10	Columbia 38399
4/23/49	**12**	15		44 **Forever And Ever**..A:12 / J:18 *I've Been Hit* 7" 33-1/3 rpm: 1-134; Male Quartet (backing vocals)	$10	Columbia 38410
5/7/49	**3**	19		45 **Baby, It's Cold Outside** A:3 / S:4 / J:6 *My One And Only Highland Fling* **DINAH SHORE and BUDDY CLARK** 7" 33-1/3 rpm: 1-200; from the movie *Neptune's Daughter* starring Esther Williams	$10	Columbia 38463
6/11/49	**22**	2		46 **A Wonderful Guy** ....A:22 / S:29 *Younger Than Springtime* 7" 33-1/3 rpm: 1-197; from the Broadway musical *South Pacific* starring **Mary Martin** and **Ezio Pinza**	$10	Columbia 38460
11/19/49+	**2**¹	18		47 **Dear Hearts And Gentle People** A:2 / S:7 / J:7 *Speak A Word Of Love (I Wish, I Wish)* 7" 33-1/3 rpm: 1-368	$10	Columbia 38605
2/11/50	**25**	1		48 **Bibbidi-Bobbidi-Boo (The Magic Song)** ....S:25 *Happy Times* 7" 33-1/3 rpm: 1-437; from the Disney animated feature movie *Cinderella*	$10	Columbia 38659
2/18/50	**20**	3		49 **It's So Nice To Have A Man Around The House**...........S:20 / A:20 / J:23 *More Than Anything Else In The World* 7" 33-1/3 rpm: 1-469	$10	Columbia 38689
9/16/50	**29**	1		50 **Can Anyone Explain? (No! No! No!)** ....J:29 *Dream A Little Dream Of Me* 7" 33-1/3 rpm: 1-759; Male Quartet (backing vocals)	$10	Columbia 38927
10/14/50	**28**	1		51 **I'll Always Love You (Querida Mia)** ....J:28 *I Didn't Know What Time It Was* 7" 33-1/3 rpm: 1-66; from the movie *My Friend Irma Goes West* starring **Dean Martin** and **Jerry Lewis**	$10	Columbia 38848
12/9/50+	**3**	19		52 **My Heart Cries For You /** A:3 / J:8 / S:11 adapted from the 18th-century French melody "Chanson de Marie Antoinette"; #38 hit for Ray Charles in 1964		
12/23/50+	**18**	3		53 **Nobody's Chasing Me** ....A:18 from the Broadway musical *Out Of This World* starring Charlotte Greenwood	$20	RCA Victor 47-3978
2/3/51	**8**	12		54 **A Penny A Kiss /** ....A:8 / J:12 / S:14 **TONY MARTIN and DINAH SHORE**		
3/3/51	**24**	2		55 **In Your Arms** ....S:24 / A:26 **DINAH SHORE and TONY MARTIN** based on Offenbach's *Barcarolle* from the opera *Tales Of Hoffman*; same melody used for Elvis Presley's "Tonight Is So Right For Love" on his 1960 album *G.I. Blues*	$20	RCA Victor 47-4019
2/24/51	**29**	1		56 **You're Just In Love** ....A:29 *Overture/Mrs. Sally Adams* (Jay Blackton) **DINAH SHORE and RUSSELL NYPE** from the Broadway musical *Call Me Madam* starring **Ethel Merman** (sung by Shore on the original cast album); available on RCA Victor's Green Label series	$20	RCA Victor 19-0001
7/7/51	**3**	17		57 **Sweet Violets** A:3 / J:3 / S:3 *If You Turn Me Down (Dee-Own-Down-Down)*	$20	RCA Victor 47-4174
9/1/51	**24**	2		58 **The Musicians** ....A:24 *How D'Ye Do And Shake Hands* **[N]** **DINAH SHORE, BETTY HUTTON, TONY MARTIN, PHIL HARRIS**	$20	RCA Victor 47-4225
6/7/52	**28**	1		59 **Delicado** ....A:28 *The World Has A Promise*	$20	RCA Victor 47-4719
10/11/52	**20**	5		60 **Blues In Advance** ....A:20 / J:22 / S:29 *Bella Musica*	$15	RCA Victor 47-4926
8/1/53	**11**	4		61 **Blue Canary** ....A:11 *Eternally*	$15	RCA Victor 47-5390
1/9/54	**12**	3		62 **Changing Partners** ....A:12 *Think*	$15	RCA Victor 47-5515
				SIMMS, Ginny **'44** Born on 5/25/15 in San Antonio. Died of a heart attack on 4/4/94 (age 78). Featured singer with **Kay Kyser** from 1934-41. Appeared in several movies and hosted own radio show.		
4/19/41	**16**	1		1 **Walkin' By The River** ....S(wc):16 *May I Never Love Again* Nat Brandwynne (orch.)	$15	Okeh 6025
4/15/44	**21**	1		2 **Irresistible You** ....J(terr.):21 *Suddenly It's Spring* from the movie *Broadway Rhythm* starring George Murphy and Simms	$10	Columbia 36693
12/2/44	**23**	1		3 **Wish You Were Waiting For Me**................................J(terr.):23 *Don't Ever Change* no instrumentation on above 2	$10	Columbia 36753

SINATRA, Frank ★5★

MEM/HOT '46

Born on 12/12/15 in Hoboken, New Jersey. Died of a heart attack on 5/14/98 (age 82). With **Harry James** from 1939-40 (first recorded for Brunswick in 1939); with **Tommy Dorsey**, 1940-42. Went solo in late 1942. Starred in several movies. Won an Oscar for the movie *From Here To Eternity* in 1953. Own TV show in 1957. Own Reprise record company in 1961, sold to Warner Bros. in 1963. Won Grammy's Lifetime Achievement Award in 1965. Married to actress Ava Gardner from 1951-57. Married to actress Mia Farrow from 1966-68. Announced his retirement in 1970, but made comeback in 1973. Regarded by many as the greatest popular singer of the 20th century.

1)Oh! What It Seemed To Be 2)Five Minutes More 3)Mam'selle 4)You'll Never Know 5)Young-At-Heart

Orchestras: Alexander, Jeff — 54
Cavanaugh, Page, Trio — 39
James, Harry — 2,10,11,13,67

Miller, Mitch — 59,60
Riddle, Nelson — 73-78

Stordahl, Axel —
1,12,14-22,24-38,40-45,47,
49-52,55-58,61-66,68-72

Winterhalter, Hugo — 53

Vocalists: Alexander, Jeff, Choir —
46,57,58,68
Charioteers, The — 23

Day, Doris — 52
Lane, Ken, Singers (Quintet) —
19,22,51,52

Modernaires, The — 55,56
Pastels, The — 53
Tucker, Bobby, Singers — 3-9

Whipoorwills, The — 61

DEBUT	PEAK	WKS		A-side	B-side	$	Label & Number
3/28/42+	**17**	3		1 **Night And Day**..S(wc):17 *The Night We Called It A Day*		$75	Bluebird 11463
				from the Broadway musical *The Gay Divorcee* starring Fred Astaire; #1 hit for **Leo Reisman** with Fred Astaire in 1932; #82 hit for Sergio Mendes & Brasil '66 in 1967			
6/19/43	**2**¹	18	●	2 **All Or Nothing At All**	S:2 *Flash* (James - R&B #10)	$15	Columbia 35587
				FRANK SINATRA with HARRY JAMES and his ORCHESTRA recorded on 9/17/39 (originally released July 1940)			
7/31/43	**2**²	13		3 **You'll Never Know /**	S:2		
				from the movie *Hello Frisco, Hello* starring Alice Faye			
10/2/43	**10**	1		4 **Close To You**..S:10		$15	Columbia 36678
9/18/43	**9**	4		5 **Sunday, Monday Or Always**..S:9 *If You Please*		$15	Columbia 36679
				from the movie *Dixie* starring **Bing Crosby**			
10/9/43	**6**	9		6 **People Will Say We're In Love /**..S:6 / J:7			
11/27/43	**15**	2		7 **Oh, What A Beautiful Mornin'**................................S(mw):15 / S(e):16		$15	Columbia 36682
				above 2 from the Broadway musical *Oklahoma!* starring **Alfred Drake**			
2/12/44	**4**	14		8 **I Couldn't Sleep A Wink Last Night /**	J:4 / S:5		
3/18/44	**15**	3		9 **A Lovely Way To Spend An Evening**................S(wc):15 / S(s):19		$15	Columbia 36687
				above 2 from the movie *Higher And Higher* (Sinatra's acting debut)			
5/27/44	**17**	2		10 **Every Day Of My Life /**..J:17			
5/13/44	**20**	1		11 **On A Little Street In Singapore**..........................J:20		$15	Columbia 36700
				FRANK SINATRA with HARRY JAMES and his Orchestra (above 2) above 2 recorded in 1939			
9/2/44	**15**	3		12 **Night And Day**..J:15 *The Lamplighter's Serenade* **[R]**		$15	Victor 20-1589
				reissue of #1 above			
10/28/44	**21**	1		13 **It's Funny To Everyone But Me**..........................J:21 *Don't Take Your Love From Me*		$15	Columbia 36738
				FRANK SINATRA with HARRY JAMES and his ORCHESTRA recorded in 1939			
12/30/44	**7**	2	●	14 **White Christmas /**..S:7 **[X]**			
				from the movie *Holiday Inn* starring Bing Crosby			
1/27/45	**19**	1		15 **If You Are But A Dream**..A:19		$15	Columbia 36756
				adapted from Anton Rubinstein's "Romance In E-Flat"			
2/3/45	**2**¹	12		16 **Saturday Night (Is The Loneliest Night In The Week) /**	A:2 / J:5 / S:6		
1/27/45	**7**	5		17 **I Dream Of You (More Than You Dream I Do)**..........S:7 / A:10 / J:12		$15	Columbia 36762
5/5/45	**14**	1		18 **What Makes The Sunset?**..A:14 *I Begged Her*		$15	Columbia 36774
				from the movie *Anchors Aweigh* starring Sinatra			
6/2/45	**5**	7		19 **Dream**..A:5 / S:7 / J:13 *There's No You*		$15	Columbia 36797
				originally heard as the closing theme for composer **Johnny Mercer**'s radio show; #19 hit for Betty Johnson in 1958			
6/23/45	**8**	2		20 **I Should Care**..A:8 *When Your Lover Has Gone*		$15	Columbia 36791
				from the movie *Thrill Of A Romance* starring Van Johnson			
9/8/45	**7**	2		21 **If I Loved You /**..A:7			
				from the Broadway musical *Carousel* starring John Raitt; #23 hit for Chad & Jeremy in 1965			
9/15/45	**9**	1		22 **You'll Never Walk Alone**..A:9		$15	Columbia 36825
				#34 hit for Patti LaBelle & Her Blue Belles in 1964; above 2 from the Broadway musical *Carousel* starring John Raitt			
11/10/45	**9**	4		23 **Don't Forget Tonight Tomorrow**..................A:9 / J:13 *Lily Belle*		$50	Columbia 36854
				FRANK SINATRA and THE CHARIOTEERS			
12/8/45	**10**	2		24 **Nancy (With The Laughing Face)**..............S:10 / A:13 *Cradle Song*		$15	Columbia 36868
				written for Frank's 4-year-old daughter			
12/15/45	**5**	4		25 **White Christmas**	A:5 *Mighty Lak' A Rose* **[X-R]**	$15	Columbia 36860
2/16/46	**❶**⁸	17		26 **Oh! What It Seemed To Be /**	A:❶⁸ / S:2 / J:3		
				#91 hit for The Castells in 1962			
2/16/46	**5**	10		27 **Day By Day**	A:5 / S:10 / J:15	$15	Columbia 36905
4/13/46	**17**	2		28 **Full Moon And Empty Arms**............................A:17 *You Are Too Beautiful*		$15	Columbia 36947
				based on Rachmaninoff's *Piano Concerto No. 2 in C-Minor*			
5/18/46	**2**¹	14		29 **They Say It's Wonderful /**	A:2 / S:8 / J:9		
6/1/46	**11**	2		30 **The Girl That I Marry**..A:11		$15	Columbia 36975
				above 2 from the Broadway musical *Annie Get Your Gun* starring **Ethel Merman**			
5/18/46	**7**	3		31 **All Through The Day**......................A:7 *Two Hearts Are Better Than One*		$15	Columbia 36962
				from the movie *Centennial Summer* starring Cornel Wilde			
7/13/46	**18**	1		32 **From This Day Forward**......................A:18 *Something Old, Something New*		$15	Columbia 36987
				title song from the movie starring Joan Fontaine			
8/3/46	**❶**⁴	22		33 **Five Minutes More**	A:❶⁴ / J:❶³ / S:❶² *How Cute Can You Be?*	$15	Columbia 37048
				featured in the movie *Sweetheart Of Sigma Chi* starring Elyse Knox			
9/28/46	**6**	12		34 **The Coffee Song (They've Got An Awful Lot Of Coffee In Brazil) /**........A:6 / S:10 / J:16			
10/26/46	**8**	6		35 **The Things We Did Last Summer**................................A:8 / J:12		$15	Columbia 37089
				#46 hit for Shelley Fabares in 1962			

DEBUT	PEAK	WKS	Gold	A-side (Chart Hit) ... B-side	$	Label & Number
				SINATRA, Frank — Cont'd		
12/21/46+	**8**	3		36 **September Song** ....A:8 *Among My Souvenirs*	$15	Columbia 37161
				from the movie *Knickerbocker Holiday* starring Nelson Eddy; #12 hit for Walter Huston in 1939; #51 hit for **Jimmy Durante** in 1963		
12/28/46	**6**	3		37 **White Christmas** ....A:6 / S:8 *Jingle Bells* **[X-R]**	$15	Columbia 37152
2/1/47	11	1		38 **This Is The Night** ....A:11 *Hugh-A-Bye Island*	$15	Columbia 37193
3/8/47	10	5		39 **That's How Much I Love You** ....A:10 *I Got A Gal I Love (In North And South Dakota)*	$15	Columbia 37231
				#2 Country hit for **Eddy Arnold** in 1946; #39 hit for Pat Boone in 1958		
5/3/47	5	6		40 **I Believe /** A:5 / J:14		
5/17/47	16	1		41 **Time After Time** A:16	$15	Columbia 37300
				#36 hit for Chris Montez in 1966; above 2 from the movie *It Happened In Brooklyn* starring Sinatra		
5/10/47	**❶**[1]	10		42 **Mam'selle** A:**❶**[1] / S:6 / J:9 *Stella By Starlight*	$15	Columbia 37343
				from the movie *The Razor's Edge* starring Tyrone Power		
9/20/47	13	2		43 **I Have But One Heart** (*O Marenariello*)..................A:13 / J:15 *Ain'tcha Ever Comin' Back*	$15	Columbia 37554
				sung in English and Italian		
11/8/47	8	1		44 **So Far** ....A:8 *A Fellow Needs A Girl*	$15	Columbia 37883
				from the Broadway musical *Allegro* starring John Battles		
4/17/48	14	1		45 **But Beautiful** ....A:14 *If I Only Had A Match*	$15	Columbia 38053
				from the movie *Road To Rio* starring **Bing Crosby** and **Bob Hope**		
5/29/48	7	4		46 **Nature Boy** ....A:7 / J:16 / S:18 *S'posin'*	$15	Columbia 38210
				#40 hit for Bobby Darin in 1961		
8/21/48	29	1		47 **Just For Now** ....A:29 *Everybody Loves Somebody*	$15	Columbia 38225
				from the movie *Whiplash* starring Dane Clark; B-side was a #1 hit for **Dean Martin** in 1964		
3/19/49	14	5		48 **Sunflower** ....A:14 / J:22 / S:25 *Once In Love With Amy*	$15	Columbia 38391
				7" 33-1/3 rpm: 1-106; a court ruling found the 1964 hit "Hello, Dolly!" to be directly based on this song		
6/11/49	6	13		49 **Some Enchanted Evening /** ....A:6 / S:25	$15	Columbia 38446
				#13 hit for Jay & The Americans in 1965		
7/2/49	18	5		50 **Bali Ha'i** ....A:18 / S:30		
				7" 33-1/3 rpm: 1-174; above 2 from the Broadway musical *South Pacific* starring **Mary Martin** and **Ezio Pinza**		
6/11/49	10	14		51 **The Huckle Buck**...S:10 / A:14 / J:19 *It Happens Every Spring*	$15	Columbia 38486
				7" 33-1/3 rpm: 1-222; based on the Charlie Parker jazz instrumental "Now's The Time"; #14 hit for Chubby Checker in 1960		
8/6/49	17	6		52 **Let's Take An Old-Fashioned Walk** ....A:17 *(Just One Way To Say) I Love You* (Sinatra)	$15	Columbia 38513
				FRANK SINATRA and DORIS DAY		
				7" 33-1/3 rpm: 1-260; from the Broadway musical *Miss Liberty* starring Eddie Albert		
10/8/49	9	12		53 **Let Her Go, Let Her Go, Let Her Go**....................A:9 / J:18 / S:21 *The Wedding Of Lilli Marlene*	$15	Columbia 38555
				7" 33-1/3 rpm: 1-315		
10/29/49	14	4		54 **That Lucky Old Sun** (Just Rolls Around Heaven All Day) ....J:14 / A:16 *Could 'Ja?*	$15	Columbia 38608
				7" 33-1/3 rpm: 1-372; #20 hit for Ray Charles in 1964		
12/24/49+	13	7		55 **The Old Master Painter** ....A:13 / J:17 / S:21 *Lost In The Stars* (Sinatra)	$10	Columbia 38650
				7" 33-1/3 rpm: 1-427		
1/21/50	28	1		56 **Sorry** ....A:28 *Why Remind Me*	$15	Columbia 38662
				FRANK SINATRA and THE MODERNAIRES (above 2)		
				7" 33-1/3 rpm: 1-440		
2/25/50	10	7		57 **Chattanoogie Shoe Shine Boy /** ....A:10 / S:24		
				#34 hit for Freddy Cannon in 1960		
2/25/50	25	1		58 **God's Country** A:25	$15	Columbia 38708
				7" 33-1/3 rpm: 1-496		
5/27/50	26	2		59 **American Beauty Rose** ....A:26 *Just An Old Stone House*	$15	Columbia 38809
				7" 33-1/3 rpm: 1-624		
8/5/50	5	12		60 **Goodnight Irene** A:5 / J:7 / S:12 *My Blue Heaven*	$25	Columbia 4-38892
				#75 hit for **Billy Williams** in 1959		
11/4/50	9	16		61 **One Finger Melody** ....A:9 *Accidents Will Happen*	$15	Columbia 39014
				45 rpm: 6-845		
12/2/50+	14	5		62 **Nevertheless (I'm In Love With You)** ....A:14 *I Guess I'll Have To Dream The Rest*	$25	Columbia 4-39044
				Billy Butterfield (trumpet solo); featured in the movie *Three Little Words* starring Fred Astaire; #5 hit for Jack Denny in 1931		
5/5/51	17	1		63 **You're The One** ....A:17 *Faithful*	$25	Columbia 4-39213
				Stan Freeman (piano solo)		
6/2/51	22	2		64 **We Kissed In A Shadow**.......................................A:22 *Hello, Young Lovers*	$25	Columbia 4-39294
				from the Broadway musical *The King And I* starring Yul Brynner		
6/23/51	14	7		65 **I'm A Fool To Want You /** A:14		
6/23/51	21	5		66 **Mama Will Bark** ....A:21 **[N]**	$25	Columbia 4-39425
				FRANK SINATRA & DAGMAR		
				Donald Bain (dog imitations)		
9/1/51	8	8		67 **Castle Rock** ....A:8 / S:26 / J:26 *Deep Night*	$25	Columbia 4-39527
				FRANK SINATRA & HARRY JAMES		
3/22/52	24	3		68 **I Hear A Rhapsody** ....A:24 *I Could Write A Book*	$25	Columbia 4-39652
9/13/52	20	4		69 **Bim Bam Baby /** ....J:20 / A:26		
9/27/52	30	1		70 **Azure - Te** (Paris Blues) A:30	$25	Columbia 4-39819
11/22/52	19	2		71 **The Birth Of The Blues** ....A:19 *Why Try To Change Me Now*	$25	Columbia 4-39882
				#1 hit for Paul Whiteman in 1926		
5/16/53	7	10		72 **I'm Walking Behind You** ....A:7 *Lean Baby*	$25	Capitol F2450
7/4/53	14	2		73 **I've Got The World On A String**.....................................A:14 *My One And Only Love*	$25	Capitol F2505
				#18 hit for **Cab Calloway** in 1932		
9/26/53	15	2		74 **From Here To Eternity** ....A:15 *Anytime - Anywhere*	$25	Capitol F2560
				melody is part of the soundtrack for the movie starring Burt Lancaster and Sinatra		
12/12/53+	18	2		75 **South Of The Border** (Down Mexico Way) ....A:18 *I Love You*	$25	Capitol F2638
				FRANK SINATRA and BILLY MAY with His Orchestra		
				Billy May's orchestra does not appear on this record — it is Nelson Riddle deliberately doing a May-style arrangement		
2/13/54	**2**[1]	22	●	76 **Young-At-Heart** S:2 / A:3 / J:5 *Take A Chance*	$20	Capitol F2703
				title song from the movie starring Sinatra		
5/8/54	17	6		77 **Don't Worry About Me** ....A:17 / S:28 *I Could Have Told You*	$20	Capitol F2787
				#5 hit for **Hal Kemp** in 1939		
5/29/54	4	13		78 **Three Coins In The Fountain** A:4 / S:7 / J:14 *Rain (Falling From The Skies)*	$20	Capitol F2816
				title song from the movie starring Clifton Webb and Dorothy McGuire		

SIX HITS AND A MISS '43
Vocal group also known as **4 Hits And A Miss**.

| 3/6/43 | 16 | 2 | | **You'd Be So Nice To Come Home To** ....S(wc):16 | | |

Would You Rather Be A Colonel With An Eagle On Your Shoulder, Or A Private With A Chicken On Your Knee? $10   Capitol 127
Gordon Jenkins (orch.); from the movie *Something To Shout About* starring Don Ameche

★114★ **SLACK, Freddie, and his Orchestra** MEM '46
Born on 8/7/10 in Westby, Wisconsin. Died of diabetes on 8/10/65 (age 55). Boogie-woogie pianist. With Ben Pollack from 1934-36, **Jimmy Dorsey** from 1936-39, and **Will Bradley** in 1940. Appeared in several movies.

| 8/22/42 | 9 | 2 | ● | 1 **Cow-Cow Boogie** ....S:9 *Here You Are* | $15 | Capitol 102 |

from the movie *Ride 'Em, Cowboy* starring Abbott & Costello

| 12/12/42 | 10 | 2 | | 2 **Mr. Five By Five** ....S:10 *The Thrill Is Gone* | $15 | Capitol 115 |

from the movie *Behind The Eight Ball* starring the Ritz Brothers; **Ella Mae Morse** (vocal, above 2)

| 3/20/43 | 10 | 1 | | 3 **That Old Black Magic** ....S:10 *Hit The Road To Dreamland* | $10 | Capitol 126 |

Margaret Whiting (vocal); #13 hit for **Sammy Davis, Jr.** in 1955

| 6/19/43 | 18 | 2 | | 4 **Riffette** ....S(wc):18 *They Didn't Believe Me* [I] | $15 | Capitol 129 |

T-Bone Walker (guitar); above 2 from the movie *Star-Spangled Rhythm* starring **Bing Crosby** and **Bob Hope**

| 7/24/43 | 19 | 2 | | 5 **Get On Board, Little Chillun** ....S(wc):19 *Old Rob Roy* | $15 | Capitol 133 |

Ella Mae Morse (vocal); same melody used in Trini Lopez's 1966 hit "I'm Comin' Home, Cindy"

| 3/4/44 | 19 | 2 | | 6 **Silver Wings In The Moonlight** ....S(terr.):19 *Furlough Fling* | $10 | Capitol 146 |

Margaret Whiting (vocal)

| 11/11/44 | 11 | 5 | | 7 **Cuban Sugar Mill** ....S(wc):11 *Small Batch O' Nod* [I] | $10 | Capitol 172 |
| 7/28/45 | 12 | 1 | | 8 **A Kiss Goodnight** ....A:12 *The Gee Chi Love Song* | $10 | Capitol 203 |

Liza Morrow (vocal)

| 5/18/46 | 8 | 13 | | 9 **The House Of Blue Lights** ....A:8 / J:15 *Hey Mr. Postman* | $15 | Capitol 251 |

Ella Mae Morse (vocal); Don Raye (jabber); #9 hit for Chuck Miller in 1955

SMITH, Eddie, And the Chief '51
Honky-tonk pianist.

| 10/20/51 | 16 | 4 | | **Down Yonder** ....J:16 *Sweet Bunch Of Daisies, Over The Waves, Medley* [I] | $20 | King 45-986 |

#5 hit for Ernest Hare & Billy Jones in 1921; #48 hit for Johnny & The Hurricanes in 1960

SMITH, Ethel, And the Bando Carioca '45
Born on 11/22/10 in Pittsburgh. Died on 5/10/96 (age 85). Organist. Billed as "The First Lady of The Organ." Appeared in several movies. Also see **Bing Crosby**'s "Just A Prayer Away."

| 1/27/45 | 14 | 1 | | **Tico-Tico** ....A:14 *Lero Lero / Bem Te Vi Atrevido* [I] | $15 | Decca 23353 |

Brazilian samba featured in the Disney movie *Saludos Amigos*

★107★ **SMITH, Jack** MEM '49
Tenor vocalist. Hosted TV's *You Asked For It!* from 1958-59. Not to be confused with 1920s vocalist "Whispering" Jack Smith.

JACK SMITH And The Clark Sisters:

| 5/31/47 | 18 | 1 | | 1 **Cu-Tu-Gu-Ru (Jack, Jack, Jack)** ....A:18 *Oh! My Achin' Heart* | $10 | Capitol 403 |

Earl Sheldon (orch.)

| 10/18/47 | 9 | 7 | | 2 **Civilization (Bongo, Bongo, Bongo)** ....A:9 / S:14 *Don't You Love Me Anymore* | $10 | Capitol 465 |

Frank DeVol (orch.); from the Broadway musical *Angel In The Wings* starring Hank Ladd

| 5/22/48 | 13 | 3 | | 3 **Baby Face** ....A:13 / S:19 / J:24 *Heartbreaker* | $10 | Capitol 15078 |

#1 hit for **Jan Garber** in 1926; #14 hit for The Wing And A Prayer Fife And Drum Corps. in 1976

| 6/19/48 | 17 | 2 | | 4 **Tea Leaves** ....J:17 / S:26 *Highways Are Happy Ways* | $10 | Capitol 15102 |

#9 hit for Nora Bayes in 1921

| 8/21/48 | 13 | 9 | ● | 5 **You Call Everybody Darling** ....S:13 / J:14 / A:16 *Cuckoo Waltz* | $10 | Capitol 15156 |

harmonica backing on above 3

| 12/4/48+ | 14 | 4 | | 6 **Cuanto Le Gusta (La Parranda)** ....A:14 / S:25 / J:26 *Cornbelt Symphony* | $10 | Capitol 15280 |

from the movie *A Date With Judy* starring Wallace Beery

| 1/22/49 | 17 | 4 | | 7 **Lavender Blue (Dilly Dilly)** ....A:17 / J:20 / S:30 *The Matador* | $10 | Capitol 15225 |

Earl Sheldon (orch.); from the Disney movie *So Dear To My Heart* starring **Burl Ives**; #3 hit for Sammy Turner in 1959

| 2/26/49 | 3 | 14 | | 8 **Cruising Down The River**   A:3 / S:14 / J:15 *Coca Roca* | $10 | Capitol 15372 |

JACK SMITH With The Crew-Chiefs:

| 4/9/49 | 13 | 4 | | 9 **Sunflower** ....A:13 / J:21 / S:27 *It's A Big Wide Wonderful World* | $10 | Capitol 15394 |

a court ruling found the 1964 hit "Hello, Dolly!" to be directly based on this song; **Frank DeVol** (orch., above 2)

★112★ **SMITH, Kate** MEM '32
Born on 5/1/07 in Greenville, Virginia. Died on 6/17/86 (age 79). Legendary soprano singer. Best known for her rendition of "God Bless America." Smith's pre-1940 #1 hits: "River, Stay 'Way From My Door" and "When The Moon Comes Over The Mountain."

| 8/3/40 | 20 | 1 | | 1 **I'm Stepping Out With A Memory To-Night** ....S(wc):20 *The Woodpecker Song* | $10 | Columbia 35398 |
| 8/17/40 | 5 | 3 | | 2 **God Bless America**   S:5 *The Star Spangled Banner* | $15 | Victor 26198 |

originally released in 1939, after Smith introduced the Irving Berlin classic on her 11/11/38 radio show; record selected for NARAS Hall of Fame; #36 hit for Connie Francis in 1959; huge surge in popularity after the 9/11 terrorist attacks

2/28/42	8	3	●	3 **Rose O'Day (The Filla-ga-dusha Song)** / S:8		
2/21/42	9	1		4 **(There'll Be Bluebirds Over) The White Cliffs Of Dover** S:9	$10	Columbia 36448
1/20/45	8	2		5 **Don't Fence Me In** / ....S:8 / J:9 / A:15		

4 Chicks and Chuck (backing vocals); from the movie *Hollywood Canteen* starring Bette Davis; #45 hit for **Tommy Edwards** in 1960

| 1/20/45 | 12 | 3 | | 6 **There Goes That Song Again** ....J:12 | $10 | Columbia 36759 |

from the movie *Carolina Blues* starring **Kay Kyser**

4/27/46	14	1		7 **Sioux City Sue** ....A:14 *I Didn't Mean A Word I Said*	$10	Columbia 36963
5/11/46	12	1		8 **Seems Like Old Times** ....A:12 *If I Had A Wishing Ring*	$10	Columbia 36950
3/20/48	12	2		9 **Now Is The Hour** ....A:12 *I'll Never Say I Love You ("To Anyone But You")*	$10	MGM 10125

based on the traditional New Zealand song "Hearera Ra"; #59 hit for Gale Storm in 1956; Jack Miller (orch., all of above)

SMITH, Keely — see **PRIMA, Louis**

SMITH, Tab

HOT '51

Born Talmadge Smith on 1/11/09 in Kinston, North Carolina. Died on 8/17/71 (age 62). Black jazz alto saxophonist. With **Count Basie** (1940-42) and **Lucky Millinder** (1942-44).

| 11/3/51 | 20 | 6 | | Because Of You ....J:20 / S:25 *Dee Jay Special* [I] | $25 | United 104 (45) |

TAB SMITH His Fabulous Alto and Orchestra
song published in 1940; featured in the 1951 movie *I Was An American Spy* starring Ann Dvorak; #71 hit for Chris Montez in 1967

SNYDER, Bill, And His Orchestra

'50

Born on 7/11/20 in Park Ridge, Illinois. Pianist/composer/bandleader.

| 4/22/50 | 3 | 19 | ● | Bewitched ....S:3 / A:5 / J:6 *Drifting Sands* [I] | $20 | Tower 45-1473 |

from the Broadway musical *Pal Joey* starring **Gene Kelly**; #50 hit for the Betty Smith Group in 1958

SONG SPINNERS, The

'43

Vocal group which enjoyed a burst of popularity during the musicians record ban. Sang on TV quiz show *Break The Bank* (1948-57).

6/19/43	❶³	11		1 Comin' In On A Wing And A Prayer /	S:❶³	
7/10/43	7	4		2 Johnny Zero S:7	$10	Decca 18553
2/10/51	18	11		3 It Is No Secret ....S:18 / A:21 / J:24 *I Hear A Choir*	$25	Decca 9-27326

Bill Kenny of THE INK SPOTS and The Song Spinners

SONS OF THE PIONEERS

MEM '48

Originally a trio consisting of Robert "Bob Nolan" Nobles (born on 4/1/08; died on 6/16/80, age 72), Leonard "Roy Rogers" Slye (born on 11/5/11; died on 7/6/98, age 86) and Vernon "Tim" Spencer (born on 7/13/08; died on 4/26/74, age 65). Formed in 1934 and first called the Pioneers; recorded for Decca in 1934. Brothers Karl (born on 4/25/09; died on 9/20/61, age 52) and Thomas "Hugh" (born on 12/6/03; died on 3/17/80, age 76) Farr were added in 1936. Group appeared in numerous western movies. Rogers and Spencer left in 1937, replaced by Lloyd Perryman (born on 1/29/17; died on 5/13/77, age 60) and Pat Brady. Spencer returned shortly thereafter. Group elected to the Country Music Hall of Fame in 1980.

| 7/24/48 | 9 | 14 | | 1 Cool Water..S:9 / J:14 / A:27 *The Legend Of Tiabi* | $15 | RCA Victor 20-2923 |

VAUGHN MONROE and Sons of the Pioneers
written in 1936; recorded by the Sons of the Pioneers in 1941 on Decca 5939 and in 1945 on RCA Victor 1724; #85 hit for Jack Scott in 1960

| 8/20/49 | 26 | 2 | | 2 Room Full Of Roses ....J:26 *Riders In The Sky* | $25 | RCA Victor 48-0060 |

78 rpm: 21-0065; #50 hit for Mickey Gilley in 1974

SOUTHERN, Jeri

MEM/HOT '51

Born Genevieve Hering on 8/5/26 in Royal, Nebraska. Died of pneumonia on 8/4/91 (one day before her 75th birthday). Jazz singer/pianist.

| 12/29/51 | 30 | 1 | | You Better Go Now..A:30 *Baby Did You Hear?* | $15 | Decca 9-27840 |

JERI SOUTHERN With MUSIC BY CAMARATA

SPITALNY, Phil — see HOUR OF CHARM CHOIR

SPIVAK, Charlie, and his Orchestra ★44★

MEM '42

Born on 2/17/06 in Kiev, Russia; raised in New Haven, Connecticut. Died of cancer on 3/1/82 (age 76). Played trumpet with Paul Specht (1925-31), Ben Pollack (1931-34), the Dorsey Brothers, **Ray Noble**, **Tommy Dorsey** (1938), and Jack Teagarden; **Glenn Miller** helped him form band in 1940. **Sonny Burke** and Nelson Riddle wrote arrangements; vocals by Garry Stevens and **The Stardusters** (including June Hutton). Band lineup in 1942 featured Willie Smith (alto sax) and Dave Tough (drums).

1)My Devotion 2)It's Been A Long, Long Time 3)Linda

Vocalists: Daye, Irene — 10,13,14   Mercer, Tommy — 17,18   **Stardusters, The** — 3,6
            Lynn, Tommy, & Choir — 19   Saunders, Jimmy — 9,11,12,15,16 Stevens, Garry — 3-5,7

| 8/2/41 | 10 | 1 | | 1 Intermezzo (A Love Story) ....S:10 *Simpatica* [I] | $10 | Okeh 6120 |

from the movie *Intermezzo* starring Ingrid Bergman

12/27/41	19	1		2 Let's Go Home ....S:(e):19 *To Your Heart's Content* [I]	$10	Okeh 6366
1/3/42	8	2		3 This Is No Laughing Matter ....S:8 *When I See An Elephant Fly*	$10	Okeh 6458
9/12/42	2²	11		4 My Devotion /	S:2	
9/19/42	8	2		5 I Left My Heart At The Stage Door Canteen..S:8	$10	Columbia 36620

from the Broadway musical *This Is The Army* starring **Burl Ives**

| 9/12/42 | 20 | 1 | | 6 Brother Bill..S(e):20 *Elegy* | $10 | Columbia 36596 |
| 11/7/42 | 18 | 5 | | 7 White Christmas ....S(s):18 *Yesterday's Gardenias* [X] | $10 | Columbia 36649 |

from the movie *Holiday Inn* starring **Bing Crosby**

| 1/6/45 | 12 | 1 | | 8 Too-Ra-Loo-Ra-Loo-Ral, That's An Irish Lullaby / ....S(mw):12 / S(s):12 [I] | | |

featured in the movie *Going My Way* starring **Bing Crosby**; #1 hit for Chauncey Olcott in 1914

| 12/23/44 | 23 | 1 | | 9 Let Me Love You To-Night ....J:23 | $10 | Victor 20-1603 |
| 4/28/45 | 16 | 1 | | 10 I Love You, I Love You, I Love You Sweetheart Of All My Dreams ....A:16 *(Yip Yip De Hootie) My Baby Said Yes* | $10 | Victor 20-1646 |

from the movie *Thirty Seconds Over Tokyo* starring Van Johnson; #5 hit for Rudy Vallee in 1929

| 5/26/45 | 6 | 6 | | 11 You Belong To My Heart / ....A:6 / S:9 / J:9 | | |

from the Disney movie *The Three Caballeros* starring Aurora Miranda

| 5/26/45 | 9 | 6 | | 12 There Must Be A Way ....A:9 / J:9 | $10 | Victor 20-1663 |

#33 hit for **Joni James** in 1959

7/14/45	16	1		13 Can't You Read Between The Lines?......................J:16 *Santa Lucia (On the Bay of Napoli)*	$10	Victor 20-1675
10/13/45	4	12		14 It's Been A Long, Long Time ....S:4 / A:6 / J:6 *If I Had A Dozen Hearts*	$10	Victor 20-1721
3/16/46	5	7		15 Oh! What It Seemed To Be ....S:5 / J:8 / A:10 *Take Care (When You Say "Te Quiero")*	$10	RCA Victor 20-1806

#91 hit for The Castells in 1962

| 12/14/46+ | 5 | 14 | | 16 (I Love You) For Sentimental Reasons ....A:5 / J:5 / S:7 *It's All Over Now* | $10 | RCA Victor 20-1981 |

#17 hit for Sam Cooke in 1958

| 3/29/47 | 5 | 11 | | 17 Linda ....J:5 / S:6 / A:10 *So They Tell Me* | $10 | RCA Victor 20-2047 |

#28 hit for Jan & Dean in 1963

SPIVAK, Charlie, and his Orchestra — Cont'd

3/20/48	14	2		18 **Now Is The Hour** (Maori Farewell Song) ....S:14 / J:14 *Who Are We To Say*	$10	RCA Victor 20-2704
				based on the traditional New Zealand song "Hearare Ra"; #59 hit for Gale Storm in 1956		
7/29/50	16	7		19 **Mona Lisa** ....A:16 / J:20 *Loveless Love*	$20	London 30073
				CHARLIE SPIVACK And His Orchestra		
				78 rpm: 619; from the movie *Captain Carey, U.S.A.* starring Alan Ladd; #25 hit for Carl Mann in 1959		

SPORTSMEN, The MEM '48

White vocal group: Bill Days, Thurl Ravenscroft, Max Smith, John Rarig and Marty Sperzel. Regulars on Jack Benny's radio show.

5/29/48	6	14		1 **You Can't Be True, Dear** / ....A:6 / S:11 / J:12		
				#75 hit for the Mary Kaye Trio in 1959		
6/12/48	11	6		2 **Toolie Oolie Doolie** (The Yodel Polka).........................A:11 / J:18 / S:20	$10	Capitol 15077
7/17/48	2⁵	9		3 **Woody Woodpecker** A:2 / S:2 / J:6 *I'd Love To Live In Loveland With A Girl Like You* (Sportsmen) **[N]**	$20	Capitol 15145
				THE SPORTSMEN and MEL BLANC And His Original Woody Woodpecker Voice		
				from the Walter Lantz cartoon		

STAFFORD, Jo ★6★   MEM/HOT '52

Born on 11/12/17 in Coalinga, California. Sang with **Tommy Dorsey**'s band, both as a solo artist and with the vocal group **The Pied Pipers**, 1940-43. Married to orchestra leader **Paul Weston**. Host of her own TV musical series, 1954-55. One of pop music's premiere female vocalists from 1944-54.

1)You Belong To Me 2)Make Love To Me! 3)Candy 4)My Darling, My Darling 5)Temptation (Tim-Tayshun)

Orchestras: Hall, Carlyle — 18
Mooney, Harold — 49
Weston, Paul — 1-10,12-17,19, 20, 22-25,29,32-48,50-71

Vocalists: Ingle, Red — 21
Laine, Frankie — 54,56,58,59,61,66
Luboff, Norman, Choir — 55,59-62,64
MacRae, Gordon — 26-28,31-33,38,42,43,45
Mercer, Johnny — 7
Murray, Lyn, Singers — 17
Pied Pipers, The — 7,10
Starlighters, The — 22,23,26,28,31,37,39-41,46

1/8/44	14	1		1 **Old Acquaintance** / ....S(e):14 / J:15 / S(wc):20		
				title song from the movie starring Bette Davis		
1/15/44	16	3		2 **How Sweet You Are** ....S(wc):16	$15	Capitol 142
				from the movie *Thank Your Lucky Stars* starring **Eddie Cantor** and Dennis Morgan		
5/13/44	6	12		3 **Long Ago** (And Far Away) / ....S:6 / J:11		
				from the movie *Cover Girl* starring Rita Hayworth		
4/29/44	8	4		4 **I Love You** ....S:8 / J:19	$10	Capitol 153
				from the Broadway musical *Mexican Hayride* starring Bobby Clark		
9/30/44	10	1		5 **It Could Happen To You** ....S:10 *Someone To Love*	$10	Capitol 158
				from the movie *And The Angels Sing* starring Dorothy Lamour; #53 hit for **Dinah Washington** in 1960		
2/17/45	14	3		6 **Let's Take The Long Way Home**.................................A:14 *I Promise You*	$10	Capitol 181
				from movie *Here Come The Waves* starring **Bing Crosby** and **Betty Hutton**		
2/24/45	❶¹	19		7 **Candy** A:❶¹ / J:❶¹ / S:2 *I'm Gonna See My Baby* (Mercer - #12)	$10	Capitol 183
				JOHNNY MERCER, JO STAFFORD		
5/12/45	7	6		8 **There's No You** / A:7		
7/28/45	9	1		9 **Out Of This World** A:9	$10	Capitol 191
				title song from the movie starring Eddie Bracken		
7/7/45	17	1		10 **On The Sunny Side Of The Street** ....J:17 *A Friend Of Yours*	$10	Capitol 199
				#2 hit for Ted Lewis in 1930		
10/27/45	4	4		11 **That's For Me** A:4 / S:9 *Gee, It's Good To Hold You*	$10	Capitol 213
				from the movie *State Fair* starring **Dick Haymes** and Dana Andrews		
12/29/45+	4	12		12 **Symphony** / S:4 / A:4 / J:8		
3/9/46	8	2		13 **Day By Day** ....A:8 / J:13	$10	Capitol 227
9/28/46	11	1		14 **This Is Always**..A:11 *I'll Be With You In Apple Blossom Time*	$10	Capitol 277
				from the movie *Three Little Girls In Blue* starring June Haver		
11/16/46	10	2		15 **The Things We Did Last Summer** / A:10		
				#46 hit for Shelley Fabares in 1962		
11/9/46	11	5		16 **You Keep Coming Back Like A Song** A:11	$10	Capitol 297
				from the movie *Blue Skies* starring Fred Astaire and **Bing Crosby**		
12/28/46	9	1		17 **White Christmas**.....................................A:9 *Silent Night* **[X]**	$10	Capitol 319
				from the movie *Holiday Inn* starring **Bing Crosby**		
1/18/47	10	5		18 **Sonata** ....A:10 *Through A Thousand Dreams*	$10	Capitol 337
6/7/47	15	1		19 **A Sunday Kind Of Love** / A:15		
				#95 hit for Jan & Dean in 1962		
5/3/47	16	4		20 **Ivy** A:16	$10	Capitol 388
				title song from the movie starring Joan Fontaine		
6/14/47	❶¹	15		21 **Temptation** (Tim-Tayshun) A:❶¹ / S:2 / J:5		
				(I Love You) For Sentimental Reasons (I Love You) For Seventy Mental Reasons **[N]**	$15	Capitol 412
				RED INGLE AND THE NATURAL SEVEN with Cinderella G. Stump (Jo Stafford)		
				novelty hillbilly version of song that was a #3 hit for **Bing Crosby** in 1934 and a #27 hit for The Everly Brothers in 1961		
8/30/47	6	11		22 **Feudin' And Fightin'** ....A:6 / J:8 / S:10 *Love And The Weather* **[N]**	$10	Capitol 443
				similar vocal as Stafford's "Cinderella G. Stump" on #21 above; from the Broadway musical *Laffing Room Only* starring **Betty Garrett**		
10/11/47	11	2		23 **Stanley Steamer** ....A:11 *When You Got A Man On Your Mind*	$10	Capitol 454
				from the movie *Summer Holiday* starring Mickey Rooney		
12/20/47	6	11		24 **Serenade Of The Bells** ....A:6 / S:6 / J:7 *The Gentleman Is A Dope*	$10	Capitol 15007
9/25/48	25	1		25 **Ev'ry Day I Love You** (Just A Little Bit More)........A:25 / S:29 *This Is The Moment*	$10	Capitol 15139
				from the movie *Two Guys From Texas* starring Dennis Morgan and Jack Carson		

STAFFORD, Jo — Cont'd

DEBUT	PEAK	WKS	Gold	A-side (Chart Hit) ... B-side	$	Label & Number
10/16/48	10	6	●	26 Say Something Sweet To Your Sweetheart / ....A:10 / S:20		
10/16/48	16	4		27 Bluebird Of Happiness ....S:16 / A:21 / J:24	$10	Capitol 15207
11/13/48+	❶¹	17		28 My Darling, My Darling A:❶¹ / S:3 / J:4 Girls Were Made To Take Care Of Boys	$10	Capitol 15270
				JO STAFFORD AND GORDON MacRAE (above 3)		
				from the Broadway musical Where's Charley? starring Ray Bolger		
1/15/49	13	11		29 Congratulations / A:13		
1/29/49	28	1		30 Here I'll Stay A:28	$10	Capitol 15319
				from the Broadway musical Love Life starring Nanette Fabray		
2/12/49	26	2		31 The Pussy Cat Song (Nyow! Nyot Nyow!) ....A:26 I'll String Along With You [N]	$10	Capitol 15342
3/19/49	4	15		32 "A" You're Adorable / ....S:4 / J:6 / A:12		
4/2/49	7	12		33 Need You ....J:7 / S:11 / A:18	$10	Capitol 15393
				JO STAFFORD AND GORDON MacRAE (above 3)		
4/23/49	16	6		34 Once And For Always ....A:16 Why Can't You Behave	$10	Capitol 15424
				from the movie A Connecticut Yankee In King Arthur's Court starring Bing Crosby		
5/14/49	4	17		35 Some Enchanted Evening A:4 / J:13 / S:21 I'm Gonna Wash That Man Right Outta My Hair	$10	Capitol 57-544
				from the Broadway musical South Pacific starring Mary Martin and Ezio Pinza; #13 hit for Jay & The Americans in 1965		
8/13/49	11	8		36 Homework / A:11		
8/20/49	12	6		37 Just One Way To Say I Love You...........................A:12	$10	Capitol 57-665
				above 2 from the Broadway musical Miss Liberty starring Eddie Albert		
8/20/49	4	23	●	38 Whispering Hope A:4 / S:6 / J:19 A Thought In My Heart	$10	Capitol 57-690
				JO STAFFORD AND GORDON MacRAE		
				#5 hit for Alma Gluck and Louise Homer in 1912		
10/15/49	9	5		39 The Last Mile Home / A:9		
9/17/49	10	7		40 Ragtime Cowboy Joe A:10	$10	Capitol 57-710
				Pat Gillham (ragtime piano solo); from the movie Hello Frisco, Hello starring Alice Faye; #1 hit for Bob Roberts in 1912; #16 hit for The Chipmunks in 1959		
11/19/49	20	2		41 If I Ever Love Again ....A:20 Red River Valley	$10	Capitol 57-742
12/24/49+	13	7		42 Bibbidi-Bobbidi-Boo (The Magic Song) / ....J:13 / A:14 / S:19		
				from the Disney animated feature movie Cinderella		
12/24/49+	18	5		43 Echoes ....J:18 / S:24 / A:28	$20	Capitol 54-782
				JO STAFFORD and GORDON MacRAE (above 2)		
1/7/50	14	4		44 Scarlet Ribbons (For Her Hair)..................A:14 Happy Times	$20	Capitol 54-785
				#13 hit for The Browns in 1959		
3/11/50	10	11		45 Dearie ....A:10 / S:12 / J:13 Monday, Tuesday, Wednesday	$20	Capitol F858
				JO STAFFORD and GORDON MacRAE		
				from the stage production The Copacabana Show Of 1950		
7/1/50	18	3		46 Play A Simple Melody ....A:18 / J:19 / S:27 Pagan Love Song	$20	Capitol F1039
				from the Broadway musical Watch Your Step starring Irene and Vernon Castle; #4 hit for Billy Murray & Elsie Baker in 1916		
8/19/50	8	11		47 No Other Love / ....S:8 / A:13 / J:27		
				melody adapted from the classical aria Chopin's "Etude No. 3 in E Major" (words by Jo's husband, Paul Weston)		
9/2/50	27	3		48 Sometime ....S:27 / A:30	$20	Capitol F1053
				#3 hit for the Green Brothers Novelty Band in 1925; George Greeley (piano, above 2)		
8/26/50	9	7		49 Goodnight, Irene ....A:9 / S:26 / J:28 Our Very Own	$20	Capitol F1142
				#75 hit for Billy Williams in 1959		
12/2/50+	7	13		50 Tennessee Waltz / ....A:7 / J:14 / S:17		
				#35 hit for Sam Cooke in 1964		
12/16/50	14	4		51 If You've Got The Money, I've Got The Time............A:14 / J:29	$20	Columbia 4-39065
				#1 Country hit for Lefty Frizzell in 1950 and Willie Nelson 1976		
1/13/51	8	18		52 If / A:8		
				#82 hit for The Paragons in 1961		
3/10/51	15	3		53 It Is No Secret ....A:15 / S:29	$20	Columbia 4-39082
5/19/51	13	10		54 Pretty Eyed Baby..................J:13 / A:16 / S:23 That's The One For Me	$20	Columbia 4-39388
				JO STAFFORD and FRANKIE LAINE		
				new lyrics to the R&B song "Satchelmouth Baby" recorded by Deek Watson & The Brown Dots on Manor 1026 in 1946		
6/2/51	12	5		55 Somebody ....A:12 Allentown Jail	$20	Columbia 4-39389
8/11/51	17	4		56 In The Cool, Cool, Cool Of The Evening..........A:17 That's Good! That's Bad!	$20	Columbia 4-39466
				JO STAFFORD & FRANKIE LAINE		
				from the movie Here Comes The Groom starring Bing Crosby and Jane Wyman		
9/15/51	20	2		57 Kissin' Bug Boogie ....J:20 Hawaiian War Chant (Ta-Hu-Wa-Hu-Wai)	$20	Columbia 4-39529
10/20/51	9	8		58 Hey, Good Lookin' / ....J:9 / A:14 / S:20		
				FRANKIE LAINE - JO STAFFORD		
10/27/51	19	4		59 Gambella (The Gamblin' Lady)..................J:19 / S:27	$20	Columbia 4-39570
				JO STAFFORD - FRANKIE LAINE		
11/10/51	2²	17	●	60 Shrimp Boats A:2 / S:2 / J:5 Love, Mystery And Adventure	$20	Columbia 4-39581
3/8/52	6	10		61 Hambone ....J:6 / S:15 / A:18 Let's Have A Party	$20	Columbia 4-39672
				FRANKIE LAINE & JO STAFFORD		
3/8/52	9	12		62 Ay-Round The Corner (Bee-hind The Bush) ....A:9 / S:22 / J:24		
				Heaven Drops Her Curtain Down (Twilight Theme Of An Autumn Fantasy)	$20	Columbia 4-39653
8/9/52	❶¹²	25	●	63 You Belong To Me A:❶¹² / S:❶⁵ / J:❶² Pretty Boy (Pretty Girl)	$20	Columbia 4-39811
				#7 hit for The Duprees in 1962		
8/30/52	3	20	●	64 Jambalaya / ....J:3 / S:3 / A:5		
				#16 hit for the Blue Ridge Rangers in 1973		
10/25/52	25	1		65 Early Autumn A:25	$20	Columbia 4-39838
10/18/52	21	3		66 Settin' The Woods On Fire...................J:21 / S:26 Piece A-Puddin'	$20	Columbia 4-39867
				JO STAFFORD - FRANKIE LAINE		
				78 rpm recording titled as "Tonight We're Setting The Woods On Fire"; Carl Fischer (piano: #54, 56, 58, 59, 61 & 66)		
11/15/52+	4	18	●	67 Keep It A Secret A:4 / J:4 / S:6 Once To Every Heart	$20	Columbia 4-39891
2/21/53	16	4		68 Now And Then, There's A Fool Such As I ....A:16 / J:16 / S:20 Just Because You're You	$20	Columbia 4-39930
				#3 Country hit for Hank Snow in 1953; #2 hit for Elvis Presley in 1959		
1/23/54	❶⁷	24	●	69 Make Love To Me! J:❶⁷ / S:❶³ / A:❶³ Adi - Adios Amigo (Il Passerotto)	$20	Columbia 4-40143
				based on the 1923 jazz instrumental "Tin Roof Blues"; issued with a picture sleeve; #96 hit for Johnny Thunder & Ruby Winters in 1967		

DEBUT	PEAK	WKS	Gold	A-side (Chart Hit)..B-side	$	Label & Number

STAFFORD, Jo — Cont'd

| 6/19/54 | 12 | 8 | | 70 **Thank You For Calling** ....A:12 / S:19 *Where Are You?* | $15 | Columbia 4-40250 |
| 11/20/54+ | 15 | 6 | | 71 **Teach Me Tonight** ....A:15 / J:16 / S:23 *Suddenly* | $15 | Columbia 4-40351 |

#25 hit for George Maharis in 1962

STANDLEY, Johnny   '52
Born on 12/6/12 in Oklahoma City. Died on 5/27/92 (age 79). Actor/comedian. With **Horace Heidt**'s stage show in the 1950s.

| 10/4/52 | **❶**² | 19 | ● | **It's In The Book (Parts 1 & 2)** ....S:**❶**² / A:4 / J:6 **[C]** | $25 | Capitol F2249 |

a parody of fundamentalist preaching; Part 1 is a monologue parody of "Little Bo Peep"; Part 2 is a hand-clapping, sing-along with **Horace Heidt** and His Musical Knights; originally released on 45 rpm on Magnolia 1063 in 1952

STAPLETON, Cyril — see GOFF, Reggie

STARDUSTERS, The   '49
Vocal group; sang background on three of **Evelyn Knight**'s hits.

| 4/2/49 | 5 | 21 | | **I Don't See Me In Your Eyes Anymore** ....J:5 / S:6 / A:24 *Because You Love Me* | $10 | Decca 24576 |

Gordon Jenkins (orch. and piano); #47 hit for Charlie Rich in 1974

STARLIGHTERS, The   MEM '50
Backing vocal group for **Jo Stafford** (regulars on Stafford's TV musical series).

2/19/49	26	1		1 **I've Got My Love To Keep Me Warm**........................A:26 *More Beer!*	$10	Capitol 15330
8/20/49	21	3		2 **Room Full Of Roses** ....A:21 *Weddin' Day*	$10	Capitol 57-617
2/18/50	12	7		3 **Rag Mop** ....A:12 *It Not Bad*	$15	Capitol F844

from the 1937 movie *On The Avenue* starring Dick Powell and Alice Faye; #3 hit for **Ray Noble** in 1937 (row 1)
#50 hit for Mickey Gilley in 1974 (row 2)
Paul Weston (orch., above 2) (row 3)

STARR, Kay ★29★   MEM/HOT '52
Born Katherine Starks on 7/21/22 in Dougherty, Oklahoma; raised in Dallas and Memphis. With Joe Venuti's orchestra at age 15, and sang briefly with **Glenn Miller**, **Charlie Barnet** and **Bob Crosby** before launching solo career in 1945. In the movies *Make Believe Ballroom* and *When You're Smiling*.

1)Wheel Of Fortune 2)Hoop-Dee-Doo 3)Side By Side 4)I'll Never Be Free 5)Bonaparte's Retreat

12/4/48+	16	8		1 **You Were Only Fooling (While I Was Falling In Love)**.......S:16 / A:20 / J:24 *A Faded Summer Love*	$10	Capitol 15226
1/15/49	7	16		2 **So Tired** ....A:7 / S:21 / J:24 *Steady Daddy*	$10	Capitol 15314
5/28/49	28	1		3 **How It Lies, How It Lies, How It Lies** ....A:28 *Wabash Cannonball*	$10	Capitol 15419
5/6/50	**2**¹	16		4 **Hoop-Dee-Doo** ....A:2 / J:6 / S:14 *A Woman Likes To Be Told*	$20	Capitol F980
5/27/50	4	27		5 **Bonaparte's Retreat** ....A:4 / J:5 / S:5 *Someday Sweetheart*	$20	Capitol F936
7/15/50	18	1		6 **Mississippi** ....A:18 *He's A Good Man To Have Around*	$20	Capitol F1072
8/19/50	3	20		7 **I'll Never Be Free /** ....S:3 / J:6 / A:8	$25	Capitol F1124
8/19/50	22	2		8 **Ain't Nobody's Business But My Own** J:22		
11/18/50	7	8		9 **Oh, Babe** ....A:7 / S:12 / J:15 *Everybody's Somebody's Fool*	$20	Capitol F1278
6/30/51	15	6		10 **Oceans Of Tears /** J:15	$25	Capitol F1567
6/30/51	22	2		11 **You're My Sugar** J:22		
8/4/51	8	9		12 **Come On-A My House**.........A:8 / S:17 / J:29 *Hold Me, Hold Me, Hold Me*	$20	Capitol F1710
10/27/51	26	1		13 **Angry** ....J:26 *Don't Tell Him What's Happened To Me*	$20	Capitol F1796
2/16/52	**❶**¹⁰	25	●	14 **Wheel Of Fortune** ....J:**❶**¹⁰ / S:**❶**⁹ / A:**❶**⁹ *I Wanna Love You*	$20	Capitol F1964
5/31/52	20	6		15 **I Waited A Little Too Long** ....J:20 / S:23 / A:29 *(Ho Ho Ha Ha) Me Too)*	$20	Capitol F2062
8/9/52	13	8		16 **Fool, Fool, Fool /** ....J:13 / A:16 / S:21		
7/26/52	18	3		17 **Kay's Lament** ....A:18 / J:20 / S:25	$20	Capitol F2151
9/27/52	9	9		18 **Comes A-Long A-Love /** ....J:9 / A:18 / S:22		
10/11/52	22	4		19 **Three Letters** J:22	$20	Capitol F2213
1/31/53	3	13		20 **Side By Side** ....A:3 / J:3 / S:7 *Noah!*	$20	Capitol F2334
6/6/53	7	15		21 **Half A Photograph /** ....J:7 / S:10 / A:10		
6/20/53	11	9		22 **Allez-Vous-En** ....A:11 / S:13	$20	Capitol F2464
10/31/53	18	1		23 **When My Dreamboat Comes Home** ....A:18 *Swamp-Fire*	$15	Capitol F2595
12/5/53+	7	13		24 **Changing Partners** ....J:7 / A:8 / S:13 *I'll Always Be In Love With You*	$15	Capitol F2657
4/24/54	4	18		25 **If You Love Me (Really Love Me) /** ....S:4 / A:4 / J:5		
4/17/54	7	17		26 **The Man Upstairs** ....S:7 / J:8 / A:9	$15	Capitol F2769
10/16/54	17	1		27 **Fortune In Dreams** ....A:17 *Am I A Toy Or A Treasure*	$15	Capitol F2887

#30 hit for **Vic Damone** in 1965 (row 1)
#9 hit for Gene Austin in 1928 (row 2)
Lou Busch (orch.); #50 hit for Billy Grammer in 1959 (row 5)
Starr's solo version charted in 1961 on Capitol 4583 (#94) (row 7)
KAY STARR and TENNESSEE ERNIE (above 2) (row 8)
Frank DeVol (orch.: #3, 4, 6 & 9) (row 9)
KAY STARR and TENNESSEE ERNIE (above 2) (row 11)
from the off-Broadway musical *The Son* (row 12)
#6 hit for Art Gillham in 1925; Dave Cavanaugh (orch., above 2) (row 13)
#83 hit for LaVern Baker in 1960 (row 14)
#1 R&B hit for The Clovers in 1951 (row 16)
The Lancers (backing vocals, above 2) (row 17)
#3 hit for both Nick Lucas and Paul Whiteman in 1927 (row 20)
from the Broadway musical *Can-Can* starring Lilo (row 22)
Dave Cavanaugh (orch.); #3 hit for Guy Lombardo in 1937; #14 hit for Fats Domino in 1956 (row 23)
introduced by Edith Piaf in 1950 as "Hymne a l'Amour" on Columbia 39027 (row 25)
same melody, but faster tempo and different words as #21 above (row 26)
Harold Mooney (orch.: #14, 18-22, 24, 25 & 27) (row 27)

DEBUT	PEAK	WKS	Gold	A-side (Chart Hit)..B-side	$	Label & Number

STEELE, Jon and Sondra   **'48**

5/15/48	2²	30	●	**My Happiness** A:2 / J:2 / S:3 *They All Recorded To Beat The Ban*	$20	Damon 11133

#2 hit for Connie Francis in 1959

STEVENS, April   **HOT '51**

Born Carol Lo Tempio on 4/29/36 in Niagara Falls, New York. Had a #1 hit in 1963 with "Deep Purple" (with brother Nino Tempo).

6/9/51	6	15		1 **I'm In Love Again**..A:6 / S:10 / J:13 *Roller Coaster*	$20	RCA Victor 47-4148

HENRI RENÉ and his Orchestra featuring April Stevens
featured in the Broadway musical *The Greenwich Village Follies Of 1925* starring Tom Howard

8/11/51	10	5		2 **Gimme A Little Kiss, Will Ya Huh?**......................A:10 / S:27 *Dreamy Melody*	$20	RCA Victor 47-4208

APRIL STEVENS with HENRI RENÉ and his Orchestra
#1 hit for "Whispering" Jack Smith in 1926

10/13/51	27	1		3 **And So To Sleep Again**...A:27 *Aw C'mon*	$20	RCA Victor 47-4283

APRIL STEVENS with HENRI RENÉ'S Orchestra and Chorus

STEWARD, Cliff, And The San Francisco Boys   **'50**

Born on 10/10/16 in Newport, Rhode Island.

5/13/50	18	5		1 **The Old Piano Roll Blues**.............................J:18 *Why Do They Always Say "No"?*	$20	Coral 9-60177

Ray Staunton (piano)

4/7/51	19	3		2 **The Aba Daba Honeymoon**.........................J:19 *Down In Jungle Town* **[N]**	$20	Coral 9-60374

from the movie *Two Weeks With Love* starring **Debbie Reynolds** and **Carleton Carpenter**; #1 hit for Arthur Collins & Byron Harlan in 1914

STEWART, Martha   **'45**

Born on 10/7/22 in Bardwell, Kentucky. Featured singer with **Claude Thornhill**. Not to be confused with the TV personality/entrepreneur of the same name.

2/17/45	12	2		**(All of a Sudden) My Heart Sings**..........................A:12 *There Goes That Song Again*	$15	Bluebird 30-0832

from the movie *Anchors Aweigh* starring **Frank Sinatra**; #15 hit for Paul Anka in 1959

STRONG, Benny, And His Orchestra   **'48**

Born on 3/17/11 in Chicago. Singer/bandleader. Former child model known as the "Milky Way Candy Boy."

9/11/48	9	14		1 **That Certain Party**..A:9 / J:9 / S:12 *My Best Girl*	$15	Tower 1271

#8 hit for Ted Lewis in 1926

5/7/49	30	1		2 **Five Foot Two, Eyes Of Blue**..............................J:30 *Dream Baby*	$15	Tower 1456

#1 hit for Gene Austin in 1926

1/14/50	19	3		3 **Dear Hearts And Gentle People**...........................J:19 / A:22 *You're The One*	$20	Capitol 54-757
4/1/50	11	6		4 **(If I Knew You Were Comin') Id've Baked A Cake**..................A:11 / J:19 *Does The Spearmint Lose Its Flavor On The Bedpost Over Night*	$20	Capitol F916

Benny Strong (vocal, all of above)

SULLIVAN, Maxine   **MEM '38**

Born Marietta Williams on 5/13/11 in Homestead, Pennsylvania. Died on 4/7/87 (age 75). Black jazz singer.

2/5/44	14	1		**My Ideal**..S(s):14 *When Your Lover Has Gone*	$15	Decca 18555

from the movie *Playboy of Paris*; #12 hit for Maurice Chevalier in 1931

SUTTON, Ellen   **'52**

2/9/52	21	2		**I Wanna Say Hello!**...J:21 *I Love The Sunshine Of Your Smile*	$25	Kem 45-2710

Sir Hubert Pimm (ragtime piano)

T

TALENT, Ziggy   **'50**

Born Zigmund Talent on 6/25/12 in Boston. Died on 6/25/97 (age 85). Novelty singer/saxophonist. With **Vaughn Monroe** from 1944-51.

11/4/50	25	2		**Please Say Goodnight To The Guy, Irene**........J:25 *Lena, The Queen A' The Uptown Arena* **[N]**	$20	RCA Victor 47-3925

answer song to **The Weavers'** "Goodnight, Irene"

TETER, Jack, Trio   **'50**

10/8/49+	6	23		**Johnson Rag**...S:6 / J:11 / A:18 *Back Of The Yards*	$20	London 30004

78 rpm: 501; Jack Teter (vocal); originally released on Sharp S2 in 1949

THARPE, Rosetta — see MILLINDER, Lucky

THOMAS, Dick   **'45**

Born Richard Thomas Goldham on 9/4/15 in Philadelphia. Singer/fiddler/accordionist/actor. Acted in several western movies.

12/15/45	16	1		**Sioux City Sue**...J:16 *Tumbling Tumbleweeds*	$20	National 5007

#1 Country hit (4 weeks)

THORNHILL, Claude, and his Orchestra   **MEM '37**

Born on 8/10/09 in Terre Haute, Indiana. Died of a heart attack on 7/1/65 (age 55). Pianist/arranger. Previously played with **Freddy Martin**, **Leo Reisman** and Paul Whiteman bands.

10/18/41	20	2		1 **Snowfall**..S(wc):20 *Where Or When* **[X-I]**	$10	Columbia 36268

Thornhill's theme song

12/27/41	20	1		2 **Autumn Nocturne**......................................S(wc):20 *Where Has My Little Dog Gone?* **[I]**	$10	Columbia 36435
2/4/50	24	4		3 **Johnson Rag**...A:24 *The Iowa Indian Song* (10 "Wuh")	$15	RCA Victor 47-3110

78 rpm: 20-3604; Joe Derise and The Snowflakes (vocals)

THREE CHUCKLES, The   **HOT '54**

Pop trio from Brooklyn, New York: Teddy Randazzo (accordion), Tom Romano (guitar) and Russ Gilberto (bass).

11/13/54	20	8		**Runaround**..S:20 *At Last You Understand*	$25	"X" 4X-0066

first released on Boulevard 100 in 1954; #23 hit for The Fleetwoods in 1960

THREE FLAMES, The　　'47

R&B group from New York City: Tiger Haynes (guitar), Roy Testamark (piano) and Averill Pollard (bass). Own NBC-TV show in 1949. Haynes acted in Broadway musicals, movies and TV since 1956, including the show *The Wiz* from 1974-78, as the Tin Man. Pollard died on 3/10/77 (age 57). Haynes died on 2/15/94 (age 86).

| 2/8/47 | ❶¹ | 8 | | **Open The Door, Richard**　　A:❶¹ / S:4 / J:5 *Nicholas (Don't Be So Ridiculous)* [N] | $20 | Columbia 37268 |

"Tiger" Haynes (vocal); #3 R&B hit

THREE SHARPS — see GRECO, Buddy

THREE SUNS, The ★77★　　MEM '47

Instrumental trio from Philadelphia: brothers Al (guitar) and Morty (accordian) Nevins, with cousin Artie Dunn (organ). Al Nevins died on 1/25/65 (age 48). Morty Nevins died on 7/23/90 (age 63). Dunn died on 1/15/96 (age 73). Al Nevins founded, with Don Kirshner, Aldon Music, the famed publishing company largely responsible for the "Brill Building" rock and roll sound.

1)Peg O' My Heart　2)Rumors Are Flying　3)How Many Hearts Have You Broken

| 7/1/44 | 16 | 1 | | 1 **Long Ago (And Far Away)** ....J:16 *And So Little Time* | $10 | Hit 7085 |

from the movie *Cover Girl* starring Rita Hayworth

| 8/12/44 | 7 | 18 | | 2 **How Many Hearts Have You Broken** /...J:7 | | |
| 11/11/44+ | 8 | 7 | | 3 **Twilight Time** ....A:8 / J:14 [I] | $10 | Hit 7092 |

the group's theme song; also released on Majestic 7092; #1 hit for The Platters in 1958

| 4/28/45 | 10 | 1 | | 4 **All Of My Life** ....A:10 *Shaga, Shuga Shuffle* | $10 | Hit 7126 |
| 9/7/46 | 7 | 13 | | 5 **Five Minutes More** ....A:7 / J:11 *By The Waters Of Minnetonka* | $10 | Majestic 7197 |

featured in the movie *Sweetheart Of Sigma Chi* starring Elyse Knox

| 11/9/46 | 7 | 6 | | 6 **Rumors Are Flying** ....A:7 / J:10 *It's All Over Now* [I] | $10 | Majestic 7205 |
| 6/21/47 | ❶³ | 19 | | 7 **Peg O' My Heart**　　J:❶³ / A:❶¹ / S:2 *Across The Alley From The Alamo* [I] | $10 | RCA Victor 20-2272 |

#1 hit for Charles Harrison in 1913; #64 hit for Robert (**Bobby**) Maxwell in 1964

| 2/28/48 | 10 | 8 | | 8 **I'm Looking Over A Four Leaf Clover** ....J:10 / S:13 *Eccentric* | $10 | RCA Victor 20-2688 |

#2 hit for Nick Lucas in 1927; Artie Dunn (vocal: #1, 2, 4, 5 & 8)

| 4/2/49 | 21 | 1 | | 9 **You, You, You Are The One** ....S:21 *Moonlight Romance* | $10 | RCA Victor 20-3322 |

Artie Dunn and The Sun Maids (vocals); adaptation of the German folk song "Du, Du Liegst Mir Im Herzen"

| 4/2/49 | 24 | 5 | | 10 **Cruising Down The River** ....S:24 / J:26 *Allah's Holiday* | $10 | RCA Victor 20-3349 |
| 7/24/54 | 24 | 4 | | 11 **Moonlight And Roses (Bring Mem'ries of You)**..S:24 *Crazy Legs* [I] | $25 | RCA Victor 47-5768 |

based on "Andantino in D Flat" by Edwin Lemare; one of the first pop hits to use a special electric guitar sound; #3 hit for John McCormack in 1925; #51 hit for Vic Dana in 1965

TILTON, Martha ★116★　　MEM '47

Born on 11/14/15 in New York City. Featured vocalist with **Benny Goodman**. Appeared in several movies.

| 7/15/44 | 4 | 24 | | 1 **I'll Walk Alone** /　　J:4 / S:5 | | |

from the movie *Follow The Boys* starring **Marlene Dietrich**

6/24/44	24	1		2 **Texas Polka** J:24	$10	Capitol 157
7/28/45	10	1		3 **Stranger In Town** /...A:10		
3/24/45	11	3		4 **I Should Care** A:11	$10	Capitol 184

from the movie *Thrill Of A Romance* starring Van Johnson; Eddie Miller (tenor sax, above 2)

| 3/8/47 | 8 | 5 | | 5 **How Are Things In Glocca Morra** ....A:8 / J:16 *Connecticut* | $10 | Capitol 345 |

from the Broadway musical *Finian's Rainbow* starring David Wayne

| 7/12/47 | 9 | 2 | | 6 **I Wonder, I Wonder, I Wonder** /...A:9 | | |
| 6/7/47 | 10 | 9 | | 7 **That's My Desire** ....A:10 | $10 | Capitol 395 |

#69 hit for The Sensations in 1962; Dean Elliott (orch., above 3)

| 10/28/50 | 23 | 1 | | 8 **I'll Always Love You** ....A:23 *There Isn't Very Much To Do Now* | $15 | Coral 9-60258 |

Lee Gordon (Singers and orch.); from the movie *My Friend Irma Goes West* starring **Dean Martin** and **Jerry Lewis**

TODD, Dick ★140★　　MEM '40

Born on 8/4/14 in Canada. Died on 5/18/73 (age 58). Vocalist with **Larry Clinton**'s band in 1938.

3/9/40	4	6		1 **The Gaucho Serenade**　　J:4 *It's The Talk Of The Town*	$10	Bluebird 10559
8/17/40	17	1		2 **Make-Believe Island** ....S(s):17 *Devil May Care*	$10	Bluebird 10729
8/31/40	20	1		3 **All This And Heaven Too**..S(wc):20 *Where Do You Keep Your Heart?*	$10	Bluebird 10789

title song from the movie starring Bette Davis

| 12/28/40 | 20 | 1 | | 4 **A Nightingale Sang In Berkeley Square** ....S(s):20 *Goodnight Mother* | $10 | Bluebird 10912 |

from the London musical *New Faces*

| 1/21/50 | 11 | 16 | | 5 **Daddy's Little Girl**..S:11 / J:13 / A:28 *Who'll Be The Next One (To Cry Over You)* | $25 | Rainbow 45-80088 |

Phil Ellis Choristers (backing vocals); **Eddie Miller** (orch.); #42 hit for **Al Martino** in 1967

| 3/14/53 | 17 | 1 | | 6 **Till I Waltz Again With You** ....A:17 *Oh, Happy Day* | $15 | Decca 9-28506 |

Jerry Jerome (orch.)

TORMÉ, Mel ★103★　　MEM/HOT '49

Born Melvin Howard on 9/13/25 in Chicago. Died of a stroke on 6/5/99 (age 73). Jazz singer/songwriter/pianist/drummer/actor. Wrote "The Christmas Song." Frequently appeared as himself on TV's *Night Court*. Nicknamed "The Velvet Fog." Won Grammy's Lifetime Achievement Award in 1999.

| 3/23/46 | 15 | 1 | | 1 **Day By Day** ....A:15 *Prove It By The Things You Do* | $15 | Decca 18746 |

BING CROSBY with MEL TORME And His Mel-Tones

| 7/20/46 | 17 | 1 | | 2 **I Got The Sun In The Morning** ....A:17 *Along With Me* | $15 | Musicraft 365 |

ARTIE SHAW and his ORCHESTRA Vocal by MEL TORME and the MELTONES
from the Broadway musical *Annie Get Your Gun* starring **Ethel Merman**

DEBUT	PEAK	WKS	Gold	A-side (Chart Hit) ....B-side	$	Label & Number

TORMÉ, Mel — Cont'd

DEBUT	PEAK	WKS		A-side	$	Label & Number
3/5/49	**❶**[1]	18		3 **Careless Hands** A:**❶**[1] / S:7 / J:11 *She's A Home Girl*	$10	Capitol 15379
				Sonny Burke (orch.)		
4/2/49	**3**	18		4 **Again /** A:3 / S:7 / J:8		
				from the movie *Road House* starring Ida Lupino and Cornel Wilde		
4/16/49	**20**	5		5 **Blue Moon** S:20	$10	Capitol 15428
				featured in the movie *Words And Music* starring Mickey Rooney and **Judy Garland**; #1 hit for **Glen Gray** in 1935; #1 hit for The Marcels in 1961		
7/2/49	**10**	8		6 **The Four Winds And The Seven Seas** A:10 / S:28 *It's Too Late Now*	$10	Capitol 57-671
				Frank DeVol (orch.)		
1/7/50	**9**	7		7 **The Old Master Painter** A:9 / J:18 *Bless You (For The Good That's In You)*	$20	Capitol F791
				PEGGY LEE and MEL TORMÉ The Mellomen (backing vocals)		
5/13/50	**8**	12		8 **Bewitched** A:8 *The Piccolino*	$20	Capitol F1000
				from the Broadway musical *Pal Joey* starring **Gene Kelly**; #50 hit for the Betty Smith Group in 1958; Pete Rugolo (orch.: #4, 5 & 8)		

DEBUT	PEAK	WKS		A-side	$	Label & Number
	★132★			**TRACE, Al, and His Orchestra** '48		
				Born on 12/25/1900 in Chicago. Died of a stroke on 8/31/93 (age 92). Orchestra leader/songwriter.		
2/19/44	**7**	6		1 **Mairzy Doats** S:7 / J:7 *Where Did You Get That Girl* **[N]**	$15	Hit 8079
				AL TRACE and his SILLY SYMPHONISTS "Red" Maddock and Al Trace and group (vocals); #75 hit for The Innocence in 1967		
6/19/48	**❶**[6]	24		2 **You Call Everybody Darlin'** J:**❶**[6] / S:**❶**[2] / A:3 *Linger Awhile*	$15	Regent 117
				AL TRACE And His New Orchestra		
9/11/48	**21**	3		3 **You Call Everybody Darlin'** J:21 *Duluth M-I-double-N*	$20	Sterling 3023
				AL TRACE and The Revelers the Sterling recording is the original version, recorded in 1946; lead vocal on both versions by Bob Vincent		
5/26/51	**21**	10		4 **Pretty Eyed Baby** J:21 / S:24 *That's The One For Me*	$20	Mercury 5609-X45
				AL TRACE and His Orchestra; Vocal by Lola Ameche new lyrics to the R&B song "Satchelmouth Baby" recorded by Deek Watson & The Brown Dots on Manor 1026 in 1946		
7/28/51	**24**	3		5 **Hitsity Hotsity** J:24 *Josephine*	$20	Mercury 5675-X45
				LOLA AMECHE; Al Trace Orchestra		

DEBUT	PEAK	WKS		A-side	$	Label & Number
	★130★			**TUBB, Ernest** MEM '50		
				Born on 2/9/14 in Crisp, Texas. Died of emphysema on 9/6/84 (age 70). Country singer/songwriter/guitarist. Known as "The Texas Troubadour." Elected to the Country Music Hall of Fame in 1965.		
1/22/44	**15**	3		1 **Try Me One More Time** J(terr.):15 *That's When It's Comin' Home To You*	$20	Decca 6093
8/19/44	**16**	2		2 **Soldier's Last Letter /** J:16	$20	Decca 6098
				#90 hit for Merle Haggard in 1971		
6/24/44	**23**	1		3 **Yesterday's Tears** J:23	$20	
9/18/48	**30**	1		4 **Forever Is Ending Today** J:30 *That Wild And Wicked Look In Your Eye* (C&W #9)	$20	Decca 46134
5/7/49	**30**	1		5 **I'm Bitin' My Fingernails And Thinking Of You** J:30 *Don't Rob Another Man's Castle* (C&W #6)	$20	Decca 24592
				ANDREWS SISTERS and ERNEST TUBB with The Texas Troubadors		
11/26/49	**17**	3		6 **Slipping Around** J:17 *My Tennessee Baby* (C&W #10)	$20	Decca 46173
12/24/49	**26**	2		7 **Blue Christmas** J:26 *White Christmas* (C&W #7) **[X]**	$20	Decca 46186
				The Troubadettes (female backing vocals); #1 hit on *Billboard's* special Christmas charts in 1964 for Elvis Presley		
8/12/50	**10**	10		8 **Goodnight Irene** J:10 *Hillbilly Fever #2* (C&W #9)	$25	Decca 9-46255
				RED FOLEY-ERNEST TUBB The Sunshine Trio (female backing vocals); #75 hit for **Billy Williams** in 1959; all of above were Top 5 Country hits		

DEBUT	PEAK	WKS		A-side	$	Label & Number
				TUCKER, Orrin, and his Orchestra MEM '40		
				Born on 2/17/11 in St. Louis. Orchestra leader/saxophonist. Featured vocalist was "Wee" Bonnie Baker (Evelyn Nelson).		
11/4/39	**2**[4]	14	●	1 **Oh Johnny, Oh Johnny, Oh!** J:2 *How Many Times*	$15	Columbia 35228
				includes 1 week at #2 on 12/23/39; #1 hit for the American Quartet in 1917		
12/23/39+	**5**	7		2 **Stop! It's Wonderful** J:5 *Lydia, The Tattooed Lady*	$10	Columbia 35249
12/30/39	**10**	2		3 **Billy** J:10 *Everybody Loves My Baby (But My Baby Don't Love Nobody But Me)*	$15	Vocalion 4914
				includes 1 week at #10 on 12/30/39; #7 hit for Kathy Linden in 1958		
2/10/40	**3**	10		4 **At The Balalaika** J:3 *Drifting And Dreaming*	$10	Columbia 35332
				Gil Mershon (vocal); from the movie *Balalaika* starring Nelson Eddy		
2/17/40	**10**	1		5 **Pinch Me** J:10 *Would Ja Mind*	$10	Columbia 35328
2/24/40	**5**	7		6 **You'd Be Surprised** J:5 *Little Girl*	$10	Columbia 35344
				from the Broadway musical *Ziegfeld Follies Of 1919* starring **Eddie Cantor**; #3 hit for Eddie Cantor in 1920; #50 hit for Kathy Linden in 1958; "Wee" Bonnie Baker (vocal: #1-3, 5 & 6)		

DEBUT	PEAK	WKS		A-side	$	Label & Number
	★136★			**TUCKER, Tommy, Time** MEM '41		
				Born on 5/18/08 in Souris, North Dakota. Died on 6/11/89 (age 81). Pianist/hotel-style band leader. Host of radio's *Sing For Your Supper with Tommy Tucker* and *30 Minutes In Hollywood*.		
1/13/40	**9**	7		1 **The Man That Comes Around** J:9 *Honestly* **[N]**	$20	Vocalion 5199
				Kerwin Somerville (vocal)		
12/7/40	**19**	3		2 **There I Go** S(mw):19 *Johnny Peddler (I Got)*	$15	Okeh 5789
				Amy Arnell (vocal)		
2/8/41	**16**	3		3 **You Walk By** S(s):16 / S(wc):18 *Walkin' Through Mockin' Bird Lane*	$15	Okeh 5973
				Amy Arnell and Don Brown (vocals)		
9/20/41	**4**	10		4 **I Don't Want To Set The World On Fire** S:4 *This Love Of Mine*	$15	Okeh 6320
				Amy Arnell & Voices Three (vocals)		
5/30/42	**18**	2		5 **Johnny Doughboy Found A Rose In Ireland** S(e):18 / S(wc):20 *I'll Pray For You*	$15	Okeh 6620
				Don Brown (vocal)		
8/25/45	**10**	3		6 **On The Atchison, Topeka And The Santa Fe** A:10 *Welcome Home*	$10	Columbia 36829
				Don Brown and The Three Two Timers (vocals); from the movie *The Harvey Girls* starring **Judy Garland**		

TURZY, Jane '51
Born in Chicago.

6/30/51	12	5		1 Good Morning Mister Echo....................A:12 / S:24 / J:28 *Be Doggone Sure You Call*	$20	Decca 9-27622
				JANE TURZY TRIO (Jane with vocal overdubbing)		
7/28/51	11	10		2 Sweet Violets ....J:11 / A:21 / S:22 *Lonely Little Robin*	$20	Decca 9-27668
11/24/51	20	4		3 I Like It ....J:20 *Yes You Are*	$20	Decca 9-27851
				Remo Biondi (orch., above 3)		

U

UNNATURAL SEVEN — see INGLE, Red

UPTOWN STRING BAND '48
String band directed by Joseph Giardino.

| 2/21/48 | 11 | 2 | | I'm Looking Over A Four Leaf Clover ....S:11 *My Little Girl* | $10 | Mercury 5100 |
| | | | | first issued on Krantz 1014; #2 hit for Nick Lucas in 1927 | | |

V

VALE, Jerry MEM/HOT '56
Born Genaro Vitaliano on 7/8/32 in the Bronx, New York. Pop ballad singer.

| 2/20/54 | 20 | 2 | | Two Purple Shadows ....J:20 *And This Is My Beloved* | $15 | Columbia 4-40131 |
| | | | | Jimmy Carroll (orch.) | | |

VALLÉE, Rudy MEM '29
Born Herbert Vallée on 7/28/01 in Island Pond, Vermont. Died of a heart attack on 7/3/86 (age 84). Legendary Depression-era singer/bandleader. Starred in several movies. Best known for singing into a megaphone. Charted 71 hits from 1929-39. Vallée's top 3 pre-1940 #1 hits: "Stein Song (University Of Maine)," "Honey" and "Brother, Can You Spare A Dime?"

| 4/24/43 | 2[1] | 10 | | **As Time Goes By** S:2 *Two In One Blues* | $10 | Victor 20-1526 |
| | | | | originally charted in 1931 (#15) on Victor 22773; from the Broadway musical *Everybody's Welcome* starring Frances Williams; revived because of the recording ban and of its inclusion in the movie *Casablanca* starring Humphrey Bogart | | |

VALLI, June MEM/HOT '53
Born on 6/30/28 in the Bronx, New York. Died of cancer on 3/12/93 (age 64). Pop singer. Voice for "Chiquita Banana" commercials.

7/19/52	23	4		1 Strange Sensation....................................A:23 *So Madly In Love*	$15	RCA Victor 47-4759
8/1/53	4	17		2 Crying In The Chapel J:4 / A:5 / S:6 *Love Every Moment You Live*	$15	RCA Victor 47-5368
				Joe Reisman (orch.); #3 hit for Elvis Presley in 1965		
6/12/54	8	12		3 I Understand ....A:8 / S:13 / J:20 *Love, Tears, And Kisses*	$15	RCA Victor 47-5740
				Hugo Winterhalter (orch. and chorus); #9 hit for The G-Clefs in 1961		
10/23/54	16	4		4 Tell Me, Tell Me....................................A:16 *Boy Wanted*	$15	RCA Victor 47-5837
				Henri René (orch. and chorus)		

VAUGHAN, Sarah ★76★ MEM/HOT '55
Born on 3/27/24 in Newark, New Jersey. Died of lung cancer on 4/3/90 (age 66). Jazz singer. Studied piano from 1931-39. Won Apollo Theater amateur contest in 1942. Vocalist for **Earl Hines** and **Billy Eckstine**. Nicknamed "The Divine One." Won Grammy's Lifetime Acievement Award in 1989.

1)Make Yourself Comfortable 2)Nature Boy 3)(I Love The Girl) I Love The Guy

Orchestras: **Faith, Percy** — 10,12,13   Lipman, Joe — 3-6   Peretti, Hugo — 14
     Leyden, Norman — 7-9   **Maltby, Richard** — 2   **Weston, Paul** — 11

7/3/48	9	1		1 Nature Boy ....A:9 *I'm Glad There Is You*	$15	Musicraft 567
				#40 hit for Bobby Darin in 1961		
8/14/48	11	11		2 It's Magic....................................A:11 / S:29 *It's You Or No One*	$15	Musicraft 557
				from the movie *Romance On The High Seas* starring **Doris Day** and Jack Carson; #91 hit for The Platters in 1962		
6/4/49	13	4		3 Black Coffee....................................A:13 *As You Desire Me*	$10	Columbia 38462
				7" 33-1/3 rpm: 1-199		
9/17/49	14	4		4 That Lucky Old Sun (Just Rolls Around Heaven All Day) / A:14		
				#20 hit for Ray Charles in 1964		
10/1/49	20	5		5 Make Believe (You Are Glad When You're Sorry)....................................A:20	$10	Columbia 38559
				7" 33-1/3 rpm: 1-321; #1 hit for Nora Bayes in 1921		
6/3/50	26	3		6 I'm Crazy To Love You ....A:26 *Summertime*	$10	Columbia 38701
				7" 33-1/3 rpm: 1-485; **Billy Butterfield** and Taft Jordan (trumpets)		
8/5/50	15	6		7 Our Very Own....................................A:15 *Don't Be Afraid*	$10	Columbia 38860
				7" 33-1/3 rpm: 1-679; title song from the movie starring Ann Blyth		
9/16/50	10	7		8 (I Love The Girl) I Love The Guy / A:10		
11/11/50	16	7		9 Thinking Of You....................................A:16	$20	Columbia 4-38925
				from the Broadway musical *The Five O'Clock Girl* starring Mary Eaton; featured in the movie *Three Little Words* starring Fred Astaire; #5 hit for Nat Shilkret in 1928		
6/2/51	11	13		10 These Things I Offer You (For A Lifetime)....................A:11 / S:21 *Deep Purple*	$20	Columbia 4-39370
8/11/51	19	2		11 Vanity ....A:19 *My Reverie*	$20	Columbia 4-39446
11/10/51	18	2		12 I Ran All The Way Home ....A:18 *Just A Moment More*	$20	Columbia 4-39576
11/8/52	22	1		13 Sinner Or Saint ....A:22 *Mighty Lonesome Feelin'*	$20	Columbia 4-39873
11/27/54+	6	15		14 Make Yourself Comfortable A:6 / S:8 / J:8 *Idle Gossip*	$15	Mercury 70469-X45

VAUGHN, Billy
HOT '55

Born Richard Vaughn on 4/12/19 in Glasgow, Kentucky. Died of cancer on 9/26/91 (age 72). Orchestra leader. Member of **The Hilltoppers**.

| 12/11/54+ | 2¹ | 27 | ● | **Melody Of Love** | S:2 / A:2 / J:3 *Joy Ride* [I] | $15 | Dot 45-15247 |

music written in 1903; lyrics added in 1954 by Tom Glazer; above version inspired by the 1940 **Wayne King** arrangement on Victor 26695

VINCENT, Anne
'48

| 7/31/48 | 6 | 16 | | **You Call Everybody Darlin'**......................................A:6 / J:11 / S:13 *Blue Bird Polka* | $10 | Mercury 5155 |

Anne Vincent and Quartet (vocals)

W

WAIN, Bea
MEM '41

Born on 4/30/17 in New York City. Featured vocalist for **Larry Clinton**'s orchestra. Hosted her own radio show.

| 8/24/40 | 15 | 2 | | 1 **I'm Nobody's Baby**..S(s):15 *Buds Won't Bud* | $10 | Victor 26603 |

Walter Gross (orch.); from the movie *Andy Hardy Meets Debutante* starring **Judy Garland** and Mickey Rooney; #3 hit for Marion Harris in 1921

| 4/12/41 | 20 | 1 | | 2 **Do I Worry?** ....S(s):20 *You Can Depend On Me* | $10 | Victor 27353 |
| 5/17/41 | 15 | 2 | | 3 **My Sister And I**..S(wc):15 *Afraid To Say Hello (Since You Said Goodbye)* | $10 | Victor 27363 |

WAKELY, Jimmy ★58★
HOT '49

Born on 2/16/14 in Mineola, Arkansas; raised in Oklahoma. Died on 9/23/82 (age 68). Singer/songwriter/guitarist/pianist. Regular on **Gene Autry**'s *Melody Ranch* radio show in the early 1940s. Known as "The Melody Kid." Starred in numerous western movies. Hosted own radio show from 1952-57. Co-hosted TV's *Five Star Jubilee* in 1961.

1)Slipping Around   2)A Bushel And A Peck   3)I'll Never Slip Around Again

| 3/20/43 | 19 | 2 | | 1 **There's A Star Spangled Banner Waving Somewhere**..................................S(wc):19 *Standing Outside Of Heaven* | $15 | Decca 6059 |

new version by Red River Dave charted in 1960 (#64)

| 10/30/48 | 10 | 8 | | 2 **One Has My Name (The Other Has My Heart)**...........J:10 *You're The Sweetest Rose In Texas* | $15 | Capitol 15162 |

#13 hit for Barry Young in 1966

| 12/18/48 | 21 | 8 | | 3 **I Love You So Much It Hurts** ....J:21 / S:30 *I Don't Want Your Sympathy* | $15 | Capitol 15243 |

#71 hit for Charlie Gracie in 1957

9/10/49	❶³	23	●	4 **Slipping Around** /	J:❶³ / S:2 / A:2		
10/22/49	30	1		5 **Wedding Bells** J:30	$15	Capitol 57-40224
11/5/49	8	10		6 **I'll Never Slip Around Again** ....J:8 / S:11 *Six Times a Week And Twice On Sunday*	$15	Capitol 57-40246

#4 & 6 are nearly identical songs

2/11/50	12	7		7 **Broken Down Merry-Go-Round** / ....J:12 / S:26		
2/25/50	17	7		8 **The Gods Were Angry With Me** J:17	$20	Capitol F800
4/15/50	13	6		9 **Let's Go To Church (Next Sunday Morning)**........................J:13 / A:18 / S:19 *Why Do You Say Those Things (That Hurt Me So)*	$20	Capitol F960

MARGARET WHITING and JIMMY WAKELY (above 6)

| 4/15/50 | 26 | 1 | | 10 **Peter Cottontail** ....A:26 *Mr. Easter Bunny* | $20 | Capitol 929 |
| 10/28/50 | 6 | 15 | | 11 **A Bushel And A Peck** ....J:6 / S:13 / A:18 *Beyond The Reef* | $20 | Capitol F1234 |

MARGARET WHITING and JIMMY WAKELY
from the Broadway musical *Guys And Dolls* starring Robert Alda and Vivian Blaine

| 1/6/51 | 12 | 13 | | 12 **My Heart Cries For You**....................J:12 / S:12 / A:15 *Music By The Angels (Lyrics By The Lord)* | $20 | Capitol F1328 |

Les Baxter Chorus (backing vocals); adapted from the 18th-century French melody "Chanson de Marie Antoinette"; #38 hit for Ray Charles in 1964

| 3/17/51 | 12 | 14 | | 13 **Beautiful Brown Eyes**....................J:12 / S:23 / A:27 *At The Close Of A Long Long Day* | $20 | Capitol F1393 |

JIMMY WAKELY and the LES BAXTER CHORUS with Orchestra

| 5/12/51 | 20 | 2 | | 14 **When You And I Were Young Maggie Blues**..................A:20 / J:25 *Till We Meet Again* | $20 | Capitol F1500 |

MARGARET WHITING and JIMMY WAKELY
#4 hit for Frank Stanley & Corrine Morgan in 1905; all of above were Top 10 hits on the Country charts (except #1)

WALD, Jerry, and his Orchestra
'45

Born on Jervis Wald on 1/15/18 in Newark, New Jersey. Died on 9/19/73 (age 55). Clarinetist/bandleader.

| 9/30/44 | 19 | 1 | | 1 **Since You Went Away** ....J(terr.):19 *Two Heavens* | $10 | Decca 4446 |

Ginnie Powell (vocal)

| 4/14/45 | 8 | 3 | | 2 **Laura** / ....A:8 | | |

Dick Merrick (vocal); title song from the movie starring Gene Tierney and Dana Andrews

| 5/19/45 | 18 | 1 | | 3 **Candy** ....A:18 | $10 | Majestic 7129 |

Kay Allen (vocal)

WALLER, "Fats"
MEM '36

Born Thomas Waller on 5/21/04 in New York City. Died of pneumonia on 12/15/43 (age 39). Highly influential jazz pianist. Charted 60 hits from 1929-39. Won Grammy's Lifetime Achievement Award in 1993. Waller's top 3 pre-1940 #1 hits: "It's A Sin To Tell A Lie," "Truckin'" and "Two Sleepy People."

| 5/25/40 | 6 | 5 | | **Little Curly Hair In A High Chair**......................J:6 *Old Grand Dad* [N] | $30 | Bluebird 10698 |

from the movie *Forty Little Mothers* starring **Eddie Cantor**

WALTERS, Teddy
'46

Sang briefly with **Jimmy Dorsey**'s orchestra.

| 4/6/46 | 4 | 12 | | **Laughing On The Outside Crying On The Inside** ....A:4 / J:14 *You I Love* | $15 | ARA 135 |

Lou Bring (orch.)

DEBUT	PEAK	WKS	Gold	A-side (Chart Hit) ....B-side	$	Label & Number

WARING, Fred — MEM '30

Born on 6/9/1900 in Tyrone, Pennsylvania. Died on 7/29/84 (age 84). Extremely popular dance band leader best known for his Pennsylvanians glee club featured on radio shows from 1933 through the 1940s. While at his peak of radio popularity, Fred ceased recording for nearly a decade after 1932; charted 50 hits from 1923-33. Hosted his own TV show from 1949-54. Waring's top 3 pre-1940 #1 hits: "Little White Lies," "Memory Lane" and "Sleep."

DEBUT	PEAK	WKS	Gold	A-side / B-side	$	Label & Number
4/15/44	16	1		1 Holiday For Strings ....S(mw):16 *Jalousie* [I]	$10	Decca 23311
				FRED WARING And His Concert Vochestra		
11/15/47	7	7	●	2 Whiffenpoof Song ....S:7 *Kentucky Babe*	$15	Decca 23990
				BING CROSBY with FRED WARING and the GLEE CLUB		
				theme song of the Yale University Glee Club since 1909; #96 Pop hit for Bob Crewe in 1960		
11/19/49	21	2		3 'Way Back Home.........................S:21 / A:30 *The Iowa Indian Song (I-O-Wuh)*	$15	Decca 24800
				BING CROSBY with FRED WARING AND HIS PENNSYLVANIANS		
				#6 hit for Victor Young in 1935		

WARREN, Fran — MEM '50

Born on 3/4/26 in the Bronx, New York. Featured singer for Claude Thornhill's orchestra.

DEBUT	PEAK	WKS	Gold	A-side / B-side	$	Label & Number
7/16/49	17	5		1 A Wonderful Guy ....A:17 *I'm Gonna Wash That Man Right Out-A My Hair*	$20	RCA Victor 47-2897
				78 rpm: 20-3403; from the Broadway musical *South Pacific* starring Mary Martin and Ezio Pinza		
10/22/49	12	9		2 Envy ....A:12 *You're In Love With Someone*	$20	RCA Victor 47-3044
				78 rpm: 20-3551		
1/21/50	3	13		3 I Said My Pajamas (And Put on My Pray'rs) A:3 / S:5 / J:8 *Have I Told You Lately That I Love You*	$20	RCA Victor 47-3119
				TONY MARTIN and FRAN WARREN		
				78 rpm: 20-3613		
3/18/50	22	5		4 Dearie ....A:22 / S:29 *Just A Girl That Men Forget* [N]	$20	RCA Victor 47-3220
				LISA KIRK and FRAN WARREN		
				78 rpm: 20-3696; from the stage production *The Copacabana Show Of 1950*		
9/2/50	22	1		5 I Love The Guy ....A:22 *Let's Make Love*	$20	RCA Victor 47-3848
				Henri René (orch., all of above)		

WASHINGTON, Dinah — MEM/HOT '60

Born as Ruth Lee Jones on 8/29/24 in Tuscaloosa, Alabama. Died of an alcohol/pill overdose on 12/14/63 (age 39). R&B singer. Inducted into the Rock and Roll Hall of Fame in 1993 as an early influence.

DEBUT	PEAK	WKS	Gold	A-side / B-side	$	Label & Number
6/17/50	22	4		I Wanna Be Loved ....J:22 *Love With Misery*	$20	Mercury 8181
				Teddy Stewart (orch.); new version by Washington charted in 1962 on Mercury 72015 (#76)		

WATSON, Paula — '49

R&B singer/pianist.

DEBUT	PEAK	WKS	Gold	A-side / B-side	$	Label & Number
11/27/48+	6	16		A Little Bird Told Me ....A:6 / J:7 / S:14 *Stick By Me Baby*	$50	Supreme 1507
				with male R&B vocal group; #2 R&B hit		

WAYNE, Bobby — MEM '52

DEBUT	PEAK	WKS	Gold	A-side / B-side	$	Label & Number
3/24/51	26	1		1 Let Me In ....A:26 *Wild Card*	$15	London 45973
				Richard Hayman (orch.)		
8/18/51	23	2		2 Belle, Belle, My Liberty Belle......................A:23 *Sweetheart Of Yesterday*	$15	Mercury 5690-X45
				George Bassman (orch.)		
12/29/51+	17	6		3 Mother At Your Feet Is Kneeling ....S:17 *Immaculate Mother*	$15	London 45968
				recorded with The Members of The Choir at the Shrine Church of St. Bernadette on 11/29/50		
2/23/52	6	13		4 Wheel Of Fortune / A:6 / S:13 / J:13		
				#83 hit for LaVern Baker in 1960		
3/15/52	29	1		5 Heart Of A Clown J:29	$15	Mercury 5779-X45
				Joe Reisman (orch., above 2)		
7/18/53	18	1		6 Love Me, Love Me ....A:18 *More Than I*	$15	Mercury 70148-X45
				Jimmy Carroll (orch.)		

WAYNE, Jerry — '49

Born in 1921 in Buffalo, New York. Vocalist on Ken Griffin's "You Can't Be True, Dear."

DEBUT	PEAK	WKS	Gold	A-side / B-side	$	Label & Number
9/4/48	14	7		1 You Call Everybody Darling......................A:14 / J:18 / S:25 *Cuckoo Waltz*	$10	Columbia 38286
1/29/49	15	5		2 A Little Bird Told Me ....A:15 / S:26 *If That Isn't Love, What Is?*	$10	Columbia 38386
				JANETTE DAVIS and JERRY WAYNE		
8/27/49	6	7		3 Room Full Of Roses ....A:6 / J:24 *I'll Keep The Lovelight Burning (In My Heart)*	$10	Columbia 38525
				Hugo Winterhalter (orch.); #50 hit for Mickey Gilley in 1974		

WEAVERS, The ★64★ — MEM '50

Legendary folk group: Pete Seeger (born on 5/3/19), Lee Hays (born on 3/14/14; died on 8/26/81, age 67), Fred Hellerman (born on 5/13/27) and female lead Ronnie Gilbert (born on 9/7/26). Political blacklisting cut short their recording career, but the group's 1955 Carnegie Hall concert helped trigger a new folk boom. The 1981 documentary movie *Wasn't That A Time?* chronicled their career.

DEBUT	PEAK	WKS	Gold	A-side / B-side	$	Label & Number
7/8/50	●13	25	●	1 Goodnight Irene / S:●13 / J:●12 / A:●8		
				#75 hit for Billy Williams in 1959		
7/1/50	2¹	17		2 Tzena Tzena Tzena S:2 / A:4 / J:5	$20	Decca 9-27077
				GORDON JENKINS and his Orchestra and THE WEAVERS (above 2)		
				adaptation of a popular Israeli song; The Weavers also issued a Hebrew version of the song on Decca 27053		
12/23/50+	11	13		3 The Roving Kind.........................J:11 / S:14 / A:16 *(The Wreck Of The)* John B	$20	Decca 9-27332
				Leroy Holmes (orch.); adapted from the English folk song "The Pirate Ship"; flip side adapted by the Beach Boys as "Sloop John B" in 1966		
1/13/51	4	14		4 So Long (It's Been Good to Know Yuh) J:4 / S:6 / A:7 *Lonesome Traveler*	$20	Decca 9-27376
				GORDON JENKINS and his Orchestra and THE WEAVERS		
3/31/51	2⁸	23	●	5 On Top Of Old Smoky J:2 / S:2 / A:2 *Across The Wide Missouri*	$20	Decca 9-27515
				THE WEAVERS and TERRY GILKYSON		
				Vic Schoen (orch.); Pete Seeger (call-outs); adaptation of a traditional Southern Highlands folk song; Tom Glazer's parody "On Top Of Spaghetti" peaked at #14 in 1963		

WEAVERS, The — Cont'd

DEBUT	PEAK	WKS	Gold	A-side	$	Label & Number
8/18/51	19	6		**6 Kisses Sweeter Than Wine /** ....S:19 / J:21 / A:25 adapted from the Irish folk song "Drimmer's Cow"; #3 hit for Jimmie Rodgers in 1957		
8/25/51	27	2		**7 When The Saints Go Marching In** ....S:27 #10 hit for **Louis Armstrong** in 1939; #18 hit for **Bill Haley & His Comets** in 1956 ("The Saints Rock 'N Roll"); Lew Diamond (orch., above 2)	$20	Decca 9-27670
2/16/52	14	11		**8 Wimoweh**..S:14 / A:19 *Old Paint (Ride Around Little Dogies)* **[F]** adapted from the South African Zulu song "Mbube"; revised version by The Tokens hit #1 in 1961 as "The Lion Sleeps Tonight"	$20	Decca 9-27928
4/26/52	19	1		**9 Around The Corner (Beneath The Berry Tree)**.....................A:19 *The Gandy Dancers' Ball* THE WEAVERS And GORDON JENKINS And His Chorus And Orchestra (above 2)	$20	Decca 9-28054

WEBER, Joan   **'55**
Born on 12/12/35 in Paulsboro, New Jersey. Died on 5/13/81 (age 45). Pop singer.

DEBUT	PEAK	WKS	Gold	A-side	$	Label & Number
12/4/54+	❶[4]	16	●	**Let Me Go Lover** A:❶[4] / J:❶[4] / S:❶[2] *Marionette* Jimmy Carroll (orch.); written in 1953 as "Let Me Go Devil" and first recorded by **Georgie Shaw**; Weber's version was an overnight sensation after being featured 6 times on the 11/15/54 *Studio One* CBS-TV production	$20	Columbia 4-40366

WEEMS, Ted, And His Orchestra ★81★   MEM **'47**
Born Wilfred Theodore Weymes on 9/26/01 in Pitcairn, Pennsylvania. Died on 5/6/63 (age 61). Leader of popular
Chicago-based dance band. **Perry Como** was featured vocalist from 1936-42. Weems' pre-1940 #1 hits: "Somebody Stole
My Gal" and "The Man From The South (With a Big Cigar in His Mouth)."

DEBUT	PEAK	WKS	Gold	A-side	$	Label & Number
2/22/41	20	1		**1 There'll Be Some Changes Made** ....S(e):20 *Moonlight* Mary Lee (vocal); featured in the 1940 movie *Play Girl* starring Kay Francis; #5 hit for Ethel Waters in 1922	$10	Decca 3044
3/15/41	20	1		**2 It All Comes Back To Me Now** ....S(wc):20 *May I Never Love Again* **Perry Como** (vocal)	$10	Decca 3627
3/1/47	❶[13]	20	●	**3 Heartaches** J:❶[13] / S:❶[12] / A:❶[11] *Oh! Monah (Decca) / Piccolo Pete (RCA Victor)* **[I]** Elmo Tanner (whistling); *Billboard* listed both the Decca and RCA versions at one chart position; the Decca version was originally recorded in 1938 and issued on Decca 2020; the RCA version was originally recorded on 8/4/33 and released on Bluebird 5131; #7 hit for The Marcels in 1961	$10	Decca 25017 and RCA Victor 20-2175
6/28/47	5	6		**4 Peg O' My Heart /** A:5 / J:12 Bob Edwards (vocal); #1 hit for Charles Harrison in 1913; #64 hit for Robert (**Bobby**) Maxwell in 1964		
6/14/47	14	1		**5 Violets**..A:14 **[I]** Elmo Tanner (whistling)	$10	Mercury 5052
8/2/47	2[5]	17		**6 I Wonder Who's Kissing Her Now** A:2 / J:2 / S:3 *That Old Gang Of Mine* TED WEEMS And His Orchestra; Perry Como, vocal *Billboard* listed both the Decca and RCA versions at one chart position (the Decca version charted alone for the first 11 weeks; it was recorded on 10/5/39 and originally issued on Decca 2919); the RCA release (Como's solo version) features Lloyd Shaffer's orchestra (B-side: "When Tonight Is Just A Memory"); title song from the 1947 movie starring June Haven; #1 hit for Henry Burr in 1909; #93 hit for Bobby Darin in 1964	$10	Decca 25078 and RCA Victor 20-2315
10/25/47	3	11	●	**7 Mickey** J:3 / A:6 / S:10 *The Martins And The Coys* Bob Edwards (vocal)	$10	Mercury 5062
9/11/48	23	4		**8 Hindustan**......................................A:23 *I Wonder Where That Man Of Mine Has Went* **[I]** #3 hit for Joseph C. Smith's Orchestra in 1919; Elmo Tanner (whistling, above 2)	$10	Mercury 5139

WEIL, Brucie   **'53**
Born in 1948.

DEBUT	PEAK	WKS	Gold	A-side	$	Label & Number
9/12/53	18	1		**God Bless Us All** ....A:18 *Little Boy Blues* Don Costa (orch.)	$25	Barbour 451

WEIR, Frank   **'54**
Saxophonist/bandleader.

DEBUT	PEAK	WKS	Gold	A-side	$	Label & Number
5/1/54	4	19		**The Happy Wanderer** S:4 / A:5 / J:5 *From Your Lips* FRANK WEIR with his Saxophone, Chorus and Orchestra German song introduced by the Oberkirchen Children's Choir; best known for its singalong "Val-da-ree, Val-da-ra" chorus	$15	London 45-1448

WELK, Lawrence, And His Orchestra ★123★   MEM/HOT **'61**
Born on 3/11/03 in Strasburg, North Dakota. Died of pneumonia on 5/17/92 (age 89). Accordion player/polka bandleader.
Band's style labeled as "champagne music." Hosted own TV musical variety show from 1955-82.

DEBUT	PEAK	WKS	Gold	A-side	$	Label & Number
2/12/44	14	1		**1 I Wish That I Could Hide Inside This Letter /** J:14		
2/5/44	17	1		**2 Cleanin' My Rifle (And Dreamin' Of You)** ....J:17 Bobby Beers (vocal)	$10	Decca 4428
3/25/44	2[1]	20		**3 Don't Sweetheart Me /** J:2 / S:8 Wayne Marsh (vocal)		
4/1/44	16	1		**4 Mairzy Doats**..J:16 Bobby Beers and Ensemble (vocals); #75 hit for The Innocence in 1967	$10	Decca 4434
4/22/44	13	5		**5 Is My Baby Blue Tonight** ....J:13 *One Little Lie Too Many* Jayne Walton (vocal: #1 & 5)	$10	Decca 4438
9/29/45	13	1		**6 Shame On You**.................................J:13 *At Mail Call Today* (C&W #3) LAWRENCE WELK AND HIS ORCHESTRA with RED FOLEY	$20	Decca 18698
1/24/53	5	10		**7 Oh, Happy Day** A:5 / J:10 / S:11 *Your Mother And Mine* LAWRENCE WELK And His Champagne Music Larry Hooper (vocal)	$15	Coral 9-60893

WESSON BROTHERS   **'49**
Comedy team from Idaho: brothers Dick and Gene Wesson. Dick was born on 2/20/19; died on 1/27/79 (age 59).
Gene was born in 1921; died on 8/22/75 (age 54).

DEBUT	PEAK	WKS	Gold	A-side	$	Label & Number
4/16/49	11	3		**All Right, Louie, Drop The Gun** ....A:11 *Oodles Of Boodle (And Batches Of Scratch)* **[N]**	$30	National 9070

WESTON, Paul ★47★   MEM '49

Born Paul Wetstein on 3/12/12 in Springfield, Massachusetts. Died on 9/20/96 (age 84). Arranger for **Tommy Dorsey** and **Bob Crosby** before becoming Capitol Record's foremost conductor/arranger (later with Columbia), backing many singers (his wife **Jo Stafford**, **Doris Day**, **Frankie Laine**, and **The Pied Pipers**) and recording "mood music" albums. Composer of the hits "I Should Care" and "Shrimp Boats." Later served as conductor for many TV shows.

    1)Nevertheless (I'm In Love With You)   2)Ole Buttermilk Sky   3)It Might As Well Be Spring

DEBUT	PEAK	WKS		A-side	B-side	$	Label & Number
10/27/45	6	11		1 **It Might As Well Be Spring**..............................S:6 / A:9 / J:12 *How Deep Is The Ocean*		$10	Capitol 214
				PAUL WESTON and his Orchestra With MARGARET WHITING
				from the movie *State Fair* starring **Dick Haymes** and Dana Andrews
11/2/46	6	13		2 **Ole Buttermilk Sky**.....................................A:6 / J:6 / S:9 *Just Squeeze Me (But Don't Tease Me)*		$10	Capitol 285
				from the movie *Canyon Passage* starring Dana Andrews; #25 hit for Bill Black's Combo in 1961
4/19/47	8	8		3 **Linda** ....A:8 / J:9 *Roses In The Rain*		$10	Capitol 362
				PAUL WESTON AND HIS ORCHESTRA With MATT DENNIS (above 2)
				#28 hit for Jan & Dean in 1963
9/4/48	15	14		4 **Clair de Lune Parts I & II** ....A:15 [I]		$10	Capitol 15153
				from the *Suite Bergamasque* by Claude Debussy; #68 hit for **Steve Lawrence** in 1961
1/15/49	20	5		5 **Deep Purple** ....A:20 *I Only Have Eyes For You* [I]		$10	Capitol 15294
				#1 hit for **Larry Clinton** in 1939; #1 hit for Nino Tempo & **April Stevens** in 1963
3/5/49	12	17		6 **The Hot Canary** ....A:12 *La Raspa* [I]		$10	Capitol 15373
				Paul Nero (violin solo)
7/16/49	9	11		7 **Some Enchanted Evening** / ....A:9 [I]
				#13 hit for Jay & The Americans in 1965
6/18/49	10	3		8 **Bali Ha'i** ....A:10 [I]		$10	Capitol 57-629
				above 2 from the Broadway musical *South Pacific* starring **Mary Martin** and **Ezio Pinza**
9/3/49	23	2		9 **Reckon I'm In Love** ....A:23 *Ooh, If You Knew*		$10	Capitol 57-697
				Pauline Byrns (vocal); from the movie *Montana* starring Errol Flynn
10/8/49	16	3		10 **Lingering Down The Lane** / A:16
11/12/49	25	2		11 **I Know, I Know, I Know** A:25		$10	Capitol 57-725
				from the movie *That Midnight Kiss* starring **Mario Lanza**
3/4/50	30	1		12 **Fairy Tales** ....A:30 *Am I Wasting My Time*		$15	Capitol F826
				The Jud Conlon Singers (vocals: #10-12)
6/24/50	12	16		13 **La Vie En Rose** ....A:12 *Les Feuilles Mortes (The Falling Leaves)* [I]		$15	Capitol F890
10/7/50	2[1]	18		14 **Nevertheless (I'm In Love With You)** A:2 / S:9 / J:14 *Beloved, Be Faithful*		$15	Columbia 4-38982
				featured in the movie *Three Little Words* starring Fred Astaire; #5 hit for Jack Denny in 1931
2/17/51	19	4		15 **Across The Wide Missouri** A:19
				adaptation of a traditional folk song (also known as "Shenandoah")
2/24/51	21	5		16 **So Long (It's Been Good To Know Yuh)** A:21		$15	Columbia 4-39160
7/7/51	16	7		17 **The Morningside Of The Mountain**...........................A:16 / J:24 *What Will I Tell My Heart*		$15	Columbia 4-39424
				#8 hit for Donny & Marie Osmond in 1975
12/1/51	30	1		18 **And So To Sleep Again** ....A:30 *The Glory Of Love*		$15	Columbia 4-39569
12/29/51+	8	6		19 **Charmaine** ....A:8 / J:29 *At Dawning (I Love You)*		$15	Columbia 4-39616
				written to promote the 1926 movie *What Price Glory?* starring Victor McLaglen; #1 hit for **Guy Lombardo** in 1927; #69 hit for The Four Freshmen in 1956; The Norman Luboff Choir (vocals: #14-19)

WHITFIELD, David   MEM/HOT '54

Born on 2/2/26 in Hull, Yorkshire, England. Classical-styled tenor.

DEBUT	PEAK	WKS		A-side	B-side	$	Label & Number
8/14/54	10	18	●	1 **Cara Mia**...S:10 / A:17 *How, When Or Where*		$20	London 45-1486
				DAVID WHITFIELD with MANTOVANI His Orchestra and Chorus
				#4 hit for Jay & The Americans in 1965
1/1/55-	19	2		2 **Santo Natale (Merry Christmas)**....................A:19 / S:27 *Adeste Fideles (O Come All Ye Faithful)* [X]		$20	London 1508
				Stanley Black (orch.)

WHITING, Margaret ★25★   MEM/HOT '49

Born on 7/22/24 in Detroit; raised in Hollywood. Vocalist with **Freddie Slack** and **Billy Butterfield**. Daughter of noted composer Richard Whiting ("Till We Meet Again"). Sister of singer/actress Barbara Whiting; starred in the 1950s TV series *Those Whiting Girls*.

    1)A Tree In The Meadow   2)Slipping Around   3)Far Away Places   4)Now Is The Hour (Maori Farewell Song)
    5)Baby, It's Cold Outside

Orchestras: Busch, Lou — 31,32   Gray, Jerry — 5-8   May, Billy — 28
              DeVol, Frank — 9-13,16,17,21,27   Kress, Carl — 2,3   Weston, Paul — 1,4,18

Vocalists: Crew Chiefs, The — 12,15   Hope, Bob — 28   Starlighters, The — 28   Wakely, Jimmy —
            DeVol, Frank — 25   Mercer, Johnny — 18   19,20,22-24,26,29,30

DEBUT	PEAK	WKS		A-side	B-side	$	Label & Number
10/27/45	6	11		1 **It Might As Well Be Spring**..............................S:6 / A:9 / J:12 *How Deep Is The Ocean*		$10	Capitol 214
				PAUL WESTON and his Orchestra With MARGARET WHITING
				from the movie *State Fair* starring **Dick Haymes** and Dana Andrews
4/13/46	11	4		2 **All Through The Day** / A:11
5/11/46	12	3		3 **In Love In Vain** A:12		$10	Capitol 240
				above 2 from the movie *Centennial Summer* starring Cornel Wilde
6/15/46	17	1		4 **Come Rain Or Come Shine**.....................................A:17 *Can't Help Lovin' Dat Man*		$10	Capitol 247
				from the Broadway musical *St. Louis Woman* starring **Pearl Bailey**; #83 hit for Ray Charles in 1960
8/31/46	13	1		5 **Along With Me** ....A:13 *When You Make Love To Me (Don't Make Believe)*		$10	Capitol 269
				from the Broadway musical *Call Me Mister* starring **Betty Garrett**
10/26/46	12	4		6 **Passé** ....A:12 *For You, For Me, For Evermore*		$10	Capitol 294

DEBUT	PEAK	WKS	Gold	A-side	$	Label & Number
				WHITING, Margaret — Cont'd		
12/7/46+	**4**	17		7 Guilty / A:4 / S:6 / J:10		
				#4 hit for Ruth Etting in 1931		
12/14/46+	**7**	7		8 Oh, But I Do A:7	$10	Capitol 324
				from the movie *The Time, The Place And The Girl* starring Dennis Morgan		
6/7/47	**11**	1		9 Old Devil Moon ....A:11 *Ask Anyone Who Knows*	$10	Capitol 410
				from the Broadway musical *Finian's Rainbow* starring David Wayne		
11/1/47	**5**	10		10 You Do A:5 / S:9 / J:13 *My Future Just Passed*	$10	Capitol 438
				from the movie *Mother Wore Tights* starring **Betty Grable**		
11/8/47	**14**	1		11 So Far ....A:14 *Lazy Countryside*	$10	Capitol 461
				from the Broadway musical *Allegro* starring John Battles		
1/3/48	**8**	1		12 Pass That Peace Pipe ....A:8 *Let's Be Sweethearts Again*	$10	Capitol 15010
				from the movie *Good News* starring June Allyson and Peter Lawford		
2/14/48	**2**¹	16		13 Now Is The Hour (Maori Farewell Song) A:2 / S:8 / J:10 *But Beautiful*	$10	Capitol 15024
				based on the traditional New Zealand song "Hearere Ra"; #59 hit for Gale Storm in 1956		
7/17/48	**❶**⁵	23	●	14 A Tree In The Meadow A:❶⁵ / S:❶² / J:2 *I'm Sorry But I'm Glad*	$10	Capitol 15122
				British song		
12/4/48+	**2**⁶	23		15 Far Away Places A:2 / S:3 / J:6 *My Own True Love*	$10	Capitol 15278
4/16/49	**5**	17		16 Forever And Ever A:5 / J:19 / S:24 *Dreamer With A Penny*	$10	Capitol 15386
				adaptation of a popular Swiss song		
5/7/49	**12**	12		17 A Wonderful Guy ....A:12 / S:12 / J:19 *Younger Than Springtime*	$10	Capitol 57-542
				from the Broadway musical *South Pacific* starring **Mary Martin** and **Ezio Pinza**		
5/14/49	**3**	19		18 Baby, It's Cold Outside A:3 / S:4 / J:8 *I Never Heard You Say*	$10	Capitol 57-567
				MARGARET WHITING AND JOHNNY MERCER		
				45 rpm: 54-582; from the movie *Neptune's Daughter* starring Esther Williams		
9/10/49	**❶**³	23	●	19 Slipping Around / J:❶³ / S:2 / A:2		
10/22/49	**30**	1		20 Wedding Bells J:30	$15	Capitol 57-40224
				MARGARET WHITING and JIMMY WAKELY (above 2)		
9/24/49	**19**	2		21 Dime A Dozen ....A:19 / J:27 *Whirlwind*	$15	Capitol 57-709
11/5/49	**8**	10		22 I'll Never Slip Around Again ....J:8 / S:11 *Six Times a Week And Twice On Sunday*	$15	Capitol 57-40246
				#19 & 22 are nearly identical songs		
2/11/50	**12**	7		23 Broken Down Merry-Go-Round / ....J:12 / S:26		
2/25/50	**17**	7		24 The Gods Were Angry With Me J:17	$20	Capitol F800
				MARGARET WHITING and JIMMY WAKELY (above 3)		
3/4/50	**21**	3		25 I Said My Pajamas (And Put On My Pray'rs) ....A:21 / S:24 *Be Mine* (Whiting)	$20	Capitol F841
				MARGARET WHITING and FRANK DeVOL (vocal duet)		
4/15/50	**13**	6		26 Let's Go To Church (Next Sunday Morning)............J:13 / A:18 / S:19 *Why Do You Say Those Things (That Hurt Me So)*	$20	Capitol F960
				MARGARET WHITING and JIMMY WAKELY		
5/6/50	**15**	8		27 My Foolish Heart ....A:15 *Stay With The Happy People*	$20	Capitol F934
				title song from the movie starring Susan Hayward		
6/17/50	**16**	4		28 Blind Date ....A:16 / S:21 *Home Cookin'* **[N]**	$20	Capitol F1042
				MARGARET WHITING & BOB HOPE		
10/28/50	**6**	15		29 A Bushel And A Peck ....J:6 / S:13 / A:18 *Beyond The Reef*	$20	Capitol F1234
				from the Broadway musical *Guys And Dolls* starring Robert Alda and Vivian Blaine		
5/12/51	**20**	2		30 When You And I Were Young Maggie Blues........A:20 / J:25 *Till We Meet Again*	$20	Capitol F1500
				MARGARET WHITING and JIMMY WAKELY (above 2)		
				#4 hit for Frank Stanley & Corrine Morgan in 1905		
7/21/51	**14**	5		31 Good Morning, Mr. Echo..............................A:14 *River Road Two-Step*	$15	Capitol F1702
3/22/52	**29**	1		32 I'll Walk Alone ....A:29 *I Could Write A Book*	$15	Capitol F2000
				featured in the movie *With A Song In My Heart* starring Susan Hayward		
				WHITMAN, Slim MEM/HOT **'52**		
				Born Otis Dewey Whitman on 1/20/24 in Tampa, Florida. Country singer/songwriter/guitarist/yodeler.		
7/26/52	**9**	14	●	Indian Love Call ....J:9 / S:10 *China Doll*	$25	Imperial 45-8156
				#2 Country hit; #3 hit for Paul Whiteman in 1925; #59 hit for Ernie Freeman in 1958		
				WILCOX, Eddie, Orch. **'52**		
				Born on 12/27/07 in Method, North Carolina. Died on 9/29/68 (age 60). Pianist/arranger for **Jimmie Lunceford** (1929-47).		
2/9/52	**13**	6		Wheel Of Fortune...........................J:13 / S:14 / A:22 *You Showed Me The Way*	$25	Derby 45-787
				EDDIE WILCOX ORCH. with SUNNY GALE		
				WILLIAMS, Billy, Quartet MEM/HOT **'57**		
				Born on 12/28/10 in Waco, Texas. Died on 10/17/72 (age 61). Lead singer of **The Charioteers**.		
8/18/51	**20**	6		1 (Why Did I Tell You I Was Going To) Shanghai ....S:20 / J:26 *The Wondrous Word (Of The Lord)*	$30	MGM K10998
				LeROY HOLMES (orch.)		
10/13/51+	**28**	2		2 (It's No) Sin ....J:28 *It's Over*	$30	MGM K11066
				WILLIAMS, Billy, and The Pecos River Rogues **'47**		
				Featured vocalist for **Sammy Kaye**'s orchestra.		
4/26/47	**13**	4		My Adobe Hacienda ....J:13 *I Ain't A-Gonna Leave My Love No More*	$15	RCA Victor 20-2150
				WILLIAMS, Cootie, and his Orchestra **'44**		
				Born Charles Williams on 7/24/08 in Mobile, Alabama. Died on 9/15/85 (age 77). Legendary black jazz trumpeter.		
				With **Duke Ellington** from 1929-40 and with **Benny Goodman** from 1940-41. Returned to Ellington's band in 1962.		
5/20/44	**19**	1		1 Tess's Torch Song (I Had A Man) ....J:19 *Now I Know*	$25	Hit 7075
				Pearl Bailey (vocal); from the movie *Up In Arms* starring **Dinah Shore** and **Danny Kaye**		
8/26/44	**18**	1		2 Red Blues..J(terr.):18 *Things Ain't What They Used To Be*	$25	Hit 7084
				Eddie "Cleanhead" Vinson (vocal); issued on Majestic 7084 as "Cherry Red-Blues"; #2 R&B hit		

WILLIAMS, Hank, With His Drifting Cowboys   MEM '52

Born Hiram King Williams on 9/17/23 in Mount Olive, Alabama. Died of alcohol/drug abuse on 1/1/53 (age 29). Highly influential country singer/songwriter/guitarist. Won Grammy's Lifetime Achievement Award in 1987. Inducted into the Rock and Roll Hall of Fame in 1987 as a forefather of rock 'n' roll. Celebrated in the movie biography *Your Cheatin' Heart*. Father of country star Hank Williams, Jr.

DEBUT	PEAK	WKS				
5/14/49	24	1	●	1 Lovesick Blues ....A:24 *Never Again (Will I Knock On Your Door)* (C&W #6)	$50	MGM 10352
				#1 Country hit (16 weeks); #44 hit for Frank Ifield in 1963		
9/6/52	20	6	●	2 Jambalaya (On The Bayou) ....J:20 / S:23 *Window Shopping*	$40	MGM K11283
				#1 Country hit (14 weeks); #16 hit for The Blue Ridge Rangers in 1973		

WILLIAMS, Tex   MEM '47

Born Sollie Paul Williams on 8/23/17 in Ramsey, Illinois. Died of cancer on 10/11/85 (age 68). Country singer/songwriter/guitarist. Acted in many western movies. Hosted own *Ranch Party* TV series in 1958.

DEBUT	PEAK	WKS				
7/5/47	❶⁶	17	●	1 Smoke! Smoke! Smoke! (That Cigarette) S:❶⁶ / J:❶⁴ / A:❶¹ *Roundup Polka* [N]	$15	Capitol Am. 40001
				TEX WILLIAMS And His Western Caravan		
				#1 Country hit (16 weeks); #94 hit for Commander Cody & His Lost Planet Airmen in 1973		
12/4/48	27	2		2 Life Gits Tee-Jus, Don't It?..S:27 *Big Hat Polka* [N]	$15	Capitol 15271
				#5 Country hit		

WILLS, Bob, and his Texas Playboys   MEM '41

Born James Robert Wills on 3/6/05 near Kosse, Texas. Died of a stroke on 5/13/75 (age 70). Country singer/songwriter/fiddle player. Known as "The King of Western Swing." Brother of **Johnnie Lee Wills**. Acted in many western movies. Elected to the Country Music Hall of Fame in 1968.

DEBUT	PEAK	WKS				
1/18/41	13	2	●	1 San Antonio Rose S(wc):13 / S(s):18 *The Convict And The Rose* [I]	$25	Okeh 04755
				recorded in 1938 and first released on Vocalion 04755		
5/10/41	16	2		2 New San Antonio Rose ....S(wc):16 *Bob Will's Special*	$25	Okeh 05694
				Tommy Duncan (vocal); vocal version of #1 above; #8 hit for Floyd Cramer in 1961		
10/14/44	11	2		3 We Might As Well Forget It / J:11		
				Leon Huff (vocal)		
10/14/44	14	3		4 You're From Texas...J:14	$25	Okeh 6722
				Leon McAuliffe (vocal); from the movie *A Tornado In The Saddle* starring Wills; above 2 were #2 Country hits		
7/13/46	20	1		5 New Spanish Two Step ....J:20 *Roly-Poly* (C&W #3)	$20	Columbia 36966
				Tommy Duncan (vocal); vocal version of Wills' 1935 instrumental recording "Spanish Two Step" on Vocalion 03230;		
				#1 Country hit (16 weeks)		

WILLS, Johnnie Lee, And His Boys   '50

Born on 9/2/12 in Jewett, Texas. Died on 10/25/84 (age 72). Country singer/fiddle player. Brother of **Bob Wills**.

DEBUT	PEAK	WKS				
2/4/50	9	11		Rag Mop ....J:9 / S:10 / A:14 *Near Me*	$20	Bullet 696
				#2 Country hit		

WILSON, Eileen   '51

Featured vocalist with **Les Brown**'s orchestra. One of the featured performers on TV's *Your Hit Parade*.

DEBUT	PEAK	WKS				
12/17/49	26	2		1 A Dreamer's Holiday ....J:26 *Tell Me Why*	$10	Decca 24738
				EILEEN WILSON And GORDON JENKINS And His Orchestra		
10/13/51	19	1		2 Cold, Cold Heart ....A:19 *Tennessee Blues*	$20	Decca 9-27761
				EILEEN WILSON With The Mellomen		
				Sonny Burke (orch.); #96 hit for **Dinah Washington** in 1962		

WINTERHALTER, Hugo ★43★   MEM/HOT '50

Born on 8/15/09 in Wilkes-Barre, Pennsylvania. Died of cancer on 9/17/73 (age 64). Conductor/arranger for RCA Records from 1950-63 (the most prolific hit orchestra conductor from 1949-54).

1)Blue Tango   2)I Can Dream, Can't I?   3)The Velvet Glove   4)Vanessa   5)The Little Shoemaker

Vocalists: Arden, Toni — 2   Five Gems, The — 4   Foster, Stuart — 11
           Fisher, Eddie — 19,20   Fontane Sisters, The — 8   Parker, Johnny — 14

HUGO WINTERHALTER and His Orchestra and Chorus:

DEBUT	PEAK	WKS				
10/15/49	10	6		1 Jealous Heart ....A:10 *Someday (You'll Want Me To Want You)*	$10	Columbia 38593
				7" 33-1/3 rpm: 1-349; #47 hit for Connie Francis in 1965		
11/19/49+	7	14		2 I Can Dream, Can't I? ....A:7 / J:29 *A Little Love, A Little Kiss*	$10	Columbia 38612
				TONI ARDEN with HUGO WINTERHALTER and his ORCHESTRA and Choir		
				7" 33-1/3 rpm: 1-377; from the Broadway musical *Right This Way* starring Guy Robertson; #5 hit for **Tommy Dorsey** in 1938		
12/24/49	9	3		3 Blue Christmas ....A:9 / J:18 / S:21 *You're All I Want For Christmas* [X]	$15	Columbia 38635
				7" 33-1/3 rpm: 1-401; #1 hit on *Billboard*'s special Christmas charts in 1964 for Elvis Presley (recorded in 1957)		
3/25/50	17	5		4 (Put Another Nickel In) Music! Music! Music! ....A:17 *The Glow-Worm*	$15	Columbia 38704
				HUGO WINTERHALTER and THE FIVE GEMS		
				7" 33-1/3 rpm: 1-489; #54 hit for The Sensations in 1961		
4/15/50	10	20		5 Count Every Star ....S:10 / A:16 / J:16 *The Flying Dutchman*	$15	RCA Victor 47-3221
				78 rpm: 20-3697; #35 hit for Donnie & The Dreamers in 1961		
4/22/50	21	4		6 The Third Man Theme ....A:21 *Come Into My Heart* [I]	$10	Columbia 38706
				7" 33-1/3 rpm: 1-492; Tony Mottola (guitar solo); from the movie *The Third Man* starring Orson Welles; #47 hit for Herb Alpert & The Tijuana Brass in 1965		
5/20/50	29	1		7 My Foolish Heart..A:29 *Leave It To Love*	$10	Columbia 38697
				7" 33-1/3 rpm: 1-478; title song from the movie starring Susan Hayward		
6/3/50	11	9		8 I Wanna Be Loved ....A:9 / J:21 / S:24 *I Didn't Know What Time It Was*	$20	RCA Victor 47-3772
				THE FONTANE SISTERS with HUGO WINTERHALTER'S Orchestra and Chorus		
10/7/50	9	7		9 Mr. Touchdown, U. S. A. ...A:9 *The Red We Want Is The Red We've Got (In the Old Red, White and Blue)*	$15	RCA Victor 47-3913
12/16/50	20	2		10 Blue Christmas ....A:20 *You're All I Want For Christmas* [X-R]	$15	Columbia 38635
2/10/51	21	4		11 Across The Wide Missouri ....S:21 / A:23 *The Seven Wonders Of The World*	$15	RCA Victor 47-4017
				adaptation of a traditional folk song (also known as "Shenandoah")		

DEBUT	PEAK	WKS	Gold	A-side (Chart Hit) .... B-side	$	Label & Number
				WINTERHALTER, Hugo — Cont'd		
11/3/51	23	3		12 Beyond The Blue Horizon ....A:23 *I Never Was Loved By Anyone Else*	$15	RCA Victor 47-4288
				#5 hit for **George Olsen** in 1930; from the movie *Monte Carlo* starring Jeanette MacDonald; #80 hit for Lou Christie in 1974		
1/5/52	18	1		13 Blue December ....A:18 *I'll See You In My Dreams*	$15	RCA Victor 47-4412
1/26/52	10	9		14 A Kiss To Build A Dream On ....A:10 / S:18 / J:21 *Love Makes The World Go 'Round*	$15	RCA Victor 47-4455
				from the movie *The Strip* starring Mickey Rooney		
3/8/52	6	18		15 Blue Tango A:6 / S:8 / J:11 *The Gypsy Trail* [I]	$15	RCA Victor 47-4518
				#16 hit for Bill Black's Combo in 1960		
6/14/52	9	14		16 Vanessa...A:9 / S:12 / J:29 *Somewhere Along The Way* [I]	$15	RCA Victor 47-4691
				composition inspired by actress Vanessa Brown		
11/1/52+	19	2		17 Blue Violins..A:19 / S:20 / J:20 *Fandango* [I]	$15	RCA Victor 47-4997
10/3/53	8	5		18 The Velvet Glove ....J:8 / S:18 / A:19 *Elaine* [I]	$15	RCA Victor 47-5405
				HENRI RENÉ and HUGO WINTERHALTER		
7/3/54	9	11		19 The Little Shoemaker / ....S:9 / A:9 / J:9		
7/31/54	25	3		20 The Magic Tango S:25	$15	RCA Victor 47-5769
				HUGO WINTERHALTER'S ORCHESTRA and CHORUS and a Friend (above 2 — Friend is **Eddie Fisher**)		
12/18/54+	25	5		21 Song Of The Barefoot Contessa / S:25		
				from the movie *The Barefoot Contessa* starring Humphrey Bogart and Ava Gardner		
12/25/54	30	1		22 Land Of Dreams..S:30 [I]	$15	RCA Victor 47-5888
				HUGO WINTERHALTER/EDDIE HEYWOOD		
				WOLCOTT, Charles, And His Orchestra HOT '44		
				Born on 9/29/06 in Flint, Michigan. Died on 1/26/87 (age 80). Pianist/composer/arranger. With Paul Whiteman, Andre Kostelanetz and Jean Goldkette bands. Music director with MGM studios from 1950-60.		
8/26/44	13	3		Tico-Tico ....S(wc):13 *Pedro From Chile* [F]	$15	Decca 23318
				Aloysio Oliveira with Bando Da Luo (vocals in Portuguese); Brazilian samba featured in the Disney movie *Saludos Amigos*		
				WOOD, Barry MEM '41		
				Born on 2/12/09 in New Haven, Connecticut. Died on 7/19/70 (age 61). Baritone who sang briefly with **Abe Lyman**.		
7/5/41	13	3		1 The Things I Love ....S(mw):13 *Talking To The Wind*	$10	Victor 27369
				#60 hit for The Fidelity's in 1958		
9/19/42	20	1		2 Put-Put-Put (Your Arms Around Me)...........S(wc):20 *Johnny Doughboy Found A Rose In Ireland* [N]	$15	Bluebird 11523
				BARRY WOOD and THE WOOD-NYMPHS		
				WOOD, Del MEM '51		
				Born Polly Adelaide Hendricks on 2/22/20 in Nashville. Died on 10/3/89 (age 69). Female honky-tonk pianist.		
9/1/51	4	25	●	Down Yonder J:4 / S:6 / A:8 *Mine, All Mine* [I]	$30	Tennessee 775 (45)
				#5 hit for Ernest Hare & Billy Jones in 1921; #48 hit for Johnny & The Hurricanes in 1960		
				WOODS, Ilene, and The Woodsmen '50		
				Singer/actress. Best known as the voice of "Cinderella" in the 1950 Disney animated classic (see **Albums Section**).		
1/14/50	22	2		Bibbidi-Bobbidi-Boo (The Magic Song) ....A:22 *So This Is Love (The Cinderella Waltz)*	$25	RCA Victor 54-0014
				78 rpm: 30-0019; Harold Mooney (orch.); record issued on RCA Victor's Bluebird Series; from the Disney animated feature movie *Cinderella*		
				WYMAN, Jane '51		
				Born Sarah Mayfield on 1/4/14 in St. Joseph, Missouri. Actress/singer. Appeared in several movies. Married to actor and future president Ronald Reagan from 1940-48.		
8/4/51	11	6		1 In The Cool, Cool, Cool Of The Evening ....A:11 / S:23 *Misto Cristofo Columbo*	$20	Decca 9-27678
				BING CROSBY And JANE WYMAN		
				Matty Matlock's All Stars (orch.); from the movie *Here Comes The Groom* starring Crosby and Wyman		
9/22/51	29	1		2 Black Strap Molasses ....J:29 / A:30 *How D' Ye Do And Shake Hands* [N]	$25	Decca 9-27748
				DANNY KAYE-JIMMY DURANTE-JANE WYMAN-GROUCHO MARX Sonny Burke (orch.); **4 Hits And A Miss** (backing vocals, above 2)		
8/9/52	18	6		3 Zing A Little Zong ....A:18 / J:28 *The Maiden Of Guadalupe*	$20	Decca 9-28255
				BING CROSBY and JANE WYMAN Jud Conlon's Rhythmaires (backing vocals); from the movie *Just For You* starring Crosby and Wyman		

Y

DEBUT	PEAK	WKS	Gold	A-side (Chart Hit) .... B-side	$	Label & Number
				YANKOVIC, Frankie, and His Yanks '49		
				Born on 7/28/15 in Davis, West Virginia; raised in Cleveland. Died on 10/14/98 (age 83). Accordionist/polka bandleader. Known as "America's Polka King."		
5/8/48	9	14		1 Just Because ....J:9 / S:14 *A Night In May*	$10	Columbia 12359-F
				Yankovic and Johnny Pecon (vocals); #99 hit for **The McGuire Sisters** in 1961		
3/5/49	12	26	●	2 Blue Skirt Waltz ....J:12 / S:14 *Charlie Was A Boxer*	$10	Columbia 12394-F
				FRANKIE YANKOVIC and his YANKS with THE MARLIN SISTERS Yankovic, The Marlin Sisters and Johnny Pecon (vocals)		
				YORGESSON, Yogi '49		
				Born Harry Skarbo on 10/21/08 in Tacoma, Washington. Died in a car crash on 5/20/56 (age 47). Also recorded as Harry Kari & His Six Saki Sippers.		
12/10/49	5	5	●	1 I Yust Go Nuts At Christmas / S:5 / A:5 / J:11 [X-N]		
				parody of "Twas The Night Before Christmas"		
12/17/49	7	4		2 Yingle Bells ....S:7 / A:7 / J:16 [X-N]	$20	Capitol 57-781
				parody of "Jingle Bells"; Johnny Duffy Trio (instrumental backing, above 2)		
				YOUNG, Eve — see CHANDLER, Karen		

YOUNG, Victor, And His Singing Strings MEM/HOT **'35**

Born on 8/8/1900 in Chicago. Died on 11/11/56 (age 56). Conductor/composer/violinist. Young's pre-1940 #1 hit: "She's A Latin From Manhattan."

★147★

DEBUT	PEAK	WKS		A-side	B-side	$	Label & Number
6/10/50	27	1		1 La Vie En Rose..S:27 *The River Seine* [I]		$15	Decca 9-24816
7/1/50	7	15		2 Mona Lisa / ....J:7 / S:10		$15	Decca 9-27048
				from the movie *Captain Carey, U.S.A.* starring Alan Ladd; #25 hit for Carl Mann in 1959			
7/8/50	22	2		3 The 3rd Man Theme..J:22 / S:25		$15	Decca 9-27048
				VICTOR YOUNG And His Orchestra And Chorus And DON CHERRY (above 2)			
				from the movie *The Third Man* starring Orson Welles; #47 hit for Herb Alpert & The Tijuana Brass in 1965			
2/24/51	29	1		4 My Heart Cries For You ....S:29 *The One Finger Melody (Yum-Dee-Da-Dee-Da)*		$15	Decca 9-27333
				VICTOR YOUNG And His Orchestra			
				Louanne Hogan, Joe Graydon and Chorus (vocals); adapted from the 18th-century French melody "Chanson de Marie Antoinette"; #38 hit for Ray Charles in 1964			
6/6/53	20	1		5 Ruby...S:20 *The Song From Moulin Rouge (Where Is Your Heart)* [I]		$15	Decca 9-28675
				George Fields (harmonica solo); theme from the movie *Ruby Gentry* starring Jennifer Jones and Charlton Heston; #28 hit for Ray Charles in 1960			
8/7/54	6	14		6 The High And The Mighty S:6 / A:11 / J:12 *Moonlight And Roses (Bring Mem'ries Of You)* [I]		$15	Decca 9-29203
				Muzzy Marcellino (whistling); title song from the movie starring John Wayne			

Z

ZABACH, Florian MEM/HOT **'51**

Born on 8/15/21 in Chicago. Violinist/composer. Hosted his own TV variety series in 1956.

DEBUT	PEAK	WKS	Gold	A-side	B-side	$	Label & Number
3/31/51	13	10	●	The Hot Canary ....S:13 / J:23 *Jalousie* [I]		$15	Decca 9-27509
				Al Rickey (orch.)			

POP ANNUAL SECTION

This section ranks, year by year, every song that <u>peaked</u> on *Billboard's* pop singles charts from 1940 through 1954. All songs are ranked in the year that they achieved their peak popularity. The only exceptions to this rule are the Christmas titles that peaked in early January, after the December holiday season. Such late-peaking Christmas songs appear within the season that they were popular (the previous December). Although these songs peaked in early January, the actual survey was taken 10 days prior to the issue date of the chart. For such seasonal titles, the date of the last chart of the previous year is shown as their peak date.

(The previous edition of *Pop Hits 1940-1954* included all songs listed on the first 1940 chart, the Record Buying Guide, which included some songs that peaked in 1939. The songs that peaked in 1939 have been omitted from the 1940 ranking in this edition.)

RANKING SYSTEM

The single's peak position is taken from the chart on which it achieved its highest ranking. Peak weeks, Top 5 weeks, Top 10 weeks and total weeks charted are taken from the chart on which the record achieved its highest total.

Following is the method used in ranking each year's hits:

1) The single's peak position

    All singles peaking at #1 are listed first, then singles that peaked at #2 are grouped together and shown secondly, then the #3s, etc., all the way through every chart position of each year.

2) Ties among each highest position grouping are broken in the following order:

    a) Total weeks single held its peak position
    b) Total weeks charted in Top 5
    c) Total weeks charted in Top 10
    d) Total weeks charted

If there are still ties among singles which peaked in the Top 10, a computerized inverse point system is used to calculate a point total for each Top 10 hit based on its weekly chart positions. For each week a record appears on the charts, it is given points based on its chart position for that week (#1 = 100 points, #2 = 99 points, etc.). These points are added together to create a raw point total for each record, which is used to break any remaining ties. Ties among non-Top 10 titles are listed alphabetically by artist name.

KEY TO COLUMNS AND SYMBOLS

PEAK POSITION:	Single's highest charted position (large bold number)
PEAK DATE:	Date single reached its peak position
WEEKS:	**CH** - Total weeks charted
	10 - Total weeks charted in the Top 10
	5 - Total weeks charted in the Top 5
	PK - Total weeks record held its peak position
RANK:	Final ranking for the year
GOLD:	● Gold single (million seller)
Songwriter(s):	The songwriter(s) of all titles appear in italics to the right of each title.
SYMBL:	[C] Comedy recording
	[F] Foreign language recording
	[I] Instrumental recording
	[N] Novelty recording
	[R] Re-entry, reissue or re-recording of a prior hit by that artist
	[S] Spoken recording
	[X] Christmas recording

DEBUT: ❶   Artist's first appearance on the Pop charts

             ✦   Artist's first and only appearance on the Pop charts

Names in parentheses next to the name of an orchestra or a band leader is their featured vocalist(s) on that song.

PEAK POSITION OF TITLE'S A- OR B-SIDE

For a two-sided hit, the peak position reached by either its A- or B-side follows the song's writer(s). The position (and year, if different) of the corresponding A- or B-side appears in brackets (< >) to the right of the title. The A-side is the side that reached the highest position.

Weekly Positions: Below every #1 hit is a week-by-week, position-by-position chronology of its entire chart life. For singles that hit #1 on one or more of the multiple charts, the chart-run of each chart the record made is shown—regardless, if it topped one or all of these charts. The chart on which it held on to the #1 spot for the most weeks is shown first, and so on. In the case of tied weeks at the peak position, the order in which the charts are listed is as follows: Best Sellers, Disc Jockey and Juke Box.

NOTES

Brief notes of special interest appear in soft brackets { } below some titles, such as a record that may have originally charted at an earlier date.

TOP 20 ARTISTS

Immediately following each year's Time Capsule is a ranking of the year's Top 20 artists. The three-digit number that appears next to these artists' names is the number of points that they earned. This is the same point system used for the All-Time Top 150 Pop Artists from 1940-54. See page 296 for an explanation of this ranking system. Photographs appear for each year's Top 3 artists.

TOP SONGWRITERS RANKING

Also appearing after each Time Capsule is a ranking of the year's Top 12 Songwriters. Songwriters' yearly rankings are based on the number of their songs that peaked in that year. Ties at number of hits are broken according to a formula for which each songwriter's hits during the year are given points based on highest charted position. For example, a #1 hit is awarded 100 points, #2 = 99 points, #3 = 98 points, and so on. Co-songwriters are each awarded the same number of points for their collaborations. Regular songwriting teams, such as Richard Rodgers and Oscar Hammerstein II, are individually awarded the same number of points. A songwriter receives credit for each separate version of a hit song. For example, Frank Loesser gets five hit songwriting credits in 1949 for "Baby, It's Cold Outside" since five separate versions of his song hit the charts that year.

TOP ARTIST DEBUTS

Following each year's listing of Top 20 Artists and Top Songwriters is a listing, in chronological order by debut date, of those new artists who made their chart debuts during the year and went on to be ranked among the Top 150 Artists of 1940-1954 or the Top 500 of our *Top Pop Singles 1955-1999* book. The number in parentheses after an artist name is the artist's rank in this book.

- † indicates the highest ranking artist of the *Top 150 Artists* debuting that year
- ★ indicates artist has a *Top 500* ranking in our **Top Pop Singles 1955-1999** book
- ◆ indicates artist has a *Top 200* ranking in our **Top R&B Singles 1942-1999** or **Top Country Singles 1944-2001** books and is <u>not</u> ranked in any of our **Pop Singles** books.

1940

NATIONAL NEWS: As war rages in Europe, Franklin D. Roosevelt (FDR) becomes the first man in American history to win a third term as President by defeating Wendell Wilkie. FDR begins to prepare a reluctant nation for possible American involvement in the war, as Congress enacts the nation's first peacetime conscription. The U.S. population now stands at 132 million.

INTERNATIONAL NEWS: German troops seize Finland, Denmark, Norway, Belgium, Holland, and — most shocking of all on June 14 — Paris. Nazi bombers launch ferocious air attacks on British cities, forcing nightly blackouts throughout England. Japan joins Germany and Italy in the Axis pact. New British Prime Minister Winston Churchill attempts to rally the free world and to bring the U.S. into the war effort.

COMMERCE AND SCIENCE: The sturdy Jeep, developed by the U.S. Army, makes its debut. Nylon stockings are commercially introduced in May, replacing silk stockings for millions of American women. A U.S. political convention is televised for the first time.

FADS AND FASHION: Sixteen years before it sweeps the U.S. record charts, Trinidad's calypso music captivates many Americans. The hobbyhorse, promoted by movie star Harold Lloyd, is a popular fad. Thanks to Walter Winchell, Jack Benny and Fred Allen, humorous takeoffs on the sayings of Confucius sweep the country.

SPORTS: The Cincinnati Reds edge the Detroit Tigers in the World Series in the seventh game. Joe Louis successfully defends his heavyweight boxing championship four times. George Halas' Chicago Bears obliterate the Washington Redskins, 73-0, in the NFL title game. Minnesota reigns as college football's #1 team. The Olympic Games are not held in 1940 or 1944 due to war.

MOVIES: *Gone With the Wind* (released the previous December) dominates American movie theaters. Among new releases, the most honored films are Alfred Hitchcock's *Rebecca* (Oscar winner for Best Picture); *The Philadelphia Story* with the matchless trio of James Stewart (selected for Best Actor), Katharine Hepburn and Cary Grant; John Ford's epic *The Grapes of Wrath* starring Henry Fonda; *Boom Town* with Clark Gable and Spencer Tracy; and Charles Chaplin's savage satire *The Great Dictator*. Walt Disney's all-time classic *Fantasia* premieres, following the huge Christmas 1939 debut of *Pinocchio*. Mae West and W.C. Fields make a superstar pairing in *My Little Chickadee*. Bing Crosby, Bob Hope and Dorothy Lamour launch their "road" series with *Road to Singapore*.

RADIO: Among the programs dominating the nation's airwaves are *The Jack Benny Program*, *The Chase and Sanborn Hour*, *Fibber McGee and Molly*, *The Shadow*, and *The Lone Ranger*.

THEATER: Laurence Olivier and Vivien Leigh win rave reviews in *Romeo and Juliet*. *Life With Father* (Nov. 1939 premiere) is en route to an amazing eight-year Broadway run, the longest ever for a non-musical. Cole Porter's *Panama Hattie* with Ethel Merman packs them in.

BOOKS: It is a year of American classics, with Ernest Hemingway's *For Whom the Bell Tolls*, John Steinbeck's *Of Mice and Men* and Richard Wright's *Native Son*.

1940 — TOP 20 ARTISTS

1. Glenn Miller
2,458

2. Tommy Dorsey
1,153

3. Bing Crosby
814

4.	468	**Ink Spots**
5.	439	**Kay Kyser**
6.	421	**Charlie Barnet**
7.	364	**Dick Jurgens**
8.	335	**Andrews Sisters**
9.	305	**Orrin Tucker**
10.	294	**Artie Shaw**
11.	234	**Jimmy Dorsey**
12.	229	**Dick Todd**
13.	223	**Sammy Kaye**
14.	217	**Will Bradley**
15.	212	**Eddy Duchin**
16.	189	**Bob Crosby**
17.	181	**Benny Goodman**
18.	164	**Erskine Hawkins**
19.	135	**Guy Lombardo**
20.	126	**Frankie Masters**

> The above ranking shows a point total for each artist. Refer to the "Top 20 Artists Point System" on page 147 for an explanation of the *Top 20 Artists* ranking.

1940 — TOP SONGWRITERS

	# of Hits	Points	
1.	10	881	**Jimmy Van Heusen**
2.	8	732	**Johnny Burke**
3.	8	703	**Mack Gordon**
4.	8	689	**Eddie DeLange**
5.	7	640	**James Monaco**
6.	7	628	**Will Grosz**
7.	7	621	**Charles Kenny**
	7	621	**Nick Kenny**
9.	7	619	**Harold Adamson**
	7	619	**Eldo DiLazzaro**
11.	7	602	**Harry Warren**
12.	5	455	**Don Raye**

1940 — TOP ARTIST DEBUTS

1.	1/13	**Tommy Tucker** (136)
2.	5/11	**Will Bradley** (117)
3.	10/12 †	**Dinah Shore** (10)
4.	12/28	**Vaughn Monroe** (13)

PEAK DATE	WEEKS CH	WEEKS 10	WEEKS 5	WEEKS PK	RANK	GOLD	Title / PEAK POSITION / Songwriter(s)	SYMBL	DEBUT	Artist

1

| 2/10 | 28 | 28 | 19 | 13 | 1 | ● | **In The Mood** .... *Joe Garland* [I] | | | **Glenn Miller** |

Juke Box: 10,8,8,9,8,8,6,1,5,5,6,5,3,3,3,1,1,1,1,1,1,1,1,1,1,10

| 12/21 | 23 | 23 | 17 | 13 | 2 | ● | **Frenesi** .... *Ray Charles/Alberto Dominguez/S.K. Russell* <B:20> [I] | | | **Artie Shaw** |

Best Seller: 10,10,9,7,1,1,1,1,1,1,1,1,1,1,1,3,1,4,4,6,5,9

| 7/27 | 18 | 18 | 14 | 12 | 3 | ● | **I'll Never Smile Again** .... *Ruth Lowe* | | | **Tommy Dorsey** (Frank Sinatra/Pied Pipers) |

Best Seller: 1,1,1,1,1,1,1,1,1,1,1,1,2,3,9
Juke Box: 9,8,8,6,6,4,4,3,2,2,2,2,1,1,1,1,1,1

| 10/19 | 16 | 16 | 16 | 9 | 4 | | **Only Forever** .... *Johnny Burke/James Monaco* | | | **Bing Crosby** |

Best Seller: 5,4,2,1,1,1,1,1,1,1,1,2,4,4,5

| 5/4 | 17 | 17 | 12 | 9 | 5 | ● | **Tuxedo Junction** .... *Julian Dash/Erskine Hawkins/William Johnson* [I] | | | **Glenn Miller** |

Juke Box: 7,7,7,7,7,5,3,2,1,1,1,1,1,1,1,1

| 7/6 | 14 | 14 | 14 | 5 | 6 | | **The Woodpecker Song** .... *Harold Adamson/Eldo DiLazzaro* | | | **Glenn Miller** (Marion Hutton) |

Juke Box: 5,5,5,3,3,2,2,2,1,1,1,1,1

| 9/14 | 12 | 12 | 9 | 4 | 7 | | **Sierra Sue** .... *Joseph Carey* | | | **Bing Crosby** |

Juke Box: 10,7,7,5,5,3,3,2,1,1,1,1
Best Seller: 9,5,4,5,4,3,4,4,4,6

| 8/10 | 11 | 11 | 7 | 2 | 8 | | **Make-Believe Island** .... *Will Grosz/Charles Kenny/Nick Kenny* | ❶ | | **Mitchell Ayres** (Mary Ann Mercer) |

Juke Box: 9,6,6,6,4,4,4,3,3,1,1
Best Seller: 10

| 8/24 | 9 | 9 | 7 | 2 | 9 | | **Where Was I?** .... *Al Dubin/W. Frank Harling* | | | **Charlie Barnet** (Mary Ann McCall) |

Juke Box: 6,5,6,5,5,3,3,1,1
Best Seller: 6

| 9/7 | 10 | 10 | 8 | 1 | 10 | | **The Breeze And I** .... *Ernesto Lecuona/Al Stillman* | | | **Jimmy Dorsey** (Bob Eberly) |

Juke Box: 10,6,7,6,6,4,4,2,2,1
Best Seller: 2,2,2,2,2,2,3,3,7

2

2/10	11	11	9	9	11		**Careless** .... *Eddy Howard/Dick Jurgens/Lew Quadling*			Glenn Miller (Ray Eberle)
10/5	14	14	11	6	12		**Maybe** .... *Allan Flynn/Frank Madden* <B:10>			Ink Spots
5/4	7	7	6	5	13		**When You Wish Upon A Star** .... *Leigh Harline/Ned Washington* <B:7>			Glenn Miller (Ray Eberle)
9/7	14	14	9	4	14		**Blueberry Hill** .... *Al Lewis/Vincent Rose/Larry Stock*			Glenn Miller (Ray Eberle)
7/6	14	14	9	3	15		**The Singing Hills** .... *Mack David/Sammy Mysels/Dick Sanford*			Bing Crosby
4/13	12	12	11	2	16		**Indian Summer** .... *Al Dubin/Victor Herbert*			Tommy Dorsey (Jack Leonard)
7/27	13	13	9	2	17		**Playmates** .... *Saxie Dowell* [N]			Kay Kyser (Sully Mason)
12/7	15	15	7	2	18		**Trade Winds** .... *Cliff Friend/Charles Tobias*			Bing Crosby
8/10	8	8	6	2	19		**Imagination** .... *Johnny Burke/Jimmy Van Heusen*			Glenn Miller (Ray Eberle)
12/28	6	6	5	2	20		**A Nightingale Sang In Berkeley Square** .... *Eric Maschwitz/Manning Sherwin*			Glenn Miller (Ray Eberle)
11/30	15	15	10	1	21		**Beat Me Daddy (Eight To The Bar) Parts I & II** .... *Hughie Prince/Don Raye/ Eleanore Sheehy*	❶		Will Bradley/Ray McKinley/ Freddie Slack

3

8/3	7	7	5	4	22		**Fools Rush In (Where Angels Fear to Tread)** .... *Rube Bloom/Johnny Mercer*			Glenn Miller (Ray Eberle)
2/10	8	8	4	4	23		**All The Things You Are** .... *Oscar Hammerstein/Jerome Kern*			Tommy Dorsey (Jack Leonard)
5/4	8	8	5	3	24		**On The Isle Of May** .... *Mack David/Andre Kostelanetz*			Connie Boswell
9/21	10	10	3	2	25		**I'm Nobody's Baby** .... *Milton Ager/Benny Davis/Lester Santly*			Judy Garland
12/7	14	14	9	1	26		**We Three (My Echo, My Shadow And Me)** .... *Nelson Cogane/Sammy Mysels/ Dick Robertson* <B:17>			Ink Spots
4/13	10	10	7	1	27		**At The Balalaika** .... *Chet Forrest/Eric Maschwitz/George Posford/Herbert Stothart/ Robert Wright*			Orrin Tucker (Gil Mershon)
12/14	6	6	1	1	28		**Pompton Turnpike** .... *Will Osborne/Dick Rogers* [I]			Charlie Barnet
12/28	5	5	1	1	29		**We Three (My Echo, My Shadow and Me)** .... *Nelson Cogane/Sammy Mysels/ Dick Robertson*			Tommy Dorsey (Frank Sinatra)

4

6/8	7	7	6	4	30		**With The Wind And The Rain In Your Hair** ...... *Clara Edwards/Jack Lawrence*			Kay Kyser (Ginny Simms)
1/20	11	11	4	3	31		**Yodelin' Jive** .... *Hughie Prince/Don Raye*			Bing Crosby & The Andrews Sisters
5/4	8	8	4	3	32		**Say "Si Si" (Para Vigo Me Voy)** .... *Ernesto Lecuona/Francis Luban/Al Stillman*			Andrews Sisters
8/31	11	11	1	1	33		**When The Swallows Come Back To Capistrano** .... *Leon Rene*			Ink Spots
4/13	6	6	1	1	34		**The Gaucho Serenade** .... *James Cavanaugh/John Redmond/Nat Simon*			Dick Todd
2/10	5	5	1	1	35		**The Little Red Fox (N'Ya N'Ya Ya Can't Catch Me)** .... *Hy Heath/James Kern/ Johnny Lange/Lew Porter* [N]			Kay Kyser
8/17	3	3	1	1	36		**Six Lessons From Madame La Zonga** .... *James Monaco/Charles Newman*			Jimmy Dorsey (Helen O'Connell)
4/20	1	1	1	1	37		**When You Wish Upon A Star** .... *Leigh Harline/Ned Washington*			Guy Lombardo (Carmen Lombardo)

5

| 3/9 | 7 | 7 | 5 | 5 | 38 | | **You'd Be Surprised** .... *Irving Berlin* | | | Orrin Tucker (Bonnie Baker) |
| 8/10 | 8 | 8 | 3 | 3 | 39 | | **The Nearness Of You** .... *Hoagy Carmichael/Ned Washington* | | | Glenn Miller (Ray Eberle) |

1940

PEAK DATE	WEEKS				RANK	GOLD	Title	PEAK POSITION Songwriter(s)	SYMBL	DEBUT	Artist
	CH	10	5	PK							

5 (cont'd)

1/20	7	7	3	3	40		Stop! It's Wonderful	Clay Boland/Bickley Reichner			Orrin Tucker (Bonnie Baker)
12/28	4	4	2	2	41		There I Go	Irving Weiser/Hy Zaret	❶		Vaughn Monroe
2/17	3	3	2	2	42		Faithful Forever	Ralph Rainger/Leo Robin			Glenn Miller (Ray Eberle)
11/16	3	3	2	2	43		Our Love Affair	Roger Edens/Arthur Freed			Tommy Dorsey (Frank Sinatra)
8/31	6	6	1	1	44	●	Pennsylvania Six-Five Thousand	Jerry Gray/Carl Sigman [I]			Glenn Miller
8/24	3	3	1	1	45		God Bless America	Irving Berlin			Kate Smith

6

10/12	6	6		4	46		Practice Makes Perfect	Ernest Gold/Don Roberts	❶		Bob Chester (Al Stuart)
6/1	5	5		2	47		Little Curly Hair In A High Chair	Nat Simon/Charles Tobias [N]			"Fats" Waller
2/17	4	4		1	48		Chatterbox	Jerome Brainin/Allan Roberts			Kay Kyser (Ginny Simms/Harry Babbitt)
1/20	3	3		1	49		Careless	Eddy Howard/Dick Jurgens/Lew Quadling			Dick Jurgens (Eddy Howard)

7

5/25	5	5		3	50		Alice Blue Gown	Joseph McCarthy/Harry Tierney			Frankie Masters (Marion Francis)
7/6	4	4		2	51		Say It	Frank Loesser/Jimmy McHugh			Glenn Miller (Ray Eberle)
5/4	3	3		2	52		With The Wind And The Rain In Your Hair	Clara Edwards/Jack Lawrence			Bob Crosby (Marion Mann)
6/15	5	5		1	53		Boog-It	Cab Calloway/Jack Palmer/Buck Ram <B:10>			Glenn Miller (Marion Hutton)
4/27	4	4		1	54		Leanin' On The Ole Top Rail	Charles Kenny/Nick Kenny			Bob Crosby
6/22	4	4		1	55		Let There Be Love	Ian Grant/Lionel Rand			Sammy Kaye (Tommy Ryan)
10/26	3	3		1	56		Only Forever	Johnny Burke/James Monaco <B:10>			Tommy Dorsey (Alan Storr)
3/2	2	2		1	57		The Gaucho Serenade	James Cavanaugh/John Redmond/Nat Simon <A:2>			Glenn Miller (Ray Eberle)
4/20	2	2		1	58		The Woodpecker Song	Harold Adamson/Eldo DiLazzaro			Andrews Sisters
12/21	2	2		1	59		Down Argentina Way	Mack Gordon/Harry Warren			Leo Reisman (Sara Horn)

8

2/17	5	5		2	60		Darn That Dream	Eddie DeLange/Jimmy Van Heusen			Benny Goodman (Mildred Bailey)
7/20	5	5		2	61		I Can't Love You Any More (Any More Than I Do)	Herb Magidson/Allie Wrubel			Benny Goodman (Helen Forrest)
3/9	3	3		2	62		In An Old Dutch Garden (By An Old Dutch Mill)	Mack Gordon/Will Grosz			Dick Jurgens (Eddy Howard)
5/25	4	4		1	63		Cecelia	Dave Dreyer/Herman Ruby [N]			Dick Jurgens (Ronnie Kemper)
12/14	3	3		1	64		Ferryboat Serenade (La Piccinina)	Harold Adamson/Eldo DiLazzaro			Andrews Sisters
11/23	2	2		1	65		Our Love Affair	Roger Edens/Arthur Freed <B:10>			Glenn Miller (Ray Eberle)
3/23	2	2		1	66		In An Old Dutch Garden (By An Old Dutch Mill)	Mack Gordon/Will Grosz <B:10>			Glenn Miller (Ray Eberle)
7/27	1	1		1	67		Imagination	Johnny Burke/Jimmy Van Heusen			Tommy Dorsey (Frank Sinatra)
8/3	1	1		1	68		Make-Believe Island	Will Grosz/Charles Kenny/Nick Kenny			Jan Savitt (George Tunnell)

9

1/13	7	7		3	69		The Man That Comes Around	John Lair/Tommy Tucker [N]	❶		Tommy Tucker Time (Kerwin Somerville)
3/9	4	4		2	70		Confucius Say	Cliff Friend/Carmen Lombardo			Guy Lombardo (Carmen Lombardo)
7/6	3	3		2	71		Slow Freight	Lupin Fien/Irving Mills/Buck Ram [I]			Glenn Miller
4/27	2	2		1	72		I've Got My Eyes On You	Cole Porter			Bob Crosby (Marion Mann)
6/1	2	2		1	73		No Name Jive (Parts 1 & 2)	Larry Wagner [I]			Glen Gray
1/6	1	1		1	74		Bluebirds In The Moonlight	Ralph Rainger/Leo Robin			Dick Jurgens (Eddy Howard)
10/5	1	1		1	75		Crosstown	James Cavanaugh/John Redmond/Nat Simon			Glenn Miller (Jack Lathrop)

10

9/21	4	4		4	76		Trade Winds	Cliff Friend/Charles Tobias <A:7>			Tommy Dorsey (Frank Sinatra)
3/9	2	2		2	77		Darn That Dream	Eddie DeLange/Jimmy Van Heusen			Blue Barron (Russ Carlyle)
6/22	2	2		2	78		April Played The Fiddle	Johnny Burke/James Monaco			Bing Crosby
4/6	2	2		2	79		It's A Blue World	Chet Forrest/Robert Wright			Tony Martin
11/30	2	2		2	80		A Handful Of Stars	Jack Lawrence/Ted Shapiro			Glenn Miller (Ray Eberle)
12/21	1	1		1	81		Down The Road A Piece	Don Raye <B:18>			Will Bradley Trio (Ray McKinley/Will Bradley)
9/14	1	1		1	82		Dolimite	William Johnson [I]			Erskine Hawkins
10/5	1	1		1	83		Whispering Grass (Don't Tell The Trees)	Doris Fisher/Fred Fisher <A:2>			Ink Spots
7/13	1	1		1	84		Shake Down The Stars	Eddie DeLange/Jimmy Van Heusen <A:7>			Glenn Miller (Ray Eberle)
4/27	1	1		1	85		Starlit Hour	Peter DeRose/Mitchell Parish <A:8>			Glenn Miller (Ray Eberle)
11/9	1	1		1	86		The Call Of The Canyon	Billy Hill <A:8>			Glenn Miller (Ray Eberle)
8/31	1	1		1	87		When The Swallows Come Back To Capistrano	Leon Rene			Glenn Miller (Ray Eberle)
2/17	1	1		1	88		Pinch Me	Everett Ralston/Joe Simay/Orrin Tucker			Orrin Tucker (Bonnie Baker)

12

| 7/27 | 1 | | | 1 | 89 | | Friendship | Cole Porter [N] | | | Kay Kyser (Ginny Simms/Harry Babbitt) |

PEAK DATE	WEEKS				RANK	GOLD	Title	PEAK POSITION / Songwriter(s)	SYMBOL	DEBUT	Artist
	CH	10	5	PK							

13

12/28	4			1	90		Down Argentina Way	Mack Gordon/Harry Warren <B:19>			Eddy Duchin (The Earbenders)
9/7	1			1	91		Six Lessons From Madame La Zonga	James Monaco/Charles Newman			Charlie Barnet (Mary Ann McCall)
8/3	1			1	92		Where Was I?	Al Dubin/W. Frank Harling <B:19>			Sammy Kaye (Clyde Burke)

14

11/9	6			2	93		A Million Dreams Ago	Eddy Howard/Dick Jurgens/Lew Quadling			Dick Jurgens (Harry Cool)
8/17	4			2	94		Boogie Woogie On St. Louis Blues	W.C. Handy [I]			Earl Hines
9/21	3			1	95		That's For Me	Johnny Burke/James Monaco			Bing Crosby

15

9/21	3			2	96		Huckleberry Duck	Raymond Scott [I]			Raymond Scott
8/10	2			2	97		All This And Heaven Too	Eddie DeLange/Jimmy Van Heusen			Tommy Dorsey (Frank Sinatra)
11/2	6			1	98		Ferry-Boat Serenade	Harold Adamson/Eldo DiLazzaro			Frankie Masters (Marion Francis)
9/28	4			1	99		The One I Love (Belongs To Somebody Else)	Isham Jones/Gus Kahn			Tommy Dorsey (Frank Sinatra/Pied Pipers)
10/12	3			1	100		Practice Makes Perfect	Ernest Gold/Don Roberts	✦		Al Kavelin (Bill Darnell)
10/12	2			1	101		Blueberry Hill	Al Lewis/Vincent Rose/Larry Stock			Kay Kyser (Harry Babbitt)
8/24	2			1	102		I'm Nobody's Baby	Milton Ager/Benny Davis/Lester Santly	❶		Bea Wain
7/27	1			1	103		The Breeze And I	Ernesto Lecuona/Al Stillman			Charlie Barnet (Mary Ann McCall)
11/23	1			1	104		Beat Me Daddy, Eight To A Bar	Hughie Prince/Don Raye/Eleanore Sheehy			Glenn Miller (Jack Lathrop)

16

9/7	3			1	105		All This And Heaven Too	Eddie DeLange/Jimmy Van Heusen			Charlie Barnet (Larry Taylor)
11/16	2			1	106		Two Dreams Met	Mack Gordon/Harry Warren			Tommy Dorsey (Connie Haines)
11/9	2			1	107		Five O'Clock Whistle	Kim Gannon/Gene Irwin/Josef Myrow [I]			Erskine Hawkins
8/3	1			1	108		Devil May Care	Johnny Burke/Harry Warren			Glenn Miller (Ray Eberle)
12/28	1			1	109		Dream Valley	Joe Burke/Charles Kenny/Nick Kenny			Eddy Duchin (Johnny Drake)
8/3	1			1	110		Whispering Grass	Doris Fisher/Fred Fisher			Erskine Hawkins (Jimmy Mitchelle)
12/14	1			1	111		Down Argentina Way	Mack Gordon/Harry Warren			Gene Krupa (Irene Daye)
8/3	1			1	112		Fools Rush In (Where Angels Fear To Tread)	Rube Bloom/Johnny Mercer			Tony Martin
8/24	1			1	113		I'm Nobody's Baby	Milton Ager/Benny Davis/Lester Santly			Ozzie Nelson (Rose Ann Stevens)

17

10/26	4			1	114		Blueberry Hill	Al Lewis/Vincent Rose/Larry Stock			Russ Morgan (Carol Kay)
8/17	2			1	115		Fools Rush In (Where Angels Fear To Tread)	Rube Bloom/Johnny Mercer			Tommy Dorsey (Frank Sinatra)
10/12	2			1	116		Maybe	Allan Flynn/Frank Madden	❶		Dinah Shore
12/28	1			1	117		Redskin Rhumba	Dale Bennett <A:17> [I]			Charlie Barnet
8/31	1			1	118		Love Lies	Ralph Freed/Joseph Meyer/Carl Sigman <B:18>			Tommy Dorsey (Frank Sinatra)
10/19	1			1	119		My Greatest Mistake	Jack Fulton/Jack O'Brien <A:3>			Ink Spots
8/10	1			1	120		I'll Never Smile Again	Ruth Lowe			Glenn Miller (Ray Eberle)
8/3	1			1	121		Sierra Sue	Joseph Carey			Glenn Miller (Ray Eberle)
8/3	1			1	122		I Can't Love You Any More (Any More Than I Do)	Herb Magidson/Allie Wrubel	✦		Terry Shand
8/17	1			1	123		Make-Believe Island	Will Grosz/Charles Kenny/Nick Kenny			Dick Todd

18

12/21	3			2	124		Down Argentine Way	Mack Gordon/Harry Warren			Shep Fields (Sonny Washburn)
8/3	2			2	125		Make-Believe Island	Will Grosz/Charles Kenny/Nick Kenny			Dick Jurgens (Harry Cool)
10/19	3			1	126		The Call Of The Canyon	Billy Hill <A:17>			Tommy Dorsey (Frank Sinatra)
9/28	2			1	127		Stop Pretending (So Hep You See)	Buddy Johnson			Ink Spots
12/28	1			1	128		There I Go	Irving Weiser/Hy Zaret			Kenny Baker
11/30	1			1	129		Celery Stalks At Midnight	Will Bradley/George Harris <A:10> [I]			Will Bradley Feat. Ray McKinley
8/10	1			1	130		The Breeze And I	Ernesto Lecuona/Al Stillman			Xavier Cugat (Dinah Shore)
10/12	1			1	131		I Could Make You Care	Sammy Cahn/Saul Chaplin			Tommy Dorsey (Frank Sinatra)
11/2	1			1	132		Only Forever	Johnny Burke/James Monaco			Eddy Duchin (June Robbins)
12/7	1			1	133		Ferry-Boat Serenade	Harold Adamson/Eldo DiLazzaro			Gray Gordon (Meredith Black)

19

12/28	3			1	134		There I Go	Irving Weiser/Hy Zaret			Tommy Tucker Time (Amy Arnell)
12/21	2			1	135		A Nightingale Sang In Berkeley Square	Eric Maschwitz/Manning Sherwin			Sammy Kaye (Tommy Ryan)
10/12	1			1	136		Beat Me Daddy, Eight To A Bar	Hughie Prince/Don Raye/Eleanore Sheehy			Andrews Sisters
10/19	1			1	137		Maybe	Allan Flynn/Frank Madden	❶		Bobby Byrne (Jimmy Palmer)
12/28	1			1	138 ●		Silent Night	Franz Gruber [X]			Bing Crosby
							{re-charted in 1941 (#16)}				
11/30	1			1	139		Two Dreams Met	Mack Gordon/Harry Warren <A:13>			Eddy Duchin (Johnny Drake)
8/17	1			1	140		The Hour Of Parting	Gus Kahn/Mischa Spoliansky [I]			Benny Goodman
7/27	1			1	141		Make Believe Island	Will Grosz/Charles Kenny/Nick Kenny <A:13>			Sammy Kaye (Tommy Ryan)
8/10	1			1	142		Where Was I?	Al Dubin/W. Frank Harling			Wayne King

1940

PEAK DATE	WEEKS				RANK	GOLD	Title	PEAK POSITION Songwriter(s)	SYMBL	DEBUT	Artist
	CH	10	5	PK							

19 (cont'd)

PEAK DATE	CH	10	5	PK	RANK	GOLD	Title	Songwriter(s)	SYMBL	DEBUT	Artist
11/16	1			1	143		Now I Lay Me Down To Dream	Ted Fiorito/Eddy Howard			Andy Kirk (Pha Terrell)
12/28	1			1	144		Ferry-Boat Serenade	Harold Adamson/Eldo DiLazzaro			Leo Reisman (Anita Boyer)

20

PEAK DATE	CH	10	5	PK	RANK	GOLD	Title	Songwriter(s)	SYMBL	DEBUT	Artist
9/21	1			1	145		I Miss You So	Jimmie Henderson	✦		The Cats & the Fiddle
8/24	1			1	146		All This And Heaven Too	Eddie DeLange/Jimmy Van Heusen			Jimmy Dorsey (Bob Eberly)
7/27	1			1	147		Woodpecker	Harold Adamson/Eldo DiLazzaro			Glahé Musette Orchestra
11/30	1			1	148		You Are My Sunshine	Jimmie Davis/Charles Mitchell <A:2>			Wayne King
8/3	1			1	149		All This And Heaven Too	Eddie DeLange/Jimmy Van Heusen	❶		Jack Leonard
9/14	1			1	150		Adios, Mariquita Linda	Marcos Jiménez <A:1>			Artie Shaw
8/3	1			1	151		I'm Stepping Out With A Memory To-Night	Herb Magidson/Allie Wrubel			Kate Smith
12/28	1			1	152		A Nightingale Sang In Berkeley Square	Eric Maschwitz/Manning Sherwin			Dick Todd
8/31	1			1	153		All This And Heaven Too	Eddie DeLange/Jimmy Van Heusen			Dick Todd

1941

NATIONAL NEWS: December 7, "a date which will live in infamy," brings the United States into World War II as 360 Japanese warplanes attack the American military base at Pearl Harbor. The U.S. declaration of war occurs nine months after President Roosevelt signed the Lend-Lease Act authorizing war supplies to the Allies. It is a year of U.S. labor strife with steel, copper and coal strikes; Henry Ford recognizes the United Auto Workers. FDR creates a federal price control office to prevent spiraling prices in wartime. Scrap iron becomes a precious metal in a national steel shortage.

INTERNATIONAL NEWS: German forces launch a massive assault on Russia; after putting Moscow and Leningrad in a state of siege, Germany faces a strong counterattack at year's end. Axis forces take over Greece and invade Yugoslavia. British and Allied troops score victories in the Middle East and East Africa. On May 7, the British royal navy sinks the feared German warship, the Bismarck, after a 1,750-mile pursuit. Joseph Stalin becomes commander-in-chief of Soviet forces.

COMMERCE AND SCIENCE: The world's largest dam, the Grand Coulee, opens in Washington state. CBS and NBC begin regular television news broadcasts, although only 6,000 TV sets are owned nationwide.

FADS AND FASHION: Jitterbugging is the nation's hottest dance.

SPORTS: In a year of historic achievement for baseball, Joe DiMaggio compiles an epic 56-game hitting streak and Ted Williams bats .406. DiMaggio's New York Yankees whip their crosstown rivals, the Brooklyn Dodgers, in a five-game World Series. Joe Louis defends his heavyweight crown seven times, although he must rally to defeat Billy Conn. The Chicago Bears repeat as NFL champions defeating the New York Giants, 37-9. Minnesota is the #1 college football team for the second straight year. Bobby Riggs wins his second U.S. tennis championship.

MOVIES: Orson Welles' *Citizen Kane* is one of the towering achievements in the history of cinema, but Oscar voters choose John Ford's *How Green Was My Valley* (Best Picture), Gary Cooper in *Sergeant York* and Joan Fontaine in *Suspicion*. Humphrey Bogart heads a stellar cast in the classic *The Maltese Falcon*. The year's animated Disney hit is *Dumbo*. Mickey Rooney is America's top box office star for the third straight year.

RADIO: Among the many popular variety shows are *Army Hour*, *Bing Crosby*, *Ed Sullivan Entertains*, *Stage Door Canteen*, and *This Is Fort Dix*. The Federal Communications Commission orders NBC to sell its Blue Network, which later becomes ABC. On December 9, an estimated 90 million people worldwide listen to FDR's "Day of Infamy" speech.

THEATER: Rodgers & Hart's *Pal Joey* is the year's top musical, while Noel Coward's *Blithe Spirit* is the season's most honored comedy. *Arsenic and Old Lace* is a comedy box-office sensation. Marian Anderson performs her historic concert at the Lincoln Memorial.

BOOKS: F. Scott Fitzgerald's *The Last Tycoon* and William Shirer's *Berlin Diary* are among the year's most acclaimed works.

1941 — TOP 20 ARTISTS

1. Glenn Miller	2. Jimmy Dorsey	3. Tommy Dorsey
1,414	1,412	1,017

4.	673	Bing Crosby	13.	283	Wayne King
5.	477	Gene Krupa	14.	272	Benny Goodman
6.	457	Freddy Martin	15.	272	Vaughn Monroe
7.	418	Horace Heidt	16.	255	Xavier Cugat
8.	408	Sammy Kaye	17.	232	Eddy Duchin
9.	315	Kay Kyser	18.	231	Will Bradley
10.	309	Artie Shaw	19.	228	Charlie Barnet
11.	304	Harry James	20.	206	Bob Crosby
12.	293	Woody Herman			

1941 — TOP SONGWRITERS

	# of Hits	Points			# of Hits	Points	
1.	15	1,336	Alex Kramer	7.	7	618	Stanley Cowan
	15	1,336	Joan Whitney	8.	7	617	Alberto Dominguez
3.	13	1,149	Hy Zaret	9.	6	516	Ben Raleigh
4.	9	780	Heinz Provost		6	516	Bernie Wayne
5.	8	714	Bobby Worth	11.	5	458	Leo Killion
6.	8	684	Robert Henning		5	458	Ted McMichael
					5	458	Jack Owens

1941 — TOP ARTIST DEBUTS

1.	5/31	Alvino Rey (93)	5.	8/02	Charlie Spivak (44)
2.	6/14	The Jesters (122)	6.	9/13	Sam Donahue (71)
3.	6/28	Tony Pastor (57)	7.	10/11 †	Les Brown (33)
4.	7/05	Four King Sisters (101)			

PEAK DATE	WEEKS				RANK	GOLD	Title	PEAK POSITION / Songwriter(s)	SYMBL	DEBUT	Artist
	CH	10	5	PK							

1

3/29	14	14	11	10	1	●	**Amapola** (Pretty Little Poppy) ....Albert Gamse/Joseph Lacalle				**Jimmy Dorsey**
							Best Seller: 7,1,1,1,1,1,1,1,1,1,1,2,6,8				(Bob Eberly/Helen O'Connell)
11/29	23	23	20	9	2	●	**Chattanooga Choo Choo** ....Mack Gordon/Harry Warren <B:19>				**Glenn Miller** (Tex Beneke)
							Best Seller: 9,6,2,3,2,2,3,2,2,2,1,1,1,2,1,1,1,1,1,1,2,6				
10/4	24	24	18	8	3	●	**Piano Concerto In B Flat** ....Pyotr Ilyich Tchaikovsky <B:17> [I]				**Freddy Martin**
							Best Seller: 8,9,9,8,7,8,5,3,1,1,1,1,1,1,1,1,2,2,3,3,3,4,3,4				
6/21	15	15	14	8	4		**Daddy** ....Bobby Troup				**Sammy Kaye**
							Best Seller: 5,3,1,3,2,1,1,1,1,1,1,2,5,7				
8/30	21	21	12	4	5	●	**Green Eyes** (Aquellos Ojos Verdes) ......Nilo Menendez/Edil Rivera/Adolfo Utrera/				**Jimmy Dorsey**
							Best Seller:6,7,8,8,8,6,9,5,7,3,3,3,2,2,1,1,1,1,4,5,8 Eddie Woods <A:1>				(Bob Eberly/Helen O'Connell)
6/14	17	17	15	2	6		**Maria Elena** ....Lorenza Barcelata <A:1>				**Jimmy Dorsey** (Bob Eberly)
							Best Seller: 9,5,3,1,2,4,1,2,2,2,2,2,3,3,6,3,5				
6/7	10	10	8	2	7		**My Sister And I** ....Alex Kramer/Joan Whitney/Hy Zaret				**Jimmy Dorsey** (Bob Eberly)
							Best Seller: 2,3,2,1,4,4,1,5,10,10				
12/20	15	15	13	1	8		**Elmer's Tune** ....Elmer Albrecht/Sammy Gallop/Dick Jurgens				**Glenn Miller** (Ray Eberle)
							Best Seller: 4,3,4,3,3,2,1,2,2,2,2,4,8,9				
9/27	14	14	7	1	9		**Blue Champagne** ....Frank Ryerson/Grady Watts				**Jimmy Dorsey** (Bob Eberly)
							Best Seller: 6,6,7,4,9,3,2,1,4,4,6,9,10				
3/15	8	8	6	1	10		**Song Of The Volga Boatmen** ....(traditional) [I]				**Glenn Miller**
							Best Seller: 9,8,4,1,4,2,5,4				

2

3/15	12	12	9	6	11		**Oh! Look At Me Now** ....John DeVries <B:16>				Tommy Dorsey (Frank Sinatra/ Connie Haines/Pied Pipers)
1/25	11	11	7	6	12		**I Hear A Rhapsody** ....Jack Baker/George Fragos/Dick Gasparre				Charlie Barnet (Bob Carroll)
10/4	11	11	9	2	13		**I Don't Want To Set The World On Fire** ....Bennie Benjamin/Eddie Durham/				Horace Heidt (Larry Cotton/Donna Wood)
							Sol Marcus/Eddie Seiler				
9/6	13	13	7	2	14		**Yours** (Quiereme Mucho) ....Albert Gamse/Gonzalo Roig/Jack Sherr				Jimmy Dorsey
											(Bob Eberly/Helen O'Connell)
5/10	9	9	6	1	15		**Dolores** ....Louis Alter/Frank Loesser				Bing Crosby
6/28	9	9	6	1	16		**The Hut-Sut Song** (A Swedish Serenade) ...Leo Killion/Ted McMichael/Jack Owens				Freddy Martin (Eddie Stone)
5/24	6	6	5	1	17		**G'bye Now** ....Ray Evans/Harold Johnson/Jay Levison/John Olsen				Horace Heidt (Ronnie Kemper)
3/8	6	6	4	1	18		**High On A Windy Hill** ....Alex Kramer/Joan Whitney <A:2>				Gene Krupa (Howard DuLany)
1/11	7	7	3	1	19		**Scrub Me, Mama, With A Boogie Beat** ....Don Raye <B:5>				Will Bradley Feat. Ray McKinley
3/22	5	5	3	1	20		**It All Comes Back To Me Now** ....Alex Kramer/Joan Whitney/Hy Zaret <A:2>				Gene Krupa (Howard DuLany)
1/4	4	4	1	1	21		**Down Argentina Way** ....Mack Gordon/Harry Warren				Bob Crosby (Bonnie King)
6/14	3	3	1	1	22		**Maria Elena** ....Lorenza Barcelata <B:20> [I]				Wayne King

3

11/22	16	16	12	4	23		**This Love Of Mine** ....Sol Parker/Henry Sanicola/Frank Sinatra				Tommy Dorsey (Frank Sinatra)
3/22	13	13	6	4	24		**Perfidia**..Alberto Dominguez/Milton Leeds [I]				Xavier Cugat
1/25	10	10	6	4	25		**I Hear A Rhapsody** ....Jack Baker/George Fragos/Dick Gasparre				Jimmy Dorsey (Bob Eberly)
7/5	6	6	4	2	26		**The Hut-Sut Song** (A Swedish Serenade) ...Leo Killion/Ted McMichael/Jack Owens				Horace Heidt (Donna Wood)
2/8	10	10	6	1	27		**Anvil Chorus–Parts 1 & 2**......................Glenn Miller/Giuseppe Verdi [I]				Glenn Miller
4/5	4	4	1	1	28		**I Dreamt I Dwelt In Harlem** ....Jerry Gray/Ben Smith/Leonard Ware/Robert Wright [I]				Glenn Miller
4/26	3	3	1	1	29		**Alexander The Swoose** (Half Swan–Half Goose) ....Glenn Burrs/Ben Forrest/				Kay Kyser (Harry Babbitt/Ginny Simms)
							Frank Furlett/Leonard Keller [N]				

4

8/9	14	14	7	8	30		**Yes Indeed!**...Sy Oliver				Tommy Dorsey (Sy Oliver/Jo Stafford)
4/19	3	3	3	2	31		**Do I Worry?** ....Stanley Cowan/Bobby Worth				Tommy Dorsey (Frank Sinatra/Pied Pipers)
10/25	10	10	2	1	32		**I Don't Want To Set The World On Fire** ....Bennie Benjamin/Eddie Durham/				Tommy Tucker Time (Amy Arnell)
							Sol Marcus/Eddie Seiler				
11/1	8	8	2	1	33		**I Don't Want To Set The World On Fire** ....Bennie Benjamin/Eddie Durham/				Ink Spots
							Sol Marcus/Eddie Seiler				
9/6	6	6	1	1	34		**You And I**...Meredith Willson				Glenn Miller (Ray Eberle)

5

5/3	11	11	5	5	35		**I'll Be With You In Apple Blossom Time** ....Neville Fleeson/Albert Von Tilzer				Andrews Sisters
6/14	13	13	4	4	36		**Souvenir De Vienne** ....Heinz Provost				Wayne King
12/20	6	6	4	4	37		**Shepherd Serenade** ....Kermit Goell/Fred Spielman				Bing Crosby
12/6	10	10	5	2	38	●	**You Made Me Love You** (I Didn't Want To Do It) ....Joseph McCarthy/				Harry James
							James Monaco <B:19> [I]				
10/11	9	9	2	2	39		**Jim**................................Caesar Petrillo/Edward Ross/Nelson Shawn				Jimmy Dorsey
											(Bob Eberly/Helen O'Connell)
11/29	8	8	2	2	40		**Tonight We Love** (Concerto No. 1, B Flat Minor).......Ray Austin/Freddy Martin/				Tony Martin
							Bobby Worth				

PEAK DATE	WEEKS CH	WEEKS 10	WEEKS 5	WEEKS PK	RANK	GOLD	Title / Peak Position / Songwriter(s)	SYMBL	DEBUT	Artist

5 (cont'd)

PEAK DATE	CH	10	5	PK	RANK	GOLD	Title / Songwriter(s)	SYM	DEB	Artist
4/26	4	4	1	1	41		Blue Flame .... *James Noble* [I]			Woody Herman
2/8	3	3	1	1	42		There I Go .... *Irving Weiser/Hy Zaret* <A:2>			Will Bradley Feat. Ray McKinley (Jimmy Valentine)
10/25	3	3	1	1	43		"Jim" .... *Caesar Petrillo/Edward Ross/Nelson Shawn*			Dinah Shore
3/15	2	2	1	1	44		It All Comes Back To Me Now .... *Alex Kramer/Joan Whitney/Hy Zaret*			Hal Kemp (Bob Allen)
12/27	2	2	1	1	45		Jingle Bells .... *James Pierpont* [X]			Glenn Miller (Tex Beneke/Ernie Caceres)

6

PEAK DATE	CH	10	5	PK	RANK	GOLD	Title / Songwriter(s)	SYM	DEB	Artist
2/22	6	6		3	46		You Walk By .... *Ben Raleigh/Bernie Wayne*			Eddy Duchin (Johnny Drake)
8/23	5	5		1	47		'Til Reveille .... *Stanley Cowan/Bobby Worth*			Bing Crosby
1/4	5	5		1	48		Ferry-Boat Serenade .... *Harold Adamson/Eldo DiLazzaro*			Kay Kyser (Harry Babbitt/Ginny Simms)
8/16	4	4		1	49		'Til Reveille .... *Stanley Cowan/Bobby Worth*			Kay Kyser (Harry Babbitt/Ginny Simms)
5/24	4	4		1	50		The Band Played On .... *John Palmer/Charles Ward*			Guy Lombardo (Kenny Gardner)
9/13	4	4		1	51		You And I .... *Meredith Willson*			Bing Crosby
1/18	3	3		1	52	●	Star Dust .... *Hoagy Carmichael/Mitchell Parish* [I]			Artie Shaw
4/26	3	3		1	53		There'll Be Some Changes Made .... *Billy Higgins/W. Benton Overstreet*			Benny Goodman (Louise Tobin)
1/11	2	2		1	54		Five O'Clock Whistle .... *Kim Gannon/Gene Irwin/Josef Myrow*			Glenn Miller (Marion Hutton)

7

PEAK DATE	CH	10	5	PK	RANK	GOLD	Title / Songwriter(s)	SYM	DEB	Artist
12/13	5	5		2	55		Shepherd Serenade .... *Kermit Goell/Fred Spielman*			Horace Heidt (Larry Cotton/Fred Lowery)
8/16	5	5		1	56		The Boogie Woogie Piggy .... *Roy Jacobs* <B:19>			Glenn Miller (Tex Beneke)
1/18	4	4		1	57		Along The Santa Fe Trail .... *Edwina Coolidge/Al Dubin/Will Grosz*			Glenn Miller (Ray Eberle)
4/12	3	3		1	58	●	New San Antonio Rose .... *Bob Wills*			Bing Crosby
7/12	3	3		1	59		The Things I Love .... *Harold Barlow/Lew Harris*			Jimmy Dorsey (Bob Eberly)
4/19	2	2		1	60		The Wise Old Owl .... *Joe Ricardel*			Al Donahue (Dee Keating)
4/26	2	2		1	61		Dolores .... *Louis Alter/Frank Loesser*			Tommy Dorsey (Frank Sinatra/Pied Pipers)
5/10	2	2		1	62		Let's Get Away From It All-Parts 1 & 2 .... *Tom Adair/Matt Dennis*			Tommy Dorsey (Frank Sinatra/ Connie Haines/Pied Pipers)
7/5	2	2		1	63		Intermezzo .... *Robert Henning/Heinz Provost*			Freddy Martin (Clyde Rogers)
8/9	2	2		1	64		The Hut-Sut Song (A Swedish Serenade) .... *Leo Killion/Ted McMichael/Jack Owens*		❶	The Four King Sisters
2/22	1	1		1	65		High On A Windy Hill .... *Alex Kramer/Joan Whitney* <B:14>			Jimmy Dorsey (Bob Eberly)
1/4	1	1		1	66		Star Dust .... *Hoagy Carmichael/Mitchell Parish*			Tommy Dorsey (Frank Sinatra/Pied Pipers)

8

PEAK DATE	CH	10	5	PK	RANK	GOLD	Title / Songwriter(s)	SYM	DEB	Artist
11/29	6	6		1	67		Elmer's Tune .... *Elmer Albrecht/Sammy Gallop/Dick Jurgens* [I]			Dick Jurgens
7/26	2	2		1	68		Good Bye Dear, I'll Be Back In A Year .... *Mack Kay*			Horace Heidt (Ronnie Kemper/Donna Wood)

9

PEAK DATE	CH	10	5	PK	RANK	GOLD	Title / Songwriter(s)	SYM	DEB	Artist
4/5	2	2		1	69	●	Dancing In The Dark .... *Howard Dietz/Arthur Schwartz* [I] {re-charted in 1944 (#21)}			Artie Shaw
2/8	1	1		1	70		High On A Windy Hill .... *Alex Kramer/Joan Whitney*			Will Bradley Feat. Ray McKinley (Jimmy Valentine)
5/3	1	1		1	71		Everything Happens To Me .... *Tom Adair/Matt Dennis*			Tommy Dorsey (Frank Sinatra)
12/20	1	1		1	72		Two In Love .... *Meredith Willson* <B:20>			Tommy Dorsey (Frank Sinatra)
1/4	1	1		1	73		Five O'Clock Whistle .... *Kim Gannon/Gene Irwin/Josef Myrow*			Ella Fitzgerald
4/12	1	1		1	74		Music Makers .... *Harry James* [I]			Harry James
8/2	1	1		1	75		Just A Little Bit South Of North Carolina .... *Bette Cannon/Arthur Shaftel/ Sunny Skylar*			Gene Krupa (Anita O'Day)
6/28	1	1		1	76		Maria Elena .... *Lorenza Barcelata*		❶	Tony Pastor (Dorsey Anderson)
3/15	1	1		1	77		I Hear A Rhapsody .... *Jack Baker/George Fragos/Dick Gasparre*			Dinah Shore

10

PEAK DATE	CH	10	5	PK	RANK	GOLD	Title / Songwriter(s)	SYM	DEB	Artist
2/15	2	2		2	78		Concerto For Clarinet (Parts 1 & 2) .... *Artie Shaw* [I]			Artie Shaw
10/25	1	1		1	79		Time Was (Duerme) .... *Miguel Prado/S.K. Russell*			Jimmy Dorsey (Bob Eberly/Helen O'Connell)
6/28	1	1		1	80		G'bye Now .... *Ray Evans/Harold Johnson/Jay Levison/John Olsen*			Woody Herman (Muriel Lane)
8/30	1	1		1	81		Lament To Love .... *Mel Torme*			Harry James (Dick Haymes)
5/24	1	1		1	82		Until Tomorrow (Goodnight My Love) .... *Sammy Kaye*			Sammy Kaye (Three Kadets)
9/6	1	1		1	83		Let Me Off Uptown .... *Earl Bostic/Redd Evans*			Gene Krupa (Anita O'Day/Roy Eldridge)
11/29	1	1		1	84		Blues In The Night .... *Harold Arlen/Johnny Mercer*			Artie Shaw ("Hot Lips" Page)
2/8	1	1		1	85	●	Summit Ridge Drive .... *Artie Shaw* [I] {re-charted in 1944 (#24)}			Artie Shaw
1/25	1	1		1	86		Yes, My Darling Daughter .... *Jack Lawrence*			Dinah Shore
8/2	1	1		1	87		Intermezzo (A Love Story) .... *Robert Henning/Heinz Provost* [I]		❶	Charlie Spivak

12

PEAK DATE	CH	10	5	PK	RANK	GOLD	Title / Songwriter(s)	SYM	DEB	Artist
4/12	2			1	88		Help Me (Cuatro Vidas) .... *Justo Carreras/Xavier Cugat/Joe Farver/Sam Ward* [F]			Abe Lyman (Dale Evans/Lucio Garcia)
3/29	1			1	89		Perfidia (Tonight) .... *Alberto Dominguez/Milton Leeds*			Benny Goodman (Helen Forrest)

PEAK DATE	CH	10	5	PK	RANK	GOLD	Title / Songwriter(s)	SYMBOL / DEBUT	Artist

13

PEAK DATE	CH	10	5	PK	RANK	GOLD	Title — Songwriter(s)	Sym/Deb	Artist
4/19	4			2	90		Perfidia ....Alberto Dominguez/Milton Leeds		Glenn Miller (Dorothy Claire)
8/2	7			1	91		Take The "A" Train ....Billy Strayhorn [I]		Duke Ellington
6/14	4			1	92		Flamingo ....Edmund Anderson/Ted Grouya		Duke Ellington (Herb Jeffries)
7/19	3			1	93		The Things I Love ....Harold Barlow/Lew Harris ◗		Barry Wood
4/5	2			1	94		Tonight (Perfidia)...............................Alberto Dominguez/Milton Leeds		Gene Krupa (Howard DuLany)
2/8	2			1	95 ●		San Antonio Rose ....Bob Wills [I] ◗		Bob Wills
6/28	1			1	96		Just A Little Bit South Of North Carolina ....Bette Cannon/Arthur Shaftel/Sunny Skylar		Mitchell Ayres (Mary Ann Mercer)
1/11	1			1	97		There I Go ....Irving Weiser/Hy Zaret		Woody Herman
3/29	1			1	98		There'll Be Some Changes Made...............Billy Higgins/W. Benton Overstreet		Gene Krupa (Irene Daye)

14

PEAK DATE	CH	10	5	PK	RANK	GOLD	Title — Songwriter(s)	Sym/Deb	Artist
5/10	11			1	99		I Understand ....Kim Gannon/Mabel Wayne <A:7>		Jimmy Dorsey (Bob Eberly)
5/24	4			1	100		Do I Worry? ....Stanley Cowan/Bobby Worth <B:17>		Ink Spots
2/8	3			1	101		So You're The One...................Alex Kramer/Joan Whitney/Hy Zaret <A:14>		Eddy Duchin (June Robbins)
1/25	2			1	102		I Give You My Word ....Al Kavelin/Merrill Lyn <A:14>		Eddy Duchin (June Robbins)
1/4	1			1	103		You've Got Me This Way ....Jimmy McHugh/Johnny Mercer		Tommy Dorsey (Pied Pipers)
1/4	1			1	104		Along The Santa Fe Trail ....Edwina Coolidge/Al Dubin/Will Grosz		Sammy Kaye (Jimmy Brown)
3/1	1			1	105		You Walk By ....Ben Raleigh/Bernie Wayne [I]		Wayne King
6/14	1			1	106		G'bye Now......................Ray Evans/Harold Johnson/Jay Levison/John Olsen		Vaughn Monroe (Marilyn Duke)
6/21	1			1	107		The Things I Love ....Harold Barlow/Lew Harris		Teddy Powell (Ruth Gaylor)

15

PEAK DATE	CH	10	5	PK	RANK	GOLD	Title — Songwriter(s)	Sym/Deb	Artist
4/5	6			1	108		You Forgot About Me....................James Hanley/Sammy Mysels/Dick Robertson		Bob Crosby
5/3	4			1	109		Boogie Woogie Bugle Boy ....Hughie Prince/Don Raye		Andrews Sisters
3/15	4			1	110		High On A Windy Hill ....Alex Kramer/Joan Whitney		Vaughn Monroe
3/1	3			1	111		You Walk By ....Ben Raleigh/Bernie Wayne		Kenny Baker
10/25	3			1	112		I Guess I'll Have To Dream The Rest....Martin Block/Harold Green/Mickey Stoner		Tommy Dorsey (Frank Sinatra/Pied Pipers)
9/20	3			1	113		Foolish..................Lorenzo Bills/Sam Ginsberg/Harry Sukman <B:17> ◗		Art Jarrett (Gale Robbins)
7/26	3			1	114		The Hut-Sut Song A Swedish Serenade .....Leo Killion/Ted McMichael/Jack Owens		The Merry Macs
3/22	2			1	115		Tonight (Perfidia) ....Alberto Dominguez/Milton Leeds [I]		Jimmy Dorsey
1/11	2			1	116		A Nightingale Sang In Berkeley Square ....Eric Maschwitz/Manning Sherwin		Ray Noble (Larry Stewart)
6/21	2			1	117		Nighty-Night ....Leslie Beacon ◗		Alvino Rey (Yvonne King)
5/24	2			1	118		My Sister And I..................Alex Kramer/Joan Whitney/Hy Zaret		Bea Wain
4/12	1			1	119		One O'Clock Jump................................Count Basie [I] ✦		Metronome All Star Band
5/17	1			1	120		Intermezzo.........................Robert Henning/Heinz Provost [I] ✦		Toscha Seidel

16

PEAK DATE	CH	10	5	PK	RANK	GOLD	Title — Songwriter(s)	Sym/Deb	Artist
10/11	3			3	121		Joltin' Joe DiMaggio................................Alan Courtney/Ben Homer [N]		Les Brown (Betty Bonney)
9/20	3			1	122		You And I..Meredith Willson		Tommy Dorsey (Frank Sinatra)
9/27	3			1	123		I Guess I'll Have To Dream The Rest...Martin Block/Harold Green/Mickey Stoner		Glenn Miller (Ray Eberle)
3/1	3			1	124		You Walk By ....Ben Raleigh/Bernie Wayne		Tommy Tucker Time (Amy Arnell/Don Brown)
8/30	2			1	125		Kiss The Boys Goodbye ....Frank Loesser/Victor Schertzinger		Tommy Dorsey (Connie Haines)
5/17	2			1	126		New San Antonio Rose ....Bob Wills		Bob Wills (Tommy Duncan)
12/27	1			1	127 ●		Silent Night......................................Franz Gruber [X-R]		Bing Crosby
1/11	1			1	128		You've Got Me This Way.............Jimmy McHugh/Johnny Mercer <B:19>		Jimmy Dorsey (Helen O'Connell)
3/22	1			1	129		You Might Have Belonged To Another ....Lucille Harmon/Pat West <A:2>		Tommy Dorsey (Frank Sinatra/Connie Haines/Pied Pipers)
2/15	1			1	130		It All Comes Back To Me Now.................Alex Kramer/Joan Whitney/Hy Zaret		Eddy Duchin (June Robbins)
1/25	1			1	131		Frenesí ....Ray Charles/Alberto Dominguez/S.K. Russell		Woody Herman
4/19	1			1	132		Walkin' By The River ....Una Carlisle/Robert Sour ◗		Ginny Simms

17

PEAK DATE	CH	10	5	PK	RANK	GOLD	Title — Songwriter(s)	Sym/Deb	Artist
8/9	4			1	133		The Reluctant Dragon....................Ed Penner/Charles Wolcott/Hee Wolcott [N]		Sammy Kaye (George Gingell/Maury Cross)
6/7	4			1	134		Intermezzo (Souvenir de Vienne) ....Robert Henning/Heinz Provost [I]		Guy Lombardo
11/15	4			1	135		Adios ....Enric Madriguera/Eddie Woods [I] {re-charted in 1948 (#28)}		Glenn Miller
3/15	2			1	136		May I Never Love Again ....Jack Erickson/Sano Marco		Bob Chester (Dolores O'Neill)
3/1	2			1	137		Java Jive ....Milton Drake/Ben Oakland <A:14>		Ink Spots
3/1	2			1	138		So You're The One................Alex Kramer/Joan Whitney/Hy Zaret <B:19>		Hal Kemp (Janet Blair)
8/23	2			1	139		Daddy ....Bobby Troup ✦		Joan Merrill
9/6	2			1	140		The Cowboy Serenade (While I'm Rollin' My Last Cigarette) ....Rich Hall		Glenn Miller (Ray Eberle)
2/8	1			1	141		Southern Fried....................................Fred Culliver <A:17> [I]		Charlie Barnet
9/20	1			1	142		Green Eyes (Ojos Verdes)....Nilo Menendez/Edil Rivera/Adolfo Utrera/Eddie Woods [I]		Xavier Cugat
5/3	1			1	143		Intermezzo (A Love Story) ....Robert Henning/Heinz Provost [I]		Benny Goodman

PEAK DATE	WEEKS				RANK	GOLD	Title	PEAK POSITION Songwriter(s)	SYMBL	DEBUT	Artist
	CH	10	5	PK							

17 (cont'd)

PEAK DATE	CH	10	5	PK	RANK	Title	Songwriter(s)	Artist
11/29	1			1	144	Shepherd Serenade	Kermit Goell/Fred Spielman <A:15>	Art Jarrett (The Smoothies)
1/18	1			1	145	I Give You My Word	Al Kavelin/Merril Lyn	Jack Leonard
8/16	1			1	146	Why Don't We Do This More Often?	Charles Newman/Allie Wrubel <A:1>	Freddy Martin (Eddie Stone)

18

PEAK DATE	CH	10	5	PK	RANK	Title	Songwriter(s)	Artist
2/8	4			2	147	So You're The One	Alex Kramer/Joan Whitney/Hy Zaret	Vaughn Monroe
3/15	2			1	148	Nona	Sam Lowe [I]	Erskine Hawkins
12/13	2			1	149	Minka	Jay Milton	Sammy Kaye (Tommy Ryan)
11/22	2			1	150	Why Don't We Do This More Often?	Charles Newman/Allie Wrubel	Kay Kyser (Ginny Simms/Harry Babbitt)
3/22	2			1	151	Frenesi	Ray Charles/Alberto Dominguez/S.K. Russell [I]	Glenn Miller
8/9	2			1	152	Yours (Quieréme Mucho)	Albert Gamse/Gonzalo Roig/Jack Sherr	Vaughn Monroe (Marilyn Duke)
2/15	1			1	153	Scrub Me Mama With A Boogie Beat	Don Raye	Andrews Sisters
3/15	1			1	154	Whatcha Know Joe	James Young	Charlie Barnet (Ford Leary)
2/15	1			1	155	Along The Santa Fe Trail	Edwina Coolidge/Al Dubin/Will Grosz	Bing Crosby
11/29	1			1	156	The Whistler's Mother-In-Law	Bert Stevens/Larry Wagner	Bing Crosby with Muriel Lane
10/25	1			1	157	Do You Care?	Jack Elliott/Lew Quadling	Bob Crosby
6/28	1			1	158	Georgia On My Mind	Hoagy Carmichael/Stuart Gorrell	Gene Krupa (Anita O'Day)
4/19	1			1	159	The Wise Old Owl	Joe Ricardel ❶	Teddy Powell (Ruth Gaylor)

19

PEAK DATE	CH	10	5	PK	RANK	Title	Songwriter(s)	Artist
2/1	3			2	160	You Walk By	Ben Raleigh/Bernie Wayne	Blue Barron (Russ Carlyle)
12/27	2			1	161	'Tis Autumn	Henry Nemo	Les Brown (Ralph Young)
6/28	2			1	162	Boulder Buff	Fred Norman/Eugene Novello <A:7> [I]	Glenn Miller
10/11	1			1	163	I Don't Want To Set The World On Fire	Bennie Benjamin/Eddie Durham/ Sol Marcus/Eddie Seiler	Mitchell Ayres (Meredith Blake)
5/31	1			1	164	My Sister And I	Alex Kramer/Joan Whitney/Hy Zaret	Bob Chester (Bill Darnell)
9/6	1			1	165	Quierme Mucho (Yours)	Albert Gamse/Gonzalo Roig/Jack Sherr	Xavier Cugat (Dinah Shore)
3/1	1			1	166	I Hear A Rhapsody	Jack Baker/George Fragos/Dick Gasparre	Al Donahue (Phil Brito)
9/13	1			1	167	Do You Care?	Jack Elliott/Lew Quadling ❶	Sam Donahue (Irene Daye)
1/11	1			1	168	The Bad Humor Man	Jimmy McHugh/Johnny Mercer <A:16> [N]	Jimmy Dorsey (Helen O'Connell)
5/17	1			1	169	My Sister And I	Alex Kramer/Joan Whitney/Hy Zaret	Benny Goodman (Helen Forrest)
8/16	1			1	170	Yours	Albert Gamse/Gonzalo Roig/Jack Sherr	Benny Goodman (Helen Forrest)
12/13	1			1	171	A Sinner Kissed An Angel	Mack David/Ray Joseph <A:5>	Harry James (Dick Haymes)
10/18	1			1	172	Trumpet Rhapsody (Parts I & II)	Harry James/Jack Matthias [I]	Harry James
5/24	1			1	173	Walkin' By The River	Una Carlisle/Robert Sour <A:17>	Hal Kemp (Janet Blair)
5/10	1			1	174	The Wise Old Owl	Joe Ricardel	Kay Kyser (Sully Mason)
6/21	1			1	175	Intermezzo (A Love Story)	Robert Henning/Heinz Provost [I]	Clyde Lucas
4/26	1			1	176	Intermezzo	Robert Henning/Heinz Provost [I]	Enric Madriguera
9/20	1			1	177	'Til Reveille	Stanley Cowan/Bobby Worth	Freddy Martin (Clyde Rogers)
7/5	1			1	178	Daddy	Bobby Troup	Frankie Masters (Swingmasters)
11/29	1			1	179	I Know Why	Mack Gordon/Harry Warren <A:1>	Glenn Miller (Paula Kelly)
7/5	1			1	180	The Things I Love	Harold Barlow/Lew Harris	Jan Savitt (Allan DeWitt)
12/27	1			1	181	Let's Go Home	Peanuts Holland/Sande Williams [I]	Charlie Spivak

20

PEAK DATE	CH	10	5	PK	RANK	Title	Songwriter(s)	Artist
10/18	2			2	182	Snowfall	Claude Thornhill [X-I]	Claude Thornhill
3/29	1			1	183	You Walk By	Ben Raleigh/Bernie Wayne	Bobby Byrne (Jerry Wayne)
9/13	1			1	184	Be Honest With Me	Gene Autry/Fred Rose	Bing Crosby
11/29	1			1	185	Clementine	Woody Harris	Bing Crosby
8/30	1			1	186	You Are My Sunshine	Jimmie Davis/Charles Mitchell	Bing Crosby
7/5	1			1	187	Intermezzo (A Love Story)	Robert Henning/Heinz Provost [I]	Xavier Cugat
12/20	1			1	188	A Sinner Kissed An Angel	Mack David/Ray Joseph <A:9>	Tommy Dorsey (Frank Sinatra)
12/6	1			1	189	By-U By-O (The Lou'siana Lullaby)	Leo Killion/Ted McMichael/Jack Owens	Woody Herman (Muriel Lane)
6/14	1			1	190	The Band Played On	John Palmer/Charles Ward ❶	The Jesters
8/23	1			1	191	'Til Reveille	Stanley Cowan/Bobby Worth	Wayne King
11/29	1			1	192	I'm Thrilled	Sylvia Dee/Sid Lippman	Glenn Miller (Ray Eberle)
11/15	1			1	193	It Happened In Sun Valley	Mack Gordon/Harry Warren	Glenn Miller (Paula Kelly/Ray Eberle/Tex Beneke)
3/1	1			1	194	There'll Be Some Changes Made	Billy Higgins/W. Benton Overstreet	Vaughn Monroe (Marilyn Duke)
7/26	1			1	195	Green Eyes (Aquellos Ojos Verdes)	Nilo Menendez/Edil Rivera/ Adolfo Utrera/Eddie Woods	Tony Pastor (Dorsey Anderson)
12/27	1			1	196	Autumn Nocturne	Kim Gannon/Josef Myrow [I]	Claude Thornhill
4/12	1			1	197	Do I Worry?	Stanley Cowan/Bobby Worth	Bea Wain
3/15	1			1	198	It All Comes Back To Me Now	Alex Kramer/Joan Whitney/Hy Zaret	Ted Weems (Perry Como)
2/22	1			1	199	There'll Be Some Changes Made	Billy Higgins/W. Benton Overstreet	Ted Weems (Mary Lee)

1942

NATIONAL NEWS: Wartime brings sacrifices on the homefront as gasoline rationing goes into effect on a natiowide basis, and FDR freezes wages, rents and farm prices. Meat, coffee, butter and shoes are scarce. Scrap metal and rubber drives are carried out to preserve precious resources, and "Victory Gardens" are grown by many families. Following a presidential order, the government begins the West Coast internment of 100,000 Japanese-Americans even when there is no evidence of disloyalty. The national landmark of Mt. Rushmore is completed.

INTERNATIONAL NEWS: A U.S. naval assault forces the Japanese navy to withdraw near Midway Island, but elsewhere in the Pacific the Japanese capture Singapore, Burma and the Philippines. The prolonged German assault into Russia continues to meet fierce resistance. The Nazi campaign in North Africa turns into a full-scale retreat following a British and U.S. counterstrike. Nazi leaders decide on their fateful "Final Solution" to round up and murder millions of Jews in concentration camps.

COMMERCE AND SCIENCE: U.S. scientists led by Enrico Fermi achieve the first controlled atomic fission reaction. Millions of American women enter the workforce; and, for the first time, many are employed in heavy industry such as steel.

FADS AND FASHION: The zoot suit is considered the height of flashy male fashion. Slacks for women become more popular.

SPORTS: The St. Louis Cardinals top the New York Yankees in the World Series five games to one. The Washington Redskins gain a measure of revenge for 1940 by defeating the Chicago Bears, 14-6, for the NFL championship. Heavyweight champ Joe Louis retires to tour Army camps after two more title defenses, although he will return four years later. Ohio State is #1 in college football. In golf, Byron Nelson outduels Ben Hogan in a playoff at the Masters.

MOVIES: The Oscar-winning *Mrs. Miniver* starring Greer Garson (Best Actress) captures the wartime spirit, and James Cagney's (Best Actor) performance in *Yankee Doodle Dandy* also stirs patriotic emotions. Gary Cooper is a memorable Lou Gehrig in *Pride of the Yankees*. Orson Welles' acclaimed followup to *Citizen Kane* is *The Magnificent Ambersons*. Katharine Hepburn and Spencer Tracy begin their long screen partnership in *Woman of the Year*. *Bambi* is another Disney animated triumph. *Holiday Inn* with Bing Crosby and Fred Astaire introduces the decade's top-selling song, *White Christmas*.

RADIO: In addition to the era's top comedies and adventure programs, long-running serial dramas are led by *One Man's Family* and *The Guiding Light*. A dispute over royalties leads to a musicians' strike against record companies; singers continue to record without bands and alter popular musical tastes with acappella vocal records.

THEATER: The year's top Broadway hits include the mystery *Angel Street* with Vincent Price, and Mike Todd's burlesque celebration *Star and Garter* featuring Gypsy Rose Lee.

BOOKS: John Steinbeck's *The Moon Is Down* is published as a novel and simultaneously staged on Broadway.

1942 — TOP 20 ARTISTS

1. **Glenn Miller**
   1,334

2. **Harry James**
   908

3. **Kay Kyser**
   839

4.	824	**Jimmy Dorsey**
5.	597	**Tommy Dorsey**
6.	555	**Benny Goodman**
7.	538	**Bing Crosby**
8.	529	**Dinah Shore**
9.	336	**Charlie Spivak**
10.	335	**Vaughn Monroe**
11.	328	**Sammy Kaye**
12.	318	**Freddy Martin**

13.	305	**Alvino Rey**
14.	236	**Woody Herman**
15.	220	**Andrews Sisters**
16.	200	**The Merry Macs**
17.	126	**Jimmie Lunceford**
18.	124	**Freddie Slack**
19.	124	**Kate Smith**
20.	115	**Horace Heidt**

1942 — TOP SONGWRITERS

	# of Hits	Points	
1.	19	1,726	**Johnny Mercer**
2.	11	1,024	**Frank Loesser**
3.	9	798	**Irving Berlin**
4.	8	708	**Charles Tobias**
5.	6	524	**Al Goodhart**
	6	524	**Kay Twomey**

	# of Hits	Points	
7.	5	470	**Harold Arlen**
8.	5	467	**Jule Styne**
9.	5	458	**Gene DePaul**
	5	458	**Don Raye**
11.	5	451	**Nat Burton**
	5	451	**Walter Kent**

1942 — TOP ARTIST DEBUTS

1.	1/31	**Lucky Millinder** (143)
2.	3/28 †	**Frank Sinatra** (5) ★
3.	8/22	**Freddie Slack** (114)

4.	8/29	**Gordon Jenkins** (34)
5.	10/24	**Spike Jones** (46)

PEAK DATE	CH	10	5	PK	RANK	GOLD	Title / Songwriter(s)	SYMBL	DEBUT	Artist

1

PEAK DATE	CH	10	5	PK	RANK	GOLD	Title / Songwriter(s)	Artist
10/31	15	15	14	11	1	●	**White Christmas** .... *Irving Berlin* [X] Best Seller: 9,3,2,1,1,1,1,1,1,1,1,1,1,1,4 {this version re-charted in 1943 (#7), 1944 (#5), 1945 (#1) and 1946 (#1)}	**Bing Crosby**
2/28	15	15	13	10	2		**Moonlight Cocktail** .... *Kim Gannon/Lucky Roberts* Best Seller: 3,7,8,5,1,1,1,1,1,1,1,1,1,4	**Glenn Miller** (Ray Eberle)
7/18	13	13	12	8	3	●	**Jingle Jangle Jingle** .... *Joseph Lilley/Frank Loesser* <B:2>	**Kay Kyser** (Harry Babbitt/Julie Conway)
9/12	18	18	15	7	4	●	**(I've Got a Gal in) Kalamazoo** .... *Mack Gordon/Harry Warren* <B:14> Best Seller: 7,4,3,4,2,3,1,1,1,1,1,1,1,3,4,4,6,7	**Glenn Miller** (Tex Beneke/Marion Hutton)
5/9	15	15	12	6	5		**Tangerine** .... *Johnny Mercer/Victor Schertzinger* Best Seller: 7,4,3,1,1,1,1,1,1,5,3,7,9,5,5	**Jimmy Dorsey** (Bob Eberly/Helen O'Connell)
6/20	18	18	14	4	6		**Sleepy Lagoon** .... *Eric Coates/Jack Lawrence* [I] Best Seller: 10,9,10,4,6,5,4,3,1,1,1,1,3,2,2,3,3,5	**Harry James**
2/7	18	18	12	2	7		**A String Of Pearls** .... *Jerry Gray* [I] Best Seller: 9,10,3,1,2,1,2,2,5,2,3,3,4,6,6,9,9 {re-charted in 1944 (#22)}	**Glenn Miller**
2/14	11	11	6	1	8		**Blues In The Night (My Mama Done Tol' Me)** ...... *Harold Arlen/Johnny Mercer* Best Seller: 7,6,4,2,4,1,3,5,9,9,7	**Woody Herman**

2

PEAK DATE	CH	10	5	PK	RANK	GOLD	Title / Songwriter(s)	Artist
6/20	22	22	17	8	9	●	**Who Wouldn't Love You** .... *Bill Carey/Carl Fischer*	**Kay Kyser** (Harry Babbitt)
10/31	13	13	13	7	10	●	**Praise The Lord And Pass The Ammunition!** .... *Frank Loesser*	**Kay Kyser**
4/25	20	20	13	6	11		**Jersey Bounce** ... *Tiny Bradshaw/Edward Johnson/Bobby Plater/Robert Wright* <B:18> [I]	**Benny Goodman**
3/14	13	13	8	5	12		**I Don't Want To Walk Without You** .... *Frank Loesser/Jule Styne*	**Harry James** (Helen Forrest)
9/5	11	11	7	4	13		**He Wears A Pair Of Silver Wings** .... *Michael Carr/Eric Maschwitz* <A:1>	**Kay Kyser** (Harry Babbitt)
6/6	13	13	8	2	14		**Don't Sit Under The Apple Tree (With Anyone Else But Me)** .... *Lew Brown/Sam Stept/Charles Tobias*	**Glenn Miller** (Marion Hutton/Tex Beneke)
10/3	11	11	7	2	15		**My Devotion** .... *Roc Hillman/Johnny Napton* <B:8>	**Charlie Spivak** (Garry Stevens)
10/10	15	15	10	1	16		**Serenade In Blue** .... *Mack Gordon/Harry Warren*	**Glenn Miller** (Ray Eberle)
12/26	16	16	8	1	17		**When The Lights Go On Again (All Over the World)** .... *Bennie Benjamin/Sol Marcus/Eddie Seiler*	**Vaughn Monroe**
2/21	10	10	6	1	18		**I Said No!** .... *Frank Loesser/Jule Styne* <B:3>	**Alvino Rey** (Yvonne King)
12/19	9	9	3	1	19		**Mister Five By Five** .... *Gene DePaul/Don Raye*	**Harry James** (Helen Forrest)

3

PEAK DATE	CH	10	5	PK	RANK	GOLD	Title / Songwriter(s)	Artist
3/7	6	6	5	2	20		**Deep In The Heart Of Texas** .... *June Hershey/Don Swander*	**Bing Crosby**
11/14	10	10	4	1	21	●	**Der Fuehrer's Face** .... *Oliver Wallace* [N] ❶	**Spike Jones** (Carl Grayson)
2/28	9	9	3	1	22		**Deep In The Heart Of Texas** .... *June Hershey/Don Swander* <A:2>	**Alvino Rey** (Bill Schallen/Skeets Herfurt)
9/19	7	7	3	1	23		**I Left My Heart At The Stage Door Canteen** .... *Irving Berlin*	**Sammy Kaye** (Don Cornell)
10/3	9	9	1	1	24		**Just As Though You Were Here** .... *John Benson Brooks/Eddie DeLange*	**Tommy Dorsey** (Frank Sinatra/Pied Pipers)
2/14	5	5	1	1	25		**Remember Pearl Harbor** .... *Sammy Kaye/Don Reid*	**Sammy Kaye**

4

PEAK DATE	CH	10	5	PK	RANK	GOLD	Title / Songwriter(s)	Artist
7/11	8	8	6	3	26		**Jingle Jangle Jingle** .... *Joseph Lilley/Frank Loesser*	**The Merry Macs**
8/1	10	10	3	1	27		**One Dozen Roses** .... *Walter Donovan/Dick Jurgens/Roger Lewis/Joe Washburne*	**Harry James** (Jimmy Saunders)
3/21	7	7	3	1	28	●	**Blues In The Night** .... *Harold Arlen/Johnny Mercer*	**Dinah Shore**
2/21	5	5	2	1	29		**Blues In The Night (My Mama Done Tol' Me) — Parts 1 & 2** .... *Harold Arlen/Johnny Mercer*	**Jimmie Lunceford**
9/5	3	3	1	1	30		**Idaho** .... *Jesse Stone* <B:10>	**Benny Goodman** (Dick Haymes)
10/10	3	3	1	1	31		**Amen** .... *Bill Hardy/Vic Schoen/Roger Segure*	**Abe Lyman** (Rose Blane)

5

PEAK DATE	CH	10	5	PK	RANK	GOLD	Title / Songwriter(s)	Artist
4/18	11	11	3	3	32		**Somebody Else Is Taking My Place** ..... *Bob Ellsworth/Dick Howard/Russ Morgan*	**Russ Morgan** (The Morganaires)
4/11	9	9	2	2	33		**Somebody Else Is Taking My Place** ..... *Bob Ellsworth/Dick Howard/Russ Morgan* {re-charted in 1948 (#30)}	**Benny Goodman** (Peggy Lee)
9/26	3	3	2	2	34		**Take Me** .... *Rube Bloom/Mack David* <B:15>	**Tommy Dorsey** (Frank Sinatra)
9/19	7	7	1	1	35		**Strictly Instrumental** .... *Edgar Battle/Bennie Benjamin/Sol Marcus/Eddie Seiler* [I]	**Harry James**
10/24	4	4	1	1	36		**My Devotion** .... *Roc Hillman/Johnny Napton*	**Vaughn Monroe**
9/12	4	4	1	1	37		**Amen** .... *Bill Hardy/Vic Schoen/Roger Segure*	**Woody Herman**
10/10	3	3	1	1	38	●	**Strip Polka** .... *Johnny Mercer*	**Kay Kyser** (Jack Martin)

6

PEAK DATE	CH	10	5	PK	RANK	GOLD	Title / Songwriter(s)	Artist
11/7	4	4		2	39		**Strip Polka** .... *Johnny Mercer* <B:17>	**Andrews Sisters**
1/24	7	7		1	40		**(There'll Be Blue Birds Over) The White Cliffs Of Dover** .... *Nat Burton/Walter Kent*	**Glenn Miller** (Ray Eberle)

1942

PEAK DATE	WEEKS				RANK	GOLD	Title — Songwriter(s)	SYMBL	DEBUT	Artist
	CH	10	5	PK						

PEAK POSITION 7

PEAK DATE	CH	10	5	PK	RANK	GOLD	Title — Songwriter(s)	SYMBL	DEBUT	Artist
9/5	6	6		4	41		Strip Polka ....*Johnny Mercer*			Johnny Mercer
5/9	11	11		3	42		Skylark ....*Hoagy Carmichael/Johnny Mercer* <B:19>			Glenn Miller (Ray Eberle)
12/26	8	8		2	43		Juke Box Saturday Night ....*Paul McGrane/Al Stillman* [N]			Glenn Miller (Marion Hutton/Tex Beneke)
2/14	4	4		1	44		Ev'rything I Love ....*Cole Porter*			Glenn Miller (Ray Eberle)
3/21	4	4		1	45	●	Deep In The Heart Of Texas ....*June Hershey/Don Swander*			Horace Heidt
1/24	3	3		1	46		(There'll Be Bluebirds Over) The White Cliffs Of Dover ....*Nat Burton/ Walter Kent*			Kay Kyser (Harry Babbitt)

PEAK POSITION 8

PEAK DATE	CH	10	5	PK	RANK	GOLD	Title — Songwriter(s)	SYMBL	DEBUT	Artist
6/20	3	3		3	47		Johnny Doughboy Found A Rose In Ireland ....*Al Goodhart/Kay Twomey*			Kay Kyser
7/11	5	5		2	48		One Dozen Roses ....*Walter Donovan/Dick Jurgens/Roger Lewis/Joe Washburne*			Dinah Shore
11/28	4	4		2	49		Praise The Lord And Pass The Ammunition! ....*Frank Loesser*			The Merry Macs
6/13	3	3		1	50		One Dozen Roses ....*Walter Donovan/Dick Jurgens/Roger Lewis/Joe Washburne*			Glen Gray (Pee Wee Hunt)
8/15	3	3		1	51		Sweet Eloise ....*Mack David/Russ Morgan*			Glenn Miller (Ray Eberle)
3/28	3	3		1	52		Miss You ....*Charles Tobias/Harry Tobias*			Dinah Shore
2/28	3	3		1	53	●	Rose O'Day (The Filla-ga-dusha Song) ....*Al Lewis/Charles Tobias* <B:9>			Kate Smith
1/10	2	2		1	54		This Is No Laughing Matter ....*Al Frisch/Buddy Kaye*			Charlie Spivak (Garry Stevens)
10/3	2	2		1	55		Strip Polka ....*Johnny Mercer* [N]			Alvino Rey (Four King Sisters)
10/17	2	2		1	56		I Left My Heart At The Stage Door Canteen ....*Irving Berlin* <A:2>			Charlie Spivak (Garry Stevens)
3/14	1	1		1	57		Blues In The Night (My Mama Done Tol' Me) ....*Harold Arlen/Johnny Mercer*			Cab Calloway
3/21	1	1		1	58		A Zoot Suit (For My Sunday Gal) ....*Ray Gilbert/Bob O'Brien*			Kay Kyser (Sully Mason)
1/17	1	1		1	59		Tonight We Love ....*Ray Austin/Freddy Martin/Bobby Worth*			Freddy Martin (Clyde Rogers)

PEAK POSITION 9

PEAK DATE	CH	10	5	PK	RANK	GOLD	Title — Songwriter(s)	SYMBL	DEBUT	Artist
8/22	2	2		2	60	●	Cow-Cow Boogie ....*Benny Carter/Gene DePaul/Don Raye*	❶		Freddie Slack (Ella Mae Morse)
4/4	1	1		1	61		I Don't Want To Walk Without You ....*Frank Loesser/Jule Styne*			Bing Crosby
6/6	1	1		1	62		Miss You ....*Charles Tobias/Harry Tobias*			Bing Crosby
4/25	1	1		1	63		I Remember You ....*Johnny Mercer/Victor Schertzinger*			Jimmy Dorsey (Bob Eberly)
6/13	1	1		1	64		Jersey Bounce............*Tiny Bradshaw/Edward Johnson/Bobby Plater/Robert Wright* [I]			Jimmy Dorsey
10/3	1	1		1	65		He's My Guy ....*Gene DePaul/Don Raye*			Harry James (Helen Forrest)
11/28	1	1		1	66		Manhattan Serenade ....*Harold Adamson/Louis Alter* <B:19>			Harry James (Helen Forrest)
6/27	1	1		1	67		Johnny Doughboy Found A Rose In Ireland ....*Al Goodhart/Kay Twomey*			Guy Lombardo (Kenny Gardner)
2/21	1	1		1	68		(There'll Be Bluebirds Over) The White Cliffs Of Dover ....*Nat Burton/ Walter Kent* <A:8>			Kate Smith

PEAK POSITION 10

PEAK DATE	CH	10	5	PK	RANK	GOLD	Title — Songwriter(s)	SYMBL	DEBUT	Artist
11/7	2	2		2	69		Daybreak....................................*Harold Adamson/Ferde Grofe* <A:1>			Tommy Dorsey (Frank Sinatra)
12/12	2	2		2	70		Mr. Five By Five ....*Gene DePaul/Don Raye*			Freddie Slack (Ella Mae Morse)
1/31	1	1		1	71		I Said No ....*Frank Loesser/Jule Styne* <B:19>			Jimmy Dorsey (Bob Eberly/Helen O'Connell)
8/29	1	1		1	72		My Devotion ....*Roc Hillman/Johnny Napton*			Jimmy Dorsey (Bob Eberly)
8/22	1	1		1	73		Take Me ....*Rube Bloom/Mack David* <A:4>			Benny Goodman (Dick Haymes)
5/23	1	1		1	74		Always In My Heart ....*Kim Gannon/Ernesto Lecuona*			Glenn Miller (Ray Eberle)
12/26	1	1		1	75		Dearly Beloved....................................*Jerome Kern/Johnny Mercer* <A:3>			Dinah Shore

PEAK POSITION 13

PEAK DATE	CH	10	5	PK	RANK	GOLD	Title — Songwriter(s)	SYMBL	DEBUT	Artist
9/12	3			2	76		My Devotion ....*Roc Hillman/Johnny Napton*			The Four King Sisters

PEAK POSITION 14

PEAK DATE	CH	10	5	PK	RANK	GOLD	Title — Songwriter(s)	SYMBL	DEBUT	Artist
10/17	8			1	77		At Last ....*Mack Gordon/Harry Warren* <A:1>			Glenn Miller (Ray Eberle)
9/19	6			1	78		Be Careful It's My Heart ....*Irving Berlin*			Bing Crosby
8/1	4			1	79		Johnny Doughboy Found A Rose In Ireland ....*Al Goodhart/Kay Twomey*			Kenny Baker
3/21	3			1	80		Deep In The Heart Of Texas ....*June Hershey/Don Swander*			The Merry Macs

PEAK POSITION 15

PEAK DATE	CH	10	5	PK	RANK	GOLD	Title — Songwriter(s)	SYMBL	DEBUT	Artist
12/19	5			1	81		Dearly Beloved....................................*Jerome Kern/Johnny Mercer*	❶		Johnnie Johnston
9/26	3			1	82		Be Careful, It's My Heart ....*Irving Berlin* <A:5>			Tommy Dorsey (Frank Sinatra)
12/12	3			1	83		Manhattan Serenade ....*Harold Adamson/Louis Alter*			Tommy Dorsey (Jo Stafford)
3/21	3			1	84		I Don't Want To Walk Without You ....*Frank Loesser/Jule Styne*			Dinah Shore

PEAK POSITION 16

PEAK DATE	CH	10	5	PK	RANK	GOLD	Title — Songwriter(s)	SYMBL	DEBUT	Artist
1/10	4			1	85		There'll Be Blue Birds Over The White Cliffs Of Dover..........*Nat Burton/ Walter Kent*			Sammy Kaye (Arthur Wright)
9/5	4			1	86		Idaho ....*Jesse Stone*			Alvino Rey (Yvonne King)
2/28	3			1	87		How About You? ....*Ralph Freed/Burton Lane*			Tommy Dorsey (Frank Sinatra)
5/30	3			1	88		Skylark ....*Hoagy Carmichael/Johnny Mercer*			Harry James (Helen Forrest)

PEAK DATE	CH	10	5	PK	RANK	GOLD	Title / PEAK POSITION / Songwriter(s)	SYMBL	DEBUT	Artist

16 (cont'd)

PEAK DATE	CH	10	5	PK	RANK	GOLD	Title / Songwriter(s)	Artist
8/15	3			1	89 ●	By The Light Of The Silv'ry Moon ....*Gus Edwards/Edward Madden* {re-charted in 1944 (#17)}	Ray Noble (Snooky Lanson)
11/14	2			1	90	White Christmas ....*Irving Berlin* **[X]**	Gordon Jenkins (Bob Carroll)
7/11	2			1	91	Johnny Doughboy Found A Rose In Ireland ....*Al Goodhart/Kay Twomey*	Freddy Martin (Clyde Rogers)
2/14	1			1	92	The White Cliffs Of Dover ....*Nat Burton/Walter Kent*	Jimmy Dorsey (Bob Eberly)
3/28	1			1	93	What Is This Thing Called Love? ....*Cole Porter*	Tommy Dorsey (Connie Haines)
8/8	1			1	94	But Not For Me ....*George Gershwin/Ira Gershwin*	Harry James (Helen Forrest)
4/11	1			1	95 ●	Easter Parade ....*Irving Berlin* **[I]**	Harry James
5/23	1			1	96	Tangerine ....*Johnny Mercer/Victor Schertzinger*	Vaughn Monroe

17

PEAK DATE	CH	10	5	PK	RANK	GOLD	Title / Songwriter(s)	Artist
9/12	4			2	97	Take Me ....*Rube Bloom/Mack David* <A:17>	Jimmy Dorsey (Helen O'Connell)
9/5	5			1	98	This Is Worth Fighting For ....*Eddie DeLange/Sam Stept* <A:17>	Jimmy Dorsey (Bob Eberly)
3/7	3			1	99	The Shrine Of Saint Cecilia ....*Bert Carroll*	Andrews Sisters
4/25	3			1	100	One Dozen Roses ....*Walter Donovan/Dick Jurgens/Roger Lewis/Joe Washburne*	Dick Jurgens (Buddy Moreno)
12/19	2			1	101	Mister Five By Five ....*Gene DePaul/Don Raye* <A:6>	Andrews Sisters
9/26	2			1	102 ●	There's A Star Spangled Banner Waving Somewhere ....*Shelby Darnell/ Paul Roberts*	❶ Elton Britt
10/17	2			1	103	Serenade In Blue ....*Mack Gordon/Harry Warren*	Benny Goodman (Dick Haymes)
2/21	2			1	104	Rose O'Day (The Filla-Ga-Dusha Song) ....*Al Lewis/Charles Tobias*	Freddy Martin (Eddie Stone)
8/15	1			1	105	Jingle Jangle Jingle ....*Joseph Lilley/Frank Loesser*	Gene Autry
1/10	1			1	106	I Got It Bad (And That Ain't Good) ....*Duke Ellington/Paul Francis Webster*	Duke Ellington (Ivie Anderson)
6/6	1			1	107	Breathless ....*Eddie Cherkose/Jacques Press*	Shep Fields (Ken Curtis)
7/11	1			1	108	Johnny Doughboy Found A Rose In Ireland ....*Al Goodhart/Kay Twomey*	Sammy Kaye (Tommy Ryan)
5/30	1			1	109	I'm Gonna Move To The Outskirts Of Town Parts 1 & 2 ....*William Weldon*	Jimmie Lunceford (Dan Grissom)
8/15	1			1	110	Jingle, Jangle, Jingle ....*Joseph Lilley/Frank Loesser*	Freddy Martin (Clyde Rogers/Stuart Wade)
1/31	1			1	111	This Is No Laughing Matter ....*Al Frisch/Buddy Kaye*	Glenn Miller (Ray Eberle)
8/22	1			1	112	I Want A Tall Skinny Papa ....*Lucky Millinder*	❶ Lucky Millinder With Rosetta Tharpe

18

PEAK DATE	CH	10	5	PK	RANK	GOLD	Title / Songwriter(s)	Artist
12/5	5			2	113	White Christmas ....*Irving Berlin* **[X]**	Charlie Spivak (Garry Stevens)
6/20	2			2	114	Three Little Sisters ....*Vic Mizzy/Irving Taylor*	Vaughn Monroe (Four V's)
6/6	2			2	115	Johnny Doughboy Found A Rose In Ireland ....*Al Goodhart/Kay Twomey*	Tommy Tucker Time (Don Brown)
4/11	3			1	116	My Little Cousin ....*Sam Braverman/Cy Coben/Happy Lewis*	Benny Goodman (Peggy Lee)
10/10	2			1	117	I Cried For You (Now It's Your Turn To Cry Over Me) ....*Gus Arnheim/ Arthur Freed/Abe Lyman*	Harry James (Helen Forrest)
1/10	2			1	118	Angeline ....*Edward Ross/Si Rothman*	Art Kassel
8/15	2			1	119	He Wears A Pair Of Silver Wings ....*Michael Carr/Eric Maschwitz*	Dinah Shore
7/25	1			1	120	Always In My Heart ....*Kim Gannon/Ernesto Lecuona*	Kenny Baker
8/8	1			1	121	I'll Take Tallulah ...........*E.Y. Harburg/Burton Lane*	Tommy Dorsey (Frank Sinatra/Pied Pipers)
1/17	1			1	122	Rose O'Day (The Filla-ga-dusha-Song) ....*Al Lewis/Charles Tobias*	The Four King Sisters
4/25	1			1	123	A String Of Pearls ....*Jerry Gray* <A:2> **[I]**	Benny Goodman
2/14	1			1	124	Blues In The Night ....*Harold Arlen/Johnny Mercer*	Benny Goodman (Peggy Lee/Lou McGarrity)
3/7	1			1	125	Rose O'Day ....*Al Lewis/Charles Tobias*	Woody Herman (Carolyn Grey)
6/20	1			1	126	Sleepy Lagoon ....*Eric Coates/Jack Lawrence*	Dinah Shore

19

PEAK DATE	CH	10	5	PK	RANK	GOLD	Title / Songwriter(s)	Artist
12/12	2			1	127	Daybreak ....*Harold Adamson/Ferde Grofe* <A:9>	Harry James (Johnny McAfee)
8/15	1			1	128	Three Little Sisters ....*Vic Mizzy/Irving Taylor*	Andrews Sisters
7/18	1			1	129	Skylark ....*Hoagy Carmichael/Johnny Mercer*	Bing Crosby
3/28	1			1	130	Arthur Murray Taught Me Dancing In A Hurry ....*Johnny Mercer/ Victor Schertzinger*	Jimmy Dorsey (Helen O'Connell)
10/31	1			1	131	Daybreak ....*Harold Adamson/Ferde Grofe* <A:17>	Jimmy Dorsey (Bob Eberly)
2/7	1			1	132	This Is No Laughing Matter ....*Al Frisch/Buddy Kaye* <A:10>	Jimmy Dorsey (Bob Eberly)
7/11	1			1	133	Jersey Bounce ....*Tiny Bradshaw/Edward Johnson/Bobby Plater/Robert Wright* **[I]**	Shep Fields
7/4	1			1	134 ●	American Patrol ....*Jerry Gray/F.W. Meacham* **[I]**	Glenn Miller
5/2	1			1	135	The Story Of A Starry Night ....*Mann Curtis/Al Hoffman/Jerry Livingston* <A:7>	Glenn Miller (Ray Eberle)
1/31	1			1	136	I Got It Bad And That Ain't Good ....*Duke Ellington/Paul Francis Webster*	Dinah Shore

20

PEAK DATE	CH	10	5	PK	RANK	GOLD	Title / Songwriter(s)	Artist
1/17	2			2	137	The Shrine Of Saint Cecilia ....*Bert Carroll*	Vaughn Monroe
6/27	1			1	138	Always In My Heart ....*Kim Gannon/Ernesto Lecuona*	Jimmy Dorsey (Bob Eberly)
10/31	1			1	139	Ev'ry Night About This Time ....*Ted Koehler/James Monaco*	Jimmy Dorsey (Bob Eberly)
6/20	1			1	140	The Last Call For Love ....*Margery Cummings/E.Y. Harburg/Burton Lane*	Tommy Dorsey (Frank Sinatra/Pied Pipers)
8/22	1			1	141	Well, Git It! ....*Sy Oliver* **[I]**	Tommy Dorsey

PEAK DATE	WEEKS				RANK	GOLD	Title	PEAK POSITION	Songwriter(s)	SYMBL	DEBUT	Artist
	CH	10	5	PK								

20 (cont'd)

PEAK DATE	CH	PK	RANK	Title	Songwriter(s)	SYMBL	Artist
6/20	1	1	142	Three Little Sisters	Vic Mizzy/Irving Taylor	[N]	Horace Heidt (Ollie O'Toole/ Red Farrington/Charles Goodman)
1/3	1	1	143	Someone's Rocking My Dream Boat	Leon Rene/Otis Rene/Emerson Scott		Ink Spots
8/29	1	1	144	He Wears A Pair Of Silver Wings	Michael Carr/Eric Maschwitz	❶	Gordon Jenkins (Connie Haines)
11/14	1	1	145	I Came Here To Talk For Joe	Lew Brown/Sam Stept/Charles Tobias		Sammy Kaye (Don Cornell)
11/7	1	1	146	I Met Her On Monday	Charles Newman/Allie Wrubel	[N]	Freddy Martin (Eddie Stone)
10/17	1	1	147 ●	White Christmas	Irving Berlin <A:15>	[X]	Freddy Martin (Clyde Rogers)
				{re-charted in 1945 (#16)}			
5/16	1	1	148	Skylark	Hoagy Carmichael/Johnny Mercer		Dinah Shore
9/12	1	1	149	Brother Bill	Louis Armstrong		Charlie Spivak (The Stardusters)
9/19	1	1	150	Put-Put-Put (Your Arms Around Me)	Al Hoffman/Manny Kurtz/Jerry Livingston	[N]	Barry Wood

1943

NATIONAL NEWS: Shoe rationing (everyone limited to three pairs per year) due to the leather shortage is followed by rationing of meats, fats, cheese and canned food. President Roosevelt's intervention ends strikes by miners and rubber workers. The Supreme Court rules unconstitutional the state practice of requiring students to salute the flag. In Washington, D.C., the Jefferson Memorial is dedicated. Race riots in Detroit end with 29 persons dead.

INTERNATIONAL NEWS: German occupying forces surrender to the Russians in Stalingrad, and the Nazis retreat following the biggest tank battle in history near Moscow. Allied forces led by Gen. George Patton triumph in Sicily and Palermo as Benito Mussolini is deposed, and the new Italian government declares war on its former German comrades. The war in North Africa ends with an Allied victory. As the Holocaust continues, Jews stage an uprising in Warsaw which is soon crushed. Japanese forces withdraw in the Solomon Islands. Britain's Royal Air Force bombs Berlin, and Americans also launch massive German air strikes.

COMMERCE AND SCIENCE: Full-scale development of penicillin is underway as a powerful anti-bacterial agent, although it will not come into general use until after the war. Nightclubs are enjoying their biggest year ever, due to a surplus of cash, a shortage of consumer items to spend it on and the desire for escape.

FADS AND FASHION: The Lindy-Hop — which originated as a variation on the Charleston in the '20s — has emerged as the nation's hottest dance craze.

SPORTS: As baseball's top stars begin leaving to join the war effort, the New York Yankees reverse 1942's result by defeating the St. Louis Cardinals in the World Series four games to one. The Chicago Bears win their third NFL championship in four years by whipping the Washington Redskins, 41-21. Notre Dame reigns atop college football. Jake LaMotta upsets Sugar Ray Robinson in the year's top boxing match.

MOVIES: Humphrey Bogart and Ingrid Bergman give a generation something to remember in the wartime classic *Casablanca*, the year's Best Picture. Other noteworthy films are *For Whom the Bell Tolls* starring Gary Cooper and Ingrid Bergman, *The Song of Bernadette* with Oscar-winner Jennifer Jones and *The Ox-Bow Incident* starring Henry Fonda. The musical *This Is the Army* is a top money-maker. Leggy Betty Grable becomes the #1 box office star and the top G.I. pin-up, a category in which Rita Hayworth and Jane Russell also rate highly.

RADIO: Popular new shows include *Inner Sanctum*, *Duffy's Tavern* and *The Red Skelton Show*.

THEATER: Rodgers & Hammerstein's *Oklahoma!* is an all-time landmark for the Broadway musical. Other top musicals this year are Kurt Weill's *One Touch of Venus* starring Mary Martin and Oscar Hammerstein's *Carmen Jones*.

BOOKS: *A Tree Grows in Brooklyn* by Betty Smith is the year's best-selling novel; Wendell Willkie's *One World* tops the nonfiction releases. Robert Frost becomes the first poet to win a Pulitzer Prize four times.

1943 — TOP 20 ARTISTS

1. Bing Crosby
819

2. Harry James
783

3. Dick Haymes
566

4.	520	**Frank Sinatra**
5.	451	**Tommy Dorsey**
6.	379	**Glenn Miller**
7.	282	**Kay Kyser**
8.	264	**Benny Goodman**
9.	245	**Dinah Shore**
10.	240	**Mills Brothers**
11.	195	**The Song Spinners**
12.	165	**Freddie Slack**

13.	156	**Freddy Martin**
14.	139	**Xavier Cugat**
15.	117	**Al Dexter**
16.	116	**Willie Kelly**
17.	114	**Andrews Sisters**
18.	111	**Jimmy Dorsey**
19.	106	**Ink Spots**
20.	105	**Dick Jurgens**

1943 — TOP SONGWRITERS

	# of Hits	Points	
1.	11	973	**Jimmy McHugh**
2.	9	803	**Frank Loesser**
3.	8	733	**Johnny Burke**
	8	733	**Jimmy Van Heusen**
5.	6	552	**Oscar Hammerstein**
	6	552	**Richard Rodgers**

	# of Hits	Points	
7.	5	476	**Mack Gordon**
	5	476	**Harry Warren**
9.	5	460	**Johnny Mercer**
10.	5	433	**Harold Adamson**
11.	4	364	**Harold Arlen**
12.	4	351	**Cole Porter**

1943 — TOP ARTIST DEBUTS

1.	1/23	**Johnny Long** (94)
2.	3/13	**Henri René** (129)
3.	3/20	**Jimmy Wakely** (58)
4.	5/08	**Ray McKinley** (138)

5.	7/03	**Dick Haymes** (14)
6.	10/16 †	**Perry Como** (3) ★
7.	12/11	**Nat "King" Cole** (17) ★
8.	12/25	**Ella Mae Morse** (97)

PEAK DATE	WEEKS				RANK	GOLD	Title / PEAK POSITION / Songwriter(s)	SYMBOL	DEBUT	Artist
	CH	10	5	PK						

1

3/6	20	20	18	13	1	●	**I've Heard That Song Before** ....*Sammy Cahn/Jule Styne* <B:17>			**Harry James** (Helen Forrest)
							Best Seller: 7,8,3,3,2,1,1,1,1,1,1,1,1,1,1,1,4,1,5			
11/6	30	30	23	12	2	●	**Paper Doll** ....*Johnny Black* <B:16>			**Mills Brothers**
							Best Seller: 10,10,10,8,6,4,7,2,2,2,2,3,2,1,1,1,1,1,1,1,1,1,1,1,3,3,4,5,8			
							Juke Box: 1,4,4,5,6,5,10,6,14,6,15,11			
9/11	18	18	15	7	3	●	**Sunday, Monday Or Always** ....*Johnny Burke/Jimmy Van Heusen* <B:17>			**Bing Crosby**
							Best Seller: 7,3,1,1,1,1,1,1,1,1,3,3,3,2,4,4,5,8,10			
1/16	24	24	15	5	4	●	**There Are Such Things** ....*Stanley Adams/Abel Baer/George Meyer* <B:10>			**Tommy Dorsey** (Frank Sinatra/Pied Pipers)
							Best Seller: 9,8,10,5,7,9,4,2,2,1,1,1,1,2,2,1,3,2,3,5,6,9,10,10			
7/24	16	16	13	4	5	●	**You'll Never Know**....................................*Mack Gordon/Harry Warren* <B:17>			**Dick Haymes**
							Best Seller: 4,2,1,1,1,1,2,4,5,2,4,8,5,8,5,7			
8/21	17	17	11	3	6		**In The Blue Of Evening** ....*Tom Adair/Al D'Artega* <B:6>			**Tommy Dorsey** (Frank Sinatra)
							Best Seller: 6,5,4,5,3,3,1,1,1,3,3,5,6,6,9,9,9			
7/3	11	11	8	3	7		**Comin' In On A Wing And A Prayer** .....*Harold Adamson/Jimmy McHugh*	❶		**The Song Spinners**
							Best Seller: 10,2,1,1,1,2,3,5,5,6,9 <B:7>			
6/12	11	11	8	3	8		**Taking A Chance On Love** ....*Vernon Duke/Ted Fetter/John Latouche*			**Benny Goodman** (Helen Forrest)
							Best Seller: 10,5,4,8,2,1,1,1,2,5,8			
2/13	18	18	12	2	9	●	**I Had The Craziest Dream** ....*Mack Gordon/Harry Warren*			**Harry James** (Helen Forrest)
							Best Seller: 9,8,5,6,4,3,2,2,2,2,1,1,3,2,4,7,9,10			
5/29	14	14	12	1	10		**That Old Black Magic** ....*Harold Arlen/Johnny Mercer*			**Glenn Miller** (Skip Nelson)
							Best Seller: 7,5,3,4,5,3,4,3,2,2,3,1,5,7			
10/30	17	17	10	1	11	●	**Pistol Packin' Mama** ....*Al Dexter* <B:22>	❶		**Al Dexter**
							Best Seller: 10,9,8,6,4,3,3,3,2,1,2,2,3,6,5,9,7			
							Juke Box: 2,5,5,-,10			

2

3/20	19	19	16	7	12		**Brazil (Aquarela Do Brasil)**...............................*Ary Barroso/S.K. Russell* [I]			Xavier Cugat
7/10	11	11	7	4	13		**It Can't Be Wrong** ....*Kim Gannon/Max Steiner* <B:7>	❶		Dick Haymes
12/4	9	9	7	4	14	●	**Pistol Packin' Mama** ....*Al Dexter* <B:6>			Bing Crosby & the Andrews Sisters
8/28	13	13	6	2	15		**You'll Never Know** ....*Mack Gordon/Harry Warren* <B:10>			Frank Sinatra
5/22	13	13	6	2	16		**Velvet Moon** ....*Eddie DeLange/Josef Myrow* <B:15> [I]			Harry James
9/4	18	18	12	1	17	●	**All Or Nothing At All** ....*Arthur Altman/Jack Lawrence*			Frank Sinatra with Harry James
11/27	14	14	11	1	18		**People Will Say We're In Love**..........*Oscar Hammerstein/Richard Rodgers* <B:5>			Bing Crosby & Trudy Erwin
5/29	16	16	6	1	19		**Don't Get Around Much Anymore** ....*Duke Ellington/Bob Russell*			Ink Spots
6/19	10	10	3	1	20		**As Time Goes By** ....*Herman Hupfeld*			Rudy Vallée

3

1/23	8	8	4	2	21		**(As Long As You're Not In Love With Anyone Else) Why Don't You Fall In Love With Me?**.......................*Al Lewis/Mabel Wayne* <B:10>			Dinah Shore
4/10	16	16	3	2	22		**As Time Goes By** ....*Herman Hupfeld*			Jacques Renard (Frank Munn)
12/25	5	5	3	2	23	●	**I'll Be Home For Christmas (If Only In My Dreams)** ....*Kim Gannon/* [X] {re-charted in 1944 (#19)} *Walter Kent/Buck Ram*			Bing Crosby
2/6	11	11	4	1	24		**Moonlight Becomes You** ....*Johnny Burke/Jimmy Van Heusen* <B:17>			Bing Crosby
4/3	10	10	1	1	25		**For Me And My Gal** ....*Ray Goetz/Edgar Leslie/George Meyer*			Judy Garland & Gene Kelly

4

10/2	18	18	8	3	26		**I Heard You Cried Last Night** ....*Ted Grouya/Jerrie Kruger*			Harry James (Helen Forrest)
3/20	12	12	7	3	27		**You'd Be So Nice To Come Home To** ....*Cole Porter*			Dinah Shore
3/27	13	13	2	2	28		**It Started All Over Again** ....*Bill Carey/Carl Fischer*			Tommy Dorsey (Frank Sinatra/Pied Pipers)
1/23	12	12	4	1	29	●	**Why Don't You Do Right** ....*Joe McCoy*			Benny Goodman (Peggy Lee)
7/3	5	5	2	1	30		**Let's Get Lost** ....*Frank Loesser/Jimmy McHugh* <B:16>			Kay Kyser (Harry Babbitt/Julie Conway)

5

12/25	9	9	1	1	31		**Oh! What A Beautiful Mornin'**...........*Oscar Hammerstein/Richard Rodgers* <A:2>			Bing Crosby & Trudy Erwin
1/30	8	8	1	1	32		**Moonlight Becomes You** ....*Johnny Burke/Jimmy Van Heusen* <B:16>			Glenn Miller (Skip Nelson)
11/27	6	6	1	1	33		**Put Your Arms Around Me, Honey (I Never Knew Any Girl Like You)** ....*Junie McCree/Albert Von Tilzer* <B:17>			Dick Haymes
1/2	4	4	1	1	34		**Dearly Beloved**..*Jerome Kern/Johnny Mercer*			Glenn Miller (Skip Nelson)
5/8	2	2	1	1	35		**"Murder," He Says** ....*Frank Loesser/Jimmy McHugh*			Dinah Shore

6

10/30	9	9		2	36		**People Will Say We're In Love** ....*Oscar Hammerstein/Richard Rodgers* <B:15>			Frank Sinatra
6/19	4	4		2	37		**You'll Never Know** ....*Mack Gordon/Harry Warren* <B:18>	❶		Willie Kelly
7/24	7	7		1	38		**It's Always You** ....*Johnny Burke/Jimmy Van Heusen* <A:1>			Tommy Dorsey (Frank Sinatra)

7

| 6/19 | 8 | 8 | | 1 | 39 | | **Don't Get Around Much Anymore** ....*Duke Ellington/Bob Russell* | | | Glen Gray (Kenny Sargent) |
| 8/21 | 7 | 7 | | 1 | 40 | | **In My Arms** ....*Ted Grouya/Frank Loesser* <A:2> | | | Dick Haymes |

PEAK DATE	WEEKS			RANK	GOLD	Title	PEAK POSITION Songwriter(s)	SYMBOL	DEBUT	Artist
	CH	10	5	PK						

7 (cont'd)

PEAK DATE	CH	10	5	PK	RANK	GOLD	Title / Songwriter(s)	Artist
7/10	4	4		1	41		Johnny Zero .... *Mack David/Vee Lawnhurst* <A:1>	The Song Spinners
12/25	1	1		1	42	●	White Christmas .... *Irving Berlin* [X-R]	Bing Crosby

8

7/3	2	2		2	43		Don't Get Around Much Anymore (Never No Lament) .... *Duke Ellington/ Bob Russell* [I]	Duke Ellington
6/12	2	2		2	44		Let's Get Lost .... *Frank Loesser/Jimmy McHugh*	Vaughn Monroe
10/23	3	3		1	45		Put Your Arms Around Me, Honey (I Never Knew Any Girl Like You) .... *Junie McCree/Albert Von Tilzer* [I] ✦	Dick Kuhn

9

| 9/18 | 4 | 4 | | 2 | 46 | | Sunday, Monday Or Always .... *Johnny Burke/Jimmy Van Heusen* | Frank Sinatra |
| 12/18 | 2 | 2 | | 1 | 47 | ● | Oklahoma! .... *Oscar Hammerstein/Richard Rodgers* ✦ | Oklahoma! Original Cast Album |

10

1/23	1	1		1	48		(As Long As You're Not In Love With Anyone Else) Why Don't You Fall In Love With Me? .... *Al Lewis/Mabel Wayne* ❶	Johnny Long (Bob Houston/Helen Young)
10/2	1	1		1	49		Close To You .... *Al Hoffman/Carl Lampl/Jerry Livingston* <A:2>	Frank Sinatra
3/20	1	1		1	50		That Old Black Magic .... *Harold Arlen/Johnny Mercer*	Freddie Slack (Margaret Whiting)

14

7/10	3			1	51		Let's Get Lost .... *Frank Loesser/Jimmy McHugh*	Jimmy Dorsey (Bob Eberly)
3/20	3			1	52		Fat Meat Is Good Meat .... *Irene Higginbotham* [I]	Jimmy Lytell (Savannah Churhill)
9/11	2			1	53		I Never Mention Your Name (Oh, No!) .. *Mack Davis/Don George/Walter Kent* <B:19>	Dick Haymes
4/24	2			1	54		That Old Black Magic .... *Harold Arlen/Johnny Mercer*	Horace Heidt (Charles Goodman)
1/16	2			1	55		When The Lights Go On Again (All Over The World) .... *Bennie Benjamin/ Sol Marcus/Eddie Seiler*	Lucky Millinder (Trevor Bacon)

15

9/11	9			2	56		Don't Cry, Baby .... *Sam Lowe/Jimmy Mitchell*	Erskine Hawkins (Jimmy Mitchelle)
6/12	6			1	57		It Can't Be Wrong .... *Kim Gannon/Max Steiner* ✦	Allen Miller
12/11	6			1	58		Rhapsody In Blue .... *George Gershwin* [I]	Glenn Miller
4/17	4			1	59		That Old Black Magic .... *Harold Arlen/Johnny Mercer* <B:22>	Charlie Barnet (Frances Wayne)
5/22	4			1	60		Prince Charming .... *Leroy Holmes* <A:2> [I]	Harry James
12/4	2			1	61		Oh, What A Beautiful Mornin' .... *Oscar Hammerstein/Richard Rodgers* <A:6>	Frank Sinatra

16

6/12	4			1	62		Big Boy .... *Milton Ager/Jack Yellen* ❶	Ray McKinley (Imogene Lynn)
3/20	3			1	63		You'd Be So Nice To Come Home To .... *Cole Porter*	Dick Jurgens (Harry Cool)
1/9	3			1	64		A Touch Of Texas .... *Frank Loesser/Jimmy McHugh*	Freddy Martin (Eddie Stone/Glenn Hughes)
1/30	2			1	65		(As Long As You're Not In Love With Anyone Else) Why Don't You Fall In Love With Me? .... *Al Lewis/Mabel Wayne*	Dick Jurgens (Harry Cool)
1/30	2			1	66		Moonlight Mood .... *Harold Adamson/Peter DeRose* <A:5>	Glenn Miller (The Modernaires)
3/6	2			1	67		You'd Be So Nice To Come Home To .... *Cole Porter* ✦	Six Hits And A Miss
10/9	1			1	68		Mission To Moscow .... *Mel Powell* [I]	Benny Goodman
7/3	1			1	69		The Fuddy Duddy Watchmaker .... *Frank Loesser/Jimmy McHugh* <A:4>	Kay Kyser (Julie Conway)
8/21	1			1	70		(Theme from the) Warsaw Concerto .... *Richard Addinsell* [I]	Freddy Martin
3/13	1			1	71		Tap The Barrel Dry .... *Demosthene Zattas* [I] ❶	René Musette Orchestra

17

12/4	3			1	72		If You Please .... *Johnny Burke/Jimmy Van Heusen* <A:1>	Bing Crosby
1/30	3			1	73		Brazil (Aquarela Do Brasil) .... *Ary Barroso/S.K. Russell* <B:19>	Jimmy Dorsey (Bob Eberly/Helen O'Connell)
10/2	3			1	74		People Will Say We're In Love .... *Oscar Hammerstein/Richard Rodgers* ✦	Hal Goodman
9/4	3			1	75		Wait For Me Mary .... *Nat Simon/Charles Tobias/Harry Tobias* <A:1>	Dick Haymes
2/27	3			1	76		Moonlight Mood .... *Harold Adamson/Peter DeRose* <B:18>	Kay Kyser
10/16	3			1	77		Night And Day .... *Cole Porter* ❶	Frank Sinatra
							{re-charted in 1944 (#15)}	
1/23	2			1	78		Moonlight Becomes You .... *Johnny Burke/Jimmy Van Heusen* <A:1>	Harry James (Johnny McAfee)
7/3	1			1	79		All Of Me .... *Gerald Marks/Seymour Simons*	Count Basie (Lynne Sherman)
2/20	1			1	80		Constantly .... *Johnny Burke/Jimmy Van Heusen* <A:3>	Bing Crosby
7/10	1			1	81		Four Or Five Times .... *Byron Gay/Marco Heilman*	Woody Herman
5/8	1			1	82		Taking A Chance On Love .... *Vernon Duke/Ted Fetter/John Latouche*	Sammy Kaye (Three Kadets)

18

4/3	3			1	83		Please Think Of Me .... *Benny Davis/Murray Mencher/Russ Morgan*	Shep Fields (Ralph Young)
7/10	2			1	84		Comin' In On A Wing And A Prayer .... *Harold Adamson/Jimmy McHugh* <A:6>	Willie Kelly
1/2	2			1	85		Can't Get Out Of This Mood .... *Frank Loesser/Jimmy McHugh* <A:17>	Kay Kyser (Harry Babbitt/Julie Conway)

PEAK DATE	WEEKS				RANK	GOLD	Title	PEAK POSITION Songwriter(s)	SYMBL	DEBUT	Artist
	CH	10	5	PK							
								18 (cont'd)			
1/9	2			1	86		**I Get The Neck Of The Chicken**......................*Frank Loesser/Jimmy McHugh*				Freddy Martin (Eddie Stone)
7/17	2			1	87		**Riffette** ....*Gay Jones/Freddie Slack* **[I]**				Freddie Slack
7/10	1			1	88		**Pushin' Sand** ....*Roc Hillman/George Simmons* **[I]**				Kay Kyser
2/20	1			1	89		**Move It Over** ....*Sunny Skylar*				Ethel Merman
								19			
3/20	2			2	90		**There's A Star Spangled Banner Waving Somewhere** ....*Shelby Darnell/ Paul Roberts*		❶		Jimmy Wakely
7/10	2			1	91		**Blue Surreal** ....*Phil Moore* **[I]**				Bob Crosby
7/31	2			1	92		**Get On Board, Little Chillun** ....*Gene DePaul/Don Raye*				Freddie Slack (Ella Mae Morse)
12/11	1			1	93		**All For You** ....*Robert Scherman*		❶		King Cole's Trio
11/13	1			1	94		**I Heard You Cried Last Night (And So Did I)** ...*Ted Grouya/Jerrie Kruger* <A:14>				Dick Haymes
1/23	1			1	95		**There Will Never Be Another You** ....*Mack Gordon/Harry Warren*				Sammy Kaye (Nancy Norman)
1/16	1			1	96		**I Lost My Sugar In Salt Lake City** ....*Johnny Lange/Leon Rene*				Johnny Mercer
								20			
10/16	1			1	97		**Goodbye, Sue**...*Jules Loman/Louis Ricca/James Rule*		❶		Perry Como
7/24	1			1	98		**Comin' In On A Wing And A Prayer**.............*Harold Adamson/Jimmy McHugh*		✦		The Four Vagabonds
4/17	1			1	99		**For Me And My Gal** ....*Ray Goetz/Edgar Leslie/George Meyer*				Guy Lombardo (Kenny Gardner)

1944

NATIONAL NEWS: Franklin D. Roosevelt is elected to a record fourth presidential term, with Sen. Harry Truman as his new running mate, defeating New York Gov. Thomas Dewey. FDR signs the G.I. Bill of Rights, which includes home and business loans and education grants. Meat rationing ends, and production of domestic appliances resumes.

INTERNATIONAL NEWS: D-Day (June 6) sees the Anglo-American invasion of Europe, under Gen. Dwight Eisenhower, launched at Normandy. Less than three months later, Paris is liberated, soon followed by several Belgian cities. Free French leader Charles DeGaulle forms a provisional government. Just before D-Day, Allied forces also liberate Rome. Gen. Douglas MacArthur's Pacific campaign leads to victory in the Philippines. The Russian Army pushes further German retreats on the Eastern Front. Nazi V-2 rockets attack London.

COMMERCE AND SCIENCE: Jet aircraft are used for the first time. Ball-point pens are introduced in the U.S.

FADS AND FASHION: Bathing suits are becoming briefer each year, due in part to the scarcity of materials.

SPORTS: The St. Louis Cardinals win a trolley-car World Series, in six games, over the St. Louis Browns, with baseball depleted of its stars by the war. The Green Bay Packers defeat the New York Giants in the NFL title game, 14-7. Appropriately for wartime, Army reigns as #1 in college football.

MOVIES: *Going My Way* is the year's sentimental #1 hit and Best Picture winner and also earns Bing Crosby an Oscar. Ingrid Bergman is honored as Best Actress for *Gaslight*. Other top films include *Double Indemnity* starring Barbara Stanwyck, *Meet Me in St. Louis* with Judy Garland, *Cover Girl* featuring Rita Hayworth, *Laura* with Gene Tierney and Laurence Olivier in *Henry V*.

RADIO: *The Adventures of Ozzie & Harriet* premieres, as does *Roy Rogers* and *The Danny Kaye Show*.

THEATER: Broadway enjoys a banner year, with multiple hits led by the Pulitzer Prize-winning *Harvey*, the Sonja Henie spectacle *Hats Off to Ice*, the sentimental *I Remember Mama* and the Harold Arlen musical *Bloomer Girl*. Aaron Copland's *Appalachian Spring* premieres.

BOOKS: Best-sellers include *Strange Fruit* by Lillian Smith, *The Robe* by Lloyd C. Douglas and *Brave Men* by Ernie Pyle.

1. Bing Crosby
1,911

2. Andrews Sisters
950

3. Jimmy Dorsey
746

4.	670	**Harry James**		13.	328	**Lawrence Welk**
5.	564	**Ink Spots**		14.	317	**Woody Herman**
6.	492	**Dick Haymes**		15.	311	**Tommy Dorsey**
7.	460	**Guy Lombardo**		16.	308	**Four King Sisters**
8.	421	**Ella Fitzgerald**		17.	306	**Jo Stafford**
9.	411	**Frank Sinatra**		18.	305	**Louis Jordan**
10.	382	**Helen Forrest**		19.	289	**Mills Brothers**
11.	368	**Ella Mae Morse**		20.	280	**The Merry Macs**
12.	344	**Glen Gray**				

1944 — TOP SONGWRITERS

	# of Hits	Points			# of Hits	Points	
1.	10	895	**Jimmy Van Heusen**	7.	7	635	**Sunny Skylar**
2.	9	803	**Johnny Burke**	8.	7	627	**Al Hoffman**
3.	9	776	**Jimmy McHugh**	9.	7	614	**Harold Adamson**
4.	8	710	**Leo Robin**	10.	6	558	**Jerome Kern**
5.	8	694	**Frank Loesser**		6	558	**Cole Porter**
6.	7	641	**Ira Gershwin**	12.	6	545	**Jule Styne**

1944 — TOP ARTIST DEBUTS

1.	1/08 †	**Jo Stafford** (6)		8.	4/29	**Helen Forrest** (75)
2.	1/22	**Ernest Tubb** (130)		9.	6/24	**Martha Tilton** (116)
3.	2/12	**Louis Jordan** (54)		10.	7/01	**The Three Suns** (77)
4.	2/19	**Al Trace** (132)		11.	7/29	**Betty Hutton** (78)
5.	4/01	**Stan Kenton** (50)		12.	8/26	**Evelyn Knight** (59)
6.	4/08	**The Pied Pipers** (65)		13.	9/30	**Red Foley** (74)
7.	4/22	**Andy Russell** (73)		14.	10/07	**Frankie Carle** (48)

PEAK DATE	WEEKS				RANK	GOLD	Title / PEAK POSITION / Songwriter(s)	SYMBOL	DEBUT	Artist
	CH	10	5	PK						

1

PEAK DATE	CH	10	5	PK	RANK	GOLD	Title / Peak Position	Artist
8/5	27	21	19	9	1	●	**Swinging On A Star**......Johnny Burke/Jimmy Van Heusen <B:12> Best Seller: 11,3,3,3,2,2,2,1,1,1,1,1,1,1,1,2,2,4,3 Juke Box: 19,19,10,11,9,11,7,8,5,5,7,4,5,2,1,1,1,1,1,1,1,2,3,-,6,19,14	**Bing Crosby**
1/15	19	19	15	9	2		**Shoo-Shoo Baby**......Phil Moore <B:17> Juke Box: 5,1,1,1,1,1,1,1,1,3,3,3,4,3,8,10,10,8 Best Seller: 7,9,3,2,4,2,3,3,5,3,5,4,3,4,9	**Andrews Sisters**
12/16	21	18	16	8	3	●	**Don't Fence Me In**......Cole Porter <B:8> Best Seller: 9,9,7,3,1,1,1,1,1,1,2,2,2,2,3,8 Juke Box: 18,7,2,1,1,1,1,1,1,1,2,2,2,2,2,2,3,10,12,17 Disc Jockey: 1,1,1,1,1,1,3,8,13	**Bing Crosby & the Andrews Sisters**
3/4	23	21	14	7	4	●	**Besame Mucho (Kiss Me Much)**......Sunny Skylar/Consuelo Velazquez <B:5> Best Seller: 10,5,2,3,2,2,1,1,1,1,1,1,1,4,5,7 Juke Box: 10,11,4,3,3,3,3,2,2,2,2,2,2,1,2,3,3,6,4,10,10,12	**Jimmy Dorsey** (Bob Eberly/Kitty Kallen)
6/10	28	23	19	6	5		**I'll Get By (As Long As I Have You)**......Fred Ahlert/Roy Turk <B:8> Juke Box: 20,10,5,5,4,5,2,4,2,1,1,1,1,1,2,2,5,3,6,4,10,5,14,9,14,11,12 Best Seller: 5,7,3,2,3,2,2,1,1,1,2,1,3,3,3,3,4,3,7,8,9	**Harry James** (Dick Haymes)
10/14	14	13	9	6	6		**(There'll Be A) Hot Time In The Town Of Berlin (When The Yanks Go Marching In)**......Joe Bushkin/John DeVries <B:2> Juke Box: 10,8,2,1,1,1,1,1,1,2,3,7,7,12	**Bing Crosby & the Andrews Sisters**
10/7	33	28	18	5	7	●	**You Always Hurt The One You Love**......Doris Fisher/Allan Roberts <B:8> Best Seller: 16,8,10,4,3,4,3,2,3,1,3,1,1,2,2,2,1,1,5,8 Juke Box: 14,14,10,8,6,6,4,8,6,6,5,5,5,4,4,4,3,3,5,4,2,2,3,3,3,4,4,6,8,11,12,10,15	**Mills Brothers**
4/29	22	18	15	5	8		**San Fernando Valley**......Gordon Jenkins <B:3> Juke Box: 17,-,13,7,5,4,3,1,1,1,1,3,1,3,2,3,5,4,4,9,10,17,-,16 Best Seller: 6,7,6,2,5,2,3,5,6,4,8,11	**Bing Crosby**
1/29	20	20	14	5	9		**My Heart Tells Me (Should I Believe My Heart?)**......Mack Gordon/Harry Warren <B:4> Best Seller: 8,7,4,5,7,2,2,2,2,1,1,1,1,1,2,4,3,8,9,9 Juke Box: 3,3,2,2,2,2,2,2,3,3,4,4,6,7,11,16,13,-,18	**Glen Gray** (Eugenie Baird)
5/6	18	14	12	5	10		**I Love You**......Cole Porter <A:1> Best Seller: 3,2,1,1,1,1,1,4,2,4,4,4,8,6 Juke Box: 19,10,9,4,3,2,1,2,1,3,2,4,2,6,6,14,11,14	**Bing Crosby**
3/18	15	11	7	5	11		**Mairzy Doats**......Milton Drake/Al Hoffman/Jerry Livingston [N] Juke Box: 15,6,4,1,1,1,1,2,6,9,7,18,11,15 Best Seller: 7,3,2,2,2,2,3,5,9	**The Merry Macs**
10/14	24	20	17	4	12		**I'll Walk Alone**......Sammy Cahn/Jule Styne <A:1> Best Seller: 7,5,8,4,3,2,3,2,3,1,3,2,1,1,1,2,3,2,9,5 Juke Box: 13,14,6,12,13,7,6,4,6,5,4,4,2,2,2,1,2,4,4,7,6,8,14,17	**Dinah Shore**
7/1	25	20	16	4	13		**I'll Be Seeing You**......Sammy Fain/Irving Kahal <A:1> Best Seller: 8,3,3,3,2,1,2,1,1,2,2,2,2,2,5,4,7,10 Juke Box: 20,12,16,11,10,7,6,5,6,5,3,2,2,2,1,4,4,6,4,6,5,6,10,-,14,7	**Bing Crosby**
8/5	25	21	12	2	14	●	**G.I. Jive**......Johnny Mercer <B:2> Juke Box: 18,14,12,9,9,7,8,6,4,3,2,3,3,1,1,4,2,2,3,9,4,9,7,-,10,18 Best Seller: 9,6,9,8,8,5,10,5,5,3,9,6,6,6	**Louis Jordan**
12/2	18	15	12	2	15	●	**Into Each Life Some Rain Must Fall**......Doris Fisher/Allan Roberts <A:1> Juke Box: 14,10,4,3,1,1,2,2,2,2,2,3,5,5,7,8,14,-,13 Best Seller: 5,6,5,5,8	**Ink Spots & Ella Fitzgerald**
12/9	17	14	11	2	16		**I'm Making Believe**......Mack Gordon/James Monaco <A:1> Best Seller: 4,4,1,1,2,2,2,2,3,4,6,5 Juke Box: 20,11,7,7,5,5,5,3,3,4,4,4,4,10,10,12 Disc Jockey: 5,6,13,-,-,10,12	**Ink Spots & Ella Fitzgerald**
4/22	19	14	8	2	17		**It's Love-Love-Love**......Mack David/Alex Kramer/Joan Whitney <B:16> Best Seller: 3,1,1,6,6,5,9,8,10,14 Juke Box: 17,14,11,6,6,4,3,5,2,3,5,3,6,5,9,13,10,7,-,-,19	**Guy Lombardo** (Skip Nelson)

2

PEAK DATE	CH	10	5	PK	RANK	GOLD	Title	Artist
4/8	19	19	12	3	18	●	**Holiday For Strings**......David Rose [I] ❶	David Rose
9/9	19	14	10	3	19		**Is You Is Or Is You Ain't (Ma' Baby)**......Billy Austin/Louis Jordan <A:1>	Louis Jordan
8/19	16	12	10	3	20		**Amor**......Gabriel Ruiz/Sunny Skylar <B:5>	Bing Crosby
12/2	14	12	9	2	21		**The Trolley Song**......Ralph Blane/Hugh Martin	The Pied Pipers
6/10	18	15	9	1	22		**Long Ago (And Far Away)**......Ira Gershwin/Jerome Kern	Helen Forrest & Dick Haymes
10/21	13	10	6	1	23		**Is You Is Or Is You Ain't (Ma' Baby)**......Billy Austin/Louis Jordan <A:1>	Bing Crosby & the Andrews Sisters
9/9	10	10	6	1	24		**Time Waits For No One**......Cliff Friend/Charles Tobias	Helen Forrest
1/15	9	9	5	1	25		**They're Either Too Young Or Too Old**......Frank Loesser/Arthur Schwartz <B:3>	Jimmy Dorsey (Kitty Kallen)
5/6	20	14	4	1	26		**Don't Sweetheart Me**......Cliff Friend/Charles Tobias <B:16>	Lawrence Welk (Wayne Marsh)

3

PEAK DATE	CH	10	5	PK	RANK	GOLD	Title	Artist
1/22	13	13	6	2	27		**Star Eyes**......Gene DePaul/Don Raye <A:2>	Jimmy Dorsey (Bob Eberly/Kitty Kallen)
11/4	12	10	4	2	28		**Together**......Lew Brown/B.G. DeSylva/Ray Henderson <B:4>	Helen Forrest & Dick Haymes
3/25	15	11	6	1	29		**Poinciana (Song Of The Tree)**......Buddy Bernier/Nat Simon <A:1>	Bing Crosby

1944

PEAK DATE	WEEKS				RANK	GOLD	Title / PEAK POSITION / Songwriter(s)	SYMBOL	DEBUT	Artist
	CH	10	5	PK						

3 (cont'd)

PEAK DATE	CH	10	5	PK	RANK	GOLD	Title / Songwriter(s)			Artist
12/9	12	7	2	1	30		Dance With A Dolly (With A Hole In Her Stockin') ....*Jimmy Eaton/ Mickey Leader/Terry Shand* <A:3>			Russ Morgan (Al Jennings)

4

10/7	24	17	6	3	31		I'll Walk Alone................*Sammy Cahn/Jule Styne* <B:24>			Martha Tilton
1/15	15	15	5	3	32		Shoo-Shoo Baby................*Phil Moore* <A:4>	❶		Ella Mae Morse
3/25	14	9	4	3	33		I Couldn't Sleep A Wink Last Night......*Harold Adamson/Jimmy McHugh* <B:15>			Frank Sinatra
10/28	12	9	3	2	34	●	Too-Ra-Loo-Ra-Loo-Ral (That's An Irish Lullaby) ....*James Shannon*			Bing Crosby
4/15	16	8	2	2	35		When They Ask About You................*Sam Stept* <B:22>			Jimmy Dorsey (Kitty Kallen)
7/29	17	10	2	1	36		I'll Be Seeing You ....*Sammy Fain/Irving Kahal*			Tommy Dorsey (Frank Sinatra)
2/12	10	5	2	1	37		Cherry................*Don Redman* <B:20>	[I]		Harry James
9/30	9	5	2	1	38		It Had To Be You................*Isham Jones/Gus Kahn* <A:3>			Dick Haymes & Helen Forrest
12/23	18	12	1	1	39		And Her Tears Flowed Like Wine......*Joe Greene/Stan Kenton/Charles Lawrence* <B:9>			Stan Kenton (Anita O'Day)
12/30	10	8	1	1	40		The Trolley Song................*Ralph Blane/Hugh Martin*			Judy Garland
5/6	11	7	1	1	41		It's Love-Love-Love................*Mack David/Alex Kramer/Joan Whitney* <B:21>			The Four King Sisters
2/19	12	5	1	1	42		No Love, No Nothin'................*Leo Robin/Harry Warren* <A:4>			Ella Mae Morse
1/22	6	4	1	1	43		My Shining Hour................*Harold Arlen/Johnny Mercer* <A:1>			Glen Gray (Eugenie Baird)

5

2/26	11	8	1	1	44		My Ideal ....*Newell Chase/Leo Robin/Richard Whiting* <A:1>			Jimmy Dorsey (Bob Eberly)
3/25	10	8	1	1	45		Speak Low................*Ogden Nash/Kurt Weill* <B:11>			Guy Lombardo (Billy Leach)
6/24	9	8	1	1	46		Amor................*Gabriel Ruiz/Sunny Skylar*			Andy Russell
3/4	8	6	1	1	47		No Love, No Nothin'................*Leo Robin/Harry Warren*			Johnny Long (Patti Dugan)
1/22	6	6	1	1	48	●	Boogie Woogie................*Clarence "Pine Top" Smith* [I] {re-charted in 1945 (#4)}			Tommy Dorsey
9/30	12	5	1	1	49		It Had To Be You................*Isham Jones/Gus Kahn* <B:7>			Betty Hutton
7/22	5	4	1	1	50		Long Ago (And Far Away) ....*Ira Gershwin/Jerome Kern* <A:2>			Bing Crosby
12/30	5	3	1	1	51		I Dream Of You................*Marjorie Goetschius/Edna Osser*			Andy Russell
12/30	3	2	1	1	52	●	White Christmas................*Irving Berlin* [X-R]			Bing Crosby

6

5/20	12	12		3	53		Long Ago (And Far Away) ....*Ira Gershwin/Jerome Kern* <B:8>			Jo Stafford
10/21	17	7		2	54		Dance With A Dolly (With A Hole In Her Stocking) ....*Jimmy Eaton/ Mickey Leader/Terry Shand*	❶		Evelyn Knight
10/7	8	7		2	55		I'll Walk Alone................*Sammy Cahn/Jule Styne*			Mary Martin
7/15	16	5		1	56		Good Night, Wherever You Are ...*Al Hoffman/Dick Robertson/Frank Weldon* <B:18>			Russ Morgan
1/8	5	5		1	57		Vict'ry Polka................*Sammy Cahn/Jule Styne* <A:2>			Bing Crosby & the Andrews Sisters
2/19	7	2		1	58		Do Nothin' Till You Hear From Me ....*Duke Ellington/Bob Russell* [I]			Duke Ellington

7

6/3	16	10		2	59		Milkman, Keep Those Bottles Quiet................*Gene DePaul/Don Raye* <B:13>			Ella Mae Morse
9/23	14	7		2	60		Pretty Kitty Blue Eyes................*Mann Curtis/Vic Mizzy*			The Merry Macs
7/29	7	7		1	61		His Rocking Horse Ran Away ....*Johnny Burke/Jimmy Van Heusen* <A:5>	❶		Betty Hutton
11/4	11	4		1	62		Smoke On The Water................*Zeke Clements/Earl Nunn*	❶		Red Foley
3/4	11	4		1	63		Do Nothin' Till You Hear From Me................*Duke Ellington/Bob Russell* <B:12>			Woody Herman
5/27	10	4		1	64		I'll Get By (As Long As I Have You)................*Fred Ahlert/Roy Turk* <B:11>			Ink Spots
9/23	18	3		1	65		How Many Hearts Have You Broken ....*Al Kaufman/Marty Symes* <B:8>			The Three Suns
10/28	11	3		1	66		Together................*Lew Brown/B.G. DeSylva/Ray Henderson*			Guy Lombardo (Tony Craig)
3/18	6	3		1	67		Mairzy Doats ....*Milton Drake/Al Hoffman/Jerry Livingston* [N]	❶		Al Trace ("Red" Maddock)
1/15	3	2		1	68		The Dreamer................*Frank Loesser/Arthur Schwartz* <B:10>	❶		Kay Armen
12/30	2	2		1	69	●	White Christmas................*Irving Berlin* <B:19> [X] {re-charted in 1945 (#5) and 1946 (#6)}			Frank Sinatra
4/8	3	1		1	70		I Love You................*Cole Porter* <B:21>			Enric Madriguera (Bob Lido)

8

9/30	5	3		3	71		Till Then................*Sol Marcus/Eddie Seiler/Guy Wood* <A:1>			Mills Brothers
9/2	8	3		1	72		Time Waits For No One................*Cliff Friend/Charles Tobias*			Johnny Long (Patti Dugan)
4/29	4	3		1	73		I Love You................*Cole Porter* <A:6>			Jo Stafford
8/5	13	2		1	74		Straighten Up And Fly Right ....*Nat "King" Cole/Irving Mills* <B:18>			Andrews Sisters
6/3	7	2		1	75		Long Ago (And Far Away) ....*Ira Gershwin/Jerome Kern* <B:16>			Perry Como
4/8	1	1		1	76		Mairzy Doats ....*Milton Drake/Al Hoffman/Jerry Livingston*	❶		The Pied Pipers

9

| 1/22 | 3 | 3 | | 1 | 77 | | Blue Rain ....*Johnny Mercer/Jimmy Van Heusen* | | | Glenn Miller (Ray Eberle) |
| 12/9 | 10 | 2 | | 1 | 78 | | Dance With A Dolly (With a Hole In Her Stocking) ....*Jimmy Eaton/ Mickey Leader/Terry Shand* | | | Tony Pastor |

PEAK DATE	WEEKS CH	10	5	PK	RANK	GOLD	Title — Songwriter(s)	SYMBL/DEBUT	Artist

9 (cont'd)

PEAK DATE	WEEKS CH	10	5	PK	RANK	Title — Songwriter(s)	Artist
7/1	5	1		1	79	Straighten Up And Fly Right ....*Nat "King" Cole/Irving Mills <B:24>*	The King Cole Trio
11/4	4	1		1	80	How Many Hearts Have You Broken ....*Al Kaufman/Marty Symes <A:4>*	Stan Kenton (Gene Howard)

10

7/29	9	3		3	81	Amor ....*Gabriel Ruiz/Sunny Skylar* **[F]**	Xavier Cugat (Carmen Castillo)
4/22	2	2		2	82	Bésame Mucho (Kiss Me Much) ....*Sunny Skylar/Consuelo Velazquez* ❶	Andy Russell
1/22	9	1		1	83	How Sweet You Are ....*Frank Loesser/Arthur Schwartz <A:7>*	Kay Armen
4/8	8	1		1	84	The Music Stopped ....*Harold Adamson/Jimmy McHugh*	Woody Herman (Frances Wayne)
4/1	8	1		1	85	Cow-Cow Boogie (Cuma-Ti-Yi-Ay) ..*Benny Carter/Gene DePaul/Don Raye <B:22>*	Ink Spots & Ella Fitzgerald
7/15	5	1		1	86	Milkman, Keep Those Bottles Quiet ....*Gene DePaul/Don Raye*	Woody Herman
10/21	5	1		1	87	The Patty Cake Man ....*Roy Jordan*	Ella Mae Morse
11/4	2	1		1	88	It Had To Be You ....*Isham Jones/Gus Kahn*	Artie Shaw
4/1	1	1		1	89	Do Nothin' 'Till You Hear From Me ....*Duke Ellington/Bob Russell* ❶	Stan Kenton (Red Dorris)
9/30	1	1		1	90	It Could Happen To You ....*Johnny Burke/Jimmy Van Heusen*	Jo Stafford

11

4/1	10			2	91	Take It Easy ....*Albert DeBru/Vic Mizzy/Irving Taylor <A:5>*	Guy Lombardo (Lombardo Trio)
3/18	6			2	92	Poinciana (Song of the Tree) ....*Buddy Bernier/Nat Simon* **[I]**	David Rose
11/18	5			2	93	Cuban Sugar Mill ....*Freddie Slack* **[I]**	Freddie Slack
10/14	2			2	94	We Might As Well Forget It ....*John Bond <B:14>*	Bob Wills (Leon Huff)
1/22	19			1	95	My Ideal ....*Newell Chase/Leo Robin/Richard Whiting* ❶	Billy Butterfield (Margaret Whiting)
8/12	10			1	96	How Blue The Night ....*Harold Adamson/Jimmy McHugh <B:22>*	Dick Haymes
7/22	4			1	97 ●	Long Ago (And Far Away) ....*Ira Gershwin/Jerome Kern <B:13>*	Guy Lombardo (Tony Craig)
7/29	1			1	98	Someday I'll Meet You Again ....*Max Steiner/Ned Washington <A:7>*	Ink Spots
12/30	1			1	99	Always ....*Irving Berlin* **[I]**	Gordon Jenkins

12

2/5	8			3	100	It Must Be Jelly ('Cause Jam Don't Shake Like That) ....*George Williams/ J. Chalmers MacGregor*	Glenn Miller
6/3	7			1	101	Suddenly It's Spring ....*Johnny Burke/Jimmy Van Heusen*	Glen Gray (Eugenie Baird)
5/13	7			1	102	By The River Of The Roses ....*Joe Burke/Marty Symes <A:7>*	Woody Herman
3/11	6			1	103	Poinciana (Song of the Tree) ....*Buddy Bernier/Nat Simon <B:23>* **[I]** ❶	Benny Carter
6/3	4			1	104	I'll Get By (As Long As I Have You) ....*Fred Ahlert/Roy Turk*	The Four King Sisters
10/7	3			1	105	Estrellita (My Little Star) ....*Manuel Ponce* **[I]**	Harry James
3/4	2			1	106	Shoo-Shoo Baby ....*Phil Moore*	Jan Garber (Liz Tilton)
9/9	1			1	107	Going My Way ....*Johnny Burke/Jimmy Van Heusen <A:1>*	Bing Crosby
10/7	1			1	108	The Day After Forever ....*Johnny Burke/Jimmy Van Heusen <B:13>*	Bing Crosby
11/11	1			1	109	Together ....*Lew Brown/B.G. DeSylva/Ray Henderson*	Dinah Shore

13

7/1	5			2	110	Milkman, Keep Those Bottles Quiet ....*Gene DePaul/Don Raye*	The Four King Sisters
9/23	4			2	111	A Fellow On A Furlough ....*Bobby Worth* ✦	Phil Hanna
8/26	3			2	112	Tico-Tico ....*Zequinha Abreu/Ervin Drake/Aloysio Oliveira* **[F]** ✦	Charles Wolcott (Aloysio Oliveira)
12/30	7			1	113	The Trolley Song ....*Ralph Blane/Hugh Martin*	The Four King Sisters
6/17	5			1	114	G.I. Jive ....*Johnny Mercer*	Johnny Mercer
6/3	5			1	115	Tess's Torch Song (I Had A Man) ....*Harold Arlen/Ted Koehler <A:7>*	Ella Mae Morse
5/20	5			1	116	Is My Baby Blue Tonight ....*Lou Handman/William Tracey*	Lawrence Welk (Jayne Walton)
9/16	3			1	117	Lili Marlene ....*Mack David/Hans Leip/Norbert Schultze*	Perry Como
4/8	2			1	118	Holiday For Strings ....*David Rose*	Jimmy Dorsey
2/12	1			1	119	The Prodigal Son ....*Floyd Jenkins*	Roy Acuff
12/16	1			1	120	It Could Happen To You ....*Johnny Burke/Jimmy Van Heusen <A:12>*	Bing Crosby
7/15	1			1	121	Humoresque ....*Anton Dvorak <A:11>* **[I]**	Guy Lombardo

14

4/8	9			1	122	Don't Believe Everything You Dream ...*Harold Adamson/Jimmy McHugh <B:17>*	Ink Spots
12/2	4			1	123	How Many Hearts Have You Broken (With Those Great Big Beautiful Eyes) ....*Al Kaufman/Marty Symes*	Tiny Hill
10/21	3			1	124	You're From Texas ....*Cindy Walker <A:11>*	Bob Wills (Leon McAuliffe)
1/15	2			1	125	Have I Stayed Away Too Long? ....*Frank Loesser*	Perry Como
9/2	2			1	126	I Learned A Lesson, I'll Never Forget ....*Joe Davis* ❶	5 Red Caps
2/26	1			1	127	My Heart Tells Me ....*Mack Gordon/Harry Warren <B:19>*	Jan Garber (Bob Davis)
8/19	1			1	128	Eager Beaver ....*Stan Kenton* **[I]**	Stan Kenton
12/16	1			1	129	The Very Thought Of You ....*Ray Noble <A:4>*	Vaughn Monroe
9/30	1			1	130	Fellow On A Furlough ....*Bobby Worth* ✦	Al Sack (Bob Matthews)
1/22	1			1	131	Old Acquaintance ....*Kim Gannon/Franz Waxman <B:16>* ❶	Jo Stafford
2/5	1			1	132	My Ideal ....*Newell Chase/Leo Robin/Richard Whiting*	Maxine Sullivan
2/12	1			1	133	I Wish That I Could Hide Inside This Letter ..*Nat Simon/Charles Tobias <B:17>*	Lawrence Welk (Jayne Walton)

PEAK DATE	WEEKS				RANK	GOLD	Title / PEAK POSITION / Songwriter(s)	SYMBL	DEBUT	Artist
	CH	10	5	PK						

15

PEAK DATE	CH	10	5	PK	RANK	GOLD	Title — Songwriter(s)	SYMBL	DEBUT	Artist
9/16	3			2	134		Night And Day .... *Cole Porter* [R]			Frank Sinatra
10/21	8			1	135		What A Diff'rence A Day Made .... *Stanley Adams/Maria Grever*			Andy Russell
3/25	3			1	136		A Lovely Way To Spend An Evening .... *Harold Adamson/Jimmy McHugh* <A:4>			Frank Sinatra
1/22	3			1	137		Try Me One More Time .... *Ernest Tubb*	●		Ernest Tubb
5/13	2			1	138		Suddenly It's Spring .... *Johnny Burke/Jimmy Van Heusen* <B:25>			Hildegarde
7/8	2			1	139		Memphis Blues .... *W.C. Handy* <B:21> [I]			Harry James
1/29	2			1	140		Sweet Slumber .... *Lucky Millinder/Al Neiburg/Henri Woode*			Lucky Millinder (Trevor Bacon)
2/19	1			1	141		Abraham .... *Irving Berlin* <B:20>			Freddy Martin (Glenn Hughes)

16

PEAK DATE	CH	10	5	PK	RANK	GOLD	Title — Songwriter(s)	SYMBL	DEBUT	Artist
5/20	3			1	142		I Love You .... *Cole Porter* <A:8>			Perry Como
1/15	3			1	143		How Sweet You Are .... *Frank Loesser/Arthur Schwartz* <A:14>			Jo Stafford
9/2	2			1	144		Soldier's Last Letter .... *Henry Stewart/Ernest Tubb* <B:23>			Ernest Tubb
4/8	1			1	145		Mexico Joe .... *Johnny Lange/Leon Rene*	✦		Ivie Anderson with Ceele Burke's Orch.
1/15	1			1	146		Tweedle-O-Twill .... *Gene Autry/Fred Rose*			Gene Autry
1/22	1			1	147		For The Good Of Your Country .... *Count Basie*			Count Basie (Jimmy Rushing)
1/8	1			1	148		Solo Flight .... *Charlie Christian/Benny Goodman/James Mundy*			Benny Goodman
9/9	1			1	149		Lili Marlene .... *Mack David/Hans Leip/Norbert Schultze*			Hildegarde
2/12	1			1	150		Ration Blues .... *Collenane Clark/Anthonio Cosey/Louis Jordan*	●		Louis Jordan
2/19	1			1	151		I'll Be Around .... *Alec Wilder* <A:1>			Mills Brothers
7/1	1			1	152		Long Ago (And Far Away) .... *Ira Gershwin/Jerome Kern*	●		The Three Suns
4/15	1			1	153		Holiday For Strings .... *David Rose* [I]			Fred Waring
4/1	1			1	154		Mairzy Doats .... *Milton Drake/Al Hoffman/Jerry Livingston* <A:2>			Lawrence Welk (Bobby Beers)

17

PEAK DATE	CH	10	5	PK	RANK	GOLD	Title — Songwriter(s)	SYMBL	DEBUT	Artist
1/29	3			2	155		Down In The Valley .... *Frank Luther* <A:1>			Andrews Sisters
1/22	3			2	156		For The First Time (I've Fallen In Love) .... *David Kapp/Charles Tobias* <A:5>			Dick Haymes
10/14	2			1	157		An Hour Never Passes .... *Jimmy Kennedy*			Jimmy Dorsey (Gladys Tell)
6/10	2			1	158		Every Day Of My Life .... *Morty Berk/Billy Hayes/Harry James*			Frank Sinatra with Harry James
9/2	1			1	159		You Belong To My Heart Solamente Una Vez .... *Ray Gilbert/Agustin Lara* <A:14>	●		Phil Brito
1/22	1			1	160		The Surrey With The Fringe On Top .... *Oscar Hammerstein/Richard Rodgers*			Alfred Drake
2/26	1			1	161		Cherry .... *Don Redman*			Erskine Hawkins (Jimmy Mitchelle)
3/11	1			1	162		A Lovely Way To Spend An Evening .... *Harold Adamson/Jimmy McHugh* <A:14>			Ink Spots
10/21	1			1	163		Let's Sing A Song About Susie .... *Mack Gordon/Will Grosz*			The Merry Macs
7/1	1			1	164		By The Light Of The Silv'ry Moon .... *Gus Edwards/Edward Madden* [R]			Ray Noble (Snooky Lanson)
2/5	1			1	165		Cleanin' My Rifle (And Dreamin' Of You) .... *Allie Wrubel* <A:14>			Lawrence Welk (Bobby Beers)

18

PEAK DATE	CH	10	5	PK	RANK	GOLD	Title — Songwriter(s)	SYMBL	DEBUT	Artist
7/1	1			1	166		Sing A Tropical Song .... *Frank Loesser/Jimmy McHugh*			Andrews Sisters
7/8	1			1	167		Tico-Tico .... *Zequinha Abreu/Ervin Drake/Aloysio Oliveira* <A:8>			Andrews Sisters
1/29	1			1	168		Cryin' The Boogie Blues .... *Emporia Scott* [I]			Will Bradley
4/1	1			1	169		Too Late To Worry .... *Al Dexter*			Al Dexter
1/22	1			1	170		Embraceable You .... *George Gershwin/Ira Gershwin*			Tommy Dorsey (Jo Stafford/Pied Pipers)
9/30	1			1	171		Hamp's Boogie Woogie .... *Milton Buckner/Lionel Hampton* [I]			Lionel Hampton
3/25	1			1	172		Friendly Tavern Polka .... *Jerry Bowne/Frank DeVol*			Horace Heidt (Jerry Bowne)
12/30	1			1	173		Let Me Love You Tonight (No Te Importe Saber) .... *Mitchell Parish/Rene Touzet*			Woody Herman (Billie Rogers)
8/12	1			1	174		It Had To Be You .... *Isham Jones/Gus Kahn*			Earl Hines (Madeline Greene)
4/8	1			1	175		When My Man Comes Home .... *Buddy Johnson/J. Mayo Williams*	●		Buddy Johnson (Ella Johnson)
10/21	1			1	176		I Dream A Lot About You .... *Trummie Young*			Jimmie Lunceford (Dan Grissom)
1/8	1			1	177		Sunrise Serenade .... *Frankie Carle* [I]			Glenn Miller
7/15	1			1	178		Louise .... *Leo Robin/Richard Whiting* <A:6>			Russ Morgan
8/26	1			1	179		Red Blues .... *Robert Haggart*			Cootie Williams (Eddie "Cleanhead" Vinson)

19

PEAK DATE	CH	10	5	PK	RANK	GOLD	Title — Songwriter(s)	SYMBL	DEBUT	Artist
4/8	2			1	180		Silver Wings In The Moonlight .... *Hugh Charles/Sonny Miller/Leo Towers*			Freddie Slack (Margaret Whiting)
12/30	1			1	181	●	I'll Be Home For Christmas (If Only In My Dreams) .... *Kim Gannon/Walter Kent/Buck Ram* [X-R]			Bing Crosby
3/25	1			1	182		Another One Of Them Things .... *Sy Oliver* [I]			Tommy Dorsey
10/21	1			1	183		Umbriago .... *Irving Caesar/Jimmy Durante* [N]			Jimmy Durante
5/13	1			1	184		No Love, No Nothin' .... *Leo Robin/Harry Warren* <A:14>			Jan Garber (Liz Tilton)
4/1	1			1	185		Back Beat Boogie .... *Harry James* [I]			Harry James
6/17	1			1	186		Arsenic And Old Face .... *Jerry Jerome* [I]	✦		Jerry Jerome
9/16	1			1	187		Sam's Got Him .... *Donald Kahn*			Johnny Mercer
9/30	1			1	188		Since You Went Away .... *Lou Forbes/Kermit Goell/Ted Grouya*	●		Jerry Wald (Ginnie Powell)
5/20	1			1	189		Tess's Torch Song (I Had A Man) .... *Harold Arlen/Ted Koehler*	●		Cootie Williams (Pearl Bailey)

PEAK DATE	WEEKS				RANK	GOLD	Title	PEAK POSITION — Songwriter(s)	SYMBL	DEBUT	Artist
	CH	10	5	PK							

20

PEAK DATE	CH	10	5	PK	RANK	GOLD	Title	Songwriter(s) / Symbol	DEBUT	Artist
7/8	2			1	190		Once Too Often	Mack Gordon/James Monaco		Ella Fitzgerald
3/11	2			1	191		I've Had This Feeling Before (But Never Like This)	Sam Stept		Johnny Long (Gene Williams)
10/7	1			1	192		Charmaine	Lew Pollack/Erno Rapee [I] ❶		Frankie Carle
11/18	1			1	193		Gee, Baby, Ain't I Good To You	Don Redman		The King Cole Trio
3/25	1			1	194		Main Stem	Duke Ellington [I]		Duke Ellington
1/8	1			1	195		Jump Town	Harry James/Jack Matthias <A:4> [I]		Harry James
6/17	1			1	196		Behind Those Swinging Doors	Fleming Allan [N]		Spike Jones (Del Porter)
4/29	1			1	197		San Fernando Valley	Gordon Jenkins		Johnny Mercer (The Barries)
4/1	1			1	198		Here We Go Again	Jerry Gray [I]		Glenn Miller
8/12	1			1	199		Hurry, Hurry	Benny Carter/Richard Larkin		Lucky Millinder (Wynonie Harris)
9/2	1			1	200		Take It, Jackson	Johnny Watson [I]		Vaughn Monroe
12/30	1			1	201		Robin Hood	Bob Miketta/Louis Prima		Tony Pastor
5/13	1			1	202		On A Little Street In Singapore	Peter DeRose/Billy Hill <A:17>		Frank Sinatra with Harry James

21

PEAK DATE	CH	10	5	PK	RANK	GOLD	Title	Songwriter(s) / Symbol	DEBUT	Artist
6/10	2			1	203		Someday I'll Meet You Again	Max Steiner/Ned Washington <A:7>		Enric Madriguera (Bob Lido)
12/30	1			1	204		I'll Forgive You But I Can't Forget	J.L. Frank/Pee Wee King		Roy Acuff
12/2	1			1	205		Sweet And Lovely	Gus Arnheim/Jules LeMare/Harry Tobias		Bing Crosby
4/29	1			1	206		Babalu	Margarita Lecuona [F]		Xavier Cugat (Miguelito Valdes)
4/15	1			1	207		Mairzy Doats And Dozy Doats (Mares Eat Oats and Does Eat Oats)	Milton Drake/Al Hoffman/Jerry Livingston <A:4> [N]		The Four King Sisters
10/7	1			1	208		Don't Take Your Love From Me	Henry Nemo		Glen Gray (Eugenie Baird)
6/17	1			1	209		She Broke My Heart In Three Places	Milton Drake/Al Hoffman/Jerry Livingston [N]		Hoosier Hot Shots
8/5	1			1	210		Sleepy Time Gal	Joseph Alden/Raymond Egan/Ange Lorenzo/Richard Whiting <A:15> [I]		Harry James
2/26	1			1	211		Besame Mucho	Sunny Skylar/Consuelo Velazquez		Abe Lyman (Rose Blane)
12/9	1			1	212		There's A New Moon Over My Shoulder	Lee Blastic/Jimmie Davis/Ekko Whelan <A:11>		Tex Ritter
3/25	1			1	213		Dancing In The Dark	Howard Dietz/Arthur Schwartz [I-R]		Artie Shaw
4/15	1			1	214		Irresistible You	Gene DePaul/Don Raye		Ginny Simms
10/28	1			1	215		It's Funny To Everyone But Me	Dave Franklin/Isham Jones		Frank Sinatra with Harry James

22

PEAK DATE	CH	10	5	PK	RANK	GOLD	Title	Songwriter(s) / Symbol	DEBUT	Artist
12/9	1			1	216		I Don't Want Anybody At All (If I Can't Have You)	Herb Magidson/Jule Styne <A:15>		Charlie Barnet (Huck Andrews)
4/22	1			1	217		Rosalita	Al Dexter <A:1>		Al Dexter
2/26	1			1	218		My First Love	Mack David/Ruth Lowe <A:4>		Jimmy Dorsey (Bob Eberly)
3/11	1			1	219		When My Sugar Walks Down The Street	Gene Austin/Jimmy McHugh/Irving Mills <A:10>		Ella Fitzgerald
3/18	1			1	220		A Journey To A Star	Leo Robin/Harry Warren		Judy Garland
12/23	1			1	221		Meet Me In St. Louis, Louis	Kerry Mills/Andrew Sterling		Judy Garland
4/29	1			1	222		Have I Stayed Away Too Long?	Frank Loesser	✦	"Tex" Grande
6/17	1			1	223		How Many Times Do I Have To Tell You	Harold Adamson/Jimmy McHugh <A:11>		Dick Haymes
11/4	1			1	224		Janie	Lee David		Dick Haymes
6/10	1			1	225		I'm In Love With Someone (Who Is Not In Love With Me)	Lew Marcus		Art Kassel (Jimmy Featherstone)
4/15	1			1	226		Back Door Stuff—Parts 1 & 2	Roger Segure [I]		Jimmie Lunceford
3/4	1			1	227		A String Of Pearls	Jerry Gray [I-R]		Glenn Miller
12/2	1			1	228		South	Thamon Hayes/Bennie Moten [I]		Bennie Moten's Kansas City Orch.
5/13	1			1	229		I'll Walk Alone	Sammy Cahn/Jule Styne		Louis Prima (Lily Ann Carol)

23

PEAK DATE	CH	10	5	PK	RANK	GOLD	Title	Songwriter(s) / Symbol	DEBUT	Artist
3/11	1			1	230		Hurry, Hurry!	Benny Carter/Richard Larkin <A:12>		Benny Carter (Savannah Churchill)
10/28	1			1	231		And The Angels Sing {originally charted in 1939 (#1)}	Ziggy Elman/Johnny Mercer [R]		Benny Goodman (Martha Tilton)
4/29	1			1	232		Amor Amor	Gabriel Ruiz/Sunny Skylar		Enric Madriguera (Bob Lido)
12/2	1			1	233		Wish You Were Waiting For Me	Bob Russell/David Saxon		Ginny Simms
12/23	1			1	234		Let Me Love You To-Night	Mitchell Parish/Rene Touzet <A:12>		Charlie Spivak (Jimmy Saunders)
6/24	1			1	235		Yesterday's Tears	Ernest Tubb <A:16>		Ernest Tubb

24

PEAK DATE	CH	10	5	PK	RANK	GOLD	Title	Songwriter(s) / Symbol	DEBUT	Artist
11/11	1			1	236		The Moment I Laid Eyes On You	Harold Arlen/Ted Koehler		Cab Calloway
5/6	1			1	237		I Can't See For Lookin'	Nadine Robinson/Doc Stanford <A:9>		The King Cole Trio
12/23	1			1	238		Moon On My Pillow	Charles Tobias/Elliott Tobias/Harry Tobias		Jimmy Dorsey (Teddy Walters)
11/25	1			1	239		Will You Still Be Mine?	Tom Adair/Matt Dennis		Tommy Dorsey (Connie Haines)
7/22	1			1	240		Swinging On A Star	Johnny Burke/Jimmy Van Heusen	✦	Gray Rains (Margie Wood)

1944

PEAK DATE	WEEKS				RANK	GOLD	Title / PEAK POSITION / Songwriter(s)	SYMBL	DEBUT	Artist
	CH	10	5	PK						

24 (cont'd)

PEAK DATE	CH	10	5	PK	RANK	GOLD	Title / Songwriter(s)	SYMBL	DEBUT	Artist
4/15	1			1	241		Summit Ridge Drive...Artie Shaw **[I-R]**			Artie Shaw
6/24	1			1	242		Texas Polka...................................Oakley Haldeman/Vick Knight/Lew Porter <A:4> ❶			Martha Tilton

25

PEAK DATE	CH	10	5	PK	RANK	GOLD	Title / Songwriter(s)	SYMBL	DEBUT	Artist
3/4	1			1	243		Leave Us Face It (We're In Love) ....Abe Burrows/Frank Loesser <A:15>			Hildegarde
11/11	1			1	244		Always ....Irving Berlin **[I]**	✦		Paul Lavalle
2/26	1			1	245		By The River Of Roses ....Joe Burke/Marty Symes			Abe Lyman (Frank Connors)
11/25	1			1	246		Oh Marie...Louis Prima <A:17>			Louis Prima (Lily Ann Carol)

1945

NATIONAL NEWS: President Franklin Delano Roosevelt dies of a cerebral hemorrhage on April 12 after twelve years in the White House, and just two months after he, Winston Churchill and Josef Stalin met at Yalta to plan the postwar future of Europe. Harry Truman takes over as President. The surrender of Germany and then Japan produces a joyous V-J Day for Americans on August 15. Rationing of gas, fuel oil, tires, meat and butter ends.

INTERNATIONAL NEWS: World War II at last is over. After Allied bombers devastate Dresden, American forces cross the Rhine and General Patton's tanks seize other German strongholds; Adolf Hitler commits suicide. The liberation of Nazi concentration camps reveals the horrors of the Holocaust. Germany surrenders on May 7. Following the bloody battle for Okinawa, the U.S. drops atomic bombs on Hiroshima and Nagasaki on August 6 and 9, leaving over 70,000 dead and forcing the unconditional surrender of Japan. The United Nations is established. Winston Churchill is defeated by Clement Attlee as Britain's prime minister. Charles DeGaulle is elected President of France.

SPORTS: Slugger Hank Greenberg and the Detroit Tigers defeat the Chicago Cubs in a seven-game World Series. The Cleveland Rams edge the Washington Redskins, 15-14, for the NFL championship. Doc Blanchard and Glenn Davis lead Army to its second straight national college football title. Oklahoma A&M is victorious in the NCAA basketball tourney. Byron Nelson wins an incredible 11 consecutive tournaments on the pro golf tour.

MOVIES: *The Lost Weekend*, with Best Actor Ray Milland, is the year's most-honored film. Joan Crawford wins the best-actress Oscar for *Mildred Pierce*. *The Bells of St. Mary's* with Bing Crosby is #1 at the box office. Alfred Hitchcock's *Spellbound* with Gregory Peck and Ingrid Bergman dazzles audiences.

THEATER: The whimsical *Harvey* is Broadway's biggest hit and also earns the Pulitzer Prize. Rodgers and Hammerstein score another musical triumph with *Carousel* starring John Raitt (Bonnie's father). Tennessee Williams' *The Glass Menagerie* provides the playwright's breakthrough on Broadway.

BOOKS: George Orwell's *Animal Farm* is published.

1945 — TOP 20 ARTISTS

1. **Bing Crosby**
1,446

2. **Sammy Kaye**
855

3. **Harry James**
800

4.	749	**Perry Como**
5.	736	**Frank Sinatra**
6.	700	**Tommy Dorsey**
7.	699	**Les Brown**
8.	657	**Dick Haymes**
9.	654	**Guy Lombardo**
10.	648	**Andrews Sisters**
11.	542	**Johnny Mercer**
12.	481	**Vaughn Monroe**
13.	450	**Kay Kyser**
14.	429	**Jo Stafford**
15.	404	**Benny Goodman**
16.	372	**Charlie Spivak**
17.	369	**Dinah Shore**
18.	364	**Freddy Martin**
19.	364	**Woody Herman**
20.	296	**Carmen Cavallaro**

1945 — TOP SONGWRITERS

	# of Hits	Points	
1.	23	2,121	**Sammy Cahn**
2.	21	1,978	**Johnny Mercer**
3.	19	1,760	**Jule Styne**
4.	11	1,037	**Oscar Hammerstein**
	11	1,037	**Richard Rodgers**
6.	11	1,009	**Harold Arlen**
7.	10	887	**Jimmy Van Heusen**
8.	9	818	**Irving Berlin**
9.	9	796	**Johnny Burke**
10.	8	754	**Harry Warren**
11.	7	657	**Moe Jaffe**
12.	6	572	**Sunny Skylar**

1945 — TOP ARTIST DEBUTS

1.	2/17	**Hal McIntyre** (131)
2.	6/30	**Carmen Cavallaro** (99)
3.	7/21	**The Modernaires** (137)
4.	10/06	**Billy Eckstine** (55)
5.	10/13 †	**Les Paul and Mary Ford** (22)
6.	10/27	**Margaret Whiting** (25)
7.	10/27	**Paul Weston** (47)
8.	11/10	**Peggy Lee** (37)
9.	11/10	**The Charioteers** (139)

1945

PEAK DATE	CH	10	5	PK	RANK	GOLD	Title / PEAK POSITION / Songwriter(s)	SYMBL / DEBUT	Artist

1

2/10 | 20 | 18 | 17 | 10 | **1 ●** | **Rum And Coca-Cola** .... *Morey Amsterdam/Paul Baron/Jeri Sullavan* <B:15> — **Andrews Sisters**
Juke Box: 20,5,2,2,2,1,1,1,1,1,1,1,1,2,3,4,10,11
Best Seller: 6,5,3,2,1,1,1,1,1,1,1,1,2,2,3,6
Disc Jockey: 3,3,2,3,3,3,3,2,3,10

9/15 | 19 | 17 | 16 | 10 | **2 ●** | **Till The End Of Time** .... *Buddy Kaye/Ted Mossman* <B:9> — **Perry Como**
Best Seller: 5,2,2,2,1,1,1,1,1,1,1,1,1,4,5,10
Disc Jockey: 7,3,3,2,1,1,1,1,1,1,1,1,2,3,4,5,11
Juke Box: 18,3,3,2,2,2,1,1,1,1,1,1,1,4,7,8,16

5/5 | 28 | 27 | 21 | 9 | **3 ●** | **Sentimental Journey** .... *Les Brown/Bud Green/Ben Homer* <B:16> — **Les Brown** (Doris Day)
Best Seller: 9,6,8,4,4,2,1,1,1,1,1,1,1,1,2,2,2,2,5,7,9,8
Disc Jockey: 14,10,9,5,9,4,5,5,6,1,6,5,3,2,2,1,1,1,1,1,1,3,2,2,3,2,4,8
Juke Box: 14,12,19,12,11,15,9,6,7,10,5,4,1,1,1,1,1,1,1,2,2,2,2,2,6,5,9

7/28 | 19 | 18 | 16 | 8 | **4** | **On The Atchison, Topeka And Santa Fe** ... *Johnny Mercer/Harry Warren* — **Johnny Mercer**
Juke Box: 10,3,2,1,1,1,1,1,1,1,1,2,2,2,2,3,3,8,11
Best Seller: 4,2,1,1,1,1,1,1,1,2,2,2,2,2,2,4
Disc Jockey: 8,4,3,1,1,1,1,1,1,2,2,2,2,2,2,2,2,3,11,12

4/7 | 16 | 13 | 12 | 7 | **5** | **My Dreams Are Getting Better All The Time** .. *Mann Curtis/Vic Mizzy* — **Les Brown** (Doris Day)
Best Seller: 2,2,1,1,1,1,1,1,1,3,8,9
Juke Box: 15,7,2,2,2,1,1,1,1,1,1,1,2,4,13,11
Disc Jockey: 8,4,1,1,1,3,2,3,3,4,3,3,7

5/12 | 29 | 23 | 16 | 6 | **6 ●** | **There! I've Said It Again** .... *Redd Evans/Dave Mann* <B:8> — **Vaughn Monroe** (Norton Sisters)
Juke Box: 11,7,7,7,5,4,1,1,1,1,1,2,2,2,2,2,2,1,5,6,7,6,5,11,8
Best Seller: 6,7,7,2,3,4,4,2,2,2,2,3,2,3,3,5,6,7,7
Disc Jockey: 18,13,12,10,6,7,7,5,4,3,2,2,3,3,2,2,2,4,3,8,12,7,5,11,10,12,-,12

12/22 | 20 | 17 | 14 | 6 | **7 ●** | **I Can't Begin To Tell You** .... *Mack Gordon/James Monaco* — **Bing Crosby with Carmen Cavallaro**
Juke Box: 15,11,9,5,4,1,2,1,1,1,1,1,3,3,4,4,4,9,11,15
Best Seller: 7,6,5,2,3,6,3,2,1,3,3,5,6,4,9,8,9
Disc Jockey: 15,12,9,11,9,3,-,2,5,4,5,8,11,4,10,13,7

11/17 | 16 | 13 | 11 | 4 | **8** | **Chickery Chick** .... *Sylvia Dee/Sid Lippman* — **Sammy Kaye** (Nancy Norman/Billy Williams)
Disc Jockey: 7,6,4,3,1,2,1,1,1,2,11,6,6,8,12,12
Best Seller: 10,4,4,1,2,2,2,1,2,1,2,3,8
Juke Box: 15,11,5,5,2,2,2,1,2,1,2,3,3,10,12

11/24 | 17 | 15 | 12 | 3 | **9** | **It's Been A Long, Long Time** .... *Sammy Cahn/Jule Styne* <B:15> — **Harry James** (Kitty Kallen)
Best Seller: 10,5,3,2,2,1,1,3,4,1,3,4,5,10
Disc Jockey: 3,5,3,2,2,3,1,2,2,2,1,2,6,7,11
Juke Box: 14,12,9,6,4,2,5,3,3,3,3,3,4,5,8,12,-,-,12

4/14 | 19 | 16 | 12 | 2 | **10** | **I'm Beginning To See The Light** .... *Duke Ellington/Don George/Johnny Hodges/Harry James* — **Harry James** (Kitty Kallen)
Disc Jockey: 13,5,5,7,5,4,4,4,7,5,2,1,3,1,6,5,8
Juke Box: 14,11,8,6,7,6,8,10,6,11,9,5,4,4,6,5,8,5,10
Best Seller: 7,10,7,7,10,5,6,4,5,5,8,8,8

3/17 | 16 | 14 | 11 | 2 | **11** | **Ac-Cent-Tchu-Ate The Positive** .... *Harold Arlen/Johnny Mercer* — **Johnny Mercer**
Disc Jockey: 2,2,3,2,2,2,2,1,1,6,3,8
Best Seller: 3,2,2,3,2,3,3,3,3,2,5,7,8
Juke Box: 13,8,6,3,3,3,3,3,3,3,2,3,7,9,14

12/1 | 16 | 14 | 10 | 2 | **12** | **It's Been A Long Long Time** .... *Sammy Cahn/Jule Styne* ❶ — **Bing Crosby with Les Paul**
Juke Box: 13,11,7,6,2,4,4,1,1,2,4,3,3,4,9,9
Best Seller: 10,7,2,3,3,3,1,3,4,4,7,7
Disc Jockey: 11,5,5,5,4,5,4,3,3,3,7,12,8,11,9

12/29 | 4 | 4 | 2 | 2 | **13 ●** | **White Christmas** .... *Irving Berlin* [X-R] — **Bing Crosby**
Disc Jockey: 10,6,**1**,**1**
Juke Box: 8,5,4,7
Best Seller: 9,9,10,9

3/31 | 19 | 17 | 12 | 1 | **14** | **Candy** .... *Mack David/Alex Kramer/Joan Whitney* <B:12> — **Johnny Mercer & Jo Stafford**
Disc Jockey: 13,9,8,4,3,1,6,2,2,2,3,3,3,3,4,5,9,11,8
Juke Box: 10,6,3,4,3,3,3,2,2,2,2,4,4,1,9,6,11,-,14
Best Seller: 9,6,6,4,3,3,3,2,2,3,2,3,5,4,7

5/5 | 18 | 17 | 9 | 1 | **15 ●** | **Dream** .... *Johnny Mercer* — **The Pied Pipers**
Disc Jockey: 14,10,4,7,9,3,4,4,1,3,3,8,7,7,5,5,6,-,-,-,-,-,-,-,9
Best Seller: 10,9,7,5,8,8,10,6,10,6,5,5,6,7,7
Juke Box: 11,14,13,11,12,11,14,13,10,7,11,9,8,7,12,11,12

2

5/26	15	15	10	2	16		**Bell Bottom Trousers** .... *Moe Jaffe* <B:11>		Tony Pastor (Ruth McCullough)
5/26	14	14	7	2	17		**Caldonia** .... *Fleecie Moore*		Woody Herman
7/28	17	17	14	1	18		**Gotta Be This Or That (Part 1)** .... *Sunny Skylar*		Benny Goodman
10/27	13	12	8	1	19		**I'll Buy That Dream** .... *Herb Magidson/Allie Wrubel* <B:9>		Helen Forrest & Dick Haymes
3/31	12	12	8	1	20		**Saturday Night (Is The Loneliest Night In The Week)** ..... *Sammy Cahn/Jule Styne* <B:7>		Frank Sinatra
9/1	15	13	7	1	21 ●		**Tampico** .... *Doris Fisher/Allan Roberts*		Stan Kenton (June Christy)
3/10	12	10	7	1	22		**Ac-Cent-Tchu-Ate The Positive** .... *Harold Arlen/Johnny Mercer*		Bing Crosby & the Andrews Sisters
7/21	13	11	5	1	23		**Bell Bottom Trousers** .... *Moe Jaffe*		Guy Lombardo (Jimmy Brown)
10/27	11	10	5	1	24		**Along The Navajo Trail** ..... *Dick Charles/Eddie DeLange/Larry Markes*		Bing Crosby & the Andrews Sisters

1945

PEAK DATE	WEEKS				RANK	GOLD	Title / PEAK POSITION / Songwriter(s)	SYMBL	DEBUT	Artist
	CH	10	5	PK						

2 (cont'd)

PEAK DATE	CH	10	5	PK	RANK	GOLD	Title / Peak Position / Songwriter(s)	SYMBL	DEBUT	Artist
11/3	14	11	3	1	25		I'll Buy That Dream ...Herb Magidson/Allie Wrubel			Harry James (Kitty Kallen)

3

PEAK DATE	CH	10	5	PK	RANK	GOLD	Title / Peak Position / Songwriter(s)	SYMBL	DEBUT	Artist
8/4	19	19	13	10	26	●	Chopin's Polonaise...Frederic Chopin	[I]	❶	Carmen Cavallaro
6/30	19	16	9	3	27		Sentimental Journey...Les Brown/Bud Green/Ben Homer	[I]		Hal McIntyre (Frankie Lester)
4/28	12	11	7	3	28		My Dreams Are Getting Better All The Time...Mann Curtis/Vic Mizzy <B:5>			Johnny Long & Dick Robertson
6/23	14	13	5	2	29		You Belong To My Heart...Ray Gilbert/Agustin Lara <B:6>			Bing Crosby & Xavier Cugat
9/29	13	9	4	2	30		Till The End Of Time...Buddy Kaye/Ted Mossman			Les Brown (Doris Day)
8/25	15	14	8	1	31		On The Atchison, Topeka And The Santa Fe...Johnny Mercer/Harry Warren			Bing Crosby
8/11	13	13	8	1	32	●	If I Loved You...Oscar Hammerstein/Richard Rodgers <B:4>			Perry Como
6/30	10	10	7	1	33		Bell Bottom Trousers...Moe Jaffe <B:10>	[N]		Kay Kyser (Ferdy & Slim)
1/13	14	10	4	1	34		There Goes That Song Again...Sammy Cahn/Jule Styne <A:3>			Russ Morgan
3/24	10	7	4	1	35		My Dreams Are Getting Better All The Time...Mann Curtis/Vic Mizzy <B:22>		❶	The Phil Moore Four
10/27	9	8	2	1	36		Till The End Of Time...Buddy Kaye/Ted Mossman <B:11>			Dick Haymes

4

PEAK DATE	CH	10	5	PK	RANK	GOLD	Title / Peak Position / Songwriter(s)	SYMBL	DEBUT	Artist
3/24	14	13	10	3	37		A Little On The Lonely Side...James Cavanaugh/Dick Robertson/Frank Weldon			Frankie Carle (Paul Allen)
1/20	7	7	4	3	38		Don't Fence Me In...Cole Porter <B:10>			Sammy Kaye (Billy Williams)
8/4	12	11	5	2	39		Sentimental Journey...Les Brown/Bud Green/Ben Homer			The Merry Macs
10/6	17	13	4	2	40		I'm Gonna Love That Gal (Like She's Never Been Loved Before)...Frances Ash <A:3>			Perry Como
1/6	7	4	2	2	41		The Trolley Song...Ralph Blane/Hugh Martin <B:14>			Vaughn Monroe (Marilyn Duke)
12/8	14	11	4	1	42		Waitin' For The Train To Come In...Martin Block/Sunny Skylar		❶	Peggy Lee
2/10	9	8	4	1	43		Cocktails For Two...Sam Coslow/Arthur Johnston <B:14>	[N]		Spike Jones (Carl Grayson)
1/27	9	8	2	1	44	●	I Dream Of You (More Than You Dream I Do)...Marjorie Goetschius/Edna Osser <B:8>			Tommy Dorsey (Freddie Stewart)
3/10	5	4	2	1	45		Rum And Coca-Cola...Morey Amsterdam/Paul Baron/Jeri Sullavan			Abe Lyman (Rose Blane)
9/22	4	4	2	1	46		Boogie Woogie...Clarence "Pine Top" Smith	[I-R]		Tommy Dorsey
5/12	12	11	1	1	47	●	Laura...Johnny Mercer/David Raksin			Woody Herman
11/17	12	11	1	1	48		It's Been A Long, Long Time...Sammy Cahn/Jule Styne			Charlie Spivak (Irene Daye)
4/28	10	10	1	1	49		Just A Prayer Away...David Kapp/Charles Tobias			Bing Crosby
4/14	10	6	1	1	50		Stuff Like That There...Ray Evans/Jay Livingston			Betty Hutton
10/27	4	2	1	1	51		That's For Me...Oscar Hammerstein/Richard Rodgers			Jo Stafford

5

PEAK DATE	CH	10	5	PK	RANK	GOLD	Title / Peak Position / Songwriter(s)	SYMBL	DEBUT	Artist
5/5	6	4	2	2	52		Chloe...Carl Hoefle/Del Porter	[N]		Spike Jones (Judy Manners/Red Ingle)
12/29	12	12	1	1	53		It Might As Well Be Spring...Oscar Hammerstein/Richard Rodgers <B:6>			Dick Haymes
3/24	13	9	1	1	54		A Little On The Lonely Side...James Cavanaugh/Dick Robertson/Frank Weldon			Guy Lombardo (Jimmy Brown)
6/30	7	5	1	1	55		Dream...Johnny Mercer			Frank Sinatra
2/10	7	5	1	1	56		Ac-cent-tchu-ate The Positive...Harold Arlen/Johnny Mercer			Artie Shaw (Imogene Lynn)
6/16	5	5	1	1	57		Laura...Johnny Mercer/David Raksin <B:9>			Johnnie Johnston
5/5	11	4	1	1	58		Candy...Mack David/Alex Kramer/Joan Whitney <B:11>			Dinah Shore
6/2	7	4	1	1	59		Yah-Ta-Ta Yah-Ta-Ta (Talk, Talk, Talk)...Johnny Burke/Jimmy Van Heusen	[N]		Bing Crosby & Judy Garland
5/19	6	3	1	1	60		I'm Beginning To See The Light...Duke Ellington/Don George/Johnny Hodges/Harry James			Ella Fitzgerald & Ink Spots
12/29	4	1	1	1	61		White Christmas...Irving Berlin	[X-R]		Frank Sinatra

6

PEAK DATE	CH	10	5	PK	RANK	GOLD	Title / Peak Position / Songwriter(s)	SYMBL	DEBUT	Artist
5/19	7	6		3	62		Laura...Johnny Mercer/David Raksin	[I]		Freddy Martin
6/2	8	4		2	63	●	Caldonia...Fleecie Moore			Louis Jordan
3/17	12	8		1	64		I'm Beginning To See The Light...Duke Ellington/Don George/Johnny Hodges/Harry James			Duke Ellington (Joya Sherrill)
6/23	11	8		1	65		I Wish...Doris Fisher/Allan Roberts <B:14>			Mills Brothers
11/17	10	8		1	66		That's For Me...Oscar Hammerstein/Richard Rodgers <A:5>			Dick Haymes
12/15	11	6		1	67		It Might As Well Be Spring...Oscar Hammerstein/Richard Rodgers		❶	Paul Weston With Margaret Whiting
12/22	10	6		1	68		Waitin' For The Train To Come In...Martin Block/Sunny Skylar <A:5>			Harry James (Kitty Kallen)
9/15	7	6		1	69		Gotta Be This Or That...Sunny Skylar <B:10>			Sammy Kaye (Nancy Norman)
8/25	6	5		1	70		On The Atchison, Topeka & Santa Fe...Johnny Mercer/Harry Warren			Tommy Dorsey (The Sentimentalists)
9/29	6	5		1	71		I Wish I Knew...Mack Gordon/Harry Warren <B:7>			Dick Haymes
11/17	9	4		1	72		It's Been A Long, Long Time...Sammy Cahn/Jule Styne			Stan Kenton (June Christy)
6/23	7	3		1	73		Good, Good, Good (That's You - That's You)...Doris Fisher/Allan Roberts			Xavier Cugat (Del Campo)
3/24	7	2		1	74		Saturday Night (Is The Loneliest Night In The Week)...Sammy Cahn/Jule Styne			Sammy Kaye (Nancy Norman)
6/16	6	2		1	75		Bell Bottom Trousers...Moe Jaffe			Louis Prima (Lily Ann Carol)
6/30	6	2		1	76		You Belong To My Heart...Ray Gilbert/Agustin Lara <B:9>			Charlie Spivak (Jimmy Saunders)
10/13	3	2		1	77		Hong Kong Blues...Hoagy Carmichael			Hoagy Carmichael
6/23	2	1		1	78		Baía...Ary Barroso/Ray Gilbert <A:3>			Bing Crosby & Xavier Cugat
8/18	2	1		1	79		June Is Bustin' Out All Over...Oscar Hammerstein/Richard Rodgers			Hildegarde with Guy Lombardo

PEAK DATE	WEEKS			RANK	GOLD	Title	PEAK POSITION *Songwriter(s)*	SYMBL	DEBUT	Artist
	CH	10	5	PK							

7

1/27	5	4		2	80		I Dream Of You (More Than You Dream I Do)......*Marjorie Goetschius/Edna Osser* <A:2>			Frank Sinatra
9/1	10	6		1	81		Who Threw The Whiskey In The Well ....*Johnny Brooks/Eddie DeLange*			Lucky Millinder (Wynonie Harris)
1/20	8	6		1	82		There Goes That Song Again ....*Sammy Cahn/Jule Styne* <B:10>			Sammy Kaye (Nancy Norman)
12/15	10	4		1	83		Waitin' For The Train To Come In......................*Martin Block/Sunny Skylar*			Johnny Long & Dick Robertson
7/28	4	4		1	84		Bell Bottom Trousers ....*Moe Jaffe* [N]	✦		Jerry Colonna
6/30	6	3		1	85		There's No You ....*Tom Adair/Hal Hopper* <B:9>			Jo Stafford
1/20	4	2		1	86		There Goes That Song Again ....*Sammy Cahn/Jule Styne*			Kay Kyser (Georgia Carroll)
7/7	3	2		1	87		The More I See You ....*Mack Gordon/Harry Warren* <A:6>			Dick Haymes
10/20	2	2		1	88		Along The Navajo Trail ......*Dick Charles/Eddie DeLange/Larry Markes*			Gene Krupa (Buddy Stewart)
9/15	2	1		1	89		Along The Navajo Trail ......*Dick Charles/Eddie DeLange/Larry Markes*			Dinah Shore
10/6	2	1		1	90		If I Loved You ....*Oscar Hammerstein/Richard Rodgers* <B:9>			Frank Sinatra
9/29	2	1		1	91		Lily Belle ....*Dave Franklin/Irving Taylor*			Freddy Martin (Gene Conklin)
3/24	1	1		1	92		(All Of A Sudden) My Heart Sings ....*Jean Blanvillain/Henri Herpin/Harold Rome*			Johnnie Johnston

8

7/14	6	3		2	93		There! I've Said It Again ....*Redd Evans/Dave Mann* <B:13>			Jimmy Dorsey (Teddy Walters)
7/28	3	3		2	94		If I Loved You ....*Oscar Hammerstein/Richard Rodgers*			Harry James (Buddy DiVito)
3/24	7	5		1	95		Twilight Time......................*Artie Dunn/Al Nevins/Morty Nevins/Buck Ram* <A:7>	[I]		The Three Suns
6/2	8	4		1	96		Candy ....*Mack David/Alex Kramer/Joan Whitney* <A:3>			Johnny Long & Dick Robertson
7/21	8	4		1	97		Dream ....*Johnny Mercer* <B:15>			Freddy Martin (Artie Wayne)
10/20	8	3		1	98		The Blond Sailor......................*Bell Leib/Mitchell Parish/Jacob Pfeil*			Andrews Sisters
9/1	6	3		1	99		If I Loved You ....*Oscar Hammerstein/Richard Rodgers*			Bing Crosby
10/6	3	3		1	100		Hong Kong Blues ....*Hoagy Carmichael*			Tommy Dorsey ("Skeets" Herfurt)
5/12	3	3		1	101		Laura ....*Johnny Mercer/David Raksin* <B:18>			Jerry Wald (Dick Merrick)
11/24	6	2		1	102		No Can Do ....*Nat Simon/Charles Tobias*			Guy Lombardo (Don Rodney/Rose Marie Lombardo)
10/27	5	2		1	103		I'll Buy That Dream ....*Herb Magidson/Allie Wrubel*			Hal McIntyre (Frankie Lester)
9/22	4	2		1	104		11:60 P.M. ....*Seger Ellis/Don George*			Harry James (Kitty Kallen)
1/20	2	2		1	105		Don't Fence Me In ....*Cole Porter* <B:12>			Kate Smith
3/3	5	1		1	106		The Three Caballeros ....*Ernesto Cortazar/Manuel Esperon/Ray Gilbert* <A:1>			Bing Crosby & the Andrews Sisters
3/24	3	1		1	107		Opus No. I ....*Sy Oliver* <A:4>	[I]		Tommy Dorsey
10/27	2	1		1	108 ●		A Cottage For Sale ....*Larry Conley/Willard Robison*	❶		Billy Eckstine
6/30	2	1		1	109		I Should Care ....*Sammy Cahn/Axel Stordahl/Paul Weston*			Frank Sinatra
2/10	1	1		1	110		Saturday Night (Is The Loneliest Night In The Week)....*Sammy Cahn/Jule Styne*			Frankie Carle (Phyliss Lynne)
6/30	1	1		1	111		Can't You Read Between The Lines?....................*Sammy Cahn/Jule Styne*			Jimmy Dorsey (Jean Cromwell)
4/7	1	1		1	112		I Don't Care Who Knows It ....*Harold Adamson/Jimmy McHugh*			Harry James (Kitty Kallen)
3/3	1	1		1	113		Rum And Coca-Cola ....*Morey Amsterdam/Paul Baron/Jeri Sullavan* <A:1>			Vaughn Monroe (Norton Sisters/Rosemary Calvin)
2/24	1	1		1	114		Sleigh Ride In July ....*Johnny Burke/Jimmy Van Heusen*			Dinah Shore

9

8/11	6	3		2	115		A Kiss Goodnight ....*Reba Herman/Freddie Slack/Floyd Victor*			Woody Herman
7/21	6	3		2	116		There Must Be A Way..................*Robert Cook/Sammy Gallop/David Saxon* <A:6>			Charlie Spivak (Jimmy Saunders)
11/3	11	2		2	117		(Did You Ever Get) That Feeling In The Moonlight ......*James Cavanaugh/ Ira Schuster/Larry Stock* <A:1>			Perry Como
5/26	8	2		1	118		Tippin' In ....*Bobby Smith* [I]			Erskine Hawkins
6/23	3	2		1	119		Laura ....*Johnny Mercer/David Raksin*			Dick Haymes
2/10	5	1		1	120		Evelina..*Harold Arlen/E.Y. Harburg*			Bing Crosby
10/27	5	1		1	121		Some Sunday Morning......*Ray Heindorf/M.K. Jerome/Ted Koehler* <A:2>			Dick Haymes & Helen Forrest
12/1	4	1		1	122		Don't Forget Tonight Tomorrow ....*Jay Milton/Ukie Sherin*			Frank Sinatra & The Charioteers
9/1	3	1		1	123		It's Only A Paper Moon ....*Harold Arlen/E.Y. Harburg/Billy Rose*			Ella Fitzgerald & Delta Rhythm Boys
9/22	2	1		1	124		Gotta Be This Or That ....*Sunny Skylar*			Glen Gray ("Fats" Daniels)
8/11	2	1		1	125		There Must Be A Way......*Robert Cook/Sammy Gallop/David Saxon* <A:5>			Johnnie Johnston
7/28	1	1		1	126		A Friend Of Yours ....*Johnny Burke/Jimmy Van Heusen*			Tommy Dorsey (Stuart Foster)
10/6	1	1		1	127		On The Atchison, Topeka And The Santa Fe ...*Johnny Mercer/Harry Warren*			Judy Garland & The Merry Macs
10/13	1	1		1	128		I'm Gonna Love That Guy......................................*Frances Ash* <B:10>			Benny Goodman (Dottie Reid)
9/15	1	1		1	129		You'll Never Walk Alone..................*Oscar Hammerstein/Richard Rodgers* <A:7>			Frank Sinatra
7/28	1	1		1	130		Out Of This World ....*Harold Arlen/Johnny Mercer* <A:7>			Jo Stafford

10

2/3	2	2		2	131		Don't Fence Me In ....*Cole Porter*			Horace Heidt (Gene Walsh)
2/3	5	1		1	132		Always ....*Irving Berlin* <B:19>			Guy Lombardo (Stuart Foster)
1/20	5	1		1	133		And Her Tears Flowed Like Wine......*Joe Greene/Stan Kenton/Charles Lawrence*			Ella Fitzgerald
11/10	5	1		1	134		I'll Be Walkin' With My Honey (Soon, Soon, Soon)....*Buddy Kaye/Sam Medoff* <B:17>			Sammy Kaye (Nancy Norman/Billy Williams)

1945

PEAK DATE	WEEKS			RANK	GOLD	Title	PEAK POSITION / Songwriter(s)	SYMBL	DEBUT	Artist
	CH	10	5	PK						

10 (cont'd)

PEAK DATE	CH	10	5	PK	RANK	GOLD	Title	Songwriter(s)	Artist
4/14	5	1		1	135		Just A Prayer Away	David Kapp/Charles Tobias <A:10>	Sammy Kaye (Billy Williams)
4/7	4	1		1	136		More And More	E.Y. Harburg/Jerome Kern	Tommy Dorsey (Bonnie Lou Williams)
1/27	4	1		1	137		Always	Irving Berlin <A:4>	Sammy Kaye (Arthur Wright)
9/1	4	1		1	138		Rosemary	Jimmie Dodd/John Jacob Loeb <B:11>	Kay Kyser (Michael Douglas)
8/25	3	1		1	139		On The Atchison, Topeka And The Santa Fe	Johnny Mercer/Harry Warren	Tommy Tucker Time (Don Brown)
1/27	3	1		1	140		You Always Hurt The One You Love	Doris Fisher/Allan Roberts <A:7>	Sammy Kaye (Billy Williams)
11/24	3	1		1	141		The Honeydripper	Joe Liggins	Jimmie Lunceford & Delta Rhythm Boys
2/10	2	1		1	142		There Goes That Song Again	Sammy Cahn/Jule Styne	Billy Butterfield (Margaret Whiting)
1/27	2	1		1	143		I Dream Of You (More Than You Dream I Do)	Marjorie Goetschius/Edna Osser <B:12>	Perry Como
12/8	2	1		1	144		Nancy (With The Laughing Face)	Phil Silvers/Jimmy Van Heusen	Frank Sinatra
10/6	1	1		1	145		Jimmy's Blues	Jimmy Rushing	Count Basie (Jimmy Rushing)
6/30	1	1		1	146		'Tain't Me	Lemuel Davis/Jack Palmer	Les Brown (Doris Day)
9/29	1	1		1	147		It's Only A Paper Moon	Harold Arlen/E.Y. Harburg/Billy Rose <A:9>	Benny Goodman (Dottie Reid)
11/24	1	1		1	148		Holiday For Strings	David Rose [I-N]	Spike Jones
4/14	1	1		1	149		All Of My Life	Irving Berlin <A:10>	Sammy Kaye (Billy Williams)
8/11	1	1		1	150		Good, Good, Good (That's You–That's You)	Doris Fisher/Allan Roberts <A:6>	Sammy Kaye (Billy Williams/Nancy Norman)
8/4	1	1		1	151		Can't You Read Between The Lines	Sammy Cahn/Jule Styne <A:3>	Kay Kyser (Dolly Mitchell)
3/10	1	1		1	152		I Wanna Get Married	Phil Charig/Milton Pascal/Dan Shapiro	Gertrude Niesen
4/28	1	1		1	153		All Of My Life	Irving Berlin	The Three Suns
7/28	1	1		1	154		Stranger In Town	Mel Torme <B:11>	Martha Tilton

11

PEAK DATE	CH	10	5	PK	RANK	GOLD	Title	Songwriter(s)	Artist
4/28	3			2	155		I Should Care	Sammy Cahn/Axel Stordahl/Paul Weston	Tommy Dorsey (Bonnie Lou Williams/The Sentimentalists)
7/21	3			2	156		Five Salted Peanuts	Charlie Abbott/Bert Wheeler <A:2>	Tony Pastor
5/12	8			1	157		Poor Little Rhode Island	Sammy Cahn/Jule Styne <B:18>	Guy Lombardo (Stuart Foster)
5/26	4			1	158		Close As Pages In A Book	Dorothy Fields/Sigmund Romberg	Benny Goodman (Jane Harvey)
1/6	4			1	159		I'm Wastin' My Tears On You	Frank Harford/Tex Ritter <B:21> ❶	Tex Ritter
6/23	3			1	160		Bell Bottom Trousers	Moe Jaffe	The Jesters
3/24	3			1	161		I Should Care	Sammy Cahn/Axel Stordahl/Paul Weston <A:10>	Martha Tilton
5/26	2			1	162		Yah-Ta-Ta, Yah-Ta-Ta	Johnny Burke/Jimmy Van Heusen	Harry James (Kitty Kallen)
4/21	2			1	163		You Can't Get That No More	Louis Jordan/Sam Theard [N]	Louis Jordan
9/15	2			1	164		Horses Don't Bet On People	John Jacob Loeb <A:10> [N]	Kay Kyser (Clyde Rogers)
9/29	1			1	165		Love Letters	Edward Heyman/Victor Young <A:3>	Dick Haymes
7/21	1			1	166		There! I've Said It Again	Redd Evans/Dave Mann ❶	The Modernaires with Paula Kelly
12/8	1			1	167		Fishin' For The Moon	Sol Marcus/Eddie Seiler/Guy Wood <B:12>	Vaughn Monroe (Norton Sisters)
4/7	1			1	168		He's Home For A Little While	Kermit Goell/Ted Shapiro <A:11>	Dinah Shore

12

PEAK DATE	CH	10	5	PK	RANK	GOLD	Title	Songwriter(s)	Artist
8/4	7			2	169		Fuzzy Wuzzy	Milton Drake/Al Hoffman/Jerry Livingston	Milt Herth Trio & The Jesters
6/16	3			2	170		Caldonia	Fleecie Moore	Erskine Hawkins (Ace Harris)
12/29	3			1	171		Here Comes Heaven Again	Harold Adamson/Jimmy McHugh <A:3>	Perry Como
3/31	3			1	172		Ev'ry Time We Say Goodbye	Cole Porter	Benny Goodman (Peggy Mann)
12/22	3			1	173		My Guy's Come Back	Ray McKinley/Mel Powell <A:2>	Benny Goodman (Liza Morrow)
8/18	3			1	174		The More I See You	Mack Gordon/Harry Warren	Harry James (Buddy DiVito)
1/27	3			1	175		There Goes That Song Again	Sammy Cahn/Jule Styne <A:3>	Kate Smith
3/17	2			1	176		Ac-Cent-Tchu-Ate The Positive	Harold Arlen/Johnny Mercer	Kay Kyser (Dolly Mitchell)
11/10	2			1	177		That's For Me	Oscar Hammerstein/Richard Rodgers	Kay Kyser (Michael Douglas)
3/31	2			1	178		I'm Gonna See My Baby	Phil Moore <A:1>	Johnny Mercer
11/17	2			1	179		Something Sentimental	Vaughn Monroe/Frank Ryerson/Irving Taylor	Vaughn Monroe (Norton Sisters)
12/29	2			1	180		Chickery Chick	Sylvia Dee/Sid Lippman	George Olsen (Judith Blair/Ray Adams)
4/21	2			1	181		(All of a Sudden) My Heart Sings	Jean Blanvillain/Henri Herpin/Harold Rome ✦	Martha Stewart
2/24	1			1	182		Robin Hood	Bob Miketta/Louis Prima <B:18>	Les Brown (Butch Stone)
3/3	1			1	183		I'm Confessin' (That I Love You)	Don Dougherty/Al Neiburg/Ellis Reynolds <A:10>	Perry Como
5/5	1			1	184		All Of My Life	Irving Berlin	Bing Crosby
7/21	1			1	185		Out Of This World	Harold Arlen/Johnny Mercer	Tommy Dorsey (Stuart Foster)
7/28	1			1	186		A Kiss Goodnight	Reba Herman/Freddie Slack/Floyd Victor	Freddie Slack (Liza Morrow)
1/6	1			1	187		Too-Ra-Loo-Ra-Loo-Ral, That's An Irish Lullaby	James Shannon <B:23> [I]	Charlie Spivak

13

PEAK DATE	CH	10	5	PK	RANK	GOLD	Title	Songwriter(s)	Artist
10/20	3			2	188 ●		The Honeydripper (Parts 1 and 2)	Joe Liggins ❶	Joe Liggins
12/29	4			1	189		In The Middle Of May	Fred Ahlert/Al Stillman <A:1>	Freddy Martin (Martin Men)
6/16	3			1	190		Dream	Johnny Mercer <A:8>	Jimmy Dorsey (Teddy Walters)

PEAK DATE	WEEKS				RANK	GOLD	Title	PEAK POSITION Songwriter(s)	SYMBL	DEBUT	Artist
	CH	10	5	PK							

13 (cont'd)

PEAK DATE	CH			PK	RANK		Title	Songwriter(s)			Artist
1/6	3			1	191		Meet Me In St. Louis, Louis	Kerry Mills/Andrew Sterling			Guy Lombardo (Lombardo Quartet)
4/21	2			1	192		I Should Care	Sammy Cahn/Axel Stordahl/Paul Weston			Jimmy Dorsey (Teddy Walters)
9/29	1			1	193		Northwest Passage	Woody Herman [I]			Woody Herman
8/18	1			1	194		Please No Squeeza Da Banana	Ben Jaffee/Louis Prima/Jack Zero			Tony Pastor
9/29	1			1	195		Shame On You	Spade Cooley			Lawrence Welk with Red Foley

14

6/16	5			2	196		Put Another Chair At The Table	Cecil Gant/Richard Nelson <A:6>			Mills Brothers
3/10	3			1	197		Sleigh Ride In July	Johnny Burke/Jimmy Van Heusen <B:15>			Bing Crosby
11/24	3			1	198		My Guy's Come Back	Ray McKinley/Mel Powell			Dinah Shore
3/10	3			1	199		Let's Take The Long Way Home	Harold Arlen/Johnny Mercer			Jo Stafford
1/27	2			1	200		I Don't Want To Love You (Like I Do)	Henry Prichard <B:17>			Phil Brito
4/21	2			1	201		More And More	E.Y. Harburg/Jerome Kern			Perry Como
4/21	2			1	202		Sweet Dreams, Sweetheart	M.K. Jerome/Ted Koehler			Ray Noble (Larry Stewart)
7/21	1			1	203		(Yip Yip De Hootie) My Baby Said Yes	Sid Robin/Teddy Walters			Bing Crosby & Louis Jordan
9/1	1			1	204		That's The Stuff You Gotta Watch	Buddy Johnson			Buddy Johnson (Ella Johnson)
3/3	1			1	205		Leave The Dishes In The Sink, Ma	Milton Berle/Gene Doyle/Spike Jones <A:4>			Spike Jones (Del Porter)
2/17	1			1	206		I'm Making Believe	Mack Gordon/James Monaco ❶			Hal McIntyre (Ruth Gaylor)
5/5	1			1	207		What Makes The Sunset?	Sammy Cahn/Jule Styne			Frank Sinatra
1/27	1			1	208		Tico-Tico	Zequinha Abreu/Ervin Drake/Aloysio Oliveira [I] ✦			Ethel Smith

15

12/1	4			2	209		A Door Will Open	John Benson Brooks/Don George <A:14>			Tommy Dorsey (Stuart Foster/ The Sentimentalists)
2/10	2			1	210		Sleigh Ride In July	Johnny Burke/Jimmy Van Heusen			Tommy Dorsey (Bonnie Lou Williams)
4/21	2			1	211		Candy	Mack David/Alex Kramer/Joan Whitney <A:15>			The Four King Sisters
10/13	2			1	212		What Do You Want To Make Those Eyes At Me For	Howard Johnson/Joseph McCarthy/James Monaco			Betty Hutton
11/3	2			1	213		Autumn Serenade	Peter DeRose/Sammy Gallop <A:1> [I]			Harry James
4/28	2			1	214		Everytime	Gordon Jenkins <A:8>			Freddy Martin (Glenn Hughes)
2/17	1			1	215		One Meat Ball	Lou Singer/Hy Zaret <A:1>			Andrews Sisters
6/16	1			1	216 ●		Temptation	Nacio Herb Brown/Arthur Freed			Perry Como
3/3	1			1	217		Like Someone In Love	Johnny Burke/Jimmy Van Heusen <A:14>			Bing Crosby
3/31	1			1	218		Saturday Night (Is The Loneliest Night In The Week)	Sammy Cahn/Jule Styne <A:15>			The Four King Sisters

16

3/17	1			1	219		Twilight Time	Artie Dunn/Al Nevins/Morty Nevins/Buck Ram <A:1> [I]			Les Brown
12/22	1			1	220		White Christmas	Irving Berlin [X-R]			Freddy Martin (Clyde Rogers)
11/17	1			1	221		Surprise Party	Walter Bishop/Bob Hilliard			Johnny Mercer
9/22	1			1	222		Lily Belle	Dave Franklin/Irving Taylor			The Pied Pipers
11/10	1			1	223		But I Did	Al Jacobs/Joseph Meyer			Dinah Shore
4/28	1			1	224		I Love You, I Love You, I Love You Sweetheart Of All My Dreams	Art Fitch/Kay Fitch/Bert Lowe			Charlie Spivak (Irene Daye)
7/14	1			1	225		Can't You Read Between The Lines?	Sammy Cahn/Jule Styne			Charlie Spivak (Irene Daye)
12/15	1			1	226		Sioux City Sue	Ray Freedman/Dick Thomas ✦			Dick Thomas

17

1/13	2			1	227		Angelina	Doris Fisher/Allan Roberts <B:25>			Louis Prima
7/14	1			1	228		Counting The Days	Alex Kramer/Hy Zaret			Frankie Carle (Paul Allen)
11/10	1			1	229		Promises	Milton Drake/Al Hoffman/Jerry Livingston <A:10>			Sammy Kaye (Billy Williams)
9/8	1			1	230		Stars In Your Eyes	Mort Greene/Ricardo Lopez Mendez/Gabriel Ruiz			Guy Lombardo (Jimmy Brown)
11/10	1			1	231		Just A Blue Serge Suit	Irving Berlin			Vaughn Monroe (Norton Sisters)
5/26	1			1	232		Captain Kidd	Roy Alfred/Marvin Fisher			Ella Mae Morse
7/7	1			1	233		On The Sunny Side Of The Street	Dorothy Fields/Jimmy McHugh			Jo Stafford

18

3/3	1			1	234		Sleigh Ride In July	Johnny Burke/Jimmy Van Heusen <A:12>			Les Brown (Gordon Drake)
2/24	1			1	235		Saturday Night (Is The Loneliest Night In The Week)	Sammy Cahn/Jule Styne			Woody Herman (Frances Wayne)
3/31	1			1	236		Oh! Moytle	Carmen Lombardo/Charles Tobias <A:11> [N]			Guy Lombardo (Jimmy Brown)
12/29	1			1	237		Aren't You Glad You're You	Johnny Burke/Jimmy Van Heusen <A:14>			The Pied Pipers
5/19	1			1	238		Candy	Mack David/Alex Kramer/Joan Whitney <A:8>			Jerry Wald (Kay Allen)

19

1/6	2			1	239		The Trolley Song	Ralph Blane/Hugh Martin <A:10>			Guy Lombardo (Stuart Foster)
2/24	1			1	240		Evelina	Harold Arlen/E.Y. Harburg			Frankie Carle (Paul Allen)
1/27	1			1	241		If You Are But A Dream	Nat Bonx/Jack Fulton/Moe Jaffe <A:7>			Frank Sinatra

PEAK DATE	WEEKS				R A N K	G O L D	Title	PEAK POSITION Songwriter(s)	S Y M B L	D E B U T	Artist
	CH	10	5	PK							
							21				
1/13	1			1	242		**Corns For My Country**..............................*Jean Barry/Dick Charles/Leah Worth*				Andrews Sisters
							22				
5/5	1			1	243		**A Little On The Lonely Side**..*James Cavanaugh/Dick Robertson/Frank Weldon <A:3>*				The Phil Moore Four

1946

NATIONAL NEWS: The transition to a peacetime economy gets off to a rough start with a wave of inflation, a severe national meat shortage, four-month strikes at General Electric and General Motors, and strikes by steel workers, maritime workers and miners. Partly as a result, Republicans gain control of Congress. President Truman ends most wage, price and salary controls. The U.S. detonates the first subsurface atomic explosion off the Bikini Islands in the Pacific.

INTERNATIONAL NEWS: The war crimes tribunals at Nuremberg and Dachau convict more than 70 members of the Nazi SS, and nine Nazi leaders are hanged. The United Nations General Assembly holds its first sessions. Winston Churchill warns that an "iron curtain" has descended upon Europe through Soviet expansionism.

COMMERCE AND SCIENCE: IBM introduces an electronic calculator that works 1,000 times faster than any previous calculator. The inventor of "xerography" patents his photocopying machine.

FADS AND FASHION: The first bikini swimsuit is modeled in Paris, just four days after the American atomic explosion at the Bikini atoll.

SPORTS: In an exciting conclusion to baseball's first full postwar season, the St. Louis Cardinals with Stan Musial edge Ted Williams' Boston Red Sox in the World Series, four games to three. The Chicago Bears' 24-14 triumph over the New York Giants gives George Halas his fifth NFL championship. Notre Dame is the nation's best in college football. Joe Louis returns to the ring after four years to successfully defend his heavyweight championship. Oklahoma A&M wins its second straight NCAA college basketball crown. Jack Kramer is the U.S. tennis champ.

MOVIES: *The Best Years of Our Lives* symbolizes American's return home from war, and wins Best Picture and Best Actor (Fredric March) Oscars. Olivia de Havilland is named Best Actress for *To Each His Own*. No 1946 film is more enduring than Frank Capra's all-time classic *It's a Wonderful Life* starring James Stewart. Other top box office hits include Disney's *Song of the South* and *The Jolson Story*, which triggers Al Jolson's amazing musical comeback.

THEATER: Ethel Merman galvanizes Broadway with Irving Berlin's *Annie Get Your Gun*. Judy Holliday bursts into stardom in *Born Yesterday*. Eugene O'Neill's *The Iceman Cometh* debuts.

BOOKS: Dr. Benjamin Spock's *The Common Sense Book of Baby and Child Care* is an all-time publishing phenomenon.

1946 — TOP 20 ARTISTS

1. **Bing Crosby**
995

2. **Frank Sinatra**
947

3. **Perry Como**
884

4.	763	**Sammy Kaye**
5.	662	**Dinah Shore**
6.	654	**Les Brown**
7.	607	**Frankie Carle**
8.	585	**Guy Lombardo**
9.	545	**Andrews Sisters**
10.	502	**Freddy Martin**
11.	489	**Nat "King" Cole**
12.	459	**Tex Beneke**
13.	459	**Glenn Miller**
14.	444	**Vaughn Monroe**
15.	428	**Ink Spots**
16.	383	**Jo Stafford**
17.	373	**Harry James**
18.	354	**Woody Herman**
19.	350	**Kay Kyser**
20.	333	**Benny Goodman**

1946 — TOP SONGWRITERS

	# of Hits	Points	
1.	20	1,860	**Irving Berlin**
2.	16	1,478	**Sammy Cahn**
3.	13	1,249	**Bennie Benjamin**
	13	1,249	**George Weiss**
5.	12	1,117	**Jule Styne**
6.	8	743	**Hoagy Carmichael**
7.	7	661	**Billy Reid**
8.	7	635	**Mack Gordon**
9.	7	634	**Sunny Skylar**
10.	6	578	**Jack Lawrence**
11.	6	553	**Johnny Burke**
	6	553	**Jimmy Van Heusen**

1946 — TOP ARTIST DEBUTS

1.	3/23	**Mel Tormé** (103)
2.	5/25	**Tex Beneke** (66)
3.	6/29 †	**Eddy Howard** (20)
4.	8/17	**Roy Milton** ◆
5.	11/02	**Merle Travis** ◆

PEAK DATE	WEEKS				RANK	GOLD	Title	PEAK POSITION / Songwriter(s)	SYMBOL	DEBUT	Artist
	CH	10	5	PK							

1

| 5/25 | 23 | 20 | 17 | 13 | 1 | ● | **The Gypsy**..Billy Reid | | | | **Ink Spots** |

Juke Box: 15,7,5,2,1,1,1,1,1,1,1,1,1,1,1,4,4,7,9,15,17
Best Seller: 6,2,1,1,1,1,1,1,1,1,1,2,3,4,5,8,10
Disc Jockey: 8,2,3,2,2,1,2,1,3,5,6,6,6,7,3,10

| 3/16 | 20 | 16 | 16 | 11 | 2 | | **Oh! What It Seemed To Be** ....Bennie Benjamin/Frankie Carle/George Weiss | | | | **Frankie Carle** (Marjorie Hughes) |

Juke Box: 11,12,5,5,2,1,1,1,1,1,1,1,1,1,1,5,5,16,16
Best Seller: 10,7,4,4,1,1,1,1,1,1,3,4,3,7,10
Disc Jockey: 10,15,12,14,6,6,4,3,2,2,2,2,2,3,4,5,2,6,10

| 10/19 | 18 | 16 | 14 | 9 | 3 | | **Rumors Are Flying**............................Bennie Benjamin/George Weiss | | | | **Frankie Carle** (Marjorie Hughes) |

Juke Box: 7,5,2,3,1,1,1,1,1,1,1,1,4,6,-,-,14
Best Seller: 7,4,2,1,1,1,1,1,1,1,1,3,4,9,9,8
Juke Box: 15,9,4,2,2,1,1,1,1,1,1,1,1,3,5,3,9,12

| 8/3 | 25 | 22 | 18 | 8 | 4 | ● | **To Each His Own** ....Ray Evans/Jay Livingston | ❶ | | **Eddy Howard** |

Disc Jockey: 14,12,6,6,4,1,1,1,1,1,1,1,1,2,2,3,2,2,2,4,3,14,10,8
Juke Box: 17,11,7,4,2,2,2,1,1,1,2,2,1,1,1,2,2,3,4,4,6,7,13
Best Seller: 9,7,2,1,1,1,2,2,2,3,3,1,1,2,2,3,4,4,9

| 5/18 | 21 | 18 | 17 | 8 | 5 | | **The Gypsy** ....Billy Reid <B:3> | | | | **Dinah Shore** |

Disc Jockey: 16,4,2,1,1,2,1,1,1,1,2,1,3,1,4,2,5,4,-,-,10
Best Seller: 8,8,5,3,2,2,3,3,2,3,5,4,3,7,10
Juke Box: 17,9,9,7,9,4,5,3,4,4,7,3,5,7,6,7,10,10,14,13,-,17

| 3/23 | 17 | 14 | 13 | 8 | 6 | | **Oh! What It Seemed To Be** ...Bennie Benjamin/Frankie Carle/George Weiss <B:5> | | | | **Frank Sinatra** |

Disc Jockey: 10,13,5,2,2,1,1,1,1,1,1,1,1,4,5,13,11
Best Seller: 8,3,2,3,2,2,2,2,2,4,3,5
Juke Box: 13,10,8,7,6,5,5,6,3,6,7,9,8,12

| 12/21 | 17 | 15 | 14 | 7 | 7 | | **The Old Lamp-Lighter** ....Nat Simon/Charles Tobias | | | | **Sammy Kaye** (Billy Williams) |

Best Seller: 5,2,2,2,2,2,1,1,1,1,1,1,1,2
Juke Box: 17,9,8,3,3,2,1,1,1,1,1,1,1,2,3,8
Disc Jockey: 11,15,10,5,3,4,3,3,2,2,2,1,2,5,5,6,7

| 12/28 | 25 | 18 | 13 | 6 | 8 | | **(I Love You) For Sentimental Reasons** ....William Best/Deek Watson <B:14> | | | | **The King Cole Trio** |

Disc Jockey: 9,6,13,4,3,5,2,1,3,1,2,1,1,1,1,3,13,8,13,5,7,14,11,-,13,-,15
Best Seller: 8,5,5,8,6,5,4,4,3,4,1,4
Juke Box: 19,-,-,10,7,7,12,8,7,4,8,5,6,8,7,7,8,15

| 1/19 | 14 | 13 | 9 | 5 | 9 | | **Let It Snow! Let It Snow! Let It Snow!**.....Sammy Cahn/Jule Styne [X] | | | | **Vaughn Monroe** (Norton Sisters) |

Best Seller: 10,5,6,3,1,1,1,1,1,2,5,6,8
Disc Jockey: 16,4,5,1,1,1,2,1,1,3,6,6,13,12
Juke Box: 17,10,7,2,2,1,1,1,1,1,3,5,14

| 9/14 | 22 | 19 | 16 | 4 | 10 | | **Five Minutes More** ....Sammy Cahn/Jule Styne | | | | **Frank Sinatra** |

Disc Jockey: 13,7,5,6,2,2,2,2,1,1,1,1,2,3,3,2,4,7,7,8,14,12
Juke Box: 20,8,8,4,2,2,2,1,1,2,1,3,3,3,2,3,3,4,4,9
Best Seller: 9,7,4,3,3,1,2,1,2,3,4,4,4,2,2,4,4,5

| 5/4 | 21 | 19 | 16 | 3 | 11 | ● | **Prisoner Of Love** ....Russ Columbo/Clarence Gaskill/Leo Robin <B:8> | | | | **Perry Como** |

Best Seller: 9,6,4,3,2,1,1,1,2,2,3,3,2,2,3,2,2,3,7
Disc Jockey: 13,-,7,12,4,2,3,5,3,1,3,3,2,3,3,4,1,2,3,8,7,11
Juke Box: 11,15,6,4,2,4,4,5,2,2,2,2,2,2,3,4,4,6,12,15

| 8/31 | 17 | 16 | 12 | 2 | 12 | | **To Each His Own** ....Ray Evans/Jay Livingston | | | | **Freddy Martin** (Stuart Wade) |

Best Seller: 3,2,1,1,4,4,5,5,6,6,6,8
Juke Box: 5,3,3,3,3,5,5,5,6,7,6,9,9,10,18,11
Disc Jockey: 13,4,5,3,3,4,4,4,4,4,5,6,7,9,-,10

| 3/2 | 15 | 15 | 12 | 2 | 13 | | **Personality** ....Johnny Burke/Jimmy Van Heusen | | | | **Johnny Mercer** |

Disc Jockey: 9,6,6,2,5,1,3,1,3,4,4,4,4,7,6
Best Seller: 9,5,2,3,2,2,1,2,3,3,3,3,5,10
Juke Box: 13,5,7,4,4,6,5,5,3,4,2,3,5,13,13

| 1/5 | 17 | 14 | 12 | 2 | 14 | | **Symphony** ....Alex Alstone/Roger Bernstein/Jack Lawrence/Andre Tabet <B:13> | | | | **Freddy Martin** (Clyde Rogers) |

Best Seller: 5,5,2,1,1,2,2,2,4,2,6,6,9
Disc Jockey: 16,7,4,4,5,3,1,2,3,2,3,4,3,4,10,11
Juke Box: 16,13,7,11,8,2,2,3,3,2,2,3,6,8,8,12

| 2/9 | 20 | 17 | 11 | 2 | 15 | | **Doctor, Lawyer, Indian Chief** ....Hoagy Carmichael/Paul Francis Webster | | | | **Betty Hutton** |

Disc Jockey: 16,-,15,10,6,12,4,2,3,1,5,2,2,1,2,5,5,8
Best Seller: 8,8,10,9,6,5,6,6,5,3,1,3,4,4,4,5,7
Juke Box: 14,-,10,-,12,9,6,6,4,4,4,5,3,2,3,2,2,2,4,7,10,14

| 12/14 | 19 | 17 | 11 | 2 | 16 | | **Ole Buttermilk Sky**................................Jack Brooks/Hoagy Carmichael | | | | **Kay Kyser** (Michael Douglas) |

Best Seller: 5,3,2,3,3,3,1,1,3,4,4,7,8
Juke Box: 15,10,9,8,5,4,2,2,2,2,2,2,2,3,6,7,6,13
Disc Jockey: 13,-,-,-,8,13,6,4,3,2,2,2,7,2,10,4,5,3,6,10

| 8/3 | 17 | 16 | 8 | 1 | 17 | | **Surrender** ....Bennie Benjamin/George Weiss <B:19> | | | | **Perry Como** |

Best Seller: 8,6,3,2,1,2,2,3,6,5,5,6,6,8,9,10
Disc Jockey: 15,13,8,9,11,2,4,2,2,5,6,5,5,-,-,-,11
Juke Box: 18,6,6,2,2,2,3,3,5,5,6,4,6,6,8,9,10

| 9/21 | 14 | 12 | 6 | 1 | 18 | ● | **To Each His Own** ....Ray Evans/Jay Livingston | | | | **Ink Spots** |

Best Seller: 6,3,1,2,7,5,5,5,7,6,7
Juke Box: 15,10,8,3,4,6,4,6,7,8,6,8,9,-,13
Disc Jockey: 8,9,5,10,8,10,14,14

PEAK DATE	WEEKS CH	WEEKS 10	WEEKS 5	WEEKS PK	RANK	GOLD	Title PEAK POSITION Songwriter(s)	SYMBL	DEBUT	Artist
							1 (cont'd)			
4/27	15	11	6	1	19		I'm A Big Girl Now ....Milton Drake/Al Hoffman/Jerry Livingston			**Sammy Kaye** (Betty Barclay)
							Best Seller: 4,**1**,2,2,5,4,10,10,10,7,8			
							Juke Box: 15,-,11,6,2,4,2,2,3,4,7,7,8,6,13,16			
							Disc Jockey: 13,-,11,-,8,5,-,9,9,-,-,14,7			
12/28	6	5	2	1	20	●	White Christmas ....Irving Berlin [X-R]			**Bing Crosby**
							Disc Jockey: 7,8,6,**1**,6			
							Best Seller: 7,2,2,7			
							Juke Box: 21,17,9,3,5,6			
							2			
4/13	15	13	7	2	21		You Won't Be Satisfied (Until You Break My Heart) ..Freddy James/Larry Stock			Les Brown (Doris Day)
							<B:11>			
4/6	10	9	6	2	22		One-Zy Two-Zy ....Dave Franklin/Irving Taylor [N]			Phil Harris
11/2	19	17	11	1	23	●	South America, Take It Away ....Harold Rome <B:14>			Bing Crosby & the Andrews Sisters
7/20	14	12	8	1	24		They Say It's Wonderful ....Irving Berlin <B:11>			Frank Sinatra
1/5	14	13	7	1	25		Symphony ....Alex Alstone/Roger Bernstein/Jack Lawrence/Andre Tabet <B:12>			Benny Goodman (Liza Morrow)
7/13	13	12	5	1	26		Doin' What Comes Natur'lly ....Irving Berlin			Freddy Martin (Glenn Hughes)
							3			
4/27	16	9	5	4	27		Sioux City Sue ....Ray Freedman/Dick Thomas			Bing Crosby & The Jesters
5/4	15	10	8	3	28		Laughing On The Outside (Crying On The Inside)...Ben Raleigh/Bernie Wayne			Dinah Shore
							<A:1>			
7/27	17	13	4	2	29		Doin' What Comes Natur'lly ....Irving Berlin			Dinah Shore with Spade Cooley
12/21	13	11	9	1	30		The Old Lamp-Lighter ....Nat Simon/Charles Tobias <B:8>			Kay Kyser (Michael Douglas)
2/9	12	9	7	1	31		Symphony ....Alex Alstone/Roger Bernstein/Jack Lawrence/Andre Tabet			Bing Crosby
1/5	14	12	6	1	32	●	Dig You Later (A Hubba-Hubba-Hubba) ......Harold Adamson/Jimmy McHugh			Perry Como
							<B:12> [N]			
6/22	17	13	5	1	33		The Gypsy ....Billy Reid			Sammy Kaye (Mary Marlow)
9/21	14	12	3	1	34		To Each His Own ....Ray Evans/Jay Livingston			The Modernaires with Paula Kelly
6/29	11	10	2	1	35		Laughing On The Outside, Crying On The Inside..............Ben Raleigh/			Sammy Kaye (Billy Williams)
							Bernie Wayne			
12/28	7	5	1	1	36	●	The Christmas Song (Merry Christmas To You)....Mel Torme/Robert Wells [X]			The King Cole Trio
							{re-charted in 1948 (#24)}			
							4			
5/18	12	8	4	3	37		Laughing On The Outside (Crying On The Inside) ....Ben Raleigh/			Andy Russell
							Bernie Wayne <B:10>			
6/29	13	8	4	2	38		They Say It's Wonderful ....Irving Berlin <B:14>			Perry Como
4/13	9	7	3	2	39		One-Zy, Two-Zy (I Love You-zy) ....Dave Franklin/Irving Taylor			Freddy Martin (Martin Men)
11/2	18	16	6	1	40		Give Me Five Minutes More ....Sammy Cahn/Jule Styne			Tex Beneke/Glenn Miller
12/14	13	10	4	1	41		Rumors Are Flying ....Bennie Benjamin/George Weiss			Andrews Sisters with Les Paul
8/31	16	12	2	1	42	●	To Each His Own ....Ray Evans/Jay Livingston			Tony Martin
6/15	9	9	2	1	43		Hey! Ba-Ba-Re-Bop ....Curley Hamner/Lionel Hampton <B:19>			Tex Beneke/Glenn Miller
1/19	12	11	1	1	44		Symphony ....Alex Alstone/Roger Bernstein/Jack Lawrence/Andre Tabet <B:8>			Jo Stafford
4/6	11	9	1	1	45		Oh! What It Seemed To Be ....Bennie Benjamin/Frankie Carle/George Weiss			Dick Haymes & Helen Forrest
5/11	12	7	1	1	46		Laughing On The Outside Crying On The Inside ......Ben Raleigh/Bernie Wayne	✦		Teddy Walters
1/19	10	7	1	1	47		It Might As Well Be Spring ....Oscar Hammerstein/Richard Rodgers			Sammy Kaye (Billy Williams)
12/28	1	1	1	1	48		Winter Wonderland ....Felix Bernard/Richard Smith <B:5> [X]			Johnny Mercer
							5			
4/13	14	11	2	2	49		You Won't Be Satisfied (Until You Break My Heart) ..Freddy James/Larry Stock			Perry Como
							<A:5>			
4/13	7	7	2	2	50		Oh! What It Seemed To Be ....Bennie Benjamin/Frankie Carle/George Weiss			Charlie Spivak (Jimmy Saunders)
11/23	11	6	2	2	51		Rumors Are Flying ....Bennie Benjamin/George Weiss	❶		Betty Rhodes
2/9	12	10	1	1	52		I Can't Begin To Tell You ....Mack Gordon/James Monaco <B:6>			Harry James (Betty Grable)
3/16	10	9	1	1	53		Day By Day ....Sammy Cahn/Axel Stordahl/Paul Weston <A:1>			Frank Sinatra
6/8	9	8	1	1	54		Cement Mixer (Put-ti Put-ti) ....Slim Gaillard/Lee Ricks			Alvino Rey (Rocky Coluccio)
12/7	10	7	1	1	55		The Old Lamplighter ....Nat Simon/Charles Tobias	✦		Hal Derwin
2/16	12	8	1	1	56	●	I'm Always Chasing Rainbows ....Harry Carroll/Joseph McCarthy <A:5>			Perry Como
11/16	3	2	1	1	57		You Keep Coming Back Like A Song ....Irving Berlin			Dinah Shore
4/27	2	1	1	1	58		One-Zy Two-Zy (I Love You-zy) ....Dave Franklin/Irving Taylor			Kay Kyser (The Moonbeams)
							6			
10/19	12	11		2	59		The Coffee Song (They've Got An Awful Lot Of Coffee In Brazil) ....Bob Hilliard/Dick Miles <B:8>			Frank Sinatra
12/28	3	2		2	60		White Christmas ....Irving Berlin [X-R]			Frank Sinatra
9/21	13	8		1	61		South America, Take It Away! ....Harold Rome			Xavier Cugat (Buddy Clark)
4/20	11	8		1	62	●	Shoo Fly Pie (And Apple Pan Dowdy) ....Sammy Gallop/Guy Wood			Stan Kenton (June Christy)

1946

PEAK DATE	WEEKS CH	10	5	PK	RANK	GOLD	Title / PEAK POSITION / Songwriter(s)	SYMBL	DEBUT	Artist
							6 (cont'd)			
12/7	13	6		1	63		Ole Buttermilk Sky ....Jack Brooks/Hoagy Carmichael			Paul Weston With Matt Dennis
11/30	11	6		1	64		The Whole World Is Singing My Song............Mann Curtis/Vic Mizzy <B:11>			Les Brown (Doris Day)
5/11	7	5		1	65		Shoo Fly Pie And Apple Pan Dowdy ....Sammy Gallop/Guy Wood <B:12>			Guy Lombardo (Don Rodney)
12/7	14	4		1	66		The Rickety Rickshaw Man...Ervin Drake			Eddy Howard
4/13	9	4		1	67		Shoo-Fly Pie And Apple Pan Dowdy ....Sammy Gallop/Guy Wood			Dinah Shore
3/30	4	4		1	68		Doctor, Lawyer, Indian Chief ....Hoagy Carmichael/Paul Francis Webster <B:15>			Les Brown (Butch Stone)
3/30	8	3		1	69		Atlanta, GA. ....Arthur Shaftel/Sunny Skylar			Sammy Kaye (Billy Williams)
11/9	7	2		1	70		Rumors Are Flying ....Bennie Benjamin/George Weiss			Billy Butterfield (Pat O'Connor)
12/21	4	1		1	71		It's All Over Now ....Don Marcotte/Sunny Skylar			Frankie Carle (Marjorie Hughes)
							7			
8/31	16	9		2	72	●	Choo Choo Ch'Boogie ....Denver Darling/Milt Gabler/Vaughn Horton			Louis Jordan
11/23	6	4		2	73		Ole Buttermilk Sky..Jack Brooks/Hoagy Carmichael	❶		Helen Carroll & The Satisfiers
5/11	14	6		1	74		The Gypsy ....Billy Reid <B:15>			Hildegarde & Guy Lombardo
11/9	6	4		1	75		Rumors Are Flying ....Bennie Benjamin/George Weiss			The Three Suns
4/6	5	3		1	76		Seems Like Old Times ....John Jacob Loeb/Carmen Lombardo			Vaughn Monroe (Norton Sisters)
12/28	4	3		1	77	●	Christmas Island..Lyle Moraine [X]			Andrews Sisters & Guy Lombardo
							{re-charted in 1948 (#26)}			
2/16	9	2		1	78		I Can't Begin To Tell You ....Mack Gordon/James Monaco			Andy Russell
8/31	6	2		1	79		Stone Cold Dead In The Market (He Had It Coming) ....Wilmoth Houdini			Ella Fitzgerald & Louis Jordan
7/20	6	2		1	80		I Don't Know Enough About You ....Dave Barbour/Peggy Lee			Peggy Lee
5/4	6	2		1	81		Bumble Boogie ....Jack Fina [I]			Freddy Martin
3/16	5	2		1	82		I'm Always Chasing Rainbows ....Harry Carroll/Joseph McCarthy			Dick Haymes & Helen Forrest
8/10	15	1		1	83		I Don't Know Enough About You ....Dave Barbour/Peggy Lee			Mills Brothers
10/26	13	1		1	84		Five Minutes More ....Sammy Cahn/Jule Styne			The Three Suns
3/30	7	1		1	85		Seems Like Old Times ....John Jacob Loeb/Carmen Lombardo <B:10>			Guy Lombardo (Don Rodney)
2/16	4	1		1	86		Let It Snow! Let It Snow! Let It Snow!.....Sammy Cahn/Jule Styne <B:11> [X]			Woody Herman
6/1	3	1		1	87		All Through The Day................................Oscar Hammerstein/Jerome Kern			Frank Sinatra
12/28	2	1		1	88		Misirlou ....Nick Roubanis [I]	❶		Jan August
							8			
7/27	10	7		3	89		Surrender ....Bennie Benjamin/George Weiss			Woody Herman
7/6	13	6		3	90		The House Of Blue Lights ....Don Raye/Freddie Slack			Freddie Slack (Ella Mae Morse)
8/17	7	4		3	91		Just The Other Day ....Johnson Croom/Redd Evans			Sam Donahue (Mynell Allen)
1/26	9	3		2	92		Aren't You Glad You're You? ....Johnny Burke/Jimmy Van Heusen <B:18>			Bing Crosby
7/27	10	5		1	93		Doin' What Comes Natur'lly ....Irving Berlin			Jimmy Dorsey (Dee Parker)
10/26	4	4		1	94		Blue Skies ....Irving Berlin			Count Basie (Jimmy Rushing)
12/14	8	3		1	95		Sooner Or Later (You're Gonna Be Comin' Around) ...Ray Gilbert/Charles Wolcott			Sammy Kaye (Betty Barclay)
							<B:11>			
12/14	6	3		1	96		The Things We Did Last Summer ....Sammy Cahn/Jule Styne <A:6>			Frank Sinatra
5/25	5	3		1	97		All Through The Day................................Oscar Hammerstein/Jerome Kern <A:1>			Perry Como
11/16	2	2		1	98		Put That Kiss Back Where You Found It ....Peter DeRose/Carl Sigman			Sam Donahue (Bill Lockwood)
6/15	4	1		1	99		In The Moon Mist...Jack Lawrence			The Pied Pipers
6/22	4	1		1	100		The Gypsy ....Billy Reid <B:17>			Hal McIntyre (Frankie Lester)
3/16	4	1		1	101		Day By Day ....Sammy Cahn/Axel Stordahl/Paul Weston <A:4>			Jo Stafford
8/3	1	1		1	102		Hawaiian War Chant (Ta-Hu-Wa-Hu-Wai) ....Ralph Freed/Johnny Noble [N]			Spike Jones
							9			
11/2	7	3		3	103		Rumors Are Flying ....Bennie Benjamin/George Weiss			Tony Martin
6/22	11	4		2	104		Prisoner Of Love................................Russ Columbo/Clarence Gaskill/Leo Robin			Ink Spots
8/3	6	3		2	105		Boogie Blues ....Ray Biondi/Gene Krupa			Gene Krupa (Anita O'Day)
4/27	8	3		1	106		Hey! Ba-Ba-Re-Bop...Curley Hamner/Lionel Hampton			Lionel Hampton
3/16	7	2		1	107		I Can't Begin To Tell You ....Mack Gordon/James Monaco			Sammy Kaye (Nancy Norman)
8/10	6	2		1	108		Dinah...Harry Akst/Sam Lewis/Joe Young [I]			Sam Donahue
11/2	9	1		1	109		Five Minutes More ....Sammy Cahn/Jule Styne	✦		Skitch Henderson (Ray Kellogg)
6/1	6	1		1	110		Laughing On The Outside (Crying On The Inside)...Ben Raleigh/Bernie Wayne			The Merry Macs
10/19	5	1		1	111		Passe ....Eddie DeLange/Joseph Meyer/Carl Sigman			Tex Beneke/Glenn Miller (Lillian Lane)
2/9	5	1		1	112		Money Is The Root Of All Evil (Take It Away, Take It Away,			
							Take It Away) ....Alex Kramer/Joan Whitney			Andrews Sisters & Guy Lombardo
2/9	5	1		1	113		Let It Snow! Let It Snow! Let It Snow! ....Sammy Cahn/Jule Styne [X]			Connee Boswell & Russ Morgan
6/1	4	1		1	114		All That Glitters Is Not Gold ....Eddie Asherman/Alice Cornett/Lee Kuhn			Dinah Shore
2/16	4	1		1	115		I'm Always Chasing Rainbows ....Harry Carroll/Joseph McCarthy			Harry James (Buddy DiVito)
8/3	3	1		1	116		I Know..Ted Brooks/John Jennings			Tex Beneke/Glenn Miller
4/6	3	1		1	117		Personality ....Johnny Burke/Jimmy Van Heusen			Bing Crosby
7/27	2	1		1	118		Who Do You Love I Hope ....Irving Berlin	❶		Elliot Lawrence (Rosalind Patton)
1/5	2	1		1	119		Buzz Me ....Danny Baxter/Fleecie Moore			Louis Jordan

PEAK DATE	CH	10	5	PK	RANK	GOLD	Title / Songwriter(s)	SYMBOL	DEBUT	Artist

9 (cont'd)

PEAK DATE	CH	10	5	PK	RANK	GOLD	Title / Songwriter(s)	SYM	DEB	Artist
8/17	1	1		1	120		Blue Skies .... *Irving Berlin* <B:12>			Benny Goodman (Art Lund)
12/28	1	1		1	121		White Christmas .... *Irving Berlin* [X]			Jo Stafford

10

PEAK DATE	CH	10	5	PK	RANK	GOLD	Title / Songwriter(s)	SYM	DEB	Artist
5/25	10	4		4	122	●	Prisoner Of Love .... *Russ Columbo/Clarence Gaskill/Leo Robin*			Billy Eckstine
6/8	10	2		2	123		The Mad Boogie........................... *Count Basie/Buster Harding* <B:14> [I]			Count Basie
9/28	8	2		2	124		Pretending .... *Al Sherman/Marty Symes*			Andy Russell
11/30	6	2		2	125		It's All Over Now .... *Don Marcotte/Sunny Skylar*			Peggy Lee
6/1	5	2		2	126		They Say It's Wonderful .... *Irving Berlin* <A:4>			Andy Russell
8/3	8	1		1	127		One More Tomorrow .... *Eddie DeLange/Ernesto Lecuona/Josef Myrow*			Frankie Carle (Marjorie Hughes)
2/16	8	1		1	128		Symphony........... *Alex Alstone/Roger Bernstein/Jack Lawrence/Andre Tabet* <A:7> [I]			Guy Lombardo
7/6	5	1		1	129		I Got The Sun In The Morning........................... *Irving Berlin*			Les Brown (Doris Day)
1/5	5	1		1	130		Chickery Chick .... *Sylvia Dee/Sid Lippman*			Gene Krupa (Anita O'Day)
1/5	5	1		1	131		Chickery Chick .... *Sylvia Dee/Sid Lippman*			Evelyn Knight & The Jesters
3/16	4	1		1	132		Personality .... *Johnny Burke/Jimmy Van Heusen*			Dinah Shore
3/30	4	1		1	133	●	McNamara's Band .... *Guy Bonham/Wamp Carlson/Dwight Latham/Shamus O'Connor/ J.J. Stamford*			Bing Crosby & The Jesters
4/6	3	1		1	134		The Dark Town Poker Club .... *Jean Havez/William Vodery/Bert Williams* [N]			Phil Harris
4/6	2	1		1	135		You Won't Be Satisfied (Until You Break My Heart) .. *Freddy James/Larry Stock*			Ella Fitzgerald & Louis Armstrong
11/16	2	1		1	136		This Is Always .... *Mack Gordon/Harry Warren*			Harry James (Buddy DiVito)
11/16	2	1		1	137		The Things We Did Last Summer .... *Sammy Cahn/Jule Styne* <B:11>			Jo Stafford
5/25	2	1		1	138		Sioux City Sue .... *Ray Freedman/Dick Thomas*			Tony Pastor
9/7	1	1		1	139		You Call It Madness (But I Call It Love) .. *Russ Columbo/Con Conrad/Gladys DuBois*			The King Cole Trio
12/28	1	1		1	140		Winter Wonderland................................ *Felix Bernard/Richard Smith* [X]			Perry Como

11

PEAK DATE	CH	10	5	PK	RANK	GOLD	Title / Songwriter(s)	SYM	DEB	Artist
12/14	2			2	141		September Song .... *Maxwell Anderson/Kurt Weill*	✦		The Dardanelle Trio
9/7	9			1	142		My Sugar Is So Refined .... *Sylvia Dee/Sid Lippman* <B:22>			Johnny Mercer
11/30	5			1	143		You Keep Coming Back Like A Song .... *Irving Berlin* <A:10>			Jo Stafford
2/9	4			1	144		Aren't You Glad You're You? .... *Johnny Burke/Jimmy Van Heusen*			Les Brown (Doris Day)
6/8	4			1	145		All Through The Day .... *Oscar Hammerstein/Jerome Kern* <B:12>			Margaret Whiting
2/9	3			1	146		Come To Baby, Do! .... *Inez James/Sidney Miller* <A:2>			Les Brown (Doris Day)
1/26	3			1	147		The Moment I Met You .... *Gail Meredith/Buck Ram*			Tommy Dorsey (The Sentimentalists)
10/5	2			1	148		I Guess I'll Get The Papers (And Go Home) .... *Hal Kanner/Hughie Prince/ Dick Rogers* <A:6>			Les Brown (Jack Haskell)
8/31	2			1	149		(Get Your Kicks On) **Route 66** .... *Bobby Troup*			The King Cole Trio
4/27	2			1	150		Atlanta, G.A. .... *Arthur Shaftel/Sunny Skylar*			Woody Herman
6/15	2			1	151		The Girl That I Marry .... *Irving Berlin* <A:2>			Frank Sinatra
5/25	1			1	152		Don't Be A Baby, Baby .... *Buddy Kaye/Howard Steiner*			Benny Goodman (Art Lund)
2/16	1			1	153		Everybody Knew But Me .... *Irving Berlin* <A:7>			Woody Herman
2/9	1			1	154		Slowly .... *Kermit Goell/David Raksin*			Kay Kyser (Michael Douglas)
10/12	1			1	155		Sherwood's Forest .... *Bobby Sherwood* [I]	✦		Bobby Sherwood
9/28	1			1	156		This Is Always.................................. *Mack Gordon/Harry Warren*			Jo Stafford

12

PEAK DATE	CH	10	5	PK	RANK	GOLD	Title / Songwriter(s)	SYM	DEB	Artist
10/19	7			2	157		I Guess I'll Get The Papers And Go Home .. *Hal Kanner/Hughie Prince/Dick Rogers*			Mills Brothers
12/28	2			2	158		The Christmas Song (Merry Christmas To You)....*Mel Torme/Robert Wells* [X]			Les Brown (Doris Day)
11/16	2			2	159		It's A Pity To Say Goodnight .... *Billy Reid*			Stan Kenton (June Christy)
6/1	8			1	160		Give Me The Moon Over Brooklyn .... *Jason Matthews/Terry Shand*			Guy Lombardo (Lombardo Trio)
11/30	5			1	161		Five Minutes More .... *Sammy Cahn/Jule Styne*			Bob Crosby
7/6	4			1	162		They Say It's Wonderful........................ *Irving Berlin*			Bing Crosby
5/4	4			1	163		Don't Be A Baby, Baby .... *Buddy Kaye/Howard Steiner*			Mills Brothers
11/2	4			1	164		Passé .... *Eddie DeLange/Joseph Meyer/Carl Sigman*			Margaret Whiting
1/26	3			1	165		I'm In The Mood For Love .... *Dorothy Fields/Jimmy McHugh*			Billy Eckstine
6/22	3			1	166		In Love In Vain .... *Jerome Kern/Leo Robin* <A:11>			Margaret Whiting
11/30	2			1	167		Rumors Are Flying .... *Bennie Benjamin/George Weiss*	✦		Harry Cool & Mindy Carson
12/14	2			1	168		You Keep Coming Back Like A Song .... *Irving Berlin*			Bing Crosby
8/17	2			1	169		In Love In Vain .... *Jerome Kern/Leo Robin*			Dick Haymes & Helen Forrest
3/16	1			1	170		Patience And Fortitude .... *Billy Moore/Blackie Warren*			Andrews Sisters
1/26	1			1	171		Jivin' Joe Jackson .... *Count Basie*			Count Basie (Ann Moore)
6/1	1			1	172		It Couldn't Be True! (Or Could It?) .... *Sylvia Dee/Sid Lippman*			Tex Beneke/Glenn Miller
10/12	1			1	173		On The Boardwalk (In Atlantic City) .... *Mack Gordon/Josef Myrow*			The Charioteers
12/7	1			1	174		The Whole World Is Singing My Song .... *Mann Curtis/Vic Mizzy*			Jimmy Dorsey (Bob Carroll)
8/3	1			1	175		I Don't Know Enough About You .... *Dave Barbour/Peggy Lee* <A:9>			Benny Goodman (Art Lund)
2/16	1			1	176		Slowly................................... *Kermit Goell/David Raksin*			Dick Haymes
8/31	1			1	177		Mabel! Mabel! .... *Ervin Drake/Jimmy Shirl*			Woody Herman
2/9	1			1	178		Someday (You'll Want Me To Want You) .... *Jimmie Hodges* [N]			Hoosier Hot Shots & Sally Foster

PEAK DATE	WEEKS				RANK	GOLD	Title	PEAK POSITION	Songwriter(s)	SYMBL	DEBUT	Artist
	CH	10	5	PK								

12 (cont'd)

PEAK DATE	CH	PK	RANK	Title	Songwriter(s)	Artist
2/16	1	1	179	Got A Right To Cry	Joe Liggins	Joe Liggins
1/26	1	1	180	Are These Really Mine?	Robert Cook/David Saxon/Sunny Skylar <A:11>	Vaughn Monroe (Norton Sisters)
12/14	1	1	181	Ole Buttermilk Sky	Jack Brooks/Hoagy Carmichael ✦	Danny O'Neil
5/11	1	1	182	Seems Like Old Times	John Jacob Loeb/Carmen Lombardo	Kate Smith

13

PEAK DATE	CH	PK	RANK	Title	Songwriter(s)	Artist
11/30	7	1	183 ●	In A Shanty In Old Shanty Town	Jack Little/John Siras/Joe Young	Johnny Long
12/14	4	1	184	The Things We Did Last Summer	Sammy Cahn/Jule Styne	Vaughn Monroe
1/26	3	1	185	Artistry Jumps	Stan Kenton <B:16> [I]	Stan Kenton
6/8	2	1	186	Cement Mixer (Put-ti, Put-ti)	Slim Gaillard/Lee Ricks [N]	Charlie Barnet (Art Robey)
9/7	2	1	187	You Call It Madness But I Call It Love	Russ Columbo/Con Conrad/ Gladys DuBois	Billy Eckstine
10/5	2	1	188	And Then It's Heaven	Al Kaufman/Sol Marcus/Eddie Seiler	Harry James (Buddy DiVito)
2/16	2	1	189	One More Dream (And She's Mine)	Buddy Kaye/Dick Manning	Johnnie Johnston
6/22	2	1	190	Cement Mixer (Put-Ti-Put-Ti)	Slim Gaillard/Lee Ricks [N]	Jimmie Lunceford (Lunceford Quartet)
2/2	1	1	191	The Bells Of St. Mary's	A. Emmett Adams/Douglas Furber	Bing Crosby
2/2	1	1	192	Come To Baby, Do!	Inez James/Sidney Miller	Duke Ellington (Joya Sherrill)
3/16	1	1	193	Give Me The Simple Life	Rube Bloom/Harry Ruby	Benny Goodman (Liza Morrow)
8/31	1	1	194	Along With Me	Harold Rome	Margaret Whiting

14

PEAK DATE	CH	PK	RANK	Title	Songwriter(s)	Artist
8/24	5	1	195	I'd Be Lost Without You	Sunny Skylar	Guy Lombardo (Don Rodney)
10/26	4	1	196	If You Were The Only Girl	Nat Ayer/Clifford Grey <A:4>	Perry Como
12/28	3	1	197	Ole Buttermilk Sky	Jack Brooks/Hoagy Carmichael	Connee Boswell
11/30	3	1	198	The Best Man	Roy Alfred/Fred Wise <A:1>	The King Cole Trio
3/23	2	1	199	Patience And Fortitude	Billy Moore/Blackie Warren <A:10>	Count Basie (Jimmy Rushing)
8/17	2	1	200	I'd Be Lost Without You	Sunny Skylar	Frankie Carle (Marjorie Hughes)
8/10	2	1	201	Get Your Kicks On "Route 66!—"	Bobby Troup <A:2>	Bing Crosby & the Andrews Sisters
2/2	2	1	202	In The Middle Of May	Fred Ahlert/Al Stillman <B:18>	The Pied Pipers
2/16	1	1	203	Let It Snow; Let It Snow; Let It Snow	Sammy Cahn/Jule Styne [X]	Bob Crosby
1/19	1	1	204	Aren't You Glad You're You?	Johnny Burke/Jimmy Van Heusen <B:15>	Tommy Dorsey (Stuart Foster)
6/22	1	1	205	The Gypsy	Billy Reid	Jan Garber (Tommy Traynor)
5/11	1	1	206	I Know	Ted Brooks/John Jennings	Andy Kirk & The Jubalaires
1/26	1	1	207	You're Nobody 'Til Somebody Loves You	James Cavanaugh/ Russ Morgan/Larry Stock <B:17>	Russ Morgan
4/27	1	1	208	Sioux City Sue	Ray Freedman/Dick Thomas	Kate Smith

15

PEAK DATE	CH	PK	RANK	Title	Songwriter(s)	Artist
10/26	5	1	209	The House Of Blue Lights	Don Raye/Freddie Slack ❶	Andrews Sisters & Eddie Heywood
8/3	3	1	210	Who Told You That Lie?	Eddie Cantor/Jack Segal/Bee Walker <B:16>	Vaughn Monroe
7/27	2	1	211	Cynthia's In Love	Billy Gish/Jack Owens/Earl White	Tex Beneke/Glenn Miller (Artie Malvin/Lillian Lane)
3/30	2	1	212	Day By Day	Sammy Cahn/Axel Stordahl/Paul Weston <A:6>	Les Brown (Doris Day)
4/13	2	1	213	One-Zy Two-Zy (I Love You-zy)	Dave Franklin/Irving Taylor <A:7>	Hildegarde & Guy Lombardo
12/7	1	1	214	The Best Man	Roy Alfred/Fred Wise	Les Brown (Butch Stone)
3/23	1	1	215	Day By Day	Sammy Cahn/Axel Stordahl/Paul Weston	Bing Crosby with Mel Torme
7/13	1	1	216	Do You Love Me	Harry Ruby	Harry James (Ginnie Powell)
1/19	1	1	217	Buzz Me	Danny Baxter/Fleecie Moore	Ella Mae Morse

16

PEAK DATE	CH	PK	RANK	Title	Songwriter(s)	Artist
8/3	5	2	218	I Don't Know Why (I Just Do)	Fred Ahlert/Roy Turk	Tommy Dorsey (Stuart Foster)
7/27	2	1	219	It's My Lazy Day	Smiley Burnette <A:15>	Vaughn Monroe
1/19	1	1	220	Give Me The Simple Life	Rube Bloom/Harry Ruby	Bing Crosby & Jimmy Dorsey
3/2	1	1	221	Guitar Polka	Al Dexter [I]	Al Dexter
12/14	1	1	222	The Old Lamp-Lighter	Nat Simon/Charles Tobias	Morton Downey
3/2	1	1	223	Just A-Sittin' And A-Rockin'	Duke Ellington/Lee Gaines/Billy Strayhorn <A:13>	Stan Kenton (June Christy)
11/2	1	1	224	You Broke The Only Heart That Ever Loved You	Barbara Belle/ Jack Little/Teddy Powell/Larry Stock	Elliot Lawrence (Jack Hunter/Rosalind Patton)

17

PEAK DATE	CH	PK	RANK	Title	Songwriter(s)	Artist
6/8	3	1	225	Cement Mixer (Put-Ti — Put-Ti)	Slim Gaillard/Lee Ricks <A:8>	Hal McIntyre (Nancy Reed)
11/2	2	1	226	Ain't That Just Like A Woman (They'll Do It Every Time)	Claude Demetrius/Fleecie Moore	Louis Jordan
4/13	2	1	227	Full Moon And Empty Arms	Buddy Kaye/Ted Mossman	Frank Sinatra
8/31	1	1	228	I Don't Know Why (I Just Do)	Fred Ahlert/Roy Turk	Andrews Sisters
2/23	1	1	229	Just A-Sittin' And A-Rockin'	Duke Ellington/Lee Gaines/Billy Strayhorn	Delta Rhythm Boys

1946

PEAK DATE	WEEKS				R A N K	G O L D	Title	PEAK POSITION	Songwriter(s)	S Y M B L	D E B U T	Artist
	CH	10	5	PK								

17 (cont'd)

PEAK DATE	CH	10	5	PK	RANK	GOLD	Title / Songwriter	Artist
1/5	1			1	230		Gee, It's Good To Hold You .... *Doris Fisher/Allan Roberts*	Woody Herman (Frances Wayne)
11/16	1			1	231		My Best To You .... *Isham Jones/Gene Willadsen*	Eddy Howard
7/6	1			1	232		There's No One But You .... *Redd Evans/Croom Johnson*	Hal McIntyre (Frankie Lester)
1/12	1			1	233		(Did You Ever Get) **That Feeling In The Moonlight** ......*James Cavanaugh/* *Ira Schuster/Larry Stock* <A:14>	Russ Morgan
7/20	1			1	234		I Got The Sun In The Morning...*Irving Berlin*	Artie Shaw & Mel Torme
6/15	1			1	235		Come Rain Or Come Shine...............................*Harold Arlen/Johnny Mercer*	Margaret Whiting

18

PEAK DATE	CH	10	5	PK	RANK	GOLD	Title / Songwriter	Artist
6/8	2			1	236		Who's Sorry Now? ....*Bert Kalmar/Harry Ruby/Ted Snyder*	Harry James (Willie Smith)
3/16	1			1	237		Doctor Lawyer Indian Chief ....*Hoagy Carmichael/Paul Francis Webster*	Hoagy Carmichael
1/5	1			1	238		In The Land Of Beginning Again ....*Grant Clarke/George Meyer* <A:8>	Bing Crosby
7/27	1			1	239		Salute To Glenn Miller.........*Elmer Albrecht/Lew Brown/Sammy Gallop/Mack Gordon/* *Dick Jurgens/Glenn Miller/Mitchell Parish/Sam Stept/Charles Tobias/Harry Warren*	The Modernaires with Paula Kelly
2/23	1			1	240		Full Moon And Empty Arms ....*Buddy Kaye/Ted Mossman*	Ray Noble (Snooky Lanson)
7/13	1			1	241		From This Day Forward ....*Mort Greene/Leigh Harline*	Frank Sinatra

19

PEAK DATE	CH	10	5	PK	RANK	GOLD	Title / Songwriter	Artist
6/22	1			1	242		The Whiffenpoof Song Baa! Baa! Baa!.........*Todd Galloway/Meade Minnigerode/* *George Pomeroy* <A:4>	Tex Beneke/Glenn Miller (Artie Malvin)
3/16	1			1	243		Wave To Me, My Lady...*Frank Loesser/Willie Stein*	Elton Britt
1/5	1			1	244		The Frim Fram Sauce ....*Redd Evans/Joe Ricardel*	The King Cole Trio
11/16	1			1	245		If I'm Lucky ....*Eddie DeLange/Josef Myrow*	Perry Como
8/17	1			1	246		More Than You Know................*Edward Eliscu/Billy Rose/Vincent Youmans* <A:1>	Perry Como

20

PEAK DATE	CH	10	5	PK	RANK	GOLD	Title / Songwriter	Artist
7/13	1			1	247		New Spanish Two Step..*Tommy Duncan/Bob Wills*	Bob Wills (Tommy Duncan)

21

PEAK DATE	CH	10	5	PK	RANK	GOLD	Title / Songwriter	Artist
5/25	1			1	248		Cement Mixer (Put-Ti-Put-Ti) ....*Slim Gaillard/Lee Ricks* [N] ✦	Slim Gaillard Trio

22

PEAK DATE	CH	10	5	PK	RANK	GOLD	Title / Songwriter	Artist
9/28	1			1	249		Ugly Chile (You're Some Pretty Doll)........................*Clarence Williams* <A:11>	Johnny Mercer

1947

NATIONAL NEWS: Congress enacts (over President Truman's veto) the controversial Taft-Hartley bill to increase government powers to end labor strikes. Truman signs legislation unifying all branches of the Armed Forces into the Department of Defense; the Central Intelligence Agency and the National Security Council are established.

INTERNATIONAL NEWS: The devastation of war over, Europe struggles with a desperate shortage of food. The Truman Administration launches its ambitious Marshall Plan to help rebuild the battered continent. After more than a year of violent demonstrations in India, the nation is granted independence from Britain, but bloody battles between Moslems and Hindus allow no opportunity for celebration.

COMMERCE AND SCIENCE: Bell Laboratories' development of the transistor promises future technological breakthroughs. Dr. Edwin Land demonstrates the Polaroid Land Camera which produces a sepia-toned print within one minute.

FADS AND FASHION: French designer Christian Dior introduces his first full fashion line, the so-called "New Look."

SPORTS: The Brooklyn Dodgers' Jackie Robinson, the first African-American player in 20th century major league baseball, makes sports and civil rights history, and is the National League's Rookie of the Year. In a thrilling seven-game World Series, Joe DiMaggio and the New York Yankees edge Robinson's Dodgers. Ted Williams wins baseball's Triple Crown. The Chicago Cardinals top the Philadelphia Eagles in the NFL title game, 28-21. Notre Dame and Michigan are college football's co-national champions. The first NBA championship is won by the Philadelphia Warriors. The NCAA basketball tournament is won by Holy Cross. Rocky Graziano wins the middleweight boxing title from Tony Zale. Jack Kramer wins Wimbledon and the U.S. tennis championship.

MOVIES: Top Oscar winners include Best Picture *Gentlemen's Agreement* starring Gregory Peck, Best Actor Ronald Colman (*A Double Life*), and Best Actress Loretta Young (*The Farmer's Daughter*). The year's most-beloved film is the holiday classic *Miracle on 34th Street*. Tops at the box office is *Welcome Stranger* with Bing Crosby.

TELEVISION: At the end of a year which saw the first televised World Series, there are still only 172,000 TV sets owned nationwide.

THEATER: At year's end, Tennessee Williams' *A Streetcar Named Desire* becomes an instant Broadway classic and a 1948 Pulitzer Prize winner, with Jessica Tandy and the historic lead performance by Marlon Brando. *Finian's Rainbow* and *Brigadoon* are the year's leading musicals.

BOOKS: James A. Michener's *Tales of the South Pacific* is a huge success, providing the basis for the musical *South Pacific*.

1947 — TOP 20 ARTISTS

1. **Eddy Howard**
650

2. **Ted Weems**
590

3. **Perry Como**
544

4.	539	**Frank Sinatra**	13.	386	**Sam Donahue**
5.	535	**Dinah Shore**	14.	355	**Count Basie**
6.	489	**Jo Stafford**	15.	346	**Margaret Whiting**
7.	476	**Vaughn Monroe**	16.	319	**Freddy Martin**
8.	471	**Bing Crosby**	17.	285	**Francis Craig**
9.	462	**Johnny Mercer**	18.	279	**Dick Haymes**
10.	443	**Guy Lombardo**	19.	262	**Art Lund**
11.	422	**Buddy Clark**	20.	249	**Hoagy Carmichael**
12.	417	**Sammy Kaye**			

1947 — TOP SONGWRITERS

	# of Hits	Points			# of Hits	Points	
1.	13	1,237	**Mack Gordon**	7.	8	739	**Frank Loesser**
2.	10	954	**Kermit Goell**	8.	7	679	**Dusty Fletcher**
3.	9	837	**Leo Robin**		7	679	**Don Howell**
	9	837	**Arthur Schwartz**		7	679	**John Mason**
5.	8	746	**Burton Lane**		7	679	**Jack McVea**
6.	8	740	**Al Hoffman**	12.	7	670	**Edmund Goulding**

1947 — TOP ARTIST DEBUTS

1.	3/22	**Johnny Desmond** (96)	6.	5/31	**Jack Smith** (107)
2.	3/29 †	**Frankie Laine** (18) ★	7.	8/09	**Francis Craig** (133)
3.	4/19	**Art Lund** (104)	8.	8/30	**Vic Damone** (28)
4.	4/26	**The Harmonicats** (110)	9.	9/20	**Jack Owens** (149)
5.	5/03	**Dennis Day** (125)	10.	11/01	**Arthur Godfrey** (80)

PEAK DATE	WEEKS				R A N K	G O L D	Title / PEAK POSITION / Songwriter(s)	S Y M B L	D E B U T	Artist
	CH	10	5	PK						

1

| 8/30 | 25 | 25 | 21 | 17 | 1 | ● | Near You ....Francis Craig/Kermit Goell | ❶ | | Francis Craig (Bob Lamm) |

Disc Jockey: 9,7,3,1,1,1,1,1,1,1,1,1,1,1,1,1,1,1,3,4,6,8
Juke Box: 16,10,8,5,2,1,1,1,1,1,1,1,1,1,1,1,1,2,4,3,10,14
Best Seller: 4,5,1,1,1,1,1,1,1,1,1,1,1,1,2,3,3,4,4,9,11

| 3/15 | 20 | 18 | 17 | 13 | 2 | ● | Heartaches ....Al Hoffman/John Klenner [I] | | | Ted Weems |

Juke Box: 12,3,2,1,1,1,1,1,1,1,1,1,1,1,1,2,11,9,9
Best Seller: 6,1,1,1,1,1,1,1,1,1,1,1,1,3,3,8
Disc Jockey: 6,2,2,1,1,1,1,1,1,1,2,1,1,2,1,1,4,5,14

| 12/13 | 22 | 21 | 18 | 10 | 3 | ● | Ballerina ....Bob Russell/Carl Sigman | | | Vaughn Monroe |

Best Seller: 4,5,2,2,2,1,1,1,1,1,1,1,2,4,4,6,8,10
Disc Jockey: 10,12,11,2,2,3,3,1,1,1,1,1,1,1,3,3,3,9,10
Juke Box: 12,8,10,5,4,2,2,2,1,1,1,1,1,1,2,2,3,5,8,10,15

| 6/21 | 26 | 24 | 13 | 8 | 4 | ● | Peg O' My Heart ....Alfred Bryan/Fred Fisher [I] | ❶ | | The Harmonicats |

Juke Box: 13,15,8,8,6,6,7,1,1,1,1,1,1,1,3,4,1,3,4,5,7,7,7,8,7,9
Best Seller: 7,7,7,6,2,1,2,3,2,1,1,1,3,2,3,6,3,5,8,6,6
Disc Jockey: 16,8,9,4,6,6,6,5,5,12,3,3,6,5,7,7,14,-,12,11

| 7/5 | 15 | 15 | 13 | 6 | 5 | | Peg O' My Heart ....Alfred Bryan/Fred Fisher | | | Buddy Clark |

Disc Jockey: 8,1,1,1,1,1,1,2,4,3,2,5,7,4,5
Best Seller: 10,9,10,9,9,4,10
Juke Box: 15,14,13,13,-,14,-,-,-,-,14,-,13

| 8/9 | 17 | 15 | 10 | 6 | 6 | ● | Smoke! Smoke! Smoke! (That Cigarette) ....Merle Travis/Tex Williams [N] | ❶ | | Tex Williams |

Best Seller: 8,6,1,1,1,1,1,1,2,2,2,4
Juke Box: 9,7,7,5,6,2,1,2,1,1,1,3,3,5,6
Disc Jockey: 15,15,3,9,8,2,1,2,6,3,2,2,2,2,4,6,10

| 8/9 | 19 | 18 | 13 | 3 | 7 | | Peg O' My Heart ....Alfred Bryan/Fred Fisher [I] | | | The Three Suns |

Juke Box: 16,8,6,4,3,3,3,1,1,3,2,1,3,3,4,4,6,6,6
Disc Jockey: 14,14,5,4,6,4,4,5,5,1,9,7,3,4,14,7,8
Best Seller: 4,2,4,3,4,7,4,5,4,3,8,2,6,7,8,7

| 2/22 | 13 | 12 | 9 | 3 | 8 | | Managua, Nicaragua..Irving Fields/Albert Gamse | | | Freddy Martin (Stuart Wade) |

Juke Box: 9,12,7,3,3,1,1,1,3,2,2,-,5,10
Best Seller: 7,4,2,1,1,3,3,3,5,5,6
Disc Jockey: 11,4,7,3,5,5,4,12,3,14,4,-,11,15

| 6/28 | 13 | 12 | 7 | 3 | 9 | ● | Chi-Baba Chi-Baba (My Bambino Go To Sleep) ......Mack David/Al Hoffman/ Jerry Livingston <B:2> | | | Perry Como |

Best Seller: 10,10,2,1,1,2,2,4,6,6,6
Juke Box: 14,15,10,4,4,2,6,6,4,6,8,10,12
Disc Jockey: 15,-,-,9,10,9,9,8,10,12,12,11

| 5/10 | 23 | 21 | 17 | 2 | 10 | | Linda ....Jack Lawrence | | | Ray Noble with Buddy Clark |

Disc Jockey: 8,9,5,7,5,12,3,3,3,2,2,1,2,2,3,2,2,1,3,4,10,12
Best Seller: 7,3,3,2,2,2,2,3,3,2,2,4,6
Juke Box: 14,13,10,7,3,3,2,3,2,3,3,2,4,3,3,6,7,10,10

| 2/8 | 15 | 14 | 10 | 2 | 11 | | Huggin' And Chalkin' ....Kermit Goell/Clancy Hayes [N] | | | Hoagy Carmichael |

Juke Box: 11,8,6,3,4,4,6,4,3,3,2,1,1,2,7
Best Seller: 10,7,6,5,7,3,3,3,4,2,5,5,9
Disc Jockey: 11,10,10,-,13,9,5,10,7,8,9

| 6/7 | 13 | 11 | 9 | 2 | 12 | ● | Mam'selle ....Mack Gordon/Edmund Goulding | ❶ | | Art Lund |

Best Seller: 9,4,3,3,2,2,3,1,1,5,9
Juke Box: 12,3,4,4,4,4,4,2,7,6,9,9,14
Disc Jockey: 5,3,3,4,4,4,4,3,9,8,7

| 3/8 | 12 | 11 | 8 | 2 | 13 | | Anniversary Song ....Saul Chaplin/Al Jolson | | | Dinah Shore |

Disc Jockey: 7,1,1,2,2,2,2,3,3,6,6,11
Best Seller: 7,5,4,4,7,7,5,10
Juke Box: 8,5,6,7,6,8,11,6,14

| 3/15 | 15 | 13 | 9 | 1 | 14 | | Managua - Nicaragua ....Irving Fields/Albert Gamse | | | Guy Lombardo (Don Rodney) |

Juke Box: 11,16,7,4,3,3,5,1,4,4,4,4,7,10,10
Best Seller: 8,8,10,8,5,10,4,4,10
Juke Box: 14,15,10,13,11,14,7,-,11,10

| 6/28 | 15 | 13 | 9 | 1 | 15 | | Temptation (Tim-Tayshun) ....Nacio Herb Brown/Arthur Freed [N] | ❶ | | Red Ingle (Jo Stafford) |

Disc Jockey: 11,5,1,2,3,2,3,6,4,4,7,11,15,-,12
Best Seller: 10,5,5,3,2,2,3,2,2,2,9,7,10
Juke Box: 16,15,13,8,5,8,7,7,7,9,9,10,10,12,15

| 3/1 | 8 | 7 | 4 | 1 | 16 | | Open The Door, Richard ....Dusty Fletcher/Don Howell/John Mason/ Jack McVea [N] | ✦ | | The Three Flames |

Disc Jockey: 6,2,2,1,2,11,6,9
Best Seller: 7,4,9
Juke Box: 13,5,6

| 2/22 | 7 | 6 | 4 | 1 | 17 | | Open The Door, Richard! ....Dusty Fletcher/Don Howell/John Mason/ Jack McVea [N] | | | Count Basie (Harry Edison/Bill Johnson) |

Best Seller: 3,1,2,4
Disc Jockey: 13,4,1,3,10,8,7
Juke Box: 6,4,2,3,10,14

| 5/31 | 10 | 9 | 3 | 1 | 18 | | Mam'selle..Mack Gordon/Edmund Goulding | | | Frank Sinatra |

Disc Jockey: 12,7,6,1,6,6,3,4,8,6
Best Seller: 7,6,8,9
Juke Box: 10,9,11,13,14,15

PEAK DATE	WEEKS				RANK	GOLD	Title / PEAK POSITION / Songwriter(s)	SYMBL	DEBUT	Artist
	CH	10	5	PK						

2

12/13	18	14	14	8	19	●	**Too Fat Polka** (I Don't Want Her) (You Can Have Her) (She's Too Fat For Me)..*Ross MacLean/Arthur Richardson* **[N]**	❶		Arthur Godfrey
3/8	14	14	10	6	20	●	**Anniversary Song** ....*Saul Chaplin/Al Jolson*			Al Jolson
8/30	17	16	12	5	21		**I Wonder Who's Kissing Her Now**.......*Frank Adams/Will Hough/Joseph Howard/ Harold Orlob*			Ted Weems (Perry Como)
6/21	19	16	10	5	22		**I Wonder, I Wonder, I Wonder**..*Daryl Hutchins*			Eddy Howard
4/26	15	13	9	5	23		**My Adobe Hacienda** ....*Louise Massey/Lee Penny*			Eddy Howard
10/18	15	13	9	5	24		**I Wish I Didn't Love You So** ....*Frank Loesser*			Vaughn Monroe
1/11	19	11	7	4	25		**Ole Buttermilk Sky** ....*Jack Brooks/Hoagy Carmichael*			Hoagy Carmichael
3/8	13	11	9	3	26		**Anniversary Song** ....*Saul Chaplin/Al Jolson*			Guy Lombardo (Kenny Gardner)
11/8	12	8	6	3	27		**I Wish I Didn't Love You So** ....*Frank Loesser*			Dinah Shore
6/28	15	12	6	2	28		**Across The Alley From The Alamo** ....*Joe Greene*			Mills Brothers
2/8	16	11	6	2	29		**(I Love You) For Sentimental Reasons** ....*William Best/Deek Watson*			Dinah Shore
9/13	22	18	9	1	30		**That's My Desire** ....*Helmy Kresa/Carroll Loveday <B:8>*			Sammy Kaye (Don Cornell)
10/25	17	13	9	1	31		**Near You** ....*Francis Craig/Kermit Goell*			Andrews Sisters
2/1	20	17	8	1	32		**(I Love You) For Sentimental Reasons** ....*William Best/Deek Watson*			Eddy Howard
12/6	11	6	4	1	33		**How Soon** (Will I Be Seeing You) ....*Carroll Lucas/Jack Owens*	❶		Jack Owens
10/11	19	15	7	1	34		**When You Were Sweet Sixteen**.............................*James Thornton <A:1>*			Perry Como
8/2	23	15	3	1	35		**I Never Knew** ....*Ted Fiorito/Gus Kahn*			Sam Donahue (Bill Lockwood)

3

10/25	13	10	8	4	36		**Near You** ....*Francis Craig/Kermit Goell*	❶		Larry Green
10/11	14	11	5	3	37		**Near You** ....*Francis Craig/Kermit Goell*			Alvino Rey (Jimmy Joyce)
6/28	17	14	7	2	38		**I Wonder, I Wonder, I Wonder**..*Daryl Hutchins*			Guy Lombardo (Don Rodney)
3/15	11	10	5	2	39		**Anniversary Song** ....*Saul Chaplin/Al Jolson*			Tex Beneke/Glenn Miller (Garry Stevens)
6/7	11	9	5	1	40		**Mam'selle** ....*Mack Gordon/Edmund Goulding*			The Pied Pipers
5/31	11	8	5	1	41		**Mam'selle** ....*Mack Gordon/Edmund Goulding*			Dick Haymes
11/22	11	9	3	1	42	●	**Mickey** ....*Charles Daniels/Harry Williams*			Ted Weems (Bob Edwards)
2/15	9	6	3	1	43		**Open The Door Richard!**...*Dusty Fletcher/Don Howell/John Mason/Jack McVea* **[N]**	✦		Jack McVea
12/27	5	4	3	1	44		**White Christmas** ....*Irving Berlin* **[X-R]**			Bing Crosby
							{this version re-charted in 1948 (#6), 1949 (#5), 1950 (#13), 1951 (#13) and 1954 (#13); shares same label number as old version}			
2/22	7	5	2	1	45	●	**Open The Door, Richard!** (Parts 1 & 2)..............*Dusty Fletcher/Don Howell/ John Mason/Jack McVea* **[N]**	✦		"Dusty" Fletcher

4

3/22	10	9	5	2	46		**Anniversary Song** ....*Saul Chaplin/Al Jolson*			Andy Russell
11/1	13	7	3	2	47		**Near You** ....*Francis Craig/Kermit Goell*			Elliot Lawrence (Rosalind Patton)
4/19	17	9	3	1	48		**Guilty** ....*Harry Akst/Gus Kahn/Richard Whiting <B:7>*			Margaret Whiting
10/4	25	12	2	1	49	●	**That's My Desire** ....*Helmy Kresa/Carroll Loveday*	❶		Frankie Laine & Mannie Klein's All Stars
7/19	13	10	2	1	50		**Peg O' My Heart** ....*Alfred Bryan/Fred Fisher*			Art Lund
9/13	12	9	2	1	51		**Feudin' And Fightin'** ....*Al Dubin/Burton Lane*	✦		Dorothy Shay
11/22	11	6	1	1	52		**You Do** ....*Mack Gordon/Josef Myrow*			Dinah Shore
11/1	8	5	1	1	53		**Sugar Blues** ....*Lucy Fletcher/Clarence Williams*			Johnny Mercer
4/12	9	4	1	1	54		**Heartaches** ....*Al Hoffman/John Klenner*			Harry James (Marion Morgan)

5

4/26	11	9	3	3	55		**Linda** ....*Jack Lawrence*			Charlie Spivak (Tommy Mercer)
10/18	12	10	2	2	56	●	**I Wish I Didn't Love You So** ....*Frank Loesser*			Betty Hutton
1/4	10	5	2	2	57		**A Gal In Calico** ....*Leo Robin/Arthur Schwartz <A:4>*			Johnny Mercer
1/11	14	9	1	1	58		**(I Love You) For Sentimental Reasons** ....*William Best/Deek Watson*			Charlie Spivak (Jimmy Saunders)
11/22	10	7	1	1	59		**You Do** ....*Mack Gordon/Josef Myrow*			Margaret Whiting
11/22	8	6	1	1	60		**You Do** ....*Mack Gordon/Josef Myrow <B:10>*			Vaughn Monroe
5/3	7	5	1	1	61		**My Melancholy Baby** ....*Ernie Burnett/George Norton* **[I]**			Sam Donahue
9/20	9	4	1	1	62		**The Lady From 29 Palms** ....*Allie Wrubel*			Freddy Martin (Martin Men)
7/19	6	4	1	1	63		**Peg O' My Heart** ....*Alfred Bryan/Fred Fisher <B:14>*			Ted Weems (Bob Edwards)
11/1	5	3	1	1	64		**An Apple Blossom Wedding** ....*Jimmy Kennedy/Nat Simon <B:17>*			Sammy Kaye (Don Cornell)
6/7	6	2	1	1	65		**I Believe** ....*Sammy Cahn/Jule Styne <B:16>*			Frank Sinatra

6

12/20	11	9		3	66		**Serenade Of The Bells** ....*Al Goodhart/Kay Twomey/Al Urbano*			Jo Stafford
3/15	8	3		2	67		**How Are Things In Gloca Mora** ...........................*E.Y. Harburg/Burton Lane*			Buddy Clark
4/12	12	8		1	68		**Managua, Nicaragua** (Manag-wa, Nicarag-wa)..........*Irving Fields/Albert Gamse*			Kay Kyser (Gloria Wood)
9/6	11	8		1	69		**Feudin' And Fightin'** ....*Al Dubin/Burton Lane* **[N]**			Jo Stafford
1/18	8	5		1	70		**A Gal In Calico** ....*Leo Robin/Arthur Schwartz <B:11>*			Tex Beneke/Glenn Miller
3/15	4	4		1	71		**Open The Door, Richard!**...*Dusty Fletcher/Don Howell/John Mason/Jack McVea* **[N]**			Louis Jordan

PEAK DATE	CH	10	5	PK	RANK	GOLD	Title / PEAK POSITION / Songwriter(s)	SYMBL	DEBUT	Artist

6 (cont'd)

PEAK DATE	CH	10	5	PK	RANK	Title / Songwriter(s)	Artist
11/8	7	2		1	72	The Whistler .... Hal Dickinson/Wilbur Hatch <B:9>	Sam Donahue (Shirley Lloyd)
1/18	6	2		1	73	A Gal In Calico .... Leo Robin/Arthur Schwartz	Benny Goodman (Eve Young)
2/15	6	2		1	74	Ain't Nobody Here But Us Chickens .... Alex Kramer/Joan Whitney	Louis Jordan
3/8	3	1		1	75	Open The Door, Richard .... Dusty Fletcher/Don Howell/John Mason/Jack McVea [N]	The Charioteers

7

PEAK DATE	CH	10	5	PK	RANK	Title / Songwriter(s)	SYMBL	Artist
5/3	8	5		3	76	Mam'selle .... Mack Gordon/Edmund Goulding	✦	Ray Dorey
12/6	9	5		2	77	You Do .... Mack Gordon/Josef Myrow		Vic Damone
10/25	7	3		2	78	I Have But One Heart "O Marinariello" .... Johnny Farrow/Marty Symes	❶	Vic Damone
12/6	7	3		1	79 ●	Whiffenpoof Song .... Todd Galloway/Meade Minnigerode/George Pomeroy		Bing Crosby with Fred Waring
2/8	7	2		1	80	Oh, But I Do .... Leo Robin/Arthur Schwartz <A:4>		Margaret Whiting
4/12	7	2		1	81	A Rainy Night In Rio .... Leo Robin/Arthur Schwartz		Sam Donahue
8/30	4	2		1	82	I Ain't Mad At You (You Ain't Mad At Me) ... Count Basie/Milton Ebbins/Freddy Green		Count Basie (Taps Miller/Ted Donnelly)
5/10	3	2		1	83	Free Eats .... Count Basie/Harry Sweets		Count Basie
11/1	3	1		1	84	Kate (Have I Come Too Early, Too Late) .... Irving Berlin		Eddy Howard
11/1	2	1		1	85	The Lady From 29 Palms .... Allie Wrubel		Andrews Sisters

8

PEAK DATE	CH	10	5	PK	RANK	Title / Songwriter(s)	SYMBL	Artist
5/31	8	3		3	86	Red Silk Stockings And Green Perfume .... Bob Hilliard/Sammy Mysels/ Dick Sanford <A:2>		Sammy Kaye (Don Cornell)
5/17	5	5		2	87	Mam'selle .... Mack Gordon/Edmund Goulding	❶	Dennis Day
11/22	8	3		2	88	You Do .... Mack Gordon/Josef Myrow <A:6>		Bing Crosby & Carmen Cavallaro
2/1	8	6		1	89	Zip-A-Dee-Doo-Dah .... Ray Gilbert/Allie Wrubel		Johnny Mercer
9/13	4	4		1	90	Smoke, Smoke, Smoke (That Cigarette) .... Merle Travis/Tex Williams [N]		Phil Harris
2/15	14	3		1	91	(I Love You) For Sentimental Reasons .... William Best/Deek Watson		Ella Fitzgerald & Delta Rhythm Boys
4/26	8	3		1	92	Linda .... Jack Lawrence		Paul Weston With Matt Dennis
1/11	9	2		1	93	Huggin' And Chalkin' .... Kermit Goell/Clancy Hayes <A:3> [N]		Kay Kyser (Jack Martin)
12/27	8	2		1	94	Civilization (Bongo, Bongo, Bongo) .... Bob Hilliard/Carl Sigman [N]		Louis Prima
2/15	7	2		1	95	Huggin' And A Chalkin' .... Kermit Goell/Clancy Hayes [N]		Johnny Mercer
2/15	6	2		1	96	A Gal In Calico .... Leo Robin/Arthur Schwartz		Bing Crosby with The Calico Kids
3/1	3	2		1	97	Open The Door Richard ..... Dusty Fletcher/Don Howell/John Mason/Jack McVea [N]		The Pied Pipers
7/5	10	1		1	98	Peg O' My Heart .... Alfred Bryan/Fred Fisher	❶	Clark Dennis
12/27	5	1		1	99	Civilization (Bongo, Bongo, Bongo) .... Bob Hilliard/Carl Sigman		Ray McKinley
3/29	5	1		1	100	How Are Things In Glocca Morra .... E.Y. Harburg/Burton Lane		Martha Tilton
7/19	4	1		1	101	One O'Clock Boogie .... Count Basie/Milton Ebbins/James Mundy [I]		Count Basie
1/4	3	1		1	102	September Song .... Maxwell Anderson/Kurt Weill		Frank Sinatra
6/7	2	1		1	103	Red Silk Stockings And Green Perfume .... Bob Hilliard/Sammy Mysels/ Dick Sanford		Tony Pastor
2/15	1	1		1	104	Sooner Or Later .... Ray Gilbert/Charles Wolcott		Les Brown (Doris Day)
11/8	1	1		1	105	So Far .... Oscar Hammerstein/Richard Rodgers		Frank Sinatra

9

PEAK DATE	CH	10	5	PK	RANK	Title / Songwriter(s)	SYMBL	Artist
11/8	7	3		1	106	I Wish I Didn't Love You So .... Frank Loesser		Dick Haymes
2/1	7	2		1	107	Sonata .... Alex Alstone/Ervin Drake/Jimmy Shirl <B:19>		Perry Como
4/5	5	2		1	108	How Are Things In Glocca Morra? .... E.Y. Harburg/Burton Lane		Tommy Dorsey (Stuart Foster)
5/24	4	2		1	109	April Showers .... B.G. DeSylva/Louis Silvers		Guy Lombardo (Jimmy Brown)
11/8	7	1		1	110	Civilization (Bongo, Bongo, Bongo) .... Bob Hilliard/Carl Sigman		Jack Smith & The Clark Sisters
3/29	5	1		1	111	How Are Things In Glocca Morra .... E.Y. Harburg/Burton Lane		Dick Haymes
5/31	4	1		1	112	My Adobe Hacienda .... Louise Massey/Lee Penny	❶	The Dinning Sisters
11/1	4	1		1	113	Feudin' And Fightin' .... Al Dubin/Burton Lane		Bing Crosby & The Jesters
11/1	4	1		1	114	An Apple Blossom Wedding .... Jimmy Kennedy/Nat Simon		Eddy Howard
4/12	2	1		1	115	Roses In The Rain .... Frankie Carle/Al Frisch/Fred Wise		Frankie Carle (Marjorie Hughes)
12/27	2	1		1	116 ●	Here Comes Santa Claus (Down Santa Claus Lane) .... Gene Autry/Oakley Haldeman [X] {re-charted in 1948 (#8) and 1949 (#24)}		Gene Autry
11/1	2	1		1	117	Red Wing .... Thurland Chattaway/F.A. Mills <A:6>		Sam Donahue (Shirley Lloyd)
7/19	2	1		1	118	I Wonder, I Wonder, I Wonder .... Daryl Hutchins <B:10>		Martha Tilton

10

PEAK DATE	CH	10	5	PK	RANK	Title / Songwriter(s)	Artist
6/14	9	3		3	119	That's My Desire .... Helmy Kresa/Carroll Loveday <A:9>	Martha Tilton
8/23	7	3		3	120	The Lady From Twenty-Nine Palms .... Allie Wrubel	Tony Pastor
5/31	3	2		2	121	Red Silk Stockings And Green Perfume .... Bob Hilliard/Sammy Mysels/ Dick Sanford	Ray McKinley
7/19	10	1		1	122	Tallahassee .... Frank Loesser	Bing Crosby & the Andrews Sisters
1/25	5	1		1	123	Sonata .... Leo Robin/Arthur Schwartz	Jo Stafford
4/19	5	1		1	124	That's How Much I Love You .... Eddy Arnold/Wally Fowler/J. Graydon Hall	Frank Sinatra

1947

PEAK DATE	CH	10	5	PK	RANK	GOLD	Title / PEAK POSITION / Songwriter(s)	SYMBOL	DEBUT	Artist
							10 (cont'd)			
7/26	4	1		1	125		Chi-Baba Chi-Baba (My Bambino Go To Sleep) ....*Mack David/Al Hoffman/ Jerry Livingston*			Peggy Lee
10/25	1	1		1	126		Kokomo, Indiana..*Mack Gordon/Josef Myrow <A:5>*			Vaughn Monroe
							11			
7/5	9			4	127		I Wonder, I Wonder, I Wonder.......................................*Daryl Hutchins*			Tony Pastor
4/19	5			1	128		Heartaches ....*Al Hoffman/John Klenner*			Eddy Howard
1/11	5			1	129		Zip-A-Dee Doo-Dah....................................*Ray Gilbert/Allie Wrubel <A:8>*			Sammy Kaye (Three Kaydets)
6/21	5			1	130		Across The Alley From The Alamo ....*Joe Greene*			Stan Kenton (June Christy)
5/10	4			1	131		Guilty..*Harry Akst/Gus Kahn/Richard Whiting*			Ella Fitzgerald & Eddie Heywood
9/27	4			1	132		I Wonder Who's Kissing Her Now ....*Frank Adams/Will Hough/Joseph Howard/ Harold Orlob*			Ray Noble (Snooky Lanson)
2/1	3			1	133		Oh, But I Do ....*Leo Robin/Arthur Schwartz <A:6>*			Tex Beneke/Glenn Miller (Artie Malvin)
1/25	3			1	134		Zip-A-Dee Doo-Dah ....*Ray Gilbert/Allie Wrubel*			The Modernaires with Paula Kelly
9/20	2			1	135		Kate (Have I Come Too Early Too Late) ....*Irving Berlin*	✦		Ray Bloch (Alan Dale)
2/15	2			1	136		The Old Lamp-Lighter ....*Nat Simon/Charles Tobias*			Kenny Baker & Russ Morgan
11/8	2			1	137		So Far ....*Oscar Hammerstein/Richard Rodgers*			Perry Como
10/11	2			1	138		Stanley Steamer ....*Ralph Blane/Harry Warren*			Jo Stafford
3/29	1			1	139		Heartaches ....*Al Hoffman/John Klenner*			Jimmy Dorsey (Bob Carroll/Dee Parker)
2/1	1			1	140		This Is The Night...*Lewis Bellin/Redd Evans*			Frank Sinatra
6/7	1			1	141		Old Devil Moon ....*E.Y. Harburg/Burton Lane*			Margaret Whiting
							12			
10/25	5			2	142		Near You ....*Francis Craig/Kermit Goell*	❶		Dick "Two Ton" Baker
6/14	2			2	143		One O'Clock Jump ....*Count Basie* **[I]**			Count Basie
3/29	3			1	144		Guilty...*Harry Akst/Gus Kahn/Richard Whiting*	❶		Johnny Desmond
5/10	2			1	145		Across The Alley From The Alamo ....*Joe Greene*			Woody Herman (Four Chips)
2/1	2			1	146		Oh, But I Do ....*Leo Robin/Arthur Schwartz*			Harry James (Buddy DiVito)
10/11	1			1	147		I Wonder Who's Kissing Her Now ....*Frank Adams/Will Hough/Joseph Howard/ Harold Orlob*			The Dinning Sisters
3/29	1			1	148		His Feet Too Big For De Bed........*Hernandez Brana/Sammy Mysels/Dick Sanford*			Stan Kenton (June Christy)
11/8	1			1	149		Harmony ....*Johnny Burke/Jimmy Van Heusen <A:12>*			Johnny Mercer & The King Cole Trio
10/25	1			1	150		Save The Bones For Henry Jones ('Cause Henry Don't Eat No Meat) ....*Danny Barker/Vernon Lee <A:12>*			Johnny Mercer & The King Cole Trio
							13			
5/10	4			1	151		My Adobe Hacienda ....*Louise Massey/Lee Penny*	✦		Billy Williams & Pecos River Rogues
9/13	3			1	152		That's My Desire ....*Helmy Kresa/Carroll Loveday*			Woody Herman (Four Chips)
8/2	3			1	153		Bloop-Bleep ....*Frank Loesser*			Alvino Rey (Rocky Coluccio)
4/12	2			1	154		I Do Do Do Like You ....*Allie Wrubel* **[N]**			Johnny Mercer
11/22	2			1	155		I Have But One Heart (O Marenariello) ....*Johnny Farrow/Marty Symes*			Frank Sinatra
11/1	1			1	156		I Wish I Didn't Love You So ....*Frank Loesser*	✦		Dick Farney
							14			
5/17	2			2	157		Mam'selle ....*Mack Gordon/Edmund Goulding*			Frankie Laine
6/7	3			1	158		Chi-Baba Chi-Baba ("My Bambino Go To Sleep")........*Mack David/Al Hoffman/ Jerry Livingston*			Blue Barron
11/8	1			1	159		An Apple Blossom Wedding ....*Jimmy Kennedy/Nat Simon*			Buddy Clark
5/3	1			1	160		Linda ....*Jack Lawrence*	✦		Larry Douglas
2/8	1			1	161		A Huggin' And A Chalkin' ....*Kermit Goell/Clancy Hayes* **[N]**	✦		Herbie Fields
2/15	1			1	162		(Oh Why, Oh Why, Did I Ever Leave) Wyoming ....*Morey Amsterdam*			Dick Jurgens (Jimmy Castle/Al Galante)
11/22	1			1	163		—And Mimi ....*Jimmy Kennedy/Nat Simon*			Art Lund
5/3	1			1	164		Moon-Faced, Starry-Eyed ....*Langston Hughes/Kurt Weill*			Freddy Martin (Murray Arnold)
6/7	1			1	165		(Baa-Baa-Baa) Whiffenpoof Song ....*Todd Galloway/Meade Minnigerode/ George Pomeroy*	✦		Robert Merrill
6/14	1			1	166		Violets ....*Harold Green/H.V. Hill/Rudy Vallee <A:5>* **[I]**			Ted Weems
11/8	1			1	167		So Far...*Oscar Hammerstein/Richard Rodgers*			Margaret Whiting
							15			
7/12	2			2	168		Tallahassee ....*Frank Loesser*			Dinah Shore & Woody Herman
12/20	1			1	169 ●		Ooh! Look-A There, Ain't She Pretty...........*Carmen Lombardo/Clarence Todd*	❶		Buddy Greco
11/22	1			1	170		—And Mimi ....*Jimmy Kennedy/Nat Simon*			Dick Haymes
1/18	1			1	171		I Love You (For Sentimental Reasons) ....*William Best/Deek Watson*			Art Kassel (Jimmy Featherstone)
11/1	1			1	172		He's A Real Gone Guy ....*Nellie Lutcher*	✦		Nellie Lutcher
3/29	1			1	173		Hoodle-Addle ....*Ray McKinley*			Ray McKinley Quartet
3/8	1			1	174		I'll Close My Eyes.......................................*Buddy Kaye/Billy Reid*			Andy Russell
6/7	1			1	175		A Sunday Kind Of Love ..*Barbara Belle/Anita Leonard/Louis Prima/Stan Rhodes <B:16>*			Jo Stafford

PEAK DATE	WEEKS			RANK	GOLD	Title	PEAK POSITION Songwriter(s)	SYMBL	DEBUT	Artist
	CH	10	5	PK						

16

PEAK DATE	CH	10	5	PK	RANK	GOLD	Title	Peak Position — Songwriter(s)	Artist
7/19	3			3	176		Chi-Baba Chi-Baba (My Bambino Go To Sleep) ....*Mack David/Al Hoffman/ Jerry Livingston*	The Charioteers
7/26	3			3	177		Ragtime Cowboy Joe......................*Maurice Abrahams/Grant Clarke/Lewis Muir*	Eddy Howard
6/7	4			1	178		Ivy ....*Hoagy Carmichael <A:15>*	Jo Stafford
4/19	2			1	179		The Egg And I ....*Harry Akst/Al Jolson/Bert Kalmar/Herman Ruby*	Dinah Shore
5/24	1			1	180		My Adobe Hacienda ....*Louise Massey/Lee Penny*	Kenny Baker & Russ Morgan
5/17	1			1	181 ●		April Showers...................................*B.G. DeSylva/Louis Silvers*	Al Jolson
5/10	1			1	182		The Egg And I ....*Harry Akst/Al Jolson/Bert Kalmar/Herman Ruby*	Sammy Kaye (Mary Marlow)
1/18	1			1	183		It's A Good Day ....*Dave Barbour/Peggy Lee*	Peggy Lee
4/26	1			1	184		Midnight Masquerade ....*Arthur Berman/Bernard Berman/Jack Manus* ❶	Monica Lewis
10/11	1			1	185		The Echo Said "No" ....*Art Kassel*	Guy Lombardo (Don Rodney)
9/13	1			1	186		Come To The Mardi Gras (Não Tenho Lagrimas)...................*Max Bulhoes/ Milton DeOliveira/Ervin Drake/Jimmy Shirl*	Freddy Martin (Stuart Wade)
6/14	1			1	187		My Adobe Hacienda ....*Louise Massey/Lee Penny* ✦	Louise Massey
10/25	1			1	188		When You Were Sweet Sixteen.....................*James Thornton*	Mills Brothers
5/17	1			1	189		Time After Time ....*Sammy Cahn/Jule Styne <A:5>*	Frank Sinatra

17

PEAK DATE	CH	10	5	PK	RANK	GOLD	Title	Peak Position — Songwriter(s)	Artist
4/26	1			1	190		That's How Much I Love You ....*Eddy Arnold/Wally Fowler/J. Graydon Hall*	Bing Crosby & Bob Crosby
4/5	1			1	191		Jalousie (Jealousy) ....*Vera Bloom/Jacob Gade* [I]	Harry James
10/4	1			1	192		When You Were Sweet Sixteen.....................*James Thornton*	Dick Jurgens (Jimmy Castle)
9/20	1			1	193		The Echo Said "No" ....*Art Kassel <A:5>*	Sammy Kaye (Don Cornell)

18

PEAK DATE	CH	10	5	PK	RANK	GOLD	Title	Peak Position — Songwriter(s)	Artist
5/31	1			1	194		Cu-Tu-Gu-Ru (Jack, Jack, Jack) ....*Armando Castro/Joe Davis* ❶	Jack Smith & The Clark Sisters

19

PEAK DATE	CH	10	5	PK	RANK	GOLD	Title	Peak Position — Songwriter(s)	Artist
2/1	1			1	195		That's The Beginning Of The End.................*Alex Kramer/Joan Whitney <A:9>*	Perry Como

23

PEAK DATE	CH	10	5	PK	RANK	GOLD	Title	Peak Position — Songwriter(s)	Artist
2/8	1			1	196		The Girl That I Marry ....*Irving Berlin*	Eddy Howard

1948

NATIONAL NEWS: President Harry Truman scores a stirring come-from-behind victory to defeat Republican presidential nominee Thomas E. Dewey. Congress is convulsed by investigations into purported Communist espionage rings in the U.S. government.

INTERNATIONAL NEWS: As Cold War tensions rise, the Soviet Union establishes a blockade in divided Berlin to force Allied nations out, but the U.S. and Britain launch a massive airlift of food and supplies into the city's Western zones. This occurs in the wake of a Communist Party coup in Czechoslovakia. After months of fierce fighting, the state of Israel is established and opens its doors to Jews around the world. India's spiritual leader Mohandas K. Gandhi is assassinated.

COMMERCE AND SCIENCE: The world's largest (200 inches) telescope is completed at the Mount Palomar Observatory in California. Columbia Records introduces the long-playing microgroove album which plays at 33-1/3 revolutions per minute, and Victor follows by offering the seven-inch 45 rpm record. The McDonald brothers open their first hamburger stand in San Bernardino, California.

SPORTS: In the first Olympic Games in 12 years, the United States dominates in London, including a gold in the decathlon for Bob Mathias. The Cleveland Indians, with a pitching staff including Bob Feller and longtime Negro league legend Satchel Paige, top Ted Williams' Boston Red Sox in a one-game American League playoff, and then defeat the Boston Braves in the World Series, four games to two. The Philadelphia Eagles edge the Chicago Cardinals, 7-0, for the NFL championship. Michigan is recognized as the nation's top college football team. The Baltimore Bullets win the NBA championship. Kentucky triumphs in the NCAA basketball tournament. Pancho Gonzales wins the U.S. tennis crown. Ben Hogan takes both the U.S. Open and the PGA in golf. Former Olympic gold medal hurdler Babe Didrickson Zaharias wins the U.S. Women's Open in golf.

MOVIES: Laurence Olivier reigns at the Academy Awards for Best Picture (*Hamlet*) and Best Actor. Jane Wyman wins best-actress honors for *Johnny Belinda*. John Huston's *The Treasure of the Sierra Madre* starring Humphrey Bogart is one of the year's most-acclaimed films. Box office hits are led by *The Red Shoes*, John Wayne in *Red River*, and *The Paleface* starring Bob Hope and Jane Russell.

TELEVISION: The first full season of network television programming introduces Milton Berle's wildly popular *Texaco Star Theater*, Ed Sullivan's *Toast of the Town*, *Candid Camera*, *Arthur Godfrey's Talent Scouts*, and Ted Macks' *Original Amateur Hour*.

THEATER: Henry Fonda triumphs on Broadway in *Mister Roberts*. Ray Bolger scores with the comedy hit *Where's Charley?*

BOOKS: Norman Mailer's *The Naked and the Dead* is a best seller, and Alfred Kinsey's *Sexual Behavior in the Human Male* generates national debate.

1948 — TOP 20 ARTISTS

1. **Andrews Sisters**
778

2. **Peggy Lee**
573

3. **Buddy Clark**
535

4.	409	**Doris Day**
5.	398	**Bing Crosby**
6.	376	**Ken Griffin**
7.	371	**Dick Haymes**
8.	361	**Kay Kyser**
9.	348	**Art Mooney**
10.	346	**Dinah Shore**
11.	341	**Eddy Arnold**
12.	330	**Margaret Whiting**
13.	327	**Vaughn Monroe**
14.	317	**Gordon MacRae**
15.	295	**Eddy Howard**
16.	292	**Sammy Kaye**
17.	280	**Nat "King" Cole**
18.	254	**The Sportsmen**
19.	239	**Freddy Martin**
20.	222	**Al Trace**

1948 — TOP SONGWRITERS

	# of Hits	Points			# of Hits	Points	
1.	11	921	**Sammy Cahn**	7.	8	726	**Hal Cotton**
	11	921	**Jule Styne**		8	726	**Gerhard Ebeler**
3.	9	808	**Ken Griffin**		8	726	**Hans Otten**
4.	9	779	**Sam Martin**	10.	7	661	**Maewa Kaihan**
	9	779	**Ben Trace**		7	661	**Clement Scott**
	9	779	**Clem Watts**		7	661	**Dorothy Stewart**

1948 — TOP ARTIST DEBUTS

1.	1/24	**Art Mooney** (61)
2.	4/10	**Ken Griffin** (111)
3.	5/15	**Eddy Arnold** (113) ★
4.	5/22	**Vera Lynn** (127)
5.	5/29	**Doris Day** (26) ★
6.	6/12	**Eddie Fisher** (21) ★
7.	6/26 †	**Patti Page** (16) ★
8.	6/26	**Pee Wee Hunt** (148)
9.	7/03	**Sarah Vaughan** (76) ★
10.	7/31	**Gordon MacRae** (52)
11.	8/21	**Ames Brothers** (36) ★
12.	12/04	**Kay Starr** (29)
13.	12/04	**Dean Martin** (115) ★

PEAK DATE	WEEKS CH	WEEKS 10	WEEKS 5	WEEKS PK	RANK	GOLD	Title / PEAK POSITION / Songwriter(s)	SYMBOL	DEBUT	Artist

1

11/6 | 25 | 19 | 17 | 10 | **1** ● | **Buttons And Bows** ....*Ray Evans/Jay Livingston* | | | **Dinah Shore**
Best Seller: 22,18,14,7,5,3,1,1,1,1,1,1,1,2,1,2,2,2,5,6,13,17
Juke Box: 25,20,5,11,4,3,1,1,1,1,1,1,1,2,2,2,3,5,10,17,22

3/13 | 21 | 19 | 19 | 9 | **2** ● | **Mañana** (Is Soon Enough For Me)................................*Dave Barbour/Peggy Lee* | | | **Peggy Lee**
Best Seller: 8,6,3,4,2,2,1,1,1,1,1,1,1,1,3,5,12,10,18,19
Disc Jockey: 11,5,3,3,2,2,2,2,1,1,1,1,1,1,2,2,5,4,12
Juke Box: 15,7,6,4,2,2,2,1,1,1,1,2,1,2,4,6,7,8,-,,25

8/28 | 32 | 23 | 16 | 8 | **3** ● | **Twelfth Street Rag** ....*Euday Bowman/Andy Razaf* [I] ❶ | | | **Pee Wee Hunt**
Best Seller: 29,13,11,15,10,7,8,7,2,1,1,1,1,1,2,2,1,1,2,2,2,3,3,6,7,15,13,22,22,29,27
Juke Box: 16,19,10,10,8,10,4,3,2,2,2,1,1,1,1,1,1,2,2,3,3,6,10,9
Disc Jockey: 16,13,10,2,3,3,1,1,2,2,1,2,2,3,2,2,5,5,10,10,20,27

5/8 | 18 | 15 | 14 | 8 | **4** ● | **Nature Boy** ....*Eden Ahbez* | | | **King Cole**
Disc Jockey: 11,5,2,1,1,1,1,1,1,1,1,2,2,5,5,10,12,20
Best Seller: 15,7,2,1,1,1,1,1,1,1,3,3,7,14,19
Juke Box: 11,4,2,2,2,2,2,3,3,4,9,13

5/22 | 23 | 17 | 11 | 7 | **5** ● | **You Can't Be True, Dear** ......*Hal Cotton/Gerhard Ebeler/Ken Griffin/Hans Otten* ❶ | | | **Ken Griffin** (Jerry Wayne)
Juke Box: 7,6,3,3,2,1,1,1,1,1,1,8,6,8,9,9,12,15,13,18,21,24
Best Seller: 10,8,4,3,4,2,2,2,2,2,2,8,6,9,13,13,15,13,22,23
Disc Jockey: 8,10,7,3,3,2,4,3,3,5,8,10,12,13,13,15,19,18

8/14 | 24 | 20 | 16 | 6 | **6** | **You Call Everybody Darlin'** ....*Sam Martin/Ben Trace/Clem Watts* | | | **Al Trace** (Bob Vincent)
Juke Box: 19,17,12,12,9,6,4,3,2,1,1,1,1,1,1,2,2,3,3,3,4,4,10,9
Best Seller: 13,18,14,11,8,6,5,1,1,2,2,4,4,3,3,4,4,5,7,6,13,16,20
Disc Jockey: 14,11,8,6,7,3,5,4,4,4,4,3,3,7,7,9,7,30
{original version also charted in 1948 (#21)}

7/3 | 15 | 13 | 9 | 6 | **7** ● | **Woody Wood-Pecker** ....*Ramez Idriss/George Tibbles* [N] | | | **Kay Kyser** (Gloria Wood)
Juke Box: 9,6,4,2,1,1,1,1,1,1,4,8,10,11
Disc Jockey: 6,5,2,1,1,1,1,1,1,3,9,11,13,18
Best Seller: 13,6,4,3,1,1,1,1,1,1,6,10,12,15,25

10/9 | 23 | 18 | 16 | 5 | **8** ● | **A Tree In The Meadow** ....*Billy Reid* | | | **Margaret Whiting**
Disc Jockey: 11,7,6,5,3,2,2,2,2,1,1,2,1,1,1,3,5,4,24,24,30,29
Best Seller: 17,19,15,11,8,6,3,4,3,2,2,2,1,1,2,2,3,3,4,7,9,14,17
Juke Box: 16,12,13,6,6,5,4,3,3,3,3,2,2,2,2,3,3,4,5,8,13,27,25

2/21 | 18 | 16 | 14 | 5 | **9** ● | **I'm Looking Over A Four Leaf Clover** ....*Mort Dixon/Harry Woods* ❶ | | | **Art Mooney**
Juke Box: 5,2,2,1,1,1,1,1,2,2,3,3,3,5,6,7,23,-,15
Disc Jockey: 6,4,2,2,1,1,1,1,2,2,2,2,3,2,7,8
Best Seller: 14,3,2,2,1,1,1,2,3,3,3,3,5,11,14

8/14 | 24 | 21 | 13 | 5 | **10** ● | **Love Somebody** ....*Alex Kramer/Joan Whitney* <B:16> ❶ | | | **Doris Day & Buddy Clark**
Disc Jockey: 12,8,5,8,7,6,10,9,4,5,3,1,1,1,1,1,3,3,5,5,6,13,10
Juke Box: 2,3,30,-,-,17,-,10,12,11,11,5,7,10,9,9,8,9,10,11,13,24,13,20
Best Seller: 11,23,9,10,9,9,10,12,9,7,7,6,10,8,7,6,7,7,6,10,8,14,15,16,28,24

4/24 | 23 | 19 | 16 | 3 | **11** ● | **Now Is The Hour** (Maori Farewell Song)...........*Maewa Kaihan/Clement Scott/Dorothy Stewart* | | | **Bing Crosby**
Juke Box: 5,5,5,3,3,3,3,2,2,1,2,1,1,2,3,3,6,7,7,11,20,-,25,27
Best Seller: 15,10,7,3,3,3,3,2,2,2,2,2,2,3,5,4,9,6,14,12,17,28
Disc Jockey: 7,9,4,5,6,5,4,4,3,3,5,4,6,6,6,11

12/25 | 8 | 6 | 6 | 3 | **12** ● | **All I Want For Christmas** (Is My Two Front Teeth) ...*Don Gardner* [X-N] | | | **Spike Jones** (George Rock)
Disc Jockey: 18,6,5,1,1,1,4
Best Seller: 17,12,4,3,2,2,1,5
Juke Box: 20,17,8,5,4,5
{re-charted in 1949 (#18)}

2

PEAK DATE	WEEKS CH	WEEKS 10	WEEKS 5	WEEKS PK	RANK	GOLD	Title / Songwriter(s)	Artist
11/27	20	17	13	7	**13** ●	**On A Slow Boat To China** ....*Frank Loesser*	Kay Kyser (Harry Babbitt/Gloria Wood)
7/10	15	13	9	7	**14** ●	**You Can't Be True, Dear** ...*Hal Cotton/Gerhard Ebeler/Ken Griffin/Hans Otten* <B:19> [I]	Ken Griffin (organ solo)
							{original instrumental version of #5 above}	
7/17	9	8	6	5	**15**	**Woody Woodpecker** ....*Ramez Idriss/George Tibbles* [N]	The Sportsmen & Mel Blanc
6/12	30	25	19	2	**16** ●	**My Happiness** ....*Borney Bergantine/Betty Peterson* ✦	Jon & Sondra Steele
5/29	23	16	12	1	**17**	**Little White Lies** ....*Walter Donaldson*	Dick Haymes
9/11	21	15	11	1	**18** ●	**It's Magic** ....*Sammy Cahn/Jule Styne*	Doris Day
1/31	18	14	11	1	**19**	**Golden Earrings** ....*Ray Evans/Jay Livingston/Victor Young* <B:11>	Peggy Lee
4/17	16	15	9	1	**20**	**Now Is The Hour** (Maori Farewell Song)..............*Maewa Kaihan/Clement Scott/Dorothy Stewart*	Margaret Whiting

3

PEAK DATE	WEEKS CH	WEEKS 10	WEEKS 5	WEEKS PK	RANK	GOLD	Title / Songwriter(s)	Artist
2/14	20	16	12	3	**21**	**Beg Your Pardon** ....*Francis Craig/Beasley Smith*	Francis Craig (Bob Lamm)
5/22	17	11	7	3	**22**	**Toolie Oolie Doolie** (The Yodel Polka) ....*Arthur Beul/Vaughn Horton* <B:14>	Andrews Sisters
7/17	21	21	10	2	**23** ●	**My Happiness** ....*Borney Bergantine/Betty Peterson*	The Pied Pipers
3/27	21	14	9	2	**24**	**Now Is The Hour** ....*Maewa Kaihan/Clement Scott/Dorothy Stewart* ❶	Gracie Fields
5/8	15	13	7	2	**25** ●	**Baby Face** ....*Harry Akst/Benny Davis*	Art Mooney
1/24	13	9	4	2	**26**	**How Soon?** (Will I Be Seeing You) ....*Carroll Lucas/Jack Owens*	Vaughn Monroe
1/3	11	9	4	2	**27**	**Civilization** (Bongo, Bongo, Bongo)................*Bob Hilliard/Carl Sigman* [N]	Danny Kaye - Andrews Sisters

PEAK DATE	CH	10	5	PK	RANK	GOLD	Title / Peak Position — Songwriter(s)	SYMBL	DEBUT	Artist

3 (cont'd)

PEAK DATE	CH	10	5	PK	RANK	GOLD	Title — Songwriter(s)	Artist
10/23	30	16	11	1	28	●	Maybe You'll Be There .... *Rube Bloom/Sammy Gallop*	Gordon Jenkins (Charles LaVere)
1/17	15	11	4	1	29		I'll Dance At Your Wedding .... *Herb Magidson/Ben Oakland*	Ray Noble with Buddy Clark
1/17	16	9	4	1	30		Serenade Of The Bells .... *Al Goodhart/Kay Twomey/Al Urbano*	Sammy Kaye (Don Cornell)
5/8	12	9	3	1	31		Sabre Dance .... *Aram Khachaturian/Lester Lee/Allan Roberts* [I]	Woody Herman

4

PEAK DATE	CH	10	5	PK	RANK	GOLD	Title — Songwriter(s)	Artist
12/4	17	12	3	2	32		On A Slow Boat To China .... *Frank Loesser*	Freddy Martin (Glenn Hughes)
11/13	21	13	2	1	33		Until .... *Bob Crosby/Jack Fulton/Hunter Kahler*	Tommy Dorsey (Harry Prime/ Clark Sisters/Town Criers)
4/17	18	6	1	1	34	●	Because .... *Guy d'Hardelot/Edward Teschemacher*	Perry Como

5

PEAK DATE	CH	10	5	PK	RANK	GOLD	Title — Songwriter(s)	Artist
11/20	16	11	3	3	35	●	Buttons And Bows .... *Ray Evans/Jay Livingston*	The Dinning Sisters
3/20	16	11	2	2	36		Beg Your Pardon .... *Francis Craig/Beasley Smith*	Frankie Carle (Marjorie Hughes)
1/17	7	5	2	2	37		Ballerina .... *Bob Russell/Carl Sigman*	Buddy Clark
5/1	17	9	1	1	38		St. Louis Blues March .... *W.C. Handy* [I]	Tex Beneke
11/6	14	8	1	1	39		Underneath The Arches .... *Reg Connelly/Bud Flanagan/Joseph McCarthy* <B:8>	Andrews Sisters
10/23	22	5	1	1	40	●	Blue Bird Of Happiness .... *Harry Davies/Sandor Harmati/Edward Heyman*	Art Mooney (Bud Brees)
5/29	11	5	1	1	41		The Dickey-Bird Song .... *Howard Dietz/Sammy Fain*	Freddy Martin (Glenn Hughes)

6

PEAK DATE	CH	10	5	PK	RANK	GOLD	Title — Songwriter(s)	SYMBL	Artist
6/26	15	8		4	42		William Tell Overture .... *Gioacchino Rossini* [N]		Spike Jones
1/24	14	9		2	43		How Soon (Will I Be Seeing You) .... *Carroll Lucas/Jack Owens* <B:8>		Bing Crosby & Carmen Cavallaro
3/20	13	9		2	44		I'm Looking Over A Four Leaf Clover .... *Mort Dixon/Harry Woods*		Russ Morgan with Milt Herth (Ames Brothers)
6/26	14	8		2	45		You Can't Be True, Dear .... *Hal Cotton/Gerhard Ebeler/Ken Griffin/Hans Otten* <B:11>	❶	The Sportsmen
10/2	16	7		2	46		Underneath The Arches .... *Reg Connelly/Bud Flanagan/Joseph McCarthy*	❶	Primo Scala with The Keynotes
12/25	12	6		2	47		I'd Love To Get You **On A Slow Boat To China** .... *Frank Loesser*		Eddy Howard
10/2	21	14		1	48		My Happiness .... *Borney Bergantine/Betty Peterson*		Ella Fitzgerald
9/18	16	10		1	49		You Call Everybody Darlin' .... *Sam Martin/Ben Trace/Clem Watts*	✦	Anne Vincent
3/6	8	6		1	50		I'm Looking Over A Four Leaf Clover .... *Mort Dixon/Harry Woods*		Alvino Rey
4/17	11	3		1	51		Sabre Dance Boogie .... *Aram Khachaturian/Lester Lee/Allan Roberts* [I]		Freddy Martin
12/25	6	3		1	52	●	White Christmas .... *Irving Berlin* [X-R]		Bing Crosby
4/10	5	2		1	53		Now Is The Hour (Maori Farewell Song) .... *Maewa Kaihan/Clement Scott/ Dorothy Stewart*		Buddy Clark & The Charioteers

7

PEAK DATE	CH	10	5	PK	RANK	GOLD	Title — Songwriter(s)	Artist
3/20	9	7		3	54		Slap 'Er Down, Agin, Paw .... *Polly Arnold/Eddie Asherman/Alice Cornett* [N]	Arthur Godfrey
12/18	13	7		1	55		My Darling My Darling .... *Frank Loesser*	Doris Day & Buddy Clark
10/16	14	4		1	56		Hair Of Gold, Eyes Of Blue .... *Sunny Skylar* <B:27>	Gordon MacRae
6/5	4	3		1	57		Nature Boy .... *Eden Ahbez*	Frank Sinatra

8

PEAK DATE	CH	10	5	PK	RANK	GOLD	Title — Songwriter(s)	SYMBL	Artist
2/28	16	10		4	58		Now Is The Hour (Maori Farewell Song) .... *Maewa Kaihan/Clement Scott/ Dorothy Stewart*		Eddy Howard
1/24	9	6		2	59		How Soon (Will I Be Seeing You) .... *Carroll Lucas/Jack Owens*		Dinah Shore
12/25	5	4		1	60		Here Comes Santa Claus (Down Santa Claus Lane) .... *Gene Autry/ Oakley Haldeman* [X-R]		Gene Autry
10/9	12	3		1	61		You Call Everybody Darling .... *Sam Martin/Ben Trace/Clem Watts* <A:5>		Andrews Sisters
4/3	7	3		1	62		Beg Your Pardon .... *Francis Craig/Beasley Smith*		Larry Green
11/13	11	2		1	63		Buttons And Bows .... *Ray Evans/Jay Livingston*	✦	Betty Garrett
7/3	10	2		1	64		Tell Me A Story .... *Terry Gilkyson*		Sammy Kaye (Don Cornell)
1/3	1	1		1	65		Pass That Peace Pipe .... *Ralph Blane/Roger Edens/Hugh Martin*		Margaret Whiting

9

PEAK DATE	CH	10	5	PK	RANK	GOLD	Title — Songwriter(s)	SYMBL	Artist
9/18	18	4		3	66		It's Magic .... *Sammy Cahn/Jule Styne*		Dick Haymes
6/19	13	3		2	67		You Can't Be True, Dear .... *Hal Cotton/Gerhard Ebeler/Ken Griffin/Hans Otten* <B:11>		Dick Haymes
9/4	17	2		2	68		It's Magic .... *Sammy Cahn/Jule Styne*	❶	Gordon MacRae
6/19	14	5		1	69		Just Because .... *Sid Robin/Bob Shelton/Joe Shelton*	❶	Frankie Yankovic
11/6	17	3		1	70		You Were Only Fooling .... *William Faber/Larry Fotine/Fred Meadows*		Blue Barron (Clyde Burke)
10/9	14	3		1	71		Cool Water .... *Bob Nolan*		Vaughn Monroe & Sons of the Pioneers
4/24	9	2		1	72	●	Shine .... *Lew Brown/Ford Dabney*		Frankie Laine
12/4	9	2		1	73		Buttons And Bows .... *Ray Evans/Jay Livingston*		Betty Rhodes
11/6	14	1		1	74		That Certain Party .... *Walter Donaldson/Gus Kahn*	❶	Benny Strong
5/22	7	1		1	75		You Can't Be True Dear .... *Hal Cotton/Gerhard Ebeler/Ken Griffin/Hans Otten*	❶	Vera Lynn
7/3	1	1		1	76		Nature Boy .... *Eden Ahbez*	❶	Sarah Vaughan

PEAK DATE	WEEKS				RANK	GOLD	Title	PEAK POSITION / Songwriter(s)	SYMBOL	DEBUT	Artist
	CH	10	5	PK							

10

1/31	6	2		2	77		I'm My Own Grandpaw	Moe Jaffe/Dwight Latham [N]			Guy Lombardo (Lombardo Trio)
4/3	8	1		1	78		I'm Looking Over A Four Leaf Clover	Mort Dixon/Harry Woods			The Three Suns
11/27	8	1		1	79		One Has My Name (The Other Has My Heart)	Hal Blair/Dearest Dean/Eddie Dean			Jimmy Wakely
1/24	8	1		1	80		Ballerina	Bob Russell/Carl Sigman			Bing Crosby
11/13	6	1		1	81 ●		Say Something Sweet To Your Sweetheart	Roy Brodsky/Sid Tepper <B:16>			Jo Stafford & Gordon MacRae
5/1	4	1		1	82		I Love You, Yes I Do	Henry Glover/Sally Nix			Sammy Kaye (Don Cornell)
12/4	1	1		1	83		Twelfth Street Rag	Euday Bowman/Andy Razaf [I]			Frankie Carle
1/17	1	1		1	84		Ballerina	Bob Russell/Carl Sigman			Jimmy Dorsey (Bob Carroll)

11

9/18	11			2	85		It's Magic	Sammy Cahn/Jule Styne			Sarah Vaughan
6/5	7			2	86		Baby Face	Harry Akst/Benny Davis			Sammy Kaye (Three Kaydets)
9/11	14			1	87		It's Magic	Sammy Cahn/Jule Styne			Tony Martin
6/19	7			1	88		Little White Lies	Walter Donaldson			Dinah Shore
7/3	6			1	89		Toolie Oolie Doolie (The Yodel Polka)	Arthur Beul/Vaughn Horton <A:6>			The Sportsmen
6/12	5			1	90		Nature Boy	Eden Ahbez <A:9>			Dick Haymes
5/29	4			1	91		Toolie Oolie Doolie The Yodel Polka	Arthur Beul/Vaughn Horton	✦		Vaughn Horton & His Polka Debs
12/25	3			1	92		You're All I Want For Christmas {re-charted in 1949 (#29)}	Seger Ellis/Glen Moore [X]			Frankie Laine
1/17	3			1	93		I'll Dance At Your Wedding	Herb Magidson/Ben Oakland <A:2>			Peggy Lee
2/21	2			1	94		I'm Looking Over A Four Leaf Clover	Mort Dixon/Harry Woods	✦		Uptown String Band

12

11/27	14			1	95		Cuanto La Gusta	Ray Gilbert/Gabriel Ruiz	❶		Carmen Miranda & Andrews Sisters
11/27	12			1	96		On A Slow Boat To China	Frank Loesser			Art Lund
7/10	8			1	97		Confess	Bennie Benjamin/George Weiss	❶		Patti Page
10/9	6			1	98		Serutan Yob (A Song For Backward Boys And Girls Under 40)	Eden Ahbez [N]			The Unnatural Seven (Karen Tedder/Enrohtwah)
3/13	3			1	99		Beg Your Pardon	Francis Craig/Beasley Smith			The Dinning Sisters
4/3	2			1	100		Now Is The Hour	Maewa Kaihan/Clement Scott/Dorothy Stewart			Kate Smith

13

9/4	27			2	101 ●		Bouquet Of Roses	Bob Hilliard/Steve Nelson <B:18>			Eddy Arnold
11/27	7			2	102		It's Too Soon To Know	Deborah Chessler	❶		The Orioles
6/26	8			2	103		Caramba! It's The Samba	Eddie Pola/Irving Taylor/George Wyle			Peggy Lee
10/16	16			1	104		You Came A Long Way (From St. Louis)	John Benson Brooks/Bob Russell			Ray McKinley
10/2	9			1	105 ●		Just A Little Lovin' (Will Go A Long, Long Way)	Eddy Arnold/Zeke Clements			Eddy Arnold
10/9	9			1	106		Underneath The Arches	Reg Connelly/Bud Flanagan/Joseph McCarthy			Andy Russell & The Pied Pipers
9/11	9			1	107 ●		You Call Everybody Darling	Sam Martin/Ben Trace/Clem Watts			Jack Smith & The Clark Sisters
5/22	3			1	108		Baby Face	Harry Akst/Benny Davis			Jack Smith & The Clark Sisters
4/24	2			1	109		Laroo Laroo Lili Bolero	Sylvia Dee/Sid Lippman/Elizabeth Moore			Peggy Lee
1/3	2			1	110		I Can't Give You Anything But Love	Dorothy Fields/Jimmy McHugh	✦		Rose Murphy
1/10	1			1	111		Too Fat Polka	Ross MacLean/Arthur Richardson [N]			Dick "Two Ton" Baker
1/3	1			1	112		Serenade Of The Bells	Al Goodhart/Kay Twomey/Al Urbano			Kay Kyser (Harry Babbitt)

14

11/13	9			1	113		Life Gits Tee-Jus Don't It	Carson Robison [N]			Carson Robison
12/18	8			1	114		Buttons And Bows	Ray Evans/Jay Livingston			Evelyn Knight
7/3	7			1	115		I Hate To Lose You	Grant Clarke/Archie Cottler <A:3>			Andrews Sisters
10/2	7			1	116		You Call Everybody Darling	Sam Martin/Ben Trace/Clem Watts	❶		Jerry Wayne
6/5	4			1	117		Baby Face	Harry Akst/Benny Davis			Henry King (Siggy Lane)
3/27	3			1	118		I'm Looking Over A Four Leaf Clover	Mort Dixon/Harry Woods			Arthur Godfrey
3/20	2			1	119		Now Is The Hour (Maori Farewell Song)	Maewa Kaihan/Clement Scott/Dorothy Stewart			Charlie Spivak (Tommy Mercer)
4/17	1			1	120		But Beautiful	Johnny Burke/Jimmy Van Heusen			Frank Sinatra

15

9/4	9			2	121		Hair Of Gold	Sunny Skylar			Jerry Murad's Harmonicats
11/27	14			1	122		Clair de Lune Parts I & II	Claude DeBussy [I]			Paul Weston
3/27	3			1	123		King Size Papa	Johnny Gomez/Paul Vance [N]	❶		Julia Lee
1/3	1			1	124		Civilization (Bongo, Bongo, Bongo)	Bob Hilliard/Carl Sigman			Woody Herman
4/24	1			1	125 ●		Cigareetes, Whuskey, And Wild, Wild Women	Tim Spencer [N]			Red Ingle

PEAK DATE	WEEKS CH	10	5	PK	RANK	GOLD	Title / PEAK POSITION / Songwriter(s)	SYMBL	DEBUT	Artist

16

PEAK DATE	CH	10	5	PK	RANK	GOLD	Title — Songwriter(s)	SYMBL	Artist
8/21	11			1	126		Confess...............Bennie Benjamin/George Weiss <A:1>		Doris Day & Buddy Clark
11/6	4			1	127		Bluebird Of Happiness..........Harry Davies/Sandor Harmati/Edward Heyman <A:10>		Jo Stafford & Gordon MacRae
12/18	3			1	128		You Started Something.............Floyd Huddleston/Al Rinker		Tony Pastor (Rosemary Clooney)
12/4	2			1	129		Brush Those Tears From Your Eyes......Oakley Haldeman/Jimmy Lee/Al Trace	✦	Barry Green

17

PEAK DATE	CH	10	5	PK	RANK	GOLD	Title — Songwriter(s)	SYMBL	Artist
12/4	11			1	130		Gloria.............Leon Rene		Mills Brothers
6/12	5			1	131		You Can't Be True.............Hal Cotton/Gerhard Ebeler/Ken Griffin/Hans Otten		Will Glahé
11/20	3			1	132		Buttons And Bows.............Ray Evans/Jay Livingston		Gene Autry
7/24	2			1	133		Tea Leaves.............Morty Berk/Frank Capano/Max Freedman		Jack Smith & The Clark Sisters
5/15	1			1	134 ●		Anytime.............Herbert Lawson <B:29>	❶	Eddy Arnold
12/4	1			1	135		A Tree In The Meadow.............Billy Reid	✦	Joe Loss (Howard Jones)

18

PEAK DATE	CH	10	5	PK	RANK	GOLD	Title — Songwriter(s)	SYMBL	Artist
7/24	6			2	136		The Woody Woodpecker.............Ramez Idriss/George Tibbles [N]		Danny Kaye - Andrews Sisters
9/4	14			1	137		Rambling Rose.............Joe Burke/Joseph McCarthy		Perry Como
8/21	10			1	138		You Call Everybody Darlin'.............Sam Martin/Ben Trace/Clem Watts	✦	Bruce Hayes
10/2	9			1	139		Hair Of Gold.............Sunny Skylar	✦	Jack Emerson
9/4	7			1	140		A Tree In The Meadow.............Billy Reid		John Laurenz
11/27	5			1	141		Recess In Heaven.............Johnny Getz	✦	Deep River Boys
7/3	1			1	142		Texarkana Baby.............Cottonseed Clark/Fred Rose <A:13>		Eddy Arnold

19

PEAK DATE	CH	10	5	PK	RANK	GOLD	Title — Songwriter(s)	SYMBL	Artist
8/7	9			1	143		The Maharajah Of Magador.............John Jacob Loeb [N]		Vaughn Monroe (Ziggy Talent)
6/26	8			1	144		Cuckoo Waltz.............Ken Griffin <A:2> [I]		Ken Griffin
7/3	4			1	145		You Can't Be True, Dear....Hal Cotton/Gerhard Ebeler/Ken Griffin/Hans Otten <B:30>	❶	The Marlin Sisters with Eddie Fisher
7/10	3			1	146 ●		Tomorrow Night.............Sam Coslow/Will Grosz	✦	Lonnie Johnson
10/23	3			1	147		Hair Of Gold.............Sunny Skylar <B:27>		Jack Lathrop
7/10	2			1	148		You Can't Be True, Dear.............Hal Cotton/Gerhard Ebeler/Ken Griffin/Hans Otten	✦	Dick James

20

PEAK DATE	CH	10	5	PK	RANK	GOLD	Title — Songwriter(s)	SYMBL	Artist
6/5	4			1	149		Just Because.............Sid Robin/Bob Shelton/Joe Shelton		Eddy Howard
10/2	4			1	150		Hair Of Gold, Eyes Of Blue.............Sunny Skylar <B:22>		Art Lund
11/27	2			1	151		A Strawberry Moon (In A Blueberry Sky).............Bob Hilliard/Sammy Mysels		Blue Barron (Clyde Burke/Dolores Hawkins)
12/4	2			1	152		In My Dreams.............Jimmie Shearer		Vaughn Monroe

21

PEAK DATE	CH	10	5	PK	RANK	GOLD	Title — Songwriter(s)	SYMBL	Artist
12/18	8			1	153		I Love You So Much It Hurts.............Floyd Tillman		Jimmy Wakely
5/22	5			1	154		Heartbreaker.............Morty Berk/Frank Catano/Max Freedman <A:21>		Andrews Sisters
6/12	3			1	155		(Every Time They Play The) Sabre Dance.............Aram Khachaturian/Lester Lee/Allan Roberts <A:21>		Andrews Sisters
9/18	3			1	156		A Tree In The Meadow.............Billy Reid		Monica Lewis & Ames Brothers
9/18	3			1	157		You Call Everybody Darlin'.............Sam Martin/Ben Trace/Clem Watts		Al Trace (Bob Vincent)
9/18	2			1	158		A Tree In The Meadow.............Billy Reid	✦	Paul Fennelly (Reggie Goff)
11/13	2			1	159		Bella Bella Marie.............Don Pelosi/Leo Towers/Gerhard Winkler		Larry Green
8/21	1			1	160		Ah But It Happens.............William Dunham/Walter Kent		Frankie Laine

22

PEAK DATE	CH	10	5	PK	RANK	GOLD	Title — Songwriter(s)	SYMBL	Artist
10/16	5			1	161		Hair Of Gold.............Sunny Skylar		John Laurenz
5/29	2			1	162		The Dickey-Bird Song.............Howard Dietz/Sammy Fain		Larry Clinton (Helen Lee)
12/4	2			1	163		Say Something Sweet To Your Sweetheart....Roy Brodsky/Sid Tepper <A:8>		Ink Spots
10/2	1			1	164		You Call Everybody Darling.............Sam Martin/Ben Trace/Clem Watts <A:20>		Art Lund
12/4	1			1	165		That Certain Party.............Walter Donaldson/Gus Kahn [N]	❶	Dean Martin & Jerry Lewis
10/30	1			1	166		Ev'rday I Love You (Just A Little Bit More).............Sammy Cahn/Jule Styne		Vaughn Monroe

23

PEAK DATE	CH	10	5	PK	RANK	GOLD	Title — Songwriter(s)	SYMBL	Artist
11/20	4			1	167		Say Something Sweet To Your Sweetheart.............Roy Brodsky/Sid Tepper		Vic Damone—Patti Page
9/25	4			1	168		Hindustan.............Oliver Wallace/Harold Weeks [I]		Ted Weems
8/28	3			1	169		Run Joe.............Louis Jordan/Walt Merrick/Joe Willoughby		Louis Jordan
11/27	2			1	170		Bella Bella Marie.............Don Pelosi/Leo Towers/Gerhard Winkler		Andrews Sisters
12/18	2			1	171		A Heart Full Of (For a handful of Kisses)...Eddy Arnold/Steve Nelson/Ray Soehnel <B:30>		Eddy Arnold
6/5	2			1	172		Haunted Heart.............Howard Dietz/Arthur Schwartz		Perry Como
11/6	2			1	173		A Hundred And Sixty Acres.............David Kapp		Bing Crosby & the Andrews Sisters
7/3	2			1	174		Put 'Em In A Box, Tie 'Em With A Ribbon (And Throw 'Em In The Deep Blue Sea).............Sammy Cahn/Jule Styne		Eddy Howard
10/2	2			1	175		Bluebird Of Happiness.............Harry Davies/Sandor Harmati/Edward Heyman	❶	Jan Peerce

PEAK DATE	CH	10	5	PK	RANK	GOLD	Title — Peak Position — Songwriter(s)	SYMBL	DEBUT	Artist
							23 (cont'd)			
7/17	1			1	176		Tea Leaves ....*Morty Berk/Frank Capano/Max Freedman*	✦		Emile Coté Serenaders
8/14	1			1	177		Ebony Rhapsody ....*Sam Coslow/Arthur Johnston*	✦		Rosetta Howard
							24			
9/18	3			2	178		A Tree In The Meadow ....*Billy Reid*	✦		Sam Browne
7/31	4			1	179		My Happiness ....*Borney Bergantine/Betty Peterson*			The Marlin Sisters
5/22	3			1	180		Time Out For Tears ....*Irving Berman/Abe Schiff*	❶		Savannah Churchill & The Four Tunes
10/16	2			1	181		Every Day I Love You ....*Sammy Cahn/Jule Styne*			Dick Haymes
12/25	1			1	182		The Christmas Song (Merry Christmas To You)....*Mel Torme/Robert Wells*			The King Cole Trio
							[X-R]			
9/18	1			1	183		It's Magic...*Sammy Cahn/Jule Styne*			Vic Damone
8/21	1			1	184		Saxa-Boogie ....*Sam Donahue <B:26>* [I]			Sam Donahue
5/15	1			1	185		I Love You Yes I Do ....*Henry Glover/Sally Nix*	✦		Bull Moose Jackson
12/25	1			1	186		Jingle Bells ....*James Pierpont <B:27>* [X]			The Keynotes with Primo Scala
							25			
10/30	3			1	187		Hair Of Gold (Eyes Of Blue)...*Sunny Skylar*	✦		Bob Eberly
12/25	1			1	188		On A Slow Boat To China ....*Frank Loesser*			Larry Clinton (Helen Lee)
12/25	1			1	189		You're All I Want For Christmas ....*Seger Ellis/Glen Moore* [X]	✦		Frank Gallagher
9/25	1			1	190		Ev'ry Day I Love You (Just A Little Bit More) ....*Sammy Cahn/Jule Styne*			Jo Stafford
							26			
11/13	3			1	191		I'll Get Along Somehow ....*Buddy Fields/Gerald Marks <A:24>*			Sam Donahue (Bill Lockwood)
8/14	2			1	192		My Happiness ....*Borney Bergantine/Betty Peterson*	❶		John Laurenz
12/25	1			1	193		Christmas Island ....*Lyle Moraine* [X-R]			Andrews Sisters & Guy Lombardo
12/11	1			1	194		September In The Rain ....*Al Dubin/Harry Warren* [I]			Sam Donahue
							27			
9/25	2			2	195		You Call Everybody Darling...............*Sam Martin/Ben Trace/Clem Watts <A:19>*	❶		Jack Lathrop
12/4	2			1	196		Life Gits Tee-Jus, Don't It?...*Carson Robison* [N]			Tex Williams
12/11	1			1	197		Dainty Brenda Lee ....*Lloyd Bryer*			Eddy Howard
11/20	1			1	198		A Tree In The Meadow...*Billy Reid*	✦		Bill Johnson
7/17	1			1	199		How High The Moon ....*Nancy Hamilton/Morgan Lewis*			Stan Kenton (June Christy)
10/23	1			1	200		Rambling Rose...*Joe Burke/Joseph McCarthy <A:7>*			Gordon MacRae
12/25	1			1	201		The Mistletoe Kiss ....*Jimmy Kennedy <A:24>* [X]			The Keynotes with Primo Scala
							28			
9/11	1			1	202		Far Cry ....*Buddy Johnson* [I]			Buddy Johnson
7/10	1			1	203		Adios...*Enric Madriguera/Eddie Woods* [I-R]			Glenn Miller
							29			
5/15	1			1	204		What A Fool I Was ....*Stu Davis <A:17>*			Eddy Arnold
8/28	1			1	205		The Darktown Strutters' Ball...*Shelton Brooks*	❶		Connie Haines & Alan Dale
12/4	1			1	206		The Mountaineer And The Jabberwock...............*Lewis Bellin/Belmont Parker*			John Laurenz
8/7	1			1	207		Bubble-Loo Bubble-Loo...............*Hoagy Carmichael/Paul Francis Webster*			Peggy Lee
8/21	1			1	208		Just For Now ....*Dick Redmond*			Frank Sinatra
12/11	1			1	209		Cuanto Le Gusta ....*Ray Gilbert/Gabriel Ruiz*			Eve Young
							30			
7/17	1			1	210		Put 'Em In A Box, Tie 'Em With A Ribbon (And Throw 'Em In The Deep Blue Sea)...*Sammy Cahn/Jule Styne*			The King Cole Trio
6/19	1			1	211		Somebody Else Is Taking My Place...............*Bob Ellsworth/Dick Howard/Russ Morgan* [R]			Benny Goodman with Peggy Lee
6/26	1			1	212		Toolie Oolie Doolie (The Yodel Polka) ....*Arthur Beul/Vaughn Horton <A:19>*			The Marlin Sisters
6/12	1			1	213		For Every Man There's A Woman ....*Harold Arlen/Leo Robin*			Tony Martin
6/19	1			1	214		Toolie-Oolie-Doolie (The Yodel Polka) ....*Arthur Beul/Vaughn Horton*			Henri René (Three-O-Niners)
9/18	1			1	215		Forever Is Ending Today ....*Johnny Bond/Ike Cargill/Ernest Tubb*			Ernest Tubb

1949

NATIONAL NEWS: President Truman criticizes what he calls the wave of anti-Communist hysteria sweeping the country. Truman introduces the first major civil rights bill since Reconstruction. Less than two months after retiring as the first Secretary of Defense, James Forrestal commits suicide. The mass-produced homes of Levittown, New York are a response to the nationwide need for housing.

INTERNATIONAL NEWS: The Soviet Union detonates its first test nuclear explosion, stirring new Cold War concerns. Nearly a year after it began, the Russians end their blockade of divided Berlin. Mao Tse-tung and his Communist Party conquer Nationalist forces and establish the People's Republic of China. The U.S., Canada, and Western European nations form the North Atlantic Treaty Organization (NATO). Israel and Egypt agree to cease hostilities, and Israel is accepted as a member of the United Nations.

COMMERCE AND SCIENCE: An American B-50 bomber completes the first non-stop flight around the world. The first rocket to reach outer space is launched at the White Sands Proving Grounds in New Mexico. 3-M announces the first tape recorder for mass production of tapes.

FADS AND FASHION: The Argentine card game Canasta attracts some 10 million Americans in barely a year.

SPORTS: The New York Yankees top the Brooklyn Dodgers (with National League Most Valuable Player Jackie Robinson) in the World Series, four games to one. The Philadelphia Eagles repeat as NFL champions by defeating the Los Angeles Rams, 14-0. Notre Dame is #1 in college football. Heavyweight champ Joe Louis retires, and Ezzard Charles wins the vacant crown. Jake LaMotta knocks out Marcel Cerdan to take the middleweight championship. The Minneapolis Lakers win the NBA title. Adolph Rupp's Kentucky Wildcats win their second straight NCAA basketball tournament. The Toronto Maple Leafs skate to their third straight National Hockey League title. Pancho Gonzales repeats as U.S. tennis champion. Sam Snead triumphs in both the Masters and the PGA.

MOVIES: *All the King's Men* earns Oscars for Best Picture and Best Actor (Broderick Crawford). Olivia de Havilland is Best Actress for *The Heiress*. The year's top box office smash is *Samson and Delilah*, with other hits including *Battleground*, *Jolson Sings Again*, and Cary Grant in *I Was a Male War Bride*. Katharine Hepburn and Spencer Tracy team again in *Adam's Rib*.

TELEVISION: Milton Berle is undisputed king of the young medium with his top-rated *Texaco Star Theater*. New shows include longtime radio favorites *The Lone Ranger*, *Hopalong Cassidy*, and *Arthur Godfrey and His Friends*.

THEATER: In a remarkable year for Broadway, Rodgers & Hammerstein's monumental *South Pacific* starring Mary Martin, *Gentlemen Prefer Blondes* with Carol Channing, and Cole Porter's *Kiss Me, Kate* are memorable musical hits. Arthur Miller's *Death of a Salesman* wins the Pulitzer Prize.

BOOKS: George Orwell's *1984* paints a foreboding vision of the future.

1. **Perry Como**	2. **Jo Stafford**	3. **Russ Morgan**
1,070	977	836

4.	772	**Bing Crosby**	13.	449	**Frank Sinatra**
5.	702	**Margaret Whiting**	14.	443	**Doris Day**
6.	657	**Vaughn Monroe**	15.	413	**Vic Damone**
7.	616	**Sammy Kaye**	16.	408	**Paul Weston**
8.	565	**Evelyn Knight**	17.	405	**Eddy Howard**
9.	561	**Guy Lombardo**	18.	405	**Dinah Shore**
10.	532	**Gordon MacRae**	19.	400	**Buddy Clark**
11.	456	**Frankie Laine**	20.	351	**Andrews Sisters**
12.	450	**Art Mooney**			

1949 — TOP SONGWRITERS

	# of Hits	Points			# of Hits	Points	
1.	20	1,753	**Richard Rodgers**	7.	8	674	**Fred Wise**
2.	17	1,508	**Oscar Hammerstein**	8.	7	658	**Dorcas Cochran**
3.	13	1,130	**Frank Loesser**		7	658	**Lionel Newman**
4.	10	869	**Irving Berlin**	10.	7	630	**Carl Sigman**
5.	8	686	**Eily Beadell**	11.	7	617	**Hy Heath**
	8	686	**Nell Tollerton**		7	617	**Johnny Lange**

1949 — TOP ARTIST DEBUTS

1.	4/30	**Kitty Kallen** (105)	5.	11/19 †	**Ray Anthony** (39)
2.	6/18	**Don Cornell** (85)	6.	11/26	**Tennessee Ernie Ford** (106)
3.	9/24	**Ralph Flanagan** (42)	7.	12/17	**Richard Hayes** (83)
4.	10/15	**Hugo Winterhalter** (43)			

PEAK DATE	WEEKS				RANK	GOLD	Title	PEAK POSITION / Songwriter(s)	SYMBL	DEBUT	Artist
	CH	10	5	PK							

1

| 5/14 | 22 | 18 | 17 | 12 | 1 ● | | **Riders In The Sky** (A Cowboy Legend) .... *Stan Jones* | | | | **Vaughn Monroe** |

Disc Jockey: 17,5,3,1,1,1,1,1,1,1,1,1,1,1,2,5,7,18,-,21
Best Seller: 30,12,4,1,1,1,1,1,1,1,1,1,1,1,2,2,2,4,4,6,17,17
Juke Box: 22,16,8,3,2,1,1,1,1,1,1,1,1,1,2,2,7,9,17,20,-,29

| 10/1 | 22 | 17 | 16 | 8 | 2 ● | | **That Lucky Old Sun** .... *Haven Gillespie/Beasley Smith* | | | | **Frankie Laine** |

Best Seller: 28,19,5,3,2,1,1,1,1,1,1,1,2,4,4,6,8,13,14,25,20
Disc Jockey: 5,5,3,3,2,1,1,1,1,1,1,2,2,4,5,6,13
Juke Box: 13,7,4,3,2,1,1,1,1,2,2,3,4,4,5,8,9,11,19

| 1/15 | 21 | 17 | 15 | 7 | 3 ● | | **A Little Bird Told Me** .... *Harvey Brooks* <B:9> | | | | **Evelyn Knight** |

Best Seller: 20,9,8,7,5,4,3,4,2,1,1,1,1,1,1,1,5,8,12,19,25
Juke Box: 11,11,4,3,3,3,2,1,1,1,1,1,1,1,2,2,4,8,11,17
Disc Jockey: 20,-,10,11,6,5,5,4,3,1,1,1,1,1,1,3,4,9,16,26

| 3/26 | 22 | 17 | 14 | 7 | 4 ● | | **Cruising Down The River** .... *Eily Beadell/Nell Tollerton* <B:5> | | | | **Russ Morgan** (The Skylarks) |

Best Seller: 15,6,4,2,1,1,1,1,1,1,1,2,3,5,6,6,10,17,10,16,23,17
Juke Box: 20,7,5,3,2,1,1,1,1,1,1,2,2,3,3,7,4,14,14,-,23
Disc Jockey: 22,14,7,8,8,8,6,4,4,9,9,10,15,22,-,-,25

| 3/12 | 20 | 16 | 13 | 7 | 5 ● | | **Cruising Down The River** .... *Eily Beadell/Nell Tollerton* <B:18> | | | | **Blue Barron** |

Disc Jockey: 28,12,15,5,4,1,1,1,1,1,1,1,2,3,2,7,5,16,16,25
Juke Box: 18,7,5,4,3,1,1,1,2,2,2,2,3,8,6,5,9,12,18,25
Best Seller: 25,12,9,4,2,2,1,1,2,2,2,2,6,6,10,12,19,26

| 11/26 | 13 | 12 | 11 | 6 | 6 ● | | **Mule Train** .... *Fred Glickman/Hy Heath/Johnny Lange* | | | | **Frankie Laine** |

Best Seller: 9,3,1,1,1,1,1,1,2,2,3,4,18
Disc Jockey: 3,1,1,1,1,1,1,2,2,2,4,14
Juke Box: 7,5,2,1,1,1,1,1,1,4,3,10,20

| 7/30 | 26 | 19 | 17 | 5 | 7 | | **Some Enchanted Evening** .... *Oscar Hammerstein/Richard Rodgers* <B:5> | | | | **Perry Como** |

Best Seller: 30,26,20,15,8,4,3,2,2,2,2,2,2,1,1,1,1,2,2,4,5,7,14,16,28
Juke Box: 25,10,8,5,4,4,2,2,2,2,2,1,1,1,1,1,2,6,6,12,17,21
Disc Jockey: 26,30,22,24,20,13,8,11,3,4,3,9,2,2,2,1,1,3,2,4,4,6,9,13

| 8/27 | 26 | 20 | 17 | 4 | 8 ● | | **You're Breaking My Heart** .... *Pat Genaro/Sunny Skylar* <B:16> | | | | **Vic Damone** |

Best Seller: 26,20,10,13,16,5,3,3,3,2,2,1,1,1,1,2,2,2,2,3,4,5,7,9,15,17
Disc Jockey: 13,13,6,3,2,1,1,2,2,1,1,2,2,2,2,3,3,6,10,8,18
Juke Box: 23,22,23,11,8,6,2,3,1,4,1,2,1,3,3,3,5,5,9,11,12,29

| 5/14 | 26 | 20 | 17 | 3 | 9 | | **Forever And Ever** .... *Malia Rosa/Franz Winkler* <B:17> | | | | **Russ Morgan** (The Skylarks) |

Juke Box: 29,15,10,10,4,3,2,2,1,1,1,2,2,2,2,3,4,4,5,4,5,7,14,14,15,-,21
Best Seller: 14,18,8,8,3,4,2,2,3,2,4,3,4,4,6,5,11,6,11,20,16,20
Disc Jockey: 30,17,21,15,15,8,8,8,6,6,13,10,16,15,26,29,22,20

| 11/19 | 23 | 20 | 16 | 3 | 10 ● | | **Slipping Around** .... *Floyd Tillman* <B:30> | | | | **Margaret Whiting & Jimmy Wakely** |

Juke Box: 28,-,14,14,7,4,4,2,2,2,1,1,1,2,2,2,2,3,3,2,5,6,6,10
Best Seller: 26,14,8,5,5,5,2,2,2,3,2,3,3,3,3,4,4,3,2,6,7,12
Disc Jockey: 10,10,5,4,4,3,2,2,2,3,3,3,3,3,4,4,3,7,7,15,20

| 9/10 | 18 | 14 | 11 | 2 | 11 | | **Someday** .... *Jimmie Hodges* | | | | **Vaughn Monroe** |

Disc Jockey: 9,5,3,1,1,2,3,3,3,4,4,6,8,13,29,19,25
Juke Box: 19,9,4,5,1,2,1,3,2,2,4,4,7,13,12,14
Best Seller: 22,13,16,7,4,3,2,3,3,3,6,8,8,13,16,20

| 5/7 | 15 | 9 | 7 | 2 | 12 | | **"A"-You're Adorable** .... *Buddy Kaye/Sid Lippman/Fred Wise* | | | | **Perry Como** (Fontane Sisters) |

Disc Jockey: 14,16,6,1,1,2,2,2,3,5,13,8,16,13
Juke Box: 27,-,16,14,9,9,7,7,6,3,11,10,12,11,16,28
Best Seller: 22,12,9,5,5,4,6,6,7,9,8,12,15,15,30

| 1/15 | 17 | 15 | 12 | 1 | 13 | | **My Darling, My Darling** .... *Frank Loesser* | | | | **Jo Stafford & Gordon MacRae** |

Disc Jockey: 24,7,4,3,2,2,2,3,2,1,2,3,3,4,7,8,21
Best Seller: 18,7,4,6,3,4,5,5,5,4,4,4,5,13,13,21
Juke Box: 23,15,8,7,4,4,4,5,4,4,6,7,8,18,19

| 3/5 | 20 | 13 | 10 | 1 | 14 | | **Powder Your Face With Sunshine** (Smile! Smile! Smile!) .... *Carmen Lombardo/Stanley Rochinski* | | | | **Evelyn Knight** |

Juke Box: 22,18,15,6,4,4,2,2,2,1,3,5,3,7,4,9,21,18,24,28
Disc Jockey: 17,13,10,6,7,3,2,6,6,7,6,10,10,13
Best Seller: 16,18,9,9,6,4,4,3,3,4,6,5,6,9,13,17,24

| 4/30 | 18 | 12 | 9 | 1 | 15 | | **Careless Hands** .... *Bob Hilliard/Carl Sigman* | | | | **Mel Tormé** |

Disc Jockey: 26,12,11,11,7,2,2,2,1,2,4,3,3,4,10,6,15,21
Best Seller: 30,19,14,10,15,7,9,9,7,8,15,16,16,24
Juke Box: 26,-,15,15,13,11,12,13,12,17,12,12,16,26,25,27

| 3/5 | 17 | 10 | 8 | 1 | 16 ● | | **I've Got My Love To Keep Me Warm** .... *Irving Berlin* [I] | | | | **Les Brown** |

Disc Jockey: 28,15,15,12,16,12,7,4,2,1,3,2,3,2,5,9,19
Best Seller: 30,11,21,19,15,10,14,10,9,8,7,10,10,10,15,17
Juke Box: 24,21,16,14,11,13,14,11,15,16,18,23

| 12/31 | 6 | 4 | 3 | 1 | 17 ● | | **Rudolph, The Red-Nosed Reindeer** .... *Johnny Marks* [X] | | | | **Gene Autry** |

Best Seller: 22,11,8,4,3,1
Disc Jockey: 28,9,3,3
Juke Box: 18,18,13,4
{re-charted in 1950 (#3), 1951 (#16) and 1952 (#13)}

1949

PEAK DATE	CH	10	5	PK	RANK	GOLD	Title	PEAK POSITION / Songwriter(s)	SYMBOL	DEBUT	Artist

2

1/29	23	16	2	6	18		Far Away Places	Alex Kramer/Joan Whitney			Margaret Whiting
5/28	23	17	12	3	19		Again	Dorcas Cochran/Lionel Newman			Gordon Jenkins (Joe Graydon)
2/12	19	14	10	3	20		Far Away Places	Alex Kramer/Joan Whitney			Bing Crosby
7/9	19	14	8	2	21		Again	Dorcas Cochran/Lionel Newman <B:22>			Doris Day
6/11	25	16	10	1	22		Forever And Ever	Malia Rosa/Franz Winkler <B:11>			Perry Como
8/27	24	16	10	1	23		Room Full Of Roses	Tim Spencer			Sammy Kaye (Don Cornell)
6/18	9	4	2	1	24		Riders In The Sky (A Cowboy Legend)	Stan Jones			Peggy Lee

3

3/12	17	10	7	5	25	●	Galway Bay	Arthur Colahan			Bing Crosby
7/23	20	13	7	2	26		Some Enchanted Evening	Oscar Hammerstein/Richard Rodgers <B:12>			Bing Crosby
4/16	22	12	5	2	27		Red Roses For A Blue Lady	Roy Brodsky/Sid Tepper			Vaughn Monroe
4/2	14	9	3	2	28		Cruising Down The River	Eily Beadell/Nell Tollerton			Jack Smith & The Clark Sisters
11/12	19	13	8	1	29		Don't Cry Joe (Let Her Go, Let Her Go, Let Her Go)	Joe Marsala			Gordon Jenkins (Betty Brewer)
7/9	19	11	8	1	30		Baby, It's Cold Outside	Frank Loesser			Margaret Whiting & Johnny Mercer
7/30	19	11	7	1	31		Baby, It's Cold Outside	Frank Loesser			Dinah Shore & Buddy Clark
5/14	22	13	5	1	32		Careless Hands	Bob Hilliard/Carl Sigman <B:13>			Sammy Kaye (Don Cornell)
4/2	25	11	5	1	33		So Tired	Russ Morgan/Jack Stuart			Russ Morgan
7/16	18	9	2	1	34		Again	Dorcas Cochran/Lionel Newman <B:20>			Mel Tormé
9/3	11	6	1	1	35		The Four Winds And The Seven Seas	Hal David/Don Rodney			Sammy Kaye (Tony Alamo)

4

9/24	26	19	7	5	36		Jealous Heart	Jenny Lou Carson	❶		Al Morgan
8/27	23	10	6	3	37		Room Full Of Roses	Tim Spencer <B:21>			Eddy Howard
2/12	16	10	6	2	38		Lavender Blue (Dilly Dilly)	Eliot Daniel/Larry Morey <B:14>			Sammy Kaye (Three Kaydets)
12/3	12	10	5	2	39		Mule Train	Fred Glickman/Hy Heath/Johnny Lange <A:2>			Bing Crosby
2/26	17	8	5	1	40		Far Away Places	Alex Kramer/Joan Whitney			Perry Como
10/8	16	14	3	1	41		You're Breaking My Heart	Pat Genaro/Sunny Skylar			Buddy Clark
2/5	14	10	2	1	42		A Little Bird Told Me	Harvey Brooks			Blue Lu Barker
10/1	23	10	1	1	43	●	Whispering Hope	Alice Hawthorne			Jo Stafford & Gordon MacRae
7/16	17	10	1	1	44		Some Enchanted Evening	Oscar Hammerstein/Richard Rodgers			Jo Stafford
4/30	15	5	1	1	45		"A" You're Adorable	Buddy Kaye/Sid Lippman/Fred Wise <B:7>			Jo Stafford & Gordon MacRae

5

10/8	15	10	2	2	46		Someday (You'll Want Me To Want You)	Jimmie Hodges			Mills Brothers
4/16	15	8	2	2	47		Sunflower	Mack David <A:1>			Russ Morgan (The Skylarks)
5/21	17	7	2	2	48		Forever And Ever	Malia Rosa/Franz Winkler			Margaret Whiting
12/31	5	3	2	2	49	●	I Yust Go Nuts At Christmas	Harry Stewart <B:7> [X-N]	❶		Yogi Yorgesson
7/23	21	10	1	1	50		I Don't See Me In Your Eyes Anymore	Bennie Benjamin/George Weiss	✦		The Starlighters
9/3	18	8	1	1	51		Maybe It's Because	Harry Ruby/Johnnie Scott			Dick Haymes
8/27	21	7	1	1	52		The Huckle-Buck	Roy Alfred/Andy Gibson <B:6>			Tommy Dorsey (Charlie Shavers)
7/9	16	5	1	1	53		Bali Ha'i	Oscar Hammerstein/Richard Rodgers <A:1>			Perry Como
12/31	4	2	1	1	54	●	White Christmas	Irving Berlin [X-R]			Bing Crosby

6

8/13	20	9		1	55		Room Full Of Roses	Tim Spencer			Dick Haymes
10/15	16	9		1	56		You're Breaking My Heart	Pat Genaro/Sunny Skylar <B:21>			Ink Spots
10/22	17	8		1	57		That Lucky Old Sun (Just Rolls Around Heaven All Day)	Haven Gillespie/Beasley Smith			Vaughn Monroe
1/15	16	7		1	58		A Little Bird Told Me	Harvey Brooks	✦		Paula Watson
5/21	21	6		1	59	●	Again	Dorcas Cochran/Lionel Newman			Vic Damone
9/17	7	2		1	60		Room Full Of Roses	Tim Spencer			Jerry Wayne
7/16	15	1		1	61		Again	Dorcas Cochran/Lionel Newman <A:5> [I]			Tommy Dorsey (Marcy Lutes)
7/30	13	1		1	62		Some Enchanted Evening	Oscar Hammerstein/Richard Rodgers <B:18>			Frank Sinatra

7

4/9	16	8		1	63		So Tired	Russ Morgan/Jack Stuart			Kay Starr
5/7	12	2		1	64		Need You	Johnny Blackburn/Teepee Mitchell/Lew Porter <A:4>			Jo Stafford & Gordon MacRae
9/24	9	2		1	65		Some Enchanted Evening	Oscar Hammerstein/Richard Rodgers	✦		Ezio Pinza
12/31	4	2		1	66		Yingle Bells	James Pierpont <A:5> [X-N]			Yogi Yorgesson
7/16	17	1		1	67		Again	Dorcas Cochran/Lionel Newman			Art Mooney (Johnny Martin/Madelyn Russell)
1/8	12	1		1	68	●	On A Slow Boat To China	Frank Loesser			Benny Goodman (Al Hendrickson)

8

| 11/26 | 10 | 6 | | 3 | 69 | | I'll Never Slip Around Again | Teepee Mitchell/Lew Porter | | | Margaret Whiting & Jimmy Wakely |
| 4/23 | 19 | 4 | | 2 | 70 | | Red Roses For A Blue Lady | Roy Brodsky/Sid Tepper <B:19> | | | Guy Lombardo (Don Rodney) |

PEAK DATE	CH	10	5	PK	RANK	GOLD	Title / PEAK POSITION / Songwriter(s)	Artist

8 (cont'd)

PEAK DATE	CH	10	5	PK	RANK	GOLD	Title	Artist
2/26	9	3		2	71		I Love You So Much It Hurts .... *Floyd Tillman <B:9>*	Mills Brothers
12/10	17	3		1	72	●	I've Got A Lovely Bunch Of Coconuts .... *Fred Heatherton* **[N]**	Freddy Martin (Merv Griffin)
4/16	12	2		1	73		Cruising Down The River (On A Sunday Afternoon) ... *Eily Beadell/Nell Tollerton*	Frankie Carle (Marjorie Hughes)
1/1	8	1		1	74		You Were Only Fooling (While I Was Falling In Love) .... *William Faber/* *Larry Fotine/Fred Meadows <B:22>*	Ink Spots

9

PEAK DATE	CH	10	5	PK	RANK	GOLD	Title	Artist
7/23	13	5		4	75		Baby, It's Cold Outside .... *Frank Loesser*	Ella Fitzgerald & Louis Jordan
9/24	14	4		4	76		Maybe It's Because .... *Harry Ruby/Johnnie Scott <B:25>*	Eddy Howard
9/3	11	4		3	77		Some Enchanted Evening .... *Oscar Hammerstein/Richard Rodgers <B:10>* **[I]**	Paul Weston
11/26	12	4		2	78		Don't Cry Joe (Let Her Go, Let Her Go, Let Her Go) .... *Joe Marsala*	Ralph Flanagan (Harry Prime)
10/29	13	2		1	79	●	I Never See Maggie Alone .... *Everett Lynton/Harry Tilsley* ✦	Kenny Roberts
4/2	11	2		1	80		I've Got My Love To Keep Me Warm .... *Irving Berlin <A:8>*	Mills Brothers
1/8	15	1		1	81		Brush Those Tears From Your Eyes ...... *Oakley Haldeman/Jimmy Lee/Al Trace <A:1>*	Evelyn Knight
11/5	12	1		1	82		Let Her Go, Let Her Go, Let Her Go .... *Joe Marsala*	Frank Sinatra
2/5	12	1		1	83		Lavender Blue (Dilly Dilly) .... *Eliot Daniel/Larry Morey*	Dinah Shore
12/17	9	1		1	84		Mule Train .... *Fred Glickman/Hy Heath/Johnny Lange* ❶	Tennessee Ernie
11/19	5	1		1	85		The Last Mile Home .... *Walton Farrar/Walter Kent <B:10>*	Jo Stafford
12/31	3	1		1	86		Blue Christmas .... *Billy Hayes/Jay Johnson* **[X]** {re-charted in 1950 (#20)}	Hugo Winterhalter

10

PEAK DATE	CH	10	5	PK	RANK	GOLD	Title	Artist
12/3	9	2		2	87		Mule Train .... *Fred Glickman/Hy Heath/Johnny Lange*	Vaughn Monroe
2/5	16	1		1	88		Sweet Georgia Brown .... *Ben Bernie/Kenneth Casey/Maceo Pinkard* **[I]** ✦	Brother Bones & His Shadows
9/3	14	1		1	89		The Huckle Buck .... *Roy Alfred/Andy Gibson*	Frank Sinatra
7/30	8	1		1	90		The Four Winds And The Seven Seas .... *Hal David/Don Rodney*	Mel Tormé
10/8	7	1		1	91		Ragtime Cowboy Joe .... *Maurice Abrahams/Grant Clarke/Lewis Muir <A:9>*	Jo Stafford
9/10	6	1		1	92		My Bolero .... *Jimmy Kennedy/Nat Simon*	Vic Damone
11/5	6	1		1	93		Jealous Heart .... *Jenny Lou Carson* ❶	Hugo Winterhalter
3/5	4	1		1	94		Powder Your Face With Sunshine (Smile! Smile! Smile!) .... *Carmen Lombardo/Stanley Rochinski*	Dean Martin
7/9	3	1		1	95		Bali Ha'i .... *Oscar Hammerstein/Richard Rodgers <A:9>* **[I]**	Paul Weston

11

PEAK DATE	CH	10	5	PK	RANK	GOLD	Title	Artist
11/5	12			2	96		Jealous Heart .... *Jenny Lou Carson*	Jack Owens
2/19	5			2	97		Grieving For You .... *Joe Gibson/Joe Gold/Joe Ribaud*	Tony Pastor (Rosemary Clooney)
7/16	15			1	98		I Don't See Me In Your Eyes Anymore ... *Bennie Benjamin/George Weiss <A:2>*	Perry Como
10/29	12			1	99		Hop-Scotch Polka (Scotch Hot) .... *Gene Rayburn/Carl Sigman/William Whitlock*	Guy Lombardo (Kenny Gardner)
3/12	9			1	100		Down By The Station .... *Slim Gaillard/Lee Ricks*	Tommy Dorsey (Denny Dennis/ Lucy Ann Polk/The Sentimentalists)
9/17	8			1	101		Homework .... *Irving Berlin <B:12>*	Jo Stafford
12/31	7			1	102		Blues Stay Away From Me .... *Alton Delmore/Rabon Delmore/Henry Glover/* ❶ *Wayne Raney*	Owen Bradley (Jack Shook/Dottie Dillard)
12/31	3			1	103		Blue Christmas .... *Billy Hayes/Jay Johnson* **[X]**	Russ Morgan
4/23	3			1	104		All Right, Louie, Drop The Gun .... *Ray Carter/Lucille Johnson* **[N]** ✦	Wesson Brothers

12

PEAK DATE	CH	10	5	PK	RANK	GOLD	Title	Artist
7/16	12			2	105		A Wonderful Guy .... *Oscar Hammerstein/Richard Rodgers*	Margaret Whiting
6/25	26			1	106	●	Blue Skirt Waltz .... *Vaclav Blaha/Mitchell Parish*	Frankie Yankovic with The Marlin Sisters
3/26	17			1	107		The Hot Canary .... *Paul Nero* **[I]**	Paul Weston
5/14	15			1	108		Forever And Ever .... *Malia Rosa/Franz Winkler*	Dinah Shore
11/26	11			1	109		A Dreamer's Holiday .... *Kim Gannon/Mabel Wayne*	Buddy Clark
7/23	10			1	110		Baby, It's Cold Outside .... *Frank Loesser* ❶	Don Cornell & Laura Leslie
5/28	10			1	111		Careless Hands .... *Bob Hilliard/Carl Sigman*	Bing Crosby
11/5	9			1	112		Envy .... *David Gussin/Eve London*	Fran Warren
5/7	8			1	113		"A"-You're Adorable (The Alphabet Song) .... *Buddy Kaye/Sid Lippman/Fred Wise*	Tony Pastor (Clooney Sisters)
6/25	7			1	114		Bali Ha'i .... *Oscar Hammerstein/Richard Rodgers <A:3>*	Bing Crosby
2/12	6			1	115		The Pussy Cat Song (Nyow! Nyot Nyow!) .... *Dick Manning* **[N]**	Patty Andrews & Bob Crosby
4/30	6			1	116		Sunflower .... *Mack David* ✦	Jack Fulton
9/10	6			1	117		Just One Way To Say I Love You .... *Irving Berlin <A:11>*	Jo Stafford

13

PEAK DATE	CH	10	5	PK	RANK	GOLD	Title	Artist
3/5	10			2	118		Powder Your Face With Sunshine .... *Carmen Lombardo/Stanley Rochinski <A:3>*	Sammy Kaye (Three Kaydets)
9/10	9			2	119		Dance Of The Hours .... *Amilcare Ponchielli* **[N]**	Spike Jones
8/20	16			1	120		Bali Ha'i .... *Oscar Hammerstein/Richard Rodgers*	Peggy Lee
2/5	11			1	121		Congratulations .... *Sid Rubin/Paul Weston <B:28>*	Jo Stafford

1949

PEAK DATE	WEEKS				RANK	GOLD	Title / PEAK POSITION / Songwriter(s)	SYMBOL	DEBUT	Artist
	CH	10	5	PK						

13 (cont'd)

PEAK DATE	CH	10	5	PK	RANK	GOLD	Title			Artist
8/6	6			1	122		Twenty-Four Hours Of Sunshine .... *Peter DeRose/Carl Sigman*			Art Mooney
4/23	4			1	123		Sunflower .... *Mack David*			Jack Smith With The Crew-Chiefs
6/18	4			1	124		Black Coffee .... *Francis Burke/Paul Francis Webster*			Sarah Vaughan
2/19	2			1	125		I Love You So Much It Hurts .... *Floyd Tillman*	✦		Reggie Goff with Cyril Stapleton
2/12	1			1	126		So In Love .... *Cole Porter*			Patti Page

14

PEAK DATE	CH	10	5	PK	RANK	GOLD	Title			Artist
6/4	10			1	127		Riders In The Sky A Cowboy Legend .... *Stan Jones*			Bing Crosby
11/5	9			1	128		You're Breaking My Heart .... *Pat Genaro/Sunny Skylar*	❶		Ralph Flanagan (Harry Prime)
12/3	8			1	129		Jealous Heart .... *Jenny Lou Carson*	✦		Bill Lawrence
3/5	8			1	130		Far Away Places .... *Alex Kramer/Joan Whitney*			Dinah Shore
8/6	7			1	131		Ain't She Sweet .... *Milton Ager/Jack Yellen* [I]	✦		Mr. Ford & Mr. Goon-Bones
1/8	6			1	132		Down Among The Sheltering Palms .... *James Brockman/Abe Olman* <A:4>			Sammy Kaye (Don Cornell)
4/2	5			1	133		Sunflower .... *Mack David*			Frank Sinatra
12/3	4			1	134		Mule Train .... *Fred Glickman/Hy Heath/Johnny Lange* <B:19>			Gordon MacRae
12/10	4			1	135		That Lucky Old Sun (Just Rolls Around Heaven All Day) .... *Haven Gillespie/Beasley Smith*			Frank Sinatra
1/22	4			1	136		Cuanto Le Gusta (La Parranda) .... *Ray Gilbert/Gabriel Ruiz*			Jack Smith & The Clark Sisters
10/1	4			1	137		That Lucky Old Sun (Just Rolls Around Heaven All Day) .... *Haven Gillespie/Beasley Smith* <B:20>			Sarah Vaughan
12/10	3			1	138		(Round Her Neck) She Wore A Yellow Ribbon .... *Mark Ottner/Leroy Parker*	✦		Eddie Miller

15

PEAK DATE	CH	10	5	PK	RANK	GOLD	Title			Artist
8/27	10			1	139		Let's Take An Old-Fashioned Walk .... *Irving Berlin* <B:23>			Perry Como
11/5	10			1	140		Canadian Capers (Cuttin' Capers) .... *Gus Chandler/Henry Cohen/Burt White*			Doris Day
2/5	5			1	141		A Little Bird Told Me .... *Harvey Brooks*	✦		Janette Davis & Jerry Wayne

16

PEAK DATE	CH	10	5	PK	RANK	GOLD	Title			Artist
5/14	7			2	142		Once In Love With Amy .... *Frank Loesser*	❶		Ray Bolger
9/17	11			1	143		Hop-Scotch Polka (Scotch Hot) .... *Gene Rayburn/Carl Sigman/William Whitlock*			Art Mooney
1/1	8			1	144		You Were Only Fooling (While I Was Falling In Love) .... *William Faber/Larry Fotine/Fred Meadows*	❶		Kay Starr
5/7	6			1	145		Once And For Always .... *Johnny Burke/Jimmy Van Heusen*			Jo Stafford
8/6	3			1	146		Four Winds And Seven Seas .... *Hal David/Don Rodney* <A:1>			Vic Damone
3/12	3			1	147		Powder Your Face With Sunshine (Smile! Smile! Smile!) .... *Carmen Lombardo/Stanley Rochinski*			Doris Day & Buddy Clark
10/8	3			1	148		Lingering Down The Lane .... *Jean Andre Brun/Charles Louis Clerc/Jack Lawrence* <B:25>			Paul Weston (Jud Conlon Singers)
2/12	1			1	149		Lavender Blue (Dilly Dilly) .... *Eliot Daniel/Larry Morey*	❶		Burl Ives with Captain Stubby & The Buccaneers

17

PEAK DATE	CH	10	5	PK	RANK	GOLD	Title			Artist
9/3	6			2	150		That's My Weakness Now .... *Bud Green/Sam Stept*			Russ Morgan
9/3	8			1	151		Did You See Jackie Robinson Hit That Ball? .... *Buddy Johnson*			Buddy Johnson (Ella Johnson)
4/23	6			1	152		You, You, You Are The One .... *Tetos Demey/Milton Leeds/Fred Wise* <A:1>			Russ Morgan (The Skylarks)
9/24	6			1	153		Let's Take An Old-Fashioned Walk .... *Irving Berlin*			Frank Sinatra & Doris Day
7/16	5			1	154		A Wonderful Guy .... *Oscar Hammerstein/Richard Rodgers*	❶		Fran Warren
2/5	4			1	155		Lavender Blue (Dilly Dilly) .... *Eliot Daniel/Larry Morey*			Jack Smith & The Clark Sisters
5/28	3			1	156		If You Stub Your Toe On The Moon .... *Johnny Burke/Jimmy Van Heusen*			Tony Martin
12/17	3			1	157		Slipping Around .... *Floyd Tillman*			Ernest Tubb
4/23	1			1	158		Similau (See-Me-Lo) .... *Arden Clar/Harry Coleman*			Peggy Lee

18

PEAK DATE	CH	10	5	PK	RANK	GOLD	Title			Artist
3/12	8			2	159		Beautiful Eyes .... *Frank Adams/Neal Madaglia/Leonard Rosen* <B:21>			Art Mooney
12/17	8			1	160		I Wanna Go Home (With You) .... *Jack Joyce* [N]			Perry Como (Fontane Sisters)
6/18	8			1	161		Merry-Go-Round Waltz .... *Arthur Finn/Jimmy Kennedy/Juventino Rosas*			Guy Lombardo (Kenny Gardner)
3/19	6			1	162		Powder Your Face With Sunshine (Smile! Smile! Smile!) .... *Carmen Lombardo/Stanley Rochinski* <A:1>			Blue Barron
7/23	5			1	163		You Told A Lie (I Believed You) .... *Teepee Mitchell/Lew Porter*	✦		Marjorie Hughes
7/9	5			1	164		Bali Ha'i .... *Oscar Hammerstein/Richard Rodgers* <A:6>			Frank Sinatra
3/12	3			1	165		Blue Room .... *Lorenz Hart/Richard Rodgers*			Perry Como
8/6	3			1	166		The Four Winds And The Seven Seas .... *Hal David/Don Rodney*	✦		Herb Jeffries
12/31	1			1	167		Merry Christmas Polka .... *Sonny Burke/Paul Francis Webster* [X]			Andrews Sisters & Guy Lombardo
12/31	1			1	168		My Two Front Teeth (All I Want for Christmas) .... *Don Gardner* [X-N-R]			Spike Jones (George Rock)

PEAK DATE	WEEKS				RANK	GOLD	Title	PEAK POSITION Songwriter(s)	SYMBL	DEBUT	Artist
	CH	10	5	PK							

19

3/12	7			2	169		Lady Of Spain	Tolchard Evans/Erell Reaves			Ray Noble (Al Bowlly)
9/24	10			1	170		You're Breaking My Heart	Pat Genaro/Sunny Skylar			Jan Garber (Bob Grabeau)
5/7	9			1	171		Everywhere You Go	Mark Fisher/Joe Goodwin/Larry Shay <A:8>			Guy Lombardo (Don Rodney)
5/21	6			1	172		Slaughter On Tenth Avenue (Parts 1 & 2)	Richard Rodgers [I]			Lennie Hayton
8/6	4			1	173		The Four Winds And The Seven Seas	Hal David/Don Rodney			Guy Lombardo (Don Rodney)
11/26	4			1	174		Toot, Toot, Tootsie (Good-Bye)	Ernie Erdman/Ted Fiorito/Gus Kahn/Robert King			Art Mooney
								<B:21>			
11/12	3			1	175		That Lucky Old Sun (Just Rolls Around Heaven All Day)	Haven Gillespie/Beasley Smith			Louis Armstrong
1/15	3			1	176		Sweet Sue, Just You	Will Harris/Victor Young			Johnny Long
4/16	3			1	177		Sunflower	Mack David			Ray McKinley (Jean Friley)
9/10	2			1	178		I'm Throwing Rice (At the Girl That I Love)	Eddy Arnold/Ed Nelson/Steve Nelson			Eddy Arnold
11/12	2			1	179		There's A Bluebird On Your Windowsill	Elizabeth Clarke			Doris Day
4/23	2			1	180		How It Lies, How It Lies, How It Lies!	Sonny Burke/Paul Francis Webster			Connie Haines
9/24	2			1	181		Dime A Dozen	Cindy Walker			Margaret Whiting
7/2	1			1	182		A Kiss And A Rose	Tommie Connor/Harold Green			The Charioteers

20

3/12	9			2	183		So In Love	Cole Porter			Gordon MacRae
3/5	5			2	184		Down By The Station	Slim Gaillard/Lee Ricks			Guy Lombardo (Lombardo Trio)
12/3	7			1	185		Why Was I Born?	Oscar Hammerstein/Jerome Kern			Vic Damone
10/1	7			1	186		(Where Are You) Now That I Need You	Frank Loesser			Doris Day
1/22	6			1	187		N'yot N'yow (The Pussycat Song)	Dick Manning			Perry Como (Fontane Sisters)
10/22	5			1	188		Now That I Need You	Frank Loesser			Frankie Laine
5/28	5			1	189		Barroom Polka	Vaughn Horton			Russ Morgan (The Rhythmaires)
4/30	5			1	190		Blue Moon	Lorenz Hart/Richard Rodgers <A:3>			Mel Tormé
10/22	5			1	191		Make Believe (You Are Glad When You're Sorry)	Benny Davis/Jack Shilkret			Sarah Vaughan
								<A:14>			
2/19	5			1	192		Deep Purple	Peter DeRose/Mitchell Parish [I]			Paul Weston
4/2	4			1	193		So In Love	Cole Porter			Dinah Shore
10/1	2			1	194		The Wedding Of Lili Marlene	Tommie Connor/Johnnie Reine <A:1>			Andrews Sisters
1/8	2			1	195		My Darling, My Darling	Frank Loesser	✦		Peter Hayes Lind
4/30	2			1	196		Candy Kisses	George Morgan			Eddy Howard
11/19	2			1	197		If I Ever Love Again	Russ Carlyle/Dick Reynolds			Jo Stafford
9/24	1			1	198		Maybe It's Because	Harry Ruby/Johnnie Scott			Connie Haines

21

4/9	5			2	199		Red Roses For A Blue Lady	Roy Brodsky/Sid Tepper			John Laurenz
8/20	3			2	200		Yes, Yes, In Your Eyes	Cliff Friend/Joseph Santly <A:4>			Eddy Howard
3/12	2			2	201		Doo De Doo On An Old Kazoo	Eddie Pola/Irving Taylor/George Wyle <A:18>			Art Mooney
5/28	6			1	202		Riders In The Sky (Cowboy Legend)	Stan Jones			Burl Ives
11/19	5			1	203 ●		Saturday Night Fish Fry (Parts I & II)	Louis Jordan/Ellis Walsh			Louis Jordan
4/2	3			1	204 ●		Blue Moon	Lorenz Hart/Richard Rodgers			Billy Eckstine
8/20	3			1	205		You're So Understanding	Ben Raleigh/Bernie Wayne <B:22>			Evelyn Knight
10/1	3			1	206		Room Full Of Roses	Tim Spencer			The Starlighters
11/19	2			1	207		'Way Back Home	Al Lewis/Tom Waring			Bing Crosby with Fred Waring
2/5	2			1	208		I've Been Waitin' For Your Phone Call For Eighteen Years (Maybe You Don't Love Me Anymore)	Chick Cohen/Fred Hillebrand [N]	✦		Beatrice Kay
7/16	1			1	209		Now! Now! Now! Is The Time	Bobby Burns/George Howe			Andrews Sisters - Russ Morgan
5/21	1			1	210		Careless Hands	Bob Hilliard/Carl Sigman	✦		Bob & Jeanne
9/24	1			1	211		Who Do You Know In Heaven (That Made You The Angel You Are?)	Peter DeRose/Al Stillman <A:6>			Ink Spots
11/19	1			1	212		I Never See Maggie Alone	Everett Lynton/Harry Tilsley <A:19>			Art Mooney (Tex Fletcher)
2/12	1			1	213		The Pussycat Song (Nyot Nyow)	Dick Manning [N]	✦		Joy Nichols & Benny Lee
2/5	1			1	214		It's Like Taking Candy From A Baby	Joel Cowan/Al Russell/Bob Russell			Tony Pastor (Rosemary Clooney)
4/2	1			1	215		You, You, You Are The One	Tetos Demey/Milton Leeds/Fred Wise			The Three Suns

22

12/31	3			2	216		Ave Maria	Franz Schubert <B:28> [X]			Perry Como
11/5	4			1	217		Don't Cry Joe (Let Her Go, Let Her Go, Let Her Go)	Joe Marsala	✦		Juanita Hall
10/29	4			1	218		Why Don't You Haul Off And Love Me	Lonnie Glosson/Wayne Raney	✦		Wayne Raney
10/15	3			1	219		Maybe It's Because	Harry Ruby/Johnnie Scott			Bob Crosby - Marion Morgan
8/13	3			1	220		A Wonderful Guy	Oscar Hammerstein/Richard Rodgers			Evelyn Knight
12/10	2			1	221		She Wore A Yellow Ribbon	Mark Ottner/Leroy Parker <A:15>			Andrews Sisters - Russ Morgan
6/18	2			1	222		It's Too Late Now	Fred Coots/Matt Furin/Tim Gayle <A:21>			Evelyn Knight
3/19	2			1	223		I've Got My Love To Keep Me Warm	Irving Berlin			Art Lund
6/25	2			1	224		A Wonderful Guy	Oscar Hammerstein/Richard Rodgers			Dinah Shore

1949

PEAK DATE	WEEKS				RANK	GOLD	Title	PEAK POSITION Songwriter(s)	SYMBL	DEBUT	Artist
	CH	10	5	PK							

22 (cont'd)

6/11	1			1	225		Everywhere You Go	Mark Fisher/Joe Goodwin/Larry Shay <A:2>			Doris Day
12/24	1			1	226		Don't Cry Joe (Let Her Go, Let Her Go, Let Her Go)	Joe Marsala			Johnny Desmond
12/17	1			1	227		Jealous Heart	Jenny Lou Carson			Jan Garber (Bob Grabeau)
3/19	1			1	228		Bouquet Of Roses	Bob Hilliard/Steve Nelson			Dick Haymes
8/20	1			1	229		Baby, It's Cold Outside	Frank Loesser [N]	❶		Homer & Jethro with June Carter

23

2/26	4			1	230		You, You, You Are The One	Tetos Demey/Milton Leeds/Fred Wise			Ames Brothers
4/9	3			1	231		For Ever And Ever	Malia Rosa/Franz Winkler			Gracie Fields
2/19	3			1	232		Again	Dorcas Cochran/Lionel Newman			Vera Lynn
5/21	3			1	233		Don't Be Afraid To Dream	Sylvia Hutton/Verlon Thompson <B:24>			Don Reid
3/19	2			1	234		Don't Rob Another Man's Castle	Jenny Lou Carson			Eddy Arnold
7/16	2			1	235		Just One Way To Say I Love You	Irving Berlin <A:15>			Perry Como
9/24	2			1	236		Give Me Your Hand	Dorothy Stewart			Perry Como
9/3	2			1	237		Reckon I'm In Love	Mack David/Al Hoffman/Jerry Livingston			Paul Weston (Pauline Byrns)
6/4	1			1	238		One Kiss Too Many	Eddy Arnold/Ed Nelson/Steve Nelson			Eddy Arnold
4/2	1			1	239		Clancy Lowered The Boom	Hy Heath/Johnny Lange			Dennis Day
3/26	1			1	240		Galway Bay	Arthur Colahan			Clark Dennis

24

4/2	5			3	241		Cruising Down The River	Eily Beadell/Nell Tollerton			The Three Suns
8/27	3			2	242		Circus	Louis Alter/Bob Russell			Tony Martin
10/22	6			1	243		Dime A Dozen	Cindy Walker			Sammy Kaye (The Kaydets)
3/26	5			1	244		Hurry! Hurry! Hurry!	Don Reid <A:23>	❶		Don Reid & the Peak-A-Boos
1/1	4			1	245		I'm Gonna Get You On A Slow Boat To China	Frank Loesser			Snooky Lanson
4/9	2			1	246		I Love You So Much It Hurts	Floyd Tillman			Buddy Clark
4/16	2			1	247		Ya Wanna Buy A Bunny?	Carl Hoefle/Del Porter [N]			Spike Jones (George Rock)
12/31	1			1	248		Here Comes Santa Claus (Down Santa Claus Lane)	Gene Autry/ Oakley Haldeman [X-R]			Gene Autry
12/24	1			1	249		Sleigh Ride	Leroy Anderson [X-I]			Boston Pops Orch./Arthur Fiedler
12/3	1			1	250		Fool's Paradise	Bob Merrill			Billy Eckstine
4/23	1			1	251		Love Me! Love Me! Love Me!	Frank Anderson/Viviane Greene/Lenny LeMarre			Eddy Howard
12/31	1			1	252		Who'll Be The Next One (To Cry Over You)	Johnny Black			Mills Brothers
5/14	1			1	253 ●		Lovesick Blues	Cliff Friend/Irving Mills/Hank Williams	❶		Hank Williams

25

9/3	2			2	254		Somehow	Mort Maser			Billy Eckstine
3/26	4			1	255		It's A Big, Wide, Wonderful World	John Rox			Buddy Clark
3/19	3			1	256		Be Mine	Harold Fields/Desmond O'Connor	❶		Anne Shelton
11/12	2			1	257		I Know, I Know, I Know	Bronislau Kaper/Bob Russell <A:16>			Paul Weston (Jud Conlon Singers)
7/2	1			1	258		Whose Girl Are You	Joseph Durlak/Albert Gamse			Blue Barron
10/29	1			1	259		Tell Me Why	Milt Gabler/Maurie Hartmann <A:9>			Eddy Howard
10/29	1			1	260		Room Full Of Roses	Tim Spencer	✦		George Morgan

26

8/20	2			1	261		Room Full Of Roses	Tim Spencer			Sons of the Pioneers
2/12	2			1	262		The Pussy Cat Song (Nyow! Nyot Nyow!)	Dick Manning [N]			Jo Stafford & Gordon MacRae
12/31	2			1	263		Blue Christmas	Billy Hayes/Jay Johnson [X]			Ernest Tubb
12/17	2			1	264		A Dreamer's Holiday	Kim Gannon/Mabel Wayne	❶		Eileen Wilson & Gordon Jenkins
12/3	1			1	265		Toot, Toot, Tootsie (Good-Bye)	Ernie Erdman/Ted Fiorito/Gus Kahn/Robert King [N]			Mel Blanc
10/1	1			1	266		You're Breaking My Heart	Pat Genaro/Sunny Skylar	✦		Russ Case (Quintones)
9/24	1			1	267		Circus	Louis Alter/Bob Russell	❶		Bill Farrell
8/20	1			1	268		Beautiful Wisconsin	Don Fina			Ken Griffin (Johnny Hill)
8/27	1			1	269		Drinkin' Wine Spo-Dee-O-Dee	Stick McGhee			"Stick" McGhee
9/3	1			1	270		I'll Keep The Love Light Burning (In My Heart)	Bennie Benjamin/George Weiss			Patti Page
2/19	1			1	271		I've Got My Love To Keep Me Warm	Irving Berlin	❶		The Starlighters
1/29	1			1	272		My Darling, My Darling	Frank Loesser			Eve Young & Jack Lathrop

27

8/6	3			2	273		Crying	Jay Chernis/Barney Ross			Billy Eckstine
11/26	2			1	274		My Hero	Stanislaus Stange/Oskar Straus [I]			Ralph Flanagan
3/12	2			1	275		Galway Bay	Arthur Colahan			Anne Shelton
4/23	1			1	276		If You Stub Your Toe On The Moon	Johnny Burke/Jimmy Van Heusen			Bing Crosby
1/1	1			1	277		Cuanto Le Gusta	Ray Gilbert/Gabriel Ruiz [I]			Xavier Cugat
3/5	1			1	278		Bewildered	Teddy Powell/Leonard Whitcup			Billy Eckstine
9/24	1			1	279		Body And Soul	Frank Eyton/John Green/Edward Heyman/Robert Sour			Billy Eckstine

PEAK DATE	WEEKS				RANK	GOLD	Title	PEAK POSITION	SYMBL	DEBUT	Artist
	CH	10	5	PK				Songwriter(s)			

27 (cont'd)

4/23	1			1	280 ●		Caravan	Duke Ellington/Irving Mills/Juan Tizol			Billy Eckstine
11/19	1			1	281		That Lucky Old Sun (Just Rolls Around Heaven All Day)	Haven Gillespie/Beasley Smith	✦		Bob Houston
5/7	1			1	282		"A" You're Adorable (The Alphabet Song)	Buddy Kaye/Sid Lippman/Fred Wise	✦		Buddy Kaye Quintet (Artie Malvin)
3/12	1			1	283		Blum Blum (I Wonder Who I Am)	Dave Barbour/Peggy Lee [N]			Peggy Lee
4/23	1			1	284		Money, Marbles And Chalk	Pop Eckler			Patti Page
3/12	1			1	285		Cruising Down The River	Eily Beadell/Nell Tollerton			Primo Scala with The Keynotes

28

12/17	2			1	286		The Lord's Prayer	Albert Hay Malotte <A:22> [X]			Perry Como
1/8	1			1	287		Bella Bella Marie	Don Pelosi/Leo Towers/Gerhard Winkler			Jan Garber (Tim Reardon)
4/30	1			1	288		Sunflower	Mack David	✦		Jack Kilty
7/16	1			1	289		Some Enchanted Evening	Oscar Hammerstein/Richard Rodgers			John Laurenz
1/29	1			1	290		Here I'll Stay	Alan Jay Lerner/Kurt Weill <A:13>			Jo Stafford
5/28	1			1	291		How It Lies, How It Lies, How It Lies	Sonny Burke/Paul Francis Webster			Kay Starr

29

4/16	1			1	292		Cruising Down The River	Eily Beadell/Nell Tollerton			Ames Brothers
4/2	1			1	293		Cruising Down The River	Eily Beadell/Nell Tollerton			Helen Carroll
9/17	1			1	294		There's Yes! Yes! In Your Eyes	Cliff Friend/Joseph Santly			Carmen Cavallaro
4/30	1			1	295		You, You, You Are The One	Tetos Demey/Milton Leeds/Fred Wise [I]			Ken Griffin
6/4	1			1	296		Red Head	Dick Rogers/Nat Simon			Eddy Howard
5/28	1			1	297		Kiss Me Sweet	Milton Drake			Sammy Kaye (Laura Leslie/Don Cornell)
8/13	1			1	298		Be Goody Good Good To Me	Hy Heath/Johnny Lange/Dick Loring			Evelyn Knight
12/31	1			1	299		You're All I Want For Christmas	Seger Ellis/Glen Moore [X-R]			Frankie Laine
4/16	1			1	300		I Didn't Like It The First Time (The Spinach Song)	Johnny Gomez/Bill Gordon [N]			Julia Lee
11/5	1			1	301		Vieni Su (Say You Love Me Too)	Johnny Cola			Vaughn Monroe
6/4	1			1	302		Merry-Go-Round Waltz	Arthur Finn/Jimmy Kennedy/Juventino Rosas			Art Mooney

30

1/29	3			3	303		More Beer!	Julian Miller			Andrews Sisters
5/7	1			1	304		I'm Bitin' My Fingernails And Thinking Of You	Ernest Benedict/Lenny Sanders/Ernest Tubb/Roy West			Andrews Sisters & Ernest Tubb
1/8	1			1	305		Then I Turned And Walked Slowly Away	Red Fortner <A:23>			Eddy Arnold
4/30	1			1	306		Kiss Me Sweet	Milton Drake	❶		Kitty Kallen
10/15	1			1	307		Homecoming Waltz	Alex Kramer/Joan Whitney <A:30>			Guy Lombardo (Lombardo Quartet)
6/11	1			1	308		Need You	Johnny Blackburn/Teepee Mitchell/Lew Porter			Guy Lombardo (Kenny Gardner)
10/22	1			1	309		The Blue Skirt Waltz	Vaclav Blaha/Mitchell Parish <A:30>			Guy Lombardo (Lombardo Quartet)
5/7	1			1	310		Five Foot Two, Eyes Of Blue	Ray Henderson/Sam Lewis/Joe Young			Benny Strong
10/22	1			1	311		Wedding Bells	Claude Boone <A:1>			Margaret Whiting & Jimmy Wakely

1950

NATIONAL NEWS: Former State Department official Alger Hiss is sentenced to five years in prison for perjury in denying that he passed government secrets to then-Communist agent Whittaker Chambers. Sen. Joseph McCarthy launches his campaign of unsubstantiated attacks on alleged Communists in the U.S. government. President Truman escapes injury in an assassination attempt by Puerto Rican nationalists. Sen. Estes Kefauver's committee launches a 15-month investigation into organized crime with nationally televised hearings. The U.S. population reaches 150 million.

INTERNATIONAL NEWS: North Korean forces cross the 38th Parallel to invade South Korea, and after a swift advance are met with a strong United Nations counterattack (labeled a "police action" by President Truman) led by Gen. Douglas MacArthur. But in November, Chinese Communist forces enter the war in support of North Korea.

COMMERCE AND SCIENCE: President Truman dedicates the Grand Coulee Dam. Diners Club introduces the first credit card. The first photocopying machines to use xerography are manufactured by the Haloid Company.

FADS AND FASHION: *Hopalong Cassidy* is not only a children's television hit, but draws 300,000 fans in public appearances and sells thousands of cowboy hats and other merchandise.

SPORTS: The New York Yankees overwhelm the Philadelphia Phillies in a four-game World Series sweep. The NFL title game is a tense 30-28 win for the Cleveland Browns over the Los Angeles Rams. Oklahoma is #1 in college football. The Minneapolis Lakers, led by towering George Mikan, repeat as NBA champions. Community College of New York is the surprise NCAA basketball champ. After recovering from a near-fatal car accident, golfer Ben Hogan wins the U.S. Open. Golfer Babe Didrickson Zaharias is named female athlete of the year.

MOVIES: *All About Eve* is the Oscar winner for Best Picture. Other top honorees are Judy Holiday (*Born Yesterday*) and Jose Ferrer (*Cyrano de Bergerac*). Billy Wilder's *Sunset Boulevard* starring William Holden and Gloria Swanson is an instant classic, as is *Harvey* with James Stewart. Box office hits include *King Solomon's Mines*, Irving Berlin's *Annie Get Your Gun*, *Cheaper By the Dozen*, *Father of the Bride* with Spencer Tracy and young Elizabeth Taylor, and Disney's *Cinderella*.

TELEVISION: One of the gems in TV's so-called Golden Age, *Your Show of Shows*, introduces viewers to the comic genius of Sid Ceasar and Imogene Coca. Groucho Marx makes the crossover to TV in *You Bet Your Life*, as do reigning king of radio Jack Benny in *The Jack Benny Program* and his friends George Burns and Gracie Allen.

THEATER: Frank Loesser's *Guys and Dolls* starring Robert Alda (Alan's dad) is a Broadway musical landmark. Carol Channing is incandescent in *Gentlemen Prefer Blondes*. Ethel Merman strikes again in Irving Berlin's *Call Me Madam*. *Come Back, Little Sheba* is the year's top drama.

BOOKS: Ray Bradbury's *The Martian Chronicles* is a sci-fi classic. *The Lonely Crowd* by David Riesman wins acclaim as a modern sociological study.

1950 — TOP 20 ARTISTS

1. Bing Crosby
1,110

2. Guy Lombardo
860

3. Ralph Flanagan
657

4.	613	**Gordon Jenkins**
5.	604	**Ames Brothers**
6.	590	**Patti Page**
7.	575	**Andrews Sisters**
8.	573	**Ray Anthony**
9.	565	**Perry Como**
10.	545	**Jo Stafford**
11.	537	**Red Foley**
12.	510	**Frankie Laine**
13.	489	**Sammy Kaye**
14.	487	**Hugo Winterhalter**
15.	469	**Kay Starr**
16.	434	**Nat "King" Cole**
17.	426	**Frank Sinatra**
18.	420	**Margaret Whiting**
19.	404	**Tony Martin**
20.	403	**Russ Morgan**

1950 — TOP SONGWRITERS

	# of Hits	Points	
1.	12	991	**Mack David**
2.	11	966	**Al Hoffman**
3.	11	912	**Bennie Benjamin**
	11	912	**George Weiss**
5.	10	881	**Bob Hilliard**
6.	10	855	**Ray Evans**
	10	855	**Jay Livingston**
8.	9	809	**Sammy Fain**
9.	9	790	**Lorenz Hart**
	9	790	**Richard Rodgers**
	9	790	**Frank Loesser**
12.	8	748	**Bert Kalmar**
	8	748	**Harry Ruby**

1950 — TOP ARTIST DEBUTS

1.	2/04	**Teresa Brewer** (63) ★
2.	3/11	**Eileen Barton** (128)
3.	3/25	**Georgia Gibbs** (67) ★
4.	6/03	**Percy Faith** (84)
5.	6/03	**The Fontane Sisters** ★
6.	6/17	**Dinah Washington** ★
7.	7/01	**The Weavers** (64)
8.	7/15	**Mitch Miller** ★
9.	7/15	**Hank Snow** ◆
10.	12/09 †	**Guy Mitchell** (53) ★
11.	12/16	**Mario Lanza** (119)

PEAK DATE	CH	10	5	PK	RANK	GOLD	Title / PEAK POSITION / Songwriter(s)	SYMBL	DEBUT	Artist

1

1 ● **The Tennessee Waltz** .... *Pee Wee King/Redd Stewart* — **Patti Page**
PEAK DATE 12/16 | CH 26 | 10 21 | 5 19 | PK 13 | RANK 1
Juke Box: 12,4,2,1,2,2,1,1,1,1,1,1,1,1,1,1,2,4,6,7,12,17,28,-,29
Best Seller: 27,8,3,2,2,2,1,1,1,1,1,1,1,1,2,4,3,4,7,10,13,18,20,29
Disc Jockey: 11,6,2,2,2,2,1,1,1,1,1,1,1,1,2,2,3,6,7,14,21,17

2 ● **Goodnight Irene** .... *Huddie Ledbetter/John Lomax* <B:2> — **Gordon Jenkins & The Weavers**
PEAK DATE 8/19 | CH 25 | 10 20 | 5 19 | PK 13 | RANK 2
Best Seller: 25,17,8,5,2,2,1,1,1,1,1,1,1,1,1,1,2,4,7,13,18,30
Juke Box: 17,15,5,3,2,2,1,1,1,1,1,1,1,1,1,1,1,2,3,3,10,23,29
Disc Jockey: 19,5,3,2,2,2,2,1,1,1,1,1,1,1,5,7,4,9,21,22

3 ● **"The Third Man" Theme** .... *Anton Karas* [I] ✦ — **Anton Karas**
PEAK DATE 4/29 | CH 27 | 10 20 | 5 17 | PK 11 | RANK 3
Best Seller: 28,23,12,7,3,3,2,1,1,1,1,1,1,1,1,1,1,2,2,3,7,7,11,19,20,11
Disc Jockey: 25,26,-,15,19,6,4,5,8,5,6,6,4,8,11,7,17,25
Juke Box: 11,9,4,5,6,5,12,5,13,6,8,11,7,13

4 ● **The 3rd Man Theme** .... *Anton Karas* [I] — **Guy Lombardo**
PEAK DATE 5/6 | CH 27 | 10 20 | 5 17 | PK 11 | RANK 4
Juke Box: 21,15,19,13,9,8,5,2,1,1,1,1,1,1,1,1,1,1,3,3,4,4,8,14,15,14
Best Seller: 16,21,22,7,11,5,5,3,4,2,2,2,2,2,2,3,5,4,7,8,14,12,21,22,17,17
Disc Jockey: 27,-,-,26,6,4,3,4,5,12,7,7,9,10,14,6,14,17,23,-,23

5 ● **If I Knew You Were Comin'** (I'd've Baked A Cake) .... *Al Hoffman/Bob Merrill/Clem Watts* ❶ — **Eileen Barton**
PEAK DATE 3/25 | CH 16 | 10 13 | 5 12 | PK 10 | RANK 5
Disc Jockey: 13,4,1,1,1,1,1,1,1,1,1,1,2,11,24,25
Juke Box: 13,10,4,3,3,1,1,1,2,2,2,2,3,7,21
Best Seller: 9,8,3,2,2,1,1,2,2,2,6,9,12,22,21

6 ● **Mona Lisa** .... *Ray Evans/Jay Livingston* — **Nat "King" Cole**
PEAK DATE 7/8 | CH 27 | 10 22 | 5 21 | PK 8 | RANK 6
Disc Jockey: 23,14,14,4,1,1,1,1,1,1,1,1,2,2,2,2,2,2,3,2,3,5,8,26,23
Best Seller: 14,14,9,5,2,1,1,1,1,1,2,2,2,2,2,2,2,2,2,3,3,10,12,16,26
Juke Box: 19,18,10,3,2,1,1,1,1,1,2,2,2,2,3,2,3,2,2,2,3,4,5,13,22,29

7 ● **Chattanoogie Shoe Shine Boy** .... *Jack Stapp/Harry Stone* <B:24> — **Red Foley**
PEAK DATE 2/11 | CH 16 | 10 15 | 5 12 | PK 8 | RANK 7
Juke Box: 7,3,1,1,1,1,1,1,1,1,2,3,3,6,8,15
Best Seller: 20,10,5,2,1,1,1,1,2,2,3,4,6,7,17
Disc Jockey: 28,9,5,3,2,1,1,3,3,4,5,5,10,10,30

8 ● **I Can Dream, Can't I?** .... *Sammy Fain/Irving Kahal* <B:20> — **Andrews Sisters**
PEAK DATE 1/7 | CH 25 | 10 20 | 5 16 | PK 5 | RANK 8
Disc Jockey: 16,11,7,5,4,5,4,5,2,2,2,1,1,1,1,2,4,9,11,18
Best Seller: 21,19,13,6,6,4,3,2,4,4,2,2,2,2,3,1,1,1,1,4,7,8,19,28
Juke Box: 24,-,16,19,16,6,7,4,3,3,4,3,3,3,3,2,2,1,1,1,3,4,5,10,19

9 ● **All My Love (Bolero)** .... *Henri Contet/Paul Durand/Mitchell Parish* — **Patti Page**
PEAK DATE 10/28 | CH 23 | 10 18 | 5 12 | PK 5 | RANK 9
Disc Jockey: 15,9,7,6,10,5,4,3,2,1,1,1,1,3,4,5,7,7,22,16,20
Juke Box: 17,19,-,14,15,7,9,9,9,9,8,4,3,2,2,4,5,5,10,10,13,18,26,29
Best Seller: 23,17,13,18,7,7,8,8,7,4,5,5,2,4,7,6,11,21,20,24,22,30

10 ● **The Thing** .... *Charles Green* [N] — **Phil Harris**
PEAK DATE 12/2 | CH 15 | 10 12 | 5 11 | PK 5 | RANK 10
Disc Jockey: 2,1,1,1,1,1,2,2,3,3,10,10,18
Best Seller: 5,1,1,1,1,2,2,2,2,3,4,6,13,14
Juke Box: 17,6,3,2,1,1,2,2,3,3,3,6,13,25

11 **Harbor Lights** .... *Will Grosz/Jimmy Kennedy* — **Sammy Kaye** (Tony Alamo)
PEAK DATE 11/18 | CH 27 | 10 19 | 5 15 | PK 4 | RANK 11
Juke Box: 14,16,9,11,7,7,5,4,4,2,1,1,1,1,3,3,3,3,4,4,4,4,7,11,17,18,20,19
Best Seller: 30,26,12,9,8,9,6,3,2,2,1,1,2,3,3,3,5,5,6,5,6,12,10,27,26
Disc Jockey: 26,27,9,9,5,3,4,2,2,3,2,4,5,4,4,13,11,13,18,18

12 ● **Music! Music! Music!** .... *Bernie Baum/Stephan Weiss* ❶ — **Teresa Brewer**
PEAK DATE 3/18 | CH 17 | 10 14 | 5 12 | PK 4 | RANK 12
Best Seller: 11,6,2,2,2,2,1,1,1,1,2,3,3,5,8,14,25
Disc Jockey: 26,11,8,7,8,2,2,3,2,2,3,3,7
Juke Box: 5,4,4,2,2,2,2,1,2,2,3,4,6,19,26

13 **I Wanna Be Loved** .... *John Green/Edward Heyman/Billy Rose* — **Andrews Sisters**
PEAK DATE 6/24 | CH 21 | 10 15 | 5 11 | PK 2 | RANK 13
Disc Jockey: 22,14,13,14,19,7,1,1,2,2,2,2,3,5,8,11,12,25,26
Juke Box: 26,19,17,12,5,6,3,2,2,3,2,2,2,3,5,6,5,7,8,19,-,18
Best Seller: 18,12,12,9,10,6,3,4,4,3,3,4,6,6,6,7,7,13,21,25

14 ● **Rag Mop** .... *Deacon Anderson/Johnnie Lee Wills* — **Ames Brothers**
PEAK DATE 2/11 | CH 14 | 10 10 | 5 9 | PK 2 | RANK 14
Disc Jockey: 18,10,2,1,1,2,4,5,8,12,23,20
Best Seller: 17,14,9,3,1,3,3,3,5,6,7,10,13,27
Juke Box: 24,21,7,4,2,2,3,3,3,3,5,5,17

15 ● **The Cry Of The Wild Goose** .... *Terry Gilkyson* — **Frankie Laine**
PEAK DATE 3/11 | CH 11 | 10 10 | 5 9 | PK 2 | RANK 15
Disc Jockey: 7,3,3,2,1,1,2,4,4,4,21
Best Seller: 11,5,4,4,4,4,8,9,11,23,21
Juke Box: 17,8,8,5,4,4,4,6,7,13,13

16 **Hoop-Dee-Doo** .... *Milton DeLugg/Frank Loesser* <B:16> — **Perry Como** (Fontane Sisters)
PEAK DATE 6/3 | CH 17 | 10 12 | 5 8 | PK 2 | RANK 16
Disc Jockey: 16,7,6,3,4,1,2,1,2,5,5,15,18,19,16,24
Best Seller: 28,13,9,9,10,7,4,4,4,6,5,10,7,15,14,17,25
Juke Box: 24,9,10,10,8,6,4,5,4,4,4,6,11,6,10,11,11,25

17 ● **Sentimental Me** .... *Jimmy Cassin/Jim Morehead* — **Ames Brothers**
PEAK DATE 6/10 | CH 27 | 10 21 | 5 11 | PK 1 | RANK 17
Disc Jockey: 24,27,14,13,13,9,13,8,4,7,5,3,4,2,4,1,3,4,2,9,6,4,7,14,17,24
Juke Box: 16,25,14,23,9,9,6,8,10,9,7,7,4,4,4,2,2,2,3,4,5,4,6,6,9,21
Best Seller: 30,22,26,24,13,13,11,11,9,9,9,7,5,7,5,3,5,5,6,3,9,4,9,18,16,18,16

PEAK DATE	CH	10	5	PK	RANK	GOLD	Title	PEAK POSITION Songwriter(s)	SYMBL	DEBUT	Artist

2

PEAK DATE	CH	10	5	PK	RANK	GOLD	Title	Songwriter(s)	SYMBL/DEBUT	Artist
4/15	24	18	11	6	18		It Isn't Fair	Richard Himber/Sylvester Sprigato/Frank Warshauer		Sammy Kaye (Don Cornell)
1/28	17	13	9	4	19	●	Dear Hearts And Gentle People	Sammy Fain/Bob Hilliard <B:4>		Bing Crosby
9/23	19	16	14	2	20		Play A Simple Melody	Irving Berlin <B:3> [N]		Gary Crosby & Friend [Bing Crosby]
2/4	27	16	10	1	21		There's No Tomorrow	Leon Carr/Leo Corday/Al Hoffman		Tony Martin
7/29	17	13	9	1	22		Tzena Tzena Tzena	Gordon Jenkins/Spencer Ross <A:1>	❶	Gordon Jenkins & The Weavers
11/4	18	13	7	1	23		Nevertheless (I'm In Love With You)	Bert Kalmar/Harry Ruby		Paul Weston (Norman Luboff Choir)
6/17	16	10	7	1	24		Hoop-Dee-Doo	Milton DeLugg/Frank Loesser		Kay Starr
11/25	20	12	5	1	25		Harbor Lights	Will Grosz/Jimmy Kennedy <B:22>		Guy Lombardo (Kenny Gardner)
1/28	12	7	2	1	26		The Old Master Painter	Haven Gillespie/Beasley Smith	❶	Richard Hayes
1/28	18	10	1	1	27		Dear Hearts And Gentle People	Sammy Fain/Bob Hilliard		Dinah Shore

3

PEAK DATE	CH	10	5	PK	RANK	GOLD	Title	Songwriter(s)	SYMBL/DEBUT	Artist
8/12	19	17	14	5	28		Sam's Song (The Happy Tune)	Jack Elliott/Lew Quadling <A:2> [N]		Gary Crosby & Friend [Bing Crosby]
12/9	18	12	6	3	29		A Bushel And A Peck	Frank Loesser [N]		Perry Como & Betty Hutton
6/17	19	13	5	1	30	●	Bewitched	Lorenz Hart/Richard Rodgers [I]	✦	Bill Snyder
11/18	20	12	5	1	31		I'll Never Be Free	Bennie Benjamin/George Weiss <B:22>		Kay Starr & Tennessee Ernie
1/21	19	13	4	1	32		A Dreamer's Holiday	Kim Gannon/Mabel Wayne		Perry Como (Fontane Sisters)
7/22	12	7	4	1	33		Tzena Tzena Tzena	Gordon Jenkins/Spencer Ross	❶	Mitch Miller
12/30	7	5	4	1	34	●	Rudolph, The Red-Nosed Reindeer	Johnny Marks [X-R]		Gene Autry
6/10	23	13	3	1	35		My Foolish Heart	Ned Washington/Victor Young		Gordon Jenkins (Sandy Evans)
2/4	13	11	3	1	36		I Said My Pajamas (And Put on My Pray'rs)	Eddie Pola/George Wyle		Tony Martin & Fran Warren
3/4	10	7	2	1	37		Rag Mop	Deacon Anderson/Johnnie Lee Wills		Ralph Flanagan

4

PEAK DATE	CH	10	5	PK	RANK	GOLD	Title	Songwriter(s)	SYMBL/DEBUT	Artist
12/16	17	13	9	3	38		Nevertheless (I'm In Love With You)	Bert Kalmar/Harry Ruby		Mills Brothers
7/15	18	11	7	2	39		Bewitched	Lorenz Hart/Richard Rodgers		Gordon Jenkins (Bonnie Lou Williams)
9/23	27	17	4	2	40		Bonaparte's Retreat	Pee Wee King		Kay Starr
7/15	21	7	2	1	41		Count Every Star	Bruno Coquatrix/Sammy Gallop		Ray Anthony (Dick Noel)
3/11	13	10	5	1	42		Chattanoogie Shoe Shine Boy	Jack Stapp/Harry Stone		Bing Crosby
12/9	21	12	3	1	43		Thinking Of You	Bert Kalmar/Harry Ruby		Don Cherry
1/28	13	7	3	1	44		The Old Master Painter	Haven Gillespie/Beasley Smith		Dick Haymes
11/18	17	8	2	1	45		Harbor Lights	Will Grosz/Jimmy Kennedy <B:9>		Ray Anthony (Ronnie Deauville)
2/4	7	1	1	1	46		Bamboo	Buddy Bernier/Nat Simon		Vaughn Monroe

5

PEAK DATE	CH	10	5	PK	RANK	GOLD	Title	Songwriter(s)	SYMBL/DEBUT	Artist
10/28	19	15	3	3	47		Can Anyone Explain? (No, No, No!)	Bennie Benjamin/George Weiss		Ames Brothers
4/29	14	7	2	2	48		Dearie	Bob Hilliard/Dave Mann		Guy Lombardo (Kenny Gardner)
10/14	13	8	1	1	49		Can Anyone Explain	Bennie Benjamin/George Weiss		Ray Anthony (Ronnie Deauville/The Skyliners)
11/11	17	7	1	1	50		Harbor Lights	Will Grosz/Jimmy Kennedy [I]		Ralph Flanagan
5/6	15	7	1	1	51		Daddy's Little Girl	Bobby Burke/Horace Gerlach		Mills Brothers
9/2	12	7	1	1	52		Goodnight Irene	Huddie Ledbetter/John Lomax		Frank Sinatra
12/16	18	4	1	1	53		Thinking Of You	Bert Kalmar/Harry Ruby		Eddie Fisher
11/4	14	4	1	1	54		Orange Colored Sky	Milton DeLugg/Willie Stein		Nat "King" Cole & Stan Kenton
5/27	12	4	1	1	55		Roses	Glenn Spencer/Tim Spencer		Sammy Kaye (The Kaydets)
4/15	10	4	1	1	56		(Put Another Nickel in) Music! Music! Music!	Bernie Baum/Stephan Weiss		Freddy Martin (Merv Griffin)
4/15	9	3	1	1	57		(Put Another Nickel In) Music! Music! Music!	Bernie Baum/Stephan Weiss		Carmen Cavallaro (Bob Lido/The Cavaliers)
4/15	5	3	1	1	58	●	Peter Cottontail {re-charted in 1951 (#19)}	Steve Nelson/Jack Rollins		Gene Autry
4/22	11	2	1	1	59		If I Knew You Were Comin' I'd've Baked A Cake	Al Hoffman/Bob Merrill/Clem Watts	❶	Georgia Gibbs

6

PEAK DATE	CH	10	5	PK	RANK	GOLD	Title	Songwriter(s)	SYMBL/DEBUT	Artist
12/16	15	4		2	60		A Bushel And A Peck	Frank Loesser		Margaret Whiting & Jimmy Wakely
6/3	19	9		1	61	●	My Foolish Heart	Ned Washington/Victor Young		Billy Eckstine
3/18	17	6		1	62		Quicksilver	Eddie Pola/Irving Taylor/George Wyle		Bing Crosby & Andrews Sisters
2/4	23	2		1	63		Johnson Rag	Guy Hall/Henry Kleinkauf/Jack Lawrence	✦	Jack Teter Trio
5/6	11	2		1	64		My Foolish Heart	Ned Washington/Victor Young <B:12>		Mindy Carson

7

PEAK DATE	CH	10	5	PK	RANK	GOLD	Title	Songwriter(s)	SYMBL/DEBUT	Artist
6/24	15	7		2	65		Sentimental Me	Jimmy Cassin/Jim Morehead		Ray Anthony (Ronnie Deauville)
8/5	11	5		2	66		Tzena, Tzena, Tzena	Gordon Jenkins/Spencer Ross		Vic Damone
3/4	10	3		2	67		Rag Mop	Deacon Anderson/Johnnie Lee Wills		Lionel Hampton (The Hamptones)
6/10	12	3		1	68		Sentimental Me	Jimmy Cassin/Jim Morehead		Russ Morgan
9/30	9	5		1	69		Cincinnati Dancing Pig	Al Lewis/Guy Wood		Red Foley
1/28	14	4		1	70		I Can Dream, Can't I?	Sammy Fain/Irving Kahal		Toni Arden with Hugo Winterhalter

PEAK DATE	CH	10	5	PK	RANK	GOLD	Title / PEAK POSITION (Songwriter(s))	SYMBOL / DEBUT	Artist

7 (cont'd)

PEAK DATE	CH	10	5	PK	RANK	GOLD	Title (Songwriter(s))	SYM	Artist
7/15	15	3		1	71		I Wanna Be Loved .... John Green/Edward Heyman/Billy Rose		Billy Eckstine
8/26	13	3		1	72		Sam's Song .... Jack Elliott/Lew Quadling ❶		Joe "Fingers" Carr
2/18	10	2		1	73		Johnson Rag .... Guy Hall/Henry Kleinkauf/Jack Lawrence		Russ Morgan
9/30	15	1		1	74		Mona Lisa .... Ray Evans/Jay Livingston <B:22>		Victor Young & Don Cherry
11/18	12	1		1	75		Patricia.. Benny Davis		Perry Como
10/21	11	1		1	76		All My Love .... Henri Contet/Paul Durand/Mitchell Parish		Percy Faith
12/2	8	1		1	77		Oh, Babe .... Milton Kabak/Louis Prima		Kay Starr
12/30	6	1		1	78	●	Frosty The Snow Man .... Steve Nelson/Jack Rollins [X]		Gene Autry
12/30	3	1		1	79		Rudolph The Red-Nosed Reindeer .... Johnny Marks [X-N]		Spike Jones (Rudolph)
							{re-charted in 1951 (#22)}		

8

PEAK DATE	CH	10	5	PK	RANK	GOLD	Title (Songwriter(s))	SYM	Artist
12/16	13	3		2	80		Harbor Lights .... Will Grosz/Jimmy Kennedy <B:26>		Bing Crosby
7/8	12	3		1	81		Bewitched .... Lorenz Hart/Richard Rodgers		Mel Tormé
4/8	6	3		1	82	●	Peter Cottontail .... Steve Nelson/Jack Rollins ✦		Mervin Shiner
7/15	12	2		1	83		Bewitched.. Lorenz Hart/Richard Rodgers [I]		Jan August & Jerry Murad's Harmonicats
9/9	11	2		1	84		No Other Love .... Bob Russell/Paul Weston <B:27>		Jo Stafford
7/22	9	2		1	85		I Don't Care If The Sun Don't Shine .... Mack David		Patti Page
4/1	7	2		1	86		Go To Sleep, Go To Sleep, Go To Sleep ..... Sammy Cahn/Fred Spielman [N]		Mary Martin & Arthur Godfrey
3/11	6	2		1	87		Chattanoogie Shoe-Shine Boy .... Jack Stapp/Harry Stone [N]		Phil Harris

9

PEAK DATE	CH	10	5	PK	RANK	GOLD	Title (Songwriter(s))	SYM	Artist
8/5	17	4		3	88		Nola .... Felix Arndt [I]		Les Paul
2/25	11	3		2	89		Rag Mop .... Deacon Anderson/Johnnie Lee Wills ✦		Johnnie Lee Wills
11/18	11	2		2	90		To Think You've Chosen Me...................... Bennie Benjamin/George Weiss		Eddy Howard
8/26	17	2		1	91		La Vie En Rose .... Mack David/Luis Guglielmi/Edith Piaf		Tony Martin
7/1	15	2		1	92		Bewitched....................................... Lorenz Hart/Richard Rodgers		Doris Day
10/7	7	2		1	93		Mr. Touchdown, U. S. A. .... William Katz/Gene Piller/Ruth Roberts		Hugo Winterhalter
12/23	16	1		1	94		One Finger Melody .... Kermit Goell/Al Hoffman/Fred Spielman		Frank Sinatra
9/2	15	1		1	95		Bonaparte's Retreat .... Pee Wee King (Bobby Soots)		Gene Krupa
11/25	14	1		1	96		Nevertheless .... Bert Kalmar/Harry Ruby <B:13>		Ralph Flanagan (Harry Prime)
12/9	14	1		1	97		Nevertheless (I'm In Love With You)............. Bert Kalmar/Harry Ruby <A:4>		Ray Anthony (Ronnie Deauville)
9/23	7	1		1	98		Goodnight, Irene .... Huddie Ledbetter/John Lomax		Jo Stafford
1/14	7	1		1	99		The Old Master Painter .... Haven Gillespie/Beasley Smith		Peggy Lee & Mel Tormé
12/30	1	1		1	100		Frosty The Snow Man .... Steve Nelson/Jack Rollins [X-N]		Nat "King" Cole

10

PEAK DATE	CH	10	5	PK	RANK	GOLD	Title (Songwriter(s))	SYM	Artist
9/23	12	4		4	101		Our Lady Of Fatima .... Gladys Gollahon		Richard Hayes & Kitty Kallen
10/21	15	3		3	102		All My Love ("Bolero") .... Henri Contet/Paul Durand/Mitchell Parish		Guy Lombardo (Bill Flanagan)
4/8	11	3		3	103		Dearie... Bob Hilliard/Dave Mann		Jo Stafford & Gordon MacRae
2/25	7	3		3	104		Chattanoogie Shoe Shine Boy .... Jack Stapp/Harry Stone <B:25>		Frank Sinatra
8/12	20	2		2	105		Count Every Star .... Bruno Coquatrix/Sammy Gallop		Hugo Winterhalter
10/7	10	2		2	106		I'm Forever Blowing Bubbles........................ John Kellette/Jean Kenbrovin		Gordon Jenkins & Artie Shaw
8/26	10	2		2	107		Goodnight Irene .... Huddie Ledbetter/John Lomax		Red Foley–Ernest Tubb
9/16	7	2		2	108		(I Love The Girl) I Love The Guy.................... Cy Coben <B:16>		Sarah Vaughan
3/25	19	1		1	109		Enjoy Yourself (It's Later Than You Think) .... Herb Magidson/Carl Sigman		Guy Lombardo (Kenny Gardner)
8/5	11	1		1	110		Count Every Star .... Bruno Coquatrix/Sammy Gallop		Dick Haymes & Artie Shaw
1/21	8	1		1	111		The Old Master Painter .... Haven Gillespie/Beasley Smith		Phil Harris
12/30	3	1		1	112		Christmas In Killarney .... James Cavanaugh/John Redmond/Frank Weldon [X]		Dennis Day

11

PEAK DATE	CH	10	5	PK	RANK	GOLD	Title (Songwriter(s))	SYM	Artist
4/1	10			3	113		Wanderin'.. Sammy Kaye		Sammy Kaye (Tony Alamo)
10/14	20			1	114		Harbor Lights .... Will Grosz/Jimmy Kennedy [I]		Ken Griffin
10/28	16			1	115		I'll Always Love You.............................. Ray Evans/Jay Livingston		Dean Martin
2/25	16			1	116		Daddy's Little Girl .... Bobby Burke/Horace Gerlach		Dick Todd
11/18	12			1	117		All My Love .... Henri Contet/Paul Durand/Mitchell Parish		Bing Crosby
2/18	11			1	118	●	With My Eyes Wide Open I'm Dreaming .... Mack Gordon/Harry Revel		Patti Page Quartet
1/28	10			1	119		A Dreamer's Holiday..................................... Kim Gannon/Mabel Wayne ❶		Ray Anthony (Dick Noel)
7/8	10			1	120		The Old Piano Roll Blues.. Cy Coben		Hoagy Carmichael & Cass Daley
11/18	10			1	121		Nevertheless .... Bert Kalmar/Harry Ruby		Frankie Laine
7/8	9			1	122		I Wanna Be Loved .... John Green/Edward Heyman/Billy Rose ❶		Fontane Sisters with Hugo Winterhalter
4/29	6			1	123		(If I Knew You Were Comin') Id've Baked A Cake .... Al Hoffman/Bob Merrill/ Clem Watts		Benny Strong
9/23	3			1	124		Cincinnati Dancing Pig................................ Al Lewis/Guy Wood		Vic Damone

PEAK DATE	WEEKS				RANK	GOLD	Title	PEAK POSITION Songwriter(s)	SYMBL	DEBUT	Artist
	CH	10	5	PK							

12

PEAK DATE	CH	PK	RANK	Title	Songwriter(s)	Artist
9/9	16	2	125	La Vie En Rose	Mack David/Luis Guglielmi/Edith Piaf [I]	Paul Weston
2/25	7	2	126	Rag Mop	Deacon Anderson/Johnnie Lee Wells	The Starlighters
1/21	12	1	127	I Can Dream, Can't I	Sammy Fain/Irving Kahal	Tex Beneke (Glenn Douglas)
4/29	11	1	128	Dearie	Bob Hilliard/Dave Mann <B:20>	Ray Bolger & Ethel Merman
1/21	8	1	129	The Old Master Painter	Haven Gillespie/Beasley Smith	Snooky Lanson
4/22	7	1	130	Candy And Cake	Bob Merrill <A:6>	Mindy Carson
12/9	7	1	131	Oh Babe!	Milton Kabak/Louis Prima	Louis Prima & Keely Smith
2/11	7	1	132	Broken Down Merry-Go-Round	Arthur Herbert/Fred Stryker <B:17>	Margaret Whiting & Jimmy Wakely
4/8	4	1	133	Swamp Girl	Michael Brown	Frankie Laine

13

PEAK DATE	CH	PK	RANK	Title	Songwriter(s)	Artist
9/9	3	2	134	The Red We Want Is The Red We've Got (In the Old Red, White and Blue)	Jimmy Kennedy/Bickley Reichner <A:9>	Ralph Flanagan
5/13	11	1	135	The Old Piano Roll Blues	Cy Coben ❶	Lawrence (Piano Roll) Cook (Jim Dandies)
2/4	11	1	136	Johnson Rag	Guy Hall/Henry Kleinkauf/Jack Lawrence	Jimmy Dorsey (Clair "Shanty" Hogan)
7/8	9	1	137	Bewitched	Lorenz Hart/Richard Rodgers	Larry Green (The Honeydreamers)
9/2	9	1	138	Music, Maestro, Please	Herb Magidson/Allie Wrubel <B:18>	Frankie Laine
1/14	7	1	139	The Old Master Painter	Haven Gillespie/Beasley Smith	Frank Sinatra & The Modernaires
1/21	7	1	140	Bibbidi-Bobbidi-Boo (The Magic Song)	Mack David/Al Hoffman/Jerry Livingston <B:18>	Jo Stafford & Gordon MacRae
4/15	6	1	141	(Put Another Nickel In) Music! Music! Music!	Bernie Baum/Stephan Weiss	Ames Brothers
10/28	6	1	142	La Vie En Rose	Mack David/Luis Guglielmi/Edith Piaf <B:22>	Bing Crosby
4/22	6	1	143	Let's Go To Church (Next Sunday Morning)	Steve Allen	Margaret Whiting & Jimmy Wakely
12/30	4	1	144 ●	White Christmas	Irving Berlin [X-R]	Bing Crosby
4/22	4	1	145	It Isn't Fair	Richard Himber/Sylvester Sprigato/Frank Warshauer	Bonny Goodman (Buddy Greco)
4/29	3	1	146	Chinese Mule Train	Fred Glickman/Hy Heath/Johnny Lange [N]	Spike Jones (Freddy Morgan)
9/9	2	1	147	Just Say I Love Her	Jimmy Dale/Martin Kalmanoff/Jack Val/Sam Ward <B:25>	Vic Damone

14

PEAK DATE	CH	PK	RANK	Title	Songwriter(s)	Artist
9/16	11	2	148	Dream A Little Dream Of Me	Fabian Andre/Gus Kahn/Wilbur Schwandt	Jack Owens
8/12	8	1	149	Mona Lisa	Ray Evans/Jay Livingston	Harry James (Dick Williams)
7/29	7	1	150	Mona Lisa	Ray Evans/Jay Livingston	Art Lund
1/28	6	1	151	Bibbidi-Bobbidi-Boo (The Magic Song)	Mack David/Al Hoffman/Jerry Livingston	Perry Como (Fontane Sisters)
12/30	4	1	152	Rudolph The Red-Nosed Reindeer	Johnny Marks [X-N]	Bing Crosby
1/14	4	1	153	Dear Hearts And Gentle People	Sammy Fain/Bob Hilliard	Dennis Day
5/27	4	1	154	Birmingham Bounce	Sid Gunter	Red Foley
12/30	4	1	155	If You've Got The Money, I've Got The Time	Jim Beck/Lefty Frizzell <A:7>	Jo Stafford
1/28	4	1	156	Scarlet Ribbons (For Her Hair)	Evelyn Danzig/Jack Segal	Jo Stafford

15

PEAK DATE	CH	PK	RANK	Title	Songwriter(s)	Artist
3/11	5	3	157	Rag Mop	Deacon Anderson/Johnnie Lee Wells	Jimmy Dorsey (Claire "Shanty" Hogan)
5/13	8	1	158	My Foolish Heart	Ned Washington/Victor Young	Margaret Whiting
3/4	6	1	159	The Cry Of The Wild Goose	Terry Gilkyson	Tennessee Ernie
1/21	6	1	160	Marta (Rambling Rose of the Wildwood)	L. Wolfe Gilbert/Moises Simons	Tony Martin
8/19	6	1	161	Our Very Own	John Elliott/Victor Young	Sarah Vaughan
1/21	4	1	162	Charley My Boy	Ted Fiorito/Gus Kahn <B:22>	Andrews Sisters - Russ Morgan
6/24	4	1	163	Hoop-Dee-Doo	Milton DeLugg/Frank Loesser	Russ Morgan
5/6	3	1	164	If I Knew You Were Comin' I'd've Baked A Cake	Al Hoffman/Bob Merrill/Clem Watts	Ethel Merman & Ray Bolger

16

PEAK DATE	CH	PK	RANK	Title	Songwriter(s)	Artist
8/26	10	2	165	Sometime	Ted Fiorito/Gus Kahn ❶	The Mariners
12/9	8	2	166	A Bushel And A Peck	Frank Loesser	Doris Day
5/20	5	2	167	On The Outgoing Tide	Lew Brown/Mabel Wayne <A:1>	Perry Como
10/28	9	1	168	Our Lady Of Fatima	Gladys Gollahon	Red Foley
1/28	7	1	169	The Wedding Samba	Abraham Ellstein/Joseph Liebowitz/Allan Small ❶	Edmundo Ros
8/19	7	1	170	Mona Lisa	Ray Evans/Jay Livingston	Charlie Spivak (Tommy Lynn)
12/2	7	1	171	Thinking Of You	Bert Kalmar/Harry Ruby <A:10>	Sarah Vaughan
8/26	5	1	172	Tzena Tzena Tzena	Gordon Jenkins/Spencer Ross	Ralph Flanagan
4/8	5	1	173	Candy And Cake	Bob Merrill	Arthur Godfrey
6/24	4	1	174	Blind Date	Sid Robin [N]	Margaret Whiting & Bob Hope
9/2	3	1	175	Mona Lisa	Ray Evans/Jay Livingston	Ralph Flanagan (Harry Prime)

17

PEAK DATE	CH	PK	RANK	Title	Songwriter(s)	Artist
8/12	13	1	176	Vagabond Shoes	Sammy Gallop/David Saxon	Vic Damone
6/10	12	1	177	Hoop-Dee-Doo	Milton DeLugg/Frank Loesser	Doris Day
9/9	8	1	178	Goodnight, Irene	Huddie Ledbetter/John Lomax <B:22>	Dennis Day

PEAK DATE	WEEKS CH	10	5	PK	RANK	GOLD	Title / Songwriter(s)	PEAK POSITION	SYMBL	DEBUT	Artist

17 (cont'd)

PEAK DATE	CH	10	5	PK	RANK	GOLD	Title — Songwriter(s)	SYMBL	DEBUT	Artist
3/18	7			1	179		The Gods Were Angry With Me .... Bill Mackintosh/Roma Mackintosh <A:12>			Margaret Whiting & Jimmy Wakely
6/24	6			1	180		The 3rd Man Theme .... Anton Karas			Freddy Martin (Merv Griffin)
5/6	5			1	181		Choo'n Gum .... Mann Curtis/Vic Mizzy [N]			Teresa Brewer with Jimmy Lytell
5/20	5			1	182		Rain .... Eugene Ford	❶		Frank Petty Trio
3/25	5			1	183		(Put Another Nickel In) Music! Music! Music! ..... Bernie Baum/Stephan Weiss			Hugo Winterhalter & The Five Gems
9/2	4			1	184		Stars Are The Windows Of Heaven .... Tommy Malie/Jimmy Steiger			Ames Brothers
3/4	3			1	185		Chattanoogie Shoe-Shine Boy .... Jack Stapp/Harry Stone	✦		Bradford & Romano
4/29	3			1	186		Joshua .... Ralph Flanagan [I]			Ralph Flanagan
8/5	3			1	187 ●		I'll Sail My Ship Alone .... Henry Bernard/Morry Burns/Lois Mann/Henry Thurston	✦		Moon Mullican
5/13	1			1	188		Juke Box Annie .... Edward Lisbona/Sidney Prosen			Kitty Kallen

18

PEAK DATE	CH	10	5	PK	RANK	GOLD	Title — Songwriter(s)	SYMBL	DEBUT	Artist
5/27	6			1	189		Valencia .... Lucien Boyer/Clifford Grey/Charles Jacques/Jose Padilla			Tony Martin
10/14	5			1	190		Dream A Little Dream Of Me .... Fabian Andre/Gus Kahn/Wilbur Schwandt <A:13>			Frankie Laine
1/14	5			1	191		Echoes .... Bennie Benjamin/George Weiss <A:13>			Jo Stafford & Gordon MacRae
7/22	5			1	192		The Old Piano Roll Blues .... Cy Coben	❶		Cliff Steward
7/1	3			1	193		Play A Simple Melody .... Irving Berlin			Jo Stafford
2/25	2			1	194		Chattanoogie Shoe Shine Boy .... Jack Stapp/Harry Stone	❶		Bill Darnel
3/11	2			1	195		(Put Another Nickel In) Music! Music! Music! ..... Bernie Baum/ Stephan Weiss [N]	❶		Mickey Katz
7/15	1			1	196		Mississippi .... Billy Simmons/Curley Williams			Kay Starr

19

PEAK DATE	CH	10	5	PK	RANK	GOLD	Title — Songwriter(s)	SYMBL	DEBUT	Artist
9/23	4			2	197		Harbor Lights .... Will Grosz/Jimmy Kennedy [I]	❶		Jerry Byrd & Jerry Murad's Harmonicats
5/13	8			1	198		Are You Lonesome Tonight .... Lou Handman/Roy Turk			Blue Barron (Bobby Beers)
7/8	4			1	199		I Didn't Slip - I Wasn't Pushed - I Fell .... Eddie Pola/George Wyle			Doris Day
9/23	3			1	200		Tenderly .... Walter Gross/Jack Lawrence	✦		Lynn Hope Quintet
9/2	3			1	201		Our Little Ranch House .... John Jacob Loeb/Carmen Lombardo			Guy Lombardo (Kenny Gardner)
1/28	3			1	202		Dear Hearts And Gentle People .... Sammy Fain/Bob Hilliard			Benny Strong
7/29	2			1	203		Roses .... Glenn Spencer/Tim Spencer			Ray Anthony (Ronnie Deauville)
1/21	2			1	204		Dear Hearts And Gentle People .... Sammy Fain/Bob Hilliard <A:14>			Gordon MacRae

20

PEAK DATE	CH	10	5	PK	RANK	GOLD	Title — Songwriter(s)	SYMBL	DEBUT	Artist
12/2	6			1	205		Oh Babe! .... Milton Kabak/Louis Prima			Ames Brothers
4/1	6			1	206		It Isn't Fair .... Richard Himber/Sylvester Sprigato/Frank Warshauer			Bill Farrell
6/3	4			1	207		I Cross My Fingers .... Walton Farrar/Walter Kent	❶		Percy Faith (Russ Emery)
5/27	4			1	208		Stars And Stripes Forever .... John Phillip Sousa			Frankie Laine
3/4	3			1	209		Quicksilver .... Eddie Pola/Irving Taylor/George Wyle			Doris Day
3/18	3			1	210		It's So Nice To Have A Man Around The House ..... Jack Elliott/Harold Spina			Dinah Shore
3/11	2			1	211		I Said My Pajamas (And Put On My Pray'rs) ...... Eddie Pola/George Wyle <A:12>			Ethel Merman & Ray Bolger
12/30	2			1	212		Blue Christmas .... Missing Song Writer [X-R]			Hugo Winterhalter
6/30	1			1	213		Bewitched .... Lorenz Hart/Richard Rodgers			Mindy Carson
7/1	1			1	214		The Picnic Song .... Carmen Dello/Teresa Dello [N]			Johnny Desmond
4/15	1			1	215		Candy And Cake .... Bob Merrill			Evelyn Knight
7/15	1			1	216		Thanks, Mister Florist .... Roy Brodsky/Sid Tepper			Vaughn Monroe

21

PEAK DATE	CH	10	5	PK	RANK	GOLD	Title — Songwriter(s)	SYMBL	DEBUT	Artist
3/11	6			1	217		I Said My Pajamas (And Put On My Pray'rs) ...... Eddie Pola/George Wyle <B:24>			Doris Day
5/20	4			1	218		The Third Man Theme .... Anton Karas [I]			Hugo Winterhalter
3/4	3			1	219		I Said My Pajamas (And Put On My Pray'rs) .... Eddie Pola/George Wyle			Margaret Whiting & Frank DeVol
6/10	2			1	220		My Foolish Heart .... Ned Washington/Victor Young			Richard Hayes
10/7	2			1	221		Goofus .... William Harold/Gus Kahn/Wayne King [I]			Les Paul
1/28	1			1	222		Sitting By The Window .... Paul Insetta			Ray Anthony (Dick Noel/The Skyliners)
7/15	1			1	223		American Beauty Rose .... Arthur Altman/Hal David/Redd Evans			Eddy Howard
6/3	1			1	224		C'est Si Bon (It's So Good) .... Henri Betti/Andre Hornez/Jerry Seelen			Danny Kaye

22

PEAK DATE	CH	10	5	PK	RANK	GOLD	Title — Songwriter(s)	SYMBL	DEBUT	Artist
6/3	2			2	225		Buffalo Billy .... James Cavanaugh/John Redmond/Frank Weldon	❶		Roberta Quinlan, Jerry Murad's Harmonicats & Jan August
3/18	5			1	226		Dearie .... Bob Hilliard/Dave Mann [N]			Lisa Kirk & Fran Warren
8/19	4			1	227		I Cross My Fingers .... Walton Farrar/Walter Kent <A:13>			Bing Crosby
11/11	4			1	228		All My Love .... Henri Contet/Paul Durand/Mitchell Parish <A:17>			Dennis Day
7/8	4			1	229		I Wanna Be Loved .... John Green/Edward Heyman/Billy Rose	❶		Dinah Washington
7/8	3			1	230		Mississippi .... Billy Simmons/Curley Williams			Red Foley
10/28	3			1	231		The Petite Waltz (La Petite Valse) .... Joe Heyne <A:2> [I]			Guy Lombardo
1/21	3			1	232		We'll Build A Bungalow .... Johnny Murphy			Johnny Long (Janet Brace)

PEAK DATE	WEEKS				RANK	GOLD	Title / Songwriter(s)	SYMBL	DEBUT	Artist
	CH	10	5	PK			PEAK POSITION			

22 (cont'd)

PEAK DATE	CH	10	5	PK	RANK	GOLD	Title / Songwriter(s)	SYMBL	DEBUT	Artist
5/13	2			1	233		It Isn't Fair .... *Richard Himber/Sylvester Sprigato/Frank Warshauer*			Les Brown (4 Hits and A Miss)
12/23	2			1	234		A Crosby Christmas (Parts 1 & 2) .... *Johnny Burke/Jimmy Van Heusen* [X]			Gary, Phillip, Dennis, Lindsay & Bing Crosby
7/8	2			1	235		I Didn't Slip, I Wasn't Pushed, I Fell .... *Eddie Pola/George Wyle*			Bing Crosby
1/7	2			1	236		You're The Only One I Care For .... *Larry Fotine/Jack Owens*			Jack Owens
9/16	2			1	237		Ain't Nobody's Business But My Own .... *Irving Taylor* <A:3>			Kay Starr & Tennessee Ernie
2/11	2			1	238		Bibbidi-Boo (The Magic Song) .... *Mack David/Al Hoffman/Jerry Livingston*	◆		Ilene Woods
7/8	2			1	239		The 3rd Man Theme .... *Anton Karas* <A:7>			Victor Young & Don Cherry
9/23	1			1	240		Can't We Talk It Over .... *Ned Washington/Victor Young*			Andrews Sisters
9/2	1			1	241		Home (When Shadows Fall) .... *Harry Clarkson/Jeff Clarkson/Peter Van Steeden*			Nat "King" Cole
9/2	1			1	242		I Love The Guy .... *Cy Coben*			Fran Warren

23

PEAK DATE	CH	10	5	PK	RANK	GOLD	Title / Songwriter(s)	SYMBL	DEBUT	Artist
10/28	5			1	243		Our Lady Of Fatima .... *Gladys Gollahon*	◆		Hour Of Charm Choir
6/3	3			1	244		The 3rd Man Theme .... *Anton Karas*			Owen Bradley
2/18	3			1	245		Sitting By The Window .... *Paul Insetta*			Billy Eckstine
1/28	3			1	246		The Wedding Samba .... *Abraham Ellstein/Joseph Leibowitz/Allan Small*			Carmen Miranda & Andrews Sisters
10/28	3			1	247		La Vie En Rose .... *Mack David/Luis Guglielmi/Edith Piaf*	❶		Edith Piaf
9/16	2			1	248		Can Anyone Explain? (No, No, No!) .... *Bennie Benjamin/George Weiss*			Dick Haymes
8/19	2			1	249		I Wanna Be Loved .... *John Green/Edward Heyman/Billy Rose*	◆		Dottie O'Brien & Jan Garber
7/1	1			1	250		M-I-S-S-I-S-S-I-P-P-I .... *Billy Simmons/Curley Williams*			Art Mooney (Allan Brooks)
10/7	1			1	251		Back In Your Own Backyard .... *Dave Dreyer/Al Jolson/Billy Rose*			Patti Page
10/28	1			1	252		I'll Always Love You .... *Ray Evans/Jay Livingston*			Martha Tilton

24

PEAK DATE	CH	10	5	PK	RANK	GOLD	Title / Songwriter(s)	SYMBL	DEBUT	Artist
2/25	4			2	253		Have I Told You Lately That I Love You? .... *Scott Wiseman* <A:6>			Bing Crosby & the Andrews Sisters
3/4	3			2	254		Enjoy Yourself (It's Later Than You Think) .... *Herb Magidson/Carl Sigman* <A:21>			Doris Day
12/16	5			1	255		The Thing .... *Charles Grean* [N]			Arthur Godfrey
10/14	4			1	256		Strangers .... *Fred Coots/Charles O'Flynn*	◆		Lorry Raine
2/4	4			1	257		Johnson Rag .... *Guy Hall/Henry Kleinkauf/Jack Lawrence*			Claude Thornhill (Joe Derise)
1/28	3			1	258		Dear Hearts And Gentle People .... *Sammy Fain/Bob Hilliard*			Ralph Flanagan (Harry Prime)
12/9	2			1	259		Orange Colored Sky .... *Milton DeLugg/Willie Stein*			Betty Hutton
10/28	1			1	260		A Rainy Day Refrain .... *Herno Gale/Eric Maschwitz*			Mindy Carson
12/30	1			1	261		A Marshmallow World .... *Peter DeRose/Carl Sigman* [X]			Bing Crosby
8/26	1			1	262		Just Say I Love Her (Dicitencello Vuie) .... *Jimmy Dale/Martin Kalmanoff/Jack Val/Sam Ward*			Johnny Desmond
2/4	1			1	263		Sugarfoot Rag .... *Hank Garland/Vaughn Horton* <A:1>			Red Foley
3/11	1			1	264		Rag Mop .... *Deacon Anderson/Johnnie Lee Wills*			Eddy Howard
1/21	1			1	265		Echoes .... *Bennie Benjamin/George Weiss*			Ink Spots
6/10	1			1	266		Tiddley Winkie Woo .... *Morton Morrow*			Guy Lombardo (Kenny Gardner)
1/14	1			1	267		Careless Kisses .... *Tim Spencer*			Russ Morgan

25

PEAK DATE	CH	10	5	PK	RANK	GOLD	Title / Songwriter(s)	SYMBL	DEBUT	Artist
3/25	2			2	268		C'est Si Bon (It's So Good) .... *Henri Betti/Andre Hornez/Jerry Seelen*			Johnny Desmond
7/29	3			1	269		May I Take Two Giant Steps? .... *Ervin Drake/Jimmy Shirl*			Eileen Barton
12/2	3			1	270		Oh Babe .... *Milton Kabak/Louis Prima*			Benny Goodman (Jimmy Ricks/Nancy Reed)
8/26	2			1	271		I Cross My Fingers .... *Walton Farrar/Walter Kent*			Perry Como (Fontane Sisters)
8/26	2			1	272		Simple Melody .... *Irving Berlin*			Georgia Gibbs & Bob Crosby
11/4	2			1	273		Please Say Goodnight To The Guy, Irene .... *Richard Adler/John Jacob Loeb* [N]	◆		Ziggy Talent
9/30	1			1	274		I Need You So .... *Ivory Joe Hunter*			Don Cornell
10/14	1			1	275		Can Anyone Explain (No! No! No!) .... *Bennie Benjamin/George Weiss* <A:13>			Vic Damone
8/19	1			1	276		Mona Lisa .... *Ray Evans/Jay Livingston*			Dennis Day
7/15	1			1	277		That Old Piano Roll Blues .... *Cy Coben*			The Jubalaires
8/19	1			1	278		All Dressed Up To Smile .... *Irving Gordon*			Evelyn Knight
9/16	1			1	279		Nola .... *Felix Arndt* [I]			Guy Lombardo
2/11	1			1	280		Bibbidi-Bobbidi-Boo (The Magic Song) .... *Mack David/Al Hoffman/Jerry Livingston*			Dinah Shore
2/25	1			1	281		God's Country .... *Haven Gillespie/Beasley Smith* <A:10>			Frank Sinatra

26

PEAK DATE	CH	10	5	PK	RANK	GOLD	Title / Songwriter(s)	SYMBL	DEBUT	Artist
5/27	2			2	282		American Beauty Rose .... *Arthur Altman/Hal David/Redd Evans*			Frank Sinatra
7/1	3			1	283		I'm Crazy To Love You .... *Larry Marino/Kay Werner/Sue Werner*			Sarah Vaughan
11/18	2			1	284		Thirsty For Your Kisses .... *Bill Ficks/Lee Morris*			Ames Brothers
9/30	2			1	285		Sometime .... *Ted Fiorito/Gus Kahn*			Ink Spots
2/4	2			1	286		I've Got A Lovely Bunch Of Cocoanuts .... *Fred Heatherton* [N]			Danny Kaye
7/1	2			1	287		Bewitched (Bothered And Bewildered) .... *Lorenz Hart/Richard Rodgers* [I]			David Rose

PEAK DATE	WEEKS				RANK	GOLD	Title	PEAK POSITION	SYMBOL	DEBUT	Artist
	CH	10	5	PK				Songwriter(s)			

26 (cont'd)

PEAK DATE	CH	10	5	PK	RANK	Title / Songwriter(s)	Artist
9/2	1			1	288	Goodnight Irene ....*Huddie Ledbetter/John Lomax* ✦	Alexander Brothers
4/22	1			1	289	Peter Cottontail ....*Steve Nelson/Jack Rollins* ❶	Fran Allison
4/1	1			1	290	I Almost Lost My Mind ....*Ivory Joe Hunter*	Nat "King" Cole
10/28	1			1	291	Beyond The Reef..*Jack Pitman <A:8>*	Bing Crosby
7/8	1			1	292	M-I-S-S-I-S-S-I-P-P-I...............................*Billy Simmons/Curley Williams*	Bill Darnel
1/28	1			1	293	Half A Heart Is All You Left Me (When You Broke My Heart In Two) ....*Al Morgan/Tubby Rives/William Walker*	Al Morgan
4/15	1			1	294	Peter Cottontail ....*Steve Nelson/Jack Rollins*	Jimmy Wakely

27

PEAK DATE	CH	10	5	PK	RANK	Title / Songwriter(s)	Artist
9/2	3			1	295	Sometime ....*Ted Fiorito/Gus Kahn <A:8>*	Jo Stafford
11/25	2			1	296	Oh Babe! ....*Milton Kabak/Louis Prima*	Ralph Flanagan (Steve Benoric)
9/9	1			1	297	Mambo Jambo ....*Perez Prado* [I] ✦	Dave Barbour
6/24	1			1	298	The Old Piano Roll Blues...*Cy Coben*	Eddie Cantor, Lisa Kirk & Sammy Kaye
3/18	1			1	299	God's Country ....*Haven Gillespie/Beasley Smith*	Vic Damone
9/23	1			1	300	La Vie En Rose ....*Mack David/Luis Guglielmi/Edith Piaf* [I]	Ralph Flanagan
6/10	1			1	301	La Vie En Rose ....*Mack David/Luis Guglielmi/Edith Piaf* [I]	Victor Young

28

PEAK DATE	CH	10	5	PK	RANK	Title / Songwriter(s)	Artist
6/3	2			1	302	Roses...*Glenn Spencer/Tim Spencer*	Dick Haymes
4/22	2			1	303	If I Knew You Were Comin' I'd've Baked A Cake................*Al Hoffman/ Bob Merrill/Clem Watts*	Art Mooney (Betty Harris)
10/14	1			1	304	La Vie En Rose ....*Mack David/Luis Guglielmi/Edith Piaf*	Louis Armstrong
9/23	1			1	305	Dream Awhile..*Johnny Mercer/Phil Ohman*	Frank DeVol
12/23	1			1	306	Christmas In Killarney ....*James Cavanaugh/John Redmond/Frank Weldon* [X]	Percy Faith (Shillelagh Singers)
6/3	1			1	307	Stars And Stripes Forever ....*John Phillip Sousa* [I]	Ralph Flanagan
10/21	1			1	308	Can Anyone Explain? (No! No! No!)..................*Bennie Benjamin/George Weiss*	Larry Green (The Honeydreamers)
2/4	1			1	309	Half A Heart Is All You Left Me (When You Broke My Heart in Two) ....*Al Morgan/Tubby Rives/William Walker*	Eddy Howard
3/25	1			1	310	Satan Wears A Satin Gown ....*Fred Katz/Frankie Laine/Jacques Wilson*	Frankie Laine
8/26	1			1	311	Show Me The Way To Get Out Of This World ('Cause That's Where Everything Is)...*Les Clark/Matt Dennis*	Peggy Lee
12/30	1			1	312	Frosty The Snowman......................................*Steve Nelson/Jack Rollins* [X]	Guy Lombardo (Kenny Gardner)
3/18	1			1	313	The Wedding Samba ....*Abraham Ellstein/Joseph Leibowitz/Allan Small*	Guy Lombardo (Kenny Gardner)
10/7	1			1	314	Beloved, Be Faithful ....*Ervin Drake/Jimmy Shirl <A:28>*	Russ Morgan
6/10	1			1	315	You Dreamer You.................................*Jack Palmer/Marty Symes <A:28>*	Russ Morgan
6/10	1			1	316	Bewitched ....*Lorenz Hart/Richard Rodgers* [I] ✦	Roy Ross
10/14	1			1	317	I'll Always Love You (Querida Mia) ....*Ray Evans/Jay Livingston*	Dinah Shore
1/21	1			1	318	Sorry...*Buddy Pepper/Richard Whiting*	Frank Sinatra & The Modernaires

29

PEAK DATE	CH	10	5	PK	RANK	Title / Songwriter(s)	Artist
12/23	1			1	319	The Thing..*Charles Grean* [N]	Ames Brothers
1/28	1			1	320	Sitting By The Window ....*Paul Insetta*	Vic Damone
12/9	1			1	321	A Bushel And A Peck ....*Frank Loesser*	Johnny Desmond
12/2	1			1	322	The Place Where I Worship (Is The Wide Open Spaces) ....*Fay Foster/ Al Goodhart/Florence Tarr*	Al Morgan
4/8	1			1	323	You're A Sweetheart....................................*Harold Adamson/Jimmy McHugh*	Jack Owens
9/16	1			1	324	Can Anyone Explain? (No! No! No!).................*Bennie Benjamin/George Weiss*	Dinah Shore
5/20	1			1	325	My Foolish Heart ....*Ned Washington/Victor Young*	Hugo Winterhalter

30

PEAK DATE	CH	10	5	PK	RANK	Title / Songwriter(s)	Artist
11/18	1			1	326	Can Anyone Explain? (No, No, No!) ....*Bennie Benjamin/George Weiss*	Ella Fitzgerald–Louis Armstrong
7/15	1			1	327	The Old Piano Roll Blues...*Cy Coben*	Jan Garber (Ernie Mathias/Bill Kleeb)
9/2	1			1	328	Simple Melody ....*Irving Berlin*	Phil Harris
11/18	1			1	329	If I Were A Bell ....*Frank Loesser*	Frankie Laine
12/2	1			1	330	Orange Colored Sky ....*Milton DeLugg/Willie Stein* [N] ✦	Jerry Lester
11/18	1			1	331	Molasses, Molasses It's Icky Sticky Goo ....*Larry Clinton* [N]	Roberta Quinlan with Jan August
3/4	1			1	332	Fairy Tales..*William Rietz*	Paul Weston (Jud Conlon Singers)

1951

NATIONAL NEWS: Julius and Ethel Rosenberg are convicted of espionage, and are subsequently sentenced to death amidst national controversy. After his firing by President Truman, Gen. Douglas MacArthur addresses a joint session of Congress. The 22nd Amendment to the Constitution is ratified, limiting Presidents to two terms.

INTERNATIONAL NEWS: President Truman fires Gen. Douglas MacArthur as commander of allied forces in Korea for challenging U.S. foreign policy by threatening to attack coastal China. United Nations forces push Communist troops back to the 38th Parallel. In November, negotiators agree on a truce, but it is short-lived. Six years after his defeat, Winston Churchill returns at 77 as Britain's Prime Minister.

COMMERCE AND SCIENCE: UNIVAC, the first commercially manufactured electronic computer, is introduced.

FADS AND FASHION: As teenage girls begin to pull their hair back with an elastic rubber band, the term "pony tail" enters the vocabulary.

SPORTS: Bobby Thompson slams "the shot heard round the world" enabling the New York Giants to score a miraculous playoff victory over the Brooklyn Dodgers for the National League pennant. But the Giants (with rookie Willie Mays) fall to the New York Yankees (featuring its own hot rookie Mickey Mantle) in the World Series, four games to two. The Los Angeles Rams defeat the Cleveland Browns, 24-17, in the NFL championship game. Tennessee is the year's best college football team. The Rochester Royals triumph in the NBA Finals. Kentucky flies high in the NCAA basketball tourney. The Toronto Maple Leafs win their sixth Stanley Cup in the past 10 years. Jersey Joe Walcott KO's Ezzard Charles to become the new heavyweight champion. Sugar Ray Robinson outslugs Jack LaMotta to win the middleweight crown. Sixteen-year-old Maureen Connolly wins the U.S. women's tennis title. Ben Hogan triumphs in both the Masters and the U.S. Open.

MOVIES: The musical classic *An American In Paris* starring Gene Kelly rules as Best Picture. Oscars also go to Humphrey Bogart (for his role opposite Katharine Hepburn in *The African Queen*) and Vivien Leigh (as Marlon Brando's co-star in *A Streetcar Named Desire*). The box-office parade is led by *Quo Vadis?*, *Show Boat* and *David and Bathsheba*. Montgomery Clift and Elizabeth Taylor star in *A Place In the Sun*. *The Day the Earth Stood Still* ushers in Hollywood's new science-fiction era.

TELEVISION: The comedy sensation of the fall season is *I Love Lucy* starring Lucile Ball and Desi Arnaz. Other ratings champs include *Arthur Godfrey's Talent Scouts* and Milton Berle's *Texaco Star Theater*. CBS begins network color broadcasts, to tiny audiences.

THEATER: Rodgers & Hammerstein once again create an enduring musical classic with *The King and I* starring Yul Brynner. Another acclaimed hit is *The Fourposter* with Jessica Tandy and Hume Cronyn.

BOOKS: J.D. Salinger's *The Catcher In the Rye* strikes a deep chord with teen and college readers. James Jones' *From Here to Eternity* and Herman Wouk's *The Caine Mutiny* are published.

1951 — TOP 20 ARTISTS

1. Les Paul & Mary Ford
974

2. Guy Mitchell
780

3. Frankie Laine
709

4.	674	**Jo Stafford**
5.	596	**Patti Page**
6.	592	**Perry Como**
7.	587	**Tony Bennett**
8.	566	**Tony Martin**
9.	494	**Rosemary Clooney**
10.	491	**Vic Damone**
11.	484	**Bing Crosby**
12.	467	**Dinah Shore**
13.	403	**The Weavers**
14.	397	**Eddy Howard**
15.	387	**Guy Lombardo**
16.	369	**Nat "King" Cole**
17.	363	**Mario Lanza**
18.	338	**Frank Sinatra**
19.	291	**Ray Anthony**
20.	288	**Richard Hayes**

1951 — TOP SONGWRITERS

	# of Hits	Points	
1.	16	1,320	**Bob Merrill**
2.	11	918	**Stanley Damerell**
	11	918	**Tolchard Evans**
	11	918	**Robert Hargreaves**
5.	10	849	**Carl Sigman**
6.	9	766	**Percy Faith**
7.	7	619	**Arthur Hammerstein**
	7	619	**Dudley Wilkinson**
9.	7	618	**Pee Wee King**
	7	618	**Redd Stewart**
11.	7	593	**L. Wolfe Gilbert**
12.	7	585	**Cy Coben**

1951 — TOP ARTIST DEBUTS

1.	2/10	**Stan Freberg** (95)
2.	2/24 †	**Rosemary Clooney** (38)
3.	3/03	**Ralph Marterie** (142)
4.	3/17	**Les Baxter** (91)
5.	6/23	**Tony Bennett** (45) ★
6.	7/28	**The Four Knights** (145)
7.	7/28	**Tommy Edwards** ★
8.	9/15	**Four Aces** (49) ★
9.	9/15	**Joe Turner** ◆
10.	11/24	**Johnnie Ray** (51)
11.	11/24	**The Four Lads** (82) ★
12.	12/29	**Cowboy Copas** ◆

PEAK DATE	WEEKS CH	10	5	PK	RANK	GOLD	Title / PEAK POSITION / Songwriter(s)	SYMBL	DEBUT	Artist

1

| 12/29 | 27 | 22 | 18 | 11 | 1 | ● | **Cry** .... *Churchill Kohlman* <B:2> | ❶ | | Johnnie Ray & The Four Lads |

Best Seller: 23,18,17,8,4,1,1,1,1,1,1,1,1,1,1,2,3,3,4,4,5,6,8,10,20,22
Disc Jockey: 16,12,11,8,3,4,1,1,1,1,1,1,1,1,1,2,2,2,4,4,7,18,19,22,21
Juke Box: 23,14,11,8,6,4,3,2,1,1,1,1,1,1,1,2,2,3,3,6,8,12,13,20

| 9/8 | 32 | 24 | 20 | 10 | 2 | ● | **Because Of You** .... *Arthur Hammerstein/Dudley Wilkinson* <B:12> | ❶ | | Tony Bennett |

Juke Box: 27,17,23,18,12,9,6,6,5,4,2,2,1,1,1,1,1,1,1,1,1,3,3,3,4,5,10,14,13,24
Best Seller: 24,19,16,13,13,7,6,6,4,2,2,1,1,1,1,1,1,1,1,2,2,2,2,3,4,6,9,11,13,16
Disc Jockey: 25,14,15,7,5,3,3,2,2,1,1,1,1,1,1,1,1,1,2,2,2,4,7,7,5,8,9,19

| 4/21 | 25 | 20 | 16 | 9 | 3 | ● | **How High The Moon** .... *Nancy Hamilton/Morgan Lewis* | | | Les Paul & Mary Ford |

Best Seller: 20,6,4,1,1,1,1,1,1,1,1,2,2,3,3,4,8,9,9,10,15,17,18,21
Disc Jockey: 16,4,2,1,1,1,1,1,1,1,1,2,2,2,3,5,6,10,15,28,23
Juke Box: 26,19,8,6,1,1,1,1,1,1,1,1,2,2,9,5,6,8,8,10,15,28

| 11/17 | 24 | 19 | 16 | 8 | 4 | ● | **Sin**.. *George Haven/Chester Shull* | | | Eddy Howard |

Disc Jockey: 18,10,5,2,2,2,2,1,1,1,1,1,1,1,1,2,2,4,7,18,10,29
Best Seller: 22,13,10,7,4,4,3,3,3,3,3,2,1,1,2,5,4,7,7,9,16,17,29
Juke Box: 17,13,8,7,5,3,3,3,3,3,2,2,1,2,2,3,5,7,7,13,20,19,27

| 3/3 | 24 | 19 | 15 | 8 | 5 | ● | **If** .... *Stanley Damerell/Tolchard Evans/Robert Hargreaves* <B:12> | | | Perry Como |

Disc Jockey: 10,8,8,4,4,3,2,1,1,1,1,1,1,23,4,7,13,13,21,29,-,24
Best Seller: 21,17,5,5,4,4,2,1,2,1,1,1,1,1,2,4,7,9,12,15,21,29
Juke Box: 16,10,8,4,3,3,3,2,2,1,1,1,1,1,4,5,5,7,8,13,21,23,30

| 7/28 | 20 | 16 | 14 | 8 | 6 | ● | **Come On-a My House** .... *William Saroyan/David Seville* | | | Rosemary Clooney |

Disc Jockey: 9,5,2,1,1,1,1,1,1,1,2,2,3,4,12,23,20
Juke Box: 17,9,7,3,1,1,1,1,1,1,1,2,2,4,5,7,11,20,30
Best Seller: 8,4,2,1,1,1,1,1,1,2,2,2,5,6,8,13,22

| 11/3 | 27 | 21 | 17 | 6 | 7 | ● | **Cold, Cold Heart** .... *Hank Williams* | | | Tony Bennett |

Best Seller: 28,22,15,13,10,9,7,6,4,2,2,2,2,1,1,1,1,1,2,2,6,6,9,17,17
Juke Box: 17,11,9,10,9,5,4,4,2,2,2,2,2,2,1,1,2,3,4,9,11,13,18,23
Disc Jockey: 29,27,18,13,17,11,7,7,6,3,4,3,3,3,3,3,4,5,8,10,8,23,19

| 6/23 | 29 | 23 | 20 | 5 | 8 | ● | **Too Young** .... *Sylvia Dee/Sid Lippman* | | | Nat "King" Cole |

Best Seller: 21,15,7,5,4,3,2,2,2,1,1,1,1,1,2,2,2,3,3,8,7,8,7,12,13,18,18
Disc Jockey: 18,15,27,10,3,2,2,2,2,2,1,1,1,1,2,2,2,3,3,4,4,7,10,25,24
Juke Box: 25,16,15,12,7,5,3,3,3,2,1,1,1,1,2,2,2,2,3,3,4,6,8,10,10,11,19

| 3/10 | 34 | 22 | 15 | 1 | 9 | ● | **Be My Love** .... *Nicholas Brodszky/Sammy Cahn* | ❶ | | Mario Lanza |

Best Seller: 22,13,10,6,5,4,4,3,3,3,3,3,1,2,2,2,2,2,4,6,6,7,7,8,13,11,14,15,16,19,18,18,20,27
Disc Jockey: 20,19,9,12,10,7,3,3,4,3,3,4,2,3,3,3,3,4,4,6,8,15,12,20,-,27
Juke Box: 22,20,30,-,26,12,6,4,5,5,6,8,8,8,8,8,10,10,11,12,13,17,20,24,25

2

4/28	23	19	13	8	10	●	**On Top Of Old Smoky** .... *Pete Seeger*			The Weavers & Terry Gilkyson
1/27	21	17	15	7	11	●	**My Heart Cries For You** .... *Percy Faith/Carl Sigman* <B:4>	❶		Guy Mitchell
3/24	24	18	12	5	12	●	**Mockin' Bird Hill** .... *Vaughn Horton*			Les Paul & Mary Ford
7/7	21	17	13	2	13	●	**Jezebel** .... *Wayne Shanklin* <B:3>			Frankie Laine
10/6	16	12	9	2	14	●	**The World Is Waiting For The Sunrise** ...... *Eugene Lockhart/Ernest Seitz* <B:7>			Les Paul & Mary Ford
12/22	17	11	7	2	15	●	**Shrimp Boats** .... *Paul Howard/Paul Weston*			Jo Stafford
12/15	21	13	11	1	16	●	**Undecided** .... *Sid Robin/Charles Shavers* <B:23>			Ames Brothers & Les Brown
5/12	22	16	9	1	17	●	**Mockin' Bird Hill** .... *Vaughn Horton*			Patti Page
7/21	19	13	9	1	18	●	**My Truly, Truly Fair** .... *Bob Merrill*			Guy Mitchell

3

10/13	30	21	10	3	19	●	**I Get Ideas** .... *Dorcas Cochran/Lenny Sanders*			Tony Martin
8/11	17	13	8	3	20	●	**Sweet Violets**.. *Cy Coben/Charles Grean*			Dinah Shore
9/1	34	23	13	2	21	●	**The Loveliest Night Of The Year** .... *Irving Aaronson/Paul Francis Webster*			Mario Lanza
12/15	14	10	6	2	22	●	**Jealousy (Jalousie)** .... *Vera Bloom/Jacob Gade*			Frankie Laine
6/2	17	11	6	1	23		**Sound Off (The Duckworth Chant)** .... *Willie Lee Duckworth*			Vaughn Monroe
3/31	17	11	4	1	24	●	**Aba Daba Honeymoon** .... *Walter Donovan/Arthur Fields*	❶		Debbie Reynolds & Carleton Carpenter
1/6	19	10	4	1	25		**My Heart Cries For You**.................................. *Percy Faith/Carl Sigman* <B:18>			Dinah Shore
7/21	19	10	3	1	26		**Rose, Rose, I Love You** .... *Chris Langdon/Wilfrid Thomas* <A:2>			Frankie Laine

4

2/24	17	12	7	4	27		**The Roving Kind** .... *Jessie Cavanaugh/Arnold Stanton* <A:2>			Guy Mitchell
3/24	19	14	4	3	28	●	**Would I Love You (Love You, Love You)** .... *Bob Russell/Harold Spina*			Patti Page
6/23	17	11	3	2	29		**My Truly, Truly Fair** .... *Bob Merrill*			Vic Damone
1/13	15	10	2	2	30		**My Heart Cries For You** .... *Percy Faith/Carl Sigman* <B:18>			Vic Damone
11/17	22	12	8	1	31	●	**Sin** .... *George Hoven/Chester Shull*	❶		Four Aces Feat. Al Alberts
11/24	25	14	3	1	32	●	**Down Yonder** .... *L. Wolfe Gilbert* [I]		✦	Del Wood
10/6	21	11	3	1	33		**Because Of You** .... *Arthur Hammerstein/Dudley Wilkinson*			Les Baxter
2/3	14	10	3	1	34		**So Long (It's Been Good to Know Yuh)** .... *Woody Guthrie*			Gordon Jenkins & The Weavers
11/10	14	9	2	1	35		**And So To Sleep Again** .... *Joe Marsala/Sunny Skylar*			Patti Page

1951

PEAK DATE	WEEKS				RANK	GOLD	Title	PEAK POSITION / Songwriter(s)	SYMBOL	DEBUT	Artist
	CH	10	5	PK							

5

2/10	17	10	3	3	36		You're Just In Love	Irving Berlin			Perry Como (Fontane Sisters)
9/29	16	11		2	37	●	Detour	Paul Westmoreland			Patti Page
11/24	13	4	2	2	38		Just One More Chance	Sam Coslow/Arthur Johnston <B:23>			Les Paul & Mary Ford
11/17	17	5	1	1	39		(It's No) Sin	George Hoven/Chester Shull			Savannah Churchill

6

1/20	17	10		3	40		Tennessee Waltz	Pee Wee King/Redd Stewart <B:29>			Guy Lombardo (Kenny Gardner)
7/21	15	9		2	41		I'm In Love Again	Cole Porter			Henri René feat. April Stevens
1/13	14	3		2	42		Tennessee Waltz	Pee Wee King/Redd Stewart <B:18>			Les Paul & Mary Ford
5/19	20	6		1	43	●	I Apologize	Al Goodhart/Al Hoffman/Ed Nelson			Billy Eckstine
9/8	9	1		1	44		While You Danced, Danced, Danced	Stephan Weiss			Georgia Gibbs

7

9/15	16	7		2	45		Whispering	Richard Coburn/Vincent Rose/John Schonberger <A:2>	[I]		Les Paul
8/18	17	5		2	46		(Why Did I Tell You I Was Going To) Shanghai	Milton DeLugg/Bob Hilliard			Doris Day
1/20	13	5		1	47		Tennessee Waltz	Pee Wee King/Redd Stewart <B:14>			Jo Stafford
5/26	8	2		1	48		Old Soldiers Never Die	Tom Glazer			Vaughn Monroe

8

6/9	16	7		3	49		On Top Of Old Smoky	Pete Seeger			Vaughn Monroe
6/30	14	7		3	50	●	Mister And Mississippi	Irving Gordon <B:26>			Patti Page
4/7	15	6		2	51		Sparrow In The Tree Top	Bob Merrill <B:27>			Guy Mitchell
4/28	15	3		2	52		Sparrow In The Tree Top	Bob Merrill			Bing Crosby & Andrews Sisters
8/25	9	3		2	53		Come On-A My House	William Saroyan/David Seville			Kay Starr
10/27	14	5		1	54		Turn Back The Hands Of Time	Jimmy Eaton/Con Hammond/Larry Wagner			Eddie Fisher
9/22	8	3		1	55		Castle Rock	Ervin Drake/Al Sears/Jimmy Shirl			Frank Sinatra & Harry James
5/5	10	2		1	56		When You And I Were Young Maggie Blues	Jack Frost/Jimmy McHugh <B:14>	[N]		Bing & Gary Crosby
6/9	10	2		1	57		Rose, Rose, I Love You	Chris Langdon/Wilfrid Thomas	❶		Buddy Morrow
2/17	18	1		1	58		If	Stanley Damerell/Tolchard Evans/Robert Hargreaves <B:15>			Jo Stafford
3/10	12	1		1	59		A Penny A Kiss	Ralph Care/Buddy Kaye <B:24>			Tony Martin & Dinah Shore

9

12/8	12	3		2	60		Domino	Louis Ferrari/Don Raye			Tony Martin
2/17	11	2		1	61		I Taut I Taw A Puddy Tat	Warren Foster/Alan Livingston/Billy May	[N]		Mel Blanc
9/8	9	2		1	62		Belle, Belle, My Liberty Belle	Bob Merrill <B:23>			Guy Mitchell
3/31	10	1		1	63		The Aba Daba Honeymoon	Walter Donovan/Arthur Fields			Richard Hayes & Kitty Kallen
12/15	9	1		1	64		Out In The Cold Again	Rube Bloom/Ted Koehler			Richard Hayes
11/17	8	1		1	65		Hey, Good Lookin'	Hank Williams <B:19>			Frankie Laine - Jo Stafford

10

4/7	17	3		3	66		Mockin' Bird Hill	Vaughn Horton	❶		The Pinetoppers (Beaver Valley Sweethearts)
12/8	19	2		2	67	●	Charmaine	Lew Pollack/Erno Rapee	[I]		Mantovani
11/10	16	1		1	68		(When We Are Dancing) I Get Ideas	Dorcas Cochran/Lenny Sanders <B:16>			Louis Armstrong
11/24	11	1		1	69		Undecided	Sid Robin/Charles Shavers			Ray Anthony (Tommy Mercer/ Gloria Craig/The Skyliners)
4/14	10	1		1	70		Would I Love You (Love You, Love You)	Bob Russell/Harold Spina			Harry James with Doris Day
5/26	9	1		1	71		On Top Of Old Smoky	Pete Seeger			Percy Faith with Burl Ives
3/10	8	1		1	72		If	Stanley Damerell/Tolchard Evans/Robert Hargreaves			Billy Eckstine
8/18	5	1		1	73		Gimme A Little Kiss, Will Ya Huh?	Maceo Pinkard/Jack Smith/Roy Turk			April Stevens with Henri René
12/29	4	1		1	74		Jingle Bells	James Pierpont	[X-I]		Les Paul

11

3/17	14			2	75		Beautiful Brown Eyes	Jerry Capehart/Alton Delmore/Arthur Smith			Rosemary Clooney
6/23	13			2	76		These Things I Offer You (For A Lifetime)	Bennie Benjamin/Morty Nevins/ George Weiss			Sarah Vaughan
2/24	13			2	77		The Roving Kind	Jessie Cavanaugh/Arnold Stanton			The Weavers
9/1	10			2	78		Sweet Violets	Cy Coben/Charles Grean			Jane Turzy
9/1	13			1	79		Vanity	Bernard Bierman/Jack Manus/Guy Wood			Don Cherry
9/29	12			1	80		Because Of You	Arthur Hammerstein/Dudley Wilkinson	✦		Gloria DeHaven & Guy Lombardo
8/4	6			1	81		In The Cool, Cool, Cool Of The Evening	Hoagy Carmichael/Johnny Mercer			Bing Crosby & Jane Wyman
8/4	5			1	82		I've Got You Under My Skin	Cole Porter <B:30>	[N]		Stan Freberg

12

8/4	17			2	83		I Won't Cry Anymore	Al Frisch/Fred Wise <A:1>			Tony Bennett
2/10	13			2	84		My Heart Cries For You	Percy Faith/Carl Sigman			Jimmy Wakely

PEAK DATE	WEEKS				RANK	GOLD	Title / PEAK POSITION / Songwriter(s)	SYMBL	DEBUT	Artist
	CH	10	5	PK						

12 (cont'd)

PEAK DATE	CH	10	5	PK	RANK	GOLD	Title / Songwriter(s)	SYMBL/DEBUT	Artist
5/12	14			1	85	●	The Syncopated Clock .... *Leroy Anderson* [I]	❶	Leroy Anderson
5/12	14			1	86		Beautiful Brown Eyes .... *Jerry Capehart/Alton Delmore/Arthur Smith*		Jimmy Wakely & Les Baxter
8/11	12			1	87		Josephine .... *Burke Bivens/Wayne King <B:18>* [I]		Les Paul
8/18	11			1	88		Longing For You .... *Walter Dana/Bernard Jansen*		Vic Damone
2/17	9			1	89		Zing Zing—Zoom Zoom .... *Sigmund Romberg/Charles Tobias <A:1>*		Perry Como (Fontane Sisters)
9/15	8			1	90		Because Of You .... *Arthur Hammerstein/Dudley Wilkinson <B:22>*		Jan Peerce
3/31	7			1	91		The Aba Daba Honeymoon .... *Walter Donovan/Arthur Fields*		Freddy Martin (Merv Griffin)
8/11	5			1	92		Laura .... *Johnny Mercer/David Raksin*		Stan Kenton
6/23	5			1	93		Somebody .... *Jack Elliott/Lew Quadling*		Jo Stafford
7/21	5			1	94		Good Morning Mister Echo .... *Belinda Putnam/Bill Putnam*	❶	Jane Turzy Trio

13

PEAK DATE	CH	10	5	PK	RANK	GOLD	Title / Songwriter(s)	SYMBL/DEBUT	Artist
2/17	16			2	95		Be My Love .... *Nicholas Brodszky/Sammy Cahn*		Ray Anthony (Ronnie Deauville)
7/14	11			1	96		Mister And Mississippi .... *Irving Gordon*		Dennis Day
12/29	10			1	97		Slow Poke .... *Pee Wee King/Chilton Price/Redd Stewart*	✦	Roberta Lee
6/30	10			1	98		Pretty Eyed Baby .... *William Johnson/Leo Mosley/Mary Lou Williams*		Jo Stafford & Frankie Laine
4/21	10			1	99	●	The Hot Canary .... *Paul Nero* [I]	❶	Florian Zabach
5/26	6			1	100		I Like The Wide Open Spaces .... *Royal Foster/Ken Murray/Charles Wick* [N]		Arthur Godfrey & Laurie Anders
1/27	5			1	101		Tennessee Waltz .... *Pee Wee King/Redd Stewart* [N]		Spike Jones (Sara Berner/Sir Fredric Gas)
12/29	3			1	102	●	White Christmas .... *Irving Berlin* [X-R]		Bing Crosby
10/20	3			1	103		Calla Calla .... *Lenny Adelson/Margarite Almeda/Eddie Samuels*		Vic Damone

14

PEAK DATE	CH	10	5	PK	RANK	GOLD	Title / Songwriter(s)	SYMBL/DEBUT	Artist
11/3	17			2	104		Down Yonder .... *L. Wolfe Gilbert* [I]		Joe "Fingers" Carr
3/10	14			2	105		Bring Back The Thrill .... *Ruth Poll/Pete Ruggolo*		Eddie Fisher
10/27	10			2	106		(It's No) Sin .... *George Hoven/Chester Shull*		The Four Knights
1/27	13			1	107	●	The Shot Gun Boogie .... *Tennessee Ernie Ford*		Tennessee Ernie
7/28	9			1	108		Lonely Little Robin .... *Cy Coben*		The Pinetoppers (Marlin Sisters/Ray Smith)
10/20	8			1	109		When I Dance With You I Get Ideas .... *Dorcas Cochran/Lenny Sanders*		Peggy Lee
3/24	7			1	110		A Penny A Kiss—A Penny A Hug .... *Ralph Care/Buddy Kaye*		Eddy Howard
6/30	7			1	111		I'm A Fool To Want You .... *Joel Herron/Frank Sinatra/Jack Wolf <B:21>*		Frank Sinatra
5/12	6			1	112		Moonlight Bay .... *Edward Madden/Percy Wenrich <A:8>* [N]		Bing & Gary Crosby
3/3	6			1	113		If .... *Stanley Damerell/Tolchard Evans/Robert Hargreaves*		Dean Martin
1/13	5			1	114		Nevertheless (I'm In Love With You) .... *Bert Kalmar/Harry Ruby*		Frank Sinatra
8/4	5			1	115		Good Morning, Mr. Echo .... *Belinda Putnam/Bill Putnam*		Margaret Whiting
8/11	1			1	116		Come On-A My House .... *William Saroyan/David Seville <B:23>*		Richard Hayes

15

PEAK DATE	CH	10	5	PK	RANK	GOLD	Title / Songwriter(s)	SYMBL/DEBUT	Artist
7/7	9			1	117		Too Young .... *Sylvia Dee/Sid Lippman*		Toni Arden
11/10	7			1	118		Down Yonder .... *L. Wolfe Gilbert*		Freddy Martin
11/17	6			1	119		Domino .... *Louis Ferrari/Don Raye*		Bing Crosby
7/21	6			1	120		Oceans Of Tears .... *Lida Dolan/Hope Ryder <B:22>*		Kay Starr & Tennessee Ernie
10/27	5			1	121		The Blues from An American In Paris .... *George Gershwin* [I]		Ralph Flanagan
3/10	3			1	122		It Is No Secret .... *Stuart Hamblen <A:8>*		Jo Stafford

16

PEAK DATE	CH	10	5	PK	RANK	GOLD	Title / Songwriter(s)	SYMBL/DEBUT	Artist
8/25	14			2	123		Because .... *Guy d'Hardelot/Edward Teschemacher*		Mario Lanza
3/24	10			2	124		Would I Love You .... *Bob Russell/Harold Spina*	❶	Helen O'Connell
11/3	11			1	125		Blue Velvet .... *Lee Morris/Bernie Wayne <B:17>*		Tony Bennett
6/23	11			1	126		Unless .... *Stanley Damerell/Tolchard Evans/Robert Hargreaves*		Guy Mitchell
5/5	10			1	127		Mockin' Bird Hill .... *Vaughn Horton*		Russ Morgan
9/8	8			1	128		Longing For You .... *Walter Dana/Bernard Jansen*		Sammy Kaye (Tony Alamo)
8/25	7			1	129		The Morningside Of The Mountain .... *Dick Manning/Larry Stock*		Paul Weston (Norman Luboff Choir)
10/27	4			1	130		Down Yonder .... *L. Wolfe Gilbert* [I]	✦	Eddie Smith & the Chief
7/7	3			1	131		Wang Wang Blues .... *Henry Busse/Buster Johnson/Gus Mueller/Leo Wood*		Ames Brothers
12/29	3			1	132		Rudolph, The Red-Nosed Reindeer .... *Johnny Marks* [X-R]		Gene Autry & The Pinafores
11/10	3			1	133		Cold, Cold Heart .... *Hank Williams*		The Fontane Sisters

17

PEAK DATE	CH	10	5	PK	RANK	GOLD	Title / Songwriter(s)	SYMBL/DEBUT	Artist
6/30	4			2	134		Because Of Rain .... *Nat "King" Cole/William Harrington/Ruth Poll*		Nat "King" Cole
11/10	16			1	135		Down Yonder .... *L. Wolfe Gilbert*		Champ Butler
6/16	11			1	136		Unless .... *Stanley Damerell/Tolchard Evans/Robert Hargreaves*		Eddie Fisher
5/26	11			1	137		September Song .... *Maxwell Anderson/Kurt Weill*		Stan Kenton
9/22	9			1	138		Sixty Minute Man .... *Rose Marks/William Ward*	❶	The Dominoes
10/13	8			1	139		Because Of You .... *Arthur Hammerstein/Dudley Wilkinson*		Johnny Desmond
3/10	7			1	140		A Penny A Kiss—A Penny A Hug .... *Ralph Care/Buddy Kaye*		Andrews Sisters

1951

PEAK DATE	WEEKS				RANK	GOLD	Title / PEAK POSITION / Songwriter(s)	SYMBL	DEBUT	Artist
	CH	10	5	PK						

17 (cont'd)

PEAK DATE	CH	PK	RANK	Title / Songwriter(s)	Artist
6/23	7	1	141	These Things I Offer You (For A Lifetime)........Bennie Benjamin/Morty Nevins/ George Weiss	Ray Anthony (Tommy Mercer/The Skyliners)
5/5	7	1	142	Down The Trail Of Achin' Hearts............Jimmy Kennedy/Nat Simon <B:24>	Patti Page
11/17	5	1	143	Solitaire............Renee Borek/King Guion/Carl Nutter <A:16>	Tony Bennett
10/6	4	1	144	Over A Bottle Of Wine............Dan Shapiro/Sam Stept	Tony Martin
8/11	4	1	145	In The Cool, Cool, Cool Of The Evening.....Hoagy Carmichael/Johnny Mercer	Jo Stafford & Frankie Laine
9/8	3	1	146	Wonderful, Wasn't It?............Hal David/Don Rodney <B:23>	Frankie Laine
5/5	1	1	147	You're The One............Ned Washington/Victor Young	Frank Sinatra

18

PEAK DATE	CH	PK	RANK	Title / Songwriter(s)	Artist
9/15	9	2	148	It's All In The Game............Charles Dawes/Carl Sigman	Tommy Edwards
3/10	11	1	149	It Is No Secret............Stuart Hamblen	Bill Kenny & The Song Spinners
9/8	9	1	150	I'll Hold You In My Heart ('Til I Can Hold You in My Arms)............Eddy Arnold/Tommy Dilbeck/Hal Horton	Eddie Fisher
12/1	9	1	151	Charmaine............Lew Pollack/Erno Rapee	Gordon Jenkins (Bob Carroll)
2/17	8	1	152	I Still Feel The Same About You............Dick Manning/Don Reid	Georgia Gibbs with Owen Bradley
6/30	7	1	153	Mr. And Mississippi............Irving Gordon	Tennessee Ernie
1/13	7	1	154	Little Rock Getaway............Joe Sullivan <A:6> [I]	Les Paul
8/4	4	1	155	I Wish I Had Never Seen Sunshine........Jimmie Davis/Johnnie Roberts <A:12>	Les Paul & Mary Ford
1/6	4	1	156	My Heart Cries For You............Percy Faith/Carl Sigman	Bill Farrell
9/15	3	1	157	Truly Truly Fair............Bob Merrill	Freddy Martin (Merv Griffin)
1/6	3	1	158	Nobody's Chasing Me............Cole Porter <A:3>	Dinah Shore
1/6	2	1	159	Music By The Angels............Arthur Altman/Marty Symes <A:4>	Vic Damone
11/24	2	1	160	I Ran All The Way Home............Bennie Benjamin/George Weiss	Sarah Vaughan
9/15	1	1	161	Vanity............Bernard Bierman/Jack Manus/Guy Wood	Tony Martin

19

PEAK DATE	CH	PK	RANK	Title / Songwriter(s)	Artist
5/5	6	2	162	Metro Polka............Willie Evans/Vaughn Horton	Frankie Laine
4/21	6	2	163	Never Been Kissed............Cy Coben/Charles Grean [N]	Freddy Martin (Merv Griffin)
8/4	8	1	164	I'm Waiting Just For You............Henry Glover/Carolyn Leigh/Lucky Millinder	Lucky Millinder (Annisteen Allen/John Carol)
6/30	6	1	165	Too Young............Sylvia Dee/Sid Lippman	Patty Andrews
4/14	6	1	166	Would I Love You (Love You, Love You).....Bob Russell/Harold Spina <B:20>	Tony Martin
9/8	6	1	167	Kisses Sweeter Than Wine............Paul Campbell/Joe Newman <B:27>	The Weavers
10/27	4	1	168	Gambella (The Gamblin' Lady)............Terry Gilkyson <A:9>	Jo Stafford - Frankie Laine
2/17	4	1	169	Across The Wide Missouri............Ervin Drake/Jimmy Shirl <B:21>	Paul Weston (Norman Luboff Choir)
12/29	3	1	170	It's Beginning To Look Like Christmas............Meredith Willson [X]	Perry Como (Fontane Sisters)
4/7	3	1	171	The Aba Daba Honeymoon............Walter Donovan/Arthur Fields [N]	Cliff Steward
3/31	2	1	172 ●	Peter Cottontail............Steve Nelson/Jack Rollins [R]	Gene Autry
6/30	2	1	173	Gone Fishin'............Charles Kenny/Nick Kenny	Bing Crosby & Louis Armstrong
9/22	2	1	174	Vanity............Bernard Bierman/Jack Manus/Guy Wood	Sarah Vaughan
10/13	1	1	175	Cold, Cold Heart............Hank Williams	Eileen Wilson

20

PEAK DATE	CH	PK	RANK	Title / Songwriter(s)	SYMBL	Artist
12/1	6	2	176	Because Of You............Arthur Hammerstein/Dudley Wilkinson [I]	❶	Tab Smith
9/15	6	1	177	(Why Did I Tell You I Was Going To) Shanghai............Milton DeLugg/Bob Hilliard	❶	Billy Williams Quartet
4/21	5	1	178	If............Stanley Damerell/Tolchard Evans/Robert Hargreaves	❶	Guy Lombardo (Bill Flanagan)
2/24	4	1	179	The Roving Kind............Jessie Cavanaugh/Arnold Stanton	❶	Rex Allen
2/10	4	1	180	Tennessee Waltz............Pee Wee King/Redd Stewart		The Fontane Sisters
12/1	4	1	181	I Like It............Manny Kurtz/Vic Mizzy		Jane Turzy
7/14	2	1	182	Too Young............Sylvia Dee/Sid Lippman		Fran Allison
3/17	2	1	183	Jet............Bennie Benjamin/Harry Revel/George Weiss		Nat "King" Cole
7/21	2	1	184	There's No Boat Like A Rowboat............Irving Gordon <B:25>		Perry Como (Fontane Sisters)
9/15	2	1	185	Kissin' Bug Boogie............Robert Allen/Allan Roberts		Jo Stafford
5/26	2	1	186	When You And I Were Young Maggie Blues......Jack Frost/Jimmy McHugh		Margaret Whiting & Jimmy Wakely
6/9	1	1	187	I Apologize............Al Goodhart/Al Hoffman/Ed Nelson <A:19>		Tony Martin
11/17	1	1	188	There's Always Room At Our House............Bob Merrill <B:28>		Guy Mitchell

21

PEAK DATE	CH	PK	RANK	Title / Songwriter(s)	Artist
3/10	5	2	189	So Long (It's Been Good To Know Yuh)............Woody Guthrie <A:19>	Paul Weston (Norman Luboff Choir)
7/7	10	1	190	Pretty Eyed Baby............William Johnson/Leo Mosley/Mary Lou Williams	Al Trace (Lola Ameche)
7/7	5	1	191	Mama Will Bark............Dick Manning <A:14> [N]	Frank Sinatra & Dagmar
9/29	4	1	192	Hawaiian War Chant (Ta-Hu-Wa-Hu-Wai)............Ralph Freed/Johnny Noble	Ames Brothers
9/29	4	1	193	I'm Waiting Just For You.........Henry Glover/Carolyn Leigh/Lucky Millinder <B:24>	Rosemary Clooney
2/10	4	1	194	Tell Me You Love Me............Sammy Kaye	Vic Damone
12/15	4	1	195	Domino............Louis Ferrari/Don Raye	Doris Day

PEAK DATE	CH	10	5	PK	RANK	GOLD	Title / Peak Position / Songwriter(s)	SYMBL	DEBUT	Artist

21 (cont'd)

PEAK DATE	CH	10	5	PK	RANK	Title / Songwriter(s)	Artist
6/30	4			1	196	Rose, Rose, I Love You ....Chris Langdon/Wilfrid Thomas <B:30>	Gordon Jenkins (Cisco Houston)
4/14	4			1	197	Across The Wide Missouri................................Ervin Drake/Jimmy Shirl	Hugo Winterhalter (Stuart Foster)
2/17	3			1	198	John And Marsha ....Stan Freberg/Billy Liebert/Cliffie Stone **[N]** ❶	Stan Freberg
3/17	3			1	199	Vesti La Giubba (On with the Play)........................Ruggiero Leoncavallo **[F]**	Mario Lanza
7/21	2			1	200	Good Morning Mister Echo................................Belinda Putnam/Bill Putnam	Georgia Gibbs
6/16	2			1	201	Tom's Tune ....Lou Busch/Lee Gillette	Georgia Gibbs
12/29	2			1	202	Charmaine ....Lew Pollack/Erno Rapee **[I]**	Jerry Murad's Harmonicats
9/8	1			1	203	Why Did I Tell You I Was Going To Shanghai ....Milton DeLugg/Bob Hilliard	Bing Crosby
9/22	1			1	204	Wonder Why..Nicholas Brodszky/Sammy Cahn	Vic Damone
2/17	1			1	205	Velvet Lips ....Manny Banks/Sammy Gallop <B:22>	Guy Lombardo (Kenny Gardner)

22

PEAK DATE	CH	10	5	PK	RANK	Title / Songwriter(s)	Artist
2/24	5			1	206	The Chicken Song (I Ain't Gonna Take It Settin' Down) ..Bob Merrill/Terry Shand <A:21>	Guy Lombardo (Cliff Grass)
6/30	5			1	207	What Is A Boy ....Alan Beck/Alec Wilder <A:12> **[S]**	Jan Peerce
1/27	4			1	208	A Bushel And A Peck...Frank Loesser	Andrews Sisters
10/13	3			1	209	Come On-A My House ....William Saroyan/David Seville **[N]**	Mickey Katz
11/17	3			1	210	Where's-A Your House? ....Roy Alfred/Al Frisch/George Mysels/Maloy Roach **[N]** ✦	Robert Q. Lewis
8/4	2			1	211	Them There Eyes ....Maceo Pinkard/Doris Tauber/William Tracey	Champ Butler
11/3	2			1	212	Down Yonder ....L. Wolfe Gilbert **[I]** (Piano Roll)	Lawrence Cook
8/18	2			1	213	Sweet Violets...Cy Coben/Charles Green ✦	Doris Drew
7/21	2			1	214	A Woman Is A Deadly Weapon ....George Campbell/Marvin Moore	Eddy Howard
6/2	2			1	215	We Kissed In A Shadow ....Oscar Hammerstein/Richard Rodgers	Frank Sinatra
6/30	2			1	216	You're My Sugar ....Irving Taylor <A:15>	Kay Starr & Tennessee Ernie
9/15	1			1	217	Mixed Emotions..Stuart Louchheim	Rosemary Clooney
7/21	1			1	218	Shanghai...Milton DeLugg/Bob Hilliard	Bob Crosby
8/11	1			1	219	Butcher Boy (Aeluna Mezzumare) ....Paolo Citorello/Lou Monte **[F]** ✦	Emil Dewan Quintones
12/29	1			1	220	Rudolph The Red-Nosed Reindeer ....Johnny Marks **[X-N-R]**	Spike Jones (Rudolph)

23

PEAK DATE	CH	10	5	PK	RANK	Title / Songwriter(s)	Artist
9/15	6			2	221	Smooth Sailing ....Arnett Cobb	Ella Fitzgerald
4/28	5			1	222	If ....Stanley Damerell/Tolchard Evans/Robert Hargreaves	Ink Spots
10/20	4			1	223	Sentimental Journey ....Les Brown/Bud Green/Ben Homer <A:2>	Les Brown & Ames Brothers
4/28	3			1	224	The Aba Daba Honeymoon ....Walter Donovan/Arthur Fields	Hoagy Carmichael & Cass Daley
11/17	3			1	225	Beyond The Blue Horizon ....W. Frank Harling/Leo Robin/Richard Whiting	Hugo Winterhalter
8/11	2			1	226	The Girl In The Wood ....Neal Gilkyson/Terry Gilkyson <A:17>	Frankie Laine
11/10	2			1	227	Jazz Me Blues ....Tom Delaney <A:5> **[I]**	Les Paul
9/1	2			1	228	Belle, Belle, My Liberty Belle ....Bob Merrill	Bobby Wayne
9/29	1			1	229	Because Of You ....Arthur Hammerstein/Dudley Wilkinson ✦	Ray Barber
7/28	1			1	230	I Love The Sunshine Of Your Smile ....Jack Hoffman/Jimmy MacDonald ❶	The Four Knights
8/11	1			1	231	Go Go Go Go ....Mack David/Jerry Livingston <A:14>	Richard Hayes
8/18	1			1	232	Sweetheart Of Yesterday........................Percy Faith/Carl Sigman <A:9>	Guy Mitchell

24

PEAK DATE	CH	10	5	PK	RANK	Title / Songwriter(s)	Artist
7/28	3			3	233	Hitsity Hotsity ....Al Hoffman/Al Trace	Lola Ameche & Al Trace
10/13	4			1	234	Rollin' Stone ....Irving Gordon <B:28>	Perry Como (Fontane Sisters)
12/22	3			1	235	Cry ....Churchill Kohlman	Georgia Gibbs
7/21	2			1	236	Red Sails In The Sunset ....Jimmy Kennedy/Hugh Williams	Nat "King" Cole
2/24	2			1	237	You're Just In Love ....Irving Berlin	Guy Mitchell & Rosemary Clooney
1/13	2			1	238	My Heart Cries For You ....Percy Faith/Carl Sigman	Al Morgan
5/19	2			1	239	Evertrue Evermore...........................Kermit Goell/Theodore Rhodes <A:17>	Patti Page
3/10	2			1	240	In Your Arms ....George Melachrino/Emile Waldteufel <A:8>	Dinah Shore & Tony Martin
9/8	2			1	241	The Musicians ....Tom Glazer/Charles Green **[N]**	Dinah Shore, Betty Hutton, Tony Martin, Phil Harris
6/30	1			1	242	I'm In Love Again ....Cole Porter	Andrews Sisters
9/22	1			1	243	If Teardrops Were Pennies ....Jenny Lou Carson <A:21>	Rosemary Clooney
7/28	1			1	244	The Morningside Of The Mountain.....................Dick Manning/Larry Stock ❶	Tommy Edwards
3/31	1			1	245	Let Me In ....Bob Merrill	The Fontane Sisters with Texas Jim Robertson
7/14	1			1	246	Too Young ....Sylvia Dee/Sid Lippman	Richard Hayes
2/24	1			1	247	Tennessee Waltz..Pee Wee King/Redd Stewart ✦	Anita O'Day

25

PEAK DATE	CH	10	5	PK	RANK	Title / Songwriter(s)	Artist
11/17	2			2	248	(It's No) Sin ....George Hoven/Chester Shull	Sammy Kaye (Kaydets)
7/28	2			1	249	There's A Big Blue Cloud (Next to Heaven)........Ervin Drake/Hans Lengsfelder/ Paul McGrane <A:20>	Perry Como
7/21	1			1	250	Lonely Little Robin ....Cy Coben	Mindy Carson

PEAK DATE	CH	10	5	PK	RANK	GOLD	Title / Peak Position / Songwriter(s)	SYMBL	DEBUT	Artist

25 (cont'd)

PEAK DATE	CH	10	5	PK	RANK	GOLD	Title — Songwriter(s)	SYMBL	Artist
9/1	1			1	251		Belle, Belle, My Liberty Belle .... *Bob Merrill*		Don Cherry & Sonny Burke
8/25	1			1	252		Belle, Belle, My Liberty Belle .... *Bob Merrill*		Merv Griffin

26

PEAK DATE	CH	10	5	PK	RANK	GOLD	Title — Songwriter(s)	SYMBL	Artist
3/17	2			2	253		If............ *Stanley Damerell/Tolchard Evans/Robert Hargreaves*		Jan Garber (Roy Cordell)
4/7	2			1	254		Be My Love.......... *Nicholas Brodszky/Sammy Cahn*		Billy Eckstine
8/4	2			1	255		These Things I Offer You......... *Bennie Benjamin/Morty Nevins/George Weiss* <A:8>		Patti Page
1/13	1			1	256		The Night Is Young And You're So Beautiful.......... *Irving Kahal/Billy Rose/ Dana Suesse*		Ray Anthony (Ronnie Deauville)
4/7	1			1	257		Let Me In .... *Bob Merrill*		Blue Barron (Johnny Goodfellow)
3/3	1			1	258		So Long (It's Been Good To Know Yuh)......... *Woody Guthrie*	❶	Ralph Marterie (Skip Farrell/Ann Andrews)
11/17	1			1	259		Down Yonder .... *L. Wolfe Gilbert* [I]		Frank Petty Trio
10/27	1			1	260		Angry .... *Henry Brunies/Merritt Brunies/Jules Cassard/Dudley Mecum*		Kay Starr
3/24	1			1	261		Let Me In .... *Bob Merrill*	❶	Bobby Wayne

27

PEAK DATE	CH	10	5	PK	RANK	GOLD	Title — Songwriter(s)	SYMBL	Artist
9/22	2			2	262		I Wish I Wuz................ *Sid Kuller/Lyn Murray*		Rosemary Clooney
8/11	2			1	263		What Is A Boy .... *Alan Beck/Alec Wilder* [S]		Arthur Godfrey
3/17	2			1	264		Christopher Columbus .... *Terry Gilkyson* <A:8>		Guy Mitchell
10/20	2			1	265		Bela Bimba .... *Oscar DeMejo/Marilou Harrington*		Patrice Munsel
9/1	2			1	266		When The Saints Go Marching In .... *James Black/Katherine Purvis* <A:19>		Weavers
9/8	1			1	267		Castle Rock............ *Ervin Drake/Al Sears/Jimmy Shirl*		The Fontane Sisters
8/4	1			1	268		The Wang Wang Blues .... *Henry Busse/Buster Johnson/Gus Mueller/Leo Wood* [I]		Benny Goodman Sextet
8/4	1			1	269		The Morningside Of The Mountain....... *Dick Manning/Larry Stock*	❶	Merv Griffin
6/2	1			1	270		What Will I Tell My Heart......... *Irving Gordon/Jack Lawrence/Peter Tinturin* <D.20>		Eddy Howard
10/27	1			1	271		Whispering .... *Richard Coburn/Vincent Rose/John Schonberger* [I]		Gordon Jenkins
10/13	1			1	272		And So To Sleep Again .... *Joe Marsala/Sunny Skylar*		April Stevens with Henri René

28

PEAK DATE	CH	10	5	PK	RANK	GOLD	Title — Songwriter(s)	SYMBL	Artist
2/10	6			3	273		My Heart Cries For You .... *Percy Faith/Carl Sigman*		Evelyn Knight & Red Foley
2/17	3			2	274		If............ *Stanley Damerell/Tolchard Evans/Robert Hargreaves*		Vic Damone
11/10	3			2	275		And So To Sleep Again .... *Joe Marsala/Sunny Skylar*		Dick Haymes
6/23	3			1	276		The Strange Little Girl .... *Richard Adler/Jerry Ross* <A:27>		Eddy Howard
4/28	2			1	278		Sparrow In The Tree Top .... *Bob Merrill*		Rex Allen
6/16	2			1	277		Syncopated Clock....................... *Leroy Anderson* [I]		Boston Pops Orch./Arthur Fiedler
4/7	2			1	279		Always You .... *Will Jason/Sid Robin*		Nat "King" Cole
12/1	2			1	280		Cold, Cold Heart .... *Hank Williams*	✦	Tony Fontane
9/22	2			1	281		Oh! How I Love You .... *Marty Bloom/Art Kassel*	❶	Gloria Hart & the Heartbeats
11/17	2			1	282		I Can't Help It (If I'm Still In Love With You) .... *Hank Williams* <A:20>		Guy Mitchell
11/17	2			1	283		Meanderin' .... *George Botsford/Cy Coben/Charles Grean*		Vaughn Monroe
7/28	1			1	284		My Truly, Truly Fair .... *Bob Merrill*		Ray Anthony (Tommy Mercer)
9/15	1			1	285		Longing For You .... *Walter Dana/Bernard Jansen*		Teresa Brewer
10/20	1			1	286		With All My Heart And Soul .... *Harry Akst/Mann Curtis/Salvatore d'Esposito/ Domenico Titomanglio* <A:24>		Perry Como
12/15	1			1	287		Alabama Jubilee .... *George Cobb/Jack Yellen*		Red Foley
9/1	1			1	288		Castle Rock .... *Ervin Drake/Al Sears/Jimmy Shirl* [I]		Johnny Hodges
12/22	1			1	289		Undecided .... *Sid Robin/Charles Shavers*		Guy Lombardo (Kenny Gardner)

29

PEAK DATE	CH	10	5	PK	RANK	GOLD	Title — Songwriter(s)	SYMBL	Artist
10/13	2			1	290		The Morningside Of The Mountain....................... *Dick Manning/Larry Stock*		Jan Garber (Roy Cordell)
2/3	2			1	291		Hot Rod Race .... *George Wilson* [N]		Tiny Hill
5/5	1			1	292		Once Upon A Nickel .... *Buddy Kaye/Tony Starr* [N]		Ray Bolger & Ethel Merman
5/26	1			1	293		I Apologize .... *Al Goodhart/Al Hoffman/Ed Nelson*	❶	Champ Butler
9/15	1			1	294		When The Saints Go Marching In .... *James Black/Katherine Purvis* <B:30>		Percy Faith
8/25	1			1	295		I Want To Be With You Always .... *Jim Beck/Lefty Frizzell*	❶	Lefty Frizzell
9/29	1			1	296		Black Strap Molasses....................... *Carmine Ennis/Marilou Harrington* [N]		Danny Kaye-Jimmy Durante-Jane Wyman-Groucho Marx
2/3	1			1	297		Get Out Those Old Records .... *John Jacob Loeb/Carmen Lombardo* <A:6>		Guy Lombardo (Kenny Gardner/Carmen Lombardo)
2/24	1			1	298		You're Just In Love....................... *Irving Berlin*		Dinah Shore & Russell Nype
2/24	1			1	299		My Heart Cries For You .... *Percy Faith/Carl Sigman*		Victor Young (Louanne Hogan/Joe Graydon)

30

PEAK DATE	CH	10	5	PK	RANK	GOLD	Title — Songwriter(s)	SYMBL	Artist
9/8	1			1	300		Way Up In North Carolina .... *Hank Beebe/Orville Campbell*	✦	Belltones Feat. David & Bebbe
6/30	1			1	301		Wondrous Word (of the Lord) .... *Ken Carson*	✦	Ken Carson
9/22	1			1	302		I Want To Be Near You....................... *Marshall Brown*		Johnny Desmond

PEAK DATE	WEEKS				R A N K	G O L D	Title	PEAK POSITION Songwriter(s)	S Y M B L	D E B U T	Artist
	CH	10	5	PK							

30 (cont'd)

PEAK DATE	CH	10	5	PK	RANK	GOLD	Title / Songwriter(s)	SYMBL	Artist
9/22	1			1	303		I Want To Be Near You ....*Marshall Brown* <A:29>		Percy Faith (Peter Hanley)
8/11	1			1	304		That's My Boy ....*Stan Freberg* <A:11> **[N]**		Stan Freberg
11/10	1			1	305		I Ran All The Way Home................................*Bennie Benjamin/George Weiss*		Buddy Greco
11/3	1			1	306		Twenty Three Starlets (And Me) ....*Tom Glazer* **[N]**		Merv Griffin
6/23	1			1	307		Unless ....*Stanley Damerell/Tolchard Evans/Robert Hargreaves* <A:21>		Gordon Jenkins (Bob Stevens)
4/7	1			1	308		You're Just In Love..*Irving Berlin*		Ethel Merman & Dick Haymes
12/29	1			1	309		You Better Go Now ....*Robert Graham/Bickley Reichner* ❶		Jeri Southern With Camarata
12/1	1			1	310		And So To Sleep Again ....*Joe Marsala/Sunny Skylar*		Paul Weston (Norman Luboff Choir)

1952

NATIONAL NEWS: Gen. Dwight Eisenhower, with running mate Richard Nixon, rolls to a landslide presidential election over Democratic nominee Adlai Stevenson. President Truman seizes steel mills in an emergency action when 600,000 steel workers go on strike, but the Supreme Court rules the seizure unconstitutional.

INTERNATIONAL NEWS: Peace talks drag on in Korea, and Allied bombing escalates to place pressure on the North Korean government. An Army coup in Egypt overthrows King Farouk. President Truman signs a peace treaty with Japan, granting that nation full sovereignty. Britain's King George VI dies of lung cancer.

COMMERCE AND SCIENCE: A mechanical heart is used for the first time in a human patient at Pennsylvania Hospital in Philadelphia. President Truman dedicates the world's first atomic submarine. General Motors offers air conditioning on some of its 1953 models.

FADS AND FASHION: Scrabble, a board game first marketed under that name in 1947, becomes a national fad.

SPORTS: The Olympic Games in Helsinki feature gold-medal performances by Emil Zapotek (the marathon, 5,000 and 10,000 meters) and repeat decathlon winner Bob Mathias. Casey Stengel's New York Yankees win their fourth straight World Series, edging the Brooklyn Dodgers four games to three. It's the Detroit Lions over the Cleveland Browns in the NFL title game, 17-7. Michigan State is the nation's best in college football. The Minneapolis Lakers are victorious in the NBA Finals. Kansas comes out on top in NCAA basketball. Rocky Marciano knocks out Jersey Joe Walcott for the world heavyweight championship. Middleweight champ Sugar Ray Robinson KO's Rocky Graziano. Young tennis phenom Maureen Connolly wins Wimbledon and the U.S. championship.

MOVIES: Gene Kelly creates what may be the finest American musical with *Singin' In the Rain*. *The Greatest Show on Earth* is Oscar's choice for Best Picture. Gary Cooper stands tall as Best Actor in *High Noon* opposite Grace Kelly, as Shirley Booth wins Best Actress honors for *Come Back, Little Sheba*. John Wayne has one of his greatest roles in John Ford's *The Quiet Man*. Other box office hits include *This Is Cinerama*, *The Snows of Kilimanjaro*, *Ivanhoe* and *Hans Christian Andersen* starring Danny Kaye.

TELEVISION: *I Love Lucy* rules the nation's airwaves, followed by a double dose of Godfrey — *Arthur Godfrey's Talent Scouts* and *Arthur Godfrey and His Friends*. *The Jackie Gleason Show*, featuring the classic *Honeymooners* sketches with Art Carney, debuts. Jack Webb's *Dragnet* is an instant smash. *The Adventures of Ozzie & Harriet* makes its TV debut after concluding its eight-year run on radio. *Your Show of Shows* repeats as Emmy winner.

THEATER: The revival of Rodgers & Hart's *Pal Joey* and the sex comedy *The Seven Year Itch* starring Tom Ewell are Broadway standouts.

BOOKS: Several enduring classics are published this year: Ernest Hemingways' *The Old Man and the Sea*, John Steinbeck's *East of Eden*, Bernard Malamaud's *The Natural* and *Anne Frank: Diary of a Young Girl*.

1952 — TOP 20 ARTISTS

1. **Eddie Fisher**
1,084

2. **Johnnie Ray**
635

3. **Patti Page**
603

4.	577	**Jo Stafford**
5.	571	**Les Paul & Mary Ford**
6.	567	**Four Aces**
7.	549	**Rosemary Clooney**
8.	505	**Kay Starr**
9.	481	**Perry Como**
10.	480	**Frankie Laine**
11.	470	**Nat "King" Cole**
12.	462	**Eddy Howard**
13.	376	**Ray Anthony**
14.	370	**Gordon Jenkins**
15.	363	**Don Cornell**
16.	347	**Guy Lombardo**
17.	344	**Doris Day**
18.	280	**Ames Brothers**
19.	275	**Georgia Gibbs**
20.	272	**Hugo Winterhalter**

1952 — TOP SONGWRITERS

	# of Hits	Points	
1.	10	890	**Chilton Price**
2.	9	811	**Pee Wee King**
	9	811	**Redd Stewart**
4.	7	608	**Sammy Cahn**
5.	6	519	**Lester Allen**
	6	519	**Robert Hill**
7.	6	491	**Irving Gordon**
8.	5	454	**John Sexton**
	5	454	**Eberhard Storch**
	5	454	**John Turner**
11.	5	452	**Bennie Benjamin**
	5	452	**George Weiss**

1952 — TOP ARTIST DEBUTS

1.	2/09	**Sunny Gale** (150)
2.	5/17	**Al Martino** ★
3.	6/14	**Steve Lawrence** ★
4.	6/14	**Fats Domino** ★
5.	6/14	**Hank Thompson** ◆
6.	8/16	† **The Hilltoppers** (88)
7.	8/23	**Kitty Wells** ◆
8.	10/18	**Joni James** (89) ★
9.	12/20	**The Gaylords** (102)

PEAK DATE	WEEKS				RANK	GOLD	Title	PEAK POSITION *Songwriter(s)*	SYMBL	DEBUT	Artist
	CH	10	5	PK							

1

| 9/13 | 25 | 22 | 17 | 12 | 1 | ● | **You Belong To Me** ....*Pee Wee King/Chilton Price/Redd Stewart* | | | | **Jo Stafford** |

Disc Jockey: 22,22,9,5,4,1,1,1,1,1,1,1,1,1,2,1,1,2,3,6,6,10,6,14
Best Seller: 23,12,8,5,2,1,1,1,1,1,2,2,2,3,5,5,5,7,12,16,17,14,19
Juke Box: 28,16,9,6,1,1,2,2,2,2,2,2,2,3,4,4,5,6,6,10,13,17

| 3/15 | 25 | 19 | 17 | 10 | 2 | ● | **Wheel Of Fortune** ....*Bennie Benjamin/George Weiss* | | | | **Kay Starr** |

Juke Box: 15,9,5,4,2,1,1,1,1,1,1,1,1,2,1,2,3,4,9,13,16,28,22,26
Best Seller: 16,6,3,2,1,1,1,1,1,1,1,1,2,2,4,5,8,13,14,21,22
Disc Jockey: 24,8,3,1,1,1,1,1,1,1,1,1,2,3,6,7,9,17

| 9/27 | 22 | 18 | 16 | 10 | 3 | ● | **I Went To Your Wedding** ....*Jessie Mae Robinson <B:4>* | | | | **Patti Page** |

Juke Box: 15,8,5,3,1,1,1,1,1,1,1,1,1,1,2,2,3,4,7,13,19,15
Best Seller: 17,7,4,2,2,2,2,1,1,1,1,1,3,4,4,5,13,12,18,12,17
Disc Jockey: 10,5,5,3,2,2,2,2,2,2,1,3,3,4,4,7,10,-,15

| 7/12 | 21 | 15 | 13 | 9 | 4 | ● | **Auf Wiederseh'n Sweetheart** ....*John Sexton/Eberhard Storch/John Turner* | | | | **Vera Lynn** |

Best Seller: 12,5,3,1,1,1,1,1,1,1,1,2,4,6,8,13,12,21,21,28
Disc Jockey: 14,9,5,7,3,1,1,1,1,1,1,3,4,4,9,9,19,-,24
Juke Box: 25,13,8,7,2,2,1,1,1,1,2,2,4,6,6,8,10,25

| 5/17 | 20 | 17 | 14 | 7 | 5 | ● | **Kiss Of Fire** ....*Lester Allen/Robert Hill* | | | | **Georgia Gibbs** |

Disc Jockey: 7,5,3,1,1,1,1,1,2,1,2,2,4,4,10,11,18,21
Juke Box: 19,10,7,6,6,3,3,1,1,1,1,1,1,5,7,7,8,16,25
Best Seller: 8,5,5,5,3,3,2,3,3,4,4,4,4,3,6,8,10,17,18,29

| 11/29 | 23 | 20 | 16 | 6 | 6 | ● | **Why Don't You Believe Me** ....*Lew Douglas/King Laney/Leroy Rodde* | ❶ | | **Joni James** |

Disc Jockey: 17,14,9,5,5,3,1,1,1,1,1,2,2,3,3,4,14,11,12,19
Best Seller: 21,17,9,7,5,4,1,1,1,2,3,3,2,2,3,3,4,7,11,13,20
Juke Box: 13,9,8,6,4,4,3,3,2,1,1,1,2,2,2,3,4,4,5,5,8,-,16,17

| 5/17 | 38 | 26 | 20 | 5 | 7 | ● | **Blue Tango** ....*Leroy Anderson* [I] | | | | **Leroy Anderson** |

Best Seller: 24,26,22,13,10,7,5,4,3,3,2,2,2,2,2,2,2,1,1,1,1,1,2,3,5,6,6,8,7,11,11,16,14,20,27,20,20
Disc Jockey: 29,-,-,-,-,25,-,29,14,9,9,6,5,2,2,3,4,3,5,4,4,2,4,5,8,5,12,10,16,19
Juke Box: 27,19,16,10,8,5,5,4,5,4,3,4,3,3,4,5,5,5,6,6,9,11,13,16,15,20

| 12/6 | 21 | 18 | 15 | 3 | 8 | ● | **The Glow-Worm** ....*Paul Lincke/Johnny Mercer/Lilla Robinson* | | | | **Mills Brothers** |

Juke Box: 18,15,4,3,3,3,2,1,1,1,2,2,3,3,4,4,6,6,12
Disc Jockey: 17,11,6,7,4,3,3,3,2,2,2,3,4,3,3,3,5,6,17,20
Best Seller: 17,11,10,9,6,4,4,2,2,3,3,3,4,4,2,4,5,5,10,17

| 7/26 | 27 | 18 | 13 | 3 | 9 | ● | **Half As Much** ....*Curley Williams* | | | | **Rosemary Clooney** |

Juke Box: 26,28,22,13,7,5,3,1,1,2,2,2,2,1,3,2,5,5,6,7,9,10,12,14
Disc Jockey: 28,-,16,14,21,13,19,6,14,6,6,4,3,3,4,2,2,2,2,3,3,5,8,8,11,13,14,18
Best Seller: 28,25,17,19,11,12,7,8,5,4,3,3,2,3,2,4,5,5,7,7,6,6,11,12,16,15

| 6/7 | 19 | 15 | 13 | 3 | 10 | ● | **Here In My Heart** ....*Bill Borrelli/Pat Genaro/Lou Levinson* | ❶ | | **Al Martino** |

Best Seller: 12,4,3,1,2,1,1,2,3,2,3,5,4,5,7,7,15,22,23
Disc Jockey: 21,4,2,2,2,1,2,1,1,2,2,3,6,5,7,11,24
Juke Box: 16,7,4,4,2,2,2,2,2,3,3,5,6,6,10,23,28

| 1/5 | 24 | 18 | 12 | 3 | 11 | ● | **Slow Poke** ....*Pee Wee King/Chilton Price/Redd Stewart* | ❶ | | **Pee Wee King** (Redd Stewart) |

Juke Box: 19,16,9,7,7,4,4,3,1,1,1,2,2,4,4,4,5,6,6,10,13,11,18,28
Best Seller: 24,24,24,13,14,14,7,10,7,3,3,4,4,4,5,5,8,8,12,15,23,30
Disc Jockey: 28,-,20,13,15,8,17,9,15,10,9,8,9,17,20,24,30

| 11/22 | 19 | 16 | 13 | 2 | 12 | ● | **It's In The Book (Parts 1 & 2)** ....*Johnny Standley/Art Thorsen* [C] | ✦ | | **Johnny Standley** |

Best Seller: 19,13,7,5,3,3,4,1,1,2,2,5,5,5,4,5,8,10,15
Disc Jockey: 22,-,14,9,7,4,4,4,4,5,5,6,15,8,9
Juke Box: 29,19,12,13,14,12,15,18,18,6,10

| 12/27 | 5 | 4 | 3 | 2 | 13 | ● | **I Saw Mommy Kissing Santa Claus** ....*Tommie Connor* [X-N] | ❶ | | **Jimmy Boyd** |

Best Seller: 13,6,2,1,1
Disc Jockey: 19,8,3,5
Juke Box: 17,7,8,3

| 9/6 | 21 | 17 | 12 | 1 | 14 | ● | **Wish You Were Here** ....*Harold Rome <B:24>* | | | | **Eddie Fisher** |

Disc Jockey: 18,10,6,3,4,4,1,2,2,2,3,3,3,3,4,6,7,12,7,15
Best Seller: 21,13,11,6,4,4,3,3,3,3,3,3,3,4,4,6,6,7,10,12,16
Juke Box: 14,16,8,5,4,4,4,4,3,3,4,4,5,7,6,7,13

| 7/5 | 22 | 16 | 12 | 1 | 15 | | **Delicado** ....*Waldyr Azevedo/Jack Lawrence* [I] | | | | **Percy Faith** |

Best Seller: 19,15,13,7,6,5,4,4,3,2,1,2,4,2,4,5,6,5,9,11,16,18
Disc Jockey: 21,20,12,8,5,6,3,4,3,4,4,8,6,8,9,12,11,18,23
Juke Box: 27,18,19,16,10,8,5,4,8,8,9,9,7,9,18,19

| 5/24 | 19 | 14 | 10 | 1 | 16 | ● | **A Guy Is A Guy** ....*Oscar Brand* | | | | **Doris Day** |

Juke Box: 21,27,8,6,2,2,2,2,1,2,2,3,4,6,9,15,-,-,28
Disc Jockey: 24,15,9,5,2,3,2,2,3,2,3,3,6,5,13,18,17
Best Seller: 23,11,6,6,6,4,4,4,4,4,5,6,7,7,8,10,16,22,28

2

1/26	24	18	13	6	17	●	**Tell Me Why** ....*Al Alberts/Marty Gold <B:14>*				**Four Aces Feat. Al Alberts**
8/2	17	12	6	3	18		**Botch-A-Me (Ba-Ba-Baciami Piccina)** ....*Luigi Astore/Riccardo Morbelli/Eddie Stanley*				**Rosemary Clooney**
4/12	30	19	13	2	19		**Any Time** ....*Herbert Lawson*				**Eddie Fisher**
1/12	22	16	11	2	20		**The Little White Cloud That Cried** ....*Johnnie Ray <A:1>*				**Johnnie Ray & The Four Lads**
4/26	15	12	8	1	21		**At Last** ....*Mack Gordon/Harry Warren*				**Ray Anthony** (Tommy Mercer)

PEAK DATE	WEEKS				RANK	GOLD	Title / PEAK POSITION / Songwriter(s)	SYMBL	DEBUT	Artist
	CH	10	5	PK						

2 (cont'd)

| 3/1 | 12 | 8 | 6 | 1 | 22 | | Tiger Rag ....Harry DeCosta/Edwin Edwards/James LaRocca/W.H. Ragas/ Anthony Sbarbaro/Larry Shields | | | Les Paul & Mary Ford |

3

4/5	22	15	9	6	23	●	The Blacksmith Blues..Jack Holmes			Ella Mae Morse
9/27	20	15	12	3	24	●	Jambalaya ....Hank Williams <B:25>			Jo Stafford
6/28	19	13	4	3	25		I'm Yours ....Robert Mellin			Eddie Fisher
8/9	18	10	5	1	26		Maybe ....Allan Flynn/Frank Madden <B:19>			Perry Como & Eddie Fisher
6/21	17	10	4	1	27	●	I'm Yours ....Robert Mellin			Don Cornell
7/12	13	8	4	1	28	●	Lover ....Lorenz Hart/Richard Rodgers			Peggy Lee & Gordon Jenkins

4

7/12	20	13	8	5	29		Walkin' My Baby Back Home ....Fred Ahlert/Roy Turk			Johnnie Ray
9/27	17	13	5	3	30		You Belong To Me ....Pee Wee King/Chilton Price/Redd Stewart <A:1>			Patti Page
5/24	21	13	3	1	31		Pittsburgh, Pennsylvania ....Bob Merrill			Guy Mitchell
8/16	16	9	3	1	32		Auf Wiederseh'n, Sweetheart.....John Sexton/Eberhard Storch/John Turner <B:26>			Eddy Howard
10/18	12	8	2	1	33		I Should Care.................Sammy Cahn/Axel Stordahl/Paul Weston			Ralph Flanagan (Harry Prime)
12/27	3	3	2	1	34		I Saw Mommy Kissing Santa Claus ....Tommie Connor [X-N]			Spike Jones (George Rock)
3/1	19	8	1	1	35	●	Tell Me Why...............................Al Alberts/Marty Gold <B:25>			Eddie Fisher

5

9/6	19	11	3	3	36	●	High Noon (Do Not Forsake Me) ....Dimitri Tiomkin/Ned Washington <B:20>			Frankie Laine
10/11	14	9	2	2	37		Meet Mister Callaghan...............................Eric Spear <B:15> [I]			Les Paul
5/24	19	9	1	1	38		I'll Walk Alone ....Sammy Cahn/Jule Styne			Don Cornell

6

3/1	18	8		4	39	●	Please, Mr. Sun ....Sid Frank/Ray Getzov <B:8>			Johnnie Ray
4/19	18	9		1	40		Blue Tango ....Leroy Anderson [I]			Hugo Winterhalter
11/8	17	9		1	41		Lady Of Spain ....Tolchard Evans/Erell Reaves <B:8>			Eddie Fisher
1/19	14	6		1	42		Slow Poke.................Pee Wee King/Chilton Price/Redd Stewart			Ralph Flanagan (Singing Winds)
6/21	15	4		1	43		Kiss Of Fire ....Lester Allen/Robert Hill			Tony Martin
2/23	14	4		1	44		Dance Me Loose ....Lee Erwin/Mel Howard <B:12>			Arthur Godfrey
3/15	13	4		1	45		Wheel Of Fortune................Bennie Benjamin/George Weiss <B:29>			Bobby Wayne
4/5	10	3		1	46		Hambone...............................Red Saunders/Leon Washington			Frankie Laine & Jo Stafford

7

2/16	16	8		4	47		Bermuda ....Cynthia Strother	❶		Bell Sisters
11/22	19	8		2	48	●	Because You're Mine................Nicholas Brodszky/Sammy Cahn			Mario Lanza
11/1	19	10		1	49		Trying ....Billy Vaughn	❶		The Hill Toppers
4/12	17	6		1	50		Forgive Me ....Milton Ager/Jack Yellen <B:10>			Eddie Fisher
12/6	17	5		1	51		Takes Two To Tango ....Al Hoffman/Dick Manning	✦		Pearl Bailey
4/19	16	4		1	52		Perfidia ....Alberto Dominguez/Milton Leeds			Four Aces Feat. Al Alberts
2/9	12	4		1	53		Be My Life's Companion ....Milton DeLugg/Bob Hilliard			Mills Brothers
8/30	14	3		1	54	●	Sugarbush ....Josef Marais			Doris Day - Frankie Laine
11/29	10	3		1	55		Yours ....Albert Gamse/Gonzalo Roig/Jack Sherr			Vera Lynn
5/17	16	2		1	56		Be Anything (But Be Mine) ....Irving Gordon			Eddy Howard
11/29	8	2		1	57		I..................Buddy Arnold/Milton Berle/Robert Mellin			Don Cornell

8

8/30	25	10		2	58		Somewhere Along The Way ....Kurt Adams/Sammy Gallop			Nat "King" Cole
2/16	15	3		2	59		Here Am I - Broken Hearted ....Lew Brown/B.G. DeSylva/Ray Henderson <A:6>			Johnnie Ray
12/13	13	3		1	60		Outside Of Heaven................Chester Conn/Sammy Gallop <A:6>			Eddie Fisher
1/26	13	3		1	61		Slow Poke ....Pee Wee King/Chilton Price/Redd Stewart			Helen O'Connell
7/12	12	2		1	62		Walkin' My Baby Back Home ....Fred Ahlert/Roy Turk <B:26>			Nat "King" Cole & Billy May
6/28	9	1		1	63		Here In My Heart ....Bill Borrelli/Pat Genaro/Lou Levinson			Vic Damone
11/29	8	1		1	64		Lady Of Spain ....Tolchard Evans/Erell Reaves <A:7> [I]			Les Paul
1/19	6	1		1	65		Charmaine...............................Lew Pollack/Erno Rapee			Paul Weston (Norman Luboff Choir)

9

4/12	19	7		6	66		Blue Tango ....Leroy Anderson [I]			Guy Lombardo
9/20	14	5		4	67	●	Indian Love Call...............Rudolf Friml/Oscar Hammerstein/Otto Harbach	❶		Slim Whitman
7/26	14	3		2	68		Vanessa ....Bernie Wayne			Hugo Winterhalter
3/1	11	2		1	69		Come What May ....Vaughn Horton <B:22>			Patti Page
8/23	11	2		1	70		Once In Awhile...............Michael Edwards/Bud Green			Patti Page
9/20	10	2		1	71		Should I ....Nacio Herb Brown/Arthur Freed			Four Aces Feat. Al Alberts
5/10	12	1		1	72		Ay-Round The Corner (Bee-hind The Bush)...............Josef Marais			Jo Stafford
11/8	9	1		1	73		Comes A-Long A-Love ....Al Sherman <B:22>			Kay Starr

PEAK DATE	CH	10	5	PK	RANK	GOLD	Title / Peak Position / Songwriter(s)	SYMBL	DEBUT	Artist
							9 (cont'd)			
12/27	2	1		1	74		The Night Before Christmas Song .... *Johnny Marks* [X]			Rosemary Clooney & Gene Autry
							10			
4/19	17	2		2	75		Blue Tango .... *Leroy Anderson* [I]			Les Baxter
1/19	11	1		1	76		Cry .... *Churchill Kohlman*			Eileen Barton
4/12	11	1		1	77		Wheel Of Fortune .... *Bennie Benjamin/George Weiss*			Bell Sisters
5/3	10	1		1	78		That's The Chance You Take .... *Sylvia Dee/Sid Lippman* <A:7>			Eddie Fisher
2/16	9	1		1	79		A Kiss To Build A Dream On............ *Oscar Hammerstein/Bert Kalmar/Harry Ruby*			Hugo Winterhalter (Johnny Parker)
6/28	4	1		1	80		As Time Goes By .... *Herman Hupfeld*			Ray Anthony (Tommy Mercer)
							11			
9/27	13			2	81		Walkin' To Missouri .... *Bob Merrill*			Sammy Kaye (Tony Russo)
4/5	14			1	82		Stolen Love .... *Marlene Feinstein/Anna Sickle*			Eddy Howard
12/20	10			1	83		Heart And Soul.................... *Hoagy Carmichael/Frank Loesser* <B:20>			Four Aces Feat. Al Alberts
9/27	7			1	84		Meet Mr. Callahan .... *Eric Spear* [I]	✦		The Harry Grove Trio
11/22	5			1	85		It's Worth Any Price You Pay.................... *Sylvia Dee/Sid Lippman*			Eddy Howard
							12			
7/26	8			2	86		Take My Heart .... *Bill Borrelli/Pat Genaro*			Al Martino
2/2	15			1	87		Unforgettable .... *Irving Gordon*			Nat "King" Cole
2/9	11			1	88		Slow Poke .... *Pee Wee King/Chilton Price/Redd Stewart* <A:6>			Arthur Godfrey
3/8	10			1	89		Please Mr. Sun .... *Sid Frank/Ray Getzov* <B:16>			Perry Como
9/20	10			1	90		You Belong To Me .... *Pee Wee King/Chilton Price/Redd Stewart*			Dean Martin
8/30	10			1	91		Doodletown Fifers........................ *William Finegan/Edward Sauter* [I]	❶		Sauter-Finegan
8/23	8			1	92		All Of Me .... *Gerald Marks/Seymour Simons*			Johnnie Ray
10/11	8			1	93		High Noon (Do Not Forsake Me) .... *Dimitri Tiomkin/Ned Washington*			Tex Ritter
9/13	6			1	94		Too Old To Cut The Mustard .... *Bill Carlisle*	✦		Marlene Dietrich & Rosemary Clooney
							13			
8/16	9			2	95		Auf Wiederseh'n Sweetheart .....*John Sexton/Eberhard Storch/John Turner* <B:20>			Guy Lombardo (Kenny Martin)
12/13	4			2	96		You Win Again .... *Hank Williams*			Tommy Edwards
6/21	11			1	97		I'm Confessin' (That I Love You) .....*Don Dougherty/Al Neiburg/Ellis Reynolds* <B:14>			Les Paul & Mary Ford
8/23	8			1	98		Aufwiederseh'n Sweetheart .... *John Sexton/Eberhard Storch/John Turner*			Ames Brothers
5/3	8			1	99		What's The Use? .... *Stuart Foster/Kermit Goell/David Seville*			Johnnie Ray
9/6	8			1	100		Fool, Fool, Fool.................................... *Ahmet Ertegun* <B:18>			Kay Starr
3/1	6			1	101		Wheel Of Fortune .... *Bennie Benjamin/George Weiss*	✦		Eddie Wilcox with Sunny Gale
11/8	5			1	102		Bunny Hop........................... *Ray Anthony/Leonard Auletti*			Ray Anthony (Tommy Mercer/Marcie Miller)
12/27	1			1	103		Rudolph, The Red-Nosed Reindeer .... *Johnny Marks* [X-R]			Gene Autry & The Pinafores
							14			
7/5	13			3	104		I'll Walk Alone .... *Sammy Cahn/Jule Styne*			Jane Froman
5/31	8			2	105		Kiss Of Fire .... *Lester Allen/Robert Hill* <B:24>			Toni Arden
1/19	11			1	106		A Garden In The Rain........................ *James Dyrenforth/Carroll Gibbons* <A:2>			Four Aces Feat. Al Alberts
4/5	11			1	107		Wimoweh .... *Paul Campbell* [F]			The Weavers & Gordon Jenkins
3/8	9			1	108		The Three Bells (Les Trois Cloches) (The Jimmy Brown Song) .... *Bert Reisfeld/Jean Villard*	❶		Les Compagnons De La Chanson
6/7	9			1	109		Carioca .... *Edward Eliscu/Gus Kahn/Vincent Youmans* <A:13> [I]			Les Paul
10/18	8			1	110		I Laughed At Love............................... *Benny Davis/Abner Silver*			Sunny Gale
7/19	7			1	111		Smoke Rings .... *H. Eugene Gifford/Ned Washington* <B:15>			Les Paul & Mary Ford
10/11	6			1	112		Mademoiselle .... *Lester Lee/Bob Russell*			Eddy Howard
9/6	6			1	113		Feet Up (Pat Him On The Po-Po)....................... *Bob Merrill*			Guy Mitchell
8/30	4			1	114		Just One Of Those Things .... *Cole Porter*			Peggy Lee & Gordon Jenkins
8/23	4			1	115		Adios............................... *Enric Madriguera/Eddie Woods*			Gisele MacKenzie
							15			
1/5	12			3	116		Don't Leave My Poor Heart Breaking............... *Henry Glover/Charles Kanter/Sydney Nathan*			Elliot Lawrence (Cowboy Copas/Rosalind Patton)
5/17	11			1	117		Junco Partner A Worthless Cajun .... *Ellen Shad*			Richard Hayes
8/2	10			1	118		Here In My Heart .... *Bill Borrelli/Pat Genaro/Lou Levinson*			Tony Bennett
10/4	8			1	119		Take Me In Your Arms And Hold Me .... *Cindy Walker* <A:5>			Les Paul & Mary Ford
7/19	7			1	120		In The Good Old Summertime ....*George Evans/Ren Shields* <A:14>			Les Paul & Mary Ford
11/1	5			1	121		My Favorite Song........................ *Moose Charlap/Jack Gold*			Ames Brothers
4/12	3			1	122		Try .... *Stan Freberg/Rubin Raksin* [N]			Stan Freberg
11/8	2			1	123		Forgetting You .... *Lew Brown/B.G. DeSylva/Ray Henderson*			Richard Hayes
							16			
6/28	13			1	124		Kiss Of Fire .... *Lester Allen/Robert Hill*			Billy Eckstine

PEAK DATE	WEEKS				R A N K	G O L D	Title	PEAK POSITION Songwriter(s)	S Y M B L	D E B U T	Artist
	CH	10	5	PK							
1/26	11			1	125		A Kiss To Build A Dream On	...Oscar Hammerstein/Bert Kalmar/Harry Ruby <A:10>			Louis Armstrong
4/19	11			1	126		Tulips And Heather	...............................Milton Carson <A:12>			Perry Como
5/17	11			1	127		Whispering Winds	...............................Corky Robbins			Patti Page
2/2	7			1	128		Shrimp Boats	...............Paul Howard/Paul Weston	✦		Dolores Gray with Camarata
9/6	6			1	129		Till The End Of The World	...............................Vaughn Horton			Bing Crosby & Grady Martin
9/13	5			1	130		Have A Good Time	...............Boudleaux Bryant/Felice Bryant			Tony Bennett
10/4	5			1	131		Because You're Mine	............Nicholas Brodszky/Sammy Cahn <B:22>			Nat "King" Cole

17

PEAK DATE	WEEKS				R A N K	G O L D	Title	PEAK POSITION Songwriter(s)	S Y M B L	D E B U T	Artist
4/12	6			2	132 ●		Tenderly	...............................Walter Gross/Jack Lawrence			Rosemary Clooney
3/15	14			1	133		Wishin'	...............Bob Hart/Ben Lewis/Teddy Simms			Eddy Howard
10/25	6			1	134		You'll Never Get Away	......Alex Kramer/Joan Whitney/Hy Zaret [N]			Don Cornell & Teresa Brewer
1/12	6			1	135		Mother At Your Feet Is Kneeling	...............................(traditional)			Bobby Wayne
10/11	3			1	136		Blues In The Night	...............Harold Arlen/Johnny Mercer			Rosemary Clooney
5/31	3			1	137		I'm Yours	...............................Robert Mellin			Four Aces Feat. Al Alberts
8/9	2			1	138		I Love Girls	...............................Jimmie Dodd [N]			Arthur Godfrey
2/2	2			1	139		Charmaine	...............Lew Pollack/Erno Rapee [I]	❶		Billy May

18

PEAK DATE	WEEKS				R A N K	G O L D	Title	PEAK POSITION Songwriter(s)	S Y M B L	D E B U T	Artist
5/10	8			1	140		One Little Candle	...............George Mysels/Maloy Roach			Perry Como
10/4	7			1	141		String Along	...............................Dave Coleman			Ames Brothers
8/9	6			1	142		Zing A Little Zong	...............Leo Robin/Harry Warren			Bing Crosby & Jane Wyman
5/10	5			1	143		Lady Love	...............Lester Lee/Bob Russell <B:20>			Vaughn Monroe
3/15	4			1	144		Silver And Gold	......Bob Crosby/Henry Prichard/Del Sharbutt			Pee Wee King (Redd Stewart)
2/16	3			1	145		Be My Life's Companion	...............Milton DeLugg/Bob Hilliard			Rosemary Clooney
8/2	3			1	146		Kay's Lament	...............Hal Stanley/Kay Starr <A:13>			Kay Starr
8/2	2			1	147		I Would Rather Look At You	...............................Art Kassel			Gloria Hart
12/6	2			1	148		Conquest	...............................Alfred Newman <A:4>			Patti Page
1/5	1			1	149		Blue December	......Arthur Berman/Ralph Care/Marvin Kahn			Hugo Winterhalter

19

PEAK DATE	WEEKS				R A N K	G O L D	Title	PEAK POSITION Songwriter(s)	S Y M B L	D E B U T	Artist
12/6	3			2	150		Nina Never Knew	...............Louis Alter/Milton Drake			Johnny Desmond
6/28	6			1	151		Watermelon Weather	......Hoagy Carmichael/Paul Francis Webster <A:3>			Perry Como & Eddie Fisher
3/29	6			1	152		Hambone	......Red Saunders/Leon Washington [N]			Phil Harris & The Bell Sisters
2/9	4			1	153		I Wanna Love You	...............Johnny Parker <B:29>			Ames Brothers
1/12	3			1	154		When It's Sleepy Time Down South	......Clarence Muse/Leon Rene/Otis Rene			Louis Armstrong & Gordon Jenkins
10/25	2			1	155		Takes Two To Tango	...............Al Hoffman/Dick Manning			Louis Armstrong
11/22	2			1	156		The Birth Of The Blues	......Lew Brown/B.G. DeSylva/Ray Henderson			Frank Sinatra
12/27	1			1	157		I Saw Mommy Kissing Santa Claus	......Tommie Connor [X-N]	✦		Molly Bee
11/1	1			1	158		To Know You (Is to Love You)	......Robert Allen/Allan Roberts			Perry Como (Fontane Sisters)
12/6	1			1	159		Greyhound	...............................Rudy Toombs			Buddy Morrow (Frankie Lester)
4/26	1			1	160		Around The Corner (Beneath The Berry Tree)	......Josef Marais			The Weavers & Gordon Jenkins

20

PEAK DATE	WEEKS				R A N K	G O L D	Title	PEAK POSITION Songwriter(s)	S Y M B L	D E B U T	Artist
5/31	6			2	161		I Waited A Little Too Long	...............Sidney Miller/Donald O'Connor			Kay Starr
10/18	6			2	162 ●		Jambalaya (On The Bayou)	...............................Hank Williams			Hank Williams
9/13	4			2	163		Bim Bam Baby	...............Sammy Mysels <B:30>			Frank Sinatra
8/23	6			1	164		Auf Wiederseh'n, Sweetheart	......John Sexton/Eberhard Storch/John Turner			Les Baxter
8/16	6			1	165		Half As Much	...............Curley Williams <A:13>			Guy Lombardo (Kenny Martin)
5/10	6			1	166		Idaho State Fair	......George Mysels/Sammy Mysels/Dick Sanford <A:18>			Vaughn Monroe
8/9	5			1	167		Rock Of Gibraltar	...............................Joe Turner <A:5>			Frankie Laine
2/23	5			1	168		Crazy Heart	...............Maurice Murray/Fred Rose			Guy Lombardo (Kenny Gardner)
11/1	5			1	169		Blues In Advance	...............................Nell Drummond			Dinah Shore
6/28	4			1	170		Just A Little Lovin' (Will Go a Long Way)	......Eddy Arnold/Zeke Clements <A:3>			Eddie Fisher
8/9	3			1	171		This Is The Beginning Of The End	...............Mack Gordon			Don Cornell
8/16	3			1	172		When I Fall In Love	...............Edward Heyman/Victor Young			Doris Day
6/7	2			1	173		Kiss Of Fire	...............Lester Allen/Robert Hill			Louis Armstrong
11/15	2			1	174		Just Squeeze Me (But Don't Tease Me)	......Duke Ellington/Lee Gaines <A:11>			Four Aces Feat. Al Alberts
8/16	2			1	175		A Sinner Am I	...............................Johnnie Ray <A:12>			Johnnie Ray
10/11	1			1	176		Marilyn	...............Ervin Drake/Jimmy Shirl			Ray Anthony (Tommy Mercer/The Skyliners)
12/13	1			1	177		A Full Time Job	...............................Gerry Teifer			Doris Day - Johnnie Ray
10/18	1			1	178		I Went To Your Wedding	...............Jessie Mae Robinson			Steve Gibson & Original Red Caps
2/2	1			1	179		Le Fiacre	...............Jean Sablon/Leon Xanroff [F]	❶		Gisele MacKenzie
4/5	1			1	180		Hambone	......Red Saunders/Leon Washington	✦		Red Saunders (Dolores Hawkins)

21

PEAK DATE	WEEKS				R A N K	G O L D	Title	PEAK POSITION Songwriter(s)	S Y M B L	D E B U T	Artist
8/2	3			3	181		Poinciana	...............Buddy Bernier/Nat Simon	❶		Steve Lawrence
4/5	7			2	182		The Gandy Dancers' Ball	......Paul Howard/Paul Weston <B:30>			Frankie Laine

PEAK DATE	WEEKS				RANK	GOLD	Title	PEAK POSITION Songwriter(s)	SYMBL	DEBUT	Artist
	CH	10	5	PK							
11/1	3			2	183		Settin' The Woods On Fire	Ed Nelson/Fred Rose			Jo Stafford - Frankie Laine
9/6	4			1	184		Slaughter On Tenth Avenue (Parts I & II)	Richard Rodgers [I]			Ray Anthony
1/19	4			1	185		Cry	Churchill Kohlman			The Four Knights
8/16	3			1	186		So Madly In Love	Kim Gannon/Mabel Wayne			Georgia Gibbs
6/7	3			1	187		Be Anything (But Be Mine)	Irving Gordon			Peggy Lee & Gordon Jenkins
2/16	2			1	188		I Wanna Say Hello!	Jack Hoffman/Jimmy MacDonald	✦		Ellen Sutton

22

PEAK DATE	CH	10	5	PK	RANK	GOLD	Title	Songwriter(s)	SYMBL	DEBUT	Artist
2/9	4			2	189		Please, Mr. Sun	Sid Frank/Ray Getzov			Tommy Edwards
10/11	4			2	190		Three Letters	Billy Rose/Hal Stanley <A:9>			Kay Starr
2/2	4			1	191		Retreat (Cries My Heart)	Anita Boyer/Nancy Farnsworth/Thomas Furtado <A:9>			Patti Page
10/25	2			1	192		Trying	Billy Vaughn			Ella Fitzgerald
10/18	1			1	193		I'm Never Satisfied	Herb Perry <A:16>			Nat "King" Cole
10/4	1			1	194		My Love And Devotion	Milton Carson			Perry Como
5/10	1			1	195		Jump Through The Ring	Jeanne Cherdak/Jack Manus/Guy Wood			Vic Damone
10/18	1			1	196		Somebody Loves Me	B.G. DeSylva/George Gershwin/Ballard MacDonald			The Four Lads
3/8	1			1	197		Mountain Laurel	Chilton Price			Vaughn Monroe
11/8	1			1	198		Sinner Or Saint	Irving Gordon			Sarah Vaughan

23

PEAK DATE	CH	10	5	PK	RANK	GOLD	Title	Songwriter(s)	SYMBL	DEBUT	Artist
8/16	4			1	199		The Mocking Bird	Anton Dvorak			The Four Lads
9/6	4			1	200		Strange Sensation	Kay Twomey/Ben Weisman/Fred Wise	❶		June Valli
5/10	3			1	201		I May Hate Myself In The Morning	Bennie Benjamin/George Weiss	✦		Bette McLaurin & Her Friends
7/26	2			1	202		Rosanne	Dick Manning/Abe Osser/Edna Osser <B:30>			Vic Damone
6/7	2			1	203		Oakie Boogie	Johnny Tyler			Ella Mae Morse
3/8	1			1	204		Noodlin' Rag	Robert Allen/Allan Roberts			Perry Como (Fontane Sisters)
7/12	1			1	205		The Mask Is Off	Arthur Ford/Elmo Russ			Richard Hayes
9/27	1			1	206		Meet Mister Callaghan	Eric Spear [I]			Mitch Miller

24

PEAK DATE	CH	10	5	PK	RANK	GOLD	Title	Songwriter(s)	SYMBL	DEBUT	Artist
10/18	4			1	207		Faith Can Move Mountains	Ben Raleigh/Guy Wood <B:25>			Nat "King" Cole
4/5	3			1	208		I Hear A Rhapsody	Jack Baker/George Fragos/Dick Gasparre			Frank Sinatra
2/23	2			1	209		Bermuda	Cynthia Strother			Ray Anthony (Tommy Mercer/Marcie Miller)
6/28	2			1	210		I'm Yours	Robert Mellin <A:14>			Toni Arden
2/23	2			1	211		Chinatown My Chinatown	William Jerome/Gene Schwartz [I]	❶		Bobby Maxwell
7/26	1			1	212		The Hand Of Fate	Pat Ballard <A:1>			Eddie Fisher
5/3	1			1	213		I'll Walk Alone	Sammy Cahn/Jule Styne			Richard Hayes
8/16	1			1	214		Some Day	Rudolf Friml/Brian Hooker <B:27>			Tony Martin

25

PEAK DATE	CH	10	5	PK	RANK	GOLD	Title	Songwriter(s)	SYMBL	DEBUT	Artist
6/7	2			1	215		Gonna Get Along Without Ya Now	Milton Kellem			Teresa Brewer
10/11	2			1	216		The Ruby And The Pearl	Ray Evans/Jay Livingston <A:24>			Nat "King" Cole
10/25	2			1	217		No Two People	Frank Loesser			Doris Day - Donald O'Connor
2/2	2			1	218		Trust In Me	Milton Ager/Jean Schwartz/Ned Wever <A:4>			Eddie Fisher
10/18	2			1	219		Wish You Were Here	Harold Rome			Jane Froman
10/25	2			1	220		My Favorite Song	Moose Charlap/Jack Gold			Georgia Gibbs
6/14	2			1	221		Delicado	Waldyr Azevedo/Jack Lawrence [I]			Stan Kenton
9/27	1			1	222		Love Me (Baby Can't You Love Me)	William Engvick/Alec Wilder			Johnnie Ray
10/25	1			1	223		Early Autumn	Ralph Burns/Woody Herman/Johnny Mercer <A:3>			Jo Stafford

26

PEAK DATE	CH	10	5	PK	RANK	GOLD	Title	Songwriter(s)	SYMBL	DEBUT	Artist
6/28	3			2	224		Lonely Wine	Roy Wells			Les Baxter
11/1	2			2	225		'Cause I Love You That's A-Why	Bob Merrill			Guy Mitchell - Mindy Carson
8/30	4			1	226		Luna Rossa (Blushing Moon)	Vincenzo DeCrescenzo/Kermit Goell/ Renato Matassa/Antonio Viscione	✦		Alan Dean
7/26	2			1	227		Delicado	Waldyr Azevedo/Jack Lawrence [I]			Ralph Flanagan
10/18	2			1	228		Wish You Were Here	Harold Rome			Guy Lombardo (Kenny Martin)
5/17	1			1	229		Be Anything (But Be Mine)	Irving Gordon			Champ Butler
8/16	1			1	230		Funny (Not Much)	Philip Broughton/Marcie Neil/Hughie Prince <A:8>			Nat "King" Cole
1/12	1			1	231		Slow Poke	Pee Wee King/Chilton Price/Redd Stewart	❶		Hawkshaw Hawkins
9/13	1			1	232		I Don't Want To Take A Chance	Bert Garr/George Haynes/Averill Pollard/ Roy Testamark <A:4>			Eddie Howard
9/20	1			1	233		Little Grass Shack	Johnny Cogswell/Thomas Harrison/Johnny Noble [I]	❶		Johnny Maddox
4/19	1			1	234		Dancing With Tears In My Eyes	Joe Burke/Al Dubin [I]			Mantovani
6/21	1			1	235		The Day Of Jubilo	Terry Gilkyson			Guy Mitchell

27

PEAK DATE	CH	10	5	PK	RANK	GOLD	Title	Songwriter(s)	SYMBL	DEBUT	Artist
8/30	2			1	236		Night Train	Jimmy Forrest [I]			Buddy Morrow
5/24	2			1	237		The Bigger The Figure	Marshall Barer/Alec Wilder [N]			Louis Prima

1952

PEAK DATE	WEEKS				RANK	GOLD	Title	PEAK POSITION / Songwriter(s)	SYMBL	DEBUT	Artist
	CH	10	5	PK							
6/14	1			1	238		Busybody	Roy Brodsky/Sid Tepper			Pee Wee King (Redd Stewart)
5/3	1			1	239		September Song	Maxwell Anderson/Kurt Weill	✦		Liberace
10/11	1			1	240		Cincinatti Ding Dong	Harry Carlson/Roy Carroll/Erwin King			Art Lund
11/8	1			1	241		Dance Of Destiny	Robert Allen/Phil Springer			Tony Martin
8/30	1			1	242		Luna Rossa (Blushing Moon)	Vincenzo DeCrescenzo/Kermit Goell/ Renato Matassa/Antonio Viscione <A:24>			Tony Martin
1/19	1			1	243		Charmaine	Lew Pollack/Erno Rapee			Vaughn Monroe
5/10	1			1	244		Be Anything (But Be Mine)	Irving Gordon			Helen O'Connell

28

PEAK DATE	WEEKS				RANK	GOLD	Title	PEAK POSITION / Songwriter(s)	SYMBL	DEBUT	Artist
8/9	2			1	245		Watermelon Weather	Hoagy Carmichael/Paul Francis Webster			Bing Crosby & Peggy Lee
1/26	2			1	246		Slow Poke	Pee Wee King/Chilton Price/Redd Stewart			Tiny Hill
10/18	2			1	247		My Favorite Song	Moose Charlap/Jack Gold	✦		The Overtures Feat. Marian Caruso
1/5	2			1	248		(It's No) Sin	George Hoven/Chester Shull			Billy Williams Quartet
10/25	1			1	249		Veradero	Bernie Wayne [I]			Music By Camarata
9/27	1			1	250		Meet Mister Callaghan	Eric Spear [I]			Carmen Cavallaro
3/1	1			1	251		Herring Boats (Shrimp Boats)	Paul Howard/Paul Weston [N]			Mickey Katz
6/7	1			1	252		You	Morton Frank/Sunny Skylar			Sammy Kaye (Tony Russo)
6/7	1			1	253		Delicado	Waldyr Azevedo/Jack Lawrence			Dinah Shore

29

PEAK DATE	WEEKS				RANK	GOLD	Title	PEAK POSITION / Songwriter(s)	SYMBL	DEBUT	Artist
3/29	1			1	254		I'll Still Love You	Redd Evans <A:19>			Ames Brothers
6/14	1			1	255		I Remember When	Percy Haid/Ed Sarche			Eddie Fisher
3/8	1			1	256		Two Little Kisses	Al Alberts/Len McCall			Four Aces Feat. Al Alberts
10/4	1			1	257		The Mermaid	Fred Peck			Frankie Laine
3/8	1			1	258		Wishin'	Bob Hart/Ben Lewis/Teddy Simms	✦		Teddy Phillips (Lynn Hoyt)
3/15	1			1	259		Heart Of A Clown	Frances Kane/Steve Nelson/Jack Hollins <A:6>			Bobby Wayne
3/22	1			1	260		I'll Walk Alone	Sammy Cahn/Jule Styne			Margaret Whiting

30

PEAK DATE	WEEKS				RANK	GOLD	Title	PEAK POSITION / Songwriter(s)	SYMBL	DEBUT	Artist
7/12	3			3	261		Take My Heart	Bill Borrelli/Pat Genaro <A:23>			Vic Damone
3/22	1			1	262		Wishin'	Bob Hart/Ben Lewis/Teddy Simms			Eileen Barton
8/23	1			1	263		It's A Blue World	Chet Forrest/Robert Wright	❶		The Four Freshmen
7/26	1			1	264		Wild Side Of Life	Arlie Carter/William Warren			Burl Ives & Grady Martin
5/17	1			1	265		When You're In Love	Gene DePaul/Johnny Mercer <A:21>			Frankie Laine
7/26	1			1	266		Kiss Of Fire	Lester Allen/Robert Hill			Guy Lombardo (Kenny Gardner)
10/25	1			1	267		The Glow Worm	Paul Lincke/Johnny Mercer/Lilla Robinson			Johnny Mercer
2/2	1			1	268		Dance Me Loose	Lee Erwin/Mel Howard			Russ Morgan
9/27	1			1	269		Azure - Te (Paris Blues)	Duke Ellington/Harold Flender/Billy Strayhorn <A:20>			Frank Sinatra

1953

NATIONAL NEWS: Julius and Ethel Rosenberg are executed. California Gov. Earl Warren is selected by President Eisenhower as Chief Justice of the Supreme Court. Sen. Joseph McCarthy outrages many Americans when he claims that former President Truman aided Communists.

INTERNATIONAL NEWS: After three years of fighting, an armistice goes into effect in Korea. Joseph Stalin dies of a stroke. Soviet authorities in East Berlin impose a military crackdown. Queen Elizabeth II is crowned in England. The long guerilla war in Vietnam escalates with a year-end French offensive. Anti-apartheid demonstrations in South Africa are violently suppressed.

COMMERCE AND SCIENCE: Dr. Jonas Salk's polio vaccine is tested successfully. In a historic genetic discovery, the structure of DNA is decoded. New Zealand's Edmund Hilary's expedition is the first to conquer Mount Everest.

FADS AND FASHION: 3-D movies become the rage, led by Vincent Price in *The House of Wax*. Toy railroads reach a peak of popularity.

SPORTS: Casey Stengel's New York Yankees (led by catcher Yogi Berra) become the first team ever to win five consecutive World Series, topping the Brooklyn Dodgers with Roy Campanella, four games to two. The Detroit Lions edge the Cleveland Browns for the NFL championship, 17-16. Maryland is #1 in college football. The Minneapolis Lakers repeat as NBA champs. Indiana triumphs in NCAA basketball. Rocky Marciano twice defends his heavyweight crown. Maureen Connolly is the first woman to win all four Grand Slam events in tennis in a single year. It's a big year for Ben Hogan as victor in the Masters, U.S. Open and British Open.

MOVIES: *From Here to Eternity* (with Best Supporting Actor Frank Sinatra) wins the Oscar for Best Picture. Other award winners are William Holden in *Stalag 17* and Audrey Hepburn in *Roman Holiday*. The box office parade is led by *The Robe* (the first motion picture in CinemaScope), the western classic *Shane*, *How to Marry a Millionaire* with Marilyn Monroe, and Disney's *Peter Pan*. Marilyn also co-stars with Jane Russell in *Gentlemen Prefer Blondes*. Fred Astaire enjoys one of his greatest musical triumphs in *The Band Wagon*.

TELEVISION: Seventy percent of the national TV audience watches Lucille Ball become a mother on *I Love Lucy*. Other ratings leaders are *Dragnet*, *Arthur Godfrey's Talent Scouts* and *You Bet Your Life* with Groucho Marx. *The Adventures of Superman* makes its TV debut.

THEATER: Broadway's top new musicals include Cole Porter's *Can-Can* and *Wonderful Town* with Rosalind Russell. The postwar comedy *The Teahouse of the August Moon* is the year's longest-running hit.

BOOKS: Ralph Ellison's *Invisible Man* is acclaimed as one of the finest works in American literature. Ray Bradbury's *Farenheit 451* is published. Ian Fleming introduces the character of James Bond in *Casino Royale*. At year's end, Hugh Hefner begins publication of *Playboy* magazine.

1. Perry Como	2. Patti Page	3. Eddie Fisher
730	664	603

4.	560	Les Paul & Mary Ford	13.	255	Vic Damone
5.	517	Joni James	14.	252	Les Baxter
6.	426	Nat "King" Cole	15.	246	Tony Bennett
7.	407	Teresa Brewer	16.	226	The Gaylords
8.	395	Frankie Laine	17.	226	Richard Hayman
9.	361	The Hilltoppers	18.	211	Frank Chacksfield
10.	289	Kay Starr	19.	201	Ames Brothers
11.	265	Percy Faith	20.	200	Ralph Marterie
12.	262	Stan Freberg			

1953 — TOP SONGWRITERS

	# of Hits	Points			# of Hits	Points	
1.	6	564	Lew Douglas	7.	5	438	Mitchell Parish
2.	6	557	Frank Lavere	8.	4	379	Walter Schumann
3.	6	540	Jimmy Kennedy	9.	4	357	Bob Merrill
4.	5	461	Artie Glenn	10.	4	354	Heinz Roemheld
5.	5	460	Al Stillman	11.	3	289	Joe Darion
6.	5	449	Paul Ferrao	12.	3	287	Larry Coleman

1953 — TOP ARTIST DEBUTS

1.	3/14	Ruth Brown ◆	3.	5/23	Bill Haley & His Comets ★
2.	4/25	Jim Reeves ★	4.	10/17	Ferlin Husky ◆

PEAK DATE	WEEKS				RANK	GOLD	Title / PEAK POSITION / Songwriter(s)	SYMBL	DEBUT	Artist
	CH	10	5	PK						

1

8/8 | 31 | 26 | 23 | 11 | **1** ● **Vaya Con Dios (May God Be With You)** ..*Inez James/Buddy Pepper/Larry Russell* — **Les Paul & Mary Ford**
Best Seller: 13,10,6,6,5,4,2,1,1,1,1,1,1,1,1,2,2,2,2,1,1,3,3,3,5,11,14,12,14,18   <B:15>
Juke Box: 13,5,4,3,3,2,2,2,1,1,1,1,1,1,1,1,1,2,2,2,2,2,3,7,7,8,14,17,18,17
Disc Jockey: 8,7,9,4,4,4,1,2,2,2,1,1,2,2,3,3,3,5,4,7,4,7,6,10,-,15

5/16 | 24 | 19 | 16 | 10 | **2** ● **The Song From Moulin Rouge (Where Is Your Heart)** ....*Georges Auric/William Engvick* — **Percy Faith** (Felicia Sanders)
Best Seller: 17,11,7,4,2,2,1,1,1,1,1,1,1,1,1,2,4,5,6,7,12,17,19
Disc Jockey: 8,4,2,1,1,1,1,1,1,1,1,2,2,2,4,6,10,15,20,17
Juke Box: 12,4,3,1,1,1,1,1,2,2,2,3,3,3,7,7,15

9/26 | 31 | 27 | 23 | 8 | **3** ● **You You You** ....*Robert Mellin/Lotar Olias* — **Ames Brothers**
Disc Jockey: 17,14,10,9,7,6,5,4,4,3,3,2,1,1,1,1,2,1,1,1,1,3,3,2,2,6,11,11,18
Juke Box: 19,13,12,9,5,5,3,3,3,2,2,2,2,2,2,1,1,1,1,1,1,2,2,3,5,6,9,10,13
Best Seller: 18,19,10,9,9,6,6,4,4,2,2,2,2,2,3,3,3,3,3,5,5,5,4,7,9,12,13,15,17,17

11/21 | 25 | 18 | 17 | 8 | **4** ● **Rags To Riches** ....*Richard Adler/Jerry Ross* — **Tony Bennett**
Juke Box: 19,15,15,12,5,5,4,4,3,1,1,1,1,1,1,1,3,4,5,9,13,15,17
Disc Jockey: 13,16,19,8,6,4,3,3,2,1,1,1,1,1,1,1,2,2,5,7,9,12,18
Best Seller: 20,13,13,11,8,7,6,5,4,1,1,1,1,1,1,2,2,2,3,5,6,7,13,17

3/21 | 21 | 18 | 15 | 8 | **5** ● **The Doggie In The Window** ....*Bob Merrill* <B:17> [N] — **Patti Page**
Best Seller: 19,11,7,6,3,3,2,1,1,1,1,1,1,1,1,2,2,5,8,8,13
Disc Jockey: 16,9,6,4,2,2,1,1,1,1,1,1,1,3,4,8,10
Juke Box: 18,6,5,4,4,3,2,1,2,1,1,1,1,1,1,2,3,9,12,17

2/14 | 24 | 19 | 18 | 7 | **6** ● **Till I Waltz Again With You** ....*Sidney Prosen* — **Teresa Brewer**
Juke Box: 18,12,15,14,4,4,3,3,2,1,1,1,1,1,1,2,1,2,2,3,4,4,11,19
Disc Jockey: 16,17,9,13,5,3,3,2,1,1,1,1,1,1,4,2,2,2,5,14,10
Best Seller: 18,11,10,6,5,3,3,2,1,1,1,1,1,2,2,2,2,5,8,8,13

7/4 | 25 | 20 | 16 | 7 | **7** ● **I'm Walking Behind You** ....*Billy Reid* — **Eddie Fisher**
Juke Box: 19,10,9,6,2,2,2,2,1,1,1,1,1,1,2,2,3,4,4,9,11,14,13,19
Disc Jockey: 19,11,8,6,2,2,2,2,2,2,1,1,1,3,3,3,5,8,12,14,20
Best Seller: 18,11,7,4,3,3,2,2,2,2,1,1,2,2,3,4,5,8,10,16,17

1/10 | 21 | 18 | 15 | 5 | **8** ● **Don't Let The Stars Get In Your Eyes** ....*Slim Willet* — **Perry Como**
Best Seller: 11,4,4,3,2,1,1,1,1,1,2,2,2,3,3,6,7,9,15,20
Juke Box: 9,4,3,4,2,1,1,1,1,2,2,2,2,6,5,7,10,13,16
Disc Jockey: 19,6,4,2,2,2,2,1,1,1,2,2,2,4,3,14,11,14,20

8/15 | 22 | 19 | 13 | 4 | **9** **No Other Love** ....*Oscar Hammerstein/Richard Rodgers* — **Perry Como**
Disc Jockey: 7,11,5,3,3,3,2,1,1,1,1,2,3,4,4,6,9,9,11,13,15,17
Best Seller: 15,9,5,5,3,3,3,3,2,3,3,3,5,5,7,9,8,10,12,12,19
Juke Box: 10,8,6,5,4,4,5,5,6,6,5,7,4,5,8,13,8,10,10,9

10/10 | 10 | 9 | 6 | 4 | **10** ● **St. George And The Dragonet** ..*Daws Butler/Stan Freberg/Walter Schumann* — **Stan Freberg**
Best Seller: 8,1,1,1,1,2,6,6,10,14   <B:9> [N]
Disc Jockey: 4,2,1,2,5,5,8
Juke Box: 13,8,9,7,10,17

2

12/19	22	20	14	6	**11** ● **That's Amore** ....*Jack Brooks/Harry Warren* — Dean Martin

12/19 | 22 | 20 | 14 | 6 | **11** ● That's Amore ....*Jack Brooks/Harry Warren* — Dean Martin
11/7 | 23 | 19 | 12 | 4 | **12** ● Ebb Tide ....*Robert Maxwell/Carl Sigman* [I] — Frank Chacksfield
5/30 | 22 | 17 | 12 | 3 | **13** April In Portugal ....*Paul Ferrao/Jimmy Kennedy* [I] — Les Baxter
4/25 | 23 | 19 | 11 | 3 | **14** ● I Believe ....*Ervin Drake/Irvin Graham/Jimmy Shirl/Al Stillman* <B:18> — Frankie Laine
4/25 | 17 | 14 | 9 | 3 | **15** ● Your Cheatin' Heart ....*Hank Williams* — Joni James
12/26 | 20 | 16 | 10 | 2 | **16** ● Ricochet (Rick-O-Shay) ....*Larry Coleman/Joe Darion/Norman Gimbel* — Teresa Brewer
3/28 | 22 | 18 | 10 | 1 | **17** ● Tell Me You're Mine ....*Dico Vasin/Ronnie Vincent* ❶ — The Gaylords
5/9 | 21 | 18 | 8 | 1 | **18** Pretend ....*Lew Douglas/Frank Lavere/Cliff Parman* — Nat "King" Cole
10/10 | 13 | 11 | 7 | 1 | **19** Dragnet ....*Walter Schumann* [I] — Ray Anthony
11/14 | 20 | 15 | 6 | 1 | **20** ● Eh, Cumpari ....*Archie Bleyer/Julius LaRosa* [F] — Julius LaRosa

3

9/12 | 25 | 20 | 16 | 11 | **21** ● Oh! ....*Byron Gay/Arnold Johnson* [I] — Pee Wee Hunt
12/19 | 19 | 15 | 12 | 6 | **22** ● Changing Partners ....*Larry Coleman/Joe Darion* — Patti Page
3/7 | 13 | 10 | 5 | 3 | **23** Side By Side ....*Harry Woods* — Kay Starr
5/30 | 19 | 14 | 11 | 2 | **24** Ruby ....*Mitchell Parish/Heinz Roemheld* [I] ❶ — Richard Hayman
6/27 | 16 | 14 | 10 | 2 | **25** Say You're Mine Again ....*Dave Heisler/Charles Nathan* <B:11> — Perry Como

4

1/24 | 16 | 11 | 5 | 4 | **26** ● Have You Heard ....*Lew Douglas/Frank Lavere/Leroy Rodde* <B:17> — Joni James
11/14 | 16 | 10 | 4 | 3 | **27** Many Times ....*Jessie Barnes/Felix Stahl* <B:18> — Eddie Fisher
1/3 | 18 | 13 | 8 | 2 | **28** Keep It A Secret ....*Jessie Mae Robinson* — Jo Stafford
8/8 | 21 | 15 | 7 | 2 | **29** ● P.S. I Love You ....*Gordon Jenkins/Johnny Mercer* <B:8> — The Hilltoppers
10/3 | 17 | 11 | 4 | 2 | **30** Crying In The Chapel ....*Artie Glenn* — June Valli
4/18 | 12 | 8 | 5 | 1 | **31** ● Tell Me A Story ....*Terry Gilkyson* [N] — Jimmy Boyd - Frankie Laine
2/21 | 9 | 6 | 2 | 1 | **32** Anywhere I Wander ....*Frank Loesser* ❶ — Julius LaRosa
1/24 | 15 | 10 | 1 | 1 | **33** ● Oh Happy Day ....*Don Howard/Nancy Reed* ✦ — Don Howard

1953

PEAK DATE	CH	10	5	PK	RANK	GOLD	Title / PEAK POSITION / Songwriter(s)	SYMBL / DEBUT	Artist
							4 (cont'd)		
1/10	13	9	1	1	34		Why Don't You Believe Me ....Lew Douglas/King Laney/Leroy Rodde <B:18>		Patti Page
12/26	5	4	1	1	35		Santa Baby ....Joan Javits/Phil Springer/Tony Springer [X]		Eartha Kitt
10/17	10	3	1	1	36		A Dear John Letter ....Billy Barton/Charles Owen/Lewis Talley ❶		Jean Shepard with Ferlin Huskey
							5		
5/2	24	16	2	2	37		Seven Lonely Days.....................Marshall Brown/Alden Schuman/Earl Schuman		Georgia Gibbs
6/27	17	10	1	1	38 ●		Anna (El N. Zumbon) ....Francesco Giordano/Armando Vatro [F] ✦		Silvana Mangano
3/7	18	8	1	1	39 ●		Hold Me, Thrill Me, Kiss Me ....Harry Noble ❶		Karen Chandler
6/20	13	7	1	1	40		Terry's Theme From "Limelight" ....Charlie Chaplin/Geoffrey Parsons [I] ❶		Frank Chacksfield
2/14	10	5	1	1	41		Oh, Happy Day ....Don Howard/Nancy Reed		Lawrence Welk (Larry Hooper)
2/28	12	4	1	1	42		Downhearted ....Bob Hilliard/Dave Mann <B:14>		Eddie Fisher
1/17	7	3	1	1	43		Bye Bye Blues.............David Bennett/Chauncey Gray/Fred Hamm/Bert Lown		Les Paul & Mary Ford
							6		
9/19	13	10		2	44		Crying In The Chapel......................Artie Glenn ✦		Darrell Glenn
8/1	18	9		2	45 ●		Gambler's Guitar.........................Jim Lowe		Rusty Draper
3/28	12	7		2	46		Wild Horses ....Johnny Burke/Robert Schumann <B:17>		Perry Como
4/25	11	7		1	47 ●		Caravan ....Duke Ellington/Irving Mills/Juan Tizol [I]		Ralph Marterie
10/24	16	5		1	48		Hey Joe! ....Boudleaux Bryant		Frankie Laine
2/7	10	2		1	49 ●		Pretend................Lew Douglas/Frank Lavere/Cliff Parman [I]		Ralph Marterie
							7		
7/18	15	6		2	50		Half A Photograph.................Bob Russell/Hal Stanley <B:11>		Kay Starr
3/28	16	4		1	51		Hot Toddy ....Ralph Flanagan [I]		Ralph Flanagan
8/22	14	4		1	52		With These Hands ....Benny Davis/Abner Silver		Eddie Fisher
6/20	12	3		1	53		Ruby ....Mitchell Parish/Heinz Roemheld [I]		Les Baxter
1/31	8	3		1	54		Even Now ....Richard Adler/Dan Howell/Jerry Ross		Eddie Fisher
6/13	10	1		1	55		I'm Walking Behind You ....Billy Reid		Frank Sinatra
1/10	10	1		1	56		My Baby's Coming Home ....Sherman Feller/John Grady/William Leavitt <B:8>		Les Paul & Mary Ford
							8		
8/15	14	8		2	57		C'est Si Bon (It's So Good) ....Henri Betti/Andre Hornez/Jerry Seelen [F] ❶		Eartha Kitt
10/10	15	6		2	58 ●		Crying In The Chapel....................Artie Glenn		Rex Allen
11/28	10	4		1	59		Love Walked In ....George Gershwin/Ira Gershwin <A:8>		The Hilltoppers
11/21	11	3		1	60		To Be Alone ....Billy Vaughn <A:8>		The Hilltoppers
6/13	10	3		1	61		The Moulin Rouge Theme (Where Is Your Heart) ....Georges Auric/ William Engvick [I]		Mantovani
10/3	12	2		1	62		My Love, My Love ....Nick Acquaviva/Bob Haymes <B:11>		Joni James
2/7	6	2		1	63		Oh, Happy Day ....Don Howard/Nancy Reed		The Four Knights
11/21	5	2		1	64		The Velvet Glove ....Harold Spina [I]		Henri René & Hugo Winterhalter
7/4	12	1		1	65		I'd Rather Die Young (Than Grow Old Without You) ....Beasley Smith/ Billy Vaughn/Randy Wood <A:4>		The Hilltoppers
5/2	6	1		1	66		Somebody Stole My Gal ....Leo Wood		Johnnie Ray
							9		
12/12	13	2		2	67		You Alone (Solo Tu)......................Robert Allen/Al Stillman <B:11>		Perry Como
6/13	9	4		1	68		The Ho Ho Song ....Red Buttons/Joe Darion/Jack Wolf <B:15> [N] ❶		Red Buttons
6/13	9	2		1	69		Almost Always ....Lew Douglas/Frank Lavere/Kathleen Lichty <B:16>		Joni James
10/10	4	1		1	70		Little Blue Riding Hood .....Daws Butler/Stan Freberg/Miklos Rozsa/Walter Schumann <A:1> [N]		Stan Freberg
							10		
1/31	7	2		2	71		Mister Tap Toe ....Richard Dehr/Terry Gilkyson/Frank Miller		Doris Day
12/5	13	1		1	72		Istanbul (Not Constantinople) ....Jimmy Kennedy/Nat Simon		The Four Lads
8/29	11	1		1	73		Butterflies.................Bob Merrill <B:20>		Patti Page
10/24	11	1		1	74		Ebb Tide ....Robert Maxwell/Carl Sigman		Vic Damone
4/25	8	1		1	75		No Help Wanted ....Bill Carlisle ❶		Rusty Draper
5/23	7	1		1	76		April In Portugal ....Paul Ferrao/Jimmy Kennedy		Vic Damone
4/18	6	1		1	77		I'm Sitting On Top Of The World ....Ray Henderson/Sam Lewis/Joe Young		Les Paul & Mary Ford
							11		
5/30	10	1		2	78		I Believe ....Ervin Drake/Irvin Graham/Jimmy Shirl/Al Stillman		Jane Froman
12/5	12			1	79		You're Fooling Someone.................Leo Fox/Wally Griffin/Frank Lavere <A:8>		Joni James
9/12	10			1	80 ●		Crying In The Chapel.................Artie Glenn		The Orioles
6/20	9			1	81		Allez-Vous-En ....Cole Porter <A:7>		Kay Starr
6/20	7			1	82		My One And Only Heart ....Robert Allen/Al Stillman <A:3>		Perry Como
12/5	5			1	83		Pa-Paya Mama.................Larry Coleman/Norman Gimbel/George Sandler <A:9>		Perry Como

PEAK DATE	WEEKS				RANK	GOLD	Title	PEAK POSITION Songwriter(s)	SYMBL	DEBUT	Artist
	CH	10	5	PK							

11 (cont'd)

8/29	4			1	84		Blue Canary .... *Vic Florino*				Dinah Shore
1/17	2			1	85		Don't Let The Stars Get In Your Eyes........................ *Slim Willet*				Gisele MacKenzie

12

6/13	11			2	86		April In Portugal .... *Paul Ferrao/Jimmy Kennedy* [I]				Richard Hayman
5/23	8			2	87		Ramona .... *L. Wolfe Gilbert/Mabel Wayne* <B:16>				The Gaylords
6/27	10			1	88		Crazy Man, Crazy .... *Bill Haley* ❶				Bill Haley With Haley's Comets
8/8	5			1	89		Eternally The Song From Limelight.................. *Charlie Chaplin/Geoffrey Parsons*				Vic Damone
6/13	4			1	90		Say Si Si .... *Ernesto Lecuona/Francis Luban/Al Stillman*				Mills Brothers
1/31	3			1	91		Teardrops On My Pillow...................... *Deborah Chessler/Fanny Wolff* <B:18>				Sunny Gale
12/12	1			1	92		Baby Baby Baby .... *Mack David/Jerry Livingston*				Teresa Brewer

13

6/27	4			2	93		Crazy, Man, Crazy .... *Bill Haley*				Ralph Marterie (Larry Ragon)
11/14	4			1	94		Don'cha Hear Them Bells .... *Les Paul*				Les Paul & Mary Ford
1/3	4			1	95		Nina Never Knew .... *Louis Alter/Milton Drake*				Sauter-Finegan (Joe Mooney)
11/28	3			1	96		I Love Paris .... *Cole Porter*				Les Baxter
12/26	3			1	97		Christmas Dragnet (Parts I & II) .... *Daws Butler/Stan Freberg/* *Walter Schumann* [X-N]				Stan Freberg
7/18	3			1	98		Terry's Theme (From Limelight) .... *Charlie Chaplin/Geoffrey Parsons* [I]				Richard Hayman
11/21	3			1	99		Sweet Mama Tree Top Tall .... *Jarrett Meacham* ❶				The Lancers
2/14	2			1	100		Sugar .... *Edna Alexander/Sidney Mitchell/Maceo Pinkard*				Vic Damone

14

9/26	8			2	101		The Story Of Three Loves .... *Sergei Rachmaninoff* [I]				Jerry Murad
1/17	7			2	102		I'm Just A Poor Bachelor .... *Jessie Mae Robinson*				Frankie Laine
11/7	14			1	103		I See The Moon .... *Meredith Willson*				The Mariners
3/14	3			1	104		Say It With Your Heart .... *Norman Kaye/Steve Nelson* ❶				Bob Carroll
3/14	2			1	105		How Do You Speak To An Angel?.................. *Bob Hilliard/Jule Styne* <A:5>				Eddie Fisher
7/4	2			1	106		I've Got The World On A String .... *Harold Arlen/Ted Koehler*				Frank Sinatra
11/28	1			1	107		Off Shore .... *Leo Diamond* [I] ❶				Leo Diamond
3/28	1			1	108		Twice As Much .... *Royce Swain*				Mills Brothers

15

11/21	7			2	109		In The Mission Of St. Augustine .... *Jack Chiarelli*				Sammy Kaye (Jeffrey Clay)
5/16	3			1	110		Strange Things Are Happening (Ho Ho, Hee Hee, Ha Ha)................... *Red Buttons/Elliot Lawrence/Allan Walker* <A:9> [N]				Red Buttons
5/30	3			1	111		April In Portugal (The Whisp'ring Serenade) ...... *Paul Ferrao/Jimmy Kennedy* [I]				Freddy Martin
4/4	2			1	112		Gomen-Nasai (Forgive Me) .... *Ryoichi Hattori/Benedict Mayers* ✦				Columbia Tokyo Orch. (Richard Bowers)
9/12	2			1	113		Crying In The Chapel... *Artie Glenn*				Ella Fitzgerald
1/10	2			1	114		Must I Cry Again .... *Lincoln Chase/Lloyd Pemberton/Jerry Valentine*				The Hilltoppers
11/14	2			1	115		Dipsy Doodle .... *Larry Clinton* [I]				Johnny Maddox
7/18	2			1	116		Johnny (Is The Boy For Me).......... *Les Paul/Paddy Roberts/Marcel Spellman* <A:1>				Les Paul & Mary Ford
10/10	2			1	117		From Here To Eternity .... *Freddie Karger/Robert Wells*				Frank Sinatra
7/25	1			1	118		Return To Paradise .... *Dimitri Tiomkin/Ned Washington*				Nat "King" Cole

16

5/23	4			1	119		Is It Any Wonder .... *Archie Gottler/Robert Hayes/Leroy Rodde* <A:9>				Joni James
3/7	4			1	120		Now And Then, There's A Fool Such As I .... *Bill Trader*				Jo Stafford
4/18	3			1	121		Can't I.. *Leroy Lovett/Ivan Mogull*				Nat "King" Cole & Billy May
11/21	3			1	122		Lover, Come Back To Me! .... *Oscar Hammerstein/Sigmund Romberg*				Nat "King" Cole & Billy May
2/14	3			1	123		In The Mood .... *Joe Garland* [I]				Johnny Maddox
1/31	3			1	124		I Don't Know .... *Willie Mabon*				Buddy Morrow (Frankie Lester)
5/16	2			1	125		The Nearness Of You .... *Hoagy Carmichael/Ned Washington* ✦				Bob Manning
4/25	1			1	126		Spinning A Web .... *Bunny Paul* <A:12>				The Gaylords
5/30	1			1	127		Oo What You Do To Me.................. *Kay Twomey/Ben Weisman/Fred Wise* <B:18>				Patti Page

17

3/21	3			1	128		Pretend .... *Lew Douglas/Frank Lavere/Cliff Parman*				Eileen Barton
6/20	3			1	129		(How Much Is) That Hound Dog In The Window .... *Bob Merrill* [N]				Homer and Jethro
4/25	3			1	130		Gomen Nasai Forgive Me .... *Ryoichi Hattori/Benedict Mayers*				Eddy Howard
4/11	2			1	131		Dancin' With Someone (Longin' For You) .... *Alex Alstone/Bennie Benjamin/* *George Weiss*				Teresa Brewer
1/24	2			1	132		Wishing Ring .... *Al Britt/Pete Maddux* <A:4>				Joni James
3/7	2			1	133		My Jealous Eyes .... *Mack David/Marge Wolpin* <A:1>				Patti Page
8/22	1			1	134		A Fool Was I.. *Kurt Adams/Roy Alfred*				Nat "King" Cole
3/28	1			1	135		I Confess.. *Tryggve Arnesson/Gunnar Hoffsten/Jack Lawrence* <A:6>				Perry Como

PEAK DATE	WEEKS				RANK	GOLD	Title / Songwriter(s)	SYMBL	DEBUT	Artist
	CH	10	5	PK			PEAK POSITION			

17 (cont'd)

PEAK DATE	CH	10	5	PK	RANK	GOLD	Title / Songwriter(s)	SYMBL	DEBUT	Artist
6/6	1			1	136		Organ Grinder's Swing ... Will Hudson/Irving Mills/Mitchell Parish			Four Aces Feat. Al Alberts
8/8	1			1	137		Down By The River Side ... (traditional)			The Four Lads
5/30	1			1	138		April In Portugal (The Whisp'ring Serenade) ... Paul Ferrao/Jimmy Kennedy			Tony Martin
8/29	1			1	139		A Dear John Letter ... Billy Barton/Charles Owen/Lewis Talley	✦		Pat O'Day
6/20	1			1	140		Candy Lips ... Fred Rose			Johnnie Ray - Doris Day
3/14	1			1	141		Till I Waltz Again With You ... Sidney Prosen			Dick Todd

18

PEAK DATE	CH	10	5	PK	RANK	GOLD	Title / Songwriter(s)	SYMBL	DEBUT	Artist
9/5	2			2	142		Please Play Our Song (Mister Record Man) ... Bob Marcus/Larry Stewart			Don Cornell
10/10	2			2	143		I Forgot More Than You'll Ever Know ... Cecil Null	✦		The Davis Sisters
1/31	2			2	144		A Stolen Waltz ... Don Larkin <A:12>			Sunny Gale
5/16	2			2	145		Your Cheatin' Heart ... Hank Williams <A:2>			Frankie Laine
1/10	1			1	146		You'll Never Know ... Mack Gordon/Harry Warren			Rosemary Clooney-Harry James
10/24	1			1	147		Just To Be With You ... Steve Nelson/Warren Spencer <A:4>			Eddie Fisher
5/2	1			1	148		A-L-B-U-Q-U-E-R-Q-U-E ... Ralph Flanagan/Herb Hendler			Ralph Flanagan
5/23	1			1	149		Now That I'm In Love ... Johnny Burke <A:16>			Patti Page
10/31	1			1	150		When My Dreamboat Comes Home ... Dave Franklin/Cliff Friend			Kay Starr
7/18	1			1	151		Love Me, Love Me ... Bill Walker			Bobby Wayne
9/12	1			1	152		God Bless Us All ... Tony Burrello/Tom Murray	✦		Brucie Weil

19

PEAK DATE	CH	10	5	PK	RANK	GOLD	Title / Songwriter(s)	SYMBL	DEBUT	Artist
6/20	2			2	153		The Breeze "That's Bringin' My Honey Back To Me" ... Al Lewis/Tony Sacco/Dick Smith	✦		Trudy Richards
5/23	2			1	154		Big Mamou ... Link Davis	✦		Pete Hanley
11/28	2			1	155		Rachmaninoff: The Eighteenth Variation (from the Rhapsody on a Theme of Paganini, Op. 43) ... Sergei Rachmaninoff [I]	✦		William Kapell
1/10	2			1	156		Blue Violins ... Ray Martin			Hugo Winterhalter
4/11	1			1	157		Gomen Nasai (Forgive Me) ... Ryoichi Hattori/Benedict Mayers ❶			Harry Belafonte
6/27	1			1	158		I Am In Love ... Cole Porter			Nat "King" Cole
6/20	1			1	159		Return To Paradise (Parts 1 & 2) ... Dimitri Tiomkin/Ned Washington [I]			Percy Faith
9/5	1			1	160		Rub-A-Dub-Dub ... Hank Thompson			Ralph Flanagan
8/15	1			1	161		Tropicana ... Bernie Wayne [I] ❶			Monty Kelly
1/31	1			1	162		She Wears Red Feathers ... Bob Merrill			Guy Mitchell

20

PEAK DATE	CH	10	5	PK	RANK	GOLD	Title / Songwriter(s)	SYMBL	DEBUT	Artist
3/7	1			1	163		Congratulations To Someone ... Roy Alfred/Al Frisch			Tony Bennett
4/4	1			1	164		Hello Sunshine ... Lee Erwin/Mel Howard	✦		Norman Brooks
1/31	1			1	165		Strange ... Marvin Fisher/John Latouche			Nat "King" Cole
9/26	1			1	166		Choo Choo Train (Ch— Ch— Foo) ... Marc Fontenoy/Jack Lawrence			Doris Day
7/18	1			1	167		Ruby ... Mitchell Parish/Heinz Roemheld [I]			Harry James
1/31	1			1	168		I Went To Your Wedding ... Jessie Mae Robinson [N]			Spike Jones (Sir Fredric Gas)
8/22	1			1	169		Song Of India ... Johnny Mercer/Nikolai Rimsky-Korsakov			Mario Lanza
8/8	1			1	170		This Is My Song ... Dick Charles <A:10>			Patti Page
8/29	1			1	171		The Moon Is Blue ... Sylvia Fine/Herschel Gilbert			Sauter-Finegan (Sally Sweetland)
6/6	1			1	172		Ruby ... Mitchell Parish/Heinz Roemheld [I]			Victor Young

1954

NATIONAL NEWS: Chief Justice Earl Warren achieves a historic unanimous U.S. Supreme Court ruling in Brown v. Board of Education that racial segregation in public schools is unconstitutional, putting an end to the "separate but equal" doctrine. Sen. Joseph McCarthy self-destructs in the televised Army-McCarthy hearings, and he is formally condemned by colleagues for conduct unbecoming a Senator. Puerto Rican radicals open fire in House chambers and injure five members of Congress. The U.S. explodes a hydrogen bomb hundreds of times more powerful than any previous weapon.

INTERNATIONAL NEWS: French troops surrender to Vietnamese Communist forces at Dien Bien Phu, leading to an armistice that divides the nation in half. The United Nations formally withdraws from Korea. Britain ends its 72-year military occupation of Egypt.

COMMERCE AND SCIENCE: School children begin receiving the first mass polio immunization shots. IBM announces an "electronic brain" capable of performing 10 million operations an hour. Nautilus, the first atomic submarine, is launched. RCA introduces the first U.S. color television sets. The first transistor radios go on sale.

FADS AND FASHION: The first stirrings of a new American youth culture, that will soon embrace the rebellious symbol of rock 'n roll, begin to emerge.

SPORTS: Concluding a remarkable season, Willie Mays leads the New York Giants to a four-game sweep over the Cleveland Indians. In one of track and field's greatest events, Roger Banniser outduels John Landy to run the first sub-four-minute mile. The Cleveland Browns crush the Detroit Lions, 56-10, for the NFL championship. Ohio State and UCLA share top honors in college football. It's three NBA titles in a row for the Minneapolis Lakers. LaSalle wins the NCAA basketball championship.

MOVIES: *On the Waterfront* dominates the Academy Awards as Best Picture and with Marlon Brando as Best Actor. Grace Kelly is honored for *The Country Girl*. It's also a year of classic performances by Humphrey Bogart (*The Caine Mutiny*) and Judy Garland (*A Star Is Born*). *White Christmas* starring Bing Crosby and Danny Kaye is the year's biggest hit, followed by *20,000 Leagues Under the Sea*, Alfred Hitchcock's *Rear Window* with James Stewart and Grace Kelly and *The Glenn Miller Story* featuring Stewart.

TELEVISION: *I Love Lucy*, *The Jackie Gleason Show* and *Dragnet* remain TV's most popular shows. Steve Allen begins a national late-night habit with the *Tonight* show.

THEATER: The year's Broadway musical are led by *The Pajama Game*, *Fanny* and *Kismet*.

BOOKS: *Lord of the Flies* by William Golding reaches an international audience.

1954 — TOP 20 ARTISTS

1. **Eddie Fisher**
716

2. **Four Aces**
457

3. **Patti Page**
448

4.	447	**Perry Como**
5.	396	**Rosemary Clooney**
6.	364	**The Gaylords**
7.	340	**The Crew-Cuts**
8.	336	**Kitty Kallen**
9.	316	**Nat "King" Cole**
10.	306	**Doris Day**
11.	303	**Frank Sinatra**
12.	289	**Kay Starr**
13.	259	**Les Paul & Mary Ford**
14.	254	**The Hilltoppers**
15.	253	**Tony Bennett**
16.	247	**Jo Stafford**
17.	213	**Frankie Laine**
18.	192	**Johnny Desmond**
19.	191	**The McGuire Sisters**
20.	182	**Ames Brothers**

1954 — TOP SONGWRITERS

	# of Hits	Points			# of Hits	Points	
1.	9	817	**Geoffrey Parsons**	7.	5	451	**Richard Adler**
2.	7	645	**John Turner**	8.	4	382	**Jimmie Crane**
3.	6	551	**Jerry Ross**		4	382	**Al Jacobs**
4.	6	536	**Ned Washington**	10.	4	359	**August Msarurgwa**
5.	5	455	**Dimitri Tiomkin**	11.	4	330	**Jimmy Kennedy**
6.	5	453	**Tom Glazer**	12.	3	288	**George Forrest**
					3	288	**Robert Wright**

1954 — TOP ARTIST DEBUTS

1.	1/23	**Eydie Gorme** ★	
2.	5/08 †	**The Crew-Cuts** (146) ★	
3.	6/26	**The McGuire Sisters** ★	
4.	8/21	**Sammy Davis, Jr.** ★	
5.	10/16	**The Drifters** ★	
6.	10/30	**The Chordettes** ★	
7.	11/20	**Webb Pierce** ◆	
8.	11/27	**Jaye P. Morgan** ★	
9.	12/11	**Billy Vaughn** ★	

PEAK DATE	WEEKS				RANK	GOLD	Title / PEAK POSITION / Songwriter(s)	SYMBL	DEBUT	Artist
	CH	10	5	PK						

1

6/5	26	20	17	9	1	●	**Little Things Mean A Lot**............................*Edith Lindeman/Carl Stutz*			**Kitty Kallen**

Best Seller: 16,11,11,10,6,2,2,1,1,1,1,1,1,1,1,2,2,4,4,4,8,12,14,15,25
Disc Jockey: 13,13,11,10,7,3,2,2,1,1,1,1,1,1,1,1,1,2,2,2,3,3,5,9,13
Juke Box: 13,9,6,7,3,2,1,1,1,1,2,1,1,1,2,2,2,4,6,10,12,12,17

| 8/7 | 20 | 18 | 15 | 9 | 2 | ● | **Sh-Boom** ....*James Edwards/Carl Feaster/Claude Feaster/James Keyes/Floyd McRae* | | | **The Crew-Cuts** |

Disc Jockey: 12,5,4,2,1,1,1,1,1,1,1,1,1,1,2,2,3,7,9,14
Juke Box: 11,10,4,3,1,1,1,1,1,1,1,1,2,3,5,7,10,11,17,-,20
Best Seller: 8,5,4,2,1,1,1,1,1,1,1,2,2,2,5,6,8,10,13,16

| 4/10 | 22 | 19 | 18 | 8 | 3 | ● | **Wanted** ....*Jack Fulton/Lois Steele* | | | **Perry Como** |

Best Seller: 20,9,4,4,2,1,1,1,1,1,1,1,1,2,3,5,5,5,6,10,17,21
Juke Box: 18,13,4,3,4,3,2,1,1,1,1,1,1,1,2,3,3,4,4,6,13
Disc Jockey: 13,7,5,4,2,2,2,1,1,1,1,1,1,1,2,3,3,4,6,7,12

| 1/2 | 19 | 17 | 13 | 8 | 4 | ● | **Oh! My Pa-Pa (O Mein Papa)** ....*Paul Burkhard/Geoffrey Parsons/John Turner* | | | **Eddie Fisher** |

Best Seller: 19,3,2,1,1,1,1,1,1,1,2,3,4,6,7,9,10,11
Disc Jockey: 6,2,2,2,1,1,1,1,1,1,1,1,3,3,7,7,8,13,20
Juke Box: 16,10,6,2,2,2,1,1,1,1,1,1,2,3,5,6,7,9,15

| 3/13 | 24 | 20 | 16 | 7 | 5 | ● | **Make Love To Me!** ....*George Brunies/Allan Copeland/Paul Mares/Walter Melrose/Bill Norvas/Benny Pollack/Leon Roppolo/Mel Stitzel* | | | **Jo Stafford** |

Juke Box: 16,9,6,5,3,1,1,1,1,1,1,2,2,2,3,4,4,7,6,7,12,12,13
Best Seller: 14,9,6,4,2,1,2,1,1,2,2,2,2,4,5,9,14,14,20,28
Disc Jockey: 16,18,11,8,5,5,2,2,2,1,1,1,2,2,2,2,5,8,4,11,16

| 11/27 | 20 | 16 | 13 | 7 | 6 | ● | **Mr. Sandman** ....*Pat Ballard* ❶ | | | **The Chordettes** |

Best Seller: 24,14,9,4,2,1,1,1,1,1,1,1,1,2,2,4,4,9,14,17,20
Disc Jockey: 14,10,7,5,1,1,1,1,1,2,1,2,1,2,4,5,8,14,17,18
Juke Box: 17,10,8,8,3,1,1,1,1,2,2,2,3,4,5,10,15,18

| 9/25 | 27 | 20 | 16 | 6 | 7 | ● | **Hey There**..*Richard Alder/Jerry Ross* <A:1> | | | **Rosemary Clooney** |

Best Seller: 28,11,7,5,4,3,2,2,2,1,1,1,1,1,1,3,2,3,7,6,11,12,18,21,23,25
Disc Jockey: 10,11,6,6,3,2,2,2,2,2,1,1,1,1,1,2,3,6,9,10,17
Juke Box: 19,12,6,5,3,2,2,2,2,1,1,1,1,2,3,3,5,7,8,14,20

| 2/27 | 22 | 15 | 10 | 4 | 8 | ● | **Secret Love** ....*Sammy Fain/Paul Francis Webster* | | | **Doris Day** |

Disc Jockey: 16,14,10,7,6,2,2,1,1,1,1,3,3,3,6,6,11,14,20
Best Seller: 17,12,8,8,4,3,2,1,1,2,1,2,4,5,6,6,8,13,15,18,22,29
Juke Box: 10,8,12,8,6,4,3,2,2,2,5,5,5,6,9,11,18

| 11/6 | 27 | 21 | 17 | 3 | 9 | | **This Ole House** ....*Stuart Hamblen* <A:1> | | | **Rosemary Clooney** |

Juke Box: 20,14,9,7,5,4,3,3,3,2,2,2,1,1,2,2,3,4,6,9,9,11,13,18
Best Seller: 25,22,12,10,8,6,5,4,4,4,3,3,3,1,3,2,3,3,4,5,4,4,5,6,15,20,27
Disc Jockey: 14,13,14,9,12,9,8,5,5,5,5,7,5,8,8,8,10,11,11,18

| 11/13 | 24 | 19 | 15 | 3 | 10 | ● | **I Need You Now** ....*Jimmie Crane/Al Jacobs* | | | **Eddie Fisher** |

Best Seller: 23,16,9,6,5,3,2,2,2,1,1,1,2,2,3,5,6,4,9,17,16,28
Disc Jockey: 11,14,10,4,4,3,2,2,2,1,1,2,2,2,1,1,3,6,9,11,13,16
Juke Box: 20,12,11,7,5,5,5,4,3,3,3,2,2,1,1,2,2,4,5,6,7,8,13,20

| 7/24 | 18 | 15 | 13 | 1 | 11 | ● | **Three Coins In The Fountain**..................*Sammy Cahn/Jule Styne* <B:26> | | | **Four Aces Feat. Al Alberts** |

Juke Box: 20,12,10,4,3,3,2,2,2,1,2,2,2,3,4,5,9,14
Disc Jockey: 16,13,3,3,2,2,2,2,2,2,4,4,5,6,10,20
Best Seller: 14,10,3,2,2,2,2,2,3,3,4,6,7,7,12,20,28,29

2

5/22	21	19	15	4	12	●	**Cross Over The Bridge**..................................*Bennie Benjamin/George Weiss*			Patti Page
7/17	17	13	10	2	13		**Hernando's Hideaway**...*Richard Adler/Jerry Ross* ❶			Archie Bleyer
2/6	19	15	7	2	14	●	**Stranger In Paradise**...*George Forrest/Robert Wright*			Tony Bennett
4/17	24	19	15	1	15	●	**I Get So Lonely (When I Dream About You)**................................*Pat Ballard*			The Four Knights
5/15	22	19	12	1	16	●	**Young-At-Heart** ....*Carolyn Leigh/Johnny Richards*			Frank Sinatra
8/21	19	14	10	1	17		**The Little Shoemaker** ....*Geoffrey Parsons/Rudi Revil/John Turner*			The Gaylords
11/20	18	12	8	1	18	●	**Hold My Hand**...*Jack Lawrence/Richard Myers*			Don Cornell

3

12/25	15	12	8	4	19	●	**The Naughty Lady Of Shady Lane** ....*Roy Bennett/Sid Tepper*			The Ames Brothers
9/25	15	11	6	3	20		**Skokiaan**...*Tom Glazer/August Msarurgwa* [I]			Ralph Marterie
11/27	17	12	6	2	21		**If I Give My Heart To You** ....*Jimmy Brewster/Jimmie Crane/Al Jacobs*			Doris Day
1/23	16	10	6	1	22	●	**Stranger In Paradise**...................................*George Forrest/Robert Wright* <B:7>			Four Aces Feat. Al Alberts

4

6/12	19	13	7	6	23		**The Happy Wanderer** ....*Friedrich Moeller/Antonia Ridge/Florenz Siegesmund* ✦			Frank Weir
11/6	18	13	8	3	24	●	**Papa Loves Mambo**...................*Al Hoffman/Dick Manning/Bickley Reichner* <B:27>			Perry Como
9/18	14	10	5	2	25	●	**In The Chapel In The Moonlight**...*Billy Hill*			Kitty Kallen
6/5	18	12	3	1	26		**If You Love Me (Really Love Me)** ....*Marguerite Monnot/Geoffrey Parsons* <B:7>			Kay Starr
7/10	13	9	3	1	27		**Three Coins In The Fountain** ....*Sammy Cahn/Jule Styne*			Frank Sinatra
9/11	13	8	1	1	28		**The High And The Mighty** ....*Dimitri Tiomkin/Ned Washington* [I]			Les Baxter

1954

PEAK DATE	WEEKS CH	10	5	PK	RANK	GOLD	Title — PEAK POSITION — Songwriter(s)	SYMBOL	DEBUT	Artist
							5			
5/15	16	9	1	1	29		Here ....Dorcas Cochran/Harold Grant			Tony Martin
7/31	16	4	1	1	30		Sh-Boom ....James Edwards/Carl Feaster/Claude Feaster/James Keyes/Floyd McRae	✦		The Chords
							6			
5/1	19	10		2	31	●	Answer Me, My Love..........................Fred Rauch/Carl Sigman/Gerhard Winkler			Nat "King" Cole
5/29	18	9		2	32		The Man With The Banjo ....Robert Mellin/Fritz Reichel			Ames Brothers
1/16	14	8		2	33		Oh, Mein Papa ....Paul Burkhard/Geoffrey Parsons/John Turner [I]	✦		Eddie Calvert
8/7	15	6		2	34	●	I Understand Just How You Feel ....Pat Best			The Four Tunes
9/11	14	10		1	35		I'm A Fool To Care ....Ted Daffan			Les Paul & Mary Ford
9/4	14	7		1	36		The High And The Mighty ....Dimitri Tiomkin/Ned Washington [I]			Victor Young
5/15	14	6		1	37		A Girl, A Girl (Zoom-Ba Di Alli Nella)......Al Bandini/Bennie Benjamin/George Weiss <B:14>			Eddie Fisher
5/22	9	4		1	38		Jilted ....Robert Colby/Dick Manning			Teresa Brewer
							7			
1/30	18	11		4	39		The Gang That Sang "Heart Of My Heart" ....Ben Ryan <A:3>			Four Aces Feat. Al Alberts
8/7	15	8		3	40		Goodnight, Sweetheart, Goodnight ....Calvin Carter/James Hudson	❶		The McGuire Sisters
11/6	27	12		2	41	●	Shake, Rattle And Roll ....Charles Calhoun			Bill Haley And His Comets
10/2	16	5		2	42		They Were Doin' The Mambo ....Don Raye			Vaughn Monroe
5/29	17	7		1	43		The Man Upstairs ....Bob Russell/Hal Stanley <A:4>			Kay Starr
2/27	14	7		1	44		Till We Two Are One ....Tom Glazer/Billy Martin/Larry Martin	❶		Georgie Shaw
1/23	13	7		1	45		Changing Partners ....Larry Coleman/Joe Darion			Kay Starr
10/9	12	6		1	46		Skokiaan (South African Song)..........Tom Glazer/August Msarurgwa			The Four Lads
2/27	12	6		1	47		From The Vine Came The Grape ....Paul Cunningham/Leonard Whitcup			The Gaylords
4/17	11	6		1	48		Darktown Strutters Ball (Italian Style).....................Shelton Brooks	❶		Lou Monte
4/24	12	4		1	49		There'll Be No Teardrops Tonight ....Hank Williams			Tony Bennett
							8			
7/3	8	2		2	50		Green Years................................Arthur Altman/Don Reid <B:15>			Eddie Fisher
3/20	11	6		1	51		From The Vine Came The Grape ....Paul Cunningham/Leonard Whitcup			The Hilltoppers
6/26	15	3		1	52		The Happy Wanderer (Val-De Ri, Val-De Ra)....Friedrich Moeller/Antonia Ridge/Florenz Siegesmund			Henri René
7/3	8	3		1	53		Steam Heat ....Richard Adler/Jerry Ross			Patti Page
7/3	18	2		1	54		Crazy 'Bout Ya Baby ....Pat Barrett/Rudi Maugeri	❶		The Crew-Cuts
7/31	12	2		1	55		I Understand...Pat Best			June Valli
10/16	14	1		1	56		If I Give My Heart To You ....Jimmy Brewster/Jimmie Crane/Al Jacobs	✦		Denise Lor
9/4	7	1		1	57		Cinnamon Sinner ....Lincoln Chase			Tony Bennett
12/25	7	1		1	58		Let Me Go, Lover! ....Jenny Lou Carson/Al Hill			Patti Page
12/25	3	1		1	59		There's No Place Like Home For The Holidays...Robert Allen/Al Stillman [X]			Perry Como
							9			
7/24	11	3		1	60		The Little Shoemaker ....Geoffrey Parsons/Rudi Revil/John Turner <B:25>			Hugo Winterhalter & a Friend [Eddie Fisher]
8/28	14	2		1	61	●	The High And The Mighty ....Dimitri Tiomkin/Ned Washington [I]	❶		Leroy Holmes
12/18	12	2		1	62	●	Mambo Italiano ....Bob Merrill			Rosemary Clooney
1/9	7	1		1	63		Woman...Dick Gleason			Johnny Desmond
1/23	6	1		1	64		What It Was, Was Football (Parts I & II)......................Andy Griffith [C]	❶		Deacon Andy Griffith
							10			
10/9	11	2		2	65		Smile.............Charlie Chaplin/Geoffrey Parsons/John Turner			Nat "King" Cole
2/20	11	2		2	66		Till Then........................Sol Marcus/Eddie Seiler/Guy Wood			The Hilltoppers
1/16	11	2		2	67		Stranger In Paradise..................George Forrest/Robert Wright			Tony Martin
11/27	12	2		2	68		Muskrat Ramble ....Ray Gilbert/Edward Ory <B:28>			The McGuire Sisters
10/30	18	1		1	69	●	Cara Mia ....Bunny Lewis/Mantovani	❶		David Whitfield with Mantovani
9/11	11	1		1	70		What A Dream................................Chuck Willis <B:13>			Patti Page
10/23	11	1		1	71		If I Give My Heart To You ....Jimmy Brewster/Jimmie Crane/Al Jacobs			Connee Boswell
1/2	10	1		1	72		The Gang That Sang "Heart Of My Heart" ....Ben Ryan			Don Cornell, Alan Dale & Johnny Desmond
10/30	9	1		1	73		Whither Thou Goest......................................Guy Singer <B:19>			Les Paul & Mary Ford
							11			
4/24	10			1	74		I Really Don't Want To Know ....Howard Barnes/Don Robertson			Les Paul & Mary Ford
11/20	7			1	75		It's A Woman's World ....Sammy Cahn/Cyril Mockridge			Four Aces Feat. Al Alberts
							12			
7/3	8			1	76		Joey ....James Kriegsmann/Herb Wiener	❶		Betty Madigan
7/10	8			1	77		Thank You For Calling ....Cindy Walker			Jo Stafford

PEAK DATE	WEEKS				RANK	GOLD	Title	PEAK POSITION Songwriter(s)	SYMBL	DEBUT	Artist
	CH	10	5	PK							

12 (cont'd)

| 5/15 | 5 | | | 1 | 78 | | Poor Butterfly | John Golden/Raymond Hubbell | | | The Hilltoppers |
| 1/9 | 3 | | | 1 | 79 | | Changing Partners | Larry Coleman/Joe Darion | | | Dinah Shore |

13

8/28	8			2	80		I Cried	Michael Elias/William Tesone <A:10>			Patti Page
4/17	15			1	81		Cuddle Me	Ronnie Gaylord			Ronnie Gaylord
11/6	7			1	82		Oop-Shoop	Shirley Gunter/Blondene Taylor			The Crew-Cuts
1/23	6			1	83	●	Marie	Irving Berlin			The Four Tunes
12/25	3			1	84	●	White Christmas	Irving Berlin [X-R]			Bing Crosby
1/2	3			1	85		C'est Si Bon (It's So Good)	Henri Betti/Andre Hornez/Jerry Seelen [N]			Stan Freberg
2/6	2			1	86		Changing Partners	Larry Coleman/Joe Darion <B:20>			Bing Crosby

14

6/5	10			3	87		Isle Of Capri	Will Grosz/Jimmy Kennedy <B:23>			The Gaylords
11/13	9			1	88		Mood Indigo	Barney Bigard/Duke Ellington/Irving Mills	❶		The Norman Petty Trio
11/27	7			1	89		Hajji Baba (Persian Lament)	Dimitri Tiomkin/Ned Washington			Nat "King" Cole
7/31	7			1	90		Some Day	Rudolf Friml/Brian Hooker			Frankie Laine
7/17	7			1	91		Hernando's Hideaway	Richard Adler/Jerry Ross			Johnnie Ray
11/13	6			1	92		That's What I Like	Bob Hilliard/Jule Styne	❶		Don, Dick & Jimmy
4/17	5			1	93		Gee	William Davis/Daniel Norton/Viola Watkins	✦		The Crows
4/17	4			1	94		Anema E Core (With All My Heart and Soul)	Harry Akst/Mann Curtis/ Salvatore d'Esposito/Domenico Titomanglio <A:6>			Eddie Fisher
8/21	4			1	95		Hernando's Hideaway	Richard Adler/Jerry Ross			Guy Lombardo (Kenny Gardner)
10/23	1			1	96		Sh-Boom	James Edwards/Carl Feaster/Claude Feaster/James Keyes/Floyd McRae [N]			Stan Freberg

15

11/20	11			1	97		(Bazoom) I Need Your Lovin'	Jerry Leiber/Mike Stoller	❶		The Cheers
8/14	10			1	98		Sway (Quien Sera)	Pablo Beltran Ruiz/Norman Gimbel			Dean Martin
7/17	8			1	99		My Friend	Ervin Drake/Jimmy Shirl <A:8>			Eddie Fisher
1/23	4			1	100		O Mein Papa (Oh! My Papa)	Paul Burkhard/Geoffrey Parsons/John Turner			Ray Anthony
7/3	3			1	101		Point Of Order	Daws Butler/Stan Freberg [N]			Stan Freberg & Daws Butler
1/23	3			1	102		The Jones Boy	Mann Curtis/Vic Mizzy			Mills Brothers
7/10	2			1	103		Hit And Run Affair	Ray Cormier/Don Roseland/Mel Van			Perry Como

16

9/4	10			2	104		Hey There	Richard Adler/Jerry Ross	❶		Sammy Davis, Jr.
5/8	4			2	105		I Speak To The Stars	Sammy Fain/Paul Francis Webster			Doris Day
2/6	7			1	106		Woman (Uh-Huh)	Dick Gleason [N]	✦		Jose Ferrer
2/27	4			1	107		Somebody Bad Stole De Wedding Bell	Bob Hilliard/Dave Mann <B:20>			Eartha Kitt
11/20	4			1	108		Tell Me, Tell Me	Bob Merrill			June Valli
5/8	2			1	109		It Happens To Be Me	Sammy Gallop/Arthur Kent			Nat "King" Cole
4/24	2			1	110		Melancholy Me	Howard Biggs/Joe Thomas			Eddy Howard
6/26	2			1	111		The Honeymoon's Over	Vaughn Horton/Charles McCarthy/Sammy Mysels			Betty Hutton & "Tennessee" Ernie Ford
1/2	1			1	112		Off Shore	Leo Diamond [I]			Richard Hayman

17

5/15	6			2	113		Don't Worry About Me	Rube Bloom/Ted Koehler			Frank Sinatra
1/30	4			2	114		Granada	Agustin Lara			Frankie Laine
9/4	3			2	115		Dream	Johnny Mercer			Four Aces Feat. Al Alberts
5/22	11			1	116		Isle Of Capri	Will Grosz/Jimmy Kennedy [I]	❶		Jackie Lee
9/18	8			1	117		Skokiaan	Tom Glazer/August Msarurgwa [I]	✦		Bulawayo Sweet Rhythms Band
8/7	5			1	118		The High And The Mighty	Dimitri Tiomkin/Ned Washington			Johnny Desmond
2/27	3			1	119		Bell Bottom Blues	Leon Carr/Hal David			Teresa Brewer
8/28	2			1	120		If I Didn't Care	Jack Lawrence			The Hilltoppers
10/16	1			1	121		Fortune In Dreams	Hal Stanley/Irving Taylor			Kay Starr

18

10/23	5			1	122		Skokiaan	Tom Glazer/August Msarurgwa [I]			Ray Anthony
3/27	4			1	123		Somebody Bad Stole De Wedding Bell (Who's Got de Ding Dong)	Bob Hilliard/Dave Mann			Georgia Gibbs
8/7	2			1	124		Happy Days And Lonely Nights	Red Fisher/Billy Rose			The Fontane Sisters
1/9	2			1	125		South Of The Border (Down Mexico Way)	Michael Carr/Jimmy Kennedy			Frank Sinatra & Billy May
7/3	1			1	126		Gilly Gilly Ossenfeffer Katzenelle Bogen By The Sea	Al Hoffman/ Dick Manning [N]			The Four Lads

1954

PEAK DATE	WEEKS				R A N K	G O L D	Title	PEAK POSITION Songwriter(s)	S Y M B L	D E B U T	Artist
	CH	10	5	PK							

19

PEAK DATE	CH	10	5	PK	RANK	GOLD	Title	Songwriter(s)	SYMBL	DEBUT	Artist
7/24	2			1	127		Make Her Mine	Chester Conn/Sammy Gallop			Nat "King" Cole
12/25	2			1	128		Santo Natale (Merry Christmas)	Missing Song Writer [X]			David Whitfield
10/9	1			1	129		Smile	Charlie Chaplin/Geoffrey Parsons/John Turner			Sunny Gale
11/27	1			1	130		Mandolino	Les Paul <A:10> [I]			Les Paul
4/17	1			1	131		Such A Night	Lincoln Chase			Johnnie Ray

20

PEAK DATE	CH	10	5	PK	RANK	GOLD	Title	Songwriter(s)	SYMBL	DEBUT	Artist
1/30	3			3	132		Y'all Come	Arlie Duff <A:13>			Bing Crosby
2/20	2			2	133		Two Purple Shadows	Sammy Mysels/Dick Sanford	❶		Jerry Vale
11/13	8			1	134		Runaround	Cirino Colacrai	❶		The Three Chuckles
12/4	3			1	135		The Mama Doll Song	Nat Simon/Charles Tobias			Patti Page
2/6	1			1	136		Sadie Thompson's Song (Blue Pacific Blues)	Lester Lee/Ned Washington [I]			Richard Hayman
3/20	1			1	137		Lovin' Spree	Joan Javits/Phil Springer <A:16>			Eartha Kitt
5/8	1			1	138		The Kid's Last Fight	Bob Merrill			Frankie Laine
12/4	1			1	139		Mr. Sandman	Pat Ballard			Buddy Morrow

21

PEAK DATE	CH	10	5	PK	RANK	GOLD	Title	Songwriter(s)	SYMBL	DEBUT	Artist
11/6	5			1	140		St. Louis Blues Mambo	W.C. Handy [I]	❶		Richard Maltby

23

PEAK DATE	CH	10	5	PK	RANK	GOLD	Title	Songwriter(s)	SYMBL	DEBUT	Artist
6/5	3			1	141		Love I You	Sam Carlisi <A:14> [N]			The Gaylords

24

PEAK DATE	CH	10	5	PK	RANK	GOLD	Title	Songwriter(s)	SYMBL	DEBUT	Artist
8/14	4			1	142		Moonlight And Roses (Bring Mem'ries of You)	Ben Black/Charles Daniels/Edwin Lemare [I]			The Three Suns

25

PEAK DATE	CH	10	5	PK	RANK	GOLD	Title	Songwriter(s)	SYMBL	DEBUT	Artist
7/31	3			1	143		The Magic Tango	Phil Bloch/Jimmy Kennedy <A:9>			Hugo Winterhalter & a Friend [Eddie Fisher]

26

PEAK DATE	CH	10	5	PK	RANK	GOLD	Title	Songwriter(s)	SYMBL	DEBUT	Artist
6/5	5			1	144		Wedding Bells (Are Breaking Up That Old Gang Of Mine)	Sammy Fain/Irving Kahal/Willie Raskin <A:1>			Four Aces Feat. Al Alberts
11/13	4			1	145		This Ole House	Stuart Hamblen	✦		Stuart Hamblen
5/29	2			1	146		If You Love Me (Really Love Me) (Hymne A L'Amour)	Marguerite Monnot/Geoffrey Parsons			Vera Lynn

27

PEAK DATE	CH	10	5	PK	RANK	GOLD	Title	Songwriter(s)	SYMBL	DEBUT	Artist
11/13	2			1	147		The Things I Didn't Do	Fred Jacobson/Ira Kosloff/Irving Reid <A:4>			Perry Como
8/14	2			1	148		Goodnight, Sweetheart, Goodnight	Calvin Carter/James Hudson			Sunny Gale
12/4	1			1	149		Yours (Quireme Mucho)	Albert Gamse/Gonzalo Roig/Jack Sherr [I]	❶		Dick Contino

28

PEAK DATE	CH	10	5	PK	RANK	GOLD	Title	Songwriter(s)	SYMBL	DEBUT	Artist
12/25	2			1	150		Ling, Ting, Tong	Mabel Godwin	❶		The Five Keys
11/6	1			1	151		Lonesome Polecat	Gene DePaul/Johnny Mercer <A:10>			The McGuire Sisters

30

PEAK DATE	CH	10	5	PK	RANK	GOLD	Title	Songwriter(s)	SYMBL	DEBUT	Artist
11/27	1			1	152		I Want You All To Myself (Just You)	Roy Carroll/John Koch			Kitty Kallen
10/23	1			1	153		Rain, Rain, Rain	Jay McConlogue			Frankie Laine & The Four Lads
12/25	1			1	154		Land Of Dreams	Norman Gimbel/Eddie Heywood <A:25> [I]			Hugo Winterhalter/Eddie Heywood

SONG TITLE INDEX

Lists, alphabetically, all titles in the Singles By Artist section. The artist's name is listed with each title along with the highest position attained and the year the song peaked on the chart.

A song with more than one charted version is listed once, with the artists' names listed below in chronological order by peak year and secondly by peak position. Many songs that have the same title, but are different tunes, are listed separately, with the most popular title listed first. This will make it easy to determine which songs are the same composition, the number of charted versions of a particular song, and which of these was the most popular.

If a title begins with the word A, An or The, that word is omitted and the title is alphabetized beginning with the second word in the title. For example, "The Old Lamp-Lighter" is alphabetized under the letter 'O' and listed as "Old Lamp-Lighter."

Cross references have been used throughout to aid in finding a title.

Please note the following when searching for titles:

> A title such as "G.I. Jive" will be found at the beginning of the first letter in its title; however, a title such as "A-L-B-U-Q-U-E-R-Q-U-E," which is a spelling of a word, is listed with regularly spelled titles.

A

A-Huggin' ..see: Huggin'
"A"-You're Adorable
1/49   *Perry Como*
4/49   *Jo Stafford & Gordon MacRae*
12/49   *Tony Pastor*
27/49   *Buddy Kaye Quintet*
Aba Daba Honeymoon
3/51   *Debbie Reynolds & Carleton Carpenter*
9/51   *Richard Hayes & Kitty Kallen*
12/51   *Freddy Martin*
19/51   *Cliff Steward*
23/51   *Hoagy Carmichael & Cass Daley*
15/44 **Abraham** *Freddy Martin*
Ac-Cent-Tchu-Ate The Positive
1/45   *Johnny Mercer*
2/45   *Bing Crosby & Andrews Sisters*
5/45   *Artie Shaw*
12/45   *Kay Kyser*
Across The Alley From The Alamo
2/47   *Mills Brothers*
11/47   *Stan Kenton*
12/47   *Woody Herman*
Across The Wide Missouri
19/51   *Paul Weston*
21/51   *Hugo Winterhalter*
Adios
17/41   *Glenn Miller*
28/48   *Glenn Miller*
14/52   *Gisele MacKenzie*
20/40 **Adios, Mariquita Linda** *Artie Shaw*
Again
2/49   *Doris Day*
2/49   *Gordon Jenkins*
3/49   *Mel Tormé*
6/49   *Vic Damone*
6/49   *Tommy Dorsey*
7/49   *Art Mooney*
23/49   *Vera Lynn*
21/48 **Ah But It Happens** *Frankie Laine*
6/47 **Ain't Nobody Here But Us Chickens**
      Louis Jordan
22/50 **Ain't Nobody's Business But My Own** *Kay Starr & Tennessee Ernie Ford*
14/49 **Ain't She Sweet**
      Mr. Ford & Mr. Goon-Bones
17/46 **Ain't That Just Like A Woman (They'll Do It Every Time)**
      Louis Jordan
28/51 **Alabama Jubilee** *Red Foley*
18/53 **A-L-B-U-Q-U-E-R-Q-U-E**
      Ralph Flanagan
3/41 **Alexander The Swoose (Half Swan–Half Goose)** *Kay Kyser*
7/40 **Alice Blue Gown** *Frankie Masters*
25/50 **All Dressed Up To Smile**
      Evelyn Knight
19/43 **All For You** *King Cole's Trio*
All I Want For Christmas (Is My Two Front Teeth)
1/48   *Spike Jones*
18/50 *Spike Jones*
All My Love
1/50   *Patti Page*
7/50   *Percy Faith*
10/50 *Guy Lombardo*
11/50 *Bing Crosby*
22/50 *Dennis Day*

(All Of A Sudden) My Heart Sings
7/45   *Johnnie Johnston*
12/45 *Martha Stewart*
All Of Me
17/43 *Count Basie*
12/52 *Johnnie Ray*
All Of My Life
10/45 *Sammy Kaye*
10/45 *Three Suns*
12/45 *Bing Crosby*
2/43 **All Or Nothing At All**
      Frank Sinatra with Harry James
11/49 **All Right, Louie, Drop The Gun**
      Wesson Brothers
9/46 **All That Glitters Is Not Gold**
      Dinah Shore
3/40 **All The Things You Are**
      Tommy Dorsey
All This And Heaven Too
15/40 *Tommy Dorsey*
16/40 *Charlie Barnet*
20/40 *Jimmy Dorsey*
20/40 *Jack Leonard*
20/40 *Dick Todd*
All Through The Day
7/46   *Frank Sinatra*
8/46   *Perry Como*
11/46 *Margaret Whiting*
11/53 **Allez-Vous-En** *Kay Starr*
9/53 **Almost Always** *Joni James*
Along The Navajo Trail
2/45   *Bing Crosby & Andrews Sisters*
7/45   *Gene Krupa*
7/45   *Dinah Shore*
Along The Santa Fe Trail
7/41   *Glenn Miller*
14/41 *Sammy Kaye*
18/41 *Bing Crosby*
13/46 **Along With Me** *Margaret Whiting*
Always
11/44 *Gordon Jenkins*
25/44 *Paul Lavalle*
10/45 *Sammy Kaye*
10/45 *Guy Lombardo*
Always In My Heart
10/42 *Glenn Miller*
18/42 *Kenny Baker*
20/42 *Jimmy Dorsey*
28/51 **Always You** *Nat "King" Cole*
1/41 **Amapola (Pretty Little Poppy)**
      Jimmy Dorsey
Amen
4/42   *Abe Lyman*
5/42   *Woody Herman*
American Beauty Rose
21/50 *Eddy Howard*
26/50 *Frank Sinatra*
19/42 **American Patrol** *Glenn Miller*
Amor
2/44   *Bing Crosby*
2/44   *Andy Russell*
10/44 *Xavier Cugat*
23/44 *Enric Madriguera*
And Her Tears Flowed Like Wine
4/44   *Stan Kenton*
10/45 *Ella Fitzgerald*
—And Mimi
14/47 *Art Lund*
15/47 *Dick Haymes*

And So To Sleep Again
4/51   *Patti Page*
27/51 *April Stevens with Henri René*
28/51 *Dick Haymes*
30/51 *Paul Weston*
23/44 **And The Angels Sing**
      Benny Goodman
13/46 **And Then It's Heaven** *Harry James*
Anema E Core (With All My Heart and Soul)
28/51 *Perry Como*
14/54 *Eddie Fisher*
17/45 **Angelina** *Louis Prima*
18/42 **Angeline** *Art Kassel*
26/51 **Angry** *Kay Starr*
5/53 **Anna (El N. Zumbon)**
      Silvana Mangano
Anniversary Song
1/47   *Dinah Shore*
2/47   *Al Jolson*
2/47   *Guy Lombardo*
3/47   *Tex Beneke/Glenn Miller*
4/47   *Andy Russell*
19/44 **Another One Of Them Things**
      Tommy Dorsey
6/54 **Answer Me, My Love**
      Nat "King" Cole
3/41 **Anvil Chorus** *Glenn Miller*
Anytime
17/48 *Eddy Arnold*
2/52   *Eddie Fisher*
4/53 **Anywhere I Wander** *Julius LaRosa*
Apple Blossom Wedding
5/47   *Sammy Kaye*
9/47   *Eddy Howard*
14/47 *Buddy Clark*
April In Portugal
2/53   *Les Baxter*
10/53 *Vic Damone*
12/53 *Richard Hayman*
15/53 *Freddy Martin*
17/53 *Tony Martin*
10/40 **April Played The Fiddle** *Bing Crosby*
April Showers
9/47   *Guy Lombardo*
16/47 *Al Jolson*
12/46 **Are These Really Mine?**
      Vaughn Monroe
19/50 **Are You Lonesome Tonight**
      Blue Barron
Aren't You Glad You're You
18/45 *Pied Pipers*
8/46   *Bing Crosby*
11/46 *Les Brown*
14/46 *Tommy Dorsey*
Around The Corner
9/52   *Jo Stafford*
19/52 *Weavers & Gordon Jenkins*
19/44 **Arsenic And Old Face** *Jerry Jerome*
19/42 **Arthur Murray Taught Me Dancing In A Hurry** *Jimmy Dorsey*
13/46 **Artistry Jumps** *Stan Kenton*
(As Long As You're Not in Love With Anyone Else) Why Don't You Fall In Love With Me?
3/43   *Dinah Shore*
10/43 *Johnny Long*
16/43 *Dick Jurgens*
As Time Goes By
2/43   *Rudy Vallée*
3/43   *Jacques Renard*
10/52 *Ray Anthony*

265

Blueberry Hill
2/40   *Glenn Miller*
15/40   *Kay Kyser*
17/40   *Russ Morgan*

Bluebird Of Happiness
5/48   *Art Mooney*
16/48   *Jo Stafford & Gordon MacRae*
23/48   *Jan Peerce*

Bluebird On Your Windowsill ..see:
   (There's A)
9/40   **Bluebirds In The Moonlight**
   Dick Jurgens
15/51   **Blues from An American In Paris**
   Ralph Flanagan
20/52   **Blues In Advance** *Dinah Shore*

Blues In The Night
10/41   *Artie Shaw*
1/42   *Woody Herman*
4/42   *Jimmie Lunceford*
4/42   *Dinah Shore*
8/42   *Cab Calloway*
18/42   *Benny Goodman*
17/52   *Rosemary Clooney*
11/49   **Blues Stay Away From Me**
   Owen Bradley
27/49   **Blum Blum (I Wonder Who I Am)**
   Peggy Lee
   (Blushing Moon) ..see: Luna Rossa
27/49   **Body And Soul** *Billy Eckstine*
   (Bolero) ..see: All My Love

Bonaparte's Retreat
4/50   *Kay Starr*
9/50   *Gene Krupa*
7/40   **Boog-It** *Glenn Miller*
9/46   **Boogie Blues** *Gene Krupa*

Boogie Woogie
5/44   *Tommy Dorsey*
4/45   *Tommy Dorsey*
15/41   **Boogie Woogie Bugle Boy**
   Andrews Sisters
14/40   **Boogie Woogie On St. Louis Blues**
   Earl Hines
7/41   **Booglie Wooglie Piggy** *Glenn Miller*
2/52   **Botch-A-Me (Ba-Ba-Baciami**
   Piccina) *Rosemary Clooney*
19/41   **Boulder Buff** *Glenn Miller*

Bouquet Of Roses
13/48   *Eddy Arnold*
22/49   *Dick Haymes*

Brazil
2/43   *Xavier Cugat*
17/43   *Jimmy Dorsey*
17/42   **Breathless** *Shep Fields*

Breeze And I
1/40   *Jimmy Dorsey*
15/40   *Charlie Barnet*
18/40   *Xavier Cugat*
19/53   **Breeze (That's Bringin' My Honey**
   Back To Me) *Trudy Richards*
14/51   **Bring Back The Thrill** *Eddie Fisher*
12/50   **Broken Down Merry-Go-Round**
   Margaret Whiting & Jimmy Wakely
20/42   **Brother Bill** *Charlie Spivak*

Brush Those Tears From Your Eyes
16/48   *Barry Green*
9/49   *Evelyn Knight*
29/48   **Bubble-Loo Bubble-Loo** *Peggy Lee*
22/50   **Buffalo Billy**
   Roberta Quinlan, Jerry Murad's
   Harmonicats & Jan August
7/46   **Bumble Boogie** *Freddy Martin*
13/52   **Bunny Hop** *Ray Anthony*

Bushel And A Peck
3/50   *Perry Como & Betty Hutton*
6/50   *Margaret Whiting & Jimmy Wakely*
16/50   *Doris Day*
29/50   *Johnny Desmond*
22/51   *Andrews Sisters*
27/52   **Busybody** *Pee Wee King*
14/48   **But Beautiful** *Frank Sinatra*
16/45   **But I Did** *Dinah Shore*
16/42   **But Not For Me** *Harry James*
22/51   **Butcher Boy (Aeluna Mezzumare)**
   Emil Dewan Quintones
10/53   **Butterflies** *Patti Page*

Buttons And Bows
1/48   *Dinah Shore*
5/48   *Dinning Sisters*
8/48   *Betty Garrett*
9/48   *Betty Rhodes*
14/48   *Evelyn Knight*
17/48   *Gene Autry*

Buzz Me
9/46   *Louis Jordan*
15/46   *Ella Mae Morse*

By The Light Of The Silv'ry Moon
16/42   *Ray Noble*
17/44   *Ray Noble*

By The River Of The Roses
12/44   *Woody Herman*
25/44   *Abe Lyman*
20/41   **By-U By-O (The Lou'siana Lullaby)**
   Woody Herman
5/53   **Bye Bye Blues** *Les Paul & Mary Ford*

C

C'est Si Bon (It's So Good)
21/50   *Danny Kaye*
25/50   *Johnny Desmond*
8/53   *Eartha Kitt*
13/54   *Stan Freberg*

Caldonia
2/45   *Woody Herman*
6/45   *Louis Jordan*
12/45   *Erskine Hawkins*

Call Of The Canyon
10/40   *Glenn Miller*
18/40   *Tommy Dorsey*
13/51   **Calla Calla** *Vic Damone*

Can Anyone Explain? (No, No, No!)
5/50   *Ames Brothers*
5/50   *Ray Anthony*
23/50   *Dick Haymes*
25/50   *Vic Damone*
28/50   *Larry Green*
29/50   *Dinah Shore*
30/50   *Ella Fitzgerald–Louis Armstrong*
18/43   **Can't Get Out Of This Mood**
   Kay Kyser
16/53   **Can't I** *Nat "King" Cole & Billy May*
22/50   **Can't We Talk It Over**
   Andrews Sisters

Can't You Read Between The
   ## Lines?
8/45   *Jimmy Dorsey*
10/45   *Kay Kyser*
16/45   *Charlie Spivak*
15/49   **Canadian Capers (Cuttin' Capers)**
   Doris Day

Candy
1/45   *Johnny Mercer & Jo Stafford*
5/45   *Dinah Shore*
8/45   *Johnny Long & Dick Robertson*
15/45   *Four King Sisters*
18/45   *Jerry Wald*

Candy And Cake
12/50   *Mindy Carson*
16/50   *Arthur Godfrey*
20/50   *Evelyn Knight*
20/49   **Candy Kisses** *Eddy Howard*
17/53   **Candy Lips** *Johnnie Ray - Doris Day*
17/45   **Captain Kidd** *Ella Mae Morse*
10/54   **Cara Mia**
   David Whitfield with Mantovani
13/48   **Caramba! It's The Samba**
   Peggy Lee

Caravan
27/49   *Billy Eckstine*
6/53   *Ralph Marterie*

Careless
2/40   *Glenn Miller*
6/40   *Dick Jurgens*

Careless Hands
1/49   *Mel Tormé*
3/49   *Sammy Kaye*
12/49   *Bing Crosby*
21/49   *Bob & Jeanne*
24/50   **Careless Kisses** *Russ Morgan*
14/52   **Carioca** *Les Paul*

Castle Rock
8/51   *Frank Sinatra & Harry James*
27/51   *Fontane Sisters*
28/51   *Johnny Hodges*
26/52   **('Cause I Love You) That's A-Why**
   Guy Mitchell - Mindy Carson
8/40   **Cecelia** *Dick Jurgens*
18/40   **Celery Stalks At Midnight**
   Will Bradley Feat. Ray McKinley

Cement Mixer (Put-ti Put-ti)
5/46   *Alvino Rey*
13/46   *Charlie Barnet*
13/46   *Jimmie Lunceford*
17/46   *Hal McIntyre*
21/46   *Slim Gaillard Trio*

Changing Partners
3/53   *Patti Page*
7/54   *Kay Starr*
12/54   *Dinah Shore*
13/54   *Bing Crosby*
15/50   **Charley My Boy**
   Andrews Sisters - Russ Morgan

Charmaine
20/44   *Frankie Carle*
10/51   *Mantovani*
18/51   *Gordon Jenkins*
21/51   *Jerry Murad's Harmonicats*
8/52   *Paul Weston*
17/52   *Billy May*
27/52   *Vaughn Monroe*
1/41   **Chattanooga Choo Choo**
   Glenn Miller

Chattanoogie Shoe Shine Boy
1/50   *Red Foley*
4/50   *Bing Crosby*
8/50   *Phil Harris*
10/50   *Frank Sinatra*
17/50   *Bradford & Romano*
18/50   *Bill Darnel*
6/40   **Chatterbox** *Kay Kyser*

Cherry
4/44   *Harry James*
17/44   *Erskine Hawkins*

267

Deadly Weapon ..see: (Woman Is A)

Dear Hearts And Gentle People
2/50 Bing Crosby
2/50 Dinah Shore
14/50 Dennis Day
19/50 Gordon MacRae
19/50 Benny Strong
24/50 Ralph Flanagan

Dear John Letter
4/53 Jean Shepard with Ferlin Husky
17/53 Pat O'Day

Dearie
5/50 Guy Lombardo
10/50 Jo Stafford & Gordon MacRae
12/50 Ray Bolger & Ethel Merman
22/50 Lisa Kirk & Fran Warren

Dearly Beloved
10/42 Dinah Shore
15/42 Johnnie Johnston
5/43 Glenn Miller

Deep In The Heart Of Texas
3/42 Bing Crosby
3/42 Alvino Rey
7/42 Horace Heidt
14/42 Merry Macs
20/49 **Deep Purple** Paul Weston

Delicado
1/52 Percy Faith
25/52 Stan Kenton
26/52 Ralph Flanagan
28/52 Dinah Shore
3/42 **Der Fuehrer's Face** Spike Jones
5/51 **Detour** Patti Page
16/40 **Devil May Care** Glenn Miller

Dickey-Bird Song
5/48 Freddy Martin
22/48 Larry Clinton

(Did You Ever Get) That Feeling In The Moonlight
9/45 Perry Como
17/46 Russ Morgan
17/49 **Did You See Jackie Robinson Hit That Ball?** Buddy Johnson

Dig You Later (A Hubba-Hubba-Hubba)
3/46 Perry Como

Dim, Dim The Lights (I Want Some Atmosphere)
11/55 Bill Haley

Dime A Dozen
19/49 Margaret Whiting
24/49 Sammy Kaye
9/46 **Dinah** Sam Donahue
15/53 **Dipsy Doodle** Johnny Maddox

Do I Worry?
4/41 Tommy Dorsey
14/41 Ink Spots
20/41 Bea Wain

Do Nothin' Till You Hear From Me
6/44 Duke Ellington
7/44 Woody Herman
10/44 Stan Kenton

Do You Care?
18/41 Bob Crosby
19/41 Sam Donahue
15/46 **Do You Love Me** Harry James

Doctor, Lawyer, Indian Chief
1/46 Betty Hutton
6/46 Les Brown
18/46 Hoagy Carmichael
1/53 **Doggie In The Window** Patti Page
       (also see: How Much Is That Hound Dog In The Window)

Doin' What Comes Natur'lly
2/46 Freddy Martin
3/46 Dinah Shore with Spade Cooley
8/46 Jimmy Dorsey
10/40 **Dolimite** Erskine Hawkins

Dolores
2/41 Bing Crosby
7/41 Tommy Dorsey

Domino
9/51 Tony Martin
15/51 Bing Crosby
21/51 Doris Day
13/53 **Don'cha Hear Them Bells**
       Les Paul & Mary Ford

Don't Be A Baby, Baby
11/46 Benny Goodman
12/46 Mills Brothers
23/49 **Don't Be Afraid To Dream** Don Reid
14/44 **Don't Believe Everything You Dream** Ink Spots
15/43 **Don't Cry, Baby** Erskine Hawkins

Don't Cry Joe (Let Her Go, Let Her Go, Let Her Go)
3/49 Gordon Jenkins
9/49 Ralph Flanagan
22/49 Johnny Desmond
22/49 Juanita Hall

Don't Fence Me In
1/44 Bing Crosby & Andrews Sisters
4/45 Sammy Kaye
8/45 Kate Smith
10/45 Horace Heidt

Don't Forget Tonight Tomorrow
9/45 Frank Sinatra & The Charioteers

Don't Get Around Much Anymore
2/43 Ink Spots
7/43 Glen Gray
8/43 Duke Ellington
15/52 **Don't Leave My Poor Heart Breaking** Elliot Lawrence

Don't Let The Stars Get In Your Eyes
1/53 Perry Como
11/53 Gisele MacKenzie
23/49 **Don't Rob Another Man's Castle** Eddy Arnold

Don't Sit Under The Apple Tree (With Anyone Else But Me)
2/42 Glenn Miller
2/44 **Don't Sweetheart Me** Lawrence Welk

Don't Take Your Love From Me
21/44 Glen Gray
       (Don't Tell The Trees) ..see: Whispering Grass
17/54 **Don't Worry About Me** Frank Sinatra
       Don't You ..see: Don'cha

Doo De Doo On An Old Kazoo
21/49 Art Mooney
12/52 **Doodletown Fifers**
       Sauter-Finegan Orchestra
15/45 **Door Will Open** Tommy Dorsey
14/49 **Down Among The Sheltering Palms**
       Sammy Kaye

Down Argentina Way
7/40 Leo Reisman
13/40 Eddy Duchin
16/40 Gene Krupa
18/40 Shep Fields
2/41 Bob Crosby
17/53 **Down By The River Side** Four Lads

Down By The Station
11/49 Tommy Dorsey
20/49 Guy Lombardo

17/44 **Down In The Valley** Andrews Sisters
10/40 **Down The Road A Piece**
       Will Bradley
17/51 **Down The Trail Of Achin' Hearts**
       Patti Page

Down Yonder
4/51 Del Wood
14/51 Joe "Fingers" Carr
15/51 Freddy Martin
16/51 Eddie Smith & the Chief
17/51 Champ Butler
22/51 Lawrence (Piano Roll) Cook
26/51 Frank Petty Trio
5/53 **Downhearted** Eddie Fisher
2/53 **Dragnet** Ray Anthony

Dream
1/45 Pied Pipers
5/45 Frank Sinatra
8/45 Freddy Martin
13/45 Jimmy Dorsey
17/54 Four Aces

Dream A Little Dream Of Me
14/50 Jack Owens
18/50 Frankie Laine
28/50 **Dream Awhile** Frank DeVol
16/40 **Dream Valley** Eddy Duchin
7/44 **Dreamer, The** Kay Armen

Dreamer's Holiday
12/49 Buddy Clark
26/49 Eileen Wilson & Gordon Jenkins
3/50 Perry Como
11/50 Ray Anthony
26/49 **Drinkin' Wine Spo-Dee-O-Dee**
       "Stick" McGhee
       (Duckworth Chant) ..see: Sound Off

E

14/44 **Eager Beaver** Stan Kenton
25/52 **Early Autumn** Jo Stafford
8/55 **Earth Angel (Will You Be Mine)**
       Penguins
16/42 **Easter Parade** Harry James

Ebb Tide
2/53 Frank Chacksfield
10/53 Vic Damone
23/48 **Ebony Rhapsody** Rosetta Howard

Echo Said "No"
16/47 Guy Lombardo
17/47 Sammy Kaye

Echoes
18/50 Jo Stafford & Gordon MacRae
24/50 Ink Spots

Egg And I
16/47 Sammy Kaye
16/47 Dinah Shore
2/53 **Eh, Cumpari** Julius LaRosa
       Eighteenth Variation ..see: Story Of Three Loves
8/45 **11:60 P.M.** Harry James

Elmer's Tune
1/41 Glenn Miller
8/41 Dick Jurgens
18/44 **Embraceable You** Tommy Dorsey

Enjoy Yourself (It's Later Than You Think)
10/50 Guy Lombardo
24/50 Doris Day
12/49 **Envy** Fran Warren

Estrellita (My Little Star)
       Harry James

I'll Get By (As Long As I Have You)
1/44   *Harry James*
7/44   *Ink Spots*
12/44   *Four King Sisters*
18/51 **I'll Hold You In My Heart ('Til I Can Hold You in My Arms)**
     Eddie Fisher
26/49 **I'll Keep The Love Light Burning (In My Heart)** *Patti Page*
3/50 **I'll Never Be Free**
     Kay Starr & Tennessee Ernie Ford
8/49 **I'll Never Slip Around Again**
     Margaret Whiting & Jimmy Wakely
I'll Never Smile Again
1/40   *Tommy Dorsey*
17/40   *Glenn Miller*
17/50 **I'll Sail My Ship Alone**
     Moon Mullican
29/52 **I'll Still Love You** *Ames Brothers*
18/42 **I'll Take Tallulah** *Tommy Dorsey*
I'll Walk Alone
1/44   *Dinah Shore*
4/44   *Martha Tilton*
6/44   *Mary Martin*
22/44   *Louis Prima*
5/52   *Don Cornell*
14/52   *Jane Froman*
24/52   *Richard Hayes*
29/52   *Margaret Whiting*
1/46 **I'm A Big Girl Now** *Sammy Kaye*
6/54 **I'm A Fool To Care**
     Les Paul & Mary Ford
14/51 **I'm A Fool To Want You**
     Frank Sinatra
I'm Always Chasing Rainbows
5/46   *Perry Como*
7/46   *Dick Haymes & Helen Forrest*
9/46   *Harry James*
I'm Beginning To See The Light
1/45   *Harry James*
5/45   *Ella Fitzgerald & Ink Spots*
6/45   *Duke Ellington*
30/49 **I'm Bitin' My Fingernails And Thinking Of You**
     Andrews Sisters & Ernest Tubb
I'm Confessin' (That I Love You)
12/45   *Perry Como*
13/52   *Les Paul & Mary Ford*
26/50 **I'm Crazy To Love You**
     Sarah Vaughan
10/50 **I'm Forever Blowing Bubbles**
     Gordon Jenkins & Artie Shaw
(I'm Gonna Get You) On A Slow Boat To China ..see: On A Slow Boat To China
I'm Gonna Love That Gal (Guy)
4/45   *Perry Como*
9/45   *Benny Goodman*
17/42 **I'm Gonna Move To The Outskirts Of Town** *Jimmie Lunceford*
12/45 **I'm Gonna See My Baby**
     Johnny Mercer
I'm In Love Again
6/51   *Henri René feat. April Stevens*
24/51   *Andrews Sisters*
22/44 **I'm In Love With Someone (Who Is Not In Love With Me)** *Art Kassel*
12/46 **I'm In The Mood For Love**
     Billy Eckstine
14/53 **I'm Just A Poor Bachelor**
     Frankie Laine

I'm Looking Over A Four Leaf Clover
1/48   *Art Mooney*
6/48   *Russ Morgan with Milt Herth*
6/48   *Alvino Rey*
10/48   *Three Suns*
11/48   *Uptown String Band*
14/48   *Arthur Godfrey*
I'm Making Believe
1/44   *Ink Spots & Ella Fitzgerald*
14/45   *Hal McIntyre*
10/48 **I'm My Own Grandpaw**
     Guy Lombardo
22/52 **I'm Never Satisfied** *Nat "King" Cole*
I'm Nobody's Baby
3/40   *Judy Garland*
15/40   *Bea Wain*
16/40   *Ozzie Nelson*
10/53 **I'm Sitting On Top Of The World**
     Les Paul & Mary Ford
20/40 **I'm Stepping Out With A Memory To-Night** *Kate Smith*
20/41 **I'm Thrilled** *Glenn Miller*
18/49 **I'm Throwing Rice (At the Girl That I Love)** *Eddy Arnold*
I'm Waiting Just For You
19/51   *Lucky Millinder*
21/51   *Rosemary Clooney*
I'm Walking Behind You
1/53   *Eddie Fisher*
7/53   *Frank Sinatra*
11/45 **I'm Wastin' My Tears On You**
     Tex Ritter
I'm Yours
3/52   *Don Cornell*
3/52   *Eddie Fisher*
17/52   *Four Aces*
24/52   *Toni Arden*
21/49 **I've Been Waitin' For Your Phone Call For Eighteen Years (Maybe You Don't Love Me Anymore)**
     Beatrice Kay
I've Got A Lovely Bunch Of Coconuts
8/49   *Freddy Martin*
26/50   *Danny Kaye*
9/40 **I've Got My Eyes On You**
     Bob Crosby
I've Got My Love To Keep Me Warm
1/49   *Les Brown*
9/49   *Mills Brothers*
22/49   *Art Lund*
26/49   *Starlighters*
14/53 **I've Got The World On A String**
     Frank Sinatra
11/51 **I've Got You Under My Skin**
     Stan Freberg
1/42 **(I've Got a Gal in) Kalamazoo**
     Glenn Miller
20/44 **I've Had This Feeling Before (But Never Like This)** *Johnny Long*
1/43 **I've Heard That Song Before**
     Harry James
Idaho
4/42   *Benny Goodman*
16/42   *Alvino Rey*
20/52 **Idaho State Fair** *Vaughn Monroe*

If
1/51   *Perry Como*
8/51   *Jo Stafford*
10/51   *Billy Eckstine*
14/51   *Dean Martin*
20/51   *Guy Lombardo*
23/51   *Ink Spots*
26/51   *Jan Garber*
28/51   *Vic Damone*
17/54 **If I Didn't Care** *Hilltoppers*
20/49 **If I Ever Love Again** *Jo Stafford*
If I Give My Heart To You
3/54   *Doris Day*
8/54   *Denise Lor*
10/54   *Connee Boswell*
If I Knew You Were Comin' (I'd've Baked A Cake)
1/50   *Eileen Barton*
5/50   *Georgia Gibbs*
11/50   *Benny Strong*
15/50   *Ethel Merman & Ray Bolger*
28/50   *Art Mooney*
If I Loved You
3/45   *Perry Como*
7/45   *Frank Sinatra*
8/45   *Bing Crosby*
8/45   *Harry James*
30/50 **If I Were A Bell** *Frankie Laine*
19/46 **If I'm Lucky** *Perry Como*
24/51 **If Teardrops Were Pennies**
     Rosemary Clooney
19/45 **If You Are But A Dream**
     Frank Sinatra
If You Love Me (Really Love Me)
4/54   *Kay Starr*
26/54   *Vera Lynn*
17/43 **If You Please** *Bing Crosby*
If You Stub Your Toe On The Moon
17/49   *Tony Martin*
27/49   *Bing Crosby*
14/46 **If You Were The Only Girl**
     Perry Como
14/50 **If You've Got The Money, I've Got The Time** *Jo Stafford*
Imagination
2/40   *Glenn Miller*
8/40   *Tommy Dorsey*
13/46 **In A Shanty In Old Shanty Town**
     Johnny Long
In An Old Dutch Garden (By An Old Dutch Mill)
8/40   *Dick Jurgens*
8/40   *Glenn Miller*
In Love In Vain
12/46   *Dick Haymes & Helen Forrest*
12/46   *Margaret Whiting*
7/43 **In My Arms** *Dick Haymes*
20/48 **In My Dreams** *Vaughn Monroe*
1/43 **In The Blue Of Evening**
     Tommy Dorsey
4/54 **In The Chapel In The Moonlight**
     Kitty Kallen
In The Cool, Cool, Cool Of The Evening
11/51   *Bing Crosby & Jane Wyman*
17/51   *Jo Stafford & Frankie Laine*
15/52 **In The Good Old Summertime**
     Les Paul & Mary Ford
18/46 **In The Land Of Beginning Again**
     Bing Crosby
In The Middle Of May
13/45   *Freddy Martin*
14/46   *Pied Pipers*

Long Ago (And Far Away)
2/44	Helen Forrest & Dick Haymes
5/44	Bing Crosby
6/44	Jo Stafford
8/44	Perry Como
11/44	Guy Lombardo
16/44	Three Suns

Longing For You
12/51	Vic Damone
16/51	Sammy Kaye
28/51	Teresa Brewer
28/49	**Lord's Prayer** Perry Como

(Lou'siana Lullaby) ..see: By-U By-O
18/44	**Louise** Russ Morgan
23/54	**Love I You** Gaylords
11/45	**Love Letters** Dick Haymes
17/40	**Love Lies** Tommy Dorsey
25/52	**Love Me (Baby Can't You Love Me)** Johnnie Ray
18/53	**Love Me, Love Me** Bobby Wayne
24/49	**Love Me! Love Me! Love Me!** Eddy Howard
1/48	**Love Somebody** Doris Day & Buddy Clark

(Love Story) ..see: Intermezzo
8/53	**Love Walked In** Hilltoppers
3/51	**Loveliest Night Of The Year** Mario Lanza

Lovely Way To Spend An Evening
15/44	Frank Sinatra
17/44	Ink Spots
3/52	**Lover** Peggy Lee & Gordon Jenkins
16/53	**Lover, Come Back To Me!** Nat "King" Cole & Billy May
24/49	**Lovesick Blues** Hank Williams
20/54	**Lovin' Spree** Eartha Kitt

Luna Rossa (Blushing Moon)
26/52	Alan Dean
27/52	Tony Martin

M

12/46	**Mabel! Mabel!** Woody Herman
10/46	**Mad Boogie** Count Basie
14/52	**Mademoiselle** Eddy Howard

(Magic Song) ..see: Bibbidi-Bobbidi-Boo
25/54	**Magic Tango** Hugo Winterhalter & Eddie Fisher
19/48	**Maharajah Of Magador** Vaughn Monroe
20/44	**Main Stem** Duke Ellington

Mairzy Doats
1/44	Merry Macs
7/44	Al Trace
8/44	Pied Pipers
16/44	Lawrence Welk
21/44	Four King Sisters

Make-Believe Island
1/40	Mitchell Ayres
8/40	Jan Savitt
17/40	Dick Todd
18/40	Dick Jurgens
19/40	Sammy Kaye
20/49	**Make Believe (You Are Glad When You're Sorry)** Sarah Vaughan
19/54	**Make Her Mine** Nat "King" Cole
1/54	**Make Love To Me!** Jo Stafford
6/55	**Make Yourself Comfortable** Sarah Vaughan

Mam'selle
1/47	Art Lund
1/47	Frank Sinatra
3/47	Dick Haymes
3/47	Pied Pipers
7/47	Ray Dorey
8/47	Dennis Day
14/47	Frankie Laine
20/54	**Mama Doll Song** Patti Page
21/51	**Mama Will Bark** Frank Sinatra & Dagmar
9/54	**Mambo Italiano** Rosemary Clooney
27/50	**Mambo Jambo** Dave Barbour
9/40	**Man That Comes Around** Tommy Tucker Time
7/54	**Man Upstairs** Kay Starr
6/54	**Man With The Banjo** Ames Brothers

Managua - Nicaragua
1/47	Guy Lombardo
1/47	Freddy Martin
6/47	Kay Kyser
1/48	**Mañana (Is Soon Enough For Me)** Peggy Lee
19/54	**Mandolino** Les Paul

Manhattan Serenade
9/42	Harry James
15/42	Tommy Dorsey
4/53	**Many Times** Eddie Fisher

(Maori Farewell Song) ..see: Now Is The Hour

Maria Elena
1/41	Jimmy Dorsey
2/41	Wayne King
9/41	Tony Pastor
13/54	**Marie** Four Tunes
20/52	**Marilyn** Ray Anthony
24/51	**Marshmallow World** Bing Crosby
15/50	**Marta (Rambling Rose of the Wildwood)** Tony Martin
23/52	**Mask Is Off** Richard Hayes

(May God Be With You) ..see: Vaya Con Dios
17/41	**May I Never Love Again** Bob Chester
25/50	**May I Take Two Giant Steps?** Eileen Barton

Maybe
2/40	Ink Spots
17/40	Dinah Shore
19/40	Bobby Byrne
3/52	Perry Como & Eddie Fisher

Maybe It's Because
5/49	Dick Haymes
9/49	Eddy Howard
20/49	Connie Haines
22/49	Bob Crosby - Marion Morgan
3/48	**Maybe You'll Be There** Gordon Jenkins
10/46	**McNamara's Band** Bing Crosby & The Jesters
28/51	**Meanderin'** Vaughn Monroe

Meet Me In St. Louis, Louis
22/44	Judy Garland
13/45	Guy Lombardo

Meet Mister Callaghan
5/52	Les Paul
11/52	Harry Grove Trio
23/52	Mitch Miller
28/52	Carmen Cavallaro
16/54	**Melancholy Me** Eddy Howard
2/55	**Melody Of Love** Billy Vaughn
15/44	**Memphis Blues** Harry James
29/52	**Mermaid** Frankie Laine

(Merry Christmas) ..see: Santo Natale
18/50	**Merry Christmas Polka** Andrews Sisters & Guy Lombardo

(Merry Christmas To You) ..see: Christmas Song

Merry-Go-Round Waltz
18/49	Guy Lombardo
29/49	Art Mooney
19/51	**Metro Polka** Frankie Laine
16/44	**Mexico Joe** Ivie Anderson with Ceele Burke's Orch.
3/47	**Mickey** Ted Weems
16/47	**Midnight Masquerade** Monica Lewis

Milkman, Keep Those Bottles Quiet
7/44	Ella Mae Morse
10/44	Woody Herman
13/44	Four King Sisters
14/40	**Million Dreams Ago** Dick Jurgens
18/41	**Minka** Sammy Kaye
7/46	**Misirlou** Jan August

Miss You
8/42	Dinah Shore
9/42	Bing Crosby
16/43	**Mission To Moscow** Benny Goodman

Mississippi
18/50	Kay Starr
22/50	Red Foley
23/50	Art Mooney
26/50	Bill Darnel

Mister And Mississippi
8/51	Patti Page
13/51	Dennis Day
18/51	Tennessee Ernie Ford

Mister Five By Five
2/42	Harry James
10/42	Freddie Slack
17/42	Andrews Sisters

Mr. Sandman
1/54	Chordettes
20/54	Buddy Morrow
5/55	Four Aces
10/53	**Mister Tap Toe** Doris Day
9/50	**Mr. Touchdown, U. S. A.** Hugo Winterhalter
27/49	**Mistletoe Kiss** Keynotes with Primo Scala
22/51	**Mixed Emotions** Rosemary Clooney

Mockin' Bird Hill
2/51	Patti Page
2/51	Les Paul & Mary Ford
10/51	Pinetoppers
16/51	Russ Morgan
23/52	**Mocking Bird** Four Lads
30/50	**Molasses, Molasses (It's Icky Sticky Goo)** Roberta Quinlan with Jan August
24/44	**Moment I Laid Eyes On You** Cab Calloway
11/46	**Moment I Met You** Tommy Dorsey

Mona Lisa
1/50	Nat "King" Cole
7/50	Victor Young & Don Cherry
14/50	Harry James
14/50	Art Lund
16/50	Ralph Flanagan
16/50	Charlie Spivack
25/50	Dennis Day
9/46	**Money Is The Root Of All Evil (Take It Away, Take It Away, Take It Away)** Andrews Sisters & Guy Lombardo

9/48	**Shine** *Frankie Laine*	
	Shoo Fly Pie And Apple Pan Dowdy	
6/46	*Stan Kenton*	
6/46	*Guy Lombardo*	
6/46	*Dinah Shore*	
	Shoo-Shoo Baby	
1/44	*Andrews Sisters*	
4/44	*Ella Mae Morse*	
12/44	*Jan Garber*	
14/51	**Shot Gun Boogie**	
	Tennessee Ernie Ford	
9/52	**Should I** *Four Aces*	
28/50	**Show Me The Way To Get Out Of This World ('Cause That's Where Everything Is)** *Peggy Lee*	
	Shrimp Boats	
2/51	*Jo Stafford*	
16/52	*Dolores Gray with Camarata*	
	(also see: Herring Boats)	
	Shrine Of Saint Cecilia	
17/42	*Andrews Sisters*	
20/42	*Vaughn Monroe*	
3/53	**Side By Side** *Kay Starr*	
	Sierra Sue	
1/40	*Bing Crosby*	
17/40	*Glenn Miller*	
	Silent Night	
19/41	*Bing Crosby*	
16/42	*Bing Crosby*	
18/52	**Silver And Gold** *Pee Wee King*	
19/44	**Silver Wings In The Moonlight**	
	Freddie Slack	
17/49	**Similau (See-Me-Lo)** *Peggy Lee*	
	Simple Melody ..see: Play A Simple Melody	
	Sin	
1/51	*Eddy Howard*	
4/51	*Four Aces*	
5/51	*Savannah Churchill*	
14/51	*Four Knights*	
25/51	*Sammy Kaye*	
28/52	*Billy Williams*	
19/44	**Since You Went Away** *Jerry Wald*	
18/44	**Sing A Tropical Song**	
	Andrews Sisters	
2/40	**Singing Hills** *Bing Crosby*	
20/52	**Sinner Am I** *Johnnie Ray*	
	Sinner Kissed An Angel	
19/41	*Harry James*	
20/41	*Tommy Dorsey*	
22/52	**Sinner Or Saint** *Sarah Vaughan*	
	Sioux City Sue	
16/45	*Dick Thomas*	
3/46	*Bing Crosby & The Jesters*	
10/46	*Tony Pastor*	
14/46	*Kate Smith*	
	Sitting By The Window	
21/50	*Ray Anthony*	
23/50	*Billy Eckstine*	
29/50	*Vic Damone*	
	Six Lessons From Madame La Zonga	
4/40	*Jimmy Dorsey*	
13/40	*Charlie Barnet*	
17/51	**Sixty Minute Man** *Dominoes*	
	Skokiaan	
3/54	*Ralph Marterie*	
7/54	*Four Lads*	
17/54	*Bulawayo Sweet Rhythms Band*	
18/54	*Ray Anthony*	

	Skylark	
7/42	*Glenn Miller*	
16/42	*Harry James*	
19/42	*Bing Crosby*	
20/42	*Dinah Shore*	
7/48	**Slap 'Er Down, Agin, Paw**	
	Arthur Godfrey	
	Slaughter On Tenth Avenue	
19/44	*Lennie Hayton*	
21/52	*Ray Anthony*	
	Sleepy Lagoon	
1/42	*Harry James*	
18/42	*Dinah Shore*	
21/44	**Sleepy Time Gal** *Harry James*	
24/49	**Sleigh Ride** *Boston Pops Orchestra*	
	Sleigh Ride In July	
8/45	*Dinah Shore*	
14/45	*Bing Crosby*	
15/45	*Tommy Dorsey*	
18/45	*Les Brown*	
	Slipping Around	
1/49	*Margaret Whiting & Jimmy Wakely*	
17/49	*Ernest Tubb*	
9/40	**Slow Freight** *Glenn Miller*	
	Slow Poke	
13/51	*Roberta Lee*	
1/52	*Pee Wee King*	
6/52	*Ralph Flanagan*	
8/52	*Helen O'Connell*	
12/52	*Arthur Godfrey*	
26/52	*Hawkshaw Hawkins*	
28/52	*Tiny Hill*	
	Slowly	
11/46	*Kay Kyser*	
12/46	*Dick Haymes*	
	Smile	
10/54	*Nat "King" Cole*	
19/54	*Sunny Gale*	
	(Smile! Smile! Smile!) ..see: Powder Your Face With Sunshine	
7/44	**Smoke On The Water** *Red Foley*	
14/52	**Smoke Rings** *Les Paul & Mary Ford*	
	Smoke! Smoke! Smoke! (That Cigarette)	
1/47	*Tex Williams*	
8/47	*Phil Harris*	
23/51	**Smooth Sailing** *Ella Fitzgerald*	
20/41	**Snowfall** *Claude Thornhill*	
	So Far	
8/47	*Frank Sinatra*	
11/47	*Perry Como*	
14/47	*Margaret Whiting*	
	So In Love	
13/49	*Patti Page*	
20/49	*Gordon MacRae*	
20/49	*Dinah Shore*	
	So Long (It's Been Good to Know Yuh)	
4/51	*Gordon Jenkins & The Weavers*	
21/51	*Paul Weston*	
26/51	*Ralph Marterie*	
21/52	**So Madly In Love** *Georgia Gibbs*	
	So Tired	
3/49	*Russ Morgan*	
7/49	*Kay Starr*	
	So You're The One	
14/41	*Eddy Duchin*	
17/41	*Hal Kemp*	
18/41	*Vaughn Monroe*	
16/44	**Soldier's Last Letter** *Ernest Tubb*	
17/51	**Solitaire** *Tony Bennett*	
16/44	**Solo Flight** *Benny Goodman*	

	Some Day	
24/52	*Tony Martin*	
14/54	*Frankie Laine*	
	Some Enchanted Evening	
1/49	*Perry Como*	
3/49	*Bing Crosby*	
4/49	*Jo Stafford*	
6/49	*Frank Sinatra*	
7/49	*Ezio Pinza*	
9/49	*Paul Weston*	
28/49	*John Laurenz*	
9/45	**Some Sunday Morning**	
	Dick Haymes & Helen Forrest	
12/51	**Somebody** *Jo Stafford*	
	Somebody Bad Stole De Wedding Bell	
16/54	*Eartha Kitt*	
18/54	*Georgia Gibbs*	
	Somebody Else Is Taking My Place	
5/42	*Benny Goodman*	
5/42	*Russ Morgan*	
30/48	*Benny Goodman with Peggy Lee*	
22/52	**Somebody Loves Me** *Four Lads*	
8/53	**Somebody Stole My Gal**	
	Johnnie Ray	
	Someday I'll Meet You Again	
11/44	*Ink Spots*	
21/44	*Enric Madriguera*	
	Someday (You'll Want Me To Want You)	
12/46	*Hoosier Hot Shots & Sally Foster*	
1/49	*Vaughn Monroe*	
5/49	*Mills Brothers*	
25/49	**Somehow** *Billy Eckstine*	
20/42	**Someone's Rocking My Dream Boat**	
	Ink Spots	
12/45	**Something Sentimental**	
	Vaughn Monroe	
	Sometime	
16/50	*Mariners*	
26/50	*Ink Spots*	
27/50	*Jo Stafford*	
8/52	**Somewhere Along The Way**	
	Nat "King" Cole	
	Sonata	
9/47	*Perry Como*	
10/47	*Jo Stafford*	
	Song From Limelight ..see: (Terry's Theme)	
	Song From Moulin Rouge (Where Is Your Heart)	
1/53	*Percy Faith*	
8/53	*Mantovani*	
20/53	**Song Of India** *Mario Lanza*	
25/55	**Song Of The Barefoot Contessa**	
	Hugo Winterhalter	
	(Song Of The Tree) ..see: Poinciana	
1/41	**Song Of The Volga Boatmen**	
	Glenn Miller	
	Sooner Or Later (You're Gonna Be Comin' Around)	
8/46	*Sammy Kaye*	
8/47	*Les Brown*	
28/50	**Sorry**	
	Frank Sinatra & The Modernaires	
3/51	**Sound Off (The Duckworth Chant)**	
	Vaughn Monroe	
22/44	**South** *Bennie Moten*	
	South America, Take It Away	
2/46	*Bing Crosby & Andrews Sisters*	
6/46	*Xavier Cugat*	

Time Waits For No One
2/44	*Helen Forrest*
8/44	*Johnny Long*
10/41	**Time Was (Duerme)** *Jimmy Dorsey*
9/45	**Tippin' In** *Erskine Hawkins*
19/41	**'Tis Autumn** *Les Brown*
8/53	**To Be Alone** *Hilltoppers*

To Each His Own
1/46	*Eddy Howard*
1/46	*Ink Spots*
1/46	*Freddy Martin*
3/46	*Modernaires with Paula Kelly*
4/46	*Tony Martin*
19/52	**To Know You (Is to Love You)** *Perry Como*
9/50	**To Think You've Chosen Me** *Eddy Howard*

Together
3/44	*Helen Forrest & Dick Haymes*
7/44	*Guy Lombardo*
12/44	*Dinah Shore*
21/51	**Tom's Tune** *Georgia Gibbs*
19/48	**Tomorrow Night** *Lonnie Johnson*

Tonight (Perfidia) ..see: Perfidia

Tonight We Love (Concerto Number 1, B Flat Minor)
1/41	*Freddy Martin*
5/41	*Tony Martin*
8/42	*Freddy Martin*

Too Fat Polka (I Don't Want Her) (You Can Have Her) (She's Too Fat For Me)
2/47	*Arthur Godfrey*
13/48	*Dick "Two Ton" Baker*
18/44	**Too Late To Worry** *Al Dexter*
12/52	**Too Old To Cut The Mustard** *Marlene Dietrich & Rosemary Clooney*

Too-Ra-Loo-Ra-Loo-Ral (That's An Irish Lullaby)
4/44	*Bing Crosby*
12/45	*Charlie Spivak*

Too Young
1/51	*Nat "King" Cole*
15/51	*Toni Arden*
19/51	*Patty Andrews*
20/51	*Fran Allison*
24/51	*Richard Hayes*

Toolie Oolie Doolie (The Yodel Polka)
3/48	*Andrews Sisters*
11/48	*Vaughn Horton*
11/48	*Sportsmen*
30/48	*Marlin Sisters*
30/48	*Henri René*

Toot, Toot, Tootsie (Good-Bye)
19/49	*Art Mooney*
26/49	*Mel Blanc*
16/43	**Touch Of Texas** *Freddy Martin*

Trade Winds
2/40	*Bing Crosby*
10/40	*Tommy Dorsey*

Tree In The Meadow
1/48	*Margaret Whiting*
17/48	*Joe Loss*
18/48	*John Laurenz*
21/48	*Paul Fennelly*
21/48	*Monica Lewis & Ames Brothers*
24/48	*Sam Browne*
27/48	*Bill Johnson*

Trolley Song
2/44	*Pied Pipers*
4/44	*Judy Garland*
13/44	*Four King Sisters*
4/45	*Vaughn Monroe*
19/45	*Guy Lombardo*
19/53	**Tropicana** *Monty Kelly*

Truly Truly Fair ..see: My Truly, Truly Fair
19/41	**Trumpet Rhapsody** *Harry James*
25/52	**Trust In Me** *Eddie Fisher*
15/52	**Try** *Stan Freberg*
15/44	**Try Me One More Time** *Ernest Tubb*

Trying
7/52	*Hilltoppers*
22/52	*Ella Fitzgerald*
16/52	**Tulips And Heather** *Perry Como*
8/51	**Turn Back The Hands Of Time** *Eddie Fisher*
1/40	**Tuxedo Junction** *Glenn Miller*
16/44	**Tweedle-O-Twill** *Gene Autry*

Twelfth Street Rag
1/48	*Pee Wee Hunt*
10/48	*Frankie Carle*
13/49	**Twenty-Four Hours Of Sunshine** *Art Mooney*
30/51	**Twenty Three Starlets (And Me)** *Merv Griffin*
14/53	**Twice As Much** *Mills Brothers*

Twilight Time
8/45	*Three Suns*
16/45	*Les Brown*

Two Dreams Met
16/40	*Tommy Dorsey*
19/40	*Eddy Duchin*
9/41	**Two In Love** *Tommy Dorsey*
29/52	**Two Little Kisses** *Four Aces*
20/54	**Two Purple Shadows** *Jerry Vale*

Tzena Tzena Tzena
2/50	*Gordon Jenkins & The Weavers*
3/50	*Mitch Miller*
7/50	*Vic Damone*
16/50	*Ralph Flanagan*

U

22/46	**Ugly Chile (You're Some Pretty Doll)** *Johnny Mercer*
19/44	**Umbriago** *Jimmy Durante*

Undecided
2/51	*Ames Brothers & Les Brown*
10/51	*Ray Anthony*
28/51	*Guy Lombardo*

Underneath The Arches
5/48	*Andrews Sisters*
6/48	*Primo Scala with The Keynotes*
13/48	*Andy Russell & The Pied Pipers*
12/52	**Unforgettable** *Nat "King" Cole*

Unless
16/51	*Guy Mitchell*
17/51	*Eddie Fisher*
30/51	*Gordon Jenkins*
4/48	**Until** *Tommy Dorsey*
10/41	**Until Tomorrow (Goodnight My Love)** *Sammy Kaye*

V

17/50	**Vagabond Shoes** *Vic Damone* **(Val-De Ri, Val-De Ra) ..see: Happy Wanderer**
18/50	**Valencia** *Tony Martin*
9/52	**Vanessa** *Hugo Winterhalter*

Vanity
11/51	*Don Cherry*
18/51	*Tony Martin*
19/51	*Sarah Vaughan*
1/53	**Vaya Con Dios (May God Be With You)** *Les Paul & Mary Ford*
8/53	**Velvet Glove** *Henri René & Hugo Winterhalter*
21/51	**Velvet Lips** *Guy Lombardo*
2/43	**Velvet Moon** *Harry James*
28/52	**Veradero** *Camarata*
14/44	**Very Thought Of You** *Vaughn Monroe*
21/51	**Vesti La Giubba (On with the Play)** *Mario Lanza* (also see: Tell Me You Love Me)
6/44	**Vict'ry Polka** *Bing Crosby & Andrews Sisters*
29/49	**Vieni Su (Say You Love Me Too)** *Vaughn Monroe*
14/47	**Violets** *Ted Weems*

W

17/43	**Wait For Me Mary** *Dick Haymes*

Waitin' For The Train To Come In
4/45	*Peggy Lee*
6/45	*Harry James*
7/45	*Johnny Long & Dick Robertson*

Walkin' By The River
16/41	*Ginny Simms*
19/41	*Hal Kemp*

Walkin' My Baby Back Home
4/52	*Johnnie Ray*
8/52	*Nat "King" Cole & Billy May*
11/52	**Walkin' To Missouri** *Sammy Kaye*
11/50	**Wanderin'** *Sammy Kaye*

Wang Wang Blues
16/51	*Ames Brothers*
27/51	*Benny Goodman*
1/54	**Wanted** *Perry Como*

Warsaw Concerto ..see: (Theme from the)

Watermelon Weather
19/52	*Perry Como & Eddie Fisher*
28/52	*Bing Crosby & Peggy Lee*
19/46	**Wave To Me, My Lady** *Elton Britt*

'Way Back Home
21/51	*Bing Crosby with Fred Waring*
30/51	**Way Up In North Carolina** *Belltones*
22/51	**We Kissed In A Shadow** *Frank Sinatra*
11/44	**We Might As Well Forget It** *Bob Wills*

We Three (My Echo, My Shadow and Me)
3/40	*Tommy Dorsey*
3/40	*Ink Spots*
22/50	**We'll Build A Bungalow** *Johnny Long*
30/49	**Wedding Bells** *Margaret Whiting & Jimmy Wakely*

Woody Wood-Pecker

1/48	Kay Kyser
2/48	Sportsmen & Mel Blanc
18/48	Danny Kaye - Andrews Sisters
2/51	**World Is Waiting For The Sunrise**
	Les Paul & Mary Ford

Would I Love You (Love You, Love You)

4/51	Patti Page
10/51	Harry James with Doris Day
16/51	Helen O'Connell
19/51	Tony Martin

Y

20/54	**Y'all Come** Bing Crosby
24/49	**Ya Wanna Buy A Bunny?**
	Spike Jones
	Yah-Ta-Ta Yah-Ta-Ta (Talk, Talk, Talk)
5/45	Bing Crosby & Judy Garland
11/45	Harry James
4/41	**Yes Indeed!** Tommy Dorsey
10/41	**Yes, My Darling Daughter**
	Dinah Shore
21/49	**Yes, Yes, In Your Eyes**
	Eddy Howard
23/44	**Yesterday's Tears** Ernest Tubb
7/49	**Yingle Bells** Yogi Yorgesson
14/45	**(Yip Yip De Hootie) My Baby Said Yes** Bing Crosby & Louis Jordan
	(Yodel Polka) ..see: Toolie Oolie Doolie
4/40	**Yodelin' Jive**
	Bing Crosby & Andrews Sisters
28/52	**You** Sammy Kaye
9/53	**You Alone (Solo Tu)** Perry Como
	You Always Hurt The One You Love
1/44	Mills Brothers
10/45	Sammy Kaye
	You And I
4/41	Glenn Miller
6/41	Bing Crosby
16/41	Tommy Dorsey
	You Are My Sunshine
20/40	Wayne King
20/41	Bing Crosby
	You Belong To Me
1/52	Jo Stafford
4/52	Patti Page
12/52	Dean Martin
	You Belong To My Heart
17/44	Phil Brito
3/45	Bing Crosby & Xavier Cugat
6/45	Charlie Spivak
30/51	**You Better Go Now**
	Jeri Southern With Camarata
16/46	**You Broke The Only Heart That Ever Loved You** Elliott Lawrence
	You Call Everybody Darlin'
1/48	Al Trace
6/48	Anne Vincent
8/48	Andrews Sisters
13/48	Jack Smith & The Clark Sisters
14/48	Jerry Wayne
18/48	Bruce Hayes
21/48	Al Trace
22/48	Art Lund
27/48	Jack Lathrop

You Call It Madness (But I Call It Love)

10/46	King Cole Trio
13/46	Billy Eckstine
13/48	**You Came A Long Way (From St. Louis)** Ray McKinley
	You Can't Be True, Dear
1/48	Ken Griffin
2/48	Ken Griffin
6/48	Sportsmen
9/48	Dick Haymes
9/48	Vera Lynn
17/48	Will Glahé
19/48	Dick James
19/48	Marlin Sisters with Eddie Fisher
11/45	**You Can't Get That No More**
	Louis Jordan
	You Do
4/47	Dinah Shore
5/47	Vaughn Monroe
5/47	Margaret Whiting
7/47	Vic Damone
8/47	Bing Crosby & Carmen Cavallaro
28/50	**You Dreamer You** Russ Morgan
15/41	**You Forgot About Me** Bob Crosby
	You Keep Coming Back Like A Song
5/46	Dinah Shore
11/46	Jo Stafford
12/46	Bing Crosby
5/41	**You Made Me Love You (I Didn't Want To Do It)** Harry James
16/41	**You Might Have Belonged To Another** Tommy Dorsey
16/48	**You Started Something** Tony Pastor
18/49	**You Told A Lie (I Believed You)**
	Marjorie Hughes
	You Walk By
6/41	Eddy Duchin
14/41	Wayne King
15/41	Kenny Baker
16/41	Tommy Tucker Time
19/41	Blue Barron
20/41	Bobby Byrne
	You Were Only Fooling (While I Was Falling In Love)
9/48	Blue Barron
8/49	Ink Spots
16/49	Kay Starr
13/52	**You Win Again** Tommy Edwards
	You Won't Be Satisfied (Until You Break My Heart)
2/46	Les Brown
5/46	Perry Como
10/46	Ella Fitzgerald & Louis Armstrong
1/53	**You You You** Ames Brothers
	You, You, You Are The One
17/49	Russ Morgan
21/49	Three Suns
23/49	Ames Brothers
29/49	Ken Griffin
	You'd Be So Nice To Come Home To
4/43	Dinah Shore
16/43	Dick Jurgens
16/43	Six Hits And A Miss
5/40	**You'd Be Surprised** Orrin Tucker
17/52	**You'll Never Get Away**
	Don Cornell & Teresa Brewer

You'll Never Know

1/43	Dick Haymes
2/43	Frank Sinatra
6/43	Willie Kelly
18/53	Rosemary Clooney-Harry James
9/45	**You'll Never Walk Alone**
	Frank Sinatra
29/50	**You're A Sweetheart** Jack Owens
	You're All I Want For Christmas
25/48	Frank Gallagher
11/49	Frankie Laine
29/50	Frankie Laine
	You're Breaking My Heart
1/49	Vic Damone
4/49	Buddy Clark
6/49	Ink Spots
14/49	Ralph Flanagan
19/49	Jan Garber
26/49	Russ Case
11/53	**You're Fooling Someone**
	Joni James
14/44	**You're From Texas** Bob Wills
	You're Just In Love
5/51	Perry Como
24/51	Guy Mitchell & Rosemary Clooney
29/51	Dinah Shore & Russell Nype
30/51	Ethel Merman & Dick Haymes
22/51	**You're My Sugar**
	Kay Starr & Tennessee Ernie
14/46	**You're Nobody 'Til Somebody Loves You** Russ Morgan
21/49	**You're So Understanding**
	Evelyn Knight
17/51	**You're The One** Frank Sinatra
22/50	**You're The Only One I Care For**
	Jack Owens
	You've Got Me This Way
14/41	Tommy Dorsey
16/41	Jimmy Dorsey
2/54	**Young-At-Heart** Frank Sinatra
	Your Cheatin' Heart
2/53	Joni James
18/53	Frankie Laine
	Yours (Quiereme Mucho)
2/41	Jimmy Dorsey
18/41	Vaughn Monroe
19/41	Xavier Cugat
19/41	Benny Goodman
7/52	Vera Lynn
27/54	Dick Contino

Z

18/52	**Zing A Little Zong**
	Bing Crosby & Jane Wyman
12/51	**Zing Zing—Zoom Zoom** Perry Como
	Zip-A-Dee-Doo-Dah
8/47	Johnny Mercer
11/47	Sammy Kaye
11/47	Modernaires with Paula Kelly
8/42	**Zoot Suit (For My Sunday Gal)**
	Kay Kyser

THE SINGLES WRAP-UP

This section lists alphabetically, in bold type, all backing performers (vocalists, orchestras, instrumentalists, etc.) that are mentioned in the numerous title notes of this book. The name(s) following the backing performer refers to the artist(s) whose title notes mention that performer. Artists who made the Top 150 ranking on their own are shown in larger type.

ACKERS, Andrew...Mindy Carson
ADAMS, Ray...George Olsen
ALAMO, Tony...Sammy Kaye
ALBA, Maria...Archie Bleyer
ALEXANDER, Jeff
   Mario Lanza
   Frank Sinatra
ALEXANDER, Van
   Molly Bee
   Lancers
ALLEN, Annisteen...
   Lucky Millinder
ALLEN, Barclay...Freddy Martin
ALLEN, Bob...Hal Kemp
ALLEN, Kay...Jerry Wald
ALLEN, Mynell...Sam Donahue
ALLEN, Paul...Frankie Carle
ALL STAR DIXIELANDERS...
   Percy Faith
AMES BROTHERS
   Milt Herth Trio
   Russ Morgan
ANDERSON, Dorsey...
   Tony Pastor
ANDERSON, Ivie...
   Duke Ellington
ANDREWS, Ann...Ralph Marterie
ANDREWS, Huck...
   Charlie Barnet
ANNIS, George...Gaylords
ARISTOKATS...Bing Crosby
ARNELL, Amy...Tommy Tucker
ARNOLD, Murray...
   Freddy Martin
AYRES, Mitchell
   Charioteers
   Buddy Clark
   Perry Como
   Eddie Fisher
   Fontane Sisters
   Betty Hutton
   Beatrice Kay
   Modernaires
BABBITT, Harry...Kay Kyser
BACON, Trevor...
   Lucky Millinder
BAILEY, Mildred...
   Benny Goodman
BAILEY, Pearl...Cootie Williams
BAIN, Donald...Frank Sinatra
BAIRD, Eugenie...Glen Gray
BAKER, Bonnie...Orrin Tucker
BAKER, Buddy...Billy Eckstine
BALLANTINE, Eddie
   Jack Fulton
   Jack Owens
BARBOUR, Dave
   Bing Crosby
   Peggy Lee
BARCLAY, Betty...Sammy Kaye
BARGY, Ray...Jimmy Durante

BARNES, George, Trio...
   Patti Page
BARON, Paul
   Ray Dorey
   Dick Farney
   Johnnie Johnston
BARRIES...Johnny Mercer
BASS, Sid...Four Tunes
BASSMAN, George
   Vic Damone
   Richard Hayes
   Bobby Wayne
BAXTER, Les
   Nat "King" Cole
   Stan Freberg
   Jimmy Wakely
BEASLEY, Alcyone, Singers
   Red Foley
   Evelyn Knight
BEAVER VALLEY SWEET-HEARTS...Pinetoppers
BEERS, Bobby
   Blue Barron
   Lawrence Welk
BELLSON, Louis...Tommy Dorsey
BENEKE, Tex...Glenn Miller
BENJAMIN, Bennie...Patti Page
BENORIC, Steve...
   Ralph Flanagan
BERGMAN, Dewey...
   Steve Lawrence
BERNER, Sara...Spike Jones
BIONDI, Remo...Jane Turzy
BLACK, Stanley
   Joy Nichols & Benny Lee
   David Whitfield
BLACKTON, Jay
   Bing Crosby
   Alfred Drake
   Oklahoma! Original Cast Album
   Dinah Shore
BLAIR, Janet...Hal Kemp
BLAIR, Judith...George Olsen
BLAKE, Meredith
   Mitchell Ayres
   Gray Gordon
BLANE, Rose...Abe Lyman
BLEYER, Archie
   Chordettes
   Arthur Godfrey
   Julius LaRosa
   Mariners
   Mary Martin
BLOCH, Ray
   Ames Brothers
   Teresa Brewer
   Alan Dale
   Larry Douglas
   Connie Haines
   Jack Leonard
   Monica Lewis

BLUE HUES...Sam Donahue
BONNEY, Betty...Les Brown
BOSTIC, Earl...Lionel Hampton
BOTKIN, Perry...Bing Crosby
BOURDON, Rosario...
   Dinah Shore
BOWERS, Richard...
   Columbia Tokyo Orch.
BOWLLY, Al...Ray Noble
BOWNE, Jerry...Horace Heidt
BOYER, Anita...Leo Reisman
BRACE, Janet...Johnny Long
BRADLEY, Owen...Four Aces
BRADLEY, Will...
   Anita O'Day
BRANDYWYNNE, Nat...
   Ginny Simms
BREES, Bud...Art Mooney
BREGMAN, Buddy...Cheers
BRENNAN, Buddy...
   Guy Lombardo
BREWER, Betty...
   Gordon Jenkins
BRING, Lou...Teddy Walters
BRITO, Phil...Al Donahue
BROADWAY, Oscar...
   Four Knights
BROOKS, Allan...Art Mooney
BROWN, Don...Tommy Tucker
BROWN, Jimmy
   Sammy Kaye
   Guy Lombardo
BRUNS, George...Stan Freberg
BURKE, Ceele...Ivie Anderson
BURKE, Clyde
   Blue Barron
   Sammy Kaye
BURKE, Sonny
   Bing Crosby
   Jimmy Durante
   Dick Haymes
   Woody Herman
   Danny Kaye
   Evelyn Knight
   Mills Brothers
   Dinah Shore
   Mel Torme
   Eileen Wilson
   Jane Wyman
BURNS, Ralph...Sunny Gale
BUSCH, Lou
   Dean Martin
   Kay Starr
   Margaret Whiting
BUTLER, Daws...Stan Freberg
BUTTERFIELD, Billy
   Will Bradley
   Benny Goodman
   Artie Shaw
   Frank Sinatra
   Sarah Vaughan

BYRNS, Pauline...Paul Weston
CACERES, Ernie...Glenn Miller
CALICO KIDS...Bing Crosby
CALVIN, Rosemary...
   Vaughn Monroe
CALYPSO BOYS...Louis Jordan
CAMARATA
   Bing Crosby
   Helen Forrest
   Dick Haymes
   Evelyn Knight
   Mary Martin
CAMPBELL, Bruce...Vera Lynn
CAMPO, Del...Xavier Cugat
CAMPUS KIDS...Kay Kyser
CANDULLO, Joe...Denise Lor
CARLYLE, Russ...Blue Barron
CAROL, John...Lucky Millinder
CAROL, Lily Ann...Louis Prima
CARR, Jerry...Don Cornell
CARROLL, Bob
   Charlie Barnet
   Jimmy Dorsey
   Gordon Jenkins
CARROLL, David
   Dick Contino
   Crew-Cuts
   Vic Damone
   Rusty Draper
   Gaylords
CARROLL, Georgia...Kay Kyser
CARROLL, Jimmy
   Richard Hayes
   Kitty Kallen
   Frankie Laine
   Patti Page
   Johnnie Ray
   Jerry Vale
   Bobby Wayne
   Joan Weber
CARTER, Benny
   Julia Lee
   Anita O'Day
CASE, Russ
   Ray Barber
   Helen Carroll
   Perry Como
   Billy Eckstine
   Bill Farrell
   Bob Houston
   Robert Merrill
   Dinah Shore
CASS COUNTY BOYS
   Gene Autry
   Bing Crosby
CASTILLO, Carmen...
   Xavier Cugat
CASTLE, Jimmy...Dick Jurgens
CATES, George...
   Johnny Desmond
CAVALIERS...Carmen Cavallaro

CAVANAUGH, Dave
Julia Lee
Helen O'Connell
Bobby Sherwood
Kay Starr
CAVANAUGH, Page, Trio
Johnny Desmond
Frank Sinatra
CHARLES, Ray, Singers
Perry Como
Dennis Day
Johnny Desmond
Ella Fitzgerald
Evelyn Knight
CHAVIGNY, Robert...Edith Piaf
CHICKADEES
Hoagy Carmichael
Bing Crosby
Bob Crosby
CHORDETTES...Arthur Godfrey
CHRISTIAN, Charlie...
Benny Goodman
CHRISTY, June...Stan Kenton
CHURCHILL, Savannah
Benny Carter
Jimmy Lytell
CLAIRE, Dorothy...Glenn Miller
CLARK, Buddy...
Xavier Cugat
CLARK SISTERS...
Tommy Dorsey
CLAY, Jeffrey...Sammy Kaye
CLOONEY, Rosemary...
Tony Pastor
CLOONEY SISTERS...
Tony Pastor
COLE, Buddy
Rosemary Clooney
Clark Dennis
Four King Sisters
Four Lads
Stan Freberg
Frankie Laine
Gisele MacKenzie
Johnnie Ray
COLUCCIO, Rocky...Alvino Rey
COLUMBIANS
Eddie Fisher
Marlin Sisters
COMO, Perry...Ted Weems
CONDON, Eddie...Bing Crosby
CONKLIN, Gene...Freddy Martin
CONLON, Jud, Singers/
Rhythmaires
Rex Allen
Bing Crosby
Frankie Laine
Peggy Lee
Paul Weston
Jane Wyman
CONWAY, Julie...Kay Kyser
COOL, Harry...Dick Jurgens
COPAS, Lloyd "Cowboy"...
Elliot Lawrence
CORDELL, Roy...Jan Garber
CORNELL, Don...
Sammy Kaye

COSTA, Don
Overtures
Brucie Weil
COTNER, Carl
Gene Autry
Rosemary Clooney
COTTON, Larry...Horace Heidt
COUNTRY COUSINS...Doris Day
CRAIG, Francis...Red Foley
CRAIG, Gloria...Ray Anthony
CRAIG, Tony...Guy Lombardo
CREW CHIEFS
Tex Beneke
Art Lund
Glenn Miller
Jack Smith
Margaret Whiting
CROMWELL, Jean...
Jimmy Dorsey
CROSBY, Bob...Bing Crosby
CROSS, Maury...Sammy Kaye
CURTIS, Ken...Shep Fields
CUTSHALL, Cutty
Jimmy Dorsey
Anita O'Day
DALE, Alan...Ray Bloch
DALE, Ted
Buddy Clark
Dinah Shore
DANA SERENADERS...
Frank Gallagher
DANIELS, Billy...Phil Moore Four
DANIELS, "Fats"...Glen Gray
DANT, Charles
Dennis Day
Betty Rhodes
DARBY, Ken, Singers...
Bing Crosby
DARNEL, Bill
Bob Chester
Al Kavelin
D'ARTEGA...Patti Page
DAVIS, Bob...Jan Garber
DAVIS, Virg...Danny O'Neil
DAVIS, Wild Bill...Bing Crosby
DAY, Doris...Les Brown
DAYE, Irene
Sam Donahue
Gene Krupa
Charlie Spivak
DEAUVILLE, Ronnie...
Ray Anthony
DeFRANCO, Buddy...
Tommy Dorsey
DELL'ISOLA, Salvatore...
Ezio Pinza
DENNIS, Denny...Tommy Dorsey
DERISE, Joe...Claude Thornhill
DERWIN, Hal...Shep Fields
DeVOL, Frank
Nat "King" Cole
Hal Derwin
Jack Smith
Kay Starr
Mel Torme
Margaret Whiting
DeWITT, Allan...Jan Savitt

DIAMOND, Lew...Weavers
DILLARD, Dottie...
Owen Bradley
DiNAPOLI, Mike...
Frank Petty Trio
DIPSY DOODLERS...
Larry Clinton
DiVITO, Buddy...Harry James
DIXIE DONS...Red Foley
DOGGETT, Bill...Ella Fitzgerald
DONNELLY, Ted...Count Basie
DORRIS, Red...Stan Kenton
DOUGLAS, Glenn...Tex Beneke
DOUGLAS, Lew
Tony Fontane
Joni James
DOUGLAS, Michael...Kay Kyser
DRAGON, Carmen...Al Jolson
DRAKE, Gordon...Les Brown
DRAKE, Johnny...Eddy Duchin
DRUGSTORE COWBOYS...
Eve Young
DUFFY, Johnny, Trio...
Yogi Yorgesson
DUGAN, Patti...Johnny Long
DUKE, Marilyn...Vaughn Monroe
DuLANY, Howard...Gene Krupa
DUNCAN, Tommy...Bob Wills
DUNN, Artie...Three Suns
EARBENDERS...Eddy Duchin
EBERLE, Ray...Glenn Miller
EBERLY, Bob...Jimmy Dorsey
EDISON, Harry...Count Basie
EDWARDS, Bob...Ted Weems
ELDRIDGE, Roy
Gene Krupa
Artie Shaw
ELLIS, Phil, Choristers
Eddie Miller
Dick Todd
ELMAN, Ziggy
Tommy Dorsey
Benny Goodman
EMERY, Russ...Percy Faith
ENROHTWAH...Red Ingle
ERWIN, Trudy...Kay Kyser
EVANS, Dale...Abe Lyman
EVANS, Sandy...Gordon Jenkins
FAITH, Percy
Toni Arden
Tony Bennett
Champ Butler
Rosemary Clooney
Doris Day
Guy Mitchell
Sarah Vaughan
FARNON, Bob
Gracie Fields
Vera Lynn
FARRELL, Skip...Ralph Marterie
FARRINGTON, Red...
Horace Heidt
FASCINATO, Jack
Fran Allison
Dinning Sisters
FEATHERSTONE, Jimmy...
Art Kassel

FELLER, Sid...Jane Froman
FERDY...Kay Kyser
FERGUSON, Maynard...
Stan Kenton
FIELDS, George...Victor Young
FIELDS, Herbie...Lionel Hampton
FINA, Jack...Freddy Martin
FISCHER, Carl
Doris Day
Frankie Laine
Jo Stafford
FLANAGAN, Bill...
Guy Lombardo
FLETCHER, Tex...Art Mooney
FONTANE SISTERS...
Perry Como
FORAY, June...Stan Freberg
FORREST, Helen
Benny Goodman
Harry James
FOSTER, Sally...
Hoosier Hot Shots
FOSTER, Stuart
Tommy Dorsey
Guy Lombardo
Hugo Winterhalter
4 CHICKS AND CHUCK...
Kate Smith
FOUR CHIPS...Woody Herman
FOUR CLOVERS...Art Mooney
4 HITS AND A MISS
Les Brown
Bing Crosby
Jimmy Durante
Connie Haines
Dick Haymes
Danny Kaye
Evelyn Knight
Jane Wyman
FOUR HORSEMEN...Pat O'Day
FOUR KING SISTERS...
Alvino Rey
FOUR LADS...Johnnie Ray
FOUR LEE SISTERS...
Vaughn Monroe
FOUR REINDEER...Spike Jones
FRANCIS, Marion...
Frankie Masters
FREEMAN, Stan
Percy Faith
Frank Sinatra
FRILEY, Jean...Ray McKinley
GALANTE, Al...Dick Jurgens
GALLI SISTERS...Art Mooney
GARCIA, Lucio...Abe Lyman
GARDNER, Kenny...
Guy Lombardo
GARLAND, Hank "Sugarfoot"...
Red Foley
GAS, Sir Frederick...
Spike Jones
GAYLOR, Ruth
Hal McIntyre
Teddy Powell
GAY SISTERS...Russ Morgan

GELLER, Harry
Rex Allen
Kitty Kallen
Frankie Laine
Patti Page
GETZ, Stan
Benny Goodman
Woody Herman
Stan Kenton
GILLESPIE, Dizzy...
Cab Calloway
GILLHAM, Pat...Jo Stafford
GINGELL, George...Sammy Kaye
GIRL FRIENDS...Buddy Clark
GOFF, Reggie...Paul Fennelly
GOODFELLOW, Johnny...
Blue Barron
GOODMAN, Charles...
Horace Heidt
GORDON, Anita
Buddy Clark
Ray Noble
GORDON, Lee, Singers
Bing Crosby
Danny Kaye
Evelyn Knight
Martha Tilton
GRABEAU, Bob...Jan Garber
GRABLE, Betty...Harry James
GRASS, Cliff...Guy Lombardo
GRAY, Jerry
Bob Crosby
Vic Damone
Margaret Whiting
GRAYDON, Joe
Gordon Jenkins
Victor Young
GRAYSON, Carl...Spike Jones
GRECO, Buddy...
Benny Goodman
GREELEY, George...Jo Stafford
GREEN, Phil...Gracie Fields
GREENE, Madeline...Earl Hines
GREY, Carolyn...Woody Herman
GRIFFIN, Merv...Freddy Martin
GRISSOM, Dan...
Jimmie Lunceford
GROSS, Walter...Bea Wain
GUARDSMEN QUARTETTE...
Bing Crosby
GUMINA, Tommy...Harry James
HACKETT, Bobby...
Johnny Desmond
HAGEN, Earle
Buddy Clark
Bill Farrell
Helen Forrest
Dick Haymes
Tony Martin
HAGGART, Bob
Louis Armstrong
Connee Boswell
Bing Crosby
Ella Fitzgerald
Jesters
Evelyn Knight

HAINES, Connie
Tommy Dorsey
Gordon Jenkins
HALL, Carlyle
Gordon MacRae
Jo Stafford
HALLORAN, Jack, Singers/Choir
Vic Damone
Rusty Draper
Doris Drew
Eddy Howard
Joni James
HAMBONE KIDS...Red Saunders
HANLEY, Peter...Percy Faith
HARMONAIRES...Danny Kaye
HARMONICA GENTLEMEN
Andrews Sisters
Art Lund
HAROLD, Lou...Norman Brooks
HARRIS, Ace...Erskine Hawkins
HARRIS, Betty...Art Mooney
HARRIS, Wynonie...
Lucky Millinder
HARVEY, Jane...
Benny Goodman
HASKELL, Jack...Les Brown
HAWKINS, Dolores
Blue Barron
Red Saunders
HAYMAN, Richard
Vic Damone
Harmonicats
Bobby Wayne
HAYMES, Dick
Benny Goodman
Harry James
HAYNES, "Tiger"...Three Flames
HAYTON, Lennie...Tony Martin
HEARTBEATS...Russ Morgan
HEATHERTONES
Bill Darnel
Buddy Greco
HEFTI, Neal
Eileen Barton
Four Lads
McGuire Sisters
HEINDORF, Ray...Doris Day
HENDERSON, Fletcher...
Benny Goodman
HENDRICKSON, Al...
Benny Goodman
HENRY, Fred...Guy Lombardo
HERFURT, "Skeets"
Tommy Dorsey
Alvino Rey
HERMAN, Woody...
Bing Crosby
HIGHLIGHTERS...Connie Haines
HILL, Johnny...Ken Griffin
HOGAN, Claire "Shanty"...
Jimmy Dorsey
HOGAN, Louanne...Victor Young

HOLMES, Leroy
Tommy Edwards
Robert Q. Lewis
Art Lund
Weavers
Billy Williams
HONEYDREAMERS...Larry Green
HOOPER, Larry...Lawrence Welk
HORN, Sara...Leo Reisman
HOUSTON, Bob...Johnny Long
HOUSTON, Cisco...
Gordon Jenkins
HOWARD, Chet...Jack Emerson
HOWARD, Eddy...
Dick Jurgens
HOWARD, Gene...Stan Kenton
HOYT, Lynn...Teddy Phillips
HUFF, Leon...Bob Wills
HUGHES, Glenn...Freddy Martin
HUGHES, Marjorie...
Frankie Carle
HUNT, Pee Wee...Glen Gray
HUNTER, Jack...Elliot Lawrence
HUSKY, Ferlin...Jean Shepard
HUTTON, Marion...Glenn Miller
INGLE, Paul...Spike Jones
JACOBS, Dick...McGuire Sisters
JEFFRIES, Herb...
Duke Ellington
JENKINS, Gordon
Andrews Sisters
Louis Armstrong
Dick Haymes
Johnnie Johnston
Ethel Merman
Dinah Shore
Six Hits & A Miss
Stardusters
JENNINGS, Al...Russ Morgan
JEROME, Jerry...Dick Todd
JIM DANDIES...
Lawrence (Piano Roll) Cook
JO, Damita...5 Red Caps
JOHNSON, Bill...Count Basie
JOHNSON, Ella...Buddy Johnson
JONES, Dick...Buddy Clark
JONES, Howard...Joe Loss
JONES, Jimmy..."Dusty" Fletcher
JORDAN, Taft...Sarah Vaughan
JOY, Leonard
Kenny Baker
Phil Hanna
Dinah Shore
JOYCE, Jimmy...Alvino Rey
KABIBBLE, Ish...Kay Kyser
KALLEN, Kitty
Jimmy Dorsey
Harry James
KAMINSKY, Max...Georgia Gibbs
KANNER, Hal...Ken Carson
KASSEL, Art...Gloria Hart
KAY, Carol...Russ Morgan
KAYE, Sammy...Don Cornell

KEARNEY, Rex...Bette McLaurin
KEATING, Dee...Al Donahue
KELLOGG, Ray...
Skitch Henderson
KELLY, Monty
Bob Manning
Al Martino
KELLY, Paula...Glenn Miller
KEMPER, Ronnie
Horace Heidt
Dick Jurgens
KERR, Anita, Singers...
Red Foley
KESSEL, Barney...Artie Shaw
KEY-TONES...Al Morgan
KING, Bonnie...Bob Crosby
KING, Yvonne...Alvino Rey
KIRKLAND, Leroy...
Ella Fitzgerald
KLEEB, Bill...Jan Garber
KLEIN, Mannie/Manny
Charioteers
Evelyn Knight
Modernaires
Bobby Sherwood
KLINK, Al...Anita O'Day
KREITZER, Fred...
Guy Lombardo
KRESS, Carl...Margaret Whiting
KUSMIAK, Eugene...
Toscha Seidel
LAMM, Bob...Francis Craig
LANCERS...Kay Starr
LANE, Frances...Johnny Long
LANE, Ken, Singers
Vic Damone
Doris Day
Frank Sinatra
LANE, Lillian
Tex Beneke
Glenn Miller
LANE, Muriel...Woody Herman
LANE, Siggy...Henry King
LANSON, Snooky...Ray Noble
LATHROP, Jack...Glenn Miller
LAVALLE, Paul...Phil Brito
LaVERE, Charles...
Gordon Jenkins
LAWRENCE, Elliot...Red Buttons
LEACH, Billy...Guy Lombardo
LEARY, Ford...Charlie Barnet
LeBRUN SISTERS...Glen Gray
LEE, Helen...Larry Clinton
LEE, Mary...Ted Weems
LEE, Peggy...Benny Goodman
LEONARD, Jack...Tommy Dorsey
LESLIE, Laura...Sammy Kaye
LESTER, Frankie
Hal McIntyre
Buddy Morrow
LEYDEN, Jimmy
Bob Carroll
Georgie Shaw

BACKING PERFORMER CROSS-REFERENCE

LEYDEN, Norman
Mindy Carson
Don Cornell
Vic Damone
Jose Ferrer
Fontane Sisters
Four Lads
Patrice Munsel
Sarah Vaughan
LEYDEN BROTHERS...
Pete Hanley
LIBERACE, George...Liberace
LIDO, Bob
Carmen Cavallaro
Enric Madriguera
LILLEY, Joseph/Joe
Bing Crosby
Judy Garland
Betty Hutton
LIPMAN, Joe
Nat "King" Cole
Alan Dean
Betty Madigan
Sarah Vaughan
LITTLE AUDREY...Kay Kyser
LLOYD, Shirley...Sam Donahue
LOCKWOOD, Bill...
Sam Donahue
LOMBARDO, Carmen...
Guy Lombardo
LOMBARDO, Rose Marie...
Guy Lombardo
LONG, Johnny...Ella Fitzgerald
LOWERY, Fred
Horace Heidt
LeRoy Holmes
LUBOFF, Norman, Choir
Jimmy Boyd
Dennis Day
Doris Day
Frankie Laine
Jo Stafford
Paul Weston
LUND, Art...Benny Goodman
LUTES, Marcy...Tommy Dorsey
LYNN, Imogene
Ray McKinley
Artie Shaw
LYNN, Tommy...Charlie Spivak
LYNNE, Phyliss...Frankie Carle
LYTELL, Jimmy...
Morton Downey
LYTTLE SISTERS...Tony Martin
MADDOCK, "Red"...Al Trace
MALTBY, Richard...
Sarah Vaughan
MALVIN, Artie
Tex Beneke
Buddy Kaye
Glenn Miller
MANN, Dave...Don Reid
MANN, Marion...Bob Crosby
MANN, Peggy...Benny Goodman
MANNING, Marty
Ames Brothers
Jan August
Roberta Quinlan

MARCELLINO, Muzzy...
Victor Young
MARINERS...Arthur Godfrey
MARLIN SISTERS...Pinetoppers
MARLOW, Mary...Sammy Kaye
MARSH, Wayne...Lawrence Welk
MARTERIE, Ralph...
Vic Damone
MARTIN, Jack...Kay Kyser
MARTIN, Kenny...Guy Lombardo
MARTIN, Skip/Skippy
Champ Butler
DeCastro Sisters
Tony Martin
MASHER, Zeb...Patti Page
MASINGILL, O.B...
DeJohn Sisters
MASON, Sully...Kay Kyser
MATHIAS, Ernie...Jan Garber
MATLOCK, Matty
Hoagy Carmichael
Bing Crosby
Cass Daley
Jane Wyman
MAY, Billy
Charlie Barnet
Mel Blanc
"Tennessee" Ernie Ford
Stan Freberg
Betty Hutton
Peggy Lee
Ella Mae Morse
Margaret Whiting
McAFEE, Johnny...Harry James
McAULIFFE, Leon...Bob Wills
McCALL, Mary Ann...
Charlie Barnet
McCORMICK, John
Blue Barron
Al Morgan
McCULLOUGH, Ruth...
Tony Pastor
McGARRITY, Lou...
Benny Goodman
McINTIRE, Dick...Bing Crosby
McINTYRE, Hal...
Mills Brothers
McKINLEY, Ray...
Will Bradley
MEADOWLARKS...Vic Damone
MELLO LARKS
Tex Beneke
Glenn Miller
MELLOMEN
Rosemary Clooney
Doris Day
Peggy Lee
Mel Torme
MELLOWMEN...Dennis Day
MENDELSOHN, Danny...
Jack Owens
MERCER, Mary Ann...
Mitchell Ayres
MERCER, Tommy
Ray Anthony
Charlie Spivak
MERRICK, Dick...Jerry Wald

MERRY MACS...Bing Crosby
MERSHON, Gil...Orrin Tucker
MILLER, Eddie
Bing Crosby
Bob Crosby
Martha Tilton
Dick Todd
MILLER, Jack...Kate Smith
MILLER, Marcie...Ray Anthony
MILLER, Mitch
Mindy Carson
Rosemary Clooney
Four Lads
Arthur Godfrey
Richard Hayes
Kitty Kallen
Frankie Laine
John Laurenz
Guy Mitchell
Patti Page
Frank Sinatra
MILLER, Taps...Count Basie
MITCHELL, Dolly...Kay Kyser
MITCHELLE, Jimmy...
Erskine Hawkins
MODERNAIRES...
Glenn Miller
MONTGOMERY, Wes...
Lionel Hampton
MOONBEAMS...Kay Kyser
MOONEY, Harold
Betty Garrett
Helen O'Connell
Jo Stafford
Kay Starr
Ilene Woods
MOONEY, Joe...Sauter-Finegan
MOON MAIDS...Vaughn Monroe
MOON MEN...Vaughn Monroe
MOORE, Ann...Count Basie
MORENO, Buddy...Dick Jurgens
MORGAN, Fleddy...Spike Jones
MORGAN, Marion...Harry James
MORROW, Liza
Benny Goodman
Freddie Slack
MORSE, Ella Mae...
Freddie Slack
MORTON, Bennie...Juanita Hall
MOTOLLA, Tony
Johnny Desmond
Hugo Winterhalter
MUNN, Frank...Jacques Renard
MURE, Billy...Anita O'Day
MURRAY, Lyn
Bing Crosby
Judy Garland
Merry Macs
Jo Stafford
MUSIC MAIDS...Bing Crosby
MUSSO, Vido...Stan Kenton
NASHVILLE DIXIELANDERS...
Red Foley
NEILSON, Paul...Eileen Barton
NELSON, Skip
Guy Lombardo
Glenn Miller

NERO, Paul...Paul Weston
NEWMAN, Emil...Dick Haymes
NEW YORKERS...Eileen Barton
NOEL, Dick...Ray Anthony
NORMAN, Loulie Jean...
Frankie Laine
NORMAN, Nancy...Sammy Kaye
NORTON SISTERS...
Vaughn Monroe
NORVO, Red...Woody Herman
O'CONNELL, Helen...
Jimmy Dorsey
O'CONNOR, Pat...Billy Butterfield
O'DAY, Anita
Stan Kenton
Gene Krupa
OLIVEIRA, Aloysio...
Charles Wolcott
OLIVER, Sy
Louis Armstrong
Ray Bolger
Don Cherry
Bing Crosby
Sammy Davis Jr.
Tommy Dorsey
Ella Fitzgerald
Ethel Merman
Mills Brothers
Jack Owens
O'NEILL, Dolores...Bob Chester
OSBORNE, Mary, Trio
Ames Brothers
Monica Lewis
OSSER, Glenn
Vic Damone
Georgia Gibbs
O'TOOLE, Ollie...Horace Heidt
OWEN, Larry...Guy Lombardo
PAGE, Bobby...Four Knights
PAGE, "Hot Lips"...Artie Shaw
PALMER, Jimmy...Bobby Byrne
PALMER BROTHERS...
Cab Calloway
PARKER, Andy...Gordon MacRae
PARKER, Dee...Jimmy Dorsey
PARKER, Johnny...
Hugo Winterhalter
PARMAN, Cliff
Doris Drew
Lorry Raine
PASTELS
Stan Kenton
Frank Sinatra
PASTOR, Stubby...Tony Pastor
PATTON, Rosalind...
Elliot Lawrence
PECON, Johnny
Marlin Sisters
Frankie Yankovic
PERETTI, Hugo...Sarah Vaughan
PIED PIPERS
Tommy Dorsey
Johnny Mercer
Jo Stafford
PIMM, Sir Hubert...Ellen Sutton
PINAFORES...Gene Autry
PINGATORE, Mike...Art Mooney

PLEIS, Jack
Eileen Barton
Teresa Brewer
Karen Chandler
Don Cornell
Alan Dale
Johnny Desmond
Four Aces
Kitty Kallen
Lancers
Jimmy Lytell
Al Morgan
POKEY...Kay Kyser
POLK, Lucy Ann...Tommy Dorsey
PORTER, Del...Spike Jones
POWELL, Ginnie
Harry James
Jerry Wald
PRIME, Harry
Tommy Dorsey
Ralph Flanagan
QUARTONES
Billy Eckstine
Bob Houston
QUINTONES
Russ Case
Johnny Desmond
RAEL, Jack...Patti Page
RAGON, Larry...Ralph Marterie
RAMBLERS...Perry Como
RARIG, John...Doris Day
RAWLEY, Al...Pat O'Day
RAYE, Don...Freddie Slack
REARDON, Tim...Jan Garber
REDMAN, Don...Pearl Bailey
REED, Nancy
Benny Goodman
Hal McIntyre
REID, Dottie...Benny Goodman
REINER, Fritz...William Kapell
REISMAN, Joe
Sunny Gale
Richard Hayes
Patti Page
Johnnie Ray
June Valli
Bobby Wayne
RENE, Henri
Bell Sisters
Mindy Carson
Perry Como
Dennis Day
Phil Harris
Betty Hutton
Lisa Kirk
Eartha Kitt
Tony Martin
Dinah Shore
June Valli
Fran Warren
REY, Alvino
Four King Sisters
Johnny Mercer
RHODES, David...Mariners
RHYTHMAIRES
Dennis Day
Russ Morgan

RICKEY, Al...Florian Zabach
RICKS, Jimmy...
Benny Goodman
RIDDLE, Nelson
Nat "King" Cole
Tommy Dorsey
Billy Eckstine
Ella Mae Morse
Frank Sinatra
ROBBINS, Gale...Art Jarrett
ROBBINS, June...Eddy Duchin
ROBERTSON, Dick...
Johnny Long
ROBERTSON, Roy...
Anne Shelton
ROBEY, Art...Charlie Barnet
ROBINSON, Eric
Vic Damone
Patti Page
ROCK, George...Spike Jones
RODNEY, Don...Guy Lombardo
RODRIGUEZ, William...
Guy Lombardo
ROGERS, Billie...
Woody Herman
ROGERS, Clyde
Kay Kyser
Freddy Martin
ROGERS, Shorty...Stan Kenton
ROMBERG, Sigmund...
Perry Como
ROSE, David
Judy Garland
Tony Martin
ROSS, Roy
Ames Brothers
Bill Darnel
Connie Haines
RUDOLPH...Spike Jones
RUGOLO, Pete
Nat "King" Cole
Billy Eckstine
Mel Torme
RUSHING, Jimmy...Count Basie
RUSSELL, Madelyn...Art Mooney
RUSSELL, Mischa...
Dorothy Shay
RUSSO, Tony...Sammy Kaye
RYAN, Tommy...Sammy Kaye
SACK, Al
Tony Martin
Andy Russell
Dinah Shore
SANDERS, Felicia...Percy Faith
SANTA CLAUS...Spike Jones
SARGENT, Kenny...Glen Gray
SATISFIERS
Helen Carroll
Perry Como
SAUNDERS, Jimmy
Harry James
Charlie Spivak
SAUTER, Eddie...Richard Hayes
SCHALLEN, Bill...Alvino Rey
SCHARF, Walter...Phil Harris

SCHOEN, Vic
Andrews Sisters
Hoagy Carmichael
Bing Crosby
Dick Haymes
Danny Kaye
Peggy Lee
Carmen Miranda
Dinah Shore
Weavers
SCHUMANN, Walter...
Stan Freberg
SCOTT, Nathan...Stan Freberg
SELBY, Ronnie...Vic Damone
SENTIMENTALISTS...
Tommy Dorsey
SEVERINSEN, Doc
Anita O'Day
Sauter-Finegan
SHAFFER, Lloyd
Perry Como
Johnnie Johnston
SHANK, Bud...Stan Kenton
SHAVERS, Charlie
Tommy Dorsey
Anita O'Day
SHAW, Roland...Vera Lynn
SHELDON, Earl...Jack Smith
SHERMAN, Lynne...Count Basie
SHERRILL, Joya...
Duke Ellington
SHERWOOD, Bobby...
Judy Garland
SHILLELAGH SINGERS...
Percy Faith
SHOOK, Jack...Owen Bradley
SHORE, Dinah...Xavier Cugat
SIMMS, Ginny...Kay Kyser
SINATRA, Frank...Tommy
Dorsey
SINATRA, Ray
Mario Lanza
Tony Martin
SINGING PUSSY CATS...
Nat "King" Cole
SINGING WINDS...
Ralph Flanagan
SIRAVO, George
Connee Boswell
Buddy Clark
Vic Damone
Doris Day
Richard Hayes
Kitty Kallen
SIX HITS AND A MISS
Bing Crosby
Jimmy Durante
SKYLARKS...Russ Morgan
SKYLINERS...Ray Anthony
SLACK, Freddie...
Johnny Mercer
SLIM...Kay Kyser
SMART, Charles...Vera Lynn
SMECK, Roy...Ames Brothers
SMITH, Beasley...Lancers
SMITH, Ethel...Bing Crosby
SMITH, Ray...Pinetoppers

SMITH, Willie...Harry James
SMOOTHIES...Art Jarrett
SNOWFLAKES...Claude Thornhill
SOMERVILLE, Kerwin...
Tommy Tucker
SONG SPINNERS
Ella Fitzgerald
Dick Haymes
Hildegarde
Guy Lombardo
SOOTS, Bobby...Gene Krupa
SOSNIK, Harry
Kenny Baker
Bing Crosby
Hildegarde
Gertrude Niesen
SPICER, Willie...Spike Jones
SPITALNY, Phil...
Hour Of Charm Choir
SPORTSMEN
Phil Harris
Ray Noble
SPORTSMEN GLEE CLUB...
Bing Crosby
STABILE, Dick...Dean Martin
STAFFORD, Jo
Tommy Dorsey
Red Ingle
STARDUSTERS
Peter Lind Hayes
Gordon Jenkins
Evelyn Knight
Charlie Spivak
STARLIGHTERS
Gordon MacRae
Tony Martin
Jo Stafford
Margaret Whiting
STAUNTON, Ray...Cliff Steward
STEELE, Ted...Perry Como
STEVENS, Bob...Gordon Jenkins
STEVENS, Garry
Tex Beneke
Glenn Miller
Charlie Spivak
STEVENS, Rose Ann...
Ozzie Nelson
STEWART, Buddy...Gene Krupa
STEWART, Freddie...
Tommy Dorsey
STEWART, Larry...Ray Noble
STEWART, Redd...Pee Wee King
STEWART, Teddy...
Dinah Washington
STOLL, Georgie...Judy Garland
STOLOFF, Morris
Al Jolson
Dinah Shore
STONE, Butch...Les Brown
STONE, Cliffie
Stan Freberg
Helen O'Connell
STONE, Eddie...Freddy Martin
STORDAHL, Axel
Bing Crosby
Doris Day
Frank Sinatra

STORR, Alan...Tommy Dorsey
STUART, Al...Bob Chester
SUNSHINE SERENADERS...
   Frankie Carle
SUNSHINE TRIO
   Red Foley
   Ernest Tubb
SWEETLAND, Sally
   Eddie Fisher
   Sauter-Finegan
SWEETLAND SINGERS...
   Ames Brothers
SWEETSWINGSTERS...
   Horace Heidt
TALENT, Ziggy...
   Vaughn Monroe
TANNER, Elmo...Ted Weems
TATTLERS...Dick Haymes
TAYLOR, Gil...Hoosier Hot Shots
TAYLOR, Larry...Charlie Barnet
TEAGARDEN, Charlie...
   Jimmy Dorsey
TEDDER, Karen...Red Ingle
TELL, Gladys...Jimmy Dorsey
TERNENT, Billy...
   Andrews Sisters
TERRELL, Pha...Andy Kirk
TERRY, Dave...Don Cherry
THOMPSON, Bert...Sam Browne
THOMPSON, Johnny...Art Lund
3 BEAUS AND A PEEP...
   Jack Owens
THREE-O-NINERS...Henri Rene
THREE TWO TIMERS...
   Tommy Tucker
THREE VARIETIES...Earl Hines
TILTON, Liz...Jan Garber
TILTON, Martha...
   Benny Goodman
TOADS...Stan Freberg
TOBIN, Louise...Benny Goodman
TOO FAT TRIO...Arthur Godfrey
TOWN CRIERS...Tommy Dorsey

TRAYNOR, Tommy...
   Jan Garber
TROTTER, John Scott...
   Louis Armstrong
   Bing Crosby
TROUBADOURS...Dick Haymes
TUCKER, Bobby, Singers...
   Frank Sinatra
TUNNELL, George...Jan Savitt
VALDES, Miguelito...
   Xavier Cugat
VALENTINE, Jimmy...
   Will Bradley
VAN DAMME, Art, Quintet...
   Dinning Sisters
VAUGHN, Billy...Fontane Sisters
VENTURA, Charlie...Gene Krupa
VENUTI, Joe
   Andrews Sisters
   Bing Crosby
VIGNEAU, Francis...
   Guy Lombardo
VINCENT, Bob...Al Trace
VINSON, Eddie "Cleanhead"...
   Cootie Williams
WADE, Stuart...Freddy Martin
WALKER, T-Bone...
   Freddie Slack
WALSH, Gene...Horace Heidt
WALTERS, Dick...Ella Mae Morse
WALTERS, Teddy...
   Jimmy Dorsey
WALTON, Jayne...Lawrence Welk
WARDOUR SINGERS...
   Anne Shelton
WASHBURN, Sonny...Shep Fields
WAYNE, Artie...Freddy Martin
WAYNE, Frances/Francis
   Charlie Barnet
   Woody Herman
WAYNE, Jerry
   Bobby Byrne
   Ken Griffin

WEAVER, Doodles...Spike Jones
WEISS, Georgie...Patti Page
WELTON, Danny...Les Baxter
WESTON, Paul
   Champ Butler
   Doris Day
   Betty Hutton
   Frankie Laine
   Gordon MacRae
   Dean Martin
   Johnny Mercer
   Pied Pipers
   Johnnie Ray
   Andy Russell
   Dinah Shore
   Jo Stafford
   Starlighters
   Sarah Vaughan
   Margaret Whiting
WHIPOORWILLS...
   Frank Sinatra
WHITING, Margaret
   Billy Butterfield
   Freddie Slack
WILCOX, Eddie...
   Trudy Richards
WILLIAMS, Billy...Sammy Kaye
WILLIAMS, Bonnie Lou
   Tommy Dorsey
   Gordon Jenkins
WILLIAMS, Cootie...
   Benny Goodman
WILLIAMS, Dick...Harry James
WILLIAMS, Gene...Johnny Long
WILLIAMS, Jack...Kay Kyser
WILLIAMS, Max...Kay Kyser
WILLIAMS BROTHERS...
   Bing Crosby
WILSON, Teddy...Anita O'Day
WINDING, Kai
   Benny Goodman
   Stan Kenton
   Sauter-Finegan

WINTERHALTER, Hugo
   Ames Brothers
   Perry Como
   Don Cornell
   Billy Eckstine
   Eddie Fisher
   Sunny Gale
   Merv Griffin
   Marjorie Hughes
   Herb Jeffries
   Tony Martin
   Lou Monte
   Jaye P. Morgan
   Jan Peerce
   Dinah Shore
   Frank Sinatra
   June Valli
   Jerry Wayne
WOOD, Donna...Horace Heidt
WOOD, Gloria...Kay Kyser
WOOD, Margie...Gray Rains
WRIGHT, Arthur...Sammy Kaye
WYLE, George...Doris Day
YALE BROTHERS...
   Georgia Gibbs
YOUNG, Eve...Benny Goodman
YOUNG, Helen...Johnny Long
YOUNG, Ralph
   Les Brown
   Shep Fields
YOUNG, Victor
   Patty Andrews
   Connee Boswell
   Bing Crosby
   Helen Forrest
   Dick Haymes
   Evelyn Knight
ZENTNER, Si
   Jimmy Dorsey
   Abe Lyman
ZIMMERMAN, Harry
   Buddy Clark
   Betty Rhodes
   Dinah Shore

TOP BACKING ARTISTS

1.	17	**Hugo Winterhalter**
2.	15	**Paul Weston**
3.	12	**Henri René**
4.	11	**Sonny Burke**
5.	11	**Mitch Miller**
6.	11	**Jack Pleis**
7.	10	**Sy Oliver**
8.	9	**Vic Schoen**
9.	8	**Mitchell Ayres**
10.	8	**Jimmy Carroll**
11.	8	**Russ Case**
12.	8	**Buddy Cole**
13.	8	**4 Hits And A Miss**
14.	8	**Gordon Jenkins**
15.	8	**Norman Leyden**
16.	8	**Billy May**
17.	7	**Ray Bloch**
18.	7	**Percy Faith**
19.	6	**Jud Conlon Singers**
20.	6	**Frank DeVol**

THE TOP ARTISTS

Top 150 Artists In Rank Order

Top 150 Artists In A-Z Order

Top 20 Artists By Half-Decade

Top Artists By Category

Top Artist Achievements:

> Most Chart Hits
> Most Top 10 Hits
> Most Top 5 Hits
> Most #1 Hits
> Most Weeks At The #1 Position
> Most Consecutive #1 Hits
> Most 2-Sided Hits
> Top Artists Who Never Hit #1

Top Artist Debuts

Top Songwriters

One-Hit Wonders

TOP 150 ARTISTS IN RANK ORDER

This section ranks the Top 150 artists from 1940-54. Each artist's accumulated point total is shown to the right of their name. This ranking includes all titles that <u>peaked</u> from 1940-1954. A picture of each Top 100 artist is shown next to their listing in the artist section of this book.

POINT SYSTEM:

Points are awarded according to the formula below. This is the same formula used to rank the artists in our *Top Pop Singles 1955-1999* book.

1. Each artist's charted singles are given points based on their highest charted position:

#1	=	100 points for its first week at #1, plus 10 points for each additional week at #1
#2	=	90 points for its first week at #2, plus 5 points for each additional week at #2
#3	=	80 points for its first week at #3, plus 3 points for each additional week at #3
#4-5	=	70 points
#6-10	=	60 points
#11-15	=	55 points
#16-20	=	50 points
#21-30	=	45 points

2. Total weeks charted are added in.

In the case of a tie, the artist listed first is determined by the following tie-breaker rules:
   1) Most charted singles
   2) Most Top 10 singles

Special Symbols:

● = **Deceased Solo Artist**

■ = **Deceased Group Member**
   (The total number of square symbols indicates the total number of deceased members.)

TOP 150 ARTISTS — 1940-54

Rank		Points
1.	Bing Crosby ●	10,758
2.	Glenn Miller ●	6,584
3.	Perry Como ●	6,547
4.	Andrews Sisters ■■	5,229
5.	Frank Sinatra ●	5,219
6.	Jo Stafford	4,935
7.	Guy Lombardo ●	4,833
8.	Tommy Dorsey ●	4,784
9.	Sammy Kaye ●	4,774
10.	Dinah Shore ●	4,532
11.	Harry James ●	4,328
12.	Jimmy Dorsey ●	3,989
13.	Vaughn Monroe ●	3,930
14.	Dick Haymes ●	3,180
15.	Kay Kyser ●	3,177
16.	Patti Page	3,161
17.	Nat "King" Cole ●	3,109
18.	Frankie Laine	3,088
19.	Freddy Martin ●	2,915
20.	Eddy Howard ●	2,843
21.	Eddie Fisher	2,808
22.	Les Paul & Mary Ford ■	2,697
23.	Benny Goodman ●	2,442
24.	Ink Spots ■■■■■	2,323
25.	Margaret Whiting	2,310
26.	Doris Day	2,268
27.	Russ Morgan ●	2,146
28.	Vic Damone	1,987
29.	Kay Starr	1,955
30.	Tony Martin	1,951
31.	Woody Herman ●	1,935
32.	Mills Brothers ■■■■	1,907
33.	Les Brown ●	1,843
34.	Gordon Jenkins ●	1,805
35.	Johnny Mercer ●	1,734

Rank		Points
36.	Ames Brothers ■	1,672
37.	Peggy Lee ●	1,594
38.	Rosemary Clooney ●	1,490
39.	Ray Anthony ●	1,457
40.	Buddy Clark ●	1,357
41.	Ella Fitzgerald ●	1,302
42.	Ralph Flanagan	1,277
43.	Hugo Winterhalter ●	1,267
44.	Charlie Spivak ●	1,222
45.	Tony Bennett	1,206
46.	Spike Jones ●	1,190
47.	Paul Weston ●	1,187
48.	Frankie Carle ●	1,186
49.	Four Aces	1,167
50.	Stan Kenton ●	1,094
51.	Johnnie Ray ●	1,092
52.	Gordon MacRae ●	1,089
53.	Guy Mitchell ●	1,076
54.	Louis Jordan ●	1,043
55.	Billy Eckstine ●	1,034
56.	Artie Shaw	1,026
57.	Tony Pastor ●	934
58.	Jimmy Wakely ●	922
59.	Evelyn Knight	918
60.	Xavier Cugat ●	905
61.	Art Mooney	891
62.	Gene Autry ●	885
63.	Teresa Brewer	880
64.	The Weavers ■	872
65.	The Pied Pipers ■■	839
66.	Tex Beneke ●	833
67.	Georgia Gibbs	820
68.	Bob Crosby ●	816
69.	Charlie Barnet ●	811
70.	Gene Krupa ●	796

Rank		Points
71.	Sam Donahue ●	772
72.	Count Basie ●	765
73.	Andy Russell ●	763
74.	Red Foley ●	761
75.	Helen Forrest ●	753
76.	Sarah Vaughan ●	751
77.	The Three Suns ■■■	748
78.	Betty Hutton ●	748
79.	The Merry Macs ■■■	747
80.	Arthur Godfrey ●	742
81.	Ted Weems ●	741
82.	The Four Lads	732
83.	Richard Hayes	724
84.	Percy Faith ●	719
85.	Don Cornell	704
86.	Horace Heidt ●	703
87.	Dick Jurgens ●	695
88.	The Hilltoppers ■■	694
89.	Joni James	690
90.	Blue Barron	688
91.	Les Baxter ●	676
92.	Phil Harris ●	670
93.	Alvino Rey	667
94.	Johnny Long ●	658
95.	Stan Freberg	646
96.	Johnny Desmond ●	643
97.	Ella Mae Morse ●	639
98.	Ray Noble ●	613
99.	Carmen Cavallaro ●	609
100.	Glen Gray ●	599
101.	Four King Sisters ■■	592
102.	The Gaylords	590
103.	Mel Tormé ●	585
104.	Art Lund ●	584
105.	Kitty Kallen	575
106.	Tennessee Ernie Ford ●	562
107.	Jack Smith	561
108.	Jan Garber ●	559
109.	Louis Armstrong ●	553
110.	The Harmonicats ■■■	543

Rank		Points
111.	Ken Griffin ●	543
112.	Kate Smith ●	537
113.	Eddy Arnold ●	532
114.	Freddie Slack ●	530
115.	Dean Martin ●	509
116.	Martha Tilton	501
117.	Will Bradley ●	499
118.	Judy Garland ●	493
119.	Mario Lanza ●	493
120.	Duke Ellington ●	480
121.	Hoagy Carmichael ●	476
122.	The Jesters	469
123.	Lawrence Welk ●	464
124.	Erskine Hawkins ●	457
125.	Dennis Day ●	452
126.	Eddy Duchin ●	444
127.	Vera Lynn	433
128.	Eileen Barton	424
129.	Henri René ●	423
130.	Ernest Tubb ●	418
131.	Hal McIntyre ●	394
132.	Al Trace ●	391
133.	Francis Craig ●	391
134.	Louis Prima ●	387
135.	Wayne King ●	385
136.	Tommy Tucker ●	368
137.	The Modernaires ■■	367
138.	Ray McKinley ●	362
139.	The Charioteers ■	352
140.	Dick Todd ●	351
141.	Hildegarde	347
142.	Ralph Marterie ●	347
143.	Lucky Millinder ●	344
144.	Jimmie Lunceford ●	343
145.	The Four Knights ■■	340
146.	The Crew-Cuts	340
147.	Victor Young ●	339
148.	Pee Wee Hunt ●	337
149.	Jack Owens ●	336
150.	Sunny Gale	332

A-Z — TOP 150 ARTISTS

1940-44

1.	**Glenn Miller**	5,859	11.	Sammy Kaye	1,061
2.	Bing Crosby	4,755	12.	Dick Haymes	1,058
3.	Tommy Dorsey	3,529	13.	Freddy Martin	987
4.	Jimmy Dorsey	3,327	14.	Frank Sinatra	931
5.	Harry James	2,665	15.	Woody Herman	897
6.	Kay Kyser	1,875	16.	Vaughn Monroe	850
7.	Andrews Sisters	1,810	17.	Guy Lombardo	825
8.	Ink Spots	1,378	18.	Artie Shaw	757
9.	Benny Goodman	1,369	19.	Charlie Barnet	754
10.	Dinah Shore	1,231	20.	Horace Heidt	641

1945-49

1.	**Bing Crosby**	4,082	11.	Margaret Whiting	1,732
2.	Perry Como	3,446	12.	Eddy Howard	1,670
3.	Sammy Kaye	2,943	13.	Les Brown	1,531
4.	Frank Sinatra	2,837	14.	Freddy Martin	1,501
5.	Andrews Sisters	2,561	15.	Johnny Mercer	1,409
6.	Jo Stafford	2,444	16.	Harry James	1,360
7.	Vaughn Monroe	2,385	17.	Buddy Clark	1,357
8.	Guy Lombardo	2,355	18.	Kay Kyser	1,302
9.	Dinah Shore	2,317	19.	Russ Morgan	1,283
10.	Dick Haymes	1,780	20.	Tommy Dorsey	1,255

1950-54

1.	**Patti Page**	2,901	11.	Ames Brothers	1,529
2.	Perry Como	2,815	12.	Rosemary Clooney	1,490
3.	Eddie Fisher	2,754	13.	Ray Anthony	1,457
4.	Les Paul & Mary Ford	2,488	14.	Frank Sinatra	1,451
5.	Frankie Laine	2,307	15.	Doris Day	1,416
6.	Jo Stafford	2,185	16.	Tony Martin	1,391
7.	Nat "King" Cole	2,015	17.	Vic Damone	1,343
8.	Bing Crosby	1,921	18.	Gordon Jenkins	1,267
9.	Kay Starr	1,775	19.	Tony Bennett	1,206
10.	Guy Lombardo	1,653	20.	Eddy Howard	1,173

TOP ARTISTS BY CATEGORY
1940-1954

Male Vocalists

1. Bing Crosby
2. Perry Como
3. Frank Sinatra
4. Vaughn Monroe
5. Dick Haymes
6. Nat "King" Cole
7. Frankie Laine
8. Eddie Fisher
9. Eddy Howard
10. Vic Damone
11. Tony Martin
12. Johnny Mercer
13. Buddy Clark
14. Tony Bennett
15. Johnnie Ray
16. Gordon MacRae
17. Guy Mitchell
18. Billy Eckstine
19. Andy Russell
20. Richard Hayes
21. Don Cornell
22. Johnny Desmond

Female Vocalists

1. Jo Stafford
2. Dinah Shore
3. Patti Page
4. Margaret Whiting
5. Doris Day
6. Kay Starr
7. Peggy Lee
8. Rosemary Clooney
9. Teresa Brewer
10. Evelyn Knight
11. Georgia Gibbs
12. Helen Forrest
13. Betty Hutton
14. Joni James
15. Ella Mae Morse
16. Kitty Kallen
17. Kate Smith
18. Martha Tilton
19. Judy Garland
20. Vera Lynn
21. Eileen Barton
22. Hildegarde

Groups

1. Andrews Sisters
2. Ink Spots
3. Mills Brothers
4. Ames Brothers
5. Four Aces
6. The Weavers
7. The Pied Pipers
8. The Three Suns
9. The Merry Macs
10. The Four Lads
11. The Hilltoppers
12. Four King Sisters
13. The Gaylords
14. The Harmonicats
15. The Jesters
16. The Fontane Sisters
17. The Modernaires
18. The Crew-Cuts
19. The Song Spinners
20. The Dinning Sisters
21. The Sportsmen
22. The McGuire Sisters

Big Bands/Orchestras: Jazz/Swing

1. Glenn Miller
2. Tommy Dorsey
3. Harry James
4. Jimmy Dorsey
5. Benny Goodman
6. Woody Herman
7. Les Brown
8. Stan Kenton
9. Artie Shaw
10. Tex Beneke
11. Bob Crosby
12. Charlie Barnet
13. Gene Krupa
14. Sam Donahue
15. Count Basie
16. Louis Armstrong
17. Freddie Slack
18. Will Bradley
19. Duke Ellington
20. Erskine Hawkins
21. Hal McIntyre
22. Louis Prima

Big Bands/Orchestras: Sweet

1. Guy Lombardo
2. Sammy Kaye
3. Kay Kyser
4. Freddy Martin
5. Russ Morgan
6. Gordon Jenkins
7. Charlie Spivak
8. Paul Weston
9. Frankie Carle
10. Tony Pastor

Jazz/R&B Vocalists

1. Ella Fitzgerald
2. Sarah Vaughan
3. Dinah Washington

R&B/Rock 'N Roll

1. Louis Jordan
2. The Charioteers
3. Lucky Millinder
4. The Four Knights
5. Delta Rhythm Boys
6. Bill Haley & His Comets
7. The Four Tunes
8. The Orioles
9. Joe Liggins
10. The Chords
11. The Dominoes
12. The Crows

Orchestras: Early '50s

1. Ray Anthony
2. Hugo Winterhalter
3. Ralph Flanagan
4. Percy Faith
5. Les Baxter
6. Ralph Marterie

Duos

1. Les Paul and Mary Ford
2. Bing Crosby/Andrews Sisters
3. Jo Stafford/Gordon MacRae
4. Dick Haymes/Helen Forrest
5. Margaret Whiting/Jimmy Wakely
6. Jo Stafford/Frankie Laine

Country

1. Jimmy Wakely
2. Gene Autry
3. Red Foley
4. Tennessee Ernie Ford
5. Eddy Arnold
6. Ernest Tubb
7. Al Dexter
8. Bob Wills
9. Tex Williams
10. Hank Williams

Novelty

1. Spike Jones
2. Arthur Godfrey
3. Phil Harris
4. Stan Freberg
5. Mel Blanc
6. Red Buttons
7. Jimmy Durante
8. Red Ingle

TOP ARTIST ACHIEVEMENTS

MOST CHART HITS

1. Bing Crosby 135
2. Glenn Miller 84
3. Perry Como 84
4. Frank Sinatra 78
5. Guy Lombardo 73
6. Andrews Sisters 71
7. Jo Stafford 71
8. Tommy Dorsey 68
9. Sammy Kaye 64
10. Dinah Shore 62
11. Harry James 58
12. Jimmy Dorsey 53
13. Vaughn Monroe 52
14. Dick Haymes 45
15. Nat "King" Cole 45
16. Frankie Laine 44
17. Freddy Martin 41
18. Eddy Howard 41
19. Kay Kyser 40
20. Patti Page 39
21. Benny Goodman 38
22. Eddie Fisher 36
23. Les Paul & Mary Ford 33
24. Margaret Whiting 32
25. Doris Day 32
26. Vic Damone 32
27. Russ Morgan 31
28. Ink Spots 30
29. Tony Martin 30
30. Woody Herman 30

MOST TOP 10 HITS

1. Bing Crosby 78
2. Glenn Miller 56
3. Frank Sinatra 40
4. Perry Como 39
5. Tommy Dorsey 37
6. Sammy Kaye 37
7. Jo Stafford 36
8. Andrews Sisters 33
9. Dinah Shore 33
10. Guy Lombardo 31
11. Harry James 30
12. Jimmy Dorsey 27
13. Dick Haymes 27
14. Kay Kyser 27
15. Vaughn Monroe 25
16. Eddie Fisher 22
17. Patti Page 20
18. Freddy Martin 19
19. Les Paul & Mary Ford 19
20. Benny Goodman 16
21. Ink Spots 16
22. Frankie Laine 15
23. Eddy Howard 15
24. Nat "King" Cole 14
25. Margaret Whiting 13
26. Kay Starr 13
27. Tony Martin 13
28. Woody Herman 13
29. Mills Brothers 13

MOST TOP 5 HITS

1. Bing Crosby 51
2. Glenn Miller 31
3. Perry Como 29
4. Tommy Dorsey 20
5. Sammy Kaye 20
6. Dinah Shore 20
7. Andrews Sisters 19
8. Harry James 18
9. Jimmy Dorsey 16
10. Kay Kyser 16
11. Frank Sinatra 15
12. Vaughn Monroe 15
13. Dick Haymes 14
14. Jo Stafford 13
15. Patti Page 12
16. Eddie Fisher 12
17. Guy Lombardo 11
18. Freddy Martin 11
19. Frankie Laine 10
20. Les Paul & Mary Ford 10
21. Ink Spots 10
22. Gordon Jenkins 9
23. Margaret Whiting 8
24. Johnny Mercer 8
25. Nat "King" Cole 7
26. Eddy Howard 7
27. Benny Goodman 7
28. Russ Morgan 7
29. Mills Brothers 7
30. Buddy Clark 7

MOST #1 HITS

1. Bing Crosby 15
2. Perry Como 11
3. Glenn Miller 10
4. Jimmy Dorsey 8
5. Andrews Sisters 6
6. Harry James 6
7. Jo Stafford 5
8. Sammy Kaye 5
9. Vaughn Monroe 5

MOST WEEKS AT THE #1 POSITION

1. Bing Crosby 82
2. Glenn Miller 58
3. Perry Como 51
4. Andrews Sisters 40
5. Patti Page 36
6. Vaughn Monroe 35
7. Jimmy Dorsey 33
8. Harry James 30
9. Nat "King" Cole 27
10. Sammy Kaye 24
11. Dinah Shore 24
12. Tony Bennett 24
13. Jo Stafford 22
14. Les Paul & Mary Ford 22
15. Tommy Dorsey 20
16. Mills Brothers 20
17. Rosemary Clooney 20
18. Frankie Carle 20

MOST CONSECUTIVE #1 HITS

1. 5   Bing Crosby (1943-44)
2. 3   Andrews Sisters (1944-45)
3. 3   Jimmy Dorsey (1941)
4. 3   Ink Spots (1944-46)
5. 3   Johnny Mercer (1945)

MOST 2-SIDED HITS

25   Perry Como
24   Bing Crosby
17   Jo Stafford
15   Frank Sinatra
14   Andrews Sisters
13   Guy Lombardo
11   Glenn Miller
11   Sammy Kaye
11   Dick Haymes
11   Eddie Fisher
10   Tommy Dorsey
10   Jimmy Dorsey
10   Les Paul & Mary Ford

TOP ARTISTS WHO NEVER HIT #1

Rank

1. 30   Tony Martin
2. 39   Ray Anthony
3. 42   Ralph Flanagan
4. 43   Hugo Winterhalter
5. 44   Charlie Spivak
6. 47   Paul Weston
7. 50   Stan Kenton

To quality, artist must rank in the Top 50.

Ties are broken according to rank in the *Top 150 Artists* section.

Following is a chronological listing of artists who debuted on the Pop charts during that year, and based on chart performance, are ranked among the *Top 150 Artists* in this book. Each artist's *Top 150* rank is shown in parentheses.

†   indicates the highest ranking artist of the *Top 150 Artists* debuting that year

★   indicates artist has a *Top 500* ranking in our **Top Pop Singles 1955-1999** book

PRE-1940 DEBUTS

Below is a chronological listing of artists who rank as a *Top 150 Artist* in this book, but debuted prior to 1940. The debut dates shown are taken from our **Pop Memories 1890-1954** book.

#	Date	Artist
1.	7/29/22	Ted Weems (81)
2.	4/4/23	Jan Garber (108)
3.	7/17/26	Louis Armstrong (109)
4.	7/2/27	Kate Smith (112)
5.	7/30/27	Duke Ellington (120)
6.	9/10/27 †	Guy Lombardo (7)
7.	3/22/30	Wayne King (135)
8.	1/3/31	Benny Goodman (23)
9.	1/17/31	Glen Gray (100)
10.	3/28/31 †	Bing Crosby (1) ★
11.	9/26/31	Ray Noble (98)
12.	10/17/31	Victor Young (147)
13.	11/21/31	Mills Brothers (32)
14.	3/26/32	Eddy Duchin (126)
15.	6/18/32 †	Hoagy Carmichael (121)

#	Date	Artist
16.	3/25/33	Phil Harris (92)
17.	9/16/33 †	Freddy Martin (19)
18.	11/18/33	Gene Autry (62)
19.	11/10/34	Jimmie Lunceford (144)
20.	5/18/35	Xavier Cugat (60)
21.	6/1/35	Louis Prima (134)
22.	6/22/35	Russ Morgan (27)
23.	6/22/35	Bob Crosby (68)
24.	6/29/35	Kay Kyser (15)
25.	7/13/35 †	Glenn Miller (2)
26.	10/26/35	Tommy Dorsey (8)
27.	12/14/35	Jimmy Dorsey (12)
28.	7/25/36 †	Ella Fitzgerald (41)
29.	8/29/36	Erskine Hawkins (124)
30.	9/19/36	Charlie Barnet (69)
31.	12/12/36	Artie Shaw (56)
32.	12/26/36	Hildegarde (141)

#	Date	Artist
33.	7/3/37	Horace Heidt (86)
34.	9/18/37	Count Basie (72)
35.	10/2/37 †	Sammy Kaye (9)
36.	12/25/37	Woody Herman (31)
37.	1/1/38 †	Andrews Sisters (4)
38.	2/19/38	Harry James (11)
39.	3/12/38	Blue Barron (90)
40.	5/7/38	Dick Todd (140)
41.	5/28/38	Gene Krupa (70)
42.	7/23/38	Buddy Clark (40)
43.	7/30/38	Tony Martin (30)
44.	8/13/38	Johnny Mercer (35)
45.	9/10/38	Lawrence Welk (123) ★
46.	3/4/39	Dick Jurgens (87)
47.	3/25/39	The Merry Macs (79)
48.	4/15/39 †	Ink Spots (24)
49.	9/9/39	Judy Garland (118)

#	Date	Artist
50.	1/13/40	Tommy Tucker (136)
51.	5/11/40	Will Bradley (117)
52.	10/12/40 †	Dinah Shore (10)
53.	12/28/40	Vaughn Monroe (13)
54.	5/13/41	Alvino Rey (93)
55.	6/14/41	The Jesters (122)
56.	6/28/41	Tony Pastor (57)
57.	7/05/41	Four King Sisters (101)
58.	8/02/41	Charlie Spivak (44)
59.	9/13/41	Sam Donahue (71)
60.	10/11/41 †	Les Brown (33)
61.	1/31/42	Lucky Millinder (143)
62.	3/28/42 †	Frank Sinatra (5) ★
63.	8/22/42	Freddie Slack (114)
64.	8/29/42	Gordon Jenkins (34)
65.	10/24/42	Spike Jones (46)
66.	1/23/43	Johnny Long (94)
67.	3/13/43	Henri René (129)
68.	3/20/43	Jimmy Wakely (58)
69.	5/08/43	Ray McKinley (138)
70.	7/03/43	Dick Haymes (14)
71.	10/16/43 †	Perry Como (3) ★
72.	12/11/43	Nat "King" Cole (17) ★
73.	12/25/43	Ella Mae Morse (97)

#	Date	Artist
74.	1/08/44 †	Jo Stafford (6)
75.	1/22/44	Ernest Tubb (130)
76.	2/12/44	Louis Jordan (54)
77.	2/19/44	Al Trace (132)
78.	4/01/44	Stan Kenton (50)
79.	4/08/44	The Pied Pipers (65)
80.	4/22/44	Andy Russell (73)
81.	4/29/44	Helen Forrest (75)
82.	6/24/44	Martha Tilton (116)
83.	7/01/44	The Three Suns (77)
84.	7/29/44	Betty Hutton (78)
85.	8/26/44	Evelyn Knight (59)
86.	9/30/44	Red Foley (74)
87.	10/07/44	Frankie Carle (48)
88.	2/17/45	Hal McIntyre (131)
89.	6/30/45	Carmen Cavallaro (99)
90.	7/21/45	The Modernaires (137)
91.	10/06/45	Billy Eckstine (55)
92.	10/13/45 †	Les Paul & Mary Ford (22)
93.	10/27/45	Margaret Whiting (25)
94.	10/27/45	Paul Weston (47)
95.	11/10/45	Peggy Lee (37)
96.	11/10/45	The Charioteers (139)

#	Date	Artist
97.	3/23/46	Mel Tormé (103)
98.	5/25/46	Tex Beneke (66)
99.	6/29/46 †	Eddy Howard (20)
100.	3/22/47	Johnny Desmond (96)
101.	3/29/47 †	Frankie Laine (18) ★
102.	4/19/47	Art Lund (104)
103.	4/26/47	The Harmonicats (110)
104.	5/03/47	Dennis Day (125)
105.	5/31/47	Jack Smith (107)
106.	8/09/47	Francis Craig (133)
107.	8/30/47	Vic Damone (28)
108.	9/20/47	Jack Owens (149)
109.	11/01/47	Arthur Godfrey (80)
110.	1/24/48	Art Mooney (61)
111.	4/10/48	Ken Griffin (111)
112.	5/15/48	Eddy Arnold (113) ★
113.	5/22/48	Vera Lynn (127)
114.	5/29/48	Doris Day (26) ★
115.	6/12/48	Eddie Fisher (21) ★
116.	6/26/48 †	Patti Page (16) ★
117.	6/26/48	Pee Wee Hunt (148)
118.	7/03/48	Sarah Vaughan (76) ★
119.	7/31/48	Gordon MacRae (52)
120.	8/21/48	Ames Brothers (36) ★
121.	12/04/48	Kay Starr (29)
122.	12/04/48	Dean Martin (115) ★

123.	4/30/49		**Kitty Kallen** (105)
124.	6/18/49		**Don Cornell** (85)
125.	9/24/49		**Ralph Flanagan** (42)
126.	10/15/49		**Hugo Winterhalter** (43)
127.	11/19/49	†	**Ray Anthony** (39)
128.	11/26/49		**Tennessee Ernie Ford** (106)
129.	12/17/49		**Richard Hayes** (83)

130.	2/04/50		**Teresa Brewer** (63) ★
131.	3/11/50		**Eileen Barton** (128)
132.	3/25/50		**Georgia Gibbs** (67) ★
133.	6/03/50		**Percy Faith** (84)
134.	7/01/50		**The Weavers** (64)
135.	12/09/50	†	**Guy Mitchell** (53) ★
136.	12/16/50		**Mario Lanza** (119)

137.	2/10/51		**Stan Freberg** (95)
138.	2/24/51	†	**Rosemary Clooney** (38)
139.	3/03/51		**Ralph Marterie** (142)
140.	3/17/51		**Les Baxter** (91)
141.	6/23/51		**Tony Bennett** (45) ★
142.	7/28/51		**The Four Knights** (145)
143.	9/15/51		**Four Aces** (49) ★
144.	11/24/51		**Johnnie Ray** (51)
145.	11/24/51		**The Four Lads** (82) ★

146.	2/09/52		**Sunny Gale** (150)
147.	8/16/52	†	**The Hilltoppers** (88)
148.	10/18/52		**Joni James** (89) ★
149.	12/20/52		**The Gaylords** (102)

| 150. | 5/08/54 | | **The Crew-Cuts** (146) ★ |

DEBUT YEAR — ARTISTS A-Z

Ames Brothers '48	Eckstine, Billy '45	Jenkins, Gordon '42	Noble, Ray '31
Andrews Sisters '38	Ellington, Duke '27	Jesters, The '41	Owens, Jack '47
Anthony, Ray '49	Faith, Percy '50	Jones, Spike '42	Page, Patti '48
Armstrong, Louis '26	Fisher, Eddie '48	Jordan, Louis '44	Pastor, Tony '41
Arnold, Eddy '48	Fitzgerald, Ella '36	Jurgens, Dick '39	Paul, Les, & Mary Ford '45
Autry, Gene '33	Flanagan, Ralph '49	Kallen, Kitty '49	Pied Pipers, The '44
Barnet, Charlie '36	Foley, Red '44	Kaye, Sammy '37	Prima, Louis '35
Barron, Blue '38	Ford, Tennessee Ernie '49	Kenton, Stan '44	Ray, Johnnie '51
Barton, Eileen '50	Forrest, Helen '44	King, Wayne '30	René, Henri '43
Basie, Count '37	Four Aces '51	Knight, Evelyn '44	Rey, Alvino '41
Baxter, Les '51	Four King Sisters '41	Krupa, Gene '38	Russell, Andy '44
Beneke, Tex '46	Four Knights, The '51	Kyser, Kay '35	Shaw, Artie '36
Bennett, Tony '51	Four Lads, The '51	Laine, Frankie '47	Shore, Dinah '40
Bradley, Will '40	Freberg, Stan '51	Lanza, Mario '50	Sinatra, Frank '42
Brewer, Teresa '50	Garber, Jan '23	Lee, Peggy '45	Slack, Freddie '42
Brown, Les '41	Garland, Judy '39	Lombardo, Guy '27	Smith, Jack '47
Carle, Frankie '44	Gale, Sunny '52	Long, Johnny '43	Smith, Kate '27
Carmichael, Hoagy '32	Gaylords, The '52	Lunceford, Jimmie '34	Spivak, Charlie '41
Cavallaro, Carmen '45	Gibbs, Georgia '50	Lund, Art '47	Stafford, Jo '44
Charioteers, The '45	Godfrey, Arthur '47	Lynn, Vera '48	Starr, Kay '48
Clark, Buddy '38	Goodman, Benny '31	MacRae, Gordon '48	Three Suns, The '44
Clooney, Rosemary '51	Gray, Glen '31	Marterie, Ralph '51	Tilton, Martha '44
Cole, Nat "King" '43	Griffin, Ken '48	Martin, Dean '48	Todd, Dick '38
Como, Perry '43	Harmonicats, The '47	Martin, Freddy '33	Tormé, Mel '46
Cornell, Don '49	Harris, Phil '33	Martin, Tony '38	Trace, Al '44
Craig, Francis '47	Hawkins, Erskine '36	McIntyre, Hal '45	Tubb, Ernest '44
Crew-Cuts, The '54	Hayes, Richard '49	McKinley, Ray '43	Tucker, Tommy` '40
Crosby, Bing '31	Haymes, Dick '43	Mercer, Johnny '38	Vaughan, Sarah '48
Crosby, Bob '35	Heidt, Horace '37	Merry Macs, The '39	Wakely, Jimmy '43
Cugat, Xavier '35	Herman, Woody '37	Miller, Glenn '35	Weavers, The '50
Damone, Vic '47	Hildegarde '36	Millinder, Lucky '42	Weems, Ted '22
Day, Dennis '47	Hilltoppers, The '52	Mills Brothers '31	Welk, Lawrence '38
Day, Doris '48	Howard, Eddy '46	Mitchell, Guy '50	Weston, Paul '45
Desmond, Johnny '47	Hunt, Pee Wee '48	Modernaires, The '45	Whiting, Margaret '45
Donahue, Sam '41	Hutton, Betty '44	Monroe, Vaughn '40	Winterhalter, Hugo '49
Dorsey, Jimmy '35	Ink Spots '39	Mooney, Art '48	Young, Victor '31
Dorsey, Tommy '35	James, Harry '38	Morgan, Russ '35	
Duchin, Eddy '32	James, Joni '52	Morse, Ella Mae '43	

TOP SONGWRITERS

# of Hits	Points		# of Hits	Points		# of Hits	Points	
1. 76	6,866	Sammy Cahn	34. 25	2,224	Bob Russell	68. 16	1,328	Steve Nelson
2. 74	6,621	Irving Berlin	35. 25	2,212	Ned Washington	69. 15	1,326	Sylvia Dee
3. 73	6,526	Frank Loesser	36. 24	2,174	Jay Livingston	70. 16	1,320	Cy Coben
4. 71	6,388	Johnny Mercer	37. 23	1,997	Jerry Livingston	71. 14	1,281	Josef Myrow
5. 64	5,794	Jule Styne	38. 22	1,985	Kermit Goell	72. 15	1,280	Paul Francis Webster
6. 55	5,053	Mack Gordon	39. 22	1,895	Gus Kahn			
7. 55	4,940	Richard Rodgers	40. 21	1,886	Will Grosz	73. 14	1,268	Al Stillman
8. 50	4,467	Bennie Benjamin	41. 21	1,862	Buddy Kaye	74. 14	1,264	Bert Kalmar
9. 49	4,455	Oscar Hammerstein	42. 20	1,798	Pee Wee King	75. 14	1,232	Al Lewis
			43. 20	1,750	Mitchell Parish	76. 14	1,231	Haven Gillespie
10. 50	4,447	Jimmy Van Heusen	44. 19	1,725	Sammy Gallop	77. 14	1,224	Clem Watts
			45. 19	1,705	Eddie DeLange	78. 14	1,211	Larry Stock
11. 49	4,393	Johnny Burke	46. 19	1,701	Harry Ruby	79. 14	1,202	Milton Drake
12. 45	3,923	Mack David	47. 19	1,700	Beasley Smith	80. 14	1,191	Fred Wise
13. 43	3,898	Harry Warren	48. 19	1,686	Sid Lippman	81. 14	1,188	Tolchard Evans
14. 43	3,810	George Weiss	49. 19	1,681	Duke Ellington	82. 14	1,173	Jimmy Shirl
15. 41	3,619	Al Hoffman	50. 19	1,679	Kim Gannon	83. 13	1,161	E.Y. Harburg
16. 41	3,609	Sunny Skylar	51. 19	1,664	Hy Zaret	84. 13	1,161	Vic Mizzy
17. 38	3,364	Bob Hilliard	52. 18	1,643	Jerome Kern	85. 13	1,156	Sammy Mysels
18. 37	3,303	Carl Sigman	53. 18	1,611	Allie Wrubel	86. 13	1,155	Ben Raleigh
19. 36	3,061	Bob Merrill	54. 19	1,602	Ervin Drake	87. 13	1,154	Guy Wood
20. 33	2,981	Alex Kramer	55. 18	1,568	Irving Taylor	88. 13	1,139	Carmen Lombardo
21. 33	2,960	Jack Lawrence	56. 17	1,553	James Monaco	89. 13	1,132	Lorenz Hart
22. 32	2,897	Joan Whitney	57. 17	1,529	Redd Stewart	90. 13	1,127	Victor Young
23. 33	2,884	Jimmy McHugh	58. 17	1,519	Billy Reid	91. 13	1,126	Walter Kent
24. 32	2,826	Jimmy Kennedy	59. 16	1,456	Arthur Schwartz	92. 13	1,125	Al Goodhart
25. 30	2,702	Charles Tobias	60. 16	1,448	Allan Roberts	93. 13	1,125	Hank Williams
26. 29	2,604	Harold Arlen	61. 16	1,441	Sammy Fain	94. 13	1,124	Milton DeLugg
27. 29	2,581	Cole Porter	62. 16	1,430	Ray Gilbert	95. 12	1,099	John Turner
28. 29	2,546	Harold Adamson	63. 17	1,413	Dick Manning	96. 12	1,090	Geoffrey Parsons
29. 27	2,451	Ray Evans	64. 16	1,411	Gene DePaul	97. 12	1,072	Herb Magidson
30. 27	2,432	Nat Simon	65. 16	1,410	Bernie Wayne	98. 12	1,071	Benny Davis
31. 27	2,428	Leo Robin	66. 16	1,390	Vaughn Horton	99. 12	1,067	Al Dubin
32. 27	2,401	Hoagy Carmichael	67. 15	1,337	Paul Weston	100. 13	1,063	Irving Gordon
33. 26	2,336	Don Raye						

ONE-HIT WONDERS

1. **Anton Karas** .... "The Third Man" Theme (1[11]/'50)
2. **Johnny Standley** .... It's In The Book (Parts 1 & 2) (1[2]/'52)
3. **The Three Flames** .... Open The Door, Richard (1[1]/'47)
4. **Jon & Sondra Steele** .... My Happiness (2[2]/'48)
5. **Jack McVea** .... Open The Door Richard! (3[1]/'47)
6. **"Dusty" Fletcher** .... Open The Door, Richard! (Parts 1 & 2) (3[1]/'47)
7. **Bill Snyder** .... Bewitched (3[1]/'50)
8. **Frank Weir** .... The Happy Wanderer (4[6]/'54)
9. **Teddy Walters** .... Laughing On The Outside (Crying On The Inside) (4[1]/'46)
10. **Dorothy Shay** .... Feudin' And Fightin' (4[1]/'47)
11. **Del Wood** .... Down Yonder (4[1]/'51)
12. **Don Howard** .... Oh Happy Day (4[1]/'52)
13. **Hal Derwin** .... The Old Lamplighter (5[1]/'46)
14. **The Stardusters** .... I Don't See Me In Your Eyes Anymore (5[1]/'49)
15. **Silvana Mangano** .... Anna (5[1]/'53)
16. **The Chords** .... Sh-Boom (5[1]/'54)

The above artists' only chart hit reached the #5 position or higher.

#9, 13 & 14 did appear as backing performers (see Cross-Reference Section).

January 6, 1945

Music Popularity Chart
Week Ending Dec. 28, 1944

MOST PLAYED JUKE BOX RECORDS
Going Strong

Reports received from The Billboard representatives and based on information given by leading juke box operators last week show the records listed below are currently receiving the most play on automatic phonographs thruout the nation. These reports stem from the country's leading operating centers and are averaged together. Thus only records that are distributed nationally will show up in the guide. Listed under the title of each most played record are the other available recordings of this number.

POSITION			
Weeks to date	Last Week	This Week	
7	1	1.	DON'T FENCE ME IN—Bing Crosby-Andrews Sisters (Vic Schoen Ork) ....Decca 23364 (The Three Suns, Hit 7114; Sammy Kaye, Victor 20-1610; Kate Smith, Columbia 36759; Gene Autry, Okeh 6728; Hal McIntyre, Bluebird 30-0834)
10	2	2.	INTO EACH LIFE SOME RAIN MUST FALL — Ink Spots-Ella Fitzgerald ....Decca 23356 (Charlie Barnet, Decca 18638)
9	3	3.	I'M MAKING BELIEVE—Ink Spots-Ella Fitzgerald.... ....Decca 23356 (The Three Suns, Hit 7105; Hal McIntyre, Bluebird 30-0831.)
5	7	4.	THERE GOES THAT SONG AGAIN—Russ Morgan.... ....Decca 18625 (Sammy Kaye, Victor 20-1606; Billy Butterfield, Capitol 182; Kay Kyser, Columbia 36757; Kate Smith, Columbia 36759; Martha Stewart, Bluebird 30-0832.)
11	4	5.	THE TROLLEY SONG—The Pied Pipers (Paul Weston Ork) ....Capitol 168 (The King Sisters, Bluebird 30-0829; Judy Garland, Decca 23361; Jack Smith, Hit 7115; Sula's Musette Ork (Don Baker), Continental C-1154; Vaughn Monroe, Victor 20-1605; Guy Lombardo, Decca 18634.)
6	8	6.	THE TROLLEY SONG—Judy Garland (Georgie Stoll Ork) (See No. 5) ....Decca 23361
8	14	7.	DANCE WITH A DOLLY (With a Hole in Her Stocking) —Russ Morgan (Al Jennings) ....Decca 18625 (Evelyn Knight, Decca 18614; Louis Prima, Hit 7107; Tony Pastor, Bluebird 30-0827)
2	16	8.	THERE GOES THAT SONG AGAIN—Sammy Kaye (Nancy Norman) (See No. 4.) ....Victor 20-16106
22	6	8.	I'LL WALK ALONE—Dinah Shore ....Victor 20-1586 (Martha Tilton, Capitol 157; Mary Martin, Decca 23340; Louis Prima, Hit 7083)
1	—	9.	I DREAM OF YOU—Tommy Dorsey (Freddie Stewart) ....Victor 20-1608 (Andy Russell, Capitol 175; Art Kassel, Hit 7110; Frank Sinatra, Columbia 36762; Jimmy Dorsey, Decca 18637; Perry Como, Victor 20-1629)
32	12	10.	YOU ALWAYS HURT THE ONE YOU LOVE—Mills Brothers ....Decca 18599 (The Three Suns, Hit 7105; Sammy Kaye, Victor 20-1606; Charlie Barnet, Decca 18638)
1	—	11.	I'M WASTIN' MY TEARS ON YOU—Tex Ritter..Capitol 174
15	17	12.	AND HER TEARS FLOWED LIKE WINE—Stan Kenton (Anita O'Day) ....Capitol 166 (Ella Fitzgerald-Johnny Long, Decca 18633)
1	—	13.	MEET ME IN ST. LOUIS, LOUIS—Guy Lombardo (The Lombardo Quartet) ....Decca 18626 (Judy Garland, Decca 23360)
1	—	13.	AC-CENT-TCHU-ATE THE POSITIVE—Johnny Mercer (The Pied Pipers-Paul Weston Ork) ....Capitol 180 (Artie Shaw, Victor 20-1612; George Paxton, Hit 7120)
4	10	14.	THE TROLLEY SONG—Vaughn Monroe (Vaughn Monroe-Marilyn Duke) ....Victor 20-1605
10	15	15.	DANCE WITH A DOLLY (With a Hole in Her Stocking) —Tony Pastor (See No. 7) ....Bluebird 30-0827
16	—	16.	DANCE WITH A DOLLY (With a Hole in Her Stocking) —Evelyn Knight (Camarata Ork) (See No. 7)....Decca 18614
3	13	17.	THE TROLLEY SONG—The King Sisters (See No. 4) ....Bluebird 30-0829

Coming Up

Reports received from The Billboard representatives last week, and based on information given them by leading juke box operators, show the records listed below are gaining in popularity all over the nation.

I DON'T WANT TO LOVE YOU—Phil Brito (Paul Lavalle Ork) ....Musicraft 15018
THE TROLLEY SONG—Guy Lombardo (The Lombardo Trio-Stuart Foster) ....Decca 18634
RUM AND COCA-COLA—Andrews Sisters (Vic Schoen Ork)....Decca 18636
AND HER TEARS FLOWED LIKE WINE—Ella Fitzgerald-Johnny Long ....Decca 18633

Territorial Favorites With Juke Box Operators

The following records are reported as favorites in various territories as indicated in reports to The Billboard from leading Juke Box Operators.
SOLDIER'S LAST LETTER—Ernest Tubb ....Decca 6098 (Fort Worth)
EVELINA—Bing Crosby (Camarata Ork) ....Decca 18635 (Buffalo)

THE TOP SINGLES

Top Singles:
>All-Time
>1940-44
>1945-49
>1950-54

Top POPular Recordings:
>Instrumental
>Novelty
>Christmas

Singles Of Longevity

Songs With Longest Titles

Songs With Most Charted Versions

MVPs — Most Valuable Platters

Academy Award-Winning Songs

Year-By-Year Synopsis

Top Record Labels

TOP 100 #1 SINGLES

ALL-TIME

Peak Year	Wks Chr	Wks T10	Wks T5	Wks @ #1	Rank	Title	Artist
47	25	25	21	17	1.	Near You	Francis Craig And His Orchestra
40	28	28	19	13	2.	In The Mood	Glenn Miller and his Orch.
50	26	21	19	13	3.	The Tennessee Waltz	Patti Page
50	25	20	19	13	4.	Goodnight Irene	Gordon Jenkins and his Orchestra and The Weavers
43	20	20	18	13	5.	I've Heard That Song Before	Harry James and his Orchestra
40	23	23	17	13	6.	Frenesi	Artie Shaw and his Orchestra
46	23	20	17	13	7.	The Gypsy	Ink Spots
47	20	18	17	13	8.	Heartaches	Ted Weems And His Orchestra
43	30	30	23	12	9.	Paper Doll	Mills Brothers
52	25	22	17	12	10.	You Belong To Me	Jo Stafford
49	22	18	17	12	11.	Riders In The Sky (A Cowboy Legend)	Vaughn Monroe and his Orchestra
40	18	18	14	12	12.	I'll Never Smile Again	Tommy Dorsey and his Orchestra
53	31	26	23	11	13.	Vaya Con Dios (May God Be With You)	Les Paul and Mary Ford
51	27	22	18	11	14.	Cry	Johnnie Ray & The Four Lads
50	27	20	17	11	15.	"The Third Man" Theme	Anton Karas
50	27	20	17	11	16.	The 3rd Man Theme	Guy Lombardo And His Royal Canadians
46	20	16	16	11	17.	Oh! What It Seemed To Be	Frankie Carle and his Orchestra
42	15	15	14	11	18.	White Christmas	Bing Crosby
51	32	24	20	10	19.	Because Of You	Tony Bennett
47	22	21	18	10	20.	Ballerina	Vaughn Monroe and his Orchestra
52	25	19	17	10	21.	Wheel Of Fortune	Kay Starr
48	25	19	17	10	22.	Buttons And Bows	Dinah Shore and her Happy Valley Boys
45	20	18	17	10	23.	Rum And Coca-Cola	Andrews Sisters
53	24	19	16	10	24.	The Song From Moulin Rouge (Where Is Your Heart)	Percy Faith & his Orch.
52	22	18	16	10	25.	I Went To Your Wedding	Patti Page
45	19	17	16	10	26.	Till The End Of Time	Perry Como
42	15	15	13	10	27.	Moonlight Cocktail	Glenn Miller and his Orchestra
50	16	13	12	10	28.	If I Knew You Were Comin' (I'd've Baked A Cake)	Eileen Barton
41	14	14	11	10	29.	Amapola (Pretty Little Poppy)	Jimmy Dorsey And His Orchestra
45	28	27	21	9	30.	Sentimental Journey	Les Brown and his Orchestra
41	23	23	20	9	31.	Chattanooga Choo Choo	Glenn Miller and his Orchestra
44	27	21	19	9	32.	Swinging On A Star	Bing Crosby
48	21	19	19	9	33.	Mañana (Is Soon Enough For Me)	Peggy Lee
54	26	20	17	9	34.	Little Things Mean A Lot	Kitty Kallen
51	25	20	16	9	35.	How High The Moon	Les Paul and Mary Ford
40	16	16	16	9	36.	Only Forever	Bing Crosby
44	19	19	15	9	37.	Shoo-Shoo Baby	Andrews Sisters
54	20	18	15	9	38.	Sh-Boom	The Crew-Cuts
46	18	16	14	9	39.	Rumors Are Flying	Frankie Carle and his Orchestra
52	21	15	13	9	40.	Auf Wiederseh'n Sweetheart	Vera Lynn And Chorus
40	17	17	12	9	41.	Tuxedo Junction	Glenn Miller and his Orch.
53	31	27	23	8	42.	You You You	Ames Brothers
50	27	22	21	8	43.	Mona Lisa	Nat "King" Cole
41	24	24	18	8	44.	Piano Concerto In B Flat	Freddy Martin and his Orchestra
46	25	22	18	8	45.	To Each His Own	Eddy Howard And His Orchestra
54	22	19	18	8	46.	Wanted	Perry Como
53	25	18	17	8	47.	Rags To Riches	Tony Bennett
46	21	18	17	8	48.	The Gypsy	Dinah Shore
48	32	23	16	8	49.	Twelfth Street Rag	Pee Wee Hunt And His Orchestra
51	24	19	16	8	50.	Sin	Eddy Howard And His Orchestra

ALL-TIME

Peak Year	Wks Chr	Wks T10	Wks T5	Wks @ #1	Rank	Title	Artist
44	21	18	16	8	51.	Don't Fence Me In	Bing Crosby and the Andrews Sisters
45	19	18	16	8	52.	On The Atchison, Topeka And Santa Fe	Johnny Mercer
49	22	17	16	8	53.	That Lucky Old Sun	Frankie Laine
51	24	19	15	8	54.	If	Perry Como
53	21	18	15	8	55.	The Doggie In The Window	Patti Page
51	20	16	14	8	56.	Come On-a My House	Rosemary Clooney
48	18	15	14	8	57.	Nature Boy	King Cole
41	15	15	14	8	58.	Daddy	Swing and Sway with Sammy Kaye
47	26	24	13	8	59.	Peg O' My Heart	The Harmonicats
54	19	17	13	8	60.	Oh! My Pa-Pa (O Mein Papa)	Eddie Fisher
46	17	14	13	8	61.	Oh! What It Seemed To Be	Frank Sinatra
50	16	15	12	8	62.	Chattanoogie Shoe Shine Boy	Red Foley
42	13	13	12	8	63.	Jingle Jangle Jingle	Kay Kyser and his Orchestra
53	24	19	18	7	64.	Till I Waltz Again With You	Teresa Brewer
53	25	20	16	7	65.	I'm Walking Behind You	Eddie Fisher
54	24	20	16	7	66.	Make Love To Me!	Jo Stafford
42	18	18	15	7	67.	(I've Got a Gal in) Kalamazoo	Glenn Miller and his Orchestra
43	18	18	15	7	68.	Sunday, Monday Or Always	Bing Crosby
49	21	17	15	7	69.	A Little Bird Told Me	Evelyn Knight
44	23	21	14	7	70.	Besame Mucho (Kiss Me Much)	Jimmy Dorsey And His Orchestra
49	22	17	14	7	71.	Cruising Down The River	Russ Morgan And His Orchestra
52	20	17	14	7	72.	Kiss Of Fire	Georgia Gibbs
46	17	15	14	7	73.	The Old Lamp-Lighter	Swing and Sway with Sammy Kaye
54	20	16	13	7	74.	Mr. Sandman	The Chordettes
49	20	16	13	7	75.	Cruising Down The River	Blue Barron and his Orchestra
45	16	13	12	7	76.	My Dreams Are Getting Better All The Time	Les Brown and his Orchestra
48	23	17	11	7	77.	You Can't Be True, Dear	Ken Griffin at the Organ
44	28	23	19	6	78.	I'll Get By (As Long As I Have You)	Harry James and his Orchestra
51	27	21	17	6	79.	Cold, Cold Heart	Tony Bennett
45	29	23	16	6	80.	There! I've Said It Again	Vaughn Monroe and his Orchestra
54	27	20	16	6	81.	Hey There	Rosemary Clooney
48	24	20	16	6	82.	You Call Everybody Darlin'	Al Trace And His New Orchestra
52	23	20	16	6	83.	Why Don't You Believe Me	Joni James
45	20	17	14	6	84.	I Can't Begin To Tell You	Bing Crosby with Carmen Cavallaro At The Piano
46	25	18	13	6	85.	(I Love You) For Sentimental Reasons	The King Cole Trio
47	15	15	13	6	86.	Peg O' My Heart	Buddy Clark
42	15	15	12	6	87.	Tangerine	Jimmy Dorsey And His Orchestra
49	13	12	11	6	88.	Mule Train	Frankie Laine and the Muleskinners
47	17	15	10	6	89.	Smoke! Smoke! Smoke! (That Cigarette)	Tex Williams And His Western Caravan
48	15	13	9	6	90.	Woody Wood-Pecker	Kay Kyser and his Orchestra
44	14	13	9	6	91.	(There'll Be A) Hot Time In The Town Of Berlin (When The Yanks Go Marching In)	Bing Crosby and the Andrews Sisters
52	38	26	20	5	92.	Blue Tango	Leroy Anderson "Pops" Concert Orchestra
51	29	23	20	5	93.	Too Young	Nat "King" Cole
44	33	28	18	5	94.	You Always Hurt The One You Love	Mills Brothers
49	26	19	17	5	95.	Some Enchanted Evening	Perry Como
50	25	20	16	5	96.	I Can Dream, Can't I?	Andrews Sisters
48	23	18	16	5	97.	A Tree In The Meadow	Margaret Whiting
43	24	24	15	5	98.	There Are Such Things	Tommy Dorsey and his Orchestra
44	22	18	15	5	99.	San Fernando Valley	Bing Crosby
53	21	18	15	5	100.	Don't Let The Stars Get In Your Eyes	Perry Como

TOP 40 #1 SINGLES

1940-44

Peak Year	Wks Chr	Wks T10	Wks T5	Wks @ #1	Rank	Title	Artist
40	28	28	19	13	1.	In The Mood	Glenn Miller and his Orch.
43	20	20	18	13	2.	I've Heard That Song Before	Harry James and his Orchestra
40	23	23	17	13	3.	Frenesi	Artie Shaw and his Orchestra
43	30	30	23	12	4.	Paper Doll	Mills Brothers
40	18	18	14	12	5.	I'll Never Smile Again	Tommy Dorsey and his Orchestra
42	15	15	14	11	6.	White Christmas	Bing Crosby
42	15	15	13	10	7.	Moonlight Cocktail	Glenn Miller and his Orchestra
41	14	14	11	10	8.	Amapola (Pretty Little Poppy)	Jimmy Dorsey And His Orchestra
41	23	23	20	9	9.	Chattanooga Choo Choo	Glenn Miller and his Orchestra
44	27	21	19	9	10.	Swinging On A Star	Bing Crosby
40	16	16	16	9	11.	Only Forever	Bing Crosby
44	19	19	15	9	12.	Shoo-Shoo Baby	Andrews Sisters
40	17	17	12	9	13.	Tuxedo Junction	Glenn Miller and his Orch.
41	24	24	18	8	14.	Piano Concerto In B Flat	Freddy Martin and his Orchestra
44	21	18	16	8	15.	Don't Fence Me In	Bing Crosby and the Andrews Sisters
41	15	15	14	8	16.	Daddy	Swing and Sway with Sammy Kaye
42	13	13	12	8	17.	Jingle Jangle Jingle	Kay Kyser and his Orchestra
42	18	18	15	7	18.	(I've Got a Gal in) Kalamazoo	Glenn Miller and his Orchestra
43	18	18	15	7	19.	Sunday, Monday Or Always	Bing Crosby
44	23	21	14	7	20.	Besame Mucho (Kiss Me Much)	Jimmy Dorsey And His Orchestra
44	28	23	19	6	21.	I'll Get By (As Long As I Have You)	Harry James and his Orchestra
42	15	15	12	6	22.	Tangerine	Jimmy Dorsey And His Orchestra
44	14	13	9	6	23.	(There'll Be A) Hot Time In The Town Of Berlin (When The Yanks Go Marching In)	Bing Crosby and the Andrews Sisters
44	33	28	18	5	24.	You Always Hurt The One You Love	Mills Brothers
43	24	24	15	5	25.	There Are Such Things	Tommy Dorsey and his Orchestra
44	22	18	15	5	26.	San Fernando Valley	Bing Crosby
44	20	20	14	5	27.	My Heart Tells Me (Should I Believe My Heart?)	Glen Gray And The Casa Loma Orchestra
40	14	14	14	5	28.	The Woodpecker Song	Glenn Miller and his Orchestra
44	18	14	12	5	29.	I Love You	Bing Crosby
44	15	11	7	5	30.	Mairzy Doats	The Merry Macs
44	24	20	17	4	31.	I'll Walk Alone	Dinah Shore
44	25	20	16	4	32.	I'll Be Seeing You	Bing Crosby
42	18	18	14	4	33.	Sleepy Lagoon	Harry James and his Orchestra
43	16	16	13	4	34.	You'll Never Know	Dick Haymes
41	21	21	12	4	35.	Green Eyes (Aquellos Ojos Verdes)	Jimmy Dorsey And His Orchestra
40	12	12	9	4	36.	Sierra Sue	Bing Crosby
43	17	17	11	3	37.	In The Blue Of Evening	Tommy Dorsey and his Orchestra
43	11	11	8	3	38.	Comin' In On A Wing And A Prayer	The Song Spinners
43	11	11	8	3	39.	Taking A Chance On Love	Benny Goodman And His Orchestra
41	17	17	15	2	40.	Maria Elena	Jimmy Dorsey And His Orchestra

TOP 40 #1 SINGLES

1945-49

Peak Year	Wks Chr	Wks T10	Wks T5	Wks @ #1	Rank	Title	Artist
47	25	25	21	17	1.	**Near You**	*Francis Craig And His Orchestra*
46	23	20	17	13	2.	**The Gypsy**	*Ink Spots*
47	20	18	17	13	3.	**Heartaches**	*Ted Weems And His Orchestra*
49	22	18	17	12	4.	**Riders In The Sky (A Cowboy Legend)**	*Vaughn Monroe and his Orchestra*
46	20	16	16	11	5.	**Oh! What It Seemed To Be**	*Frankie Carle and his Orchestra*
47	22	21	18	10	6.	**Ballerina**	*Vaughn Monroe and his Orchestra*
48	25	19	17	10	7.	**Buttons And Bows**	*Dinah Shore and her Happy Valley Boys*
45	20	18	17	10	8.	**Rum And Coca-Cola**	*Andrews Sisters*
45	19	17	16	10	9.	**Till The End Of Time**	*Perry Como*
45	28	27	21	9	10.	**Sentimental Journey**	*Les Brown and his Orchestra*
48	21	19	19	9	11.	**Mañana (Is Soon Enough For Me)**	*Peggy Lee*
46	18	16	14	9	12.	**Rumors Are Flying**	*Frankie Carle and his Orchestra*
46	25	22	18	8	13.	**To Each His Own**	*Eddy Howard And His Orchestra*
46	21	18	17	8	14.	**The Gypsy**	*Dinah Shore*
48	32	23	16	8	15.	**Twelfth Street Rag**	*Pee Wee Hunt And His Orchestra*
45	19	18	16	8	16.	**On The Atchison, Topeka And Santa Fe**	*Johnny Mercer*
49	22	17	16	8	17.	**That Lucky Old Sun**	*Frankie Laine*
48	18	15	14	8	18.	**Nature Boy**	*King Cole*
47	26	24	13	8	19.	**Peg O' My Heart**	*The Harmonicats*
46	17	14	13	8	20.	**Oh! What It Seemed To Be**	*Frank Sinatra*
49	21	17	15	7	21.	**A Little Bird Told Me**	*Evelyn Knight*
49	22	17	14	7	22.	**Cruising Down The River**	*Russ Morgan And His Orchestra*
46	17	15	14	7	23.	**The Old Lamp-Lighter**	*Swing and Sway with Sammy Kaye*
49	20	16	13	7	24.	**Cruising Down The River**	*Blue Barron and his Orchestra*
45	16	13	12	7	25.	**My Dreams Are Getting Better All The Time**	*Les Brown and his Orchestra*
48	23	17	11	7	26.	**You Can't Be True, Dear**	*Ken Griffin at the Organ*
45	29	23	16	6	27.	**There! I've Said It Again**	*Vaughn Monroe and his Orchestra*
48	24	20	16	6	28.	**You Call Everybody Darlin'**	*Al Trace And His New Orchestra*
45	20	17	14	6	29.	**I Can't Begin To Tell You**	*Bing Crosby with Carmen Cavallaro At The Piano*
46	25	18	13	6	30.	**(I Love You) For Sentimental Reasons**	*The King Cole Trio*
47	15	15	13	6	31.	**Peg O' My Heart**	*Buddy Clark*
49	13	12	11	6	32.	**Mule Train**	*Frankie Laine and the Muleskinners*
47	17	15	10	6	33.	**Smoke! Smoke! Smoke! (That Cigarette)**	*Tex Williams And His Western Caravan*
48	15	13	9	6	34.	**Woody Wood-Pecker**	*Kay Kyser and his Orchestra*
49	26	19	17	5	35.	**Some Enchanted Evening**	*Perry Como*
48	23	18	16	5	36.	**A Tree In The Meadow**	*Margaret Whiting*
48	18	16	14	5	37.	**I'm Looking Over A Four Leaf Clover**	*Art Mooney And His Orchestra*
48	24	21	13	5	38.	**Love Somebody**	*Doris Day and Buddy Clark*
46	14	13	9	5	39.	**Let It Snow! Let It Snow! Let It Snow!**	*Vaughn Monroe and his Orchestra*
49	26	20	17	4	40.	**You're Breaking My Heart**	*Vic Damone*

TOP 40 #1 SINGLES

1950-54

Peak Year	Wks Chr	Wks T10	Wks T5	Wks @ #1	Rank	Title	Artist
50	26	21	19	13	1.	The Tennessee Waltz	Patti Page
50	25	20	19	13	2.	Goodnight Irene	Gordon Jenkins and his Orchestra and The Weavers
52	25	22	17	12	3.	You Belong To Me	Jo Stafford
53	31	26	23	11	4.	Vaya Con Dios (May God Be With You)	Les Paul and Mary Ford
51	27	22	18	11	5.	Cry	Johnnie Ray & The Four Lads
50	27	20	17	11	6.	"The Third Man" Theme	Anton Karas
50	27	20	17	11	7.	The 3rd Man Theme	Guy Lombardo And His Royal Canadians
51	32	24	20	10	8.	Because Of You	Tony Bennett
52	25	19	17	10	9.	Wheel Of Fortune	Kay Starr
53	24	19	16	10	10.	The Song From Moulin Rouge (Where Is Your Heart)	Percy Faith & his Orch.
52	22	18	16	10	11.	I Went To Your Wedding	Patti Page
50	16	13	12	10	12.	If I Knew You Were Comin' (I'd've Baked A Cake)	Eileen Barton
54	26	20	17	9	13.	Little Things Mean A Lot	Kitty Kallen
51	25	20	16	9	14.	How High The Moon	Les Paul and Mary Ford
54	20	18	15	9	15.	Sh-Boom	The Crew-Cuts
52	21	15	13	9	16.	Auf Wiederseh'n Sweetheart	Vera Lynn And Chorus
53	31	27	23	8	17.	You You You	Ames Brothers
50	27	22	21	8	18.	Mona Lisa	Nat "King" Cole
54	22	19	18	8	19.	Wanted	Perry Como
53	25	18	17	8	20.	Rags To Riches	Tony Bennett
51	24	19	16	8	21.	Sin	Eddy Howard And His Orchestra
51	24	19	15	8	22.	If	Perry Como
53	21	18	15	8	23.	The Doggie In The Window	Patti Page
51	20	16	14	8	24.	Come On-a My House	Rosemary Clooney
54	19	17	13	8	25.	Oh! My Pa-Pa (O Mein Papa)	Eddie Fisher
50	16	15	12	8	26.	Chattanoogie Shoe Shine Boy	Red Foley
53	24	19	18	7	27.	Till I Waltz Again With You	Teresa Brewer
53	25	20	16	7	28.	I'm Walking Behind You	Eddie Fisher
54	24	20	16	7	29.	Make Love To Me!	Jo Stafford
52	20	17	14	7	30.	Kiss Of Fire	Georgia Gibbs
54	20	16	13	7	31.	Mr. Sandman	The Chordettes
51	27	21	17	6	32.	Cold, Cold Heart	Tony Bennett
54	27	20	16	6	33.	Hey There	Rosemary Clooney
52	23	20	16	6	34.	Why Don't You Believe Me	Joni James
52	38	26	20	5	35.	Blue Tango	Leroy Anderson "Pops" Concert Orchestra
51	29	23	20	5	36.	Too Young	Nat "King" Cole
50	25	20	16	5	37.	I Can Dream, Can't I?	Andrews Sisters
53	21	18	15	5	38.	Don't Let The Stars Get In Your Eyes	Perry Como
50	23	18	12	5	39.	All My Love (Bolero)	Patti Page
50	15	12	11	5	40.	The Thing	Phil Harris

TOP POPular RECORDINGS

TOP INSTRUMENTAL

PEAK YEAR	WKS CHR	WKS T10	WKS T5	PEAK POS	RANK	TITLE	ARTIST
40	28	28	19	1 [13]	1.	In The Mood	Glenn Miller and his Orch.
40	23	23	17	1 [13]	2.	Frenesi	Artie Shaw and his Orchestra
47	20	18	17	1 [13]	3.	Heartaches	Ted Weems And His Orchestra
50	27	20	17	1 [11]	4.	"The Third Man" Theme	Anton Karas
50	27	20	17	1 [11]	5.	The 3rd Man Theme	Guy Lombardo And His Royal Canadians
40	17	17	12	1 [9]	6.	Tuxedo Junction	Glenn Miller and his Orch.
41	24	24	18	1 [8]	7.	Piano Concerto In B Flat	Freddy Martin and his Orch.
48	32	23	16	1 [8]	8.	Twelfth Street Rag	Pee Wee Hunt And His Orchestra
47	26	24	13	1 [8]	9.	Peg O' My Heart	The Harmonicats
52	38	26	20	1 [5]	10.	Blue Tango	Leroy Anderson "Pops" Concert Orchestra
42	18	18	14	1 [4]	11.	Sleepy Lagoon	Harry James and his Orchestra
47	19	18	13	1 [3]	12.	Peg O' My Heart	The Three Suns

TOP NOVELTY

PEAK YEAR	WKS CHR	WKS T10	WKS T5	PEAK POS	RANK	TITLE	ARTIST
53	21	18	15	1 [8]	1.	The Doggie In The Window	Patti Page
47	17	15	10	1 [6]	2.	Smoke! Smoke! Smoke! (That Cigarette)	...Tex Williams And His Western Caravan
48	15	13	9	1 [6]	3.	Woody Wood-Pecker	Kay Kyser and his Orchestra
50	15	12	11	1 [5]	4.	The Thing	Phil Harris
44	15	11	7	1 [5]	5.	Mairzy Doats	The Merry Macs
53	10	9	6	1 [4]	6.	St. George And The Dragonet	Stan Freberg
48	8	6	6	1 [3]	7.	All I Want For Christmas (Is My Two Front Teeth)	...Spike Jones & his City Slickers
52	19	16	13	1 [2]	8.	It's In The Book (Parts 1 & 2)	Johnny Standley
47	15	14	10	1 [2]	9.	Huggin' And Chalkin'	Hoagy Carmichael
52	5	4	3	1 [2]	10.	I Saw Mommy Kissing Santa Claus	Jimmy Boyd
47	15	13	9	1 [1]	11.	Temptation (Tim-Tayshun)	Red Ingle & The Natural Seven
47	8	7	4	1 [1]	12.	Open The Door, Richard	The Three Flames

TOP CHRISTMAS

PEAK YEAR	WKS CHR	WKS T10	WKS T5	PEAK POS	RANK	TITLE	ARTIST
42	54	36	23	1 [14]	1.	White Christmas	Bing Crosby
45	14	13	9	1 [5]	2.	Let It Snow! Let It Snow! Let It Snow!	Vaughn Monroe and his Orchestra
48	8	6	6	1 [3]	3.	All I Want For Christmas (Is My Two Front Teeth)	Spike Jones & his City Slickers
52	5	4	3	1 [2]	4.	I Saw Mommy Kissing Santa Claus	Jimmy Boyd
49	17	9	7	1 [1]	5.	Rudolph, The Red-Nosed Reindeer	Gene Autry
43	5	5	3	3 [2]	6.	I'll Be Home For Christmas (If Only In My Dreams)	Bing Crosby
46	7	5	1	3 [1]	7.	The Christmas Song (Merry Christmas To You)	The King Cole Trio
52	3	3	2	4 [1]	8.	I Saw Mommy Kissing Santa Claus	Spike Jones & his City Slickers
53	5	4	1	4 [1]	9.	Santa Baby	Eartha Kitt
46	1	1	1	4 [1]	10.	Winter Wonderland	Johnny Mercer
49	5	3	2	5 [2]	11.	I Yust Go Nuts At Christmas	Yogi Yorgesson
41	2	2	1	5 [1]	12.	Jingle Bells	Glenn Miller and his Orchestra

SINGLES OF LONGEVITY

Singles with 26 or more total weeks charted.

PK YR	PK WKS	PK POS	WKS CHR	RANK	TITLE	ARTIST
42	14	1	54	1.	White Christmas .... *charted in eleven Christmas seasons*	*Bing Crosby*
52	5	1	38	2.	Blue Tango	*Leroy Anderson "Pops" Concert Orchestra*
51	1	1	34	3.	Be My Love	*Mario Lanza*
51	2	3	34	4.	The Loveliest Night Of The Year	*Mario Lanza*
44	5	1	33	5.	You Always Hurt The One You Love	*Mills Brothers*
51	10	1	32	6.	Because Of You	*Tony Bennett*
48	8	1	32	7.	Twelfth Street Rag	*Pee Wee Hunt And His Orchestra*
53	11	1	31	8.	Vaya Con Dios (May God Be With You)	*Les Paul and Mary Ford*
53	8	1	31	9.	You You You	*Ames Brothers*
43	12	1	30	10.	Paper Doll	*Mills Brothers*
48	2	2	30	11.	My Happiness	*Jon and Sondra Steele*
52	2	2	30	12.	Any Time	*Eddie Fisher*
51	3	3	30	13.	I Get Ideas	*Tony Martin*
48	1	3	30	14.	Maybe You'll Be There	*Gordon Jenkins And His Orchestra*
45	6	1	29	15.	There! I've Said It Again	*Vaughn Monroe and his Orchestra*
51	5	1	29	16.	Too Young	*Nat "King" Cole*
40	13	1	28	17.	In The Mood	*Glenn Miller and his Orch.*
45	9	1	28	18.	Sentimental Journey	*Les Brown and his Orchestra*
44	6	1	28	19.	I'll Get By (As Long As I Have You)	*Harry James and his Orchestra*
51	11	1	27	20.	Cry	*Johnnie Ray & The Four Lads*
50	11	1	27	21.	"The Third Man" Theme	*Anton Karas*
50	11	1	27	22.	The 3rd Man Theme	*Guy Lombardo And His Royal Canadians*
44	9	1	27	23.	Swinging On A Star	*Bing Crosby*
50	8	1	27	24.	Mona Lisa	*Nat "King" Cole*
51	6	1	27	25.	Cold, Cold Heart	*Tony Bennett*
54	6	1	27	26.	Hey There	*Rosemary Clooney*
50	4	1	27	27.	Harbor Lights	*Swing And Sway with Sammy Kaye*
54	3	1	27	28.	This Ole House	*Rosemary Clooney*
52	3	1	27	29.	Half As Much	*Rosemary Clooney*
50	1	1	27	30.	Sentimental Me	*Ames Brothers*
50	1	2	27	31.	There's No Tomorrow	*Tony Martin*
55	1	2	27	32.	Melody Of Love	*Billy Vaughn and his Orchestra*
48	2	3	27	33.	My Happiness	*The Pied Pipers*
50	2	4	27	34.	Bonaparte's Retreat	*Kay Starr*
54	2	7	27	35.	Shake, Rattle And Roll	*Bill Haley And His Comets*
48	2	13	27	36.	Bouquet Of Roses	*Eddy Arnold and his Tennessee Plowboys*
50	13	1	26	37.	The Tennessee Waltz	*Patti Page*
54	9	1	26	38.	Little Things Mean A Lot	*Kitty Kallen*
47	8	1	26	39.	Peg O' My Heart	*The Harmonicats*
49	5	1	26	40.	Some Enchanted Evening	*Perry Como*
49	4	1	26	41.	You're Breaking My Heart	*Vic Damone*
49	3	1	26	42.	Forever And Ever	*Russ Morgan And His Orchestra*
49	5	4	26	43.	Jealous Heart	*Al Morgan*
49	1	12	26	44.	Blue Skirt Waltz	*Frankie Yankovic and his Yanks with The Marlin Sisters*

SONGS WITH LONGEST TITLES

# of Char.	Title	Artist
90	I've Been Waitin' For Your Phone Call For Eighteen Years (Maybe You Don't Love Me Anymore)	Beatrice Kay
89	Rachmaninoff: The Eighteenth Variation (from the Rhapsody on a Theme of Paganini, Op. 43)	William Kapell
83	(As Long As You're Not In Love With Anyone Else) Why Don't You Fall In Love With Me	Dinah Shore
		Johnny Long And His Orchestra
		Dick Jurgens and his Orchestra
78	(There'll Be A) Hot Time In The Town Of Berlin (When The Yanks Go Marching In)	Bing Crosby and the Andrews Sisters
76	Put 'Em In A Box, Tie 'Em With A Ribbon (And Throw 'Em In The Deep Blue Sea)	Eddy Howard
		The King Cole Trio
76	Show Me The Way To Get Out Of This World ('Cause That's Where Everything Is)	Peggy Lee
74	Too Fat Polka (I Don't Want Her) (You Can Have Her) (She's Too Fat For Me)	Arthur Godfrey
72	Money Is The Root Of All Evil (Take It Away, Take It Away, Take It Away)	
		Andrews Sisters and Guy Lombardo And His Royal Canadians
69	How Many Hearts Have You Broken (With Those Great Big Beautiful Eyes)	Tiny Hill And His Orchestra
69	The Red We Want Is The Red We've Got (In the Old Red, White and Blue)	Ralph Flanagan and his Orchestra

SONGS WITH MOST CHARTED VERSIONS

Total Versions*	Title	Songwriter(s)
9	You Call Everybody Darlin'	Ben Trace-Sam Martin-Clem Watts
8	Bewitched	Lorenz Hart-Richard Rodgers
8	Cruising Down The River	Eily Beadell-Nell Tollerton
8	I'll Walk Alone	Jule Styne-Sammy Cahn
8	If	Robert Hargreaves-Tolchard Evans-Stanley Damerell
8	Intermezzo	Heinz Provost-Robert Henning
8	My Heart Cries For You	Carl Sigman-Percy Faith
8	You Can't Be True, Dear	Ken Griffin-Hal Cotton-Hans Otten
7	Again	Dorcas Cochran-Lionel Newman
7	Because Of You	Arthur Hammerstein-Dudley Wilkinson
7	Blues In The Night	Harold Arlen-Johnny Mercer
7	Can Anyone Explain? (No, No, No!)	Bennie Benjamin-George Weiss
7	Charmaine	Erno Rapee-Lew Pollack
7	Down Yonder	L. Wolfe Gilbert
7	Hair Of Gold, Eyes Of Blue	Sunny Skylar
7	Harbor Lights	Jimmy Kennedy-Hugh Williams (Will Grosz)
7	La Vie En Rose	Mack David (English)-Edith Piaf (French)-Louiguy
7	Mam'selle	Mack Gordon-Edmund Goulding
7	Mona Lisa	Jay Livingston-Ray Evans
7	Now Is The Hour (Maori Farewell Song)	Maewa Kaihant-Clement Scott-Dorothy Stewart
7	On A Slow Boat To China	Frank Loesser
7	Open The Door, Richard	Jack McVea-Don Howell
7	Rag Mop	Deacon Anderson-Johnnie Lee Wills
7	Room Full Of Roses	Tim and Glenn Spencer
7	Rumors Are Flying	George Weiss-Bennie Benjamin
7	Slow Poke	Pee Wee King-Chilton Price
7	Some Enchanted Evening	Richard Rodgers-Oscar Hammerstein II
7	Tennessee Waltz, The	Pee Wee King-Redd Stewart
7	Tree In The Meadow, A	Billy Reid
7	White Christmas	Irving Berlin

*Total does not include re-entries of the same version by an artist; however, new versions are counted.

MVP'S (Most Valuable Platters)

Following is a list of singles in this book valued at $40 or more.

YEAR	VALUE	TITLE	ARTIST
51	$500	1. Sixty Minute Man	The Dominoes
48	$200	2. It's Too Soon To Know	The Orioles
55	$150	3. Earth Angel (Will You Be Mine)	The Penguins
54	$125	4. Sh-Boom	The Chords
54	$125	5. Gee	The Crows
55	$100	6. Hearts Of Stone	The Charms
47	$100	7. I Love You (For Sentimental Reasons)	Art Kassel And His Orchestra
53	$100	8. Crying In The Chapel	The Orioles
53	$75	9. Crazy Man, Crazy	Bill Haley With Haley's Comets
49	$75	10. Drinkin' Wine Spo-Dee-O-Dee	"Stick" McGhee and His Buddies
51	$75	11. I'm Waiting Just For You	Lucky Millinder And His Orchestra
43	$75	12. Night And Day	Frank Sinatra
54	$60	13. Ling, Ting, Tong	The Five Keys
44	$60	14. Fellow On A Furlough	Albert Sack and his Orchestra
52	$60	15. Hambone	Red Saunders & his Orch.
44	$50	16. Mexico Joe	Ivie Anderson with Ceele Burke's Orch.
50	$50	17. If I Knew You Were Comin' (I'd've Baked A Cake)	Eileen Barton
41	$50	18. Joltin' Joe DiMaggio	Les Brown and his Orchestra
49	$50	19. Did You See Jackie Robinson Hit That Ball?	Buddy Johnson And His Orchestra
47	$50	20. Chi-Baba Chi-Baba (My Bambino Go To Sleep)	The Charioteers
49	$50	21. A Kiss And A Rose	The Charioteers
47	$50	22. Open The Door, Richard	The Charioteers
46	$50	23. On The Boardwalk (In Atlantic City)	The Charioteers
48	$50	24. Now Is The Hour (Maori Farewell Song)	Buddy Clark and The Charioteers
43	$50	25. Comin' In On A Wing And A Prayer	The Four Vagabonds
53	$50	26. Christmas Dragnet (Parts I & II)	Stan Freberg
45	$50	27. Don't Forget Tonight Tomorrow	Frank Sinatra and The Charioteers
49	$50	28. A Little Bird Told Me	Paula Watson
49	$50	29. Lovesick Blues	Hank Williams With His Drifting Cowboys
41	$40	30. Boogie Woogie Bugle Boy	Andrews Sisters
44	$40	31. Cryin' The Boogie Blues	Will Bradley and his Boogie Woogie Boys
51	$40	32. Wondrous Word (of the Lord)	Ken Carson
40	$40	33. I Miss You So	The Cats and the Fiddle
51	$40	34. Frosty The Snow Man	Nat "King" Cole
46	$40	35. Just A-Sittin' And A-Rockin'	Delta Rhythm Boys
52	$40	36. I Went To Your Wedding	Steve Gibson and the Original Red Caps featuring Damita Jo
52	$40	37. Cry	The Four Knights
51	$40	38. (It's No) Sin	The Four Knights
51	$40	39. I Love The Sunshine Of Your Smile	The Four Knights
54	$40	40. Marie	The Four Tunes
54	$40	41. I Understand Just How You Feel	The Four Tunes
53	$40	42. St. George And The Dragonet	Stan Freberg
53	$40	43. Little Blue Riding Hood	Stan Freberg
53	$40	44. Crying In The Chapel	Darrell Glenn
49	$40	45. Don't Cry Joe (Let Her Go, Let Her Go, Let Her Go)	Juanita Hall
48	$40	46. I Love You Yes I Do	Bull Moose Jackson and his Buffalo Bearcats
45	$40	47. The Honeydripper (Parts 1 and 2)	Joe Liggins And His Honeydrippers
46	$40	48. Got A Right To Cry	Joe Liggins And His Honeydrippers
52	$40	49. I May Hate Myself In The Morning	Bette McLaurin and Her Friends
47	$40	50. Open The Door Richard!	Jack McVea And His All Stars
52	$40	51. Jambalaya (On The Bayou)	Hank Williams

ACADEMY AWARD-WINNING SONGS

Year	Best Song	Movie	Songwriter(s)
1940	When You Wish Upon A Star	Pinocchio	Ned Washington/Leigh Harline
1941	The Last Time I Saw Paris	Lady Be Good	Oscar Hammerstein II/Jerome Kern
1942	White Christmas	Holiday Inn	Irving Berlin
1943	You'll Never Know	Hello Frisco, Hello	Mack Gordon/Harry Warren
1944	Swinging On A Star	Going My Way	Johnny Burke/Jimmy Van Heusen
1945	It Might As Well Be Spring	State Fair	Oscar Hammerstein II/Richard Rodgers
1946	On The Atchison, Topeka & Santa Fe	The Harvey Girls	Johnny Mercer/Harry Warren
1947	Zip-A-Dee-Doo-Dah	Song of the South	Ray Gilbert/Allie Wrubel
1948	Buttons And Bows	The Paleface	Ray Evans/Jay Livingston
1949	Baby, It's Cold Outside	Neptune's Daughter	Frank Loesser
1950	Mona Lisa	Captain Carey, U.S.A.	Ray Evans/Jay Livingston
1951	In The Cool Cool Cool Of The Evening	Here Comes the Groom	Johnny Mercer/Hoagy Carmichael
1952	High Noon	High Noon	Ned Washington/Dimitri Tiomkin
1953	Secret Love	Calamity Jane	Paul Francis Webster/Sammy Fain
1954	Three Coins In The Fountain	Three Coins in the Fountain	Sammy Cahn/Jule Styne

YEAR-BY-YEAR SYNOPSIS

Year	Total Ranked Hits	Wks @ #1	#1 Hit	#1 Artist
1940	153	13	In The Mood...Glenn Miller and his Orch.	Glenn Miller
1941	199	10	Amapola (Pretty Little Poppy)...Jimmy Dorsey And His Orchestra	Glenn Miller
1942	150	11	White Christmas...Bing Crosby	Glenn Miller
1943	99	13	I've Heard That Song Before...Harry James and his Orchestra	Bing Crosby
1944	246	9	Swinging On A Star...Bing Crosby	Bing Crosby
1945	243	10	Rum And Coca-Cola...Andrews Sisters	Bing Crosby
1946	249	13	The Gypsy...Ink Spots	Bing Crosby
1947	196	17	Near You...Francis Craig and His Orchestra	Eddy Howard
1948	215	10	Buttons And Bows...Dinah Shore and her Happy Valley Boys	Andrews Sisters
1949	311	12	Riders In The Sky (A Cowboy Legend)...Vaughn Monroe and his Orchestra	Perry Como
1950	332	13	The Tennessee Waltz..Patti Page	Bing Crosby
1951	310	11	Cry...Johnnie Ray & The Four Lads	Les Paul & Mary Ford
1952	269	12	You Belong To Me...Jo Stafford	Eddie Fisher
1953	172	11	Vaya Con Dios (May God Be With You)...Les Paul and Mary Ford	Perry Como
1954	154	9	Little Things Mean A Lot...Kitty Kallen	Eddie Fisher

Total: 3,298

TOP RECORD LABELS

		Total Hits
1.	Decca	836
2.	RCA Victor	699
3.	Columbia	653
4.	Capitol	530
5.	Mercury	218
6.	Bluebird	153
7.	MGM	90
8.	Coral	75
9.	Okeh	51
10.	London	44
11.	Majestic	29
12.	Hit	24
13.	Dot	16
14.	King	11
15.	National	9
16.	Vocalion	9
17.	Musicraft	8
18.	Signature	8
19.	ARA	7
20.	Cadence	5
21.	Derby	5
22.	Rondo	5
23.	Tower	5

Sample of multiple pop singles charts (6/6/53)

The Billboard Music Popularity Charts . . . **for Week Ending May 30**

TOP POPULAR RECORDS

Best Selling Singles

Records are ranked in order of their current national selling importance at the retail level. Results are based on The Billboard's weekly survey among the nation's top volume pop record dealers representing every important market area. The reverse side of each record is also listed.

This Week		Last Week	Weeks on Chart
1.	SONG FROM MOULIN ROUGE— P. Faith Swedish Rhapsody—Col 39944—BMI	1	10
2.	APRIL IN PORTUGAL—L. Baxter Suddenly—Cap 2374—ASCAP	2	10
3.	I'M WALKING BEHIND YOU— E. Fisher-H. Winterhalter Just Another Polka—V 20-5293—ASCAP	4	5
4.	RUBY—R. Hayman Love Mood—Mercury 70115—ASCAP	3	9
5.	SAY YOU'RE MINE AGAIN— Perry Como My One and Only Heart—V 20-5277—ASCAP	7	7
6.	ANNA—S. Mangano I Loved You—M-G-M 11457—BMI	8	9
7.	I BELIEVE—F. Laine Your Cheatin' Heart—Col 39938—ASCAP	6	16
8.	DOGGIE IN THE WINDOW—P. Page My Jealous Eyes—Mercury 70070—ASCAP	5	19
9.	PRETEND—Nat (King) Cole Don't Let Your Eyes Go Shopping— Cap 2346—ASCAP	9	17
10.	THE HO HO SONG—Red Buttons Strange Things Are Happening— Col 39981—ASCAP	10	6
11.	LIMELIGHT (Terry's Theme)— F. Chacksfield Limelight (Ballet Music)—London 1342—ASCAP	19	2
12.	RUBY—L. Baxter Little Love—Cap 2457—ASCAP	20	2
13.	I BELIEVE—J. Froman Ghost of a Rose—Cap 2332—ASCAP	11	6
14.	SEVEN LONELY DAYS—G. Gibbs If You Take My Heart Away— Mercury 70095—ASCAP	12	13
15.	APRIL IN PORTUGAL—R. Hayman Anna—Mercury 70114—ASCAP	13	6
16.	APRIL IN PORTUGAL—V. Damone— I'm Walking Behind You— Mercury 70128—ASCAP	—	1
17.	SONG FROM MOULIN ROUGE— Mantovani Vola Colomba—London 1328—BMI	16	3
18.	CRAZY MAN CRAZY— B. Haley's Comets What 'Cha Gonna Do?—Essex 321—BMI	17	3
19.	I'D RATHER DIE YOUNG—Hilltoppers— I Love You—Dot 15085—ASCAP	—	1
20.	RUBY—Victor Young Song From Moulin Rouge—Dec 28675—ASCAP	—	1

Most Played in Juke Boxes

Records are ranked in order of the greatest number of plays in juke boxes throut the country. Results are based on The Billboard's weekly survey among the nation's juke box operators. The reverse side of each record is also listed.

This Week		Last Week	Weeks on Chart
1.	SONG FROM MOULIN ROUGE— P. Faith Swedish Rhapsody—Col 39944—BMI	1	6
2.	I'M WALKING BEHIND YOU— E. Fisher-H. Winterhalter Just Another Polka—V 20-5293—ASCAP	6	5
3.	APRIL IN PORTUGAL—L. Baxter Suddenly—Cap 2374—ASCAP	2	7
4.	SAY YOU'RE MINE AGAIN— P. Como My One and Only Heart—V 20-5277—BMI	4	6
5.	SEVEN LONELY DAYS—G. Gibbs If You Take My Heart Away— Mercury 70095—ASCAP	7	13
6.	I BELIEVE—F. Laine Your Cheatin' Heart—Col 39938—ASCAP	4	13
7.	PRETEND—Nat (King) Cole Don't Let Your Eyes Go Shopping— Cap 2346—ASCAP	8	16
8.	YOUR CHEATIN' HEART—Joni James I'll Be Waiting for You—M-G-M 11426—BMI	9	16
9.	DOGGIE IN THE WINDOW—Patti Page My Jealous Eyes—Mercury 70070—ASCAP	3	18
10.	ALMOST ALWAYS—J. James Is It Any Wonder?—M-G-M 11470—ASCAP	11	6
11.	ANNA—S. Mangano I Loved You—M-G-M 11457—BMI	10	4
12.	HO HO SONG—R. Buttons Strange Things Are Happening— Col 39981—ASCAP	13	3
13.	RUBY—R. Hayman Love Mood—Mercury 70115—ASCAP	15	2
14.	CRAZY MAN CRAZY— B. Haley's Comets What 'Cha Gonna Do?—Essex 321—BMI	15	3
15.	APRIL IN PORTUGAL—V. Damone— I'm Walking Behind You— Mercury 70128—ASCAP	—	1
16.	RUBY—L. Baxter Little Love—Cap 2457—ASCAP	13	3
17.	ORGAN GRINDER'S SWING— Four Aces Honey in the Horn—Dec 28691—ASCAP	—	1
17.	I'D RATHER DIE YOUNG—Hilltoppers— I Love You—Dot 15085—ASCAP	—	1
19.	THAT HOUND DOG IN THE WINDOW—Homer & Jethro Pore Ol' Koo-Liger—V 20-5280—ASCAP	—	1
19.	HALF A PHOTOGRAPH—K. Starr Allez-Vous-En—Cap 2464—BMI	—	1

Most Played by Jockeys

Records are ranked in order of the greatest number of plays on disk jockey radio shows throut the country. Results are based on The Billboard's weekly survey among the nation's disk jockeys. The reverse side of each record is also listed.

This Week		Last Week	Weeks on Chart
1.	SONG FROM MOULIN ROUGE— P. Faith Swedish Rhapsody—Col 39944—BMI	1	7
2.	I'M WALKING BEHIND YOU— E. Fisher-H. Winterhalter Just Another Polka—V 20-5293—ASCAP	6	4
3.	I BELIEVE—F. Laine Your Cheatin' Heart—Col 39938—ASCAP	3	14
4.	APRIL IN PORTUGAL—L. Baxter Suddenly—Cap 2374—ASCAP	2	9
5.	RUBY—R. Hayman Love Mood—Mercury 70115—ASCAP	4	8
6.	SAY YOU'RE MINE AGAIN— Perry Como My One and Only Heart—V 20-5277—ASCAP	7	6
7.	SEVEN LONELY DAYS—G. Gibbs If You Take My Heart Away— Mercury 70095—ASCAP	5	12
8.	RUBY—L. Baxter Little Love—Cap 2457—ASCAP	13	3
9.	SONG FROM MOULIN ROUGE— Mantovani Vola Colomba—London 1328—BMI	15	4
10.	DOGGIE IN THE WINDOW—P. Page My Jealous Eyes—Mercury 70070—ASCAP	8	17
11.	PRETEND—Nat (King) Cole Don't Let Your Eyes Go Shopping— Cap 2346—ASCAP	9	14
12.	I'M WALKING BEHIND YOU— F. Sinatra Lean Baby—Cap 2450—ASCAP	14	4
12.	CARAVAN—R. Marterie White We Dream—Mercury 70097—ASCAP	20	12
14.	MY ONE AND ONLY HEART—F. Como.— Say You're Mine Again—V 20-5277—ASCAP	—	1
15.	ANNA—S. Mangano I Loved You—M-G-M 11457—BMI	—	3
16.	APRIL IN PORTUGAL—V. Damone— I'm Walking Behind You— Mercury 70128—ASCAP	11	5
17.	YOUR CHEATING HEART—J. James I'll Be Waiting for You—M-G-M 11426—BMI	10	15
17.	IS IT ANY WONDER?—J. James Almost Always—M-G-M 11470—ASCAP	18	4
19.	HO HO SONG—R. Buttons Strange Things Are Happening— Col 39981—ASCAP	—	1
20.	TELL ME A STORY— F. Laine-J. Boyd Little Boy and the Old Man—Col 39945—BMI	12	11

#1 SINGLES 1940-1954

This section lists, in chronological order, all 203 singles which hit #1 on *Billboard's* Pop charts from 1940 through 1954. These top hits have been researched extensively, and not only include the song title and artist, but also all featured vocalists, backing orchestras and songwriters.

A letter symbol appears in parentheses after the names of many contributing performers which indicate the following:

> **v** = featured vocalist
> **o** = backing orchestra
> **bv** = backing vocalist

As of January 8, 1944 *Billboard* began publishing more than one weekly pop singles chart. All #1 hits from these multiple pop charts are shown, and the chart designation and #1 weeks on each chart are listed beneath the record title. The chart designations are:

> **BS** = Best Sellers
> **JB** = Juke Box
> **DJ** = Disk Jockey

The date shown is the earliest date the record hit #1 on any of the pop charts. The weeks column lists the total weeks at #1, from the chart that it achieved its highest total. This total is not a combined total from the various pop charts.

Because of the multiple charts used for this research, some dates are duplicated, as certain #1 hits may have peaked on the same week on different charts. *Billboard* also showed ties at #1 on some of these charts; therefore, the total weeks for each year may calculate out to more than 52. For more information on these multiple pop charts please refer to the "Researching *Billboard's* Pop Charts" on page 11.

COLUMN HEADINGS

DATE: Date record first peaked at the #1 position

WKS: Total weeks record held the #1 position

> The <u>top hit</u> of each year is boxed out for quick reference. The top hit is determined by most weeks at the #1 position, followed by total weeks in the Top 5, Top 10, and total weeks charted.

#1 SINGLES

1940

	DATE	WKS	
1.	1/6	6	**Scatter-Brain** *Frankie Masters and his Orchestra — Frankie Masters (v)*

includes 2 weeks at #1 in 1939: 12/23 & 12/30

2. 1/13 5 **South Of The Border (Down Mexico Way)** *Shep Fields and his Rippling Rhythm — Hal Derwin (v)*

includes 4 weeks at #1 in 1939: 11/4, 11/18, 11/29 & 12/9

3. 2/10 13 **In The Mood [I]** *Glenn Miller and his Orch.*

includes 1 week at #1 in 1939: 12/16

4. 5/4 9 **Tuxedo Junction [I]** *Glenn Miller and his Orch.*

5. 7/6 5 **The Woodpecker Song** *Glenn Miller and his Orchestra — Marion Hutton (v)*

July 27, 1940: Billboard debuts Best Sellers chart

6. 7/27 12 **I'll Never Smile Again** *Tommy Dorsey and his Orchestra — Frank Sinatra and The Pied Pipers (v)*

#1 for 6 weeks on the Juke Box "Record Buying Guide"

7. 8/10 2 **Make-Believe Island** *Mitchell Ayres and his Fashions in Music — Mary Ann Mercer (v)*

8. 8/24 2 **Where Was I?** *Charlie Barnet and his Orchestra — Mary Ann McCall (v)*

9. 9/7 1 **The Breeze And I** *Jimmy Dorsey And His Orchestra — Bob Eberly (v)*

10. 9/14 4 **Sierra Sue** *Bing Crosby — John Scott Trotter (o)*

11. 10/19 9 **Only Forever** *Bing Crosby — John Scott Trotter (o)*

12. 12/21 13 **Frenesi [I]** *Artie Shaw and his Orchestra*

#6, 11 & 12: the #1 hit data is taken from *Billboard's* "Best Sellers" charts; the data for the other 1940 #1 hits is taken from *Billboard's* Juke Box "Record Buying Guide." Chart data was compiled for **all** records that made the Top 10 of these Juke Box charts from 1/6/40 through 7/20/40. This explains why some of the titles peaked before or after these dates.

1941

	DATE	WKS	
1.	3/15	1	**Song Of The Volga Boatmen [I]** *Glenn Miller and his Orchestra*

2. 3/29 10 **Amapola (Pretty Little Poppy)** *Jimmy Dorsey And His Orchestra — Bob Eberly and Helen O'Connell (v)*

3. 6/7 2 **My Sister And I** *Jimmy Dorsey And His Orchestra — Bob Eberle (v)*

4. 6/14 2 **Maria Elena** *Jimmy Dorsey And His Orchestra — Bob Eberly (v)*

5. 6/21 8 **Daddy** *Swing and Sway with Sammy Kaye — The Kaye Choir (v)*

6. 8/30 4 **Green Eyes (Aquellos Ojos Verdes)** *Jimmy Dorsey And His Orchestra — Bob Eberly and Helen O'Connell (v)*

7. 9/27 1 **Blue Champagne** *Jimmy Dorsey And His Orchestra — Bob Eberly (v)*

8. 10/4 8 **Piano Concerto In B Flat [I]** *Freddy Martin and his Orch. — Jack Fina (piano)*

1941 (cont'd)

9. 11/29 9 **Chattanooga Choo Choo** *Glenn Miller and his Orchestra — Tex Beneke and The Four Modernaires (v)*

10. 12/20 1 **Elmer's Tune** *Glenn Miller and his Orchestra — Ray Eberle and The Modernaires (v)*

1942

	DATE	WKS	
1.	2/7	2	**A String Of Pearls [I]** *Glenn Miller and his Orchestra*

2. 2/14 1 **Blues In The Night (My Mama Done Tol' Me)** *Woody Herman And His Orchestra — Woody Herman (v)*

3. 2/28 10 **Moonlight Cocktail** *Glenn Miller and his Orchestra — Ray Eberle and The Modernaires (v)*

4. 5/9 6 **Tangerine** *Jimmy Dorsey And His Orchestra — Bob Eberly and Helen O'Connell (v)*

5. 6/20 4 **Sleepy Lagoon [I]** *Harry James and his Orchestra*

6. 7/18 8 **Jingle Jangle Jingle** *Kay Kyser and his Orchestra — Harry Babbitt, Julie Conway and The Group (v)*

7. 9/12 7 **(I've Got a Gal in) Kalamazoo** *Glenn Miller and his Orchestra — Tex Beneke, Marion Hutton and The Modernaires (v)*

8. 10/31 11 **White Christmas** *Bing Crosby — Ken Darby Singers (bv)/John Scott Trotter (o)*

1943

	DATE	WKS	
1.	1/16	5	**There Are Such Things** *Tommy Dorsey and his Orchestra — Frank Sinatra and The Pied Pipers (v)*

2. 2/13 2 **I Had The Craziest Dream** *Harry James and his Orchestra — Helen Forrest (v)*

3. 3/6 13 **I've Heard That Song Before** *Harry James and his Orchestra — Helen Forrest (v)*

4. 5/29 1 **That Old Black Magic** *Glenn Miller and his Orchestra — Skip Nelson and The Modernaires (v)*

5. 6/12 3 **Taking A Chance On Love** *Benny Goodman And His Orchestra — Helen Forrest (v)*

6. 7/3 3 **Comin' In On A Wing And A Prayer** *The Song Spinners — a cappella*

7. 7/24 4 **You'll Never Know** *Dick Haymes — The Song Spinners (a cappella) (bv)*

8. 8/21 3 **In The Blue Of Evening** *Tommy Dorsey and his Orchestra — Frank Sinatra (v)*

recorded 6/17/42

9. 9/11 7 **Sunday, Monday Or Always** *Bing Crosby — Ken Darby Singers (a cappella) (bv)*

10. 10/30 1 **Pistol Packin' Mama** *Al Dexter and his Troopers — Al Dexter (v)*

11. 11/6 12 **Paper Doll** *Mills Brothers*

#1 for 1 week on first Juke Box chart

#1 SINGLES

January 8, 1944: Billboard debuts Juke Box chart

1. 1/15 **9** **Shoo-Shoo Baby**
   Andrews Sisters — Vic Schoen (o)
   JB: 9

2. 1/29 **5** **My Heart Tells Me (Should I Believe My Heart?)** *Glen Gray And The Casa Loma Orchestra — Eugenie Baird (v)*
   BS: 5

3. 3/4 **7** **Besame Mucho (Kiss Me Much)**
   Jimmy Dorsey And His Orchestra — Bob Eberly and Kitty Kallen (v)
   BS: 7 / JB: 1

4. 3/18 **5** **Mairzy Doats** *The Merry Macs*
   JB: 5

5. 4/22 **2** **It's Love-Love-Love**
   Guy Lombardo And His Royal Canadians — Skip Nelson and The Lombardo Trio (v)
   BS: 2

6. 4/29 **5** **San Fernando Valley**
   Bing Crosby — John Scott Trotter (o)
   JB: 5

7. 5/6 **5** **I Love You**
   Bing Crosby — John Scott Trotter (o)
   BS: 5 / JB: 2

8. 6/10 **6** **I'll Get By (As Long As I Have You)** *Harry James and his Orchestra — Dick Haymes (v)*
   JB: 6 / BS: 4

9. 7/1 **4** **I'll Be Seeing You**
   Bing Crosby — John Scott Trotter (o)
   BS: 4 / JB: 1

10. 8/5 **9** **Swinging On A Star** *Bing Crosby — Williams Brothers Quartet (bv)/ John Scott Trotter (o)*
    BS: 9 / JB: 8

11. 8/5 **2** **G.I. Jive** *Louis Jordan And His Tympany Five — Louis Jordan (v)*
    JB: 2

12. 10/7 **5** **You Always Hurt The One You Love**
    Mills Brothers — Doris Fisher-Allan Roberts (v)
    BS: 5

13. 10/14 **6** **(There'll Be A) Hot Time In The Town Of Berlin (When The Yanks Go Marching In)**
    Bing Crosby and the Andrews Sisters — Vic Schoen (o)
    JB: 6

14. 10/14 **4** **I'll Walk Alone**
    Dinah Shore — a cappella with chorus (v)
    BS: 4 / JB: 1

15. 12/2 **2** **Into Each Life Some Rain Must Fall**
    Ink Spots and Ella Fitzgerald — Allan Roberts - Doris Fisher (v)
    JB: 2

16. 12/9 **2** **I'm Making Believe**
    Ink Spots and Ella Fitzgerald
    BS: 2

17. 12/16 **8** **Don't Fence Me In** *Bing Crosby and the Andrews Sisters — Vic Schoen (o)*
    BS: 8 / JB: 8 / DJ: 7

January 27, 1945: Billboard debuts Disk Jockey chart

1. 2/10 **10** **Rum And Coca-Cola**
   Andrews Sisters — Vic Schoen (o)
   JB: 10 / BS: 8

2. 3/17 **2** **Ac-Cent-Tchu-Ate The Positive**
   Johnny Mercer — The Pied Pipers (bv)/ Paul Weston (o)
   DJ: 2

3. 3/31 **1** **Candy** *Johnny Mercer, Jo Stafford — The Pied Pipers (bv)/Paul Weston (o)*
   DJ: 1 / JB: 1

4. 4/7 **7** **My Dreams Are Getting Better All The Time** *Les Brown and his Orchestra — Doris Day (v)*
   BS: 7 / JB: 7 / DJ: 3

5. 4/14 **2** **I'm Beginning To See The Light**
   Harry James and his Orchestra — Kitty Kallen (v)
   DJ: 2

6. 5/5 **9** **Sentimental Journey** *Les Brown and his Orchestra — Doris Day (v)*
   BS: 9 / DJ: 7 / JB: 7

7. 5/5 **1** **Dream** *The Pied Pipers — Paul Weston (o)*
   DJ: 1

8. 5/12 **6** **There! I've Said It Again**
   Vaughn Monroe and his Orchestra — Vaughn Monroe and The Norton Sisters (v)
   DJ: 6

9. 7/28 **8** **On The Atchison, Topeka And Santa Fe**
   Johnny Mercer — The Pied Pipers (bv)/ Paul Weston (o)
   JB: 8 / BS: 7 / DJ: 6

10. 9/15 **10** **Till The End Of Time**
    Perry Como — Russell Case (o)
    BS: 10 / DJ: 9 / JB: 9

11. 11/17 **4** **Chickery Chick** *Swing and Sway with Sammy Kaye — Nancy Norman, Billy Williams and The Kaye Choir (v)*
    DJ: 4 / BS: 3 / JB: 2

12. 11/24 **3** **It's Been A Long, Long Time**
    Harry James and his Orchestra — Kitty Kallen (v)
    BS: 3 / DJ: 2

13. 12/1 **2** **It's Been A Long Long Time**
    Bing Crosby with Les Paul And His Trio
    BS: 2 / JB: 1

14. 12/22 **6** **I Can't Begin To Tell You** *Bing Crosby with Carmen Cavallaro At The Piano*
    JB: 6 / BS: 1

15. 12/29 **2** **White Christmas** *Bing Crosby — Ken Darby Singers (bv) /John Scott Trotter (o)*
    DJ: 2; first hit #1 on 10/31/42 – 11 weeks

#1 SINGLES

1. 1/5 **2** **Symphony** *Freddy Martin and his Orchestra*
   — Clyde Rogers (v)
   BS: 2 / DJ: 1

2. 1/19 **5** **Let It Snow! Let It Snow! Let It Snow!**
   Vaughn Monroe and his Orchestra —
   Vaughn Monroe and The Norton Sisters (v)
   BS: 5 / DJ: 5 / JB: 5

3. 2/9 **2** **Doctor, Lawyer, Indian Chief** *Betty Hutton*
   — Paul Weston (o)
   DJ: 2 / BS: 1

4. 3/2 **2** **Personality** *Johnny Mercer —*
   The Pied Pipers (bv)/Paul Weston (o)
   DJ: 2 / BS: 1

5. 3/16 **11** **Oh! What It Seemed To Be** *Frankie Carle*
   and his Orchestra — Marjorie Hughes (v)
   JB: 11 / BS: 6

6. 3/23 **8** **Oh! What It Seemed To Be**
   Frank Sinatra — Axel Stordahl (o)
   DJ: 8

7. 4/27 **1** **I'm A Big Girl Now** *Swing and Sway with*
   Sammy Kaye — Betty Barclay (v)
   BS: 1

8. 5/4 **3** **Prisoner Of Love**
   Perry Como — Russ Case (o)
   BS: 3 / DJ: 2

9. 5/18 **8** **The Gypsy** *Dinah Shore — Sonny Burke (o)*
   DJ: 8

10. 5/25 **13** **The Gypsy** *Ink Spots*
    JB: 13 / BS: 10 / DJ: 2

11. 8/3 **8** **To Each His Own** *Eddy Howard And*
    His Orchestra — Eddy Howard (v)
    DJ: 8 / JB: 6 / BS: 5

12. 8/3 **1** **Surrender** *Perry Como — Russ Case (o)*
    BS: 1

13. 8/31 **2** **To Each His Own** *Freddy Martin and*
    his Orchestra — Stuart Wade (v)
    BS: 2

14. 9/14 **4** **Five Minutes More**
    Frank Sinatra — Alex Stordahl (o)
    DJ: 4 / JB: 3 / BS: 2

15. 9/21 **1** **To Each His Own** *Ink Spots*
    BS: 1

16. 10/19 **9** **Rumors Are Flying** *Frankie Carle and*
    his Orchestra — Marjorie Hughes (v)
    DJ: 9 / BS: 8 / JB: 8

17. 12/14 **2** **Ole Buttermilk Sky**
    Kay Kyser and his Orchestra —
    Michael Douglas and The Campus Kids (v)
    BS: 2

18. 12/21 **7** **The Old Lamp-Lighter**
    Swing and Sway with Sammy Kaye —
    Billy Williams and Choir (v)
    BS: 7 / JB: 7 / DJ: 1

19. 12/28 **6** **(I Love You) For Sentimental Reasons**
    The King Cole Trio — Nat "King" Cole (v)
    DJ: 6 / BS: 1

20. 12/28 **1** **White Christmas** *Bing Crosby —*
    Ken Darby Singers (bv)/John Scott Trotter (o)
    DJ: 1; new version – original version first hit #1 on
    10/31/42 for 11 weeks, and on 12/29/45 for 2
    weeks

1. 2/8 **2** **Huggin' And Chalkin'** *Hoagy Carmichael —*
   The Chickadees (bv)/Vic Schoen (o)
   JB: 2

2. 2/22 **3** **Managua, Nicaragua** *Freddy Martin and his*
   Orchestra — Stuart Wade and Ensemble (v)
   JB: 3 / BS: 2

3. 2/22 **1** **Open The Door, Richard!**
   Count Basie and his Orchestra —
   Harry Edison and Bill Johnson (v)
   BS: 1 / DJ: 1

4. 3/1 **1** **Open The Door, Richard**
   The Three Flames — "Tiger" Haynes (v)
   DJ: 1

5. 3/8 **2** **Anniversary Song**
   Dinah Shore — Morris Stoloff (o)
   JB: 2

6. 3/15 **13** **Heartaches [I]**
   Ted Weems And His Orchestra —
   Elmo Tanner (whistling)
   JB: 13 / BS: 12 / DJ: 11; 2 versions by Weems
   charted together at one position: Decca
   (recorded 1938) and RCA (1933)

7. 3/15 **1** **Managua - Nicaragua**
   Guy Lombardo And His Royal Canadians —
   Don Rodney and The Lombardo Trio (v)
   BS: 1

8. 5/10 **2** **Linda** *Ray Noble and his Orchestra*
   with Buddy Clark
   DJ: 2

9. 5/31 **1** **Mam'selle** *Frank Sinatra — Axel Stordahl (o)*
   DJ: 1

10. 6/7 **2** **Mam'selle** *Art Lund — Johnny Thompson (o)*
    BS: 2

11. 6/21 **8** **Peg O' My Heart [I]** *The Harmonicats*
    JB: 8 / BS: 4

12. 6/28 **3** **Chi-Baba Chi-Baba (My Bambino Go To**
    Sleep) *Perry Como — The Satisfiers (bv)/*
    Lloyd Shaffer (o)
    BS: 3

13. 6/28 **1** **Temptation (Tim-Tayshun)** *Red Ingle & The*
    Natural Seven with Cinderella G. Stump —
    Red Ingle and Jo Stafford (v)
    DJ: 1

14. 7/5 **6** **Peg O' My Heart**
    Buddy Clark — Mitchell Ayres (o)
    DJ: 6

15. 8/9 **6** **Smoke! Smoke! Smoke! (That Cigarette)**
    Tex Williams And His Western Caravan
    BS: 6 / JB: 4 / DJ: 1

16. 8/9 **3** **Peg O' My Heart [I]** *The Three Suns*
    JB: 3 / DJ: 1

17. 8/30 **17** **Near You** *Francis Craig And His Orchestra*
    — Bob Lamm (v)/Francis Craig (piano)
    DJ: 17 / JB: 13 / BS: 12

18. 12/13 **10** **Ballerina** *Vaughn Monroe and his Orchestra*
    BS: 10 / DJ: 8 / JB: 7

#1 SINGLES

DATE	WKS	1948

1. 2/21 **5 I'm Looking Over A Four Leaf Clover**
   Art Mooney And His Orchestra —
   Ensemble (v)/Mike Pingatore (banjo)
   JB: 5 / DJ: 4 / BS: 3

2. 3/13 **9 Mañana (Is Soon Enough For Me)** *Peggy Lee*
   — Dave Barbour And The Brazilians (o-bv)
   BS: 9 / DJ: 7 / JB: 5

3. 4/24 **3 Now Is The Hour (Maori Farewell Song)**
   Bing Crosby — Ken Darby Choir (bv)
   JB: 3

4. 5/8 **8 Nature Boy** *King Cole — Frank DeVol (o)*
   DJ: 8 / BS: 7

5. 5/22 **7 You Can't Be True, Dear**
   Ken Griffin at the Organ — Jerry Wayne (v)
   JB: 7

6. 7/3 **6 Woody Wood-Pecker** *Kay Kyser and*
   his Orchestra — Gloria Wood (v)
   BS: 6 / DJ: 6 / JB: 6

7. 8/14 **6 You Call Everybody Darlin'** *Al Trace*
   And His New Orchestra — Bob Vincent (v)
   JB: 6 / BS: 2

8. 8/14 **5 Love Somebody** *Doris Day and Buddy Clark*
   — George Siravo (o)
   DJ: 5

9. 8/28 **8 Twelfth Street Rag [I]**
   Pee Wee Hunt And His Orchestra
   BS: 8 / JB: 6 / DJ: 4

10. 10/9 **5 A Tree In The Meadow** *Margaret Whiting*
    DJ: 5 / BS: 2

11. 11/6 **10 Buttons And Bows**
    Dinah Shore and her Happy Valley Boys
    BS: 10 / JB: 9 / DJ: 5

12. 12/25 **3 All I Want For Christmas (Is My Two Front**
    Teeth) *Spike Jones and his City Slickers —*
    George Rock (v)
    DJ: 3 / BS: 1

DATE	WKS	1949

1. 1/15 **7 A Little Bird Told Me**
   Evelyn Knight — The Stardusters (bv)
   BS: 7 / JB: 7 / DJ: 6

2. 1/15 **1 My Darling, My Darling**
   Jo Stafford And Gordon MacRae —
   The Starlighters (bv)
   DJ: 1

3. 3/5 **1 I've Got My Love To Keep Me Warm [I]**
   Les Brown and his Orchestra
   DJ: 1

4. 3/5 **1 Powder Your Face With Sunshine (Smile!**
   Smile! Smile!)
   Evelyn Knight — The Stardusters (bv)
   JB: 1

5. 3/12 **7 Cruising Down The River** *Blue Barron and*
   his Orchestra — Ensemble (v)
   DJ: 7 / JB: 3 / BS: 2

6. 3/26 **7 Cruising Down The River** *Russ Morgan*
   And His Orchestra — The Skylarks (v)
   BS: 7 / JB: 6

7. 4/30 **1 Careless Hands**
   Mel Tormé — Sonny Burke (o)
   DJ: 1

1949 (cont'd)

8. 5/7 **2 "A"-You're Adorable** *Perry Como —*
   The Fontane Sisters (bv)/Mitchell Ayres (o)
   DJ: 2

9. 5/14 **12 Riders In The Sky (A Cowboy Legend)**
   Vaughn Monroe and his Orchestra
   DJ: 12 / BS: 11 / JB: 10

10. 5/14 **3 Forever And Ever** *Russ Morgan And*
    His Orchestra — The Skylarks (v)
    JB: 3

11. 7/30 **5 Some Enchanted Evening**
    Perry Como — Mitchell Ayres (o)
    BS: 5 / JB: 5 / DJ: 2

12. 8/27 **4 You're Breaking My Heart**
    Vic Damone — Glenn Osser (o)
    BS: 4 / JB: 4 / DJ: 3

13. 9/10 **2 Someday** *Vaughn Monroe and his Orchestra*
    — Vaughn Monroe and The Moon Men (v)
    DJ: 2 / JB: 2

14. 10/1 **8 That Lucky Old Sun**
    Frankie Laine — Judd Conlon's Rhythmaires
    (bv)/Harry Geller (o)
    BS: 8 / DJ: 7 / JB: 5

15. 11/19 **3 Slipping Around**
    Margaret Whiting and Jimmy Wakely
    JB: 3

16. 11/26 **6 Mule Train**
    Frankie Laine and the Muleskinners
    BS: 6 / DJ: 6 / JB: 6

17. 12/31 **1 Rudolph, The Red-Nosed Reindeer**
    Gene Autry — The Pinafores (bv)
    BS: 1

DATE	WKS	1950

1. 1/7 **5 I Can Dream, Can't I?**
   Andrews Sisters — Gordon Jenkins (o)
   DJ: 5 / BS: 4 / JB: 3

2. 2/11 **8 Chattanoogie Shoe Shine Boy** *Red Foley*
   JB: 8 / BS: 4 / DJ: 2

3. 2/11 **2 Rag Mop** *Ames Brothers — Roy Ross (o)*
   DJ: 2 / BS: 1

4. 3/11 **2 The Cry Of The Wild Goose** *Frankie Laine*
   — Harry Geller (o)
   DJ: 2

5. 3/18 **4 Music! Music! Music!** *Teresa Brewer with*
   The Dixieland All Stars
   BS: 4 / JB: 1

6. 3/25 **10 If I Knew You Were Comin' (I'd've Baked A**
   Cake)
   Eileen Barton — The New Yorkers (bv)
   DJ: 10 / JB: 3 / BS: 3

7. 4/29 **11 "The Third Man" Theme [I]**
   Anton Karas — zither solo
   BS: 11

8. 5/6 **11 The 3rd Man Theme [I]**
   Guy Lombardo And His Royal Canadians —
   Don Rodney (guitar solo)
   JB: 11

9. 6/3 **2 Hoop-Dee-Doo**
   Perry Como — Mitchell Ayres (o)
   DJ: 2

#1 SINGLES

1950 (cont'd)

10. 6/10 **1** **Sentimental Me**
   Ames Brothers — Roy Ross (o)
   DJ: 1

11. 6/24 **2** **I Wanna Be Loved**
   Andrews Sisters — Gordon Jenkins (o)
   DJ: 2

12. 7/8 **8** **Mona Lisa** *Nat "King" Cole*
   DJ: 8 / BS: 5 / JB: 5

13. 8/19 **13** **Goodnight Irene** *Gordon Jenkins and his*
   Orchestra and The Weavers
   BS: 13 / JB: 12 / DJ: 8

14. 10/28 **5** **All My Love (Bolero)**
   Patti Page — Harry Geller (o)
   DJ: 5

15. 11/18 **4** **Harbor Lights**
   Swing And Sway with Sammy Kaye —
   Tony Alamo and The Kaydets (v)
   JB: 4 / BS: 2

16. 12/2 **5** **The Thing** *Phil Harris — Walter Scharf (o)*
   DJ: 5 / BS: 4 / JB: 2

17. 12/16 **13** The Tennessee Waltz
   Patti Page — Jack Rael (o)
   JB: 13 / BS: 9 / DJ: 8

DATE WKS 1951

1. 3/3 **8** **If** *Perry Como — Mitchell Ayres (o)*
   DJ: 8 / BS: 6 / JB: 5

2. 3/10 **1** **Be My Love** *Mario Lanza — Jeff Alexander*
   Choir (bv)/Ray Sinatra (conductor)
   BS: 1

3. 4/21 **9** **How High The Moon**
   Les Paul and Mary Ford — Mary Ford (v)
   BS: 9 / DJ: 9 / JB: 9

4. 6/23 **5** **Too Young** *Nat "King" Cole — Les Baxter (o)*
   BS: 5 / DJ: 4 / JB: 4

5. 7/28 **8** **Come On-a My House** *Rosemary Clooney*
   — Stan Freeman (harpsichord)
   DJ: 8 / JB: 8 / BS: 6

6. 9/8 **10** **Because Of You**
   Tony Bennett — Percy Faith (o)
   JB: 10 / BS: 8 / DJ: 8

7. 11/3 **6** **Cold, Cold Heart**
   Tony Bennett — Percy Faith (o)
   BS: 6 / JB: 3

8. 11/17 **8** **Sin** *Eddy Howard And His Orchestra —*
   Eddy Howard (v)
   DJ: 8 / BS: 2 / JB: 1

9. 12/29 **11** Cry *Johnnie Ray & The Four Lads*
   BS: 11 / DJ: 10 / JB: 9

DATE WKS 1952

1. 1/5 **3** **Slow Poke** *Pee Wee King and his Golden*
   West Cowboys — Redd Stewart (v)
   JB: 3

2. 3/15 **10** **Wheel Of Fortune**
   Kay Starr — Harold Mooney (o)
   JB: 10 / BS: 9 / DJ: 9

3. 5/17 **7** **Kiss Of Fire**
   Georgia Gibbs — Glenn Osser (o)
   DJ: 7 / JB: 6

4. 5/17 **5** **Blue Tango [I]**
   Leroy Anderson "Pops" Concert Orchestra
   BS: 5

5. 5/24 **1** **A Guy Is A Guy** *Doris Day — Paul Weston (o)*
   JB: 1

6. 6/7 **3** **Here In My Heart**
   Al Martino — Monty Kelly (o)
   BS: 3 / DJ: 3

7. 7/5 **1** **Delicado [I]** *Percy Faith & His Orch. —*
   Stan Freeman (harpsichord)
   BS: 1

8. 7/12 **9** **Auf Wiederseh'n Sweetheart**
   Vera Lynn And Chorus — Roland Shaw (o)
   BS: 9 / DJ: 6 / JB: 4

9. 7/26 **3** **Half As Much**
   Rosemary Clooney — Percy Faith (o)
   JB: 3

10. 9/6 **1** **Wish You Were Here**
   Eddie Fisher — Hugo Winterhalter (o)
   DJ: 1

11. 9/13 **12** You Belong To Me
   Jo Stafford — Paul Weston (o)
   DJ: 12 / BS: 5 / JB: 2

12. 9/27 **10** **I Went To Your Wedding**
   Patti Page — Jack Rael (o)
   JB: 10 / BS: 5 / DJ: 1

13. 11/22 **2** **It's In The Book (Parts 1 & 2)**
   Johnny Standley — Part 1: comedy
   monologue; Part 2: sing-along with Horace
   Heidt and His Musical Knights (o)
   BS: 2

14. 11/29 **6** **Why Don't You Believe Me**
   Joni James — Lew Douglas (o)
   DJ: 6 / BS: 4 / JB: 3

15. 12/6 **3** **The Glow-Worm**
   Mills Brothers — Hal McIntyre (o)
   JB: 3

16. 12/27 **2** **I Saw Mommy Kissing Santa Claus**
   Jimmy Boyd — Norman Luboff
   (accompaniment)
   BS: 2

#1 SINGLES

TOP 10 SINGLES CHARTS

A chronological listing of the Top 10 charts from every *Record Buying Guide* chart *Billboard* published from January 6, 1940 through July 20, 1940, and every *Best Sellers* chart *Billboard* published from July 27, 1940 through December 25, 1954.

KEY TO THE TOP 10 CHARTS

This section lists the 10 biggest pop hits of every week from the Big Band era up to the dawn of Rock 'n' Roll. This is a week-by-week chronology of *Billboard* magazine's *Record Buying Guide* chart from January 6, 1940, through July 20, 1940, and *Billboard's Best Sellers* chart from July 27, 1940, through December 25, 1954. See "Reseaching *Billboard's* Pop Singles Charts" on page 11 for a complete explanation of the Record Buying Guide and the Best Sellers charts.

The song title is shown as it appears on the recording. Each week's current and previous chart positions are listed, along with total weeks on the chart, the artist and original label and number.

TW: this week's chart position
LW: last week's chart position
WK: total weeks on the chart

A TITLE'S VARYING TYPE SIZE

The type size of most titles is consistent in size. In cases such as "Fools Rush In (Where Angels Fear to Tread)" by Glenn Miller, a portion of the title is a point size smaller to indicate that it appeared smaller on the label of the original recording.

TIES

From January 27, 1945 through June 26, 1954, *Billboard* showed singles tying at the same position.

Billboard ⊛ JANUARY 6, 1940 ⊛ Record Buying Guide

TW	LW	WK	Title	Artist...Label
1	1	8	Scatter-Brain	Frankie Masters...Vocalion 4915
2	2	12	South Of The Border (Down Mexico Way)	Shep Fields...Bluebird 10376
3	3	10	Oh Johnny, Oh Johnny, Oh!	Orrin Tucker...Columbia 35228
4	4	6	My Prayer	Glenn Miller...Bluebird 10404
5	6	7	Yodelin' Jive	Bing Crosby & Andrews Sisters...Decca 2800
6	5	12	In The Mood	Glenn Miller...Bluebird 10416
7	7	3	Stop! It's Wonderful	Orrin Tucker...Columbia 35249
8	—	1	Careless	Dick Jurgens...Vocalion 5235
9	—	1	Bluebirds In The Moonlight	Dick Jurgens...Vocalion 5181
10	10	2	Billy	Orrin Tucker...Vocalion 4914

Billboard ⊛ JANUARY 13, 1940 ⊛ Record Buying Guide

TW	LW	WK	Title	Artist...Label
1	2	13	South Of The Border (Down Mexico Way)	Shep Fields...Bluebird 10376
2	1	9	Scatter-Brain	Frankie Masters...Vocalion 4915
3	3	11	Oh Johnny, Oh Johnny, Oh!	Orrin Tucker...Columbia 35228
4	4	7	My Prayer	Glenn Miller...Bluebird 10404
5	6	13	In The Mood	Glenn Miller...Bluebird 10416
6	5	8	Yodelin' Jive	Bing Crosby & Andrews Sisters...Decca 2800
7	7	4	Stop! It's Wonderful	Orrin Tucker...Columbia 35249
8	8	2	Careless	Dick Jurgens...Vocalion 5235
9	—	1	The Man That Comes Around	Tommy Tucker Time...Vocalion 5199
10	—	1	All The Things You Are	Tommy Dorsey...Victor 26401

Billboard ⊛ JANUARY 20, 1940 ⊛ Record Buying Guide

TW	LW	WK	Title	Artist...Label
1	2	10	Scatter-Brain	Frankie Masters...Vocalion 4915
2	3	12	Oh Johnny, Oh Johnny, Oh!	Orrin Tucker...Columbia 35228
3	5	14	In The Mood	Glenn Miller...Bluebird 10416
4	6	9	Yodelin' Jive	Bing Crosby & Andrews Sisters...Decca 2800
5	7	5	Stop! It's Wonderful	Orrin Tucker...Columbia 35249
6	8	3	Careless	Dick Jurgens...Vocalion 5235
7	10	2	All The Things You Are	Tommy Dorsey...Victor 26401
8	—	2	The Little Red Fox (N'Ya N'Ya Ya Can't Catch Me)	Kay Kyser...Columbia 35295
9	—	1	Chatterbox	Kay Kyser...Columbia 35307
10	9	2	The Man That Comes Around	Tommy Tucker Time...Vocalion 5199

Billboard ⊛ JANUARY 27, 1940 ⊛ Record Buying Guide

TW	LW	WK	Title	Artist...Label
1	1	11	Scatter-Brain	Frankie Masters...Vocalion 4915
2	2	13	Oh Johnny, Oh Johnny, Oh!	Orrin Tucker...Columbia 35228
3	3	15	In The Mood	Glenn Miller...Bluebird 10416
4	4	10	Yodelin' Jive	Bing Crosby & Andrews Sisters...Decca 2800
5	5	6	Stop! It's Wonderful	Orrin Tucker...Columbia 35249
6	—	1	Careless	Glenn Miller...Bluebird 10520
7	7	3	All The Things You Are	Tommy Dorsey...Victor 26401
8	8	3	The Little Red Fox (N'Ya N'Ya Ya Can't Catch Me)	Kay Kyser...Columbia 35295
9	9	2	Chatterbox	Kay Kyser...Columbia 35307
10	10	3	The Man That Comes Around	Tommy Tucker Time...Vocalion 5199

Billboard ⊛ FEBRUARY 3, 1940 ⊛ Record Buying Guide

TW	LW	WK	Title	Artist...Label
1	1	12	Scatter-Brain	Frankie Masters...Vocalion 4915
2	2	14	Oh Johnny, Oh Johnny, Oh!	Orrin Tucker...Columbia 35228
3	3	16	In The Mood	Glenn Miller...Bluebird 10416
4	4	11	Yodelin' Jive	Bing Crosby & Andrews Sisters...Decca 2800
5	5	7	Stop! It's Wonderful	Orrin Tucker...Columbia 35249
6	6	2	Careless	Glenn Miller...Bluebird 10520
7	7	4	All The Things You Are	Tommy Dorsey...Victor 26401
8	8	4	The Little Red Fox (N'Ya N'Ya Ya Can't Catch Me)	Kay Kyser...Columbia 35295
9	—	1	Indian Summer	Tommy Dorsey...Victor 26390
10	10	4	The Man That Comes Around	Tommy Tucker Time...Vocalion 5199

TW	LW	WK	Billboard® FEBRUARY 10, 1940 Record Buying Guide
1	3	17	In The Mood .... *Glenn Miller*...Bluebird 10416
2	6	3	Careless .... *Glenn Miller*...Bluebird 10520
3	7	5	All The Things You Are .... *Tommy Dorsey*...Victor 26401
4	8	5	The Little Red Fox (N'Ya N'Ya Ya Can't Catch Me) .... *Kay Kyser*...Columbia 35295
5	9	2	Indian Summer .... *Tommy Dorsey*...Victor 26390
6	—	1	Faithful Forever .... *Glenn Miller*...Bluebird 10465
7	—	3	Chatterbox .... *Kay Kyser*...Columbia 35307
8	—	1	At The Balalaika .... *Orrin Tucker*...Columbia 35332
9	10	5	The Man That Comes Around .... *Tommy Tucker Time*...Vocalion 5199
10	—	1	Darn That Dream .... *Benny Goodman*...Columbia 35331

TW	LW	WK	Billboard® FEBRUARY 17, 1940 Record Buying Guide
1	1	18	In The Mood .... *Glenn Miller*...Bluebird 10416
2	2	4	Careless .... *Glenn Miller*...Bluebird 10520
3	3	6	All The Things You Are .... *Tommy Dorsey*...Victor 26401
4	5	3	Indian Summer .... *Tommy Dorsey*...Victor 26390
5	6	2	Faithful Forever .... *Glenn Miller*...Bluebird 10465
6	7	4	Chatterbox .... *Kay Kyser*...Columbia 35307
7	8	2	At The Balalaika .... *Orrin Tucker*...Columbia 35332
8	10	2	Darn That Dream .... *Benny Goodman*...Columbia 35331
9	9	6	The Man That Comes Around .... *Tommy Tucker Time*...Vocalion 5199
10	—	1	Pinch Me .... *Orrin Tucker*...Columbia 35328

TW	LW	WK	Billboard® FEBRUARY 24, 1940 Record Buying Guide
1	1	19	In The Mood .... *Glenn Miller*...Bluebird 10416
2	2	5	Careless .... *Glenn Miller*...Bluebird 10520
3	3	7	All The Things You Are .... *Tommy Dorsey*...Victor 26401
4	4	4	Indian Summer .... *Tommy Dorsey*...Victor 26390
5	5	3	Faithful Forever .... *Glenn Miller*...Bluebird 10465
6	7	3	At The Balalaika .... *Orrin Tucker*...Columbia 35332
7	—	1	You'd Be Surprised .... *Orrin Tucker*...Columbia 35344
8	—	1	The Gaucho Serenade .... *Glenn Miller*...Bluebird 10570
9	8	3	Darn That Dream .... *Benny Goodman*...Columbia 35331
10	9	7	The Man That Comes Around .... *Tommy Tucker Time*...Vocalion 5199

TW	LW	WK	Billboard® MARCH 2, 1940 Record Buying Guide
1	1	20	In The Mood .... *Glenn Miller*...Bluebird 10416
2	2	6	Careless .... *Glenn Miller*...Bluebird 10520
3	3	8	All The Things You Are .... *Tommy Dorsey*...Victor 26401
4	4	5	Indian Summer .... *Tommy Dorsey*...Victor 26390
5	6	4	At The Balalaika .... *Orrin Tucker*...Columbia 35332
6	7	2	You'd Be Surprised .... *Orrin Tucker*...Columbia 35344
7	8	2	The Gaucho Serenade .... *Glenn Miller*...Bluebird 10570
8	9	4	Darn That Dream .... *Benny Goodman*...Columbia 35331
9	—	1	In An Old Dutch Garden (By An Old Dutch Mill) .... *Dick Jurgens*...Vocalion 5263
10	—	1	Confucius Say .... *Guy Lombardo*...Decca 2917

TW	LW	WK	Billboard® MARCH 9, 1940 Record Buying Guide
1	1	21	In The Mood .... *Glenn Miller*...Bluebird 10416
2	2	7	Careless .... *Glenn Miller*...Bluebird 10520
3	4	6	Indian Summer .... *Tommy Dorsey*...Victor 26390
4	5	5	At The Balalaika .... *Orrin Tucker*...Columbia 35332
5	6	3	You'd Be Surprised .... *Orrin Tucker*...Columbia 35344
6	—	1	The Gaucho Serenade .... *Dick Todd*...Bluebird 10559
7	—	1	Tuxedo Junction .... *Glenn Miller*...Bluebird 10612
8	9	2	In An Old Dutch Garden (By An Old Dutch Mill) .... *Dick Jurgens*...Vocalion 5263
9	10	2	Confucius Say .... *Guy Lombardo*...Decca 2917
10	—	1	Darn That Dream .... *Blue Barron*...Bluebird 10525

TW	LW	WK	Billboard® 🎵 MARCH 16, 1940 🎵 Record Buying Guide
1	1	22	**In The Mood** .... *Glenn Miller...Bluebird 10416*
2	2	8	**Careless** .... *Glenn Miller...Bluebird 10520*
3	3	7	**Indian Summer** .... *Tommy Dorsey...Victor 26390*
4	4	6	**At The Balalaika** .... *Orrin Tucker...Columbia 35332*
5	5	4	**You'd Be Surprised** .... *Orrin Tucker...Columbia 35344*
6	6	2	**The Gaucho Serenade** .... *Dick Todd...Bluebird 10559*
7	7	2	**Tuxedo Junction** .... *Glenn Miller...Bluebird 10612*
8	8	3	**In An Old Dutch Garden (By An Old Dutch Mill)** .... *Dick Jurgens...Vocalion 5263*
9	9	3	**Confucius Say** .... *Guy Lombardo...Decca 2917*
10	10	2	**Darn That Dream** .... *Blue Barron...Bluebird 10525*

TW	LW	WK	Billboard® 🎵 MARCH 23, 1940 🎵 Record Buying Guide
1	1	23	**In The Mood** .... *Glenn Miller...Bluebird 10416*
2	2	9	**Careless** .... *Glenn Miller...Bluebird 10520*
3	3	8	**Indian Summer** .... *Tommy Dorsey...Victor 26390*
4	4	7	**At The Balalaika** .... *Orrin Tucker...Columbia 35332*
5	5	5	**You'd Be Surprised** .... *Orrin Tucker...Columbia 35344*
6	6	3	**The Gaucho Serenade** .... *Dick Todd...Bluebird 10559*
7	7	3	**Tuxedo Junction** .... *Glenn Miller...Bluebird 10612*
8	—	1	**In An Old Dutch Garden (By An Old Dutch Mill)** .... *Glenn Miller...Bluebird 10553*
9	—	5	**Darn That Dream** .... *Benny Goodman...Columbia 35331*
10	9	4	**Confucius Say** .... *Guy Lombardo...Decca 2917*

TW	LW	WK	Billboard® 🎵 MARCH 30, 1940 🎵 Record Buying Guide
1	1	24	**In The Mood** .... *Glenn Miller...Bluebird 10416*
2	2	10	**Careless** .... *Glenn Miller...Bluebird 10520*
3	3	9	**Indian Summer** .... *Tommy Dorsey...Victor 26390*
4	4	8	**At The Balalaika** .... *Orrin Tucker...Columbia 35332*
5	5	6	**You'd Be Surprised** .... *Orrin Tucker...Columbia 35344*
6	6	4	**The Gaucho Serenade** .... *Dick Todd...Bluebird 10559*
7	7	4	**Tuxedo Junction** .... *Glenn Miller...Bluebird 10612*
8	—	1	**On The Isle Of May** .... *Connie Boswell...Decca 3004*
9	—	1	**Say "Si Si" (Para Vigo Me Voy)** .... *Andrews Sisters...Decca 3013*
10	8	2	**In An Old Dutch Garden (By An Old Dutch Mill)** .... *Glenn Miller...Bluebird 10553*

TW	LW	WK	Billboard® 🎵 APRIL 6, 1940 🎵 Record Buying Guide
1	1	25	**In The Mood** .... *Glenn Miller...Bluebird 10416*
2	2	11	**Careless** .... *Glenn Miller...Bluebird 10520*
3	3	10	**Indian Summer** .... *Tommy Dorsey...Victor 26390*
4	4	9	**At The Balalaika** .... *Orrin Tucker...Columbia 35332*
5	5	7	**You'd Be Surprised** .... *Orrin Tucker...Columbia 35344*
6	6	5	**The Gaucho Serenade** .... *Dick Todd...Bluebird 10559*
7	7	5	**Tuxedo Junction** .... *Glenn Miller...Bluebird 10612*
8	8	2	**On The Isle Of May** .... *Connie Boswell...Decca 3004*
9	9	2	**Say "Si Si" (Para Vigo Me Voy)** .... *Andrews Sisters...Decca 3013*
10	—	1	**It's A Blue World** .... *Tony Martin...Decca 2932*

TW	LW	WK	Billboard® 🎵 APRIL 13, 1940 🎵 Record Buying Guide
1	1	26	**In The Mood** .... *Glenn Miller...Bluebird 10416*
2	3	11	**Indian Summer** .... *Tommy Dorsey...Victor 26390*
3	4	10	**At The Balalaika** .... *Orrin Tucker...Columbia 35332*
4	6	6	**The Gaucho Serenade** .... *Dick Todd...Bluebird 10559*
5	7	6	**Tuxedo Junction** .... *Glenn Miller...Bluebird 10612*
6	—	1	**When You Wish Upon A Star** .... *Glenn Miller...Bluebird 10570*
7	8	3	**On The Isle Of May** .... *Connie Boswell...Decca 3004*
8	9	3	**Say "Si Si" (Para Vigo Me Voy)** .... *Andrews Sisters...Decca 3013*
9	—	1	**The Woodpecker Song** .... *Andrews Sisters...Decca 3065*
10	10	2	**It's A Blue World** .... *Tony Martin...Decca 2932*

TW	LW	WK	Billboard® ✸ APRIL 20, 1940 ✸ Record Buying Guide
1	1	27	**In The Mood** ....*Glenn Miller*...Bluebird 10416
2	2	12	**Indian Summer** ....*Tommy Dorsey*...Victor 26390
3	5	7	**Tuxedo Junction** ....*Glenn Miller*...Bluebird 10612
4	—	1	**When You Wish Upon A Star** ....*Guy Lombardo*...Decca 2969
5	7	4	**On The Isle Of May** ....*Connie Boswell*...Decca 3004
6	8	4	**Say "Si Si" (Para Vigo Me Voy)** ....*Andrews Sisters*...Decca 3013
7	9	2	**The Woodpecker Song** ....*Andrews Sisters*...Decca 3065
8	—	1	**The Singing Hills** ....*Bing Crosby*...Decca 3064
9	—	1	**Leanin' On The Ole Top Rail** ....*Bob Crosby*...Decca 3027
10	—	1	**I've Got My Eyes On You** ....*Bob Crosby*...Decca 2991

TW	LW	WK	Billboard® ✸ APRIL 27, 1940 ✸ Record Buying Guide
1	1	28	**In The Mood** ....*Glenn Miller*...Bluebird 10416
2	3	8	**Tuxedo Junction** ....*Glenn Miller*...Bluebird 10612
3	—	2	**When You Wish Upon A Star** ....*Glenn Miller*...Bluebird 10570
4	5	5	**On The Isle Of May** ....*Connie Boswell*...Decca 3004
5	6	5	**Say "Si Si" (Para Vigo Me Voy)** ....*Andrews Sisters*...Decca 3013
6	8	2	**The Singing Hills** ....*Bing Crosby*...Decca 3064
7	9	2	**Leanin' On The Ole Top Rail** ....*Bob Crosby*...Decca 3027
8	—	1	**With The Wind And The Rain In Your Hair** ....*Bob Crosby*...Decca 3018
9	10	2	**I've Got My Eyes On You** ....*Bob Crosby*...Decca 2991
10	—	1	**Starlit Hour** ....*Glenn Miller*...Bluebird 10553

TW	LW	WK	Billboard® ✸ MAY 4, 1940 ✸ Record Buying Guide
1	2	9	**Tuxedo Junction** ....*Glenn Miller*...Bluebird 10612
2	3	3	**When You Wish Upon A Star** ....*Glenn Miller*...Bluebird 10570
3	4	6	**On The Isle Of May** ....*Connie Boswell*...Decca 3004
4	5	6	**Say "Si Si" (Para Vigo Me Voy)** ....*Andrews Sisters*...Decca 3013
5	—	1	**The Woodpecker Song** ....*Glenn Miller*...Bluebird 10598
6	6	3	**The Singing Hills** ....*Bing Crosby*...Decca 3064
7	8	2	**With The Wind And The Rain In Your Hair** ....*Bob Crosby*...Decca 3018
8	7	3	**Leanin' On The Ole Top Rail** ....*Bob Crosby*...Decca 3027
9	—	1	**Cecelia** ....*Dick Jurgens*...Vocalion 5405
10	—	1	**Playmates** ....*Kay Kyser*...Columbia 35375

TW	LW	WK	Billboard® ✸ MAY 11, 1940 ✸ Record Buying Guide
1	1	10	**Tuxedo Junction** ....*Glenn Miller*...Bluebird 10612
2	2	4	**When You Wish Upon A Star** ....*Glenn Miller*...Bluebird 10570
3	3	7	**On The Isle Of May** ....*Connie Boswell*...Decca 3004
4	4	7	**Say "Si Si" (Para Vigo Me Voy)** ....*Andrews Sisters*...Decca 3013
5	5	2	**The Woodpecker Song** ....*Glenn Miller*...Bluebird 10598
6	6	4	**The Singing Hills** ....*Bing Crosby*...Decca 3064
7	7	3	**With The Wind And The Rain In Your Hair** ....*Bob Crosby*...Decca 3018
8	8	4	**Leanin' On The Ole Top Rail** ....*Bob Crosby*...Decca 3027
9	10	2	**Playmates** ....*Kay Kyser*...Columbia 35375
10	9	2	**Cecelia** ....*Dick Jurgens*...Vocalion 5405

TW	LW	WK	Billboard® ✸ MAY 18, 1940 ✸ Record Buying Guide
1	1	11	**Tuxedo Junction** ....*Glenn Miller*...Bluebird 10612
2	2	5	**When You Wish Upon A Star** ....*Glenn Miller*...Bluebird 10570
3	3	8	**On The Isle Of May** ....*Connie Boswell*...Decca 3004
4	4	8	**Say "Si Si" (Para Vigo Me Voy)** ....*Andrews Sisters*...Decca 3013
5	5	3	**The Woodpecker Song** ....*Glenn Miller*...Bluebird 10598
6	6	5	**The Singing Hills** ....*Bing Crosby*...Decca 3064
7	—	1	**With The Wind And The Rain In Your Hair** ....*Kay Kyser*...Columbia 35350
8	9	3	**Playmates** ....*Kay Kyser*...Columbia 35375
9	—	1	**Alice Blue Gown** ....*Frankie Masters*...Vocalion 5455
10	10	3	**Cecelia** ....*Dick Jurgens*...Vocalion 5405

TW	LW	WK	Billboard® MAY 25, 1940 Record Buying Guide
1	1	12	Tuxedo Junction ....Glenn Miller...Bluebird 10612
2	2	6	When You Wish Upon A Star ....Glenn Miller...Bluebird 10570
3	5	4	The Woodpecker Song ....Glenn Miller...Bluebird 10598
4	6	6	The Singing Hills ....Bing Crosby...Decca 3064
5	7	2	With The Wind And The Rain In Your Hair...Kay Kyser...Columbia 35350
6	8	4	Playmates ....Kay Kyser...Columbia 35375
7	9	2	Alice Blue Gown ....Frankie Masters...Vocalion 5455
8	10	4	Cecelia ....Dick Jurgens...Vocalion 5405
9	—	1	Little Curly Hair In A High Chair ....Fats Waller...Bluebird 10698
10	—	1	Let There Be Love ....Sammy Kaye...Victor 26564

TW	LW	WK	Billboard® JUNE 1, 1940 Record Buying Guide
1	1	13	Tuxedo Junction ....Glenn Miller...Bluebird 10612
2	2	7	When You Wish Upon A Star ....Glenn Miller...Bluebird 10570
3	3	5	The Woodpecker Song ....Glenn Miller...Bluebird 10598
4	4	7	The Singing Hills ....Bing Crosby...Decca 3064
5	5	3	With The Wind And The Rain In Your Hair...Kay Kyser...Columbia 35350
6	9	2	Little Curly Hair In A High Chair ....Fats Waller...Bluebird 10698
7	7	3	Alice Blue Gown ....Frankie Masters...Vocalion 5455
8	—	1	Boog-It ....Glenn Miller...Bluebird 10689
9	—	1	No Name Jive (Parts 1 & 2) ....Glen Gray...Decca 3089
10	10	2	Let There Be Love ....Sammy Kaye...Victor 26564

TW	LW	WK	Billboard® JUNE 8, 1940 Record Buying Guide
1	1	14	Tuxedo Junction ....Glenn Miller...Bluebird 10612
2	3	6	The Woodpecker Song ....Glenn Miller...Bluebird 10598
3	4	8	The Singing Hills ....Bing Crosby...Decca 3064
4	5	4	With The Wind And The Rain In Your Hair...Kay Kyser...Columbia 35350
5	—	5	Playmates ....Kay Kyser...Columbia 35375
6	6	3	Little Curly Hair In A High Chair ....Fats Waller...Bluebird 10698
7	7	4	Alice Blue Gown ....Frankie Masters...Vocalion 5455
8	8	2	Boog-It ....Glenn Miller...Bluebird 10689
9	—	1	Make-Believe Island ....Mitchell Ayres...Bluebird 10687
10	9	2	No Name Jive (Parts 1 & 2) ....Glen Gray...Decca 3089

TW	LW	WK	Billboard® JUNE 15, 1940 Record Buying Guide
1	1	15	Tuxedo Junction ....Glenn Miller...Bluebird 10612
2	2	7	The Woodpecker Song ....Glenn Miller...Bluebird 10598
3	3	9	The Singing Hills ....Bing Crosby...Decca 3064
4	4	5	With The Wind And The Rain In Your Hair...Kay Kyser...Columbia 35350
5	5	6	Playmates ....Kay Kyser...Columbia 35375
6	9	2	Make-Believe Island ....Mitchell Ayres...Bluebird 10687
7	8	3	Boog-It ....Glenn Miller...Bluebird 10689
8	6	4	Little Curly Hair In A High Chair ....Fats Waller...Bluebird 10698
9	7	5	Alice Blue Gown ....Frankie Masters...Vocalion 5455
10	—	1	Say It ....Glenn Miller...Bluebird 10631

TW	LW	WK	Billboard® JUNE 22, 1940 Record Buying Guide
1	1	16	Tuxedo Junction ....Glenn Miller...Bluebird 10612
2	2	8	The Woodpecker Song ....Glenn Miller...Bluebird 10598
3	3	10	The Singing Hills ....Bing Crosby...Decca 3064
4	4	6	With The Wind And The Rain In Your Hair...Kay Kyser...Columbia 35350
5	5	7	Playmates ....Kay Kyser...Columbia 35375
6	6	3	Make-Believe Island ....Mitchell Ayres...Bluebird 10687
7	—	3	Let There Be Love ....Sammy Kaye...Victor 26564
8	8	5	Little Curly Hair In A High Chair ....Fats Waller...Bluebird 10698
9	—	1	Imagination ....Glenn Miller...Bluebird 10622
10	—	1	April Played The Fiddle..Bing Crosby...Decca 3161

TW	LW	WK	Billboard® ● JUNE 29, 1940 ● Record Buying Guide
1	1	17	**Tuxedo Junction** ....*Glenn Miller*...Bluebird 10612
2	2	9	**The Woodpecker Song** ....*Glenn Miller*...Bluebird 10598
3	3	11	**The Singing Hills** ....*Bing Crosby*...Decca 3064
4	4	7	**With The Wind And The Rain In Your Hair** ....*Kay Kyser*...Columbia 35350
5	5	8	**Playmates** ....*Kay Kyser*...Columbia 35375
6	6	4	**Make-Believe Island** ....*Mitchell Ayres*...Bluebird 10687
7	9	2	**Imagination** ....*Glenn Miller*...Bluebird 10622
8	—	2	**Say It** ....*Glenn Miller*...Bluebird 10631
9	7	4	**Let There Be Love** ....*Sammy Kaye*...Victor 26564
10	10	2	**April Played The Fiddle**...*Bing Crosby*...Decca 3161

TW	LW	WK	Billboard® ● JULY 6, 1940 ● Record Buying Guide
1	2	10	**The Woodpecker Song** ....*Glenn Miller*...Bluebird 10598
2	3	12	**The Singing Hills** ....*Bing Crosby*...Decca 3064
3	5	9	**Playmates** ....*Kay Kyser*...Columbia 35375
4	6	5	**Make-Believe Island** ....*Mitchell Ayres*...Bluebird 10687
5	7	3	**Imagination** ....*Glenn Miller*...Bluebird 10622
6	—	1	**Where Was I?** ....*Charlie Barnet*...Bluebird 10669
7	8	3	**Say It** ....*Glenn Miller*...Bluebird 10631
8	—	4	**Boog-It** ....*Glenn Miller*...Bluebird 10689
9	—	1	**Slow Freight** ....*Glenn Miller*...Bluebird 10740
10	—	1	**The Breeze And I**...*Jimmy Dorsey*...Decca 3150

TW	LW	WK	Billboard® ● JULY 13, 1940 ● Record Buying Guide
1	1	11	**The Woodpecker Song**..*Glenn Miller*...Bluebird 10598
2	2	13	**The Singing Hills** ....*Bing Crosby*...Decca 3064
3	3	10	**Playmates** ....*Kay Kyser*...Columbia 35375
4	4	6	**Make-Believe Island** ....*Mitchell Ayres*...Bluebird 10687
5	6	2	**Where Was I?** ....*Charlie Barnet*...Bluebird 10669
6	10	2	**The Breeze And I** ....*Jimmy Dorsey*...Decca 3150
7	7	4	**Say It** ....*Glenn Miller*...Bluebird 10631
8	8	5	**Boog-It** ....*Glenn Miller*...Bluebird 10689
9	9	2	**Slow Freight**...*Glenn Miller*...Bluebird 10740
10	—	1	**Shake Down The Stars** ....*Glenn Miller*...Bluebird 10689

TW	LW	WK	Billboard® ● JULY 20, 1940 ● Record Buying Guide
1	1	12	**The Woodpecker Song**..*Glenn Miller*...Bluebird 10598
2	2	14	**The Singing Hills** ....*Bing Crosby*...Decca 3064
3	3	11	**Playmates** ....*Kay Kyser*...Columbia 35375
4	4	7	**Make-Believe Island** ....*Mitchell Ayres*...Bluebird 10687
5	—	4	**Imagination** ....*Glenn Miller*...Bluebird 10622
6	5	3	**Where Was I?** ....*Charlie Barnet*...Bluebird 10669
7	6	3	**The Breeze And I** ....*Jimmy Dorsey*...Decca 3150
8	—	1	**I Can't Love You Any More (Any More Than I Do)** ....*Benny Goodman*...Columbia 35487
9	—	1	**I'll Never Smile Again** ....*Tommy Dorsey*...Victor 26628
10	—	1	**Sierra Sue**..*Bing Crosby*...Decca 3133

Billboard's first national "Best Selling Retail Records" chart debuts on July 27, 1940.

TW	LW	WK	Billboard®	JULY 27, 1940	Best Sellers
1	—	1	I'll Never Smile Again		*Tommy Dorsey*...Victor 26628
2	—	1	The Breeze And I		*Jimmy Dorsey*...Decca 3150
3	—	1	Imagination		*Glenn Miller*...Bluebird 10622
4	—	1	Playmates		*Kay Kyser*...Columbia 35375
5	—	1	Fools Rush In (Where Angels Fear to Tread)		*Glenn Miller*...Bluebird 10728
6	—	1	Where Was I?		*Charlie Barnet*...Bluebird 10669
7	—	1	Pennsylvania Six-Five Thousand		*Glenn Miller*...Bluebird 10754
8	—	1	Imagination		*Tommy Dorsey*...Victor 26581
9	—	1	Sierra Sue		*Bing Crosby*...Decca 3133
10	—	1	Make-Believe Island		*Mitchell Ayres*...Bluebird 10687

TW	LW	WK	Billboard®	AUGUST 3, 1940	Best Sellers
1	1	2	I'll Never Smile Again		*Tommy Dorsey*...Victor 26628
2	2	2	The Breeze And I		*Jimmy Dorsey*...Decca 3150
3	5	2	Fools Rush In (Where Angels Fear to Tread)		*Glenn Miller*...Bluebird 10728
4	3	2	Imagination		*Glenn Miller*...Bluebird 10622
5	9	2	Sierra Sue		*Bing Crosby*...Decca 3133
6	—	1	The Nearness Of You		*Glenn Miller*...Bluebird 10745
7	—	1	When The Swallows Come Back To Capistrano		*Ink Spots*...Decca 3195
8	—	1	Make-Believe Island		*Jan Savitt*...Decca 3188
9	7	2	Pennsylvania Six-Five Thousand		*Glenn Miller*...Bluebird 10754
10	—	1	Frenesi		*Artie Shaw*...Victor 26542

TW	LW	WK	Billboard®	AUGUST 10, 1940	Best Sellers
1	1	3	I'll Never Smile Again		*Tommy Dorsey*...Victor 26628
2	2	3	The Breeze And I		*Jimmy Dorsey*...Decca 3150
3	3	3	Fools Rush In (Where Angels Fear to Tread)		*Glenn Miller*...Bluebird 10728
4	5	3	Sierra Sue		*Bing Crosby*...Decca 3133
5	6	2	The Nearness Of You		*Glenn Miller*...Bluebird 10745
6	9	3	Pennsylvania Six-Five Thousand		*Glenn Miller*...Bluebird 10754
7	—	1	I'm Nobody's Baby		*Judy Garland*...Decca 3174
8	4	3	Imagination		*Glenn Miller*...Bluebird 10622
9	7	2	When The Swallows Come Back To Capistrano		*Ink Spots*...Decca 3195
10	—	1	Blueberry Hill		*Glenn Miller*...Bluebird 10768

TW	LW	WK	Billboard®	AUGUST 17, 1940	Best Sellers
1	1	4	I'll Never Smile Again		*Tommy Dorsey*...Victor 26628
2	2	4	The Breeze And I		*Jimmy Dorsey*...Decca 3150
3	3	4	Fools Rush In (Where Angels Fear to Tread)		*Glenn Miller*...Bluebird 10728
4	—	1	Six Lessons From Madame La Zonga		*Jimmy Dorsey*...Decca 3152
5	4	4	Sierra Sue		*Bing Crosby*...Decca 3133
6	7	2	I'm Nobody's Baby		*Judy Garland*...Decca 3174
7	5	3	The Nearness Of You		*Glenn Miller*...Bluebird 10745
8	—	1	God Bless America		*Kate Smith*...Victor 26198
9	9	3	When The Swallows Come Back To Capistrano		*Ink Spots*...Decca 3195
10	6	4	Pennsylvania Six-Five Thousand		*Glenn Miller*...Bluebird 10754

TW	LW	WK	Billboard®	AUGUST 24, 1940	Best Sellers
1	1	5	I'll Never Smile Again		*Tommy Dorsey*...Victor 26628
2	2	5	The Breeze And I		*Jimmy Dorsey*...Decca 3150
3	3	5	Fools Rush In (Where Angels Fear to Tread)		*Glenn Miller*...Bluebird 10728
4	5	5	Sierra Sue		*Bing Crosby*...Decca 3133
5	8	2	God Bless America		*Kate Smith*...Victor 26198
6	—	2	Blueberry Hill		*Glenn Miller*...Bluebird 10768
7	6	3	I'm Nobody's Baby		*Judy Garland*...Decca 3174
8	9	4	When The Swallows Come Back To Capistrano		*Ink Spots*...Decca 3195
9	10	5	Pennsylvania Six-Five Thousand		*Glenn Miller*...Bluebird 10754
10	—	2	Frenesi		*Artie Shaw*...Victor 26542

TW	LW	WK	Billboard® ✸ AUGUST 31, 1940 ✸	Best Sellers
1	1	6	I'll Never Smile Again	Tommy Dorsey...Victor 26628
2	2	6	The Breeze And I	Jimmy Dorsey...Decca 3150
3	4	6	Sierra Sue	Bing Crosby...Decca 3133
4	8	5	When The Swallows Come Back To Capistrano	Ink Spots...Decca 3195
5	9	6	Pennsylvania Six-Five Thousand	Glenn Miller...Bluebird 10754
6	7	4	I'm Nobody's Baby	Judy Garland...Decca 3174
7	—	2	Six Lessons From Madame La Zonga	Jimmy Dorsey...Decca 3152
8	—	4	The Nearness Of You	Glenn Miller...Bluebird 10745
9	10	3	Frenesi	Artie Shaw...Victor 26542
10	—	1	When The Swallows Come Back To Capistrano	Glenn Miller...Bluebird 10776

TW	LW	WK	Billboard® ✸ SEPTEMBER 7, 1940 ✸	Best Sellers
1	1	7	I'll Never Smile Again	Tommy Dorsey...Victor 26628
2	—	3	Blueberry Hill	Glenn Miller...Bluebird 10768
3	2	7	The Breeze And I	Jimmy Dorsey...Decca 3150
4	3	7	Sierra Sue	Bing Crosby...Decca 3133
5	8	5	The Nearness Of You	Glenn Miller...Bluebird 10745
6	6	5	I'm Nobody's Baby	Judy Garland...Decca 3174
7	4	6	When The Swallows Come Back To Capistrano	Ink Spots...Decca 3195
8	—	1	Maybe	Ink Spots...Decca 3258
9	—	6	Fools Rush In (Where Angels Fear to Tread)	Glenn Miller...Bluebird 10728
10	7	3	Six Lessons From Madame La Zonga	Jimmy Dorsey...Decca 3152

TW	LW	WK	Billboard® ✸ SEPTEMBER 14, 1940 ✸	Best Sellers
1	1	8	I'll Never Smile Again	Tommy Dorsey...Victor 26628
2	2	4	Blueberry Hill	Glenn Miller...Bluebird 10768
3	3	8	The Breeze And I	Jimmy Dorsey...Decca 3150
4	4	8	Sierra Sue	Bing Crosby...Decca 3133
5	6	6	I'm Nobody's Baby	Judy Garland...Decca 3174
6	7	7	When The Swallows Come Back To Capistrano	Ink Spots...Decca 3195
7	5	6	The Nearness Of You	Glenn Miller...Bluebird 10745
8	9	7	Fools Rush In (Where Angels Fear to Tread)	Glenn Miller...Bluebird 10728
9	—	3	God Bless America	Kate Smith...Victor 26198
10	—	1	Dolimite	Erskine Hawkins...Bluebird 10812

TW	LW	WK	Billboard® ✸ SEPTEMBER 21, 1940 ✸	Best Sellers
1	1	9	I'll Never Smile Again	Tommy Dorsey...Victor 26628
2	2	5	Blueberry Hill	Glenn Miller...Bluebird 10768
3	5	7	I'm Nobody's Baby	Judy Garland...Decca 3174
4	4	9	Sierra Sue	Bing Crosby...Decca 3133
5	7	7	The Nearness Of You	Glenn Miller...Bluebird 10745
6	6	8	When The Swallows Come Back To Capistrano	Ink Spots...Decca 3195
7	3	9	The Breeze And I	Jimmy Dorsey...Decca 3150
8	—	2	Maybe	Ink Spots...Decca 3258
9	—	1	Trade Winds	Bing Crosby...Decca 3299
10	—	1	Trade Winds	Tommy Dorsey...Victor 26666

TW	LW	WK	Billboard® ✸ SEPTEMBER 28, 1940 ✸	Best Sellers
1	1	10	I'll Never Smile Again	Tommy Dorsey...Victor 26628
2	2	6	Blueberry Hill	Glenn Miller...Bluebird 10768
3	3	8	I'm Nobody's Baby	Judy Garland...Decca 3174
4	8	3	Maybe	Ink Spots...Decca 3258
5	—	1	Only Forever	Bing Crosby...Decca 3300
6	4	10	Sierra Sue	Bing Crosby...Decca 3133
7	6	9	When The Swallows Come Back To Capistrano	Ink Spots...Decca 3195
8	9	2	Trade Winds	Bing Crosby...Decca 3299
9	—	1	Beat Me Daddy (Eight To The Bar) Parts I & II	Will Bradley...Columbia 35530
10	5	8	The Nearness Of You	Glenn Miller...Bluebird 10745

TW	LW	WK	Billboard® ❀ OCTOBER 5, 1940 ❀	Best Sellers
1	1	11	I'll Never Smile Again	Tommy Dorsey...Victor 26628
2	4	4	Maybe	Ink Spots...Decca 3258
3	2	7	Blueberry Hill	Glenn Miller...Bluebird 10768
4	5	2	Only Forever	Bing Crosby...Decca 3300
5	9	2	Beat Me Daddy (Eight To The Bar) Parts I & II	Will Bradley...Columbia 35530
6	8	3	Trade Winds	Bing Crosby...Decca 3299
7	7	10	When The Swallows Come Back To Capistrano	Ink Spots...Decca 3195
8	3	9	I'm Nobody's Baby	Judy Garland...Decca 3174
9	—	1	Crosstown	Glenn Miller...Bluebird 10832
10	—	1	Whispering Grass (Don't Tell The Trees)	Ink Spots...Decca 3258

TW	LW	WK	Billboard® ❀ OCTOBER 12, 1940 ❀	Best Sellers
1	1	12	I'll Never Smile Again	Tommy Dorsey...Victor 26628
2	4	3	Only Forever	Bing Crosby...Decca 3300
3	2	5	Maybe	Ink Spots...Decca 3258
4	3	8	Blueberry Hill	Glenn Miller...Bluebird 10768
5	6	4	Trade Winds	Bing Crosby...Decca 3299
6	—	1	Practice Makes Perfect	Bob Chester...Bluebird 10838
7	5	3	Beat Me Daddy (Eight To The Bar) Parts I & II	Will Bradley...Columbia 35530
8	8	10	I'm Nobody's Baby	Judy Garland...Decca 3174
9	—	1	We Three (My Echo, My Shadow And Me)	Ink Spots...Decca 3379
10	—	2	Trade Winds	Tommy Dorsey...Victor 26666

TW	LW	WK	Billboard® ❀ OCTOBER 19, 1940 ❀	Best Sellers
1	2	4	Only Forever	Bing Crosby...Decca 3300
2	1	13	I'll Never Smile Again	Tommy Dorsey...Victor 26628
3	4	9	Blueberry Hill	Glenn Miller...Bluebird 10768
4	3	6	Maybe	Ink Spots...Decca 3258
5	7	4	Beat Me Daddy (Eight To The Bar) Parts I & II	Will Bradley...Columbia 35530
6	5	5	Trade Winds	Bing Crosby...Decca 3299
7	6	2	Practice Makes Perfect	Bob Chester...Bluebird 10838
8	9	2	We Three (My Echo, My Shadow And Me)	Ink Spots...Decca 3379
9	—	11	When The Swallows Come Back To Capistrano	Ink Spots...Decca 3195
10	10	3	Trade Winds	Tommy Dorsey...Victor 26666

TW	LW	WK	Billboard® ❀ OCTOBER 26, 1940 ❀	Best Sellers
1	1	5	Only Forever	Bing Crosby...Decca 3300
2	4	7	Maybe	Ink Spots...Decca 3258
3	2	14	I'll Never Smile Again	Tommy Dorsey...Victor 26628
4	5	5	Beat Me Daddy (Eight To The Bar) Parts I & II	Will Bradley...Columbia 35530
5	3	10	Blueberry Hill	Glenn Miller...Bluebird 10768
6	6	6	Trade Winds	Bing Crosby...Decca 3299
7	—	1	Only Forever	Tommy Dorsey...Victor 26666
8	7	3	Practice Makes Perfect	Bob Chester...Bluebird 10838
9	8	3	We Three (My Echo, My Shadow And Me)	Ink Spots...Decca 3379
10	—	1	Pompton Turnpike	Charlie Barnet...Bluebird 10825

TW	LW	WK	Billboard® ❀ NOVEMBER 2, 1940 ❀	Best Sellers
1	1	6	Only Forever	Bing Crosby...Decca 3300
2	2	8	Maybe	Ink Spots...Decca 3258
3	4	6	Beat Me Daddy (Eight To The Bar) Parts I & II	Will Bradley...Columbia 35530
4	9	4	We Three (My Echo, My Shadow And Me)	Ink Spots...Decca 3379
5	6	7	Trade Winds	Bing Crosby...Decca 3299
6	8	4	Practice Makes Perfect	Bob Chester...Bluebird 10838
7	10	2	Pompton Turnpike	Charlie Barnet...Bluebird 10825
8	5	11	Blueberry Hill	Glenn Miller...Bluebird 10768
9	3	15	I'll Never Smile Again	Tommy Dorsey...Victor 26628
10	—	1	Ferry-Boat Serenade	Kay Kyser...Columbia 35627

TW	LW	WK	Billboard® ✹ NOVEMBER 9, 1940 ✹ Best Sellers
1	1	7	Only Forever .... *Bing Crosby*...Decca 3300
2	2	9	Maybe .... *Ink Spots*...Decca 3258
3	5	8	Trade Winds .... *Bing Crosby*...Decca 3299
4	3	7	Beat Me Daddy (Eight To The Bar) Parts I & II .... *Will Bradley*...Columbia 35530
5	4	5	We Three (My Echo, My Shadow And Me) .... *Ink Spots*...Decca 3379
6	6	5	Practice Makes Perfect .... *Bob Chester*...Bluebird 10838
7	8	12	Blueberry Hill .... *Glenn Miller*...Bluebird 10768
8	—	1	Our Love Affair .... *Tommy Dorsey*...Victor 26736
9	—	1	Our Love Affair .... *Glenn Miller*...Bluebird 10845
10	—	1	The Call Of The Canyon .... *Glenn Miller*...Bluebird 10845

TW	LW	WK	Billboard® ✹ NOVEMBER 16, 1940 ✹ Best Sellers
1	1	8	Only Forever .... *Bing Crosby*...Decca 3300
2	2	10	Maybe .... *Ink Spots*...Decca 3258
3	4	8	Beat Me Daddy (Eight To The Bar) Parts I & II .... *Will Bradley*...Columbia 35530
4	3	9	Trade Winds .... *Bing Crosby*...Decca 3299
5	8	2	Our Love Affair .... *Tommy Dorsey*...Victor 26736
6	6	6	Practice Makes Perfect .... *Bob Chester*...Bluebird 10838
7	5	6	We Three (My Echo, My Shadow And Me) .... *Ink Spots*...Decca 3379
8	—	2	Only Forever .... *Tommy Dorsey*...Victor 26666
9	—	3	Pompton Turnpike .... *Charlie Barnet*...Bluebird 10825
10	—	4	Trade Winds .... *Tommy Dorsey*...Victor 26666

TW	LW	WK	Billboard® ✹ NOVEMBER 23, 1940 ✹ Best Sellers
1	1	9	Only Forever .... *Bing Crosby*...Decca 3300
2	2	11	Maybe .... *Ink Spots*...Decca 3258
3	—	13	Blueberry Hill .... *Glenn Miller*...Bluebird 10768
4	7	7	We Three (My Echo, My Shadow And Me) .... *Ink Spots*...Decca 3379
5	5	3	Our Love Affair .... *Tommy Dorsey*...Victor 26736
6	4	10	Trade Winds .... *Bing Crosby*...Decca 3299
7	3	9	Beat Me Daddy (Eight To The Bar) Parts I & II .... *Will Bradley*...Columbia 35530
8	—	2	Our Love Affair .... *Glenn Miller*...Bluebird 10845
9	8	3	Only Forever .... *Tommy Dorsey*...Victor 26666
10	—	1	Down Argentina Way .... *Leo Reisman*...Victor 26765

TW	LW	WK	Billboard® ✹ NOVEMBER 30, 1940 ✹ Best Sellers
1	1	10	Only Forever .... *Bing Crosby*...Decca 3300
2	7	10	Beat Me Daddy (Eight To The Bar) Parts I & II .... *Will Bradley*...Columbia 35530
3	2	12	Maybe .... *Ink Spots*...Decca 3258
4	6	11	Trade Winds .... *Bing Crosby*...Decca 3299
5	4	8	We Three (My Echo, My Shadow And Me) .... *Ink Spots*...Decca 3379
6	—	1	We Three (My Echo, My Shadow and Me) .... *Tommy Dorsey*...Victor 26747
7	—	2	Ferry-Boat Serenade .... *Kay Kyser*...Columbia 35627
8	—	4	Pompton Turnpike .... *Charlie Barnet*...Bluebird 10825
9	3	14	Blueberry Hill .... *Glenn Miller*...Bluebird 10768
10	—	1	A Handful Of Stars .... *Glenn Miller*...Bluebird 10893

TW	LW	WK	Billboard® ✹ DECEMBER 7, 1940 ✹ Best Sellers
1	1	11	Only Forever .... *Bing Crosby*...Decca 3300
2	4	12	Trade Winds .... *Bing Crosby*...Decca 3299
3	5	9	We Three (My Echo, My Shadow And Me) .... *Ink Spots*...Decca 3379
4	2	11	Beat Me Daddy (Eight To The Bar) Parts I & II .... *Will Bradley*...Columbia 35530
5	3	13	Maybe .... *Ink Spots*...Decca 3258
6	8	5	Pompton Turnpike .... *Charlie Barnet*...Bluebird 10825
7	7	3	Ferry-Boat Serenade .... *Kay Kyser*...Columbia 35627
8	—	1	Scrub Me, Mama, With A Boogie Beat .... *Will Bradley*...Columbia 35743
9	—	1	Ferryboat Serenade (La Piccinina) .... *Andrews Sisters*...Decca 3328
10	6	2	We Three (My Echo, My Shadow and Me) .... *Tommy Dorsey*...Victor 26747

TW	LW	WK	Billboard® 🎵 **DECEMBER 14, 1940** 🎵	**Best Sellers**
1	1	12	Only Forever	*Bing Crosby*...Decca 3300
2	2	13	Trade Winds	*Bing Crosby*...Decca 3299
3	6	6	Pompton Turnpike	*Charlie Barnet*...Bluebird 10825
4	4	12	Beat Me Daddy (Eight To The Bar) Parts I & II	*Will Bradley*...Columbia 35530
5	3	10	We Three (My Echo, My Shadow And Me)	*Ink Spots*...Decca 3379
6	—	1	Down Argentina Way	*Bob Crosby*...Decca 3404
7	—	4	Frenesi	*Artie Shaw*...Victor 26542
8	9	2	Ferryboat Serenade (La Piccinina)	*Andrews Sisters*...Decca 3328
9	5	14	Maybe	*Ink Spots*...Decca 3258
10	8	2	Scrub Me, Mama, With A Boogie Beat	*Will Bradley*...Columbia 35743

TW	LW	WK	Billboard® 🎵 **DECEMBER 21, 1940** 🎵	**Best Sellers**
1	7	5	Frenesi	*Artie Shaw*...Victor 26542
2	1	13	Only Forever	*Bing Crosby*...Decca 3300
3	4	13	Beat Me Daddy (Eight To The Bar) Parts I & II	*Will Bradley*...Columbia 35530
4	5	11	We Three (My Echo, My Shadow And Me)	*Ink Spots*...Decca 3379
5	—	1	A Nightingale Sang In Berkeley Square	*Glenn Miller*...Bluebird 10931
6	10	3	Scrub Me, Mama, With A Boogie Beat	*Will Bradley*...Columbia 35743
7	—	2	Down Argentina Way	*Leo Reisman*...Victor 26765
8	2	14	Trade Winds	*Bing Crosby*...Decca 3299
9	—	3	We Three (My Echo, My Shadow and Me)	*Tommy Dorsey*...Victor 26747
10	—	1	Down The Road A Piece	*Will Bradley*...Columbia 35707

TW	LW	WK	Billboard® 🎵 **DECEMBER 28, 1940** 🎵	**Best Sellers**
1	1	6	Frenesi	*Artie Shaw*...Victor 26542
2	5	2	A Nightingale Sang In Berkeley Square	*Glenn Miller*...Bluebird 10931
3	9	4	We Three (My Echo, My Shadow and Me)	*Tommy Dorsey*...Victor 26747
4	2	14	Only Forever	*Bing Crosby*...Decca 3300
5	—	1	There I Go	*Vaughn Monroe*...Bluebird 10848
6	8	15	Trade Winds	*Bing Crosby*...Decca 3299
7	—	4	Ferry-Boat Serenade	*Kay Kyser*...Columbia 35627
8	4	12	We Three (My Echo, My Shadow And Me)	*Ink Spots*...Decca 3379
9	—	1	There I Go	*Will Bradley*...Columbia 35743
10	3	14	Beat Me Daddy (Eight To The Bar) Parts I & II	*Will Bradley*...Columbia 35530

TW	LW	WK	Billboard® ❀ JANUARY 4, 1941 ❀ Best Sellers
1	1	7	Frenesi...*Artie Shaw*...Victor 26542
2	—	2	Down Argentina Way..*Bob Crosby*...Decca 3404
3	2	3	A Nightingale Sang In Berkeley Square.................................*Glenn Miller*...Bluebird 10931
4	4	15	Only Forever...*Bing Crosby*...Decca 3300
5	8	13	We Three (My Echo, My Shadow And Me) ....*Ink Spots*...Decca 3379
6	7	5	Ferry-Boat Serenade..*Kay Kyser*...Columbia 35627
7	—	1	Star Dust...*Tommy Dorsey*...Victor 27233
8	3	5	We Three (My Echo, My Shadow and Me) ....*Tommy Dorsey*...Victor 26747
9	—	1	Five O'Clock Whistle...*Ella Fitzgerald*...Decca 3420
10	—	2	A Handful Of Stars..*Glenn Miller*...Bluebird 10893

TW	LW	WK	Billboard® ❀ JANUARY 11, 1941 ❀ Best Sellers
1	1	8	Frenesi...*Artie Shaw*...Victor 26542
2	—	4	Scrub Me, Mama, With A Boogie Beat...............................*Will Bradley*...Columbia 35743
3	3	4	A Nightingale Sang In Berkeley Square ....*Glenn Miller*...Bluebird 10931
4	5	14	We Three (My Echo, My Shadow And Me) ....*Ink Spots*...Decca 3379
5	4	16	Only Forever...*Bing Crosby*...Decca 3300
6	—	1	Five O'Clock Whistle..*Glenn Miller*...Bluebird 10900
7	2	3	Down Argentina Way..*Bob Crosby*...Decca 3404
8	—	1	Anvil Chorus-Parts 1 & 2...*Glenn Miller*...Bluebird 10982
9	—	1	I Hear A Rhapsody..*Charlie Barnet*...Bluebird 10934
10	—	3	Ferryboat Serenade (La Piccinina)..*Andrews Sisters*...Decca 3328

TW	LW	WK	Billboard® ❀ JANUARY 18, 1941 ❀ Best Sellers
1	1	9	Frenesi...*Artie Shaw*...Victor 26542
2	3	5	A Nightingale Sang In Berkeley Square ....*Glenn Miller*...Bluebird 10931
3	9	2	I Hear A Rhapsody..*Charlie Barnet*...Bluebird 10934
4	2	5	Scrub Me, Mama, With A Boogie Beat...............................*Will Bradley*...Columbia 35743
5	—	2	There I Go...*Vaughn Monroe*...Bluebird 10848
6	—	1	Star Dust...*Artie Shaw*...Victor 27230
7	—	1	Along The Santa Fe Trail...*Glenn Miller*...Bluebird 10970
8	6	2	Five O'Clock Whistle..*Glenn Miller*...Bluebird 10900
9	7	4	Down Argentina Way..*Bob Crosby*...Decca 3404
10	—	1	I Hear A Rhapsody..*Jimmy Dorsey*...Decca 3570

TW	LW	WK	Billboard® ❀ JANUARY 25, 1941 ❀ Best Sellers
1	1	10	Frenesi...*Artie Shaw*...Victor 26542
2	3	3	I Hear A Rhapsody..*Charlie Barnet*...Bluebird 10934
3	10	2	I Hear A Rhapsody..*Jimmy Dorsey*...Decca 3570
4	4	6	Scrub Me, Mama, With A Boogie Beat...............................*Will Bradley*...Columbia 35743
5	—	2	Anvil Chorus-Parts 1 & 2...*Glenn Miller*...Bluebird 10982
6	2	6	A Nightingale Sang In Berkeley Square ....*Glenn Miller*...Bluebird 10931
7	6	2	Star Dust...*Artie Shaw*...Victor 27230
8	—	2	There I Go...*Will Bradley*...Columbia 35743
9	7	2	Along The Santa Fe Trail...*Glenn Miller*...Bluebird 10970
10	—	1	Yes, My Darling Daughter...*Dinah Shore*...Bluebird 10920

TW	LW	WK	Billboard® ❀ FEBRUARY 1, 1941 ❀ Best Sellers
1	1	11	Frenesi...*Artie Shaw*...Victor 26542
2	2	4	I Hear A Rhapsody..*Charlie Barnet*...Bluebird 10934
3	3	3	I Hear A Rhapsody..*Jimmy Dorsey*...Decca 3570
4	—	1	Perfidia [Tonight]..*Xavier Cugat*...Victor 26334
5	5	3	Anvil Chorus-Parts 1 & 2...*Glenn Miller*...Bluebird 10982
6	4	7	Scrub Me, Mama, With A Boogie Beat...............................*Will Bradley*...Columbia 35743
7	—	3	There I Go...*Vaughn Monroe*...Bluebird 10848
8	—	1	You Walk By..*Eddy Duchin*...Columbia 35903
9	9	3	Along The Santa Fe Trail...*Glenn Miller*...Bluebird 10970
10	—	15	Beat Me Daddy (Eight To The Bar) Parts I & II ....*Will Bradley*...Columbia 35530

TW	LW	WK	Billboard ❀ FEBRUARY 8, 1941 ❀	Best Sellers
1	1	12	Frenesi	Artie Shaw...Victor 26542
2	2	5	I Hear A Rhapsody	Charlie Barnet...Bluebird 10934
3	5	4	Anvil Chorus-Parts 1 & 2	Glenn Miller...Bluebird 10982
4	3	4	I Hear A Rhapsody	Jimmy Dorsey...Decca 3570
5	—	3	There I Go	Will Bradley...Columbia 35743
6	7	4	There I Go	Vaughn Monroe...Bluebird 10848
7	4	2	Perfidia [Tonight]	Xavier Cugat...Victor 26334
8	9	4	Along The Santa Fe Trail	Glenn Miller...Bluebird 10970
9	—	1	High On A Windy Hill	Will Bradley...Columbia 35912
10	—	1	Summit Ridge Drive	Artie Shaw...Victor 26763

TW	LW	WK	Billboard ❀ FEBRUARY 15, 1941 ❀	Best Sellers
1	1	13	Frenesi	Artie Shaw...Victor 26542
2	2	6	I Hear A Rhapsody	Charlie Barnet...Bluebird 10934
3	4	5	I Hear A Rhapsody	Jimmy Dorsey...Decca 3570
4	3	5	Anvil Chorus-Parts 1 & 2	Glenn Miller...Bluebird 10982
5	—	1	High On A Windy Hill	Gene Krupa...Okeh 5883
6	—	1	It All Comes Back To Me Now	Hal Kemp...Victor 27255
7	—	2	You Walk By	Eddy Duchin...Columbia 35903
8	—	3	Star Dust	Artie Shaw...Victor 27230
9	7	3	Perfidia [Tonight]	Xavier Cugat...Victor 26334
10	—	1	Concerto For Clarinet (Parts 1 & 2)	Artie Shaw...Victor 36383

TW	LW	WK	Billboard ❀ FEBRUARY 22, 1941 ❀	Best Sellers
1	1	14	Frenesi	Artie Shaw...Victor 26542
2	2	7	I Hear A Rhapsody	Charlie Barnet...Bluebird 10934
3	5	2	High On A Windy Hill	Gene Krupa...Okeh 5883
4	4	6	Anvil Chorus-Parts 1 & 2	Glenn Miller...Bluebird 10982
5	3	6	I Hear A Rhapsody	Jimmy Dorsey...Decca 3570
6	7	3	You Walk By	Eddy Duchin...Columbia 35903
7	—	1	High On A Windy Hill	Jimmy Dorsey...Decca 3585
8	—	1	It All Comes Back To Me Now	Gene Krupa...Okeh 5883
9	—	1	Song Of The Volga Boatmen	Glenn Miller...Bluebird 11029
10	10	2	Concerto For Clarinet (Parts 1 & 2)	Artie Shaw...Victor 36383

TW	LW	WK	Billboard ❀ MARCH 1, 1941 ❀	Best Sellers
1	1	15	Frenesi	Artie Shaw...Victor 26542
2	2	8	I Hear A Rhapsody	Charlie Barnet...Bluebird 10934
3	3	3	High On A Windy Hill	Gene Krupa...Okeh 5883
4	—	4	Perfidia [Tonight]	Xavier Cugat...Victor 26334
5	8	2	It All Comes Back To Me Now	Gene Krupa...Okeh 5883
6	6	4	You Walk By	Eddy Duchin...Columbia 35903
7	5	7	I Hear A Rhapsody	Jimmy Dorsey...Decca 3570
8	9	2	Song Of The Volga Boatmen	Glenn Miller...Bluebird 11029
9	4	7	Anvil Chorus-Parts 1 & 2	Glenn Miller...Bluebird 10982
10	—	1	Oh! Look At Me Now	Tommy Dorsey...Victor 27274

TW	LW	WK	Billboard ❀ MARCH 8, 1941 ❀	Best Sellers
1	1	16	Frenesi	Artie Shaw...Victor 26542
2	3	4	High On A Windy Hill	Gene Krupa...Okeh 5883
3	7	8	I Hear A Rhapsody	Jimmy Dorsey...Decca 3570
4	8	3	Song Of The Volga Boatmen	Glenn Miller...Bluebird 11029
5	5	3	It All Comes Back To Me Now	Gene Krupa...Okeh 5883
6	2	9	I Hear A Rhapsody	Charlie Barnet...Bluebird 10934
7	4	5	Perfidia [Tonight]	Xavier Cugat...Victor 26334
8	10	2	Oh! Look At Me Now	Tommy Dorsey...Victor 27274
9	9	8	Anvil Chorus-Parts 1 & 2	Glenn Miller...Bluebird 10982
10	6	5	You Walk By	Eddy Duchin...Columbia 35903

TW	LW	WK	Billboard® ❀ MARCH 15, 1941 ❀ Best Sellers
1	4	4	Song Of The Volga Boatmen ....*Glenn Miller*...Bluebird 11029
2	8	3	Oh! Look At Me Now ....*Tommy Dorsey*...Victor 27274
3	1	17	Frenesi ....*Artie Shaw*...Victor 26542
4	9	9	Anvil Chorus-Parts 1 & 2 ....*Glenn Miller*...Bluebird 10982
5	—	2	It All Comes Back To Me Now ....*Hal Kemp*...Victor 27255
6	10	6	You Walk By ....*Eddy Duchin*...Columbia 35903
7	2	5	High On A Windy Hill..*Gene Krupa*...Okeh 5883
8	7	6	Perfidia [Tonight] ....*Xavier Cugat*...Victor 26334
9	—	1	I Hear A Rhapsody ....*Dinah Shore*...Bluebird 11003
10	—	1	Dancing In The Dark..*Artie Shaw*...Victor 27335

TW	LW	WK	Billboard® ❀ MARCH 22, 1941 ❀ Best Sellers
1	3	18	Frenesi ....*Artie Shaw*...Victor 26542
2	—	4	It All Comes Back To Me Now ....*Gene Krupa*...Okeh 5883
3	8	7	Perfidia [Tonight] ....*Xavier Cugat*...Victor 26334
4	1	5	Song Of The Volga Boatmen ....*Glenn Miller*...Bluebird 11029
5	2	4	Oh! Look At Me Now ....*Tommy Dorsey*...Victor 27274
6	—	10	I Hear A Rhapsody ....*Charlie Barnet*...Bluebird 10934
7	—	1	Amapola (Pretty Little Poppy) ....*Jimmy Dorsey*...Decca 3629
8	4	10	Anvil Chorus-Parts 1 & 2 ....*Glenn Miller*...Bluebird 10982
9	—	9	I Hear A Rhapsody ....*Jimmy Dorsey*...Decca 3570
10	—	1	I Dreamt I Dwelt In Harlem ....*Glenn Miller*...Bluebird 11063

TW	LW	WK	Billboard® ❀ MARCH 29, 1941 ❀ Best Sellers
1	7	2	Amapola (Pretty Little Poppy) ....*Jimmy Dorsey*...Decca 3629
2	4	6	Song Of The Volga Boatmen..*Glenn Miller*...Bluebird 11029
3	3	8	Perfidia [Tonight] ....*Xavier Cugat*...Victor 26334
4	1	19	Frenesi ....*Artie Shaw*...Victor 26542
5	5	5	Oh! Look At Me Now ....*Tommy Dorsey*...Victor 27274
6	10	2	I Dreamt I Dwelt In Harlem ....*Glenn Miller*...Bluebird 11063
7	—	6	High On A Windy Hill ....*Gene Krupa*...Okeh 5883
8	—	1	New San Antonio Rose ....*Bing Crosby*...Decca 3590
9	6	11	I Hear A Rhapsody ....*Charlie Barnet*...Bluebird 10934
10	9	10	I Hear A Rhapsody ....*Jimmy Dorsey*...Decca 3570

TW	LW	WK	Billboard® ❀ APRIL 5, 1941 ❀ Best Sellers
1	1	3	Amapola (Pretty Little Poppy) ....*Jimmy Dorsey*...Decca 3629
2	5	6	Oh! Look At Me Now ....*Tommy Dorsey*...Victor 27274
3	6	3	I Dreamt I Dwelt In Harlem..*Glenn Miller*...Bluebird 11063
4	4	20	Frenesi ....*Artie Shaw*...Victor 26542
5	2	7	Song Of The Volga Boatmen..*Glenn Miller*...Bluebird 11029
6	3	9	Perfidia [Tonight] ....*Xavier Cugat*...Victor 26334
7	—	1	Blue Flame ....*Woody Herman*...Decca 3643
8	—	5	It All Comes Back To Me Now ....*Gene Krupa*...Okeh 5883
9	—	2	Dancing In The Dark ....*Artie Shaw*...Victor 27335
10	—	1	There'll Be Some Changes Made ....*Benny Goodman*...Columbia 35210

TW	LW	WK	Billboard® ❀ APRIL 12, 1941 ❀ Best Sellers
1	1	4	Amapola (Pretty Little Poppy) ....*Jimmy Dorsey*...Decca 3629
2	2	7	Oh! Look At Me Now ....*Tommy Dorsey*...Victor 27274
3	6	10	Perfidia [Tonight] ....*Xavier Cugat*...Victor 26334
4	5	8	Song Of The Volga Boatmen ....*Glenn Miller*...Bluebird 11029
5	—	1	Do I Worry? ....*Tommy Dorsey*...Victor 27338
6	4	21	Frenesi..*Artie Shaw*...Victor 26542
7	—	2	New San Antonio Rose ....*Bing Crosby*...Decca 3590
8	3	4	I Dreamt I Dwelt In Harlem..*Glenn Miller*...Bluebird 11063
9	—	1	Music Makers ....*Harry James*...Columbia 35932
10	7	2	Blue Flame..*Woody Herman*...Decca 3643

TW	LW	WK	Billboard	APRIL 19, 1941	Best Sellers
1	1	5	Amapola (Pretty Little Poppy)		Jimmy Dorsey...Decca 3629
2	2	8	Oh! Look At Me Now		Tommy Dorsey...Victor 27274
3	3	11	Perfidia [Tonight]		Xavier Cugat...Victor 26334
4	5	2	Do I Worry?		Tommy Dorsey...Victor 27338
5	6	22	Frenesi		Artie Shaw...Victor 26542
6	10	3	Blue Flame		Woody Herman...Decca 3643
7	—	1	The Wise Old Owl		Al Donahue...Okeh 6037
8	—	2	There'll Be Some Changes Made		Benny Goodman...Columbia 35210
9	7	3	New San Antonio Rose		Bing Crosby...Decca 3590
10	—	1	Souvenir De Vienne [Intermezzo]		Wayne King...Victor 26659

TW	LW	WK	Billboard	APRIL 26, 1941	Best Sellers
1	1	6	Amapola (Pretty Little Poppy)		Jimmy Dorsey...Decca 3629
2	2	9	Oh! Look At Me Now		Tommy Dorsey...Victor 27274
3	—	1	Alexander The Swoose (Half Swan-Half Goose)		Kay Kyser...Columbia 36040
4	4	3	Do I Worry?		Tommy Dorsey...Victor 27338
5	6	4	Blue Flame		Woody Herman...Decca 3643
6	8	3	There'll Be Some Changes Made		Benny Goodman...Columbia 35210
7	—	1	Dolores		Tommy Dorsey...Victor 27317
8	7	2	The Wise Old Owl		Al Donahue...Okeh 6037
9	5	23	Frenesi		Artie Shaw...Victor 26542
10	—	1	Dolores		Bing Crosby...Decca 3644

TW	LW	WK	Billboard	MAY 3, 1941	Best Sellers
1	1	7	Amapola (Pretty Little Poppy)		Jimmy Dorsey...Decca 3629
2	2	10	Oh! Look At Me Now		Tommy Dorsey...Victor 27274
3	10	2	Dolores		Bing Crosby...Decca 3644
4	—	1	G'bye Now		Horace Heidt...Columbia 36026
5	—	1	I'll Be With You In Apple Blossom Time		Andrews Sisters...Decca 3622
6	3	2	Alexander The Swoose (Half Swan-Half Goose)		Kay Kyser...Columbia 36040
7	—	2	Souvenir De Vienne [Intermezzo]		Wayne King...Victor 26659
8	—	12	Perfidia [Tonight]		Xavier Cugat...Victor 26334
9	—	1	Everything Happens To Me		Tommy Dorsey...Victor 27359

TW	LW	WK	Billboard	MAY 10, 1941	Best Sellers
1	1	8	Amapola (Pretty Little Poppy)		Jimmy Dorsey...Decca 3629
2	3	3	Dolores		Bing Crosby...Decca 3644
3	2	11	Oh! Look At Me Now		Tommy Dorsey...Victor 27274
4	4	2	G'bye Now		Horace Heidt...Columbia 36026
5	5	2	I'll Be With You In Apple Blossom Time		Andrews Sisters...Decca 3622
6	6	3	Alexander The Swoose (Half Swan-Half Goose)		Kay Kyser...Columbia 36040
7	—	1	Let's Get Away From It All-Parts 1 & 2		Tommy Dorsey...Victor 27377
8	—	2	Dolores		Tommy Dorsey...Victor 27317
9	7	3	Souvenir De Vienne [Intermezzo]		Wayne King...Victor 26659
10	8	13	Perfidia [Tonight]		Xavier Cugat...Victor 26334

TW	LW	WK	Billboard	MAY 17, 1941	Best Sellers
1	1	9	Amapola (Pretty Little Poppy)		Jimmy Dorsey...Decca 3629
2	—	1	My Sister And I		Jimmy Dorsey...Decca 3710
3	4	3	G'bye Now		Horace Heidt...Columbia 36026
4	2	4	Dolores		Bing Crosby...Decca 3644
5	5	5	I'll Be With You In Apple Blossom Time		Andrews Sisters...Decca 3622
6	—	1	Green Eyes (Aquellos Ojos Verdes)		Jimmy Dorsey...Decca 3698
7	9	4	Souvenir De Vienne [Intermezzo]		Wayne King...Victor 26659
8	7	2	Let's Get Away From It All-Parts 1 & 2		Tommy Dorsey...Victor 27377
9	3	12	Oh! Look At Me Now		Tommy Dorsey...Victor 27274
10	—	1	The Band Played On		Guy Lombardo...Decca 3675

TW	LW	WK	Billboard ☢ MAY 24, 1941 ☢ Best Sellers
1	1	10	**Amapola (Pretty Little Poppy)** ....*Jimmy Dorsey*...Decca 3629
2	3	4	**G'bye Now** ....*Horace Heidt*...Columbia 36026
3	2	2	**My Sister And I** ....*Jimmy Dorsey*...Decca 3710
4	4	5	**Dolores** ....*Bing Crosby*...Decca 3644
5	5	4	**I'll Be With You In Apple Blossom Time** ....*Andrews Sisters*...Decca 3622
6	10	2	**The Band Played On** ....*Guy Lombardo*...Decca 3675
7	6	2	**Green Eyes (Aquellos Ojos Verdes)** ....*Jimmy Dorsey*...Decca 3698
8	7	5	**Souvenir De Vienne [Intermezzo]** ....*Wayne King*...Victor 26659
9	—	1	**Maria Elena** ....*Jimmy Dorsey*...Decca 3698
10	—	1	**Until Tomorrow (Goodnight My Love)** ....*Sammy Kaye*...Victor 27262

TW	LW	WK	Billboard ☢ MAY 31, 1941 ☢ Best Sellers
1	1	11	**Amapola (Pretty Little Poppy)** ....*Jimmy Dorsey*...Decca 3629
2	3	3	**My Sister And I** ....*Jimmy Dorsey*...Decca 3710
3	4	6	**Dolores** ....*Bing Crosby*...Decca 3644
4	2	5	**G'bye Now** ....*Horace Heidt*...Columbia 36026
5	9	2	**Maria Elena** ....*Jimmy Dorsey*...Decca 3698
6	5	5	**I'll Be With You In Apple Blossom Time** ....*Andrews Sisters*...Decca 3622
7	6	3	**The Band Played On** ....*Guy Lombardo*...Decca 3675
8	7	3	**Green Eyes (Aquellos Ojos Verdes)** ....*Jimmy Dorsey*...Decca 3698
9	—	1	**Yours (Quiereme Mucho)** ....*Jimmy Dorsey*...Decca 3657
10	8	6	**Souvenir De Vienne [Intermezzo]** ....*Wayne King*...Victor 26659

TW	LW	WK	Billboard ☢ JUNE 7, 1941 ☢ Best Sellers
1	2	4	**My Sister And I** ....*Jimmy Dorsey*...Decca 3710
2	1	12	**Amapola (Pretty Little Poppy)** ....*Jimmy Dorsey*...Decca 3629
3	5	3	**Maria Elena** ....*Jimmy Dorsey*...Decca 3698
4	3	7	**Dolores** ....*Bing Crosby*...Decca 3644
5	—	1	**Daddy** ....*Sammy Kaye*...Victor 27391
6	6	6	**I'll Be With You In Apple Blossom Time** ....*Andrews Sisters*...Decca 3622
7	—	1	**Maria Elena** ....*Wayne King*...Victor 26767
8	8	4	**Green Eyes (Aquellos Ojos Verdes)** ....*Jimmy Dorsey*...Decca 3698
9	10	7	**Souvenir De Vienne [Intermezzo]** ....*Wayne King*...Victor 26659
10	—	1	**The Hut-Sut Song (A Swedish Serenade)** ....*Freddy Martin*...Bluebird 11147

TW	LW	WK	Billboard ☢ JUNE 14, 1941 ☢ Best Sellers
1	3	4	**Maria Elena** ....*Jimmy Dorsey*...Decca 3698
2	7	2	**Maria Elena** ....*Wayne King*...Victor 26767
3	5	2	**Daddy** ....*Sammy Kaye*...Victor 27391
4	1	5	**My Sister And I** ....*Jimmy Dorsey*...Decca 3710
5	9	8	**Souvenir De Vienne [Intermezzo]** ....*Wayne King*...Victor 26659
6	2	13	**Amapola (Pretty Little Poppy)** ....*Jimmy Dorsey*...Decca 3629
7	4	8	**Dolores** ....*Bing Crosby*...Decca 3644
8	10	2	**The Hut-Sut Song (A Swedish Serenade)** ....*Freddy Martin*...Bluebird 11147
9	—	1	**The Hut-Sut Song (A Swedish Serenade)** ....*Horace Heidt*...Columbia 36138
10	—	4	**The Band Played On** ....*Guy Lombardo*...Decca 3675

TW	LW	WK	Billboard ☢ JUNE 21, 1941 ☢ Best Sellers
1	3	3	**Daddy** ....*Sammy Kaye*...Victor 27391
2	1	5	**Maria Elena** ....*Jimmy Dorsey*...Decca 3698
3	8	3	**The Hut-Sut Song (A Swedish Serenade)** ....*Freddy Martin*...Bluebird 11147
4	4	6	**My Sister And I** ....*Jimmy Dorsey*...Decca 3710
5	5	9	**Souvenir De Vienne [Intermezzo]** ....*Wayne King*...Victor 26659
6	9	2	**The Hut-Sut Song (A Swedish Serenade)** ....*Horace Heidt*...Columbia 36138
7	2	3	**Maria Elena** ....*Wayne King*...Victor 26767
8	—	5	**Green Eyes (Aquellos Ojos Verdes)** ....*Jimmy Dorsey*...Decca 3698
9	7	9	**Dolores** ....*Bing Crosby*...Decca 3644
10	—	6	**G'bye Now** ....*Horace Heidt*...Columbia 36026

TW	LW	WK	Billboard® · JUNE 28, 1941 ·	Best Sellers
1	4	7	My Sister And I	Jimmy Dorsey...Decca 3710
2	3	4	The Hut-Sut Song (A Swedish Serenade)	Freddy Martin...Bluebird 11147
3	1	4	Daddy	Sammy Kaye...Victor 27391
4	2	6	Maria Elena	Jimmy Dorsey...Decca 3698
5	5	10	Souvenir De Vienne [Intermezzo]	Wayne King...Victor 26659
6	8	6	Green Eyes (Aquellos Ojos Verdes)	Jimmy Dorsey...Decca 3698
7	—	7	I'll Be With You In Apple Blossom Time	Andrews Sisters...Decca 3622
8	—	14	Amapola (Pretty Little Poppy)	Jimmy Dorsey...Decca 3629
9	—	1	Maria Elena	Tony Pastor...Bluebird 11127
10	—	1	G'bye Now	Woody Herman...Decca 3745

TW	LW	WK	Billboard® · JULY 5, 1941 ·	Best Sellers
1	4	7	Maria Elena	Jimmy Dorsey...Decca 3698
2	3	5	Daddy	Sammy Kaye...Victor 27391
3	—	3	The Hut-Sut Song (A Swedish Serenade)	Horace Heidt...Columbia 36138
4	2	5	The Hut-Sut Song (A Swedish Serenade)	Freddy Martin...Bluebird 11147
5	1	8	My Sister And I	Jimmy Dorsey...Decca 3710
6	5	11	Souvenir De Vienne [Intermezzo]	Wayne King...Victor 26659
7	—	1	Intermezzo	Freddy Martin...Bluebird 11123
8	—	1	The Things I Love	Jimmy Dorsey...Decca 3737
9	6	7	Green Eyes (Aquellos Ojos Verdes)	Jimmy Dorsey...Decca 3698
10	—	1	The Hut-Sut Song (A Swedish Serenade)	The Four King Sisters...Bluebird 11154

TW	LW	WK	Billboard® · JULY 12, 1941 ·	Best Sellers
1	2	6	Daddy	Sammy Kaye...Victor 27391
2	1	8	Maria Elena	Jimmy Dorsey...Decca 3698
3	3	4	The Hut-Sut Song (A Swedish Serenade)	Horace Heidt...Columbia 36138
4	4	6	The Hut-Sut Song (A Swedish Serenade)	Freddy Martin...Bluebird 11147
5	9	8	Green Eyes (Aquellos Ojos Verdes)	Jimmy Dorsey...Decca 3698
6	—	2	Yours (Quiereme Mucho)	Jimmy Dorsey...Decca 3657
7	8	2	The Things I Love	Jimmy Dorsey...Decca 3737
8	7	2	Intermezzo	Freddy Martin...Bluebird 11123
9	—	8	I'll Be With You In Apple Blossom Time	Andrews Sisters...Decca 3622
10	—	1	Yes Indeed!	Tommy Dorsey...Victor 27421

TW	LW	WK	Billboard® · JULY 19, 1941 ·	Best Sellers
1	1	7	Daddy	Sammy Kaye...Victor 27391
2	2	9	Maria Elena	Jimmy Dorsey...Decca 3698
3	4	7	The Hut-Sut Song (A Swedish Serenade)	Freddy Martin...Bluebird 11147
4	3	5	The Hut-Sut Song (A Swedish Serenade)	Horace Heidt...Columbia 36138
5	—	12	Souvenir De Vienne [Intermezzo]	Wayne King...Victor 26659
6	10	2	Yes Indeed!	Tommy Dorsey...Victor 27421
7	5	9	Green Eyes (Aquellos Ojos Verdes)	Jimmy Dorsey...Decca 3698
8	6	3	Yours (Quiereme Mucho)	Jimmy Dorsey...Decca 3657
9	7	3	The Things I Love	Jimmy Dorsey...Decca 3737
10	—	9	My Sister And I	Jimmy Dorsey...Decca 3710

TW	LW	WK	Billboard® · JULY 26, 1941 ·	Best Sellers
1	1	8	Daddy	Sammy Kaye...Victor 27391
2	2	10	Maria Elena	Jimmy Dorsey...Decca 3698
3	7	10	Green Eyes (Aquellos Ojos Verdes)	Jimmy Dorsey...Decca 3698
4	4	6	The Hut-Sut Song (A Swedish Serenade)	Horace Heidt...Columbia 36138
5	3	8	The Hut-Sut Song (A Swedish Serenade)	Freddy Martin...Bluebird 11147
6	6	3	Yes Indeed!	Tommy Dorsey...Victor 27421
7	8	4	Yours (Quiereme Mucho)	Jimmy Dorsey...Decca 3657
8	—	1	Good Bye Dear, I'll Be Back In A Year	Horace Heidt...Columbia 36148
9	—	1	'Til Reveille	Kay Kyser...Columbia 36137
10	10	10	My Sister And I	Jimmy Dorsey...Decca 3710

TW	LW	WK	Billboard ❀ AUGUST 2, 1941 ❀	Best Sellers
1	1	9	Daddy	Sammy Kaye...Victor 27391
2	2	11	Maria Elena	Jimmy Dorsey...Decca 3698
3	3	11	Green Eyes (Aquellos Ojos Verdes)	Jimmy Dorsey...Decca 3698
4	7	5	Yours (Quiereme Mucho)	Jimmy Dorsey...Decca 3657
5	6	4	Yes Indeed!	Tommy Dorsey...Victor 27421
6	—	1	Blue Champagne	Jimmy Dorsey...Decca 3775
7	5	9	The Hut-Sut Song (A Swedish Serenade)	Freddy Martin...Bluebird 11147
8	—	1	The Booglie Wooglie Piggy	Glenn Miller...Bluebird 11163
9	—	1	Just A Little Bit South Of North Carolina	Gene Krupa...Okeh 6130
10	—	1	Intermezzo (A Love Story)	Charlie Spivak...Okeh 6120

TW	LW	WK	Billboard ❀ AUGUST 9, 1941 ❀	Best Sellers
1	1	10	Daddy	Sammy Kaye...Victor 27391
2	2	12	Maria Elena	Jimmy Dorsey...Decca 3698
3	3	12	Green Eyes (Aquellos Ojos Verdes)	Jimmy Dorsey...Decca 3698
4	5	5	Yes Indeed!	Tommy Dorsey...Victor 27421
5	—	9	I'll Be With You In Apple Blossom Time	Andrews Sisters...Decca 3622
6	6	2	Blue Champagne	Jimmy Dorsey...Decca 3775
7	—	2	The Hut-Sut Song (A Swedish Serenade)	The Four King Sisters...Bluebird 11154
8	—	1	Piano Concerto In B Flat	Freddy Martin...Bluebird 11211
9	—	2	Good Bye Dear, I'll Be Back In A Year	Horace Heidt...Columbia 36148
10	—	1	'Til Reveille	Bing Crosby...Decca 3886

TW	LW	WK	Billboard ❀ AUGUST 16, 1941 ❀	Best Sellers
1	1	11	Daddy	Sammy Kaye...Victor 27391
2	3	13	Green Eyes (Aquellos Ojos Verdes)	Jimmy Dorsey...Decca 3698
3	2	13	Maria Elena	Jimmy Dorsey...Decca 3698
4	—	6	Yours (Quiereme Mucho)	Jimmy Dorsey...Decca 3657
5	4	6	Yes Indeed!	Tommy Dorsey...Victor 27421
6	—	2	'Til Reveille	Kay Kyser...Columbia 36137
7	—	2	The Booglie Wooglie Piggy	Glenn Miller...Bluebird 11163
8	—	13	Souvenir De Vienne [Intermezzo]	Wayne King...Victor 26659
9	8	2	Piano Concerto In B Flat	Freddy Martin...Bluebird 11211
10	5	10	I'll Be With You In Apple Blossom Time	Andrews Sisters...Decca 3622

TW	LW	WK	Billboard ❀ AUGUST 23, 1941 ❀	Best Sellers
1	1	12	Daddy	Sammy Kaye...Victor 27391
2	2	14	Green Eyes (Aquellos Ojos Verdes)	Jimmy Dorsey...Decca 3698
3	3	14	Maria Elena	Jimmy Dorsey...Decca 3698
4	4	7	Yours (Quiereme Mucho)	Jimmy Dorsey...Decca 3657
5	5	7	Yes Indeed!	Tommy Dorsey...Victor 27421
6	—	2	'Til Reveille	Bing Crosby...Decca 3886
7	—	3	Blue Champagne	Jimmy Dorsey...Decca 3775
8	6	3	'Til Reveille	Kay Kyser...Columbia 36137
9	9	3	Piano Concerto In B Flat	Freddy Martin...Bluebird 11211
10	10	11	I'll Be With You In Apple Blossom Time	Andrews Sisters...Decca 3622

TW	LW	WK	Billboard ❀ AUGUST 30, 1941 ❀	Best Sellers
1	2	15	Green Eyes (Aquellos Ojos Verdes)	Jimmy Dorsey...Decca 3698
2	1	13	Daddy	Sammy Kaye...Victor 27391
3	4	8	Yours (Quiereme Mucho)	Jimmy Dorsey...Decca 3657
4	7	4	Blue Champagne	Jimmy Dorsey...Decca 3775
5	5	8	Yes Indeed!	Tommy Dorsey...Victor 27421
6	3	15	Maria Elena	Jimmy Dorsey...Decca 3698
7	8	4	'Til Reveille	Kay Kyser...Columbia 36137
8	9	4	Piano Concerto In B Flat	Freddy Martin...Bluebird 11211
9	—	3	The Booglie Wooglie Piggy	Glenn Miller...Bluebird 11163
10	—	1	Lament To Love	Harry James...Columbia 36222

TW	LW	WK	Billboard®	SEPTEMBER 6, 1941	Best Sellers
1	1	16	Green Eyes (Aquellos Ojos Verdes)..		Jimmy Dorsey...Decca 3698
2	3	9	Yours (Quiereme Mucho)..		Jimmy Dorsey...Decca 3657
3	6	16	Maria Elena...		Jimmy Dorsey...Decca 3698
4	—	1	You And I...		Glenn Miller...Bluebird 11215
5	2	14	Daddy...		Sammy Kaye...Victor 27391
6	5	9	Yes Indeed!..		Tommy Dorsey...Victor 27421
7	8	5	Piano Concerto In B Flat..		Freddy Martin...Bluebird 11211
8	9	4	The Booglie Wooglie Piggy..		Glenn Miller...Bluebird 11163
9	4	5	Blue Champagne...		Jimmy Dorsey...Decca 3775
10	—	1	Let Me Off Uptown..		Gene Krupa...Okeh 6210

TW	LW	WK	Billboard®	SEPTEMBER 13, 1941	Best Sellers
1	1	17	Green Eyes (Aquellos Ojos Verdes)..		Jimmy Dorsey...Decca 3698
2	2	10	Yours (Quiereme Mucho)..		Jimmy Dorsey...Decca 3657
3	9	6	Blue Champagne...		Jimmy Dorsey...Decca 3775
4	6	10	Yes Indeed!..		Tommy Dorsey...Victor 27421
5	3	17	Maria Elena...		Jimmy Dorsey...Decca 3698
6	—	1	You And I...		Bing Crosby...Decca 3840
7	5	15	Daddy...		Sammy Kaye...Victor 27391
8	7	6	Piano Concerto In B Flat..		Freddy Martin...Bluebird 11211
9	—	1	Chattanooga Choo Choo...		Glenn Miller...Bluebird 11230
10	—	3	'Til Reveille..		Bing Crosby...Decca 3886

TW	LW	WK	Billboard®	SEPTEMBER 20, 1941	Best Sellers
1	1	18	Green Eyes (Aquellos Ojos Verdes)..		Jimmy Dorsey...Decca 3698
2	3	7	Blue Champagne...		Jimmy Dorsey...Decca 3775
3	2	11	Yours (Quiereme Mucho)..		Jimmy Dorsey...Decca 3657
4	4	11	Yes Indeed!..		Tommy Dorsey...Victor 27421
5	8	7	Piano Concerto In B Flat..		Freddy Martin...Bluebird 11211
6	9	2	Chattanooga Choo Choo...		Glenn Miller...Bluebird 11230
7	10	4	'Til Reveille..		Bing Crosby...Decca 3886
8	—	2	You And I...		Glenn Miller...Bluebird 11215
9	6	2	You And I...		Bing Crosby...Decca 3840
10	—	1	I Don't Want To Set The World On Fire...		Tommy Tucker Time...Okeh 6320

TW	LW	WK	Billboard®	SEPTEMBER 27, 1941	Best Sellers
1	2	8	Blue Champagne...		Jimmy Dorsey...Decca 3775
2	6	3	Chattanooga Choo Choo...		Glenn Miller...Bluebird 11230
3	5	8	Piano Concerto In B Flat..		Freddy Martin...Bluebird 11211
4	1	19	Green Eyes (Aquellos Ojos Verdes)..		Jimmy Dorsey...Decca 3698
5	—	1	I Don't Want To Set The World On Fire...		Horace Heidt...Columbia 36295
6	10	2	I Don't Want To Set The World On Fire...		Tommy Tucker Time...Okeh 6320
7	4	12	Yes Indeed!..		Tommy Dorsey...Victor 27421
8	8	3	You And I...		Glenn Miller...Bluebird 11215
9	—	5	The Booglie Wooglie Piggy..		Glenn Miller...Bluebird 11163
10	3	12	Yours (Quiereme Mucho)..		Jimmy Dorsey...Decca 3657

TW	LW	WK	Billboard®	OCTOBER 4, 1941	Best Sellers
1	3	9	Piano Concerto In B Flat..		Freddy Martin...Bluebird 11211
2	5	2	I Don't Want To Set The World On Fire...		Horace Heidt...Columbia 36295
3	2	4	Chattanooga Choo Choo...		Glenn Miller...Bluebird 11230
4	1	9	Blue Champagne...		Jimmy Dorsey...Decca 3775
5	4	20	Green Eyes (Aquellos Ojos Verdes)..		Jimmy Dorsey...Decca 3698
6	7	13	Yes Indeed!..		Tommy Dorsey...Victor 27421
7	—	1	Jim..		Jimmy Dorsey...Decca 3963
8	10	13	Yours (Quiereme Mucho)..		Jimmy Dorsey...Decca 3657
9	8	4	You And I...		Glenn Miller...Bluebird 11215
10	—	5	'Til Reveille..		Bing Crosby...Decca 3886

Billboard — OCTOBER 11, 1941 — Best Sellers

TW	LW	WK	Title	Artist...Label
1	1	10	Piano Concerto In B Flat	Freddy Martin...Bluebird 11211
2	3	5	Chattanooga Choo Choo	Glenn Miller...Bluebird 11230
3	2	3	I Don't Want To Set The World On Fire	Horace Heidt...Columbia 36295
4	4	10	Blue Champagne	Jimmy Dorsey...Decca 3775
5	7	2	Jim	Jimmy Dorsey...Decca 3963
6	—	3	I Don't Want To Set The World On Fire	Tommy Tucker Time...Okeh 6320
7	9	5	You And I	Glenn Miller...Bluebird 11215
8	5	21	Green Eyes (Aquellos Ojos Verdes)	Jimmy Dorsey...Decca 3698
9	—	1	"Jim"	Dinah Shore...Bluebird 11204
10	—	1	Elmer's Tune	Dick Jurgens...Okeh 6209

Billboard — OCTOBER 18, 1941 — Best Sellers

TW	LW	WK	Title	Artist...Label
1	1	11	Piano Concerto In B Flat	Freddy Martin...Bluebird 11211
2	2	6	Chattanooga Choo Choo	Glenn Miller...Bluebird 11230
3	3	4	I Don't Want To Set The World On Fire	Horace Heidt...Columbia 36295
4	4	11	Blue Champagne	Jimmy Dorsey...Decca 3775
5	—	1	I Don't Want To Set The World On Fire	Ink Spots...Decca 3987
6	5	3	Jim	Jimmy Dorsey...Decca 3963
7	6	4	I Don't Want To Set The World On Fire	Tommy Tucker Time...Okeh 6320
8	—	14	Yes Indeed!	Tommy Dorsey...Victor 27421
9	7	6	You And I	Glenn Miller...Bluebird 11215
10	—	3	You And I	Bing Crosby...Decca 3840

Billboard — OCTOBER 25, 1941 — Best Sellers

TW	LW	WK	Title	Artist...Label
1	1	12	Piano Concerto In B Flat	Freddy Martin...Bluebird 11211
2	3	5	I Don't Want To Set The World On Fire	Horace Heidt...Columbia 36295
3	2	7	Chattanooga Choo Choo	Glenn Miller...Bluebird 11230
4	7	5	I Don't Want To Set The World On Fire	Tommy Tucker Time...Okeh 6320
5	—	2	"Jim"	Dinah Shore...Bluebird 11204
6	4	12	Blue Champagne	Jimmy Dorsey...Decca 3775
7	5	2	I Don't Want To Set The World On Fire	Ink Spots...Decca 3987
8	6	4	Jim	Jimmy Dorsey...Decca 3963
9	—	1	This Love Of Mine	Tommy Dorsey...Victor 27508
10	—	1	Time Was (Duerme)	Jimmy Dorsey...Decca 3859

Billboard — NOVEMBER 1, 1941 — Best Sellers

TW	LW	WK	Title	Artist...Label
1	1	13	Piano Concerto In B Flat	Freddy Martin...Bluebird 11211
2	3	8	Chattanooga Choo Choo	Glenn Miller...Bluebird 11230
3	2	6	I Don't Want To Set The World On Fire	Horace Heidt...Columbia 36295
4	7	3	I Don't Want To Set The World On Fire	Ink Spots...Decca 3987
5	8	5	Jim	Jimmy Dorsey...Decca 3963
6	4	6	I Don't Want To Set The World On Fire	Tommy Tucker Time...Okeh 6320
7	9	2	This Love Of Mine	Tommy Dorsey...Victor 27508
8	—	1	You Made Me Love You (I Didn't Want To Do It)	Harry James...Columbia 36296
9	—	4	You And I	Bing Crosby...Decca 3840
10	5	3	"Jim"	Dinah Shore...Bluebird 11204

Billboard — NOVEMBER 8, 1941 — Best Sellers

TW	LW	WK	Title	Artist...Label
1	1	14	Piano Concerto In B Flat	Freddy Martin...Bluebird 11211
2	2	9	Chattanooga Choo Choo	Glenn Miller...Bluebird 11230
3	3	7	I Don't Want To Set The World On Fire	Horace Heidt...Columbia 36295
4	—	1	Elmer's Tune	Glenn Miller...Bluebird 11274
5	6	7	I Don't Want To Set The World On Fire	Tommy Tucker Time...Okeh 6320
6	7	3	This Love Of Mine	Tommy Dorsey...Victor 27508
7	4	4	I Don't Want To Set The World On Fire	Ink Spots...Decca 3987
8	5	6	Jim	Jimmy Dorsey...Decca 3963
9	—	13	Blue Champagne	Jimmy Dorsey...Decca 3775
10	—	1	Tonight We Love (Concerto No. 1, B Flat Minor)	Tony Martin...Decca 3988

TW	LW	WK	Billboard® ❀ NOVEMBER 15, 1941 ❀ Best Sellers
1	1	15	Piano Concerto In B Flat ....Freddy Martin...Bluebird 11211
2	2	10	Chattanooga Choo Choo ....Glenn Miller...Bluebird 11230
3	4	2	Elmer's Tune ....Glenn Miller...Bluebird 11274
4	3	8	I Don't Want To Set The World On Fire ....Horace Heidt...Columbia 36295
5	6	4	This Love Of Mine ....Tommy Dorsey...Victor 27508
6	8	7	Jim ....Jimmy Dorsey...Decca 3963
7	7	5	I Don't Want To Set The World On Fire ....Ink Spots...Decca 3987
8	10	2	Tonight We Love (Concerto No. 1, B Flat Minor) ....Tony Martin...Decca 3988
9	5	8	I Don't Want To Set The World On Fire ....Tommy Tucker Time...Okeh 6320
10	9	14	Blue Champagne ....Jimmy Dorsey...Decca 3775

TW	LW	WK	Billboard® ❀ NOVEMBER 22, 1941 ❀ Best Sellers
1	1	16	Piano Concerto In B Flat ....Freddy Martin...Bluebird 11211
2	2	11	Chattanooga Choo Choo ....Glenn Miller...Bluebird 11230
3	5	5	This Love Of Mine ....Tommy Dorsey...Victor 27508
4	3	3	Elmer's Tune ....Glenn Miller...Bluebird 11274
5	4	9	I Don't Want To Set The World On Fire ....Horace Heidt...Columbia 36295
6	7	6	I Don't Want To Set The World On Fire ....Ink Spots...Decca 3987
7	6	8	Jim ....Jimmy Dorsey...Decca 3963
8	8	3	Tonight We Love (Concerto No. 1, B Flat Minor) ....Tony Martin...Decca 3988
9	—	2	Elmer's Tune ....Dick Jurgens...Okeh 6209
10	—	2	You Made Me Love You (I Didn't Want To Do It) ....Harry James...Columbia 36296

TW	LW	WK	Billboard® ❀ NOVEMBER 29, 1941 ❀ Best Sellers
1	2	12	Chattanooga Choo Choo ....Glenn Miller...Bluebird 11230
2	1	17	Piano Concerto In B Flat ....Freddy Martin...Bluebird 11211
3	4	4	Elmer's Tune ....Glenn Miller...Bluebird 11274
4	3	6	This Love Of Mine ....Tommy Dorsey...Victor 27508
5	8	4	Tonight We Love (Concerto No. 1, B Flat Minor) ....Tony Martin...Decca 3988
6	6	7	I Don't Want To Set The World On Fire ....Ink Spots...Decca 3987
7	5	10	I Don't Want To Set The World On Fire ....Horace Heidt...Columbia 36295
8	9	3	Elmer's Tune ....Dick Jurgens...Okeh 6209
9	—	9	I Don't Want To Set The World On Fire ....Tommy Tucker Time...Okeh 6320
10	—	1	Blues In The Night ....Artie Shaw...Victor 27609

TW	LW	WK	Billboard® ❀ DECEMBER 6, 1941 ❀ Best Sellers
1	1	13	Chattanooga Choo Choo ....Glenn Miller...Bluebird 11230
2	2	18	Piano Concerto In B Flat ....Freddy Martin...Bluebird 11211
3	3	5	Elmer's Tune ....Glenn Miller...Bluebird 11274
4	4	7	This Love Of Mine ....Tommy Dorsey...Victor 27508
5	—	3	You Made Me Love You (I Didn't Want To Do It) ....Harry James...Columbia 36296
6	5	5	Tonight We Love (Concerto No. 1, B Flat Minor) ....Tony Martin...Decca 3988
7	7	11	I Don't Want To Set The World On Fire ....Horace Heidt...Columbia 36295
8	—	1	Shepherd Serenade ....Horace Heidt...Columbia 36370
9	9	10	I Don't Want To Set The World On Fire ....Tommy Tucker Time...Okeh 6320
10	—	9	Jim ....Jimmy Dorsey...Decca 3963

TW	LW	WK	Billboard® ❀ DECEMBER 13, 1941 ❀ Best Sellers
1	1	14	Chattanooga Choo Choo ....Glenn Miller...Bluebird 11230
2	3	6	Elmer's Tune ....Glenn Miller...Bluebird 11274
3	2	19	Piano Concerto In B Flat ....Freddy Martin...Bluebird 11211
4	4	8	This Love Of Mine ....Tommy Dorsey...Victor 27508
5	6	6	Tonight We Love (Concerto No. 1, B Flat Minor) ....Tony Martin...Decca 3988
6	5	4	You Made Me Love You (I Didn't Want To Do It) ....Harry James...Columbia 36296
7	8	2	Shepherd Serenade ....Horace Heidt...Columbia 36370
8	—	1	Shepherd Serenade ....Bing Crosby...Decca 4065
9	—	8	I Don't Want To Set The World On Fire ....Ink Spots...Decca 3987
10	—	4	Elmer's Tune ....Dick Jurgens...Okeh 6209

TW	LW	WK	Billboard® ✸ DECEMBER 20, 1941 ✸ Best Sellers
1	2	7	Elmer's Tune..*Glenn Miller*...Bluebird 11274
2	1	15	Chattanooga Choo Choo..*Glenn Miller*...Bluebird 11230
3	3	20	Piano Concerto In B Flat ....*Freddy Martin*...Bluebird 11211
4	4	9	This Love Of Mine ....*Tommy Dorsey*...Victor 27508
5	8	2	Shepherd Serenade ....*Bing Crosby*...Decca 4065
6	5	7	Tonight We Love (Concerto No. 1, B Flat Minor)..*Tony Martin*...Decca 3988
7	6	5	You Made Me Love You (I Didn't Want To Do It)................................*Harry James*...Columbia 36296
8	7	3	Shepherd Serenade ....*Horace Heidt*...Columbia 36370
9	—	1	Two In Love..*Tommy Dorsey*...Victor 27611
10	10	5	Elmer's Tune ....*Dick Jurgens*...Okeh 6209

TW	LW	WK	Billboard® ✸ DECEMBER 27, 1941 ✸ Best Sellers
1	2	16	Chattanooga Choo Choo..*Glenn Miller*...Bluebird 11230
2	1	8	Elmer's Tune..*Glenn Miller*...Bluebird 11274
3	3	21	Piano Concerto In B Flat ....*Freddy Martin*...Bluebird 11211
4	4	10	This Love Of Mine ....*Tommy Dorsey*...Victor 27508
5	—	1	Jingle Bells ....*Glenn Miller*...Bluebird 11353
6	5	3	Shepherd Serenade ....*Bing Crosby*...Decca 4065
7	7	6	You Made Me Love You (I Didn't Want To Do It)................................*Harry James*...Columbia 36296
8	8	4	Shepherd Serenade ....*Horace Heidt*...Columbia 36370
9	6	8	Tonight We Love (Concerto No. 1, B Flat Minor)..*Tony Martin*...Decca 3988
10	10	6	Elmer's Tune ....*Dick Jurgens*...Okeh 6209

TW	LW	WK	Billboard ❄ JANUARY 3, 1942 ❄ Best Sellers
1	1	17	Chattanooga Choo Choo..*Glenn Miller*...Bluebird 11230
2	2	9	Elmer's Tune..*Glenn Miller*...Bluebird 11274
3	4	11	This Love Of Mine..*Tommy Dorsey*...Victor 27508
4	3	22	Piano Concerto In B Flat..*Freddy Martin*...Bluebird 11211
5	6	4	Shepherd Serenade..*Bing Crosby*...Decca 4065
6	5	2	Jingle Bells..*Glenn Miller*...Bluebird 11353
7	8	5	Shepherd Serenade..*Horace Heidt*...Columbia 36370
8	7	7	You Made Me Love You (I Didn't Want To Do It)..*Harry James*...Columbia 36296
9	—	1	This Is No Laughing Matter..*Charlie Spivak*...Okeh 6458
10	—	1	(There'll Be Blue Birds Over) The White Cliffs Of Dover..*Glenn Miller*...Bluebird 11397

TW	LW	WK	Billboard ❄ JANUARY 10, 1942 ❄ Best Sellers
1	1	18	Chattanooga Choo Choo..*Glenn Miller*...Bluebird 11230
2	2	10	Elmer's Tune..*Glenn Miller*...Bluebird 11274
3	4	23	Piano Concerto In B Flat..*Freddy Martin*...Bluebird 11211
4	3	12	This Love Of Mine..*Tommy Dorsey*...Victor 27508
5	5	5	Shepherd Serenade..*Bing Crosby*...Decca 4065
6	8	8	You Made Me Love You (I Didn't Want To Do It)..*Harry James*...Columbia 36296
7	—	1	Blues In The Night (My Mama Done Tol' Me)..*Woody Herman*...Decca 4030
8	9	2	This Is No Laughing Matter..*Charlie Spivak*...Okeh 6458
9	—	1	A String Of Pearls..*Glenn Miller*...Bluebird 11382
10	—	1	(There'll Be Bluebirds Over) The White Cliffs Of Dover..*Kay Kyser*...Columbia 36445

TW	LW	WK	Billboard ❄ JANUARY 17, 1942 ❄ Best Sellers
1	1	19	Chattanooga Choo Choo..*Glenn Miller*...Bluebird 11230
2	2	11	Elmer's Tune..*Glenn Miller*...Bluebird 11274
3	4	13	This Love Of Mine..*Tommy Dorsey*...Victor 27508
4	3	24	Piano Concerto In B Flat..*Freddy Martin*...Bluebird 11211
5	5	6	Shepherd Serenade..*Bing Crosby*...Decca 4065
6	7	2	Blues In The Night (My Mama Done Tol' Me)..*Woody Herman*...Decca 4030
7	6	9	You Made Me Love You (I Didn't Want To Do It)..*Harry James*...Columbia 36296
8	—	1	Tonight We Love..*Freddy Martin*...Bluebird 11320
9	—	2	(There'll Be Blue Birds Over) The White Cliffs Of Dover..*Glenn Miller*...Bluebird 11397
10	—	1	I Said No!..*Alvino Rey*...Bluebird 11391

TW	LW	WK	Billboard ❄ JANUARY 24, 1942 ❄ Best Sellers
1	1	20	Chattanooga Choo Choo..*Glenn Miller*...Bluebird 11230
2	2	12	Elmer's Tune..*Glenn Miller*...Bluebird 11274
3	3	14	This Love Of Mine..*Tommy Dorsey*...Victor 27508
4	6	3	Blues In The Night (My Mama Done Tol' Me)..*Woody Herman*...Decca 4030
5	7	10	You Made Me Love You (I Didn't Want To Do It)..*Harry James*...Columbia 36296
6	9	3	(There'll Be Blue Birds Over) The White Cliffs Of Dover..*Glenn Miller*...Bluebird 11397
7	—	2	(There'll Be Bluebirds Over) The White Cliffs Of Dover..*Kay Kyser*...Columbia 36445
8	10	2	I Said No!..*Alvino Rey*...Bluebird 11391
9	—	1	Ev'rything I Love..*Glenn Miller*...Bluebird 11365
10	—	2	A String Of Pearls..*Glenn Miller*...Bluebird 11382

TW	LW	WK	Billboard ❄ JANUARY 31, 1942 ❄ Best Sellers
1	1	21	Chattanooga Choo Choo..*Glenn Miller*...Bluebird 11230
2	4	4	Blues In The Night (My Mama Done Tol' Me)..*Woody Herman*...Decca 4030
3	10	3	A String Of Pearls..*Glenn Miller*...Bluebird 11382
4	2	13	Elmer's Tune..*Glenn Miller*...Bluebird 11274
5	8	3	I Said No!..*Alvino Rey*...Bluebird 11391
6	3	15	This Love Of Mine..*Tommy Dorsey*...Victor 27508
7	—	1	Remember Pearl Harbor..*Sammy Kaye*...Victor 27738
8	9	2	Ev'rything I Love..*Glenn Miller*...Bluebird 11365
9	6	4	(There'll Be Blue Birds Over) The White Cliffs Of Dover..*Glenn Miller*...Bluebird 11397
10	—	1	I Said No..*Jimmy Dorsey*...Decca 4102

TW	LW	WK	Billboard® FEBRUARY 7, 1942 Best Sellers
1	3	4	**A String Of Pearls** ....*Glenn Miller*...Bluebird 11382
2	1	22	**Chattanooga Choo Choo** ....*Glenn Miller*...Bluebird 11230
3	5	4	**I Said No!** ....*Alvino Rey*...Bluebird 11391
4	2	5	**Blues In The Night** (My Mama Done Tol' Me)..........................*Woody Herman*...Decca 4030
5	6	16	**This Love Of Mine** ....*Tommy Dorsey*...Victor 27508
6	—	1	**Blues In The Night** (My Mama Done Tol' Me) - Parts 1 & 2 ....*Jimmie Lunceford*...Decca 4125
7	7	2	**Remember Pearl Harbor** ....*Sammy Kaye*...Victor 27738
8	4	14	**Elmer's Tune**..*Glenn Miller*...Bluebird 11274
9	—	3	**(There'll Be Bluebirds Over) The White Cliffs Of Dover** ....*Kay Kyser*...Columbia 36445
10	8	3	**Ev'rything I Love** ....*Glenn Miller*...Bluebird 11365

TW	LW	WK	Billboard® FEBRUARY 14, 1942 Best Sellers
1	4	6	**Blues In The Night** (My Mama Done Tol' Me)......................................*Woody Herman*...Decca 4030
2	1	5	**A String Of Pearls** ....*Glenn Miller*...Bluebird 11382
3	7	3	**Remember Pearl Harbor** ....*Sammy Kaye*...Victor 27738
4	3	5	**I Said No!** ....*Alvino Rey*...Bluebird 11391
5	6	2	**Blues In The Night** (My Mama Done Tol' Me) - Parts 1 & 2 ....*Jimmie Lunceford*...Decca 4125
6	2	23	**Chattanooga Choo Choo** ....*Glenn Miller*...Bluebird 11230
7	10	4	**Ev'rything I Love** ....*Glenn Miller*...Bluebird 11365
8	—	5	**(There'll Be Blue Birds Over) The White Cliffs Of Dover** ....*Glenn Miller*...Bluebird 11397
9	8	15	**Elmer's Tune**..*Glenn Miller*...Bluebird 11274
10	—	1	**Deep In The Heart Of Texas** ....*Alvino Rey*...Bluebird 11391

TW	LW	WK	Billboard® FEBRUARY 21, 1942 Best Sellers
1	2	6	**A String Of Pearls** ....*Glenn Miller*...Bluebird 11382
2	4	6	**I Said No!** ....*Alvino Rey*...Bluebird 11391
3	1	7	**Blues In The Night** (My Mama Done Tol' Me)......................................*Woody Herman*...Decca 4030
4	5	3	**Blues In The Night** (My Mama Done Tol' Me) - Parts 1 & 2 ....*Jimmie Lunceford*...Decca 4125
5	—	1	**Moonlight Cocktail** ....*Glenn Miller*...Bluebird 11401
6	3	4	**Remember Pearl Harbor** ....*Sammy Kaye*...Victor 27738
7	10	2	**Deep In The Heart Of Texas** ....*Alvino Rey*...Bluebird 11391
8	—	1	**Blues In The Night** ....*Dinah Shore*...Bluebird 11436
9	—	1	**(There'll Be Bluebirds Over) The White Cliffs Of Dover** ....*Kate Smith*...Columbia 36448
10	8	6	**(There'll Be Blue Birds Over) The White Cliffs Of Dover** ....*Glenn Miller*...Bluebird 11397

TW	LW	WK	Billboard® FEBRUARY 28, 1942 Best Sellers
1	5	2	**Moonlight Cocktail** ....*Glenn Miller*...Bluebird 11401
2	1	7	**A String Of Pearls** ....*Glenn Miller*...Bluebird 11382
3	7	3	**Deep In The Heart Of Texas** ....*Alvino Rey*...Bluebird 11391
4	2	7	**I Said No!** ....*Alvino Rey*...Bluebird 11391
5	3	8	**Blues In The Night** (My Mama Done Tol' Me)......................................*Woody Herman*...Decca 4030
6	6	5	**Remember Pearl Harbor** ....*Sammy Kaye*...Victor 27738
7	4	4	**Blues In The Night** (My Mama Done Tol' Me) - Parts 1 & 2 ....*Jimmie Lunceford*...Decca 4125
8	—	1	**Rose O'Day** (The Filla-ga-dusha Song) ....*Kate Smith*...Columbia 36448
9	10	7	**(There'll Be Blue Birds Over) The White Cliffs Of Dover** ....*Glenn Miller*...Bluebird 11397
10	—	1	**I Don't Want To Walk Without You** ....*Harry James*...Columbia 36478

TW	LW	WK	Billboard® MARCH 7, 1942 Best Sellers
1	1	3	**Moonlight Cocktail** ....*Glenn Miller*...Bluebird 11401
2	2	8	**A String Of Pearls** ....*Glenn Miller*...Bluebird 11382
3	—	1	**Deep In The Heart Of Texas** ....*Bing Crosby*...Decca 4162
4	4	8	**I Said No!** ....*Alvino Rey*...Bluebird 11391
5	3	4	**Deep In The Heart Of Texas** ....*Alvino Rey*...Bluebird 11391
6	7	5	**Blues In The Night** (My Mama Done Tol' Me) - Parts 1 & 2 ....*Jimmie Lunceford*...Decca 4125
7	—	2	**Blues In The Night** ....*Dinah Shore*...Bluebird 11436
8	10	2	**I Don't Want To Walk Without You** ....*Harry James*...Columbia 36478
9	5	9	**Blues In The Night** (My Mama Done Tol' Me)......................................*Woody Herman*...Decca 4030
10	8	2	**Rose O'Day** (The Filla-ga-dusha Song) ....*Kate Smith*...Columbia 36448

TW	LW	WK	Billboard ❀ MARCH 14, 1942 ❀ Best Sellers
1	1	4	**Moonlight Cocktail** ....*Glenn Miller*...Bluebird 11401
2	8	3	**I Don't Want To Walk Without You** ....*Harry James*...Columbia 36478
3	3	2	**Deep In The Heart Of Texas**................................*Bing Crosby*...Decca 4162
4	5	5	**Deep In The Heart Of Texas** ....*Alvino Rey*...Bluebird 11391
5	2	9	**A String Of Pearls** ....*Glenn Miller*...Bluebird 11382
6	7	3	**Blues In The Night** ....*Dinah Shore*...Bluebird 11436
7	4	9	**I Said No!** ....*Alvino Rey*...Bluebird 11391
8	—	1	**Blues In The Night (My Mama Done Tol' Me)**................*Cab Calloway*...Okeh 6422
9	—	1	**Deep In The Heart Of Texas** ....*Horace Heidt*...Columbia 36525
10	10	3	**Rose O'Day (The Filla-ga-dusha Song)** ....*Kate Smith*...Columbia 36448

TW	LW	WK	Billboard ❀ MARCH 21, 1942 ❀ Best Sellers
1	1	5	**Moonlight Cocktail** ....*Glenn Miller*...Bluebird 11401
2	5	10	**A String Of Pearls** ....*Glenn Miller*...Bluebird 11382
3	2	4	**I Don't Want To Walk Without You** ....*Harry James*...Columbia 36478
4	6	4	**Blues In The Night** ....*Dinah Shore*...Bluebird 11436
5	3	3	**Deep In The Heart Of Texas**................................*Bing Crosby*...Decca 4162
6	4	6	**Deep In The Heart Of Texas** ....*Alvino Rey*...Bluebird 11391
7	9	2	**Deep In The Heart Of Texas** ....*Horace Heidt*...Columbia 36525
8	—	1	**A Zoot Suit (For My Sunday Gal)** ....*Kay Kyser*...Columbia 36517
9	—	10	**Blues In The Night (My Mama Done Tol' Me)**................*Woody Herman*...Decca 4030
10	—	1	**Miss You** ....*Dinah Shore*...Bluebird 11322

TW	LW	WK	Billboard ❀ MARCH 28, 1942 ❀ Best Sellers
1	1	6	**Moonlight Cocktail** ....*Glenn Miller*...Bluebird 11401
2	3	5	**I Don't Want To Walk Without You** ....*Harry James*...Columbia 36478
3	2	11	**A String Of Pearls** ....*Glenn Miller*...Bluebird 11382
4	5	4	**Deep In The Heart Of Texas**................................*Bing Crosby*...Decca 4162
5	4	5	**Blues In The Night** ....*Dinah Shore*...Bluebird 11436
6	—	1	**Somebody Else Is Taking My Place** ....*Benny Goodman*...Okeh 6497
7	9	11	**Blues In The Night (My Mama Done Tol' Me)**................*Woody Herman*...Decca 4030
8	10	2	**Miss You** ....*Dinah Shore*...Bluebird 11322
9	—	10	**I Said No!** ....*Alvino Rey*...Bluebird 11391
10	7	3	**Deep In The Heart Of Texas** ....*Horace Heidt*...Columbia 36525

TW	LW	WK	Billboard ❀ APRIL 4, 1942 ❀ Best Sellers
1	1	7	**Moonlight Cocktail** ....*Glenn Miller*...Bluebird 11401
2	2	6	**I Don't Want To Walk Without You** ....*Harry James*...Columbia 36478
3	3	12	**A String Of Pearls** ....*Glenn Miller*...Bluebird 11382
4	4	5	**Deep In The Heart Of Texas**................................*Bing Crosby*...Decca 4162
5	5	6	**Blues In The Night** ....*Dinah Shore*...Bluebird 11436
6	—	7	**Deep In The Heart Of Texas** ....*Alvino Rey*...Bluebird 11391
7	—	1	**Jersey Bounce** ....*Benny Goodman*...Okeh 6590
8	6	2	**Somebody Else Is Taking My Place** ....*Benny Goodman*...Okeh 6497
9	—	1	**I Don't Want To Walk Without You** ....*Bing Crosby*...Decca 4184
10	—	1	**Somebody Else Is Taking My Place** ....*Russ Morgan*...Decca 4098

TW	LW	WK	Billboard ❀ APRIL 11, 1942 ❀ Best Sellers
1	1	8	**Moonlight Cocktail** ....*Glenn Miller*...Bluebird 11401
2	2	7	**I Don't Want To Walk Without You** ....*Harry James*...Columbia 36478
3	3	13	**A String Of Pearls** ....*Glenn Miller*...Bluebird 11382
4	7	2	**Jersey Bounce** ....*Benny Goodman*...Okeh 6590
5	8	3	**Somebody Else Is Taking My Place** ....*Benny Goodman*...Okeh 6497
6	4	6	**Deep In The Heart Of Texas**................................*Bing Crosby*...Decca 4162
7	5	7	**Blues In The Night** ....*Dinah Shore*...Bluebird 11436
8	10	2	**Somebody Else Is Taking My Place** ....*Russ Morgan*...Decca 4098
9	6	8	**Deep In The Heart Of Texas** ....*Alvino Rey*...Bluebird 11391
10	—	3	**Miss You** ....*Dinah Shore*...Bluebird 11322

Billboard — APRIL 18, 1942 — Best Sellers

TW	LW	WK	Title	Artist
1	1	9	**Moonlight Cocktail**	*Glenn Miller*...Bluebird 11401
2	2	8	**I Don't Want To Walk Without You**	*Harry James*...Columbia 36478
3	4	3	**Jersey Bounce**	*Benny Goodman*...Okeh 6590
4	3	14	**A String Of Pearls**	*Glenn Miller*...Bluebird 11382
5	8	3	**Somebody Else Is Taking My Place**	*Russ Morgan*...Decca 4098
6	5	4	**Somebody Else Is Taking My Place**	*Benny Goodman*...Okeh 6497
7	—	1	**Tangerine**	*Jimmy Dorsey*...Decca 4123
8	—	1	**Who Wouldn't Love You**	*Kay Kyser*...Columbia 36526
9	—	4	**Deep In The Heart Of Texas**	*Horace Heidt*...Columbia 36525
10	9	9	**Deep In The Heart Of Texas**	*Alvino Rey*...Bluebird 11391

Billboard — APRIL 25, 1942 — Best Sellers

TW	LW	WK	Title	Artist
1	1	10	**Moonlight Cocktail**	*Glenn Miller*...Bluebird 11401
2	3	4	**Jersey Bounce**	*Benny Goodman*...Okeh 6590
3	2	9	**I Don't Want To Walk Without You**	*Harry James*...Columbia 36478
4	7	2	**Tangerine**	*Jimmy Dorsey*...Decca 4123
5	5	4	**Somebody Else Is Taking My Place**	*Russ Morgan*...Decca 4098
6	4	15	**A String Of Pearls**	*Glenn Miller*...Bluebird 11382
7	6	5	**Somebody Else Is Taking My Place**	*Benny Goodman*...Okeh 6497
8	8	2	**Who Wouldn't Love You**	*Kay Kyser*...Columbia 36526
9	—	1	**I Remember You**	*Jimmy Dorsey*...Decca 4132
10	—	1	**Sleepy Lagoon**	*Harry James*...Columbia 36549

Billboard — MAY 2, 1942 — Best Sellers

TW	LW	WK	Title	Artist
1	1	11	**Moonlight Cocktail**	*Glenn Miller*...Bluebird 11401
2	2	5	**Jersey Bounce**	*Benny Goodman*...Okeh 6590
3	4	3	**Tangerine**	*Jimmy Dorsey*...Decca 4123
4	3	10	**I Don't Want To Walk Without You**	*Harry James*...Columbia 36478
5	7	6	**Somebody Else Is Taking My Place**	*Benny Goodman*...Okeh 6497
6	6	16	**A String Of Pearls**	*Glenn Miller*...Bluebird 11382
7	8	3	**Who Wouldn't Love You**	*Kay Kyser*...Columbia 36526
8	—	1	**Don't Sit Under The Apple Tree (With Anyone Else But Me)**	*Glenn Miller*...Bluebird 11474
9	10	2	**Sleepy Lagoon**	*Harry James*...Columbia 36549
10	—	1	**Skylark**	*Glenn Miller*...Bluebird 11462

Billboard — MAY 9, 1942 — Best Sellers

TW	LW	WK	Title	Artist
1	3	4	**Tangerine**	*Jimmy Dorsey*...Decca 4123
2	2	6	**Jersey Bounce**	*Benny Goodman*...Okeh 6590
3	7	4	**Who Wouldn't Love You**	*Kay Kyser*...Columbia 36526
4	1	12	**Moonlight Cocktail**	*Glenn Miller*...Bluebird 11401
5	8	2	**Don't Sit Under The Apple Tree (With Anyone Else But Me)**	*Glenn Miller*...Bluebird 11474
6	—	5	**Somebody Else Is Taking My Place**	*Russ Morgan*...Decca 4098
7	10	2	**Skylark**	*Glenn Miller*...Bluebird 11462
8	4	11	**I Don't Want To Walk Without You**	*Harry James*...Columbia 36478
9	5	7	**Somebody Else Is Taking My Place**	*Benny Goodman*...Okeh 6497
10	9	3	**Sleepy Lagoon**	*Harry James*...Columbia 36549

Billboard — MAY 16, 1942 — Best Sellers

TW	LW	WK	Title	Artist
1	1	5	**Tangerine**	*Jimmy Dorsey*...Decca 4123
2	2	7	**Jersey Bounce**	*Benny Goodman*...Okeh 6590
3	4	13	**Moonlight Cocktail**	*Glenn Miller*...Bluebird 11401
4	10	4	**Sleepy Lagoon**	*Harry James*...Columbia 36549
5	5	3	**Don't Sit Under The Apple Tree (With Anyone Else But Me)**	*Glenn Miller*...Bluebird 11474
6	3	5	**Who Wouldn't Love You**	*Kay Kyser*...Columbia 36526
7	9	8	**Somebody Else Is Taking My Place**	*Benny Goodman*...Okeh 6497
8	7	3	**Skylark**	*Glenn Miller*...Bluebird 11462
9	—	17	**A String Of Pearls**	*Glenn Miller*...Bluebird 11382
10	6	6	**Somebody Else Is Taking My Place**	*Russ Morgan*...Decca 4098

TW	LW	WK	Billboard® MAY 23, 1942 Best Sellers
1	1	6	Tangerine .... *Jimmy Dorsey*...Decca 4123
2	2	8	Jersey Bounce .... *Benny Goodman*...Okeh 6590
3	5	4	Don't Sit Under The Apple Tree (With Anyone Else But Me) ...... *Glenn Miller*...Bluebird 11474
4	6	6	Who Wouldn't Love You .... *Kay Kyser*...Columbia 36526
5	10	7	Somebody Else Is Taking My Place .... *Russ Morgan*...Decca 4098
6	4	5	Sleepy Lagoon .... *Harry James*...Columbia 36549
7	3	14	Moonlight Cocktail .... *Glenn Miller*...Bluebird 11401
8	8	4	Skylark .... *Glenn Miller*...Bluebird 11462
9	7	9	Somebody Else Is Taking My Place .... *Benny Goodman*...Okeh 6497
10	—	1	Always In My Heart .... *Glenn Miller*...Bluebird 11438

TW	LW	WK	Billboard® MAY 30, 1942 Best Sellers
1	1	7	Tangerine .... *Jimmy Dorsey*...Decca 4123
2	2	9	Jersey Bounce .... *Benny Goodman*...Okeh 6590
3	3	5	Don't Sit Under The Apple Tree (With Anyone Else But Me) ...... *Glenn Miller*...Bluebird 11474
4	4	7	Who Wouldn't Love You .... *Kay Kyser*...Columbia 36526
5	6	6	Sleepy Lagoon .... *Harry James*...Columbia 36549
6	5	8	Somebody Else Is Taking My Place .... *Russ Morgan*...Decca 4098
7	8	5	Skylark .... *Glenn Miller*...Bluebird 11462
8	7	15	Moonlight Cocktail .... *Glenn Miller*...Bluebird 11401
9	—	18	A String Of Pearls .... *Glenn Miller*...Bluebird 11382
10	—	12	I Don't Want To Walk Without You .... *Harry James*...Columbia 36478

TW	LW	WK	Billboard® JUNE 6, 1942 Best Sellers
1	1	8	Tangerine .... *Jimmy Dorsey*...Decca 4123
2	3	6	Don't Sit Under The Apple Tree (With Anyone Else But Me) ...... *Glenn Miller*...Bluebird 11474
3	2	10	Jersey Bounce .... *Benny Goodman*...Okeh 6590
4	5	7	Sleepy Lagoon .... *Harry James*...Columbia 36549
5	4	8	Who Wouldn't Love You .... *Kay Kyser*...Columbia 36526
6	6	9	Somebody Else Is Taking My Place .... *Russ Morgan*...Decca 4098
7	—	1	One Dozen Roses .... *Harry James*...Columbia 36566
8	7	6	Skylark .... *Glenn Miller*...Bluebird 11462
9	—	1	Miss You .... *Bing Crosby*...Decca 4183
10	10	13	I Don't Want To Walk Without You .... *Harry James*...Columbia 36478

TW	LW	WK	Billboard® JUNE 13, 1942 Best Sellers
1	1	9	Tangerine .... *Jimmy Dorsey*...Decca 4123
2	2	7	Don't Sit Under The Apple Tree (With Anyone Else But Me) ...... *Glenn Miller*...Bluebird 11474
3	4	8	Sleepy Lagoon .... *Harry James*...Columbia 36549
4	5	9	Who Wouldn't Love You .... *Kay Kyser*...Columbia 36526
5	3	11	Jersey Bounce .... *Benny Goodman*...Okeh 6590
6	6	10	Somebody Else Is Taking My Place .... *Russ Morgan*...Decca 4098
7	7	2	One Dozen Roses .... *Harry James*...Columbia 36566
8	—	1	One Dozen Roses .... *Glen Gray*...Decca 4299
9	—	1	Jersey Bounce .... *Jimmy Dorsey*...Decca 4288
10	8	7	Skylark .... *Glenn Miller*...Bluebird 11462

TW	LW	WK	Billboard® JUNE 20, 1942 Best Sellers
1	3	9	Sleepy Lagoon .... *Harry James*...Columbia 36549
2	4	10	Who Wouldn't Love You .... *Kay Kyser*...Columbia 36526
3	5	12	Jersey Bounce .... *Benny Goodman*...Okeh 6590
4	2	8	Don't Sit Under The Apple Tree (With Anyone Else But Me) ...... *Glenn Miller*...Bluebird 11474
5	1	10	Tangerine .... *Jimmy Dorsey*...Decca 4123
6	7	3	One Dozen Roses .... *Harry James*...Columbia 36566
7	10	8	Skylark .... *Glenn Miller*...Bluebird 11462
8	—	1	Johnny Doughboy Found A Rose In Ireland .... *Kay Kyser*...Columbia 36558
9	—	1	One Dozen Roses .... *Dinah Shore*...Victor 27881
10	8	2	One Dozen Roses .... *Glen Gray*...Decca 4299

TW	LW	WK	Billboard 🏵 JUNE 27, 1942 🏵 Best Sellers
1	1	10	Sleepy Lagoon ....Harry James...Columbia 36549
2	2	11	Who Wouldn't Love You ....Kay Kyser...Columbia 36526
3	5	11	Tangerine ....Jimmy Dorsey...Decca 4123
4	4	9	Don't Sit Under The Apple Tree (With Anyone Else But Me) ......Glenn Miller...Bluebird 11474
5	3	13	Jersey Bounce...Benny Goodman...Okeh 6590
6	6	4	One Dozen Roses ....Harry James...Columbia 36566
7	—	11	Somebody Else Is Taking My Place ....Russ Morgan...Decca 4098
8	7	9	Skylark..Glenn Miller...Bluebird 11462
9	—	1	Johnny Doughboy Found A Rose In Ireland ....Guy Lombardo...Decca 4278
10	9	2	One Dozen Roses ....Dinah Shore...Victor 27881

TW	LW	WK	Billboard 🏵 JULY 4, 1942 🏵 Best Sellers
1	1	11	Sleepy Lagoon ....Harry James...Columbia 36549
2	2	12	Who Wouldn't Love You ....Kay Kyser...Columbia 36526
3	5	14	Jersey Bounce...Benny Goodman...Okeh 6590
4	—	1	Jingle Jangle Jingle ....Kay Kyser...Columbia 36604
5	6	5	One Dozen Roses ....Harry James...Columbia 36566
6	4	10	Don't Sit Under The Apple Tree (With Anyone Else But Me) ......Glenn Miller...Bluebird 11474
7	3	12	Tangerine ....Jimmy Dorsey...Decca 4123
8	8	10	Skylark..Glenn Miller...Bluebird 11462
9	—	1	Jingle Jangle Jingle ....The Merry Macs...Decca 18361
10	10	3	One Dozen Roses ....Dinah Shore...Victor 27881

TW	LW	WK	Billboard 🏵 JULY 11, 1942 🏵 Best Sellers
1	1	12	Sleepy Lagoon ....Harry James...Columbia 36549
2	2	13	Who Wouldn't Love You ....Kay Kyser...Columbia 36526
3	4	2	Jingle Jangle Jingle ....Kay Kyser...Columbia 36604
4	9	2	Jingle Jangle Jingle ....The Merry Macs...Decca 18361
5	5	6	One Dozen Roses ....Harry James...Columbia 36566
6	6	11	Don't Sit Under The Apple Tree (With Anyone Else But Me) ......Glenn Miller...Bluebird 11474
7	3	15	Jersey Bounce...Benny Goodman...Okeh 6590
8	10	4	One Dozen Roses ....Dinah Shore...Victor 27881
9	7	13	Tangerine ....Jimmy Dorsey...Decca 4123
10	8	11	Skylark..Glenn Miller...Bluebird 11462

TW	LW	WK	Billboard 🏵 JULY 18, 1942 🏵 Best Sellers
1	3	3	Jingle Jangle Jingle ....Kay Kyser...Columbia 36604
2	2	14	Who Wouldn't Love You ....Kay Kyser...Columbia 36526
3	1	13	Sleepy Lagoon ....Harry James...Columbia 36549
4	4	3	Jingle Jangle Jingle ....The Merry Macs...Decca 18361
5	9	14	Tangerine ....Jimmy Dorsey...Decca 4123
6	5	7	One Dozen Roses ....Harry James...Columbia 36566
7	6	12	Don't Sit Under The Apple Tree (With Anyone Else But Me) ......Glenn Miller...Bluebird 11474
8	—	2	Johnny Doughboy Found A Rose In Ireland................................Kay Kyser...Columbia 36558
9	—	3	One Dozen Roses ....Glen Gray...Decca 4299
10	7	16	Jersey Bounce...Benny Goodman...Okeh 6590

TW	LW	WK	Billboard 🏵 JULY 25, 1942 🏵 Best Sellers
1	1	4	Jingle Jangle Jingle ....Kay Kyser...Columbia 36604
2	3	14	Sleepy Lagoon ....Harry James...Columbia 36549
3	2	15	Who Wouldn't Love You ....Kay Kyser...Columbia 36526
4	4	4	Jingle Jangle Jingle ....The Merry Macs...Decca 18361
5	5	15	Tangerine ....Jimmy Dorsey...Decca 4123
6	6	8	One Dozen Roses ....Harry James...Columbia 36566
7	7	13	Don't Sit Under The Apple Tree (With Anyone Else But Me) ......Glenn Miller...Bluebird 11474
8	—	5	One Dozen Roses ....Dinah Shore...Victor 27881
9	10	17	Jersey Bounce...Benny Goodman...Okeh 6590
10	—	1	Just As Though You Were Here ....Tommy Dorsey...Victor 27903

TW	LW	WK	Billboard® 🏵 AUGUST 1, 1942 🏵 Best Sellers
1	1	5	Jingle Jangle Jingle ....Kay Kyser...Columbia 36604
2	2	15	Sleepy Lagoon ....Harry James...Columbia 36549
3	3	16	Who Wouldn't Love You ....Kay Kyser...Columbia 36526
4	6	9	One Dozen Roses ....Harry James...Columbia 36566
5	4	5	Jingle Jangle Jingle ....The Merry Macs...Decca 18361
6	10	2	Just As Though You Were Here ....Tommy Dorsey...Victor 27903
7	—	1	(I've Got a Gal in) Kalamazoo ....Glenn Miller...Victor 27934
8	—	3	Johnny Doughboy Found A Rose In Ireland ....Kay Kyser...Columbia 36558
9	9	18	Jersey Bounce ....Benny Goodman...Okeh 6590
10	—	1	Sweet Eloise...Glenn Miller...Victor 27879

TW	LW	WK	Billboard® 🏵 AUGUST 8, 1942 🏵 Best Sellers
1	1	6	Jingle Jangle Jingle ....Kay Kyser...Columbia 36604
2	3	17	Who Wouldn't Love You ....Kay Kyser...Columbia 36526
3	2	16	Sleepy Lagoon ....Harry James...Columbia 36549
4	7	2	(I've Got a Gal in) Kalamazoo ....Glenn Miller...Victor 27934
5	5	6	Jingle Jangle Jingle ....The Merry Macs...Decca 18361
6	6	3	Just As Though You Were Here ....Tommy Dorsey...Victor 27903
7	—	1	He Wears A Pair Of Silver Wings ....Kay Kyser...Columbia 36604
8	—	1	Strictly Instrumental..Harry James...Columbia 36579
9	10	2	Sweet Eloise...Glenn Miller...Victor 27879
10	9	19	Jersey Bounce ....Benny Goodman...Okeh 6590

TW	LW	WK	Billboard® 🏵 AUGUST 15, 1942 🏵 Best Sellers
1	1	7	Jingle Jangle Jingle ....Kay Kyser...Columbia 36604
2	2	18	Who Wouldn't Love You ....Kay Kyser...Columbia 36526
3	4	3	(I've Got a Gal in) Kalamazoo ....Glenn Miller...Victor 27934
4	7	2	He Wears A Pair Of Silver Wings ....Kay Kyser...Columbia 36604
5	5	7	Jingle Jangle Jingle ....The Merry Macs...Decca 18361
6	8	2	Strictly Instrumental..Harry James...Columbia 36579
7	6	4	Just As Though You Were Here ....Tommy Dorsey...Victor 27903
8	9	3	Sweet Eloise...Glenn Miller...Victor 27879
9	—	10	One Dozen Roses ....Harry James...Columbia 36566
10	10	20	Jersey Bounce ....Benny Goodman...Okeh 6590

TW	LW	WK	Billboard® 🏵 AUGUST 22, 1942 🏵 Best Sellers
1	1	8	Jingle Jangle Jingle ....Kay Kyser...Columbia 36604
2	2	19	Who Wouldn't Love You ....Kay Kyser...Columbia 36526
3	—	17	Sleepy Lagoon ....Harry James...Columbia 36549
4	3	4	(I've Got a Gal in) Kalamazoo ....Glenn Miller...Victor 27934
5	4	3	He Wears A Pair Of Silver Wings ....Kay Kyser...Columbia 36604
6	7	5	Just As Though You Were Here ....Tommy Dorsey...Victor 27903
7	6	3	Strictly Instrumental..Harry James...Columbia 36579
8	5	8	Jingle Jangle Jingle ....The Merry Macs...Decca 18361
9	—	1	Cow-Cow Boogie ....Freddie Slack...Capitol 102
10	—	1	Take Me ....Benny Goodman...Columbia 36613

TW	LW	WK	Billboard® 🏵 AUGUST 29, 1942 🏵 Best Sellers
1	1	9	Jingle Jangle Jingle ....Kay Kyser...Columbia 36604
2	4	5	(I've Got a Gal in) Kalamazoo ....Glenn Miller...Victor 27934
3	2	20	Who Wouldn't Love You ....Kay Kyser...Columbia 36526
4	5	4	He Wears A Pair Of Silver Wings ....Kay Kyser...Columbia 36604
5	3	18	Sleepy Lagoon ....Harry James...Columbia 36549
6	—	1	Idaho...Benny Goodman...Columbia 36613
7	7	4	Strictly Instrumental..Harry James...Columbia 36579
8	6	6	Just As Though You Were Here ....Tommy Dorsey...Victor 27903
9	9	2	Cow-Cow Boogie ....Freddie Slack...Capitol 102
10	—	1	My Devotion ....Jimmy Dorsey...Decca 18372

TW	LW	WK	Billboard® ❄ SEPTEMBER 5, 1942 ❄ Best Sellers
1	1	10	Jingle Jangle Jingle ....*Kay Kyser*...Columbia 36604
2	4	5	He Wears A Pair Of Silver Wings ....*Kay Kyser*...Columbia 36604
3	2	6	(I've Got a Gal in) Kalamazoo ....*Glenn Miller*...Victor 27934
4	6	2	Idaho...*Benny Goodman*...Columbia 36613
5	3	21	Who Wouldn't Love You ....*Kay Kyser*...Columbia 36526
6	—	1	Amen...*Abe Lyman*...Bluebird 11542
7	—	1	Strip Polka ....*Johnny Mercer*...Capitol 103
8	—	1	I Left My Heart At The Stage Door Canteen ....*Sammy Kaye*...Victor 27932
9	—	1	Amen...*Woody Herman*...Decca 18346
10	—	1	My Devotion ....*Vaughn Monroe*...Victor 27925

TW	LW	WK	Billboard® ❄ SEPTEMBER 12, 1942 ❄ Best Sellers
1	3	7	(I've Got a Gal in) Kalamazoo...*Glenn Miller*...Victor 27934
2	2	6	He Wears A Pair Of Silver Wings ....*Kay Kyser*...Columbia 36604
3	1	11	Jingle Jangle Jingle ....*Kay Kyser*...Columbia 36604
4	—	1	My Devotion ....*Charlie Spivak*...Columbia 36620
5	9	2	Amen...*Woody Herman*...Decca 18346
6	5	22	Who Wouldn't Love You ....*Kay Kyser*...Columbia 36526
7	4	3	Idaho...*Benny Goodman*...Columbia 36613
8	—	5	Strictly Instrumental...*Harry James*...Columbia 36579
9	7	2	Strip Polka ....*Johnny Mercer*...Capitol 103
10	8	2	I Left My Heart At The Stage Door Canteen ....*Sammy Kaye*...Victor 27932

TW	LW	WK	Billboard® ❄ SEPTEMBER 19, 1942 ❄ Best Sellers
1	1	8	(I've Got a Gal in) Kalamazoo...*Glenn Miller*...Victor 27934
2	2	7	He Wears A Pair Of Silver Wings ....*Kay Kyser*...Columbia 36604
3	10	3	I Left My Heart At The Stage Door Canteen ....*Sammy Kaye*...Victor 27932
4	3	12	Jingle Jangle Jingle ....*Kay Kyser*...Columbia 36604
5	8	6	Strictly Instrumental...*Harry James*...Columbia 36579
6	4	2	My Devotion ....*Charlie Spivak*...Columbia 36620
7	9	3	Strip Polka ....*Johnny Mercer*...Capitol 103
8	—	1	Serenade In Blue ....*Glenn Miller*...Victor 27935
9	5	3	Amen...*Woody Herman*...Decca 18346
10	—	1	I Left My Heart At The Stage Door Canteen ....*Charlie Spivak*...Columbia 36620

TW	LW	WK	Billboard® ❄ SEPTEMBER 26, 1942 ❄ Best Sellers
1	1	9	(I've Got a Gal in) Kalamazoo...*Glenn Miller*...Victor 27934
2	2	8	He Wears A Pair Of Silver Wings ....*Kay Kyser*...Columbia 36604
3	6	3	My Devotion ....*Charlie Spivak*...Columbia 36620
4	3	4	I Left My Heart At The Stage Door Canteen ....*Sammy Kaye*...Victor 27932
5	—	1	Take Me ....*Tommy Dorsey*...Victor 27923
6	5	7	Strictly Instrumental...*Harry James*...Columbia 36579
7	8	2	Serenade In Blue ....*Glenn Miller*...Victor 27935
8	4	13	Jingle Jangle Jingle ....*Kay Kyser*...Columbia 36604
9	9	4	Amen...*Woody Herman*...Decca 18346
10	—	1	Strip Polka ....*Alvino Rey*...Bluebird 11573

TW	LW	WK	Billboard® ❄ OCTOBER 3, 1942 ❄ Best Sellers
1	1	10	(I've Got a Gal in) Kalamazoo...*Glenn Miller*...Victor 27934
2	3	4	My Devotion ....*Charlie Spivak*...Columbia 36620
3	—	7	Just As Though You Were Here ....*Tommy Dorsey*...Victor 27903
4	4	5	I Left My Heart At The Stage Door Canteen ....*Sammy Kaye*...Victor 27932
5	5	2	Take Me ....*Tommy Dorsey*...Victor 27923
6	2	9	He Wears A Pair Of Silver Wings ....*Kay Kyser*...Columbia 36604
7	7	3	Serenade In Blue ....*Glenn Miller*...Victor 27935
8	10	2	Strip Polka ....*Alvino Rey*...Bluebird 11573
9	—	1	He's My Guy ....*Harry James*...Columbia 36614
10	—	1	Strip Polka ....*Kay Kyser*...Columbia 36635

TW	LW	WK	Billboard®	OCTOBER 10, 1942	Best Sellers
1	1	11	(I've Got a Gal in) **Kalamazoo**		Glenn Miller...Victor 27934
2	7	4	**Serenade In Blue**		Glenn Miller...Victor 27935
3	2	5	**My Devotion**		Charlie Spivak...Columbia 36620
4	—	2	**Amen**		Abe Lyman...Bluebird 11542
5	10	2	**Strip Polka**		Kay Kyser...Columbia 36635
6	5	3	**Take Me**		Tommy Dorsey...Victor 27923
7	4	6	**I Left My Heart At The Stage Door Canteen**		Sammy Kaye...Victor 27932
8	—	4	**Strip Polka**		Johnny Mercer...Capitol 103
9	—	1	**White Christmas**		Bing Crosby...Decca 18429
10	6	10	**He Wears A Pair Of Silver Wings**		Kay Kyser...Columbia 36604

TW	LW	WK	Billboard®	OCTOBER 17, 1942	Best Sellers
1	1	12	(I've Got a Gal in) **Kalamazoo**		Glenn Miller...Victor 27934
2	3	6	**My Devotion**		Charlie Spivak...Columbia 36620
3	9	2	**White Christmas**		Bing Crosby...Decca 18429
4	—	1	**Praise The Lord And Pass The Ammunition!**		Kay Kyser...Columbia 36640
5	2	5	**Serenade In Blue**		Glenn Miller...Victor 27935
6	10	11	**He Wears A Pair Of Silver Wings**		Kay Kyser...Columbia 36604
7	8	5	**Strip Polka**		Johnny Mercer...Capitol 103
8	—	2	**I Left My Heart At The Stage Door Canteen**		Charlie Spivak...Columbia 36620
9	7	7	**I Left My Heart At The Stage Door Canteen**		Sammy Kaye...Victor 27932
10	—	8	**Just As Though You Were Here**		Tommy Dorsey...Victor 27903

TW	LW	WK	Billboard®	OCTOBER 24, 1942	Best Sellers
1	1	13	(I've Got a Gal in) **Kalamazoo**		Glenn Miller...Victor 27934
2	3	3	**White Christmas**		Bing Crosby...Decca 18429
3	4	2	**Praise The Lord And Pass The Ammunition!**		Kay Kyser...Columbia 36640
4	5	6	**Serenade In Blue**		Glenn Miller...Victor 27935
5	—	2	**My Devotion**		Vaughn Monroe...Victor 27925
6	—	1	**Der Fuehrer's Face**		Spike Jones...Bluebird 11586
7	7	6	**Strip Polka**		Johnny Mercer...Capitol 103
8	2	7	**My Devotion**		Charlie Spivak...Columbia 36620
9	—	3	**Amen**		Abe Lyman...Bluebird 11542
10	—	3	**Strip Polka**		Kay Kyser...Columbia 36635

TW	LW	WK	Billboard®	OCTOBER 31, 1942	Best Sellers
1	2	4	**White Christmas**		Bing Crosby...Decca 18429
2	3	3	**Praise The Lord And Pass The Ammunition!**		Kay Kyser...Columbia 36640
3	1	14	(I've Got a Gal in) **Kalamazoo**		Glenn Miller...Victor 27934
4	4	7	**Serenade In Blue**		Glenn Miller...Victor 27935
5	8	8	**My Devotion**		Charlie Spivak...Columbia 36620
6	6	2	**Der Fuehrer's Face**		Spike Jones...Bluebird 11586
7	—	1	**Strip Polka**		Andrews Sisters...Decca 18470
8	5	3	**My Devotion**		Vaughn Monroe...Victor 27925
9	—	9	**Just As Though You Were Here**		Tommy Dorsey...Victor 27903
10	—	1	**When The Lights Go On Again** (All Over the World)		Vaughn Monroe...Victor 27945

TW	LW	WK	Billboard®	NOVEMBER 7, 1942	Best Sellers
1	1	5	**White Christmas**		Bing Crosby...Decca 18429
2	2	4	**Praise The Lord And Pass The Ammunition!**		Kay Kyser...Columbia 36640
3	4	8	**Serenade In Blue**		Glenn Miller...Victor 27935
4	3	15	(I've Got a Gal in) **Kalamazoo**		Glenn Miller...Victor 27934
5	6	3	**Der Fuehrer's Face**		Spike Jones...Bluebird 11586
6	7	2	**Strip Polka**		Andrews Sisters...Decca 18470
7	5	9	**My Devotion**		Charlie Spivak...Columbia 36620
8	8	4	**My Devotion**		Vaughn Monroe...Victor 27925
9	10	2	**When The Lights Go On Again** (All Over the World)		Vaughn Monroe...Victor 27945
10	—	1	**Daybreak**		Tommy Dorsey...Victor 27974

TW	LW	WK	Billboard ❀ NOVEMBER 14, 1942 ❀ Best Sellers
1	1	6	White Christmas..Bing Crosby...Decca 18429
2	2	5	Praise The Lord And Pass The Ammunition!...Kay Kyser...Columbia 36640
3	5	4	Der Fuehrer's Face..Spike Jones...Bluebird 11586
4	4	16	(I've Got a Gal in) Kalamazoo...Glenn Miller...Victor 27934
5	3	9	Serenade In Blue...Glenn Miller...Victor 27935
6	6	3	Strip Polka...Andrews Sisters...Decca 18470
7	7	10	My Devotion..Charlie Spivak...Columbia 36620
8	9	3	When The Lights Go On Again (All Over the World).....................Vaughn Monroe...Victor 27945
9	—	1	There Are Such Things..Tommy Dorsey...Victor 27974
10	—	1	Praise The Lord And Pass The Ammunition!............................The Merry Macs...Decca 18498

TW	LW	WK	Billboard ❀ NOVEMBER 21, 1942 ❀ Best Sellers
1	1	7	White Christmas..Bing Crosby...Decca 18429
2	2	6	Praise The Lord And Pass The Ammunition!...Kay Kyser...Columbia 36640
3	5	10	Serenade In Blue...Glenn Miller...Victor 27935
4	7	11	My Devotion..Charlie Spivak...Columbia 36620
5	8	4	When The Lights Go On Again (All Over the World).....................Vaughn Monroe...Victor 27945
6	4	17	(I've Got a Gal in) Kalamazoo...Glenn Miller...Victor 27934
7	3	5	Der Fuehrer's Face..Spike Jones...Bluebird 11586
8	9	2	There Are Such Things..Tommy Dorsey...Victor 27974
9	6	4	Strip Polka...Andrews Sisters...Decca 18470
10	10	2	Praise The Lord And Pass The Ammunition!............................The Merry Macs...Decca 18498

TW	LW	WK	Billboard ❀ NOVEMBER 28, 1942 ❀ Best Sellers
1	1	8	White Christmas..Bing Crosby...Decca 18429
2	2	7	Praise The Lord And Pass The Ammunition!...Kay Kyser...Columbia 36640
3	3	11	Serenade In Blue...Glenn Miller...Victor 27935
4	5	5	When The Lights Go On Again (All Over the World).....................Vaughn Monroe...Victor 27945
5	7	6	Der Fuehrer's Face..Spike Jones...Bluebird 11586
6	—	1	Mister Five By Five..Harry James...Columbia 36650
7	6	18	(I've Got a Gal in) Kalamazoo...Glenn Miller...Victor 27934
8	10	3	Praise The Lord And Pass The Ammunition!............................The Merry Macs...Decca 18498
9	—	1	Manhattan Serenade...Harry James...Columbia 36644
10	8	3	There Are Such Things..Tommy Dorsey...Victor 27974

TW	LW	WK	Billboard ❀ DECEMBER 5, 1942 ❀ Best Sellers
1	1	9	White Christmas..Bing Crosby...Decca 18429
2	2	8	Praise The Lord And Pass The Ammunition!...Kay Kyser...Columbia 36640
3	3	12	Serenade In Blue...Glenn Miller...Victor 27935
4	5	7	Der Fuehrer's Face..Spike Jones...Bluebird 11586
5	10	4	There Are Such Things..Tommy Dorsey...Victor 27974
6	6	2	Mister Five By Five..Harry James...Columbia 36650
7	4	6	When The Lights Go On Again (All Over the World).....................Vaughn Monroe...Victor 27945
8	8	4	Praise The Lord And Pass The Ammunition!............................The Merry Macs...Decca 18498
9	—	1	I Had The Craziest Dream..Harry James...Columbia 36659
10	—	2	Daybreak..Tommy Dorsey...Victor 27974

TW	LW	WK	Billboard ❀ DECEMBER 12, 1942 ❀ Best Sellers
1	1	10	White Christmas..Bing Crosby...Decca 18429
2	2	9	Praise The Lord And Pass The Ammunition!...Kay Kyser...Columbia 36640
3	7	7	When The Lights Go On Again (All Over the World).....................Vaughn Monroe...Victor 27945
4	3	13	Serenade In Blue...Glenn Miller...Victor 27935
5	6	3	Mister Five By Five..Harry James...Columbia 36650
6	4	8	Der Fuehrer's Face..Spike Jones...Bluebird 11586
7	5	5	There Are Such Things..Tommy Dorsey...Victor 27974
8	9	2	I Had The Craziest Dream..Harry James...Columbia 36659
9	—	1	Juke Box Saturday Night...Glenn Miller...Victor 20-1509
10	—	1	Mr. Five By Five...Freddie Slack...Capitol 115

TW	LW	WK	Billboard® ❀ DECEMBER 19, 1942 ❀ Best Sellers
1	1	11	White Christmas ....Bing Crosby...Decca 18429
2	5	4	Mister Five By Five ....Harry James...Columbia 36650
3	2	10	Praise The Lord And Pass The Ammunition! ....Kay Kyser...Columbia 36640
4	3	8	When The Lights Go On Again (All Over the World).....................Vaughn Monroe...Victor 27945
5	8	3	I Had The Craziest Dream...Harry James...Columbia 36659
6	—	1	Dearly Beloved...Glenn Miller...Victor 27953
7	4	14	Serenade In Blue ....Glenn Miller...Victor 27935
8	9	2	Juke Box Saturday Night ....Glenn Miller...Victor 20-1509
9	7	6	There Are Such Things ....Tommy Dorsey...Victor 27974
10	—	1	Moonlight Becomes You ....Glenn Miller...Victor 20-1520

TW	LW	WK	Billboard® ❀ DECEMBER 26, 1942 ❀ Best Sellers
1	1	12	White Christmas ....Bing Crosby...Decca 18429
2	4	9	When The Lights Go On Again (All Over the World).....................Vaughn Monroe...Victor 27945
3	3	11	Praise The Lord And Pass The Ammunition! ....Kay Kyser...Columbia 36640
4	9	7	There Are Such Things ....Tommy Dorsey...Victor 27974
5	2	5	Mister Five By Five ....Harry James...Columbia 36650
6	5	4	I Had The Craziest Dream...Harry James...Columbia 36659
7	8	3	Juke Box Saturday Night ....Glenn Miller...Victor 20-1509
8	7	15	Serenade In Blue ....Glenn Miller...Victor 27935
9	—	9	Der Fuehrer's Face...Spike Jones...Bluebird 11586
10	—	1	Dearly Beloved ....Dinah Shore...Victor 27970

Billboard ❀ JANUARY 2, 1943 ❀ Best Sellers

TW	LW	WK		
1	1	13	White Christmas	Bing Crosby...Decca 18429
2	4	8	There Are Such Things	Tommy Dorsey...Victor 27974
3	3	12	Praise The Lord And Pass The Ammunition!	Kay Kyser...Columbia 36640
4	6	5	I Had The Craziest Dream	Harry James...Columbia 36659
5	—	2	Dearly Beloved	Glenn Miller...Victor 27953
6	5	6	Mister Five By Five	Harry James...Columbia 36650
7	7	4	Juke Box Saturday Night	Glenn Miller...Victor 20-1509
8	2	10	When The Lights Go On Again (All Over the World)	Vaughn Monroe...Victor 27945
9	—	2	Moonlight Becomes You	Glenn Miller...Victor 20-1520
10	—	2	Mr. Five By Five	Freddie Slack...Capitol 115

Billboard ❀ JANUARY 9, 1943 ❀ Best Sellers

TW	LW	WK		
1	1	14	White Christmas	Bing Crosby...Decca 18429
2	2	9	There Are Such Things	Tommy Dorsey...Victor 27974
3	4	6	I Had The Craziest Dream	Harry James...Columbia 36659
4	3	13	Praise The Lord And Pass The Ammunition!	Kay Kyser...Columbia 36640
5	8	11	When The Lights Go On Again (All Over the World)	Vaughn Monroe...Victor 27945
6	6	7	Mister Five By Five	Harry James...Columbia 36650
7	5	3	Dearly Beloved	Glenn Miller...Victor 27953
8	7	5	Juke Box Saturday Night	Glenn Miller...Victor 20-1509
9	—	10	Der Fuehrer's Face	Spike Jones...Bluebird 11586
10	—	1	Why Don't You Do Right	Benny Goodman...Columbia 36652

Billboard ❀ JANUARY 16, 1943 ❀ Best Sellers

TW	LW	WK		
1	2	10	There Are Such Things	Tommy Dorsey...Victor 27974
2	3	7	I Had The Craziest Dream	Harry James...Columbia 36659
3	5	12	When The Lights Go On Again (All Over the World)	Vaughn Monroe...Victor 27945
4	1	15	White Christmas	Bing Crosby...Decca 18429
5	10	2	Why Don't You Do Right	Benny Goodman...Columbia 36652
6	—	1	(As Long As You're Not in Love With Anyone Else) Why Don't You Fall In Love With Me?	Dinah Shore...Victor 27970
7	—	1	Moonlight Becomes You	Bing Crosby...Decca 18513
8	7	4	Dearly Beloved	Glenn Miller...Victor 27953
9	6	8	Mister Five By Five	Harry James...Columbia 36650
10	8	6	Juke Box Saturday Night	Glenn Miller...Victor 20-1509

Billboard ❀ JANUARY 23, 1943 ❀ Best Sellers

TW	LW	WK		
1	1	11	There Are Such Things	Tommy Dorsey...Victor 27974
2	2	8	I Had The Craziest Dream	Harry James...Columbia 36659
3	6	2	(As Long As You're Not in Love With Anyone Else) Why Don't You Fall In Love With Me?	Dinah Shore...Victor 27970
4	5	3	Why Don't You Do Right	Benny Goodman...Columbia 36652
5	3	13	When The Lights Go On Again (All Over the World)	Vaughn Monroe...Victor 27945
6	9	9	Mister Five By Five	Harry James...Columbia 36650
7	—	3	Moonlight Becomes You	Glenn Miller...Victor 20-1520
8	7	2	Moonlight Becomes You	Bing Crosby...Decca 18513
9	10	7	Juke Box Saturday Night	Glenn Miller...Victor 20-1509
10	—	1	(As Long As You're Not In Love With Anyone Else) Why Don't You Fall In Love With Me?	Johnny Long...Decca 4375

Billboard ❀ JANUARY 30, 1943 ❀ Best Sellers

TW	LW	WK	Title	Artist / Label
1	1	12	There Are Such Things	Tommy Dorsey...Victor 27974
2	2	9	I Had The Craziest Dream	Harry James...Columbia 36659
3	3	3	(As Long As You're Not in Love With Anyone Else) Why Don't You Fall In Love With Me?	Dinah Shore...Victor 27970
4	8	3	Moonlight Becomes You	Bing Crosby...Decca 18513
5	7	4	Moonlight Becomes You	Glenn Miller...Victor 20-1520
6	4	4	Why Don't You Do Right	Benny Goodman...Columbia 36652
7	—	1	I've Heard That Song Before	Harry James...Columbia 36668
8	5	14	When The Lights Go On Again (All Over the World)	Vaughn Monroe...Victor 27945
9	—	1	For Me And My Gal	Judy Garland & Gene Kelly...Decca 18480
10	—	1	Brazil (Aquarela Do Brasil)	Xavier Cugat...Columbia 36651

Billboard ❀ FEBRUARY 6, 1943 ❀ Best Sellers

TW	LW	WK	Title	Artist / Label
1	1	13	There Are Such Things	Tommy Dorsey...Victor 27974
2	2	10	I Had The Craziest Dream	Harry James...Columbia 36659
3	4	4	Moonlight Becomes You	Bing Crosby...Decca 18513
4	10	2	Brazil (Aquarela Do Brasil)	Xavier Cugat...Columbia 36651
5	6	5	Why Don't You Do Right	Benny Goodman...Columbia 36652
6	3	4	(As Long As You're Not in Love With Anyone Else) Why Don't You Fall In Love With Me?	Dinah Shore...Victor 27970
7	5	5	Moonlight Becomes You	Glenn Miller...Victor 20-1520
8	7	2	I've Heard That Song Before	Harry James...Columbia 36668
9	8	15	When The Lights Go On Again (All Over the World)	Vaughn Monroe...Victor 27945
10	—	8	Juke Box Saturday Night	Glenn Miller...Victor 20-1509

Billboard ❀ FEBRUARY 13, 1943 ❀ Best Sellers

TW	LW	WK	Title	Artist / Label
1	2	11	I Had The Craziest Dream	Harry James...Columbia 36659
2	1	14	There Are Such Things	Tommy Dorsey...Victor 27974
3	8	3	I've Heard That Song Before	Harry James...Columbia 36668
4	3	5	Moonlight Becomes You	Bing Crosby...Decca 18513
5	6	5	(As Long As You're Not in Love With Anyone Else) Why Don't You Fall In Love With Me?	Dinah Shore...Victor 27970
6	4	3	Brazil (Aquarela Do Brasil)	Xavier Cugat...Columbia 36651
7	—	1	You'd Be So Nice To Come Home To	Dinah Shore...Victor 20-1519
8	5	6	Why Don't You Do Right	Benny Goodman...Columbia 36652
9	9	16	When The Lights Go On Again (All Over the World)	Vaughn Monroe...Victor 27945
10	—	1	It Started All Over Again	Tommy Dorsey...Victor 20-1522

Billboard ❀ FEBRUARY 20, 1943 ❀ Best Sellers

TW	LW	WK	Title	Artist / Label
1	1	12	I Had The Craziest Dream	Harry James...Columbia 36659
2	2	15	There Are Such Things	Tommy Dorsey...Victor 27974
3	3	4	I've Heard That Song Before	Harry James...Columbia 36668
4	6	4	Brazil (Aquarela Do Brasil)	Xavier Cugat...Columbia 36651
5	5	6	(As Long As You're Not in Love With Anyone Else) Why Don't You Fall In Love With Me?	Dinah Shore...Victor 27970
6	7	2	You'd Be So Nice To Come Home To	Dinah Shore...Victor 20-1519
7	4	6	Moonlight Becomes You	Bing Crosby...Decca 18513
8	8	7	Why Don't You Do Right	Benny Goodman...Columbia 36652
9	—	6	Moonlight Becomes You	Glenn Miller...Victor 20-1520
10	—	1	Don't Get Around Much Anymore	Ink Spots...Decca 18503

TW	LW	WK	Billboard® ❀ FEBRUARY 27, 1943 ❀ Best Sellers
1	2	16	There Are Such Things ....*Tommy Dorsey*...Victor 27974
2	3	5	I've Heard That Song Before ....*Harry James*...Columbia 36668
3	1	13	I Had The Craziest Dream ....*Harry James*...Columbia 36659
4	7	7	Moonlight Becomes You ....*Bing Crosby*...Decca 18513
5	6	3	You'd Be So Nice To Come Home To..*Dinah Shore*...Victor 20-1519
6	4	5	Brazil (Aquarela Do Brasil) ....*Xavier Cugat*...Columbia 36651
7	—	2	It Started All Over Again ....*Tommy Dorsey*...Victor 20-1522
8	8	8	Why Don't You Do Right ....*Benny Goodman*...Columbia 36652
9	9	7	Moonlight Becomes You ....*Glenn Miller*...Victor 20-1520
10	5	7	(As Long As You're Not in Love With Anyone Else) Why Don't You Fall In Love With Me? ....*Dinah Shore*...Victor 27970

TW	LW	WK	Billboard® ❀ MARCH 6, 1943 ❀ Best Sellers
1	2	6	I've Heard That Song Before ....*Harry James*...Columbia 36668
2	3	14	I Had The Craziest Dream ....*Harry James*...Columbia 36659
3	1	17	There Are Such Things ....*Tommy Dorsey*...Victor 27974
4	6	6	Brazil (Aquarela Do Brasil) ....*Xavier Cugat*...Columbia 36651
5	5	4	You'd Be So Nice To Come Home To..*Dinah Shore*...Victor 20-1519
6	8	9	Why Don't You Do Right ....*Benny Goodman*...Columbia 36652
7	10	8	(As Long As You're Not in Love With Anyone Else) Why Don't You Fall In Love With Me? ....*Dinah Shore*...Victor 27970
8	7	3	It Started All Over Again ....*Tommy Dorsey*...Victor 20-1522
9	—	2	For Me And My Gal ....*Judy Garland & Gene Kelly*...Decca 18480
10	9	8	Moonlight Becomes You ....*Glenn Miller*...Victor 20-1520

TW	LW	WK	Billboard® ❀ MARCH 13, 1943 ❀ Best Sellers
1	1	7	I've Heard That Song Before ....*Harry James*...Columbia 36668
2	3	18	There Are Such Things ....*Tommy Dorsey*...Victor 27974
3	4	7	Brazil (Aquarela Do Brasil) ....*Xavier Cugat*...Columbia 36651
4	2	15	I Had The Craziest Dream ....*Harry James*...Columbia 36659
5	6	10	Why Don't You Do Right ....*Benny Goodman*...Columbia 36652
6	5	5	You'd Be So Nice To Come Home To..*Dinah Shore*...Victor 20-1519
7	—	1	That Old Black Magic ....*Glenn Miller*...Victor 20-1523
8	—	8	Moonlight Becomes You ....*Bing Crosby*...Decca 18513
9	9	3	For Me And My Gal ....*Judy Garland & Gene Kelly*...Decca 18480
10	8	4	It Started All Over Again ....*Tommy Dorsey*...Victor 20-1522

TW	LW	WK	Billboard® ❀ MARCH 20, 1943 ❀ Best Sellers
1	1	8	I've Heard That Song Before ....*Harry James*...Columbia 36668
2	3	8	Brazil (Aquarela Do Brasil) ....*Xavier Cugat*...Columbia 36651
3	2	19	There Are Such Things ....*Tommy Dorsey*...Victor 27974
4	6	6	You'd Be So Nice To Come Home To..*Dinah Shore*...Victor 20-1519
5	7	2	That Old Black Magic ....*Glenn Miller*...Victor 20-1523
6	5	11	Why Don't You Do Right ....*Benny Goodman*...Columbia 36652
7	4	16	I Had The Craziest Dream ....*Harry James*...Columbia 36659
8	10	5	It Started All Over Again ....*Tommy Dorsey*...Victor 20-1522
9	8	9	Moonlight Becomes You ....*Bing Crosby*...Decca 18513
10	—	1	That Old Black Magic ....*Freddie Slack*...Capitol 126

TW	LW	WK	Billboard® ❀ MARCH 27, 1943 ❀ Best Sellers
1	1	9	I've Heard That Song Before ....*Harry James*...Columbia 36668
2	2	9	Brazil (Aquarela Do Brasil) ....*Xavier Cugat*...Columbia 36651
3	5	3	That Old Black Magic ....*Glenn Miller*...Victor 20-1523
4	8	6	It Started All Over Again ....*Tommy Dorsey*...Victor 20-1522
5	3	20	There Are Such Things ....*Tommy Dorsey*...Victor 27974
6	4	7	You'd Be So Nice To Come Home To..*Dinah Shore*...Victor 20-1519
7	—	2	Don't Get Around Much Anymore ....*Ink Spots*...Decca 18503
8	9	10	Moonlight Becomes You ....*Bing Crosby*...Decca 18513
9	7	17	I Had The Craziest Dream ....*Harry James*...Columbia 36659
10	—	1	As Time Goes By ....*Jacques Renard*...Brunswick 6205

TW	LW	WK	Billboard® APRIL 3, 1943 Best Sellers
1	1	10	I've Heard That Song Before ....Harry James...Columbia 36668
2	2	10	Brazil (Aquarela Do Brasil) ....Xavier Cugat...Columbia 36651
3	—	4	For Me And My Gal ....Judy Garland & Gene Kelly...Decca 18480
4	3	4	That Old Black Magic ....Glenn Miller...Victor 20-1523
5	6	8	You'd Be So Nice To Come Home To...Dinah Shore...Victor 20-1519
6	5	21	There Are Such Things ....Tommy Dorsey...Victor 27974
7	4	7	It Started All Over Again ....Tommy Dorsey...Victor 20-1522
8	8	11	Moonlight Becomes You ....Bing Crosby...Decca 18513
9	10	2	As Time Goes By ....Jacques Renard...Brunswick 6205
10	9	18	I Had The Craziest Dream..Harry James...Columbia 36659

TW	LW	WK	Billboard® APRIL 10, 1943 Best Sellers
1	1	11	I've Heard That Song Before ....Harry James...Columbia 36668
2	2	11	Brazil (Aquarela Do Brasil) ....Xavier Cugat...Columbia 36651
3	9	3	As Time Goes By ....Jacques Renard...Brunswick 6205
4	5	9	You'd Be So Nice To Come Home To...Dinah Shore...Victor 20-1519
5	4	5	That Old Black Magic ....Glenn Miller...Victor 20-1523
6	7	8	It Started All Over Again ....Tommy Dorsey...Victor 20-1522
7	—	12	Why Don't You Do Right ....Benny Goodman...Columbia 36652
8	—	3	Don't Get Around Much Anymore ....Ink Spots...Decca 18503
9	6	22	There Are Such Things ....Tommy Dorsey...Victor 27974
10	3	5	For Me And My Gal ....Judy Garland & Gene Kelly...Decca 18480

TW	LW	WK	Billboard® APRIL 17, 1943 Best Sellers
1	1	12	I've Heard That Song Before ....Harry James...Columbia 36668
2	2	12	Brazil (Aquarela Do Brasil) ....Xavier Cugat...Columbia 36651
3	5	6	That Old Black Magic ....Glenn Miller...Victor 20-1523
4	4	10	You'd Be So Nice To Come Home To...Dinah Shore...Victor 20-1519
5	8	4	Don't Get Around Much Anymore ....Ink Spots...Decca 18503
6	10	6	For Me And My Gal ....Judy Garland & Gene Kelly...Decca 18480
7	3	4	As Time Goes By ....Jacques Renard...Brunswick 6205
8	—	1	Velvet Moon ....Harry James...Columbia 36672
9	6	9	It Started All Over Again ....Tommy Dorsey...Victor 20-1522
10	9	23	There Are Such Things ....Tommy Dorsey...Victor 27974

TW	LW	WK	Billboard® APRIL 24, 1943 Best Sellers
1	1	13	I've Heard That Song Before ....Harry James...Columbia 36668
2	2	13	Brazil (Aquarela Do Brasil) ....Xavier Cugat...Columbia 36651
3	7	5	As Time Goes By ....Jacques Renard...Brunswick 6205
4	3	7	That Old Black Magic ....Glenn Miller...Victor 20-1523
5	4	11	You'd Be So Nice To Come Home To...Dinah Shore...Victor 20-1519
6	6	7	For Me And My Gal ....Judy Garland & Gene Kelly...Decca 18480
7	5	5	Don't Get Around Much Anymore ....Ink Spots...Decca 18503
8	—	1	As Time Goes By ....Rudy Vallée...Victor 20-1526
9	9	10	It Started All Over Again ....Tommy Dorsey...Victor 20-1522
10	8	2	Velvet Moon ....Harry James...Columbia 36672

TW	LW	WK	Billboard® MAY 1, 1943 Best Sellers
1	1	14	I've Heard That Song Before ....Harry James...Columbia 36668
2	2	14	Brazil (Aquarela Do Brasil) ....Xavier Cugat...Columbia 36651
3	4	8	That Old Black Magic ....Glenn Miller...Victor 20-1523
4	7	6	Don't Get Around Much Anymore ....Ink Spots...Decca 18503
5	3	6	As Time Goes By ....Jacques Renard...Brunswick 6205
6	10	3	Velvet Moon ....Harry James...Columbia 36672
7	9	11	It Started All Over Again ....Tommy Dorsey...Victor 20-1522
8	5	12	You'd Be So Nice To Come Home To...Dinah Shore...Victor 20-1519
9	8	2	As Time Goes By ....Rudy Vallée...Victor 20-1526
10	—	24	There Are Such Things ....Tommy Dorsey...Victor 27974

Billboard® — MAY 8, 1943 — Best Sellers

TW	LW	WK	Title	Artist...Label
1	1	15	I've Heard That Song Before	Harry James...Columbia 36668
2	3	9	That Old Black Magic	Glenn Miller...Victor 20-1523
3	2	15	Brazil (Aquarela Do Brasil)	Xavier Cugat...Columbia 36651
4	6	4	Velvet Moon	Harry James...Columbia 36672
5	—	1	"Murder," He Says	Dinah Shore...Victor 20-1525
6	4	7	Don't Get Around Much Anymore	Ink Spots...Decca 18503
7	9	3	As Time Goes By	Rudy Vallée...Victor 20-1526
8	5	7	As Time Goes By	Jacques Renard...Brunswick 6205
9	—	1	Don't Get Around Much Anymore	Glen Gray...Decca 18479
10	—	1	Taking A Chance On Love	Benny Goodman...Columbia 35869

Billboard® — MAY 15, 1943 — Best Sellers

TW	LW	WK	Title	Artist...Label
1	1	16	I've Heard That Song Before	Harry James...Columbia 36668
2	2	10	That Old Black Magic	Glenn Miller...Victor 20-1523
3	3	16	Brazil (Aquarela Do Brasil)	Xavier Cugat...Columbia 36651
4	—	12	It Started All Over Again	Tommy Dorsey...Victor 20-1522
5	10	2	Taking A Chance On Love	Benny Goodman...Columbia 35869
6	6	8	Don't Get Around Much Anymore	Ink Spots...Decca 18503
7	4	5	Velvet Moon	Harry James...Columbia 36672
8	8	8	As Time Goes By	Jacques Renard...Brunswick 6205
9	7	4	As Time Goes By	Rudy Vallée...Victor 20-1526
10	—	8	For Me And My Gal	Judy Garland & Gene Kelly...Decca 18480

Billboard® — MAY 22, 1943 — Best Sellers

TW	LW	WK	Title	Artist...Label
1	1	17	I've Heard That Song Before	Harry James...Columbia 36668
2	7	6	Velvet Moon	Harry James...Columbia 36672
3	2	11	That Old Black Magic	Glenn Miller...Victor 20-1523
4	5	3	Taking A Chance On Love	Benny Goodman...Columbia 35869
5	3	17	Brazil (Aquarela Do Brasil)	Xavier Cugat...Columbia 36651
6	4	13	It Started All Over Again	Tommy Dorsey...Victor 20-1522
7	6	9	Don't Get Around Much Anymore	Ink Spots...Decca 18503
8	8	9	As Time Goes By	Jacques Renard...Brunswick 6205
9	9	5	As Time Goes By	Rudy Vallée...Victor 20-1526
10	—	2	"Murder," He Says	Dinah Shore...Victor 20-1525

Billboard® — MAY 29, 1943 — Best Sellers

TW	LW	WK	Title	Artist...Label
1	3	12	That Old Black Magic	Glenn Miller...Victor 20-1523
2	7	10	Don't Get Around Much Anymore	Ink Spots...Decca 18503
3	5	18	Brazil (Aquarela Do Brasil)	Xavier Cugat...Columbia 36651
4	1	18	I've Heard That Song Before	Harry James...Columbia 36668
5	9	6	As Time Goes By	Rudy Vallée...Victor 20-1526
6	2	7	Velvet Moon	Harry James...Columbia 36672
7	8	10	As Time Goes By	Jacques Renard...Brunswick 6205
8	4	4	Taking A Chance On Love	Benny Goodman...Columbia 35869
9	—	2	Don't Get Around Much Anymore	Glen Gray...Decca 18479
10	—	9	For Me And My Gal	Judy Garland & Gene Kelly...Decca 18480

Billboard® — JUNE 5, 1943 — Best Sellers

TW	LW	WK	Title	Artist...Label
1	4	19	I've Heard That Song Before	Harry James...Columbia 36668
2	8	5	Taking A Chance On Love	Benny Goodman...Columbia 35869
3	2	11	Don't Get Around Much Anymore	Ink Spots...Decca 18503
4	3	19	Brazil (Aquarela Do Brasil)	Xavier Cugat...Columbia 36651
5	1	13	That Old Black Magic	Glenn Miller...Victor 20-1523
6	7	11	As Time Goes By	Jacques Renard...Brunswick 6205
7	6	8	Velvet Moon	Harry James...Columbia 36672
8	5	7	As Time Goes By	Rudy Vallée...Victor 20-1526
9	9	3	Don't Get Around Much Anymore	Glen Gray...Decca 18479
10	10	10	For Me And My Gal	Judy Garland & Gene Kelly...Decca 18480

TW	LW	WK	Billboard ❀ JUNE 12, 1943 ❀ Best Sellers
1	2	6	Taking A Chance On Love...Benny Goodman...Columbia 35869
2	7	9	Velvet Moon ....Harry James...Columbia 36672
3	3	12	Don't Get Around Much Anymore ....Ink Spots...Decca 18503
4	8	8	As Time Goes By ....Rudy Vallée...Victor 20-1526
5	1	20	I've Heard That Song Before ....Harry James...Columbia 36668
6	6	12	As Time Goes By ....Jacques Renard...Brunswick 6205
7	5	14	That Old Black Magic ....Glenn Miller...Victor 20-1523
8	—	1	Let's Get Lost ....Vaughn Monroe...Victor 20-1524
9	9	4	Don't Get Around Much Anymore ....Glen Gray...Decca 18479
10	—	1	You'll Never Know ....Willie Kelly...Hit 7046

TW	LW	WK	Billboard ❀ JUNE 19, 1943 ❀ Best Sellers
1	1	7	Taking A Chance On Love...Benny Goodman...Columbia 35869
2	4	9	As Time Goes By ....Rudy Vallée...Victor 20-1526
3	2	10	Velvet Moon ....Harry James...Columbia 36672
4	6	13	As Time Goes By ....Jacques Renard...Brunswick 6205
5	3	13	Don't Get Around Much Anymore ....Ink Spots...Decca 18503
6	10	2	You'll Never Know ....Willie Kelly...Hit 7046
7	9	5	Don't Get Around Much Anymore ....Glen Gray...Decca 18479
8	8	2	Let's Get Lost ....Vaughn Monroe...Victor 20-1524
9	—	1	All Or Nothing At All...Frank Sinatra with Harry James...Columbia 35587
10	—	1	Comin' In On A Wing And A Prayer ....The Song Spinners...Decca 18553

TW	LW	WK	Billboard ❀ JUNE 26, 1943 ❀ Best Sellers
1	1	8	Taking A Chance On Love...Benny Goodman...Columbia 35869
2	10	2	Comin' In On A Wing And A Prayer ....The Song Spinners...Decca 18553
3	9	2	All Or Nothing At All...Frank Sinatra with Harry James...Columbia 35587
4	3	11	Velvet Moon ....Harry James...Columbia 36672
5	—	1	Let's Get Lost ....Kay Kyser...Columbia 36673
6	5	14	Don't Get Around Much Anymore ....Ink Spots...Decca 18503
7	6	3	You'll Never Know ....Willie Kelly...Hit 7046
8	4	14	As Time Goes By ....Jacques Renard...Brunswick 6205
9	2	10	As Time Goes By ....Rudy Vallée...Victor 20-1526
10	7	6	Don't Get Around Much Anymore ....Glen Gray...Decca 18479

TW	LW	WK	Billboard ❀ JULY 3, 1943 ❀ Best Sellers
1	2	3	Comin' In On A Wing And A Prayer ....The Song Spinners...Decca 18553
2	1	9	Taking A Chance On Love...Benny Goodman...Columbia 35869
3	3	3	All Or Nothing At All...Frank Sinatra with Harry James...Columbia 35587
4	5	2	Let's Get Lost ....Kay Kyser...Columbia 36673
5	4	12	Velvet Moon ....Harry James...Columbia 36672
6	7	4	You'll Never Know ....Willie Kelly...Hit 7046
7	6	15	Don't Get Around Much Anymore ....Ink Spots...Decca 18503
8	—	1	Don't Get Around Much Anymore (Never No Lament)....................Duke Ellington...Victor 26610
9	8	15	As Time Goes By ....Jacques Renard...Brunswick 6205
10	—	1	It Can't Be Wrong ....Dick Haymes...Decca 18557

TW	LW	WK	Billboard ❀ JULY 10, 1943 ❀ Best Sellers
1	1	4	Comin' In On A Wing And A Prayer ....The Song Spinners...Decca 18553
2	10	2	It Can't Be Wrong ....Dick Haymes...Decca 18557
3	3	4	All Or Nothing At All...Frank Sinatra with Harry James...Columbia 35587
4	—	1	You'll Never Know ....Dick Haymes...Decca 18556
5	2	10	Taking A Chance On Love...Benny Goodman...Columbia 35869
6	—	1	In The Blue Of Evening..Tommy Dorsey...Victor 20-1530
7	—	1	Johnny Zero ....The Song Spinners...Decca 18553
8	8	2	Don't Get Around Much Anymore (Never No Lament)....................Duke Ellington...Victor 26610
9	5	13	Velvet Moon ....Harry James...Columbia 36672
10	4	3	Let's Get Lost ....Kay Kyser...Columbia 36673

JULY 17, 1943 — Billboard Best Sellers

TW	LW	WK	Title	Artist
1	1	5	Comin' In On A Wing And A Prayer	The Song Spinners...Decca 18553
2	4	2	You'll Never Know	Dick Haymes...Decca 18556
3	2	3	It Can't Be Wrong	Dick Haymes...Decca 18557
4	3	5	All Or Nothing At All	Frank Sinatra with Harry James...Columbia 35587
5	6	2	In The Blue Of Evening	Tommy Dorsey...Victor 20-1530
6	10	4	Let's Get Lost	Kay Kyser...Columbia 36673
7	—	1	It's Always You	Tommy Dorsey...Victor 20-1530
8	5	11	Taking A Chance On Love	Benny Goodman...Columbia 35869
9	—	7	Don't Get Around Much Anymore	Glen Gray...Decca 18479
10	—	16	Don't Get Around Much Anymore	Ink Spots...Decca 18503

JULY 24, 1943 — Billboard Best Sellers

TW	LW	WK	Title	Artist
1	2	3	You'll Never Know	Dick Haymes...Decca 18556
2	1	6	Comin' In On A Wing And A Prayer	The Song Spinners...Decca 18553
3	3	4	It Can't Be Wrong	Dick Haymes...Decca 18557
4	5	3	In The Blue Of Evening	Tommy Dorsey...Victor 20-1530
5	4	6	All Or Nothing At All	Frank Sinatra with Harry James...Columbia 35587
6	7	2	It's Always You	Tommy Dorsey...Victor 20-1530
7	6	5	Let's Get Lost	Kay Kyser...Columbia 36673
8	—	2	Johnny Zero	The Song Spinners...Decca 18553
9	9	8	Don't Get Around Much Anymore	Glen Gray...Decca 18479
10	—	16	As Time Goes By	Jacques Renard...Brunswick 6205

JULY 31, 1943 — Billboard Best Sellers

TW	LW	WK	Title	Artist
1	1	4	You'll Never Know	Dick Haymes...Decca 18556
2	3	5	It Can't Be Wrong	Dick Haymes...Decca 18557
3	2	7	Comin' In On A Wing And A Prayer	The Song Spinners...Decca 18553
4	5	7	All Or Nothing At All	Frank Sinatra with Harry James...Columbia 35587
5	4	4	In The Blue Of Evening	Tommy Dorsey...Victor 20-1530
6	—	1	I Heard You Cried Last Night	Harry James...Columbia 36677
7	—	1	You'll Never Know	Frank Sinatra...Columbia 36678
8	6	3	It's Always You	Tommy Dorsey...Victor 20-1530
9	8	3	Johnny Zero	The Song Spinners...Decca 18553
10	—	1	In My Arms	Dick Haymes...Decca 18557

AUGUST 7, 1943 — Billboard Best Sellers

TW	LW	WK	Title	Artist
1	1	5	You'll Never Know	Dick Haymes...Decca 18556
2	2	6	It Can't Be Wrong	Dick Haymes...Decca 18557
3	5	5	In The Blue Of Evening	Tommy Dorsey...Victor 20-1530
4	4	8	All Or Nothing At All	Frank Sinatra with Harry James...Columbia 35587
5	3	8	Comin' In On A Wing And A Prayer	The Song Spinners...Decca 18553
6	7	2	You'll Never Know	Frank Sinatra...Columbia 36678
7	8	4	It's Always You	Tommy Dorsey...Victor 20-1530
8	6	2	I Heard You Cried Last Night	Harry James...Columbia 36677
9	9	4	Johnny Zero	The Song Spinners...Decca 18553
10	—	1	Paper Doll	Mills Brothers...Decca 18318

AUGUST 14, 1943 — Billboard Best Sellers

TW	LW	WK	Title	Artist
1	1	6	You'll Never Know	Dick Haymes...Decca 18556
2	2	7	It Can't Be Wrong	Dick Haymes...Decca 18557
3	3	6	In The Blue Of Evening	Tommy Dorsey...Victor 20-1530
4	4	9	All Or Nothing At All	Frank Sinatra with Harry James...Columbia 35587
5	5	9	Comin' In On A Wing And A Prayer	The Song Spinners...Decca 18553
6	8	3	I Heard You Cried Last Night	Harry James...Columbia 36677
7	6	3	You'll Never Know	Frank Sinatra...Columbia 36678
8	—	2	In My Arms	Dick Haymes...Decca 18557
9	7	5	It's Always You	Tommy Dorsey...Victor 20-1530
10	10	2	Paper Doll	Mills Brothers...Decca 18318

Billboard — AUGUST 21, 1943 — Best Sellers

TW	LW	WK	Title	Artist
1	3	7	In The Blue Of Evening	Tommy Dorsey...Victor 20-1530
2	1	7	You'll Never Know	Dick Haymes...Decca 18556
3	2	8	It Can't Be Wrong	Dick Haymes...Decca 18557
4	4	10	All Or Nothing At All	Frank Sinatra with Harry James...Columbia 35587
5	7	4	You'll Never Know	Frank Sinatra...Columbia 36678
6	5	10	Comin' In On A Wing And A Prayer	The Song Spinners...Decca 18553
7	8	3	In My Arms	Dick Haymes...Decca 18557
8	6	4	I Heard You Cried Last Night	Harry James...Columbia 36677
9	9	6	It's Always You	Tommy Dorsey...Victor 20-1530
10	10	3	Paper Doll	Mills Brothers...Decca 18318

Billboard — AUGUST 28, 1943 — Best Sellers

TW	LW	WK	Title	Artist
1	1	8	In The Blue Of Evening	Tommy Dorsey...Victor 20-1530
2	5	5	You'll Never Know	Frank Sinatra...Columbia 36678
3	4	11	All Or Nothing At All	Frank Sinatra with Harry James...Columbia 35587
4	2	8	You'll Never Know	Dick Haymes...Decca 18556
5	8	5	I Heard You Cried Last Night	Harry James...Columbia 36677
6	3	9	It Can't Be Wrong	Dick Haymes...Decca 18557
7	—	1	Sunday, Monday Or Always	Bing Crosby...Decca 18561
8	10	4	Paper Doll	Mills Brothers...Decca 18318
9	6	11	Comin' In On A Wing And A Prayer	The Song Spinners...Decca 18553
10	—	1	Pistol Packin' Mama	Al Dexter...Okeh 6708

Billboard — SEPTEMBER 4, 1943 — Best Sellers

TW	LW	WK	Title	Artist
1	1	9	In The Blue Of Evening	Tommy Dorsey...Victor 20-1530
2	3	12	All Or Nothing At All	Frank Sinatra with Harry James...Columbia 35587
3	7	2	Sunday, Monday Or Always	Bing Crosby...Decca 18561
4	2	6	You'll Never Know	Frank Sinatra...Columbia 36678
5	4	9	You'll Never Know	Dick Haymes...Decca 18556
6	8	5	Paper Doll	Mills Brothers...Decca 18318
7	5	6	I Heard You Cried Last Night	Harry James...Columbia 36677
8	6	10	It Can't Be Wrong	Dick Haymes...Decca 18557
9	10	2	Pistol Packin' Mama	Al Dexter...Okeh 6708
10	—	7	It's Always You	Tommy Dorsey...Victor 20-1530

Billboard — SEPTEMBER 11, 1943 — Best Sellers

TW	LW	WK	Title	Artist
1	3	3	Sunday, Monday Or Always	Bing Crosby...Decca 18561
2	5	10	You'll Never Know	Dick Haymes...Decca 18556
3	1	10	In The Blue Of Evening	Tommy Dorsey...Victor 20-1530
4	6	6	Paper Doll	Mills Brothers...Decca 18318
5	2	13	All Or Nothing At All	Frank Sinatra with Harry James...Columbia 35587
6	4	7	You'll Never Know	Frank Sinatra...Columbia 36678
7	7	7	I Heard You Cried Last Night	Harry James...Columbia 36677
8	9	3	Pistol Packin' Mama	Al Dexter...Okeh 6708
9	—	4	In My Arms	Dick Haymes...Decca 18557
10	8	11	It Can't Be Wrong	Dick Haymes...Decca 18557

Billboard — SEPTEMBER 18, 1943 — Best Sellers

TW	LW	WK	Title	Artist
1	1	4	Sunday, Monday Or Always	Bing Crosby...Decca 18561
2	6	8	You'll Never Know	Frank Sinatra...Columbia 36678
3	3	11	In The Blue Of Evening	Tommy Dorsey...Victor 20-1530
4	2	11	You'll Never Know	Dick Haymes...Decca 18556
5	7	8	I Heard You Cried Last Night	Harry James...Columbia 36677
6	8	4	Pistol Packin' Mama	Al Dexter...Okeh 6708
7	4	7	Paper Doll	Mills Brothers...Decca 18318
8	5	14	All Or Nothing At All	Frank Sinatra with Harry James...Columbia 35587
9	—	1	Sunday, Monday Or Always	Frank Sinatra...Columbia 36679
10	9	5	In My Arms	Dick Haymes...Decca 18557

Billboard — SEPTEMBER 25, 1943 — Best Sellers

TW	LW	WK	Title	Artist
1	1	5	Sunday, Monday Or Always	Bing Crosby...Decca 18561
2	7	8	Paper Doll	Mills Brothers...Decca 18318
3	2	9	You'll Never Know	Frank Sinatra...Columbia 36678
4	6	5	Pistol Packin' Mama	Al Dexter...Okeh 6708
5	3	12	In The Blue Of Evening	Tommy Dorsey...Victor 20-1530
6	5	9	I Heard You Cried Last Night	Harry James...Columbia 36677
7	8	15	All Or Nothing At All	Frank Sinatra with Harry James...Columbia 35587
8	4	12	You'll Never Know	Dick Haymes...Decca 18556
9	9	2	Sunday, Monday Or Always	Frank Sinatra...Columbia 36679
10	10	6	In My Arms	Dick Haymes...Decca 18557

Billboard — OCTOBER 2, 1943 — Best Sellers

TW	LW	WK	Title	Artist
1	1	6	Sunday, Monday Or Always	Bing Crosby...Decca 18561
2	2	9	Paper Doll	Mills Brothers...Decca 18318
3	4	6	Pistol Packin' Mama	Al Dexter...Okeh 6708
4	6	10	I Heard You Cried Last Night	Harry James...Columbia 36677
5	8	13	You'll Never Know	Dick Haymes...Decca 18556
6	5	13	In The Blue Of Evening	Tommy Dorsey...Victor 20-1530
7	3	10	You'll Never Know	Frank Sinatra...Columbia 36678
8	7	16	All Or Nothing At All	Frank Sinatra with Harry James...Columbia 35587
9	10	7	In My Arms	Dick Haymes...Decca 18557
10	—	1	Close To You	Frank Sinatra...Columbia 36678

Billboard — OCTOBER 9, 1943 — Best Sellers

TW	LW	WK	Title	Artist
1	1	7	Sunday, Monday Or Always	Bing Crosby...Decca 18561
2	2	10	Paper Doll	Mills Brothers...Decca 18318
3	3	7	Pistol Packin' Mama	Al Dexter...Okeh 6708
4	4	11	I Heard You Cried Last Night	Harry James...Columbia 36677
5	7	11	You'll Never Know	Frank Sinatra...Columbia 36678
6	6	14	In The Blue Of Evening	Tommy Dorsey...Victor 20-1530
7	8	17	All Or Nothing At All	Frank Sinatra with Harry James...Columbia 35587
8	5	14	You'll Never Know	Dick Haymes...Decca 18556
9	—	1	People Will Say We're In Love	Frank Sinatra...Columbia 36682
10	—	3	Sunday, Monday Or Always	Frank Sinatra...Columbia 36679

Billboard — OCTOBER 16, 1943 — Best Sellers

TW	LW	WK	Title	Artist
1	1	8	Sunday, Monday Or Always	Bing Crosby...Decca 18561
2	2	11	Paper Doll	Mills Brothers...Decca 18318
3	3	8	Pistol Packin' Mama	Al Dexter...Okeh 6708
4	4	12	I Heard You Cried Last Night	Harry James...Columbia 36677
5	8	15	You'll Never Know	Dick Haymes...Decca 18556
6	5	12	You'll Never Know	Frank Sinatra...Columbia 36678
7	9	2	People Will Say We're In Love	Frank Sinatra...Columbia 36682
8	7	18	All Or Nothing At All	Frank Sinatra with Harry James...Columbia 35587
9	6	15	In The Blue Of Evening	Tommy Dorsey...Victor 20-1530
10	—	1	People Will Say We're In Love	Bing Crosby & Trudy Erwin...Decca 18564

Billboard — OCTOBER 23, 1943 — Best Sellers

TW	LW	WK	Title	Artist
1	1	9	Sunday, Monday Or Always	Bing Crosby...Decca 18561
2	3	9	Pistol Packin' Mama	Al Dexter...Okeh 6708
3	2	12	Paper Doll	Mills Brothers...Decca 18318
4	10	2	People Will Say We're In Love	Bing Crosby & Trudy Erwin...Decca 18564
5	4	13	I Heard You Cried Last Night	Harry James...Columbia 36677
6	6	13	You'll Never Know	Frank Sinatra...Columbia 36678
7	7	3	People Will Say We're In Love	Frank Sinatra...Columbia 36682
8	—	1	Put Your Arms Around Me, Honey (I Never Knew Any Girl Like You)	Dick Kuhn...Decca 4337
9	9	16	In The Blue Of Evening	Tommy Dorsey...Victor 20-1530
10	—	1	Boogie Woogie	Tommy Dorsey...Victor 26054

TW	LW	WK	Billboard® OCTOBER 30, 1943 Best Sellers
1	2	10	**Pistol Packin' Mama** ....*Al Dexter*...Okeh 6708
2	3	13	**Paper Doll** ....*Mills Brothers*...Decca 18318
3	1	10	**Sunday, Monday Or Always** ....*Bing Crosby*...Decca 18561
4	4	3	**People Will Say We're In Love** ....*Bing Crosby & Trudy Erwin*...Decca 18564
5	5	14	**I Heard You Cried Last Night** ....*Harry James*...Columbia 36677
6	7	4	**People Will Say We're In Love** ....*Frank Sinatra*...Columbia 36682
7	—	16	**You'll Never Know** ....*Dick Haymes*...Decca 18556
8	—	1	**Put Your Arms Around Me, Honey (I Never Knew Any Girl Like You)** ....*Dick Haymes*...Decca 18565
9	9	17	**In The Blue Of Evening** ....*Tommy Dorsey*...Victor 20-1530
10	8	2	**Put Your Arms Around Me, Honey (I Never Knew Any Girl Like You)** ....*Dick Kuhn*...Decca 4337

TW	LW	WK	Billboard® NOVEMBER 6, 1943 Best Sellers
1	2	14	**Paper Doll** ....*Mills Brothers*...Decca 18318
2	1	11	**Pistol Packin' Mama** ....*Al Dexter*...Okeh 6708
3	3	11	**Sunday, Monday Or Always** ....*Bing Crosby*...Decca 18561
4	4	4	**People Will Say We're In Love** ....*Bing Crosby & Trudy Erwin*...Decca 18564
5	5	15	**I Heard You Cried Last Night** ....*Harry James*...Columbia 36677
6	6	5	**People Will Say We're In Love** ....*Frank Sinatra*...Columbia 36682
7	8	2	**Put Your Arms Around Me, Honey (I Never Knew Any Girl Like You)** ....*Dick Haymes*...Decca 18565
8	—	1	**Pistol Packin' Mama** ....*Bing Crosby & Andrews Sisters*...Decca 23277
9	10	3	**Put Your Arms Around Me, Honey (I Never Knew Any Girl Like You)** ....*Dick Kuhn*...Decca 4337
10	—	1	**Blue Rain** ....*Glenn Miller*...Victor 20-1536

TW	LW	WK	Billboard® NOVEMBER 13, 1943 Best Sellers
1	1	15	**Paper Doll** ....*Mills Brothers*...Decca 18318
2	2	12	**Pistol Packin' Mama** ....*Al Dexter*...Okeh 6708
3	3	12	**Sunday, Monday Or Always** ....*Bing Crosby*...Decca 18561
4	4	5	**People Will Say We're In Love** ....*Bing Crosby & Trudy Erwin*...Decca 18564
5	8	2	**Pistol Packin' Mama** ....*Bing Crosby & Andrews Sisters*...Decca 23277
6	7	3	**Put Your Arms Around Me, Honey (I Never Knew Any Girl Like You)** ....*Dick Haymes*...Decca 18565
7	—	1	**Oh! What A Beautiful Mornin'** ....*Bing Crosby & Trudy Erwin*...Decca 18564
8	6	6	**People Will Say We're In Love** ....*Frank Sinatra*...Columbia 36682
9	5	16	**I Heard You Cried Last Night** ....*Harry James*...Columbia 36677
10	—	4	**Sunday, Monday Or Always** ....*Frank Sinatra*...Columbia 36679

TW	LW	WK	Billboard® NOVEMBER 20, 1943 Best Sellers
1	1	16	**Paper Doll** ....*Mills Brothers*...Decca 18318
2	3	13	**Sunday, Monday Or Always** ....*Bing Crosby*...Decca 18561
3	2	13	**Pistol Packin' Mama** ....*Al Dexter*...Okeh 6708
4	5	3	**Pistol Packin' Mama** ....*Bing Crosby & Andrews Sisters*...Decca 23277
5	4	6	**People Will Say We're In Love** ....*Bing Crosby & Trudy Erwin*...Decca 18564
6	6	4	**Put Your Arms Around Me, Honey (I Never Knew Any Girl Like You)** ....*Dick Haymes*...Decca 18565
7	9	17	**I Heard You Cried Last Night** ....*Harry James*...Columbia 36677
8	7	2	**Oh! What A Beautiful Mornin'** ....*Bing Crosby & Trudy Erwin*...Decca 18564
9	8	7	**People Will Say We're In Love** ....*Frank Sinatra*...Columbia 36682
10	—	2	**Blue Rain** ....*Glenn Miller*...Victor 20-1536

Billboard® ❀ NOVEMBER 27, 1943 ❀ Best Sellers

TW	LW	WK		
1	1	17	**Paper Doll**	Mills Brothers...Decca 18318
2	5	7	**People Will Say We're In Love**	Bing Crosby & Trudy Erwin...Decca 18564
3	4	4	**Pistol Packin' Mama**	Bing Crosby & Andrews Sisters...Decca 23277
4	2	14	**Sunday, Monday Or Always**	Bing Crosby...Decca 18561
5	6	5	**Put Your Arms Around Me, Honey (I Never Knew Any Girl Like You)**	Dick Haymes...Decca 18565
6	3	14	**Pistol Packin' Mama**	Al Dexter...Okeh 6708
7	7	18	**I Heard You Cried Last Night**	Harry James...Columbia 36677
8	—	1	**My Heart Tells Me (Should I Believe My Heart?)**	Glen Gray...Decca 18567
9	8	3	**Oh! What A Beautiful Mornin'**	Bing Crosby & Trudy Erwin...Decca 18564
10	9	8	**People Will Say We're In Love**	Frank Sinatra...Columbia 36682

Billboard® ❀ DECEMBER 4, 1943 ❀ Best Sellers

TW	LW	WK		
1	1	18	**Paper Doll**	Mills Brothers...Decca 18318
2	3	5	**Pistol Packin' Mama**	Bing Crosby & Andrews Sisters...Decca 23277
3	2	8	**People Will Say We're In Love**	Bing Crosby & Trudy Erwin...Decca 18564
4	4	15	**Sunday, Monday Or Always**	Bing Crosby...Decca 18561
5	6	15	**Pistol Packin' Mama**	Al Dexter...Okeh 6708
6	9	4	**Oh! What A Beautiful Mornin'**	Bing Crosby & Trudy Erwin...Decca 18564
7	8	2	**My Heart Tells Me (Should I Believe My Heart?)**	Glen Gray...Decca 18567
8	—	2	**Boogie Woogie**	Tommy Dorsey...Victor 26054
9	5	6	**Put Your Arms Around Me, Honey (I Never Knew Any Girl Like You)**	Dick Haymes...Decca 18565
10	—	1	**They're Either Too Young Or Too Old**	Jimmy Dorsey...Decca 18571

Billboard® ❀ DECEMBER 11, 1943 ❀ Best Sellers

TW	LW	WK		
1	1	19	**Paper Doll**	Mills Brothers...Decca 18318
2	2	6	**Pistol Packin' Mama**	Bing Crosby & Andrews Sisters...Decca 23277
3	3	9	**People Will Say We're In Love**	Bing Crosby & Trudy Erwin...Decca 18564
4	7	3	**My Heart Tells Me (Should I Believe My Heart?)**	Glen Gray...Decca 18567
5	4	16	**Sunday, Monday Or Always**	Bing Crosby...Decca 18561
6	6	5	**Oh! What A Beautiful Mornin'**	Bing Crosby & Trudy Erwin...Decca 18564
7	10	2	**They're Either Too Young Or Too Old**	Jimmy Dorsey...Decca 18571
8	—	9	**People Will Say We're In Love**	Frank Sinatra...Columbia 36682
9	8	3	**Boogie Woogie**	Tommy Dorsey...Victor 26054
10	—	1	**I'll Be Home For Christmas (If Only In My Dreams)**	Bing Crosby...Decca 18570

Billboard® ❀ DECEMBER 18, 1943 ❀ Best Sellers

TW	LW	WK		
1	1	20	**Paper Doll**	Mills Brothers...Decca 18318
2	2	7	**Pistol Packin' Mama**	Bing Crosby & Andrews Sisters...Decca 23277
3	3	10	**People Will Say We're In Love**	Bing Crosby & Trudy Erwin...Decca 18564
4	10	2	**I'll Be Home For Christmas (If Only In My Dreams)**	Bing Crosby...Decca 18570
5	4	4	**My Heart Tells Me (Should I Believe My Heart?)**	Glen Gray...Decca 18567
6	6	6	**Oh! What A Beautiful Mornin'**	Bing Crosby & Trudy Erwin...Decca 18564
7	9	4	**Boogie Woogie**	Tommy Dorsey...Victor 26054
8	5	17	**Sunday, Monday Or Always**	Bing Crosby...Decca 18561
9	—	1	**Oklahoma!**	Oklahoma! Original Cast Album...Decca 359
10	7	3	**They're Either Too Young Or Too Old**	Jimmy Dorsey...Decca 18571

Billboard® ❀ DECEMBER 25, 1943 ❀ Best Sellers

TW	LW	WK		
1	1	21	**Paper Doll**	Mills Brothers...Decca 18318
2	2	8	**Pistol Packin' Mama**	Bing Crosby & Andrews Sisters...Decca 23277
3	4	3	**I'll Be Home For Christmas (If Only In My Dreams)**	Bing Crosby...Decca 18570
4	3	11	**People Will Say We're In Love**	Bing Crosby & Trudy Erwin...Decca 18564
5	6	7	**Oh! What A Beautiful Mornin'**	Bing Crosby & Trudy Erwin...Decca 18564
6	—	1	**Shoo-Shoo Baby**	Ella Mae Morse...Capitol 143
7	5	5	**My Heart Tells Me (Should I Believe My Heart?)**	Glen Gray...Decca 18567
8	10	4	**They're Either Too Young Or Too Old**	Jimmy Dorsey...Decca 18571
9	—	16	**Pistol Packin' Mama**	Al Dexter...Okeh 6708
10	8	18	**Sunday, Monday Or Always**	Bing Crosby...Decca 18561

TW	LW	WK	Billboard ❄ JANUARY 1, 1944 ❄ Best Sellers
1	1	22	Paper Doll..*Mills Brothers*...Decca 18318
2	7	6	My Heart Tells Me (Should I Believe My Heart?) ....*Glen Gray*...Decca 18567
3	3	4	I'll Be Home For Christmas (If Only In My Dreams) ....*Bing Crosby*...Decca 18570
4	4	12	People Will Say We're In Love...............................*Bing Crosby & Trudy Erwin*...Decca 18564
5	8	5	They're Either Too Young Or Too Old...*Jimmy Dorsey*...Decca 18571
6	5	8	Oh! What A Beautiful Mornin'.............................*Bing Crosby & Trudy Erwin*...Decca 18564
7	—	1	Shoo-Shoo Baby...*Andrews Sisters*...Decca 18572
8	6	2	Shoo-Shoo Baby...*Ella Mae Morse*...Capitol 143
9	—	1	White Christmas..*Bing Crosby*...Decca 18429
10	2	9	Pistol Packin' Mama...................................*Bing Crosby & Andrews Sisters*...Decca 23277

TW	LW	WK	Billboard ❄ JANUARY 8, 1944 ❄ Best Sellers
1	1	23	Paper Doll..*Mills Brothers*...Decca 18318
2	2	7	My Heart Tells Me (Should I Believe My Heart?) ....*Glen Gray*...Decca 18567
3	5	6	They're Either Too Young Or Too Old...*Jimmy Dorsey*...Decca 18571
4	—	1	Star Eyes...*Jimmy Dorsey*...Decca 18571
5	8	3	Shoo-Shoo Baby...*Ella Mae Morse*...Capitol 143
6	6	9	Oh! What A Beautiful Mornin'.............................*Bing Crosby & Trudy Erwin*...Decca 18564
7	—	17	Pistol Packin' Mama..*Al Dexter*...Okeh 6708
8	3	5	I'll Be Home For Christmas (If Only In My Dreams) ....*Bing Crosby*...Decca 18570
9	7	2	Shoo-Shoo Baby...*Andrews Sisters*...Decca 18572
10	—	2	Oklahoma!..*Oklahoma! Original Cast Album*...Decca 359

TW	LW	WK	Billboard ❄ JANUARY 15, 1944 ❄ Best Sellers
1	1	24	Paper Doll..*Mills Brothers*...Decca 18318
2	2	8	My Heart Tells Me (Should I Believe My Heart?) ....*Glen Gray*...Decca 18567
3	9	3	Shoo-Shoo Baby...*Andrews Sisters*...Decca 18572
4	5	4	Shoo-Shoo Baby...*Ella Mae Morse*...Capitol 143
5	3	7	They're Either Too Young Or Too Old...*Jimmy Dorsey*...Decca 18571
6	4	2	Star Eyes...*Jimmy Dorsey*...Decca 18571
7	—	13	People Will Say We're In Love...............................*Bing Crosby & Trudy Erwin*...Decca 18564
8	—	5	Boogie Woogie..*Tommy Dorsey*...Victor 26054
9	—	1	My Ideal..*Jimmy Dorsey*...Decca 18574
10	—	1	Besame Mucho (Kiss Me Much)..*Jimmy Dorsey*...Decca 18574

TW	LW	WK	Billboard ❄ JANUARY 22, 1944 ❄ Best Sellers
1	1	25	Paper Doll..*Mills Brothers*...Decca 18318
2	2	9	My Heart Tells Me (Should I Believe My Heart?) ....*Glen Gray*...Decca 18567
3	6	3	Star Eyes...*Jimmy Dorsey*...Decca 18571
4	—	1	My Shining Hour...*Glen Gray*...Decca 18567
5	8	6	Boogie Woogie..*Tommy Dorsey*...Victor 26054
6	4	5	Shoo-Shoo Baby...*Ella Mae Morse*...Capitol 143
7	5	8	They're Either Too Young Or Too Old...*Jimmy Dorsey*...Decca 18571
8	7	14	People Will Say We're In Love...............................*Bing Crosby & Trudy Erwin*...Decca 18564
9	—	3	Blue Rain...*Glenn Miller*...Victor 20-1536
10	—	1	How Sweet You Are...*Kay Armen*...Decca 18566

TW	LW	WK	Billboard ❄ JANUARY 29, 1944 ❄ Best Sellers
1	2	10	My Heart Tells Me (Should I Believe My Heart?) ....*Glen Gray*...Decca 18567
2	—	4	Shoo-Shoo Baby...*Andrews Sisters*...Decca 18572
3	1	26	Paper Doll..*Mills Brothers*...Decca 18318
4	3	4	Star Eyes...*Jimmy Dorsey*...Decca 18571
5	—	2	Besame Mucho (Kiss Me Much)..*Jimmy Dorsey*...Decca 18574
6	6	6	Shoo-Shoo Baby...*Ella Mae Morse*...Capitol 143
7	7	9	They're Either Too Young Or Too Old...*Jimmy Dorsey*...Decca 18571
8	—	1	Speak Low...*Guy Lombardo*...Decca 18573
9	4	2	My Shining Hour...*Glen Gray*...Decca 18567
10	—	1	Cherry ....*Harry James*...Columbia 36683

TW	LW	WK	Billboard ● FEBRUARY 5, 1944 ● Best Sellers
1	1	11	My Heart Tells Me (Should I Believe My Heart?) ....*Glen Gray*...Decca 18567
2	5	3	Besame Mucho (Kiss Me Much)..*Jimmy Dorsey*...Decca 18574
3	3	27	Paper Doll..*Mills Brothers*...Decca 18318
4	2	5	Shoo-Shoo Baby..*Andrews Sisters*...Decca 18572
5	4	5	Star Eyes...*Jimmy Dorsey*...Decca 18571
6	6	7	Shoo-Shoo Baby...*Ella Mae Morse*...Capitol 143
7	9	3	My Shining Hour...*Glen Gray*...Decca 18567
8	—	1	No Love, No Nothin'...*Ella Mae Morse*...Capitol 143
9	—	2	My Ideal...*Jimmy Dorsey*...Decca 18574
10	—	1	Do Nothin' Till You Hear From Me...*Duke Ellington*...Victor 20-1547

TW	LW	WK	Billboard ● FEBRUARY 12, 1944 ● Best Sellers
1	1	12	My Heart Tells Me (Should I Believe My Heart?) ....*Glen Gray*...Decca 18567
2	4	6	Shoo-Shoo Baby..*Andrews Sisters*...Decca 18572
3	2	4	Besame Mucho (Kiss Me Much)..*Jimmy Dorsey*...Decca 18574
4	3	28	Paper Doll..*Mills Brothers*...Decca 18318
5	5	6	Star Eyes...*Jimmy Dorsey*...Decca 18571
6	6	8	Shoo-Shoo Baby...*Ella Mae Morse*...Capitol 143
7	8	2	No Love, No Nothin'...*Ella Mae Morse*...Capitol 143
8	7	4	My Shining Hour...*Glen Gray*...Decca 18567
9	—	1	I Couldn't Sleep A Wink Last Night...*Frank Sinatra*...Columbia 36687
10	—	2	Speak Low...*Guy Lombardo*...Decca 18573

TW	LW	WK	Billboard ● FEBRUARY 19, 1944 ● Best Sellers
1	1	13	My Heart Tells Me (Should I Believe My Heart?) ....*Glen Gray*...Decca 18567
2	3	5	Besame Mucho (Kiss Me Much)..*Jimmy Dorsey*...Decca 18574
3	2	7	Shoo-Shoo Baby..*Andrews Sisters*...Decca 18572
4	6	9	Shoo-Shoo Baby...*Ella Mae Morse*...Capitol 143
5	4	29	Paper Doll..*Mills Brothers*...Decca 18318
6	5	7	Star Eyes...*Jimmy Dorsey*...Decca 18571
7	—	1	Holiday For Strings ....*David Rose*...Victor 27853
8	—	3	My Ideal...*Jimmy Dorsey*...Decca 18574
9	—	1	Mairzy Doats ....*Al Trace*...Hit 8079
10	10	3	Speak Low...*Guy Lombardo*...Decca 18573

TW	LW	WK	Billboard ● FEBRUARY 26, 1944 ● Best Sellers
1	1	14	My Heart Tells Me (Should I Believe My Heart?) ....*Glen Gray*...Decca 18567
2	2	6	Besame Mucho (Kiss Me Much)..*Jimmy Dorsey*...Decca 18574
3	3	8	Shoo-Shoo Baby..*Andrews Sisters*...Decca 18572
4	6	8	Star Eyes...*Jimmy Dorsey*...Decca 18571
5	4	10	Shoo-Shoo Baby...*Ella Mae Morse*...Capitol 143
6	—	2	I Couldn't Sleep A Wink Last Night...*Frank Sinatra*...Columbia 36687
7	—	1	Mairzy Doats ....*The Merry Macs*...Decca 18588
8	5	30	Paper Doll..*Mills Brothers*...Decca 18318
9	7	2	Holiday For Strings ....*David Rose*...Victor 27853
10	8	4	My Ideal...*Jimmy Dorsey*...Decca 18574

TW	LW	WK	Billboard ● MARCH 4, 1944 ● Best Sellers
1	2	7	Besame Mucho (Kiss Me Much)..*Jimmy Dorsey*...Decca 18574
2	1	15	My Heart Tells Me (Should I Believe My Heart?) ....*Glen Gray*...Decca 18567
3	7	2	Mairzy Doats ....*The Merry Macs*...Decca 18588
4	5	11	Shoo-Shoo Baby...*Ella Mae Morse*...Capitol 143
5	3	9	Shoo-Shoo Baby..*Andrews Sisters*...Decca 18572
6	4	9	Star Eyes...*Jimmy Dorsey*...Decca 18571
7	9	3	Holiday For Strings ....*David Rose*...Victor 27853
8	6	3	I Couldn't Sleep A Wink Last Night...*Frank Sinatra*...Columbia 36687
9	—	2	Mairzy Doats ....*Al Trace*...Hit 8079
10	—	4	Speak Low...*Guy Lombardo*...Decca 18573

Billboard 🎯 MARCH 11, 1944 🎯 Best Sellers

TW	LW	WK	Title	Artist
1	1	8	Besame Mucho (Kiss Me Much)	*Jimmy Dorsey*...Decca 18574
2	3	3	Mairzy Doats	*The Merry Macs*...Decca 18588
3	5	10	Shoo-Shoo Baby	*Andrews Sisters*...Decca 18572
4	2	16	My Heart Tells Me (Should I Believe My Heart?)	*Glen Gray*...Decca 18567
5	7	4	Holiday For Strings	*David Rose*...Victor 27853
6	4	12	Shoo-Shoo Baby	*Ella Mae Morse*...Capitol 143
7	6	10	Star Eyes	*Jimmy Dorsey*...Decca 18571
8	10	5	Speak Low	*Guy Lombardo*...Decca 18573
9	—	1	Do Nothin' Till You Hear From Me	*Woody Herman*...Decca 18578
10	—	1	Poinciana (Song Of The Tree)	*Bing Crosby*...Decca 18586

Billboard 🎯 MARCH 18, 1944 🎯 Best Sellers

TW	LW	WK	Title	Artist
1	1	9	Besame Mucho (Kiss Me Much)	*Jimmy Dorsey*...Decca 18574
2	2	4	Mairzy Doats	*The Merry Macs*...Decca 18588
3	4	17	My Heart Tells Me (Should I Believe My Heart?)	*Glen Gray*...Decca 18567
4	5	5	Holiday For Strings	*David Rose*...Victor 27853
5	3	11	Shoo-Shoo Baby	*Andrews Sisters*...Decca 18572
6	—	4	I Couldn't Sleep A Wink Last Night	*Frank Sinatra*...Columbia 36687
7	—	3	Mairzy Doats	*Al Trace*...Hit 8079
8	8	6	Speak Low	*Guy Lombardo*...Decca 18573
9	7	11	Star Eyes	*Jimmy Dorsey*...Decca 18571
10	6	13	Shoo-Shoo Baby	*Ella Mae Morse*...Capitol 143

Billboard 🎯 MARCH 25, 1944 🎯 Best Sellers

TW	LW	WK	Title	Artist
1	1	10	Besame Mucho (Kiss Me Much)	*Jimmy Dorsey*...Decca 18574
2	2	5	Mairzy Doats	*The Merry Macs*...Decca 18588
3	4	6	Holiday For Strings	*David Rose*...Victor 27853
4	5	12	Shoo-Shoo Baby	*Andrews Sisters*...Decca 18572
5	—	2	Poinciana (Song Of The Tree)	*Bing Crosby*...Decca 18586
6	8	7	Speak Low	*Guy Lombardo*...Decca 18573
7	6	5	I Couldn't Sleep A Wink Last Night	*Frank Sinatra*...Columbia 36687
8	3	18	My Heart Tells Me (Should I Believe My Heart?)	*Glen Gray*...Decca 18567
9	10	14	Shoo-Shoo Baby	*Ella Mae Morse*...Capitol 143
10	9	12	Star Eyes	*Jimmy Dorsey*...Decca 18571

Billboard 🎯 APRIL 1, 1944 🎯 Best Sellers

TW	LW	WK	Title	Artist
1	1	11	Besame Mucho (Kiss Me Much)	*Jimmy Dorsey*...Decca 18574
2	2	6	Mairzy Doats	*The Merry Macs*...Decca 18588
3	4	13	Shoo-Shoo Baby	*Andrews Sisters*...Decca 18572
4	3	7	Holiday For Strings	*David Rose*...Victor 27853
5	7	6	I Couldn't Sleep A Wink Last Night	*Frank Sinatra*...Columbia 36687
6	6	8	Speak Low	*Guy Lombardo*...Decca 18573
7	10	13	Star Eyes	*Jimmy Dorsey*...Decca 18571
8	—	1	When They Ask About You	*Jimmy Dorsey*...Decca 18582
9	8	19	My Heart Tells Me (Should I Believe My Heart?)	*Glen Gray*...Decca 18567
10	—	1	Do Nothin' 'Till You Hear From Me	*Stan Kenton*...Capitol 145

Billboard 🎯 APRIL 8, 1944 🎯 Best Sellers

TW	LW	WK	Title	Artist
1	1	12	Besame Mucho (Kiss Me Much)	*Jimmy Dorsey*...Decca 18574
2	4	8	Holiday For Strings	*David Rose*...Victor 27853
3	2	7	Mairzy Doats	*The Merry Macs*...Decca 18588
4	3	14	Shoo-Shoo Baby	*Andrews Sisters*...Decca 18572
5	5	7	I Couldn't Sleep A Wink Last Night	*Frank Sinatra*...Columbia 36687
6	—	3	Poinciana (Song Of The Tree)	*Bing Crosby*...Decca 18586
7	—	1	I Love You	*Enric Madriguera*...Hit 7077
8	—	1	Mairzy Doats	*The Pied Pipers*...Capitol 148
9	9	20	My Heart Tells Me (Should I Believe My Heart?)	*Glen Gray*...Decca 18567
10	—	15	Shoo-Shoo Baby	*Ella Mae Morse*...Capitol 143

TW	LW	WK	Billboard® APRIL 15, 1944 Best Sellers
1	1	13	Besame Mucho (Kiss Me Much)...Jimmy Dorsey...Decca 18574
2	2	9	Holiday For Strings...David Rose...Victor 27853
3	—	1	It's Love-Love-Love..Guy Lombardo...Decca 18589
4	—	2	When They Ask About You...Jimmy Dorsey...Decca 18582
5	3	8	Mairzy Doats...The Merry Macs...Decca 18588
6	—	1	San Fernando Valley...Bing Crosby...Decca 18586
7	5	8	I Couldn't Sleep A Wink Last Night...Frank Sinatra...Columbia 36687
8	6	4	Poinciana (Song Of The Tree)..Bing Crosby...Decca 18586
9	4	15	Shoo-Shoo Baby...Andrews Sisters...Decca 18572
10	—	2	Do Nothin' Till You Hear From Me...Woody Herman...Decca 18578

TW	LW	WK	Billboard® APRIL 22, 1944 Best Sellers
1	3	2	It's Love-Love-Love..Guy Lombardo...Decca 18589
2	2	10	Holiday For Strings...David Rose...Victor 27853
3	—	1	I Love You...Bing Crosby...Decca 18595
4	1	14	Besame Mucho (Kiss Me Much)...Jimmy Dorsey...Decca 18574
5	—	1	I'll Get By (As Long As I Have You)..Harry James...Columbia 36698
6	4	3	When They Ask About You...Jimmy Dorsey...Decca 18582
7	6	2	San Fernando Valley...Bing Crosby...Decca 18586
8	8	5	Poinciana (Song Of The Tree)..Bing Crosby...Decca 18586
9	5	9	Mairzy Doats...The Merry Macs...Decca 18588
10	—	1	Bésame Mucho (Kiss Me Much)...Andy Russell...Capitol 149

TW	LW	WK	Billboard® APRIL 29, 1944 Best Sellers
1	1	3	It's Love-Love-Love..Guy Lombardo...Decca 18589
2	3	2	I Love You...Bing Crosby...Decca 18595
3	2	11	Holiday For Strings...David Rose...Victor 27853
4	6	4	When They Ask About You...Jimmy Dorsey...Decca 18582
5	4	15	Besame Mucho (Kiss Me Much)...Jimmy Dorsey...Decca 18574
6	7	3	San Fernando Valley...Bing Crosby...Decca 18586
7	5	2	I'll Get By (As Long As I Have You)..Harry James...Columbia 36698
8	—	1	I Love You...Jo Stafford...Capitol 153
9	—	1	It's Love-Love-Love..The Four King Sisters...Bluebird 30-0822
10	10	2	Bésame Mucho (Kiss Me Much)...Andy Russell...Capitol 149

TW	LW	WK	Billboard® MAY 6, 1944 Best Sellers
1	2	3	I Love You...Bing Crosby...Decca 18595
2	6	4	San Fernando Valley...Bing Crosby...Decca 18586
3	7	3	I'll Get By (As Long As I Have You)..Harry James...Columbia 36698
4	9	2	It's Love-Love-Love..The Four King Sisters...Bluebird 30-0822
5	3	12	Holiday For Strings...David Rose...Victor 27853
6	1	4	It's Love-Love-Love..Guy Lombardo...Decca 18589
7	5	16	Besame Mucho (Kiss Me Much)...Jimmy Dorsey...Decca 18574
8	—	1	Don't Sweetheart Me...Lawrence Welk...Decca 4434
9	—	1	Long Ago (And Far Away)...Helen Forrest & Dick Haymes...Decca 23317
10	8	2	I Love You...Jo Stafford...Capitol 153

TW	LW	WK	Billboard® MAY 13, 1944 Best Sellers
1	1	4	I Love You...Bing Crosby...Decca 18595
2	3	4	I'll Get By (As Long As I Have You)..Harry James...Columbia 36698
3	9	2	Long Ago (And Far Away)...Helen Forrest & Dick Haymes...Decca 23317
4	5	13	Holiday For Strings...David Rose...Victor 27853
5	2	5	San Fernando Valley...Bing Crosby...Decca 18586
6	6	5	It's Love-Love-Love..Guy Lombardo...Decca 18589
7	—	1	Long Ago (And Far Away)...Jo Stafford...Capitol 153
8	8	2	Don't Sweetheart Me...Lawrence Welk...Decca 4434
9	4	3	It's Love-Love-Love..The Four King Sisters...Bluebird 30-0822
10	—	1	Milkman, Keep Those Bottles Quiet...Ella Mae Morse...Capitol 151

TW	LW	WK	Billboard®	🏵	MAY 20, 1944	🏵	Best Sellers
1	1	5	I Love You				Bing Crosby...Decca 18595
2	5	6	San Fernando Valley				Bing Crosby...Decca 18586
3	2	5	I'll Get By (As Long As I Have You)				Harry James...Columbia 36698
4	3	3	Long Ago (And Far Away)				Helen Forrest & Dick Haymes...Decca 23317
5	6	6	It's Love-Love-Love				Guy Lombardo...Decca 18589
6	7	2	Long Ago (And Far Away)				Jo Stafford...Capitol 153
7	—	5	When They Ask About You				Jimmy Dorsey...Decca 18582
8	9	4	It's Love-Love-Love				The Four King Sisters...Bluebird 30-0822
9	4	14	Holiday For Strings				David Rose...Victor 27853
10	—	1	Long Ago (And Far Away)				Perry Como...Victor 20-1569

TW	LW	WK	Billboard®	🏵	MAY 27, 1944	🏵	Best Sellers
1	1	6	I Love You				Bing Crosby...Decca 18595
2	3	6	I'll Get By (As Long As I Have You)				Harry James...Columbia 36698
3	2	7	San Fernando Valley				Bing Crosby...Decca 18586
4	9	15	Holiday For Strings				David Rose...Victor 27853
5	4	4	Long Ago (And Far Away)				Helen Forrest & Dick Haymes...Decca 23317
6	6	3	Long Ago (And Far Away)				Jo Stafford...Capitol 153
7	—	1	I'll Get By (As Long As I Have You)				Ink Spots...Decca 18579
8	—	1	I'll Be Seeing You				Bing Crosby...Decca 18595
9	5	7	It's Love-Love-Love				Guy Lombardo...Decca 18589
10	—	3	I Love You				Jo Stafford...Capitol 153

TW	LW	WK	Billboard®	🏵	JUNE 3, 1944	🏵	Best Sellers
1	1	7	I Love You				Bing Crosby...Decca 18595
2	2	7	I'll Get By (As Long As I Have You)				Harry James...Columbia 36698
3	8	2	I'll Be Seeing You				Bing Crosby...Decca 18595
4	5	5	Long Ago (And Far Away)				Helen Forrest & Dick Haymes...Decca 23317
5	3	8	San Fernando Valley				Bing Crosby...Decca 18586
6	4	16	Holiday For Strings				David Rose...Victor 27853
7	6	4	Long Ago (And Far Away)				Jo Stafford...Capitol 153
8	9	8	It's Love-Love-Love				Guy Lombardo...Decca 18589
9	—	1	I'll Be Seeing You				Tommy Dorsey...Victor 20-1574
10	—	1	Amor				Andy Russell...Capitol 156

TW	LW	WK	Billboard®	🏵	JUNE 10, 1944	🏵	Best Sellers
1	2	8	I'll Get By (As Long As I Have You)				Harry James...Columbia 36698
2	4	6	Long Ago (And Far Away)				Helen Forrest & Dick Haymes...Decca 23317
3	3	3	I'll Be Seeing You				Bing Crosby...Decca 18595
4	1	8	I Love You				Bing Crosby...Decca 18595
5	6	17	Holiday For Strings				David Rose...Victor 27853
6	5	9	San Fernando Valley				Bing Crosby...Decca 18586
7	9	2	I'll Be Seeing You				Tommy Dorsey...Victor 20-1574
8	—	2	Long Ago (And Far Away)				Perry Como...Victor 20-1569
9	—	1	G.I. Jive				Louis Jordan...Decca 8659
10	8	9	It's Love-Love-Love				Guy Lombardo...Decca 18589

TW	LW	WK	Billboard®	🏵	JUNE 17, 1944	🏵	Best Sellers
1	1	9	I'll Get By (As Long As I Have You)				Harry James...Columbia 36698
2	4	9	I Love You				Bing Crosby...Decca 18595
3	3	4	I'll Be Seeing You				Bing Crosby...Decca 18595
4	6	10	San Fernando Valley				Bing Crosby...Decca 18586
5	2	7	Long Ago (And Far Away)				Helen Forrest & Dick Haymes...Decca 23317
6	9	2	G.I. Jive				Louis Jordan...Decca 8659
7	—	5	Long Ago (And Far Away)				Jo Stafford...Capitol 153
8	—	2	Amor				Andy Russell...Capitol 156
9	5	18	Holiday For Strings				David Rose...Victor 27853
10	—	2	Milkman, Keep Those Bottles Quiet				Ella Mae Morse...Capitol 151

TW	LW	WK	Billboard®	JUNE 24, 1944	Best Sellers
1	1	10	I'll Get By (As Long As I Have You)		Harry James...Columbia 36698
2	3	5	I'll Be Seeing You		Bing Crosby...Decca 18595
3	11	2	Swinging On A Star		Bing Crosby...Decca 18597
4	2	10	I Love You		Bing Crosby...Decca 18595
5	8	3	Amor		Andy Russell...Capitol 156
6	5	8	Long Ago (And Far Away)		Helen Forrest & Dick Haymes...Decca 23317
7	7	6	Long Ago (And Far Away)		Jo Stafford...Capitol 153
8	4	11	San Fernando Valley		Bing Crosby...Decca 18586
9	6	3	G.I. Jive		Louis Jordan...Decca 8659
10	—	3	I'll Be Seeing You		Tommy Dorsey...Victor 20-1574

TW	LW	WK	Billboard®	JULY 1, 1944	Best Sellers
1	2	6	I'll Be Seeing You		Bing Crosby...Decca 18595
2	1	11	I'll Get By (As Long As I Have You)		Harry James...Columbia 36698
3	3	3	Swinging On A Star		Bing Crosby...Decca 18597
4	4	11	I Love You		Bing Crosby...Decca 18595
5	6	9	Long Ago (And Far Away)		Helen Forrest & Dick Haymes...Decca 23317
6	7	7	Long Ago (And Far Away)		Jo Stafford...Capitol 153
7	5	4	Amor		Andy Russell...Capitol 156
8	9	4	G.I. Jive		Louis Jordan...Decca 8659
9	—	2	Straighten Up And Fly Right		The King Cole Trio...Capitol 154
10	—	19	Holiday For Strings		David Rose...Victor 27853

TW	LW	WK	Billboard®	JULY 8, 1944	Best Sellers
1	2	12	I'll Get By (As Long As I Have You)		Harry James...Columbia 36698
2	1	7	I'll Be Seeing You		Bing Crosby...Decca 18595
3	3	4	Swinging On A Star		Bing Crosby...Decca 18597
4	4	12	I Love You		Bing Crosby...Decca 18595
5	5	10	Long Ago (And Far Away)		Helen Forrest & Dick Haymes...Decca 23317
6	7	5	Amor		Andy Russell...Capitol 156
7	—	1	Amor		Bing Crosby...Decca 18608
8	8	5	G.I. Jive		Louis Jordan...Decca 8659
9	—	1	Long Ago (And Far Away)		Bing Crosby...Decca 18608
10	6	8	Long Ago (And Far Away)		Jo Stafford...Capitol 153

TW	LW	WK	Billboard®	JULY 15, 1944	Best Sellers
1	2	8	I'll Be Seeing You		Bing Crosby...Decca 18595
2	3	5	Swinging On A Star		Bing Crosby...Decca 18597
3	1	13	I'll Get By (As Long As I Have You)		Harry James...Columbia 36698
4	5	11	Long Ago (And Far Away)		Helen Forrest & Dick Haymes...Decca 23317
5	8	6	G.I. Jive		Louis Jordan...Decca 8659
6	—	2	Good Night, Wherever You Are		Russ Morgan...Decca 18598
7	7	2	Amor		Bing Crosby...Decca 18608
8	4	13	I Love You		Bing Crosby...Decca 18595
9	10	9	Long Ago (And Far Away)		Jo Stafford...Capitol 153
10	6	6	Amor		Andy Russell...Capitol 156

TW	LW	WK	Billboard®	JULY 22, 1944	Best Sellers
1	1	9	I'll Be Seeing You		Bing Crosby...Decca 18595
2	2	6	Swinging On A Star		Bing Crosby...Decca 18597
3	3	14	I'll Get By (As Long As I Have You)		Harry James...Columbia 36698
4	7	3	Amor		Bing Crosby...Decca 18608
5	—	2	Long Ago (And Far Away)		Bing Crosby...Decca 18608
6	8	14	I Love You		Bing Crosby...Decca 18595
7	10	7	Amor		Andy Russell...Capitol 156
8	—	2	You Always Hurt The One You Love		Mills Brothers...Decca 18599
9	9	10	Long Ago (And Far Away)		Jo Stafford...Capitol 153
10	5	7	G.I. Jive		Louis Jordan...Decca 8659

TW	LW	WK	Billboard ⊛ JULY 29, 1944 ⊛ Best Sellers
1	1	10	I'll Be Seeing You ....Bing Crosby...Decca 18595
2	2	7	Swinging On A Star ....Bing Crosby...Decca 18597
3	3	15	I'll Get By (As Long As I Have You)..Harry James...Columbia 36698
4	—	5	I'll Be Seeing You ....Tommy Dorsey...Victor 20-1574
5	10	8	G.I. Jive ....Louis Jordan...Decca 8659
6	4	4	Amor ....Bing Crosby...Decca 18608
7	—	1	His Rocking Horse Ran Away ....Betty Hutton...Capitol 155
8	—	3	Good Night, Wherever You Are ....Russ Morgan...Decca 18598
9	9	11	Long Ago (And Far Away) ....Jo Stafford...Capitol 153
10	7	8	Amor..Andy Russell...Capitol 156

TW	LW	WK	Billboard ⊛ AUGUST 5, 1944 ⊛ Best Sellers
1	2	8	Swinging On A Star ....Bing Crosby...Decca 18597
2	1	11	I'll Be Seeing You ....Bing Crosby...Decca 18595
3	3	16	I'll Get By (As Long As I Have You)..Harry James...Columbia 36698
4	6	5	Amor ....Bing Crosby...Decca 18608
5	5	9	G.I. Jive ....Louis Jordan...Decca 8659
6	4	6	I'll Be Seeing You ....Tommy Dorsey...Victor 20-1574
7	—	1	Time Waits For No One ....Helen Forrest...Decca 18600
8	—	3	Long Ago (And Far Away)..Bing Crosby...Decca 18608
9	—	1	I'll Walk Alone ....Martha Tilton...Capitol 157
10	9	12	Long Ago (And Far Away) ....Jo Stafford...Capitol 153

TW	LW	WK	Billboard ⊛ AUGUST 12, 1944 ⊛ Best Sellers
1	1	9	Swinging On A Star ....Bing Crosby...Decca 18597
2	2	12	I'll Be Seeing You ....Bing Crosby...Decca 18595
3	5	10	G.I. Jive ....Louis Jordan...Decca 8659
4	3	17	I'll Get By (As Long As I Have You)..Harry James...Columbia 36698
5	4	6	Amor ....Bing Crosby...Decca 18608
6	8	4	Long Ago (And Far Away)...Bing Crosby...Decca 18608
7	—	1	I'll Walk Alone ....Dinah Shore...Victor 20-1586
8	6	7	I'll Be Seeing You ....Tommy Dorsey...Victor 20-1574
9	—	2	His Rocking Horse Ran Away ....Betty Hutton...Capitol 155
10	7	2	Time Waits For No One ....Helen Forrest...Decca 18600

TW	LW	WK	Billboard ⊛ AUGUST 19, 1944 ⊛ Best Sellers
1	1	10	Swinging On A Star ....Bing Crosby...Decca 18597
2	2	13	I'll Be Seeing You ....Bing Crosby...Decca 18595
3	4	18	I'll Get By (As Long As I Have You)..Harry James...Columbia 36698
4	10	3	Time Waits For No One ....Helen Forrest...Decca 18600
5	7	2	I'll Walk Alone ....Dinah Shore...Victor 20-1586
6	5	7	Amor ....Bing Crosby...Decca 18608
7	—	2	I'll Walk Alone ....Martha Tilton...Capitol 157
8	8	8	I'll Be Seeing You ....Tommy Dorsey...Victor 20-1574
9	3	11	G.I. Jive ....Louis Jordan...Decca 8659
10	—	3	You Always Hurt The One You Love ....Mills Brothers...Decca 18599

TW	LW	WK	Billboard ⊛ AUGUST 26, 1944 ⊛ Best Sellers
1	1	11	Swinging On A Star ....Bing Crosby...Decca 18597
2	2	14	I'll Be Seeing You ....Bing Crosby...Decca 18595
3	4	4	Time Waits For No One ....Helen Forrest...Decca 18600
4	10	4	You Always Hurt The One You Love ....Mills Brothers...Decca 18599
5	8	9	I'll Be Seeing You ....Tommy Dorsey...Victor 20-1574
6	9	12	G.I. Jive ....Louis Jordan...Decca 8659
7	3	19	I'll Get By (As Long As I Have You)..Harry James...Columbia 36698
8	5	3	I'll Walk Alone ....Dinah Shore...Victor 20-1586
9	—	3	His Rocking Horse Ran Away ....Betty Hutton...Capitol 155
10	7	3	I'll Walk Alone ....Martha Tilton...Capitol 157

TW	LW	WK	Billboard ✹ SEPTEMBER 2, 1944 ✹ Best Sellers
1	1	12	Swinging On A Star ....Bing Crosby...Decca 18597
2	2	15	I'll Be Seeing You ....Bing Crosby...Decca 18595
3	4	5	You Always Hurt The One You Love ....Mills Brothers...Decca 18599
4	8	4	I'll Walk Alone ....Dinah Shore...Victor 20-1586
5	3	5	Time Waits For No One ....Helen Forrest...Decca 18600
6	6	13	G.I. Jive ....Louis Jordan...Decca 8659
7	—	1	Is You Is Or Is You Ain't (Ma' Baby) ....Louis Jordan...Decca 8659
8	7	20	I'll Get By (As Long As I Have You) ....Harry James...Columbia 36698
9	5	10	I'll Be Seeing You ....Tommy Dorsey...Victor 20-1574
10	9	4	His Rocking Horse Ran Away ....Betty Hutton...Capitol 155

TW	LW	WK	Billboard ✹ SEPTEMBER 9, 1944 ✹ Best Sellers
1	1	13	Swinging On A Star ....Bing Crosby...Decca 18597
2	5	6	Time Waits For No One ....Helen Forrest...Decca 18600
3	4	5	I'll Walk Alone ....Dinah Shore...Victor 20-1586
4	3	6	You Always Hurt The One You Love ....Mills Brothers...Decca 18599
5	2	16	I'll Be Seeing You ....Bing Crosby...Decca 18595
6	6	14	G.I. Jive ....Louis Jordan...Decca 8659
7	—	4	I'll Walk Alone ....Martha Tilton...Capitol 157
8	9	11	I'll Be Seeing You ....Tommy Dorsey...Victor 20-1574
9	8	21	I'll Get By (As Long As I Have You) ....Harry James...Columbia 36698
10	10	5	His Rocking Horse Ran Away ....Betty Hutton...Capitol 155

TW	LW	WK	Billboard ✹ SEPTEMBER 16, 1944 ✹ Best Sellers
1	1	14	Swinging On A Star ....Bing Crosby...Decca 18597
2	3	6	I'll Walk Alone ....Dinah Shore...Victor 20-1586
3	4	7	You Always Hurt The One You Love ....Mills Brothers...Decca 18599
4	5	17	I'll Be Seeing You ....Bing Crosby...Decca 18595
5	2	7	Time Waits For No One ....Helen Forrest...Decca 18600
6	—	1	Is You Is Or Is You Ain't (Ma' Baby) ....Bing Crosby & Andrews Sisters...Decca 23350
7	7	5	I'll Walk Alone ....Martha Tilton...Capitol 157
8	10	6	His Rocking Horse Ran Away ....Betty Hutton...Capitol 155
9	—	1	It Had To Be You ....Dick Haymes & Helen Forrest...Decca 23349
10	—	1	And Her Tears Flowed Like Wine ....Stan Kenton...Capitol 166

TW	LW	WK	Billboard ✹ SEPTEMBER 23, 1944 ✹ Best Sellers
1	1	15	Swinging On A Star ....Bing Crosby...Decca 18597
2	3	8	You Always Hurt The One You Love ....Mills Brothers...Decca 18599
3	2	7	I'll Walk Alone ....Dinah Shore...Victor 20-1586
4	6	2	Is You Is Or Is You Ain't (Ma' Baby) ....Bing Crosby & Andrews Sisters...Decca 23350
5	5	8	Time Waits For No One ....Helen Forrest...Decca 18600
6	7	6	I'll Walk Alone ....Martha Tilton...Capitol 157
7	4	18	I'll Be Seeing You ....Bing Crosby...Decca 18595
8	8	7	His Rocking Horse Ran Away ....Betty Hutton...Capitol 155
9	9	2	It Had To Be You ....Dick Haymes & Helen Forrest...Decca 23349
10	—	1	It Had To Be You ....Betty Hutton...Capitol 155

TW	LW	WK	Billboard ✹ SEPTEMBER 30, 1944 ✹ Best Sellers
1	1	16	Swinging On A Star ....Bing Crosby...Decca 18597
2	3	8	I'll Walk Alone ....Dinah Shore...Victor 20-1586
3	2	9	You Always Hurt The One You Love ....Mills Brothers...Decca 18599
4	9	3	It Had To Be You ....Dick Haymes & Helen Forrest...Decca 23349
5	10	2	It Had To Be You ....Betty Hutton...Capitol 155
6	6	7	I'll Walk Alone ....Martha Tilton...Capitol 157
7	4	3	Is You Is Or Is You Ain't (Ma' Baby) ....Bing Crosby & Andrews Sisters...Decca 23350
8	—	1	Till Then ....Mills Brothers...Decca 18599
9	—	2	Is You Is Or Is You Ain't (Ma' Baby) ....Louis Jordan...Decca 8659
10	—	1	It Could Happen To You ....Jo Stafford...Capitol 158

TW	LW	WK	Billboard® ❀ OCTOBER 7, 1944 ❀ Best Sellers
1	3	10	You Always Hurt The One You Love ....*Mills Brothers*...Decca 18599
2	1	17	Swinging On A Star ....*Bing Crosby*...Decca 18597
3	2	9	I'll Walk Alone ....*Dinah Shore*...Victor 20-1586
4	7	4	Is You Is Or Is You Ain't (Ma' Baby) ....*Bing Crosby & Andrews Sisters*...Decca 23350
5	4	4	It Had To Be You...*Dick Haymes & Helen Forrest*...Decca 23349
6	—	1	I'll Walk Alone ....*Mary Martin*...Decca 23340
7	—	9	Time Waits For No One ....*Helen Forrest*...Decca 18600
8	6	8	I'll Walk Alone ....*Martha Tilton*...Capitol 157
9	—	2	And Her Tears Flowed Like Wine ....*Stan Kenton*...Capitol 166
10	—	19	I'll Be Seeing You ....*Bing Crosby*...Decca 18595

TW	LW	WK	Billboard® ❀ OCTOBER 14, 1944 ❀ Best Sellers
1	3	10	I'll Walk Alone ....*Dinah Shore*...Victor 20-1586
2	2	18	Swinging On A Star ....*Bing Crosby*...Decca 18597
3	1	11	You Always Hurt The One You Love ....*Mills Brothers*...Decca 18599
4	4	5	Is You Is Or Is You Ain't (Ma' Baby) ....*Bing Crosby & Andrews Sisters*...Decca 23350
5	—	3	Is You Is Or Is You Ain't (Ma' Baby) ....*Louis Jordan*...Decca 8659
6	7	10	Time Waits For No One ....*Helen Forrest*...Decca 18600
7	6	2	I'll Walk Alone ....*Mary Martin*...Decca 23340
8	—	2	Till Then ....*Mills Brothers*...Decca 18599
9	—	1	Together ....*Helen Forrest & Dick Haymes*...Decca 23349
10	—	1	Dance With A Dolly (With A Hole In Her Stocking) ....*Evelyn Knight*...Decca 18614

TW	LW	WK	Billboard® ❀ OCTOBER 21, 1944 ❀ Best Sellers
1	3	12	You Always Hurt The One You Love ....*Mills Brothers*...Decca 18599
2	4	6	Is You Is Or Is You Ain't (Ma' Baby) ....*Bing Crosby & Andrews Sisters*...Decca 23350
3	1	11	I'll Walk Alone ....*Dinah Shore*...Victor 20-1586
4	2	19	Swinging On A Star ....*Bing Crosby*...Decca 18597
5	—	9	I'll Walk Alone ....*Martha Tilton*...Capitol 157
6	7	3	I'll Walk Alone ....*Mary Martin*...Decca 23340
7	9	2	Together ....*Helen Forrest & Dick Haymes*...Decca 23349
8	—	3	And Her Tears Flowed Like Wine ....*Stan Kenton*...Capitol 166
9	—	5	It Had To Be You...*Dick Haymes & Helen Forrest*...Decca 23349
10	—	1	The Trolley Song...*The Pied Pipers*...Capitol 168

TW	LW	WK	Billboard® ❀ OCTOBER 28, 1944 ❀ Best Sellers
1	1	13	You Always Hurt The One You Love ....*Mills Brothers*...Decca 18599
2	3	12	I'll Walk Alone ....*Dinah Shore*...Victor 20-1586
3	4	20	Swinging On A Star ....*Bing Crosby*...Decca 18597
4	—	1	Too-Ra-Loo-Ra-Loo-Ral (That's An Irish Lullaby) ....*Bing Crosby*...Decca 18621
5	2	7	Is You Is Or Is You Ain't (Ma' Baby) ....*Bing Crosby & Andrews Sisters*...Decca 23350
6	7	3	Together ....*Helen Forrest & Dick Haymes*...Decca 23349
7	6	4	I'll Walk Alone ....*Mary Martin*...Decca 23340
8	—	3	Till Then ....*Mills Brothers*...Decca 18599
9	5	10	I'll Walk Alone ....*Martha Tilton*...Capitol 157
10	10	2	The Trolley Song...*The Pied Pipers*...Capitol 168

TW	LW	WK	Billboard® ❀ NOVEMBER 4, 1944 ❀ Best Sellers
1	2	13	I'll Walk Alone ....*Dinah Shore*...Victor 20-1586
2	1	14	You Always Hurt The One You Love ....*Mills Brothers*...Decca 18599
3	6	4	Together ....*Helen Forrest & Dick Haymes*...Decca 23349
4	4	2	Too-Ra-Loo-Ra-Loo-Ral (That's An Irish Lullaby) ....*Bing Crosby*...Decca 18621
5	9	11	I'll Walk Alone ....*Martha Tilton*...Capitol 157
6	5	8	Is You Is Or Is You Ain't (Ma' Baby) ....*Bing Crosby & Andrews Sisters*...Decca 23350
7	7	5	I'll Walk Alone ....*Mary Martin*...Decca 23340
8	—	4	And Her Tears Flowed Like Wine ....*Stan Kenton*...Capitol 166
9	—	1	How Many Hearts Have You Broken ....*Stan Kenton*...Capitol 166
10	—	1	It Had To Be You...*Artie Shaw*...Victor 20-1593

Billboard — NOVEMBER 11, 1944 — Best Sellers

TW	LW	WK	Title	Artist
1	1	14	I'll Walk Alone	Dinah Shore...Victor 20-1586
2	2	15	You Always Hurt The One You Love	Mills Brothers...Decca 18599
3	—	3	The Trolley Song	The Pied Pipers...Capitol 168
4	6	9	Is You Is Or Is You Ain't (Ma' Baby)	Bing Crosby & Andrews Sisters...Decca 23350
5	3	5	Together	Helen Forrest & Dick Haymes...Decca 23349
6	8	5	And Her Tears Flowed Like Wine	Stan Kenton...Capitol 166
7	7	6	I'll Walk Alone	Mary Martin...Decca 23340
8	5	12	I'll Walk Alone	Martha Tilton...Capitol 157
9	4	3	Too-Ra-Loo-Ra-Loo-Ral (That's An Irish Lullaby)	Bing Crosby...Decca 18621
10	—	1	Dance With A Dolly (With A Hole In Her Stockin')	Russ Morgan...Decca 18625

Billboard — NOVEMBER 18, 1944 — Best Sellers

TW	LW	WK	Title	Artist
1	1	15	I'll Walk Alone	Dinah Shore...Victor 20-1586
2	2	16	You Always Hurt The One You Love	Mills Brothers...Decca 18599
3	5	6	Together	Helen Forrest & Dick Haymes...Decca 23349
4	3	4	The Trolley Song	The Pied Pipers...Capitol 168
5	9	4	Too-Ra-Loo-Ra-Loo-Ral (That's An Irish Lullaby)	Bing Crosby...Decca 18621
6	6	6	And Her Tears Flowed Like Wine	Stan Kenton...Capitol 166
7	8	13	I'll Walk Alone	Martha Tilton...Capitol 157
8	10	2	Dance With A Dolly (With A Hole In Her Stockin')	Russ Morgan...Decca 18625
9	4	10	Is You Is Or Is You Ain't (Ma' Baby)	Bing Crosby & Andrews Sisters...Decca 23350
10	7	7	I'll Walk Alone	Mary Martin...Decca 23340

Billboard — NOVEMBER 25, 1944 — Best Sellers

TW	LW	WK	Title	Artist
1	2	17	You Always Hurt The One You Love	Mills Brothers...Decca 18599
2	1	16	I'll Walk Alone	Dinah Shore...Victor 20-1586
3	4	5	The Trolley Song	The Pied Pipers...Capitol 168
4	—	1	I'm Making Believe	Ink Spots & Ella Fitzgerald...Decca 23356
5	3	7	Together	Helen Forrest & Dick Haymes...Decca 23349
6	8	3	Dance With A Dolly (With A Hole In Her Stockin')	Russ Morgan...Decca 18625
7	5	5	Too-Ra-Loo-Ra-Loo-Ral (That's An Irish Lullaby)	Bing Crosby...Decca 18621
8	7	14	I'll Walk Alone	Martha Tilton...Capitol 157
9	—	1	Don't Fence Me In	Bing Crosby & Andrews Sisters...Decca 23364
10	6	7	And Her Tears Flowed Like Wine	Stan Kenton...Capitol 166

Billboard — DECEMBER 2, 1944 — Best Sellers

TW	LW	WK	Title	Artist
1	1	18	You Always Hurt The One You Love	Mills Brothers...Decca 18599
2	3	6	The Trolley Song	The Pied Pipers...Capitol 168
3	2	17	I'll Walk Alone	Dinah Shore...Victor 20-1586
4	4	2	I'm Making Believe	Ink Spots & Ella Fitzgerald...Decca 23356
5	8	15	I'll Walk Alone	Martha Tilton...Capitol 157
6	6	4	Dance With A Dolly (With A Hole In Her Stockin')	Russ Morgan...Decca 18625
7	10	8	And Her Tears Flowed Like Wine	Stan Kenton...Capitol 166
8	7	6	Too-Ra-Loo-Ra-Loo-Ral (That's An Irish Lullaby)	Bing Crosby...Decca 18621
9	9	2	Don't Fence Me In	Bing Crosby & Andrews Sisters...Decca 23364
10	5	8	Together	Helen Forrest & Dick Haymes...Decca 23349

Billboard — DECEMBER 9, 1944 — Best Sellers

TW	LW	WK	Title	Artist
1	4	3	I'm Making Believe	Ink Spots & Ella Fitzgerald...Decca 23356
2	3	18	I'll Walk Alone	Dinah Shore...Victor 20-1586
3	6	5	Dance With A Dolly (With A Hole In Her Stockin')	Russ Morgan...Decca 18625
4	2	7	The Trolley Song	The Pied Pipers...Capitol 168
5	1	19	You Always Hurt The One You Love	Mills Brothers...Decca 18599
6	8	7	Too-Ra-Loo-Ra-Loo-Ral (That's An Irish Lullaby)	Bing Crosby...Decca 18621
7	9	3	Don't Fence Me In	Bing Crosby & Andrews Sisters...Decca 23364
8	7	9	And Her Tears Flowed Like Wine	Stan Kenton...Capitol 166
9	5	16	I'll Walk Alone	Martha Tilton...Capitol 157
10	—	1	The Trolley Song	Judy Garland...Decca 23361

TW	LW	WK	Billboard® DECEMBER 16, 1944 Best Sellers
1	1	4	I'm Making Believe ....*Ink Spots & Ella Fitzgerald*...Decca 23356
2	4	8	The Trolley Song...*The Pied Pipers*...Capitol 168
3	7	4	Don't Fence Me In ....*Bing Crosby & Andrews Sisters*...Decca 23364
4	3	6	Dance With A Dolly (With A Hole In Her Stockin') ....*Russ Morgan*...Decca 18625
5	—	1	Into Each Life Some Rain Must Fall ....*Ink Spots & Ella Fitzgerald*...Decca 23356
6	8	10	And Her Tears Flowed Like Wine ....*Stan Kenton*...Capitol 166
7	—	9	Together ....*Helen Forrest & Dick Haymes*...Decca 23349
8	5	20	You Always Hurt The One You Love ....*Mills Brothers*...Decca 18599
9	2	19	I'll Walk Alone ....*Dinah Shore*...Victor 20-1586
10	9	17	I'll Walk Alone ....*Martha Tilton*...Capitol 157

TW	LW	WK	Billboard® DECEMBER 23, 1944 Best Sellers
1	3	5	Don't Fence Me In ....*Bing Crosby & Andrews Sisters*...Decca 23364
2	1	5	I'm Making Believe ....*Ink Spots & Ella Fitzgerald*...Decca 23356
3	2	9	The Trolley Song...*The Pied Pipers*...Capitol 168
4	6	11	And Her Tears Flowed Like Wine ....*Stan Kenton*...Capitol 166
5	9	20	I'll Walk Alone ....*Dinah Shore*...Victor 20-1586
6	5	2	Into Each Life Some Rain Must Fall ....*Ink Spots & Ella Fitzgerald*...Decca 23356
7	4	7	Dance With A Dolly (With A Hole In Her Stockin') ....*Russ Morgan*...Decca 18625
8	—	1	The Trolley Song ....*Vaughn Monroe*...Victor 20-1605
9	10	18	I'll Walk Alone ....*Martha Tilton*...Capitol 157
10	—	8	Too-Ra-Loo-Ra-Loo-Ral (That's An Irish Lullaby) ....*Bing Crosby*...Decca 18621

TW	LW	WK	Billboard® DECEMBER 30, 1944 Best Sellers
1	1	6	Don't Fence Me In ....*Bing Crosby & Andrews Sisters*...Decca 23364
2	2	6	I'm Making Believe ....*Ink Spots & Ella Fitzgerald*...Decca 23356
3	3	10	The Trolley Song...*The Pied Pipers*...Capitol 168
4	—	2	The Trolley Song ....*Judy Garland*...Decca 23361
5	—	1	I Dream Of You ....*Andy Russell*...Capitol 175
6	—	1	White Christmas ....*Bing Crosby*...Decca 18429
7	—	1	White Christmas ....*Frank Sinatra*...Columbia 36756
8	10	9	Too-Ra-Loo-Ra-Loo-Ral (That's An Irish Lullaby) ....*Bing Crosby*...Decca 18621
9	9	19	I'll Walk Alone ....*Martha Tilton*...Capitol 157
10	4	12	And Her Tears Flowed Like Wine ....*Stan Kenton*...Capitol 166

TW	LW	WK	Billboard ✹ JANUARY 6, 1945 ✹ Best Sellers
1	1	7	Don't Fence Me In...Bing Crosby & Andrews Sisters...Decca 23364
2	2	7	I'm Making Believe...Ink Spots & Ella Fitzgerald...Decca 23356
3	3	11	The Trolley Song...The Pied Pipers...Capitol 168
4	—	2	The Trolley Song...Vaughn Monroe...Victor 20-1605
5	—	1	There Goes That Song Again...Russ Morgan...Decca 18625
6	—	1	I Dream Of You (More Than You Dream I Do)...Tommy Dorsey...Victor 20-1608
7	6	2	White Christmas...Bing Crosby...Decca 18429
8	4	3	The Trolley Song...Judy Garland...Decca 23361
9	7	2	White Christmas...Frank Sinatra...Columbia 36756
10	—	10	Together...Helen Forrest & Dick Haymes...Decca 23349

TW	LW	WK	Billboard ✹ JANUARY 13, 1945 ✹ Best Sellers
1	1	8	Don't Fence Me In...Bing Crosby & Andrews Sisters...Decca 23364
2	2	8	I'm Making Believe...Ink Spots & Ella Fitzgerald...Decca 23356
3	—	1	Ac-Cent-Tchu-Ate The Positive...Johnny Mercer...Capitol 180
4	4	3	The Trolley Song...Vaughn Monroe...Victor 20-1605
5	—	3	Into Each Life Some Rain Must Fall...Ink Spots & Ella Fitzgerald...Decca 23356
6	—	1	Rum And Coca-Cola...Andrews Sisters...Decca 18636
7	8	4	The Trolley Song...Judy Garland...Decca 23361
8	—	1	There Goes That Song Again...Sammy Kaye...Victor 20-1606
9	6	2	I Dream Of You (More Than You Dream I Do)...Tommy Dorsey...Victor 20-1608
10	3	12	The Trolley Song...The Pied Pipers...Capitol 168

TW	LW	WK	Billboard ✹ JANUARY 20, 1945 ✹ Best Sellers
1	1	9	Don't Fence Me In...Bing Crosby & Andrews Sisters...Decca 23364
2	3	2	Ac-Cent-Tchu-Ate The Positive...Johnny Mercer...Capitol 180
3	2	9	I'm Making Believe...Ink Spots & Ella Fitzgerald...Decca 23356
4	—	1	Don't Fence Me In...Sammy Kaye...Victor 20-1610
5	6	2	Rum And Coca-Cola...Andrews Sisters...Decca 18636
6	9	3	I Dream Of You (More Than You Dream I Do)...Tommy Dorsey...Victor 20-1608
7	—	1	There Goes That Song Again...Kay Kyser...Columbia 36757
8	—	1	Don't Fence Me In...Kate Smith...Columbia 36759
9	—	2	I Dream Of You...Andy Russell...Capitol 175
9	4	4	The Trolley Song...Vaughn Monroe...Victor 20-1605
10	—	2	There Goes That Song Again...Russ Morgan...Decca 18625

TW	LW	WK	Billboard ✹ JANUARY 27, 1945 ✹ Best Sellers
1	1	10	Don't Fence Me In...Bing Crosby & Andrews Sisters...Decca 23364
2	2	3	Ac-Cent-Tchu-Ate The Positive...Johnny Mercer...Capitol 180
3	5	3	Rum And Coca-Cola...Andrews Sisters...Decca 18636
4	4	2	Don't Fence Me In...Sammy Kaye...Victor 20-1610
4	3	10	I'm Making Believe...Ink Spots & Ella Fitzgerald...Decca 23356
4	6	4	I Dream Of You (More Than You Dream I Do)...Tommy Dorsey...Victor 20-1608
5	—	4	Into Each Life Some Rain Must Fall...Ink Spots & Ella Fitzgerald...Decca 23356
6	—	1	Cocktails For Two...Spike Jones...Victor 20-1628
7	—	1	I Dream Of You (More Than You Dream I Do)...Frank Sinatra...Columbia 36762
8	9	3	I Dream Of You...Andy Russell...Capitol 175
9	8	2	Don't Fence Me In...Kate Smith...Columbia 36759
9	7	2	There Goes That Song Again...Kay Kyser...Columbia 36757
10	10	3	There Goes That Song Again...Russ Morgan...Decca 18625
10	—	2	There Goes That Song Again...Sammy Kaye...Victor 20-1606
10	—	1	I Dream Of You (More Than You Dream I Do)...Perry Como...Victor 20-1629

TW	LW	WK	Billboard® ❀ FEBRUARY 3, 1945 ❀ Best Sellers
1	1	11	Don't Fence Me In ....Bing Crosby & Andrews Sisters...Decca 23364
2	3	4	Rum And Coca-Cola ....Andrews Sisters...Decca 18636
3	2	4	Ac-Cent-Tchu-Ate The Positive ....Johnny Mercer...Capitol 180
4	4	3	Don't Fence Me In ....Sammy Kaye...Victor 20-1610
5	4	5	I Dream Of You (More Than You Dream I Do)..Tommy Dorsey...Victor 20-1608
6	—	1	Ac-cent-tchu-ate The Positive ....Artie Shaw...Victor 20-1612
6	4	11	I'm Making Believe ....Ink Spots & Ella Fitzgerald...Decca 23356
7	6	2	Cocktails For Two ....Spike Jones...Victor 20-1628
8	5	5	Into Each Life Some Rain Must Fall ....Ink Spots & Ella Fitzgerald...Decca 23356
9	7	2	I Dream Of You (More Than You Dream I Do) ....Frank Sinatra...Columbia 36762
9	—	1	Ac-Cent-Tchu-Ate The Positive...Bing Crosby & Andrews Sisters...Decca 23379
10	—	1	Don't Fence Me In..Horace Heidt...Columbia 36761

TW	LW	WK	Billboard® ❀ FEBRUARY 10, 1945 ❀ Best Sellers
1	1	12	Don't Fence Me In ....Bing Crosby & Andrews Sisters...Decca 23364
1	2	5	Rum And Coca-Cola ....Andrews Sisters...Decca 18636
2	3	5	Ac-Cent-Tchu-Ate The Positive ....Johnny Mercer...Capitol 180
3	9	2	Ac-Cent-Tchu-Ate The Positive...Bing Crosby & Andrews Sisters...Decca 23379
4	7	3	Cocktails For Two ....Spike Jones...Victor 20-1628
5	6	2	Ac-cent-tchu-ate The Positive ....Artie Shaw...Victor 20-1612
5	6	12	I'm Making Believe ....Ink Spots & Ella Fitzgerald...Decca 23356
6	4	4	Don't Fence Me In ....Sammy Kaye...Victor 20-1610
7	9	3	I Dream Of You (More Than You Dream I Do) ....Frank Sinatra...Columbia 36762
7	—	1	I'm Beginning To See The Light ....Harry James...Columbia 36758
8	—	1	Saturday Night (Is The Loneliest Night In The Week) ....Frank Sinatra...Columbia 36777
9	—	1	A Little On The Lonely Side...Frankie Carle...Columbia 36760
10	10	2	Don't Fence Me In..Horace Heidt...Columbia 36761

TW	LW	WK	Billboard® ❀ FEBRUARY 17, 1945 ❀ Best Sellers
1	1	6	Rum And Coca-Cola ....Andrews Sisters...Decca 18636
2	1	13	Don't Fence Me In ....Bing Crosby & Andrews Sisters...Decca 23364
3	2	6	Ac-Cent-Tchu-Ate The Positive ....Johnny Mercer...Capitol 180
4	3	3	Ac-Cent-Tchu-Ate The Positive...Bing Crosby & Andrews Sisters...Decca 23379
5	6	5	Don't Fence Me In ....Sammy Kaye...Victor 20-1610
6	—	6	I Dream Of You (More Than You Dream I Do)..Tommy Dorsey...Victor 20-1608
6	—	1	Saturday Night (Is The Loneliest Night In The Week) ....Frank Sinatra...Columbia 36762
7	9	2	A Little On The Lonely Side...Frankie Carle...Columbia 36760
8	4	4	Cocktails For Two ....Spike Jones...Victor 20-1628
9	5	3	Ac-cent-tchu-ate The Positive ....Artie Shaw...Victor 20-1612
10	7	4	I Dream Of You (More Than You Dream I Do) ....Frank Sinatra...Columbia 36762

TW	LW	WK	Billboard® ❀ FEBRUARY 24, 1945 ❀ Best Sellers
1	1	7	Rum And Coca-Cola ....Andrews Sisters...Decca 18636
2	2	14	Don't Fence Me In ....Bing Crosby & Andrews Sisters...Decca 23364
3	3	7	Ac-Cent-Tchu-Ate The Positive ....Johnny Mercer...Capitol 180
4	4	4	Ac-Cent-Tchu-Ate The Positive...Bing Crosby & Andrews Sisters...Decca 23379
5	8	5	Cocktails For Two ....Spike Jones...Victor 20-1628
6	6	2	Saturday Night (Is The Loneliest Night In The Week) ....Frank Sinatra...Columbia 36762
7	6	7	I Dream Of You (More Than You Dream I Do)..Tommy Dorsey...Victor 20-1608
8	7	3	A Little On The Lonely Side...Frankie Carle...Columbia 36760
8	5	6	Don't Fence Me In ....Sammy Kaye...Victor 20-1610
9	9	4	Ac-cent-tchu-ate The Positive ....Artie Shaw...Victor 20-1612
10	—	2	I'm Beginning To See The Light ....Harry James...Columbia 36758

TW	LW	WK	Billboard®	❋	MARCH 3, 1945	❋	Best Sellers
1	1	8	Rum And Coca-Cola			*Andrews Sisters*...Decca 18636	
2	2	15	Don't Fence Me In			*Bing Crosby & Andrews Sisters*...Decca 23364	
3	3	8	Ac-Cent-Tchu-Ate The Positive			*Johnny Mercer*...Capitol 180	
4	4	5	Ac-Cent-Tchu-Ate The Positive			*Bing Crosby & Andrews Sisters*...Decca 23379	
5	5	6	Cocktails For Two			*Spike Jones*...Victor 20-1628	
6	8	4	A Little On The Lonely Side			*Frankie Carle*...Columbia 36760	
7	—	1	Rum And Coca-Cola			*Abe Lyman*...Columbia 36775	
8	—	1	Rum And Coca-Cola			*Vaughn Monroe*...Victor 20-1637	
9	—	1	Candy			*Johnny Mercer & Jo Stafford*...Capitol 183	
10	9	5	Ac-cent-tchu-ate The Positive			*Artie Shaw*...Victor 20-1612	
10	6	3	Saturday Night (Is The Loneliest Night In The Week)			*Frank Sinatra*...Columbia 36762	

TW	LW	WK	Billboard®	❋	MARCH 10, 1945	❋	Best Sellers
1	1	9	Rum And Coca-Cola			*Andrews Sisters*...Decca 18636	
2	4	6	Ac-Cent-Tchu-Ate The Positive			*Bing Crosby & Andrews Sisters*...Decca 23379	
2	2	16	Don't Fence Me In			*Bing Crosby & Andrews Sisters*...Decca 23364	
3	3	9	Ac-Cent-Tchu-Ate The Positive			*Johnny Mercer*...Capitol 180	
4	7	2	Rum And Coca-Cola			*Abe Lyman*...Columbia 36775	
5	5	7	Cocktails For Two			*Spike Jones*...Victor 20-1628	
6	9	2	Candy			*Johnny Mercer & Jo Stafford*...Capitol 183	
7	—	3	I'm Beginning To See The Light			*Harry James*...Columbia 36758	
8	6	5	A Little On The Lonely Side			*Frankie Carle*...Columbia 36760	
9	—	7	Don't Fence Me In			*Sammy Kaye*...Victor 20-1610	
10	—	1	I Wanna Get Married			*Gertrude Niesen*...Decca 23382	

TW	LW	WK	Billboard®	❋	MARCH 17, 1945	❋	Best Sellers
1	1	10	Rum And Coca-Cola			*Andrews Sisters*...Decca 18636	
2	3	10	Ac-Cent-Tchu-Ate The Positive			*Johnny Mercer*...Capitol 180	
3	2	17	Don't Fence Me In			*Bing Crosby & Andrews Sisters*...Decca 23364	
4	2	7	Ac-Cent-Tchu-Ate The Positive			*Bing Crosby & Andrews Sisters*...Decca 23379	
5	4	3	Rum And Coca-Cola			*Abe Lyman*...Columbia 36775	
6	6	3	Candy			*Johnny Mercer & Jo Stafford*...Capitol 183	
7	7	4	I'm Beginning To See The Light			*Harry James*...Columbia 36758	
8	5	8	Cocktails For Two			*Spike Jones*...Victor 20-1628	
9	—	1	I'm Beginning To See The Light			*Duke Ellington*...Victor 20-1618	
10	8	6	A Little On The Lonely Side			*Frankie Carle*...Columbia 36760	
10	—	8	I Dream Of You (More Than You Dream I Do)			*Tommy Dorsey*...Victor 20-1608	
10	—	1	Dream			*The Pied Pipers*...Capitol 185	

TW	LW	WK	Billboard®	❋	MARCH 24, 1945	❋	Best Sellers
1	1	11	Rum And Coca-Cola			*Andrews Sisters*...Decca 18636	
2	—	1	My Dreams Are Getting Better All The Time			*Les Brown*...Columbia 36779	
3	—	1	My Dreams Are Getting Better All The Time			*The Phil Moore Four*...Victor 20-1641	
4	6	4	Candy			*Johnny Mercer & Jo Stafford*...Capitol 183	
5	2	11	Ac-Cent-Tchu-Ate The Positive			*Johnny Mercer*...Capitol 180	
6	4	8	Ac-Cent-Tchu-Ate The Positive			*Bing Crosby & Andrews Sisters*...Decca 23379	
7	5	4	Rum And Coca-Cola			*Abe Lyman*...Columbia 36775	
8	3	18	Don't Fence Me In			*Bing Crosby & Andrews Sisters*...Decca 23364	
9	10	7	A Little On The Lonely Side			*Frankie Carle*...Columbia 36760	
10	7	5	I'm Beginning To See The Light			*Harry James*...Columbia 36758	

Billboard ✖ MARCH 31, 1945 ✖ Best Sellers

TW	LW	WK		
1	1	12	**Rum And Coca-Cola**	*Andrews Sisters*...Decca 18636
2	2	2	**My Dreams Are Getting Better All The Time**	*Les Brown*...Columbia 36779
3	4	5	**Candy**	*Johnny Mercer & Jo Stafford*...Capitol 183
4	3	2	**My Dreams Are Getting Better All The Time**	*The Phil Moore Four*...Victor 20-1641
5	10	6	**I'm Beginning To See The Light**	*Harry James*...Columbia 36758
6	9	8	**A Little On The Lonely Side**	*Frankie Carle*...Columbia 36760
7	5	12	**Ac-Cent-Tchu-Ate The Positive**	*Johnny Mercer*...Capitol 180
8	6	9	**Ac-Cent-Tchu-Ate The Positive**	*Bing Crosby & Andrews Sisters*...Decca 23379
9	—	2	**Dream**	*The Pied Pipers*...Capitol 185
10	—	2	**I'm Beginning To See The Light**	*Duke Ellington*...Victor 20-1618

Billboard ✖ APRIL 7, 1945 ✖ Best Sellers

TW	LW	WK		
1	2	3	**My Dreams Are Getting Better All The Time**	*Les Brown*...Columbia 36779
2	1	13	**Rum And Coca-Cola**	*Andrews Sisters*...Decca 18636
3	3	6	**Candy**	*Johnny Mercer & Jo Stafford*...Capitol 183
4	4	3	**My Dreams Are Getting Better All The Time**	*The Phil Moore Four*...Victor 20-1641
5	6	9	**A Little On The Lonely Side**	*Frankie Carle*...Columbia 36760
6	5	7	**I'm Beginning To See The Light**	*Harry James*...Columbia 36758
7	9	3	**Dream**	*The Pied Pipers*...Capitol 185
8	7	13	**Ac-Cent-Tchu-Ate The Positive**	*Johnny Mercer*...Capitol 180
8	10	3	**I'm Beginning To See The Light**	*Duke Ellington*...Victor 20-1618
9	—	1	**Sentimental Journey**	*Les Brown*...Columbia 36769
10	—	1	**A Little On The Lonely Side**	*Guy Lombardo*...Decca 18642

Billboard ✖ APRIL 14, 1945 ✖ Best Sellers

TW	LW	WK		
1	1	4	**My Dreams Are Getting Better All The Time**	*Les Brown*...Columbia 36779
2	2	14	**Rum And Coca-Cola**	*Andrews Sisters*...Decca 18636
3	3	7	**Candy**	*Johnny Mercer & Jo Stafford*...Capitol 183
4	6	8	**I'm Beginning To See The Light**	*Harry James*...Columbia 36758
5	5	10	**A Little On The Lonely Side**	*Frankie Carle*...Columbia 36760
5	7	4	**Dream**	*The Pied Pipers*...Capitol 185
5	4	4	**My Dreams Are Getting Better All The Time**	*The Phil Moore Four*...Victor 20-1641
6	8	4	**I'm Beginning To See The Light**	*Duke Ellington*...Victor 20-1618
6	9	2	**Sentimental Journey**	*Les Brown*...Columbia 36769
6	—	1	**There! I've Said It Again**	*Vaughn Monroe*...Victor 20-1637
7	—	1	**Just A Prayer Away**	*Bing Crosby*...Decca 23392
7	—	1	**My Dreams Are Getting Better All The Time**	*Johnny Long & Dick Robertson*...Decca 18661
7	—	1	**Stuff Like That There**	*Betty Hutton*...Capitol 188
8	10	2	**A Little On The Lonely Side**	*Guy Lombardo*...Decca 18642
9	—	1	**Laura**	*Woody Herman*...Columbia 36785
10	—	1	**Candy**	*Dinah Shore*...Victor 20-1632
10	—	1	**Just A Prayer Away**	*Sammy Kaye*...Victor 20-1642

Billboard ✖ APRIL 21, 1945 ✖ Best Sellers

TW	LW	WK		
1	1	5	**My Dreams Are Getting Better All The Time**	*Les Brown*...Columbia 36779
2	3	8	**Candy**	*Johnny Mercer & Jo Stafford*...Capitol 183
3	2	15	**Rum And Coca-Cola**	*Andrews Sisters*...Decca 18636
4	7	2	**My Dreams Are Getting Better All The Time**	*Johnny Long & Dick Robertson*...Decca 18661
5	4	9	**I'm Beginning To See The Light**	*Harry James*...Columbia 36758
6	5	5	**My Dreams Are Getting Better All The Time**	*The Phil Moore Four*...Victor 20-1641
7	7	2	**Just A Prayer Away**	*Bing Crosby*...Decca 23392
7	6	2	**There! I've Said It Again**	*Vaughn Monroe*...Victor 20-1637
8	5	5	**Dream**	*The Pied Pipers*...Capitol 185
9	6	5	**I'm Beginning To See The Light**	*Duke Ellington*...Victor 20-1618
10	5	11	**A Little On The Lonely Side**	*Frankie Carle*...Columbia 36760

TW	LW	WK	Billboard® ✿ APRIL 28, 1945 ✿ Best Sellers
1	1	6	My Dreams Are Getting Better All The Time.................................Les Brown...Columbia 36779
2	2	9	Candy ....Johnny Mercer & Jo Stafford...Capitol 183
3	4	3	My Dreams Are Getting Better All The Time...Johnny Long & Dick Robertson...Decca 18661
4	7	3	Just A Prayer Away ....Bing Crosby...Decca 23392
5	5	10	I'm Beginning To See The Light ....Harry James...Columbia 36758
6	3	16	Rum And Coca-Cola ....Andrews Sisters...Decca 18636
7	7	3	There! I've Said It Again ....Vaughn Monroe...Victor 20-1637
8	8	6	Dream ....The Pied Pipers...Capitol 185
8	—	3	Sentimental Journey ....Les Brown...Columbia 36769
9	9	6	I'm Beginning To See The Light.....................................Duke Ellington...Victor 20-1618
10	6	6	My Dreams Are Getting Better All The Time ....The Phil Moore Four...Victor 20-1641

TW	LW	WK	Billboard® ✿ MAY 5, 1945 ✿ Best Sellers
1	1	7	My Dreams Are Getting Better All The Time.................................Les Brown...Columbia 36779
2	7	4	There! I've Said It Again ....Vaughn Monroe...Victor 20-1637
3	2	10	Candy ....Johnny Mercer & Jo Stafford...Capitol 183
4	8	4	Sentimental Journey ....Les Brown...Columbia 36769
5	—	1	Chloe ....Spike Jones...Victor 20-1654
6	3	4	My Dreams Are Getting Better All The Time ....Johnny Long & Dick Robertson...Decca 18661
7	—	1	I'm Beginning To See The Light.....................Ella Fitzgerald & Ink Spots...Decca 23399
7	4	4	Just A Prayer Away ....Bing Crosby...Decca 23392
8	5	11	I'm Beginning To See The Light ....Harry James...Columbia 36758
8	—	1	Caldonia ....Woody Herman...Columbia 36789
9	—	2	Laura..Woody Herman...Columbia 36785
10	8	7	Dream ....The Pied Pipers...Capitol 185
10	—	1	Laura..Freddy Martin...Victor 20-1655
10	10	7	My Dreams Are Getting Better All The Time ....The Phil Moore Four...Victor 20-1641

TW	LW	WK	Billboard® ✿ MAY 12, 1945 ✿ Best Sellers
1	1	8	My Dreams Are Getting Better All The Time.................................Les Brown...Columbia 36779
2	3	11	Candy ....Johnny Mercer & Jo Stafford...Capitol 183
3	2	5	There! I've Said It Again ....Vaughn Monroe...Victor 20-1637
4	4	5	Sentimental Journey ....Les Brown...Columbia 36769
5	5	2	Chloe ....Spike Jones...Victor 20-1654
6	10	8	Dream ....The Pied Pipers...Capitol 185
7	8	2	Caldonia ....Woody Herman...Columbia 36789
8	8	12	I'm Beginning To See The Light ....Harry James...Columbia 36758
8	7	2	I'm Beginning To See The Light.....................Ella Fitzgerald & Ink Spots...Decca 23399
8	9	3	Laura..Woody Herman...Columbia 36785
9	7	5	Just A Prayer Away ....Bing Crosby...Decca 23392
9	10	2	Laura..Freddy Martin...Victor 20-1655
10	6	5	My Dreams Are Getting Better All The Time ....Johnny Long & Dick Robertson...Decca 18661

TW	LW	WK	Billboard® ✿ MAY 19, 1945 ✿ Best Sellers
1	1	9	My Dreams Are Getting Better All The Time.................................Les Brown...Columbia 36779
2	4	6	Sentimental Journey ....Les Brown...Columbia 36769
3	2	12	Candy ....Johnny Mercer & Jo Stafford...Capitol 183
4	3	6	There! I've Said It Again ....Vaughn Monroe...Victor 20-1637
5	10	6	My Dreams Are Getting Better All The Time ....Johnny Long & Dick Robertson...Decca 18661
6	7	3	Caldonia ....Woody Herman...Columbia 36789
7	9	3	Laura..Freddy Martin...Victor 20-1655
8	8	13	I'm Beginning To See The Light ....Harry James...Columbia 36758
9	5	3	Chloe ....Spike Jones...Victor 20-1654
10	—	1	Bell Bottom Trousers ....Tony Pastor...Victor 20-1661
10	6	9	Dream ....The Pied Pipers...Capitol 185

TW	LW	WK	Billboard®	MAY 26, 1945	Best Sellers
1	2	7	Sentimental Journey		*Les Brown*...Columbia 36769
2	10	2	Bell Bottom Trousers		*Tony Pastor*...Victor 20-1661
3	1	10	My Dreams Are Getting Better All The Time		*Les Brown*...Columbia 36779
4	4	7	There! I've Said It Again		*Vaughn Monroe*...Victor 20-1637
5	3	13	Candy		*Johnny Mercer & Jo Stafford*...Capitol 183
6	10	10	Dream		*The Pied Pipers*...Capitol 185
7	—	4	Laura		*Woody Herman*...Columbia 36785
8	9	4	Chloe		*Spike Jones*...Victor 20-1654
8	7	4	Laura		*Freddy Martin*...Victor 20-1655
9	6	4	Caldonia		*Woody Herman*...Columbia 36789
10	—	1	Laura		*Dick Haymes*...Decca 18666
10	—	1	You Belong To My Heart		*Charlie Spivak*...Victor 20-1663

TW	LW	WK	Billboard®	JUNE 2, 1945	Best Sellers
1	1	8	Sentimental Journey		*Les Brown*...Columbia 36769
2	4	8	There! I've Said It Again		*Vaughn Monroe*...Victor 20-1637
3	2	3	Bell Bottom Trousers		*Tony Pastor*...Victor 20-1661
4	5	14	Candy		*Johnny Mercer & Jo Stafford*...Capitol 183
5	6	11	Dream		*The Pied Pipers*...Capitol 185
6	—	1	Caldonia		*Louis Jordan*...Decca 8670
7	—	1	Dream		*Frank Sinatra*...Columbia 36797
8	3	11	My Dreams Are Getting Better All The Time		*Les Brown*...Columbia 36779
8	—	1	You Belong To My Heart		*Bing Crosby & Xavier Cugat*...Decca 23413
9	—	1	Laura		*Johnnie Johnston*...Capitol 196
10	9	5	Caldonia		*Woody Herman*...Columbia 36789

TW	LW	WK	Billboard®	JUNE 9, 1945	Best Sellers
1	1	9	Sentimental Journey		*Les Brown*...Columbia 36769
2	2	9	There! I've Said It Again		*Vaughn Monroe*...Victor 20-1637
3	3	4	Bell Bottom Trousers		*Tony Pastor*...Victor 20-1661
4	8	2	You Belong To My Heart		*Bing Crosby & Xavier Cugat*...Decca 23413
5	5	12	Dream		*The Pied Pipers*...Capitol 185
6	9	2	Laura		*Johnnie Johnston*...Capitol 196
7	4	15	Candy		*Johnny Mercer & Jo Stafford*...Capitol 183
8	10	6	Caldonia		*Woody Herman*...Columbia 36789
9	6	2	Caldonia		*Louis Jordan*...Decca 8670
9	8	12	My Dreams Are Getting Better All The Time		*Les Brown*...Columbia 36779
10	—	1	Sentimental Journey		*Hal McIntyre*...Victor 20-1643

TW	LW	WK	Billboard®	JUNE 16, 1945	Best Sellers
1	1	10	Sentimental Journey		*Les Brown*...Columbia 36769
2	2	10	There! I've Said It Again		*Vaughn Monroe*...Victor 20-1637
3	3	5	Bell Bottom Trousers		*Tony Pastor*...Victor 20-1661
4	4	3	You Belong To My Heart		*Bing Crosby & Xavier Cugat*...Decca 23413
5	6	3	Laura		*Johnnie Johnston*...Capitol 196
6	5	13	Dream		*The Pied Pipers*...Capitol 185
7	—	1	Bell Bottom Trousers		*Kay Kyser*...Columbia 36801
8	9	3	Caldonia		*Louis Jordan*...Decca 8670
9	—	2	Dream		*Frank Sinatra*...Columbia 36797
9	10	2	Sentimental Journey		*Hal McIntyre*...Victor 20-1643
10	—	1	Bell Bottom Trousers		*Louis Prima*...Majestic 7134

TW	LW	WK	Billboard® JUNE 23, 1945 Best Sellers
1	1	11	**Sentimental Journey** ....*Les Brown*...Columbia 36769
2	2	11	**There! I've Said It Again** ....*Vaughn Monroe*...Victor 20-1637
3	3	6	**Bell Bottom Trousers** ....*Tony Pastor*...Victor 20-1661
4	4	4	**You Belong To My Heart**.....................................*Bing Crosby & Xavier Cugat*...Decca 23413
5	7	2	**Bell Bottom Trousers**..*Kay Kyser*...Columbia 36801
6	—	1	**Bell Bottom Trousers** ....*Guy Lombardo*...Decca 18683
6	8	4	**Caldonia**...*Louis Jordan*...Decca 8670
7	6	14	**Dream** ....*The Pied Pipers*...Capitol 185
8	5	4	**Laura** ....*Johnnie Johnston*...Capitol 196
9	—	2	**Laura**..*Dick Haymes*...Decca 18666
10	9	3	**Sentimental Journey** ....*Hal McIntyre*...Victor 20-1643

TW	LW	WK	Billboard® JUNE 30, 1945 Best Sellers
1	1	12	**Sentimental Journey** ....*Les Brown*...Columbia 36769
2	2	12	**There! I've Said It Again** ....*Vaughn Monroe*...Victor 20-1637
3	3	7	**Bell Bottom Trousers** ....*Tony Pastor*...Victor 20-1661
3	10	4	**Sentimental Journey** ....*Hal McIntyre*...Victor 20-1643
4	4	5	**You Belong To My Heart**.....................................*Bing Crosby & Xavier Cugat*...Decca 23413
5	5	3	**Bell Bottom Trousers**..*Kay Kyser*...Columbia 36801
6	6	2	**Bell Bottom Trousers** ....*Guy Lombardo*...Decca 18683
7	7	15	**Dream** ....*The Pied Pipers*...Capitol 185
8	—	1	**Sentimental Journey** ....*The Merry Macs*...Decca 18684
9	8	5	**Laura** ....*Johnnie Johnston*...Capitol 196
10	—	1	**Chopin's Polonaise** ....*Carmen Cavallaro*...Decca 18677

TW	LW	WK	Billboard® JULY 7, 1945 Best Sellers
1	1	13	**Sentimental Journey** ....*Les Brown*...Columbia 36769
2	3	8	**Bell Bottom Trousers** ....*Tony Pastor*...Victor 20-1661
3	2	13	**There! I've Said It Again** ....*Vaughn Monroe*...Victor 20-1637
4	3	5	**Sentimental Journey** ....*Hal McIntyre*...Victor 20-1643
5	4	6	**You Belong To My Heart**.....................................*Bing Crosby & Xavier Cugat*...Decca 23413
6	6	3	**Bell Bottom Trousers** ....*Guy Lombardo*...Decca 18683
7	8	2	**Sentimental Journey** ....*The Merry Macs*...Decca 18684
8	5	4	**Bell Bottom Trousers**..*Kay Kyser*...Columbia 36801
9	—	5	**Caldonia**...*Louis Jordan*...Decca 8670
10	—	1	**Gotta Be This Or That (Part 1)**...*Benny Goodman*...Columbia 36813

TW	LW	WK	Billboard® JULY 14, 1945 Best Sellers
1	1	14	**Sentimental Journey** ....*Les Brown*...Columbia 36769
2	3	14	**There! I've Said It Again** ....*Vaughn Monroe*...Victor 20-1637
3	2	9	**Bell Bottom Trousers** ....*Tony Pastor*...Victor 20-1661
4	—	1	**On The Atchison, Topeka And Santa Fe**....................................*Johnny Mercer*...Capitol 195
4	4	6	**Sentimental Journey** ....*Hal McIntyre*...Victor 20-1643
5	8	5	**Bell Bottom Trousers**..*Kay Kyser*...Columbia 36801
6	10	2	**Gotta Be This Or That (Part 1)**...*Benny Goodman*...Columbia 36813
6	—	2	**Chopin's Polonaise** ....*Carmen Cavallaro*...Decca 18677
7	6	4	**Bell Bottom Trousers** ....*Guy Lombardo*...Decca 18683
8	5	7	**You Belong To My Heart**.....................................*Bing Crosby & Xavier Cugat*...Decca 23413
9	9	6	**Caldonia**...*Louis Jordan*...Decca 8670
9	7	3	**Sentimental Journey**...*The Merry Macs*...Decca 18684
10	—	1	**I Wish** ....*Mills Brothers*...Decca 18663
10	—	1	**Who Threw The Whiskey In The Well** ....*Lucky Millinder*...Decca 18674

TW	LW	WK	Billboard JULY 21, 1945 Best Sellers
1	1	15	Sentimental Journey ....*Les Brown*...Columbia 36769
2	4	2	On The Atchison, Topeka And Santa Fe..*Johnny Mercer*...Capitol 195
3	2	15	There! I've Said It Again ....*Vaughn Monroe*...Victor 20-1637
4	3	10	Bell Bottom Trousers ....*Tony Pastor*...Victor 20-1661
5	4	7	Sentimental Journey ....*Hal McIntyre*...Victor 20-1643
6	6	3	Chopin's Polonaise ....*Carmen Cavallaro*...Decca 18677
7	9	4	Sentimental Journey ....*The Merry Macs*...Decca 18684
8	7	5	Bell Bottom Trousers ....*Guy Lombardo*...Decca 18683
9	8	8	You Belong To My Heart..*Bing Crosby & Xavier Cugat*...Decca 23413
10	6	3	Gotta Be This Or That (Part 1)...*Benny Goodman*...Columbia 36813

TW	LW	WK	Billboard JULY 28, 1945 Best Sellers
1	2	3	On The Atchison, Topeka And Santa Fe..*Johnny Mercer*...Capitol 195
2	1	16	Sentimental Journey ....*Les Brown*...Columbia 36769
3	3	16	There! I've Said It Again ....*Vaughn Monroe*...Victor 20-1637
4	4	11	Bell Bottom Trousers ....*Tony Pastor*...Victor 20-1661
5	6	4	Chopin's Polonaise ....*Carmen Cavallaro*...Decca 18677
6	5	8	Sentimental Journey ....*Hal McIntyre*...Victor 20-1643
7	10	4	Gotta Be This Or That (Part 1)...*Benny Goodman*...Columbia 36813
8	8	6	Bell Bottom Trousers ....*Guy Lombardo*...Decca 18683
8	7	5	Sentimental Journey ....*The Merry Macs*...Decca 18684
9	—	1	If I Loved You ....*Perry Como*...Victor 20-1676
10	—	1	On The Atchison, Topeka And The Santa Fe ....*Bing Crosby*...Decca 18690

TW	LW	WK	Billboard AUGUST 4, 1945 Best Sellers
1	1	4	On The Atchison, Topeka And Santa Fe..*Johnny Mercer*...Capitol 195
2	2	17	Sentimental Journey ....*Les Brown*...Columbia 36769
3	5	5	Chopin's Polonaise ....*Carmen Cavallaro*...Decca 18677
4	7	5	Gotta Be This Or That (Part 1)...*Benny Goodman*...Columbia 36813
5	3	17	There! I've Said It Again ....*Vaughn Monroe*...Victor 20-1637
6	9	2	If I Loved You ....*Perry Como*...Victor 20-1676
7	4	12	Bell Bottom Trousers ....*Tony Pastor*...Victor 20-1661
8	10	2	On The Atchison, Topeka And The Santa Fe ....*Bing Crosby*...Decca 18690
9	—	1	Bell Bottom Trousers ....*Jerry Colonna*...Capitol 204
9	6	9	Sentimental Journey ....*Hal McIntyre*...Victor 20-1643
9	8	6	Sentimental Journey ....*The Merry Macs*...Decca 18684
9	—	1	Tampico ....*Stan Kenton*...Capitol 202
10	—	6	Bell Bottom Trousers ....*Kay Kyser*...Columbia 36801
10	—	9	You Belong To My Heart...*Bing Crosby & Xavier Cugat*...Decca 23413

TW	LW	WK	Billboard AUGUST 11, 1945 Best Sellers
1	1	5	On The Atchison, Topeka And Santa Fe..*Johnny Mercer*...Capitol 195
2	2	18	Sentimental Journey ....*Les Brown*...Columbia 36769
3	6	3	If I Loved You ....*Perry Como*...Victor 20-1676
4	3	6	Chopin's Polonaise ....*Carmen Cavallaro*...Decca 18677
5	4	6	Gotta Be This Or That (Part 1)...*Benny Goodman*...Columbia 36813
6	5	18	There! I've Said It Again ....*Vaughn Monroe*...Victor 20-1637
7	7	13	Bell Bottom Trousers ....*Tony Pastor*...Victor 20-1661
8	—	7	Bell Bottom Trousers ....*Guy Lombardo*...Decca 18683
8	—	1	On The Atchison, Topeka & Santa Fe ....*Tommy Dorsey*...Victor 20-1682
8	9	10	Sentimental Journey ....*Hal McIntyre*...Victor 20-1643
9	9	7	Sentimental Journey ....*The Merry Macs*...Decca 18684
9	—	2	You Belong To My Heart ....*Charlie Spivak*...Victor 20-1663
10	—	1	Good, Good, Good (That's You–That's You) ....*Sammy Kaye*...Victor 20-1684

TW	LW	WK	Billboard®　　　　AUGUST 18, 1945　　　　Best Sellers
1	1	6	On The Atchison, Topeka And Santa Fe..*Johnny Mercer*...Capitol 195
2	2	19	Sentimental Journey...*Les Brown*...Columbia 36769
3	4	7	Chopin's Polonaise...*Carmen Cavallaro*...Decca 18677
4	3	4	If I Loved You..*Perry Como*...Victor 20-1676
5	—	1	Till The End Of Time...*Perry Como*...Victor 20-1709
6	5	7	Gotta Be This Or That (Part 1)...*Benny Goodman*...Columbia 36813
7	6	19	There! I've Said It Again..*Vaughn Monroe*...Victor 20-1637
8	7	14	Bell Bottom Trousers..*Tony Pastor*...Victor 20-1661
8	8	8	Bell Bottom Trousers..*Guy Lombardo*...Decca 18683
9	—	3	On The Atchison, Topeka And The Santa Fe..*Bing Crosby*...Decca 18690
9	9	8	Sentimental Journey...*The Merry Macs*...Decca 18684
10	—	2	Bell Bottom Trousers...*Jerry Colonna*...Capitol 204
10	—	1	I'm Gonna Love That Gal (Like She's Never Been Loved Before).......*Perry Como*...Victor 20-1676
10	8	11	Sentimental Journey...*Hal McIntyre*...Victor 20-1643
10	—	2	Tampico...*Stan Kenton*...Capitol 202

TW	LW	WK	Billboard®　　　　AUGUST 25, 1945　　　　Best Sellers
1	1	7	On The Atchison, Topeka And Santa Fe..*Johnny Mercer*...Capitol 195
2	5	2	Till The End Of Time...*Perry Como*...Victor 20-1709
3	3	8	Chopin's Polonaise...*Carmen Cavallaro*...Decca 18677
4	4	5	If I Loved You..*Perry Como*...Victor 20-1676
5	2	20	Sentimental Journey...*Les Brown*...Columbia 36769
6	6	8	Gotta Be This Or That (Part 1)...*Benny Goodman*...Columbia 36813
6	9	4	On The Atchison, Topeka And The Santa Fe..*Bing Crosby*...Decca 18690
6	—	2	On The Atchison, Topeka & Santa Fe..*Tommy Dorsey*...Victor 20-1682
7	7	20	There! I've Said It Again..*Vaughn Monroe*...Victor 20-1637
8	10	3	Tampico...*Stan Kenton*...Capitol 202
9	8	15	Bell Bottom Trousers..*Tony Pastor*...Victor 20-1661
10	8	9	Bell Bottom Trousers..*Guy Lombardo*...Decca 18683

TW	LW	WK	Billboard®　　　　SEPTEMBER 1, 1945　　　　Best Sellers
1	1	8	On The Atchison, Topeka And Santa Fe..*Johnny Mercer*...Capitol 195
2	2	3	Till The End Of Time...*Perry Como*...Victor 20-1709
3	3	9	Chopin's Polonaise...*Carmen Cavallaro*...Decca 18677
4	6	9	Gotta Be This Or That (Part 1)...*Benny Goodman*...Columbia 36813
5	4	6	If I Loved You..*Perry Como*...Victor 20-1676
6	8	4	Tampico...*Stan Kenton*...Capitol 202
7	5	21	Sentimental Journey...*Les Brown*...Columbia 36769
8	6	5	On The Atchison, Topeka And The Santa Fe..*Bing Crosby*...Decca 18690
9	6	3	On The Atchison, Topeka & Santa Fe..*Tommy Dorsey*...Victor 20-1682
10	—	2	I'm Gonna Love That Gal (Like She's Never Been Loved Before).......*Perry Como*...Victor 20-1676

TW	LW	WK	Billboard®　　　　SEPTEMBER 8, 1945　　　　Best Sellers
1	1	9	On The Atchison, Topeka And Santa Fe..*Johnny Mercer*...Capitol 195
2	2	4	Till The End Of Time...*Perry Como*...Victor 20-1709
3	3	10	Chopin's Polonaise...*Carmen Cavallaro*...Decca 18677
4	4	10	Gotta Be This Or That (Part 1)...*Benny Goodman*...Columbia 36813
5	5	7	If I Loved You..*Perry Como*...Victor 20-1676
6	8	6	On The Atchison, Topeka And The Santa Fe..*Bing Crosby*...Decca 18690
7	6	5	Tampico...*Stan Kenton*...Capitol 202
8	9	4	On The Atchison, Topeka & Santa Fe..*Tommy Dorsey*...Victor 20-1682
9	7	22	Sentimental Journey...*Les Brown*...Columbia 36769
10	—	1	I Wish I Knew...*Dick Haymes*...Decca 18662

Billboard ❀ SEPTEMBER 15, 1945 ❀ Best Sellers

TW	LW	WK		
1	2	5	Till The End Of Time	Perry Como...Victor 20-1709
2	1	10	On The Atchison, Topeka And Santa Fe	Johnny Mercer...Capitol 195
3	3	11	Chopin's Polonaise	Carmen Cavallaro...Decca 18677
4	4	11	Gotta Be This Or That (Part 1)	Benny Goodman...Columbia 36813
5	5	8	If I Loved You	Perry Como...Victor 20-1676
6	—	1	Boogie Woogie	Tommy Dorsey...Victor 20-1715
7	8	5	On The Atchison, Topeka & Santa Fe	Tommy Dorsey...Victor 20-1682
7	7	6	Tampico	Stan Kenton...Capitol 202
8	9	23	Sentimental Journey	Les Brown...Columbia 36769
9	—	10	Bell Bottom Trousers	Guy Lombardo...Decca 18683
10	6	7	On The Atchison, Topeka And The Santa Fe	Bing Crosby...Decca 18690

Billboard ❀ SEPTEMBER 22, 1945 ❀ Best Sellers

TW	LW	WK		
1	1	6	Till The End Of Time	Perry Como...Victor 20-1709
2	2	11	On The Atchison, Topeka And Santa Fe	Johnny Mercer...Capitol 195
3	3	12	Chopin's Polonaise	Carmen Cavallaro...Decca 18677
4	6	2	Boogie Woogie	Tommy Dorsey...Victor 20-1715
5	4	12	Gotta Be This Or That (Part 1)	Benny Goodman...Columbia 36813
6	5	9	If I Loved You	Perry Como...Victor 20-1676
6	7	7	Tampico	Stan Kenton...Capitol 202
7	—	3	I'm Gonna Love That Gal (Like She's Never Been Loved Before)	Perry Como...Victor 20-1676
8	—	1	Along The Navajo Trail	Dinah Shore...Victor 20-1666
8	10	8	On The Atchison, Topeka And The Santa Fe	Bing Crosby...Decca 18690
8	—	1	11:60 P.M.	Harry James...Columbia 36827
9	7	6	On The Atchison, Topeka & Santa Fe	Tommy Dorsey...Victor 20-1682
10	—	1	Till The End Of Time	Dick Haymes...Decca 18699

Billboard ❀ SEPTEMBER 29, 1945 ❀ Best Sellers

TW	LW	WK		
1	1	7	Till The End Of Time	Perry Como...Victor 20-1709
2	2	12	On The Atchison, Topeka And Santa Fe	Johnny Mercer...Capitol 195
3	3	13	Chopin's Polonaise	Carmen Cavallaro...Decca 18677
4	6	10	If I Loved You	Perry Como...Victor 20-1676
5	6	8	Tampico	Stan Kenton...Capitol 202
6	5	13	Gotta Be This Or That (Part 1)	Benny Goodman...Columbia 36813
7	—	1	Along The Navajo Trail	Bing Crosby & Andrews Sisters...Decca 23437
8	4	3	Boogie Woogie	Tommy Dorsey...Victor 20-1715
9	7	4	I'm Gonna Love That Gal (Like She's Never Been Loved Before)	Perry Como...Victor 20-1676
9	8	9	On The Atchison, Topeka And The Santa Fe	Bing Crosby...Decca 18690
10	—	1	It's Only A Paper Moon	Benny Goodman...Columbia 36843
10	—	1	On The Atchison, Topeka And The Santa Fe	Judy Garland & The Merry Macs...Decca 23436
10	10	2	Till The End Of Time	Dick Haymes...Decca 18699

Billboard ❀ OCTOBER 6, 1945 ❀ Best Sellers

TW	LW	WK		
1	1	8	Till The End Of Time	Perry Como...Victor 20-1709
2	2	13	On The Atchison, Topeka And Santa Fe	Johnny Mercer...Capitol 195
3	3	14	Chopin's Polonaise	Carmen Cavallaro...Decca 18677
4	9	10	On The Atchison, Topeka And The Santa Fe	Bing Crosby...Decca 18690
4	10	3	Till The End Of Time	Dick Haymes...Decca 18699
4	5	9	Tampico	Stan Kenton...Capitol 202
5	7	2	Along The Navajo Trail	Bing Crosby & Andrews Sisters...Decca 23437
6	4	11	If I Loved You	Perry Como...Victor 20-1676
7	—	1	I'll Buy That Dream	Helen Forrest & Dick Haymes...Decca 23434
8	6	14	Gotta Be This Or That (Part 1)	Benny Goodman...Columbia 36813
9	8	4	Boogie Woogie	Tommy Dorsey...Victor 20-1715
10	—	1	Hong Kong Blues	Tommy Dorsey...Victor 20-1722

TW	LW	WK	Billboard® ⚅ OCTOBER 13, 1945 ⚅	Best Sellers
1	1	9	Till The End Of Time ....Perry Como...Victor 20-1709	
2	2	14	On The Atchison, Topeka And Santa Fe..Johnny Mercer...Capitol 195	
3	3	15	Chopin's Polonaise ....Carmen Cavallaro...Decca 18677	
4	4	10	Tampico...Stan Kenton...Capitol 202	
5	6	12	If I Loved You ....Perry Como...Victor 20-1676	
6	4	4	Till The End Of Time ....Dick Haymes...Decca 18699	
7	7	2	I'll Buy That Dream...Helen Forrest & Dick Haymes...Decca 23434	
8	5	3	Along The Navajo Trail ....Bing Crosby & Andrews Sisters...Decca 23437	
8	8	15	Gotta Be This Or That (Part 1)...Benny Goodman...Columbia 36813	
8	—	1	I'll Buy That Dream ....Harry James...Columbia 36833	
9	10	2	Hong Kong Blues ....Tommy Dorsey...Victor 20-1722	
10	—	1	It's Been A Long, Long Time..Charlie Spivak...Victor 20-1721	

TW	LW	WK	Billboard® ⚅ OCTOBER 20, 1945 ⚅	Best Sellers
1	1	10	Till The End Of Time ....Perry Como...Victor 20-1709	
2	2	15	On The Atchison, Topeka And Santa Fe..Johnny Mercer...Capitol 195	
3	7	3	I'll Buy That Dream...Helen Forrest & Dick Haymes...Decca 23434	
4	3	16	Chopin's Polonaise ....Carmen Cavallaro...Decca 18677	
5	8	4	Along The Navajo Trail ....Bing Crosby & Andrews Sisters...Decca 23437	
6	6	5	Till The End Of Time ....Dick Haymes...Decca 18699	
7	8	2	I'll Buy That Dream ....Harry James...Columbia 36833	
8	4	11	Tampico...Stan Kenton...Capitol 202	
9	9	3	Hong Kong Blues ....Tommy Dorsey...Victor 20-1722	
9	5	13	If I Loved You ....Perry Como...Victor 20-1676	
10	—	1	It's Been A Long, Long Time..Harry James...Columbia 36838	
10	—	1	It's Been A Long Long Time...Bing Crosby with Les Paul...Decca 18708	
10	10	2	It's Been A Long, Long Time..Charlie Spivak...Victor 20-1721	

TW	LW	WK	Billboard® ⚅ OCTOBER 27, 1945 ⚅	Best Sellers
1	1	11	Till The End Of Time ....Perry Como...Victor 20-1709	
2	3	4	I'll Buy That Dream...Helen Forrest & Dick Haymes...Decca 23434	
3	6	6	Till The End Of Time ....Dick Haymes...Decca 18699	
4	2	16	On The Atchison, Topeka And Santa Fe..Johnny Mercer...Capitol 195	
5	10	2	It's Been A Long, Long Time..Harry James...Columbia 36838	
6	8	12	Tampico...Stan Kenton...Capitol 202	
7	5	5	Along The Navajo Trail ....Bing Crosby & Andrews Sisters...Decca 23437	
7	10	2	It's Been A Long Long Time...Bing Crosby with Les Paul...Decca 18708	
8	4	17	Chopin's Polonaise ....Carmen Cavallaro...Decca 18677	
9	10	3	It's Been A Long, Long Time..Charlie Spivak...Victor 20-1721	
10	—	1	Chickery Chick ....Sammy Kaye...Victor 20-1726	

TW	LW	WK	Billboard® ⚅ NOVEMBER 3, 1945 ⚅	Best Sellers
1	1	12	Till The End Of Time ....Perry Como...Victor 20-1709	
2	7	3	It's Been A Long Long Time...Bing Crosby with Les Paul...Decca 18708	
3	5	3	It's Been A Long, Long Time..Harry James...Columbia 36838	
4	10	2	Chickery Chick ....Sammy Kaye...Victor 20-1726	
5	2	5	I'll Buy That Dream...Helen Forrest & Dick Haymes...Decca 23434	
6	—	3	I'll Buy That Dream ....Harry James...Columbia 36833	
7	3	7	Till The End Of Time ....Dick Haymes...Decca 18699	
8	—	1	That's For Me ....Dick Haymes...Decca 18706	
9	9	4	It's Been A Long, Long Time..Charlie Spivak...Victor 20-1721	
10	8	18	Chopin's Polonaise ....Carmen Cavallaro...Decca 18677	

TW	LW	WK	Billboard® ❄ NOVEMBER 10, 1945 ❄ Best Sellers
1	1	13	Till The End Of Time ....*Perry Como*...Victor 20-1709
2	3	4	It's Been A Long, Long Time ....*Harry James*...Columbia 36838
3	2	4	It's Been A Long Long Time ....*Bing Crosby with Les Paul*...Decca 18708
4	4	3	Chickery Chick ....*Sammy Kaye*...Victor 20-1726
5	5	6	I'll Buy That Dream...*Helen Forrest & Dick Haymes*...Decca 23434
6	6	4	I'll Buy That Dream ....*Harry James*...Columbia 36833
7	9	5	It's Been A Long, Long Time ....*Charlie Spivak*...Victor 20-1721
8	8	2	That's For Me ....*Dick Haymes*...Decca 18706
9	—	6	Along The Navajo Trail ....*Bing Crosby & Andrews Sisters*...Decca 23437
9	—	13	Tampico...*Stan Kenton*...Capitol 202
10	10	19	Chopin's Polonaise ....*Carmen Cavallaro*...Decca 18677

TW	LW	WK	Billboard® ❄ NOVEMBER 17, 1945 ❄ Best Sellers
1	4	4	Chickery Chick ....*Sammy Kaye*...Victor 20-1726
1	1	14	Till The End Of Time ....*Perry Como*...Victor 20-1709
2	2	5	It's Been A Long, Long Time ....*Harry James*...Columbia 36838
3	3	5	It's Been A Long Long Time ....*Bing Crosby with Les Paul*...Decca 18708
4	7	6	It's Been A Long, Long Time ....*Charlie Spivak*...Victor 20-1721
5	5	7	I'll Buy That Dream...*Helen Forrest & Dick Haymes*...Decca 23434
6	—	1	It's Been A Long, Long Time ....*Stan Kenton*...Capitol 219
7	6	5	I'll Buy That Dream ....*Harry James*...Columbia 36833
7	8	3	That's For Me ....*Dick Haymes*...Decca 18706
8	—	1	It Might As Well Be Spring ....*Dick Haymes*...Decca 18706
9	—	1	That's For Me...*Jo Stafford*...Capitol 213
10	—	8	Till The End Of Time ....*Dick Haymes*...Decca 18699

TW	LW	WK	Billboard® ❄ NOVEMBER 24, 1945 ❄ Best Sellers
1	2	6	It's Been A Long, Long Time ....*Harry James*...Columbia 36838
2	1	5	Chickery Chick ....*Sammy Kaye*...Victor 20-1726
3	3	6	It's Been A Long Long Time ....*Bing Crosby with Les Paul*...Decca 18708
4	1	15	Till The End Of Time ....*Perry Como*...Victor 20-1709
5	5	8	I'll Buy That Dream...*Helen Forrest & Dick Haymes*...Decca 23434
6	7	4	That's For Me ....*Dick Haymes*...Decca 18706
7	—	1	I Can't Begin To Tell You....................................*Bing Crosby with Carmen Cavallaro*...Decca 23457
7	7	6	I'll Buy That Dream ....*Harry James*...Columbia 36833
8	—	1	Waitin' For The Train To Come In ....*Peggy Lee*...Capitol 218
9	8	2	It Might As Well Be Spring...*Dick Haymes*...Decca 18706
9	4	7	It's Been A Long, Long Time...*Charlie Spivak*...Victor 20-1721
9	6	2	It's Been A Long, Long Time ....*Stan Kenton*...Capitol 219
10	—	1	Holiday For Strings...*Spike Jones*...Victor 20-1733
10	—	1	The Honeydripper ....*Jimmie Lunceford & Delta Rhythm Boys*...Decca 23451
10	—	1	Waitin' For The Train To Come In ....*Harry James*...Columbia 36867

TW	LW	WK	Billboard® ❄ DECEMBER 1, 1945 ❄ Best Sellers
1	1	7	It's Been A Long, Long Time ....*Harry James*...Columbia 36838
2	2	6	Chickery Chick ....*Sammy Kaye*...Victor 20-1726
3	3	7	It's Been A Long Long Time ....*Bing Crosby with Les Paul*...Decca 18708
4	5	9	I'll Buy That Dream...*Helen Forrest & Dick Haymes*...Decca 23434
5	4	16	Till The End Of Time ....*Perry Como*...Victor 20-1709
6	7	2	I Can't Begin To Tell You....................................*Bing Crosby with Carmen Cavallaro*...Decca 23457
7	7	7	I'll Buy That Dream ....*Harry James*...Columbia 36833
8	—	1	It Might As Well Be Spring ....*Paul Weston With Margaret Whiting*...Capitol 214
8	8	2	Waitin' For The Train To Come In ....*Peggy Lee*...Capitol 218
9	9	8	It's Been A Long, Long Time...*Charlie Spivak*...Victor 20-1721
9	9	3	It's Been A Long, Long Time ....*Stan Kenton*...Capitol 219
10	9	3	It Might As Well Be Spring...*Dick Haymes*...Decca 18706

TW	LW	WK	Billboard®　🏵　DECEMBER 8, 1945　🏵　Best Sellers
1	3	8	It's Been A Long Long Time...Bing Crosby with Les Paul...Decca 18708
2	2	7	Chickery Chick...Sammy Kaye...Victor 20-1726
3	1	8	It's Been A Long, Long Time..Harry James...Columbia 36838
4	4	10	I'll Buy That Dream......................................Helen Forrest & Dick Haymes...Decca 23434
5	6	3	I Can't Begin To Tell You...................Bing Crosby with Carmen Cavallaro...Decca 23457
6	8	3	Waitin' For The Train To Come In ....Peggy Lee...Capitol 218
7	10	4	It Might As Well Be Spring..Dick Haymes...Decca 18706
8	8	2	It Might As Well Be Spring...................Paul Weston With Margaret Whiting...Capitol 214
9	—	1	Dig You Later (A Hubba-Hubba-Hubba) ....Perry Como...Victor 20-1750
10	9	4	It's Been A Long, Long Time ....Stan Kenton...Capitol 219
10	—	1	Nancy (With The Laughing Face)..Frank Sinatra...Columbia 36868
10	5	17	Till The End Of Time ....Perry Como...Victor 20-1709

TW	LW	WK	Billboard®　🏵　DECEMBER 15, 1945　🏵　Best Sellers
1	2	8	Chickery Chick...Sammy Kaye...Victor 20-1726
2	5	4	I Can't Begin To Tell You...................Bing Crosby with Carmen Cavallaro...Decca 23457
3	1	9	It's Been A Long Long Time...Bing Crosby with Les Paul...Decca 18708
4	3	9	It's Been A Long, Long Time..Harry James...Columbia 36838
5	—	1	Symphony..Freddy Martin...Victor 20-1747
6	8	3	It Might As Well Be Spring...................Paul Weston With Margaret Whiting...Capitol 214
7	6	4	Waitin' For The Train To Come In ....Peggy Lee...Capitol 218
7	4	11	I'll Buy That Dream......................................Helen Forrest & Dick Haymes...Decca 23434
8	—	1	Doctor, Lawyer, Indian Chief ....Betty Hutton...Capitol 220
8	9	2	Dig You Later (A Hubba-Hubba-Hubba) ....Perry Como...Victor 20-1750
9	—	9	It's Been A Long, Long Time...Charlie Spivak...Victor 20-1721
9	—	1	White Christmas ....Bing Crosby...Decca 18429
9	—	1	Symphony..Benny Goodman...Columbia 36874
10	7	5	It Might As Well Be Spring..Dick Haymes...Decca 18706

TW	LW	WK	Billboard®　🏵　DECEMBER 22, 1945　🏵　Best Sellers
1	4	10	It's Been A Long, Long Time ....Harry James...Columbia 36838
2	1	9	Chickery Chick...Sammy Kaye...Victor 20-1726
3	2	5	I Can't Begin To Tell You...................Bing Crosby with Carmen Cavallaro...Decca 23457
4	3	10	It's Been A Long Long Time...Bing Crosby with Les Paul...Decca 18708
5	5	2	Symphony..Freddy Martin...Victor 20-1747
6	8	3	Dig You Later (A Hubba-Hubba-Hubba) ....Perry Como...Victor 20-1750
7	6	4	It Might As Well Be Spring...................Paul Weston With Margaret Whiting...Capitol 214
8	8	2	Doctor, Lawyer, Indian Chief ....Betty Hutton...Capitol 220
9	10	6	It Might As Well Be Spring..Dick Haymes...Decca 18706
9	9	2	White Christmas ....Bing Crosby...Decca 18429
10	7	5	Waitin' For The Train To Come In ....Peggy Lee...Capitol 218
10	—	1	Let It Snow! Let It Snow! Let It Snow! ....Vaughn Monroe...Victor 20-1759

TW	LW	WK	Billboard®　🏵　DECEMBER 29, 1945　🏵　Best Sellers
1	2	10	Chickery Chick...Sammy Kaye...Victor 20-1726
2	5	3	Symphony..Freddy Martin...Victor 20-1747
3	1	11	It's Been A Long, Long Time..Harry James...Columbia 36838
4	4	11	It's Been A Long Long Time...Bing Crosby with Les Paul...Decca 18708
5	6	4	Dig You Later (A Hubba-Hubba-Hubba) ....Perry Como...Victor 20-1750
5	9	7	It Might As Well Be Spring..Dick Haymes...Decca 18706
6	3	6	I Can't Begin To Tell You...................Bing Crosby with Carmen Cavallaro...Decca 23457
7	7	5	It Might As Well Be Spring...................Paul Weston With Margaret Whiting...Capitol 214
8	—	10	It's Been A Long, Long Time...Charlie Spivak...Victor 20-1721
9	—	1	It Might As Well Be Spring...Sammy Kaye...Victor 20-1738
10	8	3	Doctor, Lawyer, Indian Chief ....Betty Hutton...Capitol 220
10	9	3	White Christmas ....Bing Crosby...Decca 18429

TW	LW	WK	Billboard® ❀ JANUARY 5, 1946 ❀ Best Sellers
1	2	4	Symphony ....*Freddy Martin...Victor 20-1747*
2	1	11	Chickery Chick ....*Sammy Kaye...Victor 20-1726*
3	5	5	Dig You Later (A Hubba-Hubba-Hubba) ....*Perry Como...Victor 20-1750*
3	6	7	I Can't Begin To Tell You ....*Bing Crosby with Carmen Cavallaro...Decca 23457*
4	3	12	It's Been A Long, Long Time ....*Harry James...Columbia 36838*
5	—	2	Let It Snow! Let It Snow! Let It Snow! ....*Vaughn Monroe...Victor 20-1759*
6	8	11	It's Been A Long, Long Time..*Charlie Spivak...Victor 20-1721*
7	5	8	It Might As Well Be Spring..*Dick Haymes...Decca 18706*
7	4	12	It's Been A Long Long Time............................*Bing Crosby with Les Paul...Decca 18708*
8	7	6	It Might As Well Be Spring ....*Paul Weston With Margaret Whiting...Capitol 214*
8	—	1	I Can't Begin To Tell You ....*Andy Russell...Capitol 221*
9	—	1	I Can't Begin To Tell You ....*Harry James...Columbia 36867*
9	10	4	White Christmas ....*Bing Crosby...Decca 18429*
9	—	1	Buzz Me ....*Louis Jordan...Decca 18734*
10	—	1	Chickery Chick ....*Evelyn Knight & The Jesters...Decca 18725*
10	9	2	It Might As Well Be Spring..*Sammy Kaye...Victor 20-1738*

TW	LW	WK	Billboard® ❀ JANUARY 12, 1946 ❀ Best Sellers
1	1	5	Symphony ....*Freddy Martin...Victor 20-1747*
2	3	8	I Can't Begin To Tell You ....*Bing Crosby with Carmen Cavallaro...Decca 23457*
3	2	12	Chickery Chick ....*Sammy Kaye...Victor 20-1726*
4	3	6	Dig You Later (A Hubba-Hubba-Hubba) ....*Perry Como...Victor 20-1750*
5	4	13	It's Been A Long, Long Time ....*Harry James...Columbia 36838*
6	7	9	It Might As Well Be Spring..*Dick Haymes...Decca 18706*
6	5	3	Let It Snow! Let It Snow! Let It Snow! ....*Vaughn Monroe...Victor 20-1759*
7	7	13	It's Been A Long Long Time............................*Bing Crosby with Les Paul...Decca 18708*
8	10	3	It Might As Well Be Spring..*Sammy Kaye...Victor 20-1738*
8	—	1	Symphony ....*Bing Crosby...Decca 18735*
9	—	4	Doctor, Lawyer, Indian Chief ....*Betty Hutton...Capitol 220*
10	—	1	Symphony ....*Jo Stafford...Capitol 227*

TW	LW	WK	Billboard® ❀ JANUARY 19, 1946 ❀ Best Sellers
1	2	9	I Can't Begin To Tell You ....*Bing Crosby with Carmen Cavallaro...Decca 23457*
2	1	6	Symphony ....*Freddy Martin...Victor 20-1747*
3	6	4	Let It Snow! Let It Snow! Let It Snow! ....*Vaughn Monroe...Victor 20-1759*
4	10	2	Symphony ....*Jo Stafford...Capitol 227*
5	4	7	Dig You Later (A Hubba-Hubba-Hubba) ....*Perry Como...Victor 20-1750*
5	8	2	Symphony ....*Bing Crosby...Decca 18735*
6	9	5	Doctor, Lawyer, Indian Chief ....*Betty Hutton...Capitol 220*
7	—	2	Symphony ....*Benny Goodman...Columbia 36874*
8	3	13	Chickery Chick ....*Sammy Kaye...Victor 20-1726*
9	6	10	It Might As Well Be Spring..*Dick Haymes...Decca 18706*
10	—	2	I Can't Begin To Tell You ....*Andy Russell...Capitol 221*
10	5	14	It's Been A Long, Long Time ....*Harry James...Columbia 36838*

TW	LW	WK	Billboard® ❀ JANUARY 26, 1946 ❀ Best Sellers
1	3	5	Let It Snow! Let It Snow! Let It Snow! ....*Vaughn Monroe...Victor 20-1759*
2	2	7	Symphony ....*Freddy Martin...Victor 20-1747*
3	1	10	I Can't Begin To Tell You ....*Bing Crosby with Carmen Cavallaro...Decca 23457*
4	5	3	Symphony ....*Bing Crosby...Decca 18735*
5	6	6	Doctor, Lawyer, Indian Chief ....*Betty Hutton...Capitol 220*
6	4	3	Symphony ....*Jo Stafford...Capitol 227*
7	7	3	Symphony ....*Benny Goodman...Columbia 36874*
8	5	8	Dig You Later (A Hubba-Hubba-Hubba) ....*Perry Como...Victor 20-1750*
9	9	11	It Might As Well Be Spring..*Dick Haymes...Decca 18706*
9	—	1	Personality...*Johnny Mercer...Capitol 230*
10	—	2	I Can't Begin To Tell You ....*Harry James...Columbia 36867*

Billboard — FEBRUARY 2, 1946 — Best Sellers

TW	LW	WK		
1	1	6	Let It Snow! Let It Snow! Let It Snow!	Vaughn Monroe...Victor 20-1759
2	2	8	Symphony	Freddy Martin...Victor 20-1747
3	3	11	I Can't Begin To Tell You	Bing Crosby with Carmen Cavallaro...Decca 23457
4	4	4	Symphony	Bing Crosby...Decca 18735
5	9	2	Personality	Johnny Mercer...Capitol 230
6	5	7	Doctor, Lawyer, Indian Chief	Betty Hutton...Capitol 220
7	6	4	Symphony	Jo Stafford...Capitol 227
8	—	1	I'm Always Chasing Rainbows	Perry Como...Victor 20-1788
9	9	12	It Might As Well Be Spring	Dick Haymes...Decca 18706
9	7	4	Symphony	Benny Goodman...Columbia 36874
10	8	9	Dig You Later (A Hubba-Hubba-Hubba)	Perry Como...Victor 20-1750

Billboard — FEBRUARY 9, 1946 — Best Sellers

TW	LW	WK		
1	1	7	Let It Snow! Let It Snow! Let It Snow!	Vaughn Monroe...Victor 20-1759
2	5	3	Personality	Johnny Mercer...Capitol 230
3	4	5	Symphony	Bing Crosby...Decca 18735
4	2	9	Symphony	Freddy Martin...Victor 20-1747
5	3	12	I Can't Begin To Tell You	Bing Crosby with Carmen Cavallaro...Decca 23457
6	6	8	Doctor, Lawyer, Indian Chief	Betty Hutton...Capitol 220
6	9	5	Symphony	Benny Goodman...Columbia 36874
7	8	2	I'm Always Chasing Rainbows	Perry Como...Victor 20-1788
8	7	5	Symphony	Jo Stafford...Capitol 227
9	10	10	Dig You Later (A Hubba-Hubba-Hubba)	Perry Como...Victor 20-1750
10	—	4	It Might As Well Be Spring	Sammy Kaye...Victor 20-1738
10	—	1	I'm Always Chasing Rainbows	Dick Haymes & Helen Forrest...Decca 23472

Billboard — FEBRUARY 16, 1946 — Best Sellers

TW	LW	WK		
1	1	8	Let It Snow! Let It Snow! Let It Snow!	Vaughn Monroe...Victor 20-1759
2	4	10	Symphony	Freddy Martin...Victor 20-1747
3	2	4	Personality	Johnny Mercer...Capitol 230
4	3	6	Symphony	Bing Crosby...Decca 18735
5	6	9	Doctor, Lawyer, Indian Chief	Betty Hutton...Capitol 220
6	5	13	I Can't Begin To Tell You	Bing Crosby with Carmen Cavallaro...Decca 23457
7	6	6	Symphony	Benny Goodman...Columbia 36874
8	7	3	I'm Always Chasing Rainbows	Perry Como...Victor 20-1788
9	9	11	Dig You Later (A Hubba-Hubba-Hubba)	Perry Como...Victor 20-1750
9	8	6	Symphony	Jo Stafford...Capitol 227
10	—	1	Oh! What It Seemed To Be	Frankie Carle...Columbia 36892

Billboard — FEBRUARY 23, 1946 — Best Sellers

TW	LW	WK		
1	1	9	Let It Snow! Let It Snow! Let It Snow!	Vaughn Monroe...Victor 20-1759
2	3	5	Personality	Johnny Mercer...Capitol 230
3	5	10	Doctor, Lawyer, Indian Chief	Betty Hutton...Capitol 220
4	6	14	I Can't Begin To Tell You	Bing Crosby with Carmen Cavallaro...Decca 23457
5	7	7	Symphony	Benny Goodman...Columbia 36874
5	4	7	Symphony	Bing Crosby...Decca 18735
6	2	11	Symphony	Freddy Martin...Victor 20-1747
7	10	2	Oh! What It Seemed To Be	Frankie Carle...Columbia 36892
8	—	1	Oh! What It Seemed To Be	Frank Sinatra...Columbia 36905
9	—	3	I Can't Begin To Tell You	Harry James...Columbia 36867
10	—	1	You Won't Be Satisfied (Until You Break My Heart)	Les Brown...Columbia 36884

TW	LW	WK	Billboard ❀ MARCH 2, 1946 ❀ Best Sellers
1	3	11	Doctor, Lawyer, Indian Chief ....*Betty Hutton*...Capitol 220
2	1	10	Let It Snow! Let It Snow! Let It Snow! ....*Vaughn Monroe*...Victor 20-1759
2	2	6	Personality ....*Johnny Mercer*...Capitol 230
3	8	2	Oh! What It Seemed To Be...*Frank Sinatra*...Columbia 36905
4	7	3	Oh! What It Seemed To Be...*Frankie Carle*...Columbia 36892
4	5	8	Symphony ....*Bing Crosby*...Decca 18735
5	5	8	Symphony ....*Benny Goodman*...Columbia 36874
5	10	2	You Won't Be Satisfied (Until You Break My Heart) ....*Les Brown*...Columbia 36884
6	6	12	Symphony ....*Freddy Martin*...Victor 20-1747
7	—	12	Dig You Later (A Hubba-Hubba-Hubba) ....*Perry Como*...Victor 20-1750
8	—	1	Let It Snow! Let It Snow! Let It Snow!...................................*Woody Herman*...Columbia 36909
9	4	15	I Can't Begin To Tell You ....*Bing Crosby with Carmen Cavallaro*...Decca 23457
10	—	1	Oh! What It Seemed To Be ....*Dick Haymes & Helen Forrest*...Decca 23481
10	—	4	I'm Always Chasing Rainbows ....*Perry Como*...Victor 20-1788

TW	LW	WK	Billboard ❀ MARCH 9, 1946 ❀ Best Sellers
1	2	7	Personality ....*Johnny Mercer*...Capitol 230
2	3	3	Oh! What It Seemed To Be...*Frank Sinatra*...Columbia 36905
3	1	12	Doctor, Lawyer, Indian Chief ....*Betty Hutton*...Capitol 220
4	4	4	Oh! What It Seemed To Be...*Frankie Carle*...Columbia 36892
5	2	11	Let It Snow! Let It Snow! Let It Snow! ....*Vaughn Monroe*...Victor 20-1759
6	5	3	You Won't Be Satisfied (Until You Break My Heart) ....*Les Brown*...Columbia 36884
7	5	9	Symphony ....*Benny Goodman*...Columbia 36874
8	9	16	I Can't Begin To Tell You ....*Bing Crosby with Carmen Cavallaro*...Decca 23457
9	6	13	Symphony ....*Freddy Martin*...Victor 20-1747
10	—	1	Day By Day ....*Frank Sinatra*...Columbia 36905

TW	LW	WK	Billboard ❀ MARCH 16, 1946 ❀ Best Sellers
1	4	5	Oh! What It Seemed To Be...*Frankie Carle*...Columbia 36892
2	1	8	Personality ....*Johnny Mercer*...Capitol 230
3	2	4	Oh! What It Seemed To Be...*Frank Sinatra*...Columbia 36905
4	3	13	Doctor, Lawyer, Indian Chief ....*Betty Hutton*...Capitol 220
5	6	4	You Won't Be Satisfied (Until You Break My Heart) ....*Les Brown*...Columbia 36884
6	5	12	Let It Snow! Let It Snow! Let It Snow! ....*Vaughn Monroe*...Victor 20-1759
7	—	2	Oh! What It Seemed To Be ....*Dick Haymes & Helen Forrest*...Decca 23481
8	—	9	Symphony ....*Bing Crosby*...Decca 18735
9	8	17	I Can't Begin To Tell You ....*Bing Crosby with Carmen Cavallaro*...Decca 23457
10	—	1	Doctor, Lawyer, Indian Chief ....*Les Brown*...Columbia 36945

TW	LW	WK	Billboard ❀ MARCH 23, 1946 ❀ Best Sellers
1	1	6	Oh! What It Seemed To Be...*Frankie Carle*...Columbia 36892
2	3	5	Oh! What It Seemed To Be...*Frank Sinatra*...Columbia 36905
3	2	9	Personality ....*Johnny Mercer*...Capitol 230
4	4	14	Doctor, Lawyer, Indian Chief ....*Betty Hutton*...Capitol 220
5	5	5	You Won't Be Satisfied (Until You Break My Heart) ....*Les Brown*...Columbia 36884
6	7	3	Oh! What It Seemed To Be ....*Dick Haymes & Helen Forrest*...Decca 23481
7	—	1	Oh! What It Seemed To Be ....*Charlie Spivak*...RCA Victor 20-1806
8	6	13	Let It Snow! Let It Snow! Let It Snow! ....*Vaughn Monroe*...Victor 20-1759
9	—	1	Shoo Fly Pie (And Apple Pan Dowdy) ....*Stan Kenton*...Capitol 235
10	10	2	Doctor, Lawyer, Indian Chief ....*Les Brown*...Columbia 36945

TW	LW	WK	Billboard ❀ MARCH 30, 1946 ❀ Best Sellers
1	1	7	Oh! What It Seemed To Be...*Frankie Carle*...Columbia 36892
2	2	6	Oh! What It Seemed To Be...*Frank Sinatra*...Columbia 36905
3	3	10	Personality..*Johnny Mercer*...Capitol 230
4	4	15	Doctor, Lawyer, Indian Chief ....*Betty Hutton*...Capitol 220
5	5	6	You Won't Be Satisfied (Until You Break My Heart) ....*Les Brown*...Columbia 36884
6	10	3	Doctor, Lawyer, Indian Chief ....*Les Brown*...Columbia 36945
7	6	4	Oh! What It Seemed To Be ....*Dick Haymes & Helen Forrest*...Decca 23481
8	—	1	One-Zy, Two-Zy (I Love You-zy) ....*Freddy Martin*...RCA Victor 20-1826
9	—	1	Prisoner Of Love ....*Perry Como*...RCA Victor 20-1814
10	9	2	Shoo Fly Pie (And Apple Pan Dowdy) ....*Stan Kenton*...Capitol 235

TW	LW	WK	Billboard ❀ APRIL 6, 1946 ❀ Best Sellers
1	1	8	Oh! What It Seemed To Be...*Frankie Carle*...Columbia 36892
2	2	7	Oh! What It Seemed To Be...*Frank Sinatra*...Columbia 36905
3	3	11	Personality..*Johnny Mercer*...Capitol 230
4	7	5	Oh! What It Seemed To Be ....*Dick Haymes & Helen Forrest*...Decca 23481
5	4	16	Doctor, Lawyer, Indian Chief ....*Betty Hutton*...Capitol 220
6	9	2	Prisoner Of Love ....*Perry Como*...RCA Victor 20-1814
7	—	2	Oh! What It Seemed To Be ....*Charlie Spivak*...RCA Victor 20-1806
8	8	2	One-Zy, Two-Zy (I Love You-zy) ....*Freddy Martin*...RCA Victor 20-1826
9	6	4	Doctor, Lawyer, Indian Chief ....*Les Brown*...Columbia 36945
10	5	7	You Won't Be Satisfied (Until You Break My Heart) ....*Les Brown*...Columbia 36884

TW	LW	WK	Billboard ❀ APRIL 13, 1946 ❀ Best Sellers
1	1	9	Oh! What It Seemed To Be...*Frankie Carle*...Columbia 36892
2	2	8	Oh! What It Seemed To Be...*Frank Sinatra*...Columbia 36905
3	3	12	Personality..*Johnny Mercer*...Capitol 230
4	6	3	Prisoner Of Love ....*Perry Como*...RCA Victor 20-1814
5	7	3	Oh! What It Seemed To Be ....*Charlie Spivak*...RCA Victor 20-1806
6	10	8	You Won't Be Satisfied (Until You Break My Heart) ....*Les Brown*...Columbia 36884
7	5	17	Doctor, Lawyer, Indian Chief ....*Betty Hutton*...Capitol 220
7	4	6	Oh! What It Seemed To Be ....*Dick Haymes & Helen Forrest*...Decca 23481
7	8	3	One-Zy, Two-Zy (I Love You-zy) ....*Freddy Martin*...RCA Victor 20-1826
8	—	1	Shoo-Fly Pie And Apple Pan Dowdy ....*Dinah Shore*...Columbia 36943
9	—	1	Sioux City Sue ....*Bing Crosby & The Jesters*...Decca 23508
10	—	1	Hey! Ba-Ba-Re-Bop...*Lionel Hampton*...Decca 18754

TW	LW	WK	Billboard ❀ APRIL 20, 1946 ❀ Best Sellers
1	1	10	Oh! What It Seemed To Be...*Frankie Carle*...Columbia 36892
2	2	9	Oh! What It Seemed To Be...*Frank Sinatra*...Columbia 36905
3	4	4	Prisoner Of Love ....*Perry Como*...RCA Victor 20-1814
4	—	1	I'm A Big Girl Now ....*Sammy Kaye*...RCA Victor 20-1812
5	3	13	Personality..*Johnny Mercer*...Capitol 230
6	5	4	Oh! What It Seemed To Be ....*Charlie Spivak*...RCA Victor 20-1806
7	—	1	One-Zy Two-Zy ....*Phil Harris*...ARA 136
7	9	2	Sioux City Sue ....*Bing Crosby & The Jesters*...Decca 23508
8	7	4	One-Zy, Two-Zy (I Love You-zy) ....*Freddy Martin*...RCA Victor 20-1826
9	7	7	Oh! What It Seemed To Be ....*Dick Haymes & Helen Forrest*...Decca 23481
10	10	2	Hey! Ba-Ba-Re-Bop...*Lionel Hampton*...Decca 18754
10	6	9	You Won't Be Satisfied (Until You Break My Heart) ....*Les Brown*...Columbia 36884

Billboard 🎵 APRIL 27, 1946 🎵 Best Sellers

TW	LW	WK		
1	4	2	I'm A Big Girl Now	Sammy Kaye...RCA Victor 20-1812
2	3	5	Prisoner Of Love	Perry Como...RCA Victor 20-1814
3	1	11	Oh! What It Seemed To Be	Frankie Carle...Columbia 36892
4	2	10	Oh! What It Seemed To Be	Frank Sinatra...Columbia 36905
5	6	5	Oh! What It Seemed To Be	Charlie Spivak...RCA Victor 20-1806
6	8	5	One-Zy, Two-Zy (I Love You-zy)	Freddy Martin...RCA Victor 20-1826
7	7	3	Sioux City Sue	Bing Crosby & The Jesters...Decca 23508
8	—	3	Shoo Fly Pie (And Apple Pan Dowdy)	Stan Kenton...Capitol 235
8	—	1	Laughing On The Outside (Crying On The Inside)	Dinah Shore...Columbia 36964
9	10	3	Hey! Ba-Ba-Re-Bop	Lionel Hampton...Decca 18754
9	9	8	Oh! What It Seemed To Be	Dick Haymes & Helen Forrest...Decca 23481
10	5	14	Personality	Johnny Mercer...Capitol 230

Billboard 🎵 MAY 4, 1946 🎵 Best Sellers

TW	LW	WK		
1	2	6	Prisoner Of Love	Perry Como...RCA Victor 20-1814
2	1	3	I'm A Big Girl Now	Sammy Kaye...RCA Victor 20-1812
3	4	11	Oh! What It Seemed To Be	Frank Sinatra...Columbia 36905
4	3	12	Oh! What It Seemed To Be	Frankie Carle...Columbia 36892
5	8	2	Laughing On The Outside (Crying On The Inside)	Dinah Shore...Columbia 36964
6	7	4	Sioux City Sue	Bing Crosby & The Jesters...Decca 23508
7	—	2	Shoo-Fly Pie And Apple Pan Dowdy	Dinah Shore...Columbia 36943
8	—	1	Bumble Boogie	Freddy Martin...RCA Victor 20-1829
9	9	9	Oh! What It Seemed To Be	Dick Haymes & Helen Forrest...Decca 23481
9	5	6	Oh! What It Seemed To Be	Charlie Spivak...RCA Victor 20-1806
10	6	6	One-Zy, Two-Zy (I Love You-zy)	Freddy Martin...RCA Victor 20-1826

Billboard 🎵 MAY 11, 1946 🎵 Best Sellers

TW	LW	WK		
1	1	7	Prisoner Of Love	Perry Como...RCA Victor 20-1814
2	2	4	I'm A Big Girl Now	Sammy Kaye...RCA Victor 20-1812
3	4	13	Oh! What It Seemed To Be	Frankie Carle...Columbia 36892
4	5	3	Laughing On The Outside (Crying On The Inside)	Dinah Shore...Columbia 36964
5	3	12	Oh! What It Seemed To Be	Frank Sinatra...Columbia 36905
6	—	1	The Gypsy	Ink Spots...Decca 18817
7	8	2	Bumble Boogie	Freddy Martin...RCA Victor 20-1829
7	—	1	Laughing On The Outside (Crying On The Inside)	Andy Russell...Capitol 252
7	9	7	Oh! What It Seemed To Be	Charlie Spivak...RCA Victor 20-1806
8	—	1	The Gypsy	Dinah Shore...Columbia 36964
9	6	5	Sioux City Sue	Bing Crosby & The Jesters...Decca 23508
9	—	4	Shoo Fly Pie (And Apple Pan Dowdy)	Stan Kenton...Capitol 235
10	—	1	Cement Mixer (Put-ti Put-ti)	Alvino Rey...Capitol 248

Billboard 🎵 MAY 18, 1946 🎵 Best Sellers

TW	LW	WK		
1	1	8	Prisoner Of Love	Perry Como...RCA Victor 20-1814
2	6	2	The Gypsy	Ink Spots...Decca 18817
3	4	4	Laughing On The Outside (Crying On The Inside)	Dinah Shore...Columbia 36964
4	7	2	Laughing On The Outside (Crying On The Inside)	Andy Russell...Capitol 252
5	2	5	I'm A Big Girl Now	Sammy Kaye...RCA Victor 20-1812
6	10	2	Cement Mixer (Put-ti Put-ti)	Alvino Rey...Capitol 248
7	3	14	Oh! What It Seemed To Be	Frankie Carle...Columbia 36892
8	8	2	The Gypsy	Dinah Shore...Columbia 36964
9	9	6	Sioux City Sue	Bing Crosby & The Jesters...Decca 23508
10	—	1	The Gypsy	Sammy Kaye...RCA Victor 20-1844

TW	LW	WK	Billboard® ✸ MAY 25, 1946 ✸ Best Sellers
1	2	3	The Gypsy..*Ink Spots*...Decca 18817
2	1	9	Prisoner Of Love ....*Perry Como*...RCA Victor 20-1814
3	3	5	Laughing On The Outside (Crying On The Inside)..*Dinah Shore*...Columbia 36964
4	5	6	I'm A Big Girl Now ....*Sammy Kaye*...RCA Victor 20-1812
5	8	3	The Gypsy..*Dinah Shore*...Columbia 36964
6	6	3	Cement Mixer (Put-ti Put-ti) ....*Alvino Rey*...Capitol 248
7	10	2	The Gypsy..*Sammy Kaye*...RCA Victor 20-1844
8	4	3	Laughing On The Outside (Crying On The Inside) ....*Andy Russell*...Capitol 252
9	—	1	Laughing On The Outside, Crying On The Inside ....*Sammy Kaye*...RCA Victor 20-1856
10	7	15	Oh! What It Seemed To Be ....*Frankie Carle*...Columbia 36892
10	—	1	Hey! Ba-Ba-Re-Bop ....*Tex Beneke/Glenn Miller*...RCA Victor 20-1859

TW	LW	WK	Billboard® ✸ JUNE 1, 1946 ✸ Best Sellers
1	1	4	The Gypsy..*Ink Spots*...Decca 18817
2	2	10	Prisoner Of Love ....*Perry Como*...RCA Victor 20-1814
3	5	4	The Gypsy..*Dinah Shore*...Columbia 36964
4	8	4	Laughing On The Outside (Crying On The Inside) ....*Andy Russell*...Capitol 252
5	10	2	Hey! Ba-Ba-Re-Bop ....*Tex Beneke/Glenn Miller*...RCA Victor 20-1859
6	3	6	Laughing On The Outside (Crying On The Inside)..*Dinah Shore*...Columbia 36964
7	9	2	Laughing On The Outside, Crying On The Inside ....*Sammy Kaye*...RCA Victor 20-1856
8	7	3	The Gypsy..*Sammy Kaye*...RCA Victor 20-1844
9	6	4	Cement Mixer (Put-ti Put-ti) ....*Alvino Rey*...Capitol 248
10	4	7	I'm A Big Girl Now ....*Sammy Kaye*...RCA Victor 20-1812

TW	LW	WK	Billboard® ✸ JUNE 8, 1946 ✸ Best Sellers
1	1	5	The Gypsy..*Ink Spots*...Decca 18817
2	3	5	The Gypsy..*Dinah Shore*...Columbia 36964
3	2	11	Prisoner Of Love ....*Perry Como*...RCA Victor 20-1814
4	4	5	Laughing On The Outside (Crying On The Inside) ....*Andy Russell*...Capitol 252
5	6	7	Laughing On The Outside (Crying On The Inside)..*Dinah Shore*...Columbia 36964
6	8	4	The Gypsy..*Sammy Kaye*...RCA Victor 20-1844
7	5	3	Hey! Ba-Ba-Re-Bop ....*Tex Beneke/Glenn Miller*...RCA Victor 20-1859
8	7	3	Laughing On The Outside, Crying On The Inside ....*Sammy Kaye*...RCA Victor 20-1856
9	9	5	Cement Mixer (Put-ti Put-ti) ....*Alvino Rey*...Capitol 248
10	10	8	I'm A Big Girl Now ....*Sammy Kaye*...RCA Victor 20-1812

TW	LW	WK	Billboard® ✸ JUNE 15, 1946 ✸ Best Sellers
1	1	6	The Gypsy..*Ink Spots*...Decca 18817
2	2	6	The Gypsy..*Dinah Shore*...Columbia 36964
3	3	12	Prisoner Of Love ....*Perry Como*...RCA Victor 20-1814
4	7	4	Hey! Ba-Ba-Re-Bop ....*Tex Beneke/Glenn Miller*...RCA Victor 20-1859
5	4	6	Laughing On The Outside (Crying On The Inside) ....*Andy Russell*...Capitol 252
6	6	5	The Gypsy..*Sammy Kaye*...RCA Victor 20-1844
7	8	4	Laughing On The Outside, Crying On The Inside ....*Sammy Kaye*...RCA Victor 20-1856
8	5	8	Laughing On The Outside (Crying On The Inside)..*Dinah Shore*...Columbia 36964
9	9	6	Cement Mixer (Put-ti Put-ti) ....*Alvino Rey*...Capitol 248
10	10	9	I'm A Big Girl Now ....*Sammy Kaye*...RCA Victor 20-1812

TW	LW	WK	Billboard® ✸ JUNE 22, 1946 ✸ Best Sellers
1	1	7	The Gypsy..*Ink Spots*...Decca 18817
2	3	13	Prisoner Of Love ....*Perry Como*...RCA Victor 20-1814
3	2	7	The Gypsy..*Dinah Shore*...Columbia 36964
4	6	6	The Gypsy..*Sammy Kaye*...RCA Victor 20-1844
5	4	5	Hey! Ba-Ba-Re-Bop ....*Tex Beneke/Glenn Miller*...RCA Victor 20-1859
6	5	7	Laughing On The Outside (Crying On The Inside) ....*Andy Russell*...Capitol 252
7	10	10	I'm A Big Girl Now ....*Sammy Kaye*...RCA Victor 20-1812
8	—	1	Doin' What Comes Natur'lly ....*Dinah Shore with Spade Cooley*...Columbia 36976
9	—	1	They Say It's Wonderful..*Perry Como*...RCA Victor 20-1857
10	8	9	Laughing On The Outside (Crying On The Inside)..*Dinah Shore*...Columbia 36964

TW	LW	WK	Billboard®	🏵	JUNE 29, 1946	🏵	Best Sellers
1	1	8	**The Gypsy**			*Ink Spots*...Decca 18817	
2	2	14	**Prisoner Of Love**			*Perry Como*...RCA Victor 20-1814	
3	3	8	**The Gypsy**			*Dinah Shore*...Columbia 36964	
4	9	2	**They Say It's Wonderful**			*Perry Como*...RCA Victor 20-1857	
5	4	7	**The Gypsy**			*Sammy Kaye*...RCA Victor 20-1844	
6	5	6	**Hey! Ba-Ba-Re-Bop**			*Tex Beneke/Glenn Miller*...RCA Victor 20-1859	
7	8	2	**Doin' What Comes Natur'lly**			*Dinah Shore with Spade Cooley*...Columbia 36976	
8	7	11	**I'm A Big Girl Now**			*Sammy Kaye*...RCA Victor 20-1812	
9	—	1	**They Say It's Wonderful**			*Frank Sinatra*...Columbia 36975	
10	—	1	**Prisoner Of Love**			*Ink Spots*...Decca 18864	

TW	LW	WK	Billboard®	🏵	JULY 6, 1946	🏵	Best Sellers
1	1	9	**The Gypsy**			*Ink Spots*...Decca 18817	
2	3	9	**The Gypsy**			*Dinah Shore*...Columbia 36964	
3	2	15	**Prisoner Of Love**			*Perry Como*...RCA Victor 20-1814	
4	5	8	**The Gypsy**			*Sammy Kaye*...RCA Victor 20-1844	
5	7	3	**Doin' What Comes Natur'lly**			*Dinah Shore with Spade Cooley*...Columbia 36976	
6	6	7	**Hey! Ba-Ba-Re-Bop**			*Tex Beneke/Glenn Miller*...RCA Victor 20-1859	
7	—	1	**Doin' What Comes Natur'lly**			*Freddy Martin*...RCA Victor 20-1878	
8	—	1	**Surrender**			*Perry Como*...RCA Victor 20-1877	
9	4	3	**They Say It's Wonderful**			*Perry Como*...RCA Victor 20-1857	
10	9	2	**They Say It's Wonderful**			*Frank Sinatra*...Columbia 36975	

TW	LW	WK	Billboard®	🏵	JULY 13, 1946	🏵	Best Sellers
1	1	10	**The Gypsy**			*Ink Spots*...Decca 18817	
2	3	16	**Prisoner Of Love**			*Perry Como*...RCA Victor 20-1814	
3	2	10	**The Gypsy**			*Dinah Shore*...Columbia 36964	
4	4	9	**The Gypsy**			*Sammy Kaye*...RCA Victor 20-1844	
5	9	4	**They Say It's Wonderful**			*Perry Como*...RCA Victor 20-1857	
6	8	2	**Surrender**			*Perry Como*...RCA Victor 20-1877	
7	5	4	**Doin' What Comes Natur'lly**			*Dinah Shore with Spade Cooley*...Columbia 36976	
8	6	8	**Hey! Ba-Ba-Re-Bop**			*Tex Beneke/Glenn Miller*...RCA Victor 20-1859	
9	7	2	**Doin' What Comes Natur'lly**			*Freddy Martin*...RCA Victor 20-1878	
10	10	3	**They Say It's Wonderful**			*Frank Sinatra*...Columbia 36975	

TW	LW	WK	Billboard®	🏵	JULY 20, 1946	🏵	Best Sellers
1	1	11	**The Gypsy**			*Ink Spots*...Decca 18817	
2	2	17	**Prisoner Of Love**			*Perry Como*...RCA Victor 20-1814	
3	6	3	**Surrender**			*Perry Como*...RCA Victor 20-1877	
4	7	5	**Doin' What Comes Natur'lly**			*Dinah Shore with Spade Cooley*...Columbia 36976	
5	3	11	**The Gypsy**			*Dinah Shore*...Columbia 36964	
5	5	5	**They Say It's Wonderful**			*Perry Como*...RCA Victor 20-1857	
6	9	3	**Doin' What Comes Natur'lly**			*Freddy Martin*...RCA Victor 20-1878	
7	4	10	**The Gypsy**			*Sammy Kaye*...RCA Victor 20-1844	
8	10	4	**They Say It's Wonderful**			*Frank Sinatra*...Columbia 36975	
9	—	1	**To Each His Own**			*Eddy Howard*...Majestic 7188	
10	8	9	**Hey! Ba-Ba-Re-Bop**			*Tex Beneke/Glenn Miller*...RCA Victor 20-1859	

TW	LW	WK	Billboard®	🏵	JULY 27, 1946	🏵	Best Sellers
1	1	12	**The Gypsy**			*Ink Spots*...Decca 18817	
2	3	4	**Surrender**			*Perry Como*...RCA Victor 20-1877	
3	2	18	**Prisoner Of Love**			*Perry Como*...RCA Victor 20-1814	
4	5	12	**The Gypsy**			*Dinah Shore*...Columbia 36964	
5	6	4	**Doin' What Comes Natur'lly**			*Freddy Martin*...RCA Victor 20-1878	
6	4	6	**Doin' What Comes Natur'lly**			*Dinah Shore with Spade Cooley*...Columbia 36976	
7	9	2	**To Each His Own**			*Eddy Howard*...Majestic 7188	
8	5	6	**They Say It's Wonderful**			*Perry Como*...RCA Victor 20-1857	
9	—	1	**Stone Cold Dead In The Market** (He Had It Coming)			*Ella Fitzgerald & Louis Jordan*...Decca 23546	
10	8	5	**They Say It's Wonderful**			*Frank Sinatra*...Columbia 36975	

TW	LW	WK	Billboard® ✪ AUGUST 3, 1946 ✪ Best Sellers
1	2	5	Surrender ....*Perry Como*...RCA Victor 20-1877
2	1	13	The Gypsy ....*Ink Spots*...Decca 18817
2	7	3	To Each His Own ....*Eddy Howard*...Majestic 7188
3	4	13	The Gypsy ....*Dinah Shore*...Columbia 36964
4	8	7	They Say It's Wonderful ....*Perry Como*...RCA Victor 20-1857
5	6	7	Doin' What Comes Natur'lly ....*Dinah Shore with Spade Cooley*...Columbia 36976
6	5	5	Doin' What Comes Natur'lly ....*Freddy Martin*...RCA Victor 20-1878
7	3	19	Prisoner Of Love ....*Perry Como*...RCA Victor 20-1814
8	—	1	Hawaiian War Chant (Ta-Hu-Wa-Hu-Wai)..*Spike Jones*...RCA Victor 20-1893
9	—	1	South America, Take It Away ....*Bing Crosby & Andrews Sisters*...Decca 23569
10	9	2	Stone Cold Dead In The Market (He Had It Coming) ..*Ella Fitzgerald & Louis Jordan*...Decca 23546

TW	LW	WK	Billboard® ✪ AUGUST 10, 1946 ✪ Best Sellers
1	2	4	To Each His Own ....*Eddy Howard*...Majestic 7188
2	1	6	Surrender ....*Perry Como*...RCA Victor 20-1877
3	2	14	The Gypsy ....*Ink Spots*...Decca 18817
4	6	6	Doin' What Comes Natur'lly ....*Freddy Martin*...RCA Victor 20-1878
5	5	8	Doin' What Comes Natur'lly ....*Dinah Shore with Spade Cooley*...Columbia 36976
6	4	8	They Say It's Wonderful ....*Perry Como*...RCA Victor 20-1857
7	3	14	The Gypsy ....*Dinah Shore*...Columbia 36964
8	9	2	South America, Take It Away ....*Bing Crosby & Andrews Sisters*...Decca 23569
9	—	1	Five Minutes More ....*Frank Sinatra*...Columbia 37048
10	—	6	They Say It's Wonderful ....*Frank Sinatra*...Columbia 36975

TW	LW	WK	Billboard® ✪ AUGUST 17, 1946 ✪ Best Sellers
1	1	5	To Each His Own ....*Eddy Howard*...Majestic 7188
2	2	7	Surrender ....*Perry Como*...RCA Victor 20-1877
3	—	1	To Each His Own ....*Freddy Martin*...RCA Victor 20-1921
4	3	15	The Gypsy ....*Ink Spots*...Decca 18817
5	8	3	South America, Take It Away ....*Bing Crosby & Andrews Sisters*...Decca 23569
6	5	9	Doin' What Comes Natur'lly ....*Dinah Shore with Spade Cooley*...Columbia 36976
7	9	2	Five Minutes More ....*Frank Sinatra*...Columbia 37048
8	—	1	To Each His Own ....*Tony Martin*...Mercury 3022
9	4	7	Doin' What Comes Natur'lly ....*Freddy Martin*...RCA Victor 20-1878
10	7	15	The Gypsy ....*Dinah Shore*...Columbia 36964

TW	LW	WK	Billboard® ✪ AUGUST 24, 1946 ✪ Best Sellers
1	1	6	To Each His Own ....*Eddy Howard*...Majestic 7188
2	3	2	To Each His Own ....*Freddy Martin*...RCA Victor 20-1921
3	2	8	Surrender ....*Perry Como*...RCA Victor 20-1877
4	7	3	Five Minutes More ....*Frank Sinatra*...Columbia 37048
5	4	16	The Gypsy ....*Ink Spots*...Decca 18817
6	5	4	South America, Take It Away ....*Bing Crosby & Andrews Sisters*...Decca 23569
7	—	1	To Each His Own ....*Modernaires with Paula Kelly*...Columbia 37063
8	8	2	To Each His Own ....*Tony Martin*...Mercury 3022
9	9	8	Doin' What Comes Natur'lly ....*Freddy Martin*...RCA Victor 20-1878
10	6	10	Doin' What Comes Natur'lly ....*Dinah Shore with Spade Cooley*...Columbia 36976

TW	LW	WK	Billboard® ✪ AUGUST 31, 1946 ✪ Best Sellers
1	2	3	To Each His Own ....*Freddy Martin*...RCA Victor 20-1921
2	1	7	To Each His Own ....*Eddy Howard*...Majestic 7188
3	4	4	Five Minutes More ....*Frank Sinatra*...Columbia 37048
4	8	3	To Each His Own ....*Tony Martin*...Mercury 3022
5	7	2	To Each His Own ....*Modernaires with Paula Kelly*...Columbia 37063
6	3	9	Surrender ....*Perry Como*...RCA Victor 20-1877
7	6	5	South America, Take It Away ....*Bing Crosby & Andrews Sisters*...Decca 23569
8	5	17	The Gypsy ....*Ink Spots*...Decca 18817
9	10	11	Doin' What Comes Natur'lly ....*Dinah Shore with Spade Cooley*...Columbia 36976
10	—	1	Choo Choo Ch'Boogie ....*Louis Jordan*...Decca 23610

TW	LW	WK	Billboard® ✹ SEPTEMBER 7, 1946 ✹ Best Sellers
1	1	4	To Each His Own ....*Freddy Martin*...RCA Victor 20-1921
2	2	8	To Each His Own ....*Eddy Howard*...Majestic 7188
3	3	5	Five Minutes More ....*Frank Sinatra*...Columbia 37048
4	7	6	South America, Take It Away ....*Bing Crosby & Andrews Sisters*...Decca 23569
5	6	10	Surrender ....*Perry Como*...RCA Victor 20-1877
6	—	1	To Each His Own ....*Ink Spots*...Decca 23615
7	4	4	To Each His Own ....*Tony Martin*...Mercury 3022
8	5	3	To Each His Own ....*Modernaires with Paula Kelly*...Columbia 37063
9	—	1	Give Me Five Minutes More ....*Tex Beneke/Glenn Miller*...RCA Victor 20-1922
10	8	18	The Gypsy ....*Ink Spots*...Decca 18817

TW	LW	WK	Billboard® ✹ SEPTEMBER 14, 1946 ✹ Best Sellers
1	3	6	Five Minutes More ....*Frank Sinatra*...Columbia 37048
2	2	9	To Each His Own ....*Eddy Howard*...Majestic 7188
3	6	2	To Each His Own ....*Ink Spots*...Decca 23615
4	1	5	To Each His Own ....*Freddy Martin*...RCA Victor 20-1921
5	5	11	Surrender ....*Perry Como*...RCA Victor 20-1877
6	4	7	South America, Take It Away ....*Bing Crosby & Andrews Sisters*...Decca 23569
7	7	5	To Each His Own ....*Tony Martin*...Mercury 3022
8	8	4	To Each His Own ....*Modernaires with Paula Kelly*...Columbia 37063
9	9	2	Give Me Five Minutes More ....*Tex Beneke/Glenn Miller*...RCA Victor 20-1922
10	—	2	Choo Choo Ch'Boogie ....*Louis Jordan*...Decca 23610

TW	LW	WK	Billboard® ✹ SEPTEMBER 21, 1946 ✹ Best Sellers
1	3	3	To Each His Own ....*Ink Spots*...Decca 23615
2	1	7	Five Minutes More ....*Frank Sinatra*...Columbia 37048
3	2	10	To Each His Own ....*Eddy Howard*...Majestic 7188
4	4	6	To Each His Own ....*Freddy Martin*...RCA Victor 20-1921
5	6	8	South America, Take It Away ....*Bing Crosby & Andrews Sisters*...Decca 23569
6	5	12	Surrender ....*Perry Como*...RCA Victor 20-1877
7	9	3	Give Me Five Minutes More ....*Tex Beneke/Glenn Miller*...RCA Victor 20-1922
8	7	6	To Each His Own ....*Tony Martin*...Mercury 3022
9	10	3	Choo Choo Ch'Boogie ....*Louis Jordan*...Decca 23610
9	8	5	To Each His Own ....*Modernaires with Paula Kelly*...Columbia 37063
10	—	1	South America, Take It Away! ....*Xavier Cugat*...Columbia 37051

TW	LW	WK	Billboard® ✹ SEPTEMBER 28, 1946 ✹ Best Sellers
1	2	8	Five Minutes More ....*Frank Sinatra*...Columbia 37048
2	1	4	To Each His Own ....*Ink Spots*...Decca 23615
3	3	11	To Each His Own ....*Eddy Howard*...Majestic 7188
4	5	9	South America, Take It Away ....*Bing Crosby & Andrews Sisters*...Decca 23569
5	4	7	To Each His Own ....*Freddy Martin*...RCA Victor 20-1921
6	6	13	Surrender ....*Perry Como*...RCA Victor 20-1877
7	—	1	Rumors Are Flying ....*Frankie Carle*...Columbia 37069
8	8	7	To Each His Own ....*Tony Martin*...Mercury 3022
9	7	4	Give Me Five Minutes More ....*Tex Beneke/Glenn Miller*...RCA Victor 20-1922
10	9	4	Choo Choo Ch'Boogie ....*Louis Jordan*...Decca 23610

TW	LW	WK	Billboard® ✹ OCTOBER 5, 1946 ✹ Best Sellers
1	3	12	To Each His Own ....*Eddy Howard*...Majestic 7188
2	1	9	Five Minutes More ....*Frank Sinatra*...Columbia 37048
3	4	10	South America, Take It Away ....*Bing Crosby & Andrews Sisters*...Decca 23569
4	7	2	Rumors Are Flying ....*Frankie Carle*...Columbia 37069
5	5	8	To Each His Own ....*Freddy Martin*...RCA Victor 20-1921
6	9	5	Give Me Five Minutes More ....*Tex Beneke/Glenn Miller*...RCA Victor 20-1922
7	2	5	To Each His Own ....*Ink Spots*...Decca 23615
8	6	14	Surrender ....*Perry Como*...RCA Victor 20-1877
9	8	8	To Each His Own ....*Tony Martin*...Mercury 3022
10	—	2	South America, Take It Away! ....*Xavier Cugat*...Columbia 37051

TW	LW	WK	**Billboard** ❊ OCTOBER 12, 1946 ❊	**Best Sellers**
1	1	13	**To Each His Own**..*Eddy Howard*...Majestic 7188
2	4	3	**Rumors Are Flying**..*Frankie Carle*...Columbia 37069
3	2	10	**Five Minutes More**...*Frank Sinatra*...Columbia 37048
4	3	11	**South America, Take It Away**..................................*Bing Crosby & Andrews Sisters*...Decca 23569
5	7	6	**To Each His Own**..*Ink Spots*...Decca 23615
6	5	9	**To Each His Own**...*Freddy Martin*...RCA Victor 20-1921
7	6	6	**Give Me Five Minutes More**....................................*Tex Beneke/Glenn Miller*...RCA Victor 20-1922
8	—	5	**Choo Choo Ch'Boogie**..*Louis Jordan*...Decca 23610
9	9	9	**To Each His Own**...*Tony Martin*...Mercury 3022
9	8	15	**Surrender**...*Perry Como*...RCA Victor 20-1877
10	—	1	**Pretending**..*Andy Russell*...Capitol 271

TW	LW	WK	**Billboard** ❊ OCTOBER 19, 1946 ❊	**Best Sellers**
1	2	4	**Rumors Are Flying**..*Frankie Carle*...Columbia 37069
2	1	14	**To Each His Own**..*Eddy Howard*...Majestic 7188
3	4	12	**South America, Take It Away**..................................*Bing Crosby & Andrews Sisters*...Decca 23569
4	3	11	**Five Minutes More**...*Frank Sinatra*...Columbia 37048
5	5	7	**To Each His Own**..*Ink Spots*...Decca 23615
6	6	10	**To Each His Own**...*Freddy Martin*...RCA Victor 20-1921
7	7	7	**Give Me Five Minutes More**....................................*Tex Beneke/Glenn Miller*...RCA Victor 20-1922
8	9	10	**To Each His Own**...*Tony Martin*...Mercury 3022
9	—	6	**To Each His Own**...*Modernaires with Paula Kelly*...Columbia 37063
10	9	16	**Surrender**...*Perry Como*...RCA Victor 20-1877

TW	LW	WK	**Billboard** ❊ OCTOBER 26, 1946 ❊	**Best Sellers**
1	1	5	**Rumors Are Flying**..*Frankie Carle*...Columbia 37069
2	2	15	**To Each His Own**..*Eddy Howard*...Majestic 7188
3	3	13	**South America, Take It Away**..................................*Bing Crosby & Andrews Sisters*...Decca 23569
4	4	12	**Five Minutes More**...*Frank Sinatra*...Columbia 37048
5	5	8	**To Each His Own**..*Ink Spots*...Decca 23615
6	6	11	**To Each His Own**...*Freddy Martin*...RCA Victor 20-1921
7	7	8	**Give Me Five Minutes More**....................................*Tex Beneke/Glenn Miller*...RCA Victor 20-1922
8	8	11	**To Each His Own**...*Tony Martin*...Mercury 3022
9	—	1	**Rumors Are Flying**...*Andrews Sisters with Les Paul*...Decca 23656
10	—	1	**The Coffee Song (They've Got An Awful Lot Of Coffee In Brazil)**....*Frank Sinatra*...Columbia 37089

TW	LW	WK	**Billboard** ❊ NOVEMBER 2, 1946 ❊	**Best Sellers**
1	1	6	**Rumors Are Flying**..*Frankie Carle*...Columbia 37069
2	3	14	**South America, Take It Away**..................................*Bing Crosby & Andrews Sisters*...Decca 23569
3	2	16	**To Each His Own**..*Eddy Howard*...Majestic 7188
4	4	13	**Five Minutes More**...*Frank Sinatra*...Columbia 37048
5	—	1	**Ole Buttermilk Sky**...*Kay Kyser*...Columbia 37073
6	7	9	**Give Me Five Minutes More**....................................*Tex Beneke/Glenn Miller*...RCA Victor 20-1922
7	5	9	**To Each His Own**..*Ink Spots*...Decca 23615
8	6	12	**To Each His Own**...*Freddy Martin*...RCA Victor 20-1921
9	—	1	**Rumors Are Flying**...*Tony Martin*...Mercury 3032
10	9	2	**Rumors Are Flying**...*Andrews Sisters with Les Paul*...Decca 23656
10	8	12	**To Each His Own**...*Tony Martin*...Mercury 3022

TW	LW	WK	Billboard® ❀ NOVEMBER 9, 1946 ❀ Best Sellers
1	1	7	**Rumors Are Flying** ....*Frankie Carle*...Columbia 37069
2	4	14	**Five Minutes More** ....*Frank Sinatra*...Columbia 37048
3	5	2	**Ole Buttermilk Sky** ....*Kay Kyser*...Columbia 37073
4	3	17	**To Each His Own** ....*Eddy Howard*...Majestic 7188
5	2	15	**South America, Take It Away** ....*Bing Crosby & Andrews Sisters*...Decca 23569
6	7	10	**To Each His Own** ....*Ink Spots*...Decca 23615
7	6	10	**Give Me Five Minutes More** ....*Tex Beneke/Glenn Miller*...RCA Victor 20-1922
8	10	3	**Rumors Are Flying** ....*Andrews Sisters with Les Paul*...Decca 23656
9	9	2	**Rumors Are Flying** ....*Tony Martin*...Mercury 3032
9	—	3	**South America, Take It Away!** ....*Xavier Cugat*...Columbia 37051
10	—	1	**Rumors Are Flying** ....*Betty Rhodes*...RCA Victor 20-1944

TW	LW	WK	Billboard® ❀ NOVEMBER 16, 1946 ❀ Best Sellers
1	1	8	**Rumors Are Flying** ....*Frankie Carle*...Columbia 37069
2	2	15	**Five Minutes More** ....*Frank Sinatra*...Columbia 37048
2	3	3	**Ole Buttermilk Sky** ....*Kay Kyser*...Columbia 37073
3	5	16	**South America, Take It Away** ....*Bing Crosby & Andrews Sisters*...Decca 23569
4	4	18	**To Each His Own** ....*Eddy Howard*...Majestic 7188
5	—	1	**The Old Lamp-Lighter** ....*Sammy Kaye*...RCA Victor 20-1963
6	8	4	**Rumors Are Flying** ....*Andrews Sisters with Les Paul*...Decca 23656
7	6	11	**To Each His Own** ....*Ink Spots*...Decca 23615
8	10	2	**Rumors Are Flying** ....*Betty Rhodes*...RCA Victor 20-1944
9	—	1	**Ole Buttermilk Sky** ....*Paul Weston With Matt Dennis*...Capitol 285
9	9	3	**Rumors Are Flying** ....*Tony Martin*...Mercury 3032
10	7	11	**Give Me Five Minutes More** ....*Tex Beneke/Glenn Miller*...RCA Victor 20-1922

TW	LW	WK	Billboard® ❀ NOVEMBER 23, 1946 ❀ Best Sellers
1	1	9	**Rumors Are Flying** ....*Frankie Carle*...Columbia 37069
2	5	2	**The Old Lamp-Lighter** ....*Sammy Kaye*...RCA Victor 20-1963
3	2	4	**Ole Buttermilk Sky** ....*Kay Kyser*...Columbia 37073
4	2	16	**Five Minutes More** ....*Frank Sinatra*...Columbia 37048
5	8	3	**Rumors Are Flying** ....*Betty Rhodes*...RCA Victor 20-1944
6	6	5	**Rumors Are Flying** ....*Andrews Sisters with Les Paul*...Decca 23656
7	—	1	**Ole Buttermilk Sky** ....*Helen Carroll & The Satisfiers*...RCA Victor 20-1982
8	10	12	**Give Me Five Minutes More** ....*Tex Beneke/Glenn Miller*...RCA Victor 20-1922
9	4	19	**To Each His Own** ....*Eddy Howard*...Majestic 7188
10	3	17	**South America, Take It Away** ....*Bing Crosby & Andrews Sisters*...Decca 23569

TW	LW	WK	Billboard® ❀ NOVEMBER 30, 1946 ❀ Best Sellers
1	1	10	**Rumors Are Flying** ....*Frankie Carle*...Columbia 37069
2	2	3	**The Old Lamp-Lighter** ....*Sammy Kaye*...RCA Victor 20-1963
3	3	5	**Ole Buttermilk Sky** ....*Kay Kyser*...Columbia 37073
4	4	17	**Five Minutes More** ....*Frank Sinatra*...Columbia 37048
5	5	4	**Rumors Are Flying** ....*Betty Rhodes*...RCA Victor 20-1944
6	6	6	**Rumors Are Flying** ....*Andrews Sisters with Les Paul*...Decca 23656
7	—	1	**The Old Lamp-Lighter** ....*Kay Kyser*...Columbia 37095
8	—	1	**(I Love You) For Sentimental Reasons** ....*The King Cole Trio*...Capitol 304
9	7	2	**Ole Buttermilk Sky** ....*Helen Carroll & The Satisfiers*...RCA Victor 20-1982
10	—	1	**Ole Buttermilk Sky** ....*Hoagy Carmichael*...ARA 155

TW	LW	WK	Billboard® ✹ DECEMBER 7, 1946 ✹ Best Sellers
1	1	11	Rumors Are Flying ....*Frankie Carle*...Columbia 37069
2	2	4	The Old Lamp-Lighter ....*Sammy Kaye*...RCA Victor 20-1963
3	3	6	Ole Buttermilk Sky ....*Kay Kyser*...Columbia 37073
4	7	2	The Old Lamp-Lighter ....*Kay Kyser*...Columbia 37095
5	4	18	Five Minutes More ....*Frank Sinatra*...Columbia 37048
6	6	7	Rumors Are Flying ....*Andrews Sisters with Les Paul*...Decca 23656
7	9	3	Ole Buttermilk Sky ....*Helen Carroll & The Satisfiers*...RCA Victor 20-1982
8	5	5	Rumors Are Flying ....*Betty Rhodes*...RCA Victor 20-1944
9	—	2	Ole Buttermilk Sky ....*Paul Weston With Matt Dennis*...Capitol 285
10	—	1	Huggin' And Chalkin' ....*Hoagy Carmichael*...Decca 23675

TW	LW	WK	Billboard® ✹ DECEMBER 14, 1946 ✹ Best Sellers
1	3	7	Ole Buttermilk Sky ....*Kay Kyser*...Columbia 37073
2	2	5	The Old Lamp-Lighter ....*Sammy Kaye*...RCA Victor 20-1963
3	1	12	Rumors Are Flying ....*Frankie Carle*...Columbia 37069
4	4	3	The Old Lamp-Lighter ....*Kay Kyser*...Columbia 37095
5	—	2	(I Love You) For Sentimental Reasons...*The King Cole Trio*...Capitol 304
6	—	1	The Old Lamplighter ....*Hal Derwin*...Capitol 288
7	10	2	Huggin' And Chalkin' ....*Hoagy Carmichael*...Decca 23675
8	7	4	Ole Buttermilk Sky ....*Helen Carroll & The Satisfiers*...RCA Victor 20-1982
9	9	3	Ole Buttermilk Sky ....*Paul Weston With Matt Dennis*...Capitol 285
10	—	1	The Christmas Song (Merry Christmas To You) ....*The King Cole Trio*...Capitol 311

TW	LW	WK	Billboard® ✹ DECEMBER 21, 1946 ✹ Best Sellers
1	1	8	Ole Buttermilk Sky ....*Kay Kyser*...Columbia 37073
2	2	6	The Old Lamp-Lighter ....*Sammy Kaye*...RCA Victor 20-1963
3	4	4	The Old Lamp-Lighter ....*Kay Kyser*...Columbia 37095
4	3	13	Rumors Are Flying ....*Frankie Carle*...Columbia 37069
5	5	3	(I Love You) For Sentimental Reasons...*The King Cole Trio*...Capitol 304
6	7	3	Huggin' And Chalkin' ....*Hoagy Carmichael*...Decca 23675
7	—	1	White Christmas ....*Bing Crosby*...Decca 23778
8	—	2	Ole Buttermilk Sky ....*Hoagy Carmichael*...ARA 155
9	—	6	Rumors Are Flying ....*Betty Rhodes*...RCA Victor 20-1944
10	—	8	Rumors Are Flying ....*Andrews Sisters with Les Paul*...Decca 23656

TW	LW	WK	Billboard® ✹ DECEMBER 28, 1946 ✹ Best Sellers
1	2	7	The Old Lamp-Lighter ....*Sammy Kaye*...RCA Victor 20-1963
2	7	2	White Christmas ....*Bing Crosby*...Decca 23778
3	1	9	Ole Buttermilk Sky ....*Kay Kyser*...Columbia 37073
4	3	5	The Old Lamp-Lighter ....*Kay Kyser*...Columbia 37095
5	6	4	Huggin' And Chalkin' ....*Hoagy Carmichael*...Decca 23675
6	8	3	Ole Buttermilk Sky ....*Hoagy Carmichael*...ARA 155
7	—	2	The Christmas Song (Merry Christmas To You) ....*The King Cole Trio*...Capitol 311
8	5	4	(I Love You) For Sentimental Reasons...*The King Cole Trio*...Capitol 304
9	4	14	Rumors Are Flying ....*Frankie Carle*...Columbia 37069
10	—	1	Winter Wonderland ....*Perry Como*...RCA Victor 20-1968

Billboard ✪ JANUARY 4, 1947 ✪ Best Sellers

TW	LW	WK		
1	1	8	The Old Lamp-Lighter	Sammy Kaye...RCA Victor 20-1963
2	2	3	White Christmas	Bing Crosby...Decca 23778
3	6	4	Ole Buttermilk Sky	Hoagy Carmichael...ARA 155
4	3	10	Ole Buttermilk Sky	Kay Kyser...Columbia 37073
5	4	6	The Old Lamp-Lighter	Kay Kyser...Columbia 37095
6	8	5	(I Love You) For Sentimental Reasons	The King Cole Trio...Capitol 304
7	5	5	Huggin' And Chalkin'	Hoagy Carmichael...Decca 23675
8	—	1	White Christmas	Frank Sinatra...Columbia 37152
9	9	15	Rumors Are Flying	Frankie Carle...Columbia 37069
10	—	4	Ole Buttermilk Sky	Paul Weston With Matt Dennis...Capitol 285

Billboard ✪ JANUARY 11, 1947 ✪ Best Sellers

TW	LW	WK		
1	1	9	The Old Lamp-Lighter	Sammy Kaye...RCA Victor 20-1963
2	3	5	Ole Buttermilk Sky	Hoagy Carmichael...ARA 155
3	7	6	Huggin' And Chalkin'	Hoagy Carmichael...Decca 23675
4	4	11	Ole Buttermilk Sky	Kay Kyser...Columbia 37073
5	6	6	(I Love You) For Sentimental Reasons	The King Cole Trio...Capitol 304
6	5	7	The Old Lamp-Lighter	Kay Kyser...Columbia 37095
7	2	4	White Christmas	Bing Crosby...Decca 23778
8	9	16	Rumors Are Flying	Frankie Carle...Columbia 37069
9	—	1	A Gal In Calico	Tex Beneke/Glenn Miller...RCA Victor 20-1991
10	10	5	Ole Buttermilk Sky	Paul Weston With Matt Dennis...Capitol 285

Billboard ✪ JANUARY 18, 1947 ✪ Best Sellers

TW	LW	WK		
1	1	10	The Old Lamp-Lighter	Sammy Kaye...RCA Victor 20-1963
2	2	6	Ole Buttermilk Sky	Hoagy Carmichael...ARA 155
3	3	7	Huggin' And Chalkin'	Hoagy Carmichael...Decca 23675
4	5	7	(I Love You) For Sentimental Reasons	The King Cole Trio...Capitol 304
5	6	8	The Old Lamp-Lighter	Kay Kyser...Columbia 37095
6	9	2	A Gal In Calico	Tex Beneke/Glenn Miller...RCA Victor 20-1991
7	—	1	(I Love You) For Sentimental Reasons	Charlie Spivak...RCA Victor 20-1981
7	4	12	Ole Buttermilk Sky	Kay Kyser...Columbia 37073
8	—	1	(I Love You) For Sentimental Reasons	Eddy Howard...Majestic 7204
9	—	1	A Gal In Calico	Bing Crosby with The Calico Kids...Decca 23739
10	—	1	(I Love You) For Sentimental Reasons	Dinah Shore...Columbia 37188

Billboard ✪ JANUARY 25, 1947 ✪ Best Sellers

TW	LW	WK		
1	1	11	The Old Lamp-Lighter	Sammy Kaye...RCA Victor 20-1963
2	2	7	Ole Buttermilk Sky	Hoagy Carmichael...ARA 155
3	3	8	Huggin' And Chalkin'	Hoagy Carmichael...Decca 23675
4	4	8	(I Love You) For Sentimental Reasons	The King Cole Trio...Capitol 304
5	5	9	The Old Lamp-Lighter	Kay Kyser...Columbia 37095
6	8	2	(I Love You) For Sentimental Reasons	Eddy Howard...Majestic 7204
7	6	3	A Gal In Calico	Tex Beneke/Glenn Miller...RCA Victor 20-1991
8	7	13	Ole Buttermilk Sky	Kay Kyser...Columbia 37073
9	7	2	(I Love You) For Sentimental Reasons	Charlie Spivak...RCA Victor 20-1981
10	—	2	The Old Lamplighter	Hal Derwin...Capitol 288

Billboard ✪ FEBRUARY 1, 1947 ✪ Best Sellers

TW	LW	WK		
1	1	12	The Old Lamp-Lighter	Sammy Kaye...RCA Victor 20-1963
2	2	8	Ole Buttermilk Sky	Hoagy Carmichael...ARA 155
3	4	9	(I Love You) For Sentimental Reasons	The King Cole Trio...Capitol 304
4	3	9	Huggin' And Chalkin'	Hoagy Carmichael...Decca 23675
5	5	10	The Old Lamp-Lighter	Kay Kyser...Columbia 37095
6	6	3	(I Love You) For Sentimental Reasons	Eddy Howard...Majestic 7204
7	9	3	(I Love You) For Sentimental Reasons	Charlie Spivak...RCA Victor 20-1981
8	7	4	A Gal In Calico	Tex Beneke/Glenn Miller...RCA Victor 20-1991
9	—	2	(I Love You) For Sentimental Reasons	Dinah Shore...Columbia 37188
10	—	2	A Gal In Calico	Bing Crosby with The Calico Kids...Decca 23739

TW	LW	WK	Billboard ❄ FEBRUARY 8, 1947 ❄ Best Sellers
1	1	13	The Old Lamp-Lighter..Sammy Kaye...RCA Victor 20-1963
2	4	10	Huggin' And Chalkin'...Hoagy Carmichael...Decca 23675
3	2	9	Ole Buttermilk Sky..Hoagy Carmichael...ARA 155
4	3	10	(I Love You) For Sentimental Reasons....................................The King Cole Trio...Capitol 304
5	5	11	The Old Lamp-Lighter..Kay Kyser...Columbia 37095
6	9	3	(I Love You) For Sentimental Reasons....................................Dinah Shore...Columbia 37188
7	—	1	Managua, Nicaragua..Freddy Martin...RCA Victor 20-2026
8	6	4	(I Love You) For Sentimental Reasons....................................Eddy Howard...Majestic 7204
9	7	4	(I Love You) For Sentimental Reasons....................................Charlie Spivak...RCA Victor 20-1981
10	—	1	Open The Door, Richard! (Parts 1 & 2)...................................."Dusty" Fletcher...National 4012

TW	LW	WK	Billboard ❄ FEBRUARY 15, 1947 ❄ Best Sellers
1	4	11	(I Love You) For Sentimental Reasons....................................The King Cole Trio...Capitol 304
2	1	14	The Old Lamp-Lighter..Sammy Kaye...RCA Victor 20-1963
3	—	1	Open The Door, Richard!..Count Basie...RCA Victor 20-2127
4	7	2	Managua, Nicaragua..Freddy Martin...RCA Victor 20-2026
5	2	11	Huggin' And Chalkin'...Hoagy Carmichael...Decca 23675
6	3	10	Ole Buttermilk Sky..Hoagy Carmichael...ARA 155
7	10	2	Open The Door, Richard! (Parts 1 & 2)...................................."Dusty" Fletcher...National 4012
8	8	5	(I Love You) For Sentimental Reasons....................................Eddy Howard...Majestic 7204
9	6	4	(I Love You) For Sentimental Reasons....................................Dinah Shore...Columbia 37188
10	—	1	Anniversary Song..Al Jolson...Decca 23714

TW	LW	WK	Billboard ❄ FEBRUARY 22, 1947 ❄ Best Sellers
1	3	2	Open The Door, Richard!..Count Basie...RCA Victor 20-2127
2	4	3	Managua, Nicaragua..Freddy Martin...RCA Victor 20-2026
3	7	3	Open The Door, Richard! (Parts 1 & 2)...................................."Dusty" Fletcher...National 4012
4	1	12	(I Love You) For Sentimental Reasons....................................The King Cole Trio...Capitol 304
5	5	12	Huggin' And Chalkin'...Hoagy Carmichael...Decca 23675
6	—	1	Anniversary Song..Guy Lombardo...Decca 23799
7	—	1	Open The Door, Richard..The Three Flames...Columbia 37268
8	—	1	Managua - Nicaragua..Guy Lombardo...Decca 23782
9	—	1	Open The Door Richard!..Jack McVea...Black & White 792
10	10	2	Anniversary Song..Al Jolson...Decca 23714

TW	LW	WK	Billboard ❄ MARCH 1, 1947 ❄ Best Sellers
1	2	4	Managua, Nicaragua..Freddy Martin...RCA Victor 20-2026
2	1	3	Open The Door, Richard!..Count Basie...RCA Victor 20-2127
3	10	3	Anniversary Song..Al Jolson...Decca 23714
4	7	2	Open The Door, Richard..The Three Flames...Columbia 37268
5	3	4	Open The Door, Richard! (Parts 1 & 2)...................................."Dusty" Fletcher...National 4012
6	6	2	Anniversary Song..Guy Lombardo...Decca 23799
7	9	2	Open The Door Richard!..Jack McVea...Black & White 792
8	8	2	Managua - Nicaragua..Guy Lombardo...Decca 23782
9	5	13	Huggin' And Chalkin'...Hoagy Carmichael...Decca 23675
10	—	1	Anniversary Song..Tex Beneke/Glenn Miller...RCA Victor 20-2126

TW	LW	WK	Billboard ❄ MARCH 8, 1947 ❄ Best Sellers
1	1	5	Managua, Nicaragua..Freddy Martin...RCA Victor 20-2026
2	3	4	Anniversary Song..Al Jolson...Decca 23714
3	10	2	Anniversary Song..Tex Beneke/Glenn Miller...RCA Victor 20-2126
4	2	4	Open The Door, Richard!..Count Basie...RCA Victor 20-2127
5	6	3	Anniversary Song..Guy Lombardo...Decca 23799
6	—	1	Heartaches..Ted Weems...Decca 25017
7	—	1	Anniversary Song..Dinah Shore...Columbia 37234
8	5	5	Open The Door, Richard! (Parts 1 & 2)...................................."Dusty" Fletcher...National 4012
9	4	3	Open The Door, Richard..The Three Flames...Columbia 37268
10	8	3	Managua - Nicaragua..Guy Lombardo...Decca 23782

TW	LW	WK	Billboard ❋ MARCH 15, 1947 ❋ Best Sellers
1	6	2	Heartaches ....*Ted Weems*...Decca 25017
2	2	5	Anniversary Song ....*Al Jolson*...Decca 23714
3	1	6	Managua, Nicaragua...*Freddy Martin*...RCA Victor 20-2026
4	5	4	Anniversary Song ....*Guy Lombardo*...Decca 23799
5	7	2	Anniversary Song ....*Dinah Shore*...Columbia 37234
6	3	3	Anniversary Song ....*Tex Beneke/Glenn Miller*...RCA Victor 20-2126
7	—	1	Open The Door, Richard! ....*Louis Jordan*...Decca 23841
8	10	4	Managua - Nicaragua ....*Guy Lombardo*...Decca 23782
9	—	1	Managua, Nicaragua (Manag-wa, Nicarag-wa) ....*Kay Kyser*...Columbia 37214
10	—	1	Guilty...*Margaret Whiting*...Capitol 324

TW	LW	WK	Billboard ❋ MARCH 22, 1947 ❋ Best Sellers
1	1	3	Heartaches ....*Ted Weems*...Decca 25017
2	2	6	Anniversary Song ....*Al Jolson*...Decca 23714
3	3	7	Managua, Nicaragua...*Freddy Martin*...RCA Victor 20-2026
4	5	3	Anniversary Song ....*Dinah Shore*...Columbia 37234
5	8	5	Managua - Nicaragua ....*Guy Lombardo*...Decca 23782
6	4	5	Anniversary Song ....*Guy Lombardo*...Decca 23799
7	—	1	Anniversary Song ....*Andy Russell*...Capitol 368
8	6	4	Anniversary Song ....*Tex Beneke/Glenn Miller*...RCA Victor 20-2126
9	9	2	Managua, Nicaragua (Manag-wa, Nicarag-wa) ....*Kay Kyser*...Columbia 37214
10	7	2	Open The Door, Richard! ....*Louis Jordan*...Decca 23841

TW	LW	WK	Billboard ❋ MARCH 29, 1947 ❋ Best Sellers
1	1	4	Heartaches ....*Ted Weems*...Decca 25017
2	2	7	Anniversary Song ....*Al Jolson*...Decca 23714
3	3	8	Managua, Nicaragua...*Freddy Martin*...RCA Victor 20-2026
4	4	4	Anniversary Song ....*Dinah Shore*...Columbia 37234
5	8	5	Anniversary Song ....*Tex Beneke/Glenn Miller*...RCA Victor 20-2126
6	—	2	Guilty...*Margaret Whiting*...Capitol 324
7	—	1	Linda...*Ray Noble with Buddy Clark*...Columbia 37215
8	6	6	Anniversary Song ....*Guy Lombardo*...Decca 23799
9	—	1	How Are Things In Glocca Morra ....*Dick Haymes*...Decca 23830
10	5	6	Managua - Nicaragua ....*Guy Lombardo*...Decca 23782

TW	LW	WK	Billboard ❋ APRIL 5, 1947 ❋ Best Sellers
1	1	5	Heartaches ....*Ted Weems*...Decca 25017
2	2	8	Anniversary Song ....*Al Jolson*...Decca 23714
3	7	2	Linda...*Ray Noble with Buddy Clark*...Columbia 37215
4	10	7	Managua - Nicaragua ....*Guy Lombardo*...Decca 23782
5	3	9	Managua, Nicaragua...*Freddy Martin*...RCA Victor 20-2026
5	—	2	Anniversary Song ....*Andy Russell*...Capitol 368
6	6	3	Guilty...*Margaret Whiting*...Capitol 324
7	4	5	Anniversary Song ....*Dinah Shore*...Columbia 37234
8	8	7	Anniversary Song ....*Guy Lombardo*...Decca 23799
9	5	6	Anniversary Song ....*Tex Beneke/Glenn Miller*...RCA Victor 20-2126
10	—	1	Linda...*Charlie Spivak*...RCA Victor 20-2047

TW	LW	WK	Billboard ❋ APRIL 12, 1947 ❋ Best Sellers
1	1	6	Heartaches ....*Ted Weems*...Decca 25017
2	2	9	Anniversary Song ....*Al Jolson*...Decca 23714
3	3	3	Linda...*Ray Noble with Buddy Clark*...Columbia 37215
4	4	8	Managua - Nicaragua ....*Guy Lombardo*...Decca 23782
5	5	10	Managua, Nicaragua...*Freddy Martin*...RCA Victor 20-2026
6	—	1	My Adobe Hacienda ....*Eddy Howard*...Majestic 1117
7	7	6	Anniversary Song ....*Dinah Shore*...Columbia 37234
8	8	8	Anniversary Song ....*Guy Lombardo*...Decca 23799
9	9	7	Anniversary Song ....*Tex Beneke/Glenn Miller*...RCA Victor 20-2126
10	10	2	Linda...*Charlie Spivak*...RCA Victor 20-2047

TW	LW	WK	Billboard ✿ APRIL 19, 1947 ✿ Best Sellers
1	1	7	Heartaches ....*Ted Weems*...Decca 25017
2	3	4	Linda ....*Ray Noble with Buddy Clark*...Columbia 37215
3	2	10	Anniversary Song ....*Al Jolson*...Decca 23714
4	6	2	My Adobe Hacienda ....*Eddy Howard*...Majestic 1117
5	7	7	Anniversary Song ....*Dinah Shore*...Columbia 37234
6	5	11	Managua, Nicaragua ....*Freddy Martin*...RCA Victor 20-2026
7	10	3	Linda ....*Charlie Spivak*...RCA Victor 20-2047
8	8	9	Anniversary Song ....*Guy Lombardo*...Decca 23799
9	—	1	Mam'selle ....*Art Lund*...MGM 10011
10	4	9	Managua - Nicaragua ....*Guy Lombardo*...Decca 23782

TW	LW	WK	Billboard ✿ APRIL 26, 1947 ✿ Best Sellers
1	1	8	Heartaches ....*Ted Weems*...Decca 25017
2	2	5	Linda ....*Ray Noble with Buddy Clark*...Columbia 37215
3	3	11	Anniversary Song ....*Al Jolson*...Decca 23714
4	9	2	Mam'selle ....*Art Lund*...MGM 10011
5	4	3	My Adobe Hacienda ....*Eddy Howard*...Majestic 1117
6	7	4	Linda ....*Charlie Spivak*...RCA Victor 20-2047
7	—	1	Peg O' My Heart ....*The Harmonicats*...Vitacoustic 1
8	—	1	Heartaches ....*Harry James*...Columbia 37305
9	—	8	Anniversary Song ....*Tex Beneke/Glenn Miller*...RCA Victor 20-2126
10	8	10	Anniversary Song ....*Guy Lombardo*...Decca 23799

TW	LW	WK	Billboard ✿ MAY 3, 1947 ✿ Best Sellers
1	1	9	Heartaches ....*Ted Weems*...Decca 25017
2	2	6	Linda ....*Ray Noble with Buddy Clark*...Columbia 37215
3	4	3	Mam'selle ....*Art Lund*...MGM 10011
4	3	12	Anniversary Song ....*Al Jolson*...Decca 23714
5	5	4	My Adobe Hacienda ....*Eddy Howard*...Majestic 1117
6	—	1	Mam'selle ....*Dick Haymes*...Decca 23861
7	6	5	Linda ....*Charlie Spivak*...RCA Victor 20-2047
8	8	2	Heartaches ....*Harry James*...Columbia 37305
9	—	1	Mam'selle ....*Dennis Day*...RCA Victor 20-2211
10	—	8	Anniversary Song ....*Dinah Shore*...Columbia 37234

TW	LW	WK	Billboard ✿ MAY 10, 1947 ✿ Best Sellers
1	1	10	Heartaches ....*Ted Weems*...Decca 25017
2	2	7	Linda ....*Ray Noble with Buddy Clark*...Columbia 37215
3	3	4	Mam'selle ....*Art Lund*...MGM 10011
4	6	2	Mam'selle ....*Dick Haymes*...Decca 23861
5	5	5	My Adobe Hacienda ....*Eddy Howard*...Majestic 1117
6	4	13	Anniversary Song ....*Al Jolson*...Decca 23714
7	7	6	Linda ....*Charlie Spivak*...RCA Victor 20-2047
8	8	3	Heartaches ....*Harry James*...Columbia 37305
9	9	2	Mam'selle ....*Dennis Day*...RCA Victor 20-2211
10	—	1	Mam'selle ....*The Pied Pipers*...Capitol 396

TW	LW	WK	Billboard ✿ MAY 17, 1947 ✿ Best Sellers
1	1	11	Heartaches ....*Ted Weems*...Decca 25017
2	3	5	Mam'selle ....*Art Lund*...MGM 10011
3	2	8	Linda ....*Ray Noble with Buddy Clark*...Columbia 37215
4	4	3	Mam'selle ....*Dick Haymes*...Decca 23861
5	5	6	My Adobe Hacienda ....*Eddy Howard*...Majestic 1117
6	7	7	Linda ....*Charlie Spivak*...RCA Victor 20-2047
7	—	1	Mam'selle ....*Frank Sinatra*...Columbia 37343
8	9	3	Mam'selle ....*Dennis Day*...RCA Victor 20-2211
9	10	2	Mam'selle ....*The Pied Pipers*...Capitol 396
10	6	14	Anniversary Song ....*Al Jolson*...Decca 23714

Billboard ☢ MAY 24, 1947 ☢ Best Sellers

TW	LW	WK	Title	Artist
1	1	12	Heartaches	Ted Weems...Decca 25017
2	2	6	Mam'selle	Art Lund...MGM 10011
3	3	9	Linda	Ray Noble with Buddy Clark...Columbia 37215
4	4	4	Mam'selle	Dick Haymes...Decca 23861
5	5	7	My Adobe Hacienda	Eddy Howard...Majestic 1117
6	6	8	Linda	Charlie Spivak...RCA Victor 20-2047
7	—	2	Peg O' My Heart	The Harmonicats...Vitacoustic 1
8	8	4	Mam'selle	Dennis Day...RCA Victor 20-2211
9	—	1	Across The Alley From The Alamo	Mills Brothers...Decca 23863
10	9	3	Mam'selle	The Pied Pipers...Capitol 396

Billboard ☢ MAY 31, 1947 ☢ Best Sellers

TW	LW	WK	Title	Artist
1	1	13	Heartaches	Ted Weems...Decca 25017
2	3	10	Linda	Ray Noble with Buddy Clark...Columbia 37215
3	2	7	Mam'selle	Art Lund...MGM 10011
4	4	5	Mam'selle	Dick Haymes...Decca 23861
5	5	8	My Adobe Hacienda	Eddy Howard...Majestic 1117
6	—	2	Mam'selle	Frank Sinatra...Columbia 37343
7	7	3	Peg O' My Heart	The Harmonicats...Vitacoustic 1
8	9	2	Across The Alley From The Alamo	Mills Brothers...Decca 23863
9	6	9	Linda	Charlie Spivak...RCA Victor 20-2047
10	8	5	Mam'selle	Dennis Day...RCA Victor 20-2211

Billboard ☢ JUNE 7, 1947 ☢ Best Sellers

TW	LW	WK	Title	Artist
1	3	8	Mam'selle	Art Lund...MGM 10011
2	2	11	Linda	Ray Noble with Buddy Clark...Columbia 37215
3	1	14	Heartaches	Ted Weems...Decca 25017
4	4	6	Mam'selle	Dick Haymes...Decca 23861
5	5	9	My Adobe Hacienda	Eddy Howard...Majestic 1117
6	7	4	Peg O' My Heart	The Harmonicats...Vitacoustic 1
7	8	3	Across The Alley From The Alamo	Mills Brothers...Decca 23863
8	—	1	I Wonder, I Wonder, I Wonder	Eddy Howard...Majestic 1124
8	6	3	Mam'selle	Frank Sinatra...Columbia 37343
9	—	4	Mam'selle	The Pied Pipers...Capitol 396
10	—	1	Chi-Baba Chi-Baba (My Bambino Go To Sleep)	Perry Como...RCA Victor 20-2259

Billboard ☢ JUNE 14, 1947 ☢ Best Sellers

TW	LW	WK	Title	Artist
1	1	9	Mam'selle	Art Lund...MGM 10011
2	6	5	Peg O' My Heart	The Harmonicats...Vitacoustic 1
3	3	15	Heartaches	Ted Weems...Decca 25017
4	2	12	Linda	Ray Noble with Buddy Clark...Columbia 37215
5	7	4	Across The Alley From The Alamo	Mills Brothers...Decca 23863
6	5	10	My Adobe Hacienda	Eddy Howard...Majestic 1117
7	4	7	Mam'selle	Dick Haymes...Decca 23861
8	8	2	I Wonder, I Wonder, I Wonder	Eddy Howard...Majestic 1124
9	8	4	Mam'selle	Frank Sinatra...Columbia 37343
10	10	2	Chi-Baba Chi-Baba (My Bambino Go To Sleep)	Perry Como...RCA Victor 20-2259

Billboard ☢ JUNE 21, 1947 ☢ Best Sellers

TW	LW	WK	Title	Artist
1	2	6	Peg O' My Heart	The Harmonicats...Vitacoustic 1
2	10	3	Chi-Baba Chi-Baba (My Bambino Go To Sleep)	Perry Como...RCA Victor 20-2259
3	8	3	I Wonder, I Wonder, I Wonder	Eddy Howard...Majestic 1124
4	5	5	Across The Alley From The Alamo	Mills Brothers...Decca 23863
5	1	10	Mam'selle	Art Lund...MGM 10011
6	4	13	Linda	Ray Noble with Buddy Clark...Columbia 37215
7	7	8	Mam'selle	Dick Haymes...Decca 23861
8	3	16	Heartaches	Ted Weems...Decca 25017
9	6	11	My Adobe Hacienda	Eddy Howard...Majestic 1117
10	—	1	That's My Desire	Sammy Kaye...RCA Victor 20-2251

TW	LW	WK	Billboard® JUNE 28, 1947 Best Sellers
1	2	4	Chi-Baba Chi-Baba (My Bambino Go To Sleep) ....Perry Como...RCA Victor 20-2259
2	1	7	Peg O' My Heart..The Harmonicats...Vitacoustic 1
3	3	4	I Wonder, I Wonder, I Wonder ....Eddy Howard...Majestic 1124
4	—	1	Peg O' My Heart...The Three Suns...RCA Victor 20-2272
5	4	6	Across The Alley From The Alamo ....Mills Brothers...Decca 23863
6	10	2	That's My Desire ....Sammy Kaye...RCA Victor 20-2251
7	—	1	Peg O' My Heart..Art Lund...MGM 10037
8	—	1	I Wonder, I Wonder, I Wonder ....Guy Lombardo...Decca 23865
9	5	11	Mam'selle ....Art Lund...MGM 10011
10	—	1	Temptation (Tim-Tayshun) ....Red Ingle...Capitol 412

TW	LW	WK	Billboard® JULY 5, 1947 Best Sellers
1	1	5	Chi-Baba Chi-Baba (My Bambino Go To Sleep) ....Perry Como...RCA Victor 20-2259
2	4	2	Peg O' My Heart...The Three Suns...RCA Victor 20-2272
3	2	8	Peg O' My Heart..The Harmonicats...Vitacoustic 1
4	3	5	I Wonder, I Wonder, I Wonder ....Eddy Howard...Majestic 1124
5	6	3	That's My Desire ....Sammy Kaye...RCA Victor 20-2251
6	5	7	Across The Alley From The Alamo ....Mills Brothers...Decca 23863
7	—	1	That's My Desire ....Frankie Laine & Mannie Klein...Mercury 5007
8	7	2	Peg O' My Heart..Art Lund...MGM 10037
9	8	2	I Wonder, I Wonder, I Wonder ....Guy Lombardo...Decca 23865
10	—	1	Peg O' My Heart..Buddy Clark...Columbia 37392

TW	LW	WK	Billboard® JULY 12, 1947 Best Sellers
1	1	6	Chi-Baba Chi-Baba (My Bambino Go To Sleep) ....Perry Como...RCA Victor 20-2259
2	3	9	Peg O' My Heart..The Harmonicats...Vitacoustic 1
3	4	6	I Wonder, I Wonder, I Wonder ....Eddy Howard...Majestic 1124
4	2	3	Peg O' My Heart...The Three Suns...RCA Victor 20-2272
5	—	2	Temptation (Tim-Tayshun) ....Red Ingle...Capitol 412
6	8	3	Peg O' My Heart..Art Lund...MGM 10037
7	5	4	That's My Desire ....Sammy Kaye...RCA Victor 20-2251
8	6	8	Across The Alley From The Alamo ....Mills Brothers...Decca 23863
9	10	2	Peg O' My Heart..Buddy Clark...Columbia 37392
10	—	1	Peg O' My Heart..Clark Dennis...Capitol 346
10	7	2	That's My Desire ....Frankie Laine & Mannie Klein...Mercury 5007

TW	LW	WK	Billboard® JULY 19, 1947 Best Sellers
1	2	10	Peg O' My Heart..The Harmonicats...Vitacoustic 1
2	1	7	Chi-Baba Chi-Baba (My Bambino Go To Sleep) ....Perry Como...RCA Victor 20-2259
3	4	4	Peg O' My Heart...The Three Suns...RCA Victor 20-2272
4	3	7	I Wonder, I Wonder, I Wonder ....Eddy Howard...Majestic 1124
5	5	3	Temptation (Tim-Tayshun) ....Red Ingle...Capitol 412
6	7	5	That's My Desire ....Sammy Kaye...RCA Victor 20-2251
7	6	4	Peg O' My Heart..Art Lund...MGM 10037
8	—	3	I Wonder, I Wonder, I Wonder ....Guy Lombardo...Decca 23865
9	8	9	Across The Alley From The Alamo ....Mills Brothers...Decca 23863
10	10	3	That's My Desire ....Frankie Laine & Mannie Klein...Mercury 5007

TW	LW	WK	Billboard® JULY 26, 1947 Best Sellers
1	1	11	Peg O' My Heart..The Harmonicats...Vitacoustic 1
2	2	8	Chi-Baba Chi-Baba (My Bambino Go To Sleep) ....Perry Como...RCA Victor 20-2259
3	5	4	Temptation (Tim-Tayshun) ....Red Ingle...Capitol 412
4	3	5	Peg O' My Heart...The Three Suns...RCA Victor 20-2272
5	6	6	That's My Desire ....Sammy Kaye...RCA Victor 20-2251
6	4	8	I Wonder, I Wonder, I Wonder ....Eddy Howard...Majestic 1124
7	7	5	Peg O' My Heart..Art Lund...MGM 10037
8	—	1	Smoke! Smoke! Smoke! (That Cigarette)..........................Tex Williams...Capitol Americana 40001
9	8	4	I Wonder, I Wonder, I Wonder ....Guy Lombardo...Decca 23865
10	—	3	Peg O' My Heart..Buddy Clark...Columbia 37392

TW	LW	WK	Billboard ❀ AUGUST 2, 1947 ❀	Best Sellers
1	1	12	Peg O' My Heart ....*The Harmonicats*...Vitacoustic 1	
2	3	5	Temptation (Tim-Tayshun) ....*Red Ingle*...Capitol 412	
3	5	7	That's My Desire ....*Sammy Kaye*...RCA Victor 20-2251	
4	2	9	Chi-Baba Chi-Baba (My Bambino Go To Sleep) ....*Perry Como*...RCA Victor 20-2259	
5	6	9	I Wonder, I Wonder, I Wonder ....*Eddy Howard*...Majestic 1124	
6	8	2	Smoke! Smoke! Smoke! (That Cigarette)........................*Tex Williams*...Capitol Americana 40001	
7	4	6	Peg O' My Heart ....*The Three Suns*...RCA Victor 20-2272	
8	7	6	Peg O' My Heart ....*Art Lund*...MGM 10037	
9	—	4	That's My Desire ....*Frankie Laine & Mannie Klein*...Mercury 5007	
10	9	5	I Wonder, I Wonder, I Wonder ....*Guy Lombardo*...Decca 23865	

TW	LW	WK	Billboard ❀ AUGUST 9, 1947 ❀	Best Sellers
1	6	3	Smoke! Smoke! Smoke! (That Cigarette)........................*Tex Williams*...Capitol Americana 40001	
2	2	6	Temptation (Tim-Tayshun) ....*Red Ingle*...Capitol 412	
3	1	13	Peg O' My Heart ....*The Harmonicats*...Vitacoustic 1	
4	7	7	Peg O' My Heart ....*The Three Suns*...RCA Victor 20-2272	
5	3	8	That's My Desire ....*Sammy Kaye*...RCA Victor 20-2251	
6	4	10	Chi-Baba Chi-Baba (My Bambino Go To Sleep) ....*Perry Como*...RCA Victor 20-2259	
7	5	10	I Wonder, I Wonder, I Wonder ....*Eddy Howard*...Majestic 1124	
8	8	7	Peg O' My Heart ....*Art Lund*...MGM 10037	
9	—	4	Peg O' My Heart ....*Buddy Clark*...Columbia 37392	
10	10	6	I Wonder, I Wonder, I Wonder ....*Guy Lombardo*...Decca 23865	

TW	LW	WK	Billboard ❀ AUGUST 16, 1947 ❀	Best Sellers
1	1	4	Smoke! Smoke! Smoke! (That Cigarette)........................*Tex Williams*...Capitol Americana 40001	
2	3	14	Peg O' My Heart ....*The Harmonicats*...Vitacoustic 1	
3	2	7	Temptation (Tim-Tayshun) ....*Red Ingle*...Capitol 412	
4	5	9	That's My Desire ....*Sammy Kaye*...RCA Victor 20-2251	
5	4	8	Peg O' My Heart ....*The Three Suns*...RCA Victor 20-2272	
6	6	11	Chi-Baba Chi-Baba (My Bambino Go To Sleep) ....*Perry Como*...RCA Victor 20-2259	
7	7	11	I Wonder, I Wonder, I Wonder ....*Eddy Howard*...Majestic 1124	
8	8	8	Peg O' My Heart ....*Art Lund*...MGM 10037	
9	9	5	Peg O' My Heart ....*Buddy Clark*...Columbia 37392	
10	10	7	I Wonder, I Wonder, I Wonder ....*Guy Lombardo*...Decca 23865	

TW	LW	WK	Billboard ❀ AUGUST 23, 1947 ❀	Best Sellers
1	1	5	Smoke! Smoke! Smoke! (That Cigarette)........................*Tex Williams*...Capitol Americana 40001	
2	3	8	Temptation (Tim-Tayshun) ....*Red Ingle*...Capitol 412	
3	2	15	Peg O' My Heart ....*The Harmonicats*...Vitacoustic 1	
4	5	9	Peg O' My Heart ....*The Three Suns*...RCA Victor 20-2272	
5	4	10	That's My Desire ....*Sammy Kaye*...RCA Victor 20-2251	
6	6	12	Chi-Baba Chi-Baba (My Bambino Go To Sleep) ....*Perry Como*...RCA Victor 20-2259	
7	7	12	I Wonder, I Wonder, I Wonder ....*Eddy Howard*...Majestic 1124	
8	8	9	Peg O' My Heart ....*Art Lund*...MGM 10037	
9	—	1	Smoke, Smoke, Smoke (That Cigarette) ....*Phil Harris*...RCA Victor 20-2370	
10	—	1	When You Were Sweet Sixteen ....*Perry Como*...RCA Victor 20-2259	

TW	LW	WK	Billboard ❀ AUGUST 30, 1947 ❀	Best Sellers
1	1	6	Smoke! Smoke! Smoke! (That Cigarette)........................*Tex Williams*...Capitol Americana 40001	
2	2	9	Temptation (Tim-Tayshun) ....*Red Ingle*...Capitol 412	
3	4	10	Peg O' My Heart ....*The Three Suns*...RCA Victor 20-2272	
4	—	6	Peg O' My Heart ....*Buddy Clark*...Columbia 37392	
5	5	11	That's My Desire ....*Sammy Kaye*...RCA Victor 20-2251	
6	3	16	Peg O' My Heart ....*The Harmonicats*...Vitacoustic 1	
7	—	1	I Wonder Who's Kissing Her Now ....*Ted Weems & Perry Como*...Decca 25078	
8	—	1	I Have But One Heart "O Marinariello" ....*Vic Damone*...Mercury 5053	
9	8	10	Peg O' My Heart ....*Art Lund*...MGM 10037	
10	9	2	Smoke, Smoke, Smoke (That Cigarette) ....*Phil Harris*...RCA Victor 20-2370	

TW	LW	WK	Billboard ⚙ SEPTEMBER 6, 1947 ⚙ Best Sellers
1	1	7	Smoke! Smoke! Smoke! (That Cigarette)..........................*Tex Williams*...Capitol Americana 40001
2	2	10	Temptation (Tim-Tayshun)...*Red Ingle*...Capitol 412
3	6	17	Peg O' My Heart...*The Harmonicats*...Vitacoustic 1
4	—	1	Near You...*Francis Craig*...Bullet 1001
5	—	2	When You Were Sweet Sixteen ....*Perry Como*...RCA Victor 20-2259
6	5	12	That's My Desire...*Sammy Kaye*...RCA Victor 20-2251
7	7	2	I Wonder Who's Kissing Her Now ....*Ted Weems & Perry Como*...Decca 25078
8	3	11	Peg O' My Heart...*The Three Suns*...RCA Victor 20-2272
9	—	1	Feudin' And Fightin'...*Dorothy Shay*...Columbia 37189
10	—	13	I Wonder, I Wonder, I Wonder ....*Eddy Howard*...Majestic 1124

TW	LW	WK	Billboard ⚙ SEPTEMBER 13, 1947 ⚙ Best Sellers
1	1	8	Smoke! Smoke! Smoke! (That Cigarette)..........................*Tex Williams*...Capitol Americana 40001
2	8	12	Peg O' My Heart...*The Three Suns*...RCA Victor 20-2272
3	7	3	I Wonder Who's Kissing Her Now ....*Ted Weems & Perry Como*...Decca 25078
4	9	2	Feudin' And Fightin'...*Dorothy Shay*...Columbia 37189
5	4	2	Near You...*Francis Craig*...Bullet 1001
5	3	18	Peg O' My Heart...*The Harmonicats*...Vitacoustic 1
6	6	13	That's My Desire...*Sammy Kaye*...RCA Victor 20-2251
7	5	3	When You Were Sweet Sixteen ....*Perry Como*...RCA Victor 20-2259
8	—	3	Smoke, Smoke, Smoke (That Cigarette) ....*Phil Harris*...RCA Victor 20-2370
9	2	11	Temptation (Tim-Tayshun)...*Red Ingle*...Capitol 412
10	—	7	Peg O' My Heart...*Buddy Clark*...Columbia 37392

TW	LW	WK	Billboard ⚙ SEPTEMBER 20, 1947 ⚙ Best Sellers
1	5	3	Near You...*Francis Craig*...Bullet 1001
2	1	9	Smoke! Smoke! Smoke! (That Cigarette)..........................*Tex Williams*...Capitol Americana 40001
3	3	4	I Wonder Who's Kissing Her Now ....*Ted Weems & Perry Como*...Decca 25078
4	6	14	That's My Desire...*Sammy Kaye*...RCA Victor 20-2251
5	7	4	When You Were Sweet Sixteen ....*Perry Como*...RCA Victor 20-2259
6	2	13	Peg O' My Heart...*The Three Suns*...RCA Victor 20-2272
7	9	12	Temptation (Tim-Tayshun)...*Red Ingle*...Capitol 412
8	5	19	Peg O' My Heart...*The Harmonicats*...Vitacoustic 1
9	4	3	Feudin' And Fightin'...*Dorothy Shay*...Columbia 37189
10	—	1	I Wish I Didn't Love You So ....*Vaughn Monroe*...RCA Victor 20-2294

TW	LW	WK	Billboard ⚙ SEPTEMBER 27, 1947 ⚙ Best Sellers
1	1	4	Near You...*Francis Craig*...Bullet 1001
2	2	10	Smoke! Smoke! Smoke! (That Cigarette)..........................*Tex Williams*...Capitol Americana 40001
3	3	5	I Wonder Who's Kissing Her Now ....*Ted Weems & Perry Como*...Decca 25078
4	4	15	That's My Desire...*Sammy Kaye*...RCA Victor 20-2251
5	5	5	When You Were Sweet Sixteen ....*Perry Como*...RCA Victor 20-2259
6	8	20	Peg O' My Heart...*The Harmonicats*...Vitacoustic 1
7	6	14	Peg O' My Heart...*The Three Suns*...RCA Victor 20-2272
8	9	4	Feudin' And Fightin'...*Dorothy Shay*...Columbia 37189
9	—	4	Smoke, Smoke, Smoke (That Cigarette) ....*Phil Harris*...RCA Victor 20-2370
10	7	13	Temptation (Tim-Tayshun)...*Red Ingle*...Capitol 412
10	10	2	I Wish I Didn't Love You So ....*Vaughn Monroe*...RCA Victor 20-2294

TW	LW	WK	Billboard ⚙ OCTOBER 4, 1947 ⚙ Best Sellers
1	1	5	Near You...*Francis Craig*...Bullet 1001
2	2	11	Smoke! Smoke! Smoke! (That Cigarette)..........................*Tex Williams*...Capitol Americana 40001
3	3	6	I Wonder Who's Kissing Her Now ....*Ted Weems & Perry Como*...Decca 25078
4	5	6	When You Were Sweet Sixteen ....*Perry Como*...RCA Victor 20-2259
5	8	5	Feudin' And Fightin'...*Dorothy Shay*...Columbia 37189
6	6	21	Peg O' My Heart...*The Harmonicats*...Vitacoustic 1
7	10	3	I Wish I Didn't Love You So ....*Vaughn Monroe*...RCA Victor 20-2294
8	7	15	Peg O' My Heart...*The Three Suns*...RCA Victor 20-2272
9	4	16	That's My Desire...*Sammy Kaye*...RCA Victor 20-2251
10	—	2	I Have But One Heart "O Marinariello" ....*Vic Damone*...Mercury 5053

TW	LW	WK	Billboard® ☸ OCTOBER 11, 1947 ☸	Best Sellers
1	1	6	Near You	Francis Craig...Bullet 1001
2	4	7	When You Were Sweet Sixteen	Perry Como...RCA Victor 20-2259
3	3	7	I Wonder Who's Kissing Her Now	Ted Weems & Perry Como...Decca 25078
4	2	12	Smoke! Smoke! Smoke! (That Cigarette)	Tex Williams...Capitol Americana 40001
5	7	4	I Wish I Didn't Love You So	Vaughn Monroe...RCA Victor 20-2294
6	—	1	Near You	Andrews Sisters...Decca 24171
7	8	16	Peg O' My Heart	The Three Suns...RCA Victor 20-2272
8	5	6	Feudin' And Fightin'	Dorothy Shay...Columbia 37189
9	—	1	Near You	Elliot Lawrence...Columbia 37838
10	9	17	That's My Desire	Sammy Kaye...RCA Victor 20-2251

TW	LW	WK	Billboard® ☸ OCTOBER 18, 1947 ☸	Best Sellers
1	1	7	Near You	Francis Craig...Bullet 1001
2	5	5	I Wish I Didn't Love You So	Vaughn Monroe...RCA Victor 20-2294
3	3	8	I Wonder Who's Kissing Her Now	Ted Weems & Perry Como...Decca 25078
4	—	1	Near You	Larry Green...RCA Victor 20-2421
5	6	2	Near You	Andrews Sisters...Decca 24171
6	2	8	When You Were Sweet Sixteen	Perry Como...RCA Victor 20-2259
7	—	1	I Wish I Didn't Love You So	Betty Hutton...Capitol 409
8	—	1	An Apple Blossom Wedding	Sammy Kaye...RCA Victor 20-2330
9	8	7	Feudin' And Fightin'	Dorothy Shay...Columbia 37189
10	—	1	Feudin' And Fightin'	Jo Stafford...Capitol 443
10	9	2	Near You	Elliot Lawrence...Columbia 37838

TW	LW	WK	Billboard® ☸ OCTOBER 25, 1947 ☸	Best Sellers
1	1	8	Near You	Francis Craig...Bullet 1001
2	2	6	I Wish I Didn't Love You So	Vaughn Monroe...RCA Victor 20-2294
3	4	2	Near You	Larry Green...RCA Victor 20-2421
4	5	3	Near You	Andrews Sisters...Decca 24171
4	3	9	I Wonder Who's Kissing Her Now	Ted Weems & Perry Como...Decca 25078
5	6	9	When You Were Sweet Sixteen	Perry Como...RCA Victor 20-2259
6	7	2	I Wish I Didn't Love You So	Betty Hutton...Capitol 409
7	9	8	Feudin' And Fightin'	Dorothy Shay...Columbia 37189
8	8	2	An Apple Blossom Wedding	Sammy Kaye...RCA Victor 20-2330
9	—	1	I Wish I Didn't Love You So	Dinah Shore...Columbia 37506
9	—	1	Near You	Alvino Rey...Capitol 452
9	—	3	I Have But One Heart "O Marinariello"	Vic Damone...Mercury 5053
10	—	1	Kokomo, Indiana	Vaughn Monroe...RCA Victor 20-2361

TW	LW	WK	Billboard® ☸ NOVEMBER 1, 1947 ☸	Best Sellers
1	1	9	Near You	Francis Craig...Bullet 1001
2	2	7	I Wish I Didn't Love You So	Vaughn Monroe...RCA Victor 20-2294
3	3	3	Near You	Larry Green...RCA Victor 20-2421
4	4	4	Near You	Andrews Sisters...Decca 24171
5	4	10	I Wonder Who's Kissing Her Now	Ted Weems & Perry Como...Decca 25078
5	5	10	When You Were Sweet Sixteen	Perry Como...RCA Victor 20-2259
6	8	3	An Apple Blossom Wedding	Sammy Kaye...RCA Victor 20-2330
7	6	3	I Wish I Didn't Love You So	Betty Hutton...Capitol 409
8	9	2	I Wish I Didn't Love You So	Dinah Shore...Columbia 37506
9	7	9	Feudin' And Fightin'	Dorothy Shay...Columbia 37189
9	—	1	You Do	Vaughn Monroe...RCA Victor 20-2361
10	—	1	You Do	Bing Crosby & Carmen Cavallaro...Decca 24101
10	—	1	You Do	Margaret Whiting...Capitol 438

TW	LW	WK	Billboard ✿ NOVEMBER 8, 1947 ✿ Best Sellers
1	1	10	Near You ....*Francis Craig*...Bullet 1001
2	2	8	I Wish I Didn't Love You So ....*Vaughn Monroe*...RCA Victor 20-2294
3	3	4	Near You ....*Larry Green*...RCA Victor 20-2421
4	—	1	Ballerina ....*Vaughn Monroe*...RCA Victor 20-2433
5	4	5	Near You ....*Andrews Sisters*...Decca 24171
6	5	11	When You Were Sweet Sixteen ....*Perry Como*...RCA Victor 20-2259
7	—	1	How Soon (Will I Be Seeing You) ....*Jack Owens*...Tower 1258
8	—	1	Too Fat Polka (I Don't Want Her) (You Can Have Her)
			(She's Too Fat For Me) ....*Arthur Godfrey*...Columbia 37921
9	—	1	I Wish I Didn't Love You So..*Dick Haymes*...Decca 23977
10	10	2	You Do..*Margaret Whiting*...Capitol 438

TW	LW	WK	Billboard ✿ NOVEMBER 15, 1947 ✿ Best Sellers
1	1	11	Near You ....*Francis Craig*...Bullet 1001
2	2	9	I Wish I Didn't Love You So ....*Vaughn Monroe*...RCA Victor 20-2294
3	3	5	Near You ....*Larry Green*...RCA Victor 20-2421
4	5	6	Near You ....*Andrews Sisters*...Decca 24171
5	4	2	Ballerina ....*Vaughn Monroe*...RCA Victor 20-2433
6	7	2	How Soon (Will I Be Seeing You) ....*Jack Owens*...Tower 1258
7	6	12	When You Were Sweet Sixteen ....*Perry Como*...RCA Victor 20-2259
8	—	11	I Wonder Who's Kissing Her Now ....*Ted Weems & Perry Como*...Decca 25078
9	—	3	I Wish I Didn't Love You So ....*Dinah Shore*...Columbia 37506
10	—	1	Mickey ....*Ted Weems*...Mercury 5062
10	—	2	You Do..*Vaughn Monroe*...RCA Victor 20-2361

TW	LW	WK	Billboard ✿ NOVEMBER 22, 1947 ✿ Best Sellers
1	1	12	Near You ....*Francis Craig*...Bullet 1001
2	5	3	Ballerina ....*Vaughn Monroe*...RCA Victor 20-2433
3	2	10	I Wish I Didn't Love You So ....*Vaughn Monroe*...RCA Victor 20-2294
4	3	6	Near You ....*Larry Green*...RCA Victor 20-2421
5	4	7	Near You ....*Andrews Sisters*...Decca 24171
6	6	3	How Soon (Will I Be Seeing You) ....*Jack Owens*...Tower 1258
7	12	3	Too Fat Polka (I Don't Want Her) (You Can Have Her)
			(She's Too Fat For Me) ....*Arthur Godfrey*...Columbia 37921
8	10	3	You Do..*Vaughn Monroe*...RCA Victor 20-2361
9	14	2	Whiffenpoof Song..*Bing Crosby with Fred Waring*...Decca 23990
10	12	4	You Do..*Margaret Whiting*...Capitol 438

TW	LW	WK	Billboard ✿ NOVEMBER 29, 1947 ✿ Best Sellers
1	1	13	Near You ....*Francis Craig*...Bullet 1001
2	2	4	Ballerina ....*Vaughn Monroe*...RCA Victor 20-2433
3	3	11	I Wish I Didn't Love You So ....*Vaughn Monroe*...RCA Victor 20-2294
4	4	7	Near You ....*Larry Green*...RCA Victor 20-2421
5	7	4	Too Fat Polka (I Don't Want Her) (You Can Have Her)
			(She's Too Fat For Me) ....*Arthur Godfrey*...Columbia 37921
6	6	4	How Soon (Will I Be Seeing You) ....*Jack Owens*...Tower 1258
7	12	2	Civilization (Bongo, Bongo, Bongo) ....*Danny Kaye - Andrews Sisters*...Decca 23940
8	8	4	You Do..*Vaughn Monroe*...RCA Victor 20-2361
9	5	8	Near You ....*Andrews Sisters*...Decca 24171
9	10	5	You Do..*Margaret Whiting*...Capitol 438
10	14	3	Civilization (Bongo, Bongo, Bongo) ....*Louis Prima*...RCA Victor 20-2400

TW	LW	WK	Billboard® 🎯 DECEMBER 6, 1947 🎯 Best Sellers
1	1	14	**Near You** ....Francis Craig...Bullet 1001
2	2	5	**Ballerina** ....Vaughn Monroe...RCA Victor 20-2433
3	5	5	**Too Fat Polka (I Don't Want Her) (You Can Have Her)** (She's Too Fat For Me)...............Arthur Godfrey...Columbia 37921
4	6	5	**How Soon** (Will I Be Seeing You) ....Jack Owens...Tower 1258
5	4	8	**Near You** ....Larry Green...RCA Victor 20-2421
6	7	3	**Civilization (Bongo, Bongo, Bongo)** ....Danny Kaye - Andrews Sisters...Decca 23940
7	11	4	**Whiffenpoof Song** ....Bing Crosby with Fred Waring...Decca 23990
8	3	12	**I Wish I Didn't Love You So** ....Vaughn Monroe...RCA Victor 20-2294
9	8	5	**You Do** ....Vaughn Monroe...RCA Victor 20-2361
10	9	9	**Near You** ....Andrews Sisters...Decca 24171
10	9	6	**You Do** ....Margaret Whiting...Capitol 438

TW	LW	WK	Billboard® 🎯 DECEMBER 13, 1947 🎯 Best Sellers
1	2	6	**Ballerina** ....Vaughn Monroe...RCA Victor 20-2433
2	1	15	**Near You** ....Francis Craig...Bullet 1001
3	3	6	**Too Fat Polka (I Don't Want Her) (You Can Have Her)** (She's Too Fat For Me)...............Arthur Godfrey...Columbia 37921
4	4	6	**How Soon** (Will I Be Seeing You) ....Jack Owens...Tower 1258
5	14	4	**How Soon?** (Will I Be Seeing You) ....Vaughn Monroe...RCA Victor 20-2523
6	11	2	**White Christmas** ....Bing Crosby...Decca 23778
7	5	9	**Near You** ....Larry Green...RCA Victor 20-2421
8	8	13	**I Wish I Didn't Love You So** ....Vaughn Monroe...RCA Victor 20-2294
9	11	2	**How Soon (Will I Be Seeing You)** ....Bing Crosby & Carmen Cavallaro...Decca 24101
10	7	5	**Whiffenpoof Song** ....Bing Crosby with Fred Waring...Decca 23990

TW	LW	WK	Billboard® 🎯 DECEMBER 20, 1947 🎯 Best Sellers
1	1	7	**Ballerina** ....Vaughn Monroe...RCA Victor 20-2433
2	3	7	**Too Fat Polka (I Don't Want Her) (You Can Have Her)** (She's Too Fat For Me)...............Arthur Godfrey...Columbia 37921
3	2	16	**Near You** ....Francis Craig...Bullet 1001
4	13	5	**Civilization (Bongo, Bongo, Bongo)** ....Danny Kaye - Andrews Sisters...Decca 23940
5	6	3	**White Christmas** ....Bing Crosby...Decca 23778
6	4	7	**How Soon** (Will I Be Seeing You) ....Jack Owens...Tower 1258
7	7	10	**Near You** ....Larry Green...RCA Victor 20-2421
8	15	7	**You Do** ....Vaughn Monroe...RCA Victor 20-2361
9	5	5	**How Soon?** (Will I Be Seeing You) ....Vaughn Monroe...RCA Victor 20-2523
10	11	6	**You Do** ....Bing Crosby & Carmen Cavallaro...Decca 24101

TW	LW	WK	Billboard® 🎯 DECEMBER 27, 1947 🎯 Best Sellers
1	1	8	**Ballerina** ....Vaughn Monroe...RCA Victor 20-2433
2	2	8	**Too Fat Polka (I Don't Want Her) (You Can Have Her)** (She's Too Fat For Me)...............Arthur Godfrey...Columbia 37921
3	3	17	**Near You** ....Francis Craig...Bullet 1001
4	5	4	**White Christmas** ....Bing Crosby...Decca 23778
5	4	6	**Civilization (Bongo, Bongo, Bongo)** ....Danny Kaye - Andrews Sisters...Decca 23940
6	9	6	**How Soon?** (Will I Be Seeing You) ....Vaughn Monroe...RCA Victor 20-2523
7	13	6	**Serenade Of The Bells** ....Sammy Kaye...RCA Victor 20-2372
8	—	5	**Civilization (Bongo, Bongo, Bongo)** ....Louis Prima...RCA Victor 20-2400
9	—	1	**Here Comes Santa Claus (Down Santa Claus Lane)** ....Gene Autry...Columbia 37942
9	6	8	**How Soon (Will I Be Seeing You)** ....Jack Owens...Tower 1258
10	14	4	**How Soon (Will I Be Seeing You)** ....Bing Crosby & Carmen Cavallaro...Decca 24101

TW	LW	WK	Billboard® 🏵 JANUARY 3, 1948 🏵 Best Sellers
1	1	9	Ballerina...*Vaughn Monroe*...RCA Victor 20-2433
2	2	9	Too Fat Polka (I Don't Want Her) (You Can Have Her) (She's Too Fat For Me)...*Arthur Godfrey*...Columbia 37921
3	5	7	Civilization (Bongo, Bongo, Bongo)......................*Danny Kaye - Andrews Sisters*...Decca 23940
3	4	5	White Christmas...*Bing Crosby*...Decca 23778
4	3	18	Near You...*Francis Craig*...Bullet 1001
5	7	7	Serenade Of The Bells...*Sammy Kaye*...RCA Victor 20-2372
6	6	7	How Soon? (Will I Be Seeing You) ....*Vaughn Monroe*...RCA Victor 20-2523
7	12	3	I'll Dance At Your Wedding..*Ray Noble with Buddy Clark*...Columbia 37967
8	11	6	Golden Earrings ....*Peggy Lee*...Capitol 15009
9	15	3	Serenade Of The Bells ....*Jo Stafford*...Capitol 15007
10	9	9	How Soon (Will I Be Seeing You) ....*Jack Owens*...Tower 1258

TW	LW	WK	Billboard® 🏵 JANUARY 10, 1948 🏵 Best Sellers
1	1	10	Ballerina...*Vaughn Monroe*...RCA Victor 20-2433
2	2	10	Too Fat Polka (I Don't Want Her) (You Can Have Her) (She's Too Fat For Me)...*Arthur Godfrey*...Columbia 37921
3	3	8	Civilization (Bongo, Bongo, Bongo)......................*Danny Kaye - Andrews Sisters*...Decca 23940
4	4	19	Near You...*Francis Craig*...Bullet 1001
5	6	8	How Soon? (Will I Be Seeing You) ....*Vaughn Monroe*...RCA Victor 20-2523
6	10	10	How Soon (Will I Be Seeing You) ....*Jack Owens*...Tower 1258
7	8	7	Golden Earrings ....*Peggy Lee*...Capitol 15009
7	5	8	Serenade Of The Bells...*Sammy Kaye*...RCA Victor 20-2372
9	7	4	I'll Dance At Your Wedding..*Ray Noble with Buddy Clark*...Columbia 37967
10	—	1	Ballerina...*Buddy Clark*...Columbia 38040
10	11	6	How Soon (Will I Be Seeing You)........................*Bing Crosby & Carmen Cavallaro*...Decca 24101

TW	LW	WK	Billboard® 🏵 JANUARY 17, 1948 🏵 Best Sellers
1	1	11	Ballerina...*Vaughn Monroe*...RCA Victor 20-2433
2	2	11	Too Fat Polka (I Don't Want Her) (You Can Have Her) (She's Too Fat For Me)...*Arthur Godfrey*...Columbia 37921
3	9	5	I'll Dance At Your Wedding..*Ray Noble with Buddy Clark*...Columbia 37967
3	7	9	Serenade Of The Bells...*Sammy Kaye*...RCA Victor 20-2372
5	7	8	Golden Earrings ....*Peggy Lee*...Capitol 15009
6	5	9	How Soon? (Will I Be Seeing You) ....*Vaughn Monroe*...RCA Victor 20-2523
7	3	9	Civilization (Bongo, Bongo, Bongo)......................*Danny Kaye - Andrews Sisters*...Decca 23940
7	12	5	Serenade Of The Bells ....*Jo Stafford*...Capitol 15007
9	4	20	Near You...*Francis Craig*...Bullet 1001
10	10	7	How Soon (Will I Be Seeing You)........................*Bing Crosby & Carmen Cavallaro*...Decca 24101

TW	LW	WK	Billboard® 🏵 JANUARY 24, 1948 🏵 Best Sellers
1	1	12	Ballerina...*Vaughn Monroe*...RCA Victor 20-2433
2	2	12	Too Fat Polka (I Don't Want Her) (You Can Have Her) (She's Too Fat For Me)...*Arthur Godfrey*...Columbia 37921
3	5	9	Golden Earrings ....*Peggy Lee*...Capitol 15009
4	3	10	Serenade Of The Bells...*Sammy Kaye*...RCA Victor 20-2372
5	3	6	I'll Dance At Your Wedding..*Ray Noble with Buddy Clark*...Columbia 37967
6	7	6	Serenade Of The Bells ....*Jo Stafford*...Capitol 15007
7	6	10	How Soon? (Will I Be Seeing You) ....*Vaughn Monroe*...RCA Victor 20-2523
8	7	10	Civilization (Bongo, Bongo, Bongo)......................*Danny Kaye - Andrews Sisters*...Decca 23940
9	10	8	How Soon (Will I Be Seeing You)........................*Bing Crosby & Carmen Cavallaro*...Decca 24101
10	15	2	Ballerina...*Bing Crosby*...Decca 24278

TW	LW	WK	Billboard® ✸ JANUARY 31, 1948 ✸ Best Sellers
1	1	13	Ballerina...Vaughn Monroe...RCA Victor 20-2433
2	3	10	Golden Earrings...Peggy Lee...Capitol 15009
3	14	2	I'm Looking Over A Four Leaf Clover ....Art Mooney...MGM 10119
4	2	13	Too Fat Polka (I Don't Want Her) (You Can Have Her) (She's Too Fat For Me)...Arthur Godfrey...Columbia 37921
5	4	11	Serenade Of The Bells...Sammy Kaye...RCA Victor 20-2372
6	5	7	I'll Dance At Your Wedding...Ray Noble with Buddy Clark...Columbia 37967
7	6	7	Serenade Of The Bells ....Jo Stafford...Capitol 15007
8	9	9	How Soon (Will I Be Seeing You).........................Bing Crosby & Carmen Cavallaro...Decca 24101
8	—	1	Mañana (Is Soon Enough For Me)...Peggy Lee...Capitol 15022
10	—	1	I'm My Own Grandpaw ....Guy Lombardo...Decca 24288

TW	LW	WK	Billboard® ✸ FEBRUARY 7, 1948 ✸ Best Sellers
1	1	14	Ballerina...Vaughn Monroe...RCA Victor 20-2433
2	3	3	I'm Looking Over A Four Leaf Clover ....Art Mooney...MGM 10119
3	2	11	Golden Earrings...Peggy Lee...Capitol 15009
4	6	8	I'll Dance At Your Wedding...Ray Noble with Buddy Clark...Columbia 37967
5	4	14	Too Fat Polka (I Don't Want Her) (You Can Have Her) (She's Too Fat For Me)...Arthur Godfrey...Columbia 37921
6	8	2	Mañana (Is Soon Enough For Me)...Peggy Lee...Capitol 15022
7	5	12	Serenade Of The Bells..Sammy Kaye...RCA Victor 20-2372
8	11	4	Beg Your Pardon...Francis Craig...Bullet 1012
9	7	8	Serenade Of The Bells..Jo Stafford...Capitol 15007
10	15	2	Now Is The Hour (Maori Farewell Song) ....Bing Crosby...Decca 24279

TW	LW	WK	Billboard® ✸ FEBRUARY 14, 1948 ✸ Best Sellers
1	1	15	Ballerina...Vaughn Monroe...RCA Victor 20-2433
2	2	4	I'm Looking Over A Four Leaf Clover ....Art Mooney...MGM 10119
3	6	3	Mañana (Is Soon Enough For Me)...Peggy Lee...Capitol 15022
4	3	12	Golden Earrings...Peggy Lee...Capitol 15009
5	5	15	Too Fat Polka (I Don't Want Her) (You Can Have Her) (She's Too Fat For Me)...Arthur Godfrey...Columbia 37921
6	7	13	Serenade Of The Bells..Sammy Kaye...RCA Victor 20-2372
7	10	3	Now Is The Hour (Maori Farewell Song) ....Bing Crosby...Decca 24279
8	8	5	Beg Your Pardon...Francis Craig...Bullet 1012
9	11	3	Now Is The Hour ....Gracie Fields...London 110
10	12	3	I'm My Own Grandpaw ....Guy Lombardo...Decca 24288

TW	LW	WK	Billboard® ✸ FEBRUARY 21, 1948 ✸ Best Sellers
1	2	5	I'm Looking Over A Four Leaf Clover ....Art Mooney...MGM 10119
2	1	16	Ballerina...Vaughn Monroe...RCA Victor 20-2433
3	7	4	Now Is The Hour (Maori Farewell Song) ....Bing Crosby...Decca 24279
4	3	4	Mañana (Is Soon Enough For Me)...Peggy Lee...Capitol 15022
5	4	13	Golden Earrings...Peggy Lee...Capitol 15009
6	9	4	Now Is The Hour ....Gracie Fields...London 110
7	8	6	Beg Your Pardon...Francis Craig...Bullet 1012
8	—	2	Beg Your Pardon...Frankie Carle...Columbia 38036
9	6	14	Serenade Of The Bells..Sammy Kaye...RCA Victor 20-2372
10	14	2	Now Is The Hour (Maori Farewell Song)...Eddy Howard...Majestic 1191

TW	LW	WK	Billboard ❀ FEBRUARY 28, 1948 ❀ Best Sellers
1	1	6	I'm Looking Over A Four Leaf Clover ....*Art Mooney*...MGM 10119
2	4	5	Mañana (Is Soon Enough For Me)..*Peggy Lee*...Capitol 15022
3	3	5	Now Is The Hour (Maori Farewell Song) ....*Bing Crosby*...Decca 24279
4	2	17	Ballerina...*Vaughn Monroe*...RCA Victor 20-2433
5	7	7	Beg Your Pardon ....*Francis Craig*...Bullet 1012
6	6	5	Now Is The Hour ....*Gracie Fields*...London 110
7	8	3	Beg Your Pardon ....*Frankie Carle*...Columbia 38036
8	13	2	Slap 'Er Down, Agin, Paw ....*Arthur Godfrey*...Columbia 38066
9	15	2	I'm Looking Over A Four Leaf Clover ....*Russ Morgan with Milt Herth*...Decca 24319
10	10	3	Now Is The Hour (Maori Farewell Song)..*Eddy Howard*...Majestic 1191

TW	LW	WK	Billboard ❀ MARCH 6, 1948 ❀ Best Sellers
1	1	7	I'm Looking Over A Four Leaf Clover ....*Art Mooney*...MGM 10119
2	2	6	Mañana (Is Soon Enough For Me)..*Peggy Lee*...Capitol 15022
3	3	6	Now Is The Hour (Maori Farewell Song) ....*Bing Crosby*...Decca 24279
4	4	18	Ballerina...*Vaughn Monroe*...RCA Victor 20-2433
5	6	6	Now Is The Hour ....*Gracie Fields*...London 110
6	5	8	Beg Your Pardon ....*Francis Craig*...Bullet 1012
7	7	4	Beg Your Pardon ....*Frankie Carle*...Columbia 38036
8	10	4	Now Is The Hour (Maori Farewell Song)..*Eddy Howard*...Majestic 1191
9	8	3	Slap 'Er Down, Agin, Paw ....*Arthur Godfrey*...Columbia 38066
10	9	3	I'm Looking Over A Four Leaf Clover ....*Russ Morgan with Milt Herth*...Decca 24319

TW	LW	WK	Billboard ❀ MARCH 13, 1948 ❀ Best Sellers
1	2	7	Mañana (Is Soon Enough For Me)..*Peggy Lee*...Capitol 15022
2	1	8	I'm Looking Over A Four Leaf Clover ....*Art Mooney*...MGM 10119
3	3	7	Now Is The Hour (Maori Farewell Song) ....*Bing Crosby*...Decca 24279
4	6	9	Beg Your Pardon ....*Francis Craig*...Bullet 1012
5	5	7	Now Is The Hour ....*Gracie Fields*...London 110
6	4	19	Ballerina...*Vaughn Monroe*...RCA Victor 20-2433
7	10	4	I'm Looking Over A Four Leaf Clover ....*Russ Morgan with Milt Herth*...Decca 24319
8	7	5	Beg Your Pardon ....*Frankie Carle*...Columbia 38036
9	11	4	Now Is The Hour (Maori Farewell Song)....................................*Margaret Whiting*...Capitol 15024
10	9	4	Slap 'Er Down, Agin, Paw ....*Arthur Godfrey*...Columbia 38066

TW	LW	WK	Billboard ❀ MARCH 20, 1948 ❀ Best Sellers
1	1	8	Mañana (Is Soon Enough For Me)..*Peggy Lee*...Capitol 15022
2	3	8	Now Is The Hour (Maori Farewell Song) ....*Bing Crosby*...Decca 24279
3	2	9	I'm Looking Over A Four Leaf Clover ....*Art Mooney*...MGM 10119
4	5	8	Now Is The Hour ....*Gracie Fields*...London 110
5	4	10	Beg Your Pardon ....*Francis Craig*...Bullet 1012
6	8	6	Beg Your Pardon ....*Frankie Carle*...Columbia 38036
7	7	5	I'm Looking Over A Four Leaf Clover ....*Russ Morgan with Milt Herth*...Decca 24319
8	6	20	Ballerina...*Vaughn Monroe*...RCA Victor 20-2433
9	9	5	Now Is The Hour (Maori Farewell Song)....................................*Margaret Whiting*...Capitol 15024
10	10	5	Slap 'Er Down, Agin, Paw ....*Arthur Godfrey*...Columbia 38066

TW	LW	WK	Billboard ❀ MARCH 27, 1948 ❀ Best Sellers
1	1	9	Mañana (Is Soon Enough For Me)..*Peggy Lee*...Capitol 15022
2	2	9	Now Is The Hour (Maori Farewell Song) ....*Bing Crosby*...Decca 24279
3	3	10	I'm Looking Over A Four Leaf Clover ....*Art Mooney*...MGM 10119
4	4	9	Now Is The Hour ....*Gracie Fields*...London 110
5	5	11	Beg Your Pardon ....*Francis Craig*...Bullet 1012
6	6	7	Beg Your Pardon ....*Frankie Carle*...Columbia 38036
7	7	6	I'm Looking Over A Four Leaf Clover ....*Russ Morgan with Milt Herth*...Decca 24319
8	9	6	Now Is The Hour (Maori Farewell Song)....................................*Margaret Whiting*...Capitol 15024
9	11	4	Beg Your Pardon ....*Larry Green*...RCA Victor 20-2647
10	8	21	Ballerina...*Vaughn Monroe*...RCA Victor 20-2433

TW	LW	WK	Billboard	APRIL 3, 1948	Best Sellers
1	1	10	Mañana (Is Soon Enough For Me)		Peggy Lee...Capitol 15022
2	2	10	Now Is The Hour (Maori Farewell Song)		Bing Crosby...Decca 24279
3	3	11	I'm Looking Over A Four Leaf Clover		Art Mooney...MGM 10119
4	4	10	Now Is The Hour		Gracie Fields...London 110
5	5	12	Beg Your Pardon		Francis Craig...Bullet 1012
6	6	8	Beg Your Pardon		Frankie Carle...Columbia 38036
7	11	4	Because		Perry Como...RCA Victor 20-2653
8	9	5	Beg Your Pardon		Larry Green...RCA Victor 20-2647
9	7	7	I'm Looking Over A Four Leaf Clover	Russ Morgan with Milt Herth...Decca 24319
10	13	8	Now Is The Hour (Maori Farewell Song)		Eddy Howard...Majestic 1191
10	12	7	Slap 'Er Down, Agin, Paw		Arthur Godfrey...Columbia 38066

TW	LW	WK	Billboard	APRIL 10, 1948	Best Sellers
1	1	11	Mañana (Is Soon Enough For Me)		Peggy Lee...Capitol 15022
2	2	11	Now Is The Hour (Maori Farewell Song)		Bing Crosby...Decca 24279
3	3	12	I'm Looking Over A Four Leaf Clover		Art Mooney...MGM 10119
4	4	11	Now Is The Hour		Gracie Fields...London 110
5	5	13	Beg Your Pardon		Francis Craig...Bullet 1012
6	6	9	Beg Your Pardon		Frankie Carle...Columbia 38036
7	7	5	Because		Perry Como...RCA Victor 20-2653
8	13	2	Baby Face		Art Mooney...MGM 10156
9	9	8	I'm Looking Over A Four Leaf Clover	Russ Morgan with Milt Herth...Decca 24319
10	—	1	You Can't Be True, Dear		Ken Griffin...Rondo 228

TW	LW	WK	Billboard	APRIL 17, 1948	Best Sellers
1	1	12	Mañana (Is Soon Enough For Me)		Peggy Lee...Capitol 15022
2	2	12	Now Is The Hour (Maori Farewell Song)		Bing Crosby...Decca 24279
3	3	13	I'm Looking Over A Four Leaf Clover		Art Mooney...MGM 10119
4	7	6	Because		Perry Como...RCA Victor 20-2653
5	8	3	Baby Face		Art Mooney...MGM 10156
6	15	3	Sabre Dance Boogie		Freddy Martin...RCA Victor 20-2721
7	13	3	Sabre Dance		Woody Herman...Columbia 38102
8	10	2	You Can't Be True, Dear		Ken Griffin...Rondo 228
9	—	1	St. Louis Blues March		Tex Beneke...RCA Victor 20-2722
10	4	12	Now Is The Hour		Gracie Fields...London 110

TW	LW	WK	Billboard	APRIL 24, 1948	Best Sellers
1	1	13	Mañana (Is Soon Enough For Me)		Peggy Lee...Capitol 15022
2	2	13	Now Is The Hour (Maori Farewell Song)		Bing Crosby...Decca 24279
3	11	3	Little White Lies		Dick Haymes...Decca 24280
4	8	3	You Can't Be True, Dear		Ken Griffin...Rondo 228
5	3	14	I'm Looking Over A Four Leaf Clover		Art Mooney...MGM 10119
6	4	7	Because		Perry Como...RCA Victor 20-2653
7	5	4	Baby Face		Art Mooney...MGM 10156
8	7	4	Sabre Dance		Woody Herman...Columbia 38102
9	10	13	Now Is The Hour		Gracie Fields...London 110
10	9	2	St. Louis Blues March		Tex Beneke...RCA Victor 20-2722

TW	LW	WK	Billboard	MAY 1, 1948	Best Sellers
1	1	14	Mañana (Is Soon Enough For Me)		Peggy Lee...Capitol 15022
2	2	14	Now Is The Hour (Maori Farewell Song)		Bing Crosby...Decca 24279
3	4	4	You Can't Be True, Dear		Ken Griffin...Rondo 228
4	3	4	Little White Lies		Dick Haymes...Decca 24280
5	10	3	St. Louis Blues March		Tex Beneke...RCA Victor 20-2722
6	7	5	Baby Face		Art Mooney...MGM 10156
7	15	2	Nature Boy		King Cole...Capitol 15054
8	14	2	Toolie Oolie Doolie (The Yodel Polka)		Andrews Sisters...Decca 24380
9	8	5	Sabre Dance		Woody Herman...Columbia 38102
10	11	5	Sabre Dance Boogie		Freddy Martin...RCA Victor 20-2721

TW	LW	WK	Billboard 🏵 MAY 8, 1948 🏵	Best Sellers
1	1	15	Mañana (Is Soon Enough For Me) ....*Peggy Lee*...Capitol 15022	
2	7	3	Nature Boy ....*King Cole*...Capitol 15054	
3	2	15	Now Is The Hour (Maori Farewell Song) ....*Bing Crosby*...Decca 24279	
4	3	5	You Can't Be True, Dear ....*Ken Griffin*...Rondo 228	
5	8	3	Toolie Oolie Doolie (The Yodel Polka) ....*Andrews Sisters*...Decca 24380	
6	4	5	Little White Lies ....*Dick Haymes*...Decca 24280	
7	6	6	Baby Face ....*Art Mooney*...MGM 10156	
8	9	6	Sabre Dance ....*Woody Herman*...Columbia 38102	
9	5	4	St. Louis Blues March ....*Tex Beneke*...RCA Victor 20-2722	
10	10	6	Sabre Dance Boogie ....*Freddy Martin*...RCA Victor 20-2721	

TW	LW	WK	Billboard 🏵 MAY 15, 1948 🏵	Best Sellers
1	2	4	Nature Boy ....*King Cole*...Capitol 15054	
2	4	6	You Can't Be True, Dear ....*Ken Griffin*...Rondo 228	
3	1	16	Mañana (Is Soon Enough For Me) ....*Peggy Lee*...Capitol 15022	
4	6	6	Little White Lies ....*Dick Haymes*...Decca 24280	
5	3	16	Now Is The Hour (Maori Farewell Song) ....*Bing Crosby*...Decca 24279	
6	5	4	Toolie Oolie Doolie (The Yodel Polka) ....*Andrews Sisters*...Decca 24380	
7	7	7	Baby Face ....*Art Mooney*...MGM 10156	
8	12	2	The Dickey-Bird Song ....*Freddy Martin*...RCA Victor 20-2617	
9	9	5	St. Louis Blues March ....*Tex Beneke*...RCA Victor 20-2722	
10	11	10	Because ....*Perry Como*...RCA Victor 20-2653	

TW	LW	WK	Billboard 🏵 MAY 22, 1948 🏵	Best Sellers
1	1	5	Nature Boy ....*King Cole*...Capitol 15054	
2	2	7	You Can't Be True, Dear ....*Ken Griffin*...Rondo 228	
3	4	7	Little White Lies ....*Dick Haymes*...Decca 24280	
4	5	17	Now Is The Hour (Maori Farewell Song) ....*Bing Crosby*...Decca 24279	
5	3	17	Mañana (Is Soon Enough For Me) ....*Peggy Lee*...Capitol 15022	
6	6	5	Toolie Oolie Doolie (The Yodel Polka) ....*Andrews Sisters*...Decca 24380	
7	8	3	The Dickey-Bird Song ....*Freddy Martin*...RCA Victor 20-2617	
8	7	8	Baby Face ....*Art Mooney*...MGM 10156	
9	9	6	St. Louis Blues March ....*Tex Beneke*...RCA Victor 20-2722	
10	13	2	My Happiness ....*Jon & Sondra Steele*...Damon 11133	

TW	LW	WK	Billboard 🏵 MAY 29, 1948 🏵	Best Sellers
1	1	6	Nature Boy ....*King Cole*...Capitol 15054	
2	2	8	You Can't Be True, Dear ....*Ken Griffin*...Rondo 228	
3	3	8	Little White Lies ....*Dick Haymes*...Decca 24280	
4	6	6	Toolie Oolie Doolie (The Yodel Polka) ....*Andrews Sisters*...Decca 24380	
5	7	4	The Dickey-Bird Song ....*Freddy Martin*...RCA Victor 20-2617	
6	10	3	My Happiness ....*Jon & Sondra Steele*...Damon 11133	
7	8	9	Baby Face ....*Art Mooney*...MGM 10156	
8	9	7	St. Louis Blues March ....*Tex Beneke*...RCA Victor 20-2722	
9	4	18	Now Is The Hour (Maori Farewell Song) ....*Bing Crosby*...Decca 24279	
10	11	12	Because ....*Perry Como*...RCA Victor 20-2653	

TW	LW	WK	Billboard 🏵 JUNE 5, 1948 🏵	Best Sellers
1	1	7	Nature Boy ....*King Cole*...Capitol 15054	
2	2	9	You Can't Be True, Dear ....*Ken Griffin*...Rondo 228	
3	3	9	Little White Lies ....*Dick Haymes*...Decca 24280	
4	4	7	Toolie Oolie Doolie (The Yodel Polka) ....*Andrews Sisters*...Decca 24380	
5	6	4	My Happiness ....*Jon & Sondra Steele*...Damon 11133	
6	9	19	Now Is The Hour (Maori Farewell Song) ....*Bing Crosby*...Decca 24279	
7	5	5	The Dickey-Bird Song ....*Freddy Martin*...RCA Victor 20-2617	
8	7	10	Baby Face ....*Art Mooney*...MGM 10156	
9	8	8	St. Louis Blues March ....*Tex Beneke*...RCA Victor 20-2722	
10	12	19	Mañana (Is Soon Enough For Me) ....*Peggy Lee*...Capitol 15022	

TW	LW	WK	Billboard ⚫ JUNE 12, 1948 ⚫ Best Sellers
1	1	8	Nature Boy...*King Cole*...Capitol 15054
2	2	10	You Can't Be True, Dear...*Ken Griffin*...Rondo 228
3	3	10	Little White Lies...*Dick Haymes*...Decca 24280
4	4	8	Toolie Oolie Doolie (The Yodel Polka) ....*Andrews Sisters*...Decca 24380
5	5	5	My Happiness...*Jon & Sondra Steele*...Damon 11133
6	13	2	Woody Wood-Pecker...*Kay Kyser*...Columbia 38197
7	7	6	The Dickey-Bird Song...*Freddy Martin*...RCA Victor 20-2617
8	9	9	St. Louis Blues March...*Tex Beneke*...RCA Victor 20-2722
9	23	2	My Happiness...*The Pied Pipers*...Capitol 15094
10	—	1	William Tell Overture ....*Spike Jones*...RCA Victor 20-2861

TW	LW	WK	Billboard ⚫ JUNE 19, 1948 ⚫ Best Sellers
1	1	9	Nature Boy...*King Cole*...Capitol 15054
2	2	11	You Can't Be True, Dear...*Ken Griffin*...Rondo 228
3	3	11	Little White Lies...*Dick Haymes*...Decca 24280
4	6	3	Woody Wood-Pecker...*Kay Kyser*...Columbia 38197
5	5	6	My Happiness...*Jon & Sondra Steele*...Damon 11133
6	4	9	Toolie Oolie Doolie (The Yodel Polka) ....*Andrews Sisters*...Decca 24380
7	10	2	William Tell Overture ....*Spike Jones*...RCA Victor 20-2861
8	9	3	My Happiness...*The Pied Pipers*...Capitol 15094
9	23	3	Love Somebody...*Doris Day & Buddy Clark*...Columbia 38174
9	12	3	You Can't Be True, Dear...*Dick Haymes*...Decca 24439

TW	LW	WK	Billboard ⚫ JUNE 26, 1948 ⚫ Best Sellers
1	1	10	Nature Boy...*King Cole*...Capitol 15054
2	2	12	You Can't Be True, Dear...*Ken Griffin*...Rondo 228
3	4	4	Woody Wood-Pecker...*Kay Kyser*...Columbia 38197
4	3	12	Little White Lies...*Dick Haymes*...Decca 24280
5	5	7	My Happiness...*Jon & Sondra Steele*...Damon 11133
6	7	3	William Tell Overture ....*Spike Jones*...RCA Victor 20-2861
7	6	10	Toolie Oolie Doolie (The Yodel Polka) ....*Andrews Sisters*...Decca 24380
8	8	4	My Happiness...*The Pied Pipers*...Capitol 15094
9	9	4	You Can't Be True, Dear...*Dick Haymes*...Decca 24439
10	9	4	Love Somebody ....*Doris Day & Buddy Clark*...Columbia 38174

TW	LW	WK	Billboard ⚫ JULY 3, 1948 ⚫ Best Sellers
1	3	5	Woody Wood-Pecker...*Kay Kyser*...Columbia 38197
2	2	13	You Can't Be True, Dear...*Ken Griffin*...Rondo 228
3	1	11	Nature Boy...*King Cole*...Capitol 15054
4	4	13	Little White Lies...*Dick Haymes*...Decca 24280
5	5	8	My Happiness...*Jon & Sondra Steele*...Damon 11133
6	6	4	William Tell Overture ....*Spike Jones*...RCA Victor 20-2861
7	7	11	Toolie Oolie Doolie (The Yodel Polka) ....*Andrews Sisters*...Decca 24380
8	8	5	My Happiness...*The Pied Pipers*...Capitol 15094
9	10	5	Love Somebody ....*Doris Day & Buddy Clark*...Columbia 38174
10	9	5	You Can't Be True, Dear...*Dick Haymes*...Decca 24439

TW	LW	WK	Billboard ⚫ JULY 10, 1948 ⚫ Best Sellers
1	1	6	Woody Wood-Pecker...*Kay Kyser*...Columbia 38197
2	—	1	You Can't Be True, Dear...*Ken Griffin*...Rondo 128
3	3	12	Nature Boy...*King Cole*...Capitol 15054
4	4	14	Little White Lies...*Dick Haymes*...Decca 24280
5	5	9	My Happiness...*Jon & Sondra Steele*...Damon 11133
6	6	5	William Tell Overture ....*Spike Jones*...RCA Victor 20-2861
7	8	6	My Happiness...*The Pied Pipers*...Capitol 15094
8	2	14	You Can't Be True, Dear...*Ken Griffin*...Rondo 228
9	9	6	Love Somebody...*Doris Day & Buddy Clark*...Columbia 38174
9	7	12	Toolie Oolie Doolie (The Yodel Polka) ....*Andrews Sisters*...Decca 24380

TW	LW	WK	Billboard® JULY 17, 1948 Best Sellers
1	1	7	Woody Wood-Pecker ....Kay Kyser...Columbia 38197
2	2	2	You Can't Be True, Dear ....Ken Griffin...Rondo 128
3	5	10	My Happiness ....Jon & Sondra Steele...Damon 11133
4	7	7	My Happiness ....The Pied Pipers...Capitol 15094
5	4	15	Little White Lies ....Dick Haymes...Decca 24280
6	8	15	You Can't Be True, Dear ....Ken Griffin...Rondo 228
7	3	13	Nature Boy ....King Cole...Capitol 15054
8	—	1	Woody Woodpecker ....The Sportsmen & Mel Blanc...Capitol 15145
9	6	6	William Tell Overture ....Spike Jones...RCA Victor 20-2861
10	9	7	Love Somebody ....Doris Day & Buddy Clark...Columbia 38174

TW	LW	WK	Billboard® JULY 24, 1948 Best Sellers
1	1	8	Woody Wood-Pecker ....Kay Kyser...Columbia 38197
2	2	3	You Can't Be True, Dear ....Ken Griffin...Rondo 128
3	8	2	Woody Woodpecker ....The Sportsmen & Mel Blanc...Capitol 15145
4	3	11	My Happiness ....Jon & Sondra Steele...Damon 11133
5	4	8	My Happiness ....The Pied Pipers...Capitol 15094
6	9	7	William Tell Overture ....Spike Jones...RCA Victor 20-2861
7	5	16	Little White Lies ....Dick Haymes...Decca 24280
8	11	5	You Call Everybody Darlin' ....Al Trace...Regent 117
9	6	16	You Can't Be True, Dear ....Ken Griffin...Rondo 228
10	15	5	Twelfth Street Rag...Pee Wee Hunt...Capitol 15105

TW	LW	WK	Billboard® JULY 31, 1948 Best Sellers
1	1	9	Woody Wood-Pecker ....Kay Kyser...Columbia 38197
2	3	3	Woody Woodpecker ....The Sportsmen & Mel Blanc...Capitol 15145
3	2	4	You Can't Be True, Dear ....Ken Griffin...Rondo 128
4	4	12	My Happiness ....Jon & Sondra Steele...Damon 11133
5	5	9	My Happiness ....The Pied Pipers...Capitol 15094
6	8	6	You Call Everybody Darlin' ....Al Trace...Regent 117
7	10	6	Twelfth Street Rag...Pee Wee Hunt...Capitol 15105
8	6	8	William Tell Overture ....Spike Jones...RCA Victor 20-2861
9	12	9	Love Somebody ....Doris Day & Buddy Clark...Columbia 38174
10	7	17	Little White Lies ....Dick Haymes...Decca 24280

TW	LW	WK	Billboard® AUGUST 7, 1948 Best Sellers
1	1	10	Woody Wood-Pecker ....Kay Kyser...Columbia 38197
2	2	4	Woody Woodpecker ....The Sportsmen & Mel Blanc...Capitol 15145
3	3	5	You Can't Be True, Dear ....Ken Griffin...Rondo 128
4	5	10	My Happiness ....The Pied Pipers...Capitol 15094
5	6	7	You Call Everybody Darlin' ....Al Trace...Regent 117
6	4	13	My Happiness ....Jon & Sondra Steele...Damon 11133
7	9	10	Love Somebody ....Doris Day & Buddy Clark...Columbia 38174
8	7	7	Twelfth Street Rag...Pee Wee Hunt...Capitol 15105
9	10	18	Little White Lies ....Dick Haymes...Decca 24280
10	11	8	My Happiness ....Ella Fitzgerald...Decca 24446

TW	LW	WK	Billboard® AUGUST 14, 1948 Best Sellers
1	5	8	You Call Everybody Darlin' ....Al Trace...Regent 117
2	3	6	You Can't Be True, Dear ....Ken Griffin...Rondo 128
3	6	14	My Happiness ....Jon & Sondra Steele...Damon 11133
4	4	11	My Happiness ....The Pied Pipers...Capitol 15094
5	2	5	Woody Woodpecker ....The Sportsmen & Mel Blanc...Capitol 15145
6	1	11	Woody Wood-Pecker ....Kay Kyser...Columbia 38197
7	8	8	Twelfth Street Rag...Pee Wee Hunt...Capitol 15105
8	11	5	A Tree In The Meadow ....Margaret Whiting...Capitol 15122
9	12	5	It's Magic ....Doris Day...Columbia 38188
10	7	11	Love Somebody ....Doris Day & Buddy Clark...Columbia 38174

TW	LW	WK	Billboard ❋ AUGUST 21, 1948 ❋ Best Sellers
1	1	9	You Call Everybody Darlin' ....*Al Trace*...Regent 117
2	7	9	Twelfth Street Rag...*Pee Wee Hunt*...Capitol 15105
3	9	6	It's Magic ....*Doris Day*...Columbia 38188
4	4	12	My Happiness..*The Pied Pipers*...Capitol 15094
5	3	15	My Happiness ....*Jon & Sondra Steele*...Damon 11133
6	8	6	A Tree In The Meadow ....*Margaret Whiting*...Capitol 15122
7	2	7	You Can't Be True, Dear ....*Ken Griffin*...Rondo 128
8	10	12	Love Somebody ....*Doris Day & Buddy Clark*...Columbia 38174
9	5	6	Woody Woodpecker...*The Sportsmen & Mel Blanc*...Capitol 15145
10	6	12	Woody Wood-Pecker ....*Kay Kyser*...Columbia 38197

TW	LW	WK	Billboard ❋ AUGUST 28, 1948 ❋ Best Sellers
1	2	10	Twelfth Street Rag...*Pee Wee Hunt*...Capitol 15105
2	1	10	You Call Everybody Darlin' ....*Al Trace*...Regent 117
3	6	7	A Tree In The Meadow ....*Margaret Whiting*...Capitol 15122
4	3	7	It's Magic ....*Doris Day*...Columbia 38188
5	4	13	My Happiness..*The Pied Pipers*...Capitol 15094
6	5	16	My Happiness ....*Jon & Sondra Steele*...Damon 11133
7	8	13	Love Somebody ....*Doris Day & Buddy Clark*...Columbia 38174
8	7	8	You Can't Be True, Dear ....*Ken Griffin*...Rondo 128
9	12	11	Maybe You'll Be There ....*Gordon Jenkins*...Decca 24403
10	11	11	My Happiness ....*Ella Fitzgerald*...Decca 24446

TW	LW	WK	Billboard ❋ SEPTEMBER 4, 1948 ❋ Best Sellers
1	1	11	Twelfth Street Rag...*Pee Wee Hunt*...Capitol 15105
2	2	11	You Call Everybody Darlin' ....*Al Trace*...Regent 117
3	4	8	It's Magic ....*Doris Day*...Columbia 38188
4	3	8	A Tree In The Meadow ....*Margaret Whiting*...Capitol 15122
5	5	14	My Happiness..*The Pied Pipers*...Capitol 15094
6	7	14	Love Somebody ....*Doris Day & Buddy Clark*...Columbia 38174
7	6	17	My Happiness ....*Jon & Sondra Steele*...Damon 11133
8	10	12	My Happiness ....*Ella Fitzgerald*...Decca 24446
9	9	12	Maybe You'll Be There ....*Gordon Jenkins*...Decca 24403
10	8	9	You Can't Be True, Dear ....*Ken Griffin*...Rondo 128

TW	LW	WK	Billboard ❋ SEPTEMBER 11, 1948 ❋ Best Sellers
1	1	12	Twelfth Street Rag...*Pee Wee Hunt*...Capitol 15105
2	3	9	It's Magic ....*Doris Day*...Columbia 38188
3	4	9	A Tree In The Meadow ....*Margaret Whiting*...Capitol 15122
4	2	12	You Call Everybody Darlin' ....*Al Trace*...Regent 117
5	5	15	My Happiness..*The Pied Pipers*...Capitol 15094
6	7	18	My Happiness ....*Jon & Sondra Steele*...Damon 11133
7	6	15	Love Somebody ....*Doris Day & Buddy Clark*...Columbia 38174
8	9	13	Maybe You'll Be There ....*Gordon Jenkins*...Decca 24403
9	10	10	You Can't Be True, Dear ....*Ken Griffin*...Rondo 128
10	11	5	Cool Water..*Vaughn Monroe & Sons of the Pioneers*...RCA Victor 20-2923

TW	LW	WK	Billboard ❋ SEPTEMBER 18, 1948 ❋ Best Sellers
1	1	13	Twelfth Street Rag...*Pee Wee Hunt*...Capitol 15105
2	3	10	A Tree In The Meadow ....*Margaret Whiting*...Capitol 15122
3	4	13	You Call Everybody Darlin' ....*Al Trace*...Regent 117
4	2	10	It's Magic ....*Doris Day*...Columbia 38188
5	5	16	My Happiness..*The Pied Pipers*...Capitol 15094
6	8	14	Maybe You'll Be There ....*Gordon Jenkins*...Decca 24403
7	7	16	Love Somebody ....*Doris Day & Buddy Clark*...Columbia 38174
8	6	19	My Happiness ....*Jon & Sondra Steele*...Damon 11133
9	11	14	My Happiness ....*Ella Fitzgerald*...Decca 24446
10	11	6	Underneath The Arches..*Primo Scala with The Keynotes*...London 238

TW	LW	WK	Billboard ❀ SEPTEMBER 25, 1948 ❀ Best Sellers
1	1	14	**Twelfth Street Rag**..*Pee Wee Hunt*...Capitol 15105
2	2	11	**A Tree In The Meadow** ....*Margaret Whiting*...Capitol 15122
3	3	14	**You Call Everybody Darlin'** ....*Al Trace*...Regent 117
4	4	11	**It's Magic** ....*Doris Day*...Columbia 38188
5	6	15	**Maybe You'll Be There** ....*Gordon Jenkins*...Decca 24403
6	7	17	**Love Somebody** ....*Doris Day & Buddy Clark*...Columbia 38174
7	5	17	**My Happiness**..*The Pied Pipers*...Capitol 15094
8	9	15	**My Happiness**..*Ella Fitzgerald*...Decca 24446
9	10	7	**Underneath The Arches**..*Primo Scala with The Keynotes*...London 238
10	14	13	**Blue Bird Of Happiness** ....*Art Mooney*...MGM 10207

TW	LW	WK	Billboard ❀ OCTOBER 2, 1948 ❀ Best Sellers
1	1	15	**Twelfth Street Rag**..*Pee Wee Hunt*...Capitol 15105
2	2	12	**A Tree In The Meadow** ....*Margaret Whiting*...Capitol 15122
3	4	12	**It's Magic** ....*Doris Day*...Columbia 38188
4	3	15	**You Call Everybody Darlin'** ....*Al Trace*...Regent 117
5	5	16	**Maybe You'll Be There** ....*Gordon Jenkins*...Decca 24403
6	9	8	**Underneath The Arches**..*Primo Scala with The Keynotes*...London 238
7	7	18	**My Happiness**..*The Pied Pipers*...Capitol 15094
8	8	16	**My Happiness**..*Ella Fitzgerald*...Decca 24446
9	17	4	**Until** ....*Tommy Dorsey*...RCA Victor 20-3061
10	6	18	**Love Somebody** ....*Doris Day & Buddy Clark*...Columbia 38174

TW	LW	WK	Billboard ❀ OCTOBER 9, 1948 ❀ Best Sellers
1	2	13	**A Tree In The Meadow** ....*Margaret Whiting*...Capitol 15122
2	1	16	**Twelfth Street Rag**..*Pee Wee Hunt*...Capitol 15105
3	3	13	**It's Magic** ....*Doris Day*...Columbia 38188
4	4	16	**You Call Everybody Darlin'** ....*Al Trace*...Regent 117
5	5	17	**Maybe You'll Be There** ....*Gordon Jenkins*...Decca 24403
6	7	19	**My Happiness**..*The Pied Pipers*...Capitol 15094
7	6	9	**Underneath The Arches**..*Primo Scala with The Keynotes*...London 238
8	10	19	**Love Somebody** ....*Doris Day & Buddy Clark*...Columbia 38174
9	11	9	**Cool Water**...*Vaughn Monroe & Sons of the Pioneers*...RCA Victor 20-2923
10	9	5	**Until** ....*Tommy Dorsey*...RCA Victor 20-3061

TW	LW	WK	Billboard ❀ OCTOBER 16, 1948 ❀ Best Sellers
1	1	14	**A Tree In The Meadow** ....*Margaret Whiting*...Capitol 15122
2	2	17	**Twelfth Street Rag**..*Pee Wee Hunt*...Capitol 15105
3	3	14	**It's Magic** ....*Doris Day*...Columbia 38188
4	5	18	**Maybe You'll Be There** ....*Gordon Jenkins*...Decca 24403
5	4	17	**You Call Everybody Darlin'** ....*Al Trace*...Regent 117
6	7	10	**Underneath The Arches**..*Primo Scala with The Keynotes*...London 238
7	14	4	**Buttons And Bows** ....*Dinah Shore*...Columbia 38284
7	10	6	**Until** ....*Tommy Dorsey*...RCA Victor 20-3061
9	6	20	**My Happiness**..*The Pied Pipers*...Capitol 15094
10	9	10	**Cool Water**...*Vaughn Monroe & Sons of the Pioneers*...RCA Victor 20-2923

TW	LW	WK	Billboard ❀ OCTOBER 23, 1948 ❀ Best Sellers
1	2	18	**Twelfth Street Rag**..*Pee Wee Hunt*...Capitol 15105
2	1	15	**A Tree In The Meadow** ....*Margaret Whiting*...Capitol 15122
3	4	19	**Maybe You'll Be There** ....*Gordon Jenkins*...Decca 24403
4	3	15	**It's Magic** ....*Doris Day*...Columbia 38188
5	7	5	**Buttons And Bows** ....*Dinah Shore*...Columbia 38284
6	7	7	**Until** ....*Tommy Dorsey*...RCA Victor 20-3061
7	5	18	**You Call Everybody Darlin'** ....*Al Trace*...Regent 117
8	6	11	**Underneath The Arches**..*Primo Scala with The Keynotes*...London 238
9	20	17	**Blue Bird Of Happiness** ....*Art Mooney*...MGM 10207
10	12	7	**Underneath The Arches**..*Andrews Sisters*...Decca 24490

TW	LW	WK	Billboard® ✹ OCTOBER 30, 1948 ✹ Best Sellers
1	1	19	Twelfth Street Rag...*Pee Wee Hunt*...Capitol 15105
2	2	16	A Tree In The Meadow ....*Margaret Whiting*...Capitol 15122
3	5	6	Buttons And Bows ....*Dinah Shore*...Columbia 38284
4	3	20	Maybe You'll Be There ....*Gordon Jenkins*...Decca 24403
5	4	16	It's Magic ....*Doris Day*...Columbia 38188
6	7	19	You Call Everybody Darlin' ....*Al Trace*...Regent 117
7	6	8	Until ....*Tommy Dorsey*...RCA Victor 20-3061
8	19	2	On A Slow Boat To China...*Kay Kyser*...Columbia 38301
9	8	12	Underneath The Arches..*Primo Scala with The Keynotes*...London 238
10	9	18	Blue Bird Of Happiness ....*Art Mooney*...MGM 10207

TW	LW	WK	Billboard® ✹ NOVEMBER 6, 1948 ✹ Best Sellers
1	3	7	Buttons And Bows ....*Dinah Shore*...Columbia 38284
2	1	20	Twelfth Street Rag...*Pee Wee Hunt*...Capitol 15105
3	2	17	A Tree In The Meadow ....*Margaret Whiting*...Capitol 15122
4	4	21	Maybe You'll Be There ....*Gordon Jenkins*...Decca 24403
5	8	3	On A Slow Boat To China...*Kay Kyser*...Columbia 38301
6	5	17	It's Magic ....*Doris Day*...Columbia 38188
7	7	9	Until ....*Tommy Dorsey*...RCA Victor 20-3061
8	22	2	Buttons And Bows ....*The Dinning Sisters*...Capitol 15184
9	13	6	You Were Only Fooling ....*Blue Barron*...MGM 10185
10	10	19	Blue Bird Of Happiness ....*Art Mooney*...MGM 10207

TW	LW	WK	Billboard® ✹ NOVEMBER 13, 1948 ✹ Best Sellers
1	1	8	Buttons And Bows ....*Dinah Shore*...Columbia 38284
2	2	21	Twelfth Street Rag...*Pee Wee Hunt*...Capitol 15105
3	3	18	A Tree In The Meadow ....*Margaret Whiting*...Capitol 15122
4	5	4	On A Slow Boat To China...*Kay Kyser*...Columbia 38301
5	4	22	Maybe You'll Be There ....*Gordon Jenkins*...Decca 24403
6	7	10	Until ....*Tommy Dorsey*...RCA Victor 20-3061
7	6	18	It's Magic ....*Doris Day*...Columbia 38188
8	8	3	Buttons And Bows ....*The Dinning Sisters*...Capitol 15184
9	17	2	On A Slow Boat To China...*Freddy Martin*...RCA Victor 20-3123
10	14	11	Hair Of Gold, Eyes Of Blue ....*Gordon MacRae*...Capitol 15178
10	9	7	You Were Only Fooling ....*Blue Barron*...MGM 10185

TW	LW	WK	Billboard® ✹ NOVEMBER 20, 1948 ✹ Best Sellers
1	1	9	Buttons And Bows ....*Dinah Shore*...Columbia 38284
2	2	22	Twelfth Street Rag...*Pee Wee Hunt*...Capitol 15105
3	4	5	On A Slow Boat To China...*Kay Kyser*...Columbia 38301
4	3	19	A Tree In The Meadow ....*Margaret Whiting*...Capitol 15122
5	5	23	Maybe You'll Be There ....*Gordon Jenkins*...Decca 24403
6	9	3	On A Slow Boat To China...*Freddy Martin*...RCA Victor 20-3123
7	18	2	My Darling, My Darling..*Jo Stafford & Gordon MacRae*...Capitol 15270
7	6	11	Until ....*Tommy Dorsey*...RCA Victor 20-3061
9	8	4	Buttons And Bows ....*The Dinning Sisters*...Capitol 15184
10	7	19	It's Magic ....*Doris Day*...Columbia 38188

TW	LW	WK	Billboard® ✹ NOVEMBER 27, 1948 ✹ Best Sellers
1	1	10	Buttons And Bows ....*Dinah Shore*...Columbia 38284
2	3	6	On A Slow Boat To China...*Kay Kyser*...Columbia 38301
3	2	23	Twelfth Street Rag...*Pee Wee Hunt*...Capitol 15105
4	7	3	My Darling, My Darling..*Jo Stafford & Gordon MacRae*...Capitol 15270
5	5	24	Maybe You'll Be There ....*Gordon Jenkins*...Decca 24403
6	6	4	On A Slow Boat To China...*Freddy Martin*...RCA Victor 20-3123
7	4	20	A Tree In The Meadow ....*Margaret Whiting*...Capitol 15122
8	9	5	Buttons And Bows ....*The Dinning Sisters*...Capitol 15184
9	20	2	A Little Bird Told Me ....*Evelyn Knight*...Decca 24514
10	11	9	You Were Only Fooling ....*Blue Barron*...MGM 10185

TW	LW	WK	Billboard® DECEMBER 4, 1948 Best Sellers
1	1	11	**Buttons And Bows**...*Dinah Shore*...Columbia 38284
2	2	7	**On A Slow Boat To China**..*Kay Kyser*...Columbia 38301
3	3	24	**Twelfth Street Rag**...*Pee Wee Hunt*...Capitol 15105
4	5	25	**Maybe You'll Be There**...*Gordon Jenkins*...Decca 24403
5	6	5	**On A Slow Boat To China**.....................................*Freddy Martin*...RCA Victor 20-3123
6	4	4	**My Darling, My Darling**.................*Jo Stafford & Gordon MacRae*...Capitol 15270
7	8	6	**Buttons And Bows**..*The Dinning Sisters*...Capitol 15184
8	9	3	**A Little Bird Told Me**..*Evelyn Knight*...Decca 24514
9	7	21	**A Tree In The Meadow**..................................*Margaret Whiting*...Capitol 15122
10	11	13	**Until**...*Tommy Dorsey*...RCA Victor 20-3061

TW	LW	WK	Billboard® DECEMBER 11, 1948 Best Sellers
1	1	12	**Buttons And Bows**...*Dinah Shore*...Columbia 38284
2	2	8	**On A Slow Boat To China**..*Kay Kyser*...Columbia 38301
3	6	5	**My Darling, My Darling**.................*Jo Stafford & Gordon MacRae*...Capitol 15270
4	12	3	**All I Want For Christmas (Is My Two Front Teeth)**.....................*Spike Jones*...RCA Victor 20-3177
5	5	6	**On A Slow Boat To China**.....................................*Freddy Martin*...RCA Victor 20-3123
6	3	25	**Twelfth Street Rag**...*Pee Wee Hunt*...Capitol 15105
7	8	4	**A Little Bird Told Me**..*Evelyn Knight*...Decca 24514
8	4	26	**Maybe You'll Be There**...*Gordon Jenkins*...Decca 24403
9	11	4	**My Darling My Darling**.................*Doris Day & Buddy Clark*...Columbia 38353
10	7	7	**Buttons And Bows**..*The Dinning Sisters*...Capitol 15184

TW	LW	WK	Billboard® DECEMBER 18, 1948 Best Sellers
1	1	13	**Buttons And Bows**...*Dinah Shore*...Columbia 38284
2	2	9	**On A Slow Boat To China**..*Kay Kyser*...Columbia 38301
3	4	4	**All I Want For Christmas (Is My Two Front Teeth)**.....................*Spike Jones*...RCA Victor 20-3177
4	3	6	**My Darling, My Darling**.................*Jo Stafford & Gordon MacRae*...Capitol 15270
5	7	5	**A Little Bird Told Me**..*Evelyn Knight*...Decca 24514
6	5	7	**On A Slow Boat To China**.....................................*Freddy Martin*...RCA Victor 20-3123
7	9	5	**My Darling My Darling**.................*Doris Day & Buddy Clark*...Columbia 38353
7	6	26	**Twelfth Street Rag**...*Pee Wee Hunt*...Capitol 15105
9	18	2	**Here Comes Santa Claus (Down Santa Claus Lane)**.................*Gene Autry*...Columbia 20377
10	10	8	**Buttons And Bows**..*The Dinning Sisters*...Capitol 15184

TW	LW	WK	Billboard® DECEMBER 25, 1948 Best Sellers
1	1	14	**Buttons And Bows**...*Dinah Shore*...Columbia 38284
2	3	5	**All I Want For Christmas (Is My Two Front Teeth)**.....................*Spike Jones*...RCA Victor 20-3177
3	2	10	**On A Slow Boat To China**..*Kay Kyser*...Columbia 38301
4	5	6	**A Little Bird Told Me**..*Evelyn Knight*...Decca 24514
5	4	7	**My Darling, My Darling**.................*Jo Stafford & Gordon MacRae*...Capitol 15270
6	6	8	**On A Slow Boat To China**.....................................*Freddy Martin*...RCA Victor 20-3123
7	11	3	**White Christmas**..*Bing Crosby*...Decca 23778
8	10	9	**Buttons And Bows**..*The Dinning Sisters*...Capitol 15184
9	12	16	**Until**...*Tommy Dorsey*...RCA Victor 20-3061
10	7	6	**My Darling My Darling**.................*Doris Day & Buddy Clark*...Columbia 38353

TW	LW	WK	Billboard® JANUARY 1, 1949 Best Sellers
1	1	15	**Buttons And Bows**...*Dinah Shore*...Columbia 38284
2	2	6	**All I Want For Christmas (Is My Two Front Teeth)**......................*Spike Jones*...RCA Victor 20-3177
3	4	7	**A Little Bird Told Me**..*Evelyn Knight*...Decca 24514
4	3	11	**On A Slow Boat To China**...*Kay Kyser*...Columbia 38301
5	5	8	**My Darling, My Darling**...*Jo Stafford & Gordon MacRae*...Capitol 15270
6	6	9	**On A Slow Boat To China**...*Freddy Martin*...RCA Victor 20-3123
7	7	4	**White Christmas**..*Bing Crosby*...Decca 23778
8	14	4	**Here Comes Santa Claus (Down Santa Claus Lane)**........................*Gene Autry*...Columbia 20377
9	10	7	**My Darling My Darling**...*Doris Day & Buddy Clark*...Columbia 38353
10	21	7	**On A Slow Boat To China**..*Benny Goodman*...Capitol 15208

TW	LW	WK	Billboard® JANUARY 8, 1949 Best Sellers
1	2	7	**All I Want For Christmas (Is My Two Front Teeth)**......................*Spike Jones*...RCA Victor 20-3177
2	1	16	**Buttons And Bows**...*Dinah Shore*...Columbia 38284
3	4	12	**On A Slow Boat To China**...*Kay Kyser*...Columbia 38301
4	3	8	**A Little Bird Told Me**..*Evelyn Knight*...Decca 24514
5	5	9	**My Darling, My Darling**...*Jo Stafford & Gordon MacRae*...Capitol 15270
6	7	5	**White Christmas**..*Bing Crosby*...Decca 23778
7	29	11	**Buttons And Bows**...*The Dinning Sisters*...Capitol 15184
8	6	10	**On A Slow Boat To China**...*Freddy Martin*...RCA Victor 20-3123
9	8	5	**Here Comes Santa Claus (Down Santa Claus Lane)**........................*Gene Autry*...Columbia 20377
10	20	5	**Lavender Blue (Dilly Dilly)**...*Sammy Kaye*...RCA Victor 20-3100

TW	LW	WK	Billboard® JANUARY 15, 1949 Best Sellers
1	2	17	**Buttons And Bows**...*Dinah Shore*...Columbia 38284
2	4	9	**A Little Bird Told Me**..*Evelyn Knight*...Decca 24514
3	3	13	**On A Slow Boat To China**...*Kay Kyser*...Columbia 38301
4	5	10	**My Darling, My Darling**...*Jo Stafford & Gordon MacRae*...Capitol 15270
5	1	8	**All I Want For Christmas (Is My Two Front Teeth)**......................*Spike Jones*...RCA Victor 20-3177
6	10	6	**Lavender Blue (Dilly Dilly)**...*Sammy Kaye*...RCA Victor 20-3100
7	8	11	**On A Slow Boat To China**...*Freddy Martin*...RCA Victor 20-3123
8	—	3	**Far Away Places**..*Margaret Whiting*...Capitol 15278
9	18	3	**Powder Your Face With Sunshine (Smile! Smile! Smile!)**.................*Evelyn Knight*...Decca 24530
10	7	12	**Buttons And Bows**...*The Dinning Sisters*...Capitol 15184

TW	LW	WK	Billboard® JANUARY 22, 1949 Best Sellers
1	2	10	**A Little Bird Told Me**..*Evelyn Knight*...Decca 24514
2	1	18	**Buttons And Bows**...*Dinah Shore*...Columbia 38284
3	3	14	**On A Slow Boat To China**...*Kay Kyser*...Columbia 38301
4	4	11	**My Darling, My Darling**...*Jo Stafford & Gordon MacRae*...Capitol 15270
5	8	4	**Far Away Places**..*Margaret Whiting*...Capitol 15278
6	6	7	**Lavender Blue (Dilly Dilly)**...*Sammy Kaye*...RCA Victor 20-3100
7	7	12	**On A Slow Boat To China**...*Freddy Martin*...RCA Victor 20-3123
8	12	3	**Far Away Places**..*Bing Crosby*...Decca 24532
9	9	4	**Powder Your Face With Sunshine (Smile! Smile! Smile!)**.................*Evelyn Knight*...Decca 24530
10	18	2	**Far Away Places**...*Perry Como*...RCA Victor 20-3316

TW	LW	WK	Billboard® JANUARY 29, 1949 Best Sellers
1	1	11	**A Little Bird Told Me**..*Evelyn Knight*...Decca 24514
2	2	19	**Buttons And Bows**...*Dinah Shore*...Columbia 38284
3	3	15	**On A Slow Boat To China**...*Kay Kyser*...Columbia 38301
4	4	12	**My Darling, My Darling**...*Jo Stafford & Gordon MacRae*...Capitol 15270
5	5	5	**Far Away Places**..*Margaret Whiting*...Capitol 15278
6	9	5	**Powder Your Face With Sunshine (Smile! Smile! Smile!)**.................*Evelyn Knight*...Decca 24530
7	8	4	**Far Away Places**..*Bing Crosby*...Decca 24532
8	11	9	**So Tired**...*Russ Morgan*...Decca 24521
9	6	8	**Lavender Blue (Dilly Dilly)**...*Sammy Kaye*...RCA Victor 20-3100
10	15	6	**I've Got My Love To Keep Me Warm**...*Les Brown*...Columbia 38324

TW	LW	WK	Billboard® ✿ FEBRUARY 5, 1949 ✿ Best Sellers
1	1	12	A Little Bird Told Me ....Evelyn Knight...Decca 24514
2	2	20	Buttons And Bows ....Dinah Shore...Columbia 38284
3	7	5	Far Away Places ....Bing Crosby...Decca 24532
4	6	6	Powder Your Face With Sunshine (Smile! Smile! Smile!)................Evelyn Knight...Decca 24530
5	4	13	My Darling, My Darling...Jo Stafford & Gordon MacRae...Capitol 15270
6	5	6	Far Away Places ....Margaret Whiting...Capitol 15278
7	9	9	Lavender Blue (Dilly Dilly) ....Sammy Kaye...RCA Victor 20-3100
8	3	16	On A Slow Boat To China...Kay Kyser...Columbia 38301
9	19	7	Lavender Blue (Dilly Dilly) ....Dinah Shore...Columbia 38299
10	13	8	Sweet Georgia Brown ....Brother Bones...Tempo TR 652

TW	LW	WK	Billboard® ✿ FEBRUARY 12, 1949 ✿ Best Sellers
1	1	13	A Little Bird Told Me ....Evelyn Knight...Decca 24514
2	3	6	Far Away Places ....Bing Crosby...Decca 24532
3	6	7	Far Away Places ....Margaret Whiting...Capitol 15278
4	4	7	Powder Your Face With Sunshine (Smile! Smile! Smile!)................Evelyn Knight...Decca 24530
5	2	21	Buttons And Bows ....Dinah Shore...Columbia 38284
6	7	10	Lavender Blue (Dilly Dilly) ....Sammy Kaye...RCA Victor 20-3100
7	15	4	Galway Bay ....Bing Crosby...Decca 24295
8	11	5	Far Away Places ....Perry Como...RCA Victor 20-3316
9	12	3	Cruising Down The River ....Blue Barron...MGM 10346
10	14	8	I've Got My Love To Keep Me Warm ....Les Brown...Columbia 38324

TW	LW	WK	Billboard® ✿ FEBRUARY 19, 1949 ✿ Best Sellers
1	1	14	A Little Bird Told Me ....Evelyn Knight...Decca 24514
2	2	7	Far Away Places ....Bing Crosby...Decca 24532
3	4	8	Powder Your Face With Sunshine (Smile! Smile! Smile!)................Evelyn Knight...Decca 24530
4	9	4	Cruising Down The River ....Blue Barron...MGM 10346
5	6	11	Lavender Blue (Dilly Dilly) ....Sammy Kaye...RCA Victor 20-3100
6	5	22	Buttons And Bows ....Dinah Shore...Columbia 38284
7	13	12	So Tired ....Russ Morgan...Decca 24521
8	7	5	Galway Bay ....Bing Crosby...Decca 24295
9	10	9	I've Got My Love To Keep Me Warm ....Les Brown...Columbia 38324
10	3	8	Far Away Places ....Margaret Whiting...Capitol 15278

TW	LW	WK	Billboard® ✿ FEBRUARY 26, 1949 ✿ Best Sellers
1	1	15	A Little Bird Told Me ....Evelyn Knight...Decca 24514
2	4	5	Cruising Down The River ....Blue Barron...MGM 10346
3	3	9	Powder Your Face With Sunshine (Smile! Smile! Smile!)................Evelyn Knight...Decca 24530
4	8	6	Galway Bay ....Bing Crosby...Decca 24295
5	2	8	Far Away Places ....Bing Crosby...Decca 24532
6	11	7	Far Away Places ....Perry Como...RCA Victor 20-3316
7	7	13	So Tired ....Russ Morgan...Decca 24521
8	18	3	I Love You So Much It Hurts..Mills Brothers...Decca 24550
8	9	10	I've Got My Love To Keep Me Warm ....Les Brown...Columbia 38324
8	5	12	Lavender Blue (Dilly Dilly) ....Sammy Kaye...RCA Victor 20-3100

TW	LW	WK	Billboard® ✿ MARCH 5, 1949 ✿ Best Sellers
1	1	16	A Little Bird Told Me ....Evelyn Knight...Decca 24514
2	2	6	Cruising Down The River ....Blue Barron...MGM 10346
3	5	9	Far Away Places ....Bing Crosby...Decca 24532
4	3	10	Powder Your Face With Sunshine (Smile! Smile! Smile!)................Evelyn Knight...Decca 24530
5	4	7	Galway Bay ....Bing Crosby...Decca 24295
6	15	2	Cruising Down The River ....Russ Morgan...Decca 24568
7	8	11	I've Got My Love To Keep Me Warm ....Les Brown...Columbia 38324
8	11	7	Red Roses For A Blue Lady ....Vaughn Monroe...RCA Victor 47-2889
9	8	13	Lavender Blue (Dilly Dilly) ....Sammy Kaye...RCA Victor 20-3100
10	6	8	Far Away Places ....Perry Como...RCA Victor 20-3316

TW	LW	WK	Billboard® ✿ MARCH 12, 1949 ✿ Best Sellers
1	2	7	Cruising Down The River ....*Blue Barron*...MGM 10346
2	3	10	Far Away Places ....*Bing Crosby*...Decca 24532
3	5	8	Galway Bay ....*Bing Crosby*...Decca 24295
4	6	3	Cruising Down The River ....*Russ Morgan*...Decca 24568
5	1	17	A Little Bird Told Me ....*Evelyn Knight*...Decca 24514
6	4	11	Powder Your Face With Sunshine (Smile! Smile! Smile!)................*Evelyn Knight*...Decca 24530
7	12	15	So Tired ....*Russ Morgan*...Decca 24521
8	8	8	Red Roses For A Blue Lady ....*Vaughn Monroe*...RCA Victor 47-2889
9	11	5	I Love You So Much It Hurts ....*Mills Brothers*...Decca 24550
10	7	12	I've Got My Love To Keep Me Warm ....*Les Brown*...Columbia 38324

TW	LW	WK	Billboard® ✿ MARCH 19, 1949 ✿ Best Sellers
1	1	8	Cruising Down The River ....*Blue Barron*...MGM 10346
2	4	4	Cruising Down The River ....*Russ Morgan*...Decca 24568
3	3	9	Galway Bay ....*Bing Crosby*...Decca 24295
4	2	11	Far Away Places ....*Bing Crosby*...Decca 24532
5	6	12	Powder Your Face With Sunshine (Smile! Smile! Smile!)................*Evelyn Knight*...Decca 24530
6	8	9	Red Roses For A Blue Lady ....*Vaughn Monroe*...RCA Victor 47-2889
7	7	16	So Tired ....*Russ Morgan*...Decca 24521
8	5	18	A Little Bird Told Me ....*Evelyn Knight*...Decca 24514
9	14	6	Careless Hands ....*Sammy Kaye*...RCA Victor 20-3321
10	10	13	I've Got My Love To Keep Me Warm ....*Les Brown*...Columbia 38324

TW	LW	WK	Billboard® ✿ MARCH 26, 1949 ✿ Best Sellers
1	2	5	Cruising Down The River ....*Russ Morgan*...Decca 24568
2	1	9	Cruising Down The River ....*Blue Barron*...MGM 10346
3	3	10	Galway Bay ....*Bing Crosby*...Decca 24295
4	4	12	Far Away Places ....*Bing Crosby*...Decca 24532
5	7	17	So Tired ....*Russ Morgan*...Decca 24521
6	5	13	Powder Your Face With Sunshine (Smile! Smile! Smile!)................*Evelyn Knight*...Decca 24530
7	6	10	Red Roses For A Blue Lady ....*Vaughn Monroe*...RCA Victor 47-2889
8	13	7	I Love You So Much It Hurts ....*Mills Brothers*...Decca 24550
9	9	7	Careless Hands ....*Sammy Kaye*...RCA Victor 20-3321
10	10	14	I've Got My Love To Keep Me Warm ....*Les Brown*...Columbia 38324

TW	LW	WK	Billboard® ✿ APRIL 2, 1949 ✿ Best Sellers
1	1	6	Cruising Down The River ....*Russ Morgan*...Decca 24568
2	2	10	Cruising Down The River ....*Blue Barron*...MGM 10346
3	3	11	Galway Bay ....*Bing Crosby*...Decca 24295
4	4	13	Far Away Places ....*Bing Crosby*...Decca 24532
5	7	11	Red Roses For A Blue Lady ....*Vaughn Monroe*...RCA Victor 47-2889
6	5	18	So Tired ....*Russ Morgan*...Decca 24521
7	15	3	Forever And Ever ....*Perry Como*...RCA Victor 47-2892
8	18	3	Forever And Ever ....*Russ Morgan*...Decca 24569
9	6	14	Powder Your Face With Sunshine (Smile! Smile! Smile!)................*Evelyn Knight*...Decca 24530
10	11	4	Sunflower ....*Russ Morgan*...Decca 24568

TW	LW	WK	Billboard® ✿ APRIL 9, 1949 ✿ Best Sellers
1	1	7	Cruising Down The River ....*Russ Morgan*...Decca 24568
2	2	11	Cruising Down The River ....*Blue Barron*...MGM 10346
3	3	12	Galway Bay ....*Bing Crosby*...Decca 24295
4	4	14	Far Away Places ....*Bing Crosby*...Decca 24532
4	5	12	Red Roses For A Blue Lady ....*Vaughn Monroe*...RCA Victor 47-2889
6	7	4	Forever And Ever ....*Perry Como*...RCA Victor 47-2892
7	6	19	So Tired ....*Russ Morgan*...Decca 24521
8	8	4	Forever And Ever ....*Russ Morgan*...Decca 24569
9	11	9	Careless Hands ....*Sammy Kaye*...RCA Victor 20-3321
10	12	7	Red Roses For A Blue Lady ....*Guy Lombardo*...Decca 24549
10	14	4	Careless Hands ....*Mel Tormé*...Capitol 15379

TW	LW	WK	Billboard® ❀ APRIL 16, 1949 ❀ Best Sellers
1	1	8	Cruising Down The River .... Russ Morgan...Decca 24568
2	2	12	Cruising Down The River .... Blue Barron...MGM 10346
3	8	5	Forever And Ever .... Russ Morgan...Decca 24569
4	7	20	So Tired .... Russ Morgan...Decca 24521
5	4	13	Red Roses For A Blue Lady .... Vaughn Monroe...RCA Victor 47-2889
6	6	5	Forever And Ever .... Perry Como...RCA Victor 47-2892
7	3	13	Galway Bay .... Bing Crosby...Decca 24295
8	9	10	Careless Hands .... Sammy Kaye...RCA Victor 20-3321
9	4	15	Far Away Places .... Bing Crosby...Decca 24532
10	18	3	"A" You're Adorable .... Jo Stafford & Gordon MacRae...Capitol 15393

TW	LW	WK	Billboard® ❀ APRIL 23, 1949 ❀ Best Sellers
1	1	9	Cruising Down The River .... Russ Morgan...Decca 24568
2	2	13	Cruising Down The River .... Blue Barron...MGM 10346
3	6	6	Forever And Ever .... Perry Como...RCA Victor 47-2892
4	3	6	Forever And Ever .... Russ Morgan...Decca 24569
5	5	14	Red Roses For A Blue Lady .... Vaughn Monroe...RCA Victor 47-2889
6	4	21	So Tired .... Russ Morgan...Decca 24521
7	15	6	Careless Hands .... Mel Tormé...Capitol 15379
8	9	16	Far Away Places .... Bing Crosby...Decca 24532
9	12	3	"A"-You're Adorable .... Perry Como...RCA Victor 47-2899
10	8	11	Careless Hands .... Sammy Kaye...RCA Victor 20-3321

TW	LW	WK	Billboard® ❀ APRIL 30, 1949 ❀ Best Sellers
1	1	10	Cruising Down The River .... Russ Morgan...Decca 24568
2	4	7	Forever And Ever .... Russ Morgan...Decca 24569
3	3	7	Forever And Ever .... Perry Como...RCA Victor 47-2892
4	22	5	"A" You're Adorable .... Jo Stafford & Gordon MacRae...Capitol 15393
5	9	4	"A"-You're Adorable .... Perry Como...RCA Victor 47-2899
6	2	14	Cruising Down The River .... Blue Barron...MGM 10346
7	10	12	Careless Hands .... Sammy Kaye...RCA Victor 20-3321
8	5	15	Red Roses For A Blue Lady .... Vaughn Monroe...RCA Victor 47-2889
9	7	7	Careless Hands .... Mel Tormé...Capitol 15379
10	12	8	Sunflower .... Russ Morgan...Decca 24568

TW	LW	WK	Billboard® ❀ MAY 7, 1949 ❀ Best Sellers
1	1	11	Cruising Down The River .... Russ Morgan...Decca 24568
2	2	8	Forever And Ever .... Russ Morgan...Decca 24569
3	3	8	Forever And Ever .... Perry Como...RCA Victor 47-2892
4	12	3	Riders In The Sky (A Cowboy Legend) .... Vaughn Monroe...RCA Victor 47-2902
5	5	5	"A"-You're Adorable .... Perry Como...RCA Victor 47-2899
6	6	15	Cruising Down The River .... Blue Barron...MGM 10346
7	7	13	Careless Hands .... Sammy Kaye...RCA Victor 20-3321
8	13	3	Again .... Gordon Jenkins...Decca 24602
9	9	8	Careless Hands .... Mel Tormé...Capitol 15379
10	8	16	Red Roses For A Blue Lady .... Vaughn Monroe...RCA Victor 47-2889

TW	LW	WK	Billboard® ❀ MAY 14, 1949 ❀ Best Sellers
1	4	4	Riders In The Sky (A Cowboy Legend) .... Vaughn Monroe...RCA Victor 47-2902
2	1	12	Cruising Down The River .... Russ Morgan...Decca 24568
3	2	9	Forever And Ever .... Russ Morgan...Decca 24569
4	5	6	"A"-You're Adorable .... Perry Como...RCA Victor 47-2899
5	3	9	Forever And Ever .... Perry Como...RCA Victor 47-2892
6	8	4	Again .... Gordon Jenkins...Decca 24602
7	9	9	Careless Hands .... Mel Tormé...Capitol 15379
8	11	7	"A" You're Adorable .... Jo Stafford & Gordon MacRae...Capitol 15393
9	13	5	Again .... Mel Tormé...Capitol 15428
10	6	16	Cruising Down The River .... Blue Barron...MGM 10346

TW	LW	WK	Billboard®	MAY 21, 1949	Best Sellers
1	1	5	**Riders In The Sky (A Cowboy Legend)**.................................*Vaughn Monroe*...RCA Victor 47-2902		
2	3	10	**Forever And Ever**...*Russ Morgan*...Decca 24569		
3	2	13	**Cruising Down The River**...*Russ Morgan*...Decca 24568		
4	5	10	**Forever And Ever**...*Perry Como*...RCA Victor 47-2892		
5	6	5	**Again**...*Gordon Jenkins*...Decca 24602		
6	4	7	**"A"-You're Adorable**...*Perry Como*...RCA Victor 47-2899		
7	9	6	**Again**...*Mel Tormé*...Capitol 15428		
8	7	10	**Careless Hands**..*Mel Tormé*...Capitol 15379		
9	8	8	**"A" You're Adorable**.............................*Jo Stafford & Gordon MacRae*...Capitol 15393		
10	12	15	**Careless Hands**..*Sammy Kaye*...RCA Victor 20-3321		

TW	LW	WK	Billboard®	MAY 28, 1949	Best Sellers
1	1	6	**Riders In The Sky (A Cowboy Legend)**.................................*Vaughn Monroe*...RCA Victor 47-2902		
2	5	6	**Again**...*Gordon Jenkins*...Decca 24602		
3	4	11	**Forever And Ever**...*Perry Como*...RCA Victor 47-2892		
4	2	11	**Forever And Ever**...*Russ Morgan*...Decca 24569		
5	3	14	**Cruising Down The River**...*Russ Morgan*...Decca 24568		
6	6	8	**"A"-You're Adorable**...*Perry Como*...RCA Victor 47-2899		
7	11	8	**I Don't See Me In Your Eyes Anymore**...............................*The Stardusters*...Decca 24576		
8	15	5	**Some Enchanted Evening**...*Perry Como*...RCA Victor 47-2896		
9	9	9	**"A" You're Adorable**.............................*Jo Stafford & Gordon MacRae*...Capitol 15393		
10	7	7	**Again**...*Mel Tormé*...Capitol 15428		

TW	LW	WK	Billboard®	JUNE 4, 1949	Best Sellers
1	1	7	**Riders In The Sky (A Cowboy Legend)**.................................*Vaughn Monroe*...RCA Victor 47-2902		
2	2	7	**Again**...*Gordon Jenkins*...Decca 24602		
3	4	12	**Forever And Ever**...*Russ Morgan*...Decca 24569		
4	8	6	**Some Enchanted Evening**...*Perry Como*...RCA Victor 47-2896		
5	3	12	**Forever And Ever**...*Perry Como*...RCA Victor 47-2892		
6	5	15	**Cruising Down The River**...*Russ Morgan*...Decca 24568		
7	6	9	**"A"-You're Adorable**...*Perry Como*...RCA Victor 47-2899		
8	10	8	**Again**...*Mel Tormé*...Capitol 15428		
9	7	9	**I Don't See Me In Your Eyes Anymore**...............................*The Stardusters*...Decca 24576		
10	12	4	**Baby, It's Cold Outside**...........................*Margaret Whiting & Johnny Mercer*...Capitol 57-567		

TW	LW	WK	Billboard®	JUNE 11, 1949	Best Sellers
1	1	8	**Riders In The Sky (A Cowboy Legend)**.................................*Vaughn Monroe*...RCA Victor 47-2902		
2	2	8	**Again**...*Gordon Jenkins*...Decca 24602		
3	4	7	**Some Enchanted Evening**...*Perry Como*...RCA Victor 47-2896		
4	3	13	**Forever And Ever**...*Russ Morgan*...Decca 24569		
5	5	13	**Forever And Ever**...*Perry Como*...RCA Victor 47-2892		
6	6	16	**Cruising Down The River**...*Russ Morgan*...Decca 24568		
7	8	9	**Again**...*Mel Tormé*...Capitol 15428		
8	9	10	**I Don't See Me In Your Eyes Anymore**...............................*The Stardusters*...Decca 24576		
9	7	10	**"A"-You're Adorable**...*Perry Como*...RCA Victor 47-2899		
10	15	4	**Bali Ha'i**..*Perry Como*...RCA Victor 47-2896		

TW	LW	WK	Billboard®	JUNE 18, 1949	Best Sellers
1	1	9	**Riders In The Sky (A Cowboy Legend)**.................................*Vaughn Monroe*...RCA Victor 47-2902		
2	3	8	**Some Enchanted Evening**...*Perry Como*...RCA Victor 47-2896		
3	2	9	**Again**...*Gordon Jenkins*...Decca 24602		
4	4	14	**Forever And Ever**...*Russ Morgan*...Decca 24569		
5	5	14	**Forever And Ever**...*Perry Como*...RCA Victor 47-2892		
6	11	6	**Baby, It's Cold Outside**...........................*Margaret Whiting & Johnny Mercer*...Capitol 57-567		
7	8	11	**I Don't See Me In Your Eyes Anymore**...............................*The Stardusters*...Decca 24576		
8	9	11	**"A"-You're Adorable**...*Perry Como*...RCA Victor 47-2899		
8	7	10	**Again**...*Mel Tormé*...Capitol 15428		
10	6	17	**Cruising Down The River**...*Russ Morgan*...Decca 24568		

TW	LW	WK	Billboard® JUNE 25, 1949 Best Sellers
1	1	10	**Riders In The Sky (A Cowboy Legend)**.....................................*Vaughn Monroe*...RCA Victor 47-2902
2	2	9	**Some Enchanted Evening**...*Perry Como*...RCA Victor 47-2896
3	3	10	**Again**...*Gordon Jenkins*...Decca 24602
4	5	15	**Forever And Ever**..*Perry Como*...RCA Victor 47-2892
5	6	7	**Baby, It's Cold Outside**.................................*Margaret Whiting & Johnny Mercer*...Capitol 57-567
6	4	15	**Forever And Ever**...*Russ Morgan*...Decca 24569
7	13	7	**Baby, It's Cold Outside**...................................*Dinah Shore & Buddy Clark*...Columbia 38463
8	7	12	**I Don't See Me In Your Eyes Anymore** ....*The Stardusters*...Decca 24576
9	12	6	**Bali Ha'i**..*Perry Como*...RCA Victor 47-2896
10	8	11	**Again**..*Mel Tormé*...Capitol 15428

TW	LW	WK	Billboard® JULY 2, 1949 Best Sellers
1	1	11	**Riders In The Sky (A Cowboy Legend)**.....................................*Vaughn Monroe*...RCA Victor 47-2902
2	2	10	**Some Enchanted Evening**...*Perry Como*...RCA Victor 47-2896
3	3	11	**Again**...*Gordon Jenkins*...Decca 24602
4	5	8	**Baby, It's Cold Outside**.................................*Margaret Whiting & Johnny Mercer*...Capitol 57-567
5	6	16	**Forever And Ever**...*Russ Morgan*...Decca 24569
6	11	6	**Some Enchanted Evening**...*Bing Crosby*...Decca 24609
7	4	16	**Forever And Ever**..*Perry Como*...RCA Victor 47-2892
8	10	12	**Again**..*Mel Tormé*...Capitol 15428
9	9	7	**Bali Ha'i**..*Perry Como*...RCA Victor 47-2896
10	17	19	**Cruising Down The River**...*Russ Morgan*...Decca 24568
10	20	3	**You're Breaking My Heart**..*Vic Damone*...Mercury 5271

TW	LW	WK	Billboard® JULY 9, 1949 Best Sellers
1	1	12	**Riders In The Sky (A Cowboy Legend)**.....................................*Vaughn Monroe*...RCA Victor 47-2902
2	2	11	**Some Enchanted Evening**...*Perry Como*...RCA Victor 47-2896
3	3	12	**Again**...*Gordon Jenkins*...Decca 24602
4	4	9	**Baby, It's Cold Outside**.................................*Margaret Whiting & Johnny Mercer*...Capitol 57-567
5	9	8	**Bali Ha'i**..*Perry Como*...RCA Victor 47-2896
6	13	14	**I Don't See Me In Your Eyes Anymore** ....*The Stardusters*...Decca 24576
7	7	17	**Forever And Ever**..*Perry Como*...RCA Victor 47-2892
8	6	7	**Some Enchanted Evening**...*Bing Crosby*...Decca 24609
9	12	9	**Baby, It's Cold Outside**...................................*Dinah Shore & Buddy Clark*...Columbia 38463
10	8	13	**Again**..*Mel Tormé*...Capitol 15428

TW	LW	WK	Billboard® JULY 16, 1949 Best Sellers
1	1	13	**Riders In The Sky (A Cowboy Legend)**.....................................*Vaughn Monroe*...RCA Victor 47-2902
2	2	12	**Some Enchanted Evening**...*Perry Como*...RCA Victor 47-2896
3	3	13	**Again**...*Gordon Jenkins*...Decca 24602
4	4	10	**Baby, It's Cold Outside**.................................*Margaret Whiting & Johnny Mercer*...Capitol 57-567
5	8	8	**Some Enchanted Evening**...*Bing Crosby*...Decca 24609
6	11	18	**Forever And Ever**...*Russ Morgan*...Decca 24569
7	14	5	**The Four Winds And The Seven Seas**...............................*Sammy Kaye*...RCA Victor 47-2923
8	6	15	**I Don't See Me In Your Eyes Anymore** ....*The Stardusters*...Decca 24576
9	9	10	**Baby, It's Cold Outside**...................................*Dinah Shore & Buddy Clark*...Columbia 38463
10	16	5	**Room Full Of Roses**...*Sammy Kaye*...RCA Victor 47-2908

TW	LW	WK	Billboard® JULY 23, 1949 Best Sellers
1	1	14	**Riders In The Sky (A Cowboy Legend)**.....................................*Vaughn Monroe*...RCA Victor 47-2902
2	2	13	**Some Enchanted Evening**...*Perry Como*...RCA Victor 47-2896
3	3	14	**Again**...*Gordon Jenkins*...Decca 24602
4	9	11	**Baby, It's Cold Outside**...................................*Dinah Shore & Buddy Clark*...Columbia 38463
5	16	6	**You're Breaking My Heart**..*Vic Damone*...Mercury 5271
6	4	11	**Baby, It's Cold Outside**.................................*Margaret Whiting & Johnny Mercer*...Capitol 57-567
7	5	9	**Some Enchanted Evening**...*Bing Crosby*...Decca 24609
8	10	6	**Room Full Of Roses**...*Sammy Kaye*...RCA Victor 47-2908
9	11	8	**The Huckle-Buck**...*Tommy Dorsey*...RCA Victor 47-3028
10	20	19	**Forever And Ever**..*Perry Como*...RCA Victor 47-2892

TW	LW	WK	Billboard® JULY 30, 1949 Best Sellers
1	2	14	Some Enchanted Evening ....Perry Como...RCA Victor 47-2896
2	1	15	Riders In The Sky (A Cowboy Legend)...............................Vaughn Monroe...RCA Victor 47-2902
3	5	7	You're Breaking My Heart..Vic Damone...Mercury 5271
4	3	15	Again ....Gordon Jenkins...Decca 24602
5	6	12	Baby, It's Cold Outside.....................Margaret Whiting & Johnny Mercer...Capitol 57-567
6	4	12	Baby, It's Cold Outside...Dinah Shore & Buddy Clark...Columbia 38463
7	—	1	Jealous Heart ....Al Morgan...London 30001
8	20	11	Bali Ha'i ....Perry Como...RCA Victor 47-2896
9	7	10	Some Enchanted Evening ....Bing Crosby...Decca 24609
9	8	7	Room Full Of Roses ....Sammy Kaye...RCA Victor 47-2908

TW	LW	WK	Billboard® AUGUST 6, 1949 Best Sellers
1	1	15	Some Enchanted Evening ....Perry Como...RCA Victor 47-2896
2	2	16	Riders In The Sky (A Cowboy Legend)...............................Vaughn Monroe...RCA Victor 47-2902
3	3	8	You're Breaking My Heart..Vic Damone...Mercury 5271
4	4	16	Again ....Gordon Jenkins...Decca 24602
5	5	13	Baby, It's Cold Outside.....................Margaret Whiting & Johnny Mercer...Capitol 57-567
6	6	13	Baby, It's Cold Outside...Dinah Shore & Buddy Clark...Columbia 38463
6	9	8	Room Full Of Roses ....Sammy Kaye...RCA Victor 47-2908
8	11	10	The Huckle-Buck ....Tommy Dorsey...RCA Victor 47-3028
9	9	11	Some Enchanted Evening ....Bing Crosby...Decca 24609
10	7	2	Jealous Heart ....Al Morgan...London 30001

TW	LW	WK	Billboard® AUGUST 13, 1949 Best Sellers
1	1	16	Some Enchanted Evening ....Perry Como...RCA Victor 47-2896
2	2	17	Riders In The Sky (A Cowboy Legend)...............................Vaughn Monroe...RCA Victor 47-2902
3	3	9	You're Breaking My Heart..Vic Damone...Mercury 5271
4	5	14	Baby, It's Cold Outside.....................Margaret Whiting & Johnny Mercer...Capitol 57-567
5	6	9	Room Full Of Roses ....Sammy Kaye...RCA Victor 47-2908
6	4	17	Again ....Gordon Jenkins...Decca 24602
7	6	14	Baby, It's Cold Outside...Dinah Shore & Buddy Clark...Columbia 38463
8	10	3	Jealous Heart ....Al Morgan...London 30001
9	11	19	I Don't See Me In Your Eyes Anymore ....The Stardusters...Decca 24576
10	16	5	Maybe It's Because ....Dick Haymes...Decca 24650

TW	LW	WK	Billboard® AUGUST 20, 1949 Best Sellers
1	1	17	Some Enchanted Evening ....Perry Como...RCA Victor 47-2896
2	3	10	You're Breaking My Heart..Vic Damone...Mercury 5271
3	5	10	Room Full Of Roses ....Sammy Kaye...RCA Victor 47-2908
4	2	18	Riders In The Sky (A Cowboy Legend)...............................Vaughn Monroe...RCA Victor 47-2902
5	4	15	Baby, It's Cold Outside.....................Margaret Whiting & Johnny Mercer...Capitol 57-567
6	6	18	Again ....Gordon Jenkins...Decca 24602
7	19	12	The Huckle-Buck ....Tommy Dorsey...RCA Victor 47-3028
8	7	15	Baby, It's Cold Outside...Dinah Shore & Buddy Clark...Columbia 38463
9	8	4	Jealous Heart ....Al Morgan...London 30001
10	10	6	Maybe It's Because ....Dick Haymes...Decca 24650

TW	LW	WK	Billboard® AUGUST 27, 1949 Best Sellers
1	1	18	Some Enchanted Evening ....Perry Como...RCA Victor 47-2896
2	2	11	You're Breaking My Heart..Vic Damone...Mercury 5271
3	3	11	Room Full Of Roses ....Sammy Kaye...RCA Victor 47-2908
4	4	19	Riders In The Sky (A Cowboy Legend)...............................Vaughn Monroe...RCA Victor 47-2902
5	7	13	The Huckle-Buck ....Tommy Dorsey...RCA Victor 47-3028
6	9	5	Jealous Heart ....Al Morgan...London 30001
7	16	4	Someday ....Vaughn Monroe...RCA Victor 47-2986
8	6	19	Again ....Gordon Jenkins...Decca 24602
8	10	7	Maybe It's Because ....Dick Haymes...Decca 24650
10	8	16	Baby, It's Cold Outside...Dinah Shore & Buddy Clark...Columbia 38463

TW	LW	WK	Billboard ❀ SEPTEMBER 3, 1949 ❀ Best Sellers
1	2	12	You're Breaking My Heart..Vic Damone...Mercury 5271
2	1	19	Some Enchanted Evening..Perry Como...RCA Victor 47-2896
3	3	12	Room Full Of Roses..Sammy Kaye...RCA Victor 47-2908
4	7	5	Someday...Vaughn Monroe...RCA Victor 47-2986
5	8	8	Maybe It's Because..Dick Haymes...Decca 24650
6	4	20	Riders In The Sky (A Cowboy Legend)........................Vaughn Monroe...RCA Victor 47-2902
7	6	6	Jealous Heart...Al Morgan...London 30001
8	5	14	The Huckle-Buck...Tommy Dorsey...RCA Victor 47-3028
9	10	17	Baby, It's Cold Outside.............................Dinah Shore & Buddy Clark...Columbia 38463
10	17	11	The Huckle Buck...Frank Sinatra...Columbia 38486

TW	LW	WK	Billboard ❀ SEPTEMBER 10, 1949 ❀ Best Sellers
1	1	13	You're Breaking My Heart..Vic Damone...Mercury 5271
2	2	20	Some Enchanted Evening..Perry Como...RCA Victor 47-2896
3	4	6	Someday...Vaughn Monroe...RCA Victor 47-2986
4	3	13	Room Full Of Roses..Sammy Kaye...RCA Victor 47-2908
5	19	3	That Lucky Old Sun..Frankie Laine...Mercury 5316
6	7	7	Jealous Heart...Al Morgan...London 30001
7	5	9	Maybe It's Because..Dick Haymes...Decca 24650
8	8	15	The Huckle-Buck...Tommy Dorsey...RCA Victor 47-3028
9	19	3	You're Breaking My Heart..Ink Spots...Decca 24693
10	16	3	My Bolero..Vic Damone...Mercury 5313

TW	LW	WK	Billboard ❀ SEPTEMBER 17, 1949 ❀ Best Sellers
1	1	14	You're Breaking My Heart..Vic Damone...Mercury 5271
2	3	7	Someday...Vaughn Monroe...RCA Victor 47-2986
3	5	4	That Lucky Old Sun..Frankie Laine...Mercury 5316
4	2	21	Some Enchanted Evening..Perry Como...RCA Victor 47-2896
5	4	14	Room Full Of Roses..Sammy Kaye...RCA Victor 47-2908
6	6	8	Jealous Heart...Al Morgan...London 30001
7	7	10	Maybe It's Because..Dick Haymes...Decca 24650
8	16	2	Some Enchanted Evening...Ezio Pinza...Columbia 4578
9	13	17	Some Enchanted Evening...Bing Crosby...Decca 24609
10	8	16	The Huckle-Buck...Tommy Dorsey...RCA Victor 47-3028

TW	LW	WK	Billboard ❀ SEPTEMBER 24, 1949 ❀ Best Sellers
1	1	15	You're Breaking My Heart..Vic Damone...Mercury 5271
2	3	5	That Lucky Old Sun..Frankie Laine...Mercury 5316
3	2	8	Someday...Vaughn Monroe...RCA Victor 47-2986
4	6	9	Jealous Heart...Al Morgan...London 30001
5	4	22	Some Enchanted Evening..Perry Como...RCA Victor 47-2896
6	5	15	Room Full Of Roses..Sammy Kaye...RCA Victor 47-2908
7	8	3	Some Enchanted Evening...Ezio Pinza...Columbia 4578
8	7	11	Maybe It's Because..Dick Haymes...Decca 24650
9	14	6	Whispering Hope..Jo Stafford & Gordon MacRae...Capitol 57-690
10	11	11	Room Full Of Roses..Dick Haymes...Decca 24632

TW	LW	WK	Billboard ❀ OCTOBER 1, 1949 ❀ Best Sellers
1	2	6	That Lucky Old Sun..Frankie Laine...Mercury 5316
2	1	16	You're Breaking My Heart..Vic Damone...Mercury 5271
3	3	9	Someday...Vaughn Monroe...RCA Victor 47-2986
4	4	10	Jealous Heart...Al Morgan...London 30001
5	6	16	Room Full Of Roses..Sammy Kaye...RCA Victor 47-2908
6	9	7	Whispering Hope..Jo Stafford & Gordon MacRae...Capitol 57-690
7	5	23	Some Enchanted Evening..Perry Como...RCA Victor 47-2896
8	11	7	Someday (You'll Want Me To Want You)..Mills Brothers...Decca 24694
8	14	3	Slipping Around...........................Margaret Whiting & Jimmy Wakely...Capitol 57-40224
10	8	12	Maybe It's Because..Dick Haymes...Decca 24650
10	12	6	You're Breaking My Heart..Ink Spots...Decca 24693

TW	LW	WK	Billboard® ❀ OCTOBER 8, 1949 ❀ Best Sellers
1	1	7	That Lucky Old Sun...*Frankie Laine*...Mercury 5316
2	2	17	You're Breaking My Heart...*Vic Damone*...Mercury 5271
3	3	10	Someday...*Vaughn Monroe*...RCA Victor 47-2986
4	4	11	Jealous Heart...*Al Morgan*...London 30001
5	8	4	Slipping Around..*Margaret Whiting & Jimmy Wakely*...Capitol 57-40224
6	5	17	Room Full Of Roses...*Sammy Kaye*...RCA Victor 47-2908
7	6	8	Whispering Hope..*Jo Stafford & Gordon MacRae*...Capitol 57-690
8	8	8	Someday (You'll Want Me To Want You)..*Mills Brothers*...Decca 24694
9	10	7	You're Breaking My Heart..*Ink Spots*...Decca 24693
10	16	5	I Never See Maggie Alone...*Kenny Roberts*...Coral 64012

TW	LW	WK	Billboard® ❀ OCTOBER 15, 1949 ❀ Best Sellers
1	1	8	That Lucky Old Sun...*Frankie Laine*...Mercury 5316
2	2	18	You're Breaking My Heart...*Vic Damone*...Mercury 5271
3	3	11	Someday...*Vaughn Monroe*...RCA Victor 47-2986
4	4	12	Jealous Heart...*Al Morgan*...London 30001
5	5	5	Slipping Around..*Margaret Whiting & Jimmy Wakely*...Capitol 57-40224
6	13	4	I Can Dream, Can't I?...*Andrews Sisters*...Decca 24705
7	17	4	Don't Cry Joe (Let Her Go, Let Her Go, Let Her Go)............................*Gordon Jenkins*...Decca 24720
8	7	9	Whispering Hope..*Jo Stafford & Gordon MacRae*...Capitol 57-690
9	8	9	Someday (You'll Want Me To Want You)..*Mills Brothers*...Decca 24694
10	9	8	You're Breaking My Heart..*Ink Spots*...Decca 24693

TW	LW	WK	Billboard® ❀ OCTOBER 22, 1949 ❀ Best Sellers
1	1	9	That Lucky Old Sun...*Frankie Laine*...Mercury 5316
2	2	19	You're Breaking My Heart...*Vic Damone*...Mercury 5271
3	3	12	Someday...*Vaughn Monroe*...RCA Victor 47-2986
4	4	13	Jealous Heart...*Al Morgan*...London 30001
5	5	6	Slipping Around..*Margaret Whiting & Jimmy Wakely*...Capitol 57-40224
6	6	5	I Can Dream, Can't I?...*Andrews Sisters*...Decca 24705
7	7	5	Don't Cry Joe (Let Her Go, Let Her Go, Let Her Go)............................*Gordon Jenkins*...Decca 24720
8	8	10	Whispering Hope..*Jo Stafford & Gordon MacRae*...Capitol 57-690
9	15	7	You're Breaking My Heart..*Buddy Clark*...Columbia 38546
10	11	19	Room Full Of Roses...*Sammy Kaye*...RCA Victor 47-2908

TW	LW	WK	Billboard® ❀ OCTOBER 29, 1949 ❀ Best Sellers
1	1	10	That Lucky Old Sun...*Frankie Laine*...Mercury 5316
2	5	7	Slipping Around..*Margaret Whiting & Jimmy Wakely*...Capitol 57-40224
3	2	20	You're Breaking My Heart...*Vic Damone*...Mercury 5271
4	6	6	I Can Dream, Can't I?...*Andrews Sisters*...Decca 24705
5	4	14	Jealous Heart...*Al Morgan*...London 30001
6	3	13	Someday...*Vaughn Monroe*...RCA Victor 47-2986
7	7	6	Don't Cry Joe (Let Her Go, Let Her Go, Let Her Go)............................*Gordon Jenkins*...Decca 24720
8	8	11	Whispering Hope..*Jo Stafford & Gordon MacRae*...Capitol 57-690
9	14	8	I Never See Maggie Alone...*Kenny Roberts*...Coral 64012
10	10	20	Room Full Of Roses...*Sammy Kaye*...RCA Victor 47-2908

TW	LW	WK	Billboard® ❀ NOVEMBER 5, 1949 ❀ Best Sellers
1	1	11	That Lucky Old Sun...*Frankie Laine*...Mercury 5316
2	2	8	Slipping Around..*Margaret Whiting & Jimmy Wakely*...Capitol 57-40224
3	4	7	I Can Dream, Can't I?...*Andrews Sisters*...Decca 24705
4	3	21	You're Breaking My Heart...*Vic Damone*...Mercury 5271
5	7	7	Don't Cry Joe (Let Her Go, Let Her Go, Let Her Go)............................*Gordon Jenkins*...Decca 24720
6	5	15	Jealous Heart...*Al Morgan*...London 30001
7	8	12	Whispering Hope..*Jo Stafford & Gordon MacRae*...Capitol 57-690
8	6	14	Someday...*Vaughn Monroe*...RCA Victor 47-2986
9	13	9	You're Breaking My Heart..*Buddy Clark*...Columbia 38546
10	16	7	That Lucky Old Sun (Just Rolls Around Heaven All Day).......*Vaughn Monroe*...RCA Victor 47-3018

TW	LW	WK	Billboard® ❀ NOVEMBER 12, 1949 ❀ Best Sellers
1	1	12	That Lucky Old Sun ....Frankie Laine...Mercury 5316
2	3	8	I Can Dream, Can't I?..Andrews Sisters...Decca 24705
3	2	9	Slipping Around ....Margaret Whiting & Jimmy Wakely...Capitol 57-40224
4	5	8	Don't Cry Joe (Let Her Go, Let Her Go, Let Her Go)..Gordon Jenkins...Decca 24720
5	4	22	You're Breaking My Heart ....Vic Damone...Mercury 5271
5	6	16	Jealous Heart ....Al Morgan...London 30001
7	7	13	Whispering Hope ....Jo Stafford & Gordon MacRae...Capitol 57-690
8	8	15	Someday ....Vaughn Monroe...RCA Victor 47-2986
9	—	1	Mule Train ....Frankie Laine...Mercury 5345
10	10	8	That Lucky Old Sun (Just Rolls Around Heaven All Day) ....Vaughn Monroe...RCA Victor 47-3018

TW	LW	WK	Billboard® ❀ NOVEMBER 19, 1949 ❀ Best Sellers
1	1	13	That Lucky Old Sun ....Frankie Laine...Mercury 5316
2	3	10	Slipping Around ....Margaret Whiting & Jimmy Wakely...Capitol 57-40224
3	9	2	Mule Train ....Frankie Laine...Mercury 5345
4	2	9	I Can Dream, Can't I? ....Andrews Sisters...Decca 24705
5	4	9	Don't Cry Joe (Let Her Go, Let Her Go, Let Her Go)..Gordon Jenkins...Decca 24720
6	5	17	Jealous Heart ....Al Morgan...London 30001
7	5	23	You're Breaking My Heart ....Vic Damone...Mercury 5271
8	13	5	A Dreamer's Holiday...Perry Como...RCA Victor 47-3036
9	10	9	That Lucky Old Sun (Just Rolls Around Heaven All Day) ....Vaughn Monroe...RCA Victor 47-3018
10	—	1	Mule Train ....Bing Crosby...Decca 24798

TW	LW	WK	Billboard® ❀ NOVEMBER 26, 1949 ❀ Best Sellers
1	3	3	Mule Train ....Frankie Laine...Mercury 5345
2	1	14	That Lucky Old Sun ....Frankie Laine...Mercury 5316
3	2	11	Slipping Around ....Margaret Whiting & Jimmy Wakely...Capitol 57-40224
4	4	10	I Can Dream, Can't I? ....Andrews Sisters...Decca 24705
5	5	10	Don't Cry Joe (Let Her Go, Let Her Go, Let Her Go)..Gordon Jenkins...Decca 24720
6	10	2	Mule Train ....Bing Crosby...Decca 24798
7	6	18	Jealous Heart ....Al Morgan...London 30001
8	8	6	A Dreamer's Holiday...Perry Como...RCA Victor 47-3036
9	7	24	You're Breaking My Heart ....Vic Damone...Mercury 5271
10	11	15	Whispering Hope ....Jo Stafford & Gordon MacRae...Capitol 57-690

TW	LW	WK	Billboard® ❀ DECEMBER 3, 1949 ❀ Best Sellers
1	1	4	Mule Train ....Frankie Laine...Mercury 5345
2	4	11	I Can Dream, Can't I? ....Andrews Sisters...Decca 24705
3	3	12	Slipping Around ....Margaret Whiting & Jimmy Wakely...Capitol 57-40224
4	2	15	That Lucky Old Sun ....Frankie Laine...Mercury 5316
5	6	3	Mule Train ....Bing Crosby...Decca 24798
6	5	11	Don't Cry Joe (Let Her Go, Let Her Go, Let Her Go)..Gordon Jenkins...Decca 24720
7	8	7	A Dreamer's Holiday...Perry Como...RCA Victor 47-3036
8	7	19	Jealous Heart ....Al Morgan...London 30001
9	10	16	Whispering Hope ....Jo Stafford & Gordon MacRae...Capitol 57-690
9	11	6	I've Got A Lovely Bunch Of Coconuts...Freddy Martin...RCA Victor 47-3047

TW	LW	WK	Billboard® ❀ DECEMBER 10, 1949 ❀ Best Sellers
1	1	5	Mule Train ....Frankie Laine...Mercury 5345
2	2	12	I Can Dream, Can't I? ....Andrews Sisters...Decca 24705
3	3	13	Slipping Around ....Margaret Whiting & Jimmy Wakely...Capitol 57-40224
4	4	16	That Lucky Old Sun ....Frankie Laine...Mercury 5316
5	5	4	Mule Train ....Bing Crosby...Decca 24798
6	6	12	Don't Cry Joe (Let Her Go, Let Her Go, Let Her Go)..Gordon Jenkins...Decca 24720
7	7	8	A Dreamer's Holiday...Perry Como...RCA Victor 47-3036
8	9	7	I've Got A Lovely Bunch Of Coconuts...Freddy Martin...RCA Victor 47-3047
9	11	5	There's No Tomorrow ....Tony Martin...RCA Victor 47-3078
10	13	3	Mule Train ....Vaughn Monroe...RCA Victor 47-3106

TW	LW	WK	Billboard® ✹ DECEMBER 17, 1949 ✹ Best Sellers
1	1	6	Mule Train...Frankie Laine...Mercury 5345
2	2	13	I Can Dream, Can't I?...Andrews Sisters...Decca 24705
3	3	14	Slipping Around.................................Margaret Whiting & Jimmy Wakely...Capitol 57-40224
4	6	13	Don't Cry Joe (Let Her Go, Let Her Go, Let Her Go)..........................Gordon Jenkins...Decca 24720
5	7	9	A Dreamer's Holiday...Perry Como...RCA Victor 47-3036
6	4	17	That Lucky Old Sun...Frankie Laine...Mercury 5316
7	5	5	Mule Train..Bing Crosby...Decca 24798
8	11	3	Rudolph, The Red-Nosed Reindeer...Gene Autry...Columbia 38610
9	9	6	There's No Tomorrow ....Tony Martin...RCA Victor 47-3078
10	18	3	Mule Train...Tennessee Ernie Ford...Capitol 57-40258

TW	LW	WK	Billboard® ✹ DECEMBER 24, 1949 ✹ Best Sellers
1	1	7	Mule Train...Frankie Laine...Mercury 5345
2	2	14	I Can Dream, Can't I?...Andrews Sisters...Decca 24705
3	3	15	Slipping Around.................................Margaret Whiting & Jimmy Wakely...Capitol 57-40224
4	8	4	Rudolph, The Red-Nosed Reindeer...Gene Autry...Columbia 38610
5	7	6	Mule Train..Bing Crosby...Decca 24798
6	4	14	Don't Cry Joe (Let Her Go, Let Her Go, Let Her Go)..........................Gordon Jenkins...Decca 24720
7	5	10	A Dreamer's Holiday...Perry Como...RCA Victor 47-3036
8	6	18	That Lucky Old Sun...Frankie Laine...Mercury 5316
9	11	3	I Yust Go Nuts At Christmas...Yogi Yorgesson...Capitol 57-781
10	30	2	White Christmas ....Bing Crosby...Decca 23778

TW	LW	WK	Billboard® ✹ DECEMBER 31, 1949 ✹ Best Sellers
1	1	8	Mule Train...Frankie Laine...Mercury 5345
2	2	15	I Can Dream, Can't I?...Andrews Sisters...Decca 24705
3	4	5	Rudolph, The Red-Nosed Reindeer...Gene Autry...Columbia 38610
4	3	16	Slipping Around.................................Margaret Whiting & Jimmy Wakely...Capitol 57-40224
5	5	7	Mule Train..Bing Crosby...Decca 24798
5	9	4	I Yust Go Nuts At Christmas...Yogi Yorgesson...Capitol 57-781
7	13	3	Yingle Bells ....Yogi Yorgesson...Capitol 57-781
8	6	15	Don't Cry Joe (Let Her Go, Let Her Go, Let Her Go)..........................Gordon Jenkins...Decca 24720
9	7	11	A Dreamer's Holiday...Perry Como...RCA Victor 47-3036
10	12	10	I've Got A Lovely Bunch Of Coconuts....................................Freddy Martin...RCA Victor 47-3047

TW	LW	WK	Billboard ⬤ JANUARY 7, 1950 ⬤ Best Sellers
1	3	6	Rudolph, The Red-Nosed Reindeer...*Gene Autry*...Columbia 38610
2	1	9	Mule Train..*Frankie Laine*...Mercury 5345
3	2	16	I Can Dream, Can't I?..*Andrews Sisters*...Decca 24705
4	4	17	Slipping Around..*Margaret Whiting & Jimmy Wakely*...Capitol 57-40224
5	5	5	I Yust Go Nuts At Christmas...*Yogi Yorgesson*...Capitol 57-781
6	9	12	A Dreamer's Holiday..*Perry Como*...RCA Victor 47-3036
7	11	4	White Christmas...*Bing Crosby*...Decca 23778
8	21	5	Dear Hearts And Gentle People..*Bing Crosby*...Decca 24798
9	5	8	Mule Train..*Bing Crosby*...Decca 24798
9	7	4	Yingle Bells ....*Yogi Yorgesson*...Capitol 57-781

TW	LW	WK	Billboard ⬤ JANUARY 14, 1950 ⬤ Best Sellers
1	3	17	I Can Dream, Can't I?..*Andrews Sisters*...Decca 24705
2	2	10	Mule Train..*Frankie Laine*...Mercury 5345
3	4	18	Slipping Around..*Margaret Whiting & Jimmy Wakely*...Capitol 57-40224
4	6	13	A Dreamer's Holiday..*Perry Como*...RCA Victor 47-3036
5	8	6	Dear Hearts And Gentle People..*Bing Crosby*...Decca 24798
6	9	9	Mule Train..*Bing Crosby*...Decca 24798
7	13	7	Dear Hearts And Gentle People..*Dinah Shore*...Columbia 38605
8	12	17	Don't Cry Joe (Let Her Go, Let Her Go, Let Her Go).........*Gordon Jenkins*...Decca 24720
9	21	10	There's No Tomorrow ....*Tony Martin*...RCA Victor 47-3078
10	17	5	The Old Master Painter ....*Richard Hayes*...Mercury 5342

TW	LW	WK	Billboard ⬤ JANUARY 21, 1950 ⬤ Best Sellers
1	1	18	I Can Dream, Can't I?..*Andrews Sisters*...Decca 24705
2	3	19	Slipping Around..*Margaret Whiting & Jimmy Wakely*...Capitol 57-40224
3	2	11	Mule Train..*Frankie Laine*...Mercury 5345
4	5	7	Dear Hearts And Gentle People..*Bing Crosby*...Decca 24798
5	4	14	A Dreamer's Holiday..*Perry Como*...RCA Victor 47-3036
6	9	11	There's No Tomorrow ....*Tony Martin*...RCA Victor 47-3078
7	10	6	The Old Master Painter ....*Richard Hayes*...Mercury 5342
8	7	8	Dear Hearts And Gentle People..*Dinah Shore*...Columbia 38605
9	14	7	The Old Master Painter ....*Dick Haymes*...Decca 24801
10	6	10	Mule Train..*Bing Crosby*...Decca 24798

TW	LW	WK	Billboard ⬤ JANUARY 28, 1950 ⬤ Best Sellers
1	1	19	I Can Dream, Can't I?..*Andrews Sisters*...Decca 24705
2	4	8	Dear Hearts And Gentle People..*Bing Crosby*...Decca 24798
3	6	12	There's No Tomorrow ....*Tony Martin*...RCA Victor 47-3078
4	3	12	Mule Train..*Frankie Laine*...Mercury 5345
5	9	8	The Old Master Painter ....*Dick Haymes*...Decca 24801
6	2	20	Slipping Around..*Margaret Whiting & Jimmy Wakely*...Capitol 57-40224
7	5	15	A Dreamer's Holiday..*Perry Como*...RCA Victor 47-3036
8	8	9	Dear Hearts And Gentle People..*Dinah Shore*...Columbia 38605
9	14	3	Rag Mop ....*Ames Brothers*...Coral 60140
10	20	2	Chattanoogie Shoe Shine Boy ....*Red Foley*...Decca 46205

TW	LW	WK	Billboard ⬤ FEBRUARY 4, 1950 ⬤ Best Sellers
1	1	20	I Can Dream, Can't I?..*Andrews Sisters*...Decca 24705
2	3	13	There's No Tomorrow ....*Tony Martin*...RCA Victor 47-3078
3	9	4	Rag Mop ....*Ames Brothers*...Coral 60140
4	2	9	Dear Hearts And Gentle People..*Bing Crosby*...Decca 24798
5	10	3	Chattanoogie Shoe Shine Boy ....*Red Foley*...Decca 46205
6	12	18	Johnson Rag ....*Jack Teter Trio*...London 30004
7	6	21	Slipping Around..*Margaret Whiting & Jimmy Wakely*...Capitol 57-40224
8	5	9	The Old Master Painter ....*Dick Haymes*...Decca 24801
9	7	16	A Dreamer's Holiday..*Perry Como*...RCA Victor 47-3036
10	8	10	Dear Hearts And Gentle People..*Dinah Shore*...Columbia 38605

TW	LW	WK	Billboard® ❀ FEBRUARY 11, 1950 ❀ Best Sellers
1	3	5	Rag Mop ....*Ames Brothers*...Coral 60140
2	5	4	Chattanoogie Shoe Shine Boy ....*Red Foley*...Decca 46205
3	2	14	There's No Tomorrow ....*Tony Martin*...RCA Victor 47-3078
4	1	21	I Can Dream, Can't I? ....*Andrews Sisters*...Decca 24705
5	4	10	Dear Hearts And Gentle People ....*Bing Crosby*...Decca 24798
6	11	2	Music! Music! Music! ....*Teresa Brewer*...London 30023
7	10	11	Dear Hearts And Gentle People ....*Dinah Shore*...Columbia 38605
8	15	3	I Said My Pajamas (And Put on My Pray'rs)............*Tony Martin & Fran Warren*...RCA Victor 47-3119
9	6	19	Johnson Rag ....*Jack Teter Trio*...London 30004
9	8	10	The Old Master Painter ....*Dick Haymes*...Decca 24801

TW	LW	WK	Billboard® ❀ FEBRUARY 18, 1950 ❀ Best Sellers
1	2	5	Chattanoogie Shoe Shine Boy ....*Red Foley*...Decca 46205
2	6	3	Music! Music! Music! ....*Teresa Brewer*...London 30023
3	1	6	Rag Mop ....*Ames Brothers*...Coral 60140
4	3	15	There's No Tomorrow ....*Tony Martin*...RCA Victor 47-3078
5	11	2	The Cry Of The Wild Goose ....*Frankie Laine*...Mercury 5363-X45
6	5	11	Dear Hearts And Gentle People ....*Bing Crosby*...Decca 24798
7	4	22	I Can Dream, Can't I? ....*Andrews Sisters*...Decca 24705
8	8	4	I Said My Pajamas (And Put on My Pray'rs)............*Tony Martin & Fran Warren*...RCA Victor 47-3119
9	22	2	It Isn't Fair ....*Sammy Kaye*...RCA Victor 47-3115
10	13	2	Rag Mop ....*Lionel Hampton*...Decca 24855

TW	LW	WK	Billboard® ❀ FEBRUARY 25, 1950 ❀ Best Sellers
1	1	6	Chattanoogie Shoe Shine Boy ....*Red Foley*...Decca 46205
2	2	4	Music! Music! Music! ....*Teresa Brewer*...London 30023
3	3	7	Rag Mop ....*Ames Brothers*...Coral 60140
4	5	3	The Cry Of The Wild Goose ....*Frankie Laine*...Mercury 5363-X45
5	4	16	There's No Tomorrow ....*Tony Martin*...RCA Victor 47-3078
6	6	12	Dear Hearts And Gentle People ....*Bing Crosby*...Decca 24798
7	8	5	I Said My Pajamas (And Put on My Pray'rs)............*Tony Martin & Fran Warren*...RCA Victor 47-3119
8	7	23	I Can Dream, Can't I? ....*Andrews Sisters*...Decca 24705
9	9	3	It Isn't Fair ....*Sammy Kaye*...RCA Victor 47-3115
10	12	4	Chattanoogie Shoe Shine Boy ....*Bing Crosby*...Decca 24863

TW	LW	WK	Billboard® ❀ MARCH 4, 1950 ❀ Best Sellers
1	1	7	Chattanoogie Shoe Shine Boy ....*Red Foley*...Decca 46205
2	2	5	Music! Music! Music! ....*Teresa Brewer*...London 30023
3	3	8	Rag Mop ....*Ames Brothers*...Coral 60140
4	4	4	The Cry Of The Wild Goose ....*Frankie Laine*...Mercury 5363-X45
5	5	17	There's No Tomorrow ....*Tony Martin*...RCA Victor 47-3078
6	7	6	I Said My Pajamas (And Put on My Pray'rs)............*Tony Martin & Fran Warren*...RCA Victor 47-3119
7	9	4	It Isn't Fair ....*Sammy Kaye*...RCA Victor 47-3115
8	6	13	Dear Hearts And Gentle People ....*Bing Crosby*...Decca 24798
9	10	5	Chattanoogie Shoe Shine Boy ....*Bing Crosby*...Decca 24863
10	27	2	Rag Mop ....*Johnnie Lee Wills*...Bullet 696

TW	LW	WK	Billboard® ❀ MARCH 11, 1950 ❀ Best Sellers
1	1	8	Chattanoogie Shoe Shine Boy ....*Red Foley*...Decca 46205
2	2	6	Music! Music! Music! ....*Teresa Brewer*...London 30023
3	5	18	There's No Tomorrow ....*Tony Martin*...RCA Victor 47-3078
4	4	5	The Cry Of The Wild Goose ....*Frankie Laine*...Mercury 5363-X45
5	3	9	Rag Mop ....*Ames Brothers*...Coral 60140
6	6	7	I Said My Pajamas (And Put on My Pray'rs)............*Tony Martin & Fran Warren*...RCA Victor 47-3119
7	7	5	It Isn't Fair ....*Sammy Kaye*...RCA Victor 47-3115
8	13	5	Quicksilver ....*Bing Crosby & Andrews Sisters*...Decca 24827
9	—	1	If I Knew You Were Comin' (I'd've Baked A Cake) ....*Eileen Barton*...National 9103
10	12	4	Rag Mop ....*Ralph Flanagan*...RCA Victor 47-3212

TW	LW	WK	Billboard® 🎯 MARCH 18, 1950 🎯 Best Sellers
1	2	7	Music! Music! Music!..Teresa Brewer...London 30023
2	1	9	Chattanoogie Shoe Shine Boy..Red Foley...Decca 46205
3	3	19	There's No Tomorrow ....Tony Martin...RCA Victor 47-3078
4	4	6	The Cry Of The Wild Goose ....Frankie Laine...Mercury 5363-X45
5	6	8	I Said My Pajamas (And Put on My Pray'rs)............Tony Martin & Fran Warren...RCA Victor 47-3119
6	5	10	Rag Mop ....Ames Brothers...Coral 60140
7	7	6	It Isn't Fair ....Sammy Kaye...RCA Victor 47-3115
8	9	2	If I Knew You Were Comin' (I'd've Baked A Cake) ....Eileen Barton...National 9103
9	8	6	Quicksilver ....Bing Crosby & Andrews Sisters...Decca 24827
10	10	5	Rag Mop ....Ralph Flanagan...RCA Victor 47-3212

TW	LW	WK	Billboard® 🎯 MARCH 25, 1950 🎯 Best Sellers
1	1	8	Music! Music! Music!..Teresa Brewer...London 30023
2	2	10	Chattanoogie Shoe Shine Boy..Red Foley...Decca 46205
3	8	3	If I Knew You Were Comin' (I'd've Baked A Cake) ....Eileen Barton...National 9103
4	3	20	There's No Tomorrow ....Tony Martin...RCA Victor 47-3078
5	7	7	It Isn't Fair ....Sammy Kaye...RCA Victor 47-3115
6	5	9	I Said My Pajamas (And Put on My Pray'rs)............Tony Martin & Fran Warren...RCA Victor 47-3119
7	6	11	Rag Mop ....Ames Brothers...Coral 60140
8	4	7	The Cry Of The Wild Goose ....Frankie Laine...Mercury 5363-X45
9	9	7	Quicksilver ....Bing Crosby & Andrews Sisters...Decca 24827
10	15	10	Enjoy Yourself (It's Later Than You Think) ....Guy Lombardo...Decca 24825

TW	LW	WK	Billboard® 🎯 APRIL 1, 1950 🎯 Best Sellers
1	1	9	Music! Music! Music!..Teresa Brewer...London 30023
2	3	4	If I Knew You Were Comin' (I'd've Baked A Cake) ....Eileen Barton...National 9103
3	2	11	Chattanoogie Shoe Shine Boy..Red Foley...Decca 46205
4	4	21	There's No Tomorrow ....Tony Martin...RCA Victor 47-3078
5	5	8	It Isn't Fair ....Sammy Kaye...RCA Victor 47-3115
6	6	10	I Said My Pajamas (And Put on My Pray'rs)............Tony Martin & Fran Warren...RCA Victor 47-3119
7	12	4	"The Third Man" Theme ....Anton Karas...London 45-30005
8	14	2	Go To Sleep, Go To Sleep, Go To Sleep ....Mary Martin & Arthur Godfrey...Columbia 38744
9	8	8	The Cry Of The Wild Goose ....Frankie Laine...Mercury 5363-X45
10	7	12	Rag Mop ....Ames Brothers...Coral 60140

TW	LW	WK	Billboard® 🎯 APRIL 8, 1950 🎯 Best Sellers
1	1	10	Music! Music! Music!..Teresa Brewer...London 30023
2	2	5	If I Knew You Were Comin' (I'd've Baked A Cake) ....Eileen Barton...National 9103
3	7	5	"The Third Man" Theme ....Anton Karas...London 45-30005
4	3	12	Chattanoogie Shoe Shine Boy..Red Foley...Decca 46205
5	5	9	It Isn't Fair ....Sammy Kaye...RCA Victor 47-3115
6	4	22	There's No Tomorrow ....Tony Martin...RCA Victor 47-3078
7	22	4	The 3rd Man Theme..Guy Lombardo...Decca 24839
8	20	3	Peter Cottontail ....Mervin Shiner...Decca 9-46221
9	8	3	Go To Sleep, Go To Sleep, Go To Sleep ....Mary Martin & Arthur Godfrey...Columbia 38744
10	6	11	I Said My Pajamas (And Put on My Pray'rs)............Tony Martin & Fran Warren...RCA Victor 47-3119

TW	LW	WK	Billboard® 🎯 APRIL 15, 1950 🎯 Best Sellers
1	2	6	If I Knew You Were Comin' (I'd've Baked A Cake) ....Eileen Barton...National 9103
2	1	11	Music! Music! Music!..Teresa Brewer...London 30023
3	3	6	"The Third Man" Theme ....Anton Karas...London 45-30005
4	5	10	It Isn't Fair ....Sammy Kaye...RCA Victor 47-3115
5	15	3	Peter Cottontail ....Gene Autry...Columbia 38750
6	4	13	Chattanoogie Shoe Shine Boy..Red Foley...Decca 46205
7	6	23	There's No Tomorrow ....Tony Martin...RCA Victor 47-3078
7	20	6	My Foolish Heart..Gordon Jenkins...Decca 9-24830
9	11	9	Sentimental Me ....Ames Brothers...Coral 60173
10	8	4	Peter Cottontail ....Mervin Shiner...Decca 9-46221

APRIL 22, 1950 — Billboard Best Sellers

TW	LW	WK	Title	Artist / Label
1	1	7	If I Knew You Were Comin' (I'd've Baked A Cake)	Eileen Barton...National 9103
2	3	7	"The Third Man" Theme	Anton Karas...London 45-30005
3	2	12	Music! Music! Music!	Teresa Brewer...London 30023
4	4	11	It Isn't Fair	Sammy Kaye...RCA Victor 47-3115
5	11	6	The 3rd Man Theme	Guy Lombardo...Decca 24839
6	5	4	Peter Cottontail	Gene Autry...Columbia 38750
7	6	14	Chattanoogie Shoe Shine Boy	Red Foley...Decca 46205
9	9	10	Sentimental Me	Ames Brothers...Coral 60173
9	10	5	Peter Cottontail	Mervin Shiner...Decca 9-46221
10	7	7	My Foolish Heart	Gordon Jenkins...Decca 9-24830

APRIL 29, 1950 — Billboard Best Sellers

TW	LW	WK	Title	Artist / Label
1	2	8	"The Third Man" Theme	Anton Karas...London 45-30005
2	1	8	If I Knew You Were Comin' (I'd've Baked A Cake)	Eileen Barton...National 9103
3	3	13	Music! Music! Music!	Teresa Brewer...London 30023
4	4	12	It Isn't Fair	Sammy Kaye...RCA Victor 47-3115
5	5	7	The 3rd Man Theme	Guy Lombardo...Decca 24839
6	6	5	Peter Cottontail	Gene Autry...Columbia 38750
7	13	2	Bewitched	Bill Snyder...Tower 45-1473
8	10	8	My Foolish Heart	Gordon Jenkins...Decca 9-24830
9	9	11	Sentimental Me	Ames Brothers...Coral 60173
10	11	9	Daddy's Little Girl	Mills Brothers...Decca 9-24872

MAY 6, 1950 — Billboard Best Sellers

TW	LW	WK	Title	Artist / Label
1	1	9	"The Third Man" Theme	Anton Karas...London 45-30005
2	2	9	If I Knew You Were Comin' (I'd've Baked A Cake)	Eileen Barton...National 9103
3	5	8	The 3rd Man Theme	Guy Lombardo...Decca 24839
4	4	13	It Isn't Fair	Sammy Kaye...RCA Victor 47-3115
5	3	14	Music! Music! Music!	Teresa Brewer...London 30023
6	8	9	My Foolish Heart	Gordon Jenkins...Decca 9-24830
7	9	12	Sentimental Me	Ames Brothers...Coral 60173
8	7	3	Bewitched	Bill Snyder...Tower 45-1473
9	10	10	Daddy's Little Girl	Mills Brothers...Decca 9-24872
10	11	6	My Foolish Heart	Billy Eckstine...MGM K10623

MAY 13, 1950 — Billboard Best Sellers

TW	LW	WK	Title	Artist / Label
1	1	10	"The Third Man" Theme	Anton Karas...London 45-30005
2	2	10	If I Knew You Were Comin' (I'd've Baked A Cake)	Eileen Barton...National 9103
3	4	14	It Isn't Fair	Sammy Kaye...RCA Victor 47-3115
4	3	9	The 3rd Man Theme	Guy Lombardo...Decca 24839
5	7	13	Sentimental Me	Ames Brothers...Coral 60173
6	8	4	Bewitched	Bill Snyder...Tower 45-1473
7	6	10	My Foolish Heart	Gordon Jenkins...Decca 9-24830
8	5	15	Music! Music! Music!	Teresa Brewer...London 30023
9	13	3	Hoop-Dee-Doo	Perry Como...RCA Victor 47-3747
10	10	7	My Foolish Heart	Billy Eckstine...MGM K10623

MAY 20, 1950 — Billboard Best Sellers

TW	LW	WK	Title	Artist / Label
1	1	11	"The Third Man" Theme	Anton Karas...London 45-30005
2	4	10	The 3rd Man Theme	Guy Lombardo...Decca 24839
3	3	15	It Isn't Fair	Sammy Kaye...RCA Victor 47-3115
4	7	11	My Foolish Heart	Gordon Jenkins...Decca 9-24830
5	6	5	Bewitched	Bill Snyder...Tower 45-1473
6	2	11	If I Knew You Were Comin' (I'd've Baked A Cake)	Eileen Barton...National 9103
7	5	14	Sentimental Me	Ames Brothers...Coral 60173
8	10	8	My Foolish Heart	Billy Eckstine...MGM K10623
9	9	4	Hoop-Dee-Doo	Perry Como...RCA Victor 47-3747
10	15	4	Sentimental Me	Russ Morgan...Decca 9-24904

MAY 27, 1950 — Billboard Best Sellers

TW	LW	WK	Title	Artist
1	1	12	"The Third Man" Theme	Anton Karas...London 45-30005
2	2	11	The 3rd Man Theme	Guy Lombardo...Decca 24839
3	3	16	It Isn't Fair	Sammy Kaye...RCA Victor 47-3115
4	5	6	Bewitched	Bill Snyder...Tower 45-1473
5	7	15	Sentimental Me	Ames Brothers...Coral 60173
6	4	12	My Foolish Heart	Gordon Jenkins...Decca 9-24830
7	8	9	My Foolish Heart	Billy Eckstine...MGM K10623
8	13	5	Bewitched	Gordon Jenkins...Decca 9-24983
9	6	12	If I Knew You Were Comin' (I'd've Baked A Cake)	Eileen Barton...National 9103
10	9	5	Hoop-Dee-Doo	Perry Como...RCA Victor 47-3747

JUNE 3, 1950 — Billboard Best Sellers

TW	LW	WK	Title	Artist
1	1	13	"The Third Man" Theme	Anton Karas...London 45-30005
2	2	12	The 3rd Man Theme	Guy Lombardo...Decca 24839
3	5	16	Sentimental Me	Ames Brothers...Coral 60173
4	4	7	Bewitched	Bill Snyder...Tower 45-1473
5	3	17	It Isn't Fair	Sammy Kaye...RCA Victor 47-3115
6	7	10	My Foolish Heart	Billy Eckstine...MGM K10623
7	10	6	Hoop-Dee-Doo	Perry Como...RCA Victor 47-3747
8	6	13	My Foolish Heart	Gordon Jenkins...Decca 9-24830
9	12	4	I Wanna Be Loved	Andrews Sisters...Decca 9-27007
10	25	4	Bewitched	Doris Day...Columbia 38698

JUNE 10, 1950 — Billboard Best Sellers

TW	LW	WK	Title	Artist
1	1	14	"The Third Man" Theme	Anton Karas...London 45-30005
2	2	13	The 3rd Man Theme	Guy Lombardo...Decca 24839
3	8	14	My Foolish Heart	Gordon Jenkins...Decca 9-24830
4	7	7	Hoop-Dee-Doo	Perry Como...RCA Victor 47-3747
5	3	17	Sentimental Me	Ames Brothers...Coral 60173
6	4	8	Bewitched	Bill Snyder...Tower 45-1473
7	11	7	Bewitched	Gordon Jenkins...Decca 9-24983
8	6	11	My Foolish Heart	Billy Eckstine...MGM K10623
9	5	18	It Isn't Fair	Sammy Kaye...RCA Victor 47-3115
10	9	5	I Wanna Be Loved	Andrews Sisters...Decca 9-27007

JUNE 17, 1950 — Billboard Best Sellers

TW	LW	WK	Title	Artist
1	1	15	"The Third Man" Theme	Anton Karas...London 45-30005
2	2	14	The 3rd Man Theme	Guy Lombardo...Decca 24839
3	6	9	Bewitched	Bill Snyder...Tower 45-1473
4	4	8	Hoop-Dee-Doo	Perry Como...RCA Victor 47-3747
5	5	18	Sentimental Me	Ames Brothers...Coral 60173
6	3	15	My Foolish Heart	Gordon Jenkins...Decca 9-24830
6	10	6	I Wanna Be Loved	Andrews Sisters...Decca 9-27007
8	7	8	Bewitched	Gordon Jenkins...Decca 9-24983
9	8	12	My Foolish Heart	Billy Eckstine...MGM K10623
10	9	19	It Isn't Fair	Sammy Kaye...RCA Victor 47-3115

JUNE 24, 1950 — Billboard Best Sellers

TW	LW	WK	Title	Artist
1	1	16	"The Third Man" Theme	Anton Karas...London 45-30005
2	2	15	The 3rd Man Theme	Guy Lombardo...Decca 24839
3	6	7	I Wanna Be Loved	Andrews Sisters...Decca 9-27007
4	4	9	Hoop-Dee-Doo	Perry Como...RCA Victor 47-3747
5	3	10	Bewitched	Bill Snyder...Tower 45-1473
6	5	19	Sentimental Me	Ames Brothers...Coral 60173
7	8	9	Bewitched	Gordon Jenkins...Decca 9-24983
8	6	16	My Foolish Heart	Gordon Jenkins...Decca 9-24830
9	14	3	Mona Lisa	Nat "King" Cole...Capitol F1010
10	9	13	My Foolish Heart	Billy Eckstine...MGM K10623

TW	LW	WK	Billboard ⊛ JULY 1, 1950 ⊛ Best Sellers
1	1	17	"The Third Man" Theme...Anton Karas...London 45-30005
2	2	16	The 3rd Man Theme..Guy Lombardo...Decca 24839
3	6	20	Sentimental Me...Ames Brothers...Coral 60173
4	3	8	I Wanna Be Loved...Andrews Sisters...Decca 9-27007
5	9	4	Mona Lisa...Nat "King" Cole...Capitol F1010
6	4	10	Hoop-Dee-Doo...Perry Como...RCA Victor 47-3747
7	5	11	Bewitched...Bill Snyder...Tower 45-1473
8	7	10	Bewitched...Gordon Jenkins...Decca 9-24983
9	15	3	I Wanna Be Loved..Billy Eckstine...MGM K10716
10	10	14	My Foolish Heart...Billy Eckstine...MGM K10623

TW	LW	WK	Billboard ⊛ JULY 8, 1950 ⊛ Best Sellers
1	1	18	"The Third Man" Theme...Anton Karas...London 45-30005
2	5	5	Mona Lisa...Nat "King" Cole...Capitol F1010
3	2	17	The 3rd Man Theme..Guy Lombardo...Decca 24839
4	4	9	I Wanna Be Loved...Andrews Sisters...Decca 9-27007
5	6	11	Hoop-Dee-Doo...Perry Como...RCA Victor 47-3747
6	8	11	Bewitched...Gordon Jenkins...Decca 9-24983
7	7	12	Bewitched...Bill Snyder...Tower 45-1473
8	11	18	My Foolish Heart...Gordon Jenkins...Decca 9-24830
9	3	21	Sentimental Me...Ames Brothers...Coral 60173
10	9	4	I Wanna Be Loved..Billy Eckstine...MGM K10716

TW	LW	WK	Billboard ⊛ JULY 15, 1950 ⊛ Best Sellers
1	2	6	Mona Lisa...Nat "King" Cole...Capitol F1010
2	1	19	"The Third Man" Theme...Anton Karas...London 45-30005
3	4	10	I Wanna Be Loved...Andrews Sisters...Decca 9-27007
4	9	22	Sentimental Me...Ames Brothers...Coral 60173
5	3	18	The 3rd Man Theme..Guy Lombardo...Decca 24839
6	11	3	Tzena Tzena Tzena...Gordon Jenkins & The Weavers...Decca 9-27077
7	7	13	Bewitched...Bill Snyder...Tower 45-1473
8	6	12	Bewitched...Gordon Jenkins...Decca 9-24983
9	8	19	My Foolish Heart...Gordon Jenkins...Decca 9-24830
10	5	12	Hoop-Dee-Doo...Perry Como...RCA Victor 47-3747

TW	LW	WK	Billboard ⊛ JULY 22, 1950 ⊛ Best Sellers
1	1	7	Mona Lisa...Nat "King" Cole...Capitol F1010
2	2	20	"The Third Man" Theme...Anton Karas...London 45-30005
3	3	11	I Wanna Be Loved...Andrews Sisters...Decca 9-27007
4	5	19	The 3rd Man Theme..Guy Lombardo...Decca 24839
5	6	4	Tzena Tzena Tzena...Gordon Jenkins & The Weavers...Decca 9-27077
6	8	13	Bewitched...Gordon Jenkins...Decca 9-24983
7	10	13	Hoop-Dee-Doo...Perry Como...RCA Victor 47-3747
8	17	3	Goodnight Irene..Gordon Jenkins & The Weavers...Decca 9-27077
9	4	23	Sentimental Me...Ames Brothers...Coral 60173
10	7	14	Bewitched...Bill Snyder...Tower 45-1473

TW	LW	WK	Billboard ⊛ JULY 29, 1950 ⊛ Best Sellers
1	1	8	Mona Lisa...Nat "King" Cole...Capitol F1010
2	5	5	Tzena Tzena Tzena...Gordon Jenkins & The Weavers...Decca 9-27077
3	2	21	"The Third Man" Theme...Anton Karas...London 45-30005
4	3	12	I Wanna Be Loved...Andrews Sisters...Decca 9-27007
5	8	4	Goodnight Irene..Gordon Jenkins & The Weavers...Decca 9-27077
6	6	14	Bewitched...Gordon Jenkins...Decca 9-24983
7	4	20	The 3rd Man Theme..Guy Lombardo...Decca 24839
7	—	1	Play A Simple Melody..Gary Crosby & Bing Crosby...Decca 9-27112
9	16	7	Bonaparte's Retreat...Kay Starr...Capitol F936
10	—	1	Sam's Song (The Happy Tune).......................................Gary Crosby & Bing Crosby...Decca 9-27112

TW	LW	WK	Billboard ⚜ AUGUST 5, 1950 ⚜ Best Sellers
1	1	9	Mona Lisa...Nat "King" Cole...Capitol F1010
2	5	5	Goodnight Irene..Gordon Jenkins & The Weavers...Decca 9-27077
3	2	6	Tzena Tzena Tzena...Gordon Jenkins & The Weavers...Decca 9-27077
4	10	2	Sam's Song (The Happy Tune) ....Gary Crosby & Bing Crosby...Decca 9-27112
5	7	2	Play A Simple Melody......................................Gary Crosby & Bing Crosby...Decca 9-27112
6	4	13	I Wanna Be Loved...Andrews Sisters...Decca 9-27007
7	3	22	"The Third Man" Theme...Anton Karas...London 45-30005
8	7	21	The 3rd Man Theme...Guy Lombardo...Decca 24839
9	6	15	Bewitched ....Gordon Jenkins...Decca 9-24983
10	9	8	Bonaparte's Retreat...Kay Starr...Capitol F936

TW	LW	WK	Billboard ⚜ AUGUST 12, 1950 ⚜ Best Sellers
1	1	10	Mona Lisa...Nat "King" Cole...Capitol F1010
2	2	6	Goodnight Irene..Gordon Jenkins & The Weavers...Decca 9-27077
3	4	3	Sam's Song (The Happy Tune) ....Gary Crosby & Bing Crosby...Decca 9-27112
4	3	7	Tzena Tzena Tzena...Gordon Jenkins & The Weavers...Decca 9-27077
5	5	3	Play A Simple Melody......................................Gary Crosby & Bing Crosby...Decca 9-27112
6	6	14	I Wanna Be Loved...Andrews Sisters...Decca 9-27007
7	7	23	"The Third Man" Theme...Anton Karas...London 45-30005
8	9	16	Bewitched ....Gordon Jenkins...Decca 9-24983
9	10	9	Bonaparte's Retreat...Kay Starr...Capitol F936
10	13	14	Count Every Star ....Hugo Winterhalter...RCA Victor 47-3221

TW	LW	WK	Billboard ⚜ AUGUST 19, 1950 ⚜ Best Sellers
1	2	7	Goodnight Irene..Gordon Jenkins & The Weavers...Decca 9-27077
2	1	11	Mona Lisa...Nat "King" Cole...Capitol F1010
3	5	4	Play A Simple Melody......................................Gary Crosby & Bing Crosby...Decca 9-27112
4	3	4	Sam's Song (The Happy Tune) ....Gary Crosby & Bing Crosby...Decca 9-27112
5	4	8	Tzena Tzena Tzena...Gordon Jenkins & The Weavers...Decca 9-27077
6	6	15	I Wanna Be Loved...Andrews Sisters...Decca 9-27007
7	9	10	Bonaparte's Retreat...Kay Starr...Capitol F936
8	20	10	Sam's Song ....Joe "Fingers" Carr...Capitol F962
9	11	8	Nola ....Les Paul...Capitol F1014
10	13	6	Tzena Tzena Tzena ....Mitch Miller...Columbia 38885

TW	LW	WK	Billboard ⚜ AUGUST 26, 1950 ⚜ Best Sellers
1	1	8	Goodnight Irene..Gordon Jenkins & The Weavers...Decca 9-27077
2	2	12	Mona Lisa...Nat "King" Cole...Capitol F1010
3	3	5	Play A Simple Melody......................................Gary Crosby & Bing Crosby...Decca 9-27112
4	4	5	Sam's Song (The Happy Tune) ....Gary Crosby & Bing Crosby...Decca 9-27112
5	5	9	Tzena Tzena Tzena...Gordon Jenkins & The Weavers...Decca 9-27077
6	7	11	Bonaparte's Retreat...Kay Starr...Capitol F936
7	6	16	I Wanna Be Loved...Andrews Sisters...Decca 9-27007
8	23	5	Tzena, Tzena, Tzena..Vic Damone...Mercury 5454-X45
9	17	6	La Vie En Rose ....Tony Martin...RCA Victor 47-3819
10	14	3	Can Anyone Explain? (No, No, No!) ....Ames Brothers...Coral 9-60253

TW	LW	WK	Billboard ⚜ SEPTEMBER 2, 1950 ⚜ Best Sellers
1	1	9	Goodnight Irene..Gordon Jenkins & The Weavers...Decca 9-27077
2	2	13	Mona Lisa...Nat "King" Cole...Capitol F1010
3	4	6	Sam's Song (The Happy Tune) ....Gary Crosby & Bing Crosby...Decca 9-27112
4	3	6	Play A Simple Melody......................................Gary Crosby & Bing Crosby...Decca 9-27112
5	5	10	Tzena Tzena Tzena...Gordon Jenkins & The Weavers...Decca 9-27077
6	6	12	Bonaparte's Retreat...Kay Starr...Capitol F936
7	7	17	I Wanna Be Loved...Andrews Sisters...Decca 9-27007
8	8	6	Tzena, Tzena, Tzena..Vic Damone...Mercury 5454-X45
9	10	4	Can Anyone Explain? (No, No, No!) ....Ames Brothers...Coral 9-60253
10	12	10	Nola ....Les Paul...Capitol F1014

TW	LW	WK	Billboard ® ❀ SEPTEMBER 9, 1950 ❀ Best Sellers		
1	1	10	Goodnight Irene..Gordon Jenkins & The Weavers...Decca 9-27077		
2	2	14	Mona Lisa..Nat "King" Cole...Capitol F1010		
3	4	7	Play A Simple Melody...Gary Crosby & Bing Crosby...Decca 9-27112		
4	3	7	Sam's Song (The Happy Tune) ....Gary Crosby & Bing Crosby...Decca 9-27112		
5	5	11	Tzena Tzena Tzena ....Gordon Jenkins & The Weavers...Decca 9-27077		
6	6	13	Bonaparte's Retreat ....Kay Starr...Capitol F936		
7	9	5	Can Anyone Explain? (No, No, No!) ....Ames Brothers...Coral 9-60253		
8	16	3	No Other Love ....Jo Stafford...Capitol F1053		
9	10	11	Nola ....Les Paul...Capitol F1014		
10	13	18	Count Every Star ....Hugo Winterhalter...RCA Victor 47-3221		

TW	LW	WK	Billboard ® ❀ SEPTEMBER 16, 1950 ❀ Best Sellers		
1	1	11	Goodnight Irene..Gordon Jenkins & The Weavers...Decca 9-27077		
2	2	15	Mona Lisa..Nat "King" Cole...Capitol F1010		
3	3	8	Play A Simple Melody...Gary Crosby & Bing Crosby...Decca 9-27112		
4	4	8	Sam's Song (The Happy Tune) ....Gary Crosby & Bing Crosby...Decca 9-27112		
5	5	12	Tzena Tzena Tzena ....Gordon Jenkins & The Weavers...Decca 9-27077		
6	6	14	Bonaparte's Retreat ....Kay Starr...Capitol F936		
7	7	6	Can Anyone Explain? (No, No, No!) ....Ames Brothers...Coral 9-60253		
8	12	4	I'll Never Be Free ....Kay Starr & Tennessee Ernie Ford...Capitol F1124		
9	8	4	No Other Love ....Jo Stafford...Capitol F1053		
10	14	11	Mona Lisa ....Victor Young & Don Cherry...Decca 9-27048		

TW	LW	WK	Billboard ® ❀ SEPTEMBER 23, 1950 ❀ Best Sellers		
1	1	12	Goodnight Irene..Gordon Jenkins & The Weavers...Decca 9-27077		
2	2	16	Mona Lisa..Nat "King" Cole...Capitol F1010		
3	4	9	Sam's Song (The Happy Tune) ....Gary Crosby & Bing Crosby...Decca 9-27112		
4	3	9	Play A Simple Melody...Gary Crosby & Bing Crosby...Decca 9-27112		
5	6	15	Bonaparte's Retreat ....Kay Starr...Capitol F936		
6	5	13	Tzena Tzena Tzena ....Gordon Jenkins & The Weavers...Decca 9-27077		
7	7	7	Can Anyone Explain? (No, No, No!) ....Ames Brothers...Coral 9-60253		
8	8	5	I'll Never Be Free ....Kay Starr & Tennessee Ernie Ford...Capitol F1124		
9	13	13	Nola ....Les Paul...Capitol F1014		
10	11	3	Our Lady Of Fatima..Richard Hayes & Kitty Kallen...Mercury 5466-X45		

TW	LW	WK	Billboard ® ❀ SEPTEMBER 30, 1950 ❀ Best Sellers		
1	1	13	Goodnight Irene..Gordon Jenkins & The Weavers...Decca 9-27077		
2	2	17	Mona Lisa..Nat "King" Cole...Capitol F1010		
3	4	10	Play A Simple Melody...Gary Crosby & Bing Crosby...Decca 9-27112		
4	3	10	Sam's Song (The Happy Tune) ....Gary Crosby & Bing Crosby...Decca 9-27112		
5	5	16	Bonaparte's Retreat ....Kay Starr...Capitol F936		
6	6	14	Tzena Tzena Tzena ....Gordon Jenkins & The Weavers...Decca 9-27077		
7	18	5	All My Love (Bolero) ....Patti Page...Mercury 5455-X45		
8	7	8	Can Anyone Explain? (No, No, No!) ....Ames Brothers...Coral 9-60253		
9	12	4	Harbor Lights...Sammy Kaye...Columbia 4-38963		
10	—	9	La Vie En Rose ....Tony Martin...RCA Victor 47-3819		

TW	LW	WK	Billboard ® ❀ OCTOBER 7, 1950 ❀ Best Sellers		
1	1	14	Goodnight Irene..Gordon Jenkins & The Weavers...Decca 9-27077		
2	2	18	Mona Lisa..Nat "King" Cole...Capitol F1010		
3	3	11	Play A Simple Melody...Gary Crosby & Bing Crosby...Decca 9-27112		
4	4	11	Sam's Song (The Happy Tune) ....Gary Crosby & Bing Crosby...Decca 9-27112		
5	11	7	I'll Never Be Free ....Kay Starr & Tennessee Ernie Ford...Capitol F1124		
6	5	17	Bonaparte's Retreat ....Kay Starr...Capitol F936		
7	7	6	All My Love (Bolero) ....Patti Page...Mercury 5455-X45		
8	9	5	Harbor Lights...Sammy Kaye...Columbia 4-38963		
9	8	9	Can Anyone Explain? (No, No, No!) ....Ames Brothers...Coral 9-60253		
10	6	15	Tzena Tzena Tzena ....Gordon Jenkins & The Weavers...Decca 9-27077		
10	12	5	Our Lady Of Fatima..Richard Hayes & Kitty Kallen...Mercury 5466-X45		

TW	LW	WK	Billboard® ✹ OCTOBER 14, 1950 ✹ Best Sellers
1	1	15	**Goodnight Irene**..*Gordon Jenkins & The Weavers*...Decca 9-27077
2	2	19	**Mona Lisa**..*Nat "King" Cole*...Capitol F1010
3	4	12	**Sam's Song** (The Happy Tune) ....*Gary Crosby & Bing Crosby*...Decca 9-27112
4	3	12	**Play A Simple Melody**...*Gary Crosby & Bing Crosby*...Decca 9-27112
5	5	8	**I'll Never Be Free**...*Kay Starr & Tennessee Ernie Ford*...Capitol F1124
6	6	18	**Bonaparte's Retreat**..*Kay Starr*...Capitol F936
7	9	10	**Can Anyone Explain?** (No, No, No!) ....*Ames Brothers*...Coral 9-60253
8	7	7	**All My Love** (Bolero) ....*Patti Page*...Mercury 5455-X45
9	8	6	**Harbor Lights**..*Sammy Kaye*...Columbia 4-38963
10	10	6	**Our Lady Of Fatima**....................................*Richard Hayes & Kitty Kallen*...Mercury 5466-X45

TW	LW	WK	Billboard® ✹ OCTOBER 21, 1950 ✹ Best Sellers
1	1	16	**Goodnight Irene**..*Gordon Jenkins & The Weavers*...Decca 9-27077
2	2	20	**Mona Lisa**..*Nat "King" Cole*...Capitol F1010
3	3	13	**Sam's Song** (The Happy Tune) ....*Gary Crosby & Bing Crosby*...Decca 9-27112
4	4	13	**Play A Simple Melody**...*Gary Crosby & Bing Crosby*...Decca 9-27112
5	5	9	**I'll Never Be Free**...*Kay Starr & Tennessee Ernie Ford*...Capitol F1124
6	9	7	**Harbor Lights**..*Sammy Kaye*...Columbia 4-38963
7	6	19	**Bonaparte's Retreat**..*Kay Starr*...Capitol F936
8	8	8	**All My Love** (Bolero) ....*Patti Page*...Mercury 5455-X45
9	7	11	**Can Anyone Explain?** (No, No, No!) ....*Ames Brothers*...Coral 9-60253
10	10	7	**Our Lady Of Fatima**....................................*Richard Hayes & Kitty Kallen*...Mercury 5466-X45

TW	LW	WK	Billboard® ✹ OCTOBER 28, 1950 ✹ Best Sellers
1	1	17	**Goodnight Irene**..*Gordon Jenkins & The Weavers*...Decca 9-27077
2	2	21	**Mona Lisa**..*Nat "King" Cole*...Capitol F1010
3	6	8	**Harbor Lights**..*Sammy Kaye*...Columbia 4-38963
4	3	14	**Sam's Song** (The Happy Tune) ....*Gary Crosby & Bing Crosby*...Decca 9-27112
5	4	14	**Play A Simple Melody**...*Gary Crosby & Bing Crosby*...Decca 9-27112
6	5	10	**I'll Never Be Free**...*Kay Starr & Tennessee Ernie Ford*...Capitol F1124
7	8	9	**All My Love** (Bolero) ....*Patti Page*...Mercury 5455-X45
8	7	20	**Bonaparte's Retreat**..*Kay Starr*...Capitol F936
9	9	12	**Can Anyone Explain?** (No, No, No!) ....*Ames Brothers*...Coral 9-60253
10	11	6	**Thinking Of You**...*Don Cherry*...Decca 9-27128

TW	LW	WK	Billboard® ✹ NOVEMBER 4, 1950 ✹ Best Sellers
1	1	18	**Goodnight Irene**..*Gordon Jenkins & The Weavers*...Decca 9-27077
2	3	9	**Harbor Lights**..*Sammy Kaye*...Columbia 4-38963
3	2	22	**Mona Lisa**..*Nat "King" Cole*...Capitol F1010
4	7	10	**All My Love** (Bolero) ....*Patti Page*...Mercury 5455-X45
5	4	15	**Sam's Song** (The Happy Tune) ....*Gary Crosby & Bing Crosby*...Decca 9-27112
6	5	15	**Play A Simple Melody**...*Gary Crosby & Bing Crosby*...Decca 9-27112
7	6	11	**I'll Never Be Free**...*Kay Starr & Tennessee Ernie Ford*...Capitol F1124
8	8	21	**Bonaparte's Retreat**..*Kay Starr*...Capitol F936
9	15	4	**Harbor Lights**..*Guy Lombardo*...Decca 9-27208
10	9	13	**Can Anyone Explain?** (No, No, No!) ....*Ames Brothers*...Coral 9-60253

TW	LW	WK	Billboard® ✹ NOVEMBER 11, 1950 ✹ Best Sellers
1	1	19	**Goodnight Irene**..*Gordon Jenkins & The Weavers*...Decca 9-27077
2	2	10	**Harbor Lights**..*Sammy Kaye*...Columbia 4-38963
3	3	23	**Mona Lisa**..*Nat "King" Cole*...Capitol F1010
4	7	12	**I'll Never Be Free**...*Kay Starr & Tennessee Ernie Ford*...Capitol F1124
5	4	11	**All My Love** (Bolero) ....*Patti Page*...Mercury 5455-X45
6	5	16	**Sam's Song** (The Happy Tune) ....*Gary Crosby & Bing Crosby*...Decca 9-27112
7	6	16	**Play A Simple Melody**...*Gary Crosby & Bing Crosby*...Decca 9-27112
8	9	5	**Harbor Lights**..*Guy Lombardo*...Decca 9-27208
9	13	8	**Thinking Of You**...*Don Cherry*...Decca 9-27128
10	8	22	**Bonaparte's Retreat**..*Kay Starr*...Capitol F936

TW	LW	WK	Billboard ❀ NOVEMBER 18, 1950 ❀ Best Sellers
1	2	11	Harbor Lights..*Sammy Kaye*...Columbia 4-38963
2	1	20	Goodnight Irene...*Gordon Jenkins & The Weavers*...Decca 9-27077
3	4	13	I'll Never Be Free...*Kay Starr & Tennessee Ernie Ford*...Capitol F1124
4	8	6	Harbor Lights ....*Guy Lombardo*...Decca 9-27208
5	5	12	All My Love (Bolero) ....*Patti Page*...Mercury 5455-X45
6	9	9	Thinking Of You ....*Don Cherry*...Decca 9-27128
7	24	8	Patricia...*Perry Como*...RCA Victor 47-3905
8	6	17	Sam's Song (The Happy Tune) ....*Gary Crosby & Bing Crosby*...Decca 9-27112
9	13	4	Nevertheless (I'm In Love With You) ....*Paul Weston*...Columbia 4-38982
10	3	24	Mona Lisa ....*Nat "King" Cole*...Capitol F1010
10	21	6	Thinking Of You ....*Eddie Fisher*...RCA Victor 47-3901

TW	LW	WK	Billboard ❀ NOVEMBER 25, 1950 ❀ Best Sellers
1	1	12	Harbor Lights..*Sammy Kaye*...Columbia 4-38963
2	5	13	All My Love (Bolero) ....*Patti Page*...Mercury 5455-X45
2	4	7	Harbor Lights ....*Guy Lombardo*...Decca 9-27208
4	2	21	Goodnight Irene...*Gordon Jenkins & The Weavers*...Decca 9-27077
5	—	1	The Thing...*Phil Harris*...RCA Victor 47-3968
6	6	10	Thinking Of You ....*Don Cherry*...Decca 9-27128
7	3	14	I'll Never Be Free...*Kay Starr & Tennessee Ernie Ford*...Capitol F1124
8	27	2	The Tennessee Waltz..*Patti Page*...Mercury 5534-X45
9	9	5	Nevertheless (I'm In Love With You) ....*Paul Weston*...Columbia 4-38982
10	15	4	A Bushel And A Peck...*Perry Como & Betty Hutton*...RCA Victor 47-3930

TW	LW	WK	Billboard ❀ DECEMBER 2, 1950 ❀ Best Sellers
1	5	2	The Thing...*Phil Harris*...RCA Victor 47-3968
2	1	13	Harbor Lights..*Sammy Kaye*...Columbia 4-38963
3	8	3	The Tennessee Waltz..*Patti Page*...Mercury 5534-X45
4	2	14	All My Love (Bolero) ....*Patti Page*...Mercury 5455-X45
5	2	8	Harbor Lights ....*Guy Lombardo*...Decca 9-27208
6	6	11	Thinking Of You ....*Don Cherry*...Decca 9-27128
7	4	22	Goodnight Irene...*Gordon Jenkins & The Weavers*...Decca 9-27077
8	7	15	I'll Never Be Free...*Kay Starr & Tennessee Ernie Ford*...Capitol F1124
9	9	6	Nevertheless (I'm In Love With You) ....*Paul Weston*...Columbia 4-38982
10	10	5	A Bushel And A Peck...*Perry Como & Betty Hutton*...RCA Victor 47-3930

TW	LW	WK	Billboard ❀ DECEMBER 9, 1950 ❀ Best Sellers
1	1	3	The Thing...*Phil Harris*...RCA Victor 47-3968
2	3	4	The Tennessee Waltz..*Patti Page*...Mercury 5534-X45
3	2	14	Harbor Lights..*Sammy Kaye*...Columbia 4-38963
4	6	12	Thinking Of You ....*Don Cherry*...Decca 9-27128
5	5	9	Harbor Lights ....*Guy Lombardo*...Decca 9-27208
6	10	6	A Bushel And A Peck...*Perry Como & Betty Hutton*...RCA Victor 47-3930
7	4	15	All My Love (Bolero) ....*Patti Page*...Mercury 5455-X45
8	8	16	I'll Never Be Free...*Kay Starr & Tennessee Ernie Ford*...Capitol F1124
9	9	7	Nevertheless (I'm In Love With You) ....*Paul Weston*...Columbia 4-38982
10	11	9	Thinking Of You ....*Eddie Fisher*...RCA Victor 47-3901

TW	LW	WK	Billboard ❀ DECEMBER 16, 1950 ❀ Best Sellers
1	1	4	The Thing...*Phil Harris*...RCA Victor 47-3968
2	2	5	The Tennessee Waltz..*Patti Page*...Mercury 5534-X45
3	3	15	Harbor Lights..*Sammy Kaye*...Columbia 4-38963
4	5	10	Harbor Lights ....*Guy Lombardo*...Decca 9-27208
5	4	13	Thinking Of You ....*Don Cherry*...Decca 9-27128
6	7	16	All My Love (Bolero) ....*Patti Page*...Mercury 5455-X45
7	6	7	A Bushel And A Peck...*Perry Como & Betty Hutton*...RCA Victor 47-3930
8	19	3	Rudolph, The Red-Nosed Reindeer...*Gene Autry*...Columbia 38610
9	10	10	Thinking Of You ....*Eddie Fisher*...RCA Victor 47-3901
10	23	2	My Heart Cries For You...*Guy Mitchell*...Columbia 4-39067

TW	LW	WK	Billboard ® ✹ DECEMBER 23, 1950 ✹ Best Sellers
1	1	5	**The Thing**..*Phil Harris*...RCA Victor 47-3968
2	2	6	**The Tennessee Waltz**..*Patti Page*...Mercury 5534-X45
3	3	16	**Harbor Lights**...*Sammy Kaye*...Columbia 4-38963
4	8	4	**Rudolph, The Red-Nosed Reindeer**...................................*Gene Autry*...Columbia 38610
5	5	14	**Thinking Of You**...*Don Cherry*...Decca 9-27128
5	10	3	**My Heart Cries For You**...*Guy Mitchell*...Columbia 4-39067
7	7	8	**A Bushel And A Peck**..............................*Perry Como & Betty Hutton*...RCA Victor 47-3930
8	4	11	**Harbor Lights**...*Guy Lombardo*...Decca 9-27208
9	12	9	**Nevertheless (I'm In Love With You)** ....*Paul Weston*...Columbia 4-38982
10	23	5	**Harbor Lights**..*Bing Crosby*...Decca 9-27219

TW	LW	WK	Billboard ® ✹ DECEMBER 30, 1950 ✹ Best Sellers
1	2	7	**The Tennessee Waltz**..*Patti Page*...Mercury 5534-X45
2	1	6	**The Thing**..*Phil Harris*...RCA Victor 47-3968
3	4	5	**Rudolph, The Red-Nosed Reindeer**...................................*Gene Autry*...Columbia 38610
4	5	4	**My Heart Cries For You**...*Guy Mitchell*...Columbia 4-39067
5	3	17	**Harbor Lights**...*Sammy Kaye*...Columbia 4-38963
6	8	12	**Harbor Lights**...*Guy Lombardo*...Decca 9-27208
7	7	9	**A Bushel And A Peck**..............................*Perry Como & Betty Hutton*...RCA Victor 47-3930
8	5	15	**Thinking Of You**...*Don Cherry*...Decca 9-27128
9	12	8	**Nevertheless (I'm In Love With You)** ....*Mills Brothers*...Decca 9-27253
10	13	3	**Be My Love**..*Mario Lanza*...RCA Victor 49-1353

TW	LW	WK	Billboard® ❀ JANUARY 6, 1951 ❀ Best Sellers
1	1	8	The Tennessee Waltz..Patti Page...Mercury 5534-X45
2	2	7	The Thing..Phil Harris...RCA Victor 47-3968
3	4	5	My Heart Cries For You...Guy Mitchell...Columbia 4-39067
4	3	6	Rudolph, The Red-Nosed Reindeer...Gene Autry...Columbia 38610
5	5	18	Harbor Lights...Sammy Kaye...Columbia 4-38963
6	10	4	Be My Love...Mario Lanza...RCA Victor 49-1353
7	15	5	Frosty The Snow Man...Gene Autry...Columbia 6-742
8	7	10	A Bushel And A Peck..Perry Como & Betty Hutton...RCA Victor 47-3930
8	12	13	Thinking Of You...Eddie Fisher...RCA Victor 47-3901
10	8	16	Thinking Of You...Don Cherry...Decca 9-27128
10	18	2	Christmas In Killarney..Dennis Day...RCA Victor 47-3970

TW	LW	WK	Billboard® ❀ JANUARY 13, 1951 ❀ Best Sellers
1	1	9	The Tennessee Waltz..Patti Page...Mercury 5534-X45
2	2	8	The Thing..Phil Harris...RCA Victor 47-3968
3	3	6	My Heart Cries For You...Guy Mitchell...Columbia 4-39067
4	4	7	Rudolph, The Red-Nosed Reindeer...Gene Autry...Columbia 38610
5	6	5	Be My Love...Mario Lanza...RCA Victor 49-1353
6	5	19	Harbor Lights...Sammy Kaye...Columbia 4-38963
7	8	11	A Bushel And A Peck..Perry Como & Betty Hutton...RCA Victor 47-3930
8	16	14	Harbor Lights...Guy Lombardo...Decca 9-27208
9	10	17	Thinking Of You...Don Cherry...Decca 9-27128
10	—	1	So Long (It's Been Good to Know Yuh)...................Gordon Jenkins & The Weavers...Decca 9-27376

TW	LW	WK	Billboard® ❀ JANUARY 20, 1951 ❀ Best Sellers
1	1	10	The Tennessee Waltz..Patti Page...Mercury 5534-X45
2	2	9	The Thing..Phil Harris...RCA Victor 47-3968
3	3	7	My Heart Cries For You...Guy Mitchell...Columbia 4-39067
4	5	6	Be My Love...Mario Lanza...RCA Victor 49-1353
5	6	20	Harbor Lights...Sammy Kaye...Columbia 4-38963
6	15	6	Tennessee Waltz ....Guy Lombardo...Decca 9-27336
7	8	15	Harbor Lights...Guy Lombardo...Decca 9-27208
8	7	12	A Bushel And A Peck..Perry Como & Betty Hutton...RCA Victor 47-3930
9	9	18	Thinking Of You...Don Cherry...Decca 9-27128
10	10	2	So Long (It's Been Good to Know Yuh)...................Gordon Jenkins & The Weavers...Decca 9-27376

TW	LW	WK	Billboard® ❀ JANUARY 27, 1951 ❀ Best Sellers
1	1	11	The Tennessee Waltz..Patti Page...Mercury 5534-X45
2	3	8	My Heart Cries For You...Guy Mitchell...Columbia 4-39067
3	2	10	The Thing..Phil Harris...RCA Victor 47-3968
4	4	7	Be My Love...Mario Lanza...RCA Victor 49-1353
5	17	3	If...Perry Como...RCA Victor 47-3997
6	5	21	Harbor Lights...Sammy Kaye...Columbia 4-38963
7	10	3	So Long (It's Been Good to Know Yuh)...................Gordon Jenkins & The Weavers...Decca 9-27376
8	15	4	You're Just In Love...Perry Como...RCA Victor 47-3945
9	8	13	A Bushel And A Peck..Perry Como & Betty Hutton...RCA Victor 47-3930
10	14	7	The Roving Kind..Guy Mitchell...Columbia 4-39067

TW	LW	WK	Billboard® ❀ FEBRUARY 3, 1951 ❀ Best Sellers
1	1	12	The Tennessee Waltz..Patti Page...Mercury 5534-X45
2	2	9	My Heart Cries For You...Guy Mitchell...Columbia 4-39067
3	4	8	Be My Love...Mario Lanza...RCA Victor 49-1353
4	3	11	The Thing..Phil Harris...RCA Victor 47-3968
5	5	4	If...Perry Como...RCA Victor 47-3997
6	8	5	You're Just In Love...Perry Como...RCA Victor 47-3945
7	7	4	So Long (It's Been Good to Know Yuh)...................Gordon Jenkins & The Weavers...Decca 9-27376
8	10	8	The Roving Kind..Guy Mitchell...Columbia 4-39067
9	9	14	A Bushel And A Peck..Perry Como & Betty Hutton...RCA Victor 47-3930
10	18	8	Tennessee Waltz ....Guy Lombardo...Decca 9-27336

TW	LW	WK	Billboard ⚫ FEBRUARY 10, 1951 ⚫ Best Sellers
1	1	13	The Tennessee Waltz...Patti Page...Mercury 5534-X45
2	2	10	My Heart Cries For You..Guy Mitchell...Columbia 4-39067
3	3	9	Be My Love...Mario Lanza...RCA Victor 49-1353
4	5	5	If..Perry Como...RCA Victor 47-3997
5	6	6	You're Just In Love..Perry Como...RCA Victor 47-3945
6	4	12	The Thing..Phil Harris...RCA Victor 47-3968
7	8	9	The Roving Kind..Guy Mitchell...Columbia 4-39067
8	7	5	So Long (It's Been Good to Know Yuh) ....Gordon Jenkins & The Weavers...Decca 9-27376
9	10	9	Tennessee Waltz...Guy Lombardo...Decca 9-27336
10	12	23	Harbor Lights...Sammy Kaye...Columbia 4-38963

TW	LW	WK	Billboard ⚫ FEBRUARY 17, 1951 ⚫ Best Sellers
1	1	14	The Tennessee Waltz...Patti Page...Mercury 5534-X45
2	2	11	My Heart Cries For You..Guy Mitchell...Columbia 4-39067
3	3	10	Be My Love...Mario Lanza...RCA Victor 49-1353
4	4	6	If..Perry Como...RCA Victor 47-3997
5	5	7	You're Just In Love..Perry Como...RCA Victor 47-3945
6	7	10	The Roving Kind..Guy Mitchell...Columbia 4-39067
7	8	6	So Long (It's Been Good to Know Yuh) ....Gordon Jenkins & The Weavers...Decca 9-27376
8	9	10	Tennessee Waltz...Guy Lombardo...Decca 9-27336
9	15	4	I Taut I Taw A Puddy Tat...Mel Blanc...Capitol F1360
10	21	2	Would I Love You (Love You, Love You).......................................Patti Page...Mercury 5571-X45

TW	LW	WK	Billboard ⚫ FEBRUARY 24, 1951 ⚫ Best Sellers
1	1	15	The Tennessee Waltz...Patti Page...Mercury 5534-X45
2	4	7	If..Perry Como...RCA Victor 47-3997
3	3	11	Be My Love...Mario Lanza...RCA Victor 49-1353
4	2	12	My Heart Cries For You..Guy Mitchell...Columbia 4-39067
5	5	8	You're Just In Love..Perry Como...RCA Victor 47-3945
6	6	11	The Roving Kind..Guy Mitchell...Columbia 4-39067
7	7	7	So Long (It's Been Good to Know Yuh) ....Gordon Jenkins & The Weavers...Decca 9-27376
8	11	9	Tennessee Waltz...Les Paul & Mary Ford...Capitol F1316
9	8	11	Tennessee Waltz...Guy Lombardo...Decca 9-27336
10	10	3	Would I Love You (Love You, Love You).......................................Patti Page...Mercury 5571-X45

TW	LW	WK	Billboard ⚫ MARCH 3, 1951 ⚫ Best Sellers
1	2	8	If..Perry Como...RCA Victor 47-3997
2	1	16	The Tennessee Waltz...Patti Page...Mercury 5534-X45
3	3	12	Be My Love...Mario Lanza...RCA Victor 49-1353
4	6	12	The Roving Kind..Guy Mitchell...Columbia 4-39067
5	4	13	My Heart Cries For You..Guy Mitchell...Columbia 4-39067
6	7	8	So Long (It's Been Good to Know Yuh) ....Gordon Jenkins & The Weavers...Decca 9-27376
7	5	9	You're Just In Love..Perry Como...RCA Victor 47-3945
8	11	4	Aba Daba Honeymoon...............................Debbie Reynolds & Carleton Carpenter...MGM K30282
9	10	4	Would I Love You (Love You, Love You).......................................Patti Page...Mercury 5571-X45
10	16	3	Mockin' Bird Hill..Les Paul & Mary Ford...Capitol F1373

TW	LW	WK	Billboard ⚫ MARCH 10, 1951 ⚫ Best Sellers
1	3	13	Be My Love...Mario Lanza...RCA Victor 49-1353
2	1	9	If..Perry Como...RCA Victor 47-3997
3	5	14	My Heart Cries For You..Guy Mitchell...Columbia 4-39067
4	2	17	The Tennessee Waltz...Patti Page...Mercury 5534-X45
5	8	5	Aba Daba Honeymoon...............................Debbie Reynolds & Carleton Carpenter...MGM K30282
6	7	10	You're Just In Love..Perry Como...RCA Victor 47-3945
7	10	4	Mockin' Bird Hill..Les Paul & Mary Ford...Capitol F1373
8	9	5	Would I Love You (Love You, Love You).......................................Patti Page...Mercury 5571-X45
9	4	13	The Roving Kind..Guy Mitchell...Columbia 4-39067
10	11	7	I Taut I Taw A Puddy Tat...Mel Blanc...Capitol F1360

TW	LW	WK	Billboard® ❀ MARCH 17, 1951 ❀	Best Sellers
1	2	10	**If**	Perry Como...RCA Victor 47-3997
2	1	14	**Be My Love**	Mario Lanza...RCA Victor 49-1353
3	4	18	**The Tennessee Waltz**	Patti Page...Mercury 5534-X45
4	3	15	**My Heart Cries For You**	Guy Mitchell...Columbia 4-39067
5	5	6	**Aba Daba Honeymoon** ....Debbie Reynolds & Carleton Carpenter...MGM K30282	
6	7	5	**Mockin' Bird Hill**	Les Paul & Mary Ford...Capitol F1373
7	6	11	**You're Just In Love**	Perry Como...RCA Victor 47-3945
8	8	6	**Would I Love You (Love You, Love You)**	Patti Page...Mercury 5571-X45
9	12	3	**Sparrow In The Tree Top**	Guy Mitchell...Columbia 4-39190
10	12	4	**Mockin' Bird Hill**	Patti Page...Mercury 5595-X45

TW	LW	WK	Billboard® ❀ MARCH 24, 1951 ❀	Best Sellers
1	1	11	**If**	Perry Como...RCA Victor 47-3997
2	2	15	**Be My Love**	Mario Lanza...RCA Victor 49-1353
3	4	16	**My Heart Cries For You**	Guy Mitchell...Columbia 4-39067
4	3	19	**The Tennessee Waltz**	Patti Page...Mercury 5534-X45
5	6	6	**Mockin' Bird Hill**	Les Paul & Mary Ford...Capitol F1373
6	5	7	**Aba Daba Honeymoon** ....Debbie Reynolds & Carleton Carpenter...MGM K30282	
7	8	7	**Would I Love You (Love You, Love You)**	Patti Page...Mercury 5571-X45
8	10	5	**Mockin' Bird Hill**	Patti Page...Mercury 5595-X45
9	7	12	**You're Just In Love**	Perry Como...RCA Victor 47-3945
10	9	4	**Sparrow In The Tree Top**	Guy Mitchell...Columbia 4-39190

TW	LW	WK	Billboard® ❀ MARCH 31, 1951 ❀	Best Sellers
1	1	12	**If**	Perry Como...RCA Victor 47-3997
2	2	16	**Be My Love**	Mario Lanza...RCA Victor 49-1353
3	6	8	**Aba Daba Honeymoon** ....Debbie Reynolds & Carleton Carpenter...MGM K30282	
4	5	7	**Mockin' Bird Hill**	Les Paul & Mary Ford...Capitol F1373
5	8	6	**Mockin' Bird Hill**	Patti Page...Mercury 5595-X45
6	3	17	**My Heart Cries For You**	Guy Mitchell...Columbia 4-39067
7	4	20	**The Tennessee Waltz**	Patti Page...Mercury 5534-X45
8	7	8	**Would I Love You (Love You, Love You)**	Patti Page...Mercury 5571-X45
9	9	13	**You're Just In Love**	Perry Como...RCA Victor 47-3945
10	10	5	**Sparrow In The Tree Top**	Guy Mitchell...Columbia 4-39190

TW	LW	WK	Billboard® ❀ APRIL 7, 1951 ❀	Best Sellers
1	1	13	**If**	Perry Como...RCA Victor 47-3997
2	2	17	**Be My Love**	Mario Lanza...RCA Victor 49-1353
3	4	8	**Mockin' Bird Hill**	Les Paul & Mary Ford...Capitol F1373
4	3	9	**Aba Daba Honeymoon** ....Debbie Reynolds & Carleton Carpenter...MGM K30282	
5	5	7	**Mockin' Bird Hill**	Patti Page...Mercury 5595-X45
6	20	2	**How High The Moon**	Les Paul & Mary Ford...Capitol F1451
7	8	9	**Would I Love You (Love You, Love You)**	Patti Page...Mercury 5571-X45
8	13	2	**On Top Of Old Smoky** ....The Weavers and Terry Gilkyson...Decca 9-27515	
9	6	18	**My Heart Cries For You**	Guy Mitchell...Columbia 4-39067
10	7	21	**The Tennessee Waltz**	Patti Page...Mercury 5534-X45

TW	LW	WK	Billboard® ❀ APRIL 14, 1951 ❀	Best Sellers
1	1	14	**If**	Perry Como...RCA Victor 47-3997
2	2	18	**Be My Love**	Mario Lanza...RCA Victor 49-1353
3	3	9	**Mockin' Bird Hill**	Les Paul & Mary Ford...Capitol F1373
4	6	3	**How High The Moon**	Les Paul & Mary Ford...Capitol F1451
5	5	8	**Mockin' Bird Hill**	Patti Page...Mercury 5595-X45
6	4	10	**Aba Daba Honeymoon** ....Debbie Reynolds & Carleton Carpenter...MGM K30282	
7	8	3	**On Top Of Old Smoky** ....The Weavers and Terry Gilkyson...Decca 9-27515	
8	7	10	**Would I Love You (Love You, Love You)**	Patti Page...Mercury 5571-X45
9	11	7	**Sparrow In The Tree Top**	Guy Mitchell...Columbia 4-39190
10	12	7	**I Apologize**	Billy Eckstine...MGM K10903

TW	LW	WK	Billboard ⚜ APRIL 21, 1951 ⚜ Best Sellers
1	4	4	How High The Moon..*Les Paul & Mary Ford*...Capitol F1451
2	1	15	If..*Perry Como*...RCA Victor 47-3997
3	3	10	Mockin' Bird Hill...*Les Paul & Mary Ford*...Capitol F1373
4	2	19	Be My Love..*Mario Lanza*...RCA Victor 49-1353
5	5	9	Mockin' Bird Hill..*Patti Page*...Mercury 5595-X45
6	7	4	On Top Of Old Smoky ....*The Weavers and Terry Gilkyson*...Decca 9-27515
7	6	11	Aba Daba Honeymoon ....*Debbie Reynolds & Carleton Carpenter*...MGM K30282
8	10	8	I Apologize ....*Billy Eckstine*...MGM K10903
9	8	11	Would I Love You (Love You, Love You)..*Patti Page*...Mercury 5571-X45
10	9	8	Sparrow In The Tree Top ....*Guy Mitchell*...Columbia 4-39190

TW	LW	WK	Billboard ⚜ APRIL 28, 1951 ⚜ Best Sellers
1	1	5	How High The Moon..*Les Paul & Mary Ford*...Capitol F1451
2	6	5	On Top Of Old Smoky ....*The Weavers and Terry Gilkyson*...Decca 9-27515
3	3	11	Mockin' Bird Hill...*Les Paul & Mary Ford*...Capitol F1373
4	2	16	If..*Perry Como*...RCA Victor 47-3997
5	5	10	Mockin' Bird Hill..*Patti Page*...Mercury 5595-X45
6	4	20	Be My Love..*Mario Lanza*...RCA Victor 49-1353
7	15	3	Too Young..*Nat "King" Cole*...Capitol F1449
8	7	12	Aba Daba Honeymoon ....*Debbie Reynolds & Carleton Carpenter*...MGM K30282
9	8	9	I Apologize ....*Billy Eckstine*...MGM K10903
10	9	12	Would I Love You (Love You, Love You)..*Patti Page*...Mercury 5571-X45

TW	LW	WK	Billboard ⚜ MAY 5, 1951 ⚜ Best Sellers
1	1	6	How High The Moon..*Les Paul & Mary Ford*...Capitol F1451
2	2	6	On Top Of Old Smoky ....*The Weavers and Terry Gilkyson*...Decca 9-27515
3	3	12	Mockin' Bird Hill...*Les Paul & Mary Ford*...Capitol F1373
4	5	11	Mockin' Bird Hill..*Patti Page*...Mercury 5595-X45
5	7	4	Too Young..*Nat "King" Cole*...Capitol F1449
6	6	21	Be My Love..*Mario Lanza*...RCA Victor 49-1353
7	4	17	If..*Perry Como*...RCA Victor 47-3997
8	12	3	Sound Off (The Duckworth Chant)..*Vaughn Monroe*...RCA Victor 47-4113
9	9	10	I Apologize ....*Billy Eckstine*...MGM K10903
10	11	10	Sparrow In The Tree Top ....*Guy Mitchell*...Columbia 4-39190

TW	LW	WK	Billboard ⚜ MAY 12, 1951 ⚜ Best Sellers
1	1	7	How High The Moon..*Les Paul & Mary Ford*...Capitol F1451
2	2	7	On Top Of Old Smoky ....*The Weavers and Terry Gilkyson*...Decca 9-27515
3	4	12	Mockin' Bird Hill..*Patti Page*...Mercury 5595-X45
4	5	5	Too Young..*Nat "King" Cole*...Capitol F1449
5	3	13	Mockin' Bird Hill...*Les Paul & Mary Ford*...Capitol F1373
6	8	4	Sound Off (The Duckworth Chant)..*Vaughn Monroe*...RCA Victor 47-4113
7	6	22	Be My Love..*Mario Lanza*...RCA Victor 49-1353
8	9	11	I Apologize ....*Billy Eckstine*...MGM K10903
9	7	18	If..*Perry Como*...RCA Victor 47-3997
10	11	4	When You And I Were Young Maggie Blues ....*Bing & Gary Crosby*...Decca 9-27577

TW	LW	WK	Billboard ⚜ MAY 19, 1951 ⚜ Best Sellers
1	1	8	How High The Moon..*Les Paul & Mary Ford*...Capitol F1451
2	2	8	On Top Of Old Smoky ....*The Weavers and Terry Gilkyson*...Decca 9-27515
3	4	6	Too Young..*Nat "King" Cole*...Capitol F1449
4	3	13	Mockin' Bird Hill..*Patti Page*...Mercury 5595-X45
5	5	14	Mockin' Bird Hill...*Les Paul & Mary Ford*...Capitol F1373
6	6	5	Sound Off (The Duckworth Chant)..*Vaughn Monroe*...RCA Victor 47-4113
7	7	23	Be My Love..*Mario Lanza*...RCA Victor 49-1353
8	11	3	Jezebel...*Frankie Laine*...Columbia 4-39367
9	19	2	Old Soldiers Never Die ....*Vaughn Monroe*...RCA Victor 47-4146
10	8	12	I Apologize ....*Billy Eckstine*...MGM K10903
10	15	6	The Loveliest Night Of The Year ....*Mario Lanza*...RCA Victor 49-3300

TW	LW	WK	Billboard ❀ MAY 26, 1951 ❀ Best Sellers
1	1	9	How High The Moon...Les Paul & Mary Ford...Capitol F1451
2	2	9	On Top Of Old Smoky..The Weavers and Terry Gilkyson...Decca 9-27515
3	3	7	Too Young...Nat "King" Cole...Capitol F1449
4	6	6	Sound Off (The Duckworth Chant)..Vaughn Monroe...RCA Victor 47-4113
5	5	15	Mockin' Bird Hill..Les Paul & Mary Ford...Capitol F1373
6	4	14	Mockin' Bird Hill..Patti Page...Mercury 5595-X45
7	8	4	Jezebel..Frankie Laine...Columbia 4-39367
8	7	24	Be My Love..Mario Lanza...RCA Victor 49-1353
9	10	7	The Loveliest Night Of The Year.................................Mario Lanza...RCA Victor 49-3300
9	12	3	Rose, Rose, I Love You..Frankie Laine...Columbia 4-39367

TW	LW	WK	Billboard ❀ JUNE 2, 1951 ❀ Best Sellers
1	1	10	How High The Moon...Les Paul & Mary Ford...Capitol F1451
2	3	8	Too Young...Nat "King" Cole...Capitol F1449
3	2	10	On Top Of Old Smoky..The Weavers and Terry Gilkyson...Decca 9-27515
4	4	7	Sound Off (The Duckworth Chant)..Vaughn Monroe...RCA Victor 47-4113
5	7	5	Jezebel..Frankie Laine...Columbia 4-39367
6	5	16	Mockin' Bird Hill..Les Paul & Mary Ford...Capitol F1373
7	6	15	Mockin' Bird Hill..Patti Page...Mercury 5595-X45
8	9	8	The Loveliest Night Of The Year.................................Mario Lanza...RCA Victor 49-3300
9	9	4	Rose, Rose, I Love You..Frankie Laine...Columbia 4-39367
10	11	4	Old Soldiers Never Die...Vaughn Monroe...RCA Victor 47-4146

TW	LW	WK	Billboard ❀ JUNE 9, 1951 ❀ Best Sellers
1	1	11	How High The Moon...Les Paul & Mary Ford...Capitol F1451
2	2	9	Too Young...Nat "King" Cole...Capitol F1449
3	3	11	On Top Of Old Smoky..The Weavers and Terry Gilkyson...Decca 9-27515
4	5	6	Jezebel..Frankie Laine...Columbia 4-39367
5	4	8	Sound Off (The Duckworth Chant)..Vaughn Monroe...RCA Victor 47-4113
6	8	9	The Loveliest Night Of The Year.................................Mario Lanza...RCA Victor 49-3300
7	7	16	Mockin' Bird Hill..Patti Page...Mercury 5595-X45
8	6	17	Mockin' Bird Hill..Les Paul & Mary Ford...Capitol F1373
9	9	5	Rose, Rose, I Love You..Frankie Laine...Columbia 4-39367
10	11	6	On Top Of Old Smoky...Vaughn Monroe...RCA Victor 47-4114

TW	LW	WK	Billboard ❀ JUNE 16, 1951 ❀ Best Sellers
1	1	12	How High The Moon...Les Paul & Mary Ford...Capitol F1451
2	2	10	Too Young...Nat "King" Cole...Capitol F1449
3	3	12	On Top Of Old Smoky..The Weavers and Terry Gilkyson...Decca 9-27515
4	4	7	Jezebel..Frankie Laine...Columbia 4-39367
5	5	9	Sound Off (The Duckworth Chant)..Vaughn Monroe...RCA Victor 47-4113
6	9	6	Rose, Rose, I Love You..Frankie Laine...Columbia 4-39367
7	6	10	The Loveliest Night Of The Year.................................Mario Lanza...RCA Victor 49-3300
8	7	17	Mockin' Bird Hill..Patti Page...Mercury 5595-X45
9	14	3	My Truly, Truly Fair...Guy Mitchell...Columbia 4-39415
10	8	18	Mockin' Bird Hill..Les Paul & Mary Ford...Capitol F1373
10	10	7	On Top Of Old Smoky...Vaughn Monroe...RCA Victor 47-4114

TW	LW	WK	Billboard ❀ JUNE 23, 1951 ❀ Best Sellers
1	2	11	Too Young...Nat "King" Cole...Capitol F1449
2	1	13	How High The Moon...Les Paul & Mary Ford...Capitol F1451
3	4	8	Jezebel..Frankie Laine...Columbia 4-39367
4	3	13	On Top Of Old Smoky..The Weavers and Terry Gilkyson...Decca 9-27515
5	5	10	Sound Off (The Duckworth Chant)..Vaughn Monroe...RCA Victor 47-4113
6	7	11	The Loveliest Night Of The Year.................................Mario Lanza...RCA Victor 49-3300
7	6	7	Rose, Rose, I Love You..Frankie Laine...Columbia 4-39367
8	9	4	My Truly, Truly Fair...Guy Mitchell...Columbia 4-39415
9	10	19	Mockin' Bird Hill..Les Paul & Mary Ford...Capitol F1373
10	8	18	Mockin' Bird Hill..Patti Page...Mercury 5595-X45

TW	LW	WK	Billboard 🎵 JUNE 30, 1951 🎵 Best Sellers		
1	1	12	Too Young	Nat "King" Cole	Capitol F1449
2	2	14	How High The Moon	Les Paul & Mary Ford	Capitol F1451
3	3	9	Jezebel	Frankie Laine	Columbia 4-39367
4	4	14	On Top Of Old Smoky	The Weavers and Terry Gilkyson	Decca 9-27515
5	5	11	Sound Off (The Duckworth Chant)	Vaughn Monroe	RCA Victor 47-4113
6	6	12	The Loveliest Night Of The Year	Mario Lanza	RCA Victor 49-3300
7	7	8	Rose, Rose, I Love You	Frankie Laine	Columbia 4-39367
8	8	5	My Truly, Truly Fair	Guy Mitchell	Columbia 4-39415
9	9	20	Mockin' Bird Hill	Les Paul & Mary Ford	Capitol F1373
9	12	7	Mister And Mississippi	Patti Page	Mercury 5645-X45

TW	LW	WK	Billboard 🎵 JULY 7, 1951 🎵 Best Sellers		
1	1	13	Too Young	Nat "King" Cole	Capitol F1449
2	3	10	Jezebel	Frankie Laine	Columbia 4-39367
3	2	15	How High The Moon	Les Paul & Mary Ford	Capitol F1451
4	6	13	The Loveliest Night Of The Year	Mario Lanza	RCA Victor 49-3300
5	4	15	On Top Of Old Smoky	The Weavers and Terry Gilkyson	Decca 9-27515
6	8	6	My Truly, Truly Fair	Guy Mitchell	Columbia 4-39415
7	7	9	Rose, Rose, I Love You	Frankie Laine	Columbia 4-39367
8	—	1	Come On-a My House	Rosemary Clooney	Columbia 4-39467
9	5	12	Sound Off (The Duckworth Chant)	Vaughn Monroe	RCA Victor 47-4113
10	9	8	Mister And Mississippi	Patti Page	Mercury 5645-X45

TW	LW	WK	Billboard 🎵 JULY 14, 1951 🎵 Best Sellers		
1	1	14	Too Young	Nat "King" Cole	Capitol F1449
2	2	11	Jezebel	Frankie Laine	Columbia 4-39367
3	3	16	How High The Moon	Les Paul & Mary Ford	Capitol F1451
4	8	2	Come On-a My House	Rosemary Clooney	Columbia 4-39467
5	4	14	The Loveliest Night Of The Year	Mario Lanza	RCA Victor 49-3300
6	6	7	My Truly, Truly Fair	Guy Mitchell	Columbia 4-39415
7	5	16	On Top Of Old Smoky	The Weavers and Terry Gilkyson	Decca 9-27515
8	12	2	Sweet Violets	Dinah Shore	RCA Victor 47-4174
9	7	10	Rose, Rose, I Love You	Frankie Laine	Columbia 4-39367
10	9	13	Sound Off (The Duckworth Chant)	Vaughn Monroe	RCA Victor 47-4113

TW	LW	WK	Billboard 🎵 JULY 21, 1951 🎵 Best Sellers		
1	1	15	Too Young	Nat "King" Cole	Capitol F1449
2	4	3	Come On-a My House	Rosemary Clooney	Columbia 4-39467
3	2	12	Jezebel	Frankie Laine	Columbia 4-39367
4	3	17	How High The Moon	Les Paul & Mary Ford	Capitol F1451
5	5	15	The Loveliest Night Of The Year	Mario Lanza	RCA Victor 49-3300
6	8	3	Sweet Violets	Dinah Shore	RCA Victor 47-4174
7	6	8	My Truly, Truly Fair	Guy Mitchell	Columbia 4-39415
8	7	17	On Top Of Old Smoky	The Weavers and Terry Gilkyson	Decca 9-27515
9	11	8	I Get Ideas	Tony Martin	RCA Victor 47-4141
10	9	11	Rose, Rose, I Love You	Frankie Laine	Columbia 4-39367

TW	LW	WK	Billboard 🎵 JULY 28, 1951 🎵 Best Sellers		
1	2	4	Come On-a My House	Rosemary Clooney	Columbia 4-39467
2	1	16	Too Young	Nat "King" Cole	Capitol F1449
3	3	13	Jezebel	Frankie Laine	Columbia 4-39367
4	5	16	The Loveliest Night Of The Year	Mario Lanza	RCA Victor 49-3300
5	7	9	My Truly, Truly Fair	Guy Mitchell	Columbia 4-39415
6	6	4	Sweet Violets	Dinah Shore	RCA Victor 47-4174
7	13	6	Because Of You	Tony Bennett	Columbia 4-39362
8	4	18	How High The Moon	Les Paul & Mary Ford	Capitol F1451
9	8	18	On Top Of Old Smoky	The Weavers and Terry Gilkyson	Decca 9-27515
9	9	9	I Get Ideas	Tony Martin	RCA Victor 47-4141

TW	LW	WK	Billboard® 🎵 AUGUST 4, 1951 🎵 Best Sellers
1	1	5	Come On-a My House..Rosemary Clooney...Columbia 4-39467
2	2	17	Too Young...Nat "King" Cole...Capitol F1449
3	3	14	Jezebel...Frankie Laine...Columbia 4-39367
4	4	17	The Loveliest Night Of The Year...Mario Lanza...RCA Victor 49-3300
5	6	5	Sweet Violets...Dinah Shore...RCA Victor 47-4174
6	7	7	Because Of You..Tony Bennett...Columbia 4-39362
7	5	10	My Truly, Truly Fair..Guy Mitchell...Columbia 4-39415
8	9	10	I Get Ideas..Tony Martin...RCA Victor 47-4141
9	8	19	How High The Moon...Les Paul & Mary Ford...Capitol F1451
10	9	19	On Top Of Old Smoky.......................................The Weavers and Terry Gilkyson...Decca 9-27515

TW	LW	WK	Billboard® 🎵 AUGUST 11, 1951 🎵 Best Sellers
1	1	6	Come On-a My House..Rosemary Clooney...Columbia 4-39467
2	2	18	Too Young...Nat "King" Cole...Capitol F1449
3	5	6	Sweet Violets...Dinah Shore...RCA Victor 47-4174
4	3	15	Jezebel...Frankie Laine...Columbia 4-39367
5	4	18	The Loveliest Night Of The Year...Mario Lanza...RCA Victor 49-3300
6	6	8	Because Of You..Tony Bennett...Columbia 4-39362
7	7	11	My Truly, Truly Fair..Guy Mitchell...Columbia 4-39415
8	8	11	I Get Ideas..Tony Martin...RCA Victor 47-4141
9	9	20	How High The Moon...Les Paul & Mary Ford...Capitol F1451
10	11	10	I'm In Love Again ....Henri René feat. April Stevens...RCA Victor 47-4148

TW	LW	WK	Billboard® 🎵 AUGUST 18, 1951 🎵 Best Sellers
1	1	7	Come On-a My House..Rosemary Clooney...Columbia 4-39467
2	2	19	Too Young...Nat "King" Cole...Capitol F1449
3	3	7	Sweet Violets...Dinah Shore...RCA Victor 47-4174
4	6	9	Because Of You..Tony Bennett...Columbia 4-39362
5	5	19	The Loveliest Night Of The Year...Mario Lanza...RCA Victor 49-3300
6	4	16	Jezebel...Frankie Laine...Columbia 4-39367
7	7	12	My Truly, Truly Fair..Guy Mitchell...Columbia 4-39415
8	8	12	I Get Ideas..Tony Martin...RCA Victor 47-4141
9	11	7	(Why Did I Tell You I Was Going To) Shanghai.......................Doris Day...Columbia 4-39423
10	9	21	How High The Moon...Les Paul & Mary Ford...Capitol F1451

TW	LW	WK	Billboard® 🎵 AUGUST 25, 1951 🎵 Best Sellers
1	1	8	Come On-a My House..Rosemary Clooney...Columbia 4-39467
2	4	10	Because Of You..Tony Bennett...Columbia 4-39362
3	2	20	Too Young...Nat "King" Cole...Capitol F1449
4	5	20	The Loveliest Night Of The Year...Mario Lanza...RCA Victor 49-3300
5	3	8	Sweet Violets...Dinah Shore...RCA Victor 47-4174
6	6	17	Jezebel...Frankie Laine...Columbia 4-39367
7	8	13	I Get Ideas..Tony Martin...RCA Victor 47-4141
8	7	13	My Truly, Truly Fair..Guy Mitchell...Columbia 4-39415
9	29	2	Whispering..Les Paul...Capitol F1748
10	13	5	Cold, Cold Heart..Tony Bennett...Columbia 4-39449

TW	LW	WK	Billboard® 🎵 SEPTEMBER 1, 1951 🎵 Best Sellers
1	1	9	Come On-a My House..Rosemary Clooney...Columbia 4-39467
2	2	11	Because Of You..Tony Bennett...Columbia 4-39362
3	3	21	Too Young...Nat "King" Cole...Capitol F1449
3	4	21	The Loveliest Night Of The Year...Mario Lanza...RCA Victor 49-3300
5	5	9	Sweet Violets...Dinah Shore...RCA Victor 47-4174
6	7	14	I Get Ideas..Tony Martin...RCA Victor 47-4141
7	11	3	The World Is Waiting For The Sunrise ....Les Paul & Mary Ford...Capitol F1748
8	6	18	Jezebel...Frankie Laine...Columbia 4-39367
9	10	6	Cold, Cold Heart..Tony Bennett...Columbia 4-39449
10	8	14	My Truly, Truly Fair..Guy Mitchell...Columbia 4-39415

TW	LW	WK	Billboard® 🏵 SEPTEMBER 8, 1951 🏵	Best Sellers
1	2	12	Because Of You	Tony Bennett...Columbia 4-39362
2	1	10	Come On-a My House	Rosemary Clooney...Columbia 4-39467
3	3	22	The Loveliest Night Of The Year	Mario Lanza...RCA Victor 49-3300
4	6	15	I Get Ideas	Tony Martin...RCA Victor 47-4141
5	7	4	The World Is Waiting For The Sunrise	Les Paul & Mary Ford...Capitol F1748
6	5	10	Sweet Violets	Dinah Shore...RCA Victor 47-4174
7	9	7	Cold, Cold Heart	Tony Bennett...Columbia 4-39449
8	3	22	Too Young	Nat "King" Cole...Capitol F1449
9	11	4	Whispering	Les Paul...Capitol F1748
10	12	6	Because Of You	Les Baxter...Capitol F1760

TW	LW	WK	Billboard® 🏵 SEPTEMBER 15, 1951 🏵	Best Sellers
1	1	13	Because Of You	Tony Bennett...Columbia 4-39362
2	2	11	Come On-a My House	Rosemary Clooney...Columbia 4-39467
3	5	5	The World Is Waiting For The Sunrise	Les Paul & Mary Ford...Capitol F1748
4	3	23	The Loveliest Night Of The Year	Mario Lanza...RCA Victor 49-3300
5	4	16	I Get Ideas	Tony Martin...RCA Victor 47-4141
6	7	8	Cold, Cold Heart	Tony Bennett...Columbia 4-39449
7	8	23	Too Young	Nat "King" Cole...Capitol F1449
8	6	11	Sweet Violets	Dinah Shore...RCA Victor 47-4174
9	9	5	Whispering	Les Paul...Capitol F1748
10	10	7	Because Of You	Les Baxter...Capitol F1760

TW	LW	WK	Billboard® 🏵 SEPTEMBER 22, 1951 🏵	Best Sellers
1	1	14	Because Of You	Tony Bennett...Columbia 4-39362
2	2	12	Come On-a My House	Rosemary Clooney...Columbia 4-39467
3	3	6	The World Is Waiting For The Sunrise	Les Paul & Mary Ford...Capitol F1748
4	6	9	Cold, Cold Heart	Tony Bennett...Columbia 4-39449
5	4	24	The Loveliest Night Of The Year	Mario Lanza...RCA Victor 49-3300
6	5	17	I Get Ideas	Tony Martin...RCA Victor 47-4141
7	9	6	Whispering	Les Paul...Capitol F1748
8	7	24	Too Young	Nat "King" Cole...Capitol F1449
9	10	8	Because Of You	Les Baxter...Capitol F1760
9	8	12	Sweet Violets	Dinah Shore...RCA Victor 47-4174

TW	LW	WK	Billboard® 🏵 SEPTEMBER 29, 1951 🏵	Best Sellers
1	1	15	Because Of You	Tony Bennett...Columbia 4-39362
2	4	10	Cold, Cold Heart	Tony Bennett...Columbia 4-39449
3	3	7	The World Is Waiting For The Sunrise	Les Paul & Mary Ford...Capitol F1748
4	6	18	I Get Ideas	Tony Martin...RCA Victor 47-4141
5	2	13	Come On-a My House	Rosemary Clooney...Columbia 4-39467
6	5	25	The Loveliest Night Of The Year	Mario Lanza...RCA Victor 49-3300
7	7	7	Whispering	Les Paul...Capitol F1748
7	8	25	Too Young	Nat "King" Cole...Capitol F1449
9	9	9	Because Of You	Les Baxter...Capitol F1760
10	17	2	And So To Sleep Again	Patti Page...Mercury 5706-X45

TW	LW	WK	Billboard® 🏵 OCTOBER 6, 1951 🏵	Best Sellers
1	1	16	Because Of You	Tony Bennett...Columbia 4-39362
2	2	11	Cold, Cold Heart	Tony Bennett...Columbia 4-39449
3	3	8	The World Is Waiting For The Sunrise	Les Paul & Mary Ford...Capitol F1748
4	4	19	I Get Ideas	Tony Martin...RCA Victor 47-4141
5	6	26	The Loveliest Night Of The Year	Mario Lanza...RCA Victor 49-3300
6	5	14	Come On-a My House	Rosemary Clooney...Columbia 4-39467
7	11	4	Sin	Four Aces...Victoria 101
8	12	6	Down Yonder	Del Wood...Tennessee 775
9	9	10	Because Of You	Les Baxter...Capitol F1760
10	13	3	Sin	Eddy Howard...Mercury 5711-X45

TW	LW	WK	Billboard ⊛ OCTOBER 13, 1951 ⊛ Best Sellers
1	1	17	Because Of You ....Tony Bennett...Columbia 4-39362
2	2	12	Cold, Cold Heart ....Tony Bennett...Columbia 4-39449
3	4	20	I Get Ideas ....Tony Martin...RCA Victor 47-4141
4	3	9	The World Is Waiting For The Sunrise ....Les Paul & Mary Ford.♥Capitol F1748
5	7	5	Sin ....Four Aces...Victoria 101
6	5	27	The Loveliest Night Of The Year...Mario Lanza...RCA Victor 49-3300
7	10	4	Sin ....Eddy Howard...Mercury 5711-X45
8	6	15	Come On-a My House ....Rosemary Clooney...Columbia 4-39467
9	17	2	Turn Back The Hands Of Time ....Eddie Fisher...RCA Victor 47-4257
10	11	9	Whispering ....Les Paul...Capitol F1748

TW	LW	WK	Billboard ⊛ OCTOBER 20, 1951 ⊛ Best Sellers
1	1	18	Because Of You ....Tony Bennett...Columbia 4-39362
2	2	13	Cold, Cold Heart ....Tony Bennett...Columbia 4-39449
3	3	21	I Get Ideas ....Tony Martin...RCA Victor 47-4141
4	4	10	The World Is Waiting For The Sunrise ....Les Paul & Mary Ford...Capitol F1748
4	7	5	Sin ....Eddy Howard...Mercury 5711-X45
6	5	6	Sin ....Four Aces...Victoria 101
7	6	28	The Loveliest Night Of The Year...Mario Lanza...RCA Victor 49-3300
8	12	8	Down Yonder...Del Wood...Tennessee 775
9	9	3	Turn Back The Hands Of Time ....Eddie Fisher...RCA Victor 47-4257
10	10	10	Whispering ....Les Paul...Capitol F1748
10	11	12	Because Of You ....Les Baxter...Capitol F1760

TW	LW	WK	Billboard ⊛ OCTOBER 27, 1951 ⊛ Best Sellers
1	1	19	Because Of You ....Tony Bennett...Columbia 4-39362
2	2	14	Cold, Cold Heart ....Tony Bennett...Columbia 4-39449
3	3	22	I Get Ideas ....Tony Martin...RCA Victor 47-4141
4	4	6	Sin ....Eddy Howard...Mercury 5711-X45
5	6	7	Sin ....Four Aces...Victoria 101
6	4	11	The World Is Waiting For The Sunrise ....Les Paul & Mary Ford...Capitol F1748
7	8	9	Down Yonder...Del Wood...Tennessee 775
8	9	4	Turn Back The Hands Of Time ....Eddie Fisher...RCA Victor 47-4257
9	15	4	Undecided ....Ames Brothers & Les Brown...Coral 9-60566
10	12	6	And So To Sleep Again ....Patti Page...Mercury 5706-X45

TW	LW	WK	Billboard ⊛ NOVEMBER 3, 1951 ⊛ Best Sellers
1	2	15	Cold, Cold Heart ....Tony Bennett...Columbia 4-39449
2	1	20	Because Of You ....Tony Bennett...Columbia 4-39362
3	4	7	Sin ....Eddy Howard...Mercury 5711-X45
4	3	23	I Get Ideas ....Tony Martin...RCA Victor 47-4141
5	5	8	Sin ....Four Aces...Victoria 101
6	6	12	The World Is Waiting For The Sunrise ....Les Paul & Mary Ford...Capitol F1748
7	9	5	Undecided ....Ames Brothers & Les Brown...Coral 9-60566
8	7	10	Down Yonder...Del Wood...Tennessee 775
9	8	5	Turn Back The Hands Of Time ....Eddie Fisher...RCA Victor 47-4257
9	14	5	(It's No) Sin ....Savannah Churchill...RCA Victor 47-4280

TW	LW	WK	Billboard ⊛ NOVEMBER 10, 1951 ⊛ Best Sellers
1	1	16	Cold, Cold Heart ....Tony Bennett...Columbia 4-39449
2	2	21	Because Of You ....Tony Bennett...Columbia 4-39362
3	3	8	Sin ....Eddy Howard...Mercury 5711-X45
4	4	24	I Get Ideas ....Tony Martin...RCA Victor 47-4141
5	5	9	Sin ....Four Aces...Victoria 101
6	8	11	Down Yonder...Del Wood...Tennessee 775
7	7	6	Undecided ....Ames Brothers & Les Brown...Coral 9-60566
8	6	13	The World Is Waiting For The Sunrise ....Les Paul & Mary Ford...Capitol F1748
9	9	6	Turn Back The Hands Of Time ....Eddie Fisher...RCA Victor 47-4257
10	9	6	(It's No) Sin ....Savannah Churchill...RCA Victor 47-4280
10	16	2	Domino ....Tony Martin...RCA Victor 47-4343

TW	LW	WK	Billboard ⊛ NOVEMBER 17, 1951 ⊛ Best Sellers
1	1	17	Cold, Cold Heart ....*Tony Bennett*...Columbia 4-39449
2	2	22	Because Of You ....*Tony Bennett*...Columbia 4-39362
3	3	9	Sin ....*Eddy Howard*...Mercury 5711-X45
4	5	10	Sin ....*Four Aces*...Victoria 101
5	4	25	I Get Ideas ....*Tony Martin*...RCA Victor 47-4141
6	7	7	Undecided ....*Ames Brothers & Les Brown*...Coral 9-60566
7	16	2	Jealousy (Jalousie) ....*Frankie Laine*...Columbia 4-39585
8	6	12	Down Yonder...*Del Wood*...Tennessee 775
9	10	7	(It's No) Sin ....*Savannah Churchill*...RCA Victor 47-4280
10	8	14	The World Is Waiting For The Sunrise ....*Les Paul & Mary Ford*...Capitol F1748

TW	LW	WK	Billboard ⊛ NOVEMBER 24, 1951 ⊛ Best Sellers
1	1	18	Cold, Cold Heart ....*Tony Bennett*...Columbia 4-39449
2	2	23	Because Of You ....*Tony Bennett*...Columbia 4-39362
3	3	10	Sin ....*Eddy Howard*...Mercury 5711-X45
4	7	3	Jealousy (Jalousie) ....*Frankie Laine*...Columbia 4-39585
5	4	11	Sin ....*Four Aces*...Victoria 101
6	5	26	I Get Ideas ....*Tony Martin*...RCA Victor 47-4141
7	8	13	Down Yonder...*Del Wood*...Tennessee 775
8	6	8	Undecided ....*Ames Brothers & Les Brown*...Coral 9-60566
9	9	8	(It's No) Sin ....*Savannah Churchill*...RCA Victor 47-4280
10	12	4	Domino ....*Tony Martin*...RCA Victor 47-4343

TW	LW	WK	Billboard ⊛ DECEMBER 1, 1951 ⊛ Best Sellers
1	1	19	Cold, Cold Heart ....*Tony Bennett*...Columbia 4-39449
2	2	24	Because Of You ....*Tony Bennett*...Columbia 4-39362
3	3	11	Sin ....*Eddy Howard*...Mercury 5711-X45
4	4	4	Jealousy (Jalousie) ....*Frankie Laine*...Columbia 4-39585
5	5	12	Sin ....*Four Aces*...Victoria 101
6	8	9	Undecided ....*Ames Brothers & Les Brown*...Coral 9-60566
7	6	27	I Get Ideas ....*Tony Martin*...RCA Victor 47-4141
8	7	14	Down Yonder...*Del Wood*...Tennessee 775
9	9	9	(It's No) Sin ....*Savannah Churchill*...RCA Victor 47-4280
10	10	5	Domino ....*Tony Martin*...RCA Victor 47-4343

TW	LW	WK	Billboard ⊛ DECEMBER 8, 1951 ⊛ Best Sellers
1	1	20	Cold, Cold Heart ....*Tony Bennett*...Columbia 4-39449
2	3	12	Sin ....*Eddy Howard*...Mercury 5711-X45
3	2	25	Because Of You ....*Tony Bennett*...Columbia 4-39362
4	4	5	Jealousy (Jalousie) ....*Frankie Laine*...Columbia 4-39585
5	5	13	Sin ....*Four Aces*...Victoria 101
6	6	10	Undecided ....*Ames Brothers & Les Brown*...Coral 9-60566
7	8	15	Down Yonder...*Del Wood*...Tennessee 775
8	11	3	The Little White Cloud That Cried...........................*Johnnie Ray & The Four Lads*...Okeh 4-6840
9	7	28	I Get Ideas ....*Tony Martin*...RCA Victor 47-4141
10	12	4	Shrimp Boats ....*Jo Stafford*...Columbia 4-39581

TW	LW	WK	Billboard ⊛ DECEMBER 15, 1951 ⊛ Best Sellers
1	2	13	Sin ....*Eddy Howard*...Mercury 5711-X45
2	1	21	Cold, Cold Heart ....*Tony Bennett*...Columbia 4-39449
3	4	6	Jealousy (Jalousie) ....*Frankie Laine*...Columbia 4-39585
4	3	26	Because Of You ....*Tony Bennett*...Columbia 4-39362
5	8	4	The Little White Cloud That Cried...........................*Johnnie Ray & The Four Lads*...Okeh 4-6840
6	6	11	Undecided ....*Ames Brothers & Les Brown*...Coral 9-60566
7	14	7	Slow Poke ....*Pee Wee King*...RCA Victor 48-0489
8	17	4	Cry ....*Johnnie Ray & The Four Lads*...Okeh 4-6840
9	10	5	Shrimp Boats ....*Jo Stafford*...Columbia 4-39581
10	5	14	Sin ....*Four Aces*...Victoria 101

TW	LW	WK	Billboard® DECEMBER 22, 1951 Best Sellers
1	1	14	**Sin**..*Eddy Howard*...Mercury 5711-X45
2	2	22	**Cold, Cold Heart** ....*Tony Bennett*...Columbia 4-39449
3	3	7	**Jealousy (Jalousie)** ....*Frankie Laine*...Columbia 4-39585
4	8	5	**Cry**..*Johnnie Ray & The Four Lads*...Okeh 4-6840
5	5	5	**The Little White Cloud That Cried**...............*Johnnie Ray & The Four Lads*...Okeh 4-6840
6	4	27	**Because Of You** ....*Tony Bennett*...Columbia 4-39362
7	9	6	**Shrimp Boats**...*Jo Stafford*...Columbia 4-39581
8	6	12	**Undecided** ....*Ames Brothers & Les Brown*...Coral 9-60566
8	10	15	**Sin** ....*Four Aces*...Victoria 101
10	7	8	**Slow Poke** ....*Pee Wee King*...RCA Victor 48-0489

TW	LW	WK	Billboard® DECEMBER 29, 1951 Best Sellers
1	4	6	**Cry**..*Johnnie Ray & The Four Lads*...Okeh 4-6840
2	1	15	**Sin** ....*Eddy Howard*...Mercury 5711-X45
3	5	6	**The Little White Cloud That Cried**...............*Johnnie Ray & The Four Lads*...Okeh 4-6840
4	7	7	**Shrimp Boats**...*Jo Stafford*...Columbia 4-39581
5	3	8	**Jealousy (Jalousie)** ....*Frankie Laine*...Columbia 4-39585
6	2	23	**Cold, Cold Heart** ....*Tony Bennett*...Columbia 4-39449
7	10	9	**Slow Poke** ....*Pee Wee King*...RCA Victor 48-0489
8	8	13	**Undecided** ....*Ames Brothers & Les Brown*...Coral 9-60566
9	6	28	**Because Of You** ....*Tony Bennett*...Columbia 4-39362
10	13	4	**Any Time** ....*Eddie Fisher*...RCA Victor 47-4359

Billboard — JANUARY 5, 1952 — Best Sellers

TW	LW	WK	Title	Artist...Label
1	1	7	Cry	Johnnie Ray & The Four Lads...Okeh 4-6840
2	4	8	Shrimp Boats	Jo Stafford...Columbia 4-39581
3	7	10	Slow Poke	Pee Wee King...RCA Victor 48-0489
4	3	7	The Little White Cloud That Cried	Johnnie Ray & The Four Lads...Okeh 4-6840
5	2	16	Sin	Eddy Howard...Mercury 5711-X45
6	6	24	Cold, Cold Heart	Tony Bennett...Columbia 4-39449
7	5	9	Jealousy (Jalousie)	Frankie Laine...Columbia 4-39585
8	11	19	Down Yonder	Del Wood...Tennessee 775
9	12	5	Tell Me Why	Four Aces...Decca 9-27860
10	14	8	Charmaine	Mantovani...London 45-1020

Billboard — JANUARY 12, 1952 — Best Sellers

TW	LW	WK	Title	Artist...Label
1	1	8	Cry	Johnnie Ray & The Four Lads...Okeh 4-6840
2	4	8	The Little White Cloud That Cried	Johnnie Ray & The Four Lads...Okeh 4-6840
3	3	11	Slow Poke	Pee Wee King...RCA Victor 48-0489
4	5	17	Sin	Eddy Howard...Mercury 5711-X45
5	9	6	Tell Me Why	Four Aces...Decca 9-27860
6	2	9	Shrimp Boats	Jo Stafford...Columbia 4-39581
7	14	6	Any Time	Eddie Fisher...RCA Victor 47-4359
8	7	10	Jealousy (Jalousie)	Frankie Laine...Columbia 4-39585
9	6	25	Cold, Cold Heart	Tony Bennett...Columbia 4-39449
10	13	15	Undecided	Ames Brothers & Les Brown...Coral 9-60566

Billboard — JANUARY 19, 1952 — Best Sellers

TW	LW	WK	Title	Artist...Label
1	1	9	Cry	Johnnie Ray & The Four Lads...Okeh 4-6840
2	2	9	The Little White Cloud That Cried	Johnnie Ray & The Four Lads...Okeh 4-6840
3	5	7	Tell Me Why	Four Aces...Decca 9-27860
4	3	12	Slow Poke	Pee Wee King...RCA Victor 48-0489
5	6	10	Shrimp Boats	Jo Stafford...Columbia 4-39581
6	7	7	Any Time	Eddie Fisher...RCA Victor 47-4359
7	4	18	Sin	Eddy Howard...Mercury 5711-X45
8	11	3	Tell Me Why	Eddie Fisher...RCA Victor 47-4444
9	10	16	Undecided	Ames Brothers & Les Brown...Coral 9-60566
10	8	11	Jealousy (Jalousie)	Frankie Laine...Columbia 4-39585

Billboard — JANUARY 26, 1952 — Best Sellers

TW	LW	WK	Title	Artist...Label
1	1	10	Cry	Johnnie Ray & The Four Lads...Okeh 4-6840
2	3	8	Tell Me Why	Four Aces...Decca 9-27860
3	2	10	The Little White Cloud That Cried	Johnnie Ray & The Four Lads...Okeh 4-6840
4	4	13	Slow Poke	Pee Wee King...RCA Victor 48-0489
5	6	8	Any Time	Eddie Fisher...RCA Victor 47-4359
6	5	11	Shrimp Boats	Jo Stafford...Columbia 4-39581
7	7	19	Sin	Eddy Howard...Mercury 5711-X45
7	18	2	Tiger Rag	Les Paul & Mary Ford...Capitol F1920
9	8	4	Tell Me Why	Eddie Fisher...RCA Victor 47-4444
10	11	11	Charmaine	Mantovani...London 45-1020
10	15	4	Bermuda	The Bell Sisters...RCA Victor 47-4422

Billboard — FEBRUARY 2, 1952 — Best Sellers

TW	LW	WK	Title	Artist...Label
1	1	11	Cry	Johnnie Ray & The Four Lads...Okeh 4-6840
2	2	9	Tell Me Why	Four Aces...Decca 9-27860
3	3	11	The Little White Cloud That Cried	Johnnie Ray & The Four Lads...Okeh 4-6840
4	4	14	Slow Poke	Pee Wee King...RCA Victor 48-0489
5	5	9	Any Time	Eddie Fisher...RCA Victor 47-4359
6	6	12	Shrimp Boats	Jo Stafford...Columbia 4-39581
7	7	3	Tiger Rag	Les Paul & Mary Ford...Capitol F1920
8	9	5	Tell Me Why	Eddie Fisher...RCA Victor 47-4444
9	7	20	Sin	Eddy Howard...Mercury 5711-X45
10	10	5	Bermuda	The Bell Sisters...RCA Victor 47-4422

TW	LW	WK	Billboard ✺ FEBRUARY 9, 1952 ✺ Best Sellers
1	1	12	Cry..*Johnnie Ray & The Four Lads*...Okeh 4-6840
2	2	10	Tell Me Why...*Four Aces*...Decca 9-27860
3	5	10	Any Time...*Eddie Fisher*...RCA Victor 47-4359
4	3	12	The Little White Cloud That Cried.........................*Johnnie Ray & The Four Lads*...Okeh 4-6840
5	4	15	Slow Poke..*Pee Wee King*...RCA Victor 48-0489
6	7	4	Tiger Rag...*Les Paul & Mary Ford*...Capitol F1920
7	8	6	Tell Me Why..*Eddie Fisher*...RCA Victor 47-4444
8	10	6	Bermuda..*Bell Sisters*...RCA Victor 47-4422
9	6	13	Shrimp Boats..*Jo Stafford*...Columbia 4-39581
10	13	5	Blue Tango ....*Leroy Anderson*...Decca 9-27875

TW	LW	WK	Billboard ✺ FEBRUARY 16, 1952 ✺ Best Sellers
1	1	13	Cry..*Johnnie Ray & The Four Lads*...Okeh 4-6840
2	2	11	Tell Me Why...*Four Aces*...Decca 9-27860
3	4	13	The Little White Cloud That Cried.........................*Johnnie Ray & The Four Lads*...Okeh 4-6840
4	3	11	Any Time...*Eddie Fisher*...RCA Victor 47-4359
5	5	16	Slow Poke..*Pee Wee King*...RCA Victor 48-0489
6	6	5	Tiger Rag...*Les Paul & Mary Ford*...Capitol F1920
7	10	6	Blue Tango ....*Leroy Anderson*...Decca 9-27875
8	14	4	Please, Mr. Sun..*Johnnie Ray*...Columbia 4-39636
9	7	7	Tell Me Why..*Eddie Fisher*...RCA Victor 47-4444
10	9	14	Shrimp Boats..*Jo Stafford*...Columbia 4-39581

TW	LW	WK	Billboard ✺ FEBRUARY 23, 1952 ✺ Best Sellers
1	1	14	Cry..*Johnnie Ray & The Four Lads*...Okeh 4-6840
2	2	12	Tell Me Why...*Four Aces*...Decca 9-27860
3	4	12	Any Time...*Eddie Fisher*...RCA Victor 47-4359
4	3	14	The Little White Cloud That Cried.........................*Johnnie Ray & The Four Lads*...Okeh 4-6840
5	7	7	Blue Tango ....*Leroy Anderson*...Decca 9-27875
6	16	2	Wheel Of Fortune...*Kay Starr*...Capitol F1964
7	8	5	Please, Mr. Sun..*Johnnie Ray*...Columbia 4-39636
8	5	17	Slow Poke..*Pee Wee King*...RCA Victor 48-0489
9	6	6	Tiger Rag...*Les Paul & Mary Ford*...Capitol F1920
10	11	8	Bermuda..*Bell Sisters*...RCA Victor 47-4422

TW	LW	WK	Billboard ✺ MARCH 1, 1952 ✺ Best Sellers
1	1	15	Cry..*Johnnie Ray & The Four Lads*...Okeh 4-6840
2	2	13	Tell Me Why...*Four Aces*...Decca 9-27860
3	6	3	Wheel Of Fortune...*Kay Starr*...Capitol F1964
4	5	8	Blue Tango ....*Leroy Anderson*...Decca 9-27875
5	3	13	Any Time...*Eddie Fisher*...RCA Victor 47-4359
6	4	15	The Little White Cloud That Cried.........................*Johnnie Ray & The Four Lads*...Okeh 4-6840
7	7	6	Please, Mr. Sun..*Johnnie Ray*...Columbia 4-39636
8	8	18	Slow Poke..*Pee Wee King*...RCA Victor 48-0489
9	9	7	Tiger Rag...*Les Paul & Mary Ford*...Capitol F1920
10	10	9	Bermuda..*Bell Sisters*...RCA Victor 47-4422

TW	LW	WK	Billboard ✺ MARCH 8, 1952 ✺ Best Sellers
1	1	16	Cry..*Johnnie Ray & The Four Lads*...Okeh 4-6840
2	3	4	Wheel Of Fortune...*Kay Starr*...Capitol F1964
3	4	9	Blue Tango ....*Leroy Anderson*...Decca 9-27875
4	5	14	Any Time...*Eddie Fisher*...RCA Victor 47-4359
5	2	14	Tell Me Why...*Four Aces*...Decca 9-27860
6	7	7	Please, Mr. Sun..*Johnnie Ray*...Columbia 4-39636
7	6	16	The Little White Cloud That Cried.........................*Johnnie Ray & The Four Lads*...Okeh 4-6840
8	10	10	Bermuda..*Bell Sisters*...RCA Victor 47-4422
9	15	7	Here Am I - Broken Hearted...*Johnnie Ray*...Columbia 4-39636
10	11	10	Tell Me Why..*Eddie Fisher*...RCA Victor 47-4444

TW	LW	WK	Billboard® ❀ MARCH 15, 1952 ❀ Best Sellers
1	2	5	Wheel Of Fortune...Kay Starr...Capitol F1964
2	1	17	Cry...Johnnie Ray & The Four Lads...Okeh 4-6840
3	3	10	Blue Tango ....Leroy Anderson...Decca 9-27875
4	4	15	Any Time ....Eddie Fisher...RCA Victor 47-4359
5	5	15	Tell Me Why ....Four Aces...Decca 9-27860
6	6	8	Please, Mr. Sun...Johnnie Ray...Columbia 4-39636
7	11	5	The Blacksmith Blues ....Ella Mae Morse...Capitol F1922
8	8	11	Bermuda ....Bell Sisters...RCA Victor 47-4422
8	10	11	Tell Me Why ....Eddie Fisher...RCA Victor 47-4444
10	7	17	The Little White Cloud That Cried.......................Johnnie Ray & The Four Lads...Okeh 4-6840

TW	LW	WK	Billboard® ❀ MARCH 22, 1952 ❀ Best Sellers
1	1	6	Wheel Of Fortune...Kay Starr...Capitol F1964
2	3	11	Blue Tango ....Leroy Anderson...Decca 9-27875
3	2	18	Cry...Johnnie Ray & The Four Lads...Okeh 4-6840
4	4	16	Any Time ....Eddie Fisher...RCA Victor 47-4359
5	7	6	The Blacksmith Blues ....Ella Mae Morse...Capitol F1922
6	5	16	Tell Me Why ....Four Aces...Decca 9-27860
7	6	9	Please, Mr. Sun...Johnnie Ray...Columbia 4-39636
8	8	12	Bermuda ....Bell Sisters...RCA Victor 47-4422
9	12	5	Perfidia ....Four Aces...Decca 9-27987
10	8	12	Tell Me Why ....Eddie Fisher...RCA Victor 47-4444

TW	LW	WK	Billboard® ❀ MARCH 29, 1952 ❀ Best Sellers
1	1	7	Wheel Of Fortune...Kay Starr...Capitol F1964
2	2	12	Blue Tango ....Leroy Anderson...Decca 9-27875
3	3	19	Cry...Johnnie Ray & The Four Lads...Okeh 4-6840
4	4	17	Any Time ....Eddie Fisher...RCA Victor 47-4359
5	5	7	The Blacksmith Blues ....Ella Mae Morse...Capitol F1922
6	11	3	A Guy Is A Guy ....Doris Day...Columbia 4-39673
7	6	17	Tell Me Why ....Four Aces...Decca 9-27860
8	9	6	Perfidia ....Four Aces...Decca 9-27987
9	7	10	Please, Mr. Sun...Johnnie Ray...Columbia 4-39636
10	15	2	Forgive Me..Eddie Fisher...RCA Victor 47-4574

TW	LW	WK	Billboard® ❀ APRIL 5, 1952 ❀ Best Sellers
1	1	8	Wheel Of Fortune...Kay Starr...Capitol F1964
2	2	13	Blue Tango ....Leroy Anderson...Decca 9-27875
3	5	8	The Blacksmith Blues ....Ella Mae Morse...Capitol F1922
4	3	20	Cry...Johnnie Ray & The Four Lads...Okeh 4-6840
4	4	18	Any Time ....Eddie Fisher...RCA Victor 47-4359
6	6	4	A Guy Is A Guy ....Doris Day...Columbia 4-39673
7	7	18	Tell Me Why ....Four Aces...Decca 9-27860
8	10	3	Forgive Me..Eddie Fisher...RCA Victor 47-4574
9	8	7	Perfidia ....Four Aces...Decca 9-27987
10	13	4	Pittsburgh, Pennsylvania ....Guy Mitchell...Columbia 4-39663

TW	LW	WK	Billboard® ❀ APRIL 12, 1952 ❀ Best Sellers
1	1	9	Wheel Of Fortune...Kay Starr...Capitol F1964
2	2	14	Blue Tango ....Leroy Anderson...Decca 9-27875
3	3	9	The Blacksmith Blues ....Ella Mae Morse...Capitol F1922
4	4	21	Cry...Johnnie Ray & The Four Lads...Okeh 4-6840
5	4	19	Any Time ....Eddie Fisher...RCA Victor 47-4359
6	6	5	A Guy Is A Guy ....Doris Day...Columbia 4-39673
7	8	4	Forgive Me..Eddie Fisher...RCA Victor 47-4574
8	10	5	Pittsburgh, Pennsylvania ....Guy Mitchell...Columbia 4-39663
8	13	12	Please, Mr. Sun...Johnnie Ray...Columbia 4-39636
10	7	19	Tell Me Why ....Four Aces...Decca 9-27860

Billboard — APRIL 19, 1952 — Best Sellers

TW	LW	WK	Title	Artist	Label
1	1	10	Wheel Of Fortune	Kay Starr	Capitol F1964
2	2	15	Blue Tango	Leroy Anderson	Decca 9-27875
3	3	10	The Blacksmith Blues	Ella Mae Morse	Capitol F1922
4	6	6	A Guy Is A Guy	Doris Day	Columbia 4-39673
5	4	22	Cry	Johnnie Ray & The Four Lads	Okeh 4-6840
6	5	20	Any Time	Eddie Fisher	RCA Victor 47-4359
7	12	9	Perfidia	Four Aces	Decca 9-27987
8	—	1	Kiss Of Fire	Georgia Gibbs	Mercury 5823-X45
9	11	5	I'll Walk Alone	Don Cornell	Coral 9-60659
10	8	6	Pittsburgh, Pennsylvania	Guy Mitchell	Columbia 4-39663

Billboard — APRIL 26, 1952 — Best Sellers

TW	LW	WK	Title	Artist	Label
1	1	11	Wheel Of Fortune	Kay Starr	Capitol F1964
2	2	16	Blue Tango	Leroy Anderson	Decca 9-27875
3	3	11	The Blacksmith Blues	Ella Mae Morse	Capitol F1922
4	4	7	A Guy Is A Guy	Doris Day	Columbia 4-39673
5	8	2	Kiss Of Fire	Georgia Gibbs	Mercury 5823-X45
6	5	23	Cry	Johnnie Ray & The Four Lads	Okeh 4-6840
7	6	21	Any Time	Eddie Fisher	RCA Victor 47-4359
8	10	7	Pittsburgh, Pennsylvania	Guy Mitchell	Columbia 4-39663
9	13	6	Forgive Me	Eddie Fisher	RCA Victor 47-4574
10	9	6	I'll Walk Alone	Don Cornell	Coral 9-60659

Billboard — MAY 3, 1952 — Best Sellers

TW	LW	WK	Title	Artist	Label
1	1	12	Wheel Of Fortune	Kay Starr	Capitol F1964
2	2	17	Blue Tango	Leroy Anderson	Decca 9-27875
3	3	12	The Blacksmith Blues	Ella Mae Morse	Capitol F1922
4	4	8	A Guy Is A Guy	Doris Day	Columbia 4-39673
5	5	3	Kiss Of Fire	Georgia Gibbs	Mercury 5823-X45
6	8	8	Pittsburgh, Pennsylvania	Guy Mitchell	Columbia 4-39663
7	10	7	I'll Walk Alone	Don Cornell	Coral 9-60659
8	6	24	Cry	Johnnie Ray & The Four Lads	Okeh 4-6840
9	9	7	Forgive Me	Eddie Fisher	RCA Victor 47-4574
10	7	22	Any Time	Eddie Fisher	RCA Victor 47-4359

Billboard — MAY 10, 1952 — Best Sellers

TW	LW	WK	Title	Artist	Label
1	1	13	Wheel Of Fortune	Kay Starr	Capitol F1964
2	2	18	Blue Tango	Leroy Anderson	Decca 9-27875
3	3	13	The Blacksmith Blues	Ella Mae Morse	Capitol F1922
4	4	9	A Guy Is A Guy	Doris Day	Columbia 4-39673
5	5	4	Kiss Of Fire	Georgia Gibbs	Mercury 5823-X45
6	6	9	Pittsburgh, Pennsylvania	Guy Mitchell	Columbia 4-39663
7	7	8	I'll Walk Alone	Don Cornell	Coral 9-60659
8	9	8	Forgive Me	Eddie Fisher	RCA Victor 47-4574
8	12	9	Blue Tango	Hugo Winterhalter	RCA Victor 47-4518
10	8	25	Cry	Johnnie Ray & The Four Lads	Okeh 4-6840

Billboard — MAY 17, 1952 — Best Sellers

TW	LW	WK	Title	Artist	Label
1	2	19	Blue Tango	Leroy Anderson	Decca 9-27875
2	1	14	Wheel Of Fortune	Kay Starr	Capitol F1964
3	5	5	Kiss Of Fire	Georgia Gibbs	Mercury 5823-X45
4	4	10	A Guy Is A Guy	Doris Day	Columbia 4-39673
5	3	14	The Blacksmith Blues	Ella Mae Morse	Capitol F1922
6	11	4	I'm Yours	Don Cornell	Coral 9-60690
7	13	4	Delicado	Percy Faith	Columbia 4-39708
8	15	3	I'm Yours	Eddie Fisher	RCA Victor 47-4680
9	7	9	I'll Walk Alone	Don Cornell	Coral 9-60659
10	6	10	Pittsburgh, Pennsylvania	Guy Mitchell	Columbia 4-39663

TW	LW	WK	Billboard 🏵 MAY 24, 1952 🏵 Best Sellers
1	1	20	Blue Tango ....Leroy Anderson...Decca 9-27875
2	2	15	Wheel Of Fortune ....Kay Starr...Capitol F1964
3	3	6	Kiss Of Fire ....Georgia Gibbs...Mercury 5823-X45
4	12	2	Here In My Heart ....Al Martino...BBS 101
5	4	11	A Guy Is A Guy ....Doris Day...Columbia 4-39673
6	7	5	Delicado ....Percy Faith...Columbia 4-39708
7	5	15	The Blacksmith Blues ....Ella Mae Morse...Capitol F1922
8	6	5	I'm Yours ....Don Cornell...Coral 9-60690
9	8	4	I'm Yours ....Eddie Fisher...RCA Victor 47-4680
10	9	10	I'll Walk Alone ....Don Cornell...Coral 9-60659

TW	LW	WK	Billboard 🏵 MAY 31, 1952 🏵 Best Sellers
1	1	21	Blue Tango ....Leroy Anderson...Decca 9-27875
2	3	7	Kiss Of Fire ....Georgia Gibbs...Mercury 5823-X45
3	4	3	Here In My Heart ....Al Martino...BBS 101
4	2	16	Wheel Of Fortune ....Kay Starr...Capitol F1964
5	6	6	Delicado ....Percy Faith...Columbia 4-39708
6	5	12	A Guy Is A Guy ....Doris Day...Columbia 4-39673
7	8	6	I'm Yours ....Don Cornell...Coral 9-60690
8	9	5	I'm Yours ....Eddie Fisher...RCA Victor 47-4680
9	10	11	I'll Walk Alone ....Don Cornell...Coral 9-60659
10	7	16	The Blacksmith Blues ....Ella Mae Morse...Capitol F1922

TW	LW	WK	Billboard 🏵 JUNE 7, 1952 🏵 Best Sellers
1	1	22	Blue Tango ....Leroy Anderson...Decca 9-27875
1	3	4	Here In My Heart ....Al Martino...BBS 101
3	2	8	Kiss Of Fire ....Georgia Gibbs...Mercury 5823-X45
4	5	7	Delicado ....Percy Faith...Columbia 4-39708
5	4	17	Wheel Of Fortune ....Kay Starr...Capitol F1964
5	7	7	I'm Yours ....Don Cornell...Coral 9-60690
7	6	13	A Guy Is A Guy ....Doris Day...Columbia 4-39673
8	8	6	I'm Yours ....Eddie Fisher...RCA Victor 47-4680
9	9	12	I'll Walk Alone ....Don Cornell...Coral 9-60659
10	10	17	The Blacksmith Blues ....Ella Mae Morse...Capitol F1922

TW	LW	WK	Billboard 🏵 JUNE 14, 1952 🏵 Best Sellers
1	1	23	Blue Tango ....Leroy Anderson...Decca 9-27875
2	1	5	Here In My Heart ....Al Martino...BBS 101
3	3	9	Kiss Of Fire ....Georgia Gibbs...Mercury 5823-X45
4	4	8	Delicado ....Percy Faith...Columbia 4-39708
5	8	7	I'm Yours ....Eddie Fisher...RCA Victor 47-4680
6	5	8	I'm Yours ....Don Cornell...Coral 9-60690
7	7	14	A Guy Is A Guy ....Doris Day...Columbia 4-39673
8	5	18	Wheel Of Fortune ....Kay Starr...Capitol F1964
9	9	13	I'll Walk Alone ....Don Cornell...Coral 9-60659
10	13	7	Kiss Of Fire ....Tony Martin...RCA Victor 47-4671

TW	LW	WK	Billboard 🏵 JUNE 21, 1952 🏵 Best Sellers
1	2	6	Here In My Heart ....Al Martino...BBS 101
2	1	24	Blue Tango ....Leroy Anderson...Decca 9-27875
3	4	9	Delicado ....Percy Faith...Columbia 4-39708
4	3	10	Kiss Of Fire ....Georgia Gibbs...Mercury 5823-X45
5	5	8	I'm Yours ....Eddie Fisher...RCA Victor 47-4680
6	10	8	Kiss Of Fire ....Tony Martin...RCA Victor 47-4671
7	6	9	I'm Yours ....Don Cornell...Coral 9-60690
8	7	15	A Guy Is A Guy ....Doris Day...Columbia 4-39673
9	11	4	Walkin' My Baby Back Home ....Johnnie Ray...Columbia 4-39750
10	20	2	Maybe ....Perry Como & Eddie Fisher...RCA Victor 47-4744

Billboard — JUNE 28, 1952 — Best Sellers

TW	LW	WK	Title	Artist...Label
1	1	7	Here In My Heart	Al Martino...BBS 101
2	3	10	Delicado	Percy Faith...Columbia 4-39708
3	2	25	Blue Tango	Leroy Anderson...Decca 9-27875
4	4	11	Kiss Of Fire	Georgia Gibbs...Mercury 5823-X45
5	12	2	Auf Wiederseh'n Sweetheart	Vera Lynn...London 451227
6	5	9	I'm Yours	Eddie Fisher...RCA Victor 47-4680
7	6	9	Kiss Of Fire	Tony Martin...RCA Victor 47-4671
8	9	5	Walkin' My Baby Back Home	Johnnie Ray...Columbia 4-39750
9	7	10	I'm Yours	Don Cornell...Coral 9-60690
10	8	16	A Guy Is A Guy	Doris Day...Columbia 4-39673

Billboard — JULY 5, 1952 — Best Sellers

TW	LW	WK	Title	Artist...Label
1	2	11	Delicado	Percy Faith...Columbia 4-39708
2	1	8	Here In My Heart	Al Martino...BBS 101
3	5	3	Auf Wiederseh'n Sweetheart	Vera Lynn...London 451227
4	4	12	Kiss Of Fire	Georgia Gibbs...Mercury 5823-X45
5	3	26	Blue Tango	Leroy Anderson...Decca 9-27875
6	6	10	I'm Yours	Eddie Fisher...RCA Victor 47-4680
7	12	7	Half As Much	Rosemary Clooney...Columbia 4-39710
8	8	6	Walkin' My Baby Back Home	Johnnie Ray...Columbia 4-39750
9	7	10	Kiss Of Fire	Tony Martin...RCA Victor 47-4671
10	14	4	Maybe	Perry Como & Eddie Fisher...RCA Victor 47-4744

Billboard — JULY 12, 1952 — Best Sellers

TW	LW	WK	Title	Artist...Label
1	3	4	Auf Wiederseh'n Sweetheart	Vera Lynn...London 451227
2	1	12	Delicado	Percy Faith...Columbia 4-39708
3	2	9	Here In My Heart	Al Martino...BBS 101
4	4	13	Kiss Of Fire	Georgia Gibbs...Mercury 5823-X45
5	6	11	I'm Yours	Eddie Fisher...RCA Victor 47-4680
6	5	27	Blue Tango	Leroy Anderson...Decca 9-27875
7	8	7	Walkin' My Baby Back Home	Johnnie Ray...Columbia 4-39750
8	7	8	Half As Much	Rosemary Clooney...Columbia 4-39710
9	10	5	Maybe	Perry Como & Eddie Fisher...RCA Victor 47-4744
10	13	6	Lover	Peggy Lee & Gordon Jenkins...Decca 9-28215

Billboard — JULY 19, 1952 — Best Sellers

TW	LW	WK	Title	Artist...Label
1	1	5	Auf Wiederseh'n Sweetheart	Vera Lynn...London 451227
2	3	10	Here In My Heart	Al Martino...BBS 101
3	4	14	Kiss Of Fire	Georgia Gibbs...Mercury 5823-X45
4	2	13	Delicado	Percy Faith...Columbia 4-39708
5	8	9	Half As Much	Rosemary Clooney...Columbia 4-39710
6	6	28	Blue Tango	Leroy Anderson...Decca 9-27875
7	11	4	Botch-A-Me (Ba-Ba-Baciami Piccina)	Rosemary Clooney...Columbia 4-39767
8	5	12	I'm Yours	Eddie Fisher...RCA Victor 47-4680
9	7	8	Walkin' My Baby Back Home	Johnnie Ray...Columbia 4-39750
10	9	6	Maybe	Perry Como & Eddie Fisher...RCA Victor 47-4744

Billboard — JULY 26, 1952 — Best Sellers

TW	LW	WK	Title	Artist...Label
1	1	6	Auf Wiederseh'n Sweetheart	Vera Lynn...London 451227
2	4	14	Delicado	Percy Faith...Columbia 4-39708
3	2	11	Here In My Heart	Al Martino...BBS 101
4	5	10	Half As Much	Rosemary Clooney...Columbia 4-39710
5	7	5	Botch-A-Me (Ba-Ba-Baciami Piccina)	Rosemary Clooney...Columbia 4-39767
6	3	15	Kiss Of Fire	Georgia Gibbs...Mercury 5823-X45
7	9	9	Walkin' My Baby Back Home	Johnnie Ray...Columbia 4-39750
8	6	29	Blue Tango	Leroy Anderson...Decca 9-27875
9	8	13	I'm Yours	Eddie Fisher...RCA Victor 47-4680
10	10	7	Maybe	Perry Como & Eddie Fisher...RCA Victor 47-4744

TW	LW	WK	Billboard ❄ AUGUST 2, 1952 ❄ Best Sellers
1	1	7	Auf Wiederseh'n Sweetheart ....*Vera Lynn*...London 451227
2	5	6	Botch-A-Me (Ba-Ba-Baciami Piccina).........................*Rosemary Clooney*...Columbia 4-39767
3	4	11	Half As Much ....*Rosemary Clooney*...Columbia 4-39710
4	2	15	Delicado...*Percy Faith*...Columbia 4-39708
5	3	12	Here In My Heart ....*Al Martino*...BBS 101
6	7	10	Walkin' My Baby Back Home ....*Johnnie Ray*...Columbia 4-39750
7	8	30	Blue Tango ....*Leroy Anderson*...Decca 9-27875
8	6	16	Kiss Of Fire...*Georgia Gibbs*...Mercury 5823-X45
9	10	8	Maybe ....*Perry Como & Eddie Fisher*...RCA Victor 47-4744
10	9	14	I'm Yours ....*Eddie Fisher*...RCA Victor 47-4680

TW	LW	WK	Billboard ❄ AUGUST 9, 1952 ❄ Best Sellers
1	1	8	Auf Wiederseh'n Sweetheart ....*Vera Lynn*...London 451227
2	2	7	Botch-A-Me (Ba-Ba-Baciami Piccina).........................*Rosemary Clooney*...Columbia 4-39767
3	3	12	Half As Much ....*Rosemary Clooney*...Columbia 4-39710
4	5	13	Here In My Heart ....*Al Martino*...BBS 101
5	4	16	Delicado...*Percy Faith*...Columbia 4-39708
6	11	4	Wish You Were Here ....*Eddie Fisher*...RCA Victor 47-4830
7	6	11	Walkin' My Baby Back Home ....*Johnnie Ray*...Columbia 4-39750
8	9	9	Maybe ....*Perry Como & Eddie Fisher*...RCA Victor 47-4744
9	13	9	Somewhere Along The Way ....*Nat "King" Cole*...Capitol F2069
10	8	17	Kiss Of Fire...*Georgia Gibbs*...Mercury 5823-X45

TW	LW	WK	Billboard ❄ AUGUST 16, 1952 ❄ Best Sellers
1	1	9	Auf Wiederseh'n Sweetheart ....*Vera Lynn*...London 451227
2	3	13	Half As Much ....*Rosemary Clooney*...Columbia 4-39710
3	2	8	Botch-A-Me (Ba-Ba-Baciami Piccina).........................*Rosemary Clooney*...Columbia 4-39767
4	6	5	Wish You Were Here ....*Eddie Fisher*...RCA Victor 47-4830
5	4	14	Here In My Heart ....*Al Martino*...BBS 101
6	5	17	Delicado...*Percy Faith*...Columbia 4-39708
7	7	12	Walkin' My Baby Back Home ....*Johnnie Ray*...Columbia 4-39750
8	12	6	High Noon (Do Not Forsake Me) ....*Frankie Laine*...Columbia 4-39770
9	8	10	Maybe ....*Perry Como & Eddie Fisher*...RCA Victor 47-4744
10	14	7	Sugarbush..*Doris Day - Frankie Laine*...Columbia 4-39693

TW	LW	WK	Billboard ❄ AUGUST 23, 1952 ❄ Best Sellers
1	1	10	Auf Wiederseh'n Sweetheart ....*Vera Lynn*...London 451227
2	3	9	Botch-A-Me (Ba-Ba-Baciami Piccina).........................*Rosemary Clooney*...Columbia 4-39767
3	2	14	Half As Much ....*Rosemary Clooney*...Columbia 4-39710
4	4	6	Wish You Were Here ....*Eddie Fisher*...RCA Victor 47-4830
5	6	18	Delicado...*Percy Faith*...Columbia 4-39708
6	8	7	High Noon (Do Not Forsake Me) ....*Frankie Laine*...Columbia 4-39770
7	5	15	Here In My Heart ....*Al Martino*...BBS 101
8	12	3	You Belong To Me...*Jo Stafford*...Columbia 4-39811
9	7	13	Walkin' My Baby Back Home ....*Johnnie Ray*...Columbia 4-39750
10	9	11	Maybe ....*Perry Como & Eddie Fisher*...RCA Victor 47-4744

TW	LW	WK	Billboard ❄ AUGUST 30, 1952 ❄ Best Sellers
1	1	11	Auf Wiederseh'n Sweetheart ....*Vera Lynn*...London 451227
2	3	15	Half As Much ....*Rosemary Clooney*...Columbia 4-39710
3	4	7	Wish You Were Here ....*Eddie Fisher*...RCA Victor 47-4830
4	2	10	Botch-A-Me (Ba-Ba-Baciami Piccina).........................*Rosemary Clooney*...Columbia 4-39767
5	8	4	You Belong To Me...*Jo Stafford*...Columbia 4-39811
6	6	8	High Noon (Do Not Forsake Me) ....*Frankie Laine*...Columbia 4-39770
7	7	16	Here In My Heart ....*Al Martino*...BBS 101
8	12	12	Somewhere Along The Way ....*Nat "King" Cole*...Capitol F2069
9	5	19	Delicado...*Percy Faith*...Columbia 4-39708
10	9	14	Walkin' My Baby Back Home ....*Johnnie Ray*...Columbia 4-39750

Billboard ❀ SEPTEMBER 6, 1952 ❀ Best Sellers

TW	LW	WK		
1	1	12	Auf Wiederseh'n Sweetheart	Vera Lynn...London 451227
2	5	5	You Belong To Me	Jo Stafford...Columbia 4-39811
3	3	8	Wish You Were Here	Eddie Fisher...RCA Victor 47-4830
4	2	16	Half As Much	Rosemary Clooney...Columbia 4-39710
5	6	9	High Noon (Do Not Forsake Me)	Frankie Laine...Columbia 4-39770
6	4	11	Botch-A-Me (Ba-Ba-Baciami Piccina)	Rosemary Clooney...Columbia 4-39767
7	17	2	I Went To Your Wedding	Patti Page...Mercury 5899-X45
8	13	2	Jambalaya	Jo Stafford...Columbia 4-39838
9	10	15	Walkin' My Baby Back Home	Johnnie Ray...Columbia 4-39750
10	8	13	Somewhere Along The Way	Nat "King" Cole...Capitol F2069

Billboard ❀ SEPTEMBER 13, 1952 ❀ Best Sellers

TW	LW	WK		
1	2	6	You Belong To Me	Jo Stafford...Columbia 4-39811
2	1	13	Auf Wiederseh'n Sweetheart	Vera Lynn...London 451227
3	3	9	Wish You Were Here	Eddie Fisher...RCA Victor 47-4830
4	7	3	I Went To Your Wedding	Patti Page...Mercury 5899-X45
5	4	17	Half As Much	Rosemary Clooney...Columbia 4-39710
6	5	10	High Noon (Do Not Forsake Me)	Frankie Laine...Columbia 4-39770
7	6	12	Botch-A-Me (Ba-Ba-Baciami Piccina)	Rosemary Clooney...Columbia 4-39767
8	8	3	Jambalaya	Jo Stafford...Columbia 4-39838
9	11	3	Meet Mister Callaghan	Les Paul...Capitol F2193
10	14	8	Indian Love Call	Slim Whitman...Imperial 45-8156

Billboard ❀ SEPTEMBER 20, 1952 ❀ Best Sellers

TW	LW	WK		
1	1	7	You Belong To Me	Jo Stafford...Columbia 4-39811
2	4	4	I Went To Your Wedding	Patti Page...Mercury 5899-X45
3	3	10	Wish You Were Here	Eddie Fisher...RCA Victor 47-4830
4	2	14	Auf Wiederseh'n Sweetheart	Vera Lynn...London 451227
5	5	18	Half As Much	Rosemary Clooney...Columbia 4-39710
6	8	4	Jambalaya	Jo Stafford...Columbia 4-39838
7	6	11	High Noon (Do Not Forsake Me)	Frankie Laine...Columbia 4-39770
8	9	4	Meet Mister Callaghan	Les Paul...Capitol F2193
9	7	13	Botch-A-Me (Ba-Ba-Baciami Piccina)	Rosemary Clooney...Columbia 4-39767
10	12	3	You Belong To Me	Patti Page...Mercury 5899-X45

Billboard ❀ SEPTEMBER 27, 1952 ❀ Best Sellers

TW	LW	WK		
1	1	8	You Belong To Me	Jo Stafford...Columbia 4-39811
2	2	5	I Went To Your Wedding	Patti Page...Mercury 5899-X45
3	3	11	Wish You Were Here	Eddie Fisher...RCA Victor 47-4830
4	6	5	Jambalaya	Jo Stafford...Columbia 4-39838
5	7	12	High Noon (Do Not Forsake Me)	Frankie Laine...Columbia 4-39770
6	4	15	Auf Wiederseh'n Sweetheart	Vera Lynn...London 451227
7	5	19	Half As Much	Rosemary Clooney...Columbia 4-39710
8	8	5	Meet Mister Callaghan	Les Paul...Capitol F2193
9	10	4	You Belong To Me	Patti Page...Mercury 5899-X45
10	14	5	Trying	The Hill Toppers...Dot 45-15018

Billboard ❀ OCTOBER 4, 1952 ❀ Best Sellers

TW	LW	WK		
1	1	9	You Belong To Me	Jo Stafford...Columbia 4-39811
2	2	6	I Went To Your Wedding	Patti Page...Mercury 5899-X45
3	3	12	Wish You Were Here	Eddie Fisher...RCA Victor 47-4830
4	4	6	Jambalaya	Jo Stafford...Columbia 4-39838
5	5	13	High Noon (Do Not Forsake Me)	Frankie Laine...Columbia 4-39770
6	8	6	Meet Mister Callaghan	Les Paul...Capitol F2193
7	7	20	Half As Much	Rosemary Clooney...Columbia 4-39710
8	6	16	Auf Wiederseh'n Sweetheart	Vera Lynn...London 451227
9	10	6	Trying	The Hill Toppers...Dot 45-15018
10	9	5	You Belong To Me	Patti Page...Mercury 5899-X45

TW	LW	WK	Billboard ❀ OCTOBER 11, 1952 ❀ Best Sellers
1	1	10	You Belong To Me...*Jo Stafford*...Columbia 4-39811
2	2	7	I Went To Your Wedding..*Patti Page*...Mercury 5899-X45
3	3	13	Wish You Were Here...*Eddie Fisher*...RCA Victor 47-4830
4	4	7	Jambalaya..*Jo Stafford*...Columbia 4-39838
5	6	7	Meet Mister Callaghan..*Les Paul*...Capitol F2193
6	5	14	High Noon (Do Not Forsake Me) ....*Frankie Laine*...Columbia 4-39770
6	7	21	Half As Much ....*Rosemary Clooney*...Columbia 4-39710
8	9	7	Trying...*The Hill Toppers*...Dot 45-15018
9	10	6	You Belong To Me ....*Patti Page*...Mercury 5899-X45
10	11	3	The Glow-Worm..*Mills Brothers*...Decca 9-28384

TW	LW	WK	Billboard ❀ OCTOBER 18, 1952 ❀ Best Sellers
1	2	8	I Went To Your Wedding..*Patti Page*...Mercury 5899-X45
2	1	11	You Belong To Me...*Jo Stafford*...Columbia 4-39811
3	4	8	Jambalaya..*Jo Stafford*...Columbia 4-39838
4	3	14	Wish You Were Here...*Eddie Fisher*...RCA Victor 47-4830
5	5	8	Meet Mister Callaghan..*Les Paul*...Capitol F2193
6	6	22	Half As Much ....*Rosemary Clooney*...Columbia 4-39710
7	13	3	It's In The Book (Parts 1 & 2)..*Johnny Standley*...Capitol F2249
8	6	15	High Noon (Do Not Forsake Me) ....*Frankie Laine*...Columbia 4-39770
9	10	4	The Glow-Worm..*Mills Brothers*...Decca 9-28384
10	8	8	Trying...*The Hill Toppers*...Dot 45-15018

TW	LW	WK	Billboard ❀ OCTOBER 25, 1952 ❀ Best Sellers
1	1	9	I Went To Your Wedding..*Patti Page*...Mercury 5899-X45
2	2	12	You Belong To Me...*Jo Stafford*...Columbia 4-39811
3	3	9	Jambalaya..*Jo Stafford*...Columbia 4-39838
4	4	15	Wish You Were Here...*Eddie Fisher*...RCA Victor 47-4830
5	7	4	It's In The Book (Parts 1 & 2)..*Johnny Standley*...Capitol F2249
6	9	5	The Glow-Worm..*Mills Brothers*...Decca 9-28384
7	5	9	Meet Mister Callaghan..*Les Paul*...Capitol F2193
8	10	9	Trying...*The Hill Toppers*...Dot 45-15018
9	8	16	High Noon (Do Not Forsake Me) ....*Frankie Laine*...Columbia 4-39770
10	11	8	You Belong To Me ....*Patti Page*...Mercury 5899-X45

TW	LW	WK	Billboard ❀ NOVEMBER 1, 1952 ❀ Best Sellers
1	1	10	I Went To Your Wedding..*Patti Page*...Mercury 5899-X45
2	2	13	You Belong To Me...*Jo Stafford*...Columbia 4-39811
3	5	5	It's In The Book (Parts 1 & 2)..*Johnny Standley*...Capitol F2249
4	6	6	The Glow-Worm..*Mills Brothers*...Decca 9-28384
5	3	10	Jambalaya..*Jo Stafford*...Columbia 4-39838
6	4	16	Wish You Were Here...*Eddie Fisher*...RCA Victor 47-4830
7	8	10	Trying...*The Hill Toppers*...Dot 45-15018
8	7	10	Meet Mister Callaghan..*Les Paul*...Capitol F2193
9	17	3	Why Don't You Believe Me ....*Joni James*...MGM K11333
10	12	5	Outside Of Heaven...*Eddie Fisher*...RCA Victor 47-4953

TW	LW	WK	Billboard ❀ NOVEMBER 8, 1952 ❀ Best Sellers
1	1	11	I Went To Your Wedding..*Patti Page*...Mercury 5899-X45
2	2	14	You Belong To Me...*Jo Stafford*...Columbia 4-39811
3	3	6	It's In The Book (Parts 1 & 2)..*Johnny Standley*...Capitol F2249
4	4	7	The Glow-Worm..*Mills Brothers*...Decca 9-28384
5	5	11	Jambalaya..*Jo Stafford*...Columbia 4-39838
6	6	17	Wish You Were Here...*Eddie Fisher*...RCA Victor 47-4830
7	9	11	Why Don't You Believe Me ....*Joni James*...MGM K11333
8	7	11	Trying...*The Hill Toppers*...Dot 45-15018
9	8	11	Meet Mister Callaghan..*Les Paul*...Capitol F2193
10	16	10	You Belong To Me ....*Patti Page*...Mercury 5899-X45

TW	LW	WK	Billboard ❄ NOVEMBER 15, 1952 ❄ Best Sellers
1	1	12	I Went To Your Wedding..Patti Page...Mercury 5899-X45
2	4	8	The Glow-Worm...Mills Brothers...Decca 9-28384
3	2	15	You Belong To Me...Jo Stafford...Columbia 4-39811
4	3	7	It's In The Book (Parts 1 & 2)..Johnny Standley...Capitol F2249
5	7	5	Why Don't You Believe Me ....Joni James...MGM K11333
6	5	12	Jambalaya...Jo Stafford...Columbia 4-39838
7	6	18	Wish You Were Here ....Eddie Fisher...RCA Victor 47-4830
8	11	10	Because You're Mine ....Mario Lanza...RCA Victor 49-3914
9	8	12	Trying...The Hill Toppers...Dot 45-15018
10	15	8	Lady Of Spain ....Eddie Fisher...RCA Victor 47-4953

TW	LW	WK	Billboard ❄ NOVEMBER 22, 1952 ❄ Best Sellers
1	4	8	It's In The Book (Parts 1 & 2)..Johnny Standley...Capitol F2249
2	2	9	The Glow-Worm...Mills Brothers...Decca 9-28384
3	1	13	I Went To Your Wedding..Patti Page...Mercury 5899-X45
4	5	6	Why Don't You Believe Me ....Joni James...MGM K11333
5	3	16	You Belong To Me...Jo Stafford...Columbia 4-39811
6	6	13	Jambalaya...Jo Stafford...Columbia 4-39838
7	8	11	Because You're Mine ....Mario Lanza...RCA Victor 49-3914
8	9	13	Trying...The Hill Toppers...Dot 45-15018
8	12	5	Yours...Vera Lynn...London 451261
10	7	19	Wish You Were Here ....Eddie Fisher...RCA Victor 47-4830

TW	LW	WK	Billboard ❄ NOVEMBER 29, 1952 ❄ Best Sellers
1	4	7	Why Don't You Believe Me ....Joni James...MGM K11333
1	1	9	It's In The Book (Parts 1 & 2)..Johnny Standley...Capitol F2249
3	2	10	The Glow-Worm...Mills Brothers...Decca 9-28384
4	3	14	I Went To Your Wedding..Patti Page...Mercury 5899-X45
5	5	17	You Belong To Me...Jo Stafford...Columbia 4-39811
6	6	14	Jambalaya...Jo Stafford...Columbia 4-39838
7	7	12	Because You're Mine ....Mario Lanza...RCA Victor 49-3914
8	12	10	Takes Two To Tango ....Pearl Bailey...Coral 9-60817
9	8	14	Trying...The Hill Toppers...Dot 45-15018
10	8	6	Yours...Vera Lynn...London 451261

TW	LW	WK	Billboard ❄ DECEMBER 6, 1952 ❄ Best Sellers
1	1	8	Why Don't You Believe Me ....Joni James...MGM K11333
2	1	10	It's In The Book (Parts 1 & 2)..Johnny Standley...Capitol F2249
3	3	11	The Glow-Worm...Mills Brothers...Decca 9-28384
4	4	15	I Went To Your Wedding..Patti Page...Mercury 5899-X45
5	5	18	You Belong To Me...Jo Stafford...Columbia 4-39811
6	11	4	Keep It A Secret ....Jo Stafford...Columbia 4-39891
7	8	11	Takes Two To Tango ....Pearl Bailey...Coral 9-60817
8	6	15	Jambalaya...Jo Stafford...Columbia 4-39838
9	13	11	Lady Of Spain ....Eddie Fisher...RCA Victor 47-4953
10	7	13	Because You're Mine ....Mario Lanza...RCA Victor 49-3914

TW	LW	WK	Billboard ❄ DECEMBER 13, 1952 ❄ Best Sellers
1	1	9	Why Don't You Believe Me ....Joni James...MGM K11333
2	2	11	It's In The Book (Parts 1 & 2)..Johnny Standley...Capitol F2249
3	3	12	The Glow-Worm...Mills Brothers...Decca 9-28384
4	11	2	Don't Let The Stars Get In Your Eyes ....Perry Como...RCA Victor 47-5064
5	4	16	I Went To Your Wedding..Patti Page...Mercury 5899-X45
6	13	2	I Saw Mommy Kissing Santa Claus ....Jimmy Boyd...Columbia 4-39871
7	5	19	You Belong To Me...Jo Stafford...Columbia 4-39811
8	6	5	Keep It A Secret ....Jo Stafford...Columbia 4-39891
9	7	12	Takes Two To Tango ....Pearl Bailey...Coral 9-60817
10	10	14	Because You're Mine ....Mario Lanza...RCA Victor 49-3914

TW	LW	WK	Billboard® DECEMBER 20, 1952 Best Sellers
1	1	10	Why Don't You Believe Me ....*Joni James*...MGM K11333
2	6	3	I Saw Mommy Kissing Santa Claus..*Jimmy Boyd*...Columbia 4-39871
3	3	13	The Glow-Worm ....*Mills Brothers*...Decca 9-28384
4	4	3	Don't Let The Stars Get In Your Eyes ....*Perry Como*...RCA Victor 47-5064
5	2	12	It's In The Book (Parts 1 & 2)..*Johnny Standley*...Capitol F2249
6	8	6	Keep It A Secret ....*Jo Stafford*...Columbia 4-39891
7	13	3	Oh Happy Day ....*Don Howard*...Essex 45-311
8	9	13	Takes Two To Tango...*Pearl Bailey*...Coral 9-60817
9	10	15	Because You're Mine...*Mario Lanza*...RCA Victor 49-3914
10	11	17	Jambalaya...*Jo Stafford*...Columbia 4-39838

TW	LW	WK	Billboard® DECEMBER 27, 1952 Best Sellers
1	2	4	I Saw Mommy Kissing Santa Claus..*Jimmy Boyd*...Columbia 4-39871
2	1	11	Why Don't You Believe Me ....*Joni James*...MGM K11333
3	4	4	Don't Let The Stars Get In Your Eyes ....*Perry Como*...RCA Victor 47-5064
4	3	14	The Glow-Worm ....*Mills Brothers*...Decca 9-28384
5	5	13	It's In The Book (Parts 1 & 2)..*Johnny Standley*...Capitol F2249
6	6	7	Keep It A Secret ....*Jo Stafford*...Columbia 4-39891
7	14	2	I Saw Mommy Kissing Santa Claus ....*Spike Jones*...RCA Victor 47-5067
8	9	16	Because You're Mine...*Mario Lanza*...RCA Victor 49-3914
9	7	4	Oh Happy Day ....*Don Howard*...Essex 45-311
10	11	3	Till I Waltz Again With You ....*Teresa Brewer*...Coral 9-60873

Billboard ❂ JANUARY 3, 1953 ❂ Best Sellers

TW	LW	WK		
1	1	5	I Saw Mommy Kissing Santa Claus	Jimmy Boyd...Columbia 4-39871
2	3	5	Don't Let The Stars Get In Your Eyes	Perry Como...RCA Victor 47-5064
3	2	12	Why Don't You Believe Me	Joni James...MGM K11333
4	4	15	The Glow-Worm	Mills Brothers...Decca 9-28384
5	5	14	It's In The Book (Parts 1 & 2)	Johnny Standley...Capitol F2249
6	10	4	Till I Waltz Again With You	Teresa Brewer...Coral 9-60873
7	6	8	Keep It A Secret	Jo Stafford...Columbia 4-39891
8	14	3	Tell Me You're Mine	The Gaylords...Mercury 70067-X45
9	9	5	Oh Happy Day	Don Howard...Essex 45-311
10	8	17	Because You're Mine	Mario Lanza...RCA Victor 49-3914

Billboard ❂ JANUARY 10, 1953 ❂ Best Sellers

TW	LW	WK		
1	2	6	Don't Let The Stars Get In Your Eyes	Perry Como...RCA Victor 47-5064
2	4	16	The Glow-Worm	Mills Brothers...Decca 9-28384
3	3	13	Why Don't You Believe Me	Joni James...MGM K11333
4	5	15	It's In The Book (Parts 1 & 2)	Johnny Standley...Capitol F2249
5	6	5	Till I Waltz Again With You	Teresa Brewer...Coral 9-60873
6	9	6	Oh Happy Day	Don Howard...Essex 45-311
7	7	9	Keep It A Secret	Jo Stafford...Columbia 4-39891
8	8	4	Tell Me You're Mine	The Gaylords...Mercury 70067-X45
9	11	2	Have You Heard	Joni James...MGM K11390
9	—	15	Takes Two To Tango	Pearl Bailey...Coral 9-60817

Billboard ❂ JANUARY 17, 1953 ❂ Best Sellers

TW	LW	WK		
1	1	7	Don't Let The Stars Get In Your Eyes	Perry Como...RCA Victor 47-5064
2	3	14	Why Don't You Believe Me	Joni James...MGM K11333
3	5	6	Till I Waltz Again With You	Teresa Brewer...Coral 9-60873
4	2	17	The Glow-Worm	Mills Brothers...Decca 9-28384
5	4	16	It's In The Book (Parts 1 & 2)	Johnny Standley...Capitol F2249
6	8	5	Tell Me You're Mine	The Gaylords...Mercury 70067-X45
7	6	7	Oh Happy Day	Don Howard...Essex 45-311
8	9	3	Have You Heard	Joni James...MGM K11390
9	12	8	Hold Me, Thrill Me, Kiss Me	Karen Chandler...Coral 9-60831
10	7	10	Keep It A Secret	Jo Stafford...Columbia 4-39891

Billboard ❂ JANUARY 24, 1953 ❂ Best Sellers

TW	LW	WK		
1	1	8	Don't Let The Stars Get In Your Eyes	Perry Como...RCA Victor 47-5064
2	2	15	Why Don't You Believe Me	Joni James...MGM K11333
3	3	7	Till I Waltz Again With You	Teresa Brewer...Coral 9-60873
4	7	8	Oh Happy Day	Don Howard...Essex 45-311
5	4	18	The Glow-Worm	Mills Brothers...Decca 9-28384
6	6	6	Tell Me You're Mine	The Gaylords...Mercury 70067-X45
7	10	11	Keep It A Secret	Jo Stafford...Columbia 4-39891
8	5	17	It's In The Book (Parts 1 & 2)	Johnny Standley...Capitol F2249
9	8	4	Have You Heard	Joni James...MGM K11390
10	9	9	Hold Me, Thrill Me, Kiss Me	Karen Chandler...Coral 9-60831

Billboard ❂ JANUARY 31, 1953 ❂ Best Sellers

TW	LW	WK		
1	1	9	Don't Let The Stars Get In Your Eyes	Perry Como...RCA Victor 47-5064
2	3	8	Till I Waltz Again With You	Teresa Brewer...Coral 9-60873
3	2	16	Why Don't You Believe Me	Joni James...MGM K11333
4	6	7	Tell Me You're Mine	The Gaylords...Mercury 70067-X45
5	5	19	The Glow-Worm	Mills Brothers...Decca 9-28384
6	4	9	Oh Happy Day	Don Howard...Essex 45-311
7	9	5	Have You Heard	Joni James...MGM K11390
8	7	12	Keep It A Secret	Jo Stafford...Columbia 4-39891
9	10	10	Hold Me, Thrill Me, Kiss Me	Karen Chandler...Coral 9-60831
10	8	18	It's In The Book (Parts 1 & 2)	Johnny Standley...Capitol F2249

TW	LW	WK	Billboard ❀ FEBRUARY 7, 1953 ❀ Best Sellers
1	1	10	Don't Let The Stars Get In Your Eyes .... Perry Como...RCA Victor 47-5064
2	2	9	Till I Waltz Again With You .... Teresa Brewer...Coral 9-60873
3	3	17	Why Don't You Believe Me .... Joni James...MGM K11333
4	4	8	Tell Me You're Mine .... The Gaylords...Mercury 70067-X45
5	7	6	Have You Heard .... Joni James...MGM K11390
6	6	10	Oh Happy Day .... Don Howard...Essex 45-311
7	9	11	Hold Me, Thrill Me, Kiss Me .... Karen Chandler...Coral 9-60831
8	8	13	Keep It A Secret .... Jo Stafford...Columbia 4-39891
9	—	1	Anywhere I Wander .... Julius LaRosa...Cadence F1230
10	5	20	The Glow-Worm .... Mills Brothers...Decca 9-28384

TW	LW	WK	Billboard ❀ FEBRUARY 14, 1953 ❀ Best Sellers
1	2	10	Till I Waltz Again With You .... Teresa Brewer...Coral 9-60873
2	1	11	Don't Let The Stars Get In Your Eyes .... Perry Como...RCA Victor 47-5064
3	4	9	Tell Me You're Mine .... The Gaylords...Mercury 70067-X45
4	3	18	Why Don't You Believe Me .... Joni James...MGM K11333
5	5	7	Have You Heard .... Joni James...MGM K11390
6	9	2	Anywhere I Wander .... Julius LaRosa...Cadence F1230
7	11	3	The Doggie In The Window .... Patti Page...Mercury 70070-X45
8	7	12	Hold Me, Thrill Me, Kiss Me .... Karen Chandler...Coral 9-60831
9	6	11	Oh Happy Day .... Don Howard...Essex 45-311
10	8	14	Keep It A Secret .... Jo Stafford...Columbia 4-39891

TW	LW	WK	Billboard ❀ FEBRUARY 21, 1953 ❀ Best Sellers
1	1	11	Till I Waltz Again With You .... Teresa Brewer...Coral 9-60873
2	2	12	Don't Let The Stars Get In Your Eyes .... Perry Como...RCA Victor 47-5064
3	3	10	Tell Me You're Mine .... The Gaylords...Mercury 70067-X45
4	6	3	Anywhere I Wander .... Julius LaRosa...Cadence F1230
5	5	8	Have You Heard .... Joni James...MGM K11390
6	7	4	The Doggie In The Window .... Patti Page...Mercury 70070-X45
7	4	19	Why Don't You Believe Me .... Joni James...MGM K11333
8	12	4	Side By Side .... Kay Starr...Capitol F2334
9	8	13	Hold Me, Thrill Me, Kiss Me .... Karen Chandler...Coral 9-60831
10	9	12	Oh Happy Day .... Don Howard...Essex 45-311

TW	LW	WK	Billboard ❀ FEBRUARY 28, 1953 ❀ Best Sellers
1	1	12	Till I Waltz Again With You .... Teresa Brewer...Coral 9-60873
2	2	13	Don't Let The Stars Get In Your Eyes .... Perry Como...RCA Victor 47-5064
3	6	5	The Doggie In The Window .... Patti Page...Mercury 70070-X45
4	3	11	Tell Me You're Mine .... The Gaylords...Mercury 70067-X45
5	5	9	Have You Heard .... Joni James...MGM K11390
6	4	4	Anywhere I Wander .... Julius LaRosa...Cadence F1230
7	11	3	Pretend .... Nat "King" Cole...Capitol F2346
8	9	14	Hold Me, Thrill Me, Kiss Me .... Karen Chandler...Coral 9-60831
9	8	5	Side By Side .... Kay Starr...Capitol F2334
10	16	2	I Believe .... Frankie Laine...Columbia 4-39938

TW	LW	WK	Billboard ❀ MARCH 7, 1953 ❀ Best Sellers
1	1	13	Till I Waltz Again With You .... Teresa Brewer...Coral 9-60873
2	2	14	Don't Let The Stars Get In Your Eyes .... Perry Como...RCA Victor 47-5064
3	3	6	The Doggie In The Window .... Patti Page...Mercury 70070-X45
4	4	12	Tell Me You're Mine .... The Gaylords...Mercury 70067-X45
5	6	5	Anywhere I Wander .... Julius LaRosa...Cadence F1230
6	7	4	Pretend .... Nat "King" Cole...Capitol F2346
7	9	6	Side By Side .... Kay Starr...Capitol F2334
8	8	15	Hold Me, Thrill Me, Kiss Me .... Karen Chandler...Coral 9-60831
9	5	10	Have You Heard .... Joni James...MGM K11390
10	10	3	I Believe .... Frankie Laine...Columbia 4-39938

TW	LW	WK	Billboard ✹ MARCH 14, 1953 ✹ Best Sellers
1	1	14	Till I Waltz Again With You ....Teresa Brewer...Coral 9-60873
2	3	7	The Doggie In The Window ....Patti Page...Mercury 70070-X45
3	2	15	Don't Let The Stars Get In Your Eyes ....Perry Como...RCA Victor 47-5064
4	10	4	I Believe ....Frankie Laine...Columbia 4-39938
5	4	13	Tell Me You're Mine ....The Gaylords...Mercury 70067-X45
6	6	5	Pretend ....Nat "King" Cole...Capitol F2346
7	5	6	Anywhere I Wander ....Julius LaRosa...Cadence F1230
8	12	4	Your Cheatin' Heart...Joni James...MGM K11426
9	9	11	Have You Heard ....Joni James...MGM K11390
10	11	5	Wild Horses...Perry Como...RCA Victor 47-5152

TW	LW	WK	Billboard ✹ MARCH 21, 1953 ✹ Best Sellers
1	2	8	The Doggie In The Window ....Patti Page...Mercury 70070-X45
2	1	15	Till I Waltz Again With You ....Teresa Brewer...Coral 9-60873
3	3	16	Don't Let The Stars Get In Your Eyes ....Perry Como...RCA Victor 47-5064
4	4	5	I Believe ....Frankie Laine...Columbia 4-39938
5	5	14	Tell Me You're Mine ....The Gaylords...Mercury 70067-X45
6	6	6	Pretend ....Nat "King" Cole...Capitol F2346
7	8	5	Your Cheatin' Heart...Joni James...MGM K11426
8	10	6	Wild Horses...Perry Como...RCA Victor 47-5152
9	11	8	Side By Side ....Kay Starr...Capitol F2334
10	9	12	Have You Heard ....Joni James...MGM K11390

TW	LW	WK	Billboard ✹ MARCH 28, 1953 ✹ Best Sellers
1	1	9	The Doggie In The Window ....Patti Page...Mercury 70070-X45
2	2	16	Till I Waltz Again With You ....Teresa Brewer...Coral 9-60873
3	4	6	I Believe ....Frankie Laine...Columbia 4-39938
4	5	15	Tell Me You're Mine ....The Gaylords...Mercury 70067-X45
5	11	3	Tell Me A Story...Jimmy Boyd - Frankie Laine...Columbia 4-39945
6	3	17	Don't Let The Stars Get In Your Eyes ....Perry Como...RCA Victor 47-5064
7	8	7	Wild Horses...Perry Como...RCA Victor 47-5152
8	6	7	Pretend ....Nat "King" Cole...Capitol F2346
9	7	6	Your Cheatin' Heart...Joni James...MGM K11426
10	9	9	Side By Side ....Kay Starr...Capitol F2334

TW	LW	WK	Billboard ✹ APRIL 4, 1953 ✹ Best Sellers
1	1	10	The Doggie In The Window ....Patti Page...Mercury 70070-X45
2	2	17	Till I Waltz Again With You ....Teresa Brewer...Coral 9-60873
3	3	7	I Believe ....Frankie Laine...Columbia 4-39938
4	8	8	Pretend ....Nat "King" Cole...Capitol F2346
5	4	16	Tell Me You're Mine ....The Gaylords...Mercury 70067-X45
6	5	4	Tell Me A Story...Jimmy Boyd - Frankie Laine...Columbia 4-39945
7	6	18	Don't Let The Stars Get In Your Eyes ....Perry Como...RCA Victor 47-5064
7	9	7	Your Cheatin' Heart...Joni James...MGM K11426
9	10	10	Side By Side ....Kay Starr...Capitol F2334
10	7	8	Wild Horses...Perry Como...RCA Victor 47-5152

TW	LW	WK	Billboard ✹ APRIL 11, 1953 ✹ Best Sellers
1	1	11	The Doggie In The Window ....Patti Page...Mercury 70070-X45
2	2	18	Till I Waltz Again With You ....Teresa Brewer...Coral 9-60873
3	3	8	I Believe ....Frankie Laine...Columbia 4-39938
4	4	9	Pretend ....Nat "King" Cole...Capitol F2346
5	6	5	Tell Me A Story...Jimmy Boyd - Frankie Laine...Columbia 4-39945
6	5	17	Tell Me You're Mine ....The Gaylords...Mercury 70067-X45
7	7	8	Your Cheatin' Heart...Joni James...MGM K11426
8	10	9	Wild Horses...Perry Como...RCA Victor 47-5152
9	7	19	Don't Let The Stars Get In Your Eyes ....Perry Como...RCA Victor 47-5064
10	9	11	Side By Side ....Kay Starr...Capitol F2334

TW	LW	WK	Billboard® ❀ APRIL 18, 1953 ❀ Best Sellers
1	1	12	The Doggie In The Window ....Patti Page...Mercury 70070-X45
2	3	9	I Believe ....Frankie Laine...Columbia 4-39938
3	4	10	Pretend ....Nat "King" Cole...Capitol F2346
4	5	6	Tell Me A Story...Jimmy Boyd - Frankie Laine...Columbia 4-39945
5	2	19	Till I Waltz Again With You ....Teresa Brewer...Coral 9-60873
6	6	18	Tell Me You're Mine ....The Gaylords...Mercury 70067-X45
7	11	3	The Song From Moulin Rouge (Where Is Your Heart) ...Percy Faith...Columbia 4-39944
8	7	9	Your Cheatin' Heart ....Joni James...MGM K11426
9	8	10	Wild Horses...Perry Como...RCA Victor 47-5152
10	12	3	April In Portugal..Les Baxter...Capitol F2374

TW	LW	WK	Billboard® ❀ APRIL 25, 1953 ❀ Best Sellers
1	1	13	The Doggie In The Window ....Patti Page...Mercury 70070-X45
2	2	10	I Believe ....Frankie Laine...Columbia 4-39938
3	3	11	Pretend ....Nat "King" Cole...Capitol F2346
4	7	4	The Song From Moulin Rouge (Where Is Your Heart) ...Percy Faith...Columbia 4-39944
5	4	7	Tell Me A Story...Jimmy Boyd - Frankie Laine...Columbia 4-39945
6	6	19	Tell Me You're Mine ....The Gaylords...Mercury 70067-X45
7	8	10	Your Cheatin' Heart ....Joni James...MGM K11426
8	5	20	Till I Waltz Again With You ....Teresa Brewer...Coral 9-60873
9	13	3	Ruby ....Richard Hayman...Mercury 70115-X45
10	10	4	April In Portugal..Les Baxter...Capitol F2374

TW	LW	WK	Billboard® ❀ MAY 2, 1953 ❀ Best Sellers
1	1	14	The Doggie In The Window ....Patti Page...Mercury 70070-X45
2	4	5	The Song From Moulin Rouge (Where Is Your Heart) ...Percy Faith...Columbia 4-39944
3	2	11	I Believe ....Frankie Laine...Columbia 4-39938
4	3	12	Pretend ....Nat "King" Cole...Capitol F2346
5	5	8	Tell Me A Story...Jimmy Boyd - Frankie Laine...Columbia 4-39945
6	10	5	April In Portugal..Les Baxter...Capitol F2374
7	9	4	Ruby ....Richard Hayman...Mercury 70115-X45
8	8	21	Till I Waltz Again With You ....Teresa Brewer...Coral 9-60873
9	7	11	Your Cheatin' Heart ....Joni James...MGM K11426
10	6	20	Tell Me You're Mine ....The Gaylords...Mercury 70067-X45

TW	LW	WK	Billboard® ❀ MAY 9, 1953 ❀ Best Sellers
1	1	15	The Doggie In The Window ....Patti Page...Mercury 70070-X45
2	2	6	The Song From Moulin Rouge (Where Is Your Heart) ...Percy Faith...Columbia 4-39944
3	3	12	I Believe ....Frankie Laine...Columbia 4-39938
4	4	13	Pretend ....Nat "King" Cole...Capitol F2346
5	6	6	April In Portugal..Les Baxter...Capitol F2374
6	7	5	Ruby ....Richard Hayman...Mercury 70115-X45
7	5	9	Tell Me A Story...Jimmy Boyd - Frankie Laine...Columbia 4-39945
8	12	4	Anna (El N. Zumbon) ....Silvana Mangano...MGM K11457
9	14	3	Say You're Mine Again ....Perry Como...RCA Victor 47-5277
10	9	12	Your Cheatin' Heart ....Joni James...MGM K11426

TW	LW	WK	Billboard® ❀ MAY 16, 1953 ❀ Best Sellers
1	2	7	The Song From Moulin Rouge (Where Is Your Heart) ...Percy Faith...Columbia 4-39944
2	1	16	The Doggie In The Window ....Patti Page...Mercury 70070-X45
3	3	13	I Believe ....Frankie Laine...Columbia 4-39938
4	5	7	April In Portugal..Les Baxter...Capitol F2374
5	4	14	Pretend ....Nat "King" Cole...Capitol F2346
6	6	6	Ruby ....Richard Hayman...Mercury 70115-X45
7	8	5	Anna (El N. Zumbon) ....Silvana Mangano...MGM K11457
8	9	4	Say You're Mine Again ....Perry Como...RCA Victor 47-5277
9	7	10	Tell Me A Story...Jimmy Boyd - Frankie Laine...Columbia 4-39945
10	12	3	The Ho Ho Song ....Red Buttons...Columbia 4-39981

Billboard 🏵 MAY 23, 1953 🏵 Best Sellers

TW	LW	WK		
1	1	8	The Song From Moulin Rouge (Where Is Your Heart)	Percy Faith...Columbia 4-39944
2	2	17	The Doggie In The Window	Patti Page...Mercury 70070-X45
3	4	8	April In Portugal	Les Baxter...Capitol F2374
4	3	14	I Believe	Frankie Laine...Columbia 4-39938
5	5	15	Pretend	Nat "King" Cole...Capitol F2346
6	6	7	Ruby	Richard Hayman...Mercury 70115-X45
7	11	3	I'm Walking Behind You	Eddie Fisher...RCA Victor 47-5293
8	7	6	Anna (El N. Zumbon)	Silvana Mangano...MGM K11457
9	8	5	Say You're Mine Again	Perry Como...RCA Victor 47-5277
10	10	4	The Ho Ho Song	Red Buttons...Columbia 4-39981

Billboard 🏵 MAY 30, 1953 🏵 Best Sellers

TW	LW	WK		
1	1	9	The Song From Moulin Rouge (Where Is Your Heart)	Percy Faith...Columbia 4-39944
2	3	9	April In Portugal	Les Baxter...Capitol F2374
3	6	8	Ruby	Richard Hayman...Mercury 70115-X45
4	7	4	I'm Walking Behind You	Eddie Fisher...RCA Victor 47-5293
5	2	18	The Doggie In The Window	Patti Page...Mercury 70070-X45
6	4	15	I Believe	Frankie Laine...Columbia 4-39938
7	9	6	Say You're Mine Again	Perry Como...RCA Victor 47-5277
8	8	7	Anna (El N. Zumbon)	Silvana Mangano...MGM K11457
9	5	16	Pretend	Nat "King" Cole...Capitol F2346
10	10	5	The Ho Ho Song	Red Buttons...Columbia 4-39981

Billboard 🏵 JUNE 6, 1953 🏵 Best Sellers

TW	LW	WK		
1	1	10	The Song From Moulin Rouge (Where Is Your Heart)	Percy Faith...Columbia 4-39944
2	2	10	April In Portugal	Les Baxter...Capitol F2374
3	4	5	I'm Walking Behind You	Eddie Fisher...RCA Victor 47-5293
4	3	9	Ruby	Richard Hayman...Mercury 70115-X45
5	7	7	Say You're Mine Again	Perry Como...RCA Victor 47-5277
6	8	8	Anna (El N. Zumbon)	Silvana Mangano...MGM K11457
7	6	16	I Believe	Frankie Laine...Columbia 4-39938
8	5	19	The Doggie In The Window	Patti Page...Mercury 70070-X45
9	9	17	Pretend	Nat "King" Cole...Capitol F2346
10	10	6	The Ho Ho Song	Red Buttons...Columbia 4-39981

Billboard 🏵 JUNE 13, 1953 🏵 Best Sellers

TW	LW	WK		
1	1	11	The Song From Moulin Rouge (Where Is Your Heart)	Percy Faith...Columbia 4-39944
2	2	11	April In Portugal	Les Baxter...Capitol F2374
3	3	6	I'm Walking Behind You	Eddie Fisher...RCA Victor 47-5293
4	4	10	Ruby	Richard Hayman...Mercury 70115-X45
5	5	8	Say You're Mine Again	Perry Como...RCA Victor 47-5277
6	7	17	I Believe	Frankie Laine...Columbia 4-39938
7	6	9	Anna (El N. Zumbon)	Silvana Mangano...MGM K11457
8	8	20	The Doggie In The Window	Patti Page...Mercury 70070-X45
9	11	3	Terry's Theme From "Limelight"	Frank Chacksfield...London 45-1342
10	9	18	Pretend	Nat "King" Cole...Capitol F2346

Billboard 🏵 JUNE 20, 1953 🏵 Best Sellers

TW	LW	WK		
1	1	12	The Song From Moulin Rouge (Where Is Your Heart)	Percy Faith...Columbia 4-39944
2	3	7	I'm Walking Behind You	Eddie Fisher...RCA Victor 47-5293
3	2	12	April In Portugal	Les Baxter...Capitol F2374
4	4	11	Ruby	Richard Hayman...Mercury 70115-X45
5	5	9	Say You're Mine Again	Perry Como...RCA Victor 47-5277
6	6	18	I Believe	Frankie Laine...Columbia 4-39938
7	7	10	Anna (El N. Zumbon)	Silvana Mangano...MGM K11457
8	9	4	Terry's Theme From "Limelight"	Frank Chacksfield...London 45-1342
9	15	4	Ruby	Les Baxter...Capitol F2457
10	10	19	Pretend	Nat "King" Cole...Capitol F2346

Billboard — JUNE 27, 1953 — Best Sellers

TW	LW	WK	Title	Artist
1	1	13	The Song From Moulin Rouge (Where Is Your Heart)	Percy Faith...Columbia 4-39944
2	2	8	I'm Walking Behind You	Eddie Fisher...RCA Victor 47-5293
3	3	13	April In Portugal	Les Baxter...Capitol F2374
4	4	12	Ruby	Richard Hayman...Mercury 70115-X45
5	5	10	Say You're Mine Again	Perry Como...RCA Victor 47-5277
6	8	5	Terry's Theme From "Limelight"	Frank Chacksfield...London 45-1342
7	7	11	Anna (El N. Zumbon)	Silvana Mangano...MGM K11457
8	6	19	I Believe	Frankie Laine...Columbia 4-39938
9	15	2	No Other Love	Perry Como...RCA Victor 47-5317
10	13	2	Vaya Con Dios (May God Be With You)	Les Paul & Mary Ford...Capitol F2486

Billboard — JULY 4, 1953 — Best Sellers

TW	LW	WK	Title	Artist
1	1	14	The Song From Moulin Rouge (Where Is Your Heart)	Percy Faith...Columbia 4-39944
2	2	9	I'm Walking Behind You	Eddie Fisher...RCA Victor 47-5293
3	3	14	April In Portugal	Les Baxter...Capitol F2374
4	4	13	Ruby	Richard Hayman...Mercury 70115-X45
5	9	3	No Other Love	Perry Como...RCA Victor 47-5317
6	5	11	Say You're Mine Again	Perry Como...RCA Victor 47-5277
6	10	3	Vaya Con Dios (May God Be With You)	Les Paul & Mary Ford...Capitol F2486
8	6	6	Terry's Theme From "Limelight"	Frank Chacksfield...London 45-1342
9	8	20	I Believe	Frankie Laine...Columbia 4-39938
10	7	12	Anna (El N. Zumbon)	Silvana Mangano...MGM K11457

Billboard — JULY 11, 1953 — Best Sellers

TW	LW	WK	Title	Artist
1	1	15	The Song From Moulin Rouge (Where Is Your Heart)	Percy Faith...Columbia 4-39944
2	2	10	I'm Walking Behind You	Eddie Fisher...RCA Victor 47-5293
3	3	15	April In Portugal	Les Baxter...Capitol F2374
4	4	14	Ruby	Richard Hayman...Mercury 70115-X45
5	5	4	No Other Love	Perry Como...RCA Victor 47-5317
6	6	4	Vaya Con Dios (May God Be With You)	Les Paul & Mary Ford...Capitol F2486
7	8	7	Terry's Theme From "Limelight"	Frank Chacksfield...London 45-1342
8	12	3	P.S. I Love You	The Hilltoppers...Dot 45-15085
9	10	13	Anna (El N. Zumbon)	Silvana Mangano...MGM K11457
10	19	3	You You You	Ames Brothers...RCA Victor 47-5325

Billboard — JULY 18, 1953 — Best Sellers

TW	LW	WK	Title	Artist
1	1	16	The Song From Moulin Rouge (Where Is Your Heart)	Percy Faith...Columbia 4-39944
2	2	11	I'm Walking Behind You	Eddie Fisher...RCA Victor 47-5293
3	5	5	No Other Love	Perry Como...RCA Victor 47-5317
4	3	16	April In Portugal	Les Baxter...Capitol F2374
5	6	5	Vaya Con Dios (May God Be With You)	Les Paul & Mary Ford...Capitol F2486
6	7	8	Terry's Theme From "Limelight"	Frank Chacksfield...London 45-1342
7	4	15	Ruby	Richard Hayman...Mercury 70115-X45
8	8	4	P.S. I Love You	The Hilltoppers...Dot 45-15085
9	10	4	You You You	Ames Brothers...RCA Victor 47-5325
10	14	13	Say You're Mine Again	Perry Como...RCA Victor 47-5277

Billboard — JULY 25, 1953 — Best Sellers

TW	LW	WK	Title	Artist
1	2	12	I'm Walking Behind You	Eddie Fisher...RCA Victor 47-5293
2	1	17	The Song From Moulin Rouge (Where Is Your Heart)	Percy Faith...Columbia 4-39944
3	3	6	No Other Love	Perry Como...RCA Victor 47-5317
4	5	6	Vaya Con Dios (May God Be With You)	Les Paul & Mary Ford...Capitol F2486
5	4	17	April In Portugal	Les Baxter...Capitol F2374
6	8	5	P.S. I Love You	The Hilltoppers...Dot 45-15085
7	7	16	Ruby	Richard Hayman...Mercury 70115-X45
8	6	9	Terry's Theme From "Limelight"	Frank Chacksfield...London 45-1342
9	9	5	You You You	Ames Brothers...RCA Victor 47-5325
10	11	7	Half A Photograph	Kay Starr...Capitol F2464

TW	LW	WK	Billboard® ❀ AUGUST 1, 1953 ❀ Best Sellers
1	1	13	I'm Walking Behind You ....*Eddie Fisher*...RCA Victor 47-5293
2	4	7	Vaya Con Dios (May God Be With You) ....*Les Paul & Mary Ford*...Capitol F2486
3	3	7	No Other Love ....*Perry Como*...RCA Victor 47-5317
4	2	18	The Song From Moulin Rouge (Where Is Your Heart) ....*Percy Faith*...Columbia 4-39944
5	6	6	P.S. I Love You ....*The Hilltoppers*...Dot 45-15085
6	9	6	You You You ....*Ames Brothers*...RCA Victor 47-5325
7	5	18	April In Portugal ....*Les Baxter*...Capitol F2374
8	11	4	With These Hands ....*Eddie Fisher*...RCA Victor 47-5365
9	18	4	Oh! ....*Pee Wee Hunt*...Capitol F2442
10	16	3	C'est Si Bon (It's So Good) ....*Eartha Kitt*...RCA Victor 47-5358

TW	LW	WK	Billboard® ❀ AUGUST 8, 1953 ❀ Best Sellers
1	2	8	Vaya Con Dios (May God Be With You) ....*Les Paul & Mary Ford*...Capitol F2486
2	1	14	I'm Walking Behind You ....*Eddie Fisher*...RCA Victor 47-5293
3	3	8	No Other Love ....*Perry Como*...RCA Victor 47-5317
4	5	7	P.S. I Love You ....*The Hilltoppers*...Dot 45-15085
5	4	19	The Song From Moulin Rouge (Where Is Your Heart) ....*Percy Faith*...Columbia 4-39944
6	6	7	You You You ....*Ames Brothers*...RCA Victor 47-5325
7	9	5	Oh! ....*Pee Wee Hunt*...Capitol F2442
8	7	19	April In Portugal ....*Les Baxter*...Capitol F2374
9	10	4	C'est Si Bon (It's So Good) ....*Eartha Kitt*...RCA Victor 47-5358
10	12	6	Gambler's Guitar ....*Rusty Draper*...Mercury 70167-X45

TW	LW	WK	Billboard® ❀ AUGUST 15, 1953 ❀ Best Sellers
1	1	9	Vaya Con Dios (May God Be With You) ....*Les Paul & Mary Ford*...Capitol F2486
2	2	15	I'm Walking Behind You ....*Eddie Fisher*...RCA Victor 47-5293
3	3	9	No Other Love ....*Perry Como*...RCA Victor 47-5317
4	6	8	You You You ....*Ames Brothers*...RCA Victor 47-5325
5	4	8	P.S. I Love You ....*The Hilltoppers*...Dot 45-15085
6	5	20	The Song From Moulin Rouge (Where Is Your Heart) ....*Percy Faith*...Columbia 4-39944
7	7	6	Oh! ....*Pee Wee Hunt*...Capitol F2442
8	9	5	C'est Si Bon (It's So Good) ....*Eartha Kitt*...RCA Victor 47-5358
9	11	6	With These Hands ....*Eddie Fisher*...RCA Victor 47-5365
10	10	7	Gambler's Guitar ....*Rusty Draper*...Mercury 70167-X45

TW	LW	WK	Billboard® ❀ AUGUST 22, 1953 ❀ Best Sellers
1	1	10	Vaya Con Dios (May God Be With You) ....*Les Paul & Mary Ford*...Capitol F2486
2	3	10	No Other Love ....*Perry Como*...RCA Victor 47-5317
3	2	16	I'm Walking Behind You ....*Eddie Fisher*...RCA Victor 47-5293
4	4	9	You You You ....*Ames Brothers*...RCA Victor 47-5325
5	5	9	P.S. I Love You ....*The Hilltoppers*...Dot 45-15085
6	7	7	Oh! ....*Pee Wee Hunt*...Capitol F2442
7	6	21	The Song From Moulin Rouge (Where Is Your Heart) ....*Percy Faith*...Columbia 4-39944
8	8	6	C'est Si Bon (It's So Good) ....*Eartha Kitt*...RCA Victor 47-5358
9	13	4	Crying In The Chapel ....*June Valli*...RCA Victor 47-5368
10	9	7	With These Hands ....*Eddie Fisher*...RCA Victor 47-5365
10	10	8	Gambler's Guitar ....*Rusty Draper*...Mercury 70167-X45

TW	LW	WK	Billboard® ❀ AUGUST 29, 1953 ❀ Best Sellers
1	1	11	Vaya Con Dios (May God Be With You) ....*Les Paul & Mary Ford*...Capitol F2486
2	4	10	You You You ....*Ames Brothers*...RCA Victor 47-5325
3	2	11	No Other Love ....*Perry Como*...RCA Victor 47-5317
4	3	17	I'm Walking Behind You ....*Eddie Fisher*...RCA Victor 47-5293
5	5	10	P.S. I Love You ....*The Hilltoppers*...Dot 45-15085
6	6	8	Oh! ....*Pee Wee Hunt*...Capitol F2442
7	9	5	Crying In The Chapel ....*June Valli*...RCA Victor 47-5368
8	10	8	With These Hands ....*Eddie Fisher*...RCA Victor 47-5365
9	12	7	Crying In The Chapel ....*Darrell Glenn*...Valley 105
10	8	7	C'est Si Bon (It's So Good) ....*Eartha Kitt*...RCA Victor 47-5358

TW	LW	WK	Billboard ❀ SEPTEMBER 5, 1953 ❀ Best Sellers
1	1	12	Vaya Con Dios (May God Be With You) ....Les Paul & Mary Ford...Capitol F2486
2	2	11	You You You ....Ames Brothers...RCA Victor 47-5325
3	3	12	No Other Love ....Perry Como...RCA Victor 47-5317
4	5	11	P.S. I Love You..The Hilltoppers...Dot 45-15085
5	4	18	I'm Walking Behind You ....Eddie Fisher...RCA Victor 47-5293
6	6	9	Oh! ....Pee Wee Hunt...Capitol F2442
7	11	2	Dragnet ....Ray Anthony...Capitol F2562
8	7	6	Crying In The Chapel ....June Valli...RCA Victor 47-5368
9	10	8	C'est Si Bon (It's So Good) ....Eartha Kitt...RCA Victor 47-5358
10	13	5	Crying In The Chapel..Rex Allen...Decca 9-28758

TW	LW	WK	Billboard ❀ SEPTEMBER 12, 1953 ❀ Best Sellers
1	1	13	Vaya Con Dios (May God Be With You) ....Les Paul & Mary Ford...Capitol F2486
2	2	12	You You You ....Ames Brothers...RCA Victor 47-5325
3	3	13	No Other Love ....Perry Como...RCA Victor 47-5317
4	6	10	Oh! ....Pee Wee Hunt...Capitol F2442
5	7	3	Dragnet ....Ray Anthony...Capitol F2562
6	4	12	P.S. I Love You..The Hilltoppers...Dot 45-15085
7	8	7	Crying In The Chapel ....June Valli...RCA Victor 47-5368
8	5	19	I'm Walking Behind You ....Eddie Fisher...RCA Victor 47-5293
9	9	9	C'est Si Bon (It's So Good) ....Eartha Kitt...RCA Victor 47-5358
10	19	2	Ebb Tide..Frank Chacksfield...London 45-1358

TW	LW	WK	Billboard ❀ SEPTEMBER 19, 1953 ❀ Best Sellers
1	1	14	Vaya Con Dios (May God Be With You) ....Les Paul & Mary Ford...Capitol F2486
2	2	13	You You You ....Ames Brothers...RCA Victor 47-5325
3	4	11	Oh! ....Pee Wee Hunt...Capitol F2442
4	5	4	Dragnet ....Ray Anthony...Capitol F2562
5	3	14	No Other Love ....Perry Como...RCA Victor 47-5317
6	6	13	P.S. I Love You..The Hilltoppers...Dot 45-15085
7	7	8	Crying In The Chapel ....June Valli...RCA Victor 47-5368
8	16	2	Eh, Cumpari ....Julius LaRosa...Cadence 1232
9	10	3	Ebb Tide ....Frank Chacksfield...London 45-1358
10	8	20	I'm Walking Behind You ....Eddie Fisher...RCA Victor 47-5293

TW	LW	WK	Billboard ❀ SEPTEMBER 26, 1953 ❀ Best Sellers
1	1	15	Vaya Con Dios (May God Be With You) ....Les Paul & Mary Ford...Capitol F2486
2	2	14	You You You ....Ames Brothers...RCA Victor 47-5325
3	3	12	Oh! ....Pee Wee Hunt...Capitol F2442
4	4	5	Dragnet ....Ray Anthony...Capitol F2562
5	5	15	No Other Love ....Perry Como...RCA Victor 47-5317
6	7	9	Crying In The Chapel ....June Valli...RCA Victor 47-5368
7	9	4	Ebb Tide ....Frank Chacksfield...London 45-1358
8	6	14	P.S. I Love You..The Hilltoppers...Dot 45-15085
9	8	3	Eh, Cumpari ....Julius LaRosa...Cadence 1232
10	13	5	My Love, My Love ....Joni James...MGM K11543

TW	LW	WK	Billboard ❀ OCTOBER 3, 1953 ❀ Best Sellers
1	1	16	Vaya Con Dios (May God Be With You) ....Les Paul & Mary Ford...Capitol F2486
2	2	15	You You You ....Ames Brothers...RCA Victor 47-5325
3	4	6	Dragnet ....Ray Anthony...Capitol F2562
4	3	13	Oh! ....Pee Wee Hunt...Capitol F2442
5	7	5	Ebb Tide ....Frank Chacksfield...London 45-1358
6	9	4	Eh, Cumpari ....Julius LaRosa...Cadence 1232
7	5	16	No Other Love ....Perry Como...RCA Victor 47-5317
8	—	1	St. George And The Dragonet ....Stan Freberg...Capitol F2596
9	6	10	Crying In The Chapel ....June Valli...RCA Victor 47-5368
10	8	15	P.S. I Love You..The Hilltoppers...Dot 45-15085

TW	LW	WK	Billboard® ❀ OCTOBER 10, 1953 ❀ Best Sellers
1	8	2	St. George And The Dragonet ....Stan Freberg...Capitol F2596
2	1	17	Vaya Con Dios (May God Be With You) ....Les Paul & Mary Ford...Capitol F2486
3	2	16	You You You ....Ames Brothers...RCA Victor 47-5325
4	4	14	Oh! ....Pee Wee Hunt...Capitol F2442
5	5	6	Ebb Tide..Frank Chacksfield...London 45-1358
6	3	7	Dragnet ....Ray Anthony...Capitol F2562
7	6	5	Eh, Cumpari ....Julius LaRosa...Cadence 1232
8	9	11	Crying In The Chapel ....June Valli...RCA Victor 47-5368
9	7	17	No Other Love ....Perry Como...RCA Victor 47-5317
10	10	16	P.S. I Love You..The Hilltoppers...Dot 45-15085

TW	LW	WK	Billboard® ❀ OCTOBER 17, 1953 ❀ Best Sellers
1	1	3	St. George And The Dragonet ....Stan Freberg...Capitol F2596
2	2	18	Vaya Con Dios (May God Be With You) ....Les Paul & Mary Ford...Capitol F2486
3	3	17	You You You ....Ames Brothers...RCA Victor 47-5325
4	4	15	Oh! ....Pee Wee Hunt...Capitol F2442
5	5	7	Ebb Tide..Frank Chacksfield...London 45-1358
6	7	6	Eh, Cumpari ....Julius LaRosa...Cadence 1232
7	6	8	Dragnet ....Ray Anthony...Capitol F2562
8	9	18	No Other Love ....Perry Como...RCA Victor 47-5317
8	11	5	Rags To Riches..Tony Bennett...Columbia 4-40048
10	8	12	Crying In The Chapel ....June Valli...RCA Victor 47-5368

TW	LW	WK	Billboard® ❀ OCTOBER 24, 1953 ❀ Best Sellers
1	1	4	St. George And The Dragonet ....Stan Freberg...Capitol F2596
2	2	19	Vaya Con Dios (May God Be With You) ....Les Paul & Mary Ford...Capitol F2486
3	3	18	You You You ....Ames Brothers...RCA Victor 47-5325
4	5	8	Ebb Tide..Frank Chacksfield...London 45-1358
5	6	7	Eh, Cumpari ....Julius LaRosa...Cadence 1232
6	4	16	Oh! ....Pee Wee Hunt...Capitol F2442
7	8	6	Rags To Riches..Tony Bennett...Columbia 4-40048
8	7	9	Dragnet ....Ray Anthony...Capitol F2562
9	10	13	Crying In The Chapel ....June Valli...RCA Victor 47-5368
10	8	19	No Other Love ....Perry Como...RCA Victor 47-5317
10	18	2	Many Times ....Eddie Fisher...RCA Victor 47-5453

TW	LW	WK	Billboard® ❀ OCTOBER 31, 1953 ❀ Best Sellers
1	1	5	St. George And The Dragonet ....Stan Freberg...Capitol F2596
2	2	20	Vaya Con Dios (May God Be With You) ....Les Paul & Mary Ford...Capitol F2486
3	3	19	You You You ....Ames Brothers...RCA Victor 47-5325
4	4	9	Ebb Tide..Frank Chacksfield...London 45-1358
5	5	8	Eh, Cumpari ....Julius LaRosa...Cadence 1232
6	7	7	Rags To Riches..Tony Bennett...Columbia 4-40048
7	6	17	Oh! ....Pee Wee Hunt...Capitol F2442
8	13	3	Ricochet (Rick-O-Shay) ....Teresa Brewer...Coral 9-61043
9	8	10	Dragnet ....Ray Anthony...Capitol F2562
10	10	3	Many Times ....Eddie Fisher...RCA Victor 47-5453

TW	LW	WK	Billboard® ❀ NOVEMBER 7, 1953 ❀ Best Sellers
1	2	21	Vaya Con Dios (May God Be With You) ....Les Paul & Mary Ford...Capitol F2486
2	1	6	St. George And The Dragonet ....Stan Freberg...Capitol F2596
3	3	20	You You You ....Ames Brothers...RCA Victor 47-5325
4	4	10	Ebb Tide..Frank Chacksfield...London 45-1358
5	6	8	Rags To Riches..Tony Bennett...Columbia 4-40048
6	5	9	Eh, Cumpari ....Julius LaRosa...Cadence 1232
7	7	18	Oh! ....Pee Wee Hunt...Capitol F2442
8	10	4	Many Times ....Eddie Fisher...RCA Victor 47-5453
9	8	4	Ricochet (Rick-O-Shay) ....Teresa Brewer...Coral 9-61043
10	11	15	Crying In The Chapel ....June Valli...RCA Victor 47-5368

TW	LW	WK	Billboard® ❀ NOVEMBER 14, 1953 ❀	Best Sellers
1	1	22	Vaya Con Dios (May God Be With You)	Les Paul & Mary Ford...Capitol F2486
2	6	10	Eh, Cumpari	Julius LaRosa...Cadence 1232
3	4	11	Ebb Tide	Frank Chacksfield...London 45-1358
4	5	9	Rags To Riches	Tony Bennett...Columbia 4-40048
5	3	21	You You You	Ames Brothers...RCA Victor 47-5325
6	2	7	St. George And The Dragonet	Stan Freberg...Capitol F2596
7	7	19	Oh!	Pee Wee Hunt...Capitol F2442
8	9	5	Ricochet (Rick-O-Shay)	Teresa Brewer...Coral 9-61043
9	8	5	Many Times	Eddie Fisher...RCA Victor 47-5453
10	12	2	You Alone (Solo Tu)	Perry Como...RCA Victor 47-5447

TW	LW	WK	Billboard® ❀ NOVEMBER 21, 1953 ❀	Best Sellers
1	4	10	Rags To Riches	Tony Bennett...Columbia 4-40048
2	3	12	Ebb Tide	Frank Chacksfield...London 45-1358
3	1	23	Vaya Con Dios (May God Be With You)	Les Paul & Mary Ford...Capitol F2486
4	2	11	Eh, Cumpari	Julius LaRosa...Cadence 1232
5	5	22	You You You	Ames Brothers...RCA Victor 47-5325
6	6	8	St. George And The Dragonet	Stan Freberg...Capitol F2596
7	8	6	Ricochet (Rick-O-Shay)	Teresa Brewer...Coral 9-61043
8	9	6	Many Times	Eddie Fisher...RCA Victor 47-5453
9	7	20	Oh!	Pee Wee Hunt...Capitol F2442
10	14	2	That's Amore	Dean Martin...Capitol F2589

TW	LW	WK	Billboard® ❀ NOVEMBER 28, 1953 ❀	Best Sellers
1	1	11	Rags To Riches	Tony Bennett...Columbia 4-40048
2	2	13	Ebb Tide	Frank Chacksfield...London 45-1358
3	3	24	Vaya Con Dios (May God Be With You)	Les Paul & Mary Ford...Capitol F2486
4	4	12	Eh, Cumpari	Julius LaRosa...Cadence 1232
5	5	23	You You You	Ames Brothers...RCA Victor 47-5325
6	7	7	Ricochet (Rick-O-Shay)	Teresa Brewer...Coral 9-61043
7	8	7	Many Times	Eddie Fisher...RCA Victor 47-5453
8	9	21	Oh!	Pee Wee Hunt...Capitol F2442
9	10	3	That's Amore	Dean Martin...Capitol F2589
10	6	9	St. George And The Dragonet	Stan Freberg...Capitol F2596

TW	LW	WK	Billboard® ❀ DECEMBER 5, 1953 ❀	Best Sellers
1	1	12	Rags To Riches	Tony Bennett...Columbia 4-40048
2	2	14	Ebb Tide	Frank Chacksfield...London 45-1358
3	3	25	Vaya Con Dios (May God Be With You)	Les Paul & Mary Ford...Capitol F2486
4	5	24	You You You	Ames Brothers...RCA Victor 47-5325
5	4	13	Eh, Cumpari	Julius LaRosa...Cadence 1232
6	6	8	Ricochet (Rick-O-Shay)	Teresa Brewer...Coral 9-61043
7	9	4	That's Amore	Dean Martin...Capitol F2589
8	7	8	Many Times	Eddie Fisher...RCA Victor 47-5453
9	13	2	Changing Partners	Patti Page...Mercury 70260-X45
10	8	22	Oh!	Pee Wee Hunt...Capitol F2442
10	11	7	Istanbul (Not Constantinople)	The Four Lads...Columbia 4-40082

TW	LW	WK	Billboard® ❀ DECEMBER 12, 1953 ❀	Best Sellers
1	1	13	Rags To Riches	Tony Bennett...Columbia 4-40048
2	2	15	Ebb Tide	Frank Chacksfield...London 45-1358
3	7	5	That's Amore	Dean Martin...Capitol F2589
4	6	9	Ricochet (Rick-O-Shay)	Teresa Brewer...Coral 9-61043
5	3	26	Vaya Con Dios (May God Be With You)	Les Paul & Mary Ford...Capitol F2486
6	5	14	Eh, Cumpari	Julius LaRosa...Cadence 1232
7	4	25	You You You	Ames Brothers...RCA Victor 47-5325
8	9	3	Changing Partners	Patti Page...Mercury 70260-X45
9	20	2	Oh, Mein Papa	Eddie Calvert...Essex 336
10	16	2	Santa Baby	Eartha Kitt...RCA Victor 47-5502

TW	LW	WK	Billboard® ❀ DECEMBER 19, 1953 ❀ Best Sellers
1	1	14	**Rags To Riches**..*Tony Bennett*...Columbia 4-40048
2	3	6	**That's Amore** ....*Dean Martin*...Capitol F2589
3	19	2	**Oh! My Pa-Pa (O Mein Papa)** ....*Eddie Fisher*...RCA Victor 47-5552
4	2	16	**Ebb Tide**..*Frank Chacksfield*...London 45-1358
5	4	10	**Ricochet (Rick-O-Shay)**...*Teresa Brewer*...Coral 9-61043
6	8	4	**Changing Partners**...*Patti Page*...Mercury 70260-X45
7	10	3	**Santa Baby**..*Eartha Kitt*...RCA Victor 47-5502
8	14	2	**Stranger In Paradise**...*Tony Bennett*...Columbia 4-40121
9	7	26	**You You You** ....*Ames Brothers*...RCA Victor 47-5325
10	9	3	**Oh, Mein Papa** ....*Eddie Calvert*...Essex 336

TW	LW	WK	Billboard® ❀ DECEMBER 26, 1953 ❀ Best Sellers
1	1	15	**Rags To Riches**..*Tony Bennett*...Columbia 4-40048
2	3	3	**Oh! My Pa-Pa (O Mein Papa)** ....*Eddie Fisher*...RCA Victor 47-5552
3	2	7	**That's Amore** ....*Dean Martin*...Capitol F2589
4	5	11	**Ricochet (Rick-O-Shay)**...*Teresa Brewer*...Coral 9-61043
5	6	5	**Changing Partners**...*Patti Page*...Mercury 70260-X45
6	8	3	**Stranger In Paradise**...*Tony Bennett*...Columbia 4-40121
7	4	17	**Ebb Tide**..*Frank Chacksfield*...London 45-1358
8	7	4	**Santa Baby**..*Eartha Kitt*...RCA Victor 47-5502
9	10	4	**Oh, Mein Papa** ....*Eddie Calvert*...Essex 336
10	12	16	**Eh, Cumpari** ....*Julius LaRosa*...Cadence 1232

TW	LW	WK	Billboard® JANUARY 2, 1954 Best Sellers
1	2	4	Oh! My Pa-Pa (O Mein Papa)...*Eddie Fisher*...RCA Victor 47-5552
2	1	16	Rags To Riches...*Tony Bennett*...Columbia 4-40048
3	3	8	That's Amore ....*Dean Martin*...Capitol F2589
4	8	5	Santa Baby...*Eartha Kitt*...RCA Victor 47-5502
5	4	12	Ricochet (Rick-O-Shay)..*Teresa Brewer*...Coral 9-61043
6	5	6	Changing Partners..*Patti Page*...Mercury 70260-X45
7	6	4	Stranger In Paradise..*Tony Bennett*...Columbia 4-40121
8	7	18	Ebb Tide..*Frank Chacksfield*...London 45-1358
9	9	5	Oh, Mein Papa ....*Eddie Calvert*...Essex 336
10	11	5	Stranger In Paradise ....*Four Aces*...Decca 9-28927

TW	LW	WK	Billboard® JANUARY 9, 1954 Best Sellers
1	1	5	Oh! My Pa-Pa (O Mein Papa)...*Eddie Fisher*...RCA Victor 47-5552
2	2	17	Rags To Riches...*Tony Bennett*...Columbia 4-40048
3	3	9	That's Amore ....*Dean Martin*...Capitol F2589
4	5	13	Ricochet (Rick-O-Shay)..*Teresa Brewer*...Coral 9-61043
5	6	7	Changing Partners..*Patti Page*...Mercury 70260-X45
6	7	5	Stranger In Paradise..*Tony Bennett*...Columbia 4-40121
7	10	6	Stranger In Paradise ....*Four Aces*...Decca 9-28927
8	8	19	Ebb Tide..*Frank Chacksfield*...London 45-1358
9	9	6	Oh, Mein Papa ....*Eddie Calvert*...Essex 336
10	11	18	Eh, Cumpari ....*Julius LaRosa*...Cadence 1232

TW	LW	WK	Billboard® JANUARY 16, 1954 Best Sellers
1	1	6	Oh! My Pa-Pa (O Mein Papa)...*Eddie Fisher*...RCA Victor 47-5552
2	2	18	Rags To Riches...*Tony Bennett*...Columbia 4-40048
3	3	10	That's Amore ....*Dean Martin*...Capitol F2589
4	5	8	Changing Partners..*Patti Page*...Mercury 70260-X45
5	4	14	Ricochet (Rick-O-Shay)..*Teresa Brewer*...Coral 9-61043
6	6	6	Stranger In Paradise..*Tony Bennett*...Columbia 4-40121
7	7	7	Stranger In Paradise ....*Four Aces*...Decca 9-28927
8	8	20	Ebb Tide..*Frank Chacksfield*...London 45-1358
9	9	7	Oh, Mein Papa ....*Eddie Calvert*...Essex 336
10	13	3	Stranger In Paradise ....*Tony Martin*...RCA Victor 47-5535

TW	LW	WK	Billboard® JANUARY 23, 1954 Best Sellers
1	1	7	Oh! My Pa-Pa (O Mein Papa)...*Eddie Fisher*...RCA Victor 47-5552
2	3	11	That's Amore ....*Dean Martin*...Capitol F2589
3	2	19	Rags To Riches...*Tony Bennett*...Columbia 4-40048
4	4	9	Changing Partners..*Patti Page*...Mercury 70260-X45
5	7	8	Stranger In Paradise ....*Four Aces*...Decca 9-28927
6	6	7	Stranger In Paradise..*Tony Bennett*...Columbia 4-40121
7	5	15	Ricochet (Rick-O-Shay)..*Teresa Brewer*...Coral 9-61043
8	12	3	Secret Love...*Doris Day*...Columbia 4-40108
9	13	3	What It Was, Was Football (Parts I & II)................................*Andy Griffith*...Capitol F2693
10	11	8	The Gang That Sang "Heart Of My Heart" ....*Four Aces*...Decca 9-28927

TW	LW	WK	Billboard® JANUARY 30, 1954 Best Sellers
1	1	8	Oh! My Pa-Pa (O Mein Papa)...*Eddie Fisher*...RCA Victor 47-5552
2	2	12	That's Amore ....*Dean Martin*...Capitol F2589
3	6	8	Stranger In Paradise..*Tony Bennett*...Columbia 4-40121
4	4	10	Changing Partners..*Patti Page*...Mercury 70260-X45
5	3	20	Rags To Riches...*Tony Bennett*...Columbia 4-40048
6	5	9	Stranger In Paradise ....*Four Aces*...Decca 9-28927
7	7	16	Ricochet (Rick-O-Shay)..*Teresa Brewer*...Coral 9-61043
8	8	4	Secret Love...*Doris Day*...Columbia 4-40108
9	10	9	The Gang That Sang "Heart Of My Heart" ....*Four Aces*...Decca 9-28927
10	11	5	Stranger In Paradise ....*Tony Martin*...RCA Victor 47-5535

TW	LW	WK	Billboard ® 💿 FEBRUARY 6, 1954 💿 Best Sellers
1	1	9	Oh! My Pa-Pa (O Mein Papa)..*Eddie Fisher*...RCA Victor 47-5552
2	2	13	That's Amore..*Dean Martin*...Capitol F2589
3	3	9	Stranger In Paradise..*Tony Bennett*...Columbia 4-40121
4	8	5	Secret Love..*Doris Day*...Columbia 4-40108
5	6	10	Stranger In Paradise..*Four Aces*...Decca 9-28927
6	5	21	Rags To Riches..*Tony Bennett*...Columbia 4-40048
7	4	11	Changing Partners..*Patti Page*...Mercury 70260-X45
8	7	17	Ricochet (Rick-O-Shay)..*Teresa Brewer*...Coral 9-61043
9	9	10	The Gang That Sang "Heart Of My Heart" ....*Four Aces*...Decca 9-28927
10	—	1	From The Vine Came The Grape ....*The Gaylords*...Mercury 70296-X45

TW	LW	WK	Billboard ® 💿 FEBRUARY 13, 1954 💿 Best Sellers
1	1	10	Oh! My Pa-Pa (O Mein Papa)..*Eddie Fisher*...RCA Victor 47-5552
2	2	14	That's Amore..*Dean Martin*...Capitol F2589
3	4	6	Secret Love..*Doris Day*...Columbia 4-40108
4	3	10	Stranger In Paradise..*Tony Bennett*...Columbia 4-40121
5	7	12	Changing Partners..*Patti Page*...Mercury 70260-X45
6	5	11	Stranger In Paradise..*Four Aces*...Decca 9-28927
7	6	22	Rags To Riches..*Tony Bennett*...Columbia 4-40048
8	9	11	The Gang That Sang "Heart Of My Heart" ....*Four Aces*...Decca 9-28927
9	14	2	Make Love To Me!..*Jo Stafford*...Columbia 4-40143
10	10	2	From The Vine Came The Grape ....*The Gaylords*...Mercury 70296-X45

TW	LW	WK	Billboard ® 💿 FEBRUARY 20, 1954 💿 Best Sellers
1	1	11	Oh! My Pa-Pa (O Mein Papa)..*Eddie Fisher*...RCA Victor 47-5552
2	3	7	Secret Love..*Doris Day*...Columbia 4-40108
3	2	15	That's Amore..*Dean Martin*...Capitol F2589
4	4	11	Stranger In Paradise..*Tony Bennett*...Columbia 4-40121
5	5	13	Changing Partners..*Patti Page*...Mercury 70260-X45
6	9	3	Make Love To Me!..*Jo Stafford*...Columbia 4-40143
7	6	12	Stranger In Paradise..*Four Aces*...Decca 9-28927
8	10	3	From The Vine Came The Grape ....*The Gaylords*...Mercury 70296-X45
9	11	5	Till We Two Are One...*Georgie Shaw*...Decca 9-28937
10	12	4	Till Then..*Hilltoppers*...Dot 45-15132

TW	LW	WK	Billboard ® 💿 FEBRUARY 27, 1954 💿 Best Sellers
1	2	8	Secret Love..*Doris Day*...Columbia 4-40108
2	1	12	Oh! My Pa-Pa (O Mein Papa)..*Eddie Fisher*...RCA Victor 47-5552
3	3	16	That's Amore..*Dean Martin*...Capitol F2589
4	6	4	Make Love To Me!..*Jo Stafford*...Columbia 4-40143
5	4	12	Stranger In Paradise..*Tony Bennett*...Columbia 4-40121
6	5	14	Changing Partners..*Patti Page*...Mercury 70260-X45
7	12	4	I Get So Lonely (When I Dream About You) [Oh, Baby Mine] ....*The Four Knights*...Capitol F2654
8	15	2	Young-At-Heart..*Frank Sinatra*...Capitol F2703
9	9	6	Till We Two Are One...*Georgie Shaw*...Decca 9-28937
10	11	13	The Gang That Sang "Heart Of My Heart" ....*Four Aces*...Decca 9-28927

TW	LW	WK	Billboard ® 💿 MARCH 6, 1954 💿 Best Sellers
1	1	9	Secret Love..*Doris Day*...Columbia 4-40108
2	4	5	Make Love To Me!..*Jo Stafford*...Columbia 4-40143
3	2	13	Oh! My Pa-Pa (O Mein Papa)..*Eddie Fisher*...RCA Victor 47-5552
4	3	17	That's Amore..*Dean Martin*...Capitol F2589
5	5	13	Stranger In Paradise..*Tony Bennett*...Columbia 4-40121
6	7	5	I Get So Lonely (When I Dream About You) [Oh, Baby Mine] ....*The Four Knights*...Capitol F2654
7	6	15	Changing Partners..*Patti Page*...Mercury 70260-X45
8	9	7	Till We Two Are One...*Georgie Shaw*...Decca 9-28937
9	8	3	Young-At-Heart..*Frank Sinatra*...Capitol F2703
10	11	5	From The Vine Came The Grape ....*The Gaylords*...Mercury 70296-X45

TW	LW	WK	Billboard® ❀ MARCH 13, 1954 ❀ Best Sellers
1	2	6	Make Love To Me! ....*Jo Stafford*...Columbia 4-40143
2	1	10	Secret Love ....*Doris Day*...Columbia 4-40108
3	6	6	I Get So Lonely (When I Dream About You) [Oh, Baby Mine] ....*The Four Knights*...Capitol F2654
4	3	14	Oh! My Pa-Pa (O Mein Papa) ....*Eddie Fisher*...RCA Victor 47-5552
5	9	4	Young-At-Heart ....*Frank Sinatra*...Capitol F2703
6	12	3	Cross Over The Bridge..*Patti Page*...Mercury 70302-X45
7	4	18	That's Amore ....*Dean Martin*...Capitol F2589
8	5	14	Stranger In Paradise...*Tony Bennett*...Columbia 4-40121
9	20	2	Wanted..*Perry Como*...RCA Victor 47-5647
10	7	16	Changing Partners..*Patti Page*...Mercury 70260-X45

TW	LW	WK	Billboard® ❀ MARCH 20, 1954 ❀ Best Sellers
1	2	11	Secret Love ....*Doris Day*...Columbia 4-40108
2	1	7	Make Love To Me! ....*Jo Stafford*...Columbia 4-40143
3	3	7	I Get So Lonely (When I Dream About You) [Oh, Baby Mine] ....*The Four Knights*...Capitol F2654
4	9	3	Wanted..*Perry Como*...RCA Victor 47-5647
5	5	5	Young-At-Heart ....*Frank Sinatra*...Capitol F2703
6	4	15	Oh! My Pa-Pa (O Mein Papa) ....*Eddie Fisher*...RCA Victor 47-5552
7	6	4	Cross Over The Bridge..*Patti Page*...Mercury 70302-X45
8	8	15	Stranger In Paradise...*Tony Bennett*...Columbia 4-40121
9	7	19	That's Amore ....*Dean Martin*...Capitol F2589
10	17	3	Answer Me, My Love ....*Nat "King" Cole*...Capitol F2687

TW	LW	WK	Billboard® ❀ MARCH 27, 1954 ❀ Best Sellers
1	2	8	Make Love To Me! ....*Jo Stafford*...Columbia 4-40143
2	1	12	Secret Love ....*Doris Day*...Columbia 4-40108
3	3	8	I Get So Lonely (When I Dream About You) [Oh, Baby Mine] ....*The Four Knights*...Capitol F2654
4	4	4	Wanted..*Perry Como*...RCA Victor 47-5647
5	5	6	Young-At-Heart ....*Frank Sinatra*...Capitol F2703
6	7	5	Cross Over The Bridge..*Patti Page*...Mercury 70302-X45
7	6	16	Oh! My Pa-Pa (O Mein Papa) ....*Eddie Fisher*...RCA Victor 47-5552
8	10	4	Answer Me, My Love ....*Nat "King" Cole*...Capitol F2687
9	9	20	That's Amore ....*Dean Martin*...Capitol F2589
10	11	8	From The Vine Came The Grape ....*The Gaylords*...Mercury 70296-X45

TW	LW	WK	Billboard® ❀ APRIL 3, 1954 ❀ Best Sellers
1	1	9	Make Love To Me! ....*Jo Stafford*...Columbia 4-40143
2	4	5	Wanted..*Perry Como*...RCA Victor 47-5647
3	6	6	Cross Over The Bridge..*Patti Page*...Mercury 70302-X45
4	2	13	Secret Love ....*Doris Day*...Columbia 4-40108
5	3	9	I Get So Lonely (When I Dream About You) [Oh, Baby Mine] ....*The Four Knights*...Capitol F2654
6	5	7	Young-At-Heart ....*Frank Sinatra*...Capitol F2703
7	8	5	Answer Me, My Love ....*Nat "King" Cole*...Capitol F2687
8	16	2	A Girl, A Girl (Zoom-Ba Di Alli Nella) ....*Eddie Fisher*...RCA Victor 47-5675
9	7	17	Oh! My Pa-Pa (O Mein Papa) ....*Eddie Fisher*...RCA Victor 47-5552
10	10	9	From The Vine Came The Grape ....*The Gaylords*...Mercury 70296-X45

TW	LW	WK	Billboard® ❀ APRIL 10, 1954 ❀ Best Sellers
1	2	6	Wanted..*Perry Como*...RCA Victor 47-5647
2	1	10	Make Love To Me! ....*Jo Stafford*...Columbia 4-40143
3	5	10	I Get So Lonely (When I Dream About You) [Oh, Baby Mine] ....*The Four Knights*...Capitol F2654
4	3	7	Cross Over The Bridge..*Patti Page*...Mercury 70302-X45
5	4	14	Secret Love ....*Doris Day*...Columbia 4-40108
6	6	8	Young-At-Heart ....*Frank Sinatra*...Capitol F2703
7	7	6	Answer Me, My Love ....*Nat "King" Cole*...Capitol F2687
8	8	3	A Girl, A Girl (Zoom-Ba Di Alli Nella) ....*Eddie Fisher*...RCA Victor 47-5675
9	12	3	Here ....*Tony Martin*...RCA Victor 47-5665
10	9	18	Oh! My Pa-Pa (O Mein Papa) ....*Eddie Fisher*...RCA Victor 47-5552

Billboard — APRIL 17, 1954 — Best Sellers

TW	LW	WK	Title	Artist...Label
1	1	7	Wanted	Perry Como...RCA Victor 47-5647
2	2	11	Make Love To Me!	Jo Stafford...Columbia 4-40143
3	4	8	Cross Over The Bridge	Patti Page...Mercury 70302-X45
4	3	11	I Get So Lonely (When I Dream About You) [Oh, Baby Mine]	The Four Knights...Capitol F2654
5	6	9	Young-At-Heart	Frank Sinatra...Capitol F2703
6	5	15	Secret Love	Doris Day...Columbia 4-40108
7	7	7	Answer Me, My Love	Nat "King" Cole...Capitol F2687
8	8	4	A Girl, A Girl (Zoom-Ba Di Alli Nella)	Eddie Fisher...RCA Victor 47-5675
9	9	4	Here	Tony Martin...RCA Victor 47-5665
10	13	3	The Man With The Banjo	Ames Brothers...RCA Victor 47-5644

Billboard — APRIL 24, 1954 — Best Sellers

TW	LW	WK	Title	Artist...Label
1	1	8	Wanted	Perry Como...RCA Victor 47-5647
2	2	12	Make Love To Me!	Jo Stafford...Columbia 4-40143
3	4	12	I Get So Lonely (When I Dream About You) [Oh, Baby Mine]	The Four Knights...Capitol F2654
4	3	9	Cross Over The Bridge	Patti Page...Mercury 70302-X45
5	5	10	Young-At-Heart	Frank Sinatra...Capitol F2703
6	6	16	Secret Love	Doris Day...Columbia 4-40108
7	8	5	A Girl, A Girl (Zoom-Ba Di Alli Nella)	Eddie Fisher...RCA Victor 47-5675
8	7	8	Answer Me, My Love	Nat "King" Cole...Capitol F2687
9	9	5	Here	Tony Martin...RCA Victor 47-5665
10	10	4	The Man With The Banjo	Ames Brothers...RCA Victor 47-5644

Billboard — MAY 1, 1954 — Best Sellers

TW	LW	WK	Title	Artist...Label
1	1	9	Wanted	Perry Como...RCA Victor 47-5647
2	2	13	Make Love To Me!	Jo Stafford...Columbia 4-40143
3	4	10	Cross Over The Bridge	Patti Page...Mercury 70302-X45
4	5	11	Young-At-Heart	Frank Sinatra...Capitol F2703
5	3	13	I Get So Lonely (When I Dream About You) [Oh, Baby Mine]	The Four Knights...Capitol F2654
6	8	9	Answer Me, My Love	Nat "King" Cole...Capitol F2687
7	7	6	A Girl, A Girl (Zoom-Ba Di Alli Nella)	Eddie Fisher...RCA Victor 47-5675
8	6	17	Secret Love	Doris Day...Columbia 4-40108
9	10	5	The Man With The Banjo	Ames Brothers...RCA Victor 47-5644
10	9	6	Here	Tony Martin...RCA Victor 47-5665

Billboard — MAY 8, 1954 — Best Sellers

TW	LW	WK	Title	Artist...Label
1	1	10	Wanted	Perry Como...RCA Victor 47-5647
2	2	14	Make Love To Me!	Jo Stafford...Columbia 4-40143
3	3	11	Cross Over The Bridge	Patti Page...Mercury 70302-X45
4	5	14	I Get So Lonely (When I Dream About You) [Oh, Baby Mine]	The Four Knights...Capitol F2654
5	4	12	Young-At-Heart	Frank Sinatra...Capitol F2703
6	6	10	Answer Me, My Love	Nat "King" Cole...Capitol F2687
7	10	7	Here	Tony Martin...RCA Victor 47-5665
8	7	7	A Girl, A Girl (Zoom-Ba Di Alli Nella)	Eddie Fisher...RCA Victor 47-5675
9	9	6	The Man With The Banjo	Ames Brothers...RCA Victor 47-5644
10	11	4	Little Things Mean A Lot	Kitty Kallen...Decca 9-29037

Billboard — MAY 15, 1954 — Best Sellers

TW	LW	WK	Title	Artist...Label
1	1	11	Wanted	Perry Como...RCA Victor 47-5647
2	5	13	Young-At-Heart	Frank Sinatra...Capitol F2703
3	3	12	Cross Over The Bridge	Patti Page...Mercury 70302-X45
4	2	15	Make Love To Me!	Jo Stafford...Columbia 4-40143
5	4	15	I Get So Lonely (When I Dream About You) [Oh, Baby Mine]	The Four Knights...Capitol F2654
6	10	5	Little Things Mean A Lot	Kitty Kallen...Decca 9-29037
7	9	7	The Man With The Banjo	Ames Brothers...RCA Victor 47-5644
8	6	11	Answer Me, My Love	Nat "King" Cole...Capitol F2687
9	11	4	If You Love Me (Really Love Me)	Kay Starr...Capitol F2769
10	12	5	The Man Upstairs	Kay Starr...Capitol F2769

TW	LW	WK	Billboard® MAY 22, 1954 Best Sellers
1	1	12	Wanted..*Perry Como*...RCA Victor 47-5647
2	6	6	Little Things Mean A Lot...*Kitty Kallen*...Decca 9-29037
3	2	14	Young-At-Heart..*Frank Sinatra*...Capitol F2703
4	5	16	I Get So Lonely (When I Dream About You) [Oh, Baby Mine] ....*The Four Knights*...Capitol F2654
5	4	16	Make Love To Me!...*Jo Stafford*...Columbia 4-40143
6	9	5	If You Love Me (Really Love Me) ....*Kay Starr*...Capitol F2769
7	3	13	Cross Over The Bridge..*Patti Page*...Mercury 70302-X45
8	10	6	The Man Upstairs..*Kay Starr*...Capitol F2769
9	13	4	The Happy Wanderer...*Frank Weir*...London 45-1448
10	7	8	The Man With The Banjo ....*Ames Brothers*...RCA Victor 47-5644

TW	LW	WK	Billboard® MAY 29, 1954 Best Sellers
1	1	13	Wanted..*Perry Como*...RCA Victor 47-5647
2	2	7	Little Things Mean A Lot...*Kitty Kallen*...Decca 9-29037
3	3	15	Young-At-Heart..*Frank Sinatra*...Capitol F2703
4	4	17	I Get So Lonely (When I Dream About You) [Oh, Baby Mine] ....*The Four Knights*...Capitol F2654
5	7	14	Cross Over The Bridge..*Patti Page*...Mercury 70302-X45
6	6	6	If You Love Me (Really Love Me) ....*Kay Starr*...Capitol F2769
7	8	7	The Man Upstairs..*Kay Starr*...Capitol F2769
8	9	5	The Happy Wanderer...*Frank Weir*...London 45-1448
9	5	17	Make Love To Me!...*Jo Stafford*...Columbia 4-40143
10	14	2	Three Coins In The Fountain ....*Four Aces*...Decca 9-29123

TW	LW	WK	Billboard® JUNE 5, 1954 Best Sellers
1	2	8	Little Things Mean A Lot...*Kitty Kallen*...Decca 9-29037
2	1	14	Wanted..*Perry Como*...RCA Victor 47-5647
3	10	3	Three Coins In The Fountain ....*Four Aces*...Decca 9-29123
4	6	7	If You Love Me (Really Love Me) ....*Kay Starr*...Capitol F2769
5	8	6	The Happy Wanderer...*Frank Weir*...London 45-1448
6	3	16	Young-At-Heart..*Frank Sinatra*...Capitol F2703
7	4	18	I Get So Lonely (When I Dream About You) [Oh, Baby Mine] ....*The Four Knights*...Capitol F2654
8	5	15	Cross Over The Bridge..*Patti Page*...Mercury 70302-X45
9	14	2	Hernando's Hideaway ....*Archie Bleyer*...Cadence 1241
10	7	8	The Man Upstairs..*Kay Starr*...Capitol F2769

TW	LW	WK	Billboard® JUNE 12, 1954 Best Sellers
1	1	9	Little Things Mean A Lot...*Kitty Kallen*...Decca 9-29037
2	3	4	Three Coins In The Fountain ....*Four Aces*...Decca 9-29123
3	2	15	Wanted..*Perry Como*...RCA Victor 47-5647
4	5	7	The Happy Wanderer...*Frank Weir*...London 45-1448
5	9	3	Hernando's Hideaway ....*Archie Bleyer*...Cadence 1241
6	4	8	If You Love Me (Really Love Me) ....*Kay Starr*...Capitol F2769
7	6	17	Young-At-Heart..*Frank Sinatra*...Capitol F2703
8	11	15	Answer Me, My Love..*Nat "King" Cole*...Capitol F2687
9	7	19	I Get So Lonely (When I Dream About You) [Oh, Baby Mine] ....*The Four Knights*...Capitol F2654
10	10	9	The Man Upstairs..*Kay Starr*...Capitol F2769

TW	LW	WK	Billboard® JUNE 19, 1954 Best Sellers
1	1	10	Little Things Mean A Lot...*Kitty Kallen*...Decca 9-29037
2	2	5	Three Coins In The Fountain ....*Four Aces*...Decca 9-29123
3	5	4	Hernando's Hideaway ....*Archie Bleyer*...Cadence 1241
4	4	8	The Happy Wanderer...*Frank Weir*...London 45-1448
5	3	16	Wanted..*Perry Como*...RCA Victor 47-5647
6	6	9	If You Love Me (Really Love Me) ....*Kay Starr*...Capitol F2769
7	7	18	Young-At-Heart..*Frank Sinatra*...Capitol F2703
8	10	10	The Man Upstairs..*Kay Starr*...Capitol F2769
9	16	3	Three Coins In The Fountain ....*Frank Sinatra*...Capitol F2816
10	9	20	I Get So Lonely (When I Dream About You) [Oh, Baby Mine] ....*The Four Knights*...Capitol F2654

TW	LW	WK	Billboard® JUNE 26, 1954 Best Sellers
1	1	11	Little Things Mean A Lot..*Kitty Kallen*...Decca 9-29037
2	2	6	Three Coins In The Fountain ....*Four Aces*...Decca 9-29123
3	3	5	Hernando's Hideaway ....*Archie Bleyer*...Cadence 1241
4	4	9	The Happy Wanderer ....*Frank Weir*...London 45-1448
5	5	17	Wanted...*Perry Como*...RCA Victor 47-5647
6	6	10	If You Love Me (Really Love Me) ....*Kay Starr*...Capitol F2769
7	9	4	Three Coins In The Fountain...*Frank Sinatra*...Capitol F2816
8	15	7	The Happy Wanderer (Val-De Ri, Val-De Ra) ....*Henri René*...RCA Victor 47-5715
9	13	14	Here...*Tony Martin*...RCA Victor 47-5665
9	17	8	Crazy 'Bout Ya Baby ....*The Crew-Cuts*...Mercury 70341-X45

TW	LW	WK	Billboard® JULY 3, 1954 Best Sellers
1	1	12	Little Things Mean A Lot..*Kitty Kallen*...Decca 9-29037
2	2	7	Three Coins In The Fountain ....*Four Aces*...Decca 9-29123
3	3	6	Hernando's Hideaway ....*Archie Bleyer*...Cadence 1241
4	4	10	The Happy Wanderer ....*Frank Weir*...London 45-1448
5	5	18	Wanted...*Perry Como*...RCA Victor 47-5647
6	6	11	If You Love Me (Really Love Me) ....*Kay Starr*...Capitol F2769
7	7	5	Three Coins In The Fountain...*Frank Sinatra*...Capitol F2816
8	9	9	Crazy 'Bout Ya Baby ....*The Crew-Cuts*...Mercury 70341-X45
9	14	12	The Man Upstairs..*Kay Starr*...Capitol F2769
10	8	8	The Happy Wanderer (Val-De Ri, Val-De Ra) ....*Henri René*...RCA Victor 47-5715

TW	LW	WK	Billboard® JULY 10, 1954 Best Sellers
1	1	13	Little Things Mean A Lot..*Kitty Kallen*...Decca 9-29037
2	2	8	Three Coins In The Fountain ....*Four Aces*...Decca 9-29123
3	3	7	Hernando's Hideaway ....*Archie Bleyer*...Cadence 1241
4	4	11	The Happy Wanderer ....*Frank Weir*...London 45-1448
5	6	12	If You Love Me (Really Love Me) ....*Kay Starr*...Capitol F2769
6	5	19	Wanted...*Perry Como*...RCA Victor 47-5647
7	7	6	Three Coins In The Fountain...*Frank Sinatra*...Capitol F2816
8	—	1	Sh-Boom..*The Crew-Cuts*...Mercury 70404-X45
9	12	2	The Little Shoemaker...*Gaylords*...Mercury 70403-X45
10	13	7	I Understand Just How You Feel..*The Four Tunes*...Jubilee 45-5132

TW	LW	WK	Billboard® JULY 17, 1954 Best Sellers
1	1	14	Little Things Mean A Lot..*Kitty Kallen*...Decca 9-29037
2	3	8	Hernando's Hideaway ....*Archie Bleyer*...Cadence 1241
3	2	9	Three Coins In The Fountain ....*Four Aces*...Decca 9-29123
4	4	12	The Happy Wanderer ....*Frank Weir*...London 45-1448
5	8	2	Sh-Boom..*The Crew-Cuts*...Mercury 70404-X45
6	9	3	The Little Shoemaker...*Gaylords*...Mercury 70403-X45
7	5	13	If You Love Me (Really Love Me) ....*Kay Starr*...Capitol F2769
8	7	7	Three Coins In The Fountain...*Frank Sinatra*...Capitol F2816
9	13	3	Sh-Boom...*The Chords*...Cat 45-104
10	6	20	Wanted...*Perry Como*...RCA Victor 47-5647

TW	LW	WK	Billboard® JULY 24, 1954 Best Sellers
1	1	15	Little Things Mean A Lot..*Kitty Kallen*...Decca 9-29037
2	2	9	Hernando's Hideaway ....*Archie Bleyer*...Cadence 1241
3	3	10	Three Coins In The Fountain ....*Four Aces*...Decca 9-29123
4	5	3	Sh-Boom..*The Crew-Cuts*...Mercury 70404-X45
5	6	4	The Little Shoemaker...*Gaylords*...Mercury 70403-X45
6	4	13	The Happy Wanderer ....*Frank Weir*...London 45-1448
7	7	14	If You Love Me (Really Love Me) ....*Kay Starr*...Capitol F2769
8	11	9	I Understand Just How You Feel..*The Four Tunes*...Jubilee 45-5132
9	18	2	The Little Shoemaker..................................*Hugo Winterhalter & Eddie Fisher*...RCA Victor 47-5769
10	9	4	Sh-Boom...*The Chords*...Cat 45-104

JULY 31, 1954 — Billboard Best Sellers

TW	LW	WK	Title	Artist
1	1	16	Little Things Mean A Lot	Kitty Kallen...Decca 9-29037
2	4	4	Sh-Boom	The Crew-Cuts...Mercury 70404-X45
3	2	10	Hernando's Hideaway	Archie Bleyer...Cadence 1241
4	3	11	Three Coins In The Fountain	Four Aces...Decca 9-29123
5	5	5	The Little Shoemaker	Gaylords...Mercury 70403-X45
6	6	14	The Happy Wanderer	Frank Weir...London 45-1448
7	11	3	Hey There	Rosemary Clooney...Columbia 4-40266
8	12	3	In The Chapel In The Moonlight	Kitty Kallen...Decca 9-29130
9	8	10	I Understand Just How You Feel	The Four Tunes...Jubilee 45-5132
10	7	15	If You Love Me (Really Love Me)	Kay Starr...Capitol F2769

AUGUST 7, 1954 — Billboard Best Sellers

TW	LW	WK	Title	Artist
1	2	5	Sh-Boom	The Crew-Cuts...Mercury 70404-X45
2	1	17	Little Things Mean A Lot	Kitty Kallen...Decca 9-29037
3	5	6	The Little Shoemaker	Gaylords...Mercury 70403-X45
4	3	11	Hernando's Hideaway	Archie Bleyer...Cadence 1241
5	7	4	Hey There	Rosemary Clooney...Columbia 4-40266
6	4	12	Three Coins In The Fountain	Four Aces...Decca 9-29123
7	8	4	In The Chapel In The Moonlight	Kitty Kallen...Decca 9-29130
8	6	15	The Happy Wanderer	Frank Weir...London 45-1448
9	11	6	Goodnight, Sweetheart, Goodnight	The McGuire Sisters...Coral 9-61187
10	13	4	I'm A Fool To Care	Les Paul & Mary Ford...Capitol F2839

AUGUST 14, 1954 — Billboard Best Sellers

TW	LW	WK	Title	Artist
1	1	6	Sh-Boom	The Crew-Cuts...Mercury 70404-X45
2	2	18	Little Things Mean A Lot	Kitty Kallen...Decca 9-29037
3	3	7	The Little Shoemaker	Gaylords...Mercury 70403-X45
4	5	5	Hey There	Rosemary Clooney...Columbia 4-40266
5	4	12	Hernando's Hideaway	Archie Bleyer...Cadence 1241
6	7	5	In The Chapel In The Moonlight	Kitty Kallen...Decca 9-29130
7	6	13	Three Coins In The Fountain	Four Aces...Decca 9-29123
8	9	7	Goodnight, Sweetheart, Goodnight	The McGuire Sisters...Coral 9-61187
9	8	16	The Happy Wanderer	Frank Weir...London 45-1448
10	18	2	The High And The Mighty	Victor Young...Decca 9-29203

AUGUST 21, 1954 — Billboard Best Sellers

TW	LW	WK	Title	Artist
1	1	7	Sh-Boom	The Crew-Cuts...Mercury 70404-X45
2	3	8	The Little Shoemaker	Gaylords...Mercury 70403-X45
3	4	6	Hey There	Rosemary Clooney...Columbia 4-40266
4	2	19	Little Things Mean A Lot	Kitty Kallen...Decca 9-29037
5	6	6	In The Chapel In The Moonlight	Kitty Kallen...Decca 9-29130
6	5	13	Hernando's Hideaway	Archie Bleyer...Cadence 1241
7	7	14	Three Coins In The Fountain	Four Aces...Decca 9-29123
8	13	4	The High And The Mighty	Les Baxter...Capitol F2845
9	8	8	Goodnight, Sweetheart, Goodnight	The McGuire Sisters...Coral 9-61187
10	10	3	The High And The Mighty	Victor Young...Decca 9-29203

AUGUST 28, 1954 — Billboard Best Sellers

TW	LW	WK	Title	Artist
1	1	8	Sh-Boom	The Crew-Cuts...Mercury 70404-X45
2	3	7	Hey There	Rosemary Clooney...Columbia 4-40266
3	2	9	The Little Shoemaker	Gaylords...Mercury 70403-X45
4	4	20	Little Things Mean A Lot	Kitty Kallen...Decca 9-29037
5	5	7	In The Chapel In The Moonlight	Kitty Kallen...Decca 9-29130
6	8	5	The High And The Mighty	Les Baxter...Capitol F2845
7	6	14	Hernando's Hideaway	Archie Bleyer...Cadence 1241
8	9	9	Goodnight, Sweetheart, Goodnight	The McGuire Sisters...Coral 9-61187
9	13	5	The High And The Mighty	Leroy Holmes...MGM K11761
10	12	4	This Ole House	Rosemary Clooney...Columbia 4-40266

TW	LW	WK	Billboard ✸ SEPTEMBER 4, 1954 ✸ Best Sellers
1	1	9	Sh-Boom ....The Crew-Cuts...Mercury 70404-X45
2	2	8	Hey There ....Rosemary Clooney...Columbia 4-40266
3	3	10	The Little Shoemaker ....Gaylords...Mercury 70403-X45
4	4	21	Little Things Mean A Lot ....Kitty Kallen...Decca 9-29037
5	5	8	In The Chapel In The Moonlight ....Kitty Kallen...Decca 9-29130
6	11	5	The High And The Mighty ....Victor Young...Decca 9-29203
7	18	2	Skokiaan ....Ralph Marterie...Mercury 70432-X45
8	10	5	This Ole House ....Rosemary Clooney...Columbia 4-40266
9	6	6	The High And The Mighty ....Les Baxter...Capitol F2845
10	8	10	Goodnight, Sweetheart, Goodnight...............................The McGuire Sisters...Coral 9-61187

TW	LW	WK	Billboard ✸ SEPTEMBER 11, 1954 ✸ Best Sellers
1	1	10	Sh-Boom...The Crew-Cuts...Mercury 70404-X45
2	2	9	Hey There..Rosemary Clooney...Columbia 4-40266
3	3	11	The Little Shoemaker ....Gaylords...Mercury 70403-X45
4	7	3	Skokiaan ....Ralph Marterie...Mercury 70432-X45
5	5	9	In The Chapel In The Moonlight ....Kitty Kallen...Decca 9-29130
6	8	6	This Ole House ....Rosemary Clooney...Columbia 4-40266
7	6	6	The High And The Mighty ....Victor Young...Decca 9-29203
8	4	22	Little Things Mean A Lot ....Kitty Kallen...Decca 9-29037
9	9	7	The High And The Mighty ....Les Baxter...Capitol F2845
10	15	2	Skokiaan (South African Song) ....The Four Lads...Columbia 4-40306

TW	LW	WK	Billboard ✸ SEPTEMBER 18, 1954 ✸ Best Sellers
1	1	11	Sh-Boom...The Crew-Cuts...Mercury 70404-X45
2	2	10	Hey There..Rosemary Clooney...Columbia 4-40266
3	3	12	The Little Shoemaker ....Gaylords...Mercury 70403-X45
4	4	4	Skokiaan ....Ralph Marterie...Mercury 70432-X45
5	6	7	This Ole House ....Rosemary Clooney...Columbia 4-40266
6	5	10	In The Chapel In The Moonlight ....Kitty Kallen...Decca 9-29130
7	7	7	The High And The Mighty ....Victor Young...Decca 9-29203
8	10	3	Skokiaan (South African Song) ....The Four Lads...Columbia 4-40306
9	16	3	I Need You Now ....Eddie Fisher...RCA Victor 47-5830
10	11	8	The High And The Mighty ....Leroy Holmes...MGM K11761

TW	LW	WK	Billboard ✸ SEPTEMBER 25, 1954 ✸ Best Sellers
1	2	11	Hey There ....Rosemary Clooney...Columbia 4-40266
2	1	12	Sh-Boom ....The Crew-Cuts...Mercury 70404-X45
3	4	5	Skokiaan ....Ralph Marterie...Mercury 70432-X45
4	5	8	This Ole House ....Rosemary Clooney...Columbia 4-40266
5	3	13	The Little Shoemaker ....Gaylords...Mercury 70403-X45
6	9	4	I Need You Now ....Eddie Fisher...RCA Victor 47-5830
7	7	8	The High And The Mighty ....Victor Young...Decca 9-29203
8	8	4	Skokiaan (South African Song) ....The Four Lads...Columbia 4-40306
9	6	11	In The Chapel In The Moonlight ....Kitty Kallen...Decca 9-29130
10	13	3	Hold My Hand ....Don Cornell...Coral 9-61206

TW	LW	WK	Billboard ✸ OCTOBER 2, 1954 ✸ Best Sellers
1	1	12	Hey There ....Rosemary Clooney...Columbia 4-40266
2	2	13	Sh-Boom ....The Crew-Cuts...Mercury 70404-X45
3	3	6	Skokiaan ....Ralph Marterie...Mercury 70432-X45
4	4	9	This Ole House ....Rosemary Clooney...Columbia 4-40266
5	6	5	I Need You Now ....Eddie Fisher...RCA Victor 47-5830
6	10	4	Hold My Hand ....Don Cornell...Coral 9-61206
7	15	4	If I Give My Heart To You ....Doris Day...Columbia 4-40300
8	5	14	The Little Shoemaker ....Gaylords...Mercury 70403-X45
9	11	7	Shake, Rattle And Roll ....Bill Haley...Decca 29204
10	7	9	The High And The Mighty ....Victor Young...Decca 9-29203

TW	LW	WK	Billboard® OCTOBER 9, 1954 Best Sellers
1	1	13	Hey There..Rosemary Clooney...Columbia 4-40266
2	2	14	Sh-Boom...The Crew-Cuts...Mercury 70404-X45
3	5	6	I Need You Now ....Eddie Fisher...RCA Victor 47-5830
4	4	10	This Ole House...Rosemary Clooney...Columbia 4-40266
5	3	7	Skokiaan...Ralph Marterie...Mercury 70432-X45
6	7	5	If I Give My Heart To You ....Doris Day...Columbia 4-40300
7	11	6	Skokiaan (South African Song) ....The Four Lads...Columbia 4-40306
8	6	5	Hold My Hand ....Don Cornell...Coral 9-61206
9	9	8	Shake, Rattle And Roll ....Bill Haley...Decca 29204
10	8	15	The Little Shoemaker ....Gaylords...Mercury 70403-X45

TW	LW	WK	Billboard® OCTOBER 16, 1954 Best Sellers
1	1	14	Hey There..Rosemary Clooney...Columbia 4-40266
2	3	7	I Need You Now ....Eddie Fisher...RCA Victor 47-5830
3	4	11	This Ole House...Rosemary Clooney...Columbia 4-40266
4	6	6	If I Give My Heart To You ....Doris Day...Columbia 4-40300
5	2	15	Sh-Boom...The Crew-Cuts...Mercury 70404-X45
6	5	8	Skokiaan...Ralph Marterie...Mercury 70432-X45
7	8	6	Hold My Hand ....Don Cornell...Coral 9-61206
8	9	9	Shake, Rattle And Roll ....Bill Haley...Decca 29204
9	15	3	Papa Loves Mambo ....Perry Como...RCA Victor 47-5857
10	7	7	Skokiaan (South African Song) ....The Four Lads...Columbia 4-40306

TW	LW	WK	Billboard® OCTOBER 23, 1954 Best Sellers
1	1	15	Hey There..Rosemary Clooney...Columbia 4-40266
2	2	8	I Need You Now ....Eddie Fisher...RCA Victor 47-5830
3	3	12	This Ole House...Rosemary Clooney...Columbia 4-40266
4	4	7	If I Give My Heart To You ....Doris Day...Columbia 4-40300
5	7	7	Hold My Hand ....Don Cornell...Coral 9-61206
6	5	16	Sh-Boom...The Crew-Cuts...Mercury 70404-X45
7	6	9	Skokiaan...Ralph Marterie...Mercury 70432-X45
8	9	4	Papa Loves Mambo ....Perry Como...RCA Victor 47-5857
9	8	10	Shake, Rattle And Roll ....Bill Haley...Decca 29204
10	10	8	Skokiaan (South African Song) ....The Four Lads...Columbia 4-40306

TW	LW	WK	Billboard® OCTOBER 30, 1954 Best Sellers
1	1	16	Hey There..Rosemary Clooney...Columbia 4-40266
2	2	9	I Need You Now ....Eddie Fisher...RCA Victor 47-5830
3	3	13	This Ole House...Rosemary Clooney...Columbia 4-40266
4	4	8	If I Give My Heart To You ....Doris Day...Columbia 4-40300
5	5	8	Hold My Hand ....Don Cornell...Coral 9-61206
6	8	5	Papa Loves Mambo ....Perry Como...RCA Victor 47-5857
7	7	10	Skokiaan...Ralph Marterie...Mercury 70432-X45
8	6	17	Sh-Boom...The Crew-Cuts...Mercury 70404-X45
9	9	11	Shake, Rattle And Roll ....Bill Haley...Decca 29204
10	11	11	Cara Mia...David Whitfield with Mantovani...London 45-1486

TW	LW	WK	Billboard® NOVEMBER 6, 1954 Best Sellers
1	3	14	This Ole House...Rosemary Clooney...Columbia 4-40266
2	2	10	I Need You Now ....Eddie Fisher...RCA Victor 47-5830
3	1	17	Hey There..Rosemary Clooney...Columbia 4-40266
4	6	6	Papa Loves Mambo ....Perry Como...RCA Victor 47-5857
5	5	9	Hold My Hand ....Don Cornell...Coral 9-61206
6	4	9	If I Give My Heart To You ....Doris Day...Columbia 4-40300
7	9	12	Shake, Rattle And Roll ....Bill Haley...Decca 29204
8	12	5	Teach Me Tonight ....DeCastro Sisters...Abbott 3001
9	7	11	Skokiaan...Ralph Marterie...Mercury 70432-X45
10	8	18	Sh-Boom...The Crew-Cuts...Mercury 70404-X45

TW	LW	WK	Billboard® ❋ NOVEMBER 13, 1954 ❋ Best Sellers
1	2	11	I Need You Now ....Eddie Fisher...RCA Victor 47-5830
2	3	18	Hey There ....Rosemary Clooney...Columbia 4-40266
3	1	15	This Ole House ....Rosemary Clooney...Columbia 4-40266
4	4	7	Papa Loves Mambo ....Perry Como...RCA Victor 47-5857
5	6	10	If I Give My Heart To You ....Doris Day...Columbia 4-40300
6	5	10	Hold My Hand ....Don Cornell...Coral 9-61206
7	7	13	Shake, Rattle And Roll ....Bill Haley...Decca 29204
8	8	6	Teach Me Tonight ....DeCastro Sisters...Abbott 3001
9	14	3	Mr. Sandman ....The Chordettes...Cadence 1247
10	9	12	Skokiaan ....Ralph Marterie...Mercury 70432-X45

TW	LW	WK	Billboard® ❋ NOVEMBER 20, 1954 ❋ Best Sellers
1	1	12	I Need You Now ....Eddie Fisher...RCA Victor 47-5830
2	3	16	This Ole House ....Rosemary Clooney...Columbia 4-40266
3	2	19	Hey There ....Rosemary Clooney...Columbia 4-40266
4	9	4	Mr. Sandman ....The Chordettes...Cadence 1247
5	4	8	Papa Loves Mambo ....Perry Como...RCA Victor 47-5857
6	6	11	Hold My Hand ....Don Cornell...Coral 9-61206
7	5	11	If I Give My Heart To You ....Doris Day...Columbia 4-40300
8	8	7	Teach Me Tonight ....DeCastro Sisters...Abbott 3001
9	7	14	Shake, Rattle And Roll ....Bill Haley...Decca 29204
10	15	2	Mambo Italiano ....Rosemary Clooney...Columbia 4-40361

TW	LW	WK	Billboard® ❋ NOVEMBER 27, 1954 ❋ Best Sellers
1	1	13	I Need You Now ....Eddie Fisher...RCA Victor 47-5830
2	4	5	Mr. Sandman ....The Chordettes...Cadence 1247
3	2	17	This Ole House ....Rosemary Clooney...Columbia 4-40266
4	5	9	Papa Loves Mambo ....Perry Como...RCA Victor 47-5857
5	8	8	Teach Me Tonight ....DeCastro Sisters...Abbott 3001
6	6	12	Hold My Hand ....Don Cornell...Coral 9-61206
7	3	20	Hey There ....Rosemary Clooney...Columbia 4-40266
8	7	12	If I Give My Heart To You ....Doris Day...Columbia 4-40300
9	9	15	Shake, Rattle And Roll ....Bill Haley...Decca 29204
10	10	3	Mambo Italiano ....Rosemary Clooney...Columbia 4-40361

TW	LW	WK	Billboard® ❋ DECEMBER 4, 1954 ❋ Best Sellers
1	2	6	Mr. Sandman ....The Chordettes...Cadence 1247
2	1	14	I Need You Now ....Eddie Fisher...RCA Victor 47-5830
3	3	18	This Ole House ....Rosemary Clooney...Columbia 4-40266
4	5	9	Teach Me Tonight ....DeCastro Sisters...Abbott 3001
5	4	10	Papa Loves Mambo ....Perry Como...RCA Victor 47-5857
6	7	21	Hey There ....Rosemary Clooney...Columbia 4-40266
7	6	13	Hold My Hand ....Don Cornell...Coral 9-61206
8	9	16	Shake, Rattle And Roll ....Bill Haley...Decca 29204
9	8	13	If I Give My Heart To You ....Doris Day...Columbia 4-40300
10	11	6	Count Your Blessings (Instead of Sheep) ....Eddie Fisher...RCA Victor 47-5871

TW	LW	WK	Billboard® ❋ DECEMBER 11, 1954 ❋ Best Sellers
1	1	7	Mr. Sandman ....The Chordettes...Cadence 1247
2	2	15	I Need You Now ....Eddie Fisher...RCA Victor 47-5830
3	14	2	Let Me Go Lover ....Joan Weber...Columbia 4-40366
4	3	19	This Ole House ....Rosemary Clooney...Columbia 4-40266
5	4	10	Teach Me Tonight ....DeCastro Sisters...Abbott 3001
6	5	11	Papa Loves Mambo ....Perry Como...RCA Victor 47-5857
7	10	7	Count Your Blessings (Instead of Sheep) ....Eddie Fisher...RCA Victor 47-5871
8	8	17	Shake, Rattle And Roll ....Bill Haley...Decca 29204
9	7	14	Hold My Hand ....Don Cornell...Coral 9-61206
10	11	3	The Naughty Lady Of Shady Lane ....The Ames Brothers...RCA Victor 47-5897

TW	LW	WK	Billboard® DECEMBER 18, 1954 Best Sellers
1	1	8	Mr. Sandman ....The Chordettes...Cadence 1247
2	3	3	Let Me Go Lover ....Joan Weber...Columbia 4-40366
3	2	16	I Need You Now ....Eddie Fisher...RCA Victor 47-5830
4	5	11	Teach Me Tonight ....DeCastro Sisters...Abbott 3001
5	4	20	This Ole House ....Rosemary Clooney...Columbia 4-40266
6	7	8	Count Your Blessings (Instead of Sheep) ....Eddie Fisher...RCA Victor 47-5871
7	6	12	Papa Loves Mambo ....Perry Como...RCA Victor 47-5857
8	10	4	The Naughty Lady Of Shady Lane ....The Ames Brothers...RCA Victor 47-5897
9	13	4	Mister Sandman ....Four Aces...Decca 9-29344
10	8	18	Shake, Rattle And Roll ....Bill Haley...Decca 29204

TW	LW	WK	Billboard® DECEMBER 25, 1954 Best Sellers
1	1	9	Mr. Sandman ....The Chordettes...Cadence 1247
2	2	4	Let Me Go Lover ....Joan Weber...Columbia 4-40366
3	4	12	Teach Me Tonight ....DeCastro Sisters...Abbott 3001
4	5	21	This Ole House ....Rosemary Clooney...Columbia 4-40266
5	3	17	I Need You Now ....Eddie Fisher...RCA Victor 47-5830
6	8	5	The Naughty Lady Of Shady Lane ....The Ames Brothers...RCA Victor 47-5897
7	6	9	Count Your Blessings (Instead of Sheep) ....Eddie Fisher...RCA Victor 47-5871
8	7	13	Papa Loves Mambo ....Perry Como...RCA Victor 47-5857
9	9	5	Mister Sandman ....Four Aces...Decca 9-29344
10	17	3	Hearts Of Stone ....The Fontane Sisters...Dot 45-15265

THE ALBUMS

First Best-Selling Popular Record Albums chart (3/24/45)

BEST-SELLING POPULAR RECORD ALBUMS

Albums listed are those selling best in the nation's retail record stores (dealers). List is based on reports received from more than 200 dealers in all sections of the country. Albums are listed numerically according to greatest sales.

Weeks to date	Last Week	This Week		
1	—	1.	King Cole Trio Collection of Favorites	Capitol A-8
1	—	2.	Glenn Miller — Glenn Miller and Ork	Victor P-148
1	—	3.	Meet Me in St. Louis — Judy Garland	Decca A-380
1	—	4.	Hit Parade — Mark Warnow	Victor P-121
1	—	5.	Getting Sentimental — Tommy Dorsey	Victor P-80
1	—	5.	Three Caballeros — Charles Wolcott and Ork	Decca A-373
1	—	6.	Danny Kaye — Danny Kaye	Columbia C-91
1	—	7.	Oklahoma — Original Cast	Decca A-359
1	—	8.	Eight to the Bar — Johnson & Ammons	Victor P-69
1	—	8.	Up Swing — Benny Goodman, Tommy Dorsey, Artie Shaw, Glenn Miller	Victor P-146

Sample of 33-1/3 R.P.M. and 45 R.P.M. charts (12/16/50)

Best Selling Pop Albums
... based on reports received December 6, 7 and 8

Because all labels are not issued on all speeds it is difficult to conduct a pop album survey that is statistically accurate. Furthermore, separate inventory systems make it almost impossible for the average large dealer to fill out The Billboard's pop chart questionnaires so a comparison may be drawn between their 33 pop album sales and their 45 pop album sales. Therefore, The Billboard is no longer attempting to show comparative sales volume between 45 and 33 pop albums.

Best Selling 33⅓ R.P.M.

Last Week	This Week		
1	1.	THREE LITTLE WORDS — Original Cast	MGM(78)53; (33)E-516
2	2.	SOUTH PACIFIC — Mary Martin-Ezio Pinza	Col(78)MM-850; (33)ML-4180
4	3.	MERRY CHRISTMAS — Bing Crosby-Andrews Sisters	Dec(78)A-550; (33)DL-5019
3	4.	TEA FOR TWO — Doris Day	Col(78)C-215; (33)CL-6149
9	5.	CALL ME MADAM — E. Merman-D. Haymes-E. Wilson-G. Jenkins	Dec(78)A-813; (33)DL-5304
5	6.	AL JOLSON, VOL. I — A. Jolson	Dec(78)A-469; (33)DLP-5030
7	7	VOICE OF THE XTABAY — Yma Sumac	Cap(78)CD-244; (33)H-244
6	8.	YOUNG MAN WITH A HORN — Doris Day-H. James	Col(78)C-198; (33)CL-6106
8	9.	JOLSON SINGS AGAIN — A. Jolson	Dec(78)716; (33)DLP-5006
—	10.	MUSIC FOR THE FIRESIDE — P. Weston	Cap(78)CC-245; (33)H-245

Best Selling 45 R.P.M.

Last Week	This Week		
2	1.	MERRY CHRISTMAS (Four Records) — Bing Crosby-Andrews Sisters	Dec(78)A-550; (45)9-65
1	2	THREE LITTLE WORDS (Four Records) — Original Cast	MGM(78)53; (45)K53
5	3.	SOUTH PACIFIC (Seven Records) — M. Martin-E. Pinza	Col(78)MM-850; (45)A-850
4	4.	JOLSON SINGS AGAIN (Four Records) — A. Jolson	Dec(78)716; (45)9-4
3	5.	AL JOLSON, VOL. I (Four Records) — A. Jolson	Dec(78)A-469; (45)9-9
6	6.	TOAST OF NEW ORLEANS (Two Records) — M. Lanza	V(45)WDM-1417
—	7.	MERRY CHRISTMAS MUSIC — P. Como	V(78)P-161; (45)WP-161
8	8.	ANNIE GET YOUR GUN (Four Records) — B. Hutton-H. Keel	MGM(78)50; (45)G-1001
—	9.	G. LOMBARDO TWIN PIANO (Four Records) — G. Lombardo	Dec(78)A-512; (45)9-11
10	10.	STAN KENTON PRESENTS (Three Records) — S. Kenton	Cap(78)ECD-248; (45)KCF-248

Sample of LP'S and EP'S charts (3/27/54)

Best Selling Popular Albums

Albums are ranked in order of their national sales strength at the retail level according to The Billboard's weekly survey of top dealers in all key markets.

LP'S

1. THE GLENN MILLER STORY—Sound Track ...Decca DL 5519
2. GLENN MILLER PLAYS SELECTIONS FROM "THE GLENN MILLER STORY" ....RCA Victor LPT 3057
3. MUSIC FOR LOVERS ONLY—Jackie Gleason ...Capitol H 352
4. TAWNY—Jackie Gleason ....Capitol H 471
5. SONGS FOR YOUNG LOVERS—Frank Sinatra..Capitol H 488
6. CALAMITY JANE—Doris Day, Howard Keel...........Columbia CL 6273
7. KISMET—Original Cast ....Columbia ML 4850
8. MUSIC TO MAKE YOU MISTY—Jackie Gleason ....Capitol H 455
9. THAT BAD EARTHA—Eartha Kitt ...RCA Victor LPM 3187
10. MAY I SING TO YOU?—Eddie Fisher ...RCA Victor LPM 3185

EP'S

1. THE GLENN MILLER STORY—Sound Track ....Decca ED 2124-5
2. GLENN MILLER PLAYS SELECTIONS FROM "THE GLENN MILLER STORY" ...RCA Victor EPBT 3057
3. MUSIC FOR LOVERS ONLY—Jackie Gleason ....Capitol EBF 352
4. TAWNY—Jackie Gleason ....Capitol EBF 471
5. MAY I SING TO YOU?—Eddie Fisher ...RCA Victor EPB 3185
6. CALAMITY JANE—Doris Day, Howard Keel ....Columbia B 347
7. SONGS FOR YOUNG LOVERS—Frank Sinatra ....Capitol EBF 488
8. THAT BAD EARTHA—Eartha Kitt ...RCA Victor EPB 3187
9. I BELIEVE—Perry Como ...RCA Victor EPB 3188
10. MUSIC TO MAKE YOU MISTY—Jackie Gleason ....Capitol EBF 455

Billboard magazine began publishing a weekly *Best-Selling Popular Record Albums* chart on March 24, 1945. The chart listed those albums selling best in the nation's retail record stores (dealers). The list was based on reports received from more than 200 dealers in all sections of the country. By September 1946 the survey included over 4,000 dealers. The chart data in this section begins with the very first chart on March 24, 1945, and continues through December 25, 1954.

During the first few years of this chart, an album consisted of a bound-volume package of 78 rpm records (usually four). By June 1949, a number of new album formats had been introduced by various labels and the format battle began. By 1954 the familiar 33-1/3 rpm 12" vinyl album had won the format war. An extensive breakdown of the history of these charts, the various album formats and their associated labels follows. In the chart synopsis below, **Date** refers to the debut date of the chart or the date of change to the chart title and/or the chart size (number of positions).

Date	
3/24/45	**BEST SELLING POPULAR RECORD ALBUMS**
	(the first album chart — a Top 10 chart — then a Top 5 chart from 3/31/45-8/7/48)
5/22/48	*Began showing the number of '78' records in an album package*
8/14/48	*Chart expands to a Top 10*
6/11/49	*Began showing Columbia's 78 rpm and 33-1/3 rpm catalog numbers*
8/20/49	*Began showing '78', '45' and 'LP' symbols*
	(Columbia and Decca: '78' & 'LP'; RCA and Capitol: '78' & '45')
10/8/49	**POP ALBUMS**
4/8/50	*Began showing '33' symbol in place of 'LP' symbol*
	(Capitol first label to list '78', '45' & '33' catalog numbers for one title)
7/22/50	*Two separate Top 10 charts under the POP ALBUMS heading:*
	BEST SELLING 33-1/3 R.P.M.
	(Columbia/Decca/MGM) (Capitol on 11/4/50; RCA Victor on 1/6/51)
	BEST SELLING 45 R.P.M.
	(RCA Victor/Capitol/MGM) (Decca on 10/7/50; Columbia on 12/9/50)
11/4/50	**BEST SELLING POP ALBUMS** *(new heading for 33-1/3 and 45 charts)*
11/15/52	**BEST SELLING POPULAR ALBUMS** *(new heading for 33-1/3 and 45 charts)*
12/6/52	*'78' catalog numbers no longer shown on either chart*
3/21/53	*Number of records in a '45' package no longer shown on the 45 R.P.M. chart*
8/29/53 – 12/19/53	*No album chart published*
12/26/53	*Two separate Top 10 charts:*
	BEST SELLING POPULAR LP'S
	BEST SELLING POPULAR EP'S *(EP: extended play '45')*
2/20/54	**BEST SELLING POPULAR ALBUMS** *(Main Heading)*
	LP'S
	EP'S
5/29/54 – 7/3/54	*EP chart discontinued; resumed again on 7/10/54*
5/29/54	*Began bi-weekly chart and expanded chart to a Top 15*
	[no charts published for the following dates in 1954 (prior to 5/29): 1/02, 1/09, 1/16, 4/10, 5/15]

ALBUM FORMATS

The various album formats included in this research are:

78:	78 rpm album package (also listed are the number of discs in the package)
45:	45 rpm album package (also listed are the number of discs in the package)
33/10":	10" 33-1/3 rpm album (smaller version of the later-day 12" long-play album)
LP/12":	12" 33-1/3 rpm album
45/EP:	7" 45 rpm Extended Play album

As mentioned in the chart synopsis, *Billboard* published two Pop Album charts (based on album format) beginning on July 22, 1950. In many cases an album was released in multiple album formats and made both charts. If an album made only one chart, the album format and number of discs in the album are shown across from the album title (ex.: 78^5 indicates that the charted version was a 78 rpm album containing 5 discs). If an album made more than one chart, the album format, number of discs [shown in square backets], label number with prefix, and peak position attained (shown in parentheses) are listed for both formats below the title. The format which peaked the highest is the one shown as the label & number and the one listed first in the title notes. For example the album *Houseparty Hop* by Ray Anthony made the '45' chart and the '33' chart; and, therefore, the following note is shown below the title: '45'[3] KCF-292 (#8) / '33' [10"] L-292 (#10).

TIES

Ties were common on *Billboard's* early Pop Albums charts. From March 24, 1945 through August 7, 1948, ties were shown as follows: 1-2-2-3-4-5. Because of this numbering system, often the Top 5 chart would list 6 to 8 hits. When the chart expanded to a Top 10 on August 14, 1948, ties were shown as follows: 5-6-6-8-9-10, making the chart size more consistent.

USER'S GUIDE TO ALBUMS BY ARTIST SECTION

The Artist Section lists by artist name, alphabetically, every album that charted on *Billboard* magazine's Pop Albums charts from March 24, 1945, through December 25, 1954. (See page 513 for a chart synopsis.) Each artist's charted hits are listed in chronological order and are sequentially numbered. All Top 3 hits are shaded for quick identification. Listed below each album are its tracks in order of their appearance on the album.

EXPLANATION OF COLUMNAR HEADINGS

DEBUT: Date album first charted; taken from the chart on which it first appeared. The date shown is *Billboard's* issue date.

PEAK: Highest charted position (highlighted in **bold type**) taken from the chart on which it achieved its highest ranking. All #1 albums are identified by a special #1 symbol (➊).

WKS: Total weeks charted; taken from the chart on which it achieved its highest total.

Gold: ●   Gold album (million seller)*

Sym: Symbol (see "Letters In Brackets After Titles" below)

$: Current value of near-mint commercial album

Label & Number: Original label and number of album when first charted

> *Before the Recording Industry Association of America (RIAA) began certifying gold albums in 1958, *Billboard* and other entertainment trade magazines would periodically publish a list of million-selling albums. These lists were primarily compiled from reports submitted by the record companies; they were not audited.

EXPLANATION OF SYMBOLS AND NUMBERS

★34★   Number next to an artist name denotes an artist's ranking among the Top 40 Album Artists

2^1 Superscript number to the right of the #1 or #2 peak position is the total weeks the album held that position

+   Beside debut date indicates that the album peaked in the year after it first charted

78^5 Album format designation listed to the right of a title (78 rpm, 45 rpm, 33 rpm, 10" or 12"). The superscript number indicates the total number of discs in the album. If an album charted in two formats, the format information is listed below the title (see Album Formats on page 514).

PICTURES OF THE TOP 20 ARTISTS

A picture of each of the Top 20 artists is shown next to their listing in the artist section. Each Top 20 artist's overall ranking is listed to the right of their name. The overall ranking of artists from 21 through 40 is listed to the left of their name.

LETTER(S) IN BRACKETS AFTER TITLES (Sym column)

C - Comedy
EP - 7" Extended Play Album
F - Foreign Language
G - Greatest Hits
I - Instrumental Recording
K - Compilation
L - Live Recording
M - Musical (Soundtracks section only)

N - Novelty
R - Reissue or re-release **with a new label number** of a previously charted album or Christmas re-release of album with or without the same label number
S - Movie Soundtrack
T - Talk/Spoken Word Recording
X - Christmas Recording

ARTIST & TITLE NOTES

Pertinent biographical information is shown below nearly every artist name. Directly under some album titles are notes indicating the different formats on which an album was released, the backing orchestra, the location of a live recording, etc. Duets and other important name variations, as they appear on the record label, are shown in bold capital letters. All movie titles, Broadway shows and other major works, appear in italics. In the title notes, '#' refers to peak chart position.

Names of artists mentioned in the artist and title notes that have pop-charted albums of their own listed in this section are highlighted in bold type. For example, since **Benny Goodman** is mentioned in Glenn Miller's artist biography, his name is shown in bold type. A name is only shown in bold the <u>first</u> time it appears in an artist's biography and in bold every time it appears in a title note.

LISTING OF TRACKS

Below each album is a listing of its tracks in order of their appearance on the album.

All tracks that charted on *Billboard's* Pop Singles chart are highlighted in bold type with their peak position listed to the right in brackets in bold, italics type. If an artist other than the main artist appears on a track, their name is shown in brackets and italics after the track title.

If the spelling on a Pop Singles-charted single differs from the spelling listed on the album, the title's spelling is listed as it appears on the single (and thus, as it appears in the Singles section of this book).

If a track's spelling on the album label and album jacket conflict, the spelling on the label is shown unless the label spelling is proven incorrect.

COMPLETE ALBUM PRICE GUIDE

This is our first price guide for albums of the pre-rock era. The prices reflect the current estimated value of the record(s) and the jacket in near-mint condition. You will note that the very collectible albums such as hard-to-find early jazz and R&B albums reflect a much higher price than most.

Generally, albums by vocalists such as Peggy Lee and Jo Stafford are more collectible than albums by orchestra leaders such as Jackie Gleason and Paul Weston. Soundtrack and Original Cast albums are always in high demand, especially those that were released on hard-to-find 10" (33-1/3) albums in the early '50s. Prices can vary widely depending mainly, of course, on the condition of the album package and the availability of a particular format. For example, the 7" 45 rpm album packages generally fetch more money than their counterpart 78 rpm album packages.

ALBUMS BY ARTIST

Lists, alphabetically by artist name, every album that made
Billboard's Pop Albums charts from 1945-1954.

KEY

Here's a quick reference guide to our symbols. Refer to *RESEARCHING BILLBOARD'S POP ALBUMS CHARTS* and *USER'S GUIDE* for complete descriptions. (The artist and titles below are NOT real.)

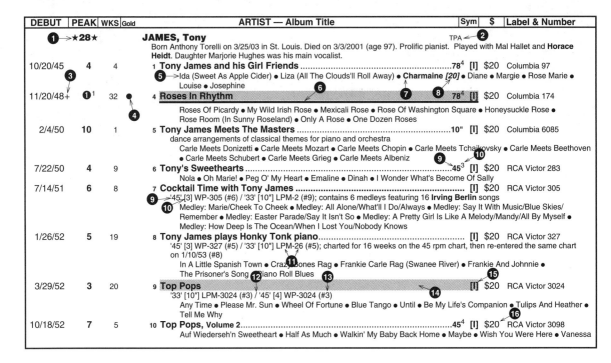

1. artist's ranking within the Top 40 artists
2. has additional hits in our *Top Pop Albums* book
3. peaked in the following year
4. gold album • (million seller)
5. album tracks in order of appearance on album
6. artist's biggest hit (underlined)
7. track charted on *Billboard's* Pop Singles chart (highlighted in bold type)
8. peak position attained on Pop Singles chart

9. album format (45, 78, 33, 10", 12") — listed across from title if album hit only one chart
10. number of discs in album package
11. prefix and label number of alternate album format
12. slash divides the two charted album formats
13. peak position (from '33' or '45' chart)
14. Top 3 hit (shaded)
15. instrumental album [I]
16. current value of near-mint album

A

AMMONS, Albert
Born on 9/23/07 in Chicago. Died on 12/2/49 (age 42). Black boogie-woogie pianist. Father of renowned jazz tenor saxophonist Gene Ammons. Formed duo with **Pete Johnson** in 1938. Temporary paralysis in both hands during the mid-1940s.

3/24/45	2[1]	11		**8 To The Bar (Two Piano Boogie Woogie For Dancing)** 78[4] [I] $150 RCA Victor 69			

PETE JOHNSON and ALBERT AMMONS
originally released September, 1941
Cuttin' The Boogie • Barrel House Boogie • Boogie Woogie Man • Walkin' The Boogie • Sixth Avenue Express • Pine Creek • Foot Pedal Boogie • Movin' The Boogie

ANDREWS SISTERS, The   TPA
Vocal trio from Minneapolis: sisters Patty Andrews (born on 2/26/18), Maxene Andrews (born on 1/13/16; died on 10/21/95, age 79) and LaVerne Andrews (born on 7/6/11; died on 5/8/67, age 55). The trio appeared together in several movies; Patty and Maxene starred in the 1974 Broadway musical *Over There*.

9/14/46	5	1		**The Andrews Sisters** ....78[5] [G] $40 Decca 458			

Vic Schoen (orch.); 1938-1941 recordings
Bei Mir Bist Du Schön *[Bobby Hackett, trumpet solo] [1/'38]* • **Joseph! Joseph!** *[18/'38]* • **Hold Tight, Hold Tight** *[w/Jimmy Dorsey Orch.] [2/'39]* • **Well All Right! (Tonight's The Night)** *[5/'39]* • **Beat Me Daddy, Eight To The Bar** *[19]* • **Scrub Me Mama With A Boogie Beat** *[18]* • **(I'll Be With You) In Apple Blossom Time** *[5]* • **Rhumboogie** *[11]* • **Beer Barrel Polka** *[4/'39]* • **Pennsylvania Polka** *[17]*

ANTHONY, Ray   TPA
Born Raymond Antonini on 1/20/22 in Bentleyville, Pennsylvania; raised in Cleveland. Trumpeter/bandleader. Joined Al Donahue in 1939; then with **Glenn Miller** and **Jimmy Dorsey** from 1940-42. Led U.S. Army band. Own band in 1946. Own TV series in 1956. Appeared in the movie *Daddy Long Legs*. Wrote "Bunny Hop." Married for a time to actress Mamie Van Doren.

3/22/52	8	4		1 **Houseparty Hop** .... [I] $30 Capitol 292			

'45' [3] KCF-292 (#8) / '33' [10"] L-292 (#10)
I Get A Kick Out Of You • Houseparty Hop • Begin The Beguine • Perdido *[10" only]* • Dinah • Sentimental Journey • My Blue Heaven • Wagon Wheels *[10" only]*

2/13/54	6	9		2 **'I Remember Glenn Miller'** .... [I] $30 Capitol 476			

'33' [10"] H-476 (#6) / '45' [EP] EBF-476 (#6); all instrumentals except 3 cuts
Tuxedo Junction • Chattanooga Choo Choo *[w/The Skyliners]* • Serenade In Blue • Elmer's Tune *[w/The Skyliners]* • In The Mood • I Know Why *[w/The Skyliners]* • Ida • Moonlight Serenade

ARMSTRONG, Louis, and The All Stars   TPA
Born Daniel Louis Armstrong on 8/4/01 in New Orleans. Died of heart failure on 7/6/71 (age 69). Legendary jazz singer/trumpet player. Nicknamed "Satchmo." Moved to Chicago in 1922 to join King Oliver's band. Formed own band in 1926. Known for his uniquely raspy, scat-tinged vocals. Numerous appearances on radio, TV and in movies. Won Grammy's Lifetime Achievement Award in 1972. Inducted into the Rock and Roll Hall of Fame in 1990. Also see **Various Artist Compilations**.

7/7/51	10	1		1 **Satchmo At Symphony Hall** ....33[2] [L] $75 Decca DX-108			

recorded live at Symphony Hall in Boston on 11/30/47; 11 of 18 cuts are instrumentals featuring Jack Teagarden (trombone) and Barney Bigard (clarinet); Decca DX-108 is a box set of two 12" 33 rpm records (Decca DL-8037-38)
King Porter Stomp • (What Did I Do To Be So) Black And Blue • Royal Garden Blues • Lover • Stars Fell On Alabama • I Cried For You • Since I Fell For You • Tea For Two • Body And Soul • Muskrat Ramble • Steak Face • On The Sunny Side Of The Street • High Society • That's My Desire • "C" Jam Blues • Baby, Won't You Please Come Home • How High The Moon • Boff Boff

10/18/52	9	2		2 **Satchmo At Pasadena, Vol. 1** ....45[4] [I-L] $50 Decca 9-336			

recorded live at Pasadena Civic Auditorium on 1/30/51; all but 1 cut are instrumentals featuring Jack Teagarden, Barney Bigard, Earl Hines, Cozy Cole, Arvell Shaw and Velma Middleton (vocals); 33 rpm: Decca DL-8041
(Back Home Again in) Indiana (2 Parts) • Star Dust • The Hucklebuck • Baby, It's Cold Outside (2 Parts) • 'Way Down Yonder in New Orleans (2 Parts)

ARNOLD, Eddy   ★34★   TPA
Born Richard Edward Arnold on 5/15/18 in Henderson, Tennessee. Legendary country singer/songwriter/guitarist. Lead singer of **Pee Wee King**'s Golden West Cowboys from 1940-43. Hosted own TV show from 1952-56. Nicknamed "The Tennessee Plowboy" on all RCA recordings through 1954. Elected to the Country Music Hall of Fame in 1966.

1/17/48	5	2		1 **All Time Hits from the Hills** ....78[3] $40 RCA Victor 195			

charted 1 week on 1/17/48 and 1 week on 3/4/50 (#9)
Rockin' Alone (In An Old Rocking Chair) • I'm Thinking Tonight Of My Blue Eyes • It Makes No Difference Now • Molly Darling • The Prisoner's Song • Seven Years With The Wrong Woman

4/9/49	2[4]	10		2 **To Mother** 78[3] $40 RCA Victor 239			

That Wonderful Mother Of Mine • M-O-T-H-E-R (A Word That Means The World To Me) • I Wouldn't Trade The Silver In My Mother's Hair (For All The Gold In The World) • My Mother's Sweet Voice • Bring Your Roses To Her Now • I Wish I Had A Girl Like You, Mother

1/14/50	5	3		3 **Eddy Arnold Sings** ....45[3] $50 RCA Victor 260			

4 songs from the movie *Feudin' Rhythm* and 2 songs from the movie *Hoedown*, both starring Arnold
The Cattle Call *[original 1945 version]* • The Nearest Thing To Heaven • **I'm Throwing Rice (At The Girl That I Love)** *[19]* • **Just A Little Lovin' (Will Go A Long, Long Way)** *[13]* • You Know How Talk Gets Around • There's No Wings On My Angel

ASTAIRE, Fred — see MOVIE SOUNDTRACKS ("Blue Skies"/"Royal Wedding"/ "Three Little Words")

B

BAUM, Charles — see SONGS OF OUR TIMES ("1933"/"1940")

BAXTER, Les, and Orchestra   TPA

Born on 3/14/22 in Mexia, Texas. Died of a heart attack on 1/15/96 (age 73). Orchestra leader/arranger. Began as a conductor on radio shows in the 1930s. Member of Mel Torme's vocal group, the Mel-Tones. Musical arranger for Capitol Records in the 1950s. Composed numerous movie scores. Also see **Yma Sumac**.

| 1/1/49 | 7 | 1 | | Perfume Set to Music ....78³ [I] | | $20 | RCA Victor 231 |

Orchestra and Chorus under the direction of Leslie Baxter
> Dr. Samuel Hoffman plays the Theremin (exotic musical instrument); tunes inspired by the French Corday perfumes
> Toujours Moi (Always Me) ● Fame ● Tzigane (Gypsy) ● Jet ● Possession ● L'Ardente Nuit (Ardent Night)

BENEKE, Tex

Born Gordon Beneke on 2/12/14 in Fort Worth, Texas. Died of respiratory failure on 5/30/2000 (age 86). Featured tenor saxophonist for **Glenn Miller** from 1938-42. Fronted Miller's band for one year after Miller's death. Went on to form his own band which continued to play in the Miller style. Also see **Various Artist Compilations**.

| 10/11/47 | 3 | 4 | | Prom Date | 78⁴ [I] | $40 | RCA Victor 183 |

TEX BENEKE with The Miller Orchestra
> features famous college songs in dance tempo (5 of 8 cuts are instrumentals)
> The Sweetheart Of Sigma Chi ● Washington And Lee Swing ● Alma Mater-Cornell ● The Eyes Of Texas ● Rambling Wreck From Georgia Tech ● Anchors Aweigh (The Song of The Navy) ● On Wisconsin ● The Victory March Of Notre Dame

BENSON, Ray — see SONGS OF OUR TIMES ("1918")

BERLIN, Irving — see CARLE, Frankie / KAYE, Sammy / KING, Wayne /
MOVIE SOUNDTRACKS ("Blue Skies"/"White Christmas") /
ORIGINAL CASTS ("Annie Get Your Gun"/"Call Me Madam"/"Miss Liberty")

BOYD, Bill — see CASSIDY, Hopalong

BRADLEY, Will, and his Orchestra

Born Wilbur Schwichtenberg on 7/12/11 in Newton, New Jersey. Died on 7/15/89 (age 78). Played trombone with Red Nichols and Ray Noble, among other bands, before starting his own in 1939, featuring boogie-woogie pianist **Freddie Slack** and drummer/vocalist Ray McKinley. Later played with the *Tonight Show* band.

| 4/19/47 | 2² | 6 | | Boogie Woogie | 78⁴ [G] | $50 | Columbia 123 |

> featuring Ray McKinley (vocals, drums) and **Freddie Slack** (piano); 1940-41 recordings
> **Beat Me Daddy (Eight To The Bar) (Part 1)** *[2]* ● **Beat Me Daddy (Eight To The Bar) (Part 2)** *[2]* ● **Scrub Me, Mama, With A Boogie Beat** *[2]* ● Boogie Woogie Conga ● Down The Road A Piece *[10]* ● Celery Stalks At Midnight *[18]* ● Fry Me Cookie, With A Can Of Lard ● Chicken Gumboog(ie)

BRANDWYNNE, Nat — see SONGS OF OUR TIMES ("1935")

| | ★37★ | | | **BROWN, Les, And His Orchestra**   TPA | | | |

Born on 3/14/12 in Reinerton, Pennsylvania. Died of cancer on 1/4/2001 (age 88). Clarinetist/bandleader. Worked as an arranger for **Jimmy Dorsey**, Larry Clinton, and other bands before his own orchestra took off. Brown's leading musicians during the 1940s included trumpeter **Billy Butterfield**, tenor saxophonist Ted Nash, and trombonists Si Zentner and Warren Covington. Vocalist **Doris Day** was the band's biggest star. In the 1950s, Les' band was featured on Steve Allen's TV show, and has since accompanied **Bob Hope** on Bob's TV shows and overseas tours. Theme song: "Leap Frog."

| 7/26/47 | 5 | 3 | | 1 **a Sentimental Journey with Les Brown** ....78⁴ [I] | | $25 | Columbia 131 |

> **Sentimental Journey** *[w/Doris Day]* *[1]* ● Twilight Time *[16]* ● Bizet Has His Day ● Good Man Is Hard To Find *[w/Butch Stone]* ● Mexican Hat Dance ● Leap Frog ● Out Of Nowhere ● Daybreak Serenade

| 7/22/50 | 4 | 13 | | 2 **Your Dance Date with Les Brown and his Band of Renown** ....10" [I] | | $25 | Columbia 6123 |

> also see **Tony Pastor**'s "Your Dance Date with..."
> Medley: A Foggy Day/Easy To Love/Drifting And Dreaming/Ebony Rhapsody ● Medley: 'S Wonderful/I Could Write A Book/Cabin In The Sky/Tico Tico

| 8/11/51 | 9 | 4 | | 3 **Over The Rainbow - A Panorama Of Color** .... [I] | | $40 | Coral 9-8023 |

> '45' [4] 9-8023 (#9) / '33' [10"] CRL-56026 (#10)
> Over The Rainbow ● That Old Black Magic ● Green Eyes ● Blue Moon ● The Moon Was Yellow ● Deep Purple ● Red Wing ● Azure

BRUBECK, Dave, Quartet   TPA

Born David Warren on 12/6/20 in Concord, California. Leader of jazz quartet consisting of Brubeck (piano), Paul Desmond (alto sax), Eugene Wright (bass) and Joe Morello (drums). One of America's all-time most popular jazz groups on college campuses. Desmond died on 5/30/77 (age 52). Brubeck won Grammy's Lifetime Achievement Award in 1996.

| 10/30/54 | 8 | 18 | | Jazz Goes To College .... [I-L] | | $50 | Columbia 566 |

> LP: Columbia CL-566 (#8); EP: Columbia B-435-6 (#10); recorded at three Midwestern universities in early 1954
> Balcony Rock ● Out Of Nowhere ● Le Souk ● Take The "A" Train ● The Song Is You ● Don't Worry 'Bout Me ● I Want To Be Happy

BUTTERFIELD, Billy, And His Orchestra   TPA

Born Charles William Butterfield on 1/14/17 in Middleton, Ohio. Died on 3/18/88 (age 71). Legendary trupeter. Played with Bob Crosby, **Artie Shaw**, **Benny Goodman** and **Les Brown**.

| 9/15/45 | 4 | 2 | | Gershwin ....78⁴ | | $40 | Capitol 10 |

> **Margaret Whiting**, Johnny Mercer, Tommy Taylor and Sue Allen (vocals); all songs written by George Gershwin
> Someone To Watch Over Me ● Oh Lady Be Good ● Somebody Loves Me ● Nice Work If You Can Get It ● Maybe ● It Ain't Necessarily So ● Do It Again ● They Can't Take That Away From Me

C

CANTOR, Eddie — see MOVIE SOUNDTRACKS ("The Eddie Cantor Story")

DEBUT	PEAK	WKS	Gold	ARTIST — Album Title	Sym	$	Label & Number

CARLE, Frankie ★8★
Born Francis Carlone on 3/25/03 in Providence, Rhode Island. Died on 3/7/2001 (age 97). Prolific pianist. Played with Mal Hallet and **Horace Heidt**. Daughter Marjorie Hughes was his main vocalist.

| 10/20/45 | 4 | 4 | | **1 Frankie Carle and his Girl Friends** ....78[4] [I] | | $20 | Columbia 97 |

Ida (Sweet As Apple Cider) • Liza (All The Clouds'll Roll Away) • **Charmaine** *[20]* • Diane • Margie • Rose Marie • Louise • Josephine

| 3/2/46 | 4 | 1 | | **2 At The Piano**...78[4] [I] | | $20 | Columbia 23 |

originally released in 1943
Medley: A Lover's Lullaby/Sunrise Serenade • Hindustan • Stumbling • Estelle • **Twelfth Street Rag** *[10]* • Sweet Lorraine • Barcarolle • Prelude In C Sharp Minor

| 6/28/47 | 2[2] | 19 | | **3 Carle Comes Calling** | 78[4] [I] | $20 | Columbia 129 |

Star Dust • Canadian Capers • I'll Get By • Deep Purple • Penthouse Serenade (When We're Alone) • I Want A Girl (Just Like The Girl That Married Dear Old Dad) • Chopin's Polonaise In Boogie • If You Were The Only Girl

| 11/20/48+ | ❶[1] | 32 | | **4 Roses In Rhythm** | 78[4] [I] | $20 | Columbia 174 |

Roses Of Picardy • My Wild Irish Rose • Mexicali Rose • Rose Of Washington Square • Honeysuckle Rose • Rose Room (In Sunny Roseland) • Only A Rose • One Dozen Roses

| 2/4/50 | 10 | 1 | | **5 Frankie Carle Meets The Masters** ....10" [I] | | $20 | Columbia 6085 |

dance arrangements of classical themes for piano and orchestra
Carle Meets Donizetti • Carle Meets Mozart • Carle Meets Chopin • Carle Meets Tchaikovsky • Carle Meets Beethoven • Carle Meets Schubert • Carle Meets Grieg • Carle Meets Albeniz

| 7/22/50 | 4 | 9 | | **6 Frankie Carle's Sweethearts**..45[3] [I] | | $20 | RCA Victor 283 |

Nola • Oh Marie! • Peg O' My Heart • Emaline • Dinah • I Wonder What's Become Of Sally

| 7/14/51 | 6 | 8 | | **7 Cocktail Time with Frankie Carle** .... [I] | | $20 | RCA Victor 305 |

'45' [3] WP-305 (#6) / '33' [10"] LPM-2 (#9); contains 6 medleys featuring 16 **Irving Berlin** songs
Medley: Marie/Cheek To Cheek • Medley: All Alone/What'll I Do/Always • Medley: Say It With Music/Blue Skies/Remember • Medley: Easter Parade/Say It Isn't So • Medley: A Pretty Girl Is Like A Melody/Mandy/All By Myself • Medley: How Deep Is The Ocean/When I Lost You/Nobody Knows

| 1/26/52 | 5 | 19 | | **8 Frankie Carle plays Honky Tonk piano**............................... [I] | | $20 | RCA Victor 327 |

'45' [3] WP-327 (#5) / '33' [10"] LPM-26 (#5); charted for 16 weeks on the 45 rpm chart, then re-entered the same chart on 1/10/53 (#8)
In A Little Spanish Town • Crazy Bones Rag • Frankie Carle Rag (Swanee River) • Frankie And Johnnie • The Prisoner's Song • Piano Roll Blues

| 3/29/52 | 3 | 20 | | **9 Top Pops** | [I] | $20 | RCA Victor 3024 |

'33' [10"] LPM-3024 (#3) / '45' [4] WP-3024 (#3)
Any Time • Please Mr. Sun • Wheel Of Fortune • Blue Tango • Until • Be My Life's Companion • Tulips And Heather • Tell Me Why

| 10/18/52 | 7 | 5 | | **10 Top Pops, Volume 2**..45[4] [I] | | $20 | RCA Victor 3098 |

Auf Wiederseh'n Sweetheart • Half As Much • Walkin' My Baby Back Home • Maybe • Wish You Were Here • Vanessa • Botch-A-Me • Somewhere Along The Way

CASSIDY, Hopalong
Born William Boyd on 6/5/1895 in Hendrysburg, Ohio. Died on 9/12/72 (age 77). Legendary western movie hero.

| 4/22/50 | 7 | 4 | | **Hopalong Cassidy And The Singing Bandit** ....45[2] [T] | | $40 | Capitol 3058 |

read-along Western story for children; includes a 34-page illustrated booklet

CAVALLARO, Carmen
Born on 5/6/13 in New York City. Died of cancer on 10/12/89 (age 76). Classically-trained pianist. Played in the 1930s with Al Kavelin, Rudy Vallee and Abe Lyman. Provided the 1956 movie soundtrack The **Eddy Duchin** Story. Also see **Songs Of Our Times** ("1921" and "1932").

| 3/9/46 | 4 | 4 | | **1 Serenade - Italian Folk Songs** ....78[4] [I] | | $20 | Decca 415 |

Serenade • Tango Of Roses • Come Back To Sorrento • Oh, Marie • Ciribiribin • Funiculi Funicula • O Sole Mio • Santa Lucia

| 7/6/46 | ❶[4] | 11 | | **2 Dancing In The Dark** | 78[5] [I] | $20 | Decca 441 |

originally released in 1940 on Decca album 122; reissued in 1947 on Decca 602
Cocktails For Two • The Very Thought Of You • If I Had You • Smoke Gets In Your Eyes • Dancing In The Dark • Lover • Body And Soul • You're Mine, You! • Alone Together • Night And Day

CHORDETTES, The
Female vocal group from Sheboygan, Wisconsin: Janet Ertel, Carol Buschman, Lynn Evans and Margie Needham. With **Arthur Godfrey** from 1949-53. Ertel married Cadence owner **Archie Bleyer** in 1954; her daughter Jackie was married to Phil Everly of The Everly Brothers. Ertel died of cancer on 11/22/88 (age 75).

| 6/10/50 | 3 | 18 | | **Harmony Time** | 10" | $50 | Columbia 6111 |

barbershop-harmony vocals (no instrumental backing)
When You Were Sweet Sixteen • Moonlight Bay • Carry Me Back To Old Virginny • Ballin' The Jack • Shine On Harvest Moon • Tell Me Why • I'd Love To Live In Loveland • When Day Is Done

CHRISTY, June   TPA
Born Shirley Luster on 11/20/25 in Springfield, Illinois. Died of kidney failure on 6/21/90 (age 64). Jazz singer. Achieved national fame with the **Stan Kenton** band.

| 10/2/54+ | 8 | 22 | | **Something Cool**... | | $40 | Capitol 516 |

LP: Capitol H-516 (#8); EP: Capitol EBF-516 (#8); Pete Rugolo (orch.)
Something Cool • It Could Happen To You • Lonely House • This Time The Dream's On Me • The Night We Called It A Day • Midnight Sun • I'll Take Romance • A Stranger Called The Blues • I Should Care • Softly, As In A Morning Sunrise • I'm Thrilled

CITIES SERVICE BAND OF AMERICA, The

Brass band consisting of 48 members formed in 1948 by Paul Lavalle.

8/11/51   5   13

America's Favorite Marches .... **[I]** $20   RCA Victor 315

'45' [4] WP-315 (#5) / '33' [10"] LPM-6 (#10)

Band Of America March ● El Capitan ● The Washington Grays ● Barnum And Bailey's Favorite ● Colonel Bogey March ● Washington Post March ● Onward, Christian Soldiers ● Stars And Stripes Forever

CLOONEY, Rosemary   TPA

Born on 5/23/28 in Maysville, Kentucky. Died of cancer on 6/29/2002 (age 74). Sang with her sister Betty in **Tony Pastor**'s orchestra in the late 1940s. Became one of the most popular singers of the early 1950s. Acted in several movies including *White Christmas*. Re-emerged in the late 1970s as a successful jazz and ballad singer and as a TV commercial actress. Married twice to actor Jose Ferrer (1953-61 and 1964-67); their son Gabriel married Debby Boone. Her nephew, George Clooney, is a popular TV and movie actor. Won Grammy's Lifetime Achievement Award in 2002.

12/6/52+   3   8

Hollywood's Best .... $40   Columbia 6224

ROSEMARY CLOONEY AND HARRY JAMES

'33' [10"] CL-6224 (#3) / '45' [4] B-319 (#7); all songs are Academy Award-winning 'Best Songs'

You'll Never Know ● On The Atchison, Topeka And The Santa Fe ● It Might As Well Be Spring ● Over The Rainbow ● Sweet Leilani ● The Continental ● When You Wish Upon A Star ● In The Cool, Cool, Cool Of The Evening

COLE, Buddy

Born Edwin Cole on 12/15/16 in Irving, Illinois. Died of a heart attack on 11/5/64 (age 47). Pianist/orchestra leader. Worked with Alvino Rey, **Bing Crosby** and **Johnnie Ray**.

5/18/46   5   5

Piano Cocktails ....78⁴ **[I]** $40   Capitol 24

Smoke Gets In Your Eyes ● Temptation ● Begin The Beguine ● Body And Soul ● Stardust ● Night And Day ● The Song Is You ● I've Got You Under My Skin

COLE, Nat "King"   ★7★   TPA

Born Nathaniel Adams Coles on 3/17/17 in Montgomery, Alabama; raised in Chicago. Died of cancer on 2/15/65 (age 47). First recorded in 1936 in band led by brother Eddie. Toured the "Shuffle Along" musical revue. Formed **The King Cole Trio** in 1939: Cole (piano), Oscar Moore (guitar) and Wesley Prince (bass; replaced several years later by Johnny Miller). Long series of top-selling records led to his solo career in 1950. Appeared in several movies. Hosted own TV variety series from 1956-57. Father of Natalie Cole. Won Grammy's Lifetime Achievement Award in 1990. Inducted into the Rock and Roll Hall of Fame in 2000 as an early influence.

KING COLE TRIO:

3/24/45   ❶¹²   35

1 **The King Cole Trio**   78⁴ $60   Capitol 8

the #1 album on *Billboard*'s first album chart; 3 of 8 cuts feature Cole's vocals

Sweet Lorraine ● Embraceable You ● The Man I Love ● Body And Soul ● Prelude In C Sharp Minor ● What Is This Thing Called Love? ● It's Only A Paper Moon ● Easy Listenin' Blues

8/3/46   ❶⁴   14

2 **King Cole Trio, Volume 2**   78⁴ $60   Capitol 29

This Way Out ● What Can I Say After I Say I'm Sorry ● I Know That You Know ● I Don't Know Why ● I'm In The Mood For Love ● To A Wild Rose ● Look What You've Done To Me ● I'm Thru With Love

1/24/48   4   9

3 **King Cole Trio, Volume 3** ....78³ $60   Capitol 59

Makin' Whoopee ● Too Marvelous For Words ● Honeysuckle Rose ● I'll String Along With You ● Rhumba Azul ● This Is My Night To Dream

8/6/49   10   1

4 **King Cole Trio, Volume 4** ....78³ $60   Capitol 139

Bop Kick ● I Used To Love You, But It's All Over Now ● 'Tis Autumn ● Yes Sir, That's My Baby ● Laugh! Cool Clown ● For All We Know

NAT "KING" COLE:

10/25/52   10   1

5 **Penthouse Serenade** .... **[I]** $40   Capitol 332

NAT "KING" COLE at the piano

'33' [10"] H-332 (#10) / '45' [4] CBF-332 (#10)

Penthouse Serenade (When We're Alone) ● Somebody Loves Me ● Laura ● Once In A Blue Moon ● Polka Dots And Moonbeams ● Down By The Old Mill Stream ● If I Should Lose You ● Rose Room

1/23/54   6   12

6 **Nat 'King' Cole Sings for Two In Love** .... $40   Capitol 420

'45' [4] EBF-420 (#6) / '33' [10"] H-420 (#8); Nelson Riddle (orch.)

Love Is Here To Stay ● A Handful Of Stars ● This Can't Be Love ● A Little Street Where Old Friends Meet ● There Goes My Heart ● Dinner For One Please, James ● Almost Like Being In Love ● Tenderly

7/10/54   7   12

7 **10th Anniversary** .... **[K]** $40   Capitol 514

EP: Capitol EAP-514 (#7); LP: Capitol W-514 (#7); previously unreleased King Cole Trio recordings and Cole's recordings with orchestral backing

Dream A Little Dream Of Me ● There I've Said It Again ● Lulubelle ● I'm An Errand Boy For Rhythm ● The Love Nest ● But All I've Got Is Me ● Peaches ● I Can't Be Bothered ● Too Soon ● Rough Ridin' ● The Story Of My Wife ● Sleeping Beauty ● Lovelight ● Where Were You ● Mother Nature And Father Time ● Wish I Were Somebody Else

11/27/54+   5   20

8 **Nat 'King' Cole sings** .... **[EP]** $40   Capitol 9120

4-song EP compiled from #9 below

If I Give My Heart To You ● Hold My Hand ● Papa Loves Mambo ● Teach Me Tonight

12/25/54   14   2

9 **Today's Top Hits, Vol. 12** ....12" **[K]** $40   Capitol 9122

LES PAUL and MARY FORD/NAT "KING" COLE

If I Give My Heart To You *[Cole]* ● Mister Sandman *[Paul & Ford]* ● Hajji Baba *[Cole] [14]* ● Take Me In Your Arms And Hold Me *[Paul & Ford] [15]* ● It's Crazy *[Cole]* ● That's What I Like *[Paul & Ford]* ● Mandolino *[Paul & Ford] [19]* ● Hold My Hand *[Cole]* ● Whither Thou Goest *[Paul & Ford] [10]* ● Papa Loves Mambo *[Cole]* ● Things I Didn't Do *[Paul & Ford]* ● Make Her Mine *[Cole] [19]* ● I Need You Now *[Paul & Ford]* ● Teach Me Tonight *[Cole]* ● Nola *[Paul & Ford]* ● Answer Me, My Love *[Cole] [6]*

DEBUT	PEAK	WKS	Gold	ARTIST — Album Title	Sym	$	Label & Number

COMO, Perry ★18★   TPA

Born Pierino Como on 5/18/12 in Canonsburg, Pennsylvania. Died on 5/12/2001 (age 88). Owned barbershop in hometown. With Freddy Carlone band in 1933; with Ted Weems from 1936-42. Appeared in several movies. Hosted own TV shows from 1948-63. One of the most popular singers of the 20th century. Won Grammy's Lifetime Achievement Award in 2002.

11/16/46	❶[1]	9		1 **Merry Christmas Music** 78[4] **[X]** $25 RCA Victor 161
				That Christmas Feeling ● **Winter Wonderland** [w/The Satisfiers] [10] ● I'll Be Home For Christmas ● Santa Claus Is Comin' To Town [w/The Satisfiers] ● Silent Night ● White Christmas ● O Come, All Ye Faithful ● Jingle Bells
11/29/47	2[4]	6		2 **Merry Christmas Music** 78[4] **[X-R]** $25 RCA Victor 161
2/14/48	❶[3]	10		3 **A Sentimental Date With Perry** 78[4] $30 RCA Victor 187
				When Day Is Done ● When Your Hair Has Turned To Silver ● Carolina Moon ● Body And Soul ● If We Can't Be The Same Old Sweethearts ● **I'm Always Chasing Rainbows** [w/The Satisfiers] [5] ● What'll I Do? ● Love Me Or Leave Me
12/11/48	3	5		4 **Merry Christmas Music** 78[4] **[X-R]** $25 RCA Victor 161
3/12/49	4	17		5 **Supper Club Favorites** **[G]** $30 RCA Victor 237
				'78' [3] P-237 (#4) / '45' [3] WP-237 (#5); charted 15 weeks on the Pop Albums chart (#4); re-charted on 7/22/50 for 2 weeks (#5) on the 45 rpm chart; album titled after Como's Chesterfield Supper Club radio shows
				Prisoner Of Love [1] ● **Because** [4] ● **When You Were Sweet Sixteen** [2] ● Song Of Songs ● Till The End Of Time [1] ● **Temptation** [15]
11/26/49	4	6		6 **Merry Christmas Music** 78[4] **[X-R]** $25 RCA Victor 161
12/16/50+	5	4		7 **Merry Christmas Music** 45[4] **[X-R]** $30 RCA Victor 161
1/5/52	10	1		8 **Merry Christmas Music** 45[4] **[X-R]** $30 RCA Victor 161
5/24/52	7	13		9 **TV Favorites** 45[4] $35 RCA Victor 334
				songs sung by Como on his Chesterfield TV show
				You'll Never Walk Alone ● Over The Rainbow ● Black Moonlight ● I Concentrate On You ● If There Is Someone Lovelier Than You ● My Heart Stood Still ● Summertime ● While We're Young
2/6/54	6	13		10 **I Believe** $30 RCA Victor 3188
				'33' [10"] LPM-3188 (#6) / '45' [EP] EPB-3188 (#6)
				I Believe ● Onward, Christian Soldiers ● Goodnight, Sweet Jesus ● Act Of Contrition ● Eli, Eli ● Kol Nidrei ● Nearer, My God, To Thee ● Abide With Me

CONTINO, Dick

Born on 1/17/30 in Fresno, California. Accordion virtuoso. Discovered by bandleader **Horace Heidt** and featured on his radio show in the late 1940s.

5/28/49	3	28		**Horace Heidt presents Dick Contino** 78[4] **[I]** $30 Magnolia 501
				DICK CONTINO with HORACE HEIDT and His Musical Knights
				Contino Boogie ● Twilight Time ● Lady Of Spain ● Sorrento ● Czardas ● Canadian Capers ● Sunrise Serenade ● Chiribiribin

CREW-CUTS, The

Vocal group from Toronto: brothers John and Ray Perkins, Pat Barrett and Rudi Maugeri.

| 11/27/54 | 14 | 2 | | **Crewcuts on the Campus**   10" $60 Mercury 25200 |
| | | | | Down The Old Ox Road ● The Whiffenpoof Song ● We're Working Our Way Thru College ● The Varsity Drag ● Buckle Down, Winsocki ● Betty Co-Ed ● You Gotta Be A Football Hero ● Collegiate |

CROSBY, Bing ★2★   TPA

Born Harry Lillis Crosby on 5/3/03 in Tacoma, Washington. Died of a heart attack on 10/14/77 (age 74). Bing and singing partner Al Rinker were hired in 1926 by Paul Whiteman; with Harry Barris they became the Rhythm Boys and gained an increasing following. The trio split from Whiteman in 1930, and Bing sang briefly with Gus Arnheim's band. It was his early-1931 smash with Arnheim, "I Surrender, Dear," which earned Bing a CBS radio contract and launched an unsurpassed solo career. Over the next three decades the mellow Crosby baritone and breezy persona sold more than 300 million records and was featured in over 50 movies (won Academy Award for Going My Way, 1944). Won Grammy's Lifetime Achievement Award in 1962. Ranked as the #1 artist in Joel Whitburn's Pop Memories 1890-1954 book, Bing had over 150 hits from 1931-39. Married to actress Dixie Lee from 1930 until her death in 1952; their son Gary Crosby began recording in 1950. Married to actress Kathryn Grant from 1957 until his death; their daughter Mary became an actress. Bing's youngest brother, Bob Crosby, was a popular swing-era bandleader. Also see **Original Casts** ("South Pacific" on Decca).

10/13/45	❶[6]	13		1 **Going My Way** 78[3] **[S]** $50 Decca 405
				Going My Way [12] ● Swinging On A Star [1] ● Too-Ra-Loo-Ra-Loo-Ral [4] ● The Day After Forever [12] ● Ave Maria [Schubert version] ● Home Sweet Home
12/1/45	❶[6]	7	●	2 **Merry Christmas** 78[5] **[X]** $20 Decca 403
				this album, in various configurations from 1945-57, spent a total of 39 weeks at the #1 position
				White Christmas [1] ● Let's Start The New Year Right ● Silent Night, Holy Night ● **Adeste Fideles** [45/'60] ● Faith Of Our Fathers ● God Rest Ye Merry Gentlemen ● **I'll Be Home For Christmas** [3] ● Danny Boy ● Jingle Bells [w/Andrews Sisters] ● Santa Claus Is Comin' To Town [w/Andrews Sisters]
3/16/46	❶[2]	9		3 **The Bells Of St. Mary's** 78[2] **[S]** $50 Decca 410
				Aren't You Glad You're You? [8] ● In The Land Of Beginning Again [18] ● The Bells Of St. Mary's [13] ● I'll Take You Home Again, Kathleen
3/16/46	2[6]	15		4 **Don't Fence Me In** (Songs Of The Wide Open Spaces) 78[6] $50 Decca 417
				Don't Fence Me In [w/Andrews Sisters] [1] ● **Pistol Packin' Mama** [w/Andrews Sisters] [2] ● **New San Antonio Rose** [7] ● It Makes No Difference Now ● **Be Honest With Me** [20] ● Goodbye, Little Darlin', Goodbye ● **You Are My Sunshine** [20] ● Ridin' Down The Canyon ● I'm Thinking Tonight Of My Blue Eyes [w/Woody Herman] ● I Only Want A Buddy-Not A Sweetheart ● Walking The Floor Over You ● Nobody's Darlin' But Mine
11/2/46	2[1]	10		5 **Blue Skies** 78[5] **[S]** $50 Decca 481
				Blue Skies ● I'll See You In Cuba [w/Trudy Erwin] ● **You Keep Coming Back Like A Song** [12] ● (Running Around In Circles) Getting Nowhere ● Old-Fashioned Girl ● Everybody Step ● All By Myself ● I've Got My Captain Working For Me Now ● Couple Of Song And Dance Men [w/Fred Astaire] ● Puttin' On The Ritz [Fred Astaire]

CROSBY, Bing — Cont'd

DEBUT	PEAK	WKS	Album	Sym	$	Label & Number
11/9/46	❶⁷	10	6 **Merry Christmas**	78⁵ [X-R]	$20	Decca 403
3/8/47	3	4	7 **St. Patrick's Day**	78⁵	$40	Decca 495

MacNamara's Band [10] ● Dear Old Donegal ● Who Threw The Overalls In Mrs. Murphy's Chowder ● It's The Same Old Shillelagh ● Did Your Mother Come From Ireland? ● Where The River Shannon Flows ● The Rose Of Tralee ● When Irish Eyes Are Smiling ● **Too-Ra-Loo-Ra-Loo-Ral [4]** ● I'll Take You Home Again, Kathleen

11/1/47	❶⁸	10	8 **Merry Christmas**	78⁴ [X-R]	$20	Decca 550

reissue of #2 & 6 above (minus "Danny Boy" and "Let's Start The New Year Right"); includes a new recording of "White Christmas"

2/21/48	3	1	9 **St. Valentine's Day**	78⁴	$40	Decca 621

I Love You Truly ● Just A-Wearyin' For You ● The Sweetest Story Ever Told ● Mighty Lak' A Rose ● **You And I [6]** ● **Miss You [9]** ● **I'll Be Seeing You [1]** ● **I Love You [1]**

2/28/48	❶²	5	10 **St. Patrick's Day**	78⁵ [R]	$40	Decca 495
7/17/48	2²	14	11 **The Emperor Waltz**	78² [S]	$50	Decca 620

Friendly Mountains ● The Kiss In Your Eyes ● I Kiss Your Hand, Madame ● Emperor Waltz

11/6/48	❶⁹	11	12 **Merry Christmas**	78⁴ [X-R]	$20	Decca 550
11/13/48	10	1	13 **Stardust**	78⁴	$40	Decca 678

originally released in 1942 on Decca 181

Star Dust ● Deep Purple ● I Cried For You ● My Melancholy Baby ● The One Rose ● Moonlight And Shadows ● A Blues Serenade ● S'posin'

2/12/49	8	2	14 **St. Valentine's Day**	78⁴ [R]	$40	Decca 621
3/12/49	3	3	15 **St. Patrick's Day**	78⁵ [R]	$40	Decca 495
5/7/49	5	8	16 **A Connecticut Yankee** In King Arthur's Court	78³ [S]	$50	Decca 699

Once And For Always ● **If You Stub Your Toe On The Moon [27]** ● Busy Doing Nothing [w/William Bendix & Sir Cedric Hardwicke] ● 'Twixt Myself And Me [Murvyn Vye] ● Once And For Always [w/Rhonda Fleming] ● When Is Sometime [Rhonda Fleming]

6/18/49	4	9	17 **South Pacific**	78⁴	$40	Decca 714

BING CROSBY/DANNY KAYE/EVELYN KNIGHT/ELLA FITZGERALD
selections from the Broadway musical of the same title (not the Original Cast)
Bali Ha'i [Crosby] ● Some Enchanted Evening [Crosby] ● There Is Nothin' Like A Dame [Kaye] ● Honey Bun [Kaye] ● A Wonderful Guy [Knight] ● A Cock-Eyed Optimist [Knight] ● I'm Gonna Wash That Man Right Outa My Hair [Fitzgerald] ● Happy Talk [Fitzgerald]

11/19/49	❶³	8	18 **Merry Christmas**	78⁴ [X-R]	$20	Decca 550
12/10/49	4	5	19 **Christmas Greetings**	78³ [X]	$40	Decca 715

Here Comes Santa Claus [w/Andrews Sisters] ● Twelve Days Of Christmas [w/Andrews Sisters] ● You're All I Want For Christmas ● The First Nowell ● Christmas Carols-Part 1 ● Christmas Carols-Part 2

12/2/50	❶⁵	8	20 **Merry Christmas**	[X-R]	$30	Decca 9-65

'45' [4] 9-65 (#1/5 wks.) / '33' [10"] DL-5019 (#1/2 wks.); 45 rpm and 33 rpm issue of #8, 12 & 18 above

1/13/51	9	1	21 **Christmas Greetings**	45³ [X-R]	$40	Decca 9-66

45 rpm issue of #19 above

1/27/51	10	1	22 **Mr. Music**	[S]	$50	Decca 5284

'33' [10"] DL-5284 (#10) / '45' [4] 9-101 (#10)
High On The List [w/Andrews Sisters] ● Life Is So Peculiar [w/Andrews Sisters] ● Accidents Will Happen ● And You'll Be Home ● Wouldn't It Be Funny ● Once More The Blue And White ● Accidents Will Happen [w/Dorothy Kirsten] ● Milady [w/Dorothy Kirsten]

3/31/51	10	1	23 **St. Patrick's Day**	[R]	$50	Decca 5037

'33' rpm [10"] issue of #7, 10 & 15 above

12/8/51+	2¹	5	24 **Merry Christmas**	[X-R]	$30	Decca 9-65

'45' [4] 9-65 (#2) / '33' [10"] DL-5019 (#2); issued with a new red cover instead of the traditional light blue cover

12/22/51+	8	2	25 **Christmas Greetings**	[X-R]	$40	Decca 5020

'33' rpm [10"] issue of #19 & 21 above, with 2 additional songs ("The Christmas Song" and "O Fir Tree Dark")

12/20/52+	2¹	3	26 **Merry Christmas**	[X-R]	$30	Decca 9-65

'45' [4] 9-65 (#2) / '33' [10"] DL-5019 (#3)

12/26/53	6	1	27 **Merry Christmas**	[X-R]	$40	Decca ED-547

two-pocket EP (Extended Play '45') issue of #26 above

10/2/54	9	14	28 **Bing** (A Musical Autobiography)	[G]	$200	Decca DX-151 [5]

LP: Decca DX-151 (#9); EP: ED-1700 (#14); a very special deluxe set of five 33 rpm 12" albums (or 17 45 rpm's in a lock-box); Crosby introduces each of the 89 songs, in chronological order, from his first hit with Paul Whiteman in 1927 ("Muddy Water") to his 1954 hit "Y'all Come"; the songs from 1927 through 1940 (except for "Small Fry") are re-recordings with instrumental backing by **Buddy Cole**'s Trio; beginning with "You Are My Sunshine," all the rest are Crosby's original recordings

Muddy Water ● Mississippi Mud ● My Kinda Love ● I Surrender Dear ● It Must Be True ● Wrap Your Troubles In Dreams ● Out Of Nowhere ● Just One More Chance ● Star Dust ● Sweet And Lovely ● Where The Blue Of The Night Meets The Gold Of The Day ● Paradise ● Please ● Just An Echo In The Valley ● I Don't Stand A Ghost Of A Chance With You ● Learn To Croon ● Down The Old Ox Road ● Thanks ● Black Moonlight ● The Day You Came Along ● After Sundown ● Temptation ● Love Thy Neighbor ● May I? ● Love In Bloom ● I Love You Truly ● June In January ● Love Is Just Around The Corner ● It's Easy To Remember ● Soon ● I Wished On The Moon ● Silent Night ● I'm An Old Cowhand ● I Can't Escape From Me ● Song Of The Islands ● Pennies From Heaven ● Sweet Leilani ● Blue Hawaii ● The One Rose ● There's A Gold Mine In The Sky ● My Heart Is Taking Lessons ● I've Got A Pocketful Of Dreams ● **Small Fry** [w/Johnny Mercer] [3/'38] ● Mexicali Rose ● That Sly Old Gentleman ● Alla En El Rancho Grande ● Tumbling Tumbleweeds ● Only Forever ● Did Your Mother Come From Ireland? ● Yes Indeed [w/Connee Boswell] ● Brahms' Lullaby ● **You Are My Sunshine [20]** ● The Waiter And The Porter And The Upstairs Maid [w/Mary Martin & Jack Teagarden] ● **Deep In The Heart Of Texas [3]** ● Wait Till The Sun Shines, Nellie [w/Mary Martin] ● Walking The Floor Over You ● **White Christmas [1]** ● **Moonlight Becomes You** [w/Bob Hope] ● **Sunday, Monday Or Always [1]** ● **Pistol Packin' Mama** [w/Andrews Sisters] [2] ● **San Fernando Valley [1]** ● I'll Be Seeing You [1] ● **Swinging On A Star [1]** ● **Too-Ra-Loo-Ra-Loo-Ral [4]** ● **Don't Fence Me In** [w/Andrews Sisters] [1] ● **Yah-Ta-Ta Yah-Ta-Ta** [w/Judy Garland] [5] ● It's Been A Long Long Time [w/Les Paul] ● **The Bells Of St. Mary's [13]** ● Put It There, Pal [w/Bob Hope] ● **MacNamara's Band** [w/The Jesters] [10] ● **Sioux City Sue** [w/The Jesters] [3] ●

CROSBY, Bing — Cont'd

Begin The Beguine ● South America, Take It Away *[w/Andrews Sisters]* ● Blue Skies ● Alexander's Ragtime Band *[w/Al Jolson]* ● **The Whiffenpoof Song** *[w/Fred Waring]* **[7]** ● **Now Is The Hour** *[1]* ● **Galway Bay** *[3]* ● Far Away Places *[2]* ● Mule Train *[4]* ● Dear Hearts And Gentle People *[2]* ● Rock Of Ages ● Sunshine Cake *[w/Carole Richards]* ● Play A Simple Melody *[w/Gary Crosby]* **[2]** ● **Sam's Song** *[w/Gary Crosby]* **[3]** ● Gone Fishin' *[w/Louis Armstrong]* **[19]** ● **The Cool, Cool, Cool Of The Evening** *[w/Jane Wyman]* **[11]** ● Y'all Come **[20]**

| 11/27/54 | 2² | 8 | | 29 White Christmas | **[S]** | $40 | Decca 8083 |

BING CROSBY - DANNY KAYE - PEGGY LEE
EP: Decca ED-819 (#2); LP: Decca DL-8083 (#4); Peggy Lee (who was not in the movie) re-recorded **Rosemary Clooney**'s part (who was in the movie but was not allowed to perform on Decca because of her Columbia contract)
Medley: Old Man/Gee, I Wish I Was Back In The Army *[Crosby & Kaye]* ● Sisters *[Lee]* ● Best Things Happen While You're Dancing *[Kaye]* ● Snow *[w/Trudy Stevens]* ● Medley: Blue Skies/Mandy *[Crosby & Kaye]* ● Choreography *[Kaye]* ● Count Your Blessings Instead Of Sheep *[Crosby]* ● Love, You Didn't Do Right By Me *[Lee]* ● What Can You Do With A General *[Crosby]* ● White Christmas (Finale) *[w/Trudy Stevens]*

| 12/25/54+ | 7 | 4 | | 30 Merry Christmas..10" | **[X-R]** | $30 | Decca 5019 |

EP: Decca ED-547 (#7); LP: Decca DL-5019 (#9)

CUGAT, Xavier, and his Waldorf-Astoria Orchestra

Born on 1/1/1900 in Barcelona, Spain; raised in Havana, Cuba. Died of heart failure on 10/27/90 (age 90). Bandleader/vocalist/composer/arranger. Specialized in Latin American music since forming own band in the late 1920s. Many appearances in movies, on radio and TV. Married to Abbe Lane (1952-63) and Charo (1964-78).

| 11/24/45 | 3 | 9 | | **Cugat's Favorite Rhumbas** | 78⁴ | $40 | Columbia 110 |

Del Campo and Hermanas Boyd (vocals); 3 songs are instrumentals
Begin The Beguine ● Say "Si Si" ● Estrellita (My Little Star) ● La Golondrina (The Swallow) ● **Green Eyes** *[17]* ● Besamé Mucho (Kiss Me Much) ● La Paloma (The Dove) ● Cielito Lindo (Blue Skies)

D

DAILY('S), Pete, Dixieland Band

Born on 5/5/11 in Portland, Indiana. Coronet player/bandleader. With Ozzie Nelson's band from 1945-47.

| 3/11/50 | 3 | 13 | | **Pete Daily's Dixieland Band** | **[I]** | $40 | Capitol 183 |

'45' [3] CCF-183 (#3) / '33' [10"] H-183 (#8); charted 3 weeks on the Pop Albums chart (#8); re-charted on 7/22/50 for 10 weeks (#3) on the 45 rpm chart
Original Dixieland One-Step ● Sensation ● Dixieland Shuffle ● Careless Love ● At A Georgia Camp Meeting ● When The Saints Go Marching In ● What's Your Story? ● I Want To Linger

DAY, Dennis

Born Eugene Dennis McNulty on 5/21/18 in New York City. Died of ALS (Lou Gehrig's disease) on 6/22/88 (age 70). Tenor who sang and performed in comedy sketches on Jack Benny's radio and TV shows from 1939-65; also appeared in several movies.

| 3/27/48 | 4 | 1 | | **My Wild Irish Rose** ....78⁴ | | $25 | RCA Victor 191 |

7 of 8 songs were featured in the 1947 movie *My Wild Irish Rose*, a biography of singer/songwriter Chauncey Olcott
My Wild Irish Rose ● By The Light Of The Silvery Moon ● Mother Machree ● Remember When You Sang "Oh Promise Me" ● When Irish Eyes Are Smiling ● My Nellie's Blue Eyes ● A Little Bit Of Heaven ● Hush-A-Bye, Wee Rose Of Killarney

DAY, Doris ★5★

Born Doris Kappelhoff on 4/3/22 in Cincinnati. Sang briefly with Bob Crosby in 1940 and shortly thereafter became a major star with the Les Brown band (she had 12 charted hits with Les). Starred in several movies; own TV series from 1968-73. Her husband, Marty Melcher, owned Arwin Records; their son, Terry, was a member of the Rip Chords and Bruce & Terry, and a prolific producer (The Beach Boys).

TPA

| 10/8/49 | 5 | 8 | | 1 **You're My Thrill** ....10" | | $40 | Columbia 6071 |

You're My Thrill ● **Bewitched** *[9]* ● I'm Confessin' (That I Love You) ● Sometime's I'm Happy ● You Go To My Head ● I Didn't Know What Time It Was ● When Your Lover Has Gone ● That Old Feeling

| 4/8/50 | ❶¹² | 50 | | 2 Young Man With A Horn | **[S]** | $40 | Columbia 6106 |

DORIS DAY and HARRY JAMES
'33' [10"] CL-6106 (#1) / '45' [4] B-198 (#9); movie loosely based on the career of jazz great Bix Beiderbecke
I May Be Wrong ● Get Happy *[James]* ● Man I Love *[James]* ● Too Marvelous For Words ● The Very Thought Of You ● Limehouse Blues *[James]* ● Melancholy Rhapsody *[James]* ● With A Song In My Heart

| 10/28/50 | 3 | 19 | | 3 Tea For Two | **[S]** | $40 | Columbia 6149 |

'33' [10"] CL-6149 (#3) / '45' [4] B-215 (#4); movie is based on the musical comedy *No, No, Nanette*
Crazy Rhythm ● Here In My Arms ● I Know That You Know ● I Want To Be Happy ● Do Do Do ● I Only Have Eyes For You ● Oh Me! Oh My! ● Tea For Two

| 4/7/51 | ❶³ | 24 | | 4 Lullaby Of Broadway | **[S]** | $40 | Columbia 235 |

'45' [4] B-235 (#1/3 wks.) / '33' [10"] CL-6168 (#2/5 wks.)
Lullaby Of Broadway ● Fine And Dandy ● In A Shanty In Old Shanty Town ● Somebody Loves Me ● Just One Of Those Things ● You're Getting To Be A Habit With Me ● I Love The Way You Say Goodnight ● Please Don't Talk About Me When I'm Gone

| 8/11/51 | 2¹ | 21 | | 5 On Moonlight Bay | **[S]** | $40 | Columbia 267 |

'45' [4] B-267 (#2) / '33' [10"] CL-6186 (#3)
Moonlight Bay ● Till We Meet Again ● Love Ya *[w/Jack Smith]* ● Christmas Story ● I'm Forever Blowing Bubbles *[w/Jack Smith]* ● Cuddle Up A Little Closer ● Every Little Movement ● Tell Me (Tell Me Why)

DEBUT	PEAK	WKS	Gold	ARTIST — Album Title	Sym	$	Label & Number

DAY, Doris — Cont'd

| 2/2/52 | ❶⁴ | 24 | | 6 **I'll See You In My Dreams** | [S] | $40 | Columbia 289 |

'45' [4] B-289 (#1/4 wks.) / '33' [10"] CL-6198 (#1/1 wk.); movie is based on the life of songwriter Gus Kahn as played by **Danny Thomas**
Ain't We Got Fun *[w/Danny Thomas]* ● The One I Love (Belongs To Somebody Else) ● I Wish I Had A Girl ● It Had To Be You ● Nobody's Sweetheart ● My Buddy ● Makin' Whoopee! *[w/Danny Thomas]* ● I'll See You In My Dreams

| 5/2/53 | 3 | 17 | | 7 **By The Light Of The Silvery Moon** | [S] | $40 | Columbia 334 |

'45' [4] B-334 (#3) / '33' [10"] CL-6248 (#4); movie is a sequel to #5 above
By The Light Of The Silv'ry Moon ● Your Eyes Have Told Me So ● Just One Girl ● Ain't We Got Fun? ● If You Were The Only Girl ● Be My Little Baby Bumble Bee ● I'll Forget You ● King Chanticleer

| 12/26/53+ | 2³ | 24 | | 8 **Calamity Jane** | [S] | $40 | Columbia 347 |

DORIS DAY and HOWARD KEEL
'45' [EP] B-347 (#2) / '33' [10"] CL-6273 (#3); except for #8, all of above Doris Day '[S]' albums are not actual movie soundtrack recordings
Deadwood Stage *[Day]* ● I Can Do Without You ● Black Hills Of Dakota *[Day]* ● Just Blew In From The Windy City *[Day]* ● Woman's Touch *[Day]* ● Higher Than A Hawk (Deeper Than A Well) *[Keel]* ● 'Tis Harry I'm Plannin' To Marry *[Day]* ● Secret Love *[Day]* [1]

DINNING SISTERS, The

Vocal trio from Wichita, Oklahoma: twin sisters Jean and Ginger Dinning, with Jayne Bundeson (had replaced Lucille Dinning in 1946). Regulars on radio's *National Barn Dance*. Their brother Mark hit #1 in 1960 with "Teen Angel."

| 6/2/45 | 3 | 4 | | **Songs By The Dinning Sisters** | 78⁴ | $30 | Capitol 7 |

Jack Fascinato (orch.)
Please Don't Talk About Me When I'm Gone ● (He's Just A) Sentimental Gentleman From Georgia ● Where Or When ● Aunt Hagar's Blues ● Once In A While ● You're A Character, Dear ● The Way You Look Tonight ● Brazil

DORSEY, Jimmy, And His Orchestra   TPA

Born on 2/29/04 in Shenandoah, Pennsylvania. Died of cancer on 6/12/57 (age 53). Legendary alto sax and clarinet soloist/bandleader. Recorded with his brother **Tommy Dorsey** in the Dorsey Brothers Orchestra from 1928-35 and 1953-56.

| 5/11/46 | 4 | 1 | | 1 **Latin American Favorites** ....78⁴ | [G] | $40 | Decca 427 |

Bob Eberly and Helen O'Connell (vocals)
Green Eyes (Aquellos Ojos Verdes) *[1]* ● **The Breeze And I** *[1]* ● **Amapola (Pretty Little Poppy)** *[1]* ● **Maria Elena** *[1]* ● **Yours (Quiereme Mucho)** *[2]* ● **Always In My Heart** *[20]* ● **Brazil (Aquarela Do Brasil)** *[17]* ● At The Cross-Roads (Malagueña)

| 1/21/50 | 4 | 34 | | 2 **Dixie By Dorsey** ....10" | [I] | $50 | Columbia 6095 |

JIMMY DORSEY and his Original "Dorseyland" Jazz Band
Charlie Teagarden (trumpet); Cutty Cutshall (trombone)
Jazz Me Blues ● Panama ● Struttin' With Some Barbecue ● Chimes Blues ● Muskrat Ramble ● High Society ● South Rampart Street Parade ● Tin Roof Blues

DORSEY, Tommy, and his Orchestra ★12★   TPA

Born on 11/19/05 in Mahanoy Plane, Pennsylvania. Choked to death on 11/26/56 (age 51). Legendary trombonist/bandleader. Tommy and brother **Jimmy Dorsey** recorded together as the Dorsey Brothers Orchestra from 1928-35 and 1953-56. They hosted a musical variety TV show, *Stage Show*, 1954-56. Warren Covington fronted band after Tommy's death. Also see **Various Artist Compilations**.

| 3/24/45 | 4 | 3 | | 1 **Getting Sentimental With Tommy Dorsey** ....78⁴ | [G] | $40 | Victor 80 |

recordings are from 1935-40; charted 1 week (#5); re-charted on 10/6/45 for 1 week (#4); re-charted again on 4/20/46 for 1 week (#5)
I'm Gettin' Sentimental Over You *[8/'36]* ● Royal Garden Blues ● **Marie** *[1/'37]* ● Who? ● **Star Dust** *[Frank Sinatra, vocal]* *[7]* ● **Song Of India** *[5/'37]* ● **I'll Never Smile Again** *[Frank Sinatra, vocal]* *[1]* ● Little White Lies

| 2/23/46 | 2³ | 10 | | 2 **Show Boat** | 78⁴ | $40 | Victor 152 |

Dorsey's version of the famous Jerome Kern/Oscar Hammerstein II musical
Make Believe ● I Still Suits Me ● Ol' Man River ● Bill ● Can't Help Lovin' Dat Man ● You Are Love ● Why Do I Love You ● Nobody Else But Me

| 2/22/47 | 2⁴ | 16 | | 3 **Tommy Dorsey All Time Hits** | 78⁴ | [G] | $40 | RCA Victor 163 |

4 instrumentals and 4 vocals
Boogie Woogie *[3/'38]* ● On The Sunny Side Of The Street *[The Sentimentalists, vocals]* ● Somewhere A Voice Is Calling *[Frank Sinatra, vocal]* ● Hawaiian War Chant ● **Embraceable You** *[Jo Stafford, vocal]* *[18]* ● After You've Gone ● Chicago *[Sy Oliver, vocal]* ● **Opus No. 1** *[8]*

| 10/9/48 | 3 | 8 | | 4 **Tommy Dorsey's Clambake Seven** | 78⁴ | $40 | RCA Victor 220 |

The Music Goes 'Round And 'Round *[1/'35]* ● Sailing At Midnight ● At The Codfish Ball ● **Josephine** *[3/'37]* ● **The Lady Is A Tramp** *[15/'37]* ● The Sheik Of Araby ● Allá En El Rancho Grande ● Chinatown, My Chinatown

| 10/8/49 | 9 | 1 | | 5 **And The Band Sings Too** ....78³ | | $40 | RCA Victor 247 |

5 vocals by Jack Leonard and 1 by Frank Sinatra
East Of The Sun (And West Of The Moon) *[Frank Sinatra, vocal]* ● I'll See You In My Dreams ● **Sweet Sue-Just You** *[13/'39]* ● Yearning (Just For You) *[3/'38]* ● Blue Moon ● **How Am I To Know?** *[13/'39]*

| 4/15/50 | 3 | 15 | | 6 **Tommy Dorsey plays Cole Porter for dancing** | 45³ | [I] | $40 | RCA Victor 263 |

Just One Of Those Things ● Love For Sale ● Why Shouldn't I ● You Do Something To Me ● I Get A Kick Out Of You ● It's Delovely

| 7/22/50 | 6 | 5 | | 7 **Tommy Dorsey's Dixieland for Dancing** ....45³ | [I] | $40 | RCA Victor 279 |

Panama ● Washboard Blues ● Down Home Rag ● Davenport Blues ● Milenberg Joys - Part 1 ● Milenberg Joys - Part 2

DUCHIN, Eddy

Born on 4/10/10 in Cambridge, Massachusetts. Died of leukemia on 2/9/51 (age 40). The famous pianist/bandleader first became known with Leo Reisman before starting his own orchestra. Five years after his death Hollywood produced *The Eddy Duchin Story*. Son Peter Duchin became a successful society pianist/bandleader. Eddy's famous theme "My Twilight Dream" (based on Chopin's "Nocturne In E-Flat") was recorded in 1939. *The Eddy Duchin Story* movie soundtrack album charted on 5/26/56.

9/22/45	4	1		1 Duchin - Gershwin ....78⁴ [I]		$30	Columbia 52

released in 1943; Eddy Duchin plays the music of George Gershwin

The Man I Love ● Someone To Watch Over Me ● Love Walked In ● Embraceable You ● 'S Wonderful ● Somebody Loves Me ● Summertime ● They Can't Take That Away From Me

9/29/45	2¹	3		2 Duchin Reminisces	78⁴ [I]	$30	Columbia 105

April Showers ● You're My Everything ● Keep Smiling At Trouble ● Till We Meet Again ● Alice Blue Gown ● I'll See You In My Dreams ● If I Could Be With You ● It Had To Be You ● I Kiss Your Hand, Madame ● When Day Is Done ● You Do Something To Me ● Can't We Talk It Over ● Sometimes I'm Happy ● Pretty Baby ● The Blue Room ● Am I Blue?

E

ECKSTINE, Billy   TPA

Born on 7/8/14 in Pittsburgh. Died of heart failure on 3/8/93 (age 78). R&B singer/guitarist/trumpeter. One of the most distinctive baritones in popular music. Sang with Earl Hines from 1939-43. Nicknamed "Mr. B." His son Ed was president of Mercury Records.

2/11/50	4	7		Songs By Billy Eckstine 78³		$50	MGM 48

Someone To Watch Over Me ● Nobody Knows De Trouble I've Seen ● My Old Flame ● I Don't Want To Cry Any More ● You Go To My Head ● Over The Rainbow

F

FAITH, Percy, and his Orchestra   ★40★   TPA

Born on 4/7/08 in Toronto. Died of cancer on 2/9/76 (age 67). Orchestra leader. Moved to the U.S. in 1940. Joined Columbia Records in 1950 as conductor/arranger.

7/25/53	2¹	5		1 Music From Hollywood	[I]	$20	Columbia 6255

'33' [10"] CL-6255 (#2) / '45' [2] B-1692/3 (#6)

Return To Paradise *[19]* ● Ruby ● **The Song From Moulin Rouge** *[no vocal] [1]* ● Theme From "The Bad And The Beautiful" (Love Is For The Very Young)

7/24/54	14	4		2 Kismet	[I]	$25	Columbia 550

Faith's version of the Broadway show which opened in New York's Ziegfeld Theater on 12/3/53

Sands Of Time ● Stranger In Paradise ● Fate ● And This Is My Beloved ● Not Since Nineveh ● Baubles, Bangles And Beads ● He's In Love! ● Bazaar Of The Caravans ● Zubbediya, Samaris' Dance ● Rhymes Have I ● Rahadlakum ● Night Of My Nights

12/25/54	10	2		3 Music Of Christmas	[X-I]	$30	Columbia 588

LP: Columbia CL-588 (#10); EP: Columbia B-1903-5 (#13)

Joy To The World ● Silent Night, Holy Night ● Deck The Hall With Boughs Of Holly ● It Came Upon The Midnight Clear ● Good King Wenceslas ● Hark! The Herald Angels Sing ● The First Noel ● Medley: Lo, How A Rose E'er Blooming/O Little Town Of Bethlehem ● O Holy Night ● Medley: The Holly And The Ivy/Here We Go A-Caroling ● God Rest Ye Merry, Gentlemen ● O Come, All Ye Faithful

FINGERLE, Marlene — see SONGS OF OUR TIMES ("1926"/"1929")

FISHER, Eddie   ★10★   TPA

Born Edwin Jack Fisher on 8/10/28 in Philadelphia. At Copacabana night club in New York at age 17. With Buddy Morrow and Charlie Ventura in 1946. On Eddie Cantor's radio show in 1949. In the Armed Forces Special Services, 1952-53. Married to Debbie Reynolds from 1955-59. Other marriages to Elizabeth Taylor and Connie Stevens. Daughter with Debbie is actress/author Carrie Fisher. Daughters with Connie are singer Tricia Leigh Fisher and actress Joely Fisher. Own *Coke Time* 15-minute TV series, 1953-57. In movies *All About Eve* (1950), *Bundle Of Joy* (1956) and *Butterfield 8* (1960). Fisher was the #1 idol of bobbysoxers during the early 1950's.

5/10/52	3	32		1 Eddie Fisher Sings		$30	RCA Victor 3025

'45' [4] WP-3025 (#3) / '33' [10"] LPM-3025 (#5)

Just Say I Love Her ● Sorry ● A Little Bit Independent ● If You Should Leave Me ● **I Remember When** *[29]* ● Am I Wasting My Time On You ● I Love You Because ● **Thinking Of You** *[5]*

10/18/52	❶¹⁵	25		2 I'm In The Mood For Love		$30	RCA Victor 3058

'45' [4] WP-3058 (#1) / '33' [10"] LPM-3058 (#3)

I'm In The Mood For Love ● You'll Never Know ● Hold Me ● Everything I Have Is Yours ● That Old Feeling ● Full Moon And Empty Arms ● Paradise ● I've Got You Under My Skin

12/13/52+	❶¹	4		3 Christmas With Eddie Fisher	[X]	$30	RCA Victor 3065

'45' EPB-3065 (#1) / '33' [10"] LPM-3065 (#2)

Silent Night ● White Christmas ● You're All I Want For Christmas ● Christmas Day ● That's What Christmas Means To Me ● Here Comes Santa Claus ● Jingle Bells ● O Come All Ye Faithful

1/30/54	2¹	15		4 May I Sing To You		$30	RCA Victor 3185

'45' [EP] EPB-3185 (#2) / '33' [10"] LPM-3185 (#4)

April Showers ● I'm Just A Vagabond Lover ● You Call It Madness But I Call It Love ● Where The Blue Of The Night Meets The Gold Of The Day ● Night And Day ● Nature Boy ● Begin The Beguine ● May I Sing To You

8/21/54	10	2		5 Broadway Classics	[EP]	$25	RCA Victor EPA 561

And This Is My Beloved ● Alone Too Long ● Lazy Afternoon ● Lost In Loveliness

FITZGERALD, Ella — see CROSBY, Bing ("South Pacific")

★22★ **FLANAGAN, Ralph, and his Orchestra**

Born on 4/7/19 in Lorain, Ohio. Pianist/arranger for **Sammy Kaye**. Also arranged for various other bands and singers. His band was credited with stimulating a 1950s revival of the **Glenn Miller** sound. Voted America's #1 Band in *Billboard's* 1953 Disk Jockey poll.

| 3/18/50 | ❶³ | 35 | | 1 Ralph Flanagan plays Rodgers & Hammerstein II for dancing 45³ [I] $25 RCA Victor 268 |

Some Enchanted Evening ● People Will Say We're In Love ● The Surrey With The Fringe On Top ● It Might As Well Be Spring ● If I Loved You ● Oh, What A Beautiful Mornin'

| 6/16/51 | 10 | 1 | | 2 Ralph Flanagan favorites 45³ [I] $25 RCA Victor 308 |

My Hero *[27]* ● Swing To 45 ● Penthouse Serenade ● Where Or When ● **Joshua** *[17]* ● Giannina Mia

| 7/7/51 | 7 | 4 | | 3 Let's Dance Again with Flanagan 45³ $25 RCA Victor 311 |

I'm Dancing With Tears In My Eyes *[Harry Prime, vocal]* ● Dancing On The Ceiling ● I Won't Dance ● Let's Face The Music And Dance ● Save The Last Dance For Me *[Harry Prime, vocal]* ● Dancing In The Dark

| 7/5/52 | 5 | 14 | | 4 Dance To The Top Pops [I] $25 RCA Victor 3084 |

'33' [10"] LPM-3084 (#5) / '45' [4] WP-3084 (#6)
I'll Walk Alone ● Be Anything (But Be Mine) ● Kiss Of Fire ● The Blacksmith Blues ● **Delicado** *[26]* ● I'm Yours ● Forgive Me ● Just A Little Lovin' (Will Go A Long Way)

FOMEEN, Basil — see SONGS OF OUR TIMES ("1925"/"1928")

FOUR ACES featuring Al Alberts

Vocal group from Chester, Pennsylvania: Al Alberts (lead singer), Dave Mahoney (tenor), Sol Vaccaro (baritone) and Lou Silvestri (bass). Worked Ye Olde Mill near Philadelphia, late 1940s. First recorded for Victoria in 1951. Group has undergone several personnel changes over the years.

| 11/8/52 | 4 | 17 | | The Four Aces $50 Decca 9-361 |

'45' [4] 9-361 (#4) / '33' [10"] DL-5429 (#5)
Squeeze Me *[20]* ● **Heart And Soul** *[11]* ● My Devotion ● I'll Never Smile Again ● Ti-Pi-Tin ● Heaven Can Wait ● La Rosita ● Take Me In Your Arms

FOUR FRESHMEN, The   TPA

Vocal group from Indianapolis: brothers Ross and Don Barbour, their cousin Bob Flanigan and Ken Albers. Don Barbour died in a car crash on 10/5/61 (age 32).

| 9/4/54 | 7 | 18 | | Voices In Modern $40 Capitol 522 |

EP: Capitol EPF-522 (#7); LP: Capitol H-522 (#8)
After You ● Over The Rainbow ● My Heart Stood Still ● The Nearness Of You ● Holiday ● Stormy Weather ● Street Of Dreams ● We'll Be Together Again ● Circus ● Mood Indigo ● It Happened Once Before ● **It's A Blue World** *[30]*

★24★ **FROMAN, Jane**

Born Ellen Jane Froman on 11/10/07 in University City, Missouri. Died on 4/22/80 (age 72). Featured in many Broadway musicals and radio programs during the 1930s and 1940s. Recovered from serious injuries in a 1943 plane crash. Honored by Hollywood in the 1952 movie *With A Song In My Heart*.

| 3/29/52 | ❶²⁵ | 44 | | With A Song In My Heart... [S] $40 Capitol 309 |

'45' [4] KDF-309 (#1/25 wks.) / '33' [10"] L-309 (#1/23 wks.); Susan Hayward portrayed Froman in the movie
It's A Good Day ● Tea For Two ● Blue Moon ● Embraceable You ● Get Happy ● Medley: **I'll Walk Alone** *[14]*/ They're Either Too Young Or Too Old ● Medley: An American Medley/With A Song In My Heart

G

GARBER, Jan, and his Orchestra

Born on 11/5/1897 in Morristown, Pennsylvania. Died on 10/5/77 (age 79). Popular dance bandleader in mellow "sweet" style. Had over 50 charted hits from 1923-39.

| 10/16/48 | 2¹ | 6 | | 1 College Medleys 78⁴ $25 Capitol 95 |

Rambling Wreck From Georgia Tech ● Fight Alabama ● Maryland, My Maryland ● Hark The Sound Of The Tar Heel Voices ● Yale "Boola" Song ● The Princeton Cannon Song ● On Brave Old Army Team ● Anchors Aweigh ● Washington And Lee Swing ● Glory To Old Georgia ● Maine Stein Song ● Hail To Old O.S.C. ● Fordham "Ram" ● Hail To Pitt ● Lights Out ● Strike Up The Band

| 10/15/49 | 7 | 2 | | 2 More College Medleys 78³ $25 Capitol 173 |

University Of Minnesota Rouser ● On Wisconsin! ● Notre Dame Victory March ● Go U Northwestern ● We're Loyal To You, Illinois ● Across The Field ● The Eyes Of Texas Are Upon You ● Iowa Corn Song ● Indiana, Our Indiana ● Hail Purdue ● The Victors ● Fight Song

★32★ **GARLAND, Judy**   TPA

Born Frances Gumm on 6/10/22 in Grand Rapids, Minnesota. Died of an accidental sleeping pill overdose on 6/22/69 (age 47). Star of MGM movie musicals from 1935-54. Most famous movie role was "Dorothy" in 1939's *The Wizard Of Oz*. Hosted own TV variety series, 1963-64. Married to director Vincente Minnelli from 1945-51; their daughter is Liza Minnelli. Won Grammy's Lifetime Achievement Award in 1997. Also see **Movie Soundtracks** ("Words And Music").

| 3/24/45 | 2¹ | 5 | | 1 Meet Me In St. Louis 78³ [S] $75 Decca 380 |

Meet Me In St. Louis, Louis *[22]* ● Skip To My Lou ● **The Trolley Song** *[4]* ● Boys And Girls Like You *[not in movie]* ● Have Yourself A Merry Little Christmas ● The Boy Next Door

| 9/30/50 | 3 | 10 | | 2 Summer Stock [S] $50 MGM 56 |

JUDY GARLAND ● GENE KELLY
'45' [4] K-56 (#3) / '33' [10"] E-519 (#5)
(Howdy Neighbor) Happy Harvest *[Garland]* ● If You Feel Like Singing, Sing *[Garland]* ● You Wonderful You *[Kelly]* ● Mem'ry Island *[Gloria De Haven & Pete Roberts]* ● Dig-Dig-Dig Dig For Your Dinner *[Gene Kelly w/Phil Silvers]* ● Heavenly Music *[Gene Kelly & Phil Silvers]* ● Friendly Star*[Garland]* ● Get Happy *[Garland]*

| 10/30/54 | 4 | 14 | | 3 A Star Is Born [S] $50 Columbia 1201 |

EP: Columbia BA-1201 (#4); LP: Columbia BL-1201 (#5); BL-1201 ('33) is a deluxe boxed edition that includes a booklet
Gotta Have Me Go With You ● The Man That Got Away ● Born In A Trunk (Medley): I'll Get By/You Took Advantage Of Me/Black Bottom/The Peanut Vendor/My Melancholy Baby/Swanee ● Here's What I'm Here For ● It's A New World ● Someone At Last ● Lose That Long Face

GERSHWIN, George — see **BUTTERFIELD, Billy / DUCHIN, Eddy / KOSTELANETZ, Andre / SHORE, Dinah / SPIVAK, Charlie / MOVIE SOUNDTRACKS** ("An American In Paris") / **ORIGINAL CASTS** ("Porgy & Bess")

GLEASON, Jackie ★4★   TPA

Born Herbert John Gleason on 2/26/16 in Brooklyn, New York. Died of cancer on 6/24/87 (age 71). Legendary movie and TV comedian. Father of actress Linda Miller. Grandfather of actor Jason Patric. His albums featured dreamy "mood music" played by studio orchestras, conducted by Gleason with trumpet solos by Bobby Hackett and Pee Wee Erwin; much of the music was written by Gleason.

| 1/17/53 | ❶²³ | 149 | | 1 **Music For Lovers Only**   [I] | $25 | Capitol 352 |
'45' [EP] EBF-352 (#1/23 wks.) / '33' [10"] H-352 (#1/18 wks.); charted from 1/17/53 through 11/26/55; off charts for 5 years; re-entered on 1/30/61 (#89); final chart date: 7/9/61
     Alone Together ● My Funny Valentine ● But Not For Me ● Love Is Here To Stay ● I Only Have Eyes For You ● I'm In The Mood For Love ● Body And Soul ● Love (Your Spell Is Everywhere)

| 6/27/53 | 7 | 5 | | 2 **Lovers' Rhapsody**   [I] | $25 | Capitol 366 |
'45' [EP] EBF-366 (#7) / '33' [10"] H-366 (#9)
     Desire ● Flirtation ● Temptation ● Enchantment ● When Your Lover Has Gone ● Tenderly ● I'm Thru With Love ● Dark Is The Night (C'est Fini)

| 12/26/53+ | 2⁴ | 36 | | 3 **Music To Make You Misty**   [I] | $25 | Capitol 455 |
'33' [10"] H-455 (#2/4 wks.) / '45' [EP] EBF-455 (#2/2 wks.); #1 & 3 re-charted as a double album in 1956
     Say It Isn't So ● I Guess I'll Have To Change My Plan ● It Happened In Monterey ● It All Depends On You ● The Man I Love ● Mickey ● I Hadn't Anyone Till You ● You Were Meant For Me

| 2/20/54 | ❶¹ | 26 | | 4 **Tawny**   [I] | $25 | Capitol 471 |
'33' [10"] H-471 (#1) / '45' [EP] EBF-471 (#2/1 wk.); "Tawny" was introduced on TV as a musical and ballet dance production
     The Girl ● The Boy ● The Dance ● The Affair ● Little Girl ● I Cover The Waterfront ● Some Day ● If I Had You

| 9/4/54 | ❶⁴ | 57 | | 5 **Music, Martinis, and Memories**   [I] | $25 | Capitol 509 |
LP: Capitol W-509 (#1); EP: Capitol EAP-509 (#2/6 wks.)
     I Got It Bad And That Ain't Good ● My Ideal ● I Remember You ● Shangri-La ● It Could Happen To You ● Somebody Loves Me ● The Song Is Ended ● Once In A While ● I Can't Get Started ● Yesterdays ● I'll Be Seeing You ● Time On My Hands

| | ★39★ | | | **GODFREY, Arthur** | | |

Born on 8/31/03 in New York City. Died on 3/16/83 (age 79). One of the best-known stars in TV and radio history. His CBS radio show *Arthur Godfrey Time* and his CBS-TV shows *Arthur Godfrey And His Friends* and *Talent Scouts* were all top-rated shows in the 1950s.

| 3/28/53 | ❶¹ | 15 | | 1 **Arthur Godfrey's TV Calendar Show** | $30 | Columbia 355 |
'45' [EP] B-355 (#1) / '33' CL-521 (#2/5 wks.); concept album first presented on 1/28/53 on Godfrey's CBS-TV show; Godfrey introduces each tune, featuring regulars from his show, which represent the spirit of each month of the year
     Look Ahead *[The Mariners]* ● I'm In Love Again *[Marion Marlowe]* ● It's The Irish In Me *[Frank Parker]* ● Easter In Waikiki *[w/Haleloke]* ● If It Wasn't For Your Father *[w/The Chordettes]* ● Everything That's Yours Is Mine *[Janette Davis & Julius La Rosa]* ● Rockaway Beach *[Lu Ann Simms]* ● Summer's Symphony *[Julius La Rosa]* ● It's Autumn Again *[Marion Marlowe & Frank Parker]* ● Give A Cheer *[Janette Davis]* ● Appreciation ● The First Snow Of Winter ● Look Ahead (Reprise)

| 11/28/53 | ❶² | 2 | | 2 **Christmas With Arthur Godfrey And All The Little Godfreys**   [X] | $30 | Columbia 540 |
'33' CL-540 (#1) / '45' [EP] B-348 (#2/2 wks.)
     White Christmas *[w/cast]* ● Santa Claus Is Comin' To Town ● The Christmas Song *[Julius La Rosa]* ● Rudolph, The Red-Nosed Reindeer *[The Mariners]* ● Mele Kalikimaka *[Haleloke]* ● Winter Wonderland *[Janette Davis]* ● Frosty, The Snowman *[McGuire Sisters]* ● Medley: God Rest Ye Merry, Gentlemen/Deck The Hall With Boughs Of Holly *[The Mariners]* ● Here Comes Santa Claus *[Lu Ann Simms]* ● Jingle Bells ● Adeste Fideles ● Silent Night, Holy Night *[Marion Marlowe]* ● The First Nowell ● It Came Upon The Midnight Clear *[Marion Marlowe & Frank Parker]* ● Away In A Manger ● O Holy Night *[Frank Parker]* ● O Little Town Of Bethlehem *[Frank Parker & Marion Marlowe]* ● Hark! The Herald Angels Sing

| | ★28★ | | | **GOODMAN, Al, and his Orchestra** | | |

Born on 8/12/1890 in Nikopol, Russia. Died on 1/10/72 (age 81). Pianist-bandleader. Orchestra conductor for Broadway shows and for the historic movie *The Jazz Singer*. Later worked as a radio conductor/arranger.

| 1/26/46 | 2² | 7 | | 1 **Polonaise**   78⁴ | $30 | Victor 145 |
Earl Wrightson, Rose Inghram and Mary Martha Briney (vocals); songs from the operetta *Polonaise*, based on the music of Chopin
     Polonaise ● O Heart Of My Country ● Mazurka ● Just For To-Night ● Now I Know Your Face By Heart ● The Next Time I Care (I'll Be Careful) ● I Wonder As I Wander ● Finale

| 9/10/49 | 6 | 6 | | 2 **South Pacific** | $30 | RCA Victor BN-3 |
'78' [4] BN-3 (#6) / '45' [4] WK-18 (#6); charted for 6 weeks, re-charted on 8/19/50 on the 45 rpm chart; Goodman's version of songs from the Broadway musical; Dickinson Eastham and Sandra Deel (featured vocalists)
     A Cock-Eyed Optimist ● Some Enchanted Evening ● There Is Nothin' Like A Dame ● Bali Ha'i ● (I'm Gonna) Wash That Man (Right Out-A My Hair) ● A Wonderful Guy ● Younger Than Springtime ● This Nearly Was Mine

| 9/24/49 | 9 | 2 | | 3 **Miss Liberty**   78⁴ | $30 | RCA Victor BN-4 |
Goodman's version of songs from Irving Berlin's Broadway musical; Martha and Bob Wright (featured vocalists); above 2 albums released on RCA Victor's Bluebird Series
     Little Fish In A Big Pond ● Let's Take An Old Fashioned Walk ● Homework ● Paris Wakes Up And Smiles ● Only For Americans! ● (Just One Way To Say) I Love You ● You Can Have Him ● Give Me Your Tired, Your Poor

DEBUT	PEAK	WKS	Gold	ARTIST — Album Title	Sym	$	Label & Number

GOODMAN, Al, and his Orchestra — Cont'd

2/11/50 | 8 | 1 | | 4 **The Student Prince** ....45[4] | | $30 | RCA Victor WK-8

Goodman's version of songs from Sigmund Romberg's Broadway musical; Donald Dame and Frances Greer (vocalists)
Overture To The Student Prince ● Golden Days ● Drinking Song ● Student's March Song ● Deep In My Heart Dear-Part 1 ● Deep In My Heart Dear-Part 2 ● Serenade ● Just We Two

GOODMAN, Benny ★16★   TPA

Born on 5/30/09 in Chicago. Died of a heart attack on 6/13/86 (age 77). Nicknamed "The King of Swing." Clarinetist/bandleader since the 1930s. Fletcher Henderson arranged many of his early 1930s hits. Won Grammy's Lifetime Achievement Award in 1986. Also see **Various Artist Compilations**.

4/14/45 | 3 | 1 | | 1 **Hot Jazz By Benny Goodman**   78[4] **[I]** | | $50 | Victor HJ-2

4 trio and 4 quartet recordings from 1935-37 with Teddy Wilson (piano), **Lionel Hampton** (vibraphone) and Gene Krupa (drums); #2 in a series of 6 'Hot Jazz' albums released March, 1945 by different jazz artists
Body And Soul *[5/'35]* ● Tiger Rag ● **After You've Gone** *[20/'35]* ● Oh, Lady Be Good ● Dinah ● Vibraphone Blues ● **Stompin' At The Savoy** *[4/'37]* ● Runnin' Wild

5/18/46 | ❶[3] | 10 | | 2 **Benny Goodman Sextet Session**   78[4] **[I]** | | $50 | Columbia 113

with Red Norvo (vibraphone), Mel Powell and Teddy Wilson (piano), Morey Feld (drums), Mike Bryan (guitar) and Slam Stewart (bass)
Tiger Rag ● Ain't Misbehavin' ● She's Funny That Way *[Jane Harvey, vocal]* ● I Got Rhythm ● Just One Of Those Things ● China Boy ● Shine ● Rachel's Dream

12/23/50+ | 2[1] | 52 | | 3 **Carnegie Hall Jazz Concert**   **[I-L]** | | $100 | Columbia 160 [2]

'33' [2] SL-160 (#2) / '45' [12] B-250 (#5); The Goodman band's historic January 16, 1938 concert, featuring **Harry James**, Gene Krupa, Teddy Wilson, **Lionel Hampton**, Cootie Williams, Bobby Hackett, **Count Basie**, Ziggy Elman, Johnny Hodges and Lester Young
Don't Be That Way ● One O'Clock Jump ● Sensation Rag ● I'm Coming Virginia ● When My Baby Smiles At Me ● Shine ● Blue Reverie ● Life Goes To A Party ● Honeysuckle Rose ● Body And Soul ● Avalon ● The Man I Love ● I Got Rhythm ● Blue Skies ● Loch Lomond *[Martha Tilton, vocal]* ● Blue Room ● Swingtime In The Rockies ● Bei Mir Bist Du Schon ● China Boy ● Stompin' At The Savoy ● Dizzy Spells ● Sing Sing Sing ● Big John's Special

11/29/52 | ❶[8] | 20 | | 4 **1937/38 Jazz Concert No. 2**   **[I-L]** | | $75 | Columbia 180 [2]

'33' SL-180 (#1) / '45' A-1040 (#4); recordings of radio broadcasts during Goodman's performing tours, featuring **Harry James**, **Lionel Hampton**, **Gene Krupa**, Teddy Wilson and Ziggy Elman
Let's Dance ● Ridin' High ● Nice Work If You Can Get It ● Vibraphone Blues ● The Sheik Of Araby ● Peckin' ● Sunny Disposish ● Nagasaki ● St. Louis Blues ● Sugar Foot Stomp ● Moonglow ● I'm A Ding Dong Daddy From Dumas ● I Hadn't Anyone Till You ● Always ● Down South Camp Meetin' ● Sweet Leilani ● Sometimes I'm Happy ● Roll 'Em ● King Porter Stomp ● Have You Met Miss Jones ● Shine ● Minnie The Moocher's Wedding Day ● Runnin' Wild ● You Turned The Tables On Me ● Darktown Strutters' Ball ● My Gal Sal ● Bugle Call Rag ● Clarinet Marmalade ● Time On My Hands ● Stardust ● Benny Sent Me ● Everybody Loves My Baby ● Josephine ● Killer Diller ● Someday Sweetheart ● Caravan ● Goodbye

GOULD, Morton, and his Orchestra   TPA

Born on 12/10/13 in Richmond Hill, New York. Died on 2/21/96 (age 82). Conductor/arranger.

4/14/45 | 2[2] | 14 | | **After Dark**   78[4] **[I]** | | $40 | Columbia 107

78 rpm album set contains four large 12" records
Temptation ● Speak Low ● Dancing In The Dark ● Besame Mucho ● That Old Black Magic ● I Get A Kick Out Of You ● I've Got You Under My Skin ● The Very Thought Of You

GRANT, Bob — see SONGS OF OUR TIMES ("1917"/"1922"/"1927"/"1934"/"1938")

GRAY, Jerry, and His Orchestra

Born on 7/3/15 in Boston. Died on 8/10/76 (age 61). Orchestra leader/arranger.

2/9/52 | 6 | 9 | | **A Tribute To Glenn Miller** .... **[I]** | | $25 | Decca 9-286

'45' [4] 9-286 (#6) / '33' [10"] DL-5375 (#9)
St. Louis Blues ● Jeep Jockey Jump ● The Dipsy Doodle ● Who's Sorry Now? ● Shine On Harvest Moon ● Flag Waver ● Introduction To A Waltz ● V Hop

GRIFFIN, Ken   ★38★

Born on 12/28/09 in Columbia, Missouri. Died on 3/11/56 (age 46). Organist.

8/14/48 | 4 | 4 | | 1 **The Wizard Of The Organ**..78[3] **[I]** | | $20 | Rondo 1007

Doodle-Ee-Do ● American Patrol ● Every Little Movement ● Valencia ● If I Had You ● Little Brown Jug

12/11/48 | 4 | 5 | | 2 **Christmas Music** ....78[3] **[X-I]** | | $20 | Broadcast 500

Silent Night ● Joy To The World ● Santa Claus Is Comin' To Town ● White Christmas ● O Little Town Of Bethlehem ● Adeste Fideles (O Come, All Ye Faithful)

12/24/49 | 10 | 1 | | 3 **Merry Christmas**..78[3] **[X-I]** | | $20 | Rondo 1010

Hark The Herald Angels Sing ● It Came Upon A Midnight Clear ● Star Of The East ● O Christmas Tree (Oh Tannenbaum) ● Jingle Bells ● Our Christmas Waltz ● Winter Wonderland ● Up On The Housetop

H

HAMPTON, Lionel, All Stars

Born on 4/20/08 in Louisville, Kentucky; raised in Birmingham and Chicago. Died of heart failure on 8/31/2002 (age 94). Legendary jazz vibraphonist. First recorded with the Reb Spikes band for Hollywood in 1924. Started as a drummer; added vibes in 1930. Worked with Les Hite, then **Benny Goodman** from 1936-40; own band thereafter. The first jazz musician to feature vibes. Acted in several movies. All Stars: Charlie Shavers (trumpet), Barney Kessel (guitar), Slam Stewart (bass), Willie Smith (alto sax), Corky Corcoran (tenor sax), Tommy Todd (piano), and Lee Young and Jackie Mills (drums). Also see **Various Artist Compilations**.

| 1/26/52 | 10 | 1 | | **Gene Norman presents Just Jazz**..45^4 **[I-L]** | **$100** | Decca 9-154 |

recorded on 8/4/47 at the Pasadena Civic Auditorium; Hampton performs on "Star Dust" but not on "The Man I Love"

Star Dust (4 Parts) ● The Man I Love (4 Parts)

HARRIS, Phil

Born on 6/24/04 in Linton, Indiana. Died of heart failure on 8/11/95 (age 91). Bandleader/drummer/radio-TV-movie personality. Co-hosted a radio program with his wife, actress Alice Faye, from 1947-54.

| 4/3/48 | 5 | 1 | | **On The Record By Phil Harris**...78^3 **[N]** | $40 | RCA Victor 199 |

That's What I Like About The South ● Look Out Stranger I'm A Texas Ranger *[w/The Sportsmen]* ● **The Dark Town Poker Club** *[10]* ● 44 Sycamore ● Pappy's Little Jug ● Minnie The Mermaid (A Love Song in Fish Time)

HAYMES, Dick

Born on 9/13/16 in Buenos Aires, Argentina; raised in America. Died of cancer on 3/28/80 (age 63). Ballad singer with **Harry James**, **Benny Goodman** and **Tommy Dorsey** in the early 1940s. Appeared in various movies from 1944-53. Married to actress Rita Hayworth from 1953-55. His daughter Stephanie Haymes (with his fifth wife, singer Fran Jeffries) married rock songwriter Bernie Taupin in 1993. Also see **Ethel Merman** ("Call Me Madam").

| 2/16/46 | ❶^4 | 8 | | **State Fair** | 78^3 | $40 | Decca 412 |

although Haymes starred in the movie *State Fair*, this album is not from the movie soundtrack

That's For Me *[6]* ● **It Might As Well Be Spring** *[5]* ● Isn't It Kinda Fun ● The Lord's Been Good To Me *[not from movie]* ● It's A Grand Night For Singing ● All I Owe Ioway

HEIDT, Horace — see CONTINO, Dick

HERMAN, Woody

Born on 5/16/13 in Milwaukee. Died of heart failure on 10/29/87 (age 74). Played clarinet and saxophone for Harry Sosnik, Gus Arnheim and Isham Jones before assembling his own "Band That Plays The Blues" in 1936. Sax stars Stan Getz and Zoot Sims led his famous jazz ensemble in the late 1940s. Won Grammy's Lifetime Achievement Award in 1987. One of the most innovative and contemporary of all bandleaders..

TPA

| 3/5/49 | 6 | 8 | | 1 **Sequence In Jazz**...78^3 **[I]** | $30 | Columbia 177 |

Summer Sequence ● Lady McGowan's Dream ● Everywhere ● Back Talk

| 10/11/52 | 9 | 1 | | 2 **Woody Herman (And The Herd) At Carnegie Hall, 1946-Vol. 1**.............10" **[I-L]** | $50 | MGM 158 |

March 25, 1946 concert featuring Flip Phillips (tenor sax), Shorty Rogers (trumpet), Bill Harris (trombone) and Red Norvo (vibraharp)

Red Top ● Sweet And Lovely ● Superman With A Horn ● Bijou ● Wild Root ● Four Men On A Horse ● Your Father's Mustache

HOUR OF CHARM

Female choir conducted by Russian-born bandleader Phil Spitalny who came to the U.S. in 1917. In 1934, he formed an "all-girl" orchestra. His *Hour Of Charm* radio show was a long-running hit through the 1940s. Phil was born on 11/7/1890; died on 10/11/70 (age 79).

| 9/15/45 | 4 | 1 | | 1 **Favorite Melodies from the Hour Of Charm**...78^4 | $40 | Columbia 108 |

The Battle Hymn Of The Republic ● National Emblem March ● Onward Christian Soldiers ● The Lord's Prayer ● The Rosary ● Love's Old Sweet Song ● Ave Maria ● The Lost Chord

| 12/18/48+ | 4 | 4 | | 2 **Christmas Carols by the Hour of Charm**...78^3 **[X]** | $50 | Charm 1 |

Silent Night ● Carol Of The Bells ● God Rest Ye Merry, Gentlemen ● 'Twas The Night Before Christmas ● Joy To The World ● The First Noël ● Adeste Fidelis (Oh Come, All Ye Faithful) ● Hark! The Herald Angels Sing ● Oh Little Town Of Bethlehem

HOWARD, Eddy, And His Orchestra

Born on 9/12/14 in Woodland, California. Died on 5/23/63 (age 48). Singer with the Dick Jurgens band from 1934-40. Composer of "My Last Goodbye" and "Careless."

| 4/5/47 | 3 | 15 | | **Romance with Eddy Howard** | 78^3 | $25 | Majestic 15 |

Goodbye Girls, I'm Through ● Till We Meet Again ● Once In A While ● Paradise ● **Heartaches** *[11]* ● Don't Tell Her What Happened To Me

HUTTON, Betty — see MOVIE SOUNDTRACKS ("Annie Get Your Gun")

I

INK SPOTS

R&B vocal group from Indianapolis: Ivory "Deek" Watson, Charlie Fuqua, Orville "Hoppy" Jones and Bill Kenny. Jones died on 10/18/44 (age 39); replaced by Bill Kenny's brother, Herb Kenny. Watson left in 1945 to form The Four Tunes. The Kenny brothers left in 1952. Watson died on 11/4/69 (age 60). Fuqua died on 12/21/71 (age 61). Bill Kenny died on 3/23/78 (age 67). Herb Kenny died on 7/11/92 (age 78). Group inducted into the Rock and Roll Hall of Fame in 1989 as forefathers of rock 'n' roll.

| 9/21/46 | ❶^7 | 15 | | **Ink Spots** | 78^4 **[G]** | $60 | Decca 477 |

charted for 13 weeks; re-charted on 8/20/49 for 2 more weeks (#8); 1939-41 recordings

If I Didn't Care *[2/'39]* ● **Whispering Grass (Don't Tell The Trees)** *[10]* ● **Do I Worry?** *[14]* ● **Java Jive** *[17]* ● We Three (My Echo, My Shadow And Me) *[3]* ● Maybe *[2]* ● I'll Never Smile Again ● (It Will Have To Do) Until The Real Thing Comes Along

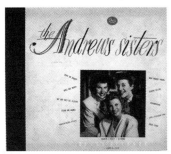

The Andrews Sisters
The Andrews Sisters ('46)

Louis Armstrong and The All Stars
Satchmo At Symphony Hall ('51)

Tex Beneke with The Miller Ochestra
Prom Date ('47)

Les Brown and His Band of Renown
Over The Rainbow ('51)

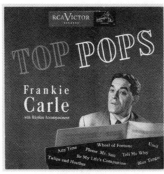

Frankie Carle
Top Pops ('52)

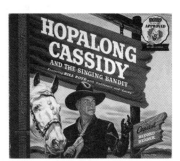

Hopalong Cassidy...*Hopalong Cassidy And The Singing Bandit ('50)*

Rosemary Clooney and Harry James
Hollywood's Best ('52)

Buddy Cole
Piano Cocktails ('46)

The Crew-Cuts
Crewcuts on the Campus ('54)

Bing Crosby...*A Connecticut Yankee In King Arthur's Court ('49)*

Bing Crosby/Danny Kaye/Evelyn Knight/ Ella Fitzgerald...*South Pacific ('49)*

Bing Crosby - Danny Kaye - Peggy Lee
White Christmas ('54)

Jimmy Dorsey and his Orchestra
Latin American Favorites ('46)

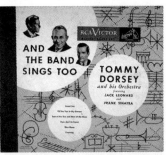

Tommy Dorsey and his Orchestra
And The Band Sings Too ('49)

Tommy Dorsey And His Orchestra
Showboat ('46)

Billy Eckstine
Songs By Billy Eckstine ('50)

Eddie Fisher
Eddie Fisher Sings ('52)

Ralph Flanagan and his Orchestra
Let's Dance Again with Flanagan ('51)

Judy Garland - Gene Kelly
Summer Stock ('50)

Arthur Godfrey
Arthur Godfrey's TV Calendar Show ('53)

Al Jolson
Jolson Sings Again ('49)

Spike Jones and his City Slickers
Musical Depreciation ('46)

Mario Lanza
The Toast Of New Orleans ('50)

Peggy Lee
Rendezvous with Peggy Lee ('48)

J

★21★ **JAMES, Harry** TPA
Born on 3/15/16 in Albany, Georgia. Died of cancer on 7/5/83 (age 67). Star trumpet player/bandleader. Achieved fame playing with **Benny Goodman** in the late 1930s. James's own band was immensely popular during the 1940s. Married to movie star Betty Grable from 1943-65.

12/7/46+ **❶**[1] **9** 1 **All-Time Favorites by Harry James** 78[4] **[G-I]** $40 Columbia 117
recordings from 1938-42
Ciribiribin *[10]* ● Sleepy Lagoon *[1]* ● One O'Clock Jump *[7/'38]* ● Two O'Clock Jump ● **You Made Me Love You (I Didn't Want To Do It)** *[5]* ● Music Makers *[9]* ● **The Flight Of The Bumble Bee** *[20]* ● Concerto For Trumpet

4/8/50 **❶**[12] **50** 2 **Young Man With A Horn** **[S]** $40 Columbia 6106
DORIS DAY and HARRY JAMES
'33' [10"] CL-6106 (#1) / '45' [4] B-198 (#9); movie loosely based on the career of jazz great Bix Beiderbecke
I May Be Wrong *[James]* ● Get Happy *[James]* ● Man I Love *[James]* ● Too Marvelous For Words ● The Very Thought Of You ● Limehouse Blues *[James]* ● Melancholy Rhapsody *[James]* ● With A Song In My Heart

12/6/52+ **3** **8** 3 **Hollywood's Best** $40 Columbia 6224
ROSEMARY CLOONEY and HARRY JAMES
'33' [10"] CL-6224 (#3) / '45' [4] B-319 (#7); all songs are Academy Award-winning 'Best Songs'
You'll Never Know ● On The Atchison, Topeka And The Santa Fe ● It Might As Well Be Spring ● Over The Rainbow ● Sweet Leilani ● The Continental ● When You Wish Upon A Star ● In The Cool, Cool, Cool Of The Evening

JAMES, Joni TPA
Born Joan Carmello Babbo on 9/22/30 in Chicago. Worked as a dancer from age 12; model during high school. Toured Canada as a dancer in the late 1940s. First recorded for Sharp in 1952. Married her orchestral arranger/conductor (1958-61) Tony Acquaviva (died on 9/27/86, age 61).

12/26/53+ **5** **7** **Let There Be Love** .... $75 MGM 222
'45' [EP] X-222 (#5) / '33' [10"] E-222 (#6); Lew Douglas (orch.)
Let There Be Love ● My Romance ● The Nearness Of You ● You're Mine You ● You're My Everything ● You're Nearer ● Love Is Here To Stay ● I'll Be Seeing You

JENKINS, Gordon TPA
Born on 5/12/10 in Webster Groves, Missouri. Died of ALS (Lou Gehrig's disease) on 5/1/84 (age 73). Pianist/arranger/ composer in the early 1930s with Isham Jones, **Benny Goodman** and others. Musical director/conductor for Decca Records beginning in 1945.

1/23/54 **8** **1** **Gordon Jenkins' "Seven Dreams"** .... $30 Decca 9011
'33' DL-9011 (#8) / '45' [EP] ED-900 (#10); a seven-part Broadway-type musical show produced for records
The Professor ● The Conductor ● The Caretaker ● The Cocktail Party ● The Pink Houseboat ● The Nightmare ● The Girl On The Rock

JOHNSON, Pete
Born Kermit Johnson on 3/24/04 in Kansas City, Missouri. Died of a heart attack on 3/23/67 (age 62). Pianist/drummer. Formed duo with **Albert Ammons** in 1938.

3/24/45 **2**[1] **11** 8 **To The Bar** (Two Piano Boogie Woogie For Dancing) 78[4] **[I]** $150 RCA Victor 69
PETE JOHNSON and ALBERT AMMONS
originally released September, 1941
Cuttin' The Boogie ● Barrel House Boogie ● Boogie Woogie Man ● Walkin' The Boogie ● Sixth Avenue Express ● Pine Creek ● Foot Pedal Boogie ● Movin' The Boogie

JOLSON, Al ★6★ TPA
Born Asa Yoelson on 3/26/1886 in St. Petersburg, Russia; raised in Washington DC. Died on 10/23/50 (age 64). One of the most popular entertainers of the 20th century. Starred in several movies and Broadway shows. Married to actress Ruby Keeler from 1928-39.

1/18/47 **❶**[25] **61** 1 **Al Jolson in songs he made famous** **[S]** $30 Decca 469
'78' [4] A-469 (#1) / '45' [4] 9-9 (#3); new recordings of Jolson's biggest hits from 1913-28 for inclusion in the movie soundtrack *The Jolson Story*; on and off the charts for 4 years: charted 51 weeks (#1), re-charted: 11/13/48 (#9, 1 week), 4/30/49 (#9, 1 week), 3/11/50 (#9, 1 week), 11/18/50 (#5, 7 weeks)
April Showers *[16]* ● Swanee ● California, Here I Come ● Rock-A-Bye Your Baby With A Dixie Melody ● You Made Me Love You (I Didn't Want To Do It) ● Ma Blushin' Rosie (Ma Posie Sweet) ● Sonny Boy *[not in movie]* ● My Mammy

8/16/47 **❶**[10] **28** 2 **Al Jolson Souvenir Album** **[S]** $30 Decca 575
'78' [4] A-575 (#1) / '45' [4] 9-8 (#10-charted only 1 week on 11/18/50); Morris Stoloff (orch.); includes more new recordings of Jolson's 1920's hits from the movie soundtrack *The Jolson Story*
Waiting For The Robert E. Lee ● When You Were Sweet Sixteen ● Golden Gate ● I'm Sitting On Top Of The World ● Toot, Toot, Tootsie! ● Back In Your Own Back Yard ● Carolina In The Morning ● Liza (All The Clouds'll Roll Away)

7/10/48 **❶**[14] **21** 3 **Al Jolson - Volume Three** 78[4] $30 Decca 649
Morris Stoloff (orch.); more new recordings of Jolson's early hits
I Want A Girl (Just Like The Girl That Married Dear Old Dad) ● Where The Black Eyed Susans Grow ● When The Red, Red, Robin Comes Bob, Bob, Bobbin' Along ● Someone Else May Be There While I'm Gone ● For Me And My Gal ● When I Leave The World Behind ● There's A Rainbow 'Round My Shoulder ● About A Quarter To Nine

9/10/49 **2**[16] **49** 4 **Jolson Sings Again** **[S]** $30 Decca 716
'78' [4] A-716 (#2/16 wks.) / '45' [4] 9-4 (#2/2 wks.); sequel to the movie *The Jolson Story* starring Larry Parks as Jolson (also see #1 & 2 above)
Pretty Baby ● I'm Looking Over A Four Leaf Clover ● Baby Face ● Give My Regards To Broadway ● I'm Just Wild About Harry ● After You've Gone ● Chinatown, My Chinatown ● I Only Have Eyes For You ● Is It True What They Say About Dixie?

JONES, Allan

Born on 10/14/07 in Scranton, Pennsylvania. Died of cancer on 6/27/92 (age 84). Singer/actor. Starred in several Hollywood musicals from 1935-45. Married to actress Irene Hervey from 1936-57; their son is popular singer Jack Jones.

| 8/31/46 | 5 | 1 | | **Night and Day and other Cole Porter show hits** ....78[4] | | $50 | Victor 1033 |

Ray Sinatra (orch.); 78 rpm album set released on Victor's 12" Red Seal Records

Night And Day ● I've Got You Under My Skin ● Begin The Beguine ● Why Shouldn't I ● What Is This Thing Called Love ● Rosalie ● Easy To Love ● In The Still Of The Night

★33★ JONES, Spike, and his City Slickers TPA

Born Lindley Armstrong Jones on 12/14/11 in Long Beach, California. Died of emphysema on 5/1/65 (age 53). Novelty bandleader. Known as "The King of Corn." His City Slickers included Red Ingle, Mickey Katz, Carl Grayson, Freddie Morgan, George Rock and Doodles Weaver.

| 1/5/46 | 2[4] | 9 | | **1 Spike Jones presents for the Kiddies The Nutcracker Suite**
with apologies to Tchaikovsky | [X-N] | $100 | Victor 143 |

Jones parodies the classic Tchaikovsky *Nutcracker Suite* ballet

The Little Girl's Dream ● Land Of The Sugar Plum Fairy ● The Fairy Ball ● The Mysterious Room ● Back To The Fairy Ball ● End Of The Little Girl's Dream

| 7/27/46 | 4 | 4 | | **2 Musical Depreciation** ....78[5] | [N] | $75 | RCA Victor no # |

RCA Victor did not give this album set a catalog number because different Jones' '78' singles were mixed in with each album set

| 6/10/50 | 6 | 8 | | **3 Spike Jones plays The Charleston for dancing** ....45[3] | [N] | $75 | RCA Victor 277 |

The Charleston ● Black Bottom ● I Wonder Where My Baby Is Tonight ● Varsity Drag ● Doin' The New Raccoon ● Charlestono-Mio

K

KAYE, Danny ★17★

Born David Daniel Kaminsky on 1/18/13 in Brooklyn, New York. Died of heart failure on 3/3/87 (age 74). Legendary comedic actor/singer. Acted in numerous movies and Broadway shows. Married lyricist Sylvia Fine in 1940.

| 3/24/45 | 3 | 2 | | **1 Columbia presents Danny Kaye** | 78[4] [N] | $40 | Columbia 91 |

Johnny Green (orch.)

Let's Not Talk About Love ● Minnie The Moocher ● Farming ● Anatole Of Paris ● The Babbitt And The Bromide ● The Fairy Pipers ● Eileen ● Dinah

| 6/18/49 | 4 | 9 | | **2 South Pacific** ....78[4] | | $40 | Decca 714 |

BING CROSBY/DANNY KAYE/EVELYN KNIGHT/ELLA FITZGERALD

selections from the Broadway musical of the same title (not the Original Cast)

Bali Ha'i *[Crosby]* ● Some Enchanted Evening *[Crosby]* ● There Is Nothin' Like A Dame *[Kaye]* ● Honey Bun *[Kaye]* ● A Wonderful Guy *[Knight]* ● A Cock-Eyed Optimist *[Knight]* ● I'm Gonna Wash That Man Right Outa My Hair *[Fitzgerald]* ● Happy Talk *[Fitzgerald]*

| 1/17/53 | ❶[17] | 32 | | **3 Hans Christian Andersen** | [S] | $40 | Decca 5433 |

'33' [10"] DL-5433 (#1/17 wks.) / '45' [4] 9-364 (#1/10 wks.); Gordon Jenkins (orch.)

I'm Hans Christian Andersen ● Anywhere I Wander ● The Ugly Duckling ● Inchworm ● Thumbelina ● No Two People *[w/Jane Wyman]* ● The King's New Clothes ● Wonderful Copenhagen

| 11/27/54 | 2[2] | 8 | | **4 White Christmas** | [S] | $40 | Decca 8083 |

BING CROSBY - DANNY KAYE - PEGGY LEE

EP: Decca ED-819 (#2); LP: Decca DL-8083 (#4); Peggy Lee (who was not in the movie) re-recorded **Rosemary Clooney's** part (who was in the movie but was not allowed to perform on Decca because of her Columbia contract)

Medley: Old Man/Gee, I Wish I Was Back In The Army *[Crosby & Kaye]* ● Sisters *[Lee]* ● Best Things Happen While You're Dancing *[Kaye]* ● Snow *[w/Trudy Stevens]* ● Medley: Blue Skies/Mandy *[Crosby & Kaye]* ● Choreography *[Kaye]* ● Count Your Blessings Instead Of Sheep *[Crosby]* ● Love, You Didn't Do Right By Me *[Lee]* ● What Can You Do With A General *[Crosby]* ● White Christmas (Finale) *[w/Trudy Stevens]*

★30★ KAYE, Sammy, and his Orchestra TPA

Born on 3/13/10 in Rocky River, Ohio. Died of cancer on 6/2/87 (age 77). Leader of popular "sweet" dance band with the slogan "Swing and Sway with Sammy Kaye." Also played clarinet and alto sax. Also see **Various Artist Compilations**.

| 9/15/45 | 3 | 1 | | **1 Stephen Foster Favorites** | 78[5] | $25 | Victor 140 |

Billy Williams, Nancy Norman & The Five Kaydets (vocals)

My Old Kentucky Home ● Swanee River ● Beautiful Dreamer ● Old Black Joe ● I Dream Of Jeanie With The Light Brown Hair ● Massa's In The Cold, Cold Ground ● Come Where My Love Lies Dreaming ● Oh Susanna ● Camptown Races ● Foster Medley: Swanee River/Old Black Joe

| 11/20/48 | 3 | 15 | | **2 Dusty Manuscripts** | 78[4] | $25 | RCA Victor 228 |

Don Cornell and Laura Leslie (vocals); readings by Sammy Kaye

I Want A Girl (Just Like the Girl That Married Dear Old Dad) ● Cuddle Up A Little Closer, Lovey Mine ● The World Is Waiting For The Sunrise ● Down Among The Sheltering Palms ● There But For You Go I ● My Son ● I Still Love You ● We Just Couldn't Say Good Bye

| 4/8/50 | 4 | 19 | | **3 Sammy Kaye plays Irving Berlin for dancing** ....45[3] | | $25 | RCA Victor 266 |

Tony Alamo (vocal); half of the cuts are instrumentals

Blue Skies ● Always ● How Deep Is The Ocean ● Say It Isn't So ● A Pretty Girl Is Like A Melody ● Alexander's Ragtime Band

KEEL, Howard — see DAY, Doris ("Calamity Jane") / MOVIE SOUNDTRACKS
("Annie Get Your Gun"/"Kiss Me Kate"/"Lovely To Look At"/"Pagan Love Song"/
"Rose Marie"/"Seven Brides For Seven Brothers"/"Show Boat")

KELLY, Gene — see GARLAND, Judy / MOVIE SOUNDTRACKS ("An American In Paris"/"Brigadoon"/"Singin' In The Rain")

KENTON, Stan, And His Orchestra ★11★   TPA

Born on 2/19/12 in Wichita, Kansas. Died of a stroke on 8/25/79 (age 67). One of the most consistently successful bandleaders of the postwar era. Began as a pianist for Gus Arnheim and other bands before becoming composer ("Artistry In Rhythm") and arranger to his own big band. A leader in the "progressive jazz" movement; his orchestras always featured top musicians and vocalists (particularly **June Christy**). Third person named to the Jazz Hall of Fame.

12/21/46+	2[1]	7		1 **Artistry in Rhythm**	78[4] [I]	$50	Capitol 39

Come Back To Sorrento ● Artistry In Bolero ● Willow Weep For Me *[June Christy, vocal]* ● Fantasy ● Safranski ● Opus In Pastels ● Ain't No Misery In Me *[June Christy, vocal]* ● Artistry In Percussion

5/29/48	❶[8]	27		2 **A Presentation Of Progressive Jazz**	78[4] [I]	$50	Capitol 79

Monotony ● Cuban Carnival ● Lament ● Lonely Woman *[June Christy, vocal]* ● Elegy For Alto ● Impressionism ● Fugue For Rhythm Section ● This Is My Theme *[June Christy, vocal]*

2/19/49	2[2]	16		3 **Stan Kenton Encores**	78[4] [I]	$50	Capitol 113

Peg O' My Heart ● He's Funny That Way *[June Christy, vocal]* ● Capitol Punishment ● Painted Rhythm ● Lover ● Somnambulism ● Abstraction ● Chorale For Brass, Piano And Bongo

3/25/50	3	15		4 **Innovations In Modern Music,** Volume One	[I]	$40	Capitol 189

'33' P-189 (#3) / '45' [4] KDM-189 (#10)

Trajectories ● Theme For Sunday ● Conflict ● Incident In Jazz ● Lonesome Road *[June Christy, vocal]* ● Mirage ● Solitaire ● Cuban Episode

11/25/50	8	4		5 **Stan Kenton Presents:**	[I]	$40	Capitol 248

'45' [3] KCF-248 (#8) / '33' [10'] L-248 (#9); featuring Art Pepper (saxophones), Maynard Ferguson (trumpet) and Shelly Manne (drums)

Art Pepper ● Maynard Ferguson ● The Halls Of Brass ● June Christy ● The House Of Strings ● Shelly Manne

5/2/53	8	5		6 **New Concepts** of artistry in rhythm	[I]	$40	Capitol 383

'45' [4] EBF-383 (#8) / '33' [10'] H-383 (#8)

23°N-82°W ● Portrait Of A Count ● Invention For Guitar And Trumpet ● My Lady ● Young Blood ● Frank Speaking ● Prologue (This is an Orchestra!) ● Improvisation

KING, Wayne, and his Orchestra   ★36★

Born on 2/16/01 in Savannah, Illinois. Died on 7/16/85 (age 84). Known as "The Waltz King." Alto saxophonist/vocalist. Featured orchestra for years at Chicago's Aragon Ballroom. Theme song: "The Waltz You Saved For Me." Also see **Various Artist Compilations**.

9/14/46	2[1]	5		1 **Irving Berlin Melodies**	78[4]	$20	RCA Victor 159

Earl Randall and Nancy Evans (vocals)

Always ● Blue Skies ● All Alone ● Say It With Music ● Remember ● A Pretty Girl Is Like A Melody ● What'll I Do ● Alexander's Ragtime Band

5/10/47	2[1]	8		2 **Wayne King Waltzes** - Volume 2	78[4] [I]	$20	RCA Victor 171

Song Of The Islands *[12/'30]* ● (I'll Be With You) In Apple Blossom Time ● **Mexicali Rose** ● **Maria Elena** *[2]* ● Carolina Moon ● The Anniversary Waltz ● Roses Of Picardy ● 'Til The Sands Of The Desert Grow Cold

4/8/50	9	4		3 **Wayne King plays Johann Strauss for dancing**	45[3] [I]	$20	RCA Victor 270

The Blue Danube ● Tales From The Vienna Woods ● You And You ● Voices Of Spring ● Emperor Waltz ● Wine, Woman And Song

KITT, Eartha

Born on 1/17/27 in Columbia, South Carolina. Black singer/actress. Appeared in several movies and as "Catwoman" on TV's *Batman*.

8/1/53	2[2]	9		1 **RCA Victor Presents Eartha Kitt**		$50	RCA Victor 3062

'45' [EP] EPB-3062 (#2) / '33' [10'] LPM-3062 (#4); Kitt sings in French, Spanish, Turkish, Swahili and English

I Want To Be Evil ● **C'est Si Bon (It's So Good)** *[8]* ● Angelitos Negros ● Avril Au Portugal (The Whisp'ring Serenade) ● Uska Dara - A Turkish Tale ● African Lullaby ● Mountain High, Valley Low ● Lilac Wine (Dance Me a Song)

2/13/54	5	12		2 **That Bad Eartha**		$50	RCA Victor 3187

'33' [10'] LPM-3187 (#5) / '45' [EP] EPB-3187 (#7); Henri Rene (orch., above 2)

Under The Bridges Of Paris ● Let's Do It ● The Blues ● My Heart Belongs To Daddy ● Sandy's Tune ● Señor ● Smoke Gets In Your Eyes ● Salanga Dou

KNIGHT, Evelyn — see CROSBY, Bing ("South Pacific")

KOSTELANETZ, Andre, and his Orchestra   TPA

Born on 12/22/01 in St. Petersburg, Russia. Died on 1/13/80 (age 78). Conductor/arranger.

10/13/45	5	2		**Music of George Gershwin**	78[4] [I]	$25	Columbia 559

78 rpm album set released on Columbia's classical Masterworks label

Embraceable You ● Fascinatin' Rhythm ● The Man I Love ● 'S Wonderful ● Medley: Someone To Watch Over Me/ Oh, Lady Be Good ● Maybe ● Soon

L

LAINE, Frankie — TPA

Born Frank Paul LoVecchio on 3/30/13 in Chicago. To Los Angeles in the early 1940s. First recorded for Exclusive in 1945. Signed to the Mercury label in 1947. Dynamic singer whose popularity lasted well into the rock era.

| 2/2/52 | 8 | 4 | | **One For My Baby** ....45[4] | | $35 | Columbia 287 |

Paul Weston (orch.)

Tomorrow Mountain ● Song Of The Islands ● She Reminds Me Of You ● To Be Worthy Of You ● When It's Sleepy Time Down South ● Love Is Such A Cheat ● Necessary Evil ● One For My Baby

LANZA, Mario ★3★ — TPA

Born Alfredo Cocozza on 1/31/21 in Philadelphia. Died of a heart attack on 10/7/59 (age 38). Became the most popular operatic tenor since Caruso, with his voice featured in seven movies, though no theatrical operas.

| 10/29/49 | 2[1] | 27 | | 1 **That Midnight Kiss** | 78[3] **[S]** | $50 | RCA Victor 1330 |

78 rpm album set released on RCA Victor's 12" classical Red Seal label

Che Gelida Manina ● Celeste Aida ● Mamma Mia Che Vo' Sape? ● Core 'Ngrato ● I Know, I Know, I Know ● They Didn't Believe Me

| 11/4/50+ | ❶[6] | 38 | | 2 **The Toast Of New Orleans** | 45[2] **[S]** | $50 | RCA Victor 1417 |

four popular songs (non-classical) from the movie; Ray Sinatra (orch.); issued in a softcover double-pocket 45 rpm package with a four-page bound-in booklet; Lanza also released a classical 45 rpm package on RCA 1395

Toast Of New Orleans ● The Bayou Lullaby ● Boom Biddy Boom ● Tina-Lina

| 3/31/51 | ❶[10] | 48 | | 3 **The Great Caruso** | **[S]** | $35 | RCA Victor 1127 |

'33' LM-1127 (#1/10 wks.) / '45' [4] WDM-1506 (#1/10 wks.); Constantine Callinicos (orch.)

Questa O Quella ● La Donna É Mobile ● Parmi Veder Le Lagrime ● Recondita Armonia ● E Lucevan Le Stelle ● Una Furtiva Lagrima ● Cielo E Mar! ● **Vesti La Giubba** [21]

| 11/17/51 | ❶[3] | 8 | | 4 **Mario Lanza sings Christmas songs** | **[X]** | $30 | RCA Victor 1649 |

'45' [4] WDM-1649 (#1/3 wks.) / '33' [10"] LM-155 (#1/3 wks.); Ray Sinatra (orch.); reissued in 1956 on RCA Victor 2029 with an additional seven songs as *Lanza Sings Christmas Carols*

The Lords Prayer ● The First Noel ● O Come, All Ye Faithful ● Away In A Manger ● We Three Kings Of Orient Are ● Oh! Little Town Of Bethlehem ● Silent Night ● Guardian Angels

| 11/1/52 | ❶[4] | 20 | | 5 **Because You're Mine** | **[S]** | $40 | RCA Victor 7015 |

'33' [10"] LM-7015 (#1) / '45' [4] WDM-7015 (#2/5 wks.); Constantine Callinicos (orch.)

Addio Alla Madre (Cavalleria Rusticana) ● Mamma Mia Che Vo' Sape? ● You Do Something To Me ● **Because You're Mine** [7] ● The Song Angels Sing ● Lee-Ah-Loo ● The Lord's Prayer ● Granada

| 12/20/52 | 4 | 3 | | 6 **Mario Lanza sings Christmas songs** .... | **[X-R]** | $30 | RCA Victor 1649 |

'45' [4] WDM-1649 (#4) / '33' [10"] LM-155 (#5)

| 7/10/54 | ❶[42] | 151 | ● | 7 **The Student Prince** and other great musical comedies | **[S]** | $30 | RCA Victor 1837 |

EP: RCA Victor ERB-1837 (#1/42 wks.); LP: RCA Victor LM-1837 (#1/36 wks.); Lanza's voice dubbed in for actor Edmund Purdom in this movie version of Sigmund Romberg's musical; side 2 contains songs from other famous musicals; after several lengthy absences from the charts, its last chart date was 9/3/61; Constantine Callinicos (orch.)

Orchestral Introduction *[Constantine Callinicos]* ● Serenade ● Golden Days ● Drink, Drink, Drink ● Summertime In Heidelberg *[w/Elizabeth Doubleday]* ● Beloved ● Gaudeamus Igitur ● Deep In My Heart, Dear *[w/Elizabeth Doubleday]* ● I'll Walk With God ● Yours Is My Heart Alone ● Romance ● I'll See You Again ● If I Loved You ● I'll Be Seeing You ● One Night Of Love

LEE, Peggy ★31★ — TPA

Born Norma Jean Egstrom on 5/26/20 in Jamestown, North Dakota. Died of a heart attack on 1/21/2002 (age 81). Jazz singer with Jack Wardlow band (1936-40), Will Osborne (1940-41) and **Benny Goodman** (1941-43). Went solo in March 1943. In movies *Mister Music* (1950), *The Jazz Singer* (1953) and *Pete Kelly's Blues* (1955). Co-wrote many songs with husband Dave Barbour (married, 1943-52). Awarded nearly $4 million in court for her singing in the animated movie *Lady And The Tramp*.

| 4/24/48 | 2[1] | 8 | | 1 **Rendezvous with Peggy Lee** | 78[3] | $60 | Capitol 72 |

Dave Barbour (orch.)

I Can't Give You Anything But Love ● Why Don't You Do Right (Get Me Some Money Too) ● Stormy Weather (Keeps Rainin' All The Time) ● Them There Eyes ● 'Deed I Do ● Don't Smoke In Bed

| 6/25/49 | 4 | 6 | | 2 **South Pacific** ....78[4] | | $40 | Capitol 162 |

PEGGY LEE/MARGARET WHITING/GORDON MacRAE

selections from the Broadway musical of the same title (not the Original Cast)

A Wonderful Guy *[Whiting]* ● Some Enchanted Evening *[MacRae]* ● Bali Ha'i *[Lee]* ● Medley: Happy Talk/Honey Bun *[Frank DeVol Orch.]* ● Younger Than Springtime *[MacRae]* ● A Cock-Eyed Optimist *[Whiting]* ● There Is Nothin' Like A Dame *[Dave Barbour]* ● I'm Gonna Wash That Man Right Outta My Hair *[Lee]*

| 11/27/54 | 2[2] | 8 | | 3 **White Christmas** | **[S]** | $40 | Decca 8083 |

BING CROSBY - DANNY KAYE - PEGGY LEE

EP: Decca ED-819 (#2); LP: Decca DL-8083 (#4); Peggy Lee (who was not in the movie) re-recorded **Rosemary Clooney**'s part (who was in the movie but was not allowed to perform on Decca because of her Columbia contract)

Medley: Old Man/Gee, I Wish I Was Back In The Army *[Crosby & Kaye]* ● Sisters *[Lee]* ● Best Things Happen While You're Dancing *[Kaye]* ● Snow *[w/Trudy Stevens]* ● Medley: Blue Skies/Mandy *[Crosby & Kaye]* ● Choreography *[Kaye]* ● Count Your Blessings Instead Of Sheep *[Crosby]* ● Love, You Didn't Do Right By Me *[Lee]* ● What Can You Do With A General *[Crosby]* ● White Christmas (Finale) *[w/Trudy Stevens]*

LeGRAND, Michel, and his Orchestra   TPA
Born on 2/24/32 in Paris. Conductor/arranger/pianist.

11/13/54+ **9** 20 **I Love Paris** .... [I] $25 Columbia 555

I Love Paris ● Mademoiselle De Paris ● Paris ● Autumn Leaves ● Under The Bridges Of Paris ● La Seine ●
Paris In The Spring ● Paris Canaille ● April In Paris ● Á Paris ● La Vie En Rose ● Under Paris Skies ● Paris Je T'Aime
(Paris, Stay The Same) ● The Song From Moulin Rouge ● The Last Time I Saw Paris

LIBERACE ★15★
Born Wladziu Valentino Liberace on 5/16/19 in Milwaukee. Died of AIDS on 2/4/87 (age 67). The flamboyant pianist became
a nationwide sensation in 1952 when he hosted his own TV musical show.

9/13/52 **❶²** 59 1 **Liberace at the piano** .... [I] $40 Columbia 308

'45' [4] B-308 (#1/2 wks.) / '33' [10"] CL-6217 (#1/1 wk.)
Stardust ● Liebestraum ● Carioca ● Polish National Dance In E-Flat Minor ● "Moonlight" Sonata ● Warsaw Concerto ●
As Time Goes By ● Malaguena

7/11/53 **3** 24 2 **Liberace By Candlelight** .... [I] $40 Columbia 336

'45' [4] B-336 (#3) / '33' [10"] CL-6251 (#5)
Tchaikovsky's Piano Concerto No. 1 ● I Don't Care (As Long As You Care For Me) ● Autumn Nocturne ● Tales From
The Vienna Woods ● I'll Be Seeing You ● Concerto No. 2 In A Major For Piano And Orchestra ● Jalousie (Jealousy) ●
September Song [27]

12/26/53 **7** 5 3 **Concertos for You** .... [I] $40 Columbia 6269

LIBERACE with PAUL WESTON And His Orchestra
"Popular LP'S" chart ('33') listed both 10" (CL-6269) and 12" (ML-4764-Masterworks) configurations; Masterworks version
contains an additional five selections: "The Dream Of Olwen," "Stella By Starlight," "Laura," "Spellbound Concerto," and
"Rachmaninoff's Fantasia
Warsaw Concerto ● Cornish Rhapsody ● Grieg's Piano Concerto ● Chopin Fantasia

2/6/54 **8** 1 4 **an evening with Liberace** .... [I] $40 Columbia 329

'45' [EP] B-329 (#8) / '33' [10"] CL-6239 (#10)
"Yakety Yak" Polka ● Begin The Beguine ● Cement Mixer ● Slaughter On Tenth Avenue ● Cumana ● Lover ●
Chopsticks ● The Old Piano Roll Blues

7/24/54 **10** 6 5 **Sincerely, Liberace** .... [I] $75 Columbia 1001 [2]

EP: Columbia BB-1001 (#10); LP: Columbia BL-1001 (#11); 10" double album packaged in a special felt-covered easel
box with a giant photo of Liberace on the front and includes an eight-page booklet; George Liberace (Liberace's brother;
orch., all of above, except #3)
Tico-Tico ● Sophisticated Lady ● Johnson Rag ● (I Wonder Why?) You're Just In Love ● Mexican Hat Dance ●
Indian Love Call ● Macarenas (La Virgin De La Macarena) ● Get Happy ● The Birth Of The Blues ● El Cumbanchero ●
(All Of A Sudden) My Heart Sings ● Bye Bye Blues ● Minuet In G ● Start The Day With A Smile ● Blue Tango ●
Sweet Sue - Just You

11/13/54 **15** 2 6 **Liberace plays Chopin** .... [EP] $30 Columbia B-448/449 [4]

issued as two separate double EPs (price is for each EP)
Polonaise In A-Flat Major, Opus 53, No. 6 ● Etude No. 3 In E Major, Opus 10 ● Waltz No. 6 In D-Flat Major, Opus 64,
No. 1 ("Minute" Waltz) ● Prelude No. 4 In E Minor, Opus 28 ● Etude In F Minor, Opus 10, No. 9 ● Prelude No. 7 In A
Major, Opus 28 ● Grande Valse, Opus 42 ● Waltz In C-Sharp Minor, Opus 64, No. 2 ● Nocturne No. 5 In F-Sharp Major
● Fantaisie - Impromptu, Opus 66 ● Nocturne No. 2 In E-Flat Major, Opus 9 ● Etude In A-Flat Major, Opus 25, No. 1 ●
Polonaise In A Major, Opus 40, No. 1

LOMBARDO, Guy, And His Royal Canadians ★20★   TPA
Born on 6/19/02 in London, Ontario, Canada. Died on 11/5/77 (age 75). The Lombardo brothers formed their band in 1925, with
Guy as leader and Carmen as lead saxophonist/singer; gained fame by decade's end for playing "The Sweetest Music This Side
of Heaven." Charted over 140 hits from 1927 to 1940 (including 21 #1 hits). The only dance band ever to sell more than 100
million records. Most remembered for their annual New Year's Eve broadcasts, always climaxed by his theme "Auld Lang Syne."

8/17/46 **5** 10 1 **Lombardoland** .... $20 Decca 570

'78' [4] A-436 (#5) / '78' [4] A-570 (#9) / '33' [10"] DL-5041 (#9) / '45' [4] 9-35 (#10); first released in 1942 on Decca 255;
charted for 1 week (#5) on Decca 436; re-charted on 1/14/50 for 8 weeks (#9) on Decca 570 and 5041; final chart entry on
1/27/51 on 45 rpm chart (#10) on Decca 9-35
I'm Always Chasing Rainbows ● Make Believe ● Smoke Gets In Your Eyes ● The Very Thought Of You ● Time On My
Hands (You In My Arms) ● Dancing In The Dark ● At Dawning ● When Day Is Done

2/15/47 **3** 15 2 **Guy Lombardo And His Royal Canadians featuring The Twin Pianos** .... [I] $20 Decca 512

'78' [4] A-512 (#3) / '33' [10"] DL-5002 (#7) / '45' [4] 9-11 (#4)
Humoresque [13] ● Tales From The Vienna Woods ● Just One Of Those Things ● Who? ● Swanee River ● Irish
Washerwoman ● Barcarolle ● Doll Dance

5/3/47 **4** 11 3 **Waltzes** ....78[4] $20 Decca 509

The Sweetheart Of Sigma Chi ● Carolina Moon ● The Merry Widow ● Russian Lullaby ● When I Grow Too Old To
Dream ● **Charmaine [1/'27]** ● **Shadow Waltz [11/'33]** ● Beautiful Love

5/27/50 **5** 20 4 **Guy Lombardo featuring the Twin Pianos, Volume Two** .... [I] $20 Decca 5193

'33' [10"] DL-5193 (#5) / '45' [4] 9-32 (#8); #2 & 5 feature the piano duo of Fred Kreitzer and Buddy Brennan or Frank
Vigneau
Canadian Capers ● Stumbling ● National Emblem March ● The Cannon Ball ● Raindrop Serenade ● La Golondrina ●
Wunderbar ● Mademoiselle Hortensia

LOMBARDO, Guy, And His Royal Canadians — Cont'd

| 7/22/50 | 5 | 15 | | 5 **Guy Lombardo and His Royal Canadians Silver Jubilee, 1925-1950** ...... [G] | $20 | Decca 5235 |

'33' [10"] DL-5235 (#5) / '45' [4] 9-28 (#6)

St. Louis Blues *[11/'39]* ● You're Driving Me Crazy *[1/'30]* ● Boo-Hoo *[1/'37]* ● A Sailboat In The Moonlight *[1/'37]* ● Swingin' In A Hammock *[3/'30]* ● Moonlight Saving Time *[1/'31]* ● Little Dutch Mill *[13/'34]* ● When The Organ Played At Twilight

LUTCHER, Nellie, And Her Rhythm
Born on 10/15/15 in Lake Charles, Louisiana. R&B singer/songwriter/pianist.

| 4/3/48 | 4 | 6 | | **Nellie Lutcher** ....78[3] | $75 | Capitol 70 |

The One I Love Belongs To Somebody Else ● Chi-Chi-Chi-Chicago ● There's Another Mule In Your Stall ● Reaching For The Moon ● Sleepy Lagoon ● Lake Charles Boogie

M

MacARTHUR, Douglas, General
Born on 1/26/1880 in Little Rock, Arkansas. Died on 4/3/64 (age 84). Famous WWII military leader. Fired in April 1951 by President Harry Truman.

| 5/12/51 | 6 | 8 | | 1 **General of the Army Douglas MacArthur's Report to Congress** .... [T] | $30 | RCA Victor 5 |

'33' [10"] LPM-5 (#6) / '45' [3] WP-317 (#6)

| 5/19/51 | 9 | 4 | | 2 **General of the Army Douglas A. MacArthur's Speech to Congress** ..12" [T] | $30 | Columbia 4410 |
| 6/2/51 | 8 | 2 | | 3 **General MacArthur's Farewell Address** ....45[3] [T] | $30 | Capitol 274 |

above 3 are recordings of his "Old soldiers never die, they just fade away" speech to Congress on April 19, 1951

MacDONALD, Jeanette TPA
Born on 6/18/03 in Philadelphia. Died of a heart attack on 1/14/65 (age 63). Star of numerous movie musicals.

| 5/26/45 | 2[3] | 5 | | **Up In Central Park** 78[3] | $40 | Victor Red Seal 991 |

JEANETTE MacDONALD with Robert Merrill
a studio version of the Sigmund Romberg Broadway musical; Robert Russell Bennett (orch.)

Carrousel In The Park ● It Doesn't Cost You Anything To Dream ● Close As Pages In A Book ● The Fireman's Bride ● The Big Back Yard ● When You Walk In The Room

MacRAE, Gordon
Born on 3/12/21 in East Orange, New Jersey. Died of cancer on 1/24/86 (age 64). Sang with **Horace Heidt** (1942-43) and recorded numerous duets with **Jo Stafford**, late 1940s. Starred in the movie musicals *Oklahoma!* and *Carousel*. Married to actress Sheila MacRae from 1941-67; their daughter is actress Meredith MacRae.

| 4/30/49 | 9 | 2 | | 1 **Kiss Me, Kate** ....78[4] | $40 | Capitol 144 |

JO STAFFORD and GORDON MacRAE
a studio version of the Cole Porter Broadway musical; Paul Weston (orch.); 45 rpm four-record package released on CDF-157; also see the 1949 Original Cast and the 1954 Movie Soundtrack versions

Wunderbar ● Too Darn Hot *[Paul Weston]* ● Were Thine That Special Face *[MacRae]* ● I Hate Men *[Stafford]* ● Always True To You In My Fashion *[Stafford]* ● Bianca *[MacRae]* ● So In Love *[MacRae] [20]* ● Why Can't You Behave *[Stafford]*

| 6/25/49 | 4 | 6 | | 2 **South Pacific** ....78[4] | $40 | Capitol 162 |

PEGGY LEE/MARGARET WHITING/GORDON MacRAE
selections from the Broadway musical of the same title (not the Original Cast)

A Wonderful Guy *[Whiting]* ● Some Enchanted Evening *[MacRae]* ● Bali Ha'i *[Lee]* ● Medley: Happy Talk/Honey Bun *[Frank DeVol Orch.]* ● Younger Than Springtime *[MacRae]* ● A Cock-Eyed Optimist *[Whiting]* ● There Is Nothin' Like A Dame *[Dave Barbour]* ● I'm Gonna Wash That Man Right Outta My Hair *[Lee]*

| 7/22/50 | 10 | 1 | | 3 **Favorite selections from New Moon** ....10" | $40 | Capitol 219 |

GORDON MacRAE with Lucille Norman
a studio version of the Sigmund Romberg, Oscar Hammerstein II musical; Paul Weston (orch.)

Overture *[Paul Weston]* ● Medley: Stout Hearted Men/Marianne *[MacRae]* ● Wanting You ● Softly, As In A Morning Sunrise *[MacRae]* ● Lover, Come Back To Me *[Norman]* ● Finale

| | ★35★ | | | **MANTOVANI And His Orchestra** TPA | | |

Born Annunzio Paolo Mantovani on 11/15/05 in Venice, Italy. Died on 3/29/80 (age 74). Played classical violin in England before forming his own orchestra in the early 1930s. Had first U.S. chart hit in 1935, "Red Sails In The Sunset." Achieved international fame 20 years later with his 40-piece orchestra and distinctive "cascading strings" sound.

| 10/4/52+ | 8 | 1 | | 1 **A Collection Of Favorite Waltzes** .... [I] | $20 | London 570 |

Dear Love, My Love ● Greensleeves ● Mexicali Rose ● It Happened In Monterey ● My Moonlight Madonna (Poeme) ● I Love You Truly ● Lovely Lady ● Love, Here Is My Heart ● At Dawning ● Was It A Dream? ● Love Makes The World Go 'Round ● Dancing With Tears In My Eyes *[26]*

| 5/16/53 | ❶[2] | 14 | | 2 **The Music of Victor Herbert** [I] | $20 | London 746 |

'33' [12"] LL-746 (#1) / '45' [4] BEP-6074 (#4)

Ah! Sweet Mystery of Life ● When You're Away ● Neapolitan Love Song ● March Of The Toys ● I'm Falling In Love With Someone ● Gypsy Love Song ● Kiss Me Again ● Indian Summer ● To The Land Of My Own Romance ● Italian Street Song ● A Kiss In The Dark ● Habanera ● Sweethearts ● The Irish Have A Great Day Tonight

| 12/25/54+ | 6 | 4 | | 3 **Christmas Carols** .... [X-I] | $15 | London 913 |

LP: London LL-913 (#6); EP: London BET-A5 (#10); re-charted 1957-61

Adeste Fideles ● Hark! The Herald Angels Sing ● God Rest Ye Merry, Gentlemen ● White Christmas ● Good King Wenceslas ● O Holy Night ● The First Nowell ● Joy To The World ● Silent Night, Holy Night ● O Tannenbaum ● Midnight Waltz ● Nazareth ● O Little Town Of Bethlehem ● The Skaters Waltz

MARLOWE, Marion, and Frank Parker
Marlowe was born on 3/7/29 in St. Louis. Parker was born on 7/1/29 in Darby, Pennsylvania. Both were regulars on **Arthur Godfrey**'s TV show.

| 2/28/53 | 2[2] | 17 | | **Sweethearts** | $35 | Columbia 331 |

'45' [4] B-331 (#2) / '33' [10"] CL-6241 (#3); Archie Bleyer (orch.)

Take Me In Your Arms ● Tenderly *[Parker]* ● Hello, Young Lovers *[Marlowe]* ● Moonlight and Roses ● I Love You Truly ● We Kiss In A Shadow *[Marlowe]* ● For You *[Parker]* ● The Sweetest Story Ever Told

MARTIN, Freddy, and his Orchestra

Born on 12/9/06 in Cleveland. Died on 9/30/83 (age 76). Leader of one of the most popular "sweet" bands, his tenor saxophone style led to the nickname "Mr. Silvertone." Pianist Jack Fina was a featured sideman and Merv Griffin was his late-1940s singing star. Also see **Various Artist Compilations**.

| 12/29/45 | 5 | 1 | | 1 **Tchaikovsky's Nutcracker Suite** in Dance Tempo ....78[4] **[X-I]** | $20 | RCA Victor 124 |

Martin's version of the classic Tchaikovsky *Nutcracker Suite* ballet

Overture Miniature ● March ● Dance Of The Sugar-Plum Fairies ● Russian Dance ● Arab Dance ● Chinese Dance ● Dance Of The Reed Flutes ● Waltz Of The Flowers

| 3/22/47 | 2[4] | 10 | | 2 **Concertos for Dancing** 78[4] **[I]** | $20 | RCA Victor 169 |

featuring Jack Fina (piano)

Tchaikovsky Piano Concerto No. 1 *[1]* ● Cornish Rhapsody Theme ● Grieg Piano Concerto ● Night And Day ● Rachmaninoff Piano Concerto No. 2 ● Symphonie Moderne ● **(Theme from the) Warsaw Concerto** *[16]* ● Intermezzo

MARTIN, Tony

Born Alvin Morris on 12/25/12 in San Francisco. Singer/actor. Appeared in several movies. Hosted own TV show from 1954-56. Married actress/dancer Cyd Charisse in 1948.

| 1/14/50 | 10 | 1 | | 1 **Oh You Beautiful Doll** ....45[3] | $50 | RCA Victor 252 |

Martin's version of songs from the movie about songwriter Fred Fisher; with The Pied Pipers and Skip Martin orch.

Oh You Beautiful Doll ● I Want You To Want Me (To Want You) ● Peg O' My Heart ● When I Get You Alone Tonight ● There's A Broken Heart For Every Light On Broadway ● Come, Josephine In My Flying Machine

| 5/26/51 | 10 | 2 | | 2 **The King And I**.. | $40 | RCA Victor 1022 |

DINAH SHORE/PATRICE MUNSEL/TONY MARTIN/ROBERT MERRILL

'33' [LP] LK-1022 (#10) / '45' [5] WK-30 (#10); selections from the Broadway show; not the original cast; cd: **Al Goodman** and Henri René

Overture *[Al Goodman Orch.]* ● Shall We Dance *[Shore & Merrill]* ● I Whistle A Happy Tune *[Shore]* ● I Have Dreamed *[Martin & Munsel]* ● My Lord And Master *[Munsel]* ● Something Wonderful *[Munsel]* ● Hello, Young Lovers *[Shore]* ● We Kiss In A Shadow *[Martin & Munsel]* ● A Puzzlement *[Merrill]* ● Getting To Know You *[Shore]*

MAY, Billy, And His Orchestra   ★29★   TPA

Born on 11/10/16 in Pittsburg. Arranger/conductor/sideman for many of the big bands. After leading his own band in the early 1950s, he went on to arrange/conduct for **Frank Sinatra** and compose movie scores. Also see **Movie Soundtracks** ("So Dear To My Heart").

| 5/31/52 | 3 | 30 | | 1 **Big Band Bash!** **[I]** | $25 | Capitol 329 |

'33' [10"] L-329 (#3/12 wks.) / '45' [3] KCF-329 (#3/6 wks.)

You're Driving Me Crazy ● When Your Lover Has Gone ● Perfidia ● My Last Affair ● Diane ● Please Be Kind ● Tenderly ● Orchids In The Moonlight

| 8/16/52 | 7 | 5 | | 2 **A Band Is Born!** .... **[I]** | $25 | Capitol 349 |

'45' [3] CCF-349 (#7) / '33' [10"] H-349 (#8)

Charmaine *[17]* ● Lean, Baby ● Fat Man Boogie ● There Is No Greater Love ● I Guess I'll Have To Change My Plan ● When My Sugar Walks Down The Street

| 3/14/53 | 5 | 8 | | 3 **Bacchanalia!**... **[I]** | $25 | Capitol 374 |

'45' [2] EBF-374 (#5) / '33' [10"] H-374 (#5)

Top Hat, White Tie And Tails ● Cocktails For Two ● Cheek To Cheek ● You And The Night And The Music ● Little Brown Jug ● Makin' Whoopee! ● Bacchanalia! ● Let's Put Out The Lights (And Go To Sleep)

McCOY, Clyde, His Trumpet and Orchestra

Born on 12/29/03 in New York City. Died on 6/11/90 (age 86). Trumpeter known for his "wah-wah" sound.

| 9/13/52 | 10 | 1 | | **Clyde McCoy's Sugar Blues**..10" **[I]** | $25 | Capitol 311 |

includes new version of McCoy's giant #2 hit of "Sugar Blues" in 1931

Sugar Blues ● Basin Street Blues ● Limehouse Blues ● Farewell Blues ● Blues In The Night ● Wabash Blues ● St. Louis Blues ● Memphis Blues

MELACHRINO STRINGS AND ORCHESTRA, The   ★25★   TPA

Born George Militiades on 5/1/09 in London (Greek parents). Died on 6/18/65 (age 56). Orchestra leader.

| 3/28/53 | 7 | 32 | | 1 **Music for Dining**... **[I]** | $20 | RCA Victor 1000 |

'33' [12"] LPM-1000 (#7) / '45' [EP] EPB-1000 (#8); charted for 16 weeks on the 33 rpm chart; re-charted on 8/24/59 for 16 more weeks (#21)

Diane (I'm In Heaven When I See You Smile) ● Too Young ● September Song ● Clopin Clopant ● Warsaw Concerto ● Domino ● Tenderly ● Charmaine ● Faithfully Yours ● Chansonette ● Dark Secret ● Legend Of The Glass Mountain

| 8/1/53 | 10 | 23 | | 2 **Music for Reading**... **[I]** | $20 | RCA Victor 1002 |

charted for 2 weeks on the 33 rpm chart; re-charted on 1/18/60 for 21 more weeks (#16)

Clair De Lune ● Greensleeves ● Festival ● Dream Of Olwen ● Song Of My Love ● Mattinata ('Tis The Day) ● Amoureuse ● Waltz In C-Sharp Minor ● Serenade ● Flirtation Waltz ● Cavatina ● Love's Roundelay

| 10/16/54 | 15 | 2 | | 3 **Music for Two People Alone**.. **[I]** | $20 | RCA Victor 1027 |

Why Do I Love You ● Embraceable You ● I Love Thee ● Yours (Quiéreme Mucho) ● Lover ● Two Sleepy People ● Liebestraum ● You Were Meant For Me ● Two Cigarettes In The Dark ● Blue Room

| 10/30/54 | 13 | 6 | | 4 **Music for Daydreaming**.. **[I]** | $20 | RCA Victor 1028 |

Dusk ● Serenade In The Night ● Moonlight And Roses ● Star Dust ● Evensong ● In The Still Of The Night ● To A Wild Rose ● Barcarolle ● Indian Summer ● By The Sleepy Lagoon

MELCHIOR, Lauritz

Born on 3/20/1890 in Copenhagen, Denmark. Died on 3/18/73 (age 82). Operatic tenor.

| 7/28/45 | 2[3] | 7 | | **Thrill Of A Romance** 78[3] | $30 | RCA Victor 990 |

not the actual soundtrack recording, although Melchior does appear in the movie

I Love You ● Lonely Night ● Serenade ● Vive L'Amour ● Please Don't Say No ● I Want What I Want When I Want It

MERMAN, Ethel

Born Ethel Zimmerman on 1/16/08 in Astoria, Queens, New York. Died on 2/15/84 (age 76). Legendary Broadway actress. Starred in such shows as *Anything Goes*, *Call Me Madam*, *Annie Get Your Gun* (which provided her trademark song, "There's No Business Like Show Business"), and *Gypsy*. Also see **Original Casts** ("Annie Get Your Gun"/"Call Me Madam").

| 12/9/50+ | 2¹ | 27 | | **Call Me Madam** | | $30 | Decca 5304 |

'33' [10"] DL-5304 or LP [12"] DL-8035 (#2) / '45' [4] 9-153 or '45' [6] 9-166 (#5); with **Dick Haymes**, Eileen Wilson and **Gordon Jenkins** (orch.); although Ethel starred in the 1950 Original Broadway Cast, this album features a studio cast; also see the Original Cast version on RCA Victor and the 1953 Movie Soundtrack on Decca

The Hostess With The Mostes' On The Ball (12") ● Washington Square Dance (12") *[Gordon Jenkins]* ● Can You Use Any Money Today? (12") ● Marrying For Love ● (Dance To The Music Of) The Ocarina *[Gordon Jenkins]* ● It's A Lovely Day Today *[Dick Haymes & Eileen Wilson]* ● The Best Thing For You ● Something To Dance About ● Once Upon A Time Today *[Dick Haymes]* ● They Like Ike (12") *[Gordon Jenkins]* ● **You're Just In Love** *[w/Haymes] [30]*

MERRILL, Robert — see MacDONALD, Jeanette / SHORE, Dinah

MILLER, Glenn, and his Orchestra ★1★   TPA

Born Alton Glenn Miller on 3/1/04 in Clarinda, Iowa. Disappeared on a flight over the English Channel on 12/15/44 (age 40). Leader of the most universally beloved of all big bands. He played trombone for Ben Pollack, Red Nichols, **Benny Goodman**, and the **Dorsey** Brothers, became de facto leader of Ray Noble's 1935 American band, and did arrangements for Glen Gray and others before starting his own band in 1937. It failed, as did a 1938 successor, but in 1939 Glenn developed his trademark reed sound (4 saxophones and clarinet) and soared to the top. Vital ingredients in the band's staggering success were arrangers **Jerry Gray** and Bill Finegan, and featured soloists Bobby Hackett, **Tex Beneke**, **Billy May** and Hal McIntyre. At the band's peak after four years of extraordinary popularity, Glenn left to enlist in the Army Air Force in September 1942, and formed the war's most famous service band. Tex Beneke carried on the legacy with a new Miller orchestra, and Hollywood's 1954 *The Glenn Miller Story* further immortalized the music and the man. Also see **Ray Anthony**, **Jerry Gray** and **Various Artist Compilations**.

| 3/24/45 | ❶¹⁶ | 130 | | 1   **Glenn Miller** | [G-I] | $50 | Victor 148 |

'78' [4] P-148 (#1) / '45' [4] WP-148 (#3); 45 rpm album package first charted on 8/12/50

American Patrol *[19]* ● **Song Of The Volga Boatmen** *[1]* ● **Tuxedo Junction** *[1]* ● **In The Mood** *[1]* ● **Little Brown Jug** *[10/'39]* ● **Moonlight Serenade** *[3/'39]* ● Star Dust ● **Pennsylvania Six-Five Thousand** *[5]*

| 10/11/47 | 3 | 4 | | 2   **Prom Date** | 78⁴ [I] | $40 | RCA Victor 183 |

TEX BENEKE with The Miller Orchestra
features famous college songs in dance tempo (5 of 8 cuts are instrumentals)

The Sweetheart Of Sigma Chi ● Washington And Lee Swing ● Alma Mater-Cornell ● The Eyes Of Texas ● Rambling Wreck From Georgia Tech ● Anchors Aweigh (The Song of The Navy) ● On Wisconsin ● The Victory March Of Notre Dame

| 10/25/47 | ❶⁶ | 32 | | 3   **Glenn Miller Masterpieces** | 78⁴ [G-I] | $50 | RCA Victor 189 |

Missouri Waltz ● Pavanne ● **My Isle Of Golden Dreams** *[15/'39]* ● **Perfidia** *[13]* ● **Runnin' Wild** *[12/'39]* ● Bugle Call Rag ● **Chattanooga Choo Choo** *[1]* ● Johnson Rag

| 10/22/49 | 5 | 10 | | 4   **Starlight Serenades** .... | 78³ [G] | $50 | RCA Victor 255 |

Ray Eberle (vocals)

The Story Of A Starry Night *[19]* ● **Stairway To The Stars** *[1/'39]* ● When You Wish Upon A Star *[2]* ● Starlit Hour *[10]* ● A Handful Of Stars *[10]* ● Shake Down The Stars *[10]*

| 12/1/51+ | 2¹ | 27 | | 5   **Glenn Miller Concert** (Volume I) | [I-L] | $50 | RCA Victor 25 |

'45' [4] WPT-25 (#2) / '33' [10"] LPT-16 (#3)

One O'Clock Jump ● Going Home ● St. Louis Blues ● Tiger Rag ● Everybody Loves My Baby ● Georgia On My Mind ● Jersey Bounce ● My Blue Heaven

| 5/10/52 | 6 | 8 | | 6   **Glenn Miller Concert** (Vol. 2) .... | [I-L] | $50 | RCA Victor 30 |

'33' [10"] LPT-30 (#6) / '45' [4] WPT-39 (#6); above 2 albums consist of live radio broadcast performances by the band from 1940-41

Anchors Aweigh ● My Buddy ● I Got Rhythm ● I Dream Of Jeanie With The Light Brown Hair ● Vilia ● Limehouse Blues ● On The Alamo ● On Army Team

| 12/26/53 | 3 | 3 | | 7   **Glenn Miller And His Orchestra** - Limited Edition | [K] | $300 | RCA Victor 6700 [5] |

'33' [5] LPT-6700 (#4) / '45' [20] EPOT-6700 (#3-EP); collectors issue of an anthology of Miller RCA Victor recordings and radio broadcasts for Chesterfield Cigarettes; features 69 recordings from 4/10/39 through 9/15/42 on five 12" records (or 20 7" records), packaged in a deluxe softcover album case which includes a 16-page booklet

Perfidia ● Wonderful One ● Weekend Of A Private Secretary ● **Always In My Heart** *[10]* ● **Boulder Buff** *[19]* ● Caribbean Clipper ● Make Believe ● Say Si Si ● Introduction To A Waltz ● Medley: Japanese Sandman/What's The Matter With Me/Let's Dance/Blue Room ● Down For The Count ● Rainbow Rhapsody ● Little Brown Jug ● **Imagination** *[2]* ● It Must Be Jelly ● **Devil May Care** *[16]* ● Chip Off The Old Block ● American Patrol ● Ida ● I Guess I'll Have To Change My Plan ● Glen Island Special ● Medley: My Darling/Blueberry Hill/I Can't Get Started ● Bugle Call Rag ● On A Little Street In Singapore ● Oh So Good ● Baby Me *[Kay Starr, vocal]* ● There'll Be Some Changes Made ● Medley: Moon Over Miami/A Million Dreams Ago/Aloha ● Sun Valley Jump ● String Of Pearls ● Love With A Capitol "You" *[Kay Starr, vocal]* ● **Wishing Will Make It So** *[1/'39]* ● Rug Cutter's Swing ● Angel Child ● King Porter Stomp ● Chattanooga Choo Choo ● Medley: My Melancholy Baby/Moon Love/Stomping At The Savoy/Blue Moon ● Sleepy Town Train ● My Devotion ● Fresh As A Daisy ● One O'Clock Jump ● Don't Sit Under The Apple Tree ● Lady Be Good ● **Fools Rush In** *[3]* ● Twenty-Four Robbers ● The Hop ● **Careless** *[1]* ● Naughty Sweetie Blues ● Bless You ● **Sweet Eloise** *[8]* ● **Rhapsody In Blue** *[15]* ● Sliphorn Jive ● **Here We Go Again** *[20]* ● Mister Meadowlark ● Just A Little Bit South Of North Carolina ● Under A Blanket Of Blue ● The Lamplighter's Serenade ● Farewell Blues

| 2/6/54 | ❶¹¹ | 78 | | 8   **Glenn Miller Plays Selections From The Film "The Glenn Miller Story"** | [I] | $50 | RCA Victor 3057 |

'33' [10"] LPT-3057 (#1/11 wks.) / '45' [EP] EPBT-3057 (#1/9 wks.); original Miller recordings, not from the movie soundtrack

Moonlight Serenade *[3/'39]* ● **American Patrol** *[19]* ● **Pennsylvania Six-Five Thousand** *[5]* ● **In The Mood** *[1]* ● **Tuxedo Junction** *[1]* ● St. Louis Blues ● String Of Pearls ● Little Brown Jug

| 2/20/54 | ❶¹⁰ | 40 | ● | 9   **The Glenn Miller Story** | [S] | $50 | Decca 5519 |

'33' [10"] DL-5519 (#1/10 wks.) / 'EP' [2] ED-2124/5 (#1/8 wks.); all Miller selections are new recordings, featuring eight members of his original band; Joseph Gershenson (conductor)

Moonlight Serenade ● Tuxedo Junction ● Little Brown Jug ● St. Louis Blues ● In The Mood ● A String Of Pearls ● Pennsylvania 6-5000 ● American Patrol

DEBUT	PEAK	WKS	Gold	ARTIST — Album Title	Sym	$	Label & Number

MILLER, Glenn, and his Orchestra — Cont'd

10/30/54   **4**   16

10 **Glenn Miller And His Orchestra - Limited Edition, Volume Two**............................. **[K]** $200 RCA Victor 6701 [5]
LP: RCA Victor LPT-6701 (#4); EP: RCA Victor EPOT-6701 (#6); collectors issue (volume 2) of an anthology of 60 Miller radio broadcasts from 6/20/38 through 9/1/42 on five 12" records (or 15 7" records), packaged in a deluxe softcover album case which includes a 16-page booklet

Along The Santa Fe Trail ● Swingin' At The Seance ● In A Sentimental Mood ● Frenesi ● Isn't That Just Like Love ● I Dreamt I Dwelt In Harlem ● You Walk By ● Are You Jumpin' Jack? ● A Million Dreams Ago ● Daisy Mae ● Falling Leaves ● Crosstown ● At Sundown ● My Last Goodbye ● Hallelujah ● The Hour Of Parting ● I'm Sorry For Myself ● The Jumpin' Jive ● Twilight Interlude ● And The Angels Sing ● Sunrise Serenade ● Blue Orchids ● We Can Life On Love ● Pagan Love Song ● We've Come A Long Way Together ● Get Out Of Town ● Blue Skies ● Heaven Can Wait ● Bluebirds In The Moonlight ● I Want To Be Happy ● My Heart Belongs To Daddy ● Deep Purple ● After All ● St. Louis Blues ● Indian Summer ● Tiger Rag ● Georgia On My Mind ● Be Happy ● I Don't Want To Walk Without You ● Limehouse Blues ● Daddy ● Deep In The Heart Of Texas ● Doin' The Jive ● This Can't Be Love ● A Stone's Throw From Heaven ● Humoresque ● So Little Time ● Down South Camp Meetin' ● Anchors Aweigh ● Body And Soul ● Let's Have Another Cup Of Coffee ● The Rhumba Jumps ● How Deep Is The Ocean ● Measure For Measure ● On The Alamo ● April In Paris ● Dancing In A Dream ● Sophisticated Lady ● I'll Never Smile Again ● V For Victory Hop

MILLS BROTHERS, The   TPA

Legendary family vocal group from Piqua, Ohio: father John Mills (born on 2/11/1889; died on 12/8/67, age 78), with sons Herbert (born on 4/2/12; died on 4/12/89, age 77), Harry (born on 8/19/13; died on 6/28/82, age 68) and Donald (born on 4/29/15; died on 11/13/99, age 84). Group appeared in several movies. Won Grammy's Lifetime Achievement Award in 1998.

10/12/46   **3**   3

1 **Famous Barber Shop Ballads, Volume One**   78[5] $50   Decca 476
first released in 1942 on Decca 336 as *My Gal Sal*
You Tell Me Your Dream I'll Tell You Mine ● Sweet Adeline ● My Gal Sal ● Just A Dream Of You, Dear ● Meet Me Tonight In Dreamland ● Can't You Hear Me Callin', Caroline ● Moonlight Bay ● On The Banks Of The Wabash ● Way Down Home ● **When You Were Sweet Sixteen** *[16]*

8/6/49   **9**   2

2 **Mills Brothers Souvenir Album** ....78[4] **[G]** $50   Decca 668
Paper Doll *[1]* ● **I'll Be Around** *[16]* ● **You Always Hurt The One You Love** *[1]* ● **Till Then** *[8]* ● Too Many Irons In The Fire ● **I Guess I'll Get THe Papers (And Go Home)** *[12]* ● You Never Miss The Water Till The Well Runs Dry ● After You

1/21/50   **8**   3

3 **Famous Barber Shop Ballads, Volume Two** ....10" $50   Decca 5051
If I Had My Way ● Sweet Genevieve ● Till We Meet Again ● Honey, Dat I Love So Well ● Love's Old Sweet Song ● Long Long Ago ● On The Banks Of The Wabash ● Moonlight Bay

MONROE, Vaughn, and his Orchestra   ★9★

Born on 10/7/11 in Akron, Ohio. Died on 5/21/73 (age 61). Big-voiced baritone/trumpeter/bandleader. Very popular on radio, and featured in several movies. Also see **Various Artist Compilations**.

10/20/45   **❶**[6]   24

1 **On The Moon-Beam**   78[5] $40   Victor 142
Moonlight And Roses ● It's Only A Paper Moon ● Moonglow ● Moon Of Monakoora ● Blue Moon ● Shine On Harvest Moon ● Carolina Moon ● Moon Love ● Moon Over Miami ● Racing With The Moon

11/23/46+   **2**[1]   14

2 **Vaughn Monroe's Dreamland Special**   78[4] $40   RCA Victor 160
I'll See You In My Dreams ● Drifting And Dreaming ● Meet Me Tonight In Dreamland ● My Isle Of Golden Dreams ● Did You Ever See A Dream Walking ● I've Got A Pocketful Of Dreams ● Dream ● My Dreams Are Getting Better All The Time

4/3/48   **❶**[6]   16

3 **Down Memory Lane**   78[4] $40   RCA Victor 202
Memory Lane ● Memories ● Memories Of You ● Just A Memory ● Remember ● Thanks For The Memory ● It's Easy To Remember ● Roses For Remembrance

1/15/49   **❶**[2]   23

4 **Vaughn Monroe Sings**   78[4] $40   RCA Victor 234
Begin The Beguine ● The Moon Was Yellow ● Anniversary Song ● Something Sentimental ● Oh Promise Me ● Because ● The Whiffenpoof Song ● Without A Song

8/20/49   **3**   18

5 **Silver Lining Songs**   78[3] $35   RCA Victor 246
songs from the 1949 movie *Look For The Silver Lining*
Look For The Silver Lining ● A Kiss In The Dark ● Who? ● Shine On Harvest Moon ● Time On My Hands ● Avalon

11/11/50   **10**   1

6 **Vaughn Monroe Sings A Medley Of College Songs**...................................45[4] $35   RCA Victor 299
Medley: The Gridiron Song/Yale Bingo/Boola Boola ● Medley: The Victors/Across The Field ● Medley: Song Of Troy/Fight On/The Cardinal Is Waving ● Medley: Ramblin' Wreck/Hail To Georgia ● Medley: The Red And The Blue/Roar, Lion, Roar ● Medley: Horned Frogs, We Are All For You/The Eyes Of Texas ● Medley: On Army Team/Navy Blue And Gold ● Medley: Indiana, Our Indiana/The Victory March Of Notre Dame

MUNSEL, Patrice — see SHORE, Dinah

MURROW, Edward R.

Born Egbert Roscoe Murrow on 4/25/08 in Greensboro, North Carolina. Died of cancer on 4/27/65 (age 57). The most legendary of all broadcast journalists, with CBS News radio and television from 1935-61. Host of TV's *See It Now* from 1951-58.

1/8/49   **3**   25   ●

"I Can Hear It Now..." 1933-1945   12" **[T]** $40   Columbia 4095
recordings from historic speeches and events, narrated by Murrow
Will Rogers/Roosevelt Inauguration/Huey Long/Duke Of Windsor ● La Guardia/Landon/Roosevelt/John L. Lewis/Hindenburg Disaster ● Czech Crisis/Chamberlain/Hitler/Louis-Schmeling Fight/Gehrig Farewell ● Britain Enters The War/Lindbergh/Al Smith/Hugh Johnson/Roosevelt/Mussolini ● Reynaud/Surrender At Compiegne/Chamberlain/Churchill/Princesses Elizabeth & Margaret Rose ● Joseph Martin & Wendell Wilkie/Roosevelt/Churchill/Pearl Harbor Announcement ● Declaration Of War/D-Day (Eisenhower, De Gaulle, King Haakon) ● Invasion Craft/Stalin/Dewey/F.D.R. ● Roosevelt's Death & Funeral/Truman Speaks To Congress/Opening Of U.N./Announcement of German Surrender ● Chaplain's Prayer Before First Atom Bomb Mission/Hiroshima Attack/Japan Surrender/MacArthur

N

NEWMAN, Alfred — see MOVIE SOUNDTRACKS ("Stars And Stripes Forever")

NORMAN, Lucille — see MacRAE, Gordon

P

PARKER, Charlie
Born on 8/29/20 in Kansas City, Kansas. Died of pneumonia on 3/12/55 (age 34). Legendary alto saxophonist. Founder of progressive jazz. Nicknames: "Bird" and "Yardbird." Won Grammy's Lifetime Achievement Award in 1984.

6/10/50 | 9 | 1 | **Charlie Parker With Strings**...10" **[I]** $500 Mercury 501
nine-member backing orchestra includes **Buddy Rich** (drums), Ray Brown (bass), Stan Freeman (piano) and **Mitch Miller** (oboe); arranged and conducted by Jimmy Carroll
April In Paris ● Summertime ● If I Should Lose You ● I Didn't Know What Time It Was ● Everything Happens To Me ● Just Friends

PARKER, Frank — see MARLOWE, Marion

PASTOR, Tony, and his Orchestra
Born Antonio Pestritto on 10/26/07 in Middletown, Connecticut. Died on 10/31/69 (age 62). Former tenor saxophonist/singer with Irving Aaronson (1928-30), Vincent Lopez, and most importantly **Artie Shaw** (1936-39). Johnny McAfee (alto sax) his featured sideman, with late-1940s arrangements by **Ralph Flanagan**. During later period Betty and **Rosemary Clooney** were band's vocalists.

8/12/50 | 10 | 1 | **Your Dance Date with Tony Pastor and his Orchestra**........................10" **[I]** $25 Columbia 6122
also see **Les Brown**'s *Your Dance Date with...*
Medley: Exactly Like You/Beyond The Blue Horizon/Time On My Hands/You're Driving Me Crazy ● Medley: Little White Lies/It Happened In Monterey/On The Sunny Side Of The Street/You Brought A New Kind Of Love To Me

PAUL, Les, and Mary Ford ★13★
Pop duo. Paul was born Lester Polsfuss on 6/9/15 in Waukesha, Wisconsin. Ford was born Colleen Summers on 7/7/24 in Pasadena, California; died on 9/30/77 (age 49). Les Paul was an innovator in electric guitar and multi-track recordings. Married to vocalist Mary Ford from 1949-63. Les Paul won the Grammy's Trustees Award in 1983 and he was inducted into the Rock and Roll Hall of Fame in 1988.

9/15/51 | 5 | 17 | 1 **The New Sound!**.. **[I]** $60 Capitol 226
'45' [4] CCF-226 (#5) / '33' [10"] H-226 (#7); Les Paul instrumental recordings only
Brazil ● Hip-Billy Boogie ● The Swiss Woodpecker ● Caravan ● Lover ● The Man On The Flying Trapeze ● By The Light Of The Silvery Moon ● What Is This Thing Called Love

9/8/51 | 2² | 27 | 2 **Les Paul's New Sound, Vol. 2, with Mary Ford** $60 Capitol 286
'45' [3] CCF-286 (#2) / '33' [10"] H-286 (#3)
In The Good Old Summertime *[15]* ● Three Little Words ● The Lonesome Road ● I'm Forever Blowing Bubbles ● Moon Of Manakoora ● La Rosita

12/13/52+ | 2² | 18 | 3 **Bye Bye Blues!** $50 Capitol 356
'33' [10"] H-356 (#2/2 wks.) / '45' [4] CBF-356 (#2/1 wk.)
Wabash Blues ● **Bye Bye Blues *[5]*** ● Blues Stay Away From Me ● Frankie And Johnnie ● Don't Cry Baby ● Deep In The Blues ● Mammy's Boogie ● St. Louis Blues

6/27/53 | 10 | 1 | 4 **The Hit Makers!** .... **[G]** $50 Capitol 416
'33' [10"] H-416 (#10) / '45' [EP] EBF-416 (#10)
How High The Moon *[1]* ● Josephine *[12]* ● Mockin' Bird Hill *[2]* ● Whispering *[7]* ● The World Is Waiting For The Sunrise *[2]* ● Meet Mister Callaghan *[5]* ● Tiger Rag *[2]* ● Tennessee Waltz *[6]*

12/11/54 | 15 | 2 | 5 **I'm A Fool To Care** .... **[EP]** $40 Capitol EAP 1-554
I'm A Fool To Care ● I Really Don't Want To Know ● Auctioneer ● It's A Lonesome Old Town

12/25/54 | 14 | 2 | 6 **Today's Top Hits, Vol. 12** ....12" **[K]** $40 Capitol 9122
LES PAUL and MARY FORD/NAT "KING" COLE
If I Give My Heart To You *[Cole]* ● Mister Sandman *[Paul & Ford]* ● **Hajji Baba** *[Cole]* *[14]* ● **Take Me In Your Arms And Hold Me** *[Paul & Ford]* *[15]* ● It's Crazy *[Cole]* ● That's What I Like *[Paul & Ford]* ● **Mandolino** *[Paul & Ford]* *[19]* ● Hold My Hand *[Cole]* ● **Whither Thou Goest** *[Paul & Ford]* *[10]* ● Papa Loves Mambo *[Cole]* ● Things I Didn't Do *[Paul & Ford]* ● **Make Her Mine** *[Cole]* *[19]* ● I Need You Now *[Paul & Ford]* ● Teach Me Tonight *[Cole]* ● Nola *[Paul & Ford]* ● **Answer Me, My Love** *[Cole]* *[6]*

12/25/54+ | 7 | 16 | 7 **Les Paul and Mary Ford** .... **[EP]** $50 Capitol 9121
4-song EP compiled from #6 above
Mister Sandman ● That's What I Like ● I Need You Now ● The Things I Didn't Do

PORTER, Cole — see JONES, Allan / ROSE, David / SHAW, Artie /
ORIGINAL CASTS ("Can-Can"/"Kiss Me Kate"/"Out Of This World")

PREVIN, Andre   TPA

Born on 4/6/29 in Berlin. Pianist/conductor/arranger/composer. Musical director for several MGM movies. In the 1970s, served as resident conductor of the London Symphony Orchestra. Married to actress Mia Farrow from 1970-79. Also see **Movie Soundtracks** ("Kiss Me Kate"/"Three Little Words").

8/28/48   **6**   6   1 **Andre Previn at the Piano** ....78⁴ **[I]** $30   RCA Victor 214

Hallelujah ● But Not For Me ● My Shining Hour ● This Can't Be Love ● Just One Of Those Things ● Mad About The Boy ● I Didn't Know What Time It Was ● Should I

9/30/50   **4**   5   2 **Three Little Words** ....45³ **[I]** $40   RCA Victor 291

also see the 1950 MGM Movie Soundtrack album on which Previn conducts and plays the piano

Three Little Words ● Thinking Of You ● All Alone Monday ● Who's Sorry Now ● Where Did You Get That Girl ● Nevertheless

R

RAY, Johnnie   TPA

Born on 1/10/27 in Dallas, Oregon. Died of liver failure on 2/25/90 (age 63). Wore hearing aid since age 14. First recorded for Okeh in 1951. Famous for emotion-packed delivery, with R&B influences. Appeared in three movies.

4/19/52   **2⁵**   24   **Johnnie Ray** $60   Columbia 288

'45' [4] B-288 (#2/5 wks.) / '33' [10"] CL-6199 (#2/1 wk.)

Don't Blame Me ● **Walkin' My Baby Back Home** [4] ● Don't Take Your Love From Me ● **All Of Me** [12] ● Give Me Time ● The Lady Drinks Champagne ● Out In The Cold Again ● Coffee And Cigarettes

REYNOLDS, Debbie — see MOVIE SOUNDTRACKS ("I Love Melvin"/"Singin' In The Rain"/"Two Weeks With Love")

RODGERS, Jimmie

Born on 9/8/1897 in Meridian, Mississippi. Died of tuberculosis on 5/26/33 (age 35). Singer/songwriter/guitarist. Known as "America's Blue Yodeler," "The Singing Brakeman," and "The Father of Country Music." Elected to the Country Music Hall of Fame in 1961. Inducted into the Rock and Roll Hall of Fame in 1986 as an early influence of rock and roll.

6/18/49   **4**   8   **Yodelingly Yours - A Memorial Album** ....78⁴ **[K]** $200   RCA Victor 244

Blue Yodel No. 1 (T for Texas) [2/'28] ● Away Out On The Mountain ● Never No Mo' Blues ● Daddy And Home ● Frankie And Johnny ● **The Brakeman's Blues** [7/'28]

RODGERS & HAMMERSTEIN — see MOVIE SOUNDTRACKS ("State Fair") / ORIGINAL CASTS ("Carousel"/"The King And I"/"Me And Juliet"/"Oklahoma"/ "South Pacific")

ROSE, David, and his Orchestra   TPA

Born on 6/15/10 in London; raised in Chicago. Died of heart failure on 8/23/90 (age 80). Conductor/composer/arranger. Married to Martha Raye (1938-41) and Judy Garland (1941-45). Also see **Movie Soundtracks** ("Rich, Young, And Pretty").

8/24/46   **❶²**   5   **a Cole Porter review**   78⁴ **[I]** $40   RCA Victor 158

songs from the movie *Night And Day* starring Cary Grant as Cole Porter

What Is This Thing Called Love? ● I've Got You Under My Skin ● Begin The Beguine ● Love For Sale ● Night And Day ● Easy To Love ● I Get A Kick Out Of You ● In The Still Of The Night

S

ST. LUKE'S CHORISTERS

Sixty-member male choral group organized in 1930 at St. Luke's Episcopal Church in Long Beach, California; William Ripley Dorr, conductor.

1/5/46   **4**   1   1 **Christmas Carols** ....78⁴ **[X]** $30   Capitol BD-2

first released in December, 1944

Hark, The Herald Angels Sing ● It Came Upon A Midnight Clear ● The First Nowel ● O Little Town Of Bethlehem ● Deck The Halls ● Christmas Eve Is Here ● Away In A Manger ● O Come, All Ye Faithful (Adeste, Fidelis) ● Silent Night

1/7/50   **10**   1   2 **Christmas Carols** ....78⁴ **[X-R]** $30   Capitol BD-2

SCHAFER, Kermit   TPA

Born on 3/24/23 in New York City. Died on 3/8/79 (age 55). Compiled several albums made up of radio and TV bloopers.

8/7/54   **7**   20   1 **Pardon My Blooper! Vol. 1** ....10" **[C]** $25   Jubilee LP-2

LP: Jubilee LP-2 (#9); EP: Jubilee EP-5011 (#7)

10/16/54   **12**   6   2 **Pardon My Blooper! Vol. 2** ....10" **[C]** $25   Jubilee LP-3

LP: Jubilee LP-3 (#12); EP: Jubilee EP-5012 (#12)

SCHUMANN, Walter, The Voices of

Born on 10/8/13 in New York City. Died on 8/21/58 (age 44). Leader of own choral group. Composer of the theme for TV's *Dragnet*.

12/22/51   **8**   3   1 **Christmas in the Air!** ....45⁴ **[X]** $20   Capitol 9016

Christmas In The Air! ● Jingle Bells ● Silent Night ● Carol Of The Bells ● Winter Wonderland ● Adeste Fideles ● White Christmas ● Patapan ● Wonderful Counselor ● Wolcum Yole ● Mary, Mary

10/25/52   **9**   1   2 **Romance in the Air!** ....10" $20   Capitol 347

Romance In The Air ● Love ● My Heart Stood Still ● 'S Wonderful ● I Guess I'll Have To Change My Plan ● When Your Lover Has Gone ● Taking A Chance On Love ● Medley: Love Is Sweeping The Country/Finale

SCHUTT, Arthur — see SONGS OF OUR TIMES ("1926"/"1929")

SHAW, Artie, and his Orchestra

Born Arthur Arshawsky on 5/23/10 in New York City. Famed clarinetist/bandleader/theatrical producer. Married eight times; wives included actresses Lana Turner and Ava Gardner. Also see **Various Artist Compilations**.

7/28/45	4	2		1 **Artie Shaw** .... [G-I]		$30	Victor 85

'78' [4] P-85 (#4) / '45' [4] WP-85 (#8); first released in 1943; charted 1 week on 7/28/45 and 1 week (#10) on 1/14/50; entered the 45 rpm chart on 11/17/51

Frenesi [1] ● **Begin The Beguine [1/'38]** ● Star Dust [6] ● Back Bay Shuffle [8/'38] ● Dancing In The Dark [9] ● Traffic Jam [9/'39] ● Moonglow ● Serenade To A Savage

9/16/50	9	1		2 **Artie Shaw plays Cole Porter** 45⁴		$40	MGM 54

originally released in 1946 as a 78 rpm album set on Musicraft S2; vocals by Mel Torme, Kitty Kallen and Teddy Walters; songs featured in the movie *Night And Day* starring Cary Grant as Cole Porter

What Is This Thing Called Love ● Night And Day ● In The Still Of The Night ● My Heart Belongs To Daddy ● Get Out Of Town ● I've Got You Under My Skin ● You Do Something To Me ● Love For Sale

SHAW, Robert, Chorale   TPA

Born on 4/30/16 in Red Bluff, California. Died of a stroke on 1/25/99 (age 82). Conductor/music director. Led the **Fred Waring** Glee Clubs, 1938-45; organized own singing group in 1948. Music director of Atlanta Symphony Orchestra and Chorus, 1967-87.

12/10/49+	5	5		1 **Christmas Hymns and Carols** ....45⁴ [X]		$35	RCA Victor 1077

Medley: Joy To The World/It Came Upon A Midnight Clear/Angels We Have Heard On High ● Medley: O Come, O Come, Emanuel/O Little Town Of Bethlehem/Silent Night ● Medley: O Come, All Ye Faithful (Adeste Fideles)/Luther's Cradle Hymn (Away In A Manger)/God Rest You Merry, Gentlemen ● Medley: We Three Kings/The First Noel/Hark! The Herald Angels Sing ● Medley: Shepherd's Carol/Coventry Carol/Patapan ● Medley: My Dancing Day/I Wonder As I Wander/Bring A Torch, Jeanette, Isabella ● Medley: Carol Of The Bells/Lo, How A Rose E'er Blooming/Go Tell It On The Mountain ● Medley: I Sing Of A Maiden/Echo Hymn/Wassail Song/Deck The Halls With Boughs Of Holly

12/30/50	9	2		2 **Christmas Hymns and Carols** .... [X-R]		$25	RCA Victor 1077

'45' [4] WMO-1077 (#9) / '33' [12"] LM-1112 (#10)

12/29/51	7	2		3 **Christmas Hymns and Carols** .... [X-R]		$25	RCA Victor 1112

ROBERT SHAW and his RCA VICTOR CHORALE (above 3)
re-charted in 1957 and 1958 on RCA Victor 1711

SHAY, Dorothy   ★23★

Born Dorothy Sims on 4/11/21 in Jacksonville, Florida. Died of a heart attack on 10/22/78 (age 57). Singer/actress. Known as "The Park Avenue Hillbillie." Acted in the movie *Comin' 'Round The Mountain*.

2/22/47	❶⁵	35		1 **Dorothy Shay (The Park Avenue Hillbillie) Sings** 78⁴ [N]		$40	Columbia 119

Feudin' And Fightin' [4] ● Say That We're Sweethearts Again ● Mountain Gal ● Efficiency ● Flat River, Missouri ● I've Been To Hollywood ● Uncle Fud ● I'm In Love With A Married Man

11/15/47+	❶¹	13		2 **Dorothy Shay (The Park Avenue Hillbillie) Goes To Town** 78⁴ [N]		$40	Columbia 155

Mischa Russell (orch., above 2)

Just A Friendly Feeling ● Mountain Lullaby ● He's The One ● The Style To Which I'm Accustomed ● With A Little Indiscretion On The Side ● It's The Little Things That Count ● Agnes Clung ● The Drainpipe Song (Your Baby Has Gone Down The Drainpipe)

12/18/48+	4	8		3 **Coming 'Round The Mountain** ....78⁴ [N]		$40	Columbia 171

Mitchell Ayres (orch.); Shay starred with Abbott & Costello in the 1951 movie of the same title

Joan Of Arkansaw ● Pure As The Driven Snow ● Why Don't Someone Marry Mary Anne ● No Ring On Her Finger ● Since Mother Was A Girl ● Love Isn't Born (It's Made) ● Grandpa's Gettin' Younger Ev'ry Day ● The Old Apple Tree

SHEARING, George, Quintet   TPA

Born on 8/13/19 in London. Jazz pianist. Blind since birth.

10/14/50	6	7		1 **You're Hearing George Shearing and his Quintet**.. [I]		$50	MGM 518

'33' [10"] E-518 (#6) / '45' [4] K-55 (#7)

Tenderly ● Strolling ● November Sea Scape ● September In The Rain ● Summertime ● Changing With The Times ● As Long As There's Music ● East Of The Sun (West Of The Moon)

11/10/51	9	1		2 **Touch Of Genius!**..45⁴ [I]		$40	MGM 90

My Silent Love ● I'll Never Smile Again ● They All Laughed ● We'll Be together Again ● Midnight Mood ● If You Were The Only Girl In The World ● Minoration ● Loose Leaf

SHORE, Dinah

Born Frances Rose Shore on 3/1/17 in Winchester, Tennessee. Died of cancer on 2/24/94 (age 76). One of the most popular female vocalists of the 1940 to mid-1950s era. Sang with Xavier Cugat from 1939-40. Hostess of the 15-minute, award-winning early evening TV variety *The Dinah Shore Show* from 1951-57; then hosted the very popular *Dinah Shore Chevy Show* from 1956-63. Own morning talk show *Dinah's Place*, 1970-80. Married to actor George Montgomery from 1943-62. Also see **Original Casts** ("Call Me Madam" on RCA Victor).

8/25/45	4	1		1 **Victor Showpiece Presents Dinah Shore in Gershwin Show Hits**....................78²		$75	RCA Victor SP-5

Albert Sack (orch.); special softcover gatefold sleeve has pockets for two 78 rpms (also see **Charlie Spivak**)

The Man I Love ● Do It Again ● Love Walked In ● Someone To Watch Over Me

9/15/45	4	1		2 **Musical Orchids** 78⁴		$30	RCA Victor 139

first released in December, 1943

Memphis Blues ● Somebody Loves Me ● Smoke Gets In Your Eyes ● Mad About Him, Sad Without Him, How Can I Be Glad Without Him Blues ● **Blues In The Night [4]** ● How Come You Do Me Like You Do? ● My Man ● Honeysuckle Rose

5/26/51	10	2		3 **The King And I**		$40	RCA Victor 1022

DINAH SHORE/PATRICE MUNSEL/TONY MARTIN/ROBERT MERRILL
'33' [LP] LK-1022 (#10) / '45' [5] WK-30 (#10); selections from the Broadway show; not the original cast; cd: **Al Goodman** and Henri René

Overture [Al Goodman Orch.] ● Shall We Dance [Shore & Merrill] ● I Whistle A Happy Tune [Shore] ● I Have Dreamed [Martin & Munsel] ● My Lord And Master [Munsel] ● Something Wonderful [Munsel] ● Hello, Young Lovers [Shore] ● We Kiss In A Shadow [Martin & Munsel] ● A Puzzlement [Merrill] ● Getting To Know You [Shore]

Peggy Lee/Margaret Whiting/Gordon MacRae..._South Pacific ('49)_

Liberace
Sincerely, Liberace ('54)

Nellie Lutcher And Her Rhythm
Nellie Lutcher ('48)

Tony Martin And The Pied Pipers
Oh You Beautiful Doll ('50)

Edward R. Murrow
"I Can Hear It Now..." 1935-1945 ('49)

Johnnie Ray
Johnnie Ray ('52)

Jimmie Rodgers
Yodelingly Yours - A Memorial Album ('49)

Artie Shaw
Artie Shaw plays Cole Porter ('50)

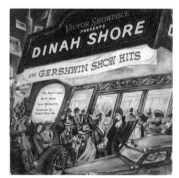

Dinah Shore..._Victor Showpiece Presents Dinah Shore in Gershwin Show Hits ('45)_

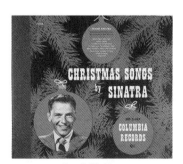

Frank Sinatra
Christmas Songs by Sinatra ('49)

Charlie Spivak..._plays selections from Gershwin's Folk-Opera Porgy and Bess ('45)_

Yma Sumac
Voice Of The Xtabay ('50)

Danny Thomas
The Jazz Singer ('53)

The Three Suns
The Three Suns in ¾ time ('51)

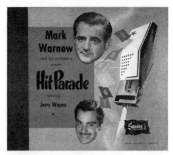

Mark Warnow and his Orchestra
Hit Parade ('45)

Soundtrack
Alice in Wonderland ('51)

Soundtrack
Show Boat ('51)

Soundtrack
Singin' In The Rain ('52)

Soundtrack
Words And Music ('49)

Original Cast
Gentlemen Prefer Blondes ('50)

Original Cast
A Tree Grows In Brooklyn ('51)

Songs Of Our Times
Song Hits Of 1932 ('48)

Various Artists...*Jazz At The Philharmonic, volume eight ('48)*

Various Artists
Theme Songs ('48)

DEBUT	PEAK	WKS	Gold	ARTIST — Album Title	Sym	$	Label & Number

SINATRA, Frank ★14★   TPA
Born Francis Albert Sinatra on 12/12/15 in Hoboken, New Jersey. Died of a heart attack on 5/14/98 (age 82). With **Harry James** from 1939-40, first recorded for Brunswick in 1939; with **Tommy Dorsey**, 1940-42. Went solo in late 1942. Starred in several movies. Won an Oscar for the movie *From Here To Eternity* in 1953. Own TV show in 1957. Own Reprise record company in 1961, sold to Warner Bros. in 1963. Won Grammy's Lifetime Achievement Award in 1965. Married to actress Ava Gardner from 1951-57. Married to actress Mia Farrow from 1966-68. Announced his retirement in 1970, but made comeback in 1973. Regarded by many as the greatest popular singer of the 20th century. Also see **Tommy Dorsey**.

3/23/46	❶[7]	18		1 **The Voice of Frank Sinatra** 78[4] $75 Columbia 112
				You Go To My Head ● I Don't Know Why (I Just Do) ● These Foolish Things (Remind Me Of You) ● (I Don't Stand) A Ghost Of A Chance (With You) ● Why Shouldn't I? ● Try A Little Tenderness ● Someone To Watch Over Me ● Paradise
5/17/47	2[2]	7		2 **Songs By Sinatra** 78[4] $75 Columbia 124
				I'm Sorry I Made You Cry ● I Concentrate On You ● How Deep Is The Ocean ● That Old Black Magic ● Over The Rainbow ● All The Things You Are ● She's Funny That Way ● Embraceable You
1/1/49	7	1		3 **Christmas Songs by Sinatra** ....78[4] [X] $100 Columbia 167
				Alex Stordahl (orch., above 3)
				Silent Night, Holy Night ● Adeste Fideles (O, Come All Ye Faithful) ● **White Christmas [5]** ● Jingle Bells ● O Little Town Of Bethlehem ● It Came Upon The Midnight Clear ● Have Yourself A Merry Little Christmas ● Santa Claus Is Comin' To Town
2/27/54	3	31		4 **Songs for Young Lovers** 10" $50 Capitol 488
				'33' [10"] H-488 (#3) / '45' [EP] EBF-488 (#4)
				My Funny Valentine ● The Girl Next Door ● A Foggy Day ● Like Someone In Love ● I Get A Kick Out Of You ● Little Girl Blue ● They Can't Take That Away From Me ● Violets For Your Furs
9/4/54	3	32		5 **Swing Easy!** 10" $50 Capitol 528
				LP: Capitol H-528 (#3); EP: Capitol EBF-528 (#5)
				Just One Of Those Things ● I'm Gonna Sit Right Down And Write Myself A Letter ● Sunday ● Wrap Your Troubles In Dreams ● Taking A Chance On Love ● Jeepers Creepers ● Get Happy ● All Of Me

SLACK, Freddie
Born on 8/7/10 in Westby, Wisconsin. Died of diabetes on 8/10/65 (age 55). Boogie-woogie pianist. WIth Ben Pollack from 1934-36, **Jimmy Dorsey** from 1936-39, and **Will Bradley** in 1940. Also see **Will Bradley**.

9/1/45	❶[5]	14		**Freddie Slack's Boogie Woogie** 78[4] [I] $50 Capitol 12
				Rib Joint ● Behind The Eight Beat ● Southpaw Serenade ● Strange Cargo ● A Cat's Ninth Life ● Blackout Boogie ● Bashful Baby Blues ● Kitten On The Keys

SONGS OF OUR TIMES — see after ORIGINAL CASTS

SPITALNY, Phil — see HOUR OF CHARM

SPIVAK, Charlie, and his Orchestra
Born on 2/17/06 in Kiev, Russia; raised in New Haven, Connecticut. Died of cancer on 3/1/82 (age 76). Played trumpet with Paul Specht (1925-31), Ben Pollack (1931-34), the Dorsey Brothers, Ray Noble, **Tommy Dorsey** (1938), and Jack Teagarden; **Glenn Miller** helped him form band in 1940. Sonny Burke and Nelson Riddle wrote arrangements; vocals by Garry Stevens and The Stardusters (including June Hutton). Band lineup in 1942 featured Willie Smith (alto sax) and Dave Tough (drums).

8/18/45	3	4		**Charlie Spivak plays selections from Gershwin's Folk-Opera Porgy and Bess** 78[2] [I] $75 RCA Victor SP-6
				special softcover gatefold sleeve has pockets for two 78 rpms (also see **Dinah Shore**'s *Gershwin Show Hits*)
				Summertime ● I Got Plenty O' Nuttin' ● Bess You Is My Woman ● It Ain't Necessarily So

STAFFORD, Jo   TPA
Born on 11/12/17 in Coalinga, California. Member of **Tommy Dorsey**'s vocal group The Pied Pipers, 1940-43. Married to orchestra leader **Paul Weston**; recorded together as the novelty duo, Jonathan & Darlene Edwards. Stafford also recorded as the hillbilly Cinderella G. Stump in 1947. Jo Stafford and **Dinah Shore** rank as the top 2 female vocalists of the pre-rock era.

4/30/49	9	2		**Kiss Me, Kate** ....78[4] $40 Capitol 144
				JO STAFFORD and GORDON MacRAE
				a studio version of the Cole Porter Broadway musical; **Paul Weston** (orch.); 45 rpm four-record package released on CDF-157; also see the 1949 Original Cast and the 1954 Movie Soundtrack versions
				Wunderbar ● Too Darn Hot *[Paul Weston]* ● Were Thine That Special Face *[MacRae]* ● I Hate Men *[Stafford]* ● Always True To You In My Fashion *[Stafford]* ● Bianca *[MacRae]* ● **So In Love** *[MacRae]* **[20]** ● Why Can't You Behave *[Stafford]*

STARR, Kay
Born Katherine Starks on 7/21/22 in Dougherty, Oklahoma; raised in Dallas and Memphis. With Joe Venuti's orchestra at age 15; sang briefly with **Glenn Miller**, Charlie Barnet and Bob Crosby before launching solo career in 1945. In the movies *Make Believe Ballroom* and *When You're Smiling*.

2/14/53	2[1]	19		**The Kay Starr Style** $60 Capitol 363
				'45' [4] CBF-363 (#2) / '33' [10"] H-363 (#3); Harold Mooney (orch.)
				Side By Side *[3]* ● It's The Talk Of The Town ● Waiting At The End Of The Road ● I Just Couldn't Take It Baby ● The Breeze (That's Bringin' My Honey Back To Me) ● To-Night You Belong To Me ● Too Busy! ● What Can I Say After I Say I'm Sorry

STEINER, Max — see MOVIE SOUNDTRACKS ("Gone With The Wind")

STONE, Cliffie, And His Square Dance Band
Born Clifford Snyder on 3/1/17 in Burbank, California. Died on 1/16/98 (age 80). Country singer/songwriter/bassist/bandleader. Elected to the Country Music Hall of Fame in 1989.

5/21/49	4	24		**Square Dances** ....78[4] [I] $30 Capitol 44
				originally released in March, 1947; includes an eight-page square dance instruction booklet
				Special Instructions For Square Dancing ● Soldier's Joy ● Sally Good'in' ● Cripple Creek ● The Gal I Left Behind Me ● Bake Them Hoecakes Brown ● Ragtime Annie ● Golden Slippers

★26★ SUMAC, Yma
Born Zoila Castillo on 9/10/27 in Ichocan, Peru. Female singer. Known for her four-octave singing voice.

| 11/4/50 | ❶⁶ | 59 | | 1 **Voice Of The Xtabay** | [F] | $60 | Capitol 244 |

'33' [10"] H-244 (#1/6 wks.) / '45' [4] CDF-244 (#1/6 wks.)
Virgin Of The Sun God (Taita Inty) ● High Andes! (Ataypúra!) ● Chant Of The Chosen Maidens (Accla Taqui) ● Earthquake! (Trumpa!) ● Dance Of The Moon Festival (Choladas) ● Dance Of The Winds (Wayra) ● Monkeys (Monos) ● Lure Of The Unknown Love (Xtabay)

| 2/23/52 | 5 | 10 | | 2 **Legend Of The Sun Virgin** .... | [F] | $60 | Capitol 299 |

'33' [10"] L-299 (#5) / '45' [4] KDF-299 (#6); **Les Baxter** (orch., above 2)
Karibe Taki ● Witallia! ● Lament ● Zana ● Kuyaway ● Suray Surita ● No Es Vida ● Mamallay!

T

THOMAS, Danny
Born Amos Jahoob on 1/16/14 in Deerfield, Michigan. Died of a heart attack on 2/6/91 (age 77). Actor. Star of TV's *Make Room For Daddy*. Father of actress Marlo Thomas and TV producer Tony Thomas. Also see **Doris Day** ("I'll See You In My Dreams").

| 4/4/53 | 7 | 5 | | **The Jazz Singer** .... | | $50 | RCA Victor 3118 |

'45' [EP] EPB-3118 (#7) / '33' [10"] LPM-3118 (#10);
Frank DeVol (orch.); Thomas sings hits from the movie he starred in, a remake of the 1927 first talking movie
Hush-A-Bye ● Oh Moon ● Living The Life I Love ● The Birth Of The Blues ● This Is A Very Special Day ● I Hear The Music Now ● Kol Nidre ● Hashkivenu

THREE SUNS, The ★19★   TPA
Instrumental trio from Philadelphia: brothers Al (guitar) and Morty (accordian) Nevins, with cousin Artie Dunn (organ). Al Nevins died on 1/25/65 (age 48). Morty Nevins died on 7/23/90 (age 63). Dunn died on 1/15/96 (age 73). Al Nevins founded, with Don Kirshner, Aldon Music, the famed publishing company largely responsible for the "Brill Building" rock and roll sound. Also see **Various Artist Compilations**.

| 7/20/46+ | 2¹ | 17 | | 1 Twilight Time | 78³ [I] | $20 | Majestic 2 |

Star Dust ● **Twilight Time** *[8]* ● Barcarolle ● Girl Of My Dreams ● Who's Sorry Now? ● Once In A While

| 9/28/47 | 3 | 4 | | 2 **The Three Suns Present** | 78⁴ [I] | $20 | RCA Victor 185 |

Twilight Time *[8]* ● Hindustan ● Dardanella ● Deep Purple ● When Day Is Done ● I'll Never Wish For More Than This ● The Breeze And I ● Sunrise Serenade

| 4/17/48 | ❶¹ | 24 | | 3 Busy Fingers | 78⁴ [I] | $20 | RCA Victor 206 |

Dancing Tambourine ● Dizzy Fingers ● The Doll Dance ● Canadian Capers ● The Wedding Of The Painted Doll ● Nola ● Eccentric ● Stumbling

| 12/3/49 | 5 | 6 | | 4 **Your Christmas Favorites** .... | 78³ [X-I] | $20 | RCA Victor 250 |

Santa Claus Is Comin' To Town ● Adeste Fideles (O Come, All Ye Faithful) ● White Christmas ● Winter Wonderland ● Silent Night ● Jingle Bells

| 8/5/50 | 6 | 3 | | 5 **Raggin' The Scales with The Three Suns**................................ | 45³ [I] | $30 | RCA Victor 278 |

Ragging The Scale ● Goofus ● Josephine ● Parade Of The Wooden Soldiers ● The Glow-Worm ● The Darktown Strutters' Ball

| 1/6/51 | 6 | 1 | | 6 **Your Christmas Favorites**.. | 45³ [X-I-R] | $25 | RCA Victor 250 |
| 8/4/51 | 10 | 1 | | 7 **The Three Suns in 3/4 time** | 45³ [I] | $30 | RCA Victor 313 |

The THREE SUNS with Larry Green at the piano
Waltz Serenade ● Waltz In A-Flat ● Rosenkavalier Waltz ● Two Hearts In Three-Quarter Time ● The Sleeping Beauty Waltz ● Coppelia Waltz

V

VAN DAMME, Art, Quintette
Born on 4/9/20 in Norway, Michigan. Jazz accordionist.

| 2/5/49 | 10 | 1 | | **Cocktail Capers** .... | 10" [I] | $25 | Capitol 178 |

Dark Eyes ● I've Got You Under My Skin ● The Breeze And I ● Meadowland ● Lover ● If I Had You ● I Know That You Know ● The Man I Love

W

WARING, Fred, and his Pennsylvanians   TPA
Born on 6/9/1900 in Tyrone, Pennsylvania. Died on 7/29/84 (age 84). Extremely popular dance band leader best known for his Pennsylvanians glee club featured on radio shows from 1933 through the '40s. While at his peak of radio popularity, Fred ceased recording for nearly a decade after 1932; charted 50 hits from 1923-33. Host of his own TV show from 1949-54.

| 12/28/46 | 5 | 1 | ● | 1 'Twas The Night Before Christmas .... | 78⁴ [X] | $20 | Decca 480 |

first released Christmas, 1942 on Decca 350
'Twas The Night Before Christmas ● Medley: Silent Night/Come Unto Him ● Oh Gathering Clouds ● Adeste Fideles (Oh, Come, All Ye Faithful) ● Cantique De Noel (O Holy Night) ● Medley: The First Nowell/O, Little Town Of Bethlehem/Carol Of The Bells ● Beautiful Saviour

| 12/20/47 | 4 | 3 | | 2 'Twas The Night Before Christmas .... | 78⁴ [X-R] | $20 | Decca 480 |
| 12/4/48 | 2⁶ | 7 | | 3 'Twas The Night Before Christmas | 78⁴ [X-R] | $20 | Decca 480 |

DEBUT	PEAK	WKS	Gold	ARTIST — Album Title	Sym	$	Label & Number

WARING, Fred, and his Pennsylvanians — Cont'd

DEBUT	PEAK	WKS		ARTIST — Album Title	Sym	$	Label & Number
12/3/49	3	6		4 'Twas The Night Before Christmas	78⁴ [X-R]	$20	Decca 480
12/23/50	4	4		5 'Twas The Night Before Christmas	[X-R]	$25	Decca 9-67

'45' [4] 9-67 (#4) / '33' [10"] DL-5021 (#5)

12/29/51	7	2		6 'Twas The Night Before Christmas	45⁴ [X-R]	$25	Decca 9-67

above 6 albums are all the same version

WARNOW, Mark, and his Orchestra
Born in 1892 in Brooklyn, New York. Died on 10/16/49 (age 57). Orchestra conductor on CBS radio's *The Saturday Night Hit Parade* from 1937-47. Older brother of bandleader Raymond Scott.

3/24/45	4	1		Hit Parade	78⁴	$30	Sonòra 470

Jerry Wayne and Vera Barton (vocals)
Let's Take The Long Way Home • I Didn't Know About You • I'm Making Believe • I'll Walk Alone • Ac-Cent-Tchu-Ate The Positive • The Very Thought Of You • Every Time We Say Goodbye • Time Waits For No One

★27★ WESTON, Paul, and his Orchestra   TPA
Born Paul Wetstein on 3/12/12 in Springfield, Massachusetts. Died on 9/20/96 (age 84). Arranger for **Tommy Dorsey** and Bob Crosby before becoming Capitol Record's foremost conductor/arranger (later with Columbia), backing many singers (his wife **Jo Stafford**, **Doris Day**, **Frankie Laine**, and The Pied Pipers) and recording "mood music" albums. Composer of the hits "I Should Care" and "Shrimp Boats." Later served as conductor for many TV shows. Also see **Jo Stafford** ("Kiss Me, Kate").

7/7/45	3	7		1 Music For Dreaming	78⁴ [I]	$20	Capitol 9

charted for 6 weeks; re-charted for 1 week (#9) on 8/26/50 on the 45 rpm chart (Capitol ADF-164)
I Only Have Eyes For You • So Beats My Heart For You • If I Love Again • Rain • Don't Blame Me • You Came Along From Out Of Nowhere • I'm In The Mood For Love • My Blue Heaven

7/23/49	3	11		2 Songs Without Words	78³ [I]	$20	Capitol 170

6 new melodies written by 6 top contemporary composers
Melody by Johnny Mercer • Melody by Isham Jones • Melody by Ray Noble • Melody by Jimmy McHugh • Melody by Paul Weston • Melody by Livingston and Evans

12/2/50	9	2		3 Music For The Fireside	10" [I]	$20	Capitol 245

Love Walked In • Something To Remember You By • Tenderly • September In The Rain • I Cover The Waterfront • Where Or When • If I Could Be With You • Stars Fell On Alabama

12/26/53	7	5		4 Concertos for You	[I]	$40	Columbia 6269

LIBERACE with PAUL WESTON And His Orchestra
"Popular LP'S" chart ('33') listed both 10" (CL-6269) and 12" (ML-4764-Masterworks) configurations; Masterworks version contains an additional five selections: "The Dream Of Olwen," "Stella By Starlight," "Laura," "Spellbound Concerto," and "Rachmaninoff's Fantasia"
Warsaw Concerto • Cornish Rhapsody • Grieg's Piano Concerto • Chopin Fantasia

WHITING, Margaret   TPA
Born on 7/22/24 in Detroit; raised in Hollywood. Vocalist with **Freddie Slack** and **Billy Butterfield**. Daughter of noted composer Richard Whiting ("Till W Meet Again"). Sister of singer/actress Barbara Whiting; starred in the 1950s TV series *Those Whiting Girls*. Also see **Billy Butterfield**.

6/25/49	4	6		South Pacific	78⁴	$40	Capitol 162

PEGGY LEE/MARGARET WHITING/GORDON MacRAE
selections from the Broadway musical of the same title (not the Original Cast)
A Wonderful Guy *[Whiting]* • Some Enchanted Evening *[MacRae]* • Bali Ha'i *[Lee]* • Medley: Happy Talk/Honey Bun *[Frank DeVol Orch.]* • Younger Than Springtime *[MacRae]* • A Cock-Eyed Optimist *[Whiting]* • There Is Nothin' Like A Dame *[Dave Barbour]* • I'm Gonna Wash That Man Right Outta My Hair *[Lee]*

WOLCOTT, Charles, and his Orchestra
Born on 9/29/06 in Flint, Michigan. Died on 1/26/87 (age 80). Pianist/composer/arranger. With Paul Whiteman, **Andre Kostelanetz** and Jean Goldkette bands. Music director with MGM studios from 1950-60.

3/24/45	3	5		The Three Caballeros	78³	$40	Decca 373

songs from the live-action/animated movie of the same title (not the original soundtrack)
The Three Caballeros (Ay Jalisco No Te Rajes) • Jesusita (En Chihuahua) • Baía (Na Baixa Do Sapateiro) • Os Quindins De Yayá • You Belong To My Heart (Solamente Una Vez) • Mexico

WOODS, Ilene — see MOVIE SOUNDTRACKS ("Cinderella")

Y

YOUNG, Victor, And His Singing Strings
Born on 8/8/1900 in Chicago. Died on 11/11/56 (age 56). Conductor/composer/violinist.

8/5/50	10	1		April in Paris	10" [I]	$25	Decca 5259

April In Paris (Avril A Paris) • Dancing With You (Danse Avec Moi) • Speak To Me Of Love (Parlez-Moi D'Amour) • Pigalle • Beyond The Sea (La Mer) • Comme Ci, Comme Ca (Clopin, Clopant) • The River Seine (La Seine) • **La Vie En Rose** *[27]*

ALBUMS BY CATEGORY

The following categories list charted albums that are not listed in the Albums By Artist section.

THE CATEGORIES

Movie Soundtracks / Original Casts / Songs Of Our Times / Various Artist Compilations

CROSS REFERENCES

Many albums are cross referenced in their respective sections and refer back to an artist in the Albums By Artist section of this book A Movie Soundtrack or Original Cast album is listed in the Albums By Artist section if one artist contributed a major portion of the album's cuts.

CUTS INDEX GUIDELINES

If various artists contributed songs to an album, then the contributing artist is listed in brackets after the cut title.

The following are unique to Movie Soundtrack and/or Original Cast albums:

ABBREVIATIONS IN THE TITLE NOTES

cp:	Composer	ly:	Lyricist	pf:	Performer
cd:	Conductor	mu:	Music writer		

MOVIE SOUNDTRACK/ORIGINAL CAST STARS

The Movie Soundtrack and Original Cast stars are listed below their respective titles. This information is also included below the Movie Soundtrack and Original Cast cross references.

MOVIE SOUNDTRACKS

9/1/51 · **8** · **1** · 1 **Alice in Wonderland**...45² **[N]** $50 · RCA Victor 437
a giant 10" x 13" 24-page hardcover booklet which includes two yellow vinyl 45 rpms; adapted from the 1951 Walt Disney animated movie featuring the voices of Kathryn Beaumont as Alice and Ed Wynn as the Mad Hatter; also see *Cinderella*
In A World Of My Own ● I'm Late ● The Caucus Race ● How Do You Do And Shake Hands ● The Walrus And The Carpenter ● All In The Golden Afternoon ● The Unbirthday Song ● Very Good Advice ● 'Twas Brillig ● Painting The Roses Red ● March Of The Cards ● Alice In Wonderland

10/27/51+ · **❶¹⁶** · **65** · ● · 2 **American In Paris, An** · **[M]** $60 · MGM 93
'33' [10"] E-93 (#1/16 wks.) / '45' [4] K-93 (#1/12 wks.); **Gene Kelly**/Leslie Caron/Oscar Levant; cp: George & Ira Gershwin; cd: Johnny Green
'S Wonderful *[Gene Kelly & Georges Guetary]* ● Love Is Here To Stay *[Gene Kelly]* ● I'll Build A Stairway To Paradise *[Georges Guetary]* ● I Got Rhythm *[Gene Kelly]* ● An American In Paris Ballet

6/10/50 · **❶⁸** · **27** · 3 **Annie Get Your Gun** · **[M]** $50 · MGM 1001
'45' [4] G-1001 (#1) / '33' [10"] E-509 (#3); Betty Hutton/**Howard Keel**; cp: **Irving Berlin**; cd: Adolph Deutsch; also see the 1946 Original Cast; re-charted in 1973 as one in a series of *Those Glorious MGM Musicals*
I've Got The Sun In The Morning *[Betty Hutton]* ● They Say It's Wonderful *[Betty Hutton & Howard Keel]* ● You Can't Get A Man With A Gun *[Betty Hutton]* ● My Defenses Are Down *[Howard Keel]* ● Doin' What Comes Natur'lly *[Betty Hutton]* ● The Girl That I Marry *[Howard Keel]* ● Anything You Can Do *[Betty Hutton & Howard Keel]* ● There's No Business Like Show Business *[Betty Hutton/Howard Keel/L. Calhern/Keenan Wynn]*

Because You're Mine — see LANZA, Mario
Mario Lanza/Doretta Morrow/James Whitmore; cd: Constantine Callinicos

Bells Of St. Mary's, The — see CROSBY, Bing
Bing Crosby (as Father O'Malley)/Ingrid Bergman; cd: John Scott Trotter

Blue Skies — see CROSBY, Bing
Bing Crosby/Fred Astaire; cp: **Irving Berlin**; cd: John Scott Trotter

11/13/54 · **8** · **8** · 4 **Brigadoon**... **[M]** $35 · MGM 3135
EP: MGM X-263 (#8); LP: MGM E-3135 (#15); **Gene Kelly**/Cyd Charisse/Van Johnson; ly: Alan Jay Lerner; mu: Frederick Loewe; cd: Johnny Green; also see the 1947 Original Cast
Medley: Prologue/Once In The Highlands ● Down On Mac Connachy Square ● Heather On The Hill *[Gene Kelly]* ● Waitin' For My Dearie *[Carol Richards]* ● I'll Go Home With Bonnie Jean *[Van Johnson & John Gustafson]* ● Come To Me, Bend To Me *[John Gustafson]* ● Almost Like Being In Love *[Gene Kelly]* ● The Heather On The Hill ● There But For You Go I *[Gene Kelly]* ● Brigadoon

By The Light Of The Silvery Moon — see DAY, Doris
Doris Day/Gordon MacRae; cd: Paul Weston

Calamity Jane — see DAY, Doris
Doris Day/Howard Keel; mu: Sammy Fain; ly: Paul Francis Webster; cd: Ray Heindorf

5/23/53 · **5** · **9** · 5 **Call Me Madam**... **[M]** $35 · Decca 5465
'33' [10"] DL-5465 (#5) / '45' [EP] ED-508 (#5); **Ethel Merman**/Donald O'Connor/George Sanders; cp: **Irving Berlin**; cd: Alfred Newman; also see **Ethel Merman**'s 1950 version and the 1951 Original Cast
The Hostess With The Mostes' On The Ball ● Can You Use Any Money Today? ● Marrying For Love ● It's A Lovely Day Today ● International Rag ● You're Just In Love ● (Dance To The Music of) The Ocarina ● What Chance Have I With Love ● Something To Dance About ● The Best Thing For You ● Call Me Madam

3/4/50 · **❶²** · **22** · 6 **Cinderella** · 45² **[N]** $50 · RCA Victor 399
a storybook album adapted from the 1950 Walt Disney animated movie featuring 3 songs by Ilene Woods as Cinderella; album includes a colorful read-along 24-page booklet; re-charted in 1995 with the original score and remakes of songs by contemporary artists; also see *Alice in Wonderland*
A Dream Is A Wish Your Heart Makes ● The Cinderella Work Song ● Bibbidi-Bobbidi-Boo (The Magic Song) ● So This Is Love

Connecticut Yankee In King Arthur's Court, A — see CROSBY, Bing
Bing Crosby/Rhonda Fleming/William Bendix; mu: Jimmy Van Heusen; ly: Johnny Burke; cd: **Victor Young**

2/6/54 · **7** · **1** · 7 **Eddie Cantor Story, The**...10" **[M]** $40 · Capitol 467
Keefe Brasselle (star and voice of Cantor)/Marilyn Erskine; cd: Ray Heindorf
Now's The Time To Fall In Love ● When I'm The President ● If You Knew Susie ● Ida! Sweet As Apple Cider ● Josephine Please No Lean On The Bell ● Medley: Pretty Baby/You Must Have Been A Beautiful Baby/Yes Sir, That's My Baby ● Makin' Whoopee ● Ma (He's Making Eyes At Me) ● Bye, Bye Blackbird ● Margie ● Row, Row, Row ● How 'Ya Gonna Keep 'Em Down On The Farm ● One Hour With You

Emperor Waltz, The — see CROSBY, Bing
Bing Crosby/Joan Fontaine; cd: **Victor Young**

8/15/53 · **5** · **8** · 8 **Gentlemen Prefer Blondes**.. **[M]** $100 · MGM 208
'45' [EP] X-208 (#5) / '33' [10"] E-208 (#7); Marilyn Monroe/Jane Russell; mu: Jule Styne; ly: Leo Robin; cd: Lionel Newman; also see the 1950 Original Cast
Bye Bye Baby *[Jane Russell]* ● A Little Girl From Little Rock *[Jane Russell & Marilyn Monroe]* ● Diamonds Are A Girl's Best Friend *[Marilyn Monroe]* ● Ain't There Anyone Here For Love? *[Jane Russell]* ● When Love Goes Wrong (Nothing Goes Right) *[Jane Russell & Marilyn Monroe]* ● Bye Bye Baby *[Marilyn Monroe]*

Glenn Miller Story, The — see MILLER, Glenn
James Stewart/June Allyson; cd: Joseph Gershenson

Going My Way — see CROSBY, Bing
Bing Crosby (as Father O'Malley)/Barry Fitzgerald; mu: Jimmy Van Heusen; ly: Johnny Burke

10/2/54 · **10** · **4** · 9 **Gone With The Wind** ....10" **[I]** $50 · RCA Victor 3227
LP: RCA Victor LPM-3227 (#10); EP: RCA Victor EPB-3227 (#13); new recording of movie soundtrack; cp/cd: **Max Steiner**; re-charted in 1961 (#64) on RCA Camden 625
Gone With The Wind ● Tara ● Invitation To The Dance ● Melanie's Theme ● Ashley ● The Prayer ● Bonnie Blue Flag ● Scarlet O'Hara ● Scarlet's Agony ● War ● Return To Tara ● Bonnie's Death ● Rhett Butler ● Bonnie's Theme ● Ashley And Melanie (Love Theme) ● The Oath

MOVIE SOUNDTRACKS — Cont'd

DEBUT	PEAK	WKS	Gold	ARTIST — Album Title	Sym	$	Label & Number
1/31/48	2[4]	14		10 Good News .... 78[4]	[M]	$30	MGM 17

June Allyson/Peter Lawford/Joan McCracken; mu: Ray Henderson; ly: B.G. DeSylva and Lew Brown; cd: Lennie Hayton
Good News (Tait College) *[Joan McCracken]* ● Lucky In Love *[Pat Marshall, Peter Lawford & June Allyson]* ● Just Imagine *[June Allyson]* ● French Lesson *[June Allyson & Peter Lawford]* ● The Best Things In Life Are Free *[June Allyson & Peter Lawford]* ● He's A Ladies Man *[Peter Lawford]* ● Pass That Peace Pipe *[Joan McCracken]* ● The Varsity Drag *[June Allyson & Peter Lawford]*

Great Caruso, The — see LANZA, Mario
Mario Lanza/Ann Blyth

Hans Christian Andersen — see KAYE, Danny
Danny Kaye/Farley Granger; cp: Frank Loesser; cd: **Gordon Jenkins**

DEBUT	PEAK	WKS	Gold	ARTIST — Album Title	Sym	$	Label & Number
4/18/53	8	2		11 I Love Melvin .... 10"	[M]	$50	MGM 190

Donald O'Connor/Debbie Reynolds; mu: Josef Myrow; ly: Mack Gordon; cd: Georgie Stoll
I Wanna Wander *[Donald O'Connor]* ● Where Did You Learn To Dance *[Donald O'Connor & Debbie Reynolds]* ● We Have Never Met As Yet *[Donald O'Connor & Debbie Reynolds]* ● And There You Are ● Life Has Its Funny Little Ups And Down *[Noreen Corcoran]* ● A Lady Loves *[Debbie Reynolds]* ● Saturday Afternoon Before The Game ● I Wanna Wander:

I'll See You In My Dreams — see DAY, Doris
Doris Day/Danny Thomas; cd: **Paul Weston**

Jazz Singer, The — see THOMAS, Danny
Danny Thomas/Peggy Lee; cd: Frank DeVol

Jolson Sings Again — see JOLSON, Al
Larry Parks (as Jolson); cd: Morris Stoloff and Matty Malneck

Jolson Story, The — see JOLSON, Al (LP #1 & 2)
Larry Parks (as Jolson); cd: Morris Stoloff and Carmen Dragon

DEBUT	PEAK	WKS	Gold	ARTIST — Album Title	Sym	$	Label & Number
1/23/54	7	3		12 Kiss Me Kate .... 45[3]	[M]	$40	MGM 223

Kathryn Grayson/**Howard Keel**/Ann Miller; cp: Cole Porter; cd: **Andre Previn**; also see Jo Stafford & Gordon MacRae's 1949 version and the 1949 Original Cast
Too Darn Hot *[Ann Miller]* ● So In Love *[Kathryn Grayson & Howard Keel]* ● We Open In Venice *[Kathryn Grayson/Howard Keel/Ann Miller/Tommy Rall]* ● Were Thine That Special Face *[Howard Keel]* ● Wunderbar *[Kathryn Grayson & Howard Keel]* ● Always True To You In My Fashion *[Ann Miller & Tommy Rall]* ● I Hate Men *[Kathryn Grayson]* ● From This Moment On *[Tommy Rall/Ann Miller/Bobby Van/Bob Fosse]* ● Brush Up Your Shakespeare *[Keenan Wynn & James Whitmore]* ● Kiss Me Kate *[Kathryn Grayson & Howard Keel]*

Look For The Silver Lining — see MONROE, Vaughn
June Haver/Ray Bolger/**Gordon MacRae**; mu: Jerome Kern; ly: B.G. DeSylva

DEBUT	PEAK	WKS	Gold	ARTIST — Album Title	Sym	$	Label & Number
7/12/52	2[11]	22		13 Lovely To Look At	[M]	$40	MGM 150

'45' [4] K-150 (#2/11 wks.) / '33' [10"] E-150 (#2/9 wks.); Kathryn Grayson/**Howard Keel**/Red Skelton/Ann Miller; mu: Jerome Kern; ly: Otto Harbach; cd: Carmen Dragon
Smoke Gets In Your Eyes *[Kathryn Grayson]* ● Yesterdays *[Kathryn Grayson]* ● You're Devastating *[Kathryn Grayson & Howard Keel]* ● The Touch Of Your Hand *[Kathryn Grayson & Howard Keel]* ● Lovely To Look At ● I Won't Dance *[Marge & Gower Champion]* ● Lafayette *[Red Skelton, Howard Keel & Gower Champion]* ● Lovely To Look At *[Howard Keel]* ● The Most Exciting Night *[Howard Keel]* ● I'll Be Hard To Handle *[Ann Miller]*

Lullaby Of Broadway — see DAY, Doris
Doris Day/Gene Nelson; cd: **Frank Comstock**

Meet Me In St. Louis — see GARLAND, Judy
Judy Garland/Margaret O'Brien; cd: Georgie Stoll

DEBUT	PEAK	WKS	Gold	ARTIST — Album Title	Sym	$	Label & Number
9/20/52	❶[4]	17		14 Merry Widow, The	[M]	$40	MGM 157

'33' [10"] E-157 (#1) / '45' [4] K-157 (#3); Fernando Lamas/Lana Turner/Richard Haydn; mu: Franz Lehar; ly: Paul Francis Webster; cd: Jay Blackton; Trudy Erwin performed Lana Turner's vocals in the movie
Merry Widow Waltz - Part 1 ● Merry Widow Waltz - Part 2 ● Maxim's *[Fernando Lamas]* ● Vilia *[Fernando Lamas]* ● Girls, Girls, Girls *[Fernando Lamas]* ● Merry Widow Waltz *[Fernando Lamas & Trudy Erwin]* ● Night *[Fernando Lamas]* ● Medley: Gypsy Music/Can Can

Mr. Music — see CROSBY, Bing
Bing Crosby/Charles Coburn; mu: Jimmy Van Heusen; ly: Johnny Burke

My Wild Irish Rose — see DAY, Dennis
Dennis Morgan/Andrea King/Arlene Dahl

Night And Day — see ROSE, David / SHAW, Artie
Cary Grant/Alexis Smith; cp: Cole Porter

Oh You Beautiful Doll — see MARTIN, Tony
June Haver/Mark Stevens

On Moonlight Bay — see DAY, Doris
Doris Day/Gordon MacRae; cd: **Paul Weston**

DEBUT	PEAK	WKS	Gold	ARTIST — Album Title	Sym	$	Label & Number
2/3/51	9	4		15 Pagan Love Song .... 45[3]	[M]	$30	MGM 64

Esther Williams/**Howard Keel**; mu: Harry Warren; ly: Arthur Freed; cd: Adolph Deutsch
Pagan Love Song ● House Of Singing Bamboo ● Why Is Love So Crazy ● Singing In The Sun *[Howard Keel & Esther Williams]* ● Sea Of The Moon *[Esther Williams]* ● Tahiti

DEBUT	PEAK	WKS	Gold	ARTIST — Album Title	Sym	$	Label & Number
3/1/52	4	6		16 Quo Vadis		$40	MGM 103

'33' [10"] E-103 (#4) / '45' [4] K-103 (#6); Robert Taylor/Deborah Kerr/Peter Ustinov; cp/cd: Miklos Rozsa
Quo Vadis Prelude ● Assyrian Dance ● Lygia ● Roman Bacchanal ● Siciliana Antica ● Hymn Of The Vestal Virgins ● Hail Nero, Triumphal March ● Jesu, Lord ● Chariot Chase ● Invocation To Venus ● Petronius' Meditation And Death ● Miracle ● Finale

DEBUT	PEAK	WKS	Gold	ARTIST — Album Title	Sym	$	Label & Number
9/8/51	4	11		17 Rich, Young, And Pretty	[M]	$60	MGM 86

'45' [4] K-86 (#4) / '33' [10"] E-86 (#4); Jane Powell/Danielle Darrieux/Fernando Lamas; mu: Nicholas Brodszky; ly: Sammy Cahn; cd: **David Rose**
I Can See You *[Jane Powell]* ● Dark Is The Night (C'est Fini) *[Jane Powell]* ● Paris *[Fernando Lamas]* ● We Never Talk Much *[Danielle Darrieux & Fernando Lamas]* ● Wonder Why *[Jane Powell]* ● My Little Nest Of Heavenly Blue *[Jane Powell]* ● There's Danger In Your Eyes, Cherie *[Danielle Darrieux]* ● L'Amour Toujours (Tonight For Sure) *[Danielle Darrieux]*

MOVIE SOUNDTRACKS — Cont'd

4/17/54 | **4** | **25** — 18 **Rose Marie** .... **[M]** $60 MGM 229

'33' [10"] E-229 (#4) / '45' [EP] X-229 (#4); Ann Blyth/**Howard Keel**/Fernando Lamas; mu: Rudolf Friml; ly: Otto Harbach and Oscar Hammerstein II; cd: Georgie Stoll
The Right Place For A Girl [Howard Keel] ● Free To Be Free [Ann Blyth] ● Love And Kisses [Bert Lahr & Marjorie Main] ● Indian Love Call [Ann Blyth & Fernando Lamas] ● Rose Marie [Howard Keel] ● I'm A Mountie Who Never Got His Man [Bert Lahr] ● I Have The Love [Ann Blyth & Fernando Lamas] ● Mounties [Howard Keel]

4/14/51 | **3** | **16** — 19 **Royal Wedding** | **[M]** $60 MGM 70

'45' [4] K-70 (#3) / '33' [10"] E-543 (#6); Fred Astaire/Jane Powell; mu: Burton Lane; ly: Alan Jay Lerner; cd: Johnny Green
How Could You Believe Me When I Said I Loved You When You Know I've Been A Liar All My Life [Fred Astaire & Jane Powell] ● Too Late Now [Jane Powell] ● You're All The World To Me [Fred Astaire] ● I Left My Hat In Haiti [Fred Astaire] ● Happiest Day Of My Life [Jane Powell] ● Open Your Eyes [Jane Powell] ● Every Night At Seven [Fred Astaire] ● Sunday Jumps [Johnny Green Orch.]

9/4/54 | **2⁴** | **32** — 20 **Seven Brides For Seven Brothers** | **[M]** $60 MGM 244

EP: MGM X-244 (#2); LP [10"]: MGM E-244 (#3); Jane Powell/**Howard Keel**; ly: Johnny Mercer; mu: Gene de Paul; cd: Adolph Deutsch
Bless Yore Beautiful Hide [Howard Keel] ● Wonderful, Wonderful Day [Jane Powell] ● Lament [Bill Lee] ● Goin' Co'tin' [Jane Powell] ● Sobbin' Women [Howard Keel] ● June Bride [Virginia Gibson] ● Spring, Spring, Spring ● When You're In Love [Jane Powell & Howard Keel]

7/21/51 | **❶¹⁹** | **75** — 21 **Show Boat** | **[M]** $60 MGM 84

'45' [4] K-84 (#1/19 wks.) / '33' [10"] E-559 (#1/18 wks.); Kathryn Grayson/**Howard Keel**/Ava Gardner; mu: Jerome Kern; ly: Oscar Hammerstein II; cd: Adolph Deutsch; Grammy's Hall of Fame Award winner in 1991; also see **Tommy Dorsey**'s 1946 version; re-charted in 1973 as one in a series of *Those Glorious MGM Musicals*
Make Believe [Kathryn Grayson & Howard Keel] ● Bill [Ava Gardner] ● Life Upon The Wicked Stage [Marge & Gower Champion] ● You Are Love [Kathryn Grayson & Howard Keel] ● Can't Help Lovin' Dat Man [Ava Gardner] ● I Might Fall Back On You [Marge & Gower Champion] ● Why Do I Love You [Kathryn Grayson & Howard Keel] ● Ol' Man River [William Warfield]

4/19/52 | **2¹¹** | **26** — 22 **Singin' In The Rain** | **[M]** $60 MGM 113

'33' [10"] E-113 (#2/11 wks.) / '45' [4] K-113 (#2/8 wks.); **Gene Kelly**/Donald O'Connor/**Debbie Reynolds**; mu: Herb Nacio Brown; ly: Arthur Freed; cd: Lennie Hayton; re-charted in 1973 as one in a series of *Those Glorious MGM Musicals*
Singin' In The Rain [Gene Kelly] ● You Were Meant For Me [Gene Kelly] ● All I Do Is Dream Of You [Debbie Reynolds] ● Fit As A Fiddle [Gene Kelly & Donald O'Connor] ● Make 'Em Laugh [Donald O'Connor] ● Good Morning [Gene Kelly/Donald O'Connor/Debbie Reynolds] ● Moses [Gene Kelly & Donald O'Connor] ● You Are My Lucky Star [Gene Kelly] ● All I Do Is Dream Of You [Gene Kelly]

2/26/49 | **10** | **1** — 23 **So Dear To My Heart** ....78⁴ **[T]** $50 Capitol 124

Bobby Driscoll/Burl Ives; a storybook adaptation of the movie, with narration by John Beal and featuring members of the original cast; music arranged and conducted by **Billy May**; released on Capitol's Children's Series BD-124 or on DD-109 (Superflex unbreakable 78 rpms)

Song Is Born, A — see VARIOUS ARTIST COMPILATIONS ("Giants Of Jazz")
Danny Kaye/Virginia Mayo

Star Is Born, A — see GARLAND, Judy
Judy Garland/James Mason; mu: Harold Arlen; ly: Ira Gershwin; cd: Ray Heindorf

1/10/53 | **❶²** | **24** — 24 **Stars And Stripes Forever** | **[I]** $50 MGM 176

'45' [4] K-176 (#1) / '33' [10"] E-176 (#2/7 wks.); Clifton Webb/Debra Paget/Ruth Hussey; Webb stars as legendary composer/conductor John Philip Sousa; Alfred Newman conducts the 20th Century-Fox Studio Orchestra
Stars And Stripes Forever ● Light Cavalry Overture ● Turkey In The Straw ● Washington Post March ● Semper Fidelis ● El Capitan ● Medley: Hail To The Chief/Dixie ● Battle Hymn Of The Republic [vocal]

State Fair — see HAYMES, Dick
Jeanne Crain/Dana Andrews/**Dick Haymes**; mu: Richard Rodgers; ly: Oscar Hammerstein II

Student Prince, The — see LANZA, Mario / GOODMAN, Al
Edmund Purdom/Ann Blyth; mu: Sigmund Romberg

Summer Stock — see GARLAND, Judy
Judy Garland/Gene Kelly; mu: Harry Warren; ly: Mack Gordon; cd: Johnny Green

That Midnight Kiss — see LANZA, Mario
Mario Lanza/Kathryn Grayson

Three Caballeros — see WOLCOTT, Charles
Donald Duck with Panchito, Gauchito and Jose Carioca

9/2/50 | **❶¹¹** | **36** — 25 **Three Little Words** | **[M]** $50 MGM 516

'33' [10"] E-516 (#1/11 wks.) / '45' [4] K-53 (#1/10 wks.); Fred Astaire/Red Skelton/Vera-Ellen; mu: Harry Ruby; ly: Bert Kalmar; cd: **Andre Previn**; also see **Andre Previn**'s 1950 version; movie is based on the story of songwriters Ruby and Kalmar
Three Little Words [Fred Astaire & Red Skelton] ● Where Did You Get That Girl [Fred Astaire & Anita Ellis] ● Thinking Of You [Anita Ellis] ● My Sunny Tennessee [Fred Astaire & Red Skelton] ● So Long! Oo-Long [Fred Astaire & Red Skelton] ● Nevertheless I'm In Love With You [Fred Astaire & Red Skelton & Anita Ellis] ● I Wanna Be Loved By You [Helen Kane] ● Who's Sorry Now? [Gloria DeHaven] ● All Alone Monday [Gale Robbins] ● I Love You So Much [Arlene Dahl]

Thrill Of A Romance — see MELCHIOR, Lauritz
Van Johnson/Esther Williams

3/29/47 | **3** | **3** — 26 **Till The Clouds Roll By** | 78⁴ **[M]** $75 MGM 1

Robert Walker/Van Heflin and many great musical stars; cd: Lennie Hayton; movie is a biography of songwriter Jerome Kern; MGM's first album featuring movie recordings taken directly from the movie soundtrack
Till The Clouds Roll By ● Who Cares If My Boat Goes Upstream? [Tony Martin] ● Make Believe [Kathryn Grayson & Tony Martin] ● Look For The Silver Lining [Judy Garland] ● Life Upon The Wicked Stage [Virginia O'Brien] ● Can't Help Lovin' Dat Man [Lena Horne] ● Who? [Judy Garland] ● Medley: Leave It To Jane/Cleopatterer [June Allyson] ● Ol' Man River [Caleb Peterson]

Toast Of New Orleans, The — see LANZA, Mario
Mario Lanza/Kathryn Grayson/David Niven

MOVIE SOUNDTRACKS — Cont'd

| 1/27/51 | 3 | 21 | | 27 **Two Weeks With Love** | [M] | $60 | MGM 61 |

'45' [3] K-61 (#3) / '33' [10"] E-530 (#5); Jane Powell/Ricardo Montalban; cd: Georgie Stoll

My Hero *[Jane Powell]* ● A Heart That's Free *[Jane Powell]* ● Oceana Roll *[Jane Powell]* ● By The Light Of The Silvery Moon *[Jane Powell]* ● **Aba Daba Honeymoon** *[Debbie Reynolds & Carleton Carpenter]* **[3]** ● Row, Row, Row *[Carleton Carpenter & Debbie Reynolds]*

| 1/23/54 | 6 | 29 | ● | 28 **Victory At Sea** | [I] | $25 | RCA Victor 1779 |

an orchestral suite from the NBC-TV series which documented the naval action of World War II; cp: Richard Rodgers; cd: Robert Russell Bennett; pf: NBC Symphony Orchestra; Vol. 2 charted in 1958 (#2); Vol. 3 in 1961 (#7)

The Song Of The High Seas ● The Pacific Boils Over ● Guadalcanal March ● D-Day ● Hardwork And Horseplay ● Theme Of The Fast Carriers ● Beneath The Southern Cross ● Mare Nostrum ● Victory At Sea

White Christmas — see CROSBY, Bing / KAYE, Danny / LEE, Peggy
Bing Crosby/Danny Kaye/Rosemary Clooney; cp: **Irving Berlin**; cd: Joseph Lilley

With A Song In My Heart — see FROMAN, Jane
Susan Hayward/Rory Calhoun; cd: George Greeley

| 1/22/49 | ❶⁶ | 22 | | 29 **Words And Music** | 78⁴ [M] | $50 | MGM 37 |

Mickey Rooney/Tom Drake and many great musical stars; cd: Lennie Hayton; movie is a biography of songwriters Richard Rodgers and Lorenz Hart

Manhattan *[Mickey Rooney]* ● Johnny One Note *[Judy Garland]* ● The Lady Is A Tramp *[Lena Horne]* ● Where Or When *[Lena Horne]* ● I Wish I Were In Love Again *[Judy Garland & Mickey Rooney]* ● Thou Swell *[June Allyson]* ● There's A Small Hotel *[Betty Garrett]* ● Where's That Rainbow *[Ann Sothern]*

Young Man With A Horn — see DAY, Doris / JAMES, Harry
Kirk Douglas (horn playing dubbed by **Harry James**)/Lauren Becall/**Doris Day**

ORIGINAL CASTS

| 7/27/46 | 2⁵ | 11 | | 1 **Annie Get Your Gun** | 78⁶ | $30 | Decca 468 |

Ethel Merman (as Annie Oakley)/Ray Middleton; cp: **Irving Berlin**; cd: Jay Blackton; also see the 1950 Movie Soundtrack

Doin' What Comes Natur'lly ● Moonshine Lullaby ● You Can't Get A Man With A Gun ● I'm An Indian Too ● They Say It's Wonderful ● Anything You Can Do ● I Got Lost In His Arms ● I Got The Sun In The Morning ● The Girl That I Marry ● My Defenses Are Down ● Who Do You Love I Hope ● There's No Business Like Show Business

| 6/14/47 | 4 | 1 | | 2 **Brigadoon** | 78⁵ | $30 | RCA Victor 178 |

David Brooks/Marion Bell/Pamela Britton/Lee Sullivan; ly: Alan Jay Lerner; mu: Frederick Loewe; cd: Franz Allers; also see the 1954 Movie Soundtrack

Overture ● Once In The Highlands ● Brigadoon ● Down On Mac Connachy Square ● Waitin' For My Dearie ● I'll Go Home With Bonnie Jean ● The Heather On The Hill ● Come To Me, Bend To Me ● Almost Like Being In Love ● There But For You Go I ● My Mother's Wedding Day ● From This Day On

| 1/13/51 | 6 | 13 | | 3 **Call Me Madam** | | $60 | RCA Victor 1000 |

'33' [LP] LOC-1000 (#6) / '45' [5] WOC-1 (#7); Ethel Merman/Paul Lukas/Russell Nype; cp: **Irving Berlin**; cd: Jay Blackton; the Original Broadway Cast, with **Dinah Shore** singing in place of **Ethel Merman** because of Merman's exclusive Decca recording contract; Dinah was not a member of the original cast; also see **Ethel Merman**'s 1950 version and the 1953 Movie Soundtrack

Overture ● Mrs. Sally Adams ● The Hostess With The Mostes' On The Ball ● Washington Square Dance ● Welcome To Lichtenburg ● Can You Use Any Money Today? ● Marrying For Love ● (Dance To The Music Of) The Ocarina ● It's A Lovely Day Today ● The Best Thing For You ● Something To Dance About ● Once Upon A Time Today ● They Like Ike ● You're Just In Love *[29]*

| 7/11/53 | 3 | 7 | | 4 **Can-Can** | | $40 | Capitol 452 |

'33' [LP] S-452 (#3) / '45' [4] EDM-452 (#8); Lilo/Peter Cookson/Hans Conreid/Gwen Verdon/Erik Rhodes; cp: Cole Porter; cd: Milton Rosenstock; movie soundtrack issued in 1960 on Capitol 1301

Medley: Introduction/Maidens Typical Of France ● Never Give Anything Away ● Quadrille ● C'est Magnifique ● Come Along With Me ● Live And Let Live ● I Am In Love ● If You Loved Me Truly ● Montmart ● Allez-Vous-En, Go Away ● Never, Never Be An Artist ● It's All Right With Me ● Every Man Is A Stupid Man ● I Love Paris ● Can-Can

| 7/21/45 | ❶⁶ | 15 | | 5 **Carousel** | 78⁵ | $40 | Decca 400 |

John Raitt/Jan Clayton/Christine Johnson/Jean Darling; mu: Richard Rodgers; ly: Oscar Hammerstein II; cd: Joseph Littau; movie soundtrack issued in 1956 on Capitol 694

The Carousel Waltz ● Medley: You're A Queer One, Julie Jordan/Mister Snow ● If I Loved You ● Soliloquy ● June Is Bustin' Out All Over ● When The Children Are Asleep ● Medley: Blow High, Blow Low/This Was A Real Nice Clambake ● Medley: There's Nothin' So Bad For A Woman/What's The Use Of Wond'rin' ● Medley: The Highest Judge Of All/You'll Never Walk Alone

| 2/4/50 | 2⁴ | 18 | | 6 **Gentlemen Prefer Blondes** | 12" | $40 | Columbia 4290 |

Carol Channing/Yvonne Adair/Jack McCauley; mu: Jule Styne; ly: Leo Robin; cd: Milton Rosenstock; also see the 1953 Movie Soundtrack

Overture ● It's High Time ● Bye Bye Baby ● A Little Girl From Little Rock ● Just A Kiss Apart ● I Love What I'm Doing ● Scherzo ● It's Delightful Down In Chile ● You Say You Care ● I'm A'Tingle, I'm A'Glow ● Sunshine ● Diamonds Are A Girl's Best Friend ● Mamie Is Mimi ● Homesick Blues ● Medley: Gentlemen Prefer Blondes/Keeping Cool With Coolidge

| 1/20/51 | ❶¹ | 37 | | 7 **Guys And Dolls** | | $40 | Decca 8036 |

'33' [LP] DL-8036 (#1) / '45' [7] 9-203 (#4); Robert Alda/Vivian Blaine/Sam Levene; cp: Frank Loesser; cd: Irving Actman; a new original cast version issued in 1992 on RCA Victor 61317

Medley: Runyonland Music/Fugue For Tinhorns/Follow The Fold ● The Oldest Established ● I'll Know ● A Bushel And A Peck ● Adelaide's Lament ● Guys And Dolls ● If I Were A Bell ● My Time Of Day ● I've Never Been In Love Before ● Take Back Your Mink ● More I Cannot Wish You ● Luck Be A Lady ● Sue Me ● Sit Down, You're Rockin' The Boat ● Marry The Man Today

| 5/26/51 | 2¹ | 54 | | 8 **King And I, The** | | $40 | Decca 9008 |

'33' [LP] DL-9008 (#2) / '45' [6] 9-260 (#3); Yul Brynner/Gertrude Lawrence/Dorothy Sarnoff; mu: Richard Rodgers; ly: Oscar Hammerstein II; cd: Frederick Dvonch; also see **Dinah Shore** and **Tony Martin**'s studio version; movie soundtrack issued in 1956 on Capitol 740

Overture ● I Whistle A Happy Tune ● My Lord And Master ● Hello Young Lovers ● March Of The Siamese Children ● A Puzzlement ● Getting To Know You ● We Kiss In A Shadow ● Shall I Tell You What I Think Of You? ● Something Wonderful ● I Have Dreamed ● Shall We Dance?

DEBUT	PEAK	WKS	Gold	ARTIST — Album Title	Sym	$	Label & Number

ORIGINAL CASTS — Cont'd

1/30/54   **4**   **23**   9 **Kismet** .... $40   Columbia 4850
'33' [12"] ML-4850 (#4) / '45' [EP] A-1100 (#10); Alfred Drake/Doretta Morrow/Joan Diener/Richard Kiley; mu: Alexander Borodin; ly: Robert Wright and George Forrest; cd: Louis Adrian; also see **Percy Faith**'s 1954 version
Medley: Overture/Sands Of Time/Rhymes Have I • Fate • Bazaar Of The Caravans • Not Since Nineveh • Baubles, Bangles And Beads • Stranger In Paradise • He's In Love! • Gesticulate • Night Of My Nights • Was I Wazir? • Rahadlakum • And This Is My Beloved • The Olive Tree • Zubbediya, Samaris' Dance • Medley: Finale/Sands Of Time

2/26/49   **❶**[10]   **61**   10 **Kiss Me, Kate**   78[6] $50   Columbia 200
Alfred Drake/Patricia Morrison/Harold Lang/Lisa Kirk; cp: Cole Porter; cd: Pembrooke Davenport; also see **Jo Stafford & Gordon MacRae**'s 1949 version and the 1954 Movie Soundtrack; album issued with large 12" 78 rpms; charted for 60 weeks; re-entered the chart on 12/2/57 (#25) for 1 week on Columbia OL-4140 (33-1/3 LP)
Medley: Overture/Another Op'nin', Another Show • Why Can't You Behave • Wunderbar • So In Love • We Open In Venice • Tom, Dick Or Harry • I've Come To Wive It Wealthily In Padua • I Hate Men • Were Thine That Special Face • Too Darn Hot • Where Is The Life That Late I Led? • Always True To You (In My Fashion) • Bianca • So In Love (Reprise) • Brush Up Your Shakespeare • Medley: I Am Ashamed That Women Are So Simple/Finale (So Kiss Me, Kate)

7/4/53   **2**[1]   **8**   11 **Me And Juliet** $60   RCA Victor 1012
'33' [12"] LOC-1012 (#2) / '45' [EP] EOC-1012 (three-pocket EP); Isabel Bigley/Bill Hayes/Joan McCracken/Ray Walston; mu: Richard Rodgers; ly: Oscar Hammerstein II; cd: Salvatore Dell-Isola
Overture • Medley: A Very Special Day/That's The Way It Happens • Marriage Type Love • Keep It Gay • No Other Love • The Big Black Giant • It's Me • It Feels Good • Intermission Talk • We Deserve Each Other • I'm Your Girl • Finale

9/3/49   **2**[4]   **14**   12 **Miss Liberty**   78[6] $50   Columbia 860
Eddie Albert/Mary McCarty/Allyn McLerie; cp: **Irving Berlin**; cd: Jay Blackton; also see **Al Goodman**'s 1949 version
Overture • I'd Like My Picture Took • The Most Expensive Statue In The World • Little Fish In A Big Pond • Let's Take An Old-Fashioned Walk • Homework • Paris Wakes Up And Smiles • Only For Americans • I Love You • You Can Have Him • The Policemen's Ball • Falling Out Of Love Can Be Fun • Give Me Your Tired, Your Poor

New Moon — see MacRAE, Gordon
mu: Sigmund Romberg; ly: Oscar Hammerstein II

3/24/45   **4**   **24**   ●   13 **Oklahoma!**.. $30   Decca 359
'78' [6] A-359 (#4) / '45' [6] 9-6 (#5); Alfred Drake/Joan Roberts/Howard da Silva/Celeste Holm/Lee Dixon; mu: Richard Rodgers; ly: Oscar Hammerstein II; cd: Jay Blackton; first released after its Broadway debut on 3/31/43; America's first significant popular album; the only album in history to show *Billboard*'s pop singles chart (#9 on 12/18/43); off and on the album chart for seven years—its last appearance on 1/12/52 on Decca DL-8000 (LP); movie soundtrack issued in 1955 on Capitol 595
Oklahoma Overture • Oh, What A Beautiful Mornin' [Alfred Drake] • **The Surrey With The Fringe On Top** [Alfred Drake] **[17]** • Kansas City [Lee Dixon] • I Cain't Say No [Celeste Holm] • Many A New Day [Joan Roberts] • People Will Say We're In Love [Alfred Drake & Joan Roberts] • Pore Jud Is Daid [Alfred Drake & Howard da Silva] • Out Of My Dreams [Joan Roberts] • All Er Nothin' [Celeste Holm & Lee Dixon] • Oklahoma [Alfred Drake] • Finale [Alfred Drake & Joan Roberts]

2/24/51   **6**   **7**   14 **Out Of This World** .... $40   Columbia 4390
'33' [12"] ML-4390 (#6) / '45' [7] A-980 (#10); Charlotte Greenwood/William Eythe/Priscilla Gillette; cp: Cole Porter; cd: Pembroke Davenport
Medley: Overture/Out Of This World/I Jupiter, I Rex • Use Your Imagination • Medley: Entrance Of Juno/Hail, Hail, Hail/I Got Beauty • Where, Oh, Where • I Am Loved • They Couldn't Compare To You • What Do You Think About Men? • I Sleep Easier Now • Climb Up The Mountain • No Lover For Me • Cherry Pies Ought To Be You • Hark To The Song Of The Night • Medley: Nobody's Chasing Me/Finale

1/12/52   **7**   **12**   15 **Paint Your Wagon** .... $40   RCA Victor 1006
'33' [LP] LOC-1006 (#7) / '45' [5] WOC-6 (#7); James Barton/Olga San Juan/Tony Bavaar; ly: Alan Jay Lerner; mu: Frederick Loewe; cd: Franz Allers; movie soundtrack issued in 1969 on Paramount 1001
I'm On My Way • Rumson • What's Goin' On Here? • I Talk To The Trees • They Call The Wind Maria • I Still See Elisa • How Can I Wait? • In Between • Whoop-Ti-Ay! • Carino Mio • There's A Coach Comin' In • Hand Me Down That Can O' Beans • Another Autumn • All For Him • Wand'rin' Star

7/10/54   **4**   **24**   16 **Pajama Game, The** .... $40   Columbia 4840
LP: Columbia ML-4840 (#4); EP: Columbia A-1098 (#5); John Raitt/Janis Paige/Eddie Foy Jr./Carol Haney; cp: Richard Adler and Jerry Ross; cd: Hal Hastings; movie soundtrack issued in 1957 on Columbia 5210
Overture • Medley: The Pajama Game/Racing With The Clock • A New Town Is A Blue Town • I'm Not At All In Love • I'll Never Be Jealous Again • Hey There • Her Is • Once-A-Year-Day! • Small Talk • There Once Was A Man • Steam Heat • Think Of The Time I Save • Hernando's Hideaway • Seven-And-A-Half Cents • Finale

Porgy And Bess — see SPIVAK, Charlie
mu: George Gershwin; ly: Ira Gershwin and DuBose Heyward (movie soundtrack issued in 1959)
Show Boat
mu: Jerome Kern; ly: Oscar Hammerstein II; first performance was at New York's Ziegfeld Theater on 12/27/27; also see **Tommy Dorsey**'s 1946 version and the 1951 Movie Soundtrack

3/31/45   **❶**[2]   **11**   17 **Song of Norway**   78[6] $60   Decca 382
Lawrence Brooks/Kitty Carlisle/Helena Bliss/Robert Shafer; cd: Arthur Kay; an operetta based on the life and music of Norwegian classical composer Edvard Grieg; musical adaptation and lyrics by Robert Wright and George Forrest; album issued with large 12" 78 rpms and includes a 28-page booklet; movie soundtrack issued in 1971 on ABC 14
Prelude And Legend • Hill Of Dreams • Freddy And His Fiddle • Now • Strange Music • Medley: Midsummer's Eve/March Of The Trollgers • Medley: Hymn Of Bethrothal (To Spring)/Finale Of Act I • Bon Vivant • Medley: Three Loves/Finaletto: Part 2: Nordraak's Farewell/Reprise Of Three Loves • Medley: I Love You/At Christmastime (Woodland Wanderings) • Song Of Norway-Finale

5/21/49   **❶**[69]   **400**   18 **South Pacific** $40   Columbia 4180
'33' [LP] ML-4180 (#1/69 wks.) / '45' [7] A-850 (#1/5 wks.); Mary Martin/Ezio Pinza/Juanita Hall/William Tabbert/Barbara Luna; mu: Richard Rodgers; ly: Oscar Hammerstein II; cd: Salvatore Dell-Isola; the longest running #1 pop album in history; charted for 98 weeks at #1 or #2; on 5/19/58 the *South Pacific* Movie Soundtrack hit #1, with the Original Cast holding down the #2 position; held down the #1, #2 or #3 position from 5/28/49 through 5/19/51; also see 1949 versions by **Bing Crosby/Danny Kaye**/Evelyn Knight/Ella Fitzgerald on Decca, **Peggy Lee/Margaret Whiting/Gordon MacRae** on Capitol, and **Al Goodman** on RCA Victor
Overture • Dites Moi • A Cock-Eyed Optimist • Twin Soliloquies (Wonder how it feels) • Some Enchanted Evening • Bloody Mary • There Is Nothin' Like A Dame • Bali Ha'i • I'm Gonna Wash That Man Right Outa My Hair • A Wonderful Guy • Younger Than Springtime • Happy Talk • Honey Bun • Carefully Taught • This Nearly Was Mine • Finale

ORIGINAL CASTS — Cont'd

Student Prince — see GOODMAN, AL / LANZA, Mario

Tea For Two — see DAY, Doris

Doris Day/Gordon MacRae/Gene Nelson; cd: Alex Stordahl

6/16/51 · **7** · 7 · **19 Tree Grows In Brooklyn, A** ....12" **$50** Columbia 4405

Shirley Booth/Johnny Johnston/Marcia Van Dyke; mu: Arthur Schwartz; ly: Dorothy Fields; cd: Max Goberman

Overture ● Medley: Payday/Mine 'Til Monday ● Make The Man Love Me ● I'm Like A New Broom ● Look Who's Dancing ● Love Is The Reason ● If You Haven't Got A Sweetheart ● I'll Buy You A Star ● That's How It Goes ● He Had Refinement ● Growing Pains ● Is That My Prince? ● Halloween Ballet ● Don't Be Afraid ● Finale

Up In Central Park — see MacDONALD, Jeanette

Wilbur Evans/Maureen Cannon/Noah Beery; mu: Sigmund Romberg; ly: Dorothy Fields

9/6/52 · **5** · 10 · **20 Wish You Were Here** .... **$40** RCA Victor 1007

'33' [12"] LOC-1007 (#5) / '45' [5] WOC-1007 (#7);

Sheila Bond/Patricia Marand/Jack Cassidy/Sidney Armus; cp: Harold Rome; cd: Jay Blackton

Overture ● Camp Kare-Free Song ● Goodbye Love ● Ballad Of A Social Director ● Shopping Around ● Mix And Mingle ● Could Be ● Tripping The Light Fantastic ● Where Did The Night Go ● Certain Individuals ● They Won't Know Me ● Summer Afternoon ● Don José Of Far Rockaway ● Everybody Love Everybody ● Wish You Were Here ● Relax ● Flattery ● Finale

5/30/53 · **5** · 6 · **21 Wonderful Town** ....12" **$40** Decca 9010

Rosalind Russell/George Gaynes/Edith Adams/Jordan Bentley; mu: Leonard Bernstein; ly: Betty Comden and Adolph Green; cd: Lehman Engel

Christopher Street ● Ohio ● One Hundred Easy Ways ● What A Waste ● A Little Bit In Love ● Pass The Football ● Conversation Piece ● A Quiet Girl ● Conga! ● My Darlin' Eileen ● Swing! ● It's Love ● Ballet At The Village Vortex ● Wrong Note Rag

SONGS OF OUR TIMES

A series of 27 albums issued by Decca in 1948 (of which 15 charted), featuring medleys of the most popular songs, year by year, 1917-1943; orchestra conductors (and their total contribution of albums for this series): Charles Baum (3), Ray Benson (2), Nat Brandwynne (3), Carmen Cavallaro (2), Basil Fomeen (3), Bob Grant (8), Roy Ross (1), Ted Straeter (2), and the piano duo of Marlene Fingerle & Arthur Schutt (3); on the 6/5/48 album chart, 5 of the top 6 albums were from this series; and on 8/21/48, 8 of the top 12.

9/4/48 · **9** · 1 · **1 Song Hits of 1917** ....78[4] **$20** Decca 1917

BOB GRANT and His Orchestra

Medley: Over There/Smiles/Tiger Rag ● Medley: I Don't Know Where I'm Going But I'm On My Way/I Don't Want To Get Well/Goodbye Broadway, Hello France ● Medley: The Darktown Strutters' Ball/They Go Wild Simply Wild Over Me/Beale Street Blues ● Medley: I'm All Bound 'Round With The Mason Dixon Line/There's Egypt In Your Dreamy Eyes/Indiana ● Medley: Sweet Emalina, My Gal/For Me And My Gal/The Bells Of St. Mary's ● Medley: Where The Black-Eyed Susans Grow/Huckleberry Finn/I'd Love To Be A Monkey In A Zoo ● Medley: The Siren's Song/Wait Till The Cows Come Home/Oh Johnny, Oh Johnny, Oh! ● Medley: Will You Remember/Dear Little Mother O' Mine

9/4/48 · **6** · 2 · **2 Song Hits of 1918** ....78[4] **$20** Decca 1918

RAY BENSON and His Orchestra

Medley: Hinky Dinky Parlay Voo/Oh! How I Hate To Get Up In The Morning/Where Do We Go From Here? ● Medley: Oh! Frenchy/Madelon/Oui Oui, Marie ● Medley: They Were All Out Of Step But Jim/Rock-A-Bye Your Baby With A Dixie Melody/Good Morning, Mr. Zip-Zip-Zip! ● Medley: Just A Baby's Prayer At Twilight/The Rose Of No Man's Land/Sunrise And You ● Medley: Ja-Da/After You've Gone/Hindustan ● Medley: My Belgian Rose/Mickey/K-K-Katy ● Medley: Dear Old Pal Of Mine/Dear Little Boy Of Mine/I'm Sorry I Made You Cry ● Medley: That Wonderful Mother Of Mine/Till We Meet Again/Beautiful Ohio

8/21/48 · **7** · 3 · **3 Song Hits of 1921** ....78[4] **[I]** **$20** Decca 1921

CARMEN CAVALLARO

Medley: Say It With Music/Tuck Me To Sleep In My Old 'Tucky Home/My Mammy ● Medley: My Man/Ka-Lu-A/I Found A Rose In The Devil's Garden ● Medley: The Sheik Of Araby/Bandana Days/Shuffle Along ● Medley: The Wang Wang Blues/Dear Old Southland/Wabash Blues ● Medley: Ten Little Fingers And Ten Little Toes/Ain't We Got Fun/Dapper Dan ● Medley: Ma - He's Making Eyes At Me/Yoo-Hoo/I'm Just Wild About Harry ● Medley: Sweet Lady/Make Believe (You Are Glad When You're Sorry)/April Showers ● Medley: Peggy O'Neil/When Francis Dances With Me/Song Of Love

8/28/48 · **7** · 1 · **4 Song Hits of 1922** ....78[4] **$20** Decca 1922

BOB GRANT and His Orchestra

Medley: A Kiss In The Dark/Wonderful One/Three O'Clock In The Morning ● Medley: Lady Of The Evening/Crinoline Days/A Pretty Girl Is Like A Melody ● Medley: Carolina In The Morning/'Way Down Yonder In New Orleans/Lovin' Sam ● Medley: All Over Nothing At All/Some Sunny Day/Somebody Stole My Gal ● Medley: My Buddy/Blue/In The Little Red School House ● Medley: Kitten On The Keys/Stumbling ● Medley: Rose Of The Rio Grande/Who Cares?/China Boy ● Medley: Chicago/Toot, Toot, Tootsie!/Mister Gallagher And Mister Shean

8/21/48 · **8** · 1 · **5 Song Hits of 1925** ....78[4] **$20** Decca 1925

BASIL FOMEEN and His Orchestra

Medley: Dinah/Don't Bring Lulu/If I Had A Girl Like You ● Medley: Brown Eyes - Why Are You Blue?/Drifting And Dreaming/Only A Rose ● Medley: Collegiate/Save Your Sorrow/Alabamy Bound ● Medley: Five Foot Two, Eyes Of Blue/Moonlight And Roses/I'm Sitting On Top Of The World ● Medley: Remember/Always ● Medley: Who?/Just A Cottage Small/Here In My Arms ● Medley: Yes Sir, That's My Baby/Yearning ● Medley: The Vagabond King Waltz/Neapolitan Nights/Down By The Winegar Woiks

6/19/48 · **5** · 1 · **6 Song Hits of 1926** ....78[4] **[I]** **$20** Decca 1926

MARLENE FINGERLE and ARTHUR SCHUTT

Medley: I Know That You Know/Baby Face/Bye Bye Blackbird ● Medley: The Blue Room/The Girl Is You And The Boy Is Me/The Girl Friend ● Medley: Valencia/Where Do You Work-A, John?/Yankee Rose/Horses ● Medley: In A Little Spanish Town/Mary Lou/Where'd You Get Those Eyes?/Gimme A Little Kiss Will "Ya" Huh ● Medley: After I Say I'm Sorry/The Little White House/Tamiami Trail/When The Red, Red Robin Comes Bob, Bob, Bobbin' Along ● Medley: The Birth Of The Blues/Muddy Water/Black Bottom ● Medley: The Desert Song/Lonesome And Sorry/One Alone ● Medley: When Day Is Done/Charmaine/Someone To Watch Over Me

DEBUT	PEAK	WKS	Gold	ARTIST — Album Title	Sym	$	Label & Number

SONGS OF OUR TIMES — Cont'd

6/5/48 | 5 | 9 7 **Song Hits of 1927** .... 78[4] $20 Decca 1927
BOB GRANT and his Orchestra
Medley: Blue Skies/Me And My Shadow/Russian Lullaby ● Medley: Chloe/Let A Smile Be Your Umbrella/Mississippi Mud ● Medley: Why Do I Love You?/Make Believe/Ol' Man River ● Medley: Thou Swell/My Heart Stood Still/'S Wonderful ● Medley: Diane/Girl Of My Dreams/Ramona ● Medley: My Blue Heaven/A Night In June/At Sundown ● Medley: Among My Souvenirs/The Best Things In Life Are Free/The Varsity Drag ● Medley: Hallelujah!/Just A Memory/Sometimes I'm Happy

5/29/48 | 5 | 4 8 **Song Hits of 1928** .... 78[4] $20 Decca 1928
BASIL FOMEEN and his Orchestra
Medley: Sonny Boy/Angela Mia/Where The Shy Little Violets Grow ● Medley: Carolina Moon/Jeannine/Chiquita ● Medley: Let's Do It/Sweethearts On Parade/You Took Advantage Of Me ● Medley: Lover, Come Back To Me!/Button Up Your Overcoat/You're The Cream In My Coffee ● Medley: Laugh! Clown! Laugh!/I Can't Give You Anything But Love, Baby!/I Ain't Got Nobody ● Medley: Diga Diga Doo/Nagasaki/I Faw Down An' Go Boom! ● Medley: Honey/Sweet Sue - Just You/That's My Weakness Now ● Medley: Back In Your Own Back Yard/I'll Get By/Marie

5/22/48 | 4 | 6 9 **Song Hits of 1929** .... 78[4] [I] $20 Decca 1929
MARLENE FINGERLE and ARTHUR SCHUTT
Medley: The Wedding Of The Painted Doll/Tip-Toe Through The Tulips With Me/Singin' In The Rain ● Medley: Sunny Side Up/Jericho/Aren't We All?/Happy Days Are Here Again ● Medley: Why Was I Born?/More Than You Know/With A Song In My Heart ● Medley: Can't We Be Friends?/My Kinda Love/Moanin' Low ● Medley: Pagan Love Song/Love/Chant Of The Jungle/Siboney ● Medley: When It's Springtime In The Rockies/When The Organ Played At Twilight/Beside An Open Fireplace/Wedding Bells Are Breaking Up That Old Gang Of Mine ● Medley: Ain't Misbehavin'/Little By Little/Weary River/I've Got A Feeling I'm Falling ● Medley: Romance/Should I/Deep Night/Am I Blue?

5/15/48 | ❶[1] | 25 10 **Song Hits of 1932** 78[4] [I] $20 Decca 1932
CARMEN CAVALLARO
Medley: Star Dust/Lullaby Of The Leaves/How Deep Is The Ocean ● Medley: In A Shanty In Old Shanty Town/Speak To Me Of Love/Play Fiddle Play/Paradise ● Medley: Forty-Second Street/Of Thee I Sing/Shuffle Off To Buffalo ● Medley: Louisiana Hayride/You're Getting To Be A Habit With Me/Alone Together ● Medley: April In Paris/I've Told Ev'ry Little Star/The Song Is You ● Medley: Soft Lights And Sweet Music/Night And Day/Underneath The Harlem Moon ● Medley: Brother, Can You Spare A Dime?/Just An Echo In The Valley/Let's Put Out The Lights ● Medley: Mimi/If I Love Again/You're An Old Smoothie

8/21/48 | 8 | 1 11 **Song Hits of 1933** .... 78[4] $20 Decca 1933
CHARLES BAUM and His Orchestra
Medley: Who's Afraid Of The Big Bad Wolf?/Easter Parade/Annie Doesn't Live Here Anymore ● Medley: In The Valley Of The Moon/The Old Spinning Wheel/The Last Round-Up ● Medley: Temptation/Everything I Have Is Yours/Orchids In The Moonlight ● Medley: Shadow Waltz/My Moonlight Madonna/Lover ● Medley: Love Is The Sweetest Thing/Yesterdays/Smoke Gets In Your Eyes ● Medley: Carioca/Let's Fall In Love/Heat Wave ● Medley: Lazybones/I Cover The Waterfront/Stormy Weather ● Medley: The Gold Diggers' Song/Did You Ever See A Dream Walking?/By A Waterfall

6/5/48 | 3 | 3 12 **Song Hits of 1934** 78[4] $20 Decca 1934
BOB GRANT and His Orchestra
Medley: June In January/Love Thy Neighbor/Love In Bloom ● Medley: You Oughta Be In Pictures/With My Eyes Wide Open I'm Dreaming/Stay As Sweet As You Are ● Medley: The Object Of My Affection/Little Man You've Had A Busy Day/The Beat O' My Heart ● Medley: The Moon Was Yellow/Isle Of Capri/The Continental ● Medley: You're The Top/I Get A Kick Out Of You/Be Still, My Heart! ● Medley: I'll Follow My Secret Heart/The Champagne Waltz ● Medley: Wagon Wheels/Cocktails For Two/Two Cigarettes In The Dark ● Medley: Solitude/The Very Thought Of You/Lost In A Fog

7/10/48 | 5 | 4 13 **Song Hits of 1935** .... 78[4] $20 Decca 1935
NAT BRANDWYNNE and His Orchestra (died on 3/8/78)
Medley: I'm In The Mood For Love/Thanks A Million/Lullaby Of Broadway ● Medley: What's The Reason/Take Me Back To My Boots And Saddle/The Music Goes 'Round And Around ● Medley: When I Grow Too Old To Dream/A Beautiful Lady In Blue/Tell Me That You Love Me ● Medley: On Treasure Island/Red Sails In The Sunset/In A Little Gypsy Tea Room ● Medley: Begin The Beguine/East Of The Sun ● Medley: These Foolish Things/You Are My Lucky Star/Love And A Dime ● Medley: Lovely To Look At/Isn't This A Lovely Day/Summer Time ● Medley: Cheek To Cheek/I'm Gonna Sit Right Down And Write Myself A Letter/On The Good Ship Lollipop

10/30/48 | 10 | 1 14 **Song Hits of 1938** .... 78[4] $20 Decca 1938
BOB GRANT and His Orchestra
Medley: Ti-Pi-Tin/Mexicali Rose/The Moon Of Manakoora ● Medley: Cathedral In The Pines/There's A Gold Mine In The Sky/Alexander's Ragtime Band ● Medley: Music, Maestro, Please!/Whistle While You Work/Heigh-Ho ● Medley: So Help Me/Says My Heart/Ten Pretty Girls ● Medley: I Double Dare You/Bei Mir Bist Du Schön/You're A Sweetheart ● Medley: The Flat Foot Floogee/A-Tisket A-Tasket/The Dipsy Doodle ● Medley: My Reverie/Thanks For The Memory/Josephine ● Medley: You Go To My Head/Where Or When/Love Walked In

8/21/48 | 8 | 2 15 **Song Hits of 1940** .... 78[4] $20 Decca 1940
CHARLES BAUM and His Orchestra
Medley: Ferry-Boat Serenade/When The Swallows Come Back To Capistrano/The Woodpecker Song ● Medley: Only Forever/Blueberry Hill/With The Wind And The Rain In Your Hair ● Medley: Perfidia/Say "Si Si"/The Breeze And I ● Medley: Six Lessons From Madame La Zonga/I'm Nobody's Baby/Tuxedo Junction ● Medley: I Didn't Know What Time It Was/I'll Never Smile Again/Trade Winds ● Medley: Make-Believe Island/When You Wish Upon A Star/Sierra Sue ● Medley: Indian Summer/Embraceable You/The Donkey Serenade ● Medley: I Dream Of Jeanie With The Light Brown Hair/All The Things You Are/On The Isle Of May

VARIOUS ARTIST COMPILATIONS

12/11/54 · **13** · 2

1 Confederacy 1861-1865, The..78³ · **$150** · Columbia 220
National Gallery Orch., conducted by Richard Bales; with Cantata Choir; featuring Florence Kopleff & Thomas Pyle; based on music of the South during the Civil War; a lavish 32-page historical pictorial booklet is bound in this 14" x 12" album package
General Lee's Grand March ● All Quiet Along The Potomac Tonight ● The Bonnie Blue Flag ● Lorena ● The Yellow Rose Of Texas ● Somebody's Darling ● We All Went Down To New Orleans For Bales ● General Robert E. Lee's Farewell Order To The Army Of Northern Virginia ● The Conquered Banner ● Dixie's Land

3/10/51 · **10** · 1

2 Dance Band Hits...45³ · **$50** · RCA Victor WPT-2
also see *Theme Songs* (#9 & 10 below)
Boogie Woogie [Tommy Dorsey] **[3/'38]** ● **Martha** [Larry Clinton (Bea Wain, vocal)] **[2/'38]** ● **Song Of The Volga Boatmen** [Glenn Miller] **[1]** ● **Heartaches** [Ted Weems (Elmo Tanner, whistling)] **[1]** ● **Mood Indigo** [Duke Ellington] **[3/'31]** ● **Got A Date With An Angel** [Hal Kemp (Skinnay Ennis, vocal)] **[16/'34]**

1/29/49 · **9** · 4

3 Giants Of Jazz...78³ · **$50** · Capitol 106
songs and artists featured in the movie *A Song Is Born*; participating artists include: **Louis Armstrong**, **Benny Goodman**, **Tommy Dorsey**, Charlie Barnet, Mel Powell, Page Cavanaugh, Jeri Sullivan, Golden Gate Quartet, and The Brazilians; benefit album for the Damon Runyon Memorial Fund
A Song Was Born (Part I & II) (jam sessions) ● Stealin' Apples [Benny Goodman Septet] ● Muskrat Ramble [Mel Powell Septet] ● The Redskin Rhumba [Charlie Barnet Orch.] ● Daddy-O (I'm Gonna Teach You Some Blues) [Page Cavanaugh Trio]

5/27/50 · **5** · 10

4 Honky-Tonk Piano..45³ · **[I]** · **$30** · Capitol 187
featuring honky-tonk pianists Marvin Ash, Ray Turner and Lou Busch (also known as Joe "Fingers" Carr)
Maple Leaf Rag [Marvin Ash] ● Cannon Ball Rag [Marvin Ash] ● Two Dollar Rag [Lou Busch] ● Kitten On The Keys [Lou Busch] ● The Entertainer's Rag [Ray Turner] ● Jim Jams [Ray Turner]

11/20/48 · **7** · 11

5 Jazz at the Philharmonic, volume eight..78³ · **[I]** · **$60** · Mercury 8
jazz improvisations on the song "Perdido"; Illinois Jacquet and Flip Phillips (tenor saxes), Bill Harris (trombone), Howard McGhee (trumpet), Jo Jones (drums), Ray Brown (bass) and Hank Jones (piano); volumes 8, 9 and 10 consists of an entire jazz concert performed at Carnegie Hall in November, 1947

3/26/49 · **4** · 9

6 Jazz at the Philharmonic, vol. 9...78³ · **[I]** · **$60** · Mercury 9
jazz improvisations on the song "Mordido"; same personnel as above

10/22/49 · **5** · 5

7 Jazz at the Philharmonic, vol. 10...78³ · **[I]** · **$60** · Mercury 10
jazz improvisations on the songs "Endido" and "I Surrender Dear"; same personnel as above 2; above 3 albums shown as *Norman Granz' Jazz at the Philharmonic* (an 18 volume series) (Granz died on 11/22/01, age 83)

1/23/54 · **8** · 1

8 Show Biz... **$40** · RCA Victor 1011
snippets of voices and songs of dozens of great entertainers from vaudeville to TV; from Caruso to **Eddie Fisher**; narrated by George Jessel; gleaned from a book *Show Biz (Vaude to Video)* by *Variety* magazine editor Abel Green with Joe Laurie, Jr.
Part 1 - 1904 to 1920 When Vaudeville Was King ● Part 2 - 1920 to 1929 The Roaring Twenties ● Part 3 - 1929 to 1940 When Wall Street Laid An Egg ● Part 4 - 1940 to date From TV To 3-D

9/4/48 · **❶³** · 31

9 Theme Songs... **$40** · RCA Victor 217
'78' [4] P-217 (#1) / '45' [4] WP-217 (#6); theme songs of eight RCA Victor popular bands
I'm Getting Sentimental Over You [Tommy Dorsey] **[8/'36]** ● **Moonlight Serenade** [Tex Beneke] ● **Tchaikovsky Piano Concerto No. 1** [Freddy Martin] **[1]** ● **Racing With The Moon** [Vaughn Monroe] ● **The Waltz You Saved For Me** [Wayne King] **[4/'30]** ● **Twilight Time** [Three Suns] **[8]** ● Kaye's Melody [Sammy Kaye] ● My Promise To You [Larry Green]

3/17/51 · **10** · 2

10 Theme Songs..45³ · **[I]** · **$50** · RCA Victor WPT-2
more theme songs of six RCA Victor popular bands; also see *Dance Band Hits*
Nightmare [Artie Shaw] **[7/'38]** ● **Good-Bye** [Benny Goodman] **[20/'36]** ● **Take The "A" Train** [Duke Ellington] **[13]** ● **Cherokee** [Charlie Barnet] **[15/'39]** ● **Flying Home** [Lionel Hampton] **[25/'40]** ● When It's Sleepy Time Down South [Louis Armstrong]

3/8/52 · **6** · 6

11 Today's Top Hits, Volume 1..10" · **$50** · Capitol 9101
the first "current hit" music compilation album
The World Is Waiting For The Sunrise [Les Paul & Mary Ford] **[2]** ● **Too Young** [Nat "King" Cole] **[1]** ● **Because Of You** [Les Baxter] **[4]** ● **(Why Did I Tell You I Was Going To) Shanghai** [Bob Crosby] **[22]** ● **September Song** [Stan Kenton] **[17]** ● **Whispering** [Les Paul] **[7]** ● **Come On-A My House** [Kay Starr] **[8]** ● **(When I Dance With You) I Get Ideas** [Peggy Lee] **[14]**

Today's Top Hits, Vol. 12 — see COLE, Nat "King" / PAUL, Les, & Mary Ford

3/24/45 · **4** · 3

12 Up Swing...78⁴ · **[I]** · **$50** · RCA Victor 146
big band hits by **Glenn Miller**, **Tommy Dorsey**, **Benny Goodman** and **Artie Shaw**
Stompin' At The Savoy [Benny Goodman] **[4/'37]** ● **Don't Be That Way** [Benny Goodman] **[1/'38]** ● **Song Of India** [Tommy Dorsey] **[5/'37]** ● **Yes Indeed!** [Tommy Dorsey] **[4]** ● **Begin The Beguine** [Artie Shaw] **[1/'38]** ● Oh, Lady Be Good [Artie Shaw] ● **Tuxedo Junction** [Glenn Miller] **[1]** ● **A String Of Pearls** [Glenn Miller] **[1]**

THE ALBUMS WRAP-UP

Top 40 Artists In Rank Order

Top 40 Artists In A-Z Order

Top Artist Achievements:

> **Most Chart Albums**
> **Most #1 Albums**
> **Most Weeks At The #1 Position**
>
> **Top 5 MVP Photos**

MVPs — Most Valuable Platters

Albums Of Longevity

Top 50 #1 Albums

> **Photos of the Top 24 #1 Albums**

TOP 40 ARTISTS IN RANK ORDER

POINT SYSTEM:

Next to each artist's name is their point total. Each artist's points are accumulated according to the following formula:

1. Highest chart position each album reached:

> #1 = 50 points for its first week at #1, plus 5 points for each additional week at #1
> #2 = 45 points for its first week at #2, plus 3 points for each additional week at #2
> #3-5 = 40 points
> #6-10 = 35 points
> #11-15 = 30 points

2. Total weeks charted.

Christmas albums [X] are awarded points for their peak position for their <u>first</u> chart appearance only. Their seasonal re-entries are awarded points for their weeks charted only.

Special Symbols:

● **Deceased Solo Artist**

■ **Deceased Group Member**
> The total number of square symbols indicates the total number of deceased members.

TOP 40 ARTISTS

Rank		Points		Rank		Points
1.	Glenn Miller ●	983		21.	Harry James ●	262
2.	Bing Crosby ●	964		22.	Ralph Flanagan	224
3.	Mario Lanza ●	890		23.	Dorothy Shay ●	216
4.	Jackie Gleason ●	637		24.	Jane Froman ●	214
5.	Doris Day	633		25.	Melachrino Strings ■	193
6.	Al Jolson ●	629		26.	Yma Sumac	184
7.	Nat "King" Cole ●	526		27.	Paul Weston ●	175
8.	Frankie Carle ●	521		28.	Al Goodman ●	169
9.	Vaughn Monroe ●	421		29.	Billy May	158
10.	Eddie Fisher	368		30.	Sammy Kaye ●	155
11.	Stan Kenton ●	362		31.	Peggy Lee ●	155
12.	Tommy Dorsey ◉	353		32.	Judy Garland ●	154
13.	Les Paul & Mary Ford ■	349		33.	Spike Jones ●	150
14.	Frank Sinatra ●	332		34.	Eddy Arnold	149
15.	Liberace ●	327		35.	Mantovani ●	144
16.	Benny Goodman ●	313		36.	Wayne King ●	142
17.	Danny Kaye ●	309		37.	Les Brown ●	135
18.	Perry Como ●	304		38.	Ken Griffin ●	125
19.	The Three Suns ■ ■ ■	301		39.	Arthur Godfrey ●	122
20.	Guy Lombardo ●	271		40.	Percy Faith ●	121

A-Z — TOP 40 ARTISTS

TOP ARTIST ACHIEVEMENTS

MOST CHART ALBUMS

1. Bing Crosby 30
2. Glenn Miller 10
3. Frankie Carle 10
4. Perry Como 10
5. Nat "King" Cole 9
6. Doris Day 8
7. Mario Lanza 7
8. Tommy Dorsey 7
9. Les Paul & Mary Ford 7
10. The Three Suns 7
11. Vaughn Monroe 6
12. Stan Kenton 6
13. Liberace 6
14. Fred Waring 6
15. Jackie Gleason 5
16. Eddie Fisher 5
17. Frank Sinatra 5
18. Guy Lombardo 5

MOST #1 ALBUMS

1. Mario Lanza 5
2. Glenn Miller 4
3. Bing Crosby 3
4. Jackie Gleason 3
5. Doris Day 3
6. Al Jolson 3
7. Vaughn Monroe 3
8. Nat "King" Cole 2
9. Eddie Fisher 2
10. Benny Goodman 2
11. Perry Como 2
12. Harry James 2
13. Dorothy Shay 2
14. Arthur Godfrey 2

MOST WEEKS AT THE #1 POSITION

1. Mario Lanza 65
2. Al Jolson 49
3. Glenn Miller 43
4. Jackie Gleason 28
5. Jane Froman 25
6. Doris Day 19
7. Danny Kaye 17
8. Nat "King" Cole 16
9. Eddie Fisher 16
10. Bing Crosby 14
11. Vaughn Monroe 14
12. Harry James 13
13. Benny Goodman.................... 11
14. Stan Kenton 8
15. Frank Sinatra 7
16. Ink Spots............................. 7
17. Dorothy Shay 6
18. Yma Sumac 6

TOP 5 MVP PHOTOS

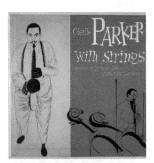

Charlie Parker With Strings
Charlie Parker
$500

**Glenn Miller And His Orchestra –
Limited Edition**
Glenn Miller
$300

**Glenn Miller And His Orchestra –
Limited Edition, Volume Two**
Glenn Miller
$200

Bing (A Musical Autobiography)
Bing Crosby
$200

**Yodelingly Yours –
A Memorial Album**
Jimmie Rodgers
$200

MVP'S (Most Valuable Platters)

Following is a list of albums in this book valued at $60 or more.

YEAR	VALUE	TITLE	ARTIST
50	$500	1. **Charlie Parker With Strings**................	*Charlie Parker*
53	$300	2. **Glenn Miller And His Orchestra - Limited Edition**..........	*Glenn Miller & His Orchestra*
54	$200	3. **Glenn Miller And His Orchestra - Limited Edition, Volume Two**..	*Glenn Miller & His Orchestra*
54	$200	4. **Bing (A Musical Autobiography)**................	*Bing Crosby*
49	$200	5. **Yodelingly Yours – A Memorial Album**.............	*Jimmie Rodgers*
45	$150	6. **8 To The Bar** (Two Piano Boogie Woogie For Dancing)........	*Pete Johnson and Albert Ammons*
54	$150	7. **The Confederacy 1861-1865**................	*Various Artist Compilation*
51	$100	8. **Carnegie Hall Jazz Concert**................	*Benny Goodman*
52	$100	9. **Gene Norman presents Just Jazz**............	*Lionel Hampton All Stars*
46	$100	10. **Spike Jones presents for the Kiddies The Nutcracker Suite** with apologies to Tchaikovsky ...*Spike Jones & His City Slickers*	
49	$100	11. **Christmas Songs by Sinatra**................	*Frank Sinatra*
53	$100	12. **Gentlemen Prefer Blondes**	*Movie Soundtrack*
51	$75	13. **Satchmo At Symphony Hall**................	*Louis Armstrong And The All Stars*
45	$75	14. **Meet Me In St. Louis**................	*Judy Garland*
52	$75	15. **1937/38 Jazz Concert No. 2**............	*Benny Goodman and his orchestra, trio and quartet*
54	$75	16. **Let There Be Love**	*Joni James*
46	$75	17. **Musical Depreciation**................	*Spike Jones & His City Slickers*
50	$75	18. **Spike Jones plays The Charleston for dancing**............	*Spike Jones & His City Slickers*
54	$75	19. **Sincerely, Liberace**................	*Liberace*
48	$75	20. **Nellie Lutcher**................	*Nellie Lutcher*
45	$75	21. **Victor Showpiece presents Dinah Shore in Gershwin Show Hits**	*Dinah Shore*
47	$75	22. **Songs By Sinatra**	*Frank Sinatra*
46	$75	23. **The Voice of Frank Sinatra**................	*Frank Sinatra*
45	$75	24. **Charlie Spivak plays selections from Gershwin's Folk-Opera Porgy and Bess** ...*Charlie Spivak and his Orchestra*	
47	$75	25. **Till The Clouds Roll By**	*Movie Soundtrack*
45	$60	26. **The King Cole Trio**................	*The King Cole Trio*
46	$60	27. **King Cole Trio**, Volume 2................	*The King Cole Trio*
48	$60	28. **King Cole Trio**, Volume 3................	*The King Cole Trio*
49	$60	29. **King Cole Trio**, Volume 4................	*Nat "King" Cole And The Trio*
54	$60	30. **Crewcuts on the Campus**	*The Crew-Cuts*
46	$60	31. **Ink Spots**................	*Ink Spots*
48	$60	32. **Rendezvous with Peggy Lee**................	*Peggy Lee*
51	$60	33. **The New Sound!**	*Les Paul & Mary Ford*
51	$60	34. **Les Paul's New Sound, Vol. 2, with Mary Ford**	*Les Paul & Mary Ford*
52	$60	35. **Johnnie Ray**	*Johnnie Ray With The Buddy Cole Quartet*
53	$60	36. **The Kay Starr Style**	*Kay Starr*
50	$60	37. **Voice Of The Xtabay**................	*Yma Sumac*
52	$60	38. **Legend Of The Sun Virgin**	*Yma Sumac*
52	$60	39. **An American In Paris**	*Movie Soundtrack*
51	$60	40. **Rich, Young, And Pretty**	*Movie Soundtrack*
54	$60	41. **Rose Marie**	*Movie Soundtrack*
51	$60	42. **Royal Wedding**	*Movie Soundtrack*
54	$60	43. **Seven Brides For Seven Brothers**	*Movie Soundtrack*
51	$60	44. **Show Boat**................	*Movie Soundtrack*
52	$60	45. **Singin' In The Rain**	*Movie Soundtrack*
51	$60	46. **Two Weeks With Love**	*Movie Soundtrack*
51	$60	47. **Call Me Madam**	*Original Cast*
53	$60	48. **Me And Juliet**	*Original Cast*
45	$60	49. **Song of Norway**	*Original Cast*
48	$60	50. **Jazz at the Philharmonic**, volume eight	*Various Artist Compilation*
49	$60	51. **Jazz at the Philharmonic**, vol. 9................	*Various Artist Compilation*
49	$60	52. **Jazz at the Philharmonic**, vol. 10................	*Various Artist Compilation*

ALBUMS OF LONGEVITY

Albums with 28 or more total weeks charted.

PK YR	PK WKS	PK POS	WKS CHR	RANK	TITLE	ARTIST
49	69	1	400	1.	**South Pacific**..*Original Cast*	
54	42	1	151	2.	**The Student Prince and other great musical comedies**...............................*Mario Lanza*	
53	23	1	149	3.	**Music For Lovers Only**..*Jackie Gleason*	
45	16	1	130	4.	**Glenn Miller** .... *Glenn Miller and his Orchestra*	
54	11	1	78	5.	**Glenn Miller Plays Selections From The Film "The Glenn Miller Story"** ...*Glenn Miller & His Orchestra*	
51	19	1	75	6.	**Show Boat** .... *Movie Soundtrack*	
52	16	1	65	7.	**An American In Paris** .... *Movie Soundtrack*	
47	25	1	61	8.	**Al Jolson in songs he made famous** .... *Al Jolson*	
49	10	1	61	9.	**Kiss Me, Kate** ....*Original Cast*	
50	6	1	59	10.	**Voice Of The Xtabay** ....*Yma Sumac*	
52	2	1	59	11.	**Liberace at the piano** .... *Liberace*	
54	4	1	57	12.	**Music, Martinis, and Memories** ....*Jackie Gleason*	
51	1	2	54	13.	**The King And I** ....*Original Cast*	
51	1	2	52	14.	**Carnegie Hall Jazz Concert** ....*Benny Goodman*	
50	12	1	50	15.	**Young Man With A Horn** ....*Doris Day and Harry James*	
49	16	2	49	16.	**Jolson Sings Again** .... *Al Jolson*	
51	10	1	48	17.	**The Great Caruso** ....*Mario Lanza*	
52	25	1	44	18.	**With A Song In My Heart...** ....*Jane Froman*	
54	10	1	40	19.	**The Glenn Miller Story** .... *Movie Soundtrack*	
51	6	1	38	20.	**The Toast Of New Orleans** ....*Mario Lanza*	
51	1	1	37	21.	**Guys And Dolls** ....*Original Cast*	
50	11	1	36	22.	**Three Little Words** .... *Movie Soundtrack*	
54	4	2	36	23.	**Music To Make You Misty** ....*Jackie Gleason*	
45	12	1	35	24.	**The King Cole Trio** .... *The King Cole Trio*	
47	5	1	35	25.	**Dorothy Shay (The Park Avenue Hillbillie) Sings** ....*Dorothy Shay*	
50	3	1	35	26.	**Ralph Flanagan plays Rodgers & Hammerstein II for dancing** ...*Ralph Flanagan and his Orchestra*	
50	1	4	34	27.	**Dixie By Dorsey** ....*Jimmy Dorsey and his Original "Dorseyland" Jazz Band*	
53	17	1	32	28.	**Hans Christian Andersen** .... *Danny Kaye*	
47	6	1	32	29.	**Glenn Miller Masterpieces** ....*Glenn Miller & His Orchestra*	
49	1	1	32	30.	**Roses In Rhythm**.. *Frankie Carle with Rhythm Section*	
54	4	2	32	31.	**Seven Brides For Seven Brothers** .... *Movie Soundtrack*	
54	3	3	32	32.	**Swing Easy!**...*Frank Sinatra*	
52	1	3	32	33.	**Eddie Fisher Sings** .... *Eddie Fisher*	
53	1	7	32	34.	**Music for Dining**.............................. *The Melachrino Strings And Orchestra*	
48	3	1	31	35.	**Theme Songs** .... *Various Artist Compilation*	
54	1	3	31	36.	**Songs for Young Lovers** ....*Frank Sinatra*	
52	12	3	30	37.	**Big Band Bash!** ....*Billy May*	
54	1	6	29	38.	**Victory At Sea** .... *Television Soundtrack*	
47	10	1	28	39.	**Al Jolson Souvenir Album** .... *Al Jolson*	
49	12	3	28	40.	**Horace Heidt presents Dick Contino** ...*Dick Contino with Horace Heidt and His Musical Knights*	

TOP 50 #1 ALBUMS

Peak Year	Wks Chr	Wks @ #1	Rank	Title	Artist
49	400	69	1.	**South Pacific**	*Original Cast*
54	151	42	2.	**The Student Prince and other great musical comedies**	*Mario Lanza*
47	61	25	3.	**Al Jolson** in songs he made famous	*Al Jolson*
52	44	25	4.	**With A Song In My Heart...**	*Jane Froman/Movie Soundtrack*
53	149	23	5.	**Music For Lovers Only**	*Jackie Gleason*
51	75	19	6.	**Show Boat**	*Movie Soundtrack*
53	32	17	7.	**Hans Christian Andersen**	*Danny Kaye*
45	25	17	8.	**Merry Christmas**	*Bing Crosby*
45	130	16	9.	**Glenn Miller**	*Glenn Miller and his Orchestra*
52	65	16	10.	**An American In Paris**	*Movie Soundtrack*
52	25	15	11.	**I'm In The Mood For Love**	*Eddie Fisher*
48	21	14	12.	**Al Jolson – Volume Three**	*Al Jolson*
50	50	12	13.	**Young Man With A Horn**	*Doris Day and Harry James/Movie Soundtrack*
45	35	12	14.	**The King Cole Trio**	*The King Cole Trio*
54	78	11	15.	**Glenn Miller Plays Selections From The Film "The Glenn Miller Story"**	*...Glenn Miller & His Orchestra*
50	36	11	16.	**Three Little Words**	*Movie Soundtrack*
49	61	10	17.	**Kiss Me, Kate**	*Original Cast*
51	48	10	18.	**The Great Caruso**	*Mario Lanza*
54	40	10	19.	**The Glenn Miller Story**	*Movie Soundtrack*
47	28	10	20.	**Al Jolson Souvenir Album**	*Al Jolson*
48	27	8	21.	**A Presentation Of Progressive Jazz**	*Stan Kenton and His Orchestra*
50	27	8	22.	**Annie Get Your Gun**	*Movie Soundtrack*
52	20	8	23.	**1937/38 Jazz Concert No. 2**	*Benny Goodman and his orchestra, trio and quartet*
46	18	7	24.	**The Voice of Frank Sinatra**	*Frank Sinatra*
46	15	7	25.	**Ink Spots**	*Ink Spots*
50	59	6	26.	**Voice Of The Xtabay**	*Yma Sumac*
51	38	6	27.	**The Toast Of New Orleans**	*Mario Lanza*
47	32	6	28.	**Glenn Miller Masterpieces**	*Glenn Miller & His Orchestra*
45	24	6	29.	**On The Moon-Beam**	*Vaughn Monroe and his Orchestra*
49	22	6	30.	**Words And Music**	*Movie Soundtrack*
48	16	6	31.	**Down Memory Lane**	*Vaughn Monroe and his Orchestra*
45	15	6	32.	**Carousel**	*Original Cast*
45	13	6	33.	**Going My Way**	*Bing Crosby*
47	35	5	34.	**Dorothy Shay (The Park Avenue Hillbillie) Sings**	*Dorothy Shay*
45	14	5	35.	**Freddie Slack's Boogie Woogie**	*Freddie Slack and his Orchestra*
54	57	4	36.	**Music, Martinis, and Memories**	*Jackie Gleason*
52	24	4	37.	**I'll See You In My Dreams**	*Doris Day*
52	20	4	38.	**Because You're Mine**	*Mario Lanza*
52	17	4	39.	**The Merry Widow**	*Movie Soundtrack*
46	14	4	40.	**King Cole Trio, Volume 2**	*The King Cole Trio*
46	11	4	41.	**Dancing In The Dark**	*Carmen Cavallaro*
46	8	4	42.	**State Fair**	*Dick Haymes*
50	35	3	43.	**Ralph Flanagan plays Rodgers & Hammerstein II for dancing**	*...Ralph Flanagan and his Orchestra*
48	31	3	44.	**Theme Songs**	*Various Artist Compilation*
51	24	3	45.	**Lullaby Of Broadway**	*Doris Day*
48	10	3	46.	**A Sentimental Date With Perry**	*Perry Como*
46	10	3	47.	**Benny Goodman Sextet Session**	*Benny Goodman Sextet*
52	59	2	48.	**Liberace at the piano**	*Liberace*
53	24	2	49.	**Stars And Stripes Forever**	*Movie Soundtrack*
49	23	2	50.	**Vaughn Monroe Sings**	*Vaughn Monroe and his Orchestra*

1. South Pacific...
Original Cast
#1/69 wks - 1949

2. The Student Prince and other great musical comedies...*Mario Lanza*
#1/42 wks - 1954

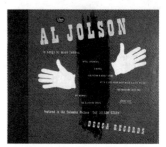

3. Al Jolson in songs he made famous...
Al Jolson
#1/25 wks - 1947

4. With A Song In My Heart... ...
Jane Froman/Movie Soundtrack
#1/25 wks - 1952

5. Music For Lovers Only...
Jackie Gleason
#1/23 wks - 1953

6. Show Boat...
Movie Soundtrack
#1/19 wks - 1951

7. Hans Christian Andersen...
Danny Kaye
#1/17 wks - 1953

8. Merry Christmas...
Bing Crosby
#1/17 wks - 1945

9. Glenn Miller...
Glenn Miller and his Orchestra
#1/16 wks - 1945

10. An American In Paris...
Movie Soundtrack
#1/16 wks - 1952

11. I'm In The Mood For Love...
Eddie Fisher
#1/15 wks - 1952

12. Al Jolson - Volume Three...
Al Jolson
#1/14 wks - 1948

13. Young Man With A Horn...*Doris Day
and Harry James/Movie Soundtrack*
#1/12 wks - 1950

14. The King Cole Trio...
The King Cole Trio
#1/12 wks - 1945

**15. Glenn Miller Plays Selections From The
Film "The Glenn Miller Story"**...Glenn Miller
& His Orchesta — #1/11 wks - 1954

16. Three Little Words...
Movie Soundtrack
#1/11 wks - 1950

17. Kiss Me, Kate...
Original Cast
#1/10 wks - 1949

18. The Great Caruso...
Mario Lanza/Movie Soundtrack
#1/10 wks - 1951

19. The Glenn Miller Story...
Movie Soundtrack
#1/10 wks - 1954

20. Al Jolson Souvenir Album...
Al Jolson
#1/10 wks - 1947

21. A Presentation Of Progressive Jazz...
Stan Kenton And His Orchestra
#1/8 wks - 1948

22. Annie Get Your Gun...
Movie Soundtrack
#1/8 wks - 1950

23. 1937/38 Jazz Concert No. 2...*Benny
Goodman and his orchestra, trio and quartet*
#1/8 wks - 1952

24. The Voice of Frank Sinatra...
Frank Sinatra
#1/7 wks - 1946

#1 ALBUMS
1945-1954

This section lists, in chronological order, all 73 albums which hit #1 on *Billboard's* Pop Albums charts from 1945 through 1954.

As of July 22, 1950 *Billboard* began publishing two weekly pop albums charts: *Best Selling 33-1/3 R.P.M.* and *Best Selling 45 R.P.M.* All #1 albums from these two pop charts are shown, and the chart designation and #1 weeks on each chart are listed beneath the album title. On December 26, 1953 the '33' chart became the *Best Selling Popular LP's* chart and the '45' chart became the *Best Selling Popular EP's* chart.

Chart Designations:

'33'	=	Best Selling 33-1/3 R.P.M.
'45'	=	Best Selling 45 R.P.M.
LP	=	Best Selling Popular LP's
EP	=	Best Selling Popular EP's

The date shown is the earliest date the album hit #1 on either of these two pop charts. The weeks column lists the total weeks at #1, from the chart that it achieved its highest total. This total is not a combined total from the two pop charts.

Because two charts are used, some dates are duplicated, as certain #1 albums may have peaked on the same week on both charts. *Billboard* also showed ties at #1 on some of these charts; therefore, the total weeks for each year may calculate out to more than 52. For more information on these pop charts please refer to the "Researching *Billboard's* Pop Albums Charts" on page 513.

COLUMN HEADINGS

DATE: Date album first peaked at the #1 position

WKS: Total weeks album held the #1 position

> The <u>top album</u> of each year is boxed out for quick reference. The top album is determined by most weeks at the #1 position, followed by total weeks in the Top 3, Top 5, and total weeks charted.

#1 ALBUMS

1945

	DATE	WKS	
1.	3/24	12	**The King Cole Trio**
			The King Cole Trio
2.	4/14	2	**Song of Norway** *Original Cast*
3.	5/12	16	**Glenn Miller**
			Glenn Miller and his Orchestra
4.	8/11	6	**Carousel** *Original Cast*
5.	9/15	5	**Freddie Slack's Boogie Woogie**
			Freddie Slack and his Orchestra
6.	10/20	6	**Going My Way**
			Bing Crosby/Movie Soundtrack
7.	12/1	6	**On The Moon-Beam**
			Vaughn Monroe and his Orchestra
8.	12/8	6	**Merry Christmas** *Bing Crosby*

1946

	DATE	WKS	
1.	2/23	4	**State Fair** *Dick Haymes*
2.	3/23	2	**The Bells Of St. Mary's**
			Bing Crosby/Movie Soundtrack
3.	4/6	7	**The Voice of Frank Sinatra**
			Frank Sinatra
4.	5/25	3	**Benny Goodman Sextet Session**
			Benny Goodman Sextet
5.	7/20	4	**Dancing In The Dark** *Carmen Cavallaro*
6.	8/17	4	**King Cole Trio, Volume 2**
			The King Cole Trio
7.	8/31	2	**a Cole Porter review**
			David Rose and his Orchestra
8.	9/28	7	**Ink Spots** *Ink Spots*
9.	11/16	1	**Merry Christmas Music** *Perry Como*
10.	11/23	7	**Merry Christmas** *Bing Crosby*

1947

	DATE	WKS	
1.	1/11	1	**All-Time Favorites by Harry James**
			Harry James and his Orchestra
2.	2/1	25	**Al Jolson in songs he made famous**
			Al Jolson
3.	8/2	5	**Dorothy Shay (The Park Avenue Hillbillie) Sings** *Dorothy Shay*
4.	8/16	10	**Al Jolson Souvenir Album** *Al Jolson*
5.	11/8	6	**Glenn Miller Masterpieces**
			Glenn Miller & His Orchestra
6.	11/15	8	**Merry Christmas** *Bing Crosby*

1948

	DATE	WKS	
1.	1/24	1	**Dorothy Shay (The Park Avenue Hillbillie) Goes To Town**
			Dorothy Shay
2.	2/28	3	**A Sentimental Date With Perry** *Perry Como*
3.	3/20	2	**St. Patrick's Day** *Bing Crosby*
4.	4/3	6	**Down Memory Lane**
			Vaughn Monroe and his Orchestra
5.	5/15	1	**Busy Fingers** *The Three Suns*
6.	5/22	1	**Song Hits of 1932**
			Songs Of Our Times/Carmen Cavallaro

1948 (cont'd)

7.	5/29	8	**A Presentation Of Progressive Jazz**
			Stan Kenton and His Orchestra
8.	7/24	14	**Al Jolson - Volume Three** *Al Jolson*
9.	10/16	3	**Theme Songs**
			Various Artist Compilation
10.	11/20	9	**Merry Christmas** *Bing Crosby*

1949

	DATE	WKS	
1.	1/22	2	**Vaughn Monroe Sings**
			Vaughn Monroe and his Orchestra
2.	1/29	1	**Roses In Rhythm**
			Frankie Carle with Rhythm Section
3.	2/12	6	**Words And Music** *Movie Soundtrack*
4.	3/19	10	**Kiss Me, Kate** *Original Cast*
5.	6/4	69	**South Pacific** *Original Cast*
6.	12/24	3	**Merry Christmas** *Bing Crosby*

1950

	DATE	WKS	
1.	5/6	2	**Cinderella** *Movie Soundtrack*
2.	5/13	12	**Young Man With A Horn**
			Doris Day and Harry James/Movie Soundtrack

July 22, 1950: Billboard debuts both a Best Selling 33-1/3 R.P.M. and Best Selling 45 R.P.M. chart

3.	7/22	3	**Ralph Flanagan plays Rodgers & Hammerstein II for dancing**
			Ralph Flanagan and his Orchestra
			'45': 3
4.	8/12	8	**Annie Get Your Gun** *Movie Soundtrack*
			'45': 8
5.	9/30	11	**Three Little Words** *Movie Soundtrack*
			'33': 11 / '45': 10
6.	12/16	5	**Merry Christmas** *Bing Crosby*
			'45': 5 / '33': 2

1951

	DATE	WKS	
1.	2/24	6	**The Toast Of New Orleans**
			Mario Lanza/Movie Soundtrack
			'45': 6
2.	3/17	1	**Guys And Dolls** *Original Cast*
			'33': 1
3.	4/7	6	**Voice Of The Xtabay** *Yma Sumac*
			'33': 6 / '45': 6
4.	4/21	3	**Lullaby Of Broadway**
			Doris Day/Movie Soundtrack
			'45': 3
5.	6/2	10	**The Great Caruso**
			Mario Lanza/Movie Soundtrack
			'33': 10 / '45': 10
6.	8/11	19	**Show Boat** *Movie Soundtrack*
			'45': 19 / '33': 18
7.	12/22	3	**Mario Lanza sings Christmas songs**
			Mario Lanza
			'45': 3 / '33': 3

#1 ALBUMS

The Charts From Top To Bottom

When the talk turns to music, more people turn to Joel Whitburn's Record Research Collection than to any other reference source.

That's because these are the **only** books that get right to the bottom of *Billboard's* major charts, with **complete, fully accurate chart data on every record ever charted**. So they're quoted with confidence by DJ's, music show hosts, program directors, collectors and other music enthusiasts worldwide.

Each book lists every record's significant chart data, such as peak position, debut date, peak date, weeks charted, label, record number and much more, all conveniently arranged for fast, easy reference. Most books also feature artist biographies, record notes, RIAA Platinum/Gold Record certifications, top artist and record achievements, all-time artist and record rankings, a chronological listing of all #1 hits, and additional in-depth chart information.

TOP POP SINGLES 1955-1999
Over 23,000 pop singles — every "Hot 100" hit — arranged by artist. Features thousands of artist biographies and countless titles notes. Also includes the B-side title of every "Hot 100" hit. 960 pages. $79.95 Hardcover / $69.95 Softcover.

POP ANNUAL 1955-1999
A year-by-year ranking, based on chart performance, of over 23,000 pop hits. Also includes, for the first time, the songwriters for every "Hot 100" hit. 912 pages. $79.95 Hardcover / $69.95 Softcover.

HIT LIST 1955-1999
An accurate checklist of every title that appears in both our Top Pop Singles 1955-1999 and Pop Annual 1955-1999. Features a check box for each record and picture sleeve (where applicable), debut year, and record label and number on an ample 11" x 8 1/2" page format. 304 pages. Spiral-bound softcover. $39.95.

POP HITS SINGLES & ALBUMS 1940-1954
Four big books in one: an artist-by-artist anthology of early pop classics, a year-by year ranking of Pop's early hits, the complete story of the early pop albums and the top 10 singles charts of every *Billboard* "Best Selling Singles" chart. Filled with artist bios, title notes, and many special sections. 576 pages. Hardcover. $69.95.

POP MEMORIES 1890-1954
Unprecedented in depth and dimension. An artist-by-artist, title-by-title chronicle of the 65 formative years of recorded popular music. Fascinating facts and statistics on over 1,600 artists and 12,000 recordings, compiled directly from America's popular music charts, surveys and record listings. 660 pages. Hardcover. $59.95.

TOP POP ALBUMS 1955-2001
An artist-by-artist history of the over 22,000 albums that ever appeared on *Billboard's* pop albums charts, with a complete A-Z listing below each artist of tracks from every charted album by that artist. 1,208 pages. Hardcover. $99.95.

ALBUM CUTS 1955-2001
A companion guide to our Top Pop Albums 1955-2001 book — an A-Z list of cut titles along with the artist name and chart debut year of the album on which the cut is first found. 720 pages. Hardcover. $44.95.

BILLBOARD HOT 100/POP SINGLES CHARTS:

THE NINETIES 1990-1999
THE EIGHTIES 1980-1989
THE SEVENTIES 1970-1979
THE SIXTIES 1960-1969

Four complete collections of the actual weekly "Hot 100" charts from each decade; black-and-white reproductions at 70% of original size. Over 550 pages each. Deluxe Hardcover. $79.95 each.

POP CHARTS 1955-1959

Reproductions of every weekly pop singles chart *Billboard* published from 1955 through 1959 ("Best Sellers," "Jockeys," "Juke Box," "Top 100" and "Hot 100"). 496 pages. Deluxe Hardcover. $59.95.

BILLBOARD POP ALBUM CHARTS 1965-1969
The greatest of all album eras...straight off the pages of *Billboard*! Every weekly *Billboard* pop albums chart, shown in its entirety, from 1965 through 1969. Black-and-white reproductions at 70% of original size. 496 pages. Deluxe Hardcover. $59.95.

TOP ADULT CONTEMPORARY 1961-2001
Artist-by-artist listing of the nearly 8,000 singles and over 1,900 artists that appeared on *Billboard's* "Easy Listening" and "Hot Adult Contemporary" singles charts from July 17, 1961 through December 29, 2001. 352 pages. Hardcover. $44.95.

TOP COUNTRY SINGLES 1944-2001
The complete history of the most genuine of American musical genres, with an artist-by-artist listing of every "Country" single ever charted. 608 pages. Hardcover. $69.95.

COUNTRY ANNUAL 1944-1997
A year-by-year ranking, based on chart performance, of over 16,000 Country hits. 704 pages. Hardcover. $64.95.

TOP COUNTRY ALBUMS 1964-1997
First edition! A music industry first and a Record Research exclusive — features an artist-by-artist listing of every album to appear on *Billboard's* Top Country Albums chart from its first appearance in 1964 through September, 1997. Includes complete listings of all tracks from every Top 10 Country album. 304 pages. Hardcover. $49.95.

A CENTURY OF POP MUSIC
This unique book chronicles the biggest Pop hits of the past 100 years, in yearly rankings of the Top 40 songs of every year from 1900 through 1999. Includes complete artist and title sections, pictures of the top artists, top hits and top artists by decade, and more. 256 pages. Softcover. $39.95.

TOP R&B SINGLES 1942-1999
Revised edition of our R&B bestseller — loaded with new features! Every "Soul," "Black," "Urban Contemporary" and "Rhythm & Blues" charted single, listed by artist. 688 pages. Hardcover. $69.95.

TOP R&B ALBUMS 1965-1998
First edition! An artist-by-artist listing of each of the 2,177 artists and 6,940 albums to appear on *Billboard's* "Top R&B Albums" chart. Includes complete listings of all tracks from every Top 10 R&B album. 360 pages. Hardcover. $49.95.

ROCK TRACKS
Two artist-by-artist listings of the over 3,700 titles that appeared on *Billboard's* "Album Rock Tracks" chart from March, 1981 through August, 1995 and the over 1,200 titles that appeared on *Billboard's* "Modern Rock Tracks" chart from September, 1988 through August, 1995. 288 pages. Softcover. $34.95.

BUBBLING UNDER SINGLES AND ALBUMS 1998 Edition
All "Bubbling Under The Hot 100" (1959-1997) and "Bubbling Under The Top Pop Albums" (1970-1985) charts covered in full and organized artist by artist. Also features a photo section of every EP that hit *Billboard's* "Best Selling Pop EP's" chart (1957-1960). 416 pages. Softcover. $49.95.

BILLBOARD TOP 10 SINGLES CHARTS 1955-2000
A complete listing of each weekly Top 10 singles chart from *Billboard's* "Best Sellers" chart (1955-July 28, 1958) and "Hot 100" chart from its inception (August 4, 1958) through 2000. Each chart shows each single's current and previous week's positions, total weeks charted on the entire chart, original label & number, and more. 712 pages. Hardcover. $49.95.

BILLBOARD TOP 10 ALBUM CHARTS 1963-1998
This books contains more than 1,800 individual Top 10 charts from over 35 years of *Billboard's* weekly Top Albums chart (currently titled The Billboard 200). Each chart shows each album's current and previous week's positions, total weeks charted on the entire Top Albums chart, original label & number, and more. 536 pages. Hardcover. $39.95.

BILLBOARD SINGLES REVIEWS 1958
Reproductions of every weekly 1958 record review *Billboard* published for 1958. Reviews of nearly 10,000 record sides by 3,465 artists. 280 pages. Softcover. $29.95.

BILLBOARD TOP 1000 x 5 1996 Edition
Includes five complete separate rankings — from #1 through #1000 — of the all-time top charted hits of Pop & Hot 100 Singles 1955-1996, Pop Singles 1940-1954, Adult Contemporary Singles 1961-1996, R&B Singles 1942-1996, and Country Singles 1944-1996. 288 pages. Softcover. $29.95.

DAILY #1 HITS 1940-1992
A desktop calendar of a half-century of #1 pop records. Lists one day of the year per page of every record that held the #1 position on the pop singles charts on that day for each of the past 53+ years. 392 pages. Spiral-bound softcover. $24.95.

MUSIC YEARBOOKS 2001/2000/1999/1998/1997/1996/1995/1994/1993/1992/1991/1990
A complete review of each year's charted music — as well as a superb supplemental update of our Record Research Pop Singles and Albums, Country Singles, R&B Singles, Adult Contemporary Singles, and Bubbling Under Singles books. Various page lengths. Softcover. 1999 thru 2001 editions $39.95 each / 1995 thru 1998 editions $34.95 each / 1990 thru 1994 editions $29.95 each.

Order Information

Shipping/Handling Extra — If you do not order through our online Web site (see below), please contact us for shipping rates.

Order By:

☎ **U.S. Toll-Free**: 1-800-827-9810
(orders only please – Mon-Fri 8 AM-12 PM, 1 PM-5 PM CST)

Foreign Orders: 1-262-251-5408

Questions?: 1-262-251-5408 or **Email**: books@recordresearch.com

💻 **Online at our Web site**: www.recordresearch.com

▤ **Fax** (24 hours): 1-262-251-9452

📫 **Mail**: Record Research Inc.
P.O. Box 200
Menomonee Falls, WI 53052-0200
U.S.A.

U.S. orders are shipped **via UPS**; please allow **7-10 business days** for delivery.

Canadian and **Foreign** orders are shipped **via surface mail**; please allow **8-12 weeks** for delivery. Orders must be paid in U.S. dollars and drawn on a U.S. bank.

For faster delivery, contact us for other shipping options/rates. We now offer **UPS Worldwide Express** service for Canadian and Foreign orders as well as airmail service through the postal system.

Payment methods accepted: MasterCard, VISA, American Express, Money Order, or Check (personal checks may be held up to 10 days for bank clearance).